The Pan CROSSWORD Dictionary

Compilers of crosswords are a law unto themselves. When filling in designs, preparatory to clueing, they are unrestricted in their choice of words, phrases, etc. A number of 15-letter examples, chosen at random, follow to illustrate the vast fields open to the compilers – fields that have never before been covered by a single reference book –

ANOREXIA NERVOSA, BULLDOG DRUMMOND, DANCE OF THE HOURS, ERNEST HEMINGWAY, FISH AND CHIP SHOP, GREEN REVOLUTION, HANSEL AND GRETEL, ITALIAN VERMOUTH, KITTEN ON THE KEYS, LOOK BACK IN ANGER, MOLOTOV COCKTAIL, NUREMBERG TRIALS, PLOUGHMAN'S LUNCH, QUICK OFF THE MARK, ROOM TO SWING A CAT, SUNDAY NEWSPAPER, TOE THE PARTY LINE, UNDER LOCK AND KEY, VENGEANCE IS MINE, WISDOM OF SOLOMON, YOURS FAITHFULLY

The Pan Crossword Dictionary covers all these 'phrases' and more than 50,000 others. Together with the word section at the end of the book, it will prove to be of inestimable value to solvers and compilers alike.

Mike Hutchinson was born in Bournemouth in 1960. After studying sociology at the London School of Economics, he began compiling crosswords for national newspapers in 1985.

His compilations have appeared in the *Daily Mail*, *Mail on Sunday*, *Daily Express*, *Daily Mirror*, *Sun*, *People*, *News of the World*, London *Evening Standard*, and even on the back of cornflakes packets.

In his position as Editor of the crosswords agency Morley Adams, he is responsible for the crosswords appearing in many top national and local newspapers.

Also available in Pan Books

The *Daily Telegraph* How to Crack a Cryptic Crossword
The *Daily Telegraph* Big Book of Quick Crosswords Vols 1–3
The *Daily Telegraph* Big Book of Cryptic Crosswords Vols 1–3
The *Daily Telegraph* Book of Quick Crosswords Vols 6–17
The *Daily Telegraph* Book of Cryptic Crosswords Vols 17–31
The *Sunday Telegraph* Book of Quick Crosswords Vol 1
The *Sunday Telegraph* Book of Cryptic Crosswords Vol 1

The Pan CROSSWORD Dictionary

Edited by Mike Hutchinson

PAN BOOKS

First published 1967 by Pan Books Ltd and revised 1988
This revised edition published 1995 by Pan Books
an imprint of Macmillan Publishers Limited
25 Eccleston Place, London SW1W 9NF
and Basingstoke

Associated companies throughout the world

ISBN 0-330-341251

9 8 7 6 5 4 3 2 1

Photoset by Parker Typesetting Service, Leicester
Printed and bound in Great Britain by Cox & Wyman Ltd, Reading

FOREWORD

People often ask me whether I consider it cheating to use reference books as an aid to solving puzzles. My reply is that you can be sure that the compilers themselves will be using as many reference books as they see fit.

As editor of the oldest and most prolific crossword agency in the world, I can confirm that many of the country's leading compilers regard the *Pan Crossword Dictionary* as an essential tool for filling in a crossword grid.

It is some confort to compilers that new words enter our vocabulary each year. Since Norman Pulsford completed the first Pan crossword dictionary in 1967, the contents of the home have changed. Apart from the ever-increasing number of labour-saving devices and gadgets, television has greatly increased the number of American, and more recently Australian, words and phrases that have become part of everyday speech. Computers are no longer the preserve of boffins and schoolchildren, but are now essential features of almost all offices and many homes. As a result of all these changes, over 2,000 phrases and words have been added to this new edition.

The phrases are listed according to the number of letters they contain, from 8 to 15 letters, and then in alphabetical order.

In order to save space, plurals are only listed when the plural form is more common than the singular. Present participles have also been omitted.

The word section at the end of the book contains words of between 3 and 9 letters.

I should like to acknowledge the contributions made by the late Norman Pulsford, Mike Grimshaw, Frank Copperstone and Kosar Hussain.

Mike Hutchinson

CONTENTS

PHRASES

A BAD TIME
A BIT MUCH
ABOVE ALL
ABOVE PAR
ACCEPT IT
ACES HIGH
ACES WILD
ACID BATH
ACID DROP
ACID HEAD
ACID RAIN
ACID ROCK
ACID TEST
ACT A PART
ACT BADLY
ACT OF GOD
ACT OF WAR
ACT THREE
ACUTE EAR
ADAM BEDE
ADAM'S ALE
ADAM'S RIB
ADDING UP
ADD WATER
ADMIT ONE
ADMIT TWO
A FAIR COP
A FAST ONE
AFTER ALL
AFTER TEA
AFTER YOU
AGE GROUP
A GOOD BUY
A GOOD FEW
A GOOD RUN
AIM A BLOW
AIR BRUSH
AIR COVER
AIR FORCE
AIR LINER
AIR MILES
AIR POWER
AIR RAIDS
AIR ROUTE
AIR SENSE
AIR SPACE
A LA CARTE

AL CAPONE
AL FRESCO
AL JOLSON
ALL ALIKE
ALL ALONE
ALL ALONG
ALL ASKEW
ALL AT SEA
ALL BLACK
ALL CLEAR
ALLEY CAT
ALL FARES
ALL FOUND
ALL FOURS
ALL HANDS
ALL HOURS
ALL IN ALL
ALL IN ONE
ALL KINDS
ALL MY EYE
ALL NIGHT
'ALLO 'ALLO
ALL QUIET
ALL READY
ALL RIGHT
ALL ROADS
ALL ROUND
ALL'S FAIR
ALL SIDES
ALL SORTS
ALL SOULS
ALL'S WELL
ALL THE GO
ALL THERE
ALL WRONG
ALPHA RAY
ALTER EGO
ANDY CAPP
A NEW LEAF
ANTS' NEST
ANZAC DAY
APPLE PIE
APPLE PIP
APTLY PUT
ARC LAMPS
ARC LIGHT
AREA CODE
ARK ROYAL
ARMED MAN

ARM IN ARM
ARMS BEND
ARMS RACE
ARMY CAMP
ARMY LIFE
ARMY LIST
ARMY RANK
ARMY TYPE
ART CLASS
ART PAPER
ARTS CLUB
ARTY TYPE
ARUM LILY
AS A WHOLE
ASCOT HAT
AS GOOD AS
ASH GROVE
ASH TREES
ASIAN FLU
AS IT WERE
ASK FOR IT
ASK LEAVE
ASK MERCY
AS STATED
ASWAN DAM
AS WELL AS
AT A GUESS
AT ANCHOR
AT A PARTY
AT A PINCH
AT A PRICE
AT BOTTOM
AT DINNER
AT HARROW
AT LENGTH
AT LOW EBB
AT NO TIME
ATOM BOMB
AT OXFORD
AT RANDOM
AT SCHOOL
AT SUNSET
AT THE BAR
AT THE END
AT THE OFF
AT THE TOP
AT THE ZOO
ATTIC WIT
AUDIT ALE

AUGER BIT
AU GRATIN
AUNT EDNA
AU REVOIR
AUTO DA FE
AVE MARIA
AWAY GAME
AWAY TEAM
AWAY WINS

B – 8

BABE RUTH
BABY BOOM
BABY CARE
BABY CARS
BABY DOLL
BABY FACE
BABY FOOD
BABY GIRL
BABY LOVE
BABY MINE
BABY SHOW
BABY TALK
BABY WOOL
BACK AWAY
BACK AXLE
BACK DOOR
BACK DOWN
BACKED UP
BACK HAIR
BACK KICK
BACK PAGE
BACK RENT
BACK ROOM
BACK SEAT
BACKS OUT
BACK SPIN
BACK STUD
BACK VIEW
BACK YARD
BACON FAT
BAD ACTOR
BAD BLOOD
BAD BOOKS
BAD CAUSE
BAD COUGH
BAD DEBTS
BAD DREAM
BAD FAITH
BAD GRACE
BAD HABIT
BAD HEART
BAD IMAGE
BAD LANDS
BAD LAYER

BAD LIGHT
BAD LIVER
BAD LOGIC
BAD LOSER
BADLY OFF
BAD MARKS
BAD MIXER
BAD MONEY
BAD NIGHT
BAD ODOUR
BAD PATCH
BAD PENNY
BAD POINT
BAD PRESS
BAD SCORE
BAD SHAPE
BAD SHOTS
BAD SIGHT
BAD SMELL
BAD SPORT
BAD START
BAD STATE
BAD STORY
BAD TASTE
BAD TERMS
BAD THING
BAD TIMES
BAD TOOTH
BAD TRADE
BALD HEAD
BALD PATE
BALES OUT
BALL BOYS
BALL GAME
BALL GOWN
BANK DOWN
BANK LOAN
BANK NOTE
BANK ON IT
BANK RATE
BARE FEET
BARE HEAD
BARE IDEA
BARE LEGS
BARE NECK
BARE WORD
BASE COIN
BASS CLEF
BASS DRUM
BASS HORN
BASS NOTE
BATH BUNS
BATH CHAP
BATH CUBE
BATH ROBE
BATH SOAP

BATTLE ON
BAY HORSE
BAY TREES
BEACH HUT
BEADY EYE
BEAR ARMS
BEAR DOWN
BEAR LEFT
BEAR PAIN
BEARS OUT
BEAR WITH
BE A SPORT
BEAT BACK
BEAT DOWN
BEATEN UP
BEAT IT UP
BEAT TIME
BEAU NASH
BED GUARD
BED LINEN
BEEF STEW
BEER HALL
BEE STING
BEG LEAVE
BE IN DEBT
BE IN LOVE
BELL TENT
BELOW PAR
BE MY LOVE
BEND DOWN
BEND OVER
BEN NEVIS
BE NO MORE
BENT BACK
BE ON CALL
BE ON EDGE
BE POLITE
BE SEATED
BE SILENT
BEST CUTS
BEST DAYS
BEST EVER
BEST FORM
BEST GIRL
BEST LOVE
BEST PART
BEST SUIT
BEST TEAM
BEST TIME
BEST TOGS
BEST WINE
BETEL NUT
BE UNKIND
BEVIN BOY
BID PRICE
BIG APPLE

BIG BREAK	BLIND MAN	BOTTLE UP
BIG BUILD	BLOCK OUT	BOTTOM UP
BIG BULLY	BLOOD RED	BOUGHT IN
BIG CHIEF	BLOOD TIE	BOUGHT UP
BIG CROWD	BLOTS OUT	BOUNCE IN
BIG DEALS	BLOW AWAY	BOUNCE UP
BIG DRINK	BLOW COLD	BOW BELLS
BIG FIGHT	BLOW DOWN	BOWL OVER
BIG FILMS	BLOW HARD	BOXER DOG
BIG GIRLS	BLOWN OUT	BOYS' CLUB
BIG HOUSE	BLOW OVER	BOY SCOUT
BIG IDEAS	BLUE BABY	BRAIN BOX
BIG MATCH	BLUE BIRD	BRAIN FAG
BIG MONEY	BLUE BOOK	BRAND NEW
BIG MOUTH	BLUE EYES	BRASS HAT
BIG NOISE	BLUE FUNK	BRAVE MAN
BIG RACES	BLUE LAMP	BREAD BIN
BIG SCORE	BLUE MOON	BREAK OFF
BIG SHOTS	BLUE NILE	BREAK OUT
BIG STAND	BLUE ROOM	BREAKS IN
BIG STICK	BLUE RUIN	BREAKS UP
BIG STORM	BLUE STAR	BREN GUNS
BIG STUFF	BLUE SUIT	BRIAN RIX
BIG WHEEL	BLUNT END	BRICK RED
BILLY BOY	BLURT OUT	BRIM OVER
BILLY CAN	BOARD OUT	BRING OFF
BIND OVER	BOAT CLUB	BRING OUT
BIRD CALL	BOAT RACE	BRINGS IN
BIRD LIFE	BOBBY PIN	BRINGS ON
BIRD LORE	BOB DYLAN	BRINGS TO
BIRD SEED	BODE EVIL	BRINGS UP
BIRD SONG	BODY BLOW	BROKEN IN
BIT BY BIT	BODY HEAT	BROKEN UP
BITE INTO	BODY LINE	BROWN ALE
BITER BIT	BOIL AWAY	BROWN COW
BIT OF FUN	BOIL DOWN	BROWN EGG
BLACK ART	BOIL OVER	BROWN OWL
BLACK BAG	BOLD DEED	BROWN RAT
BLACK BAT	BOLD FACE	BRUCE LEE
BLACK BOX	BOLD MOVE	BRUSH OFF
BLACK CAB	BOLD TYPE	BUBBLE UP
BLACK CAP	BOMB SITE	BUCKLE ON
BLACK CAT	BONA FIDE	BUCKLE TO
BLACK DOG	BONAR LAW	BUCKLE UP
BLACK EYE	BONE IDLE	BULL NECK
BLACK INK	BOOB TUBE	BULL'S EYE
BLACK KEY	BOOK CLUB	BULLY OFF
BLACK MAN	BOOKED UP	BUMP INTO
BLACK OUT	BOOK ENDS	BUMPS OFF
BLACK RAT	BOOK SHOP	BUN FIGHT
BLACK ROD	BOOM TOWN	BUNGED UP
BLACK SEA	BORN DEAD	BUNNY HUG
BLACK TEA	BORN FOOL	BUOYED UP
BLACK TIE	BORN RICH	BURN AWAY
BLESS YOU	BOTH ENDS	BURN DOWN
BLIND EYE	BOTH WAYS	BURNT OAK

BURNT OUT	CALL UPON	CHEESE IT
BURST OUT	CALM DOWN	CHESS SET
BUS DEPOT	CAME DOWN	CHEW OVER
BUS FARES	CAMP FIRE	CHEZ NOUS
BUSH FIRE	CAMP SITE	CHINA CUP
BUS QUEUE	CANON LAW	CHINA EGG
BUS STOPS	CAPE HORN	CHINA SEA
BUSY BEES	CAPE TOWN	CHINA TEA
BUSY LIFE	CAP IT ALL	CHIN CHIN
BUSY TIME	CAR ALARM	CHIP HEAD
BUSY TOWN	CAR CRASH	CHIP SHOT
BUTTED IN	CARD GAME	CHOIR BOY
BUTTER UP	CARD VOTE	CHOKE OFF
BUTTON UP	CARE A LOT	CHOP DOWN
BUY BLIND	CAR FERRY	CHOP SUEY
BUY CHEAP	CAR PARKS	CHUCK KEY
BUZZ BOMB	CAR PHONE	CHURN OUT
BUZZ WORD	CAR RALLY	CIDER CUP
BY A FLUKE	CARRY OFF	CIGAR ASH
BY CHANCE	CARRY OUT	CIGAR BOX
BY CHEQUE	CAR SMASH	CISCO KID
BY GEORGE	CART AWAY	CITY DESK
BY HALVES	CARVE OUT	CITY GENT
BY INCHES	CASE BOOK	CITY HALL
BY ITSELF	CASH BOOK	CITY LIFE
BY LETTER	CASH DESK	CITY WALL
BY MYSELF	CASH DOWN	CIVIL LAW
BY MY WILL	CASHED IN	CIVIL WAR
BY NATURE	CASH SALE	CLASS WAR
BY RETURN	CAST A FLY	CLAY PIPE
BY RIGHTS	CAST A NET	CLEAN CUT
BY STAGES	CAST AWAY	CLEAN OUT
BY THE ARM	CAST DICE	CLEANS UP
BY THE SEA	CAST DOWN	CLEAR DAY
BY THE WAY	CAST IRON	CLEAR OFF
	CAST LOTS	CLEAR OUT
	CASTS OFF	CLEAR SKY
C – 8	CASTS OUT	CLEARS UP
	CATCH OUT	CLEAR WIN
CABIN BOY	CAT LOVER	CLOCK END
CABLE CAR	CATS' EYES	CLOCK OUT
CAB RANKS	CATS' HOME	CLOCKS IN
CAFE NOIR	CAT SHOWS	CLOSED IN
CALF LOVE	CAT'S MEAT	CLOSE FIT
CALL A CAB	CAUGHT ON	CLOSE RUN
CALL AWAY	CAUGHT UP	CLOSE SET
CALL BACK	CD PLAYER	CLOSES UP
CALL BOYS	CELL MATE	CLOSE TIE
CALL DOWN	CHALK OUT	CLOTH CAP
CALLED IN	CHANCE IT	CLUB BORE
CALLED UP	CHAT SHOW	CLUB FEES
CALL GIRL	CHECK OFF	CLUB LIFE
CALL OVER	CHECK OUT	COAL CART
CALLS FOR	CHECKS IN	COAL DUST
CALLS OFF	CHECKS UP	COAL FIRE
CALLS OUT	CHEERS UP	COAL MINE
CALL TIME		

COAL SEAM	COSY CHAT	**D – 8**
COCA COLA	COT DEATH	
CODE NAME	COTTON ON	DAD'S ARMY
CODE WORD	COUGHS UP	DAILY USE
CODS' ROES	COUNT OUT	DAIRY COW
COKE FIRE	COUNT TEN	DAMP DOWN
COLD BATH	COUPLE UP	DANNY BOY
COLD BEEF	COVERS UP	DARK AGES
COLD CURE	COW'S MILK	DARK BLUE
COLD DISH	CRACKS UP	DARK DAYS
COLD DUCK	CRASH OUT	DARK DEED
COLD FEET	CRASH PAD	DARK GREY
COLD FISH	CREAM BUN	DARK HAIR
COLD FOOD	CREAM TEA	DARK LADY
COLD LAMB	CREEP OFF	DARK ROOM
COLD MEAL	CREEP OUT	DARK SIDE
COLD MEAT	CREW CUTS	DARK SKIN
COLD MILK	CRIED OUT	DARK STAR
COLD PACK	CRIES OFF	DARK SUIT
COLD PORK	CROCKS UP	DART PAST
COLD ROOM	CROSS NOW	DASH AWAY
COLD SNAP	CROSS OFF	DASH DOWN
COLD WAVE	CROSS OUT	DASH INTO
COLD WIND	CROWN HIM	DATE PALM
COLOUR UP	CROW OVER	DAVE KING
COME AWAY	CRUDE OIL	DAVID LOW
COME BACK	CRUEL ACT	DAVIS CUP
COME DOWN	CRUEL SEA	DAVY LAMP
COME HERE	CRUET SET	DAWN RAID
COME HOME	CRY ALOUD	DAY BOOKS
COME INTO	CRY 'HAVOC'	DAY BY DAY
COME LAST	CRY OF JOY	DAY DREAM
COME NEAR	CRY QUITS	DAY NURSE
COME NEXT	CRY 'SHAME'	DAY OR TWO
COME OVER	CUBE ROOT	DAY SHIFT
COMES OFF	CUP FINAL	DAY'S WORK
COMES OUT	CUP OF TEA	DEAD BALL
COME TRUE	CURLED UP	DEAD BEAT
COME UPON	CUSHY JOB	DEAD BODY
COME UP TO	CUT A DASH	DEAD CALM
COMING IN	CUT GLASS	DEAD CERT
COMING ON	CUT GRASS	DEAD DUCK
COMING TO	CUT IN TWO	DEAD EASY
CON AMORE	CUT IT OFF	DEAD FLAT
COOL CARD	CUT IT OUT	DEAD HAND
COOL DOWN	CUT LOOSE	DEAD HEAT
COOL FISH	CUT NO ICE	DEAD KEEN
COOL HAND	CUT PRICE	DEAD LEAF
COOL HEAD	CUT RATES	DEAD LOSS
COOPED UP	CUT ROUND	DEAD NUTS
COPE WITH	CUTS BACK	DEAD SHOT
COPY DOWN	CUTS DEAD	DEAD SLOW
CORK TIPS	CUTS DOWN	DEAD SOUL
CORN CURE	CUTS FINE	DEAD SPIT
CORN LAWS	CUT SHORT	DEAD SURE
COSY CAFE		DEAD WOOD

DEAF AIDS
DEAF EARS
DEAF MUTE
DEAL WITH
DEAR DEAR!
DEAR JOHN
DEAR LIFE
DEAR SIRS
DEATH BED
DEATH RAY
DEATH ROW
DEBT SWAP
DEED POLL
DEEP BLUE
DEEP COMA
DEEP DOWN
DEEP NOTE
DEEP SIGH
DEEP SNOW
DEEP TONE
DEER PARK
DEFY TIME
DE GAULLE
DE LA MARE
DENSE FOG
DERBY DAY
DEREK ROY
DESK WORK
DE VALERA
DEVON MAN
DICE GAME
DID RIGHT
DID WRONG
DIED AWAY
DIED DOWN
DIED HARD
DIE HAPPY
DIET PILL
DIG A HOLE
DIG A MINE
DIGS DEEP
DIM LIGHT
DINED OUT
DINE LATE
DIRTY DEN
DIRTY DOG
DIRTY SKY
DISHED UP
DIVAN BED
DO A TRICK
DO BATTLE
DO BETTER
DOCTOR NO
DOG FIGHT
DOGGY BAG
DOG LATIN

DOG LOVER
DOGS' HOME
DOG SHOWS
DOG'S LIFE
DOG'S NOSE
DOG'S TAIL
DOG TEAMS
DOG TRACK
DOG WATCH
DO HOMAGE
DOLLED UP
DONE DOWN
DO NO GOOD
DO NO HARM
DON'T KNOW
DORIS DAY
DO SCALES
DO THE LOT
DOUBLE UP
DOVE GREY
DO WISELY
DOW JONES
DOWN BEAT
DOWN LINE
DOWN TOWN
DOWN WIND
DRAG DOWN
DRAG HUNT
DRAGS OUT
DRAIN DRY
DRAW AWAY
DRAW BACK
DRAW LOTS
DRAW NEAR
DRAW NIGH
DRAWN OFF
DRAWN OUT
DRAW REIN
DRAW WELL
DREAM MAN
DRIED EGG
DRIED OUT
DRILL BIT
DRINKS UP
DRIVE MAD
DRIVE OFF
DRIVE OUT
DROP AWAY
DROP DEAD
DROP DOWN
DROPS OFF
DROPS OUT
DROP ZONE
DRY BONES
DRY BREAD
DRY CELLS

DRY COUGH
DRY FACTS
DRY FRUIT
DRY GOODS
DRYING UP
DRY PLATE
DRY TOAST
DR. WATSON
DUCK DOWN
DUCK POND
DUCK'S EGG
DUCK SOUP
DUE NORTH
DUE SOUTH
DULL ACHE
DULL PAIN
DULL THUD
DULL WORK
DUMB SHOW
DUMMY RUN
DUST BOWL
DUST TRAP
DUTCH GIN
DUTCH HOE
DUTY CALL
DUTY FREE
DUTY LIST
DUTY PAID
DUVET SET
DYED HAIR
DYING BED
DYING DAY
DYING MAN
DYING OUT

E – 8

EAGLE EYE
EARL HAIG
EARLY AGE
EARLY MAN
EARN FAME
EARN LESS
EARN MORE
EAR PLUGS
EASED OFF
EASED OUT
EASE OVER
EAST SIDE
EAST WIND
EAST WING
EASY BEAT
EASY COME
EASY DROP
EASY GAME
EASY LIFE

EASY MIND
EASY PACE
EASY PREY
EASY ROAD
EASY TASK
EASY TIME
EASY WORD
EAT A MEAL
EATS AWAY
EATS DIRT
EAU DE VIE
ECCE HOMO
EDGE AWAY
EGG FLIPS
EGG PLANT
EGG SALAD
EGG SAUCE
EGG SPOON
EGG TIMER
EIGHT MEN
ELDER SON
EL DORADO
ELM TREES
EMIT RAYS
EMPTY BOX
EMPTY CAN
EMPTY TIN
END HOUSE
END IT ALL
END SEATS
END TO END
ENEMY SPY
ENOLA GAY
ENTRY FEE
EPIC FILM
EPIC POEM
EPIC POET
EQUAL PAY
ERNIE ELS
ESSEX MAN
ET CETERA
ETON CROP
ETON SUIT
EVEN BEAT
EVEN DATE
EVEN KEEL
EVEN MORE
EVEN PACE
EVEN TIME
EVERY BIT
EVERY DAY
EVERY ONE
EVERY WAY
EVIL DAYS
EVIL DEED
EVIL HOUR

EVIL LIFE
EVIL OMEN
EVIL STAR
EXCUSE ME
EXIT POLL
EXTRA MAN
EXTRA PAY
EXTRA RUN
EYES LEFT
EYE TO EYE

F – 8

FACE CARD
FACE DOWN
FACE LIFT
FACE ODDS
FACE PACK
FACE RUIN
FACE UP TO
FADE AWAY
FADED OUT
FAIR COPY
FAIR DEAL
FAIR GAME
FAIR HAIR
FAIR HAND
FAIR ISLE
FAIR LADY
FAIR MAID
FAIR NAME
FAIR PLAY
FAIR SKIN
FAIR SWOP
FAIR WAGE
FAIR WIND
FALL AWAY
FALL BACK
FALL DOWN
FALL FLAT
FALL FOUL
FALL OPEN
FALL OVER
FALL SICK
FALLS ILL
FALLS OFF
FALLS OUT
FALL UPON
FALSE GOD
FALSE RIB
FAN CLUBS
FANCY BOX
FAN DANCE
FAR ABOVE
FAR AHEAD
FAR APART

FAR BELOW
FARM EGGS
FARM HAND
FARM LAND
FAR NORTH
FAR SIGHT
FAR SOUTH
FAST AWAY
FAST CARS
FAST DAYS
FAST FOOD
FAST LIFE
FAST RACE
FAST TIME
FAST WORK
FATAL DAY
FAT FRYER
FAT STOCK
FATTEN UP
FAT WOMAN
FAWN UPON
FEAST DAY
FEED WELL
FEEL BLUE
FEEL COLD
FEEL EASY
FEEL FINE
FEEL GOOD
FEEL HURT
FEEL LAZY
FEEL LIKE
FEEL PAIN
FEEL SAFE
FEEL SICK
FEELS ILL
FEEL SORE
FEEL SURE
FEEL WARM
FEEL WELL
FELL AN OX
FELL BACK
FELL DOWN
FELL FLAT
FELO DE SE
FELT HATS
FENCED IN
FETCH OUT
FEW WORDS
FIELD DAY
FIERY RED
FIFTH DAY
FIFTH ROW
FIFTH SET
FIFTH TEE
FIGHT FOR
FIGHT OFF

FIGHT SHY	FISH CAKE	FOAM BATH
FILE AWAY	FISH DISH	FOG BOUND
FILE DOWN	FISH FORK	FOGGY DAY
FILE PAST	FISH POND	FOIST OFF
FILL A GAP	FISH SHOP	FOLD ARMS
FILLED IN	FISH TANK	FOLD BACK
FILM FANS	FISH TEAS	FOLD DOWN
FILM NOIR	FIT STATE	FOLDED UP
FILM PLAY	FITS WELL	FOLD OVER
FILM SHOW	FITTED IN	FOLK LORE
FILM STAR	FITTED UP	FOLK ROCK
FINAL BID	FIVE DAYS	FOLK SONG
FINAL DAY	FIVE DEEP	FOLK TALE
FIND A JOB	FIVE FEET	FOLLOW ON
FIND A WAY	FIVE QUID	FOLLOW UP
FIND BAIL	FIVE SETS	FOND HOPE
FIND ROOM	FIX A DATE	FOOD FISH
FINDS OUT	FIX A TIME	FOOL AWAY
FIND TIME	FLAG DAYS	FOR A JOKE
FINE AIRS	FLAG DOWN	FOR A LARK
FINE ARTS	FLARED UP	FOR A SONG
FINE BIRD	FLAT BEER	FOR A TERM
FINE CHAP	FLAT FACE	FOR A TIME
FINE DAYS	FLAT FEET	FORCE OUT
FINE DOWN	FLAT FISH	FORGET IT
FINE EDGE	FLAT NOSE	FOR KEEPS
FINE FARE	FLAT PACK	FOR KICKS
FINE GAEL	FLAT RACE	FORKS OUT
FINE GOLD	FLAT RATE	FOR SHAME
FINE LADY	FLAT ROOF	FORT KNOX
FINE RAIN	FLAT SPIN	FORTY ALL
FINE SHOW	FLAT TYRE	FOUL BLOW
FINE VIEW	FLAT WASH	FOUL DEED
FINISH UP	FLEA PITS	FOUL PLAY
FIR CONES	FLEE FROM	FOUND OUT
FIRE AWAY	FLEET ARM	FOUR ACES
FIRE DAMP	FLEW AWAY	FOUR DAYS
FIRE RISK	FLEW HIGH	FOUR DEEP
FIRE UPON	FLEW HOME	FOUR FEET
FIRM DATE	FLEW SOLO	FOUR LAPS
FIRM GRIP	FLICK OFF	FOUR ONES
FIRM HAND	FLIES OFF	FOUR QUID
FIRM HOLD	FLING OFF	FOUR TENS
FIRM HOPE	FLING OUT	FOUR TWOS
FIRST ACT	FLIP SIDE	FOWL PEST
FIRST AID	FLIT PAST	FREAK OUT
FIRST BID	FLOP DOWN	FREE BEER
FIRST BUS	FLOUR BIN	FREE CITY
FIRST DAY	FLOW BACK	FREE COPY
FIRST LAP	FLOW OVER	FREE FALL
FIRST MAN	FLUFF OUT	FREE FLOW
FIRST OUT	FLUSH OUT	FREE GIFT
FIRST ROW	FLY ABOUT	FREE HAND
FIRST SET	FLY A KITE	FREE KICK
FIRST TEE	FLY APART	FREE LIFT
FIR TREES	FLY BLIND	FREE LIST

FREE LOVE
FREE MEAL
FREE MILK
FREE PASS
FREE PLAY
FREE PORT
FREE RIDE
FREE SEAT
FREE TIME
FREE TO GO
FREE VOTE
FREE WILL
FRESH AIR
FRESH EGG
FRESH TEA
FRET AWAY
FRIED EGG
FROM AFAR
FRONT MAN
FRONT ROW
FROZEN UP
FRUIT PIE
FUEL BILL
FUEL TANK
FULL BLUE
FULL CREW
FULL FACE
FULL LIFE
FULL LOAD
FULL MEAL
FULL MOON
FULL OF GO
FULL PLAY
FULL SAIL
FULL SIZE
FULL STOP
FULL TIDE
FULL TILT
FULL TIME
FULL TOSS
FULL WELL
FU MANCHU
FUMED OAK
FUN FAIRS
FUNNY HAT
FUNNY MAN
FUR COATS
FUR STOLE
FUR TRADE
FUR WRAPS
FUSE WIRE
FUSS OVER

G – 8

GAD ABOUT

GAG BOOKS
GAIN TIME
GAIN UPON
GAME BIRD
GAME LAWS
GAME PIES
GAMMA RAY
GAMMY LEG
GANG SHOW
GAOL BIRD
GAS BOARD
GAS FIRES
GAS METER
GAS PLANT
GAS POKER
GAS STOVE
GATHER IN
GATHER UP
GAVE A TUG
GAVE AWAY
GAVE BACK
GAY PRIDE
GENE BANK
GET ABOUT
GET A GOAL
GET AHEAD
GET A LIFT
GET ALONG
GET ANGRY
GET A RISE
GET BELOW
GET CLEAR
GET CROSS
GET DRUNK
GET FRESH
GET GOING
GET IDEAS
GET LEAVE
GET LOOSE
GET OLDER
GET RATTY
GET READY
GET RID OF
GET RIGHT
GET ROUGH
GET ROUND
GETS AWAY
GETS BACK
GETS EVEN
GETS OVER
GETS RICH
GETS WELL
GET THERE
GET TIRED
GET TOUGH
GET UPSET

GET WORSE
GI BRIDES
GIFT GOAL
GIFT SHOP
GIN AND IT
GINGER UP
GINNED UP
GIN RUMMY
GIN SLING
GIVE AWAY
GIVE BACK
GIVE HEED
GIVE HOPE
GIVE IN TO
GIVE IT UP
GIVEN OUT
GIVE ODDS
GIVE OVER
GIVE PAIN
GIVES EAR
GIVES WAY
GIVE VENT
GIVING UP
GLAD HAND
GLAD NEWS
GLAD RAGS
GLAM ROCK
GLASS EYE
GLASS JAW
GLEE CLUB
GLUM FACE
GNAT BITE
GNAW AWAY
GO ABOARD
GO ABROAD
GO ABSENT
GO ACROSS
GO ADRIFT
GO ALL OUT
GO AND SEE
GO AROUND
GO ASHORE
GO ASTERN
GO ASTRAY
GOBBLE UP
GO BEHIND
GO BEYOND
GO BY BOAT
GO BY RAIL
GO BY ROAD
GO BY SHIP
GO BY TAXI
GO BY TRAM
GO BY TUBE
GOD BLESS
GO DIRECT

GOD OF WAR	GOOD FEED	GO SURETY
GOD'S ACRE	GOOD FIRE	GO TO GAOL
GOD SPEED	GOOD FOLK	GO TO HELL
GOD SQUAD	GOOD FOOD	GO TOO FAR
GOD'S WILL	GOOD FORM	GO TO SEED
GOES AWAY	GOOD GAME	GO TO TOWN
GOES BACK	GOOD GATE	GO TO WORK
GOES DOWN	GOOD GIRL	GOUGE OUT
GOES OVER	GOOD HAND	GRADE ONE
GOES SLOW	GOOD HAUL	GRADE TWO
GOES WEST	GOOD HOPE	GRAF SPEE
GOES WITH	GOOD HOST	GRAND AIR
GO FOR HIM	GOOD IDEA	GRAND SUM
GO HALVES	GOOD KING	GRAY'S INN
GO HUNGRY	GOOD LADY	GREAT AGE
GO IN FEAR	GOOD LAND	GREAT AUK
GOING MAD	GOOD LIFE	GREAT DAY
GOING OFF	GOOD LUCK	GREAT FUN
GOING OUT	GOOD MEAL	GREAT GUY
GOINGS ON	GOOD MOOD	GREAT HIT
GO IN RAGS	GOOD MOVE	GREAT JOY
GO INSIDE	GOOD NAME	GREAT MAN
GOLD CARD	GOOD NEWS	GREAT TOM
GOLD COIN	GOOD OMEN	GREAT WAR
GOLD DUST	GOOD PACE	GREAT WIT
GOLD FOIL	GOOD PALS	GREEK ART
GOLD LACE	GOOD PART	GREEK GOD
GOLD LEAF	GOOD PLAN	GREEK URN
GOLD MINE	GOOD SEAT	GREEN EYE
GOLD RING	GOOD SHOT	GREEN FEE
GOLD REEF	GOOD SHOW	GREEN FLY
GOLD RUSH	GOOD SIGN	GREEN HAT
GOLD VASE	GOOD SOIL	GREEN INK
GOLD VEIN	GOOD SORT	GREEN MAN
GOLD WIRE	GOOD SOUL	GREEN TEA
GOLF BALL	GOOD TIME	GREY AREA
GOLF CLUB	GOOD TIPS	GREY COAT
GO MODERN	GOOD TRIM	GREY DAWN
GO NATIVE	GOOD TURN	GREY EYES
GONE AWAY	GOOD TYPE	GREY HAIR
GONE DOWN	GOOD VIEW	GREY MARE
GONE WEST	GOOD WASH	GREY SUIT
GOOD BALL	GOOD WIFE	GRIM FACE
GOOD BOOK	GOOD WILL	GRIM JOKE
GOOD CASE	GOOD WINE	GRIM LOOK
GOOD CAST	GOOD WORD	GRIM TASK
GOOD CHAP	GOOD WORK	GRIM VIEW
GOOD COOK	GOOD YEAR	GRIP HARD
GOOD COPY	GO ON DECK	GROPE FOR
GOOD CROP	GO ON FOOT	GROW COLD
GOOD DEAL	GOON SHOW	GROW COOL
GOOD DEBT	GO PLACES	GROW DARK
GOOD DEED	GO PURPLE	GROW LESS
GOOD DRAW	GO RACING	GROWN MAN
GOOD FACE	GO SHARES	GROW PALE
GOOD FARE	GO STEADY	GROW PEAS

GROW RICH
GROWS OLD
GROW UPON
GROW WEAK
GROW WILD
GUARD DOG
GUESS HOW
GUESS WHO
GUIDE DOG
GULP DOWN
GUN FIGHT
GUNGA DIN
GUN METAL
GYM DRESS
GYM SHOES
GYM SLIPS

H – 8

HAD WORDS
HAIL A BUS
HAIL A CAB
HAIL MARY
HAIRY APE
HALF A CUP
HALF A MAN
HALF A TON
HALF DEAD
HALF EACH
HALF FARE
HALF FULL
HALF MILE
HALF MOON
HALF OVER
HALF TIME
HALL MARK
HALT SIGN
HAM ACTOR
HAM HOUSE
HAMMER IN
HAM ROLLS
HAM SALAD
HAND BACK
HAND DOWN
HAND IT IN
HAND OVER
HAND PUMP
HANDS OFF
HANDS OUT
HANG BACK
HANG DOWN
HANG FIRE
HANG FIVE
HANG ON TO
HANG OVER
HANGS OUT

HAPPY BOY
HAPPY MAN
HARD AT IT
HARD BALL
HARD BLOW
HARD CASE
HARD CASH
HARD COAL
HARD COPY
HARD CORE
HARD DISK
HARD DRUG
HARD FACT
HARD FATE
HARD GAME
HARD HEAD
HARD KICK
HARD LIFE
HARD LOOK
HARD LUCK
HARD ROCK
HARD ROES
HARD SEAT
HARD SELL
HARD TACK
HARD TASK
HARD TIME
HARD TONE
HARD UPON
HARD WEAR
HARD WORD
HARD WORK
HARK BACK
HARM'S WAY
HARP UPON
HAT TRICK
HAUL BACK
HAUL DOWN
HAULED IN
HAVE A BET
HAVE A FAG
HAVE A FIT
HAVE A JOB
HAVE A NAP
HAVE A PEW
HAVE A ROW
HAVE A RUN
HAVE A TRY
HAVE DONE
HAVE LIFE
HAVE PITY
HAY FEVER
HAZEL NUT
HEAD BACK
HEAD CASE
HEAD COOK

HEAD GIRL
HEADS OFF
HEAD WIND
HEAR HEAR!
HEAT SPOT
HEAT WAVE
HEAVED TO
HEAVY DAY
HEAVY DEW
HEAVY SEA
HEAVY TAX
HEEL OVER
HELD BACK
HELD OVER
HELP DOWN
HELP OVER
HELPS OUT
HEMMED IN
HEN NIGHT
HEN PARTY
HEN'S EGGS
HERE GOES
HERE WE GO
HER GRACE
HERNE BAY
HIDE AWAY
HIGH AIMS
HIGH BALL
HIGH CARD
HIGH COST
HIGH DIVE
HIGHER UP
HIGH FEES
HIGH GEAR
HIGH HAND
HIGH HATS
HIGH HOPE
HIGH JUMP
HIGH KICK
HIGH LAND
HIGH LIFE
HIGH MASS
HIGH NECK
HIGH NOON
HIGH NOTE
HIGH RANK
HIGH RATE
HIGH RENT
HIGH RISE
HIGH ROAD
HIGH SEAS
HIGH SPOT
HIGH TEAS
HIGH TECH
HIGH TIDE
HIGH TIME

HIGH TONE
HIGH WAGE
HIGH WALL
HIGH WIND
HILL FARM
HILL FOLK
HIND FOOT
HIND LEGS
HIP FLASK
HIRED BUS
HIRED CAR
HIRED MAN
HIRED OUT
HIRED VAN
HIS GRACE
HIT IT OFF
HITS BACK
HITS HARD
HIT TO LEG
HOB COVER
HOCK SHOP
HOG'S BACK
HOLD BACK
HOLD DEAR
HOLD DOWN
HOLD FAST
HOLD GOOD
HOLD HARD
HOLD ON TO
HOLD OVER
HOLDS OFF
HOLDS OUT
HOLD SWAY
HOLD WITH
HOLED OUT
HOLY CITY
HOLY FEAR
HOLY LAND
HOLY LOCH
HOLY WARS
HOLY WEEK
HOLY WRIT
HOME FARM
HOME GAME
HOME HELP
HOME LIFE
HOME NEWS
HOME PARK
HOME RULE
HOME RUNS
HOME SAFE
HOME TEAM
HOME TIES
HOME TOWN
HOME WINS
HONEY BEE

HONEY POT
HONG KONG
HOOKED IT
HOP ABOUT
HOP ALONG
HOP FIELD
HOT BATHS
HOT BLOOD
HOT CAKES
HOT COALS
HOT DRINK
HOT JOINT
HOT LUNCH
HOT MEALS
HOT MONEY
HOT MUSIC
HOT NIGHT
HOT PANTS
HOT PLATE
HOT PUNCH
HOT SCENT
HOT SPELL
HOT STOVE
HOT STUFF
HOTTED UP
HOT TODDY
HOT WATER
HOUR HAND
HOUSE BOY
HOUSE DOG
HOUSE FLY
HOWL DOWN
HOW'S THAT
HULL CITY
HULL DOWN
HUMAN CRY
HUM AND HA
HUNT BALL
HUNT DOWN
HURRY OFF
HURRY OUT
HURT LOOK
HUSHED UP
HYDE PARK
HYMN BOOK
HYMN TUNE

I – 8

IAN SMITH
ICE CREAM
ICE CUBES
ICED CAKE
ICY BLAST
ICY PATCH
ICY STARE

ICY WASTE
ICY WATER
IDEAL MAN
IDEAS MAN
IDÉE FIXE
IDLE JACK
IDLE RICH
IDLE TALK
ILEX TREE
ILL GRACE
ILL TASTE
ILL USAGE
IN ACCORD
IN A CROWD
IN A CRUSH
IN ACTION
IN A DREAM
IN A FAINT
IN A FEVER
IN A FIELD
IN A FLASH
IN A FRAME
IN A GROUP
IN A HURRY
IN A JIFFY
IN AMBUSH
IN AND OUT
IN A PADDY
IN A PANIC
IN ARABIC
IN ARMOUR
IN A SENSE
IN A SLING
IN A SNARE
IN A STATE
IN A SWEAT
IN A SWOON
IN A TRICE
IN A WHIRL
IN CAMERA
IN CHAINS
IN CHARGE
IN CHORUS
IN CHURCH
IN CLOVER
IN COLOUR
IN COLUMN
IN COMMON
IN CONVOY
IN CREDIT
IN DANGER
IN DEMAND
IN DETAIL
INDY CARS
IN EFFECT
IN EMBRYO

IN EXCESS	IN THE AIR	JAR OF JAM
IN FAVOUR	IN THE ARK	JAZZ BAND
IN FLAMES	IN THE BAG	JAZZ CLUB
IN FLIGHT	IN THE BAR	JAZZ FUNK
IN FLOWER	IN THE BOX	JAZZ ROCK
INFRA DIG	IN THE CUP	JEAN MUIR
INFRA RED	IN THE END	JEST BOOK
IN FRENCH	IN THE GYM	JET BLACK
IN GERMAN	IN THE NET	JET PLANE
IN GROUPS	IN THEORY	JEW'S HARP
IN HEAVEN	IN THE PIT	JIVE TALK
IN HIDING	IN THE RAW	JOE LOUIS
IN HORROR	IN THE RED	JOG ALONG
INK SPOTS	IN THE SEA	JOHN ADAM
INK STAIN	IN THE SKY	JOHN BULL
IN LAYERS	IN THE SUN	JOHN DORY
IN LEAGUE	IN THE VAN	JOHN KNOX
IN LUXURY	IN THE WAR	JOHN NASH
IN MEMORY	IN THE WAY	JOHN PEEL
IN MID AIR	IN THE WET	JOINED IN
IN MOTION	IN THE ZOO	JOKE BOOK
IN MY VIEW	IN TIGHTS	JUMBO JET
INNER MAN	IN UNISON	JUMP AT IT
IN NO TIME	IRISH ELK	JUMP BACK
IN NO WISE	IRISH JIG	JUMP DOWN
INN SIGNS	IRISH SEA	JUMP INTO
IN OFFICE	IRON BAND	JUMP LEAD
IN OFF RED	IRON BARS	JUMP OVER
IN ONE WAY	IRON BOOT	JUMP SUIT
IN ORDERS	IRON DUKE	JUMP TO IT
IN PENCIL	IRON FIST	JUMP UPON
IN PENURY	IRON GATE	JUNK BOND
IN PERSON	IRON GRIP	JUNK FOOD
IN PIECES	IRON HAND	JUNK MAIL
IN POCKET	IRON HEEL	JUNK SHOP
IN PRISON	IRON LADY	JURY LIST
IN PUBLIC	IRON LUNG	JUST A BIT
IN PURDAH	IRON MASK	JUST A FEW
IN QUIRES	IRON MINE	JUST A SEC
IN QUOTES	IRON RULE	JUST GONE
IN REASON	IRON SHOT	JUST LOSE
IN RECESS	IRON WILL	JUST MISS
IN RELIEF	IT'S A CERT	JUST THEN
IN REPAIR	IT'S A FACT	
IN REPOSE		
IN REVOLT		**K – 8**
IN SAFETY	**J – 8**	KARL MARX
IN SEASON		KEEL OVER
IN SECRET	JACK CADE	KEEN EDGE
IN SERIES	JACK PLUG	KEEN TYPE
IN SCHOOL	JACK RUBY	KEEN WIND
IN SHREDS	JAMMED IN	KEEP A CAT
IN SPASMS	JAM PUFFS	KEEP A DOG
IN SPIRIT	JAM ROLLS	KEEP A LOG
IN TERROR	JAM TARTS	KEEP AT IT
IN THE ACT	JAM TIGHT	KEEP AWAY
	JANE EYRE	

KEEP BACK
KEEP CALM
KEEP CAVE
KEEP COOL
KEEP DARK
KEEP DOWN
KEEP FINE
KEEP GOAL
KEEP HOLD
KEEP IT UP
KEEP LEFT
KEEP OPEN
KEEP PACE
KEEP SAFE
KEEPS FIT
KEEP SHOP
KEEPS MUM
KEEPS OFF
KEEPS OUT
KEEP STEP
KEEP TIME
KEEP WARM
KEEP WELL
KEMO SABE
KEMP TOWN
KEPT BACK
KEPT BUSY
KEW GREEN
KEY ISSUE
KEY MONEY
KEY MOVES
KEY POINT
KEY POSTS
KICK BACK
KICK OVER
KICKS OFF
KICKS OUT
KID STUFF
KILL PAIN
KILLS OFF
KILL TIME
KIM NOVAK
KIND DEED
KIND FACE
KIND HOST
KIND LOOK
KIND SOUL
KIND WORD
KING COLE
KING JOHN
KING KONG
KING LEAR
KING'S CUP
KING SIZE
KISS AWAY
KNEE DEEP

KNEE GRIP
KNEE JERK
KNOCK OFF
KNOCK OUT
KNOCKS UP
KNOW BEST
KNOW WELL

L – 8

LA BOHÈME
LADLE OUT
LADY BIRD
LADY HELP
LADY LUCK
LAID BACK
LAID FLAT
LAKE COMO
LAKE ERIE
LAMB CHOP
LAME DOGS
LAME DUCK
LAND AHOY
LAND A JOB
LAND ARMY
LAND CRAB
LAND GIRL
LAND LINE
LAND'S END
LA PALOMA
LARGE EGG
LARGE GAP
LARGE GIN
LARGE RUM
LARGE SUM
LAST BALL
LAST BELL
LAST BOUT
LAST CALL
LAST CAST
LAST DAYS
LAST DROP
LAST GASP
LAST HEAT
LAST HOLE
LAST HOME
LAST HOPE
LAST HOUR
LAST JULY
LAST JUNE
LAST LEGS
LAST LINE
LAST LOOK
LAST LOVE
LAST MEAL
LAST MOVE

LAST NAME
LAST OVER
LAST PAGE
LAST PART
LAST POST
LAST RACE
LAST REST
LAST ROSE
LAST SEEN
LASTS OUT
LAST TERM
LAST TEST
LAST TIME
LAST TO GO
LAST WEEK
LAST WILL
LAST WORD
LAST YEAR
LAS VEGAS
LATE BIRD
LATE CALL
LATE HOUR
LATE MEAL
LATE NEWS
LATE PASS
LATE POST
LATE SHOW
LATE WIFE
LATIN TAG
LAUGH OFF
LAW AGENT
LAW COURT
LAW SUITS
LAY ABOUT
LAY A FIRE
LAY AN EGG
LAY ASIDE
LAY A TRAP
LAYS BARE
LAYS DOWN
LAY SIEGE
LAYS OPEN
LAY WASTE
LEAD MINE
LEAD PIPE
LEAD SHOT
LEADS OFF
LEAD UP TO
LEAK AWAY
LEAKS OUT
LEAN BACK
LEAN DIET
LEAN MEAT
LEAN OVER
LEAP OVER
LEAP YEAR

LEAST BIT	LIFE SPAN	LONG GONE
LEAVE OFF	LIFE WORK	LONG HAIR
LEAVE OUT	LIGHT ALE	LONG HAUL
LEEK SOUP	LIGHT CAR	LONG JUMP
LEE SHORE	LIGHT GUN	LONG LANE
LEFT BACK	LIGHT PEN	LONG LEAD
LEFT BANK	LIGHT RAY	LONG LEGS
LEFT FACE	LIGHTS UP	LONG LIFE
LEFT FLAT	LIGHT TEA	LONG LINE
LEFT FOOT	LIKE A MAN	LONG LIST
LEFT HALF	LIKE BEST	LONG LOST
LEFT HAND	LIKE FURY	LONG NOTE
LEFT HOME	LILY POND	LONG ODDS
LEFT HOOK	LILY PONS	LONG PLAY
LEFT OVER	LIMBER UP	LONG POEM
LEFT SIDE	LINEN BIN	LONG PULL
LEFT TURN	LINE PROP	LONG PUTT
LEFT WING	LINGER ON	LONG RACE
LEGAL AGE	LINKED UP	LONG READ
LEGAL AID	LION CUBS	LONG REST
LEG BREAK	LIONS DEN	LONG RIDE
LEG DRIVE	LIP SALVE	LONG ROAD
LEG STUMP	LISTEN IN	LONG ROOM
LEMON LAW	LITA ROZA	LONG ROPE
LEMON TEA	LITTLE ME	LONG SHOT
LEMON PIE	LITTLE MO	LONG SLIP
LEND TONE	LIVE A LIE	LONG STAY
LENT TERM	LIVE BAIT	LONG STOP
LET ALONE	LIVE COAL	LONG SUIT
LET BLOOD	LIVED OUT	LONG TAIL
LET DRIVE	LIVE DOWN	LONG TERM
LET IT LIE	LIVE IT UP	LONG TIME
LET IT RIP	LIVE RAIL	LONG VIEW
LET LOOSE	LIVE SHOW	LONG WAIT
LET ME SEE	LIVE UP TO	LONG WALK
LETS DOWN	LIVE WELL	LONG WAVE
LETS FALL	LIVE WIRE	LONG WORD
LETS FREE	LIVING IN	LOOK ARCH
LET SLIDE	LOAN CLUB	LOOK AWAY
LETS PASS	LOCAL INN	LOOK BACK
LETS SLIP	LOCAL LAD	LOOK BLUE
LEVEL OFF	LOCAL PUB	LOOK COOL
LEVEL OUT	LOCAL RAG	LOOK DOWN
LEVELS UP	LOCAL TAX	LOOKED AT
LEWIS GUN	LOCH NESS	LOOKED IN
LIAR DICE	LOCK AWAY	LOOKED ON
LIE ABOUT	LOCKED IN	LOOKED UP
LIE AWAKE	LOCKED UP	LOOK GLUM
LIE CLOSE	LOG CABIN	LOOK GOOD
LIE DOGGO	LOG FIRES	LOOK GRIM
LIE HEAVY	LOIN CHOP	LOOK HERE
LIE IN BED	LONE HAND	LOOK INTO
LIES DOWN	LONE WOLF	LOOK IT UP
LIES FLAT	LONG ACRE	LOOK LEFT
LIE STILL	LONG DROP	LOOK LIKE
LIFE PEER	LONG FACE	LOOK OVER

LOOK PALE	LOW RIDER	MAKE A HIT
LOOKS BIG	LOW SCORE	MAKE A PUN
LOOKS FOR	LOW SOUND	MAKE A ROW
LOOK SICK	LOW SPEED	MAKE A VOW
LOOKS OUT	LOW TIDES	MAKE BOLD
LOOK SPRY	LOW VOICE	MAKE EYES
LOOK TRUE	LOW WAGES	MAKE FAST
LOOK UP TO	LOW WATER	MAKE FIRM
LOOK WELL	LUCKY BOY	MAKE FREE
LOOM OVER	LUCKY DAY	MAKE GOOD
LOOP LINE	LUCKY DIP	MAKE IT UP
LOOSE BOX	LUCKY DOG	MAKE LAWS
LOOSE END	LUCKY HIT	MAKE LOVE
LOOSEN UP	LUCKY JIM	MAKE NEWS
LORD AVON	LUCKY MAN	MAKE OVER
LORD'S DAY	LUCKY RUN	MAKE PLAY
LOSE A LEG	LUCKY WIN	MAKE PORT
LOSE FACE	LUG ABOUT	MAKE PUNS
LOSE HOPE	LUMP SUMS	MAKE REAL
LOSE TIME	LUNCH BOX	MAKE ROOM
LOST BALL	LUNCH OUT	MAKE RUNS
LOST CITY	LUTON HOO	MAKE SAFE
LOST GAME	LYING LOW	MAKE SAIL
LOST LOVE	LYNCH LAW	MAKES HAY
LOST SOUL	LYRE BIRD	MAKES OFF
LOST TIME		MAKES OUT
LOT'S WIFE		MAKE SURE
LOUD BANG	**M – 8**	MAKES WAY
LOUD BOOM		MAKE TIME
LOUD PEAL	MADE EASY	MAKE UP TO
LOUD RING	MADE OVER	MALCOLM X
LOVED ONE	MAD PARTY	MAL DE MER
LOVE GAME	MAGIC BOX	MALE HEIR
LOVE NEST	MAGIC EYE	MAN ALIVE
LOVE POEM	MAIL BOAT	MAN A SHIP
LOVE SONG	MAIL BOMB	MAN OF GOD
LOVE SUIT	MAIN BODY	MAN OF LAW
LOW BIRTH	MAIN CROP	MAN POWER
LOW CARDS	MAIN DECK	MAN'S CLUB
LOW CLASS	MAIN DISH	MAN TO MAN
LOW DIVES	MAIN FILM	MANX CATS
LOW DUTCH	MAIN HALL	MANY A ONE
LOWER JAW	MAIN IDEA	MANY MORE
LOWER LIP	MAIN ITEM	MARCH OFF
LOWER SET	MAIN LINE	MARCH OUT
LOW GRADE	MAIN MEAL	MARK DOWN
LOW HEELS	MAIN PART	MARKS OFF
LOW JOINT	MAIN ROAD	MARKS OUT
LOW LATIN	MAIN ROOM	MARK TIME
LOW MARKS	MAINS HUM	MARK WELL
LOW PITCH	MAJOR KEY	MARRY OFF
LOW POINT	MAJOR TOM	MARSH GAS
LOW POWER	MAJOR WAR	MARY RAND
LOW PRICE	MAKE A BED	MARY ROSE
LOW RATES	MAKE A BET	MATA HARI
LOW RENTS	MAKE A BID	MAXIM GUN
	MAKE A BOW	

MAY QUEEN
MEAN TIME
MEAN WELL
MEAT BALL
MEAT DISH
MEAT LOAF
MEAT PIES
MEAT SAFE
MELT AWAY
MELT DOWN
MEN OF OLD
MEN'S WEAR
MERE IDEA
MERE LUCK
MERRY MEN
MESS BILL
MESSED UP
MESS ROOM
METAL BOX
METAL CAP
MEWS FLAT
MILD BEER
MILE RACE
MILES OUT
MILK BARS
MILK BILL
MILK DIET
MILK JUGS
MILK LOAF
MILK MAID
MILK PAIL
MILKY WAY
MILL GIRL
MILL HILL
MILL POND
MIME SHOW
MIND'S EYE
MINE HOST
MING VASE
MINK COAT
MINK FARM
MINK WRAP
MINOR KEY
MINUS ONE
MINUS TWO
MISS OTIS
MIXED BAG
MIXED LOT
MOBY DICK
MODEL HAT
MONA LISA
MOOT CASE
MOPPED UP
MORAL LAW
MORE TIME
MORT SAHL

MOSS ROSE
MOTH BALL
MOT JUSTE
MOTOR OIL
MOURN FOR
MOUSE MAT
MOVE AWAY
MOVE BACK
MOVED OFF
MOVED OUT
MOVE FAST
MOVE OVER
MOVIE FAN
MOVING UP
MOWN DOWN
MUCH LESS
MUCH MORE
MUCH ROOM
MUCH TIME
MUD BATHS
MUDDLE ON
MUFFLE UP
MUG'S GAME
MUSE UPON
MUSK ROSE
MUTE SWAN
MY CHOICE
MY FRIEND
MY OLD MAN
MY PUBLIC
MYRA HESS
MYRNA LOY

N – 8

NAG'S HEAD
NAIL A LIE
NAIL BOMB
NAIL DOWN
NAIL FILE
NAKED APE
NAKED EYE
NAKED MAN
NAME PART
NATAL DAY
NAVAL ARM
NAVAL GUN
NAVAL MAN
NAVY BLUE
NAVY LIST
NAVY WEEK
NEAP TIDE
NEAR BEER
NEAR EAST
NEAR HERE
NEAR HOME

NEAR MISS
NEAR ONES
NEAR SIDE
NEON LAMP
NEON SIGN
NEON TUBE
NEST EGGS
NET PRICE
NET SALES
NET VALUE
NEVER END
NEW ANGLE
NEW BALLS
NEW BIRTH
NEW BLOOD
NEW BRAND
NEW BREAD
NEW BREED
NEW BROOM
NEW CROSS
NEW DELHI
NEW DRESS
NEW FACES
NEW FLINT
NEW FRANC
NEW HEART
NEW HOUSE
NEW IDEAS
NEW ISSUE
NEW LAMPS
NEW LIGHT
NEW MODEL
NEW MONEY
NEW NOVEL
NEW ORDER
NEW OWNER
NEW PENNY
NEW PUPIL
NEW SHOES
NEW SHOOT
NEWS ITEM
NEWS ROOM
NEW STAGE
NEW STOCK
NEW STYLE
NEW SUITS
NEW TOWNS
NEW TRAIL
NEW TRIAL
NEW TRICK
NEW TYRES
NEW VISTA
NEW WOMAN
NEW WORLD
NEXT BEST
NEXT DOOR

NEXT MOVE	NOT AS YET	OLD FLAME
NEXT PAGE	NOT AT ALL	OLD FOGEY
NEXT RACE	NOT A WHIT	OLD FOLKS
NEXT STEP	NOTE DOWN	OLD FRUIT
NEXT TIME	NOTE WELL	OLD GIRLS
NEXT WEEK	NO THANKS	OLD GLORY
NEXT YEAR	NOT LEAST	OLD GUARD
NICE MESS	NOT OFTEN	OLD HABIT
NICE TIME	NOT QUITE	OLD HANDS
NICE WORK	NO TRUMPS	OLD HARRY
NIGHT AIR	NOT SO BAD	OLD HAUNT
NIGHT OFF	NOT SO HOT	OLD HEADS
NIGHT OUT	NOT TODAY	OLD MAIDS
NINE DAYS	NOT VALID	OLD MOORE
NINE DEEP	NO WAY OUT	OLD ORDER
NINE ELMS	NOW FOR IT	OLD ROGER
NINE FEET	NO WONDER	OLD SALTS
NINE QUID	NUT BROWN	OLD SARUM
NINTH DAY	NUT CASES	OLD SCORE
NINTH ROW		OLD SCREW
NINTH TEE		OLD STOCK
NIP OF GIN	**O – 8**	OLD STORY
NO ACCENT		OLD STYLE
NOAH'S ARK	OAK CHEST	OLD SWEAT
NO ANSWER	OAK TREES	OLD THING
NO APPEAL	OCEAN BED	OLD TIMER
NO BETTER	ODD MONEY	OLD TIMES
NOBLE ART	ODD SIGHT	OLD TRICK
NO BOTHER	ODD TRICK	OLD TUNES
NO CHANCE	OF COURSE	OLD WITCH
NO CHANGE	OFF AND ON	OLD WOMAN
NO CHARGE	OFF BREAK	OLD WORLD
NO CHOICE	OFF DRINK	OLIVE OIL
NO COLOUR	OFF DRIVE	ON A BINGE
NO DESIRE	OFF GUARD	ON A CHAIR
NO EFFECT	OFF PITCH	ON A LEVEL
NO EFFORT	OFF SALES	ON AND OFF
NO ESCAPE	OFF SHORE	ON A PLATE
NO EXCUSE	OFF STAGE	ON A SLOPE
NO FUTURE	OFF STUMP	ON A TABLE
NO-GO AREA	OFF TO BED	ON A VISIT
NO LONGER	OFF TO SEA	ONCE A DAY
NO MATTER	OIL DRUMS	ONCE MORE
NONE LEFT	OIL LAMPS	ONCE ONLY
NO NERVES	OIL STOVE	ONCE OVER
NO OBJECT	OIL WELLS	ON COURSE
NO OPTION	OLD BIRDS	ON CREDIT
NO QUORUM	OLD BLUES	ON DEMAND
NO REMEDY	OLD BONES	ONE BY ONE
NO RETURN	OLD BOOTS	ONE DOZEN
NORTH END	OLD CHINA	ONE ENTRY
NORTH SEA	OLD CROCK	ONE FIFTH
NO SECRET	OLD CRONY	ONE GROSS
NOSED OUT	OLD DEBTS	ONE HEART
NOTA BENE	OLD DRESS	ONE IN SIX
NOT A SOUL	OLD DUTCH	ONE IN TEN
	OLD FACES	

ONE IN TWO	ON THE SEA	P – 8
ONE MATCH	ON THE SET	
ONE MONTH	ON THE SLY	PACK A GUN
ONE NINTH	ON THE TOP	PACKED UP
ONE OR TWO	ON THE WAY	PACK IT IN
ONE OUNCE	ON TIP-TOE	PACK IT UP
ONE PENNY	ON VELVET	PAGAN GOD
ONE PIECE	ON WHEELS	PAGE FIVE
ONE POINT	OPEN ARMS	PAGE FOUR
ONE POUND	OPEN BOAT	PAGE NINE
ONE QUART	OPEN BOOK	PAID BACK
ONE ROUND	OPEN CITY	PAID CASH
ONE'S DUTY	OPEN DOOR	PAID LESS
ONE'S HOST	OPENED UP	PAID MORE
ONE SIXTH	OPEN EYES	PAINT OUT
ONE SPADE	OPEN FIRE	PAINT POT
ONE STONE	OPEN GAME	PAIR BOND
ONE'S WORD	OPEN GATE	PAIRS OFF
ONE TENTH	OPEN GOAL	PALE BLUE
ONE THIRD	OPEN HAND	PALE FACE
ONE TOUCH	OPEN LAND	PALE PINK
ONE TRICK	OPEN MIND	PALL MALL
ONE UNDER	OPEN NOTE	PALM TREE
ONE VERSE	OPEN ROAD	PANDA CAR
ONE VOICE	OPEN SHOP	PAPER BAG
ONE WHEEL	OPENS OUT	PAPER HAT
ON FRIDAY	OPEN TART	PAPER WAR
ONLY A FEW	OPEN TOWN	PARDON ME
ONLY HOPE	OPEN VOTE	PARK LANE
ONLY JUST	OPEN WIDE	PART SONG
ONLY ONCE	OPEN WORK	PART TIME
ON MONDAY	OPERA HAT	PART WITH
ON MY LIFE	OPIUM DEN	PARTY MAN
ON ONE LEG	OPTED OUT	PAR VALUE
ON PARADE	ORB OF DAY	PASS A LAW
ON PAROLE	ORDER OFF	PASS AWAY
ON PATROL	ORDER OUT	PASS BACK
ON POINTS	ORDER TEA	PASS BOOK
ON RECORD	OUT AT SEA	PASS DOWN
ON REMAND	OUT FIRST	PASSED BY
ON SAFARI	OUT OF BED	PASSED ON
ON SKATES	OUT OF GAS	PASSED UP
ON STILTS	OUT OF OIL	PASS IT ON
ON STRIKE	OUT OF USE	PASS LAWS
ON SUNDAY	OUT TO WIN	PASS OVER
ON TARGET	OVEN BIRD	PAST CURE
ON THE AIR	OVEN DOOR	PAST HELP
ON THE DOT	OVERDO IT	PAST HOPE
ON THE EBB	OVER HERE	PAST LIFE
ON THE HOB	OVER MUCH	PAST TIME
ON THE HOP	OVER SEAS	PAST WORK
ON THE JOB	OVER WE GO	PAUL MUNI
ON THE MAP	OWE MONEY	PAY A CALL
ON THE MAT	OX TONGUE	PAY A FINE
ON THE NOD		PAY CLAIM
ON THE RUN		PAY CORPS

PAY COURT	PIPE DOWN	POOR LAND
PAY EXTRA	PLACE BET	POOR LAWS
PAY FOR IT	PLAIN BOX	POOR MAKE
PAY PAUSE	PLAIN MAN	POOR RATE
PAYS BACK	PLANT OUT	POOR RISK
PAYS CASH	PLAN WELL	POOR SHOT
PAY SHEET	PLAY AWAY	POOR SHOW
PAY WAGES	PLAY BACK	POOR SIDE
PEA GREEN	PLAY BALL	POOR SOIL
PEAK FORM	PLAY DICE	POOR SOUL
PEAK HOUR	PLAY DOWN	POOR VIEW
PEAR TREE	PLAYED ON	POPE JOHN
PEAT FIRE	PLAY FAIR	POPE PAUL
PEAT MOSS	PLAY FLAT	POP MUSIC
PEDAL BIN	PLAY GOLF	POPPY DAY
PEER GYNT	PLAY HARD	POP SONGS
PEGGY LEE	PLAY HIGH	POP STARS
PEGS AWAY	PLAY HOST	PORE OVER
PEN NAMES	PLAY POLO	PORK CHOP
PENNY BUN	PLAY SAFE	PORK PIES
PEP PILLS	PLAY SNAP	PORT ARMS
PEP TALKS	PLAYS OFF	PORT BEAM
PER ANNUM	PLAY SOLO	PORT ERIN
PERKED UP	PLAY TRAY	PORT SAID
PETER MAY	PLAY UP TO	PORT SIDE
PETER OUT	PLAY WELL	PORT WINE
PETER PAN	PLAY WITH	POST FREE
PET HOBBY	PLEASE GO	POT HERBS
PET NAMES	PLUG AWAY	POT OF JAM
PET SHOPS	PLUM CAKE	POT OF TEA
PHASE ONE	PLUM DUFF	POT ROAST
PHASE TWO	PLUNGE IN	POT SHOTS
PHONE BOX	PLUS SIGN	POURS OUT
PHONE-INS	POINT MAN	POWER CUT
PIANO KEY	POINT OUT	PRAISE BE
PICKED UP	POKED FUN	PRESS BOX
PICK IT UP	POLE JUMP	PREY UPON
PICKS OFF	POLE STAR	PRICE CUT
PICKS OUT	POLISH UP	PRICE WAR
PIE MAKER	POLKA DOT	PRIME CUT
PIG SWILL	POLO NECK	PRIX FIXE
PILE ARMS	POLO PONY	PRO FORMA
PILE IT ON	PONY CLUB	PROUD DAY
PINE AWAY	PONY RACE	PROUD MAN
PINE CONE	POOL ROOM	PUB CRAWL
PINE TREE	POOLS WIN	PUB HOURS
PINK COAT	POOR CAST	PUFF AWAY
PINK GINS	POOR CHAP	PUFFED UP
PINK GLOW	POOR CROP	PULL AWAY
PINK SPOT	POOR DEAL	PULL BACK
PIN MONEY	POOR DEAR	PULL DOWN
PINNED IN	POOR FISH	PULLED IN
PINNED UP	POOR FOLK	PULLED UP
PINS DOWN	POOR GAME	PULL HARD
PINT POTS	POOR HAND	PULL OVER
PINT SIZE	POOR JOHN	PULLS OFF

PULLS OUT	RAG TRADE	RED SOCKS
PUMPED UP	RAIN HARD	RED SPOTS
PUMP IRON	RAINY DAY	RED STAMP
PUNK ROCK	RAKE OVER	RED SUITS
PUPPY FAT	RAMS HOME	REEF KNOT
PURE GOLD	RANK HIGH	REELS OFF
PURE WOOL	RAP GROUP	REG DIXON
PUSH AWAY	RAP SHEET	RELY UPON
PUSH BACK	RARA AVIS	RENT ACTS
PUSH DOWN	RARE BIRD	RENT BOOK
PUSH HARD	RARE GIFT	RENT FREE
PUSH OVER	RAT'S TAIL	RENT ROLL
PUSH PAST	RATTLE ON	REST CAMP
PUSSY CAT	RAW DEALS	REST CURE
PUT ABOUT	RAW EDGES	REST HOME
PUT ASIDE	RAW STEAK	RHUM BABA
PUT FORTH	REACH OUT	RICE CROP
PUT ON TOP	READ OVER	RICE DISH
PUT RIGHT	READ WELL	RICH AUNT
PUTS AWAY	READY CUT	RICH FARE
PUTS BACK	READY FOR	RICH FOLK
PUTS DOWN	READY PEN	RICH FOOD
PUTS OVER	READY WIT	RICH HAUL
PUTS UPON	REAL GOLD	RICH JOKE
PUT TO BED	REAL LIFE	RICH LAND
PUT TO SEA	REAL SELF	RICH MILK
PUT TO USE	REAL SILK	RICH SEAM
PUT-UP JOB	REAL TEST	RICH SOIL
	REAR RANK	RICH VEIN
	REAR VIEW	RICH WIFE
Q – 8	RECKON ON	RIDE AWAY
	RECKON UP	RIDE DOWN
QUART POT	RED ADAIR	RIDE HARD
QUEEN ANT	RED ALERT	RIDE OVER
QUEEN BEE	RED BARON	RIGHT ARM
QUEEN MAB	RED BERET	RIGHT EAR
QUEUED UP	RED BERRY	RIGHT EYE
QUICK EAR	RED BIDDY	RIGHT LEG
QUICK EYE	RED BLOOD	RIGHT MAN
QUICK ONE	RED BRICK	RIGHT OFF
QUICK WIT	RED CHINA	RIGHT OUT
QUIET END	RED CROSS	RIGHT SET
QUILL PEN	RED DWARF	RIGHT WAY
QUITE MAD	RED FACES	RING ROAD
QUIT RENT	RED LABEL	RINGS OFF
QUIZ GAME	RED LIGHT	RINGS OUT
QUIZ KIDS	RED MAPLE	RING TRUE
QUIZ TEAM	RED OCHRE	RINSE OUT
QUO VADIS?	RED PAINT	RIPE CORN
	RED PERIL	RIPE LIPS
	RED PIECE	RISE LATE
R – 8	RED QUEEN	RISEN SUN
	RED ROSES	RIVER CAM
RACE AWAY	RED SAILS	RIVER DAM
RACE CARD	RED SCARE	RIVER DEE
RADIO HAM	RED SHIRT	RIVER DON
RADIO SET		
RAG DOLLS		

RIVER EXE
RIVER GOD
RIVER TAY
RIVER USK
RIVER WYE
ROAD FUND
ROAD HOGS
ROAD HUMP
ROAD MAPS
ROAD RACE
ROAD SHOW
ROAD SIGN
ROAD TEST
ROAST PIG
ROB A BANK
ROCK CAKE
ROD LAVER
ROLE PLAY
ROLL BACK
ROLL CALL
ROLLED IN
ROLLED UP
ROLL OVER
ROMAN GOD
ROMAN LAW
ROMP HOME
ROOM MATE
ROOT CROP
ROOTS OUT
ROPED OFF
ROPE'S END
ROSE BOWL
ROSE BUSH
ROSE PINK
ROSY GLOW
ROUGH CUT
ROUGH MAP
ROUGH OUT
ROUGH SEA
ROUND BOX
ROUND OFF
ROUND ONE
ROUND PEG
ROUND SIX
ROUND SUM
ROUNDS UP
ROUND TEN
ROUND TIN
ROUND TWO
ROW A RACE
ROYAL BOX
ROYAL OAK
RUB ALONG
RUBBED IN
RUB NOSES
RUBS DOWN

RUBS IT IN
RUBY LIPS
RUBY PORT
RUDE WORD
RULED OUT
RUM PUNCH
RUM START
RUN ABOUT
RUN AFTER
RUN AHEAD
RUN ALONG
RUN A MILE
RUN AMUCK
RUN A RACE
RUN A RISK
RUN FOR IT
RUN RISKS
RUN ROUND
RUNS AWAY
RUNS BACK
RUNS DOWN
RUNS HARD
RUN SHORT
RUNS INTO
RUNS OVER
RUNS RIOT
RUNS WILD
RUN THIRD
RUN TO FAT
RUSH AWAY
RUSH HOUR
RUSH INTO
RUSH MATS
RYDER CUP
RYE BREAD

S – 8

SABRE JET
SACK RACE
SADDLE UP
SAD HEART
SAD SIGHT
SAD SONGS
SAD STORY
SAD TO SAY
SAD WORLD
SAFE AREA
SAFE SEAT
SAFE SIDE
SAIL AWAY
SAINT DAY
SALAD OIL
SALE ROOM
SALES TAX
SALT AWAY

SALT BEEF
SALT LAKE
SALT MINE
SALT PORK
SAME DATE
SAME KIND
SAME MIND
SAME NAME
SAME TIME
SAME VEIN
SAM SMALL
SAND DUNE
SANK DOWN
SAVE FACE
SAVE TIME
SAVING UP
SAXE BLUE
SAY GRACE
SCALED UP
SCENE ONE
SCENE TWO
SCENT OUT
SCOOP OUT
SCORE OFF
SCORE OUT
SCOT FREE
SCOUT OUT
SCRAPE UP
SCRUB OUT
SEA COAST
SEA FEVER
SEA FLOOR
SEA GREEN
SEALED UP
SEA LORDS
SEA NYMPH
SEA POWER
SEA SCOUT
SEA SPRAY
SEA STORY
SEAT BELT
SEA WATER
SEA WINDS
SEE ABOUT
SEE AFTER
SEE AHEAD
SEED CAKE
SEE IT ALL
SEE IT OUT
SEEKS OUT
SEEM REAL
SEE NO ONE
SEES LIFE
SEE STARS
SEIZED UP
SELF HELP

SELL DEAR
SELLS OFF
SELLS OUT
SELL WELL
SEND AWAY
SEND BACK
SEND DOWN
SEND HELP
SEND HOME
SEND WORD
SENNA POD
SENNA TEA
SERVE ILL
SERVE OUT
SET ABOUT
SET AFOOT
SET APART
SET ASIDE
SET A TRAP
SET BOOKS
SET FORTH
SET GOING
SET IDEAS
SET LUNCH
SET MEALS
SET PAPER
SET PIECE
SET PLANS
SET POINT
SET PRICE
SET RIGHT
SET SCENE
SETS DOWN
SETS FOOT
SETS FREE
SET SMILE
SETS SAIL
SET STARE
SETS UPON
SET TERMS
SETTLE IN
SETTLE UP
SEVEN MEN
SEWER RAT
SHAKEN UP
SHAKE OFF
SHAKE OUT
SHARE OUT
SHARP EAR
SHARP END
SHARP EYE
SHARP WIT
SHEER OFF
SHELL OUT
SHIN BONE
SHIP AHOY

SHIP OARS
SHIP'S LOG
SHOE HORN
SHOE LANE
SHOE RACK
SHOE SHOP
SHOO AWAY
SHOOT LOW
SHOOT OUT
SHOOTS UP
SHOP BELL
SHOP GIRL
SHORT CUT
SHORT LEG
SHORT ONE
SHORT RUN
SHOT AWAY
SHOT DEAD
SHOT DOWN
SHOT SILK
SHOUT OUT
SHOVE OFF
SHOW A LEG
SHOW BOAT
SHOW CASE
SHOW DOWN
SHOWED UP
SHOW FEAR
SHOW GIRL
SHOWN OFF
SHOWN OUT
SHOW OVER
SHOW PITY
SHOW ROOM
SHRUG OFF
SHUT DOWN
SHUTS OFF
SHUTS OUT
SHY CHILD
SHY SMILE
SHY THING
SHY WOMAN
SICK JOKE
SICK LIST
SICK ROOM
SIDE ARMS
SIDE BETS
SIDE DISH
SIDE DOOR
SIDE DRUM
SIDE GATE
SIDE LINE
SIDE ROAD
SIDE SHOW
SIDE VIEW
SIDE WIND

SIDE WITH
SIEGE CAP
SIGN AWAY
SIGNED ON
SIGN HERE
SIGNS OFF
SILK GOWN
SILLY ASS
SING HIGH
SING SING
SINGS OUT
SINK BACK
SINK DOWN
SINN FEIN
SIT ABOUT
SIT ERECT
SIT IT OUT
SITS BACK
SITS DOWN
SIT STILL
SIT TIGHT
SIT UNDER
SITZ BATH
SIX CLUBS
SIX DOZEN
SIX GROSS
SIX HOLES
SIX HOURS
SIX MILES
SIX PARTS
SIX PINTS
SIX SCORE
SIXTH DAY
SIXTH ROW
SIXTH TEE
SIX TIMES
SIX WEEKS
SIX YEARS
SIZE FIVE
SIZE FOUR
SIZE NINE
SKI BOOTS
SKIM OVER
SKIN DEEP
SKIN GAME
SKI PANTS
SKIP OVER
SKIVE OFF
SKY PILOT
SLACK OFF
SLAG HEAP
SLAM DUNK
SLAP DOWN
SLEEP OFF
SLEEP OUT
SLEEPS IN

SLEEPS ON	SOBER MAN	SPIN A WEB
SLING OFF	SOB STORY	SPINS OUT
SLING OUT	SOB STUFF	SPION KOP
SLINGS IN	SOFT BALL	SPLIT PIN
SLIP AWAY	SOFT DRUG	SPLITS UP
SLIP BACK	SOFTEN UP	SPONGE ON
SLIP INTO	SOFT EYES	SPOON FED
SLIP KNOT	SOFT HAIR	SPORT AID
SLIP PAST	SOFT ROCK	SPOT CASH
SLIPS OFF	SOFT ROES	SPRING UP
SLIPS OUT	SOFT SEAT	SPRUCE UP
SLIT OPEN	SOFT SELL	SPUN GOLD
SLOG AWAY	SOFT SKIN	SPUN SILK
SLOPE OFF	SOFT SOAP	SPUN YARN
SLOPES UP	SOFT SPOT	SQUAD CAR
SLOP OVER	SOFT TOYS	SQUARE UP
SLOW BALL	SOFT WORD	STAFF CAR
SLOW BOAT	SOHO FAIR	STAGE ONE
SLOW DOWN	SOLD A PUP	STAGE SET
SLOWED UP	SOLE HEIR	STAG HUNT
SLOW PACE	SOLO CALL	STAKE OUT
SLOW TIME	SOME GOOD	ST ALBANS
SLUM AREA	SOME MORE	STALE AIR
SLY JOKES	SONG BIRD	STALE BUN
SMALL ADS	SONG HITS	STALL OFF
SMALL BOY	SONNY BOY	STAMP ACT
SMALL CAR	SON OF GOD	STAMP OUT
SMALL EGG	SORE EYES	STAND FOR
SMALL FRY	SORE FEET	STAND OFF
SMALL GIN	SORE HEAD	STAND OUT
SMALL MAN	SORE NEED	STAND PAT
SMALL RUM	SORRY END	ST ANDREW
SMALL SUM	SORTS OUT	STANDS BY
SMALL WAY	SO SIMPLE	STANDS IN
SMART LAD	SOUL FOOD	STANDS TO
SMART MAN	SOUND BET	STANDS UP
SMART SET	SOUND BID	STAR PART
SMASH HIT	SOUND BOX	START OFF
SMELL OUT	SOUND MAN	START OUT
SMOG MASK	SOUR LOOK	STAR TREK
SMOKE OUT	SOUR MILK	STARTS UP
SNACK BAR	SOUTH SEA	STAR TURN
SNAKE PIT	SOYA BEAN	STAR WARS
SNAP VOTE	SPACE AGE	STAVE OFF
SNATCH UP	SPACE MAN	STAY AWAY
SNEAK OFF	SPACE OUT	STAY COOL
SNEAK OUT	SPARE BED	STAY DOWN
SNEAKS IN	SPARE MAN	STAYED IN
SNEAKS UP	SPARE RIB	STAYED UP
SNOWED IN	SPARK OFF	STAY HERE
SNOWED UP	SPEAK FOR	STAY OPEN
SNOW HILL	SPEAK OUT	STAYS PUT
SNOW LINE	SPEAKS UP	ST BRIDE'S
SNUB NOSE	SPEED COP	ST DAVID'S
SNUFF BOX	SPELL OUT	STEAK PIE
SNUFF OUT	SPILT INK	STEEL BAR

STEEL NIB
STEN GUNS
STEP BACK
STEP DOWN
STEP INTO
STEP IT UP
STEP ON IT
STEP OVER
STEPS OUT
ST GEORGE
ST GILES'S
ST HELENA
ST HELEN'S
ST HELIER
STICK OUT
STICKS TO
STICKS UP
STIFF LEG
ST JAMES'S
ST MORITZ
STOCK CAR
STONE AGE
STOP AWAY
STOP DEAD
STOP HERE
STOP HOME
STOP OVER
STOP PLAY
STOPS OFF
STOPS OUT
STOP WORK
STOUT MAN
STOW AWAY
ST PETER'S
STRAW HAT
STRAY CAT
STRAY DOG
STREAK BY
STREAK IN
STREAM BY
STREAM IN
STRIKE UP
STRING UP
STRIP OFF
STROLL BY
STRUCK ON
STRUNG UP
STUD BOOK
STUD FARM
STUDY ART
STUDY LAW
STUMPS UP
STUNT MAN
SUGAR RAY
SUMMED UP
SUMMON UP

SUMS IT UP
SUM TOTAL
SUNNY DAY
SUNNY JIM
SUN SPOTS
SUN'S RAYS
SURE CURE
SURE GAIN
SURE LOSS
SURE SHOT
SWAN LAKE
SWAN SONG
SWAP NEWS
SWAT TEAM
SWEAR OFF
SWEARS IN
SWEEP OUT
SWEEPS UP
SWEET AIR
SWEET PEA
SWEET SUE
SWEET TEA
SWELL MOB
SWELL OUT
SWELLS UP
SWIM SUIT
SWINE FLU
SWING LOW
SWITCH ON

T – 8

TABBY CAT
TABLE BAY
TAG ALONG
TAIL AWAY
TAIL COAT
TAIL WIND
TAJ MAHAL
TAKE A BOW
TAKE A BUS
TAKE A CAB
TAKE A NAP
TAKE A NIP
TAKE A PEW
TAKE A TIP
TAKE A VOW
TAKE AWAY
TAKE BACK
TAKE BETS
TAKE CARE
TAKE DOWN
TAKE FIRE
TAKE FOOD
TAKE HEED
TAKE HOLD

TAKE IT IN
TAKE IT UP
TAKE LIFE
TAKEN ILL
TAKEN OFF
TAKE NOTE
TAKEN OUT
TAKE ODDS
TAKE OVER
TAKE PART
TAKE PITY
TAKE ROOT
TAKES AIM
TAKE SILK
TAKES OFF
TAKES OUT
TAKE THAT
TAKE THIS
TAKE TIME
TAKE TOLL
TAKE VOWS
TAKE WINE
TAKE WING
TAKING IN
TALK A LOT
TALK BACK
TALK BOSH
TALK DOWN
TALK OVER
TALKS BIG
TALK SHOP
TALL GIRL
TALL TALE
TALL TALK
TALL TREE
TANK TRAP
TAPAS BAR
TAP DANCE
TAPER OFF
TAP WATER
TAUT ROPE
TAWNY OWL
TAX BREAK
TAX EXILE
TAX HAVEN
TAXI FARE
TAXI RANK
TEA BREAK
TEA CADDY
TEACH ART
TEA DANCE
TEA IN BED
TEAMED UP
TEAM GAME
TEAM MATE
TEAM WORK

TEA PARTY	THE CHAIR	THE SHORE
TEAR DOWN	THE CHASE	THE SOMME
TEAR IT UP	THE CLOTH	THE SOUTH
TEAR OPEN	THE CONGO	THE SPURS
TEA ROSES	THE COUNT	THE STAGE
TEARS OFF	THE CREED	THE STAKE
TEA SHOPS	THE CROWN	THE STARS
TEDDY BOY	THE DALES	THE SUDAN
TED HEATH	THE DERBY	THE THING
TEE SHOTS	THE DEVIL	THE TIMES
TELL A FIB	THE DOWNS	THE TOWER
TELL A LIE	THE DRAMA	THE TWINS
TELL LIES	THE DUTCH	THE TWIST
TELLS OFF	THE EARTH	THE URALS
TEN CENTS	THE ELITE	THE USUAL
TEN DOZEN	THE ENEMY	THE VOLGA
TEN GROSS	THE FACTS	THE WAITS
TEN HOURS	THE FATES	THE WAY IN
TEN MARKS	THE FIELD	THE WEALD
TEN MILES	THE FILMS	THE WELSH
TEN PARTS	THE FIRST	THE WILDS
TEN SCORE	THE FLEET	THE WOLDS
TENSED UP	THE FLOOD	THE WORLD
TENTH DAY	THE GOODS	THE WORKS
TENTH MAN	THE GOONS	THE WORST
TENTH ROW	THE GRAVE	THICK EAR
TENTH TEE	THE GREAT	THICK FOG
TEN TIMES	THE GREYS	THIN COAT
TEN TO ONE	THE GROOM	THIN DOWN
TEN TO SIX	THE HAGUE	THIN EDGE
TEN TO TEN	THE HAVES	THIN HAIR
TEN TO TWO	THE HOUSE	THINK BIG
TEN WEEKS	THE IDEAL	THINK FIT
TEN YEARS	THE IDIOT	THINK OUT
TERM TIME	THE IRISH	THINKS UP
TEST CASE	THE JOKER	THIN SKIN
TEST TUBE	THE KORAN	THIN TIME
TEXAS TEA	THE LIMIT	THIN WIRE
TEXT BOOK	THE LOCAL	THIRD ACT
THANK GOD	THE LORDS	THIRD AGE
THANK YOU	THE LOSER	THIRD DAY
THAT SIDE	THE MAFIA	THIRD MAN
THE ANDES	THE MITRE	THIRD ROW
THE ANGEL	THE MOORS	THIRD SET
THE ASHES	THE MUSES	THIRD TEE
THE BELLS	THE NORTH	THIS IS IT
THE BENCH	THE NOVEL	THIS SIDE
THE BIBLE	THE PANEL	THIS TIME
THE BLIND	THE POINT	THIS WEEK
THE BLITZ	THE POOLS	THIS YEAR
THE BLUES	THE PRESS	THREE MEN
THE BRAVE	THE RAINS	THROWN IN
THE BRIDE	THE RIGHT	THROW OFF
THE BRINY	THE ROPES	THROW OUT
THE BRONX	THE SAINT	THUMBS UP
THE BUFFS	THE SHAKE	TICK OVER

TICKS OFF	TOO LARGE	TRAP FIVE
TIDE MARK	TOON ARMY	TRAP FOUR
TIDE OVER	TOO QUICK	TRIAL RUN
TIDIED UP	TOO SHARP	TRIED OUT
TIDY MIND	TOO SMALL	TRIM AWAY
TIE A KNOT	TOO STEEP	TRIP OVER
TIED DOWN	TOOTH OUT	TROOP OFF
TIED GAME	TOP BRASS	TROOP OUT
TIGER BAY	TOP FLOOR	TROTS OFF
TIGER CUB	TOP FORTY	TROTS OUT
TIGER RAG	TOP LAYER	TRUE BILL
TIGHT FIT	TOP MARKS	TRUE BLUE
TILL THEN	TOP NOTCH	TRUE COPY
TILT OVER	TOP NOTES	TRUE HEIR
TIME BASE	TOPPED UP	TRUE LOVE
TIME BOMB	TOP PLACE	TRUE TIME
TIME CARD	TOP PRICE	TRUE WORD
TIME FUSE	TOP PRIZE	TRY AGAIN
TIME IS UP	TOP RATES	TRY FOR IT
TIME TEST	TOP SCORE	TRY IT OUT
TIME TO GO	TOP SHELF	TRY TO SAY
TIMOR SEA	TOP SPEED	TUB CHAIR
TIN LIZZY	TOP SPOTS	TUCK AWAY
TIN MINES	TOP STAIR	TUCKED IN
TINY HAND	TOP TABLE	TUCKED UP
TINY MITE	TOP TO TOE	TUCK SHOP
TINY TOTS	TORY GAIN	TUG ALONG
TIPPED UP	TORY LOSS	TUG OF WAR
TIP TO TOE	TOSS AWAY	TUNA WARS
TIP TO WIN	TOSSED UP	TURN AWAY
TIRED MAN	TOTAL SUM	TURN BACK
TIRED OUT	TOTAL WAR	TURN BLUE
TIRED TIM	TOTE A GUN	TURN COLD
TO A FAULT	TOTE ODDS	TURN DOWN
TO AND FRO	TO THE BAD	TURNED IN
TO BE SURE	TO THE END	TURNED ON
TOBY JUGS	TO THE TOP	TURNED UP
TODDLE IN	TOT OF RUM	TURN GREY
TODDLE UP	TOTTED UP	TURN INTO
TOE TO TOE	TOTTER UP	TURN IT IN
TOLL CALL	TOUCH OFF	TURN IT ON
TOM BROWN	TOUGH GUY	TURN IT UP
TOM HANKS	TOUGH JOB	TURN LEFT
TOM JONES	TOUGH NUT	TURN OVER
TOMMY GUN	TOW ALONG	TURN PALE
TOMMY ROT	TOWN HALL	TURNS OFF
TOM PINCH	TOWN LIFE	TURN SOFT
TOM THUMB	TOWN TALK	TURN SOUR
TOM WALLS	TOY MAKER	TURNS OUT
TO MY MIND	TOY SHOPS	TURN TAIL
TONE DEAF	TOY TRAIN	TURN UPON
TONE DOWN	TRADE GAP	TV AERIAL
TONE POEM	TRAD JAZZ	TWICE ONE
TON-UP BOY	TRAIL OFF	TWICE SHY
TOO EAGER	TRAIN SET	TWICE SIX
TOO EARLY	TRAM STOP	TWICE TEN

TWICE TWO
TWIN BEDS
TWIN BOYS
TWO BRACE
TWO BY TWO
TWO CARDS
TWO CLUBS
TWO DOZEN
TWO GROSS
TWO HANDS
TWO HEADS
TWO HOLES
TWO HOURS
TWO IN ONE
TWO LUMPS
TWO MILES
TWO MINDS
TWO PAGES
TWO PAIRS
TWO PARTS
TWO PINTS
TWO PUTTS
TWO RANKS
TWO SCORE
TWO SIDES
TWO STARS
TWO TO ONE
TWO WEEKS
TWO WIVES
TWO WORDS
TWO YARDS
TWO YEARS
TYPE SIZE

U – 8

UGLY FACE
UGLY LOOK
UGLY MOOD
UGLY SCAR
UNCLE MAC
UNCLE SAM
UNCLE TOM
UNCUT GEM
UNDER AGE
UNDER PAR
UNDER WAY
UNTIL NOW
UPAS TREE
UP AT DAWN
UP IN ARMS
UP ON HIGH
UPON OATH
UPPER AIR
UPPER CUT
UPPER JAW

UPPER LIP
UPPER SET
UPPER TEN
UP STREAM
UP TO DATE
UP TO FORM
UP TO TIME
USED CARS
USED HALF
USED TO IT
USE FORCE
USHER OUT
USHERS IN
USUAL WAY
UTTER CAD

V – 8

VAIN HOPE
VAIN SHOW
VAST SIZE
VEER AWAY
VEER LEFT
VERA CRUZ
VERA LYNN
VERSED IN
VERY BEST
VERY COLD
VERY DEAR
VERY FAIR
VERY FULL
VERY GOOD
VERY HARD
VERY KEEN
VERY KIND
VERY LATE
VERY MANY
VERY MUCH
VERY NEAR
VERY NICE
VERY POOR
VERY RICH
VERY SLOW
VERY SOFT
VERY SOON
VERY TRUE
VERY WARM
VERY WELL
VINE LEAF
VIVA VOCE
VIVID RED
VOTE DOWN
VOTE TORY
VOUCH FOR

W – 8

WADE INTO
WAGE BILL
WAGED WAR
WAIT A BIT
WAITED ON
WAIT HERE
WAIT UPON
WALK AWAY
WALK BACK
WALK DOWN
WALK INTO
WALK OVER
WALK PAST
WALKS OFF
WALKS OUT
WALLED UP
WALL GAME
WALTZ OUT
WANGLE IT
WAN SMILE
WANT A LOT
WANT MORE
WAR CRIME
WAR DANCE
WARDS OFF
WAR FEVER
WAR HOUSE
WAR LORDS
WARMED UP
WARM OVEN
WARM WORK
WAR PAINT
WAR PARTY
WAR POEMS
WAR POETS
WAR SCARE
WART HOGS
WAR YEARS
WASH AWAY
WASH DOWN
WASHED UP
WATCH OUT!
WATER ICE
WATER JUG
WATER RAT
WAT TYLER
WAVE AWAY
WAVY HAIR
WAVY LINE
WAVY NAVY
WAX MATCH
WAX MERRY
WAX MODEL
WAX VESTA

WAY AHEAD
WEAK CASE
WEAK CHIN
WEAK EYES
WEAK HEAD
WEAK LINK
WEAK SIDE
WEAK SPOT
WEAK WILL
WEAR AWAY
WEAR DOWN
WEARS OFF
WEARS OUT
WEAR WELL
WEE FREES
WEIGHS UP
WELL AWAY
WELL DONE
WELL HELD
WELL MADE
WELL OVER
WELL PAID
WELL READ
WELL SAID
WELL TO DO
WELL UP IN
WELL USED
WELL WELL!
WENT AWAY
WENT BACK
WENT DOWN
WENT EAST
WENT FREE
WENT OVER
WENT WELL
WENT WEST
WEST BANK
WEST DOOR
WEST SIDE
WEST WIND
WEST WING
WET PAINT
WET PLATE
WET SHEET
WET SPELL
WHALE OIL
WHAT A FAG
WHAT IS IT
WHAT NEXT?
WHAT OF IT?
WHAT'S NEW?
WHEEL OFF
WHEEL OUT
WHICH WAY?
WHIP HAND
WHISK OFF

WHITE ANT
WHITE EGG
WHITE HOT
WHITE KEY
WHITE LIE
WHITE MAN
WHITE SEA
WHITE TIE
WHIT WEEK
WHO DUN IT?
WHOLE HOG
WHOLE LOT
WHO'S NEXT?
WHY WORRY?
WIDE BALL
WIDE BOYS
WIDE FAME
WIDE GULF
WIDE OPEN
WIDE ROAD
WIDE VIEW
WILD BIRD
WILD BLOW
WILD BOAR
WILD DUCK
WILD FOWL
WILD GOAT
WILD LIFE
WILD LOOK
WILD OATS
WILD ROSE
WILD TALK
WILD WEST
WILD WIND
WILY BIRD
WIN A GAME
WIN A RACE
WIND SOCK
WINDY DAY
WINE BARS
WINE GUMS
WINE LAKE
WINE LIST
WINE SHOP
WING HALF
WIN GLORY
WIN MONEY
WINS OVER
WIPE AWAY
WIPED OUT
WIRE MESH
WIRE WOOL
WISE GUYS
WISE HEAD
WISE MOVE
WITH CARE

WITH EASE
WITH LOVE
WITTY MAN
WOLF CALL
WOLF CUBS
WOOD FIRE
WOOD PULP
WORD GAME
WORKED UP
WORK EVIL
WORK HARD
WORK LATE
WORK OVER
WORKS OFF
WORKS OUT
WORLD CUP
WORLD WAR
WORN DOWN
WRAP IT UP
WRING DRY
WRING OUT
WRITE OFF
WRITE OUT
WRITES UP
WRONG DAY
WRONG MAN
WRONG WAY
WRY SMILE
WYCH ELMS

X – 8

X-RAY UNIT

Y – 8

YALE LOCK
YEAR BOOK
YEARN FOR
YEARS AGO
YES AND NO
YET AGAIN
YOU AND ME
YOUNG BOY
YOUNG MAN
YOUNG ONE
YOUR CALL
YOUR DEAL
YOUR MOVE
YOUR TURN
YULE LOGS

Z – 8

ZANE GREY
ZERO HOUR

ZOOM LENS
ZOOT SUIT

A – 9

AARON'S ROD
A BIT FISHY
A BIT STEEP
A BIT STIFF
A BIT THICK
ABLE TO FLY
ABLE TO PAY
ABOUT FACE
ABOUT TIME
ABOUT TURN
ABOVE ZERO
ACID HOUSE
ACID REPLY
ACKER BILK
ACT AS HOST
ACTED WELL
ACT FAIRLY
ACTING FOR
ACTION MAN
ACT OF LOVE
ACT WISELY
ACUTE PAIN
ADAM SMITH
ADAM STYLE
ADAM'S WINE
ADD A RIDER
ADD A TOUCH
ADD COLOUR
ADD FRILLS
ADDLED EGG
AD NAUSEAM
A DOG'S LIFE
AD VALOREM
AEGEAN SEA
AER LINGUS
AFTER DARK
AFTER TIME
AGILE MIND
AGONY AUNT
A GOOD DEAL
A GOOD MANY
AGREE WITH
AHOY THERE
AIMED HIGH
AIM HIGHER
AIM TO KILL
AIR BATTLE
AIR BRIDGE
AIR FILTER
AIR LETTER
AIR LOSSES

AIR PIRACY
AIR POCKET
AIR TRAVEL
ALARM BELL
ALARM CALL
ALEC WAUGH
ALERT MIND
ALICE BAND
ALICE BLUE
ALIEN CORN
ALIEN RACE
ALL ABOARD
ALL ACTION
ALL ADRIFT
ALL AGREED
ALL AROUND
ALL ASHORE
ALL AT ONCE
ALL BEHIND
ALL BLACKS
ALL BUT ONE
ALL CHANGE
ALL COMERS
ALL FOR ONE
ALL IN VAIN
ALL IS LOST
ALL IS WELL
ALL ON DECK
ALL ON EDGE
ALLOW BAIL
ALL SAINTS
ALL SERENE
ALL SQUARE
ALL THE DAY
ALL THE LOT
ALL THE WAY
ALL THUMBS
ALL TIED UP
ALLY PALLY
ALMA COGAN
ALMA MATER
ALMOND OIL
ALMOST ALL
ALPHA PLUS
ALPHA RAYS
AMPLE ROOM
AMPLE TIME
ANCHOR LEG
ANCHOR MAN
ANDY PANDY
ANGEL CAKE
ANGEL DUST
ANGEL FACE
ANGEL FISH
ANGORA CAT
ANGRY LOOK

ANIMAL CRY
ANIMAL FAT
ANIMAL OIL
ANITA LOOS
ANKLE DEEP
ANNE FRANK
ANNUAL FEE
ANY MOMENT
ANY OFFERS?
ANY TO COME
APPIAN WAY
APPLE A DAY
APPLE CART
APPLE TART
APPLE TREE
APRIL FOOL
ARAB HORSE
ARAB STEED
ARCH ENEMY
ARCH KNAVE
ARCH ROGUE
ARCH SMILE
AREA STEPS
ARID WASTE
ARMED BAND
ARMS DEPOT
ARMS LOWER
ARMS RAISE
ARMY BOOTS
ARMY CADET
ARMY CORPS
ARMY GROUP
ARMY ISSUE
ARNOLD BAX
ART CRITIC
ART DEALER
ART EDITOR
ARTIE SHAW
ART MASTER
ART MUSEUM
ART SCHOOL
ART STUDIO
AS A RESULT
ASCOT MILE
ASCOT WEEK
ASH BLONDE
ASIA MINOR
AS IT COMES
ASK ADVICE
ASK A PRICE
ASK NICELY
ASK PARDON
ASK THE WAY
AS ORDERED
ASPEN LEAF
AS PER PLAN

AS PLANNED
AS THEY SAY
AS YOU WERE
AT A CANTER
AT A GALLOP
AT A GLANCE
AT A LOW EBB
AT AN ANGLE
AT ANY RATE
AT ANY TIME
AT A PROFIT
AT LEISURE
AT LIBERTY
AT LOW TIDE
ATOMIC AGE
ATOMIC WAR
AT ONE BLOW
AT ONE TIME
AT PRESENT
AT THE BACK
AT THE BANK
AT THE BEST
AT THE DOOR
AT THE FAIR
AT THE HEAD
AT THE HELM
AT THE MAIN
AT THE MOST
AT THE NETS
AT THE OVAL
AT THE PEAK
AT THE POST
AT THE REAR
AT THE SIDE
AT THE TIME
ATTIC SALT
AUGUR WELL
AU NATUREL
AUNT SALLY
AWAY MATCH
AZURE BLUE

B – 9

BABY GRAND
BABY LINEN
BACK AGAIN
BACK ALLEY
BACK BACON
BACKED OUT
BACK OUT OF
BACK PEDAL
BACK SLANG
BACK STAGE
BACK TEETH
BACK TOOTH

BACK WATER
BACK WHEEL
BACON RIND
BAD ADVICE
BAD ATTACK
BAD CREDIT
BAD CUSTOM
BAD DRIVER
BAD ENOUGH
BAD EXCUSE
BAD FIGURE
BAD FOR ONE
BAD FRIEND
BAD HABITS
BAD HEALTH
BAD HUMOUR
BAD INTENT
BADLY DONE
BADLY DOWN
BADLY HURT
BAD MARKET
BAD MEMORY
BAD PLAYER
BAD POINTS
BAD POLICY
BAD RECORD
BAD REPORT
BAD REPUTE
BAD RESULT
BAD REVIEW
BAD SAILOR
BAD SCRAPE
BAD SEAMAN
BAD SECOND
BAD SPIRIT
BAD TEMPER
BAD TIMING
BAG OF GOLD
BAG O' NAILS
BAG THE LOT
BAKE A CAKE
BAKE A LOAF
BAKE BREAD
BALANCE UP
BALD FACTS
BALD PATCH
BALD TRUTH
BALLET FAN
BALLOT BOX
BALSA WOOD
BALTIC SEA
BAND WAGON
BANDY LEGS
BANK CLERK
BANK PAPER
BAR CODING

BARE FACTS
BARE FISTS
BARE KNEES
BARE TRUTH
BARE WALLS
BARE WORDS
BARGE INTO
BARLEY MOW
BAR MAGNET
BARMY ARMY
BARN DANCE
BAR OF IRON
BAR OF SOAP
BAR PRINTER
BARROW BOY
BAR THE WAY
BASE METAL
BASIC NEED
BASIC PLAN
BASIC WAGE
BAS RELIEF
BASS NOTES
BASS VOICE
BATH BRICK
BATH NIGHT
BATH SALTS
BATH TOWEL
BATH WATER
BATTLE BUS
BATTLE CRY
BAY LEAVES
BAY OF PIGS
BAY WINDOW
BEACH SUIT
BEACH WEAR
BE ADVISED
BE A MARTYR
BE AN ANGEL
BEAR FRUIT
BEARING UP
BEAR RIGHT
BE AT A LOSS
BE AT FAULT
BEAT MUSIC
BEAU GESTE
BEAU IDEAL
BEAU MONDE
BE A YES-MAN
BE CAREFUL
BE CERTAIN
BECOME DUE
BECOME ONE
BED CANOPY
BEDDED OUT
BED OF PAIN
BED SHEETS

BEECH TREE
BEEF CURRY
BEER MONEY
BEER ON TAP
BEER STAIN
BEET SUGAR
BEFORE ALL
BEFORE NOW
BEFORE TEA
BE FRIENDS
BEGGED OFF
BEG IN VAIN
BEGIN WELL
BEGIN WORK
BEG PARDON
BEL ESPRIT
BELL METAL
BELL TOWER
BELOW COST
BELOW ZERO
BELT ALONG
BEN JONSON
BEN LOMOND
BENNY HILL
BE ONE'S AGE
BE ONESELF
BE ON GUARD
BE PRESENT
BE PRUDENT
BERTA RUCK
BERYL GREY
BERYL REID
BE SERIOUS
BEST CHINA
BEST DRESS
BEST ENTRY
BEST GRADE
BEST OF ALL
BEST SCORE
BEST TASTE
BEST THING
BEST VALUE
BE SWEET ON
BÊTE NOIRE
BE THE BEST
BETTER MAN
BETTER OFF
BETTER 'OLE
BETTY BOOP
BETWEEN US
BEVIN BOYS
BEYOND ONE
BIG BERTHA
BIG CHANCE
BIG CHEESE
BIG DEMAND

BIG DIPPER
BIG EFFORT
BIG FREEZE
BIG HEADED
BIG MARGIN
BIG PROFIT
BIG TALKER
BILL SIKES
BILLY FURY
BILLY GOAT
BILLY LIAR
BINGO CLUB
BINGO HALL
BIRCH TREE
BIRD BRAIN
BIRD'S NEST
BIRTH MARK
BIRTH RATE
BITE TO EAT
BITING WIT
BIT OF A JOB
BIT OF A LAD
BIT OF LUCK
BITTER CUP
BITTER END
BJORN BORG
BLACK ARTS
BLACK BALL
BLACK BEAR
BLACK BELT
BLACK BESS
BLACK BOOK
BLACK FLAG
BLACK GOLD
BLACK HAIR
BLACK HAND
BLACK HOLE
BLACK JACK
BLACK KING
BLACK LACE
BLACK LEAD
BLACK LION
BLACK LIST
BLACK LOOK
BLACK MARK
BLACK MASS
BLACK MONK
BLACK MOOD
BLACK NOTE
BLACK OPAL
BLACK PAWN
BLACK ROOK
BLACK RUIN
BLACK SPOT
BLACK SUIT
BLACK SWAN

BLANK FILE
BLANK LOOK
BLANK MIND
BLANK PAGE
BLANK WALL
BLAZE AWAY
BLIND DATE
BLIND ROAD
BLIND SIDE
BLIND SPOT
BLOCK PERM
BLOCK VOTE
BLOND HAIR
BLOOD BANK
BLOOD BATH
BLOOD CLOT
BLOOD FEUD
BLOOD HEAT
BLOOD TEST
BLOOD TYPE
BLOW A FUSE
BLOW ALONG
BLOWING UP
BLUE ANGEL
BLUE BLOOD
BLUE CHIPS
BLUE GRASS
BLUE JEANS
BLUE LIGHT
BLUE MEANY
BLUE MOVIE
BLUE PAINT
BLUE PETER
BLUE PRINT
BLUE RINSE
BLUE SKIES
BLUE SOCKS
BLUES ROCK
BLUE STAMP
BLUE STEEL
BLUE STORY
BLUE WATER
BLUE WHALE
BLUNT EDGE
BOARD A BUS
BOARDED UP
BOARD GAME
BOARD ROOM
BOAR'S HEAD
BOAT DRILL
BOAT TRAIN
BOB SAWYER
BODY OF MEN
BOIL AN EGG
BOILED EGG
BOILED HAM

BOLD FRONT
BOLD LINES
BOLD PRINT
BOLSTER UP
BONA FIDES
BON CHANCE
BONE CHINA
BON MARCHÉ
BON VIVANT
BON VIVEUR
BON VOYAGE
BOOBY TRAP
BOOGIE BOX
BOOK A ROOM
BOOK A SEAT
BOOK LOVER
BOOK OF JOB
BOOK SEATS
BOOK STORE
BOOK TITLE
BOOK TOKEN
BORE A HOLE
BORN ACTOR
BORN AGAIN
BORN ALIVE
BORN MIMIC
BORN MIXER
BORN SLAVE
BOSSA NOVA
BOTANY BAY
BOTH HANDS
BOTH SIDES
BOTTLE OUT
BOTTOM DOG
BOTTOMS UP
BOUGHT OFF
BOUGHT OUT
BOUNCE OUT
BOUND BOOK
BOUND OVER
BOVVER BOY
BOWED DOWN
BOWED HEAD
BOWL ALONG
BOWLED OUT
BOWLER HAT
BOW STREET
BOW TO FATE
BOW WINDOW
BOX AND COX
BOX CAMERA
BOX CLEVER
BOXING DAY
BOX NUMBER
BOX OFFICE
BOX OF FIGS

BOY FRIEND
BOY GEORGE
BOYLE'S LAW
BRAIN WAVE
BRAKE DRUM
BRANCH OFF
BRANCH OUT
BRASS BALL
BRASS BAND
BRASS RING
BRASS TACK
BRAVE DEED
BRAVE FACE
BRAZEN OUT
BRAZIL NUT
BREAD LINE
BREAD ROLL
BREAK A LEG
BREAK AWAY
BREAK BACK
BREAK BAIL
BREAK CAMP
BREAK DOWN
BREAK EVEN
BREAK IT UP
BREAK JAIL
BREAK OPEN
BREAK STEP
BREATHE IN
BRENDA LEE
BRIAR PIPE
BRICK WALL
BRIDAL BED
BRIDE TO BE
BRIGHT BOY
BRIGHT LAD
BRIGHT RED
BRING BACK
BRING DOWN
BRING HOME
BRING OVER
BRING WORD
BRISK WALK
BRISTLE UP
BROAD BACK
BROAD BEAM
BROAD BEAN
BROAD GRIN
BROAD HINT
BROAD JOKE
BROAD MIND
BROAD VIEW
BROKEN ARM
BROKEN LEG
BROKEN MAN
BROKEN RIB

BROKEN SET
BROKE OPEN
BRONZE AGE
BROOD MARE
BROODY HEN
BROUGHT UP
BROWN BEAR
BROWN BESS
BROWN COAL
BROWN EYES
BROWN HAIR
BROWN LOAF
BROWN STEW
BROWN SUIT
BRUSH AWAY
BRUSHED UP
BRUSH DOWN
BRUSH OVER
BRUSH PAST
BUBBLE CAR
BUBBLE GUM
BUCK TEETH
BUDGET DAY
BUGLE CALL
BUGS BUNNY
BULLY BEEF
BUMBLE BEE
BUMPED OFF
BUNNY GIRL
BURGER BAR
BURGER BUN
BURKE'S LAW
BURMA ROAD
BURMA STAR
BURN A HOLE
BURN ALIVE
BURNT COKE
BURNT DOWN
BURST OPEN
BURST PIPE
BURST TYRE
BUS DRIVER
BUSH HOUSE
BUSH SKIRT
BUS STRIKE
BUS TICKET
BUSY PLACE
BUTLER ACT
BUY A HOUSE
BUY A ROUND
BUY ON TICK
BUY SHARES
BUZZ ABOUT
BUZZ ALONG
BY ACCLAIM
BY AIR MAIL

BY AUCTION	CARD PARTY	CHANCE HIT
BY COMMAND	CARD SENSE	CHASE AWAY
BY CONSENT	CARD TABLE	CHEAP FARE
BY DEFAULT	CARD TRICK	CHEAP GIFT
BY DEGREES	CARE ORDER	CHEAP JACK
BY HERSELF	CARGO SHIP	CHEAP LINE
BY HIMSELF	CARL LEWIS	CHEAP MILK
BY NO MEANS	CAROL REED	CHEAP RATE
BY NUMBERS	CARPET BAG	CHEAP SHOT
BY ONESELF	CARRIED ON	CHEAP TRIP
BY REQUEST	CARRY AWAY	CHEAP WINE
BY STEALTH	CARRY CASE	CHECK MATE
BY THE ACRE	CARRY OVER	CHECK OVER
BY THE BOOK	CARRY SAIL	CHEERED UP
BY THE HOUR	CAR STEREO	CHERRY PIE
BY THE NOSE	CAR TRIALS	CHESS CLUB
BY THE YARD	CAR WINDOW	CHIEF COOK
BY THUNDER	CARY GRANT	CHIEF HOPE
	CASHEW NUT	CHIEF MEAL
	CASH PRICE	CHIEF PART
C – 9	CASH PRIZE	CHIEF PORT
	CASH TERMS	CHIEF WHIP
CAB DRIVER	CAST ABOUT	CHILD CARE
CADDIE CAR	CAST A LOOK	CHILD STAR
CAFÉ ROYAL	CAST AN EYE	CHILD WIFE
CALF'S HEAD	CAST A SHOE	CHINA CLAY
CALL AGAIN	CAST A SHOW	CHINA DOLL
CALL A HALT	CAST ASIDE	CHINA ROSE
CALL A TAXI	CAST A SLUR	CHINA SHOP
CALLED FOR	CAST A VOTE	CHIPPED IN
CALLED OFF	CAST DOUBT	CHOICE BIT
CALLED OUT	CAST FORTH	CHOKE BACK
CALL FORTH	CAST LOOSE	CHOKE DAMP
CALL HEADS	CASTOR OIL	CHOKE DOWN
CALL IT OFF	CAT AND DOG	CHOP HOUSE
CALL MONEY	CATCH A BUS	CHOPPY SEA
CALL TAILS	CATCH COLD	CHOSEN FEW
CALM CHEEK	CATCH FIRE	CHUMP CHOP
CAME APART	CATCH FISH	CIRCUS ACT
CAME LOOSE	CAT FAMILY	CITY GATES
CAMEL WALK	CATTLE PEN	CITY STATE
CAMERA SHY	CAUGHT OUT	CIVIC DUTY
CAMP DAVID	CAUSE LIST	CIVIL CASE
CAMPED OUT	CAUSE PAIN	CIVIL CODE
CANAL BANK	CEASE FIRE	CIVIL LIFE
CANAL TURN	CEASE TO BE	CIVIL LIST
CANAL ZONE	CEASE WORK	CIVIL SUIT
CANCEL OUT	CEDAR TREE	CLAIM BACK
CANE CHAIR	CEYLON TEA	CLAMP DOWN
CANE SUGAR	CHA CHA CHA	CLAP HANDS
CANNY SCOT	CHAIN DOWN	CLARA BUTT
CAN OF BEER	CHAIN GANG	CLARET CUP
CAN OPENER	CHAIN MAIL	CLASH WITH
CAPE DUTCH	CHALKED UP	CLEAN BILL
CAPE WRATH	CHALK FARM	CLEAN BLOW
CAP IN HAND	CHALK IT UP	CLEAN DOWN
CARD INDEX		

CLEANED UP	COLD CREAM	CORAL REEF
CLEAN LIFE	COLD DRINK	CORDON OFF
CLEAR AWAY	COLD FRAME	CORNY JOKE
CLEAR CASE	COLD FRONT	COSMIC RAY
CLEARED UP	COLD HANDS	COST PRICE
CLEAR HEAD	COLD HEART	COT BUMPER
CLEAR LEAD	COLD JOINT	COT MOBILE
CLEAR MIND	COLD NIGHT	COUGHED UP
CLEAR NOTE	COLD PLATE	COUNT DOWN
CLEAR ROAD	COLD SCENT	COUNT UPON
CLEAR SOUP	COLD SNACK	COUP D'ÉTAT
CLEAR VIEW	COLD SOBER	COURT CARD
CLEVER DOG	COLD SPELL	COURT CASE
CLEVER MAN	COLD STEEL	COVERED UP
CLIMB DOWN	COLD SWEAT	COVER GIRL
CLIMB OVER	COLD WATER	COVER OVER
CLING FILM	COLLIE DOG	COWES WEEK
CLIP JOINT	COLOUR BAR	CRAB SALAD
CLOCHE HAT	COLWYN BAY	CRACK A NUT
CLOCKED IN	COME ABOUT	CRACKED UP
CLOCK GOLF	COME AFTER	CRACK OPEN
CLOG DANCE	COME AGAIN	CRACK SHOT
CLOSE CALL	COME ALIVE	CRASH DOWN
CLOSE COPY	COME ALONG	CRAZY GANG
CLOSE CROP	COME AND GO	CREAM CAKE
CLOSED CAR	COME APART	CREAM PUFF
CLOSE DOWN	COME CLEAN	CREEP AWAY
CLOSE GAME	COME CLOSE	CRESTA RUN
CLOSE LOOK	COME EARLY	CRIED DOWN
CLOSE RACE	COME FIRST	CRIED WOLF
CLOSE UPON	COME FORTH	CRIME WAVE
CLOSING IN	COME LOOSE	CROPPED UP
CLOTH EARS	COME OF AGE	CROSS FIRE
CLOTH FAIR	COME OFF IT	CROSS KEYS
CLOUD OVER	COME RIGHT	CROSS OVER
CLOUDY SKY	COME ROUND	CROSS WIND
CLUB MONEY	COME THIRD	CROUCH END
CLUB NIGHT	COME UNDER	CROUCH LOW
COACH TOUR	COMIC CUTS	CROWD WORK
COACH TRIP	COMIC MASK	CROWN CORK
COAL BLACK	COMIC MUSE	CROWN LAND
COAL BOARD	COMIC SONG	CROW'S FEET
COAL FIELD	COMING MAN	CROW'S NEST
COAL TRUCK	COMING OUT	CRUDE JOKE
COAST ROAD	COMMON END	CRUDE SALT
COCKED HAT	COMMON LAW	CRUEL BLOW
COCK ROBIN	COMMON LOT	CRUEL FATE
COCOA BEAN	COMMON MAN	CRUMPLE UP
CODE OF LAW	CONGER EEL	CRUSH DOWN
COFFEE BAR	CONJURE UP	CRY FOR JOY
COFFEE CUP	COOL CHEEK	CUBAN HEEL
COFFEE POT	COOL DRINK	CUBE SUGAR
COIN A WORD	COOLED OFF	CUBIC FOOT
COIN MONEY	COOL WATER	CUBIC INCH
COLD AS ICE	COPIED OUT	CUBIC YARD
COLD BLOOD	COPPER AGE	CUB MASTER

CUFF LINKS
CUPID'S BOW
CUP OF MILK
CURB CHAIN
CURIO SHOP
CURTAIN UP
CURTIS CUP
CURLY CORD
CURLY HAIR
CURLY KALE
CUT A CAPER
CUT ACROSS
CUT ADRIFT
CUT AND RUN
CUT A TOOTH
CUT CAPERS
CUT IN HALF
CUT IT FINE
CUTTING IN
CUTTY SARK
CUT UP WELL
CYCLE TOUR

D – 9

DAFFY DUCK
DAILY HELP
DAILY MAIL
DAILY WORK
DAIRY FARM
DAIRY HERD
DAIRY MAID
DAISY BELL
DALAI LAMA
DAMON HILL
DAMP PATCH
DAMP SQUIB
DAMSON JAM
DANCE A JIG
DANCE AWAY
DANCE BAND
DANCE HALL
DANCE STEP
DANCE TUNE
DANDY DICK
DANNY KAYE
DARK BLUES
DARK BROWN
DARK CLOUD
DARK DEEDS
DARK DRESS
DARK GREEN
DARK HORSE
DARK NIGHT
DARTED OUT
DARTS TEAM

DASHED OFF
DASHED OUT
DATE STAMP
DATUM LINE
DAVY JONES
DAWN OF DAY
DAY BEFORE
DAY IS DONE
DAY OF DOOM
DAY OF REST
DAY SCHOOL
DAYS OF OLD
DEAD AHEAD
DEAD DRUNK
DEAD FAINT
DEAD LUCKY
DEADLY SIN
DEAD MARCH
DEAD QUIET
DEAD RIGHT
DEAD SLEEP
DEAD SOBER
DEAD TIRED
DEAD WATER
DEAD WRONG
DEAL A BLOW
DEAL TABLE
DEAN SWIFT
DEAR ENEMY
DEAR HEART
DEAR MADAM
DEATH BLOW
DEATH CELL
DEATH DUTY
DEATH MASK
DEATH RATE
DEATH ROLL
DEATH SEAT
DEATH STAR
DEATH TRAP
DEATH WISH
DEBIT SIDE
DECK GAMES
DECOY DUCK
DEEP COVER
DEEP GRIEF
DEEP RIVER
DEEP SLEEP
DEEP SOUTH
DEEP VOICE
DEEP WATER
DELTA WING
DEMON KING
DEN OF VICE
DEPOT ONLY
DEPOT SHIP

DE QUINCEY
DEREK BOND
DEREK HART
DE RIGUEUR
DESERT AIR
DESERT FOX
DESERT RAT
DEVIL'S OWN
DIANA DORS
DIANA ROSS
DIESEL OIL
DIET SHEET
DIG DEEPER
DIG DEEPLY
DIME NOVEL
DIM MEMORY
DINING CAR
DINING OUT
DINNER SET
DIRECT HIT
DIRECT TAX
DIRT CHEAP
DIRT TRACK
DIRTY DICK
DIRTY LOOK
DIRTY PLAY
DIRTY WORD
DIRTY WORK
DISH CLOUT
DISHED OUT
DISH OF TEA
DISK DRIVE
DIXIE LAND
DO A BAD JOB
DO A FAVOUR
DO AS ASKED
DOCK BRIEF
DOCK GREEN
DOCTOR WHO
DODGE CITY
DOG COLLAR
DOG EAT DOG
DOG KENNEL
DOG RACING
DOGS OF WAR
DOG'S TOOTH
DOING FINE
DOING GOOD
DOING TIME
DOING WELL
DO IT AGAIN
DO JUSTICE
DOLLAR GAP
DOLL'S PRAM
DOLLY BIRD
DONE BROWN

DONE THING
DO NOTHING
DON'T GET UP
DON'T WORRY
DO ONE DOWN
DO ONE'S BIT
DOOR CHIME
DOPE FIEND
DO PENANCE
DORA BRYAN
DO REPAIRS
DORSAL FIN
DO THE DEED
DO THE TOWN
DOT MATRIX
DO TO DEATH
DOUBLE ACT
DOUBLE BED
DOUBLED UP
DOUBLE GIN
DOUBLE ONE
DOUBLE ROW
DOUBLE RUM
DOUBLE SIX
DOUBLE TEN
DOUBLE TOP
DOUBLE TWO
DOVER ROAD
DOVER SOLE
DO WITHOUT
DOWN BELOW
DOWN GRADE
DOWN IN ONE
DOWN IN TWO
DOWN QUILT
DOWN RIVER
DOWN SOUTH
DOWN STAGE
DOWN THERE
DOWN TOOLS
DOWN TRAIN
DOWN UNDER
DO YOU MIND?
DRAIN AWAY
DRAW A BEAD
DRAW A LINE
DRAW APART
DRAW A VEIL
DRAW BLANK
DRAW BLOOD
DRAW FORTH
DRAW LEVEL
DRAW MONEY
DRAWN FACE
DRAWN GAME
DRAW TEARS

DRAW TIGHT
DRAW WATER
DRAY HORSE
DREAM BOAT
DREAM GIRL
DREAM LAND
DRESS COAT
DRESS DOWN
DRESSED UP
DRESS RING
DRESS SHOW
DRESS SUIT
DRESS WELL
DRIED EGGS
DRIED FIGS
DRIED MILK
DRIED PEAS
DRIFT AWAY
DRILL HALL
DRINK DEEP
DRIVE A BUS
DRIVE A CAR
DRIVE AWAY
DRIVE BACK
DRIVE HARD
DRIVE HOME
DRIVEN MAD
DRIVE PAST
DR JOHNSON
DR KILDARE
DROP A BOMB
DROP A HINT
DROP A LINE
DROP A NOTE
DROP OF GIN
DROP OF TEA
DROPPED IN
DROP SHORT
DRUG FIEND
DRUG HABIT
DRUG STORE
DRUM MAJOR
DRURY LANE
DRY AS DUST
DRY GINGER
DRY HUMOUR
DRY REMARK
DRY SEASON
DRY SHERRY
DRY SUMMER
DRY WICKET
DUBLIN BAY
DUD CHEQUE
DUDE RANCH
DUE NOTICE
DUE REWARD

DULL LIGHT
DULL SOUND
DU MAURIER
DUNCE'S CAP
DUST STORM
DUSTY ROAD
DUTCH BARN
DUTCH DOLL
DUTCH OVEN
DUTCH WIFE
DUTY BOUND
DUTY CALLS
DUTY FIRST
DUTY NURSE
DWARF BEAN
DWELL UPON
DYING DOWN
DYING DUCK
DYING RACE
DYING SWAN
DYING TO GO
DYING WISH
DYING YEAR

E – 9

EACH OF TWO
EACH OTHER
EARLY BIRD
EARLY CALL
EARLY DAYS
EARLY DOOR
EARLY HOUR
EARLY LIFE
EARLY PART
EARLY WORM
EARN A NAME
EARN MONEY
EAR OF CORN
EASILY LED
EAST COAST
EASTER DAY
EASTER EGG
EASTER EVE
EAST INDIA
EAST LYNNE
EAST SHEEN
EASY AS PIE
EASY CATCH
EASY DEATH
EASY FIRST
EASY GOING
EASY MONEY
EASY PITCH
EASY RIDER
EASY TERMS

EASY THING
EASY TIMES
EASY TO RUN
EASY TO SEE
EATEN AWAY
EATING OUT
EAT NO MEAT
EDGED TOOL
EDGE ROUND
EDGE TOOLS
EIGHT DAYS
EIGHT DEEP
EIGHT FEET
EIGHTH DAY
EIGHTH MAN
EIGHTH ROW
EIGHTH TEE
EIGHT QUID
EITHER WAY
EL ALAMEIN
ELBOW ROOM
ELDER WINE
ELDEST SON
ELEVEN MEN
ELMER RICE
ELTON JOHN
EMBER DAYS
EMILE ZOLA
EMIT WAVES
EMMY AWARD
EMPIRE DAY
EMPTY LIFE
EMPTY NEST
EMPTY ROOM
EMPTY SEAT
EMPTY SHOW
EMPTY TALK
EMPTY TANK
END IN GAOL
END IN VIEW
END OF PLAY
END OF TERM
END OF TIME
ENEMY FIRE
ENERGY GAP
EN FAMILLE
ENJOY LIFE
EN PASSANT
EN PENSION
EN RAPPORT
ENTER INTO
ENTRE NOUS
ENTRY CARD
ENTRY FORM
EPIC VERSE
EQUAL RANK

ERASE HEAD
ERIC SYKES
'ER INDOORS
ERRAND BOY
ESKIMO DOG
ESSEX GIRL
ESTATE CAR
ET TU BRUTE
EVA BARTOK
EVENIN' ALL
EVEN MONEY
EVEN SCORE
EVEN TENOR
EVER AFTER
EVER SINCE
EVERY HOUR
EVERY INCH
EVERY SIDE
EVERY TIME
EVERY WEEK
EVERY WORD
EVERY YEAR
EXACT COPY
EXACT FARE
EXACT TIME
EXIT OMNES
EX OFFICIO
EXTRA COPY
EXTRA FOOD
EXTRA GOOD
EXTRA HELP
EXTRA ROOM
EXTRA SEAT
EXTRA TIME
EXTRA WORK
EYE APPEAL
EYE LOTION
EYE MAKE-UP
EYES FRONT
EYES RIGHT
EYE STRAIN
EZRA POUND

F – 9

FACE ABOUT
FACE CREAM
FACE DEATH
FACE FACTS
FACE IT OUT
FACE NORTH
FACE PAINT
FACE SOUTH
FACE TOWEL
FACE VALUE
FADING OUT

FAGGED OUT
FAIL TO ACT
FAIL TO SEE
FAIL TO WIN
FAINT HOPE
FAINT LINE
FAIR BREAK
FAIR FIELD
FAIR FIGHT
FAIR JUDGE
FAIRLY NEW
FAIR OFFER
FAIR PRICE
FAIR'S FAIR
FAIR SHARE
FAIR START
FAIR TRADE
FAIR TRIAL
FAIR VALUE
FAIR WORDS
FAIRY CAKE
FAIRY DOLL
FAIRY FOLK
FAIRY KING
FAIRY RING
FAIRY TALE
FAIRY WAND
FAITH CURE
FAKE ALIBI
FALL AMONG
FALL APART
FALLEN OUT
FALL FOR IT
FALL OF MAN
FALL SHORT
FALL UNDER
FALSE CARD
FALSE CASE
FALSE COIN
FALSE GODS
FALSE HAIR
FALSE IDEA
FALSE MOVE
FALSE NAME
FALSE NOSE
FALSE NOTE
FALSE OATH
FALSE PLEA
FALSE STEP
FAMILY CAR
FAMILY MAN
FAMILY PEW
FAMILY ROW
FAMOUS MAN
FANCY CAKE
FANCY FREE

FANCY WORK
FAN DANCER
FAN HEATER
FANNED OUT
FANNY HILL
FAR AFIELD
FAR BEHIND
FAR BETTER
FAR BEYOND
FAR CORNER
FAR ENOUGH
FARE STAGE
FAR FROM IT
FARMED OUT
FARM HORSE
FARTHER UP
FAR TOO FEW
FAST TRAIN
FAST WOMAN
FATAL BLOW
FATAL DOSE
FATAL HOUR
FATAL MOVE
FATAL URGE
FAT CATTLE
FAT CHANCE
FAT PROFIT
FEED A COLD
FEEL A NEED
FEEL ANGRY
FEEL CHEAP
FEEL FAINT
FEEL FRESH
FEEL FUNNY
FEEL GIDDY
FEEL GREAT
FEEL HAPPY
FEEL QUEER
FEEL RIGHT
FEEL SEEDY
FEEL SHAME
FEEL SMALL
FEEL SORRY
FEE SIMPLE
FEET APART
FEET FIRST
FELL APART
FELT A FOOL
FELT SILLY
FEMALE SEX
FEMME SOLE
FENCED OUT
FERRET OUT
FERRY OVER
FEUDAL LAW
FEUDAL TAX

FEVER HEAT
FIELD ARMY
FIELD GREY
FIELD TEST
FIFTH FORM
FIFTH HOLE
FIFTH PART
FIFTH RACE
FIFTH TEST
FIFTH TIME
FIFTY QUID
FIGHT BACK
FIGHT FAIR
FIGHT WITH
FIG LEAVES
FIGURE ONE
FIGURE OUT
FIGURE TEN
FIGURE TWO
FILE A SUIT
FILM ACTOR
FILM EXTRA
FILM STILL
FILM STUNT
FILTER TIP
FINAL BOUT
FINAL HEAT
FINAL HOPE
FINAL MOVE
FINALS DAY
FINAL STEP
FINAL TEST
FIND A CLUE
FIND A FLAT
FIND A HOME
FIND A WIFE
FIND FAULT
FIND MEANS
FIND PEACE
FIND WORDS
FINE BIRDS
FINE BLADE
FINE GRAIN
FINE LINEN
FINE POINT
FINE PRINT
FINE SPORT
FINE SPRAY
FINE TIMES
FINE TOUCH
FINE VOICE
FINE WOMAN
FINISH OFF
FIRE ALARM
FIRE A SHOT
FIRE AT SEA

FIRE DRILL
FIRE POWER
FIRM BASIS
FIRM FAITH
FIRM GOING
FIRM OFFER
FIRM PRICE
FIRM STAND
FIRST ARMY
FIRST BALL
FIRST BASE
FIRST BELL
FIRST BLOW
FIRST BORN
FIRST COAT
FIRST COME
FIRST COPY
FIRST COST
FIRST CROP
FIRST FOOT
FIRST FORM
FIRST GEAR
FIRST HALF
FIRST HAND
FIRST HEAT
FIRST HOLE
FIRST HOME
FIRST LADY
FIRST LEAD
FIRST LINE
FIRST LORD
FIRST LOVE
FIRST MATE
FIRST MEAL
FIRST MOVE
FIRST NAME
FIRST PAGE
FIRST PART
FIRST POST
FIRST RACE
FIRST RATE
FIRST SHOT
FIRST SIGN
FIRST SLIP
FIRST STEP
FIRST TEAM
FIRST TERM
FIRST TEST
FIRST TIME
FIRST TO GO
FIRST TURN
FIRST WORD
FIRST YEAR
FISHED OUT
FISH KNIFE
FISH PASTE

FISH SLICE	FLIT ABOUT	FOUR IN ONE
FISH STEAK	FLOAT DOWN	FOUR JACKS
FISHY EYED	FLOOD TIDE	FOUR KINGS
FISHY LOOK	FLOOR PLAN	FOUR LUMPS
FISHY TALE	FLOOR SHOW	FOUR MILES
FIT FOR USE	FLOOR TILE	FOUR NINES
FIT OF RAGE	FLOUR MILL	FOUR PAIRS
FIT PERSON	FLOW OF WIT	FOUR PARTS
FITTED OUT	FLY AT ZERO	FOUR PINTS
FIT TO BUST	FLYING FOX	FOUR SCORE
FIT TO DROP	FLYING LOW	FOUR SIDES
FIVE CARDS	FLYING MAN	FOUR SIXES
FIVE CLUBS	FLY TO ARMS	FOURTH DAY
FIVE DOZEN	FOBBED OFF	FOURTH ROW
FIVE GROSS	FOG SIGNAL	FOURTH SET
FIVE HOLES	FOLK DANCE	FOURTH TEE
FIVE HOURS	FOLK MUSIC	FOUR TIMES
FIVE LUMPS	FOLLOW OUT	FOUR TO ONE
FIVE MILES	FONDUE SET	FOUR WEEKS
FIVE OR SIX	FOOD STORE	FOUR WINDS
FIVE PARTS	FOOD VALUE	FOUR YEARS
FIVE PINTS	FOOL ABOUT	FRANK MUIR
FIVE SCORE	FOOL'S MATE	FRANS HALS
FIVE TIMES	FOOT FAULT	FRED EMNEY
FIVE TO ONE	FORAGE CAP	FRED KARNO
FIVE TO TEN	FOR A START	FRED PERRY
FIVE TO TWO	FOR A WHILE	FREE AGENT
FIVE TOWNS	FORCE OPEN	FREE AS AIR
FIVE WEEKS	FOR EFFECT	FREE BOARD
FIVE YEARS	FOREST LAW	FREE CHINA
FIX A PRICE	FOR EXPORT	FREE DRINK
FIXED GAZE	FORKED OUT	FREE ENTRY
FIXED IDEA	FORK LUNCH	FREE FIELD
FIXED LINK	FORM A CORE	FREE FIGHT
FIXED LOOK	FORMAL BOW	FREE HOUSE
FIXED ODDS	FORM A RING	FREE LUNCH
FIXED RATE	FORM FOURS	FREE OFFER
FIXED STAR	FOR MY PART	FREE OF TAX
FIXED TIME	FORTY DAYS	FREE PLACE
FIXED TYPE	FORTY LOVE	FREE PRESS
FIXED WAYS	FOR VALOUR	FREE RANGE
FIZZLE OUT	FOSTER SON	FREE SCOPE
FLAKED OUT	FOUL CRIME	FREE SPACE
FLARE PATH	FOUL FIEND	FREE STATE
FLASH BULB	FOUL SMELL	FREE STYLE
FLAT BROKE	FOUL THROW	FREE TRADE
FLAT SHARE	FOUR AWAYS	FREE UNION
FLAT TO LET	FOUR BY TWO	FREE VERSE
FLAY ALIVE	FOUR CARDS	FREE WHEEL
FLESH PINK	FOUR CLUBS	FREE WORLD
FLESH TINT	FOUR DOZEN	FREEZE OUT
FLICK AWAY	FOUR FIVES	FRESH BAIT
FLING AWAY	FOUR FOURS	FRESH EGGS
FLING DOWN	FOUR GROSS	FRESHEN UP
FLING OPEN	FOUR HOLES	FRESH FACE
FLIRT WITH	FOUR HOURS	FRESH FISH

FRESH FOOD
FRESH LOAF
FRESH MEAT
FRESH MILK
FRESH NEWS
FRESH PEAS
FRESH ROLL
FRESH WIND
FRIAR TUCK
FRIED FISH
FRIED FOOD
FRIED RICE
FRIGID BOW
FROCK COAT
FROM BELOW
FROM BIRTH
FROM NOW ON
FRONT DOOR
FRONT LINE
FRONT PAGE
FRONT RANK
FRONT ROOM
FRONT SEAT
FRONT STEP
FRONT STUD
FRONT VIEW
FROWN DOWN
FROWN UPON
FROZEN SEA
FRUIT BOWL
FRUIT CAKE
FRUIT TART
FRUIT TREE
FULL BLAST
FULL BLOOM
FULL BOARD
FULL COVER
FULL DRESS
FULL GLASS
FULL GROWN
FULL HEART
FULL HOUSE
FULL MARKS
FULL OF FUN
FULL OF JOY
FULL OF PEP
FULL OF WOE
FULL PITCH
FULL PURSE
FULL QUOTA
FULL SCOPE
FULL SCORE
FULL SKIRT
FULL SPEED
FULL STEAM
FULL STORY

FULL SWING
FULL TABLE
FULL TITLE
FULL VALUE
FULLY CLAD
FULLY PAID
FULLY RIPE
FUND OF WIT
FUNNY BONE
FUNNY FACE
FUNNY FILM
FUNNY HA-HA
FUNNY IDEA
FUNNY JOKE
FUNNY LIFE
FUNNY TIME
FUN PALACE
FUR COLLAR
FUR GLOVES
FUR LINING
FUR MARKET
FURTHER ON
FURTHER UP
FUR TRADER
FUSED PLUG

G – 9

GAG WRITER
GAIN POWER
GALA DRESS
GALA NIGHT
GALE FORCE
GALLOP OFF
GALWAY BAY
GAME CHIPS
GAMES ROOM
GAMING ACT
GAMMA RAYS
GANG AGLEY
GARDEN BED
GAS AND AIR
GAS ATTACK
GAS COOKER
GAS ENGINE
GAS ESCAPE
GAS HEATER
GAS MANTLE
GATE HOUSE
GATE MONEY
GATHER WAY
GAVE CHASE
GAZA STRIP
GENDER GAP
GENE AUTRY
GENOA CAKE

GENTLE SEX
GEORGE FOX
GET A CHILL
GET ACROSS
GET AROUND
GET A START
GET BEHIND
GET BETTER
GET CREDIT
GET KILLED
GET MOVING
GET THE PIP
GETTING ON
GETTING UP
GET TO HEAR
GET TO KNOW
GET UP LATE
GET WIND OF
GET WITH IT
GHOST TOWN
GIDDY GOAT
GIFTED MAN
GIFT HORSE
GIFT TOKEN
GIN AND PEP
GIN BOTTLE
GINGER ALE
GINGER CAT
GINGER POP
GINGER TOM
GIN PALACE
GIPSY LOVE
GIPSY MOTH
GIRL GUIDE
GIRLS' HOME
GIVE A HAND
GIVE A HINT
GIVE A LEAD
GIVE A LIFT
GIVE A TALK
GIVE BIRTH
GIVE CHASE
GIVE EAR TO
GIVE FORTH
GIVEN NAME
GIVEN TIME
GIVE PAUSE
GIVE PLACE
GIVE TERMS
GIVE VOICE
GIVING OUT
GIVING WAY
GLANCE OFF
GLASS CASE
GLASS TUBE
GLASS VASE

GLIDE AWAY
GLIDE PATH
GLOAT OVER
GLOBAL WAR
GLOOMY DAY
GLORY HOLE
GLOSS OVER
GNAW IN TWO
GO AGAINST
GO A-MAYING
GO AND LOOK
GOAT'S HAIR
GOAT'S MILK
GO BEGGING
GO BERSERK
GO BETWEEN
GO BOATING
GO BY COACH
GO BY PLANE
GO BY TRAIN
GO BY WATER
GO DANCING
GOD FORBID
GOD OF FIRE
GOD OF LOVE
GOD OF WINE
GOD'S IMAGE
GOD'S TRUTH
GOES ABOUT
GOES AFTER
GOES AHEAD
GOES BELOW
GOES IN FOR
GOES ROUND
GOES TO BED
GOES TO POT
GOES TO SEA
GOES TO SEE
GOES UNDER
GOES WRONG
GO FISHING
GO FLAT OUT
GO FOR A CAB
GO FOR A DIP
GO FOR A RUN
GO FOR HELP
GO FORWARD
GO HALF-WAY
GO HAYWIRE
GO HUNTING
GO INDOORS
GO IN FRONT
GOING AWAY
GOING BACK
GOING BALD
GOING DOWN

GOING GREY
GOING HOME
GOING OVER
GOING SLOW
GOING WELL
GOING WEST
GO IN ORBIT
GO IT ALONE
GOLD BRAID
GOLD BRICK
GOLD CHAIN
GOLD COAST
GOLDEN AGE
GOLDEN BOY
GOLDEN EGG
GOLDEN KEY
GOLDEN ROD
GOLD FEVER
GOLD INGOT
GOLD MEDAL
GOLD MINER
GOLD PAINT
GOLD PLATE
GOLD TOOTH
GOLD WATCH
GOLF CLUBS
GOLF LINKS
GOLF MATCH
GOLF SHOES
GOLF WIDOW
GONE TO BED
GONE TO POT
GONE UNDER
GOOD ACTOR
GOOD ALIBI
GOOD ANGEL
GOOD BOOKS
GOOD CATCH
GOOD CAUSE
GOOD CHEER
GOOD CLASS
GOOD DEBTS
GOOD DODGE
GOOD EATER
GOOD FAIRY
GOOD FAITH
GOOD FAULT
GOOD FIELD
GOOD FIGHT
GOOD GOING
GOOD GOLLY
GOOD GRACE
GOOD GRIEF
GOOD GUESS
GOOD GUIDE
GOOD HABIT

GOOD HANDS
GOOD HEART
GOOD HOTEL
GOOD HOURS
GOOD HOUSE
GOOD IMAGE
GOOD JUDGE
GOOD LAYER
GOOD LIGHT
GOOD LINES
GOOD LIVER
GOOD LOOKS
GOOD LOSER
GOOD LUNCH
GOOD LUNGS
GOOD MARKS
GOOD MATCH
GOOD MIXER
GOOD MONEY
GOOD MUSIC
GOOD NIGHT
GOOD ODOUR
GOOD OFFER
GOOD ORDER
GOOD PATCH
GOOD POINT
GOOD PRICE
GOOD REPLY
GOOD SCORE
GOOD SENSE
GOOD SHAPE
GOOD SHAVE
GOOD SIGHT
GOODS LIFT
GOOD SPEED
GOOD SPORT
GOOD START
GOOD STATE
GOOD STOCK
GOOD STORY
GOOD STUFF
GOOD TABLE
GOOD TASTE
GOOD TERMS
GOOD THING
GOOD TIMES
GOOD TO EAT
GOOD TONIC
GOOD TO SEE
GOOD TRADE
GOOD USAGE
GOOD VALUE
GOOD VOICE
GOOD WAGES
GOOD WOMAN
GOOD WORKS

GOOD YIELD
GO OFF DUTY
GO ON A DIET
GO ON AND ON
GO ON BOARD
GO ONE'S WAY
GO ON LEAVE
GOOSE FAIR
GO OUTSIDE
GO QUIETLY
GO SAILING
GO SKATING
GO THE PACE
GO THROUGH
GO TO EARTH
GO TO GLORY
GO TO GRASS
GO TO HADES
GO TO PRESS
GO TO SLEEP
GO TOWARDS
GO TO WASTE
GO WITHOUT
GRACE NOTE
GRAND DUKE
GRAND JURY
GRAND LAMA
GRAND PRIX
GRAND SLAM
GRAND TIME
GRAND TOUR
GRAND VIEW
GRASS PLOT
GRAVEL PIT
GRAVE NEWS
GRAVE NOTE
GREAT AUNT
GREAT BEAR
GREAT BLOW
GREAT CARE
GREAT DANE
GREAT DEAL
GREAT DEED
GREAT DRAW
GREAT FAME
GREAT FEAT
GREAT FIRE
GREAT FOLK
GREAT GAIN
GREAT GUNS
GREAT HALL
GREAT HELP
GREAT IDEA
GREAT LIFE
GREAT LOSS
GREAT MANY

GREAT MIND
GREAT NAME
GREAT NEWS
GREAT PAIN
GREAT PITY
GREAT SCOT
GREAT SEAL
GREAT SHIP
GREAT TIME
GREEDY PIG
GREEK CITY
GREEK FIRE
GREEK FLAG
GREEK GIFT
GREEK MYTH
GREEK PLAY
GREEN BELT
GREEN CARD
GREEN EYES
GREEN FEES
GREEN FIGS
GREEN FLAG
GREEN HILL
GREEN LINE
GREEN PARK
GREEN PEAS
GREEN ROOM
GREY CLOUD
GREY GOOSE
GREY HAIRS
GREY HORSE
GREY SKIES
GRILL ROOM
GRIM DEATH
GRIM SMILE
GRIM TRUTH
GRIND DOWN
GRIP TIGHT
GROUND NUT
GROW ANGRY
GROW APART
GROW FRUIT
GROWING UP
GROW OLDER
GROW PEARS
GROW STALE
GROW TIRED
GROW WEARY
GUARD DUTY
GUARD ROOM
GUARDS' TIE
GUARD'S VAN
GUESS WHEN
GUEST ROOM
GUEST STAR
GUIDE BOOK

GUILTY ACT
GUILTY MAN
GUINEA HEN
GUINEA PIG
GUM ARABIC
GUN BATTLE
GUN TURRET
GUY FAWKES
GYPSY BAND

H – 9

HAIL A TAXI
HAIR CREAM
HAIR SHIRT
HAIR STYLE
HAIR TONIC
HALF A LOAF
HALF AN EYE
HALF A PINT
HALF A QUID
HALF A TICK
HALF AWAKE
HALF A YARD
HALF CROWN
HALF DRUNK
HALF HITCH
HALF LIGHT
HALF PRICE
HALF SHARE
HALF SPEED
HALF TRUTH
HALF WAY UP
HALL TABLE
HAM AND EGG
HAM COMMON
HAMMER OUT
HAND BASIN
HAND IT OUT
HAND MOWER
HAND OF GOD
HAND ROUND
HANDS DOWN
HANDS FREE
HAND'S TURN
HAND TOWEL
HANDY ANDY
HANG ABOUT
HANG HEAVY
HANGING ON
HANG IT ALL
HANG LOOSE
HANG ROUND
HANSOM CAB
HAPPY DAYS
HAPPY GIRL
HAPPY HOME

HAPPY HOUR	HAVE A SEAT	HIGH ALTAR
HAPPY IDEA	HAVE A SHOT	HIGH BIRTH
HAPPY LIFE	HAVE A STAB	HIGH BOOTS
HAPPY MEAN	HAVE A TRIM	HIGH CHAIR
HAPPY OMEN	HAVE A WISH	HIGH COURT
HAPPY PAIR	HAVE FAITH	HIGH DUTCH
HAPPY TRIO	HAVE IT OUT	HIGHER PAY
HARD APORT	HAVE LUNCH	HIGH FEVER
HARD CATCH	HAVE MERCY	HIGH GRADE
HARD CLIMB	HAVE ROOTS	HIGH HEELS
HARD COURT	HAVE SENSE	HIGH HOPES
HARD FACTS	HAVE TASTE	HIGH HORSE
HARD FIGHT	HAVE VIEWS	HIGH JINKS
HARD FRANC	HAVE WORDS	HIGH LEVEL
HARD FROST	HAVING FUN	HIGH MARKS
HARD FRUIT	HAZEL EYES	HIGH PITCH
HARD GOING	HEAD COVER	HIGH PLANE
HARD GRIND	HEAD FIRST	HIGH PRICE
HARD HEART	HEADS I WIN	HIGH SCORE
HARD KNOCK	HEAD TO TOE	HIGH SPEED
HARD LINES	HEAP ABUSE	HIGH SPOTS
HARDLY ANY	HEAVE AWAY	HIGH STOOL
HARD MONEY	HEAVE COAL	HIGH TABLE
HARD STEEL	HEAVY BLOW	HIGH TOWER
HARD STUFF	HEAVY COLD	HIGH VALUE
HARD TIMES	HEAVY COST	HIGH VOICE
HARD TO GET	HEAVY FALL	HIGH WAGES
HARD TO SAY	HEAVY FINE	HIGH WATER
HARD TO SEE	HEAVY GUNS	HIGH WORDS
HARD USAGE	HEAVY HAND	HILL TRIBE
HARD VOICE	HEAVY LIDS	HIRE A MAID
HARD WATER	HEAVY LOAD	HIRED HAND
HARD WORDS	HEAVY LOSS	HIRED HELP
HARE'S FOOT	HEAVY MEAL	HIRED THUG
HARRY LIME	HEAVY MIST	HIS HONOUR
HARRY TATE	HEAVY ODDS	HIT AND RUN
HARSH NOTE	HEAVY POLL	HITCH HIKE
HARSH TONE	HEAVY POST	HIT FOR SIX
HARSH WORD	HEAVY RAIN	HIT NUMBER
HAVE A BALL	HEAVY SEAS	HIT OR MISS
HAVE A BASH	HEAVY SNOW	HIT PARADE
HAVE A BATH	HEAVY TASK	HIT SINGLE
HAVE A BITE	HEAVY TYPE	HIT THE HAY
HAVE A CARE	HEAVY WIND	HIT WICKET
HAVE A CASE	HEAVY WORK	HIT WILDLY
HAVE A CHAT	HELL TO PAY	HOG THE LOT
HAVE A COLD	HELP ALONG	HOI POLLOI
HAVE A DATE	HELPED OUT	HOIST SAIL
HAVE A GAME	HEM STITCH	HOLD ALOFT
HAVE A HOPE	HENRY FORD	HOLD ALOOF
HAVE A LARK	HENRY HALL	HOLD A SALE
HAVE A LOOK	HERE BELOW	HOLD AT BAY
HAVE A MEAL	HERNE HILL	HOLD CHEAP
HAVE AN EGG	HEROIC AGE	HOLD COURT
HAVE A PLAN	HEY PRESTO	HOLD FORTH
HAVE A REST	HIGH ABOVE	HOLD HANDS

HOLDING ON
HOLD STILL
HOLD TIGHT
HOLD UNDER
HOLD WATER
HOLE IN ONE
HOLLOW OUT
HOLLY BUSH
HOLY BIBLE
HOLY GHOST
HOLY GRAIL
HOLY MOSES
HOLY PLACE
HOLY SMOKE
HOLY WATER
HOME AGAIN
HOME FIRES
HOME FLEET
HOME FRONT
HOME GROWN
HOME GUARD
HOME JAMES
HOME LOVER
HOMELY WIT
HOME MATCH
HOME OF MAN
HOME TRADE
HOME TRUTH
HONEST MAN
HOOT OF JOY
HOPE CHEST
HOP GARDEN
HOP PICKER
HORSE FAIR
HORSE RACE
HORSE SHOW
HOT AIR GUN
HOT AS HELL
HOTEL BILL
HOTEL ROOM
HOT NUMBER
HOT POTATO
HOT SHOWER
HOT SPRING
HOT SUMMER
HOT TEMPER
HOUND DOWN
HOUSE BOAT
HOUSE FULL
HOUSE NAME
HOUSE RENT
HOUSE ROOM
HOW ABSURD!
HOW AND WHY
HOW ARE YOU?
HOW GOES IT?

HUDSON BAY
HUE AND CRY
HUM AND HAW
HUMAN LIFE
HUMAN RACE
HUMAN SOUL
HUMBLE PIE
HUNGRY MAN
HUNTED AIR
HURL ABUSE
HURRIED UP
HURRY AWAY
HURRY BACK
HURRY DOWN
HURRY HOME
HURRY OVER
HURST PARK
HURT PRIDE
HUSH MONEY

I – 9

IAN BOTHAM
ICE CORNET
ICED DRINK
ICED WATER
ICE HOCKEY
ICY MANNER
ICY REMARK
IDA LUPINO
IDEAL GIFT
IDEAL HOME
IDEAL TIME
IDEAL TYPE
IDEAL WIFE
IDLE BOAST
IDLE FANCY
IDLE HANDS
IDLE HOURS
IDLE STORY
IDLE TEARS
ILL AT EASE
ILL CHANCE
ILL EFFECT
ILL FAVOUR
ILL HEALTH
ILL HUMOUR
ILL REPORT
ILL REPUTE
IMRAN KHAN
IN A BAD WAY
IN A BIG WAY
IN A BUNKER
IN A CANTER
IN A CLINCH
IN A CORNER

IN A CRISIS
IN ADVANCE
IN A FRENZY
IN A GROOVE
IN A HUDDLE
IN A MINUTE
IN A MOMENT
IN A MUDDLE
IN ANY CASE
IN A PICKLE
IN ARREARS
IN A SCRAPE
IN A SECOND
IN A STUPOR
IN A TANGLE
IN A TEMPER
IN A TRANCE
IN A VACUUM
IN BAD FORM
IN BAD PART
IN BETWEEN
IN BILLETS
IN BLOSSOM
IN CIRCLES
IN CIVVIES
INCOME TAX
IN COMFORT
IN COMMAND
IN COMPANY
IN CONCERT
IN CONTACT
IN CONTROL
IN COPPERS
IN COSTUME
IN COUNCIL
IN CUSTODY
IN DEFAULT
IN DEFENCE
IN DESPAIR
IN DIALECT
INDIAN INK
INDIAN TEA
IN DISGUST
IN DISPUTE
IN DRY DOCK
IN DUE TIME
IN EARNEST
IN ECHELON
IN ENGLISH
INERT MASS
IN FASHION
IN FETTERS
IN FRONT OF
IN FULL CRY
IN GENERAL
INGLE NOOK

IN HARBOUR
IN HARMONY
IN HARNESS
IN INFANCY
IN ITALIAN
IN ITALICS
INK BOTTLE
IN KEEPING
INK ERASER
INLAND SEA
INNER CITY
INNER EDGE
INNER ROOM
INNER SELF
INNER TUBE
IN NEUTRAL
IN NO DOUBT
IN ONE MOVE
IN ONE WORD
IN OUTLINE
IN PASSING
IN POVERTY
IN PRIVATE
IN PROFILE
IN PROTEST
IN PURSUIT
IN REALITY
IN RESERVE
IN RESPECT
IN RETREAT
IN REVERSE
IN RUSSIAN
IN SERVICE
IN SESSION
INSIDE JOB
INSIDE OUT
IN SILENCE
IN SLAVERY
IN SOCIETY
IN SOME WAY
IN SPANISH
IN SUPPORT
IN TATTERS
INTER ALIA
IN THE ALPS
IN THE AREA
IN THE ARMY
IN THE BAND
IN THE BANK
IN THE BATH
IN THE BUSH
IN THE CART
IN THE CITY
IN THE COLD
IN THE DARK
IN THE DOCK

IN THE DUSK
IN THE EAST
IN THE FACE
IN THE FALL
IN THE FILE
IN THE FIRE
IN THE FOLD
IN THE FRAY
IN THE GODS
IN THE HOLD
IN THE HOME
IN THE KNOW
IN THE LAKE
IN THE LEAD
IN THE LIFT
IN THE LOFT
IN THE MAIL
IN THE MAIN
IN THE MASS
IN THE MIND
IN THE MINE
IN THE MODE
IN THE MOOD
IN THE MOON
IN THE NAVY
IN THE NECK
IN THE NEST
IN THE NEWS
IN THE NUDE
IN THE OPEN
IN THE OVEN
IN THE PACK
IN THE PARK
IN THE PAST
IN THE PINK
IN THE POST
IN THE RAIN
IN THE REAR
IN THE RING
IN THE ROAD
IN THE SAFE
IN THE SNOW
IN THE SOUP
IN THE SWIM
IN THE TEAM
IN THE TILL
IN THE TOWN
IN THE VEIN
IN THE WAKE
IN THE WARS
IN THE WASH
IN THE WEST
IN THE WIND
INTO FOCUS
IN TOP FORM
IN TOP GEAR

IN TORMENT
INTO TOUCH
IN TRAFFIC
IN TRANSIT
IN TRIUMPH
IN TROUBLE
IN UNIFORM
INVOKE AID
IN WAITING
IN WRITING
IONIAN SEA
IPSO FACTO
IRISH BULL
IRISH EYES
IRISH FLAG
IRISH PEER
IRISH STEW
IRON CROSS
IRONED OUT
IRON FRAME
IRON GUARD
IRON HORSE
IRON NERVE
IRON TONIC
IRON WORKS
ILSE OF ELY
ISLE OF MAN
IT'S A CINCH
IVORY GATE
IVY LEAGUE

J – 9

JACK BENNY
JACK FROST
JACK HOBBS
JACK JONES
JACK KETCH
JACK PAYNE
JACK SPRAT
JACK TRAIN
JADE GREEN
JAMES BOND
JAMES DEAN
JAMES WATT
JAM SPONGE
JANE FONDA
JANE WYMAN
JAY WALKER
JELLY BABY
JELLY BEAN
JENNY LIND
JENNY WREN
JERSEY COW
JESUS WEPT
JET ENGINE

JET FLIGHT
JEWEL CASE
JOAN OF ARC
JOAN REGAN
JOB CENTRE
JOB OF WORK
JOE BLOGGS
JOE PUBLIC
JO GRIMOND
JOHN ADAMS
JOHN BLUNT
JOHN BROWN
JOHN CABOT
JOHN KEATS
JOHN MAJOR
JOHN MILLS
JOHN SMITH
JOHN WAYNE
JOIN HANDS
JOIN ISSUE
JOINT HEIR
JOINT WILL
JOLLY GOOD
JOLLY TIME
JOLLY WELL
JONAH WORD
JOT IT DOWN
JUDAS KISS
JUDAS TREE
JUDGE'S CAP
JUDGE WELL
JUG KETTLE
JUG OF MILK
JUMP ABOUT
JUMP AHEAD
JUMP CLEAR
JUMP LEADS
JUMP START
JUNE BRIDE
JUNGLE LAW
JUST A DROP
JUST CAUSE
JUST CLAIM
JUST FANCY
JUST PRICE
JUST RIGHT
JUST THINK

K – 9

KEEN FIGHT
KEEN FROST
KEEN MATCH
KEEN PRICE
KEEN SIGHT
KEEP A DATE

KEEP AHEAD
KEEP ALIVE
KEEP APART
KEEP ASIDE
KEEP AT BAY
KEEP CLEAR
KEEP CLOSE
KEEP COUNT
KEEP FAITH
KEEP FRESH
KEEP GOING
KEEP GUARD
KEEP HOUSE
KEEP ON ICE
KEEP ORDER
KEEP QUIET
KEEP SCORE
KEEP SHORT
KEEP SOBER
KEEP STILL
KEEP STOCK
KEEP UNDER
KEEP VIGIL
KEEP WATCH
KEG BITTER
KELLY'S EYE
KEPT AT BAY
KEPT ON ICE
KEPT WOMAN
KERRY BLUE
KEW BRIDGE
KEW PALACE
KEY MOMENT
KEY WORKER
KICKED OFF
KICKED OUT
KID GLOVES
KIEL CANAL
KILLER BEE
KIM PHILBY
KIND HEART
KINDLY ACT
KIND WORDS
KING CAROL
KING COBRA
KING DAVID
KING HENRY
KING MIDAS
KING PRIAM
KING'S HEAD
KING'S LYNN
KING'S PAWN
KING'S ROAD
KING'S ROOK
KING STORK
KIPPER TIE

KIRBY GRIP
KISS HANDS
KNEEL DOWN
KNEES BEND
KNOCK COLD
KNOCK DOWN
KNOCKED UP
KNOCK HARD
KNOCK ONCE
KNOCK OVER
KNOW AGAIN
KNOW NO LAW
KOREAN WAR
KUBLA KHAN

L – 9

LABOUR DAY
LACK DRIVE
LADIES' BAR
LADIES' DAY
LADIES' MAN
LADY'S MAID
LAG BEHIND
LAGER BEER
LAGER LOUT
LA GUARDIA
LAID WASTE
LAKE HURON
LAKE POETS
LAMB'S WOOL
LAMP SHADE
LAND A BLOW
LAND AGENT
LAND AHEAD
LAND FORCE
LAND OF NOD
LAND ROVER
LAND SPEED
LAP RECORD
LARGE AREA
LARGE ARMY
LARGE BEER
LARGE BILL
LARGE CAST
LARGE CITY
LARGE FLAT
LARGE HEAD
LARGE LOAF
LARGE PORT
LARGE ROOM
LARGE SIZE
LARGE TOWN
LARGE TYPE
LARK ABOUT
LASER BEAM

LASER DISC
LASER SHOW
LASHED OUT
LAS PALMAS
LAST APRIL
LAST CRUMB
LAST DANCE
LAST DITCH
LAST DREGS
LAST DRINK
LAST EVENT
LAST FLING
LAST HOURS
LAST LAUGH
LAST NIGHT
LAST MAN IN
LAST MARCH
LAST MATCH
LAST MONTH
LAST NIGHT
LAST OF ALL
LAST OFFER
LAST OF SIX
LAST OF TEN
LAST ORDER
LAST PENNY
LAST PLACE
LAST RITES
LAST ROUND
LAST SCENE
LAST SHIFT
LAST STAGE
LAST STAND
LAST STRAW
LAST TANGO
LAST THING
LAST THROW
LAST TRAIN
LAST TRUMP
LAST VERSE
LAST VISIT
LAST WALTZ
LAST WORDS
LATE CROPS
LATE ENTRY
LATE EXTRA
LATE FROST
LATE HOURS
LATE NIGHT
LATER DATE
LATE RISER
LATE SHIFT
LATE STAGE
LATE START
LATIN CRIB
LATIN RACE

LATTER END
LAUGH AWAY
LAUGH DOWN
LAUGH LINE
LAUGH OVER
LAUNCH OUT
LAVA BREAD
LAWFUL ACT
LAWFUL AGE
LAWN MOWER
LAW OFFICE
LAW REFORM
LAW REPORT
LAW SCHOOL
LAZY BONES
LEAD OXIDE
LEAF MOULD
LEAN YEARS
LEASE LEND
LEAST SAID
LEAVE A GAP
LEAVE A TIP
LEAVE HOME
LEAVE OPEN
LEAVE OVER
LEAVE ROOM
LEAVE WORD
LEAVE WORK
LE BOURGET
LED ASTRAY
LEFT ALONE
LEFT BRAIN
LEFT FLANK
LEFT TO DIE
LEFT TO ROT
LEFT WHEEL
LEGAL CODE
LEGAL FARE
LEGAL HEIR
LEGAL MIND
LEGAL TERM
LEGER LINE
LEG GLANCE
LEG OF LAMB
LEG OF PORK
LEGS APART
LEG THEORY
LEIGH HUNT
LEMON CURD
LEMON PEEL
LEMON SOLE
LENA HORNE
LEND A HAND
LEND AN EAR
LEND MONEY
LEN HUTTON

LENS COVER
LESSON ONE
LESSON SIX
LESSON TEN
LESSON TWO
LESS SPEED
LET HER RIP
LE TOUQUET
LETTER BOX
LETTING UP
LET US PRAY
LEVEL BEST
LEYDEN JAR
LIBEL CASE
LIBEL SUIT
LIE ASLEEP
LIE AT REST
LIE DIRECT
LIE FALLOW
LIE HIDDEN
LIE IN WAIT
LIFE CLASS
LIFE CYCLE
LIFE FORCE
LIFE STORY
LIFE STUDY
LIFE'S WORK
LIFT A HAND
LIGHT BLUE
LIGHT BULB
LIGHT DIET
LIGHT MEAL
LIGHT RAIN
LIGHT SHOW
LIGHT SIDE
LIGHTS OUT
LIGHT SUIT
LIGHT TANK
LIGHT UPON
LIGHT WAVE
LIGHT WINE
LIGHT WORK
LIGHT YEAR
LIKE A BIRD
LIKE A BOMB
LIKE A CORK
LIKE A DUCK
LIKE A FOOL
LIKE A LAMB
LIKE A LION
LIKE A MULE
LIKE A SHOT
LIKELY LAD
LIKE MAGIC
LIKE MUSIC
LIKE SMOKE

LIKE WATER	LONG GRASS	LOSE AN EYE
LILAC TIME	LONG HOURS	LOSE COUNT
LILAC TREE	LONG LEASE	LOSE FAITH
LIME GREEN	LONG MARCH	LOSE HEART
LIME GROVE	LONG NIGHT	LOSE MONEY
LIME JUICE	LONG PANTS	LOSER PAYS
LION'S CAGE	LONG PURSE	LOSE TOUCH
LION'S MANE	LONG QUEUE	LOSE TRACK
LION'S SKIN	LONG RANGE	LOSING BET
LION'S TAIL	LONG REACH	LOSING RUN
LION TAMER	LONG REIGN	LOST AT SEA
LIP READER	LONG SIEGE	LOST CAUSE
LIQUID AIR	LONG SIGHT	LOST CHORD
LIQUOR LAW	LONG SINCE	LOST COUNT
LIST PRICE	LONG SKIRT	LOST HABIT
LITTER BIN	LONG SLEEP	LOST SCENT
LITTER BUG	LONG SPELL	LOST SHEEP
LITTLE BIT	LONG STAGE	LOST SKILL
LITTLE BOY	LONG STORY	LOT OF GOOD
LITTLE DOG	LONG TRAIN	LOTS OF FUN
LITTLE MAN	LONG TRIAL	LOUD KNOCK
LITTLE ONE	LONG VISIT	LOUD LAUGH
LITTLE TOE	LONG VOWEL	LOUD MUSIC
LITTLE WAY	LONG WAVES	LOUD NOISE
LIVE AGAIN	LONG WHIST	LOUD PEDAL
LIVE ALONE	LOOK A FOOL	LOUD SOUND
LIVE IN SIN	LOOK AFTER	LOUD VOICE
LIVE ISSUE	LOOK AHEAD	LOUNGE BAR
LIVE ON AIR	LOOK ALIVE	LOVE APPLE
LIVE OR DIE	LOOK A MESS	LOVE BEADS
LIVE ROUGH	LOOK BLACK	LOVE CHILD
LIVING LIE	LOOK BLANK	LOVED ONES
LOADED GUN	LOOKED FOR	LOVE FORTY
LOAD OF HAY	LOOK FRESH	LOVELY DAY
LOAF SUGAR	LOOK GRAVE	LOVE LYRIC
LOATH TO GO	LOOKING UP	LOVE MATCH
LOCAL CALL	LOOK NIPPY	LOVE MY DOG
LOCAL NAME	LOOK RIGHT	LOVE OF WAR
LOCAL NEWS	LOOK ROUND	LOVE STORY
LOCAL TIME	LOOK SEEDY	LOVE TOKEN
LOCAL VETO	LOOK SHARP	LOVING CUP
LOCKED OUT	LOOK SILLY	LOW BRIDGE
LOFTY AIMS	LOOK SMALL	LOW CHURCH
LOGIC BOMB	LOOK SMART	LOW COMEDY
LOG OF WOOD	LOOK THERE	LOW DEGREE
LONDON BUS	LOOM LARGE	LOWER CASE
LONDON ZOO	LOON PANTS	LOWER DECK
LONG AFTER	LOONY LEFT	LOWER DOWN
LONG BEACH	LOOSE BALL	LOWER FORM
LONG BEARD	LOOSE CASH	LOWER LIFE
LONG CHALK	LOOSE TALK	LOWER LIMB
LONG DELAY	LOOSE TILE	LOWER PART
LONG DOZEN	LORD BYRON	LOW FELLOW
LONG DRESS	LORD DERBY	LOW GERMAN
LONG DRINK	LORD MAYOR	LOW GROUND
LONG DRIVE	LOSE A LIMB	LOW INCOME

LOW IN TONE
LOW NUMBER
LOW PERSON
LOW RELIEF
LOW RESORT
LOW RETURN
LOW SALARY
LOW STAKES
LOW STATUS
LUCID MIND
LUCKY DRAW
LUCKY FIND
LUCKY GIRL
LUCKY MOVE
LUCKY OMEN
LUCKY SHOT
LUCKY STAR
LUMP SUGAR
LUNACY ACT
LUNAR YEAR
LUNCH DATE
LUNCH HOUR
LUNCH TIME
LURID PAST
LYING DOWN
LYME REGIS
LYRIC POEM
LYRIC POET

M – 9

MADE OF TIN
MADE READY
MAD HATTER
MAD SCHEME
MAGGIE MAY
MAGIC LAMP
MAGIC RING
MAGIC SIGN
MAGIC WAND
MAGIC WORD
MAIDA VALE
MAIL ORDER
MAIL PLANE
MAIL TRAIN
MAIN FORCE
MAIN ISSUE
MAIN POINT
MAIN THEME
MAIN THING
MAJOR DOMO
MAJOR PART
MAJOR POET
MAJOR ROAD
MAJOR SNAG
MAJOR SUIT

MAJOR WORK
MAKE A BACK
MAKE A BOOK
MAKE A CAKE
MAKE A CALL
MAKE A COPY
MAKE A DATE
MAKE A DEAL
MAKE A FACE
MAKE A FIRE
MAKE A FUSS
MAKE A HOLE
MAKE A JOKE
MAKE A KILL
MAKE A LIST
MAKE A LOSS
MAKE A MESS
MAKE A MOVE
MAKE A NOTE
MAKE A PASS
MAKE A PILE
MAKE A PLAN
MAKE A RING
MAKE A SHOW
MAKE A SIGN
MAKE A SLIP
MAKE A STIR
MAKE A TART
MAKE A WILL
MAKE A WISH
MAKE CLEAR
MAKE FACES
MAKE FUN OF
MAKE HASTE
MAKE IT BIG
MAKE KNOWN
MAKE LEGAL
MAKE MERRY
MAKE MONEY
MAKE MUSIC
MAKE MY DAY
MAKE NOTES
MAKE OR MAR
MAKE PEACE
MAKE PLAIN
MAKE PLANS
MAKE READY
MAKE SENSE
MAKE TERMS
MAKE TIGHT
MAKE-UP MAN
MAKE-UP SET
MAKE VALID
MAKE WHOLE
MAKE WORSE
MAKING HAY

MALE CHOIR
MALE MODEL
MALE NURSE
MALE SCREW
MALE VOICE
MAN AND BOY
MAN FRIDAY
MAN OF IRON
MAN OF KENT
MAN OF MARK
MAN OF NOTE
MAN OF RANK
MANOR FARM
MANOR PARK
MANY A SLIP
MANY A TIME
MANY HANDS
MANY TIMES
MANY WORDS
MANY YEARS
MAPLE LEAF
MAPLE TREE
MAP OF ROME
MAPPED OUT
MARCH AWAY
MARCH HARE
MARCH PAST
MARCH WIND
MARCO POLO
MARDI GRAS
MARE'S NEST
MARIA MONK
MARKED MAN
MARKET DAY
MARK TWAIN
MARRY WELL
MARY QUANT
MASKED MAN
MASS MEDIA
MASTER KEY
MASTER SPY
MATCH PLAY
MATE IN ONE
MATE IN TWO
MATT MONRO
MAX ADRIAN
MAX MILLER
MEANS TEST
MEAN TO SAY
MEANT WELL
MEASLY LOT
MEAT JELLY
MEAT PASTE
MEDAL PLAY
MEDIA HYPE
MEDIUM DRY

MEIN KAMPF
MEL FERRER
MEN AT WORK
MEND A FUSE
MENTAL AGE
MERCY SEAT
MERE TRUTH
MERE WORDS
MERRY QUIP
MERRY TUNE
MESS ABOUT
METAL DISC
METAL RING
METAL TUBE
METER MAID
METRIC TON
MID-DAY SUN
MIDDLE AGE
MIDDLE WAY
MIGHTY FEW
MIGHTY MAN
MIKE TYSON
MILD STEEL
MILES AWAY
MILK CHURN
MILK DRINK
MILK FLOAT
MILK PUNCH
MILK ROUND
MILK SHAKE
MILK STOUT
MILK TEETH
MILL ABOUT
MILLS BOMB
MINE SHAFT
MINI SKIRT
MINK STOLE
MINOR PART
MINOR POET
MINOR ROAD
MINOR ROLE
MINOR SUIT
MINT JULEP
MINT SAUCE
MINUS SIGN
MINUTE MAN
MISSED OUT
MISS WORLD
MIX A DRINK
MIXED NUTS
MOCK TRIAL
MODEL FARM
MODEL GIRL
MODERN ART
MONEY DOWN
MONIED MAN

MONKEY NUT
MONT BLANC
MOON ABOUT
MOON BOOTS
MOON BUGGY
MOON RIVER
MOOT POINT
MORAL CODE
MORAL EVIL
MORAL TONE
MORE HASTE
MORE LIGHT
MORE MONEY
MORE SCOPE
MORSE CODE
MORTAL SIN
MOSAIC LAW
MOSS GREEN
MOST NOBLE
MOST OF ALL
MOTHER WIT
MOTOR RACE
MOTOR ROAD
MOTOR SHOW
MOTOR TOUR
MOUNTED UP
MOUNT ETNA
MOUTH WASH
MOVE ABOUT
MOVE ALONG
MOVE APART
MOVE HOUSE
MOVE ROUND
MOVIE STAR
MOWED DOWN
MR NICE GUY
MRS BEATON
MRS GRUNDY
MR SPEAKER
MUCH ALIKE
MUCH LATER
MUCH MOVED
MUCH NOISE
MUCH SPACE
MUCH WORSE
MUFFIN MAN
MUFFLED UP
MUG OF BEER
MUM AND DAD
MUSIC CASE
MUSIC HALL
MUSIC ROOM
MUTINY ACT
MUTTON FAT
MUTUAL AID
MUTUAL AIM

MY DARLING
MY DEAR SIR
MY HUSBAND
MY OPINION

N – 9

NAKED CITY
NAKED LADY
NANNY GOAT
NARROW WIN
NASTY BLOW
NASTY MESS
NASTY TYPE
NASTY WORD
NATIVE WIT
NAVAL BASE
NAVAL RANK
NAVAL TYPE
NAZI PARTY
NEARLY ALL
NEAR SIGHT
NEAR THING
NEAT DRINK
NEAT TRICK
NEEDS MUST
NEON LIGHT
NET AMOUNT
NET LOSSES
NET PROFIT
NET RESULT
NET RETURN
NEVER A ONE
NEVER FEAR
NEVER MIND
NEVER MORE
NEVER REST
NEVER SEEN
NEVER STOP
NEVER VARY
NEW BARNET
NEW BONNET
NEW CUSTOM
NEW DEALER
NEW ENERGY
NEW FOREST
NEW FRIEND
NEW GROUND
NEW GUINEA
NEW JERSEY
NEW MASTER
NEW MEMBER
NEW METHOD
NEW MEXICO
NEW PLANET
NEW POLICY

NEW POTATO	NOBLE LORD	NUMBER TEN
NEW READER	NOBLE PART	NUMBER TWO
NEW RECORD	NOBLE PILE	NUTS IN MAY
NEW REGIME	NO CHICKEN	
NEW ROMNEY	NO COMMENT	
NEW SCHOOL	NOD ASSENT	O – 9
NEW SERIES	NO DEFENCE	
NEWS FLASH	NO EFFECTS	OAST HOUSE
NEWS SHEET	NO FISHING	OBJET D'ART
NEW STREET	NO FLOWERS	OCEAN LANE
NEWS VALUE	NO FOOLING	OCEAN WAVE
NEW YORKER	NO FURTHER	OCTANE GAS
NEXT APRIL	NO GROUNDS	ODD CHOICE
NEXT ISSUE	NO HAWKERS	ODD CORNER
NEXT MAN IN	NO INKLING	ODD COUPLE
NEXT MARCH	NOISES OFF	ODD JOB MAN
NEXT MONTH	NO KIDDING	ODD MAN OUT
NEXT OF KIN	NO MANNERS	ODD MOMENT
NEXT STAGE	NO MEANING	ODD NUMBER
NEXT TRAIN	NO MISTAKE	ODD OR EVEN
NEXT WORLD	NO MODESTY	ODD PERSON
NICE POINT	NO ONE ELSE	OFF CENTRE
NICE SLEEP	NO PARKING	OFF CHANCE
NICE TASTE	NO QUARTER	OFF COLOUR
NICE TO SEE	NO REGRETS	OFF COURSE
NICK FALDO	NORTH CAPE	OFFICE BOY
NICK PRICE	NORTH POLE	OFFICE CAT
NIGHT BELL	NORTH SIDE	OFF MOMENT
NIGHT CLUB	NORTH STAR	OFF SEASON
NIGHT DUTY	NORTH WIND	OFF TARGET
NIGHT LIFE	NORTH ZONE	OFF THE AIR
NIGHT SPOT	NOSMO KING	OFF THE MAP
NIGHT WORK	NO SMOKING	OFF THE PEG
NILE DELTA	NO SPIRITS	OFF THE SET
NILE GREEN	NO STRINGS	OF NO AVAIL
NINE CARAT	NOT AT HOME	OF NO WORTH
NINE DOZEN	NOT FAR OFF	OF ONE MIND
NINE GROSS	NOT GUILTY	OF THAT ILK
NINE HOLES	NOTHING ON	OIL COOKER
NINE HOURS	NOT HUNGRY	OILED SILK
NINE LIVES	NOT IN TIME	OIL HEATER
NINE MILES	NOT LATELY	OIL TANKER
NINE MUSES	NOT LIKELY	OIL TYCOON
NINE OR TEN	NOT PROVEN	OLD AND NEW
NINE PARTS	NOTRE DAME	OLD AS ADAM
NINE SCORE	NO TROUBLE	OLD AS TIME
NINE TIMES	NOT SO GOOD	OLD BAILEY
NINE TO ONE	NOT STRONG	OLD BRANDY
NINE WEEKS	NOT TOO BAD	OLD BUFFER
NINE YEARS	NOT UP TO IT	OLD CODGER
NINTH HOLE	NOT WANTED	OLD COUPLE
NINTH PART	NOVEL ITEM	OLD CROCKS
NINTH TIME	NO WAITING	OLD CUSTOM
NISSEN HUT	NO WARNING	OLD EMPIRE
NOBLE LADY	NUMBER ONE	OLDEN DAYS
NOBLE LINE	NUMBER SIX	OLD FAMILY
		OLD FELLOW

OLD FOSSIL	ONE STROKE	ON THE TOTE
OLD FRIEND	ONE TO COME	ON THE TOWN
OLD MASTER	ONE TOO FEW	ON THE TROT
OLD METHOD	ONE WICKET	ON THE TURF
OLD PEOPLE	ON HALF PAY	ON THE TURN
OLD POSSUM	ON HOLIDAY	ON THE WALL
OLD RECORD	ON IMPULSE	ON THE WANE
OLD REEKIE	ONION SKIN	ON THE WING
OLD RÉGIME	ONION SOUP	ON THIN ICE
OLD ROWLEY	ONLY CHILD	ON TUESDAY
OLD SAYING	ONLY HUMAN	OPEN A SHOP
OLD SCHOOL	ON MY RIGHT	OPEN COURT
OLD SCORES	ON ONE SIDE	OPEN DRAIN
OLD STAGER	ON ONE'S OWN	OPEN EVENT
OLD STREET	ON ONE'S WAY	OPEN FIELD
OLIVE TREE	ON PURPOSE	OPEN GRATE
ON ACCOUNT	ON RATIONS	OPEN GRAVE
ON A CHARGE	ON RUNNERS	OPEN HEART
ON A PICNIC	ON SUNDAYS	OPEN HOUSE
ON ARRIVAL	ON THE BALL	OPEN MATCH
ON A STRING	ON THE BEAM	OPEN MOUTH
ON A TANDEM	ON THE BEAT	OPEN ORDER
ON AVERAGE	ON THE BOIL	OPEN PORES
ON BALANCE	ON THE BONE	OPEN PURSE
ONCE AGAIN	ON THE CHIN	OPEN SHIRT
ONCE A WEEK	ON THE DOLE	OPEN SKIES
ONCE A YEAR	ON THE EDGE	OPEN SPACE
ONCE ROUND	ON THE FARM	OPEN TO ALL
ON DEPOSIT	ON THE FIRE	OPEN WOUND
ON DISPLAY	ON THE FLAT	OPTING OUT
ON DRAUGHT	ON THE HEAD	ORANGE GIN
ON DRY LAND	ON THE HOOF	ORANGE PIP
ONE ACROSS	ON THE HOUR	ORDER ARMS
ONE AND ALL	ON THE HUNT	ORDER BOOK
ONE BETTER	ON THE JURY	ORDER FORM
ONE DEGREE	ON THE LAKE	ORGAN LOFT
ONE DOLLAR	ON THE LAND	ORGAN STOP
ONE EIGHTH	ON THE LEAD	ORLOP DECK
ONE FOR ALL	ON THE LEFT	ORRIS ROOT
ONE FOURTH	ON THE LINE	OTHER DAYS
ONE GALLON	ON THE LIST	OTHER HALF
ONE GUINEA	ON THE MAKE	OTHER SELF
ONE IN FIVE	ON THE MARK	OTHER SIDE
ONE IN FOUR	ON THE MEND	OUR CHOICE
ONE IN NINE	ON THE MENU	OUR FATHER
ONE LENGTH	ON THE MOON	OUT AND OUT
ONE-MAN DOG	ON THE MOVE	OUT AT HEEL
ONE MINUTE	ON THE NAIL	OUTER EDGE
ONE MOMENT	ON THE NOSE	OUTER SKIN
ONE NATION	ON THE PIER	OUTER TUBE
ONE O'CLOCK	ON THE RACK	OUT FOR TEA
ONE OCTAVE	ON THE RISE	OUT OF A JOB
ONE OF MANY	ON THE ROAD	OUT OF BOND
ONE SECOND	ON THE ROOF	OUT OF DATE
ONE'S EQUAL	ON THE SIDE	OUT OF DEBT
ONE STRIPE	ON THE SPOT	OUT OF FORM

OUT OF GEAR
OUT OF HAND
OUT OF LINE
OUT OF LOVE
OUT OF LUCK
OUT OF MIND
OUT OF PAIN
OUT OF PITY
OUT OF PLAY
OUT OF STEP
OUT OF TIME
OUT OF TOWN
OUT OF TRIM
OUT OF TRUE
OUT OF TUNE
OUT OF TURN
OUT OF WORK
OUT ON BAIL
OUT WITH IT
OUT YONDER
OVER AGAIN
OVER FORTY
OVER PROOF
OVER THERE
OVER TO YOU
OWEN NARES
OWEN TUDOR
OWN A HOUSE
OXFORD DON
OYSTER BAR
OYSTER BED

P – 9

PACKED OUT
PADDED OUT
PAGE EIGHT
PAGE PROOF
PAGE SEVEN
PAGE THREE
PAINT OVER
PAIRED OFF
PALE BROWN
PALE GREEN
PALE HANDS
PALM BEACH
PALMY DAYS
PANAMA HAT
PANEL GAME
PANT AFTER
PAPAL BULL
PAPER BACK
PAPER BILL
PAPER CLIP
PAPER DOLL
PAPER GAME

PAPER MILL
PAPER OVER
PAPER RACK
PAPER WORK
PARCEL OUT
PARIAH DOG
PARI PASSU
PARIS GOWN
PARK BENCH
PARKED CAR
PARK ROYAL
PARTY GAME
PARTY LINE
PARTY MOOD
PARTY RULE
PARTY WALL
PARTY WHIP
PAS DE DEUX
PAS DU TOUT
PASS ALONG
PASSED OFF
PASSED OUT
PASSING BY
PASSING ON
PASS ROUND
PAST GLORY
PAST SHAME
PAST TENSE
PATCHED UP
PATCH IT UP
PATNA RICE
PATROL CAR
PAUL MOREL
PAUL SIMON
PAVED ROAD
PAVED WALK
PAWN'S MOVE
PAY A VISIT
PAY DOUBLE
PAY HOMAGE
PAY IN FULL
PAYING OUT
PAY IN KIND
PAY OFFICE
PAY ON CALL
PAY ONE OUT
PAY PACKET
PAY RANSOM
PEACE PACT
PEACE SIGN
PEACH TREE
PEAKED CAP
PEARL BUCK
PEAR MELBA
PEGGED OUT
PENAL CODE

PENAL LAWS
PENAL WORK
PEN AND INK
PEN FRIEND
PENNY BANK
PENNY POST
PENNY WISE
PEPPER POT
PEP UP PILL
PER CAPITA
PER CENTUM
PER CONTRA
PERRY COMO
PETAL SOFT
PETER COOK
PETER WEST
PET FEEDER
PETIT FOUR
PET NOTION
PETROL CAN
PETROL TAX
PET THEORY
PETTY CASH
PETTY JURY
PEWTER POT
PHONE CALL
PHONEY WAR
PHOTO CALL
PIANO DUET
PIANO LEGS
PIANO SOLO
PICK A LOCK
PICK A TEAM
PICKED MAN
PICKED OFF
PICKED OUT
PICK FRUIT
PICK HOLES
PICKING UP
PICK OAKUM
PICNIC RUG
PICNIC SET
PIECE RATE
PIED PIPER
PIER GLASS
PIGEON PIE
PIGGY BANK
PIG MARKET
PILAU RICE
PILLAR BOX
PILOT FISH
PINE AFTER
PINE BENCH
PINE TABLE
PINK FLOYD
PINK ICING

PINK PEARL	PLUS FOURS	POUR FORTH
PIN-UP GIRL	PLY A TRADE	POWDER KEG
PIOUS DUTY	POETIC ART	POWER DIVE
PIOUS HOPE	POINT DUTY	POWER PACK
PIPE DREAM	POISON GAS	POWER PLAY
PIPE MAJOR	POISON IVY	POWER TOOL
PIPE MUSIC	POISON PEN	POWER UNIT
PIPING HOT	POKE FUN AT	PRAY ALOUD
PISTON ROD	POKER DICE	PRESS BACK
PITCH DARK	POKER FACE	PRESS CLUB
PITCHED IN	POKER HAND	PRESS DATE
PITCH INTO	POLA NEGRI	PRESS DOWN
PITCH UPON	POLAR BEAR	PRESSED ON
PIT PONIES	POLE VAULT	PRESS GANG
PIT STALLS	POLICE BOX	PRESS HARD
PIT WORKER	POLICE CAR	PRESS HOME
PIXIE RING	POLICE DOG	PRESS LAWS
PLACE A BET	POLISH OFF	PRESS ROOM
PLACE KICK	POLITE ACT	PRESS SEAT
PLACE NAME	POLO MATCH	PRESS SHOW
PLAIN CAKE	POODLE CUT	PRETTY BAD
PLAIN COOK	POOK'S HILL	PRETTY BIG
PLAIN FACT	POOR CATCH	PRICE LIST
PLAIN FOOD	POOR CHILD	PRICE RING
PLAIN JANE	POOR CLASS	PRIME BEEF
PLAIN WORK	POOR DEVIL	PRIME COST
PLAN AHEAD	POOR GRADE	PRISON VAN
PLANE TREE	POOR GUIDE	PRIVY SEAL
PLANT LIFE	POOR HOUSE	PRIZE BULL
PLATE RACK	POOR JUDGE	PRIZE CREW
PLAY ABOUT	POOR LIGHT	PRIZE DRAW
PLAY A CARD	POOR MARKS	PRIZE LIST
PLAY A FISH	POOR MATCH	PRIZE POEM
PLAY A JOKE	POOR SCORE	PRIZE RING
PLAY AN ACE	POOR SPORT	PROOF COPY
PLAY A NOTE	POOR START	PRO PATRIA
PLAY A PART	POOR STUFF	PROPER DAY
PLAY BINGO	POOR TABLE	PROPER MAN
PLAY BOWLS	POOR TASTE	PROPER WAY
PLAY BY EAR	POOR THING	PROPPED UP
PLAY CARDS	POOR THROW	PROSE POEM
PLAY CHESS	POOR VALUE	PROUD STEP
PLAY DARTS	POOR VOICE	PROVE TRUE
PLAYED OUT	POOR WOMAN	PRUNE AWAY
PLAY FALSE	POOR YIELD	PUBLIC EYE
PLAY GAMES	POP NUMBER	PUFFED OUT
PLAY HAVOC	POPPED OFF	PULL A FACE
PLAY POKER	POP RECORD	PULL AHEAD
PLAY ROUGH	POP SINGER	PULL APART
PLAY SHARP	PORCH LAMP	PULL ASIDE
PLAY TO WIN	PORT LIGHT	PULLED OFF
PLAY WHIST	POST EARLY	PULLED OUT
PLEASE SIR	POT THE RED	PULL FACES
PLOD ALONG	POUND AWAY	PULL IT OFF
PLUGGED IN	POUND COIN	PULL IT OUT
PLUMP DOWN	POUND NOTE	PULL ROUND

PULL TIGHT
PULL WIRES
PUNCH BOWL
PUNCH LINE
PUNIC WARS
PUPPY LOVE
PURE SPITE
PURE WATER
PURE WHITE
PURE WOMAN
PUSH ASIDE
PUSHED OFF
PUSHED OUT
PUT ACROSS
PUT AT EASE
PUT IN GAOL
PUT IN GEAR
PUT IN HAND
PUT IN JAIL
PUT IN MIND
PUT IN QUOD
PUT IT DOWN
PUT IT OVER
PUT ON AIRS
PUT ON OATH
PUT ON SALE
PUT ON SHOW
PUT ON SIDE
PUT ON TAPE
PUT PAID TO
PUT TO ROUT
PUT TO WORK
PUT UP BAIL
PUT UP WITH
PUZZLE OUT

Q – 9

QUEEN ANNE
QUEEN BESS
QUEEN MARY
QUEEN BIRD
QUEEN CARD
QUEER COVE
QUEER FISH
QUEUE HERE
QUICK FIRE
QUICK SALE
QUICK STEP
QUICK TIME
QUICK WITS
QUICK WORK
QUIET LIFE
QUIET READ
QUIET TIME
QUIET TONE

QUITE A FEW
QUITE FULL
QUITE GOOD
QUITE NEAR
QUITE NICE
QUITE SURE
QUITE WELL
QUIZ NIGHT

R – 9

RABBIT PIE
RACE AHEAD
RACE RIOTS
RACE TRACK
RACING CAR
RACING MAN
RACING SET
RACING TIP
RACY STYLE
RADAR TRAP
RADIO CITY
RADIO MAST
RADIO PLAY
RADIO STAR
RADIO WAVE
RAIN BLOWS
RAIN CHECK
RAIN CLOUD
RAIN COVER
RAIN GAUGE
RAIN WATER
RAISE CAIN
RAISE HELL
RALPH LYNN
RAM RAIDER
RAPID FIRE
RAPID RATE
RA-RA SKIRT
RAREE SHOW
RARE EVENT
RARE STAMP
RARE STEAK
RARE TREAT
RATE OF PAY
RAT POISON
RATTLE OFF
RAVEN HAIR
RAVING MAD
RAW CARROT
RAW COTTON
RAW SPIRIT
RAW TOMATO
RAY OF HOPE
REACH HOME
REACH LAND

READ A BOOK
READ ALOUD
READ IN BED
READ MORSE
READ MUSIC
READ VERSE
READY CASH
READY TO GO
REAL CREAM
REAL DOUBT
REAL SPORT
REAL THING
REAL TONIC
REAL TRUTH
REAL WORLD
REAR LIGHT
REAR WHEEL
REASON WHY
REBEL ARMY
RECORD BID
RECORD RUN
RECORD SUM
RED ARROWS
RED CARPET
RED CHEEKS
RED CHEESE
RED CIRCLE
RED COTTON
RED DEVILS
RED DRAGON
RED DUSTER
RED ENSIGN
RED GROUSE
RED GUARDS
RED INDIAN
RED LETTER
RED MENACE
RED MULLET
RED PENCIL
RED PEPPER
RED PLANET
RED RIBAND
RED RIBBON
RED SETTER
RED SQUARE
RED SPIDER
REED ORGAN
REELED OFF
REFUSE BIN
RELAY RACE
RELIEF BUS
RELIEF MAP
RENT A FLAT
REPAIR JOB
REPLY PAID
REP PLAYER

RESCUE BID	RIVAL FIRM	ROUGH CAST
RHINE WINE	RIVER AVON	ROUGH COAT
RIB OF BEEF	RIVER BANK	ROUGH COPY
RICE PAPER	RIVER BOAT	ROUGH EDGE
RICH UNCLE	RIVER FISH	ROUGHED IT
RICH WIDOW	RIVER NILE	ROUGH GAME
RICH WOMAN	RIVER STYX	ROUGH IDEA
RIDE IT OUT	RIVER TEST	ROUGH LUCK
RIDE ROUGH	RIVER TRIP	ROUGH PLAN
RIDING CAP	ROAD AGENT	ROUGH PLAY
RIDING KIT	ROAD ATLAS	ROUGH ROAD
RIFLE FIRE	ROAD BLOCK	ROUGH SKIN
RIFLE SHOT	ROAD DRILL	ROUGH TIME
RIGHT AWAY	ROAD METAL	ROUGH TYPE
RIGHT BACK	ROAD SENSE	ROUGH WORK
RIGHT BANK	ROAD TO RIO	ROUND FACE
RIGHT CARD	ROAD WORKS	ROUND GAME
RIGHT DOWN	ROAST BEEF	ROUND HAND
RIGHT FACE!	ROAST DUCK	ROUND HEAD
RIGHT FOOT	ROAST LAMB	ROUND HOLE
RIGHT FORM	ROAST MEAT	ROUND OATH
RIGHT HALF	ROAST PORK	ROUND POND
RIGHT HAND	ROAST VEAL	ROUND SHOT
RIGHT HOOK	ROBIN HOOD	ROUND TOUR
RIGHT IDEA	ROCK 'N' ROLL	ROUND TRIP
RIGHT LINE	ROCK OPERA	ROUTED OUT
RIGHT MOOD	ROCK PLANT	ROVING EYE
RIGHT MOVE	ROD OF IRON	ROWAN TREE
RIGHT NAME	ROLE MODEL	ROWING MAN
RIGHT NOTE	ROLL ALONG	ROYAL ARMS
RIGHT ROAD	ROLLING UP	ROYAL BLUE
RIGHT RULE	ROLL OF FAT	ROYAL DUKE
RIGHT SIDE	ROMAN BATH	ROYAL LINE
RIGHT SIZE	ROMAN CAMP	ROYAL MAIL
RIGHT TIME	ROMAN NOSE	ROYAL MILE
RIGHT TURN	ROMAN ORGY	ROYAL MINT
RIGHT VIEW	ROMAN POET	ROYAL NAVY
RIGHT WING	ROMAN ROAD	ROYAL PARK
RIGHT WORD	ROMAN TYPE	ROYAL ROAD
RING A BELL	ROMAN WALL	ROYAL ROBE
RING AGAIN	ROMANY RYE	ROYAL SCOT
RING A PEAL	ROOK RIFLE	ROYAL SEAT
RING CRAFT	ROOK'S MOVE	ROYAL TOUR
RING FALSE	ROOK'S NEST	ROY CASTLE
RING FENCE	ROOK'S PAWN	ROY ROGERS
RING ROUND	ROOM TO LET	RUBBED OUT
RIN TIN TIN	ROOT CAUSE	RUB GENTLY
RIO GRANDE	ROOTED OUT	RUDE WORDS
RIOT SQUAD	ROPE ONE IN	RUE THE DAY
RIPE FRUIT	ROPE TRICK	RUGBY BALL
RISE ABOVE	ROSE MARIE	RUGBY TEAM
RISE EARLY	ROSE PETAL	RUINED MAN
RISING AIR	ROSE WATER	RULE OF LAW
RISING MAN	ROSS ON WYE	RUM AND PEP
RISING SUN	ROTTEN EGG	RUM BOTTLE
RITUAL ACT	ROTTEN ROW	RUMP STEAK

RUM RATION	SAME STAMP	SECOND TRY
RUM RUNNER	SAME TO YOU	SECRET ART
RUN ACROSS	SAM WELLER	SECURE JOB
RUN A HORSE	SANDY LYLE	SEE A GHOST
RUN AROUND	SANDY SOIL	SEE DOUBLE
RUN ASHORE	SAN MARINO	SEED PEARL
RUN IT FINE	SANS SOUCI	SEEING RED
RUNNING IN	SANTA CRUZ	SEEK A CLUE
RUNNING ON	SARAH GAMP	SEEK AFTER
RUN OF LUCK	SAVAGE DOG	SEEK PEACE
RUN SECOND	SAVE MONEY	SEEK SCOPE
RUN TOO FAR	SAVE SPACE	SEE NO EVIL
RUN TO SEED	SAVILE ROW	SEE REASON
RURAL DEAN	SAW THE AIR	SEE THINGS
RUSH ABOUT	SAX ROHMER	SEIZE UPON
RUSH ORDER	SAY CHEESE	SELECT FEW
RUS IN URBE	SAY LITTLE	SELL BADLY
RYE WHISKY	SAY NO MORE	SELL SHORT
	SAY PLEASE	SELL SPACE
S – 9	SCALE DOWN	SEND A CHIT
	SCAPA FLOW	SEND A WIRE
SABLE COAT	SCART LEAD	SEND FORTH
SACRED COW	SCENT GAME	SENIOR BOY
SAD ENDING	SCHOOL AGE	SENIOR MAN
SAD PLIGHT	SCHOOL CAP	SENNA PODS
SAFE CATCH	SCHOOL TIE	SERGE SUIT
SAFE HANDS	SCORE A TRY	SERVE TIME
SAFE HAVEN	SCORE CARD	SERVE WELL
SAFE HOUSE	SCORE DRAW	SET ADRIFT
SAFE PLACE	SCOTCH EGG	SET ALIGHT
SAFEST WAY	SCOTCH FIR	SET AT EASE
SAFETY NET	SCOTS PINE	SET AT ODDS
SAGE GREEN	SCRAPE OFF	SET AT REST
SAIL NORTH	SCRAP IRON	SET A WATCH
SAIL FORTH	SCREAM OUT	SET COURSE
SAILOR BOY	SCREW DOWN	SET EYES ON
SAILOR HAT	SCRUM HALF	SET FIRE TO
SAIL ROUND	SEA BATTLE	SET IN HAND
SAINT IVES	SEA BOTTOM	SET MOVING
SAINT JOAN	SEA BREEZE	SET ON EDGE
SAINT JOHN	SEALED OFF	SET ON FIRE
SAINT PAUL	SEAMY SIDE	SET ON FOOT
SAINT'S DAY	SEARCH FEE	SET PHRASE
SALAD BOWL	SEARCH FOR	SET SPEECH
SALAD DAYS	SEARCH OUT	SET SQUARE
SALE PRICE	SEA SHANTY	SET THEM UP
SALES TALK	SEAT COVER	SETTING IN
SALLY LUNN	SEA TRAVEL	SETTING UP
SALOON BAR	SEA URCHIN	SETTLED IN
SALOON CAR	SEA VOYAGE	SETTLED UP
SALT FLATS	SECOND ACT	SET TO WORK
SALT SPOON	SECOND CUP	SET UP SHOP
SALT TALKS	SECOND DAY	SEVEN AGES
SALT WATER	SECOND ROW	SEVEN DAYS
SAM BROWNE	SECOND SET	SEVEN DEEP
SAME AGAIN	SECOND TEE	SEVEN FEET

SEVEN QUID	SHORT NOTE	SIMPLE SUM
SEVEN SEAS	SHORT ODDS	SIMPLY FAB
SEX APPEAL	SHORT POEM	SING A SONG
SEX KITTEN	SHORT PUTT	SINGLE BED
SEX OBJECT	SHORT READ	SINGLE MAN
SEX SYMBOL	SHORT REST	SINGLE OUT
SHADY DEAL	SHORT SLIP	SING SMALL
SHADY NOOK	SHORT SPAN	SINK A PUTT
SHADY SIDE	SHORT STAY	SINK A WELL
SHADY TREE	SHORT STEP	SIREN SONG
SHAGGY DOG	SHORT TAIL	SIREN SUIT
SHAKE A LEG	SHORT TERM	SIT AT HOME
SHAKE DOWN	SHORT TIME	SITTING UP
SHAKY HAND	SHORT VIEW	SIT UP LATE
SHAM FIGHT	SHORT WALK	SIX-DAY WAR
SHAM SLEEP	SHORT WAVE	SIX HEARTS
SHANGRI LA	SHORT WORD	SIX MONTHS
SHAPE WELL	SHORT WORK	SIX O'CLOCK
SHARP BEND	SHOUT DOWN	SIX OUNCES
SHARP BLOW	SHOVEL HAT	SIX POINTS
SHARP EDGE	SHOVE PAST	SIX POUNDS
SHARP EYES	SHOW CAUSE	SIX SPADES
SHARP FALL	SHOWED OFF	SIXTH FORM
SHARP NOTE	SHOWED OUT	SIXTH HOLE
SHARP PAIN	SHOW FIGHT	SIXTH PART
SHARP RISE	SHOW MERCY	SIXTH RACE
SHARP TURN	SHOW ONE IN	SIXTH TIME
SHARP WITS	SHOW PIECE	SIX TO FOUR
SHARP WORK	SHOW PLACE	SIX TRICKS
SHED A TEAR	SHOW ROUND	SIX WHEELS
SHED BLOOD	SHOW SIGNS	SIZE EIGHT
SHED LIGHT	SHOW STYLE	SIZE SEVEN
SHEEP FARM	SHRIEK OUT	SIZE THREE
SHEER DROP	SHRILL CRY	SKATE OVER
SHEER LUCK	SHRIVEL UP	SKETCH MAP
SHEER SILK	SHUT TIGHT	SKETCH OUT
SHEET IRON	SICK LEAVE	SKIM ALONG
SHELF LIFE	SICKLY HUE	SKIN DIVER
SHELL SUIT	SIDE ISSUE	SKIN FLICK
SHELL PEAS	SIGHT GAME	SKINS GAME
SHIP'S BELL	SIGHT LAND	SKIP A MEAL
SHIP'S BOAT	SIGNAL BOX	SLACK ROPE
SHIP'S GUNS	SIGN A PACT	SLACK TIME
SHOCK WAVE	SIGN BELOW	SLANG WORD
SHOE BRUSH	SIGNED OFF	SLATE CLUB
SHOOT DOWN	SILK PURSE	SLAVE AWAY
SHOP FLOOR	SILK SCARF	SLAVE CAMP
SHOP FRONT	SILK SOCKS	SLEEP ON IT
SHOP HOURS	SILLY FOOL	SLEEP WELL
SHOP TO LET	SILLY TALK	SLEEPY AIR
SHORN LAMB	SILVER CUP	SLIDE BACK
SHORT HAIR	SILVER FIR	SLIDE DOWN
SHORT HEAD	SILVER FOX	SLIM WAIST
SHORT HOLE	SILVER SEA	SLINK PAST
SHORT LIFE	SILVER URN	SLIP COVER
SHORT LIST	SIMON PURE	SLIPPED IN

SLIPPED UP	SMOKE A LOT	SOLID FOOD
SLIT SKIRT	SMOKE BOMB	SOLID FUEL
SLOP BASIN	SMOKED EEL	SOLID GOLD
SLOPE ARMS	SMOKED HAM	SOLID MASS
SLOPE DOWN	SMOKE RING	SOLID MEAL
SLOPPY JOE	SMOKY CITY	SOLID TYRE
SLOUCH HAT	SMOKY FIRE	SOLID VOTE
SLOW DEATH	SMOKY ROOM	SOLO DANCE
SLOW MARCH	SMOOTH OUT	SOLO WHIST
SLOW MATCH	SMOOTH SEA	SOME HOPES
SLOW MUSIC	SMUGGLE IN	SONG CYCLE
SLOW PULSE	SNAIL PACE	SONG TITLE
SLOW START	SNAKE BITE	SONIC BOOM
SLOW TEMPO	SNAPPED UP	SON OF A GUN
SLOW TRAIN	SNEAK AWAY	SOON AFTER
SLOW WALTZ	SNEAK PAST	SORE PLACE
SLUSH FUND	SNOB VALUE	SORE POINT
SLY AS A FOX	SNOW QUEEN	SORE TRIAL
SLY CORNER	SNOW SCENE	SO TO SPEAK
SLY HUMOUR	SNOW STORM	SOTTO VOCE
SMALL ARMS	SNOW WHITE	SOUL MUSIC
SMALL BEER	SNUGGLE UP	SOUL OF WIT
SMALL BORE	SOAP OPERA	SOUND BODY
SMALL COAL	SOAR ABOVE	SOUND MIND
SMALL COIN	SOBER DOWN	SOUND TYPE
SMALL DEBT	SOBER FACT	SOUND WAVE
SMALL DOOR	SOB SISTER	SOUP LADLE
SMALL FEET	SOCIAL WAR	SOUP PLATE
SMALL FLAT	SOCKET SET	SOUP SPOON
SMALL GAME	SODA WATER	SOUR CREAM
SMALL HEAD	SOFT DRINK	SOUR TASTE
SMALL HOLE	SOFT FOCUS	SOUTH BANK
SMALL ITEM	SOFT FRUIT	SOUTH POLE
SMALL LOAF	SOFT GOING	SOUTH SEAS
SMALL LOAN	SOFT GOODS	SOUTH WIND
SMALL MIND	SOFT HEART	SOUTH ZONE
SMALL PART	SOFT LIGHT	SPACE RACE
SMALL PORT	SOFT MUSIC	SPACE SHIP
SMALL RISK	SOFT PEDAL	SPACE SUIT
SMALL ROOM	SOFT THING	SPACE WALK
SMALL SIZE	SOFT TOUCH	SPARE CASH
SMALL SLAM	SOFT VOICE	SPARE COPY
SMALL SPOT	SOFT WATER	SPARE PART
SMALL TALK	SOFT WORDS	SPARE ROOM
SMALL TOWN	SO IT SEEMS	SPARE TIME
SMALL TWIG	SOLAR CELL	SPARE TYRE
SMALL TYPE	SOLAR TIME	SPARKS FLY
SMART ALEC	SOLAR YEAR	SPEAK WELL
SMART BOMB	SOLDIER ON	SPEECH DAY
SMART CARD	SOLE AGENT	SPEEDED UP
SMARTEN UP	SOLEMN VOW	SPEED HUMP
SMART GIRL	SOLE OWNER	SPEED IT UP
SMART PACE	SO LET IT BE	SPEED KING
SMART SUIT	SOLE TRUST	SPEND TIME
SMART WALK	SOLID BALL	SPERM BANK
SMELL A RAT	SOLID BODY	SPILL OVER

SPILL SALT	STAND FIRM	STILL MORE
SPILT MILK	STAND HIGH	STILL OPEN
SPIN A COIN	STAND IDLE	STILL ROOM
SPIN A DISC	STAND OVER	STILL WINE
SPIN A YARN	ST ANDREWS	STINK BOMB
SPIN DRIER	STAND UP TO	STIR CRAZY
SPIN ROUND	STAPLE GUN	STIRRED UP
SPIT IT OUT	STAR ACTOR	ST MATTHEW
SPLIT OPEN	STARE DOWN	ST MICHAEL
SPLIT PEAS	STAR PUPIL	STOCK FARM
SPLIT VOTE	STARRY SKY	STOCK LIST
SPONGE BAG	STAR SHELL	STOCK PART
SPONGE MOP	START A ROW	STOCK PILE
SPONGE OUT	START A WAR	STOCK SHOT
SPORTS BAG	START BACK	STOCK SIZE
SPORTS CAR	STARTED UP	STOKE CITY
SPORTS DAY	START TO GO	STOLE AWAY
SPORTS FAN	START WITH	STONE COLD
SPOT CHECK	START WORK	STONE DEAD
SPOT DANCE	STARVE OUT	STONE DEAF
SPOT OF INK	STATE FAIR	STONE WALL
SPOT PRIZE	STATE FARM	STOOP DOWN
SPOT TO EAT	STATUS QUO	STOP A BLOW
SPREAD OUT	STAY ALIVE	STOP A LEAK
SPRING OUT	STAY AWAKE	STOP AND GO
SPUN GLASS	STAYED OUT	STOP IN BED
SQUARE JAW	STAYED PUT	STOPPED UP
SQUARE LEG	STAY IN BED	STOP PRESS
SQUARE OFF	STAY STILL	STOP SHORT
SQUARE ONE	ST BERNARD	STOP THIEF!
SQUARE PEG	STEAL AWAY	STOP VALVE
SQUAT DOWN	STEAL PAST	STORE AWAY
SQUEEZE IN	STEAL UP ON	STORM CONE
STABLE BOY	STEAM BATH	STORMY SEA
STAFF FUND	STEAM IRON	ST PANCRAS
STAFF ROOM	STEAM OPEN	ST PATRICK
STAFF WORK	STEEL BAND	STRAP DOWN
STAGE DOOR	STEEL BILL	STRAW POLL
STAGE NAME	STEEL MILL	STRAW VOTE
STAGE PLAY	STEEL TAPE	STRAY AWAY
STAGE SHOW	STEEP HILL	STREAK OUT
STAGGER IN	STEP ASIDE	STREAM OUT
STAG NIGHT	STEP DANCE	STREET MAP
STAG PARTY	STEP SHORT	STRETCH UP
STALE CAKE	STEP STOOL	STRIDE OFF
STALE JOKE	STEVE CRAM	STRIDE OUT
STALE LOAF	STICK AT IT	STRIKE OFF
STALE NEWS	STICK 'EM UP	STRIKE OIL
STAMP DOWN	STICK FAST	STRIKE OUT
STAMP DUTY	STICK IT ON	STRIKE PAY
STAND AWAY	STICK TO IT	STRING BAG
STAND BACK	STICKY END	STRING OUT
STAND BAIL	STIFF GALE	STRIP BARE
STAND DOWN	STIFF NECK	STRIP CLUB
STAND EASY	STIFF TEST	STRONG ALE
STAND FAST	STILL LIFE	STRONG ARM

STRONG BOX
STRONG MAN
STRONG TEA
STRUCK OFF
STRUCK OUT
STRUNG OUT
STUD HORSE
STUDIO ONE
STUD POKER
STUDY FORM
STUDY HARD
SUB JUDICE
SUDDEN END
SUDDEN FIT
SUEZ CANAL
SUGAR BEET
SUGAR CANE
SUGAR PLUM
SUIT AT LAW
SULTRY AIR
SUMMING UP
SUN BONNET
SUNDAY TEA
SUN HELMET
SUNK FENCE
SUN LOUNGE
SUNNY SIDE
SUN VALLEY
SUN YAT-SEN
SUPER BOWL
SUPPOSE SO
SURE THING
SURE TO WIN
SURVEY MAP
SUSAN SHAW
SWAGGER IN
SWALLOW UP
SWARM OVER
SWEAR BY IT
SWEAR WORD
SWEEP AWAY
SWEEP DOWN
SWEEP PAST
SWEET CORN
SWEET DISH
SWEET NELL
SWEET PEAS
SWEET SHOP
SWEET SONG
SWEET WINE
SWELL IDEA
SWELL TIME
SWEPT AWAY
SWING BACK
SWING HIGH
SWISS ALPS

SWISS CITY
SWISS NAVY
SWISS ROLL
SWITCH OFF
SWOOP DOWN

T – 9

TAB HUNTER
TABLE BIRD
TABLE FISH
TABLE LAMP
TABLE SALT
TABLE TALK
TABLE WINE
TAKE ABACK
TAKE A BATH
TAKE A CARD
TAKE A CASE
TAKE A COPY
TAKE A CURE
TAKE A DROP
TAKE A FALL
TAKE AFTER
TAKE A HAND
TAKE A HINT
TAKE A LOOK
TAKE A MEAL
TAKE AMISS
TAKE AN ELL
TAKE A NOTE
TAKE APART
TAKE A PEEP
TAKE A PILL
TAKE A REST
TAKE A RISK
TAKE A SEAT
TAKE A SNAP
TAKE A TAXI
TAKE A TEST
TAKE A TOSS
TAKE A TRAM
TAKE A TRIP
TAKE A TURN
TAKE A VIEW
TAKE A VOTE
TAKE A WALK
TAKE A WIFE
TAKE COVER
TAKE DRUGS
TAKE HEART
TAKE IN TOW
TAKE ISSUE
TAKE LEAVE
TAKE LUNCH
TAKE MY TIP

TAKEN DOWN
TAKE NOTES
TAKE ON OIL
TAKE PAINS
TAKE PLACE
TAKE PRIDE
TAKE RISKS
TAKE ROOMS
TAKE SHAPE
TAKE SIDES
TAKE SNUFF
TAKE STEPS
TAKE STOCK
TAKE TURNS
TAKE UP ART
TAKING OFF
TAKING OUT
TALE OF WOE
TALK ABOUT
TALKED BIG
TALKED OUT
TALK ROUND
TALK SENSE
TALK TRIPE
TALL ORDER
TALL POPPY
TALL STORY
TALL WOMAN
TANK CORPS
TAR BARREL
TAROT CARD
TASK FORCE
TASMAN SEA
TAWNY PORT
TAX DEMAND
TAX FIDDLE
TAX REBATE
TAX RELIEF
TAY BRIDGE
TEA FOR TWO
TEA GARDEN
TEA KETTLE
TEA LEAVES
TEAR ABOUT
TEAR ALONG
TEAR APART
TEA RATION
TEAR IN TWO
TEDDY BEAR
TEDDY GIRL
TELL NO LIE
TELL NO ONE
TELL TALES
TEMPLE BAR
TEMPT FATE
TENDER AGE

TEN MONTHS	THE GIPPER	THE SOLENT
TENNIS ACE	THE GOSPEL	THE SPHINX
TENNIS NET	THE GRACES	THE SPLITS
TEN O'CLOCK	THE GUARDS	THE SPOILS
TENOR CLEF	THE HILTON	THE SPRING
TENOR DRUM	THE ICE AGE	THE SQUIRE
TENOR OBOE	THE JACKAL	THE STATES
TEN OUNCES	THE JET AGE	THE STITCH
TEN POINTS	THE JUNGLE	THE STOCKS
TEN POUNDS	THE KAISER	THE STONES
TEN ROUNDS	THE LANCET	THE STRAND
TENTH HOLE	THE LATEST	THE SUMMER
TENTH PART	THE LATTER	THE TATLER
TENTH TIME	THE LEVANT	THE TEMPLE
TEST MATCH	THE LIVING	THE THAMES
TEST PAPER	THE LIZARD	THE TICKET
TEST PIECE	THE LOSERS	THE TIVOLI
TEST PILOT	THE LOUVRE	THE UMPIRE
TEXAS CITY	THE MAQUIS	THE UNSEEN
THAT'S LIFE	THE MASSES	THE WAY OUT
THAT'S THAT	THE MASTER	THE WINNER
THE ALBANY	THE MEDWAY	THE WINTER
THE ALBION	THEME PARK	THEY'RE OFF!
THE ALLIES	THEME SONG	THICK HAIR
THE AMAZON	THE METHOD	THICK HEAD
THE ARMADA	THE MIKADO	THICK MIST
THE AUTUMN	THE MINUET	THICK SKIN
THE AZORES	THE MORGUE	THICK SNOW
THE BALTIC	THE MOVIES	THICK SOUP
THE BIG TOP	THE OCCULT	THICK WIRE
THE BOARDS	THE OLD VIC	THIN BLOOD
THE BOTTOM	THE OLD WAY	THINK BACK
THE BOUNTY	THE ORIENT	THINK BEST
THE BOURSE	THE PAPERS	THINK FAST
THE BOWERY	THE PEOPLE	THING HARD
THE BROADS	THE PLAGUE	THINK LONG
THE BUDGET	THE PLOUGH	THINK OVER
THE CINEMA	THE POLICE	THIN ON TOP
THE CLERGY	THE PUBLIC	THIN SHELL
THE COLBYS	THE QUEENS	THIN SLICE
THE CREEPS	THE RABBLE	THIN TWINE
THE CRIMEA	THE RED SEA	THIRD FORM
THE DALEKS	THE RINGER	THIRD GEAR
THE DANUBE	THE RIVALS	THIRD HAND
THE DELUGE	THE ROCKET	THIRD HEAT
THE DESERT	THE RUBBER	THIRD HOLE
THE EMPIRE	THE RUSHES	THIRD JUMP
THE FALLEN	THE SCOTCH	THIRD LINE
THE FINISH	THE SCRIPT	THIRD PART
THE FLICKS	THESE DAYS	THIRD RACE
THE FLOODS	THE SENATE	THIRD RATE
THE FRENCH	THE SEVERN	THIRD TEAM
THE FÜHRER	THE SHAKES	THIRD TERM
THE FUTURE	THE SHIRES	THIRD TEST
THE GANGES	THE SIGHTS	THIRD TIME
THE GENTRY	THE SMITHS	THIRD WEEK

THIRD YEAR	TIN LIZZIE	TOTAL COST
THIRST FOR	TIN OF SOUP	TOTAL LOSS
THIRTY ALL	TIN OPENER	TOTEM POLE
THIS EARTH	TIP AND RUN	TOTE PRICE
THIS MONTH	TIPPED OFF	TO THE BONE
THIS WAY IN	TIPSY CAKE	TO THE BRIM
THIS WAY UP	TIP-UP SEAT	TO THE EAST
THORPE BAY	TIRED EYES	TO THE FORE
THRASH OUT	TIRING JOB	TO THE FULL
THREE ACES	TIT FOR TAT	TO THE GOOD
THREE ACTS	TITHE BARN	TO THE HILT
THREE DAYS	TITIAN RED	TO THE LAST
THREE DEEP	TITLE DEED	TO THE LEFT
THREE EGGS	TITLE PAGE	TO THE LIFE
THREE FEET	TITLE ROLE	TO THE MOON
THREE LAPS	TITO GOBBI	TO THE WEST
THREE PIPS	TO A DEGREE	TO THIS DAY
THREE QUID	TOAST RACK	TOUCH DOWN
THREE SETS	TO BE BRIEF	TOUCHED UP
THREE STAR	TODAY WEEK	TOUCH UPON
THREE TENS	TODDLE OFF	TOUCH WOOD
THROW A FIT	TOGGED OUT	TOUGHEN UP
THROW AWAY	TOILET SET	TOUGH LUCK
THROW BACK	TOKEN VOTE	TOUGH MEAT
THROW DOWN	TOKYO ROSE	TOUGH SKIN
THROWN OUT	TO LEEWARD	TOUGH SPOT
THROW OPEN	TOM PEARSE	TOWEL BALE
THROW OVER	TOM SAWYER	TOWER HILL
TICKED OFF	TOM WATSON	TOWER OVER
TIC-TAC MAN	TON OF COAL	TOWER UNIT
TIDAL FLOW	TON OF COKE	TOWN CLERK
TIDAL RACE	TON OF LEAD	TOWN CRIER
TIDAL WAVE	TON OF SALT	TOWN HOUSE
TIED HOUSE	TON WEIGHT	TOWN MOUSE
TIE IN A BOW	TONY AWARD	TOY POODLE
TIGER HUNT	TONY BLAIR	TRACE BACK
TIGER LILY	TOOK PLACE	TRACK DOWN
TIGER MOTH	TOOL CHEST	TRACK SUIT
TIGHTEN UP	TOO LITTLE	TRADE BOOM
TIGHT GRIP	TO ONE SIDE	TRADE FAIR
TIGHT HAND	TOO STRONG	TRADE MARK
TIGHT REIN	TOP DRAWER	TRADE NAME
TIGHT SPOT	TOP PEOPLE	TRADE WIND
TILL POINT	TOP SECRET	TRAIL ARMS
TIME BEING	TOP STOREY	TRAIL BOSS
TIME CHECK	TOP THIRTY	TRAIN FARE
TIME FLIES	TOP TO TAIL	TRAIN LOAD
TIME LIMIT	TOP TWENTY	TRAM DEPOT
TIME OF DAY	TOP WEIGHT	TRAMPLE ON
TIME OF WAR	TORCH SONG	TRAP THREE
TIME STUDY	TORY PARTY	TREAD DOWN
TIME TAKEN	TOSS ABOUT	TREE HOUSE
TIME TO EAT	TOSS A COIN	TREE STUMP
TIME TO PAY	TOSS ASIDE	TRIAL GAME
TINDER BOX	TOSS FOR IT	TRIAL JURY
TIN HELMET	TOSSING UP	TRIAL SPIN

TRIAL TRIP
TRIBAL LAW
TRIBAL WAR
TRICKY BIT
TRICKY JOB
TRIED HARD
TRIED IT ON
TRILBY HAT
TRIM WAIST
TRIPPED UP
TROJAN WAR
TROT ALONG
TROT IT OUT
TRUDGE OFF
TRUE VALUE
TRUE WORTH
TRUMP CARD
TRUNK CALL
TRUNK LINE
TRUNK ROAD
TRUSSED UP
TRUST DEED
TRUST FUND
TRUTH DRUG
TRUTH GAME
TRY HARDER
TRY IN VAIN
TRY TO STOP
TSETSE FLY
TUBAL CAIN
TUBE TRAIN
TUCK ONE IN
TUCK ONE UP
TUDOR ROSE
TUG OF LOVE
TULIP TREE
TULSE HILL
TUMBLE OFF
TUMBLE OUT
TUMMY ACHE
TUMMY TUCK
TUNNY FISH
TUN OF BEER
TUN OF WINE
TURFED OUT
TURK'S HEAD
TURN ABOUT
TURN AGAIN
TURN A HAIR
TURN ASIDE
TURNED OFF
TURNED OUT
TURN GREEN
TURNING IN
TURNING UP
TURN IT OFF

TURN LOOSE
TURN NASTY
TURN RIGHT
TURN ROUND
TURN TO ICE
TURN WHITE
TWEED SUIT
TWELVE MEN
TWICE A DAY
TWICE FIVE
TWICE FOUR
TWICE NINE
TWICE OVER
TWICE TOLD
TWIGGED IT
TWIN GIRLS
TWIN SCREW
TWIN SOULS
TWO A PENNY
TWO COPIES
TWO FIFTHS
TWO FOR ONE
TWO FOR TEA
TWO HALVES
TWO HEARTS
TWO LOAVES
TWO MONTHS
TWO NINTHS
TWO O'CLOCK
TWO OUNCES
TWO POINTS
TWO POUNDS
TWO QUARTS
TWO ROUNDS
TWO SPADES
TWO STOOLS
TWO STRAWS
TWO THIRDS
TWO TO COME
TWO TRICKS
TWO VERSES
TWO VOICES
TWO WHEELS

U – 9

UGLY AS SIN
UGLY CROWD
UNCLE TOBY
UNDER A BAN
UNDER ARMS
UNDER FIRE
UNDER OATH
UNDER SAIL
UNDER SEAL
UNHEARD OF

UNHOLY JOY
UNHOLY ROW
UNION CARD
UNION FLAG
UNION JACK
UNIT TRUST
UP AGAINST
UP AND AT 'EM
UP AND AWAY
UP AND DOWN
UP AND OVER
UP COUNTRY
UP FOR SALE
UPPER CASE
UPPER DECK
UPPER FORM
UPPER HAND
UPPER LIMB
UPPER PART
UP THE HILL
UP THE LINE
UP THE POLE
UP THE WALL
UP TO SNUFF
URBAN AREA
URBAN MYTH
URCHIN CUT
URIAH HEEP
URSA MAJOR
URSA MINOR
USE AS A PEG
USUAL TEXT
UTTER LOSS
UTTER RUIN

V – 9

VACANT LOT
VADE MECUM
VAGUE HOPE
VAGUE IDEA
VAIN ABUSE
VAIN BOAST
VAIN GLORY
VANITY BAG
VAST FRAME
VAULT OVER
VEER RIGHT
VEER ROUND
VENIAL SIN
VERSE FORM
VERS LIBRE
VERY IMAGE
VERY LGHT
VERY OFTEN
VERY QUICK

VERY STEEP
VERY SWEET
VEX A SAINT
VICE SQUAD
VICE VERSA
VICKI BAUM
VIC OLIVER
VIDEO DISC
VIDEO SHOP
VIDEO TAPE
VILLA PARK
VIN DU PAYS
VINGT ET UN
VIOLIN BOW
VISUAL AID
VITAL PART
VITAL ROLE
VIVE LE ROI
VIVID BLUE
VOID SPACE
VOLTE FACE
VOLUME ONE
VOLUME SIX
VOLUME TEN
VOLUME TWO
VOTING AGE
VOTING DAY
VOX HUMANA
VOX POPULI

W – 9

WAGE CLAIM
WAGE PAUSE
WAGES BILL
WAGE SCALE
WAGE SLAVE
WAIST HIGH
WAIT ABOUT
WAIT FOR IT!
WAIT FOR ME!
WAIT TABLE
WAIT THERE
WAKE EARLY
WAKES WEEK
WALK ABOUT
WALKED OFF
WALKED OUT
WALKER CUP
WALK ON AIR
WALK OUT ON
WALL LIGHT
WALTZ HOME
WALTZ KING
WALTZ TIME
WALTZ TUNE

WANDER OFF
WANDER OUT
WANTED MAN
WAR DAMAGE
WAR EFFORT
WAR GRAVES
WAR HEROES
WAR LEADER
WARM HEART
WARM NIGHT
WARM PLACE
WARM SPELL
WAR MUSEUM
WARM WATER
WARNED OFF
WAR OFFICE
WAR ON WANT
WAR POLICY
WAR RECORD
WAR VICTIM
WAR WORKER
WASH CLEAN
WASHED OUT
WASPS' NEST
WASP STING
WASP WAIST
WASTE AWAY
WASTE FOOD
WASTE LAND
WASTE TIME
WATCH OVER
WATER BABY
WATER DOWN
WATER FOWL
WATER HOLE
WATER JUMP
WATER LILY
WATER MAIN
WATER POLO
WATER RATE
WATER TANK
WAVE ASIDE
WAVE A WAND
WAVE POWER
WAX CANDLE
WAX EFFIGY
WAX FIGURE
WAX STRONG
WAY BEHIND
WAY OF LIFE
WEAK CHEST
WEAKER SEX
WEAK HEART
WEAK POINT
WEAK STATE
WEAK STYLE

WEAK THING
WEAK VOICE
WEAK WOMAN
WEALTH TAX
WEAR A HALO
WEAR A MASK
WEAR BLACK
WEAVE A WEB
WEB OF LIES
WEEDED OUT
WEIGH DOWN
WEIGHED IN
WELCOME IN
WELL AGAIN
WELL AHEAD
WELL AIRED
WELL BEGUN
WELL BELOW
WELL OILED
WELL SET UP
WELL SPENT
WELL TAPED
WELSH BARD
WELSH HARP
WENT AHEAD
WENT BELOW
WENT FORTH
WENT ROUND
WENT TO BED
WENT TO POT
WENT TO SEA
WENT TO WAR
WENT UNDER
WENT WRONG
WEST COAST
WEST FRONT
WEST POINT
WEST WALES
WET AND DRY
WET SEASON
WET SPONGE
WET WICKET
WHALE MEAT
WHAT A LARK!
WHAT A LIFE!
WHAT A PITY!
WHAT'S WHAT
WHEAT GERM
WHEEL AWAY
WHERE IS IT?
WHIP ROUND
WHISK AWAY
WHITE BEAR
WHITE CITY
WHITE FISH
WHITE FLAG

WHITE GOLD
WHITE HAIR
WHITE HEAT
WHITE HOPE
WHITE KING
WHITE LADY
WHITE LEAD
WHITE LINE
WHITE LOAF
WHITE MARK
WHITE MEAT
WHITE MICE
WHITE NILE
WHITE NOTE
WHITE PAWN
WHITE PINE
WHITE PORT
WHITE RACE
WHITE ROOK
WHITE ROSE
WHITE SALE
WHITE SPOT
WHITE STAR
WHITE WINE
WHOLE SKIN
WICKED LIE
WICKED ONE
WIDE APART
WIDE AWAKE
WIDE BERTH
WIDE FIELD
WIDE GUESS
WIDE RANGE
WIDE SCOPE
WIDE SWEEP
WIDE WORLD
WIGAN PIER
WILD BEAST
WILD GEESE
WILD GOOSE
WILD GRASS
WILD GUESS
WILD HORSE
WILD NIGHT
WILD PARTY
WILD STATE
WILD THYME
WILL POWER
WILL TO WIN
WIN A FIGHT
WIN A MATCH
WIN A POINT
WIN A PRIZE
WIND GAUGE
WINDING UP
WIND POWER

WIND SCALE
WINDY SIDE
WIN EASILY
WINE GLASS
WINE PARTY
WINE TABLE
WIN FAVOUR
WINGED ANT
WINKLE OUT
WIN OR LOSE
WIN RENOWN
WIN THE CUP
WIN THE DAY
WIPE CLEAN
WIRE BRUSH
WIRE FENCE
WISE WOMAN
WITCH HUNT
WITH A BANG
WITH A WILL
WITH SKILL
WITH SUGAR
WOMAN'S MAN
WOMEN ONLY
WOMEN'S LIB
WONDER WHY
WOODEN BOX
WOODEN LEG
WOOD GREEN
WOOD NYMPH
WORD MAGIC
WORK BENCH
WORKED OUT
WORKER BEE
WORK ETHIC
WORK IT OUT
WORK LOOSE
WORK OF ART
WORK PARTY
WORKS BAND
WORK STUDY
WORKS WELL
WORK TABLE
WORLD BANK
WORLD FAIR
WORLD'S END
WORLD TOUR
WORSE LUCK
WORST PART
WORST TEAM
WORTH A LOT
WORTH A TRY
WORTHY AIM
WRAPPED UP
WRAP ROUND
WRENCH OUT

WRITE BACK
WRITE DOWN
WRITE HOME
WRITE WELL
WRONG DATE
WRONG DOOR
WRONG IDEA
WRONG MOVE
WRONG NAME
WRONG RATE
WRONG ROAD
WRONG SIDE
WRONG STEP
WRONG TIME
WRONG TURN
WRONG VIEW
WRONG WORD
WROUGHT UP
WYATT EARP
WYE VALLEY

Y – 9

YACHT CLUB
YACHT RACE
YARD OF ALE
YEA AND NAY
YELLOW DOG
YELLOW SEA
YES PLEASE
YET TO COME
YORKED OUT
YOUNG BIRD
YOUNG GIRL
YOUNG FOLK
YOUNG IDEA
YOUNG LOVE
YOUNG THUG
YOUR FAULT
YOUR GRACE
YOUR SHARE
YOUTH CLUB
YUPPIE FLU

Z – 9

ZOO INMATE
ZUYDER ZEE

A – 10

ABE LINCOLN
A BIT PAST IT
ABJECT FEAR
ABLE FELLOW
ABLE SEAMAN

ABLE TO COPE	AIR CUSHION	AMBER LIGHT
ABOARD SHIP	AIR DEFENCE	AMBLE ALONG
ABOVE BOARD	AIR DISPLAY	AMEN CORNER
ABOVE IT ALL	AIR FREIGHT	AMPLE CAUSE
ABOVE PRICE	AIR HOSTESS	AMPLE MEANS
ABOVE WATER	AIR MARSHAL	AMPLE SCOPE
ABRUPT EXIT	AIR SERVICE	AMY JOHNSON
ACCESS TIME	AIR WARFARE	AND ALL THAT
ACE OF CLUBS	ALAIN PROST	AND SO FORTH
ACE SERVICE	ALARM CLOCK	AND SO TO BED
ACETIC ACID	ALARM WATCH	AND THE LIKE
ACHING FEET	ALBERT HALL	AND THE REST
ACHING VOID	ALBUM CHART	ANGEL CHILD
ACID REMARK	ALF GARNETT	ANGLED SHOT
ACID TONGUE	ALF'S BUTTON	ANGORA GOAT
ACT AS AGENT	ALI SHUFFLE	ANGORA WOOL
ACT AS COACH	ALL BUT A FEW	ANGRY SCENE
ACT AS GUIDE	ALL COLOURS	ANGRY WORDS
ACTIVE CELL	ALL CORRECT	ANILINE DYE
ACTIVE LIFE	ALL DAY LONG	ANIMAL FARM
ACTIVE LIST	ALL FORLORN	ANIMAL FOOD
ACTIVE MIND	ALL FOR LOVE	ANIMAL GRAB
ACTIVE PART	ALL HALLOWS	ANIMAL LIFE
ACT OF FAITH	ALL HAYWIRE	ANKLE SOCKS
ACT OF FOLLY	ALL IN A HEAP	ANNABEL LEE
ACT OF GRACE	ALL IN ORDER	ANNE BOLEYN
ACT OF MERCY	ALL KEYED UP	ANNO DOMINI
ACT OF PIETY	ALL MIXED UP	ANNUAL RENT
ACT OF UNION	ALL MOD CONS	ANOTHER DAY
ACT THE FOOL	ALL OF A GLOW	ANOTHER WAY
ACT THE GOAT	ALL OF A HEAP	ANSWER BACK
ACT THE HERO	ALL OF A KIND	ANY OLD IRON
ACT THE HOST	ALL PARTIES	ANY OLD TIME
ACT THE PART	ALL PRESENT	APPLE GREEN
ACUTE ANGLE	ALL SET TO GO	APPLE SAUCE
ADAM AND EVE	ALL THE BEST	APPLIED ART
ADAM'S APPLE	ALL THE LUCK	APRICOT JAM
ADD A CLAUSE	ALL THE MORE	APRON STAGE
ADDIS ABABA	ALL THE RAGE	APT ANALOGY
ADELE LEIGH	ALL THE REST	APT SCHOLAR
ADOPTED SON	ALL THE SAME	AQUA FORTIS
ADVANCE MAN	ALL THE TIME	ARABIAN SEA
ADVICE NOTE	ALL THE YEAR	ARAB LEAGUE
ADVISE WELL	ALL THROUGH	ARABLE FARM
AERIAL VIEW	ALL-TIME LOW	ARAB LEGION
AFRICA STAR	ALL TOO SOON	ARABLE LAND
AFTER A TIME	ALL TOO WELL	ARAB STATES
AFTER DEATH	ALMOND CAKE	ARCHED BACK
AFTER HOURS	ALMOND TREE	ARENA STAGE
AFTER LUNCH	ALMOST DEAD	ARMED FORCE
AFTER TODAY	ALMOST FULL	ARMED GUARD
A GREAT DEAL	ALMOST OVER	ARMED TRUCE
A GREAT MANY	ALPACA COAT	ARMS AKIMBO
AID AND ABET	ALPINE CLUB	ARM'S LENGTH
AIM TOO HIGH	ALPINE RACE	ARMY DOCTOR
AIR CLEANER	ALTAR CLOTH	ARMY ORDERS

ARRIVE LATE
ART GALLERY
ARTHUR DENT
ARTHUR RANK
ART STUDENT
ART SUBJECT
ART THEATRE
AS ARRANGED
ASCOT HEATH
ASCOT RACES
AS INTENDED
ASK A FAVOUR
ASK FOR HELP
ASK FOR MORE
ASK FOR TIME
ASK TOO MUCH
AS MAN TO MAN
AS PER USUAL
AS PROMISED
ASTON VILLA
ASTRAL BODY
AT ALL COSTS
AT ALL HOURS
AT ALL TIMES
AT ANY PRICE
AT A PREMIUM
AT A STRETCH
AT A TANGENT
AT A VENTURE
AT DAYBREAK
AT DAYLIGHT
AT FULL TIDE
AT GUN-POINT
AT HALF-MAST
AT ITS WORST
AT LONG LAST
ATOMIC BOMB
ATOMIC PILE
AT ONE'S BEST
AT ONE SCOOP
AT ONE'S DOOR
AT ONE'S EASE
AT ONE'S FEET
AT ONE'S POST
AT ONE'S SIDE
AT SEA LEVEL
ATTEND MASS
AT THE ALTAR
AT THE DERBY
AT THE FRONT
AT THE LOCAL
AT THE OPERA
AT THE READY
AT THE SLOPE
AT THE WHEEL
AT THE WORST

AT VARIANCE
AT WHAT TIME?
AUBURN HAIR
AULD REEKIE
AU PAIR GIRL
AUTO-REPEAT
AUTUMN WIND
AVA GARDNER
AVANT GARDE
AVERAGE AGE
AVERAGE MAN
AVERAGE OUT
AVID DESIRE
AWFUL SIGHT
AWKWARD AGE
AXE TO GRIND
AXLE GREASE

B – 10

BABE IN ARMS
BABE UNBORN
BABY BOOMER
BABY FARMER
BABY'S DUMMY
BABY SITTER
BABY WALKER
BACK A HORSE
BACK A LOSER
BACK GARDEN
BACK IN TIME
BACK MARKER
BACK NUMBER
BACK RASHER
BACK STAIRS
BACK STITCH
BACK STREET
BACK STROKE
BACK TO BACK
BACK TO BASE
BACK TO WORK
BACON CURER
BAD ACCOUNT
BAD ACTRESS
BAD BARGAIN
BAD CLIMATE
BAD COMPANY
BAD CONDUCT
BAD DICTION
BAD EXAMPLE
BAD FORTUNE
BAD GRAMMAR
BAD HARVEST
BAD HUSBAND
BAD LEARNER
BAD LOOKOUT

BAD MANAGER
BAD MANNERS
BAD MISTAKE
BAD OUTLOOK
BAD QUALITY
BAD SERVANT
BAD SERVICE
BAD SOCIETY
BAD TACTICS
BAD THEATRE
BAD WEATHER
BAD WRITING
BAG OF BONES
BAG OF FLOUR
BAG OF NAILS
BAGS OF TIME
BAITED TRAP
BAKED APPLE
BAKED BEANS
BAKER'S SHOP
BALANCE DUE
BALLET SHOE
BALL OF FIRE
BALL OF WOOL
BALTIC PORT
BANANA BELT
BANANA BOAT
BANANA SKIN
BAND LEADER
BAND OF HOPE
BAND OF IRON
BANDY WORDS
BANK RAIDER
BANK ROBBER
BANK TO BANK
BANK VAULTS
BANNED BOOK
BANTAM COCK
BAN THE BOMB
BARBARY APE
BARBED WIRE
BARBIE DOLL
BARD OF AVON
BARE BOARDS
BARE CHANCE
BARELY PASS
BARIUM MEAL
BARLEY WINE
BAR PARLOUR
BARREN LAND
BASE MOTIVE
BASIC TRUTH
BASIL BRUSH
BAT AND BALL
BATH OLIVER
BATTEN DOWN

BATTER DOWN
BATTERY HEN
BAWDY HOUSE
BEACH BUNNY
BEACH GAMES
BEACHY HEAD
BEACON FIRE
BEAK STREET
BEARER BOND
BEAR GARDEN
BEAR IN MIND
BEAR MALICE
BEAR WITH ME
BEAT HOLLOW
BEAT THE AIR
BEAT THE RAP
BEAUTY SHOP
BEAUTY SPOT
BE CHAIRMAN
BECKY SHARP
BECOME LESS
BECOME SANE
BEDDED DOWN
BED OF NAILS
BED OF ROSES
BEEF CATTLE
BEER BARREL
BEER BOTTLE
BEER CELLAR
BEER GARDEN
BEFORE DAWN
BEFORE DUSK
BEFORE LONG
BEFORE NOON
BEFORE TIME
BEG A FAVOUR
BEG FOR MORE
BEG FOR TIME
BEGGAR MAID
BEGIN AGAIN
BEHAVE WELL
BEHIND BARS
BEHIND TIME
BE INFERIOR
BELL THE CAT
BELOW DECKS
BELTED EARL
BELT SANDER
BE MERCIFUL
BE MISTAKEN
BENDED KNEE
BENEATH ONE
BENT DOUBLE
BEN TRAVERS
BE PREPARED
BERLIN WALL

BE SENSIBLE
BE SOCIABLE
BEST BITTER
BEST CHANCE
BEST EFFORT
BEST FRIEND
BEST OF FIVE
BEST OF PALS
BEST PEOPLE
BEST POLICY
BEST SELLER
BEST SILVER
BEST WAY OUT
BEST WISHES
BE SUPERIOR
BE TOO SMART
BETTE DAVIS
BETTER DAYS
BETTER DEAD
BETTER HALF
BETTER HOLE
BETTER IDEA
BETTER SELF
BETTER SORT
BETTING ACT
BETTING MAN
BEYOND HOPE
BE YOURSELF
BIBLE CLASS
BID AGAINST
BIG BAD WOLF
BIG BROTHER
BIGGER SIZE
BIGGIN HILL
BIG HELPING
BIG SUCCESS
BIG SWINDLE
BIJOU VILLA
BILL AND COO
BILL BENBOW
BILL OF FARE
BILL OF SALE
BINARY CODE
BING CROSBY
BINGO NIGHT
BIRD IN HAND
BIRD OF PREY
BISCUIT BOX
BISCUIT TIN
BISHOP'S HAT
BITE THE LIP
BITING WIND
BIT OF A MESS
BIT OF FLUFF
BIT PATTERN
BITTER BEER

BITTER BLOW
BITTER PILL
BITTER RICE
BLACK ADDER
BLACK ANGUS
BLACK ARROW
BLACK AS INK
BLACK AS JET
BLACK BEARD
BLACK BEAST
BLACK BOOKS
BLACK BOOTS
BLACK BREAD
BLACK CLOUD
BLACK DEATH
BLACK DRESS
BLACKED OUT
BLACK FRIAR
BLACK HEART
BLACK HORSE
BLACK LACES
BLACK LOOKS
BLACK MAGIC
BLACK MARIA
BLACK PAINT
BLACK PAPER
BLACK PATCH
BLACK PIECE
BLACK POWER
BLACK QUEEN
BLACK SHEEP
BLACK SHIRT
BLACK SHOES
BLACK SOCKS
BLACK WATCH
BLACK WIDOW
BLANK PAPER
BLANK SHEET
BLANK SPACE
BLANK STARE
BLANK VERSE
BLASTED OAK
BLAZE A PATH
BLAZING SUN
BLEAK HOUSE
BLEED WHITE
BLEW THE LOT
BLIND ALLEY
BLIND DRUNK
BLIND FAITH
BLIND GUESS
BLITZ KRIEG
BLOCK OF ICE
BLONDE HAIR
BLOOD COUNT
BLOOD DONOR

BLOOD GROUP
BLOOD HORSE
BLOOD MONEY
BLOOD ROYAL
BLOOD SERUM
BLOOD SPORT
BLOODY MARY
BLOTTED OUT
BLOW BY BLOW
BLOW ME DOWN
BLUE AND RED
BLUE CHEESE
BLUE DANUBE
BLUE DEVILS
BLUE ENSIGN
BLUE GROTTO
BLUE HELMET
BLUE LAGOON
BLUE MONDAY
BLUE MURDER
BLUE ORCHID
BLUE PENCIL
BLUE RIBAND
BLUE RIBBON
BLUE STREAK
BLUNT WORDS
BOAT PEOPLE
BOAT RACING
BOBBED HAIR
BOBBY MOORE
BODILY HARM
BODILY PAIN
BODY SWERVE
BOGGED DOWN
BOILED BEEF
BOILED FISH
BOILED RICE
BOILER ROOM
BOILER SUIT
BOILING HOT
BOILING OIL
BOLD DESIGN
BOLD RELIEF
BOLD STROKE
BOMBAY DUCK
BOMB CRATER
BOMB DAMAGE
BONDED DEBT
BOND STREET
BONE TO PICK
BONUS ISSUE
BOOBY PRIZE
BOOK A TABLE
BOOK CRITIC
BOOKING FEE
BOOK OF FATE

BOOK REVIEW
BOOK RIGHTS
BOOT POLISH
BORED STIFF
BORING WORK
BORN LEADER
BORN TO RULE
BORSTAL BOY
BOSTON REEL
BO TO A GOOSE
BOTTLE BANK
BOTTLED ALE
BOTTOM GEAR
BOTTOM LINE
BOTTOM RUNG
BOUGHT OVER
BOULDER DAM
BOUNCE BACK
BOUND TC WIN
BOWIE KNIFE
BOWL A BREAK
BOWLED OVER
BOWL OF RICE
BOWL OF SOUP
BOW THE KNEE
BOX BARRAGE
BOXING RING
BOX OF DATES
BOX OF PILLS
BOY AND GIRL
BOYS IN BLUE
BRACING AIR
BRAIN CHILD
BRAIN DEATH
BRAIN DRAIN
BRAIN FEVER
BRAIN STORM
BRANCH LINE
BRASS PLATE
BRASS TACKS
BRAVE FRONT
BRAVE IT OUT
BREAD FRUIT
BREAD ROUND
BREAD SAUCE
BREAK A BONE
BREAK A DATE
BREAK A FALL
BREAK AN ARM
BREAK BREAD
BREAK COVER
BREAK DANCE
BREAK FAITH
BREAK FORTH
BREAK IN TWO
BREAK IT OFF

BREAK LOOSE
BREAK OF DAY
BREAK RANKS
BREAK SHORT
BREAST PUMP
BREATHE OUT
BRER RABBIT
BRETT YOUNG
BRIDAL GOWN
BRIDAL VEIL
BRIDGE A GAP
BRIDGE CLUB
BRIDGE HAND
BRIDGE OVER
BRIDGE ROLL
BRIDLE PATH
BRIDLE REIN
BRIEF VISIT
BRIGHT BLUE
BRIGHT EYES
BRIGHT IDEA
BRIGHT SIDE
BRIGHT SPOT
BRIGHT STAR
BRING ABOUT
BRING A CASE
BRING A SUIT
BRING FORTH
BRING ROUND
BRING TO BAY
BRISK TRADE
BROAD ACRES
BROAD ARROW
BROAD BEANS
BROAD GAUGE
BROKEN BACK
BROKEN BONE
BROKEN DOWN
BROKEN HOME
BROKEN LINE
BROKEN NECK
BROKEN NOSE
BROKEN REED
BROKEN WORD
BROKER'S MAN
BRONX CHEER
BROUGHT LOW
BROWN BOOTS
BROWN BREAD
BROWNED OFF
BROWN GOODS
BROWN LACES
BROWN PAINT
BROWN PAPER
BROWN SHIRT
BROWN SHOES

BROWN STONE
BROWN STUDY
BROWN SUGAR
BRUSH ASIDE
BRUTE FORCE
BUBBLE BATH
BUBBLE OVER
BUCKET SEAT
BUCKET SHOP
BUCK RABBIT
BUCK ROGERS
BULK BUYING
BULLET HEAD
BULLET HOLE
BULL MARKET
BUMPER CROP
BUMPING CAR
BUMP SUPPER
BURNE JONES
BURN RUBBER
BURNT AMBER
BURNT BLACK
BURNT TOAST
BURST FORTH
BUSHEY PARK
BUS SHELTER
BUS STATION
BUSY AS A BEE
BUSY PERSON
BUSY STREET
BUSY WOPKER
BUTTER DISH
BUTTONED UP
BUY AND SELL
BUY BRITISH
BY ACCIDENT
BY ALL MEANS
BY AND LARGE
BY ANY MEANS
BY CONTRAST
BY DAYLIGHT
BY GASLIGHT
BYGONE DAYS
BY INSTINCT
BY SNATCHES
BY SURPRISE
BY THE CLOCK
BY THE DOZEN
BY THE RIVER
BY TRANSFER
BY YOURSELF

C – 10

CABIN TRUNK
CADET CORPS

CADET FORCE
CADGE A LIFT
CAFÉ AU LAIT
CAKE OF SOAP
CALDER HALL
CALL A TRUCE
CALL BY NAME
CALLED AWAY
CALL IT A DAY
CALL OF DUTY
CALL OPTION
CALL SPADES
CALL TO ARMS
CALL TO MIND
CALL TRUMPS
CAMDEN TOWN
CAME IN LAST
CAME IN VIEW
CAMEL CORPS
CAMEL'S HUMP
CAMEL'S MILK
CAMEL TRAIN
CAMPING OUT
CANDY FLOSS
CANNED BEER
CANNED FOOD
CANNEL COAL
CANNON BALL
CAP AND GOWN
CAPE COLONY
CAPER SAUCE
CARBON COPY
CARD PLAYER
CAREER GIRL
CARGO SPACE
CAR LICENCE
CAROLE CARR
CARRIED OFF
CARRIER BAG
CARRY COALS
CARRY IT OFF
CARSON CITY
CAR SURFING
CART GREASE
CASE A JOINT
CASE OF WINE
CASE RECORD
CASHEW NUTS
CASH IN HAND
CASK OF WINE
CASPIAN SEA
CAST A CLOUT
CAST ANCHOR
CAST A SPELL
CASTING OFF
CASUAL WARD

CASUS BELLI
CAT BURGLAR
CATCH A BALL
CATCH A COLD
CATCH A CRAB
CATCH A TRAM
CATCHY TUNE
CATHODE RAY
CATO STREET
CAT SCANNER
CAT'S CRADLE
CATTLE FARM
CATTLE FOOD
CATTLE SHOW
CAUGHT COLD
CAUGHT FIRE
CAUSE ALARM
CAUSE A RIOT
CAUSE A STIR
CAUSTIC WIT
CAVERN CLUB
CAXTON HALL
CELERY SALT
CENTRE HALF
CERAMIC HOB
CERTAIN DAY
CHAIN SMOKE
CHAIN STORE
CHAIR COVER
CHALET GIRL
CHANCE SHOT
CHANGE ENDS
CHANGE GEAR
CHANGE OVER
CHANGE STEP
CHAPEL FOLK
CHAPTER ONE
CHAPTER SIX
CHAPTER TWO
CHARGE CARD
CHARGE HAND
CHAT-UP LINE
CHEAP MONEY
CHEAP PAPER
CHEAP SKATE
CHEAT DEATH
CHECK POINT
CHEESE DISH
CHEESED OFF
CHEESE RIND
CHEESE ROLL
CHELSEA BUN
CHELSEA SET
CHEQUE BOOK
CHERRY LIPS
CHERRY RIPE

CHERRY TART
CHERRY TREE
CHESS BOARD
CHESS MATCH
CHESS PIECE
CHEST OF TEA
CHEVY CHASE
CHEWING GUM
CHEW THE CUD
CHEW THE FAT
CHEW THE RAG
CHEYNE WALK
CHICKEN RUN
CHIEF CLERK
CHIEF POINT
CHIEF SCOUT
CHILD BRIDE
CHILD'S PLAY
CHILLY ROOM
CHIMNEY TOP
CHINA PLATE
CHINESE BOX
CHIPPING IN
CHORUS GIRL
CHOSEN RACE
CHURCH ARMY
CHURCH DOOR
CHURN IT OUT
CIDER APPLE
CIGAR SMOKE
CIGAR STORE
CILLA BLACK
CINQUE PORT
CIRCUS RING
CITRIC ACID
CITY CENTRE
CITY EDITOR
CITY FATHER
CITY LIGHTS
CITY LIMITS
CITY OF BATH
CITY OFFICE
CITY POLICE
CITY STREET
CITY TEMPLE
CITY WORKER
CIVIC CROWN
CIVIC PRIDE
CIVIL COURT
CIVIL STATE
CIVIL WRONG
CLAP EYES ON
CLAP HOLD OF
CLAP ON SAIL
CLARK GABLE
CLASP HANDS

CLASSY DAME
CLAUSE FOUR
CLAY PIGEON
CLEAN BREAK
CLEANED OUT
CLEAN FIGHT
CLEAN HABIT
CLEAN HANDS
CLEAN LINEN
CLEAN LIVER
CLEAN SHAVE
CLEAN SHEET
CLEAN SLATE
CLEAN SWEEP
CLEAN TOWEL
CLEAN WATER
CLEAR AS DAY
CLEAR AS MUD
CLEAR FIELD
CLEAR IMAGE
CLEAR LIGHT
CLEAR PRINT
CLEAR ROUND
CLEAR SPACE
CLEAR STYLE
CLEAR VOICE
CLEAR WATER
CLEFT STICK
CLEVER DICK
CLEVER IDEA
CLEVER MOVE
CLEVER SAVE
CLIMB A HILL
CLIMB A TREE
CLIVE JAMES
CLIVE LLOYD
CLOCK RADIO
CLOCK TOWER
CLOSED BOOK
CLOSED DOOR
CLOSED MIND
CLOSED SHOP
CLOSE GRIPS
CLOSE MATCH
CLOSE OF DAY
CLOSE ORDER
CLOSE SHAVE
CLOSE STUDY
CLOSE THING
CLOSE WATCH
CLOSING BID
CLOVE HITCH
CLOVEN FOOT
CLOVEN HOOF
CLOVER LEAF
CLUB MEMBER

CLUMSY HAND
CLUNK CLICK
COACH PARTY
COAL CELLAR
COARSE FISH
COARSE JOKE
COARSE MIND
COAST ALONG
COAT OF ARMS
COAT OF MAIL
COAT POCKET
COBALT BLUE
COBALT BOMB
COCK A SNOOK
COCONUT OIL
COCONUT SHY
CODDLED EGG
COFFEE BEAN
COFFEE ROOM
COFFIN NAIL
COIL MAGNET
COLD BUFFET
COLD FAXING
COLD FUSION
COLD REASON
COLD REGION
COLD SEASON
COLD SHOWER
COLD TONGUE
COLD TURKEY
COLD WINTER
COLE PORTER
COLLEGE BOY
COLLEGE RAG
COLOUR FILM
COLOUR TONE
COME ACROSS
COME ADRIFT
COME AND SEE
COME AROUND
COME ASHORE
COME AT ONCE
COME CLOSER
COMEDY HOUR
COME HITHER
COME IN LAST
COME INSIDE
COME NEARER
COME SECOND
COME TO BITS
COME TO HAND
COME TO HARM
COME TO HEEL
COME TO KNOW
COME TO LIFE
COME TO PASS

COME TO REST
COME TO STAY
COME UNDONE
COMIC OPERA
COMIC PAPER
COMIC STRIP
COMIC VERSE
COMMON BOND
COMMON COLD
COMMON FORM
COMMON FUND
COMMON GOOD
COMMON HERD
COMMON JEST
COMMON LAND
COMMON NAME
COMMON NOUN
COMMON ROOM
COMMON SALT
COMMON SEAL
COMMON SORT
COMMON TALK
COMMON TASK
COMMON TIME
COMMON TYPE
COMPANY LAW
COMPANY TAX
CONAN DOYLE
CONTACT MAN
CONTOUR MAP
COOKED MEAT
COPPER BELT
COPPER COIN
COPPER MINE
COPPER WIRE
COPYING INK
COPY TYPIST
COR ANGLAIS
CORDON BLEU
CORD REWIND
CORNED BEEF
CORNER FLAG
CORNER KICK
CORNER POST
CORNER SEAT
CORNER SHOP
CORNER SITE
CORNER UNIT
CORNET SOLO
COS LETTUCE
COSMIC RAYS
COSTA BRAVA
COSY CORNER
COTTAGE PIE
COTTON CLUB
COTTON MILL

COTTON REEL
COTTON YARN
COUNCIL TAX
COUNTED OUT
COUNT HANDS
COUNT HEADS
COUNT ME OUT
COUNTRY INN
COUNTRY PUB
COUNT SHEEP
COUNTY CORK
COUNTY DOWN
COUNTY HALL
COUNTY MAYO
COUNTY TOWN
COUP DE MAIN
COURT DRESS
COURT OF LAW
COURT ORDER
COURT SCENE
COURT USHER
COVER DRIVE
COVERED WAY
COVER POINT
COWBOY SUIT
COW PARSLEY
COX'S ORANGE
CRACK A CRIB
CRACK A JOKE
CRACKED EGG
CRACK HOUSE
CRADLE SONG
CRASH DUMMY
CRAWL ABOUT
CREDIT CARD
CREDIT NOTE
CREDIT SIDE
CRÊPE PAPER
CRÊPE SOLES
CRICKET BAT
CRICKET CAP
CRIMEAN WAR
CRIME STORY
CROOKED MAN
CROP CIRCLE
CROSS IT OFF
CROSS IT OUT
CROSS PATHS
CROSS WORDS
CROUCH DOWN
CROWDED OUT
CROWD ROUND
CROWD SCENE
CROWN AGENT
CROWN DERBY
CROWN GLASS

CROWN LEASE
CROWN PIECE
CRUDE FACTS
CRUDE FORCE
CRUDE METAL
CRUEL SHAME
CRUSTY LOAF
CRUSTY PORT
CRY FOR HELP
CRYING FOUL
CRY OF AGONY
CRY OUT LOUD
CRYSTAL SET
CRY TOO SOON
CUCKOO PINT
CUNARD LINE
CUP AND BALL
CUPID'S DART
CUP OF COCOA
CUP OF WATER
CUP WINNERS
CURATE'S EGG
CURED BACON
CURL THE LIP
CURRANT BUN
CURRENT HIT
CURRY HOUSE
CURRY SAUCE
CURTAIN OFF
CURTAIN ROD
CURT ANSWER
CURVED LINE
CURZON LINE
CUSTARD PIE
CUT A FIGURE
CUT ASUNDER
CUT A TUNNEL
CUT CORNERS
CUT FLOWERS
CUT FOR DEAL
CUT IT SHORT
CUT THE CAKE
CUT THE COST
CUT THE KNOT
CUT THE TAPE
CUT THROUGH
CUTTING OUT
CUTTLE FISH
CUT UP ROUGH
CYCLE LIGHT
CYCLE RALLY

D – 10

DAB OF PAINT
DAILY BREAD

DAILY DOZEN	DEAD SEASON	DEVIL TO PAY
DAILY EVENT	DEAD SECRET	DICK BARTON
DAILY GRIND	DEAD WEIGHT	DICK TURPIN
DAILY HABIT	DEAL GENTLY	DIE FOR LOVE
DAILY PAPER	DEALT A BLOW	DIE OF GRIEF
DAILY PRESS	DEAN MARTIN	DIE OF SHOCK
DAILY ROUND	DEAR BRUTUS	DIEPPE RAID
DAINTY DISH	DEAR FRIEND	DIESEL FUEL
DAIRY CREAM	DEAR READER	DIG A TRENCH
DAIRY FRESH	DEATH HOUSE	DIG FOR GOLD
DAISY CHAIN	DEATH KNELL	DILLY DALLY
DAISY WHEEL	DEATH METAL	DINAH SHORE
DAMASK ROSE	DEATH SCENE	DINE AT HOME
DAMP COURSE	DEATH'S DOOR	DINING CLUB
DANCE MUSIC	DEATH'S HEAD	DINING HALL
DANCING MAN	DEATH SQUAD	DINING ROOM
DANGER LINE	DEBIT ENTRY	DINNER BELL
DANGER LIST	DEBT CRISIS	DINNER GONG
DANISH BLUE	DECENT TYPE	DINNER HOUR
DARK CLOUDS	DECK QUOITS	DINNER SUIT
DARK COLOUR	DECK TENNIS	DINNER TIME
DARK CORNER	DECLARE OFF	DIP THE FLAG
DARK MATTER	DECLARE WAR	DIRECT LINE
DARK PURPLE	DECREE NISI	DIRTY HABIT
DARK SECRET	DEEP BREATH	DIRTY LINEN
DARTS BOARD	DEEPEST DYE	DIRTY MONEY
DARTS MATCH	DEEP FREEZE	DIRTY STORY
DASH OF SODA	DEEP IN DEBT	DIRTY TRICK
DAS KAPITAL	DEEP LITTER	DIRTY WATER
DATA SOURCE	DEEPLY HURT	DISC JOCKEY
DATIVE CASE	DEEP PURPLE	DISC BRAKES
DAVID FROST	DEEP REGRET	DISH AERIAL
DAVID JASON	DEEP SECRET	DISH WASHER
DAVID NIVEN	DEEP SORROW	DISPEL FEAR
DAWN ATTACK	DEEP THROAT	DIVE BOMBER
DAWN CHORUS	DEEP WATERS	DIVINE KING
DAWN FRENCH	DEEP YELLOW	DIVING BIRD
DAWN OF HOPE	DEER FOREST	DIZZY ROUND
DAWN OF LIFE	DELFT CHINA	DIZZY SPELL
DAWN OF LOVE	DEL CHANNON	DIZZY WHIRL
DAWN PATROL	DEMAND NOTE	DO A BAD TURN
DAY DREAMER	DEMON RUMMY	DO A STRETCH
DAY NURSERY	DEN OF LIONS	DO AWAY WITH
DAY OF GRACE	DENSE CROWD	DO BUSINESS
DAYS GONE BY	DENVER BOOT	DOCK LABOUR
DAYS OF YORE	DENY ACCESS	DOCK MASTER
DAYS TO COME	DEODAR TREE	DOCTOR FELL
DAY TRIPPER	DEPTH GUIDE	DOCTOR'S FEE
DEAD CENTRE	DERBY CHINA	DOG BISCUIT
DEADEN PAIN	DERBY HORSE	DOG EATS DOG
DEAD GROUND	DERBY SWEEP	DOGGER BANK
DEAD LETTER	DERNIER CRI	DOG LICENCE
DEADLY BLOW	DESERT SONG	DOG'S CHANCE
DEADLY DULL	DEUCES WILD	DOG'S DINNER
DEAD MATTER	DEVIL'S DYKE	DOG TRAINER
DEAD ON TIME	DEVIL'S LUCK	DOING RIGHT

DOING WRONG
DO IN THE EYE
DO IT AT ONCE
DO LIKEWISE
DOLLAR AREA
DOLLAR BILL
DOLL'S HOUSE
DONALD DUCK
DON BRADMAN
DONE BY HAND
DONEGAL BAY
DONKEY WORK
DO NOT TOUCH!
DON QUIXOTE
DON'T BE RUDE!
DON'T CALL US
DON'T WAIT UP
DO ONE PROUD
DO ONE'S BEST
DO ONE'S DUTY
DO ONE'S HAIR
DOOR HANDLE
DOOR TO DOOR
DO OVERTIME
DOPE ADDICT
DOPE PEDLAR
DO PORRIDGE
DORIAN GRAY
DOROTHY BAG
DO THE HALLS
DO THE TANGO
DO THE TRICK
DO THE TWIST
DOTTED LINE
DOTTED NOTE
DOUBLE BACK
DOUBLE BASS
DOUBLE BLUE
DOUBLE CHIN
DOUBLE DATE
DOUBLE FIVE
DOUBLE FOUR
DOUBLE LIFE
DOUBLE LOCK
DOUBLE NINE
DOUBLE ROOM
DOUBLE STAR
DOUBLE TAKE
DOUBLE TALK
DOUBLE TIME
DOUBLING UP
DOUBLY SURE
DOUGLAS FIR
DO VIOLENCE
DOWER HOUSE
DOWN AND OUT

DOWN AT HEEL
DOWN THE PIT
D'OYLY CARTE
DRAG ARTIST
DRAKE'S DRUM
DRAUGHT ALE
DRAW A BLANK
DRAW A PRIZE
DRAW BREATH
DRAWING INK
DRAW IT FINE
DRAW IT MILD
DRAWN MATCH
DRAWN SWORD
DRAW ONE OUT
DRAW STUMPS
DRAW SWORDS
DR BARNARDO
DR DOLITTLE
DREAM HOUSE
DREAM WORLD
DREAMY EYES
DREAMY LOOK
DRESS SENSE
DRESS SHIRT
DRIED FRUIT
DRIFT ALONG
DRIFT APART
DRINK MONEY
DRINK VODKA
DRINK WATER
DRIVEN SNOW
DROP A BRICK
DROP A CATCH
DROP ANCHOR
DROP ASTERN
DROP BEHIND
DROP BY DROP
DROP OF RAIN
DROPPED OFF
DROPPED OUT
DROP THE HEM
DROWNED OUT
DROWNED RAT
DRUG ADDICT
DRUG DEALER
DRUG PUSHER
DRUMMED OUT
DRUMMER BOY
DRY AS A BONE
DRY BATTERY
DRY CANTEEN
DRY CLIMATE
DRY MARTINI
DRY MEASURE
DRY ONESELF

DRY SHAMPOO
DRY THE EYES
DRY WEATHER
DUEL OF WITS
DUE RESPECT
DUFFEL COAT
DUKE OF KENT
DUKE OF YORK
DULCE DOMUM
DULL COLOUR
DULL MOMENT
DUMB ANIMAL
DUMB BLONDE
DUMB CRAMBO
DUMB WAITER
DUMMY WHIST
DUNDEE CAKE
DUSKY BRIDE
DUSTBIN LID
DUST JACKET
DUST TO DUST
DUTCH BULBS
DUTCH PARTY
DUTCH TREAT
DUTCH UNCLE
DUTY ROSTER
DWARF BEANS
DWARF PLANT
DYING CAUSE
DYING WORDS

E – 10

EACH AND ALL
EACH TO EACH
EACH-WAY BET
EAGLE'S NEST
EARL'S COURT
EARLY DOORS
EARLY HOURS
EARLY LUNCH
EARLY NIGHT
EARLY RISER
EARLY STAGE
EARLY START
EARLY TO BED
EARLY TRAIN
EARLY TUDOR
EARLY VISIT
EARLY WORKS
EARTHA KITT
EAR TRUMPET
EASILY DONE
EAST AFRICA
EAST ANGLIA
EAST BERLIN

EASTER TERM
EASTER TIME
EASTER WEEK
EAST INDIAN
EAST INDIES
EAST IS EAST
EAST LONDON
EAST OF EDEN
EAST OF SUEZ
EAST RIDING
EAST TO WEST
EASY ACCESS
EASY DOES IT
EASY GALLOP
EASY IN MIND
EASY MANNER
EASY MARKET
EASY STAGES
EASY STREET
EASY TARGET
EASY TO COPY
EASY VIRTUE
EASY WAY OUT
EASY WICKET
EASY WINNER
EAT ONE'S HAT
EBB AND FLOW
ECCLES CAKE
EDAM CHEESE
EDISON BELL
EDMUNDO ROS
EDWARD LEAR
EDWIN DROOD
EFFECTS MAN
EGG CUSTARD
EGG ON CHIPS
EGG ON TOAST
EGG POACHER
EGG SHAMPOO
EIGHT BELLS
EIGHT DOZEN
EIGHT DRAWS
EIGHT GROSS
EIGHTH ARMY
EIGHTH HOLE
EIGHT HOURS
EIGHTH PART
EIGHTH RACE
EIGHTH TIME
EIGHT MILES
EIGHT PARTS
EIGHT PINTS
EIGHT SCORE
EIGHTS WEEK
EIGHT TIMES
EIGHT TO ONE

EIGHT WEEKS
EIGHTY DAYS
EIGHT YEARS
EL CORDOBES
ELEVEN DAYS
ELEVEN FEET
ELEVEN PLUS
ELEVEN QUID
ELINOR GLYN
ELLEN TERRY
EMERY CLOTH
EMERY PAPER
EMPIRE GOWN
EMPTY BOAST
EMPTY CHAIR
EMPTY CURSE
EMPTY GLASS
EMPTY HOUSE
EMPTY PURSE
EMPTY SHELL
EMPTY SOUND
EMPTY SPACE
EMPTY TRUCK
EMPTY WORDS
END IN SMOKE
END PRODUCT
ENEMY AGENT
ENEMY ALIEN
ENEMY FLEET
ENEMY LINES
ENGAGE A CAB
ENGINE ROOM
ENID BLYTON
ENJOY PEACE
ENOCH ARDEN
ENOUGH ROOM
ENOUGH SAID
ENOUGH TIME
ENOUGH TO DO
ENTICE AWAY
ENTRY MONEY
EPIC POETRY
EPSOM DOWNS
EPSOM RACES
EPSOM SALTS
EQUAL PARTS
EQUAL SHARE
EQUALS SIGN
EQUAL TERMS
EQUAL VALUE
ERIC AMBLER
ERIC BARKER
ERIC COATES
ERRING WIFE
ERROL FLYNN
ESCORT DUTY

ESTATE DUTY
ETHEL M. DELL
ETON COLLAR
ETON JACKET
EUSTON ROAD
EVE BOSWELL
EVELYN LAYE
EVEN CHANCE
EVEN HIGHER
EVEN NUMBER
EVEN TEMPER
EVER SO MANY
EVER SO MUCH
EVERY MONTH
EVERY OTHER
EVERY WOMAN
EVIL GENIUS
EVIL INTENT
EVIL SPIRIT
EVIL TEMPER
EXACT IMAGE
EXACT SENSE
EXCESS FARE
EXCISE BILL
EXCISE DUTY
EX DIVIDEND
EXETER CITY
EXIT PERMIT
EXPERT SHOT
EXPIRY DATE
EXPORT ONLY
EXPRESS FEE
EXTRA COVER
EXTRA MONEY
EXTRA POWER
EYES OF BLUE
EYE WITNESS

F – 10

FACE DANGER
FACE DEFEAT
FACE POWDER
FACE TO FACE
FACE UP TO IT
FACTORY ACT
FADED YOUTH
FAIL TO COME
FAIL TO MEET
FAIL TO MOVE
FAIL TO OBEY
FAINT HEART
FAINT LIGHT
FAINT SOUND
FAIR AMOUNT
FAIR CHANCE

FAIR ENOUGH
FAIR EXCUSE
FAIR INCOME
FAIRLY GOOD
FAIRLY WARM
FAIRLY WELL
FAIR OF FACE
FAIR REPORT
FAIR SAMPLE
FAIR SHARES
FAIR TACKLE
FAIRY QUEEN
FAIRY STORY
FAIRY WORLD
FALL ASLEEP
FALL ASTERN
FALL BEHIND
FALLEN IDOL
FALL FOUL OF
FALLING OFF
FALL IN LINE
FALL IN LOVE
FALL IN WITH
FALL OF SNOW
FALL OF TROY
FALLOW DEER
FALLOW LAND
FALL SILENT
FALL TO BITS
FALSE ALARM
FALSE ALIBI
FALSE BEARD
FALSE CLAIM
FALSE CREED
FALSE FRONT
FALSE HOPES
FALSE IMAGE
FALSE LIGHT
FALSE LOGIC
FALSE PRIDE
FALSE SCENT
FALSE SHAME
FALSE START
FALSE TEETH
FAMILY FEUD
FAMILY FIRM
FAMILY LIFE
FAMILY NAME
FAMILY SEAT
FAMILY TIES
FAMILY TREE
FAMOUS DEED
FAMOUS NAME
FAMOUS WORK
FANCY DRESS
FANCY GOODS

FANCY PRICE
FANCY SOCKS
FANNY ADAMS
FAN THE FIRE
FAR AND AWAY
FAR AND NEAR
FAR AND WIDE
FAR BETWEEN
FAR COUNTRY
FARE DODGER
FARM ANIMAL
FARM BUTTER
FARMER'S BOY
FARM WORKER
FAR-OFF LAND
FAR THE BEST
FAR TOO MANY
FAR TOO MUCH
FAST ASLEEP
FAST BOWLER
FAST COLOUR
FAST READER
FAST WICKET
FAST WORKER
FATAL CAUSE
FATAL CRASH
FATAL ERROR
FATAL WOUND
FAT AND LEAN
FATHER'S DAY
FATHER TIME
FATS WALLER
FATTED CALF
FAX MACHINE
FAY COMPTON
FEARFUL DIN
FEATHER BED
FEATHER BOA
FEAT OF ARMS
FEEBLE JOKE
FEEBLE MIND
FEED THE CAT
FEED THE DOG
FEEL AT EASE
FEEL AT HOME
FEEL BETTER
FEEL CHILLY
FEEL DEEPLY
FEEL GROGGY
FEEL HUNGRY
FEELING ILL
FEELING SAD
FEEL NO PITY
FEEL RELIEF
FEEL SECURE
FEEL SLEEPY

FEEL UNWELL
FEEL UP TO IT
FEET OF CLAY
FELL INTENT
FELT-TIP PEN
FENCE ROUND
FEN COUNTRY
FETTER LANE
FEUDAL LORD
FEVER PITCH
FIANNA FAIL
FIBRE GLASS
FIELD EVENT
FIELD SPORT
FIERY CROSS
FIERY STEED
FIESTA TIME
FIFTEEN ALL
FIFTEEN MEN
FIFTH FLOOR
FIFTH GREEN
FIFTH OF MAY
FIFTH PLACE
FIFTH ROUND
FIFTY MILES
FIFTY TIMES
FIFTY TO ONE
FIFTY YEARS
FIGHT A DUEL
FIGHT FOR IT
FIGHT IT OUT
FIGHT SHY OF
FILE A CLAIM
FILIAL DUTY
FILL IN TIME
FILL THE AIR
FILL THE GAP
FILM ADDICT
FILM CENSOR
FILM COLONY
FILM CRITIC
FILM OF DUST
FILM REVIEW
FILM RIGHTS
FILM STUDIO
FILTHY TALK
FINAL CAUSE
FINAL CLAIM
FINAL COUNT
FINAL EVENT
FINAL FLING
FINAL ISSUE
FINAL OFFER
FINAL POINT
FINAL PROOF
FINAL SCENE

FINAL SCORE
FINAL STAGE
FINAL TERMS
FINAL TOUCH
FINANCE ACT
FIND A BASIS
FIND A PLACE
FIND FAVOUR
FIND GUILTY
FIND RELIEF
FIND THE WAY
FINE CHANCE
FINE FELLOW
FINE FETTLE
FINE FIGURE
FINE PERSON
FINE SHOWER
FINEST HOUR
FINE VELLUM
FINE WRITER
FINGER WAVE
FINISH LAST
FINITE VERB
FIRE A SALVO
FIRE BUCKET
FIRE ESCAPE
FIREMAN SAM
FIRE POLICY
FIRE SCREEN
FIRING LINE
FIRM ADVICE
FIRM BELIEF
FIRM DEMAND
FIRM DENIAL
FIRM FRIEND
FIRM GROUND
FIRST BATCH
FIRST BLOOD
FIRST BLUSH
FIRST CAUSE
FIRST CHILD
FIRST CLAIM
FIRST DANCE
FIRST DRAFT
FIRST ENTRY
FIRST EVENT
FIRST FLOOR
FIRST FLUSH
FIRST GREEN
FIRST HOUSE
FIRST ISSUE
FIRST LIGHT
FIRST MAN IN
FIRST MATCH
FIRST NIGHT
FIRST NOVEL

FIRST OF ALL
FIRST OF MAY
FIRST PLACE
FIRST PRIZE
FIRST PROOF
FIRST ROUND
FIRST SHIFT
FIRST SIGHT
FIRST STAGE
FIRST STEPS
FIRST TEETH
FIRST THING
FIRST THROW
FIRST TO ACT
FIRST VERSE
FIRST WATCH
FIRST WATER
FIRST WOMAN
FIRST WORLD
FIRTH OF TAY
FISH COURSE
FISH DINNER
FISH FINGER
FISHING NET
FISH KETTLE
FISH MARKET
FISH SUPPER
FISHY STORY
FIT AND WELL
FIT OF ANGER
FIT OF BLUES
FIT THE BILL
FIT TO BURST
FIT TO PLEAD
FIVE AND ONE
FIVE AND SIX
FIVE AND TEN
FIVE AND TWO
FIVE A PENNY
FIVE FIFTHS
FIVE HEARTS
FIVE MONTHS
FIVE NINTHS
FIVE O'CLOCK
FIVE OUNCES
FIVE POINTS
FIVE POUNDS
FIVE QUARTS
FIVE ROUNDS
FIVES COURT
FIVE SENSES
FIVE SIXTHS
FIVE SPADES
FIVE STONES
FIVE TO FOUR
FIVE TRICKS

FIXED ABODE
FIXED IDEAS
FIXED POINT
FIXED PRICE
FIXED SMILE
FIXED STARS
FIX THE DATE
FIX THE TIME
FLAG WAVING
FLAK JACKET
FLAMING RED
FLASH FLOOD
FLASH HARRY
FLASH POINT
FLAT DENIAL
FLAT GROUND
FLAT IN TOWN
FLAT RACING
FLAT SCREEN
FLAT SEASON
FLATTEN OUT
FLAXEN HAIR
FLEA CIRCUS
FLESH WOUND
FLICK KNIFE
FLIGHT DECK
FLING ABOUT
FLING ASIDE
FLINT GLASS
FLOAT ABOUT
FLOAT A LOAN
FLOAT ON AIR
FLOODED OUT
FLOOD GATES
FLOOD LEVEL
FLOOD WATER
FLOOR SPACE
FLOPPY DISK
FLOUNCE OUT
FLOWER SHOW
FLOWER VASE
FLUID OUNCE
FLY FOR HELP
FLYING BOAT
FLYING BOMB
FLYING CLUB
FLYING FISH
FLYING HIGH
FLYING JUMP
FLYING KICK
FLYING LEAP
FLYING SHOT
FLY THE FLAG
FOAM RUBBER
FOCAL POINT
FOGGY NIGHT

FOG WARNING
FOLDED ARMS
FOLK DANCER
FOLK SINGER
FOLLOW SUIT
FOND BELIEF
FOND PARENT
FOOD PARCEL
FOOD SLICER
FOOD SUPPLY
FOOD TABLET
FOOD WARMER
FOOL AROUND
FOOT BY FOOT
FOR A CHANGE
FOR ALL THAT
FOR ALL TIME
FOR A SEASON
FORCE A DRAW
FORCE APART
FORCED LOAN
FORCED SALE
FORCE OF LAW
FOR CERTAIN
FOR CHARITY
FORE AND AFT
FOREIGN LAW
FOREST FIRE
FOREST HILL
FOREST LAND
FOREST TREE
FOR EXAMPLE
FORGE AHEAD
FORGED NOTE
FORK SUPPER
FORMAL CALL
FORM A QUEUE
FORMER DAYS
FORMER LAND
FORM MASTER
FOR NOTHING
FOR THE BEST
FOR TWO PINS
FORTY MILES
FORTY TIMES
FORTY WINKS
FORTY YEARS
FOSTER HOPE
FOUL MANNER
FOUL MOTIVE
FOUL STROKE
FOUL TEMPER
FOUR-ALE BAR
FOUR AND SIX
FOUR AND TEN
FOUR AND TWO

FOUR A PENNY
FOUR BY FOUR
FOUR EIGHTS
FOUR FIFTHS
FOUR HEARTS
FOUR IN HAND
FOUR KNAVES
FOUR MONTHS
FOUR NINTHS
FOUR O'CLOCK
FOUR OR FIVE
FOUR OUNCES
FOUR POINTS
FOUR POUNDS
FOUR QUARTS
FOUR QUEENS
FOUR SEVENS
FOUR SPADES
FOURTH FORM
FOURTH HAND
FOURTH HOLE
FOURTH PART
FOURTH RACE
FOUR THREES
FOURTH TEST
FOURTH TIME
FOUR TRICKS
FOUR WHEELS
FOX HUNTING
FOX TERRIER
FRANK BRUNO
FRANZ KAFKA
FRANZ LEHAR
FRANZ LISZT
FRAUD SQUAD
FRAYED EDGE
FREE ACCESS
FREE ACTION
FREE ADVICE
FREE CHOICE
FREE CHURCH
FREE DRINKS
FREE FOR ALL
FREE FRENCH
FREE LABOUR
FREE LIVING
FREE MARKET
FREE OF COST
FREE OF DEBT
FREE OF DUTY
FREE ON RAIL
FREE PARDON
FREE SAMPLE
FREE SPEECH
FREE TICKET
FREEZE HARD

FREEZE ON TO
FREEZE OVER
FRENCH ALPS
FRENCH BEAN
FRENCH BRED
FRENCH HORN
FRENCH LOAF
FRENCH PORT
FRENCH ROLL
FRENCH WINE
FRESH BLOOD
FRESH BREAD
FRESH CREAM
FRESH FRUIT
FRESH HOPES
FRESH LIGHT
FRESH PAINT
FRESH SLANT
FRESH SPURT
FRESH START
FRESH WATER
FRESH WOUND
FRIED BACON
FRIED BREAD
FRIGID TONE
FRIGID ZONE
FROM ABROAD
FROM BEHiND
FROM MEMORY
FROM THE AIR
FROM THE TOP
FRONT BENCH
FRONT COVER
FRONT TEETH
FRONT TOOTH
FRONT WHEEL
FROZEN FISH
FROZEN FOOD
FROZEN OVER
FROZEN PEAS
FROZEN SNOW
FRUGAL DIET
FRUGAL MEAL
FRUIT DRINK
FRUIT JELLY
FRUIT JUICE
FRUIT LOLLY
FRUIT SALAD
FUEL CRISIS
FULL BELIEF
FULL BOTTLE
FULL CHORUS
FULL CIRCLE
FULL EXTENT
FULL FIGURE
FULL GALLOP

FULL GROWTH
FULL IMPORT
FULL LENGTH
FULL OF HATE
FULL OF HOPE
FULL OF LIFE
FULL OF LOVE
FULL OF NEWS
FULL OF ZEAL
FULL OF ZEST
FULL PARDON
FULL REPORT
FULL SISTER
FULL TRAVEL
FULL VOLUME
FULLY ARMED
FULLY AWARE
FULLY WOUND
FUNDED DEBT
FUND RAISER
FUNKY MUSIC
FUNNY STORY
FUNNY THING
FUSSY STYLE

G – 10

GAIETY GIRL
GAIN ACCESS
GAIN CREDIT
GAIN FAVOUR
GAIN GROUND
GAIN HEIGHT
GAIN THE DAY
GAIN WEIGHT
GALLANT ACT
GALLUP POLL
GAMBLE AWAY
GAME AND SET
GAME OF DICE
GAME OF LIFE
GAME THEORY
GAME WARDEN
GAMING LAWS
GANG OF FOUR
GARAGE BAND
GARAGE HAND
GARAGE SALE
GARBAGE MAN
GARDEN CITY
GARDEN FETE
GARDEN FLAT
GARDEN GATE
GARDEN HOSE
GARDEN PATH
GARDEN PEAS

GARDEN PEST
GARDEN SEAT
GARDEN WALL
GARLIC SALT
GARY COOPER
GAS CHAMBER
GAS COMPANY
GAS COUNCIL
GAS GUZZLER
GAS LIGHTER
GAS ONESELF
GAS TURBINE
GAS WARFARE
GATHER FOOD
GATHER WOOL
GATLING GUN
GAVE GROUND
GAVE NOTICE
GAVE VENT TO
GAY COLOURS
GAY GORDONS
GEISHA GIRL
GENE PITNEY
GENERAL LEE
GENERAL RUN
GENE TUNNEY
GENIAL HOST
GENTLE BLOW
GENTLE HEAT
GENTLE PUSH
GEORGE BEST
GEORGE SAND
GERMAN BAND
GERMAN MARK
GET A LIVING
GET A LOOK IN
GET A MOVE ON
GET A WICKET
GET DRESSED
GET ELECTED
GET ENGAGED
GET EXCITED
GET HITCHED
GET IN A MESS
GET IN TOUCH
GET MARRIED
GET NOWHERE
GET RATTLED
GET SPLICED
GET STARTED
GET THE BIRD
GET THE BOOT
GET THE FEEL
GET THE HUMP
GET THE PUSH
GET THE SACK

GET THROUGH
GETTING HOT
GETTING OFF
GETTING OLD
GETTING OUT
GET TO GRIPS
GET UP EARLY
GET UP STEAM
GET WEAVING
GHOST STORY
GHOST TRAIN
GIANT CRANE
GIANT PANDA
GIDDY LIMIT
GIDDY SPELL
GIFT COUPON
GIFT OF LIFE
GIFT PARCEL
GILDED CAGE
GIN AND LIME
GINGER BEER
GINGER WINE
GIPSY DANCE
GIPSY QUEEN
GIRL FRIDAY
GIRL FRIEND
GIVE A CATCH
GIVE ADVICE
GIVE A LEG UP
GIVE AN INCH
GIVE A PARTY
GIVE A SHOUT
GIVE BATTLE
GIVE BY WILL
GIVE COLOUR
GIVE CREDIT
GIVE FREELY
GIVE GROUND
GIVE IT A TRY
GIVEN A LIFT
GIVEN LEAVE
GIVE NOTICE
GIVE ORDERS
GIVE PRAISE
GIVE RISE TO
GIVE THANKS
GIVE THE CUE
GIVE TONGUE
GIVE UP HOPE
GIVE UP WORK
GLANCE BACK
GLANCE DOWN
GLANCE OVER
GLASS BEADS
GLASS COACH
GLASS OF ALE

GLASS PRISM
GLASSY LOOK
GLAZED EYES
GLAZED LOOK
GLEE SINGER
GLIB TONGUE
GLOVE MONEY
GO ALL FUNNY
GO A LONG WAY
GO BACKWARD
GO BANKRUPT
GOBI DESERT
GO CRACKERS
GOD OF MERCY
GO DOWNHILL
GO DOWN WELL
GOD WILLING
GO FOR A BLOW
GO FOR A RIDE
GO FOR A SAIL
GO FOR A SPIN
GO FOR A SWIM
GO FOR A TRIP
GO FOR A WALK
GO FOR BROKE
GO GINGERLY
GO-GO DANCER
GO IN AND OUT
GO IN AND WIN
GO IN EASILY
GOING BADLY
GOING CHEAP
GOING FORTH
GOING ROUND
GOING SOUTH
GOING UNDER
GOLD BANGLE
GOLDEN CALF
GOLDEN DAYS
GOLDEN DISC
GOLDEN GATE
GOLDEN GIRL
GOLDEN HAIR
GOLDEN HIND
GOLDEN HORN
GOLDEN HOUR
GOLDEN MEAN
GOLDEN MILE
GOLDEN RAIN
GOLDEN ROSE
GOLDEN RULE
GOLD NUGGET
GOLD SHARES
GOLD STRIKE
GOLD THREAD
GOLF COURSE

GOLF STROKE
GONE TO SEED
GOOD ACCORD
GOOD ADVICE
GOOD AND ILL
GOOD AND BAD
GOOD AS GOLD
GOOD BRAINS
GOOD CARVER
GOOD CELLAR
GOOD CHANCE
GOOD CINEMA
GOOD DINNER
GOOD DRIVER
GOOD EATING
GOOD EFFECT
GOOD EFFORT
GOOD ENDING
GOOD ENOUGH
GOOD EXCUSE
GOOD FAMILY
GOOD FARMER
GOOD FELLOW
GOOD FIGURE
GOOD FOR ONE
GOOD FOR YOU
GOOD FRIDAY
GOOD FRIEND
GOOD GRACES
GOOD GROUND
GOOD HABITS
GOOD HEALTH
GOOD HIDING
GOOD HUMOUR
GOOD INCOME
GOOD INTENT
GOOD JUMPER
GOOD LENGTH
GOOD LIVING
GOOD MARGIN
GOOD MARKET
GOOD MEMORY
GOOD MORALS
GOOD MORROW
GOOD NATURE
GOOD NOTICE
GOOD NUMBER
GOOD PEOPLE
GOOD PLAYER
GOOD POLICY
GOOD REASON
GOOD RECORD
GOOD REPORT
GOOD REPUTE
GOOD RESULT
GOOD RETURN

GOOD SAILOR
GOOD SEAMAN
GOOD SECOND
GOOD SELLER
GOOD SERMON
GOOD SPEECH
GOOD STAYER
GOOD STRAIN
GOODS TRAIN
GOOD STROKE
GOOD SUPPLY
GOODS WAGON
GOOD TEMPER
GOOD TENANT
GOOD TIMING
GOOD TIPPER
GOOD TO HEAR
GOOD TO KNOW
GOOD WICKET
GOOD WISHES
GOOD WORKER
GO ON A BLIND
GO ON A SPREE
GO ON TIPTOE
GO ON WHEELS
GOOSE GREEN
GO OVERSEAS
GO SCOT-FREE
GO SHOOTING
GO SHOPPING
GO SLUMMING
GO STRAIGHT
GO SWIMMING
GO THE LIMIT
GOTHIC ARCH
GO TO BLAZES!
GO TO CHURCH
GO TOGETHER
GO TO GROUND
GO TO HEAVEN
GO TO MARKET
GO TO PIECES
GO TO PRISON
GO TO SCHOOL
GO TO THE BAD
GO TO THE BAR
GO TO THE TOP
GO TO THE ZOO
GOT THE SACK
GO UPSTAIRS
GRACE KELLY
GRAND CANAL
GRAND CROSS
GRAND DUCHY
GRAND HOTEL
GRAND LODGE

GRAND MARCH
GRAND OPERA
GRAND PIANO
GRAND SCALE
GRAND STAND
GRAND STYLE
GRAND TOTAL
GRANNY BOND
GRANNY FLAT
GRANNY KNOT
GRANT A LOAN
GRANT A WISH
GRAPE JUICE
GRAPHIC ART
GRASS COURT
GRASS SKIRT
GRASS SNAKE
GRASS VERGE
GRASS WIDOW
GRASSY BANK
GRAVE DOUBT
GRAVE FEARS
GRAVEL PATH
GRAVELY ILL
GRAVE WORDS
GRAVY TRAIN
GRAY'S ELEGY
GREASY POLE
GREASY ROAD
GREAT ASSET
GREAT CATCH
GREAT GROSS
GREAT HEART
GREAT HOPES
GREAT JUDGE
GREAT LAKES
GREAT MERIT
GREAT MINDS
GREAT MOGUL
GREAT NIECE
GREAT POWER
GREAT SAINT
GREAT SHOCK
GREAT SPEED
GREAT TREAT
GREAT UNCLE
GREAT VALUE
GREAT WHEEL
GREAT WOMAN
GRECIAN URN
GREEK CROSS
GREEK DRAMA
GREEK VERSE
GREEN AUDIT
GREEN BAIZE
GREEN CLOTH

GREEN FIELD
GREEN FLASH
GREEN GRASS
GREEN LIGHT
GREEN MONEY
GREEN PAINT
GREEN POUND
GREEN SALAD
GREEN STAMP
GREEN STUFF
GREEN TABLE
GRETA GARBO
GREG NORMAN
GREY FRIARS
GREY FUTURE
GREY MARKET
GREY MATTER
GREY STREAK
GREY TOPPER
GRID SYSTEM
GRILLED HAM
GRIP OF IRON
GROSS ERROR
GROSS VALUE
GROUND ARMS
GROUND BAIT
GROUND CORN
GROUND CREW
GROUND DOWN
GROUND PLAN
GROUND RENT
GROUND RICE
GROUND WAVE
GROUP OF SIX
GROUP OF TEN
GROUSE MOOR
GROW A BEARD
GROW APPLES
GROW BETTER
GROW BIGGER
GROWING BOY
GROWING OLD
GROW LARGER
GROW LONGER
GROWN WOMAN
GROW TALLER
GRUB STREET
GRUFF VOICE
GUESS AGAIN
GUESS RIGHT
GUESS WRONG
GUEST HOUSE
GUEST NIGHT
GUEST TOWEL
GUILTY LOOK
GUILTY MIND

GUINEA FOWL
GUITAR SOLO
GULF OF ADEN
GULF OF SUEZ
GULF STREAM
GUN LICENCE
GUST OF WIND

H – 10

HACKNEY CAB
HACK WRITER
HAIR LOTION
HALF A CROWN
HALF A DOZEN
HALF A GLASS
HALF A GROSS
HALF A JIFFY
HALF AN ACRE
HALF AN HOUR
HALF AN INCH
HALF A POUND
HALF A SCORE
HALF A SHAKE
HALF ASLEEP
HALF AS MUCH
HALF BOTTLE
HALF DOLLAR
HALF LENGTH
HALF OF MILD
HALF SHARES
HALF STEWED
HALF VOLLEY
HALF YEARLY
HALL OF FAME
HALL PORTER
HALOGEN HOB
HAM AND EGGS
HAMMER AWAY
HAMMER DOWN
HAMMER HOME
HAMMER TOES
HAND IN HAND
HAND IT OVER
HAND LOTION
HAND OF TIME
HAND SIGNAL
HAND TO HAND
HANG AROUND
HANG BEHIND
HAPPY BREED
HAPPY CHILD
HAPPY EVENT
HAPPY KNACK
HAPPY WOMAN
HARBOUR BAR

HARD AS IRON
HARD AS TEAK
HARD ASTERN
HARD AT WORK
HARD CENTRE
HARD CHEESE
HARD GROUND
HARD HITTER
HARD KERNEL
HARD KNOCKS
HARD LABOUR
HARD LESSON
HARD LIQUOR
HARDLY EVER
HARD MASTER
HARD NATURE
HARD PENCIL
HARD RIDING
HARD SCHOOL
HARD TO BEAR
HARD TO HOLD
HARD TO TAKE
HARD WINTER
HARD WORKER
HARPOON GUN
HARRY WORTH
HARSH SOUND
HARSH VOICE
HASTY WORDS
HATCH AN EGG
HATCH A PLOT
HAVE A CHAIR
HAVE A CRACK
HAVE A DRINK
HAVE A FIGHT
HAVE A FLING
HAVE A GUESS
HAVE A HEART
HAVE A HUNCH
HAVE AN IDEA
HAVE A PARTY
HAVE A SMOKE
HAVE A SNACK
HAVE BRAINS
HAVE DINNER
HAVE DOUBTS
HAVE EFFECT
HAVE FAULTS
HAVE IN HAND
HAVE IN MIND
HAVE IN VIEW
HAVE NO FEAR
HAVE NO HOPE
HAVE NO VOTE
HAVE QUALMS
HEAD HONCHO

HEAD HUNTER
HEAD KEEPER
HEAD OFFICE
HEAD OF HAIR
HEAD TO FOOT
HEAD TO TAIL
HEAD WAITER
HEAD WARDER
HEADY DRINK
HEALING ART
HEALTH CURE
HEALTH FARM
HEALTH FOOD
HEALTH KICK
HEAP OF WORK
HEARING AID
HEAR NO EVIL
HEART OF OAK
HEART'S EASE
HEARTY MEAL
HEAR VOICES
HEAT STROKE
HEAVE A SIGH
HEAVY CHILL
HEAVY CLOUD
HEAVY GOING
HEAVY HEART
HEAVY METAL
HEAVY NIGHT
HEAVY SLEEP
HEAVY STORM
HEAVY STUFF
HEAVY STYLE
HEAVY SWELL
HEAVY TOUCH
HEAVY TREAD
HEAVY WATER
HECTIC TIME
HEDY LAMARR
HEEL AND TOE
HELEN WILLS
HELLO DOLLY
HELL'S BELLS
HENNA RINSE
HENRY FONDA
HENRY JAMES
HENRY MOORE
HENRY TUDOR
HERB GARDEN
HERD OF DEER
HERE AND NOW
HERE YOU ARE
HER MAJESTY
HERMIT CRAB
HEROIC DEED
HEROIC POEM

HERR HITLER
HIDDEN HAND
HIGH AND DRY
HIGH AND LOW
HIGH CASTLE
HIGH CHURCH
HIGH COLLAR
HIGH COLOUR
HIGH COMEDY
HIGH DEGREE
HIGHER RANK
HIGH ESTEEM
HIGH FAVOUR
HIGH FIGURE
HIGH FLYING
HIGH GERMAN
HIGH GROUND
HIGH IDEALS
HIGH INCOME
HIGH LIVING
HIGHLY PAID
HIGH MORALE
HIGH NUMBER
HIGH OCTANE
HIGH OFFICE
HIGH PLACES
HIGH POLISH
HIGH PRAISE
HIGH PRIEST
HIGH REGARD
HIGH RELIEF
HIGH REPUTE
HIGH SALARY
HIGH SCHOOL
HIGH STAKES
HIGH STATUS
HIGH STREET
HIGH SUMMER
HILARY TERM
HINDER PART
HIS AND HERS
HIS MAJESTY
HIS WORSHIP
HIT AND MISS
HIT THE MARK
HIT THE POST
HOBBY HORSE
HOCKEY BALL
HOCKEY CLUB
HOCKEY TEAM
HOCUS POCUS
HOKEY COKEY
HOLD A PARTY
HOLD NO HOPE
HOLD OFFICE
HOLD THE KEY

HOLIDAY PAY
HOLLOW TREE
HOLY FATHER
HOLY GROUND
HOLY ISLAND
HOLY OFFICE
HOLY ORDERS
HOLY SPIRIT
HOLY TEMPLE
HOLY TERROR
HOME AND DRY
HOME CINEMA
HOME CIRCLE
HOME COUNTY
HOME FORCES
HOME FOR TEA
HOME GROUND
HOME MARKET
HOME OFFICE
HOME TRUTHS
HOME WATERS
HONEST FACE
HONEST FOLK
HONEST JOHN
HONEST LOOK
HONEST TOIL
HONEST WORK
HONOURS MAN
HOOK AND EYE
HOOKED NOSE
HOPPING MAD
HORNED MOON
HORNED TOAD
HORROR FILM
HORSE LAUGH
HORSE OPERA
HORSE SENSE
HORSE THIEF
HOSTILE ACT
HOT AND COLD
HOT AS HADES
HOT CLIMATE
HOT COCKLES
HOTEL STAFF
HOTEL SUITE
HOT PURSUIT
HOT WEATHER
HOUR BY HOUR
HOUR OF DOOM
HOUR OF NEED
HOURS ON END
HOUSE AGENT
HOUSE GUEST
HOUSE MUSIC
HOUSE OF GOD
HOUSE ORGAN

HOUSE PARTY
HOUSE RULES
HOUSE TO LET
HOUSING ACT
HOVER ABOUT
HOVER MOWER
HOW DARE YOU!
HOW DO YOU DO?
HOW ON EARTH
HUBBLE'S LAW
HUGE PROFIT
HUG ONESELF
HUG THE LAND
HUMAN BEING
HUMAN CHAIN
HUMAN ERROR
HUMAN FRAME
HUMAN SKILL
HUMAN VOICE
HUMBLE FARE
HUMBLE FOLK
HUMBLE HOME
HUMMING TOP
HUNDRED MEN
HUNGRY LOOK
HUNTING DOG
HUNTING KIT
HUNT THE FOX
HURDLE RACE
HURRY ALONG
HUSKY VOICE
HYBRID RACE
HYMN OF HATE

I – 10

IAN FLEMING
IAN WOOSNAM
ICED COFFEE
ICE SKATING
ICING SUGAR
ICY COLD DAY
ICY SURFACE
IDEAL PLACE
IDEAL WOMAN
IDLE GOSSIP
IDLE MOMENT
IDLE RUMOUR
IDLE THREAT
IF POSSIBLE
ILKLEY MOOR
ILL CONTENT
ILLEGAL ACT
ILL FEELING
ILL FORTUNE
ILL MANNERS

IMPORT DUTY
IMPOSE A BAN
IMPOSE UPON
IN A BAD MOOD
IN ABEYANCE
IN ADDITION
IN A DECLINE
IN A DILEMMA
IN A DRAUGHT
IN A FAIR WAY
IN A FASHION
IN A FERMENT
IN A FLUTTER
IN A GOOD WAY
IN ALLIANCE
IN AN UPROAR
IN ANY EVENT
IN A PASSION
IN A TANTRUM
IN AT THE END
IN A TURMOIL
IN A WHISPER
IN BAD ODOUR
IN BAD SHAPE
IN BAD TASTE
IN BARRACKS
IN BOOK FORM
IN BRACKETS
IN BUSINESS
IN CHAMBERS
IN CHANCERY
INCH BY INCH
IN CONFLICT
IN CONTEMPT
IN CONTRAST
IN DARKNESS
IN DAYLIGHT
IN DEFIANCE
INDEX TABLE
INDIAN ARMY
INDIAN CLUB
INDIAN CORN
INDIAN FILE
INDIAN HEMP
INDIAN MEAL
INDIA PAPER
INDIGO BLUE
IN DISARRAY
IN DISGRACE
IN DISGUISE
IN DISORDER
IN DISTRESS
INDOOR GAME
IN EVERY WAY
IN EVIDENCE
IN EXCHANGE

IN EXTREMIS
IN FAVOUR OF
IN FULL SAIL
IN FULL VIEW
IN GOOD FORM
IN GOOD PART
IN GOOD TIME
IN GOOD TRIM
IN HOSPITAL
IN HOT BLOOD
IN HOT WATER
INIGO JONES
IN JEOPARDY
INJURY TIME
INLAND BILL
INLAND PORT
INLAND TOWN
INLET VALVE
IN LONGHAND
IN LOW WATER
IN MANY WAYS
IN MEMORIAM
IN MOURNING
IN NAME ONLY
INNER HOUSE
INNER LIGHT
INNER VOICE
IN OFF WHITE
IN ONE PIECE
IN ONE'S CUPS
IN ONE SENSE
IN ONE'S HEAD
IN ONE'S MIND
IN ONE'S ROOM
IN PARADISE
IN PARALLEL
IN POLITICS
IN POSITION
IN PRACTICE
IN PROGRESS
IN PROSPECT
IN QUESTION
IN REAL LIFE
IN RESPONSE
IN ROTATION
INS AND OUTS
INSANE IDEA
IN SEQUENCE
INSIDE EDGE
INSIDE LEFT
INSIDE SEAT
IN SLOW TIME
IN SOME WAYS
IN STERLING
IN STITCHES
IN SUSPENSE

IN SYMPATHY
INTENT LOOK
IN THE ATTIC
IN THE BLOOD
IN THE CHAIR
IN THE CHOIR
IN THE CLEAR
IN THE DERBY
IN THE DITCH
IN THE DOUGH
IN THE DRINK
IN THE DUMPS
IN THE EVENT
IN THE FIELD
IN THE FILES
IN THE FINAL
IN THE FLESH
IN THE FRONT
IN THE GRAVE
IN THE HOUSE
IN THE INDEX
IN THE KITTY
IN THE LIGHT
IN THE LOCAL
IN THE LURCH
IN THE MONEY
IN THE NIGHT
IN THE NORTH
IN THE OCEAN
IN THE PAPER
IN THE PRESS
IN THE QUEUE
IN THE RANKS
IN THE RIGHT
IN THE RIVER
IN THE ROUGH
IN THE ROUND
IN THE SCRUM
IN THE SHADE
IN THE SLIPS
IN THE SLUMS
IN THE SOUTH
IN THE STAND
IN THE STARS
IN THE STUDY
IN THE SWING
IN THE TOWER
IN THE TRADE
IN THE TRAIN
IN THE VOGUE
IN THE WATER
IN THE WILDS
IN THE WINGS
IN THE WOODS
IN THE WORLD
IN THE WRONG

INTO BATTLE
IN TRAINING
IN TWO MINDS
IN TWO TICKS
INVALID OUT
IN WHISPERS
IRISH LINEN
IRISH SWEEP
IRISH TWEED
IRON HOLDER
IRON MAIDEN
IRON RATION
ISLAND RACE
ISLE OF BUTE
ISLE OF DOGS
ISLE OF ELBA
ISLE OF MULL
ISLE OF SARK
ISLE OF SKYE
ISSUE A WRIT
ISSUE FORTH
ISSUE PRICE
ITALIAN CUT
ITALIC TYPE
IT'S A WANGLE
IVORY BLACK
IVORY COAST
IVORY PAINT
IVORY TOWER
IVY LEAGUER

J – 10

JACK ARCHER
JACK HORNER
JACK HYLTON
JACK LONDON
JACK SOCKET
JACK SPRATT
JAGGED EDGE
JAMAICA INN
JAMAICA RUM
JAMES AGATE
JAMES JOYCE
JAMES MASON
JAM SESSION
JANE AUSTEN
JAR OF HONEY
JERSEY LILY
JESUS FREAK
JIMMY YOUNG
JOCKEY CLUB
JOCKEY'S CAP
JOE BECKETT
JOHN ARLOTT
JOHN BRIGHT

JOHN BUCHAN
JOHN BUNYAN
JOHN CALVIN
JOHN CLEESE
JOHN DRYDEN
JOHN GILPIN
JOHN LENNON
JOHN MILTON
JOHN O'GAUNT
JOHN RUSKIN
JOHN WESLEY
JOIN BATTLE
JOIN FORCES
JOINT STOCK
JOLLY ROGER
JOSE FERRER
JO STAFFORD
JOYS OF LIFE
JUDO EXPERT
JUDO LESSON
JUGGED HARE
JULES VERNE
JUMBLE SALE
JUMP A CLAIM
JUMP FOR JOY
JUMP THE GUN
JUNGLE BOOK
JUNIOR MISS
JURY SYSTEM
JUST AN IDEA
JUST AS WELL
JUST BEFORE
JUST ENOUGH
JUST FOR FUN
JUST FOR NOW
JUST IN CASE
JUST IN TIME
JUST REWARD

K – 10

KANSAS CITY
KATHY KIRBY
KAY HAMMOND
KAY KENDALL
KEEN GLANCE
KEEN MEMBER
KEEP A DIARY
KEEP AFLOAT
KEEPING FIT
KEEP IN HAND
KEEP IN MIND
KEEP IN PAWN
KEEP IN PLAY
KEEP IN STEP
KEEP IN TUNE

KEEP IN VIEW
KEEP IT DARK
KEEP MOVING
KEEP POSTED
KEEP SCHTUM
KEEP SECRET
KEEP SILENT
KEEP STEADY
KEEP TABS ON
KEEP TRYING
KEEP WICKET
KEIR HARDY
KENNEL CLUB
KENNEL MAID
KENNY BAKER
KENNY LYNCH
KENTISH COB
KENTISH MAN
KETTLE DRUM
KEW GARDENS
KEY WITNESS
KHMER ROUGE
KICK UP A ROW
KID BROTHER
KIDNEY BEAN
KID ONESELF
KILL OR CURE
KIND HEARTS
KIND PERSON
KINETIC ART
KING ALFRED
KING ARTHUR
KING CANUTE
KING EDWARD
KING GEORGE
KING HAROLD
KING OF ARMS
KING'S BENCH
KING'S COURT
KING'S CROSS
KING'S PRIZE
KING'S SCOUT
KING WILLOW
KINKY BOOTS
KISS CANNON
KISS ME KATE
KISS OF LIFE
KISS THE ROD
KITCHEN BOY
KITH AND KIN
KNIFE WOUND
KNOCK ABOUT
KNOCKED OUT
KNOCK KNOCK
KNOT OF HAIR
KNOW BETTER

KNOW THE LAW
KNOW THE WAY
KU KLUX KLAN

L – 10

LABOUR CAMP
LABOUR CLUB
LABOUR POOL
LABOUR VOTE
LACE STITCH
LACK BRAINS
LACK FINISH
LACK OF FOOD
LACK OF FORM
LACK OF NEWS
LACK OF TIME
LACK OF ZEAL
LACK SPIRIT
LADIES' MAID
LADY BE GOOD
LADY DOCKER
LADY DOCTOR
LADY GODIVA
LA GIOCONDA
LAID TO REST
LAKE GENEVA
LAKE LUGANO
LAKE SCHOOL
LAMB CUTLET
LAMB'S TALES
LAME EXCUSE
LAND AGENCY
LAND AND SEA
LAND FORCES
LAND IN GAOL
LAND OF SONG
LAND REFORM
LAND TENURE
LAND TRAVEL
LARA'S THEME
LARCENY ACT
LARGE CROWD
LARGE DRINK
LARGE FLEET
LARGE HOUSE
LARGE ORDER
LARGE PARTY
LARGE PIECE
LARGE POWER
LARGE PRINT
LARGE SCALE
LARGE SPACE
LARGE STAFF
LARGE STOCK
LARGE STONE

LARGE VODKA
LARGE WAIST
LARRY ADLER
LASSA FEVER
LAST AUTUMN
LAST BREATH
LAST BUT ONE
LAST BUT TWO
LAST CHANCE
LAST COURSE
LAST DEMAND
LAST EASTER
LAST FRIDAY
LAST GLANCE
LAST HURRAH
LAST IN LINE
LAST LESSON
LAST LETTER
LAST MAN OUT
LAST MINUTE
LAST MOMENT
LAST MONDAY
LAST NUMBER
LAST OF FIVE
LAST OF FOUR
LAST OF NINE
LAST ORDERS
LAST PERSON
LAST REFUGE
LAST RESORT
LAST RUBBER
LAST SEASON
LAST SERIES
LAST SPRING
LAST STROKE
LAST SUMMER
LAST SUNDAY
LAST SUPPER
LAST TO COME
LA STUPENDA
LAST VOLUME
LAST WINTER
LATE AUTUMN
LATE DINNER
LATE FOR TEA
LATE GOTHIC
LATE IN LIFE
LATENT HEAT
LATE SPRING
LATEST NEWS
LATEST WORD
LATE SUMMER
LATE SUPPER
LATIN PROSE
LATIN VERSE
LA TRAVIATA

LATTER HALF
LAUGH IT OFF
LAVISH CARE
LAWFUL WIFE
LAWN TENNIS
LAW OFFICER
LAW OF LIBEL
LAW SOCIETY
LAW STUDENT
LAWYER'S FEE
LAY A COURSE
LAY BROTHER
LAY CLAIM TO
LAY HANDS ON
LAY IN DRINK
LAY IN RUINS
LAY IN STOCK
LAY SIEGE TO
LAY THE DUST
LAY THE FIRE
LAY THE ODDS
LAZY PERSON
LEAD A PARTY
LEAD ASTRAY
LEAD A TRUMP
LEADED TYPE
LEADEN FEET
LEADER PAGE
LEADING MAN
LEAD PENCIL
LEAD THE WAY
LEAD TRUMPS
LEAD WEIGHT
LEAP FOR JOY
LEARNED MAN
LEARN MUSIC
LEARN TO FLY
LEAST OF ALL
LEATHER BAG
LEAVE ALONE
LEAVE A MARK
LEAVE A NOTE
LEAVE A WILL
LEAVE EARLY
LED TO AGREE
LEE TREVINO
LEFT BEHIND
LEFT INSIDE
LEFT WINGER
LEGAL CLAIM
LEGAL COSTS
LEGAL EAGLE
LEGAL FORCE
LEGAL ISSUE
LEGAL LIGHT
LEGAL OWNER

LEGAL RIGHT
LEGAL TITLE
LEGAL TRIAL
LEGS ELEVEN
LEMON DRINK
LEMON JUICE
LEND COLOUR
LEND WEIGHT
LENIN'S TOMB
LENTIL SOUP
LESSER EVIL
LESSON FIVE
LESSON FOUR
LESSON NINE
LETHAL DOSE
LET IT SLIDE
LET IT STAND
LET ONE KNOW
LET'S FACE IT
LETTER BOMB
LETTER CARD
LETTER CASE
LETTER FILE
LETTER POST
LETTER RATE
LETTING OFF
LETTING OUT
LEVEL SCORE
LIB-LAB PACT
LIE DORMANT
LIE IN STATE
LIE IN STATE
LIFE MEMBER
LIFE OF EASE
LIFE POLICY
LIFE'S BLOOD
LIFE TO COME
LIGHT A FIRE
LIGHT A PIPE
LIGHT AS AIR
LIGHT AS DAY
LIGHT BLUES
LIGHT BROWN
LIGHT GREEN
LIGHT HEART
LIGHT LUNCH
LIGHT MUSIC
LIGHT OF DAY
LIGHT OPERA
LIGHT SLEEP
LIGHT SNACK
LIGHT TOUCH
LIGHT TREAD
LIGHT VERSE
LIKE A CHARM
LIKE A FLASH

LIKE A THIEF
LIKELY SPOT
LIKELY TALE
LIME STREET
LIMPET MINE
LINDEN TREE
LINEN CHEST
LINEN SHELF
LINE OF DUTY
LINE OF FIRE
LINE OF LIFE
LINE OF TYPE
LINSEED OIL
LIONEL BART
LION'S MOUTH
LION'S SHARE
LIP READING
LIP SERVICE
LIQUID DIET
LIQUID FIRE
LIQUID FOOD
LIQUID FUEL
LIQUID MEAL
LIQUOR LAWS
LITTER LOUT
LITTLE BEAR
LITTLE BIRD
LITTLE DROP
LITTLE FISH
LITTLE FOLK
LITTLE GAIN
LITTLE GIRL
LITTLE GOOD
LITTLE HOPE
LITTLE JOHN
LITTLE LAMB
LITTLE LESS
LITTLE MARY
LITTLE MORE
LITTLE NELL
LITTLE ROCK
LITTLE ROOM
LITTLE SHIP
LITTLE SLAM
LITTLE TIME
LITTLE USED
LIVE ABROAD
LIVE AFLOAT
LIVE AT EASE
LIVE IN DIGS
LIVE IN FEAR
LIVE IN HOPE
LIVE IN WANT
LIVE IT DOWN
LIVELY MIND
LIVELY TUNE

LIVE UP TO IT
LIVING ROOM
LIVING SOUL
LIVING WAGE
LIVING WILL
LLOYDS BANK
LLOYDS LIST
LOADED DICE
LOADING BAY
LOAD OF COAL
LOAD OF COKE
LOBSTER POT
LOCAL BOARD
LOCAL IDIOM
LOCAL PAPER
LOCAL RADIO
LOCAL RATES
LOCAL TRAIN
LOCAL VICAR
LOCH LOMOND
LOCK AND KEY
LOCKED DOOR
LOCK OF HAIR
LOCK-UP SHOP
LONDON AREA
LONDON TOWN
LONDON WALL
LONELY LIFE
LONE RANGER
LONG CAREER
LONG CREDIT
LONG CRUISE
LONG ENOUGH
LONGER ODDS
LONGEST DAY
LONGEST WAY
LONG FIGHT
LONG ISLAND
LONG LADDER
LONG LETTER
LONG MEMORY
LONG PERIOD
LONG PLAYER
LONG SPEECH
LONG TUNNEL
LONG VISION
LONG VOYAGE
LONG WINTER
LOOK AGHAST
LOOK AROUND
LOOK AT LIFE
LOOK A TREAT
LOOK A WRECK
LOOK DOWN ON
LOOK GUILTY
LOOK INSIDE

LOOK INTO IT
LOOK IN VAIN
LOOK LIVELY
LOOK-OUT MAN
LOOK SLIPPY
LOOK YONDER
LOOSE COVER
LOOSE LIVER
LOOSE STATE
LOOSE TOOTH
LOOSE WOMAN
LORD ATTLEE
LORD CURZON
LORD HAW-HAW
LORD HELP US!
LORD LISTER
LORD NELSON
LORD'S TABLE
LORD WARDEN
LORNA DOONE
LOS ANGELES
LOSE A TRICK
LOSE COLOUR
LOSE CREDIT
LOSE FAVOUR
LOSE GROUND
LOSE HEIGHT
LOSE NO TIME
LOSE THE DAY
LOSE THE WAY
LOSE WEIGHT
LOSING GAME
LOSING HAND
LOSING SIDE
LOSING TEAM
LOSING TOSS
LOSS LEADER
LOSS OF FACE
LOSS OF HOPE
LOSS OF LIFE
LOSS OF TIME
LOST BATTLE
LOST CHANCE
LOST LABOUR
LOST LEADER
LOST TO VIEW
LOST TRIBES
LOTS OF LUCK
LOTS OF ROOM
LOTS OF TIME
LOUD CHEERS
LOUD COLOUR
LOUD OUTCRY
LOUD PRAISE
LOUD REPORT
LOUIS SEIZE

LOUNGE SUIT
LOVE AFFAIR
LOVE DEARLY
LOVE EMBLEM
LOVE LETTER
LOVELY GRUB
LOVELY TIME
LOVE OF LIFE
LOVE POTION
LOVERS' KNOT
LOVERS' LANE
LOVERS' LEAP
LOVERS' TIFF
LOVERS' VOWS
LOVE THIRTY
LOVING CARE
LOW CEILING
LOW COMPANY
LOW CONTENT
LOW CUNNING
LOW DENSITY
LOWER A FLAG
LOWER CLASS
LOWER FARES
LOWER HOUSE
LOWER LIMIT
LOWER PITCH
LOWER RANKS
LOWER SIXTH
LOWER WAGES
LOWER WORLD
LOW IN PRICE
LOW OPINION
LOW QUALITY
LOW SPIRITS
LOW STATION
LOW STATURE
LOW TENSION
LUCID STYLE
LUCKY BREAK
LUCKY CHARM
LUCKY GUESS
LUCKY PATCH
LUCKY PENNY
LUCKY STARS
LUCKY START
LUGGAGE VAN
LUMP OF CLAY
LUMP OF LEAD
LUNAR MONTH
LUNCH BREAK
LUNCH SCORE
LUPINO LANE
LURID LIGHT
LURID STYLE
LUTINE BELL

LUXURY FLAT
LYING KNAVE
LYRIC DRAMA
LYRIC VERSE

M – 10

MACHINE AGE
MACH NUMBER
MADE BY HAND
MADE FAMOUS
MADE TO LAST
MADE-UP DISH
MADE USEFUL
MAD WITH JOY
MAGIC FLUTE
MAGIC POWER
MAGIC RITES
MAGIC SPELL
MAGIC SWORD
MAGIC TOUCH
MAGIC TRICK
MAGIC WORDS
MAGIC WORLD
MAGNA CARTA
MAGNUM OPUS
MAIDEN AUNT
MAIDEN LANE
MAIDEN NAME
MAIDEN OVER
MAID MARIAN
MAILED FIST
MAIL PACKET
MAIN ARTERY
MAIN CHANCE
MAIN CHARGE
MAIN CLAUSE
MAIN COURSE
MAIN OFFICE
MAIN REASON
MAIN SOURCE
MAIN STREAM
MAIN STREET
MAIN SWITCH
MAJOR CHORD
MAJOR ISSUE
MAJOR SCALE
MAJOR THIRD
MAKE A BREAK
MAKE A CATCH
MAKE A CLAIM
MAKE A GUESS
MAKE A JOINT
MAKE A MATCH
MAKE AMENDS
MAKE AN EXIT

MAKE A NOISE
MAKE A POINT
MAKE A SCENE
MAKE A STAND
MAKE A START
MAKE BETTER
MAKE EYES AT
MAKE GAME OF
MAKE IT A DAY
MAKE NO SIGN
MAKE PASSES
MAKE PUBLIC
MAKE SPARKS
MAKE THE BED
MAKE THE TEA
MAKE TRACKS
MAKE-UP ROOM
MAKE UP TIME
MALE CHORUS
MALE DANCER
MALTED MILK
MALT LIQUOR
MAN AND WIFE
MAN OF DEEDS
MAN OF IDEAS
MAN OF MONEY
MAN OF MOODS
MAN OF PARTS
MAN OF PEACE
MAN OF STEEL
MAN OF STRAW
MAN OF TASTE
MAN ON TRIAL
MANOR HOUSE
MAN OR MOUSE?
MAN'S ESTATE
MAN THE GUNS
MAN TO WATCH
MANUAL WORK
MANY THANKS
MAO-TSE TUNG
MAPLE SUGAR
MAPLE SYRUP
MAP OF SPAIN
MAP READING
MARBLE ARCH
MARCEL WAVE
MARCH FORTH
MARCH TO WAR
MARCH WINDS
MARIA BUENO
MARIE CURIE
MARIE LLOYD
MARIO LANZA
MARK ANTONY
MARKET HALL

MARKET TOWN	MEMORY TEST	MINOR POINT
MARKING INK	MENIAL WORK	MINOR SCALE
MARK OF CAIN	MENTAL CASE	MINOR THIRD
MARK WYNTER	MENTAL HOME	MINUS THREE
MARRIED MAN	MENTAL PAIN	MINUTE BOOK
MARRY YOUNG	MENTAL TEST	MINUTE HAND
MARTIAL ART	MENTAL WARD	MIRACLE MAN
MARTIAL LAW	MERE NOTION	MISERLY PAY
MARTIN AMIS	MERE NOVICE	MISS A CATCH
MARY MARTIN	MERINO WOOL	MISS A TRICK
MARY STUART	MERRY DANCE	MISS MARPLE
MASKED BALL	MERRY HEART	MISS MUFFET
MASONRY BIT	MERRY MONTH	MISS POINTS
MASS APPEAL	MERRY PRANK	MISS THE BUS
MASS ATTACK	MERRY WIDOW	MIXED BLOOD
MASS MARKET	MERRY WIVES	MIXED BREED
MASS MURDER	MERSEY BEAT	MIXED BUNCH
MASTER MIND	MESS JACKET	MIXED DRINK
MASTER PLAN	METAL PLATE	MIXED GRILL
MASTER PLUG	MEXICO CITY	MIXED HERBS
MASTER RACE	MIAMI BEACH	MIXED PARTY
MATCH POINT	MICE AND MEN	MIXED SAUNA
MATCH TRICK	MICKEY FINN	MIXED TRAIN
MATINÉE HAT	MICK JAGGER	MIXED-UP KID
MATING CALL	MIDAS TOUCH	MIXING DESK
MATT DILLON	MIDDAY MEAL	MOBILE UNIT
MATTED HAIR	MIDDLE AGES	MOCK TURTLE
MATURE MIND	MIDDLE DECK	MODEL DRESS
MAXIM GORKY	MIDDLE EAST	MODEL PLANE
MAY BLOSSOM	MIDDLE LIFE	MODEL TRAIN
MAY FLOWERS	MIDDLE PART	MODEL YACHT
MAY MORNING	MIDDLE ROAD	MODE OF LIFE
MAZE PRISON	MIDDLE TERM	MODERN GIRL
MEADOW LAND	MIDDLE WEST	MODERN MISS
MEAGRE DIET	MIDI SYSTEM	MOIST SUGAR
MEAL TICKET	MIGHTY ATOM	MONDAY CLUB
MEAN NO HARM	MIGHTY DEEP	MONEYED MAN
MEAN STREAK	MIGHTY FINE	MONEY ORDER
MEASURE OUT	MIKE HAMMER	MONEY PRIZE
MEAT COURSE	MILD ANSWER	MONEY TALKS
MEAT MARKET	MILD AS MILK	MONKEY SUIT
MEAT RATION	MILD REBUKE	MONK'S HABIT
MEDIA EVENT	MILD SPOKEN	MONTE CARLO
MEDICAL ART	MILD WINTER	MONTEGO BAY
MEDICAL MAN	MILES APART	MONTE VIDEO
MEDIUM DONE	MILK BOTTLE	MOON AROUND
MEDIUM RARE	MILL AROUND	MOORING FEE
MEDIUM SIZE	MILLED EDGE	MORAL BLAME
MEDIUM WAVE	MINCED MEAT	MORAL FIBRE
MEET THE BUS	MINCED OATH	MORAL ISSUE
MEET THE EYE	MINCE WORDS	MORAL LAPSE
MELBA TOAST	MINERAL OIL	MORAL POWER
MELTING POT	MINER'S LAMP	MORAL RIGHT
MELT THE ICE	MINI SYSTEM	MORAL SENSE
MEMORY CHIP	MINOR CANON	MORAY FIRTH
MEMORY LANE	MINOR CHORD	MORBID FEAR

MORDANT WIT
MORE OR LESS
MORE TO COME
MORNING SUN
MORNING TEA
MORTAL BLOW
MORTAL COIL
MORTAL FEAR
MORTAL SPAN
MOSAIC WORK
MOSS STITCH
MOST LIKELY
MOST PEOPLE
MOTHER LOVE
MOTHER'S BOY
MOTHER'S DAY
MOTHER SHIP
MOTOR COACH
MOTOR RALLY
MOUNT GUARD
MOUNT KENYA
MOUNT SINAI
MOUTH ORGAN
MOVE ACROSS
MOVE IN A RUT
MOVE SLOWLY
MOVE TROOPS
MOVING BELT
MOVING PART
MOW THE LAWN
MR MICAWBER
MRS SQUEERS
MR UNIVERSE
MUCH BETTER
MUCH SORROW
MUDDY BOOTS
MUDDY WATER
MUFFIN BELL
MULLED WINE
MUMBO JUMBO
MURDER CASE
MURPHY'S LAW
MUSICAL BOX
MUSICAL EAR
MUSIC LOVER
MUSIC STAND
MUSIC STOOL
MUSKET FIRE
MUSTARD GAS
MUSTARD POT
MUTE APPEAL
MUTTON CHOP
MUTUAL LOVE
MY CUP OF TEA
MY DEAR CHAP
MY FAIR LADY

MY GOODNESS!
MY HEARTIES
MY OLD DUTCH
MY OLD WOMAN
MYSTERY MAN

N – 10

NAIL POLISH
NAKED FACTS
NAKED FLAME
NAKED LIGHT
NAKED STEEL
NAKED SWORD
NAKED TRUTH
NAME THE DAY
NARROW DOWN
NARROW MIND
NARROW MISS
NARROW PATH
NARROW ROAD
NARROW VIEW
NASAL ORGAN
NASAL TWANG
NASTY HABIT
NASTY KNOCK
NASTY SHOCK
NASTY SPILL
NASTY TASTE
NASTY TRICK
NATIVE LAND
NATIVE RACE
NATIVE SOIL
NATURAL GAS
NATURAL KEY
NATURAL LAW
NATURAL WIT
NATURE CURE
NAUGHTY BOY
NAUTCH GIRL
NAVAL CADET
NAVAL CRAFT
NAVAL POWER
NAVAL STORE
NAVY LEAGUE
NAZI RÉGIME
NEAR AND FAR
NEAR AT HAND
NEAR ENOUGH
NEAR FRIEND
NEAR FUTURE
NEARLY OVER
NEAR THE END
NEAR THE SEA
NEAR THE TOP
NEAT AS A PIN

NEAT FIGURE
NEAT SCOTCH
NEAT STROKE
NEAT WHISKY
NECK OF LAMB
NECK OF LAND
NECK PILLOW
NEEDLE'S EYE
NEGRO MUSIC
NELSON EDDY
NERVE TONIC
NERVOUS TIC
NESTLE DOWN
NEVER AGAIN
NEVER LEARN
NEVER NEVER
NEVER WAVER
NEVER WORRY
NEVER WRONG
NEVIL SHUTE
NEVIS RANGE
NEW ADDRESS
NEW ARRIVAL
NEW CHAPTER
NEW CLOTHES
NEW COINAGE
NEW COLLEGE
NEW CONVERT
NEW EDITION
NEW ENGLAND
NEW FASHION
NEW HORIZON
NEW-LAID EGG
NEW-MOWN HAY
NEW ORLEANS
NEW PROCESS
NEW RECRUIT
NEW RESOLVE
NEWS AGENCY
NEWS CINEMA
NEWS EDITOR
NEWS LETTER
NEW SPEAKER
NEWS REPORT
NEW UNIFORM
NEW VERSION
NEW ZEALAND
NEXT AUTUMN
NEXT BUT ONE
NEXT BUT TWO
NEXT DOOR TO
NEXT FRIDAY
NEXT IN LINE
NEXT MONDAY
NEXT PERSON
NEXT PLEASE

NEXT SEASON	NONE OF THAT!	O – 10
NEXT SPRING	NO NONSENSE	
NEXT SUMMER	NON-STOP RUN	OBEY ORDERS
NEXT SUNDAY	NOODLE SOUP	OCEAN LINER
NEXT TO COME	NOONDAY SUN	OCEAN WAVES
NEXT VICTIM	NO PATIENCE	ODD AND EVEN
NEXT WINTER	NO RESPONSE	OEDIPUS REX
NICE ENOUGH	NORMAL LIFE	OF A PATTERN
NICE PEOPLE	NORMAL LOAD	OFF BALANCE
NICE TO KNOW	NORMAL PACE	OFFER TO PAY
NICK CARTER	NORTH COAST	OFFICE DESK
NICKEL COIN	NORTH DEVON	OFFICE GIRL
NICK OF TIME	NORTH DOWNS	OFFICE SAFE
NIGHT FROST	NORTH WALES	OFFICE WORK
NIGHT NURSE	NOSE TO TAIL	OFF LICENCE
NIGHT SHIFT	NO SHORTAGE	OFF ONE'S NUT
NIGHT SIGHT	NO SOLUTION	OFFSIDE LAW
NIGHT TRAIN	NO STANDING	OFF THE BEAM
NIGHT WATCH	NO STRANGER	OFF THE CUFF
NINE AND ONE	NO SUCH LUCK	OFF THE CUSH
NINE AND SIX	NOSY PARKER	OFF THE HOOK
NINE AND TEN	NOT A CHANCE	OFF THE LAND
NINE AND TWO	NOT CRICKET	OFF THE MARK
NINE MONTHS	NOTE OF HAND	OFF THE MENU
NINE O'CLOCK	NOT FAR AWAY	OFF THE REEL
NINE OUNCES	NOT FOR SALE	OFF THE WALL
NINE POINTS	NO THANK YOU	OIL COMPANY
NINE POUNDS	NOTHING NEW	OLD AND MILD
NINE TENTHS	NOT JUST NOW	OLD AND TRUE
NINTH GREEN	NOT LONG AGO	OLD BRIGADE
NINTH OF MAY	NOT ONE OF US	OLD CLOTHES
NINTH PLACE	NOT PRESENT	OLD COUNTRY
NINTH ROUND	NOT SO DUSTY	OLD EDITION
NIP ON AHEAD	NOT THE SAME	OLD ENGLAND
NITRIC ACID	NOT THE TYPE	OLD ENGLISH
NO APPETITE	NOT TO WORRY	OLDEN TIMES
NOBEL PRIZE	NOT VISIBLE	OLD ETONIAN
NOBLE BIRTH	NOT WORKING	OLD OAK TREE
NOBLE BLOOD	NOT WORTH IT	OLD PALS ACT
NOBLE HOUSE	NOVA SCOTIA	OLD ROUTINE
NOBODY ELSE	NOVEL TITLE	OLD SO-AND-SO
NO DECISION	NOW AND THEN	OLD SOLDIER
NO DISTANCE	NO WEAKNESS	OLD VERSION
NOD THE HEAD	NOW OR NEVER	OLD VETERAN
NOEL COWARD	NUCLEAR WAR	OLD WARRIOR
NO ENTRANCE	NUDE FIGURE	OLD WINDBAG
NO FRICTION	NUDIST CAMP	OLD YEAR OUT
NO HARM DONE	NUDIST CLUB	OLIVE GREEN
NO INTEREST	NUMBER FIVE	OLIVE GROVE
NO LEFT TURN	NUMBER FOUR	OL' MAN RIVER
NO LOVE LOST	NUMBER NINE	ON A CRUSADE
NO MAN'S LAND	NUT AND BOLT	ON ALL FOURS
NOM DE PLUME	NUTS AND MAY	ON ALL HANDS
NO MEAN CITY	NUTTY SLACK	ON ALL SIDES
NOMINAL FEE		ON APPROVAL
NOMINAL SUM		ON BAD TERMS

ON BUSINESS	ON THE BRAIN	OPEN ARREST
ONCE A MONTH	ON THE BRINK	OPEN BREACH
ONCE BITTEN	ON THE CARDS	OPEN CHEQUE
ONCE IN A WAY	ON THE CHEAP	OPEN CREDIT
ON CRUTCHES	ON THE CLOCK	OPEN DRAWER
ON DELIVERY	ON THE CLYDE	OPEN GROUND
ON EACH SIDE	ON THE COAST	OPEN HEARTH
ONE-ACT PLAY	ON THE CREST	OPENING BID
ONE AND FIVE	ON THE CROSS	OPENING DAY
ONE AND FOUR	ON THE FENCE	OPEN LETTER
ONE AND NINE	ON THE FILES	OPEN MARKET
ONE AND ONLY	ON THE FLANK	OPEN PRISON
ONE ANOTHER	ON THE FLOOR	OPEN REVOLT
ONE AT A TIME	ON THE GREEN	OPEN SEASON
ONE BILLION	ON THE HALLS	OPEN SECRET
ONE DIAMOND	ON THE HOUSE	OPEN SESAME
ONE FINE DAY	ON THE LATCH	OPEN THE BOX
ONE FURLONG	ON THE LEVEL	OPEN TO VIEW
ONE HUNDRED	ON THE LINKS	OPEN WINDOW
ONE IN EIGHT	ON THE LOOSE	OPERA GLASS
ONE IN SEVEN	ON THE MARCH	OPERA HOUSE
ONE IN THREE	ON THE PANEL	OPERA MUSIC
ONE-MAN BAND	ON THE PHONE	OPIUM EATER
ONE MILLION	ON THE PROWL	OPIUM HABBIT
ONE NO-TRUMP	ON THE QUIET	OPIUM POPPY
ONE PER CENT	ON THE RADIO	OPTIC NERVE
ONE QUARTER	ON THE RAILS	ORANGE PEEL
ONE SEVENTH	ON THE RHINE	ORANGE TREE
ONE'S OWN WAY	ON THE RIGHT	ORANGE WINE
ONE SQUARED	ON THE RIVER	ORDER A MEAL
ONE SWALLOW	ON THE ROCKS	ORDER PAPER
ONE TOO MANY	ON THE SANDS	ORGAN MUSIC
ONE TWELFTH	ON THE SCENT	ORIENT LINE
ONE WAY ONLY	ON THE SHELF	ORION'S BELT
ON FURLOUGH	ON THE SLANT	OSCAR AWARD
ONION SAUCE	ON THE SLATE	OSCAR WILDE
ON LOCATION	ON THE SOMME	OSTRICH EGG
ONLY CHANCE	ON THE SPREE	OTHER RANKS
ONLY CHOICE	ON THE STAFF	OTHER WORLD
ON MORTGAGE	ON THE STAGE	OUIJA BOARD
ON MY HONOUR	ON THE STAND	OUR BETTERS
ON OCCASION	ON THE TABLE	OUR VERSION
ON ONE'S BACK	ON THE TELLY	OUT AND HOME
ON ONE'S FEET	ON THE TILES	OUT AT ELBOW
ON ONE'S LEGS	ON THE TRACK	OUTER COVER
ON ONE'S TOES	ON THE TRAIL	OUTER SPACE
ON SATURDAY	ON THE VERGE	OUTER WORLD
ON SCHEDULE	ON THE WAGON	OUT IN FORCE
ON SENTRY-GO	ON THE WATCH	OUT IN FRONT
ON THE ALERT	ON THE WATER	OUT OF COURT
ON THE BEACH	ON THE WAY IN	OUT OF DOORS
ON THE BENCH	ON THE WAY UP	OUT OF FOCUS
ON THE BIBLE	ON THE WHOLE	OUT OF FUNDS
ON THE BOARD	ON THIS SIDE	OUT OF HOURS
ON THE BOOKS	ON THURSDAY	OUT OF JOINT
ON THE BOOZE	ON VACATION	OUT OF MONEY

OUT OF MY WAY
OUT OF ORBIT
OUT OF ORDER
OUT OF PLACE
OUT OF PRINT
OUT OF RANGE
OUT OF REACH
OUT OF SCALE
OUT OF SHAPE
OUT OF SIGHT
OUT OF SORTS
OUT OF SPITE
OUT OF STOCK
OUT OF TOUCH
OUT OF WATER
OUT ON A LIMB
OUT PATIENT
OUT TO LUNCH
OUTWARD EYE
OVAL OFFICE
OVER AND OUT
OVER EXPOSE
OVER POLITE
OVER THE AIR
OVER THE BAR
OVER THE SEA
OVER THE TOP
OVER THE WAY
OWE LOYALTY
OWNER'S RISK
OX-EYE DAISY
OXFORD BAGS
OXFORD BLUE
OXTAIL SOUP
OXYGEN MASK
OXYGEN TENT
OZONE LAYER

P – 10

PACK ANIMAL
PACK A PUNCH
PACK OF LIES
PADDED CELL
PADDY FIELD
PAGE ELEVEN
PAGE TWELVE
PAID A VISIT
PAIL OF MILK
PAINED LOOK
PAIR OF ACES
PAIR OF OARS
PAIR OF TENS
PAIR OF TWOS
PALE AND WAN
PALE YELLOW

PALM SUNDAY
PANCAKE DAY
PAPAL COURT
PAPER CHAIN
PAPER MONEY
PAPER ROUND
PAPER TIGER
PARCEL BOMB
PARCEL POST
PAR CONTEST
PARENT BIRD
PARENTS' DAY
PARENT SHIP
PARENT TREE
PARI MUTUEL
PARISH PUMP
PARK AVENUE
PARKING BAY
PARKING FEE
PARKING LOT
PART BY PART
PARTED LIPS
PARTY DRESS
PARTY FROCK
PARTY FUNDS
PARTY PIECE
PARTY TRICK
PASS FRIEND
PASSING FAD
PASS MUSTER
PASS ORDERS
PASS THE CAN
PASS THE HAT
PAST BELIEF
PAST CARING
PAST MASTER
PAST RECORD
PASTRY CHEF
PASTRY COOK
PATH OF DUTY
PATROL DUTY
PAUL DOMBEY
PAUL REVERE
PAUL TEMPLE
PAVE THE WAY
PAVLOV'S DOG
PAWN TICKET
PAY A REWARD
PAY AS YOU GO
PAY CORKAGE
PAY DAMAGES
PAYING GAME
PAY-OFF LINE
PAY ONE'S WAY
PAY ON SIGHT
PAY THE BILL

PAY THE RENT
PAY TRIBUTE
PEACE CORPS
PEACE OFFER
PEACE PARTY
PEACE TERMS
PEACH MELBA
PEAK PERIOD
PEARL DIVER
PEARLY KING
PEAS IN A POD
PEA-SOUP FOG
PECKHAM RYE
PECK OF DIRT
PEDDLE DOPE
PEEPING TOM
PEGGED DOWN
PEGGY MOUNT
PENALTY BOX
PENCIL CASE
PENNY BLACK
PENNY PIECE
PENNY PLAIN
PENNY SHARE
PENNY STAMP
PENSION OFF
PEPPER MILL
PEPYS' DIARY
PERFECT FIT
PERIOD PLAY
PERRY MASON
PERSIAN CAT
PERSIAN MAT
PERSIAN RUG
PET CARRIER
PETE MURRAY
PETER FINCH
PETER PIPER
PETER SCOTT
PETIT POINT
PETITS POIS
PETROL DUMP
PETROL PUMP
PETROL TANK
PETTY CRIME
PETTY THEFT
PETTY THIEF
PHIL ARCHER
PHIL HARRIS
PHRASE BOOK
PIANO STOOL
PIANO TUNER
PICK A FIGHT
PICKET LINE
PICK FAULTS
PICK STRAWS

PICK UP NEWS
PICNIC SITE
PICTURE HAT
PIED-À-TERRE
PIER MASTER
PIGEON POST
PIG IN A POKE
PILLOW SHAM
PILOT LIGHT
PINA COLADA
PINE FOREST
PINK RIBBON
PINNED DOWN
PINT OF BEER
PINT OF MILD
PINT OF MILK
PIOUS HOPES
PIOUS TRUTH
PIPED MUSIC
PIPES OF PAN
PIRATE FLAG
PIRATE SHIP
PISTOL SHOT
PITCH A TENT
PITCH A YARN
PITCH BLACK
PITH HELMET
PLACED LAST
PLACE MONEY
PLACE ON END
PLAGUE SPOT
PLAID CYMRU
PLAIN FACTS
PLAIN FOLLY
PLAIN PAPER
PLAIN SKIRT
PLAIN SOCKS
PLAIN TERMS
PLAIN TO SEE
PLAIN TRUTH
PLAIN WORDS
PLANE CRASH
PLANT A TREE
PLANT STAND
PLASTIC ART
PLASTIC BAG
PLASTIC MAC
PLASTIC TOY
PLAT DU JOUR
PLATE GLASS
PLAY A CHORD
PLAY A SCALE
PLAY AT HOME
PLAY A TRICK
PLAY A WALTZ
PLAY BO-PEEP

PLAY BRIDGE
PLAY HAMLET
PLAY HOCKEY
PLAY HOOKEY
PLAY IT COOL
PLAY POSSUM
PLAY PRANKS
PLAY RUGGER
PLAY SCALES
PLAY SOCCER
PLAY SQUASH
PLAY STREET
PLAY TENNIS
PLAY THE MAN
PLAY THE WAG
PLAY TRICKS
PLAY TRUANT
PLAY TRUMPS
PLENTY MORE
PLENTY TO DO
PLOT OF LAND
PLOUGH BACK
PLOVER'S EGG
PLUCKY CHAP
PLUMB CRAZY
PLY FOR HIRE
POACHED EGG
POCKET COMB
POETIC VEIN
POINT BLANK
POINT OF LAW
POISON PILL
POKER PARTY
POLES APART
POLE TO POLE
POLICE BALL
POLICE RAID
POLICE TRAP
POLLING DAY
POLO GROUND
POLO PLAYER
POMPOUS ASS
PONDER'S END
POOR BEGGAR
POOR CHANCE
POOR CHOICE
POOR EXCUSE
POOR FELLOW
POOR GROUND
POOR HEALTH
POOR PEOPLE
POOR PLAYER
POOR RELIEF
POOR RESULT
POOR RETURN
POOR SAILOR

POOR SECOND
POOR SERMON
POOR STAYER
POOR WRETCH
POOR YORICK
POPLAR TREE
POPULAR AIR
PORK FILLET
PORK-PIE HAT
PORT ARTHUR
PORT DARWIN
PORT ENGINE
PORTION OUT
PORT NELSON
PORT OF CALL
PORTON DOWN
PORT TALBOT
POSTAL RATE
POSTMAN PAT
POST MORTEM
POST OFFICE
POTATO PEEL
POT HUNTING
POT OF HONEY
POT OF MONEY
POT OF PAINT
POTTED MEAT
POTTER'S BAR
POT THE BLUE
POT THE PINK
POUNCE UPON
POUND OF TEA
POULTRY RUN
POURING WET
POWDER BLUE
POWDER BOWL
POWDER PUFF
POWDER ROOM
POWER HOUSE
POWER PLANT
POWER POINT
POWER PRESS
PRAIRIE DOG
PRAWN CURRY
PRAWN SALAD
PRAYER BOOK
PREP. SCHOOL
PRESENT DAY
PRESS AGENT
PRESS AHEAD
PRESS BARON
PRETTY FACE
PRETTY FAIR
PRETTY GIRL
PRETTY GOOD
PRETTY MESS

PRETTY PASS	PUBLIC PATH	PUZZLED AIR
PRETTY POLL	PUBLIC ROAD	PUZZLE OVER
PRETTY SURE	PUBLIC ROOM	
PRETTY TUNE	PUBLIC SALE	
PRETTY WELL	PUBLIC WEAL	Q – 10
PRICE INDEX	PUERTO RICO	
PRICE LABEL	PUFF OF WIND	QUACK, QUACK
PRICE LEVEL	PUFF PASTRY	QUAI D'ORSAY
PRIMA DONNA	PUGIL STICK	QUAINT IDEA
PRIMA FACIE	PULLMAN CAR	QUAKER GIRL
PRIME CAUSE	PUNCH DRUNK	QUARTER DAY
PRIME MOVER	PUPPET SHOW	QUEEN'S HALL
PRINCE IGOR	PURE ACCENT	QUEEN'S HEAD
PRINT DRESS	PURE CHANCE	QUEEN'S PAWN
PRIOR CLAIM	PURE COLOUR	QUEEN'S ROOK
PRISON BARS	PURE REASON	QUEER SOUND
PRISON CAMP	PURE SILVER	QUICK LUNCH
PRISON CELL	PURSED LIPS	QUICK MARCH
PRISON DIET	PUSH AROUND	QUICK TEMPO
PRISON FARE	PUSH BUTTON	QUICK TRICK
PRISON GATE	PUSH TOO FAR	QUID PRO QUO
PRISON YARD	PUT AND TAKE	QUIET START
PRIVATE BAR	PUT AN END TO	QUITE CLEAR
PRIVATE BUS	PUT A STOP TO	QUITE CLOSE
PRIVATE CAR	PUT ASUNDER	QUITE EMPTY
PRIVATE EYE	PUT FORWARD	QUITE HAPPY
PRIVATE LAW	PUT IN A BOOK	QUITE RIGHT
PRIVATE WAR	PUT IN A CELL	QUITE STILL
PRIVATE WAY	PUT IN A WORD	QUITE WRONG
PRIVY PURSE	PUT IN FRONT	QUIT OFFICE
PRIZE COURT	PUT IN IRONS	QUIZ LEAGUE
PRIZE ENTRY	PUT IN ORDER	QUIZ MASTER
PRIZE ESSAY	PUT IN POWER	
PRIZE FIGHT	PUT IN RHYME	
PRIZE IDIOT	PUT IN VERSE	R – 10
PRIZE MONEY	PUT IN WORDS	
PROFITS TAX	PUT ON AN ACT	RABBIT SKIN
PROMPT BOOK	PUT ON A SHOW	RACE HATRED
PROPER CARE	PUT ON BLACK	RACING CARD
PROPER MIND	PUT ON BOARD	RACING FORM
PROPER NAME	PUT ONE OVER	RACING NEWS
PROPER NOUN	PUT ONE WISE	RACING TOUT
PROPER TIME	PUT ON FLESH	RADIATE JOY
PROSE WORKS	PUT ON SPEED	RADIO DRAMA
PRO TEMPORE	PUT ON TRIAL	RADIO TIMES
PROUD BOAST	PUT THE SHOT	RADIUM BOMB
PROUD FLESH	PUT THROUGH	RAGGED EDGE
PROUD HEART	PUTTING OFF	RAILWAY ACT
PROUD SIGHT	PUTTING OUT	RAISE A DUST
PROVEN FACT	PUT TO DEATH	RAISE A HAND
PROWL ABOUT	PUT TO MUSIC	RAISE A LOAN
PRYING EYES	PUT TO SHAME	RAISE ALOFT
PSYCHIC BID	PUT TO SLEEP	RAISE MONEY
PUBLIC GOOD	PUTTY MEDAL	RAISE STEAM
PUBLIC LIFE	PUT UP A SHOW	RAISE TAXES
PUBLIC PARK	PUT UP A SIGN	RALLY ROUND
		RAM RAIDING
		RANCH HOUSE

RANDOM SHOT
RAPID PULSE
RARE CHANCE
RARING TO GO
RASH BELIEF
RATHER COOL
RATHER FLAT
RATHER GOOD
RATHER LATE
RATION BOOK
RATION CARD
RATTLE AWAY
RAW RECRUIT
RAY CHARLES
RAYNES PARK
RAY OF LIGHT
RAZOR BLADE
RAZOR'S EDGE
RAZOR SHARP
RAZOR STROP
READ A STORY
READ DEEPLY
READ MY LIPS
READY FOR IT
READY MONEY
READY REPLY
READY TO CRY
READY TO DIE
READY TO EAT
REAL DANGER
REAL ESTATE
REAL FRIEND
REALLY MEAN
REAL MADRID
REAL OBJECT
REAL PERSON
REAL SCHOOL
REAL TENNIS
REAR WINDOW
RECALL TEST
RECENT DATE
RECENT PAST
RECIPE BOOK
RECORD CROP
RECORD GATE
RECORD ROOM
RECORD SALE
RECORD SHOP
RECORD TIME
RED ADMIRAL
RED AS A ROSE
RED BALLOON
RED BIRETTA
RED CABBAGE
RED CURRANT
RED FLANNEL

RED HERRING
RED PIGMENT
RED, RED ROSE
REFINED OIL
REFORM BILL
REFORM CLUB
REFUSE BAIL
REFUSE DUMP
REFUSE TO GO
RELIEF FUND
REMAIN CALM
REMAIN DUMB
REMAND HOME
REMOTE AGES
REMOVAL VAN
RENEW A BOOK
RENT A HOUSE
RENT STRIKE
REPAIR BILL
REPAY A LOAN
REPORT BACK
REPORT SICK
RESCUE SHIP
RESCUE TEAM
RESCUE WORK
REST AWHILE
REST CENTRE
REST PERIOD
RETAIL SHOP
RETIRED PAY
RETIRE HURT
RETURN FARE
RETURN GAME
RETURN HALF
RETURN HOME
REVIEW COPY
RICHARD ROE
RICH PEOPLE
RICH REWARD
RICH SOURCE
RICH SUPPLY
RIDING COAT
RIDING CROP
RIDING HIGH
RIDING SEAT
RIDING WHIP
RIFLE CORPS
RIFLE RANGE
RIGHT ABOUT
RIGHT AHEAD
RIGHT ANGLE
RIGHT BRAIN
RIGHT DRESS
RIGHT FLANK
RIGHT LINES
RIGHT OF WAY

RIGHT ON TOP
RIGHT PLACE
RIGHT ROUND
RIGHT ROYAL
RIGHT THING
RIGHT TO BUY
RIGHT TOTAL
RIGHT TRACK
RIGHT TRAIL
RIGHT WAY UP
RIGHT WHEEL
RIGHT WOMAN
RING FINGER
RING MASTER
RINGO STARR
RIOT POLICE
RIOT SHIELD
RIPEN EARLY
RIPE OLD AGE
RIPE TOMATO
RISE HIGHER
RISE IN ARMS
RISING COST
RISING TIDE
RIVAL CAMPS
RIVAL CAUSE
RIVAL CLAIM
RIVER BASIN
RIVER CLYDE
RIVER CRAFT
RIVER LEVEL
RIVER MOUTH
RIVER PLATE
RIVER RHINE
RIVER RHONE
RIVER TRENT
RIVER TROUT
RIVER TWEED
ROAD SAFETY
ROAD TO FAME
ROAD TO HELL
ROAD TO RUIN
ROAD-UP SIGN
ROAST ALIVE
ROBBER BAND
ROBERT ADAM
ROBERT PEEL
ROBIN ADAIR
ROB THE TILL
ROCK BOTTOM
ROCKET BASE
ROCKET SITE
ROCK GARDEN
ROCK HUDSON
ROCK OF AGES
ROCKS AHEAD

ROCK SALMON
ROCK STEADY
ROCKY COAST
ROD AND LINE
RODEO DRIVE
ROD STEWART
ROGER BACON
ROGER MOORE
ROLLED GOLD
ROLLED OATS
ROLLS OF FAT
ROMAN EAGLE
ROMAN FORUM
ROMAN RUINS
ROMAN TUNIC
ROMAN VILLA
ROMPER SUIT
ROOF GARDEN
ROOM NUMBER
ROOM TO MOVE
ROOM TO TURN
ROPE A STEER
ROPE LADDER
ROSE COLOUR
ROSE GARDEN
ROSY CHEEKS
ROTARY CLUB
ROTTEN HAND
ROTTEN IDEA
ROTTEN LUCK
ROUGH CIDER
ROUGH DRAFT
ROUGH GOING
ROUGH GUESS
ROUGH GUIDE
ROUGH HANDS
ROUGH HOUSE
ROUGH NIGHT
ROUGH STATE
ROUGH STONE
ROUGH STUFF
ROUGH TRACK
ROUGH USAGE
ROUGH WATER
ROUGH WORDS
ROUND ABOUT
ROUND DANCE
ROUND DOZEN
ROUND GUESS
ROUND ROBIN
ROUND SCORE
ROUND TABLE
ROUND TERMS
ROUND TOWER
ROUTE MARCH
ROWING BLUE

ROWING BOAT
ROWING CLUB
ROW OF BEANS
ROW OF TREES
ROW UPON ROW
ROYAL ASCOT
ROYAL BARGE
ROYAL BIRTH
ROYAL BLOOD
ROYAL FLUSH
ROYAL HOUSE
ROYAL LODGE
ROYAL SCOTS
ROYAL SUITE
ROYAL TRAIN
ROYAL VISIT
ROYAL YACHT
ROY EMERSON
ROY ORBISON
RUB AGAINST
RUBBER BALL
RUBBER BAND
RUBBER HOSE
RUBBER SOLE
RUBBER TUBE
RUBBER TYRE
RUBIKS CUBE
RUBY MURRAY
RUDE ANSWER
RUDE HEALTH
RUDE PERSON
RUDE REMARK
RUDOLF HESS
RUGBY FIELD
RUGBY MATCH
RUGBY PITCH
RUGBY SCRUM
RUGBY TRIAL
RUGBY UNION
RUGGER BLUE
RUM AND LIME
RUN ABREAST
RUN AGAINST
RUN AGROUND
RUN A MINUTE
RUN AT A LOSS
RUN ERRANDS
RUN FOR HELP
RUN FOR PORT
RUN IN PAIRS
RUN LIKE MAD
RUNNER BEAN
RUNNING DOG
RUNNING OUT
RUN THE RISK
RUN THE SHOW

RUN THROUGH
RUN TO EARTH
RUN TO WASTE
RUN UP A BILL
RUPERT BEAR
RURAL SCENE
RUSS CONWAY
RUSSIAN EGG
RUSSIAN TEA
RUSTIC ARCH
RUSTIC SEAT
RUSTIC WORK

S – 10

SABBATH DAY
SABLE STOLE
SACK OF COAL
SACK OF COKE
SACK OF CORN
SACK THE LOT
SACRED BOOK
SACRED RITE
SACRED WRIT
SAD OUTLOOK
SAD TIDINGS
SAFARI PARK
SAFARI SUIT
SAFE IN PORT
SAFE METHOD
SAFE POLICY
SAFE REFUGE
SAFETY BELT
SAFETY LAMP
SAIL A YACHT
SAILING AID
SAILOR SUIT
SAINT LOUIS
SAINT PETER
SALAD CREAM
SALE OF WORK
SALES STAFF
SALLY FORTH
SALMON PINK
SALT CELLAR
SALTED AWAY
SALTED BEEF
SALT OF LIFE
SALT TREATY
SAM GOLDWYN
SAMPLE BOOK
SAND CASTLE
SANDIE SHAW
SANDS OF DEE
SANDY BEACH
SANE ENOUGH

SANTA CLAUS
SANTA LUCIA
SARAH MILES
SARDINE TIN
SATIN DRESS
SAUCER EYES
SAVAGE BLOW
SAVAGE CLUB
SAVAGE RACE
SAVE A TRICK
SAVE LABOUR
SAVE THE DAY
SAVING GAME
SAVOY HOTEL
SAY A PRAYER
SAY GOOD-BYE
SAY NOTHING
SAY THE WORD
SCALDED CAT
SCALE MODEL
SCAMPER OFF
SCARLET HAT
SCARS OF WAR
SCENE THREE
SCENT SPRAY
SCHOOL BELL
SCHOOL BOOK
SCHOOL DAYS
SCHOOL FEES
SCHOOL SONG
SCHOOL TERM
SCHOOL YEAR
SCORE A BULL
SCORE A DUCK
SCORE A GOAL
SCOTCH KALE
SCOTCH MIST
SCOTCH PINE
SCOTCH REEL
SCOTS GREYS
SCOUT ROUND
SCRAPE AWAY
SCRAPE HOME
SCRAP METAL
SCRAP PAPER
SCRATCH MAN
SCRATCH OUT
SCREECH OWL
SCREEN IDOL
SCREEN TEST
SCREW LOOSE
SCRIP ISSUE
SCUBA DIVER
SCUFF GUARD
SCUTTLE OFF
SEA ANEMONE

SEA BATHING
SEA CAPTAIN
SEALED BOOK
SEALED KNOT
SEALED LIPS
SEA MONSTER
SEAN O'CASEY
SEA OF FACES
SEA PASSAGE
SEA SERPENT
SECOND BELL
SECOND BEST
SECOND COAT
SECOND COPY
SECOND CROP
SECOND FORM
SECOND GEAR
SECOND HALF
SECOND HAND
SECOND HEAT
SECOND HOLE
SECOND HOME
SECOND JUMP
SECOND LEAD
SECOND LINE
SECOND MATE
SECOND NAME
SECOND PART
SECOND POST
SECOND RACE
SECOND RANK
SECOND SELF
SECOND SLIP
SECONDS OUT
SECOND TEAM
SECOND TERM
SECOND TEST
SECOND TIME
SECOND WEEK
SECOND WIFE
SECOND WIND
SECOND YEAR
SECRET CODE
SECRET DOOR
SECRET FILE
SECRET PACT
SECRET SIGN
SECRET VICE
SECRET VOTE
SEDAN CHAIR
SEE ABOUT IT
SEE A DOCTOR
SEE A LAWYER
SEE CLEARLY
SEEING LIFE
SEEK ACCORD

SEEK ADVICE
SEEK OFFICE
SEEK REFUGE
SEEK SAFETY
SEE NOTHING
SEE ONE'S WAY
SEE SERVICE
SEE THE JOKE
SEE THROUGH
SEE VISIONS
SEIZE POWER
SELECT CLUB
SELL AN IDEA
SELL-BY DATE
SELL IN BULK
SELL SHARES
SELSEY BILL
SEND A CABLE
SEND BY HAND
SEND BY POST
SEND FLYING
SENIOR GIRL:
SENSE ORGAN
SENT FLYING
SENTRY DUTY
SERENE LOOK
SERIOUS AIR
SERVE A MEAL
SERVE AN ACE
SERVE A WRIT
SERVE BADLY
SERVING MAN
SET A COURSE
SET AGAINST
SET AT LARGE
SET FORMULA
SET IN ORDER
SET IN PLACE
SET OF BELLS
SET OF CHESS
SET OF CLUBS
SET OF DARTS
SET OF EIGHT
SET OF RULES
SET OF SEVEN
SET OF STUDS
SET OF TEETH
SET OF THREE
SET OF TOOLS
SET PROBLEM
SET PURPOSE
SET STORE BY
SET THE PACE
SETTING OFF
SETTING OUT
SETTING SUN

SETTLE DOWN	SHEER FOLLY	SHREWD TURN
SET TO MUSIC	SHEER FORCE	SHRILL NOTE
SET UP HOUSE	SHEER WASTE	SHRILL TONE
SEVEN A SIDE	SHEET GLASS	SHRINK AWAY
SEVEN CLUBS	SHEET METAL	SHRINK BACK
SEVEN DIALS	SHEET MUSIC	SHUFFLE OFF
SEVEN DOZEN	SHEET OF ICE	SHUFFLE OUT
SEVEN GROSS	SHELL SHOCK	SHUTTING UP
SEVEN HOURS	SHIFT ABOUT	SHUT UP SHOP
SEVEN KINGS	SHINE FORTH	SIAMESE CAT
SEVEN MILES	SHIN OF BEEF	SICK AS A DOG
SEVEN PARTS	SHIP'S CARGO	SICK HUMOUR
SEVEN PINTS	SHIRE HORSE	SICKLE CELL
SEVEN SCORE	SHOE A HORSE	SICKLY LOOK
SEVEN STARS	SHOE POLISH	SICK OF WORK
SEVENTH DAY	SHOOT AHEAD	SICK PARADE
SEVENTH ROW	SHOOT A LINE	SICK PERSON
SEVENTH TEE	SHOOT FORTH	SIDE BY SIDE
SEVEN TIMES	SHOOT IT OUT	SIDE EFFECT
SEVEN TO ONE	SHOP WINDOW	SIDE OF BEEF
SEVEN VEILS	SHORE LEAVE	SIDE POCKET
SEVEN WEEKS	SHORT BURST	SIDE STAKES
SEVEN YEARS	SHORT DRINK	SIDE STREET
SEVERE BLOW	SHORT DRIVE	SIDE TO SIDE
SEVERE LOOK	SHORT HAIRS	SIDE WINDOW
SEVERE LOSS	SHORT HOURS	SIDLE ALONG
SEVERE PAIN	SHORT LEASE	SIGH DEEPLY
SEVERE TEST	SHORT LEAVE	SIGH NO MORE
SEVERN BORE	SHORT PANTS	SIGNAL LAMP
SEWAGE FARM	SHORT PRICE	SIGNED COPY
SEX PISTOLS	SHORT QUEUE	SIGNET RING
SEX THERAPY	SHORT RANGE	SIGN MANUAL
SHABBY DEAL	SHORT SIGHT	SIGN OF LIFE
SHACKING UP	SHORT SKIRT	SILENT FILM
SHADY PLACE	SHORT SLEEP	SILKEN HAIR
SHADY TRICK	SHORT SOCKS	SILKEN HOSE
SHAKE HANDS	SHORT SPELL	SILK FABRIC
SHAKE IT OFF	SHORT STAGE	SILK GLOVES
SHALLOW END	SHORT STORY	SILK SQUARES
SHANK'S PONY	SHORT VISIT	SILLY BILLY
SHANTY TOWN	SHOT AT DAWN	SILLY DEVIL
SHAPE BADLY	SHOVE ASIDE	SILLY GOOSE
SHARE A FLAT	SHOW A LIGHT	SILLY IDIOT
SHARE A TAXI	SHOWER BATH	SILLY MID-ON
SHARE ISSUE	SHOW FAVOUR	SILLY POINT
SHARP FROST	SHOW NO PITY	SILVER BAND
SHARP KNIFE	SHOW NO SIGN	SILVER COIN
SHARP POINT	SHOW SPIRIT	SILVER DISC
SHARP TASTE	SHOW TALENT	SILVER FOIL
SHARP TWIST	SHOW THE WAY	SILVER HAIR
SHARP VOICE	SHOW UP WELL	SILVER MINE
SHARP WORDS	SHOW VALOUR	SILVER RING
SHAVING SET	SHREWD BLOW	SILVER STAR
SHED A LIGHT	SHREWD FACE	SILVER TRAY
SHEEP'S EYES	SHREWD IDEA	SILVER WIRE
SHEER FLUKE	SHREWD MOVE	SIMMER DOWN

SIMNEL CAKE	SIZE ELEVEN	SMART WOMAN
SIMON PETER	SIZE OF TYPE	SMILE AGAIN
SIMPLE DIET	SIZE TWELVE	SMOKE ALARM
SIMPLE FARE	SKETCH BOOK	SMOKE A PIPE
SIMPLE IDEA	SKIPPED OFF	SMOKED FISH
SIMPLE LIFE	SKIPPED OUT	SMOKING CAP
SIMPLE MIND	SKIRT ROUND	SMOKING HOT
SIMPLE PAST	SKITTLE OUT	SMOOTH AWAY
SIMPLE SOUL	SLACKEN OFF	SMOOTH CHIN
SINE QUA NON	SLACK WATER	SMOOTH DOWN
SING A DIRGE	SLAP-UP MEAL	SMOOTH FACE
SING FOR JOY	SLATE LOOSE	SMOOTH HAIR
SING IN TUNE	SLAVE DANCE	SMOOTH OVER
SINGLE BLOW	SLAVE STATE	SMOOTH SKIN
SINGLE FARE	SLAVE TRADE	SMUGGLE OUT
SINGLE FILE	SLEEP IT OFF	SNAIL'S PACE
SINGLE LIFE	SLEEP ROUGH	SNAP ANSWER
SINGLE LINE	SLEEP TIGHT	SNAP INTO IT
SINGLE MIND	SLEIGH RIDE	SNATCH AWAY
SINGLE NOTE	SLICED LOAF	SNEAK ABOUT
SINGLE ROOM	SLICK CHICK	SNEAK ROUND
SINGLES BAR	SLIDE VALVE	SNEAK THIEF
SINGLE VOTE	SLIGHT BLOW	SNOW AND ICE
SINK A SHAFT	SLIGHT COLD	SNOW MAIDEN
SINK OR SWIM	SLIM CHANCE	SNOWY WHITE
SIRE AND DAM	SLIM FIGURE	SNUFF MOVIE
SIR GALAHAD	SLIM VOLUME	SOAKING WET
SIR OR MADAM	SLIP OF A BOY	SOAP BUBBLE
SISTER SHIP	SLIPPED OFF	SOAP FLAKES
SIT AND FUME	SLIPPED OUT	SOAP POWDER
SITTING OUT	SLOW BOWLER	SOAP RATION
SIX BILLION	SLOW COOKER	SOAPY WATER
SIX COURSES	SLOW GROWTH	SOBER TRUTH
SIX DEGREES	SLOW MOTION	SOCCER TEAM
SIX DOLLARS	SLOW POISON	SOCIAL CLUB
SIX FATHOMS	SLOW WICKET	SOCIAL EVIL
SIX GALLONS	SMALL BLAME	SOCIAL ILLS
SIX HUNDRED	SMALL BUILD	SOCIAL LIFE
SIX MINUTES	SMALL CHILD	SOCIAL RANK
SIX OCTAVES	SMALL CRAFT	SOCIAL RUIN
SIX OF CLUBS	SMALL CROWD	SOCIAL WORK
SIX OR SEVEN	SMALL HOPES	SODIUM LAMP
SIX PER CENT	SMALL HOURS	SOFT ANSWER
SIX SHOOTER	SMALL HOUSE	SOFT AS SILK
SIX SQUARED	SMALL MEANS	SOFT AS SOAP
SIX STROKES	SMALL ORDER	SOFT CENTRE
SIXTH FLOOR	SMALL PIECE	SOFT COLLAR
SIXTH GREEN	SMALL PRINT	SOFT COLOUR
SIXTH OF MAY	SMALL SCALE	SOFT GROUND
SIXTH PLACE	SMALL THING	SOFT NUMBER
SIXTH ROUND	SMALL VOICE	SOFT PALATE
SIXTH SENSE	SMALL WAIST	SOFT PENCIL
SIXTY MILES	SMALL WOMAN	SOFT TONGUE
SIXTY TIMES	SMALL WORLD	SOFT WICKET
SIXTY YEARS	SMART HOUSE	SOHO SQUARE
SIX WICKETS	SMART MONEY	SOLAR MONTH

SOLAR POWER	SPELL CHECK	STAGE FEVER
SOLEMN FACE	SPELL IT OUT	STAGGER OFF
SOLEMN LOOK	SPEND MONEY	STAGGER OUT
SOLEMN OATH	SPENT FORCE	STAKE MONEY
SOLE RIGHTS	SPICED WINE	STALE BREAD
SOLE TRADER	SPICY STORY	STAMP ALBUM
SOLID BUILD	SPIDER'S WEB	STAND ABOUT
SOLID FACTS	SPIKE JONES	STAND ALONE
SOLID IVORY	SPILL BLOOD	STAND ALOOF
SOLID SENSE	SPINAL CORD	STAND APART
SOLID STATE	SPIN BOWLER	STAND ASIDE
SOLID WATER	SPIN DOCTOR	STAND AT BAY
SOLO EFFORT	SPIRAL DOWN	STAND CLEAR
SOLO FLIGHT	SPIRIT AWAY	STAND ERECT
SON AND HEIR	SPIRIT LAMP	STAND FOR IT
SONG OF LOVE	SPLIT HAIRS	STAND GUARD
SONG WRITER	SPLIT IN TWO	STAND IN AWE
SONJA HENIE	SPODE CHINA	STANDING BY
SONNIE HALE	SPOKEN WORD	STANDING UP
SOON ENOUGH	SPONGE CAKE	STAND ON END
SOOTH TO SAY	SPONGE DOWN	STAND READY
SORDID GAIN	SPORTS CLUB	STAND STILL
SORE THROAT	SPORTS COAT	STAND TO WIN
SORRY SIGHT	SPORTS PAGE	STAND TREAT
SORRY STATE	SPOTTED DOG	STAND TRIAL
SORRY TO SAY	SPREAD FEAR	STAND UP FOR
SOUND BASIS	SPREAD SAIL	STAPLE DIET
SOUND RADIO	SPRING AWAY	STARK NAKED
SOUND SENSE	SPRING BACK	STARLIT SKY
SOUND SLEEP	SPRING DOWN	STAR OF HOPE
SOUND TRACK	SPRING OPEN	STAR PLAYER
SOUND VIEWS	SPRING OVER	START A FIRE
SOUND WAVES	SPRING SALE	START AGAIN
SOUP COURSE	SPRING SONG	START A RIOT
SOUP TICKET	SPRING TIDE	START YOUNG
SOUR GRAPES	SPUN SILVER	STATE A CASE
SOUR NATURE	SQUAD DRILL	STATE COACH
SOUTH COAST	SQUARE CHIN	STATED TIME
SOUTH DEVON	SQUARE DEAL	STATE GRANT
SOUTH DOWNS	SQUARE FOOT	STATE NURSE
SOUTH WALES	SQUARE GAME	STATE OF WAR
SOW THE SEED	SQUARE HOLE	STATE TRIAL
SPACE PROBE	SQUARE INCH	STATE VISIT
SPANISH FLY	SQUARE MEAL	STATUTE LAW
SPAN OF LIFE	SQUARE MILE	STAY AT HOME
SPARE FRAME	SQUARE ROOT	STAY BEHIND
SPARE WHEEL	SQUARE SAIL	STAY IN A RUT
SPEAK ALOUD	SQUARE UP TO	STAY INSIDE
SPEAK DUTCH	SQUARE YARD	STAY UP LATE
SPEAK WELSH	SQUEEZE DRY	ST DUNSTAN'S
SPECIAL BUS	SQUEEZE OUT	STEADY BEAM
SPECIAL DAY	STABLE DOOR	STEADY FLOW
SPEED FIEND	STABLE MATE	STEADY HAND
SPEED GAUGE	STACK OF HAY	STEADY PACE
SPEED LIMIT	STAFF NURSE	STEADY RAIN
SPEED TRIAL	STAG BEETLE	STEADY SALE

STEADY WIND
STEAK HOUSE
STEAL A KISS
STEAL ALONG
STEALING BY
STEALING UP
STEAM NAVVY
STEAM ORGAN
STEAM POWER
STEAM RADIO
STEAM TRAIN
STEAM VALVE
STEAM YACHT
STEEL WORKS
STEELY LOOK
STEEP CLIMB
STEEP PRICE
STEER CLEAR
STEFFI GRAF
STEP ASHORE
STEP BY STEP
STEP INSIDE
STEP LADDER
STEP LIVELY
STEPPED OUT
STERN CHASE
STERN TRUTH
STERN WORDS
STEWED BEEF
STEWED EELS
STEWED LAMB
STEWED MEAT
STICK IT OUT
STICK TIGHT
STICK UP FOR
STICKY BOMB
STICKY MESS
STIFF CLIMB
STIFF DRINK
STIFF FENCE
STIFF PRICE
STILL OWING
STILL THERE
STILL WATER
STIRRUP CUP
STIR THE POT
STITCHED UP
ST LAWRENCE
ST LUKE'S DAY
STOCK REPLY
STOCK STILL:
STODGY FOOD
STOKE POGES
STOLE A KISS
STONE STEPS
STONE WALLS

STONY BROKE
STONY HEART
STONY STARE
STOOD TRIAL
STOP AT HOME
STOP A TOOTH
STOP AT WILL
STOP CRYING
STOP FOR TEA
STOP IN TIME
STOPPED ONE
STOPPED OUT
STOP THE BUS
STOP THE GAP
STOP THE ROT
STORAGE BOX
STORE OF WIT
STORK'S NEST
STORMY LIFE
STOUT HEART
STOUT WOMAN
STRAIGHT BY
STRAIGHT IN
STRAIGHT ON
STRAIGHT UP
STRANGE MAN
STREAK AWAY
STREAK PAST
STREET ARAB
STREET CRED
STREET DOOR
STREET LAMP
STRETCH OUT
STRICT DIET
STRICT TIME
STRIKE BACK
STRIKE CAMP
STRIKE DOWN
STRIKE DUMB
STRIKE GOLD
STRIKE HARD
STRIKE HOME
STRIKE SAIL
STRING BAND
STRING TRIO
STRING VEST
STRIP POKER
STRIP TEASE
STROKE PLAY
STRONG BREW
STRONG CASE
STRONG GRIP
STRONG HAND
STRONG HEAD
STRONG LINE
STRONG MEAT

STRONG MIND
STRONG PULL
STRONG ROOM
STRONG SIDE
STRONG SUIT
STRONG WILL
STRONG WIND
STRUCK DOWN
STRUCK DUMB
STRUGGLE BY
STRUGGLE ON
ST STEPHEN'S
STUDIO DESK
STUDIO FLAT
STUDY MUSIC
STUFFED OWL
STUFFY ROOM
STUMP ALONG
STUMPED OUT
STUMPY TAIL
STURDY LEGS
SUCH IS LIFE
SUCKING PIG
SUDDEN BANG
SUDDEN BLOW
SUDDEN FEAR
SUDDEN HUSH
SUDDEN STOP
SUEDE SHOES
SUEZ CRISIS
SUFFER LOSS
SUFFER PAIN
SUGAR CANDY
SUGAR DADDY
SUMMER CAMP
SUMMER HEAT
SUMMER RAIN
SUMMER SALE
SUMMER TERM
SUMMER TIME
SUM OF MONEY
SUN AND MOON
SUNDAY BEST
SUNDAY SUIT
SUN GLASSES
SUNKEN REEF
SUNNY SMILE
SUNNY SOUTH
SUN-RAY LAMP
SUNSET GLOW
SUPERB VIEW
SUPPER TIME
SUPPLY BASE
SUPPLY SHIP
SURE AS FATE
SURE ENOUGH

SURE GROUND
SURGE AHEAD
SURPLUS FAT
SWAGGER OUT
SWAN OF AVON
SWEARING IN
SWEAT BLOOD
SWEAT IT OUT
SWEEP ALONG
SWEEP ASIDE
SWEEP CLEAN
SWEET DRINK
SWEET HERBS
SWEET MUSIC
SWEET SLEEP
SWEET SMELL
SWEET SMILE
SWEET SOUND
SWEET SYRUP
SWEET TOOTH
SWEET VOICE
SWEET WORDS
SWERVE PAST
SWIM ACROSS
SWINE FEVER
SWING ALONG
SWING FOR IT
SWING MUSIC
SWING ROUND
SWISS GUARD
SWISS WATCH
SWITCH BACK
SWITCHED ON
SWITCH OVER
SWIVEL HOSE
SWORD DANCE
SWORN ENEMY

T – 10

TABLE D'HÔTE
TABLE KNIFE
TABLE LINEN
TABLE MONEY
TABLE WATER
TAKE A BRIEF
TAKE A CHAIR
TAKE ACTION
TAKE A DEKKO
TAKE ADVICE
TAKE AN OATH
TAKE A PHOTO
TAKE A PUNCH
TAKE A SHARE
TAKE A SNACK
TAKE AS READ

TAKE A STAND
TAKE A TITLE
TAKE A TRAIN
TAKE CHARGE
TAKE CREDIT
TAKE EFFECT
TAKE FLIGHT
TAKE FRIGHT
TAKE IN HAND
TAKE IN SAIL
TAKE IN VAIN
TAKE IT BACK
TAKE IT EASY
TAKE IT HARD
TAKE KINDLY
TAKE MY HAND
TAKE MY WORD
TAKEN ABACK
TAKE NO PART
TAKE NOTICE
TAKE OFFICE
TAKE ON A JOB
TAKE ORDERS
TAKE PITY ON
TAKE POISON
TAKE REFUGE
TAKE THE AIR
TAKE THE CUP
TAKE THE RAP
TAKE TO ARMS
TAKE TO TASK
TAKE UP ARMS
TAKE UP TIME
TAKING WAYS
TALENT SHOW
TALE OF A TUB
TALK AWHILE
TALK IT OVER
TALK TURKEY
TALLEST BOY
TALLEST MAN
TAME AFFAIR
TAME ANIMAL
TANGLED WEB
TANK ENGINE
TAP LIGHTLY
TAP THE LINE
TAP THE WIRE
TARGET AREA
TARGET DATE
TARGET SHIP
TARIFF WALL
TARTAN KILT
TART ANSWER
TASK IN HAND
TASTE BLOOD

TASTY SNACK
TATTOO MARK
TAUT NERVES
TAX EVASION
TAXI DRIVER
T-BONE STEAK
TEACH CLASS
TEACH MUSIC
TEA CLIPPER
TEA DRINKER
TEAM OF FOUR
TEAM SPIRIT
TEA PLANTER
TEAR IN HALF
TEAR TO BITS
TEA SERVICE
TEENY WEENY
TELL A STORY
TELLING OFF
TEN BILLION
TEN DEGREES
TENDER CARE
TENDER LOVE
TENDER MEAT
TENDER SPOT
TEN DOLLARS
TEN FATHOMS
TEN GALLONS
TEN GUINEAS
TEN MILLION
TEN MINUTES
TENNIS BALL
TENNIS CLUB
TENNIS STAR
TEN OF CLUBS
TENOR VOICE
TEN PAST ONE
TEN PAST SIX
TEN PAST TWO
TEN PER CENT
TEN SECONDS
TEN SQUARED
TENTH GREEN
TENTH OF MAY
TENTH PLACE
TENTH ROUND
TEN TO EIGHT
TEN TO SEVEN
TEN TO THREE
TEN WICKETS
TEPID WATER
TERRA COTTA
TERRA FIRMA
TERRY WOGAN
TEST FLIGHT
TEST OF TIME

TEST RESULT
TEST WICKET
TEXAS WEDGE
THE ACCUSED
THE AMAZONS
THE ANIMALS
THE ARCHERS
THE ARSENAL
THEATRE BAR
THEATRE FAN
THE BACKING
THE BAHAMAS
THE BALKANS
THE BEATLES
THE BEST MAN
THE BIG BANG
THE BIG FIVE
THE BOER WAR
THE BRAVEST
THE BRONTËS
THE CABINET
THE CAPITAL
THE CHANNEL
THE COLD WAR
THE COMMONS
THE CRITICS
THE CURRAGH
THE CUSTOMS
THÉ DANSANT
THE DEAD SEA
THE DEEP END
THE DYNASTS
THE EAST END
THE ENGLISH
THE ETERNAL
THE EVIL EYE
THE EVIL ONE
THE EXPERTS
THE FAIR SEX
THE FAR EAST
THE FIDGETS
THE FIFTIES
THE FORTIES
THE GALLERY
THE GALLOWS
THE GESTAPO
THE GIGGLES
THE GLAD EYE
THE GORBALS
THE GUNNERS
THE HARD WAY
THE HEIRESS
THE HOLLIES
THE HORRORS
THE JACKPOT
THE JONESES

THE KNOW-HOW
THE KREMLIN
THE LANCERS
THE LAST BUS
THE LAST LAP
THE LINCOLN
THE LOW-DOWN
THE MAESTRO
THE MARINES
THE MAZURKA
THEME MUSIC
THE MENDIPS
THE MESSIAH
THE MILITIA
THE MIXTURE
THE NEEDFUL
THE NEEDLES
THE NEW LOOK
THE ODYSSEY
THE OLD ADAM
THE OLD FIRM
THE ORKNEYS
THE PEERAGE
THE PLANETS
THE PRELUDE
THE PREMIER
THE QUAKERS
THE QUALITY
THE RED ARMY
THE RED FLAG
THE REGENCY
THE RENT ACT
THERE THERE!
THE REVENGE
THE RIOT ACT
THE RIVIERA
THE ROCKERS
THE ROCKIES
THE SABBATH
THE SAME KEY
THE SAPPERS
THE SEASONS
THE SHADOWS
THE SHIVERS
THE SIXTIES
THE SPEAKER
THE STARTER
THE STEPPES
THE ST LEGER
THE SUBURBS
THE SWEENEY
THE TAIL-END
THE TEMPEST
THE THEATRE
THE THINKER
THE THIN MAN

THE TITANIC
THE TROPICS
THE TWELFTH
THE UNITIES
THE UNKNOWN
THE VATICAN
THE VICTORY
THE VIKINGS
THE WAY IT IS
THE WEATHER
THE WEST END
THE WILLIES
THICK SKULL
THICK SLICE
THICK TWINE
THIN EXCUSE
THING OR TWO
THINK ABOUT
THINK AGAIN
THINK AHEAD
THINK ALIKE
THINK ALOUD
THINK IT OUT
THINK TWICE
THINNED OUT
THIN STRING
THIRD CHILD
THIRD CLASS
THIRD FLOOR
THIRD GREEN
THIRD MONTH
THIRD OF MAY
THIRD PARTY
THIRD PLACE
THIRD POWER
THIRD PRIZE
THIRD REICH
THIRD ROUND
THIRD STAGE
THIRD VERSE
THIRD WORLD
THIRTY DAYS
THIRTY LOVE
THIS FRIDAY
THIS MONDAY
THIS OR THAT
THIS SEASON
THIS SIDE UP
THIS SPRING
THIS SUMMER
THIS SUNDAY
THIS WAY OUT
THIS WINTER
THOMAS GRAY
THOMAS HOOD
THORNY PATH

THREE BALLS	TIGHT SKIRT	TONY CURTIS
THREE BEARS	TILLER GIRL	TONY WELLER
THREE BRACE	TIMBER TREE	TOO FAR GONE
THREE CARDS	TIME A PUNCH	TOOL SETTER
THREE CLUBS	TIME ENOUGH	TO ONE'S FACE
THREE DARTS	TIME FACTOR	TOOTING BEC
THREE DOZEN	TIME FOR BED	TOP AND TAIL
THREE DRAWS	TIME FOR TEA	TOP BILLING
THREE FATES	TIME IN HAND	TOP HONOURS
THREE FIVES	TIMELY EXIT	TOPPLE DOWN
THREE FOURS	TIMELY WORD	TOPPLE OVER
THREE GROSS	TIME OF LIFE	TOP QUALITY
THREE HOLES	TIME OF YEAR	TOP THE BILL
THREE HOURS	TIME, PLEASE	TORRID ZONE
THREE IN ONE	TIME SIGNAL	TORY LEADER
THREE JACKS	TIME SWITCH	TOTAL BLANK
THREE KINGS	TIME TO COME	TOTAL WRECK
THREE LUMPS	TIME TO KILL	TO THE ALTAR
THREE MILES	TIME TO LOSE	TO THE NORTH
THREE NINES	TIME TO STOP	TO THE POINT
THREE PAIRS	TINKER BELL	TO THE RIGHT
THREE PARTS	TINKER WITH	TO THE SOUTH
THREE PINTS	TINNED CRAB	TOUCH AND GO
THREE PUTTS	TINNED FISH	TOUCH JUDGE
THREE SCORE	TINNED FOOD	TOUCH LUCKY
THREE SIDES	TINNED MEAT	TOUGH BREAK
THREE SIXES	TINNED MILK	TOUGH FIGHT
THREE STARS	TINNED SOUP	TOUR AROUND
THREE TIMES	TINNY NOISE	TOURING CAR
THREE TO ONE	TINNY SOUND	TOUR OF DUTY
THREE WEEKS	TIN OF BEANS	TO WINDWARD
THREE YEARS	TIN OF COCOA	TOWN CENTRE
THRIFT CLUB	TIN OF FRUIT	TOWN SQUARE
THROW ABOUT	TIN OF PAINT	TOY SOLDIER
THROW A KISS	TINSEL TOWN	TOY SPANIEL
THROW ASIDE	TIN SOLDIER	TOY TERRIER
THRUST DOWN	TIN WHISTLE	TRACKER DOG
THRUST HOME	TIP A WINNER	TRACK EVENT
THRUST OPEN	TIP THE WINK	TRADE CYCLE
THRUST PAST	TITIAN HAIR	TRADE PAPER
THUMB A LIFT	TITLED RANK	TRADE PRICE
THUMB A RIDE	TITLE FIGHT	TRADER HORN
THUMB INDEX	TITUS OATES	TRADE ROUTE
THUMBS DOWN	TOBACCO ROW	TRADE TERMS
TIDAL BASIN	TODAY'S DATE	TRADE UNION
TIDAL POWER	TOE THE LINE	TRADE WINDS
TIDAL RIVER	TOE THE MARK	TRAFFIC COP
TIDY INCOME	TOILET SOAP	TRAFFIC JAM
TIE IN KNOTS	TOKEN MONEY	TRAGIC MASK
TIE-ON LABEL	TOLL BRIDGE	TRAGIC MUSE
TIES OF RACE	TOMATO SOUP	TRAGIC NEWS
TIE THE KNOT	TOM BOWLING	TRAGIC TALE
TIGHT DRESS	TONIC SOLFA	TRAIN CRASH
TIGHT GRASP	TONIC WATER	TRAINED EYE
TIGHT MONEY	TONS OF LOVE	TRAINED MAN
TIGHT PLACE	TONS OF TIME	TRAIN FERRY

TRAIN SMASH
TRAM DRIVER
TRAMPLED ON
TRAM TICKET
TRAPEZE ACT
TRAVEL BOOK
TRAVEL IRON
TRAVEL PLUG
TREAD ON AIR
TREAD WATER
TREAT BADLY
TREATY PORT
TREBLE CLEF
TREE DOCTOR
TREE OF LIFE
TREE PRUNER
TRENCH COAT
TRENCH FEET
TRIAL MATCH
TRIAL SCENE
TRICK OR TWO
TRIFLE WITH
TRIGGER OFF
TRIM ANKLES
TRIM FIGURE
TRIP ABROAD
TRIPLE STAR
TRIPLE TIME
TRIP TO TOWN
TRIVIA QUIZ
TROLLEY BUS
TROOP TRAIN
TROTTED OFF
TROTTED OUT
TROY WEIGHT
TRUDGE PAST
TRUE CHARGE
TRUE FRIEND
TRUE REPORT
TRUE SAMPLE
TRUE TO FORM
TRUE TO LIFE
TRUE TO TYPE
TRULY RURAL
TRUSS OF HAY
TRUSTEE ACT
TRUST HOUSE
TRY A NEW WAY
TRYING TIME
TUDOR HOUSE
TUDOR KINGS
TUDOR STYLE
TUFT OF HAIR
TUMBLE DOWN
TUMBLE OVER
TUNING FORK

TUNNEL INTO
TURKEY TROT
TURN ADRIFT
TURN AROUND
TURN COLOUR
TURN IT DOWN
TURN OF DUTY
TURN THE KEY
TURN TO DUST
TURN TO GOLD
TURN TURTLE
TURN YELLOW
TURTLE DOVE
TURTLE SOUP
TWELFTH DAY
TWELFTH MAN
TWELFTH ROW
TWELVE DAYS
TWELVE FEET
TWELVE QUID
TWENTY QUID
TWICE A WEEK
TWICE A YEAR
TWICE DAILY
TWICE EIGHT
TWICE ROUND
TWICE SEVEN
TWICE THREE
TWINE ROUND
TWIN SISTER
TWIRL ROUND
TWIST ABOUT
TWIST DRILL
TWIST MY ARM
TWIST ROUND
TWO AND FIVE
TWO AND FOUR
TWO AND NINE
TWO AT A TIME
TWO BILLION
TWO COLOURS
TWO COURSES
TWO DEGREES
TWO DOLLARS
TWO FATHOMS
TWO GALLONS
TWO GUINEAS
TWO HUNDRED
TWO LENGTHS
TWO MASTERS
TWO MILLION
TWO MINUTES
TWO NATIONS
TWO OCTAVES
TWO OF A KIND
TWO OF CLUBS

TWO OR THREE
TWO PER CENT
TWO RASHERS
TWO SECONDS
TWO SQUARED
TWO STRIPES
TWO STROKES
TWO WICKETS
TYBURN TREE
TYPING POOL

U – 10

UGLY RUMOUR
UGLY SISTER
UGLY THREAT
ULTRA VIRES
UNCLE REMUS
UNCUT PAGES
UNCUT STONE
UNDER A TREE
UNDER COVER
UNDER GLASS
UNDER PROOF
UNDER STEAM
UNDER TRIAL
UNDER WATER
UNDUE HASTE
UNION BOARD
UNION CHIEF
UNION RULES
UNIQUE CASE
UNIT OF HEAT
UNIT OF TIME
UNIT OF WORK
UNKIND DEED
UNKIND WORD
UNPAID BILL
UNSOLD BOOK
UNTIDY MIND
UNTIE A KNOT
UP A GUM TREE
UP ALL NIGHT
UP AND ABOUT
UP AND DOING
UP AT OXFORD
UP FOR TRIAL
UPHILL TASK
UPHILL WALK
UPHILL WORK
UP IN A PLANE
UP IN THE AIR
UP IN THE SKY
UPON MY SOUL
UPON MY WORD
UPPER BERTH

UPPER CLASS
UPPER CRUST
UPPER HOUSE
UPPER LIMIT
UPPER SIXTH
UPPER STORY
UPRIGHT MAN
UPSIDE DOWN
UP THE AISLE
UP THE CREEK
UP THE RIVER
UP THE SPOUT
UP TO A POINT
UP TO NO GOOD
UP TO SAMPLE
UP TO THE HUB
USE FINESSE
USEFUL HINT
USE THE POST
USUAL THING
UTTERLY BAD
UTTER TRIPE

V – 10

VACANT LOOK
VACANT POST
VACUUM PUMP
VAIN EFFORT
VAIN PERSON
VAIN REGRET
VALE AND LEA
VALID POINT
VALLEY GIRL
VAMPIRE BAT
VANILLA ICE
VANITY CASE
VANITY FAIR
VANTAGE OUT
VAPOUR BATH
VARIETY ACT
VAST EXTENT
VAST PLAINS
VEAL AND HAM
VEAL CUTLET
VENTURE OUT
VERY HUNGRY
VERY LIKELY
VERY LITTLE
VERY NEARLY
VERY SELDOM
VETERAN CAR
VICHY WATER
VICIOUS LIE
VICTOR HUGO
VICTORY DAY

VIDEO LIGHT
VIDEO NASTY
VIETNAM WAR
VILE BODIES
VILLAGE INN
VINEGAR JOE
VINE GROWER
VINTAGE CAR
VIOLENT END
VIOLIN CASE
VIOLIN SOLO
VIRGIN CLAY
VIRGIN LAND
VIRGIN MARY
VIRGIN SOIL
VITAL ERROR
VITAL FLAME
VITAL FORCE
VITAL POINT
VITAL POWER
VITAL SPARK
VITAL WOUND
VIVID GREEN
VOCAL CORDS
VOCAL GROUP
VOCAL MUSIC
VOCAL ORGAN
VOLLEY BALL
VOTE LABOUR
VOTING LIST
VOUCH FOR IT
VOWEL SOUND
VULGAR HERD

W – 10

WADE ACROSS
WADING BIRD
WAD OF MONEY
WAD OF NOTES
WAGE FREEZE
WAGE PACKET
WAGES CLERK
WAGES OF SIN
WAGON TRAIN
WAG THE HEAD
WAIT AND SEE
WAIT AROUND
WAIT AWHILE
WALK ACROSS
WALK AROUND
WALK BEHIND
WALK IN FEAR
WALK OF LIFE
WALK SLOWLY
WALK SOFTLY

WALL OF FIRE
WALL STREET
WALNUT TREE
WALT DISNEY
WALTZ MUSIC
WALTZ ROUND
WANDER AWAY
WANING MOON
WANT OF CARE
WANT OF LOVE
WANT OF ZEAL
WARD SISTER
WAR FOOTING
WAR MEMOIRS
WARM FRIEND
WARMING PAN
WARNING CRY
WAR OF WORDS
WARPED MIND
WAR SAVINGS
WARSAW PACT
WASH AND DRY
WASHING DAY
WASP'S STING
WASTE MONEY
WASTE PAPER
WASTE WORDS
WATCH CHAIN
WATCHED POT
WATCH FOR IT
WATER BOARD
WATER LEVEL
WATER MELON
WATER MUSIC
WATER NYMPH
WATER ON TAP
WATER POWER
WATER'S EDGE
WATER TOWER
WAVE LENGTH
WAX AND WANE
WAXED PAPER
WAXING MOON
WAY IN FRONT
WAY OFF BEAM
WAYSIDE INN
WAY THROUGH
WEAK EXCUSE
WEAK STROKE
WEAK WILLED
WEALTHY MAN
WEARY WORLD
WEATHER EYE
WEATHER MAP
WEBBED FEET
WEDDED PAIR

WEDDED WIFE	WHIPPED OFF	WILY PERSON
WEDDING DAY	WHIRL ROUND	WIN A RUBBER
WEED KILLER	WHIST DRIVE	WIN BY A GOAL
WEEK BY WEEK	WHISTLE FOR	WIN BY A HEAD
WEEKLY RENT	WHITE BREAD	WIN BY A NECK
WEEKLY WAGE	WHITE CARGO	WINDOW PANE
WEEP FOR JOY	WHITE CHALK	WINE BIBBER
WEEP NO MORE	WHITE FRIAR	WINE CELLAR
WEIGH HEAVY	WHITE FROST	WINE TASTER
WEIGHING IN	WHITE GOODS	WINE TAVERN
WELCOME END	WHITE HORSE	WINE WAITER
WELL BEATEN	WHITE HOUSE	WIN FREEDOM
WELL BEHIND	WHITE LIGHT	WING COLLAR
WELL CAUGHT	WHITE MAGIC	WIN HONOURS
WELL ENOUGH	WHITE METAL	WINNING BET
WELL I NEVER!	WHITE MOUSE	WINNING HIT
WELL IN HAND	WHITE NOISE	WINNING RUN
WELL OF LIFE	WHITE PAINT	WINNING TRY
WELL PLACED	WHITE PAPER	WIN ON MERIT
WELL PLAYED	WHITE PIECE	WINTER COAT
WELLS FARGO	WHITE QUEEN	WINTER FEED
WELL VERSED	WHITE SAUCE	WINTER SALE
WELSH CORGI	WHITE SHEET	WINTER TIME
WELSH WALES	WHITE SHIRT	WINTER WEAR
WENDY HOUSE	WHITE SLAVE	WIN THE GAME
WENT AROUND	WHITE SUGAR	WIN THE RACE
WENT DIRECT	WHITE TRASH	WIN THE TOSS
WENT TO TOWN	WHIT MONDAY	WIN THROUGH
WEST AFRICA	WHIT SUNDAY	WIRE BASKET
WEST BERLIN	WHOLE TRUTH	WIRE PUZZLE
WEST INDIAN	WHOLE WORLD	WISE CHOICE
WEST INDIES	WICKED DEED	WISE OLD OWL
WEST IS WEST	WICKED WAYS	WISH IN VAIN
WEST LONDON	WIDE APPEAL	WISH UNDONE
WEST RIDING	WIDE CHOICE	WITCH HAZEL
WESTWARD HO!	WIDE CIRCLE	WITH A SMILE
WET BATTERY	WIDELY HELD	WITHER AWAY
WET BLANKET	WIDE MARGIN	WITHIN CALL
WET CANTEEN	WIDE SCREEN	WITHIN HAIL
WET CLOTHES	WIDE VISION	WITHOUT END
WET SHAMPOO	WIDOW'S MITE	WITH REGRET
WET THROUGH	WIDOW'S PEAK	WITNESS BOX
WET WEATHER	WIDOW WOMAN	WIZARD OF OZ
WHAT AM I BID?	WIELD POWER	WOMAN HATER
WHAT A NERVE!	WIFE BEATER	WOMAN'S HOUR
WHAT A SHAME!	WIG AND GOWN	WOMAN'S WORK
WHAT GOES ON?	WILD ANIMAL	WOMEN'S ARMY
WHAT'S UP DOC?	WILD CHEERS	WOMEN'S PAGE
WHAT'S YOURS?	WILD CHERRY	WOMEN'S WEAR
WHEAT FIELD	WILD FLOWER	WON BY A HEAD
WHEEL ABOUT	WILD HORSES	WON BY A NECK
WHEEL CLAMP	WILD SCHEME	WONDER DRUG
WHEELIE BIN	WILL OF IRON	WOODEN CLUB
WHEEL ROUND	WILLOW TREE	WOODEN SEAT
WHELK STALL	WILL TO LIVE	WOODEN SHOE
WHIFF OF AIR	WILLY NILLY	WOOD STREET

WOODY ALLEN
WOOLLY HAIR
WORD MAKING
WORD OF A LIE
WORD PUZZLE
WORD SQUARE
WORKING DAY
WORKING MAN
WORKING OUT
WORK IN HAND
WORK IN VAIN
WORK ON HAND
WORK PERMIT
WORK TO RULE
WORK UNDONE
WORLD ATLAS
WORLD CLASS
WORLD COURT
WORLD MUSIC
WORLD POWER
WORLD TITLE
WORLD TRADE
WORRIED MAN
WORRY BEADS
WORST OF ALL
WORST TASTE
WORTH WHILE
WOUNDED MAN
WREAK HAVOC
WRIGGLE OUT
WRITE A BOOK
WRITE ABOUT
WRITE AGAIN
WRITE A NOTE
WRITE A POEM
WRITE A SONG
WRITE BADLY
WRITE BOOKS
WRITE IN INK
WRITE IT OFF
WRITE MUSIC
WRITE NOTES
WRITE PLAYS
WRITE VERSE
WRITING INK
WRITTEN LAW
WRONG LINES
WRONG PLACE
WRONG TOTAL
WRONG TRACK
WRONG WOMAN

X – 10

X-RAY CAMERA

Y – 10

YARD BY YARD
YEAR BY YEAR
YEARLY RENT
YEAR TO YEAR
YELLOW BOOK
YELLOW CARD
YELLOW FLAG
YELLOW JACK
YELLOW RACE
YELLOW ROSE
YELLOW STAR
YIELD CROPS
YIELD FRUIT
YOB CULTURE
YOUNG BLOOD
YOUNG CHILD
YOUNG FOGEY
YOUNGER SON
YOUNG IDEAS
YOUNG TURKS
YOUNG WOMAN
YOUR CHOICE
YOUR HONOUR
YOURS TRULY
YOU'VE HAD IT
YUL BRYNNER

Z – 10

ZIG-ZAG LINE
ZOO ANIMALS

A – 11

AARON'S BEARD
ABANDON HOPE
ABANDON SHIP
ABIDE WITH ME
ABLE TO SPEAK
ABODE OF LOVE
ABOVE GROUND
ABOVE NORMAL
ABOVE RUBIES
ABOVE THE LAW
ABSTRACT ART
ACCENT GRAVE
ACCOUNT BOOK
ACCOUNT PAID
ACE OF HEARTS
ACE OF SPADES
ACE OF TRUMPS
ACHING HEART
ACHING TOOTH
ACT AS A BRAKE

ACT IN UNISON
ACTION LEVEL
ACTIVE VOICE
ACT OF HOMAGE
ACT ON ADVICE
ACT TOGETHER
ACUTE ACCENT
ACUTE ATTACK
ADD A CODICIL
ADDRESS BOOK
ADDRESS CARD
ADEQUATE SUM
AD INFINITUM
ADMIRAL'S CUP
ADMIT BEARER
ADMIT DEFEAT
ADOLF HITLER
ADOPTION ACT
ADRIATIC SEA
ADVANCE BASE
ADVANCE COPY
ADVANCED AGE
ADVANCE DATE
ADVANCE FATE
AEOLIAN HARP
AFFECTED AIR
AFGHAN HOUND
AFRICA HOUSE
AFTER A WHILE
AFTER CHURCH
AFTER DINNER
AFTER SCHOOL
AFTER SUNSET
AFTER SUPPER
AFTER THE WAR
AGAINST TIME
AGENT ORANGE
AGE OF WISDOM
AGES AND AGES
AGONY COLUMN
AHEAD OF TIME
AID TO BEAUTY
AID TO MEMORY
AIM STRAIGHT
AIM TO PLEASE
AIR MINISTER
AIR MINISTRY
AIR PURIFIER
AIR TERMINAL
AIR TERMINUS
A LA MODE BEEF
ALAN BENNETT
ALAN SHEARER
ALARM SIGNAL
ALDGATE PUMP
ALFRED MARKS

ALFRED NOYES
ALASTAIR SIM
ALIVE OR DEAD
ALLAN BORDER
ALL COCK-EYED
ALL CREATION
ALL FALL DOWN
ALL FOOL'S DAY
ALL FOR MONEY
ALL GOES WELL
ALL HOPE GONE
ALL IN FAVOUR
ALL OF A PIECE
ALL OF A SHAKE
ALL ONE CAN DO
ALLOT SHARES
ALL-OUT DRIVE
ALLOW CREDIT
ALL QUARTERS
ALL SOULS' DAY
ALL STANDING
ALL-STAR CAST
ALL STRAIGHT
ALL THAT JAZZ
ALL THE SIGNS
ALL THE VOGUE
ALL THE WHILE
ALL THE WORLD
ALL TOGETHER
ALL TOGGED UP
ALL TO PIECES
ALL VERY FINE
ALL VERY WELL
ALL WASHED-UP
ALL WEEK LONG
ALMIGHTY GOD
ALMOND PASTE
ALMOST THERE
ALONE I DID IT
ALPINE GUIDE
ALSATIAN DOG
ALTER COURSE
AMATEUR SIDE
AMATEUR TEAM
AMERICAN BAR
AMERICAN WAR
AMERICA'S CUP
AMOS AND ANDY
AMOUR PROPRE
AN APPLE A DAY
ANCIENT CITY
ANCIENT ROME
ANDRE AGASSI
ANDY STEWART
ANGELIC HOST
ANGELIC LOOK

ANGLING CLUB
ANIMAL HOUSE
ANIMAL TAMER
ANIMAL WORLD
ANISEED BALL
ANITA EKBERG
ANNA LUCASTA
ANNA PAVLOVA
ANNE SHELTON
ANN HATHAWAY
ANNIE BESANT
ANNIE LAURIE
ANNIE OAKLEY
ANN SHERIDAN
ANNUAL EVENT
ANNUAL LEAVE
ANNUAL TREAT
ANN VERONICA
ANOTHER TIME
ANTHONY EDEN
ANTHONY HOPE
ANTIQUE SHOP
ANTI-TANK GUN
ANVIL CHORUS
ANXIOUS TIME
APACHE DANCE
APPEAL COURT
APPEAL JUDGE
APPLE-PIE BED
APRIL SHOWER
ARCTIC OCEAN
ARE YOU READY?
ARMED ATTACK
ARMED BANDIT
ARMED COMBAT
ARMED ESCORT
ARMED FORCES
ARM OF THE LAW
ARM OF THE SEA
ARMOURED CAR
ARMOUR PLATE
ARMS AND LEGS
ARMS COUNCIL
ARMS STRETCH
ARMS TRAFFIC
ARMY BLANKET
ARMY CANTEEN
ARMY OFFICER
ARMY RESERVE
ARMY SURPLUS
AROMATIC GUM
ARRIVE EARLY
ARSENE LUPIN
ART DIRECTOR
ARTEMUS WARD
ARTFUL DODGE

ARTHUR ASKEY
ARTHUR'S SEAT
ARTS COUNCIL
ARTS THEATRE
ASCOT STAKES
AS DRY AS DUST
AS EASY AS PIE
AS GOOD AS NEW
ASK FOR A RISE
ASK FOR MERCY
ASK FOR TERMS
ASK THE PRICE
AS MUCH AGAIN
AS NICE AS PIE
ASSUME A RÔLE
ASSUMED NAME
A STAR IS BORN
ASTRAL PLANE
AS UGLY AS SIN
AS YOU LIKE IT
AT A DISCOUNT
AT A DISTANCE
AT ALL EVENTS
AT ALL POINTS
AT A LOOSE END
AT ATTENTION
AT CAMBRIDGE
AT FIRST HAND
AT FULL SPEED
AT GREAT RISK
AT HALF PRICE
A THING OR TWO
ATHOLE BROSE
AT INTERVALS
ATOMIC CLOCK
ATOMIC POWER
AT ONE'S ELBOW
AT ONE'S HEEL
AT ONE'S PERIL
AT ONE'S WORST
ATTACHÉ CASE
AT THE BOTTOM
AT THE CINEMA
AT THE CIRCUS
AT THE DOUBLE
AT THE FINISH
AT THE MOMENT
AT THE SUMMIT
AT THE TILLER
AT THE WICKET
AT THE ZENITH
AT WHAT PLACE?
AT WHICH TIME?
AUCTION ROOM
AUCTION SALE
AUTHOR'S NOTE

AUTUMN TINTS
AVERAGE HAND
AVERAGE TYPE
AVERAGE WAGE
AVERTED EYES
AVOCADO PEAR
AVOID DEFEAT
AVON CALLING
AWAY WITH YOU!
AWKWARD TIME
AYES AND NOES

B – 11

BABY BOUNCER
BABY BUNTING
BABY CLOTHES
BABY MONITOR
BACK A WINNER
BACK HEAVILY
BACK PAYMENT
BACK-ROOM BOY
BACK TO FRONT
BACKWARD BOY
BACON AND EGG
BACON SLICER
BAD BUSINESS
BADEN POWELL
BAD EYESIGHT
BAD FEELINGS
BAD FOR TRADE
BADGE OF RANK
BAD JUDGEMENT
BAD LANGUAGE
BAD LIKENESS
BADLY PLACED
BADLY SHAKEN
BADLY WANTED
BAD PRACTICE
BAD TEACHING
BAG OF CRISPS
BAG OF NERVES
BAG OF SWEETS
BAG OF TRICKS
BAGS OF MONEY
BAIT THE TRAP
BAKED POTATO
BAKER'S DOZEN
BAKER STREET
BALCONY SEAT
BALD AS A COOT
BALLOT PAPER
BANANA SKIN
BANBURY CAKE
BANG THE DOOR
BANK ACCOUNT

BANK BALANCE
BANK CHARGES
BANK DEPOSIT
BANK HOLIDAY
BANK MANAGER
BANK THE FIRE
BARBED ARROW
BARBED SHAFT
BARBED WORDS
BARBER'S POLE
BARBER'S SHOP
BARE MIDRIFF
BARE MINIMUM
BARGAIN SALE
BARKING DOGS
BARLEY SUGAR
BARLEY WATER
BARNARD'S INN
BARON OF BEEF
BARON'S COURT
BARRACK ROOM
BARREL ORGAN
BARREN HEATH
BARREN WASTE
BARRIER REEF
BAR SINISTER
BART SIMPSON
BASEBALL CAP
BASIC RIGHTS
BASIL FAWLTY
BASKET CHAIR
BAT AN EYELID
BATED BREATH
BATHING POOL
BATTING SIDE
BATTLE ABBEY
BATTLE ARRAY
BATTLE DRESS
BATTLE ORDER
BATTLE ROYAL
BATTLE SCENE
BAY OF BENGAL
BAY OF BISCAY
BAY OF NAPLES
BEAD CUSHION
BEAM OF LIGHT
BEAR A GRUDGE
BEAR BAITING
BEARDED LADY
BEARER BONDS
BEAR ILL-WILL
BEARING REIN
BEARSKIN RUG
BEAR THE COST
BEAR THE NAME
BEAR WITNESS

BEAST OF PREY
BEAT A TATTOO
BEATEN TRACK
BEAT THE BAND
BEAT THE BANK
BEAT THE BOOK
BEAT THE DRUM
BEAU BRUMMEL
BEAU SABREUR
BEAUTY QUEEN
BEAUTY SALON
BEAUTY SLEEP
BEBE DANIELS
BECK AND CALL
BECOME AWARE
BECOME SOLID
BED AND BOARD
BE DIFFERENT
BED OF THE SEA
BED OF THORNS
BEDSIDE LAMP
BEEF EXTRACT
BEER SHAMPOO
BEER TANKARD
BEES' WEDDING
BEFORE LUNCH
BEG FOR MERCY
BEGGING BOWL
BEGIN TO PALL
BEG TO DIFFER
BEHAVE BADLY
BELGIAN PORT
BELGIAN TOWN
BELINDA FAIR
BELLY DANCER
BELOW GROUND
BELOW STAIRS
BELT OF TREES
BEND FORWARD
BEND THE KNEE
BEND THE MIND
BENGAL LIGHT
BENGAL TIGER
BE OF SERVICE
BE REALISTIC
BERNARD SHAW
BERNESE ALPS
BEST CIRCLES
BEST CLOTHES
BEST EDITION
BEST OF TASTE
BEST OF TERMS
BEST OF THREE
BEST QUALITY
BEST REGARDS
BETTER BY FAR

BETTER TERMS	BLACK LETTER	BOMBER PILOT
BETTER TIMES	BLACK MARKET	BOMB SHELTER
BETTER VALUE	BLACK MONDAY	BOND OF UNION
BETTER WAGES	BLACK PEPPER	BONNE BOUCHE
BETTING SHOP	BLACK PRINCE	BONNY DUNDEE
BETTING SLIP	BLACK SQUARE	BOOKER PRIZE
BETTY GRABLE	BLACK TO MOVE	BOOKING HALL
BETTY HUTTON	BLACK TO PLAY	BOOK OF VERSE
BETTY MARTIN	BLACK VELVET	BOOK OF WORDS
BETWEEN MAID	BLANK CHEQUE	BOOK VOUCHER
BEYOND A JOKE	BLANKET BATH	BORACIC ACID
BEYOND DOUBT	BLAZE A TRAIL	BORIS BECKER
BEYOND PRICE	BLAZING FIRE	BORN ACTRESS
BICYCLE BELL	BLESS MY SOUL!	BORN AND BRED
BID DEFIANCE	BLESS THE DAY	BORROW A BOOK
BID FAREWELL	BLIND AS A BAT	BORROW MONEY
BIG BUSINESS	BLIND CHANCE	BOSOM FRIEND
BIG TURNOVER	BLIND CORNER	BOSS THE SHOW
BILL CLINTON	BLIND FLYING	BOSTON BEANS
BILLIARD CUE	BLOCK LETTER	BOTTLED BEER
BILL OF COSTS	BLOCK OF WOOD	BOTTLE GREEN
BILLY BUNTER	BLOCK THE WAY	BOTTLE OF GIN
BILLY COTTON	BLOOD ORANGE	BOTTLE OF INK
BILLY THE KID	BLOOD STREAM	BOTTLE OF RUM
BILLY WALKER	BLOOD VESSEL	BOTTLE PARTY
BINGO CALLER	BLOODY TOWER	BOTTOM LAYER
BIRD FANCIER	BLOSSOM TIME	BOTTOM MARKS
BIRD WATCHER	BLOW BUBBLES	BOTTOM TEETH
BISHOP'S MOVE	BLOW FOR BLOW	BOUND TO LOSE
BISHOP'S PAWN	BLOW ME TIGHT!	BOVVER BOOTS
BITE ONE'S LIP	BLOW ONE'S TOP	BOW AND ARROW
BITE THE DUST	BLOW SKY-HIGH	BOWL A YORKER
BITS AND BOBS	BLOW THE FIRE	BOWL OF FRUIT
BITTER ALOES	BLOW THE GAFF	BOWL OF PUNCH
BITTER ENEMY	BLUE-COAT BOY	BOXER SHORTS
BITTER GRIEF	BLUE-EYED BOY	BOXING BOOTH
BITTER LEMON	BLUE FOR A BOY	BOXING GLOVE
BITTER SWEET	BLUE HORIZON	BOXiNG MATCH
BITTER TASTE	BLUNT REMARK	BOX OF BRICKS
BITTER TEARS	BLUSH UNSEEN	BOX OF CIGARS
BITTER WORDS	BOARD SCHOOL	BOX OF PAINTS
BLACK AND TAN	BOATING SONG	BOX OF TRICKS
BLACK AS COAL	BOB CRATCHIT	BOY NEXT DOOR
BLACK AS SOOT	BODY AND SOUL	BOYS' BRIGADE
BLACK BEAUTY	BODY POLITIC	BRACE AND BIT
BLACK BEETLE	BODY SCANNER	BRACING WIND
BLACK BISHOP	BOGNOR REGIS	BRAIN DAMAGE
BLACK BOTTOM	BOILED BACON	BRAIN INJURY
BLACK CASTLE	BOILED SHIRT	BRAINS TRUST
BLACK COFFEE	BOILED SWEET	BRAISED BEEF
BLACK COTTON	BOLD AS A LION	BRANDS HATCH
BLACK FRIARS	BOLD AS BRASS	BRANDY GLASS
BLACK FRIDAY	BOLD ATTEMPT	BRASS FENDER
BLACK FOREST	BOLD OUTLINE	BRASS MONKEY
BLACK GRAPES	BOLT THE DOOR	BRASSY VOICE
BLACK KNIGHT	BOLT UPRIGHT	BRAVE EFFORT

BRAVE PERSON
BRAZEN IT OUT
BREAD AND JAM
BREAD OF LIFE
BREAD RATION
BREAD STREET
BREAD WINNER
BREAK A HABIT
BREAK BOUNDS
BREAK FOR TEA
BREAK GROUND
BREAK STONES
BREAK THE ICE
BREAK THE LAW
BREATHE FIRE
BREATHE HARD
BREATH OF AIR
BREEZE BLOCK
BRENNER PASS
BREWER'S DRAY
BRIAN CLOUGH
BRIAN INGLIS
BRIAN WALDEN
BRIDAL MARCH
BRIDAL PARTY
BRIDAL SUITE
BRIDAL TRAIN
BRIDGE DRIVE
BRIDGE FIEND
BRIDGE PARTY
BRIDGE TABLE
BRIDLE STRAP
BRIEF MOMENT
BRIEF SKETCH
BRIGHT CHILD
BRIGHT GREEN
BRIGHT LIGHT
BRIGHT PUPIL
BRIGHT SPARK
BRING TO BEAR
BRING TO BOOK
BRING TO HEEL
BRING TO LIFE
BRING TO MIND
BRING TO PASS
BRING TO REST
BRING TO RUIN
BRISTOL CITY
BRISTOL MILK
BRITISH ARMY
BRITISH CAMP
BRITISH FLAG
BRITISH LION
BRITISH MADE
BRITISH NAVY
BRITISH RAIL

BRITISH RULE
BRITISH SOIL
BRITISH WARM
BRITISH ZONE
BROAD ACCENT
BROAD COMEDY
BROAD SCOTCH
BROADSIDE ON
BROAD STREET
BROGUE SHOES
BROKE GROUND
BROKEN ANKLE
BROKEN BONES
BROKEN GLASS
BROKEN HEART
BRONZED SKIN
BRONZE MEDAL
BROTHER LOVE
BROUGHT HOME
BROWN BOMBER
BROWN RIBBON
BROWN SHERRY
BROWN SHIRTS
BRUCE WILLIS
BRUNO WALTER
BRYAN ROBSON
BUDDING POET
BUD FLANAGAN
BUENOS AIRES
BUFFALO BILL
BUFFER STATE
BUILD A HOUSE
BUILT ON SAND
BUILT TO LAST
BUILT-UP AREA
BULGING EYES
BULL AND BUSH
BULL AT A GATE
BULL BAITING
BULLET TRAIN
BULLET WOUND
BULL TERRIER
BULLY FOR YOU!
BUMPING RACE
BUNCH OF KEYS
BUNDLE OF FUN
BUNNY RABBIT
BURGLAR BILL
BURIAL AT SEA
BURIAL PLACE
BURIED ALIVE
BURIED AT SEA
BURKINA FASO
BURNING BUSH
BURNT ALMOND
BURNT EFFIGY

BURN TO ASHES
BURNT SIENNA
BURST OF FIRE
BURY ONESELF
BUSHEY HEATH
BUSINESS END
BUSINESS MAN
BUS TERMINUS
BUTTER BEANS
BUYING PRICE
BUYING SPREE
BUY ON CREDIT
BUY OUTRIGHT
BY AUTHORITY
BY FAIR MEANS
BYGONE TIMES
BY LAMPLIGHT
BY MAIN FORCE
BY MESSENGER
BY MISCHANCE
BY MOONLIGHT
BY THAT MEANS
BY THIS TOKEN
BY TRADITION
BY YOUR LEAVE

C – 11

CABARET STAR
CABBAGE LEAF
CABBAGE MOTH
CABBAGE ROSE
CABINET SIZE
CABIN WINDOW
CABLE STITCH
CAESAR'S WIFE
CAFÉ DE PARIS
CAFÉ SOCIETY
CAGED ANIMAL
CAIN AND ABEL
CAKE MIXTURE
CAKES AND ALE
CALCUTTA CUP
CALL FOR HELP
CALLING CARD
CALL IT QUITS
CALL ME MADAM
CALLOW YOUTH
CALL THE ROLL
CALL THE TIME
CALL THE TUNE
CALL TO A HALT
CALL TO ORDER
CALM WEATHER
CALVIN KLEIN
CALYPSO BAND

CAME FORWARD
CAMOMILE TEA
CAMPING SITE
CANADA HOUSE
CANCEL LEAVE
CANDIED PEEL
CANDY KISSES
CANDY STRIPE
CANINE TOOTH
CANNED BEANS
CANNED FRUIT
CANNED GOODS
CANNED MUSIC
CANNING TOWN
CAN OF PETROL
CAP AND BELLS
CAPE KENNEDY
CAPITAL CITY
CAPITAL FUND
CAPITAL GAIN
CAPITAL IDEA
CAPITAL LEVY
CAPITAL SHIP
CAPTAIN AHAB
CAPTAIN COOK
CAPTAIN HOOK
CAPTAIN KIDD
CAPTAIN WEBB
CARAVAN SITE
CARAWAY SEED
CARBON PAPER
CAR BOOT SALE
CARDIGAN BAY
CARDINAL RED
CARDINAL SIN
CAREER WOMAN
CARGO VESSEL
CAR INDUSTRY
CARLTON CLUB
CARMEN JONES
CAROL SINGER
CAR POLISHER
CARRION CROW
CARRY ACROSS
CARRY A TORCH
CARRY ON FILM
CARRY THE CAN
CARRY THE DAY
CARRY TOO FAR
CARRY WEIGHT
CASE HISTORY
CASE IN POINT
CASH ACCOUNT
CASH A CHEQUE
CASH BETTING
CASH CHEMIST

CASH PAYMENT
CASSIUS CLAY
CAST A GLANCE
CAST AN EYE ON
CAST A SHADOW
CASTILE SOAP
CASTING VOTE
CASTOR SUGAR
CASUAL VISIT
CAT AND MOUSE
CATCH A CHILL
CATCH ALIGHT
CATCH A PLANE
CATCH A THIEF
CATCH A TRAIN
CATCH PHRASE
CATCH THE EYE
CATHODE RAYS
CATS AND DOGS
CATS' CONCERT
CAT'S WHISKER
CATTLE RANCH
CATTLE THIEF
CATTY REMARK
CAUSE DAMAGE
CAUSTIC SODA
CAVALRY UNIT
CAVE DRAWING
CAVE DWELLER
CEASE TO LIVE
CECIL BEATON
CECIL RHODES
CELLAR STEPS
CELLO PLAYER
CELL THERAPY
CELTIC CROSS
CEMENT MIXER
CENTRAL ASIA
CENTRAL HALL
CENTRAL IDEA
CENTRAL LINE
CENTRAL PARK
CENTRE COURT
CENTRE PARTY
CEREAL PLANT
CERTAIN CURE
CERTAIN HOPE
CHAFING DISH
CHAIN LETTER
CHAIN SMOKER
CHAIN STITCH
CHALK CLIFFS
CHALK GARDEN
CHANCERY INN
CHANGE A NOTE
CHANGE BUSES

CHANGE HANDS
CHANGE OF AIR
CHANGE ROUND
CHANGE SEATS
CHANGE SIDES
CHANGING BAG
CHANGING MAT
CHANNEL FOUR
CHAOS THEORY
CHAPEL ROYAL
CHAPTER FIVE
CHAPTER FOUR
CHARGE EXTRA
CHARGE SHEET
CHARIOT RACE
CHARITY BALL
CHARLES LAMB
CHARLIE CHAN
CHARMED LIFE
CHARM SCHOOL
CHEAP AS DIRT
CHEAP LABOUR
CHEAP REMARK
CHEAP RETURN
CHEAP THRILL
CHEAP TICKET
CHEEK BY JOWL
CHEEKY DEVIL
CHEER LEADER
CHEESE SALAD
CHEESE STRAW
CHEMIN DE FER
CHERRY STONE
CHESHIRE CAT
CHESS PLAYER
CHEVAL GLASS
CHICKEN COOP
CHICKEN FARM
CHICKEN FEED
CHICKEN SOUP
CHIEF PRIEST
CHIEF STOKER
CHILD LABOUR
CHILLED BEEF
CHINA ORANGE
CHINESE FOOD
CHINESE JUNK
CHINESE MEAL
CHINESE SILK
CHIT OF A GIRL
CHOICE OF TWO
CHOIR MASTER
CHOOSE A WIFE
CHOOSE SIDES
CHU CHIN CHOW
CHURCH BELLS

CHURCH CHOIR
CHURCH HOUSE
CHURCH LANDS
CHURCH MOUSE
CHURCH MUSIC
CHURCH ORGAN
CHURCH SPIRE
CHURCH TOWER
CINDER TRACK
CINEMA QUEUE
CINEMA USHER
CINEMA WORLD
CINQUE PORTS
CIRCLE ROUND
CIRCULAR SAW
CIRCUS RIDER
CITIZEN KANE
CITRUS FRUIT
CITY COMPANY
CITY COUNCIL
CITY FATHERS
CIVIC CENTRE
CIVIC RIGHTS
CIVIL ACTION
CIVIL ANSWER
CIVIL RIGHTS
CIVIL TONGUE
CIVVY STREET
CLAIM TO FAME
CLAIM TO KNOW
CLAIRE BLOOM
CLAM CHOWDER
CLAP IN IRONS
CLARET GLASS
CLARION CALL
CLASH OF ARMS
CLASS ACTION
CLASS HATRED
CLASSIC RACE
CLASS SYMBOL
CLAUDE DUVAL
CLEAN AIR ACT
CLEAN BOWLED
CLEAN BREAST
CLEAN COLLAR
CLEAN FORGOT
CLEAN RECORD
CLEAR A HEDGE
CLEARLY SEEN
CLEAR OF DEBT
CLEAR PROFIT
CLEAR THE AIR
CLEAR THE WAY
CLEFT PALATE
CLEVER DODGE
CLEVER STUFF

CLEVER TRICK
CLINCH A DEAL
CLOSE ARREST
CLOSE AT HAND
CLOSE BEHIND
CLOSE COMBAT
CLOSED DOORS
CLOSED PURSE
CLOSE FINISH
CLOSE FRIEND
CLOSE OF PLAY
CLOSE SEASON
CLOSE SECOND
CLOSE SECRET
CLOSE THE GAP
CLOSING DATE
CLOSING TIME
CLOTHES LINE
CLOTH OF GOLD
CLOT OF BLOOD
CLOUD OF DUST
CLUB COLOURS
CLUB STEWARD
CLUB TO DEATH
CLUMSY STYLE
CLUSTER BOMB
COACHING INN
COAL SCUTTLE
COALS OF FIRE
COARSE CLOTH
COARSE GRAIN
COARSE GRASS
COARSE VOICE
COASTAL ROAD
COAT OF PAINT
COAT THE PILL
COAXING WAYS
COCK AND BULL
COCK ONE'S EYE
COCK SPARROW
COCKTAIL BAR
COCOA BUTTER
COCONUT PALM
CODE MESSAGE
COD-LIVER OIL
COFFEE BEANS
COFFEE BREAK
COFFEE CREAM
COFFEE HOUSE
COFFEE MAKER
COFFEE SPOON
COFFEE STALL
COFFEE TABLE
COIN A PHRASE
COLD AS DEATH
COLD CLIMATE

COLD COMFORT
COLD DRAUGHT
COLD SHIVERS
COLD STORAGE
COLD WEATHER
COLD WELCOME
COLLECT DUST
COLLEGE GIRL
COLNEY HATCH
COLOMBO PLAN
COLONIAL WAR
COLOUR BLIND
COLOUR CHART
COLOURED MAN
COLOUR PHOTO
COLOUR PLATE
COME BETWEEN
COME FORWARD
COME IN FIRST
COME IN FRONT
COME IN HANDY
COMELY WENCH
COME OFF BEST
COME OFF WELL
COME OUT BEST
COME OUTSIDE
COME THIS WAY
COME THROUGH
COME TO A HALT
COME TO A HEAD
COME TO AN END
COME TO A STOP
COME TO BLOWS
COME TO EARTH
COME TO GRIEF
COME TO GRIPS
COME TO LIGHT
COME TO ORDER
COME TO POWER
COME TO TERMS
COME UNSTUCK
COME WHAT MAY
COMIC RELIEF
COMME IL FAUT
COMMON CAUSE
COMMON CHORD
COMMON ENEMY
COMMON FAULT
COMMON FRONT
COMMON PLEAS
COMMON PURSE
COMMON SENSE
COMMON STOCK
COMMON THIEF
COMMON TO ALL
COMMON TOUCH

COMMON USAGE
COMPACT DISC
COMPLETE ASS
COMPLETE SET
COMPOST HEAP
COMPUTER AGE
CONCERT HALL
CONEY ISLAND
CONSOLE GAME
CONSTANT USE
CONTACT LENS
CONTACT MINE
CONTOUR LINE
CONTRACT OUT
CONTROL ROOM
CONVERT A TRY
COOKERY BOOK
COOK GENERAL
COOL AND CALM
COOL HUNDRED
COPPER BEACH
COPPER'S NARK
CORAL ISLAND
CORDON ROUGE
CORFE CASTLE
CORNERED RAT
CORNER TABLE
CORN IN EGYPT
CORN PLASTER
CORPS D'ÉLITE
CORRECT TIME
COSTA BLANCA
COSTA DEL SOL
COSTA DORADA
COSTUME BALL
COSTUME PLAY
COTTAGE LOAF
COTTON CLOTH
COTTON DRESS
COTTON FIELD
COTTON FROCK
COTTON GOODS
COTTON PLANT
COTTON SOCKS
COTTON WASTE
COUCH POTATO
COUNCIL FLAT
COUNTER HAND
COUNTRY CLUB
COUNTRY CODE
COUNTRY FOLK
COUNTRY LANE
COUNTRY LIFE
COUNTRY SEAT
COUNTRY TOWN
COUNTRY WALK

COUNTY CLARE
COUNTY COURT
COUNTY MATCH
COUP DE GRÂCE
COURT DEFEAT
COURT JESTER
COVER A STORY
COVER CHARGE
COVER GROUND
COWSLIP WINE
CRACK OF DAWN
CRACK OF DOOM
CRACK PLAYER
CRACK TROOPS
CRANE DRIVER
CRASH COURSE
CRASH HELMET
CRAWLER LANE
CRAZY NOTION
CRAZY PAVING
CREAM CHEESE
CREAMED RICE
CREATE A NEED
CREATE A RÔLE
CREATE A STIR
CREATE HAVOC
CREDIT ENTRY
CREDIT TERMS
CREDIT TITLE
CRÊPE RUBBER
CREVICE TOOL
CRICKET BALL
CRICKET CLUB
CRICKET TEAM
CRIMINAL LAW
CRIMSON LAKE
CRITICAL AGE
CROCK OF GOLD
CROOKED DEAL
CROOKED PATH
CROP FAILURE
CROPPED HAIR
CROQUET BALL
CROQUET CLUB
CROQUET HOOP
CROQUET LAWN
CROSSBOW MAN
CROSS STITCH
CROSS SWORDS
CROSS THE BAR
CROSS THE SEA
CROWDED HOUR
CROWDED ROOM
CROWN A TOOTH
CROWN COLONY
CROWNED HEAD

CROWN JEWELS
CROWN OFFICE
CROWN PRINCE
CRUCIAL TEST
CRUEL TYRANT
CRUMBLE AWAY
CRY FOR MERCY
CRYING SHAME
CRYPTIC CLUE
CRYSTAL BALL
CUB REPORTER
CUCKOO CLOCK
CULINARY ART
CUPID'S ARROW
CUP OF COFFEE
CUP OF POISON
CUP OF SORROW
CUPPED HANDS
CURDLED MILK
CURE OF SOULS
CURLING CLUB
CURLING IRON
CURL OF SMOKE
CURL ONE'S LIP
CURRANT CAKE
CURRANT LOAF
CURRENT DATE
CURRENT NEWS
CURRENT WEEK
CURRENT YEAR
CURRY FAVOUR
CURRY POWDER
CURSE OF CAIN
CURTAIN CALL
CUSTARD TART
CUSTOM HOUSE
CUSTOMS DUTY
CUT A LECTURE
CUT AND DRIED
CUT-AWAY COAT
CUT BOTH WAYS
CUT IN SALARY
CUT OFF SHORT
CUT OF HIS JIB
CUT ONE'S HAIR
CUT THE CARDS
CUT THE GRASS
CUT THE SCENE
CUTTING EDGE
CUTTING WIND
CUT TO PIECES
CYCLE HELMET
CYCLE TO WORK
CYCLING CLUB
CYNICAL FOUL

D – 11

DAILY MARKET
DAILY MIRROR
DAILY RECORD
DAILY REPORT
DAILY SKETCH
DAILY WORKER
DAIRY CATTLE
DAME FORTUNE
DAMON RUNYON
DANA ANDREWS
DANCE A TANGO
DANCE A WALTZ
DANCE FOR JOY
DANCING BEAR
DANCING GIRL
DANGER MONEY
DANGER POINT
DANIEL DEFOE
DANISH BACON
DARK CLOTHES
DARKEST HOUR
DARK GLASSES
DARK LANTERN
DART FORWARD
DARTING PAIN
DARTS PLAYER
DASHED HOPES
DASH FORWARD
DASH THROUGH
DATE OF BIRTH
DATE OF DEATH
DAVID JACOBS
DAWN GODDESS
DAY AFTER DAY
DAY AND NIGHT
DAY IN, DAY OUT
DAY LABOURER
DAY OF ACTION
DAY OF PRAYER
DAYS AND DAYS
DAY'S JOURNEY
DAYS OF GRACE
DAZZLING WIT
DEAD AGAINST
DEAD AND GONE
DEAD AS A DODO
DEAD CERTAIN
DEAD EARNEST
DEADEN SOUND
DEAD FAILURE
DEAD FLOWERS
DEADLY CRIME
DEADLY ENEMY
DEADLY PERIL

DEADLY RIVAL
DEAD OF NIGHT
DEAD OR ALIVE
DEAD SILENCE
DEAD TO SHAME
DEAF AND DUMB
DEAF AS A POST
DEAF TO MUSIC
DEAR BELOVED
DEAR OCTOPUS
DEAR OLD PALS
DEATH COLUMN
DEATHLY HUSH
DEATHLY PALE
DEATH NOTICE
DEATH RATTLE
DEBORAH KERR
DEB'S DELIGHT
DECK OF CARDS
DEED OF MERCY
DEEP BLUE SEA
DEEP CONCERN
DEEP FEELING
DEEP IN A BOOK
DEEP INSIGHT
DEEP MYSTERY
DEEP REMORSE
DEEP THINKER
DEEP THOUGHT
DEFENCE WORK
DEFERRED PAY
DEFY THE WHIP
DELIVERY MAN
DELLA ROBBIA
DE-LUXE MODEL
DEMON BARBER
DEMON BOWLER
DENIS NORDEN
DENMARK HILL
DENNIS NOBLE
DENSE FOREST
DENTAL CHAIR
DE PROFUNDIS
DEPTH CHARGE
DERBY COUNTY
DERBY STAKES
DERBY WINNER
DESERT SANDS
DESERT STORM
DESERT WASTE
DESERVE WELL
DEVIL OF A JOB
DEVIL'S ELBOW
DEVOTED WIFE
DIAMOND MINE
DIAMOND RING

DICK BENTLEY
DICK VAN DYKE
DO THE TWIST
DIE BY INCHES
DIE FIGHTING
DIE LIKE A DOG
DIE OF FRIGHT
DIE OF HUNGER
DIESEL TRAIN
DIET OF WORMS
DIG AND DELVE
DINNER DANCE
DINNER PARTY
DINNER WAGON
DIRECT DEBIT
DIRECT ROUTE
DIRECT STYLE
DIRE STRAITS
DIRK BOGARDE
DIRTY OLD MAN
DIRTY TRICKS
DISMAL JIMMY
DISPATCH BOX
DISPLAY CARD
DISTAFF SIDE
DISTANT PAST
DISTANT VIEW
DISUSED WELL
DIVIDE BY SIX
DIVIDE BY TEN
DIVIDE BY TWO
DIVINE BEING
DIVINE GRACE
DIVINE RIGHT
DIVINING ROD
DIVISION ONE
DIVISION SUM
DIVISION TWO
DIVORCE CASE
DIVORCE LAWS
DIVORCE SUIT
DIZZY HEIGHT
DO A GOOD TURN
DO ALL ONE CAN
DO A MISCHIEF
DO A WAR-DANCE
DOCTOR OF LAW
DOFF ONE'S HAT
DOING NICELY
DO IT IN STYLE
DOLEFUL LOOK
DOLEFUL TALE
DOLLY VARDEN
DO ME A FAVOUR
DOMESTIC PET
DONALD PEERS

DONE TO A TURN
DONE TO DEATH
DOOMED TO DIE
DO ONE'S WORST?
DO REVERENCE
DORIC COLUMN
DORIS ARCHER
DOT AND CARRY
DO THE ROUNDS
DO THE SPLITS
DOUBLE AGENT
DOUBLE BLANK
DOUBLE CROSS
DOUBLE DOORS
DOUBLE DUMMY
DOUBLE DUTCH
DOUBLE EAGLE
DOUBLE EIGHT
DOUBLE ENTRY
DOUBLE EVENT
DOUBLE FAULT
DOUBLE FIRST
DOUBLE MARCH
DOUBLE SEVEN
DOUBLE SHARE
DOUBLE SHIFT
DOUBLE THREE
DOUBLE TRACK
DOVE OF PEACE
DOVER CASTLE
DOVER PATROL
DOWN AT HEART
DOWN IN PRICE
DOWN PAYMENT
DOWN THE AGES
DOWN THE HILL
DOWN THE LINE
DOWN THE MINE
DOWN THE ROAD
DOWN THE SINK
DOWN THE WELL
DOWN TO EARTH
DOWN YOUR WAY
DRAGON LIGHT
DRAMA CRITIC
DRAMA SCHOOL
DRAMATIC ART
DRAUGHT BEER
DRAW A CIRCLE
DRAW A SALARY
DRAWING ROOM
DRAW RATIONS
DRAW THE CORK
DRAW THE LINE
DRAW TO AN END
DRAW TO SCALE

DRAW UP A PLAN
DREAM DREAMS
DREAM TICKET
DREAMY MUSIC
DRESS CIRCLE
DRESSED CRAB
DRESS TO KILL
DREYFUS CASE
DRINK ADDICT
DRINK A PINTA
DRINK A TOAST
DRINKING DEN
DRIPPING WET
DRIVE AROUND
DRIVE INSANE
DRIVE ONE MAD
DRIVE SLOWLY
DRIVING RAIN
DRIVING TEST
DROP A CURTSY
DROP A LETTER
DROP AN AITCH
DROP A REMARK
DROP A SITTER
DROP A STITCH
DROP IN PRICE
DROP ME A LINE
DROP OF BLOOD
DROP OF WATER
DROPPED GOAL
DROP THE MASK
DROP TOO MUCH
DROWNING MAN
DRUG PEDDLER
DRUG TRAFFIC
DRUNKEN ORGY
DRY AS A STICK
DRY CLEANERS
DRY CLEANING
DRY ONE'S EYES
DUAL CONTROL
DUAL PURPOSE
DUCHESSE SET
DUCK-EGG BLUE
DULCET TONES
DULL READING
DULL SCHOLAR
DULL WEATHER
DUMB CHARADE
DUMB DESPAIR
DUMB FRIENDS
DUMPER TRUCK
DURANCE VILE
DUSTY MILLER
DUTCH CHEESE
DUTCH SCHOOL

DUTCH TULIPS
DUTY OFFICER
DWINDLE AWAY
DYE ONE'S HAIR
DYING BREATH
DYING EMBERS
DYING TO KNOW
DYLAN THOMAS

E – 11

EAGER BEAVER
EAR FOR MUSIC
EARL MARSHAL
EARL OF ARRAN
EARLY AUTUMN
EARLY CHURCH
EARLY GOTHIC
EARLY IN LIFE
EARLY RISING
EARLY SPRING
EARLY SUMMER
EARLY TO RISE
EARN A LIVING
EARTH'S CRUST
EARTH TREMOR
EASE THE PAIN
EASILY MOVED
EAST AND WEST
EASTERN BLOC
EAST GERMANY
EAST LOTHIAN
EASY PROBLEM
EASY TO GRASP
EASY VICTORY
EAT AND DRINK
EAT AND SLEEP
EATING HOUSE
EAT LIKE A PIG
EAT ONE'S FILL
ECONOMIC AID
ECONOMY SIZE
EDDIE FISHER
EDGE ONE'S WAY
EDGEWARE ROAD
EDIBLE FUNGI
EDITH CAVELL
EDMUND BURKE
EDUCATED MAN
EDWARD HEATH
EDWARD MY SON
EGG AND BACON
EGG AND CHIPS
EGG SANDWICH
EIFFEL TOWER
EIGHTH FLOOR

EIGHTH GREEN
EIGHTH MONTH
EIGHTH OF MAY
EIGHTH PLACE
EIGHTH ROUND
EIGHT MONTHS
EIGHT NINTHS
EIGHT O'CLOCK
EIGHT OR NINE
EIGHT OUNCES
EIGHT POINTS
EIGHT POUNDS
EIGHT ROUNDS
EIGHTY MILES
EIGHTY TIMES
EIGHTY YEARS
EILEEN JOYCE
ELASTIC BAND
ELBOW GREASE
ELDERS FIRST
ELDER SISTER
ELDEST CHILD
ELECTION DAY
ELECTRIC EEL
ELECTRIC EYE
ELECTRIC FAN
ELECTRIC RAY
ELECTRIC VAN
ELECTRON GUN
ELEPHANT BOY
ELEPHANT GUN
ELEVEN A SIDE
ELEVEN DOZEN
ELEVEN GROSS
ELEVEN HOURS
ELEVEN MILES
ELEVEN PARTS
ELEVEN SCORE
ELEVENTH DAY
ELEVENTH ROW
ELEVEN TIMES
ELEVEN WEEKS
ELLERY QUEEN
ELLIS ISLAND
EMERALD ISLE
EMERALD RING
EMPIRE STYLE
EMPIRE TRADE
EMPTY BOTTLE
EMPTY LARDER
EMPTY POCKET
EMPTY STREET
EMPTY THE BAG
EMPTY THREAT
EMPTY WALLET
EN CASSEROLE

ENDLESS BAND
ENDLESS BELT
ENDLESS TIME
END OF THE DAY
END OF THE WAR
END ONE'S DAYS
END ONE'S LIFE
ENEMY ACTION
ENEMY PATROL
ENEMY TROOPS
ENEMY VESSEL
ENGAGED TONE
ENGINE HOUSE
ENGINE POWER
ENGLISH HORN
ENGLISH POET
ENGLISH PORT
ENGLISH ROSE
ENLARGE UPON
ENLISTED MAN
ENOCH POWELL
ENTER A PHASE
ENTER A STAGE
ENTRANCE FEE
EQUAL CHANCE
EQUAL HEIGHT
EQUAL RIGHTS
EQUAL SHARES
EQUAL WEIGHT
ERECT FIGURE
ERIC CANTONA
ERIC CLAPTON
ERIC PORTMAN
ERMINE STOLE
ERNEST BEVIN
ESCAPE DEATH
ESCAPE HATCH
ESCAPE ROUTE
ESCAPING GAS
ESTATE AGENT
ETERNAL CITY
ETERNAL HOME
ETERNAL LIFE
ETERNAL REST
ETHEL MERMAN
ETON COLLEGE
EVADE THE LAW
EVELYN WAUGH
EVENING MEAL
EVENING NEWS
EVENING STAR
EVER AND A DAY
EVER AND ANON
EVER AND EVER
EVERY EXCUSE
EVERY MINUTE

EVERY VIRTUE
EVIL CONDUCT
EVIL THOUGHT
EXACT AMOUNT
EXALTED RANK
EXEUNT OMNES
EXHAUST PIPE
EXPLAIN AWAY
EXPORT DRIVE
EXPORT ORDER
EXPORT TRADE
EXPRESS LIFT
EXPRESS POST
EXTRA CHARGE
EXTRA STRONG
EXTREME CASE
EXTREME EDGE
EXTREME PAIN
EYE FOR AN EYE
EYES AND EARS

F – 11

FACE MASSAGE
FACE REALITY
FACE THE ODDS
FACE UPWARDS
FACTORY ACTS
FACTORY BAND
FACTORY HAND
FACTS OF LIFE
FADED BEAUTY
FADING HOPES
FADING LIGHT
FAIL THE TEST
FAIL TO AGREE
FAIL TO REPLY
FAIL TO SCORE
FAINT EFFORT
FAINTING FIT
FAINT PRAISE
FAIR COMMENT
FAIR FORTUNE
FAIR HEARING
FAIRLY CLOSE
FAIR WARNING
FAIR WEATHER
FAIRY CIRCLE
FAIRY LIGHTS
FAITH HEALER
FALL ASUNDER
FALLEN ANGEL
FALL IN DROPS
FALLING STAR
FALL IN PLACE
FALL IN PRICE

FALL IN RUINS	FEEDING TIME	FIJI ISLANDS
FALL IN VALUE	FEEL CERTAIN	FILING CLERK
FALL THROUGH	FEEL NO SHAME	FILL AN ORDER
FALL TO EARTH	FEEL NOTHING	FILLET STEAK
FALSE BOTTOM	FEEL ONE'S WAY	FILL THE BILL
FALSE CHARGE	FEEL PECKISH	FILL THE TILL
FALSE COLOUR	FEEL REMORSE	FILM ACTRESS
FALSE FRIEND	FEEL STRANGE	FILM COMPANY
FALSE REPORT	FEEL THE COLD	FILTHY LUCRE
FALSE RUMOUR	FEEL THE HEAT	FINAL ANSWER
FALSE VALUES	FEEL THE URGE	FINAL CHOICE
FALSE VANITY	FEEL THE WIND	FINAL CLAUSE
FAMILY ALBUM	FELIX AYLMER	FINAL DEFEAT
FAMILY BIBLE	FELIX THE CAT	FINAL DEMAND
FAMILY CARES	FELL THROUGH	FINAL NOTICE
FAMILY CREST	FEMALE SCREW	FINAL REPORT
FAMILY HOTEL	FEMALE VOICE	FINAL RESULT
FAMILY MOTTO	FEMME FATALE	FINAL SPEECH
FAMILY PARTY	FEN DISTRICT	FINAL STROKE
FAMILY PRIDE	FERTILE LAND	FINANCE BILL
FAMILY TREAT	FERTILE MIND	FIND A REFUGE
FAMILY VAULT	FERTILE SOIL	FIND A REMEDY
FAMINE PRICE	FERVENT HOPE	FIND A WAY OUT
FAMOUS WOMEN	FESTIVE MOOD	FIND FREEDOM
FAN THE FLAME	FEVERED BROW	FIND ONESELF
FAR-AWAY LOOK	FIBRE OPTICS	FIND ONE'S WAY
FAR DISTANCE	FIBRE-TIP PEN	FIND SHELTER
FARES PLEASE	FIDDLE ABOUT	FIND THE LADY
FAR FROM HERE	FIDEL CASTRO	FIND THE TIME
FAR FROM HOME	FIELD EVENTS	FINE FLAVOUR
FARMER GILES	FIELD OF CORN	FINE RAIMENT
FARMER'S WIFE	FIELD OF PLAY	FINE SOLDIER
FARMING TYPE	FIELD OF VIEW	FINE TEXTURE
FARM MANAGER	FIELD SPORTS	FINE WEATHER
FARM PRODUCE	FIERCE GLARE	FINE WRITING
FASHION SHOW	FIERY DRAGON	FINGAL'S CAVE
FAST BOWLING	FIERY ORDEAL	FINISH EARLY
FAST BREEDER	FIERY SPEECH	FINISH FIRST
FAST COLOURS	FIERY SPIRIT	FINNISH BATH
FAST FRIENDS	FIERY TEMPER	FIRE AND FURY
FATAL ATTACK	FIFTEEN LOVE	FIRE A SALUTE
FATAL INJURY	FIFTH AVENUE	FIRE A VOLLEY
FATA MORGANA	FIFTH BEATLE	FIRE BRIGADE
FAT AS BUTTER	FIFTH COLUMN	FIRE CURTAIN
FATHER BROWN	FIFTH LETTER	FIRE SERVICE
FATHER IMAGE	FIFTH OF JULY	FIRE STATION
FATHERLY EYE	FIFTH OF JUNE	FIRING PARTY
FATIGUE DUTY	FIFTH STOREY	FIRING SQUAD
FATTY TISSUE	FIFTH VOLUME	FIRM AS A ROCK
FEARFUL BORE	FIGHT FOR AIR	FIRM BACKING
FEARFUL ODDS	FIGHTING FIT	FIRM CONTROL
FEAR OF DEATH	FIGHTING MAD	FIRM FRIENDS
FEAR TO TREAD	FIGHTING MAN	FIRM PROMISE
FEATURE FILM	FIGURE EIGHT	FIRM RESOLVE
FEEBLE BRAIN	FIGURE IT OUT	FIRST CHARGE
FEEBLE GRASP	FIGURE OF FUN	FIRST CHOICE

FIRST COURSE	FIVE FATHOMS	FLOW THROUGH
FIRST COUSIN	FIVE FINGERS	FLOW TOWARDS
FIRST DEGREE	FIVE GALLONS	FLUID INTAKE
FIRST ELEVEN	FIVE GUINEAS	FLUSH OF DAWN
FIRST FIDDLE	FIVE HUNDRED	FLUSH OF HOPE
FIRST FINGER	FIVE MINUTES	FLUTTER DOWN
FIRST FLIGHT	FIVE OCTAVES	FLY AWAY PAUL
FIRST FRUITS	FIVE OF CLUBS	FLYING CORPS
FIRST GLANCE	FIVE PER CENT	FLYING FIELD
FIRST IN LINE	FIVE SQUARED	FLYING SPEED
FIRST LEADER	FIVE STROKES	FLYING SQUAD
FIRST LEAGUE	FIVE WICKETS	FLYING START
FIRST LESSON	FIX BAYONETS	FLYING VISIT
FIRST LETTER	FIXED AMOUNT	FOLDED HANDS
FIRST MAN OUT	FIXED ASSETS	FOLK DANCING
FIRST OF JULY	FIXED BELIEF	FOLLOW AFTER
FIRST OF JUNE	FIXED CHARGE	FOLLOW A PLAN
FIRST PERSON	FIXED INCOME	FOND EMBRACE
FIRST REMOVE	FIXED SALARY	FONDEST LOVE
FIRST RUBBER	FIX THE PRICE	FOND OF A DRAM
FIRST SEASON	FIX THE TERMS	FOND REGARDS
FIRST SERIES	FIXTURE LIST	FOOD COUNTER
FIRST SERVED	FLAG CAPTAIN	FOOD SUBSIDY
FIRST SINGLE	FLAG OFFICER	FOOLISH IDEA
FIRST SKETCH	FLAG OF TRUCE	FOOLISH TALK
FIRST STOREY	FLAKY PASTRY	FOOL'S ERRAND
FIRST STRIKE	FLAME COLOUR	FOOLS RUSH IN
FIRST STRING	FLAMING JUNE	FOOTBALL FAN
FIRST STROKE	FLANK ATTACK	FOOT THE BILL
FIRST TO COME	FLASH A SMILE	FOR ALL TO SEE
FIRST TO LAND	FLASH GORDON	FOR A PURPOSE
FIRST TO LAST	FLASK OF WINE	FORCE A WAY IN
FIRST VIOLIN	FLAT FOR SALE	FORCED ENTRY
FIRST VOLUME	FLAT HUNTING	FORCED LAUGH
FIRST WICKET	FLAT REFUSAL	FORCED MARCH
FISHER OF MEN	FLAT SURFACE	FORCED SMILE
FISH FINGERS	FLEET AIR-ARM	FORCE OF ARMS
FISHING BIRD	FLEET OF CABS	FOR DEAR LIFE
FISHING BOAT	FLEET OF CARS	FOREIGN BODY
FISHING LINE	FLEET OF FOOT	FOREIGN COIN
FISSION BOMB	FLEET PRISON	FOREIGN FILM
FIT FOR A KING	FLEET STREET	FOREIGN LAND
FIT OF ENERGY	FLESH COLOUR	FOREIGN NAME
FIT OF NERVES	FLESH TIGHTS	FOREIGN NEWS
FIT OF TEMPER	FLIMSY PAPER	FOREIGN RULE
FIT OF TERROR	FLOATING RIB	FOREIGN SOIL
FITTING ROOM	FLOOD DAMAGE	FOREIGN TOUR
FITTING SHOP	FLOOR POLISH	FOREST HILLS
FITTING TIME	FLORAL DANCE	FOR INSTANCE
FIT TO BE SEEN	FLORA ROBSON	FORLORN HOPE
FIVE AT A TIME	FLORID STYLE	FORMAL DRESS
FIVE-BAR GATE	FLOWER POWER	FORMAL OFFER
FIVE COURSES	FLOWING BOWL	FORMAL VISIT
FIVE-DAY WEEK	FLOWING HAND	FORM AN IMAGE
FIVE DOLLARS	FLOWING TIDE	FORMER PUPIL
FIVE EIGHTHS	FLOW OF WORDS	FORMER TIMES

FOR PLEASURE
FOR SOME TIME
FORSYTE SAGA
FORTH BRIDGE
FOR THE NONCE
FOR THE WORSE
FORT WILLIAM
FORTY NIGHTS
FORTY THIRTY
FORWARD LINE
FORWARD MOVE
FORWARD PLAY
FOSTER CHILD
FOUL JOURNEY
FOUL THE LINE
FOUL WEATHER
FOUND A PARTY
FOUNDERS' DAY
FOUND GUILTY
FOUNTAIN PEN
FOUR AT A TIME
FOUR CORNERS
FOUR COURSES
FOUR-DAY WEEK
FOUR DEGREES
FOUR DOLLARS
FOUR FATHOMS
FOUR FIGURES
FOUR GALLONS
FOUR GUINEAS
FOUR HUNDRED
FOUR JUST MEN
FOUR MINUTES
FOUR OCTAVES
FOUR OF CLUBS
FOUR PER CENT
FOUR SEASONS
FOUR SQUARED
FOUR STROKES
FOURTH FLOOR
FOURTH GREEN
FOURTH OF MAY
FOURTH PLACE
FOURTH ROUND
FOUR WICKETS
FOX AND GEESE
FRAME OF MIND
FRANK AVOWAL
FRANTIC PACE
FRANTIC RUSH
FRED ASTAIRE
FRED COUPLES
FREE AND EASY
FREE AS A BIRD
FREE CITIZEN
FREE COUNTRY

FREE ECONOMY
FREE LIBRARY
FREE ON BOARD
FREE ONESELF
FREE PARKING
FREE PASSAGE
FREE SERVICE
FREE SPENDER
FREE THINKER
FREE THOUGHT
FREE TO SPEAK
FREE TRIBUTE
FRENCH BEANS
FRENCH BREAD
FRENCH CHALK
FRENCH COAST
FRENCH FARCE
FRENCH FRANC
FRENCH FRIED
FRENCH FRIES
FRENCH LEAVE
FRENCH MONEY
FRENCH NOVEL
FRENCH SALON
FRENCH TOAST
FRESH BREEZE
FRESH BUTTER
FRESH FIELDS
FRESH GROUND
FRESH SALMON
FRESH TROOPS
FRET AND FUME
FRIDAY NIGHT
FRIED ONIONS
FRIENDLY ACT
FRIENDLY TIP
FRIEND OF MAN
FRIEND OR FOE
FRIGHTEN OFF
FRITTER AWAY
FROM SCRATCH
FROM THE EAST
FROM THE WEST
FROM THE WOOD
FROM WITHOUT
FRONT GARDEN
FRONT LIGHTS
FRONT WINDOW
FROSTED LENS
FROSTY SMILE
FROZEN NORTH
FROZEN PIPES
FROZEN SOLID
FROZEN STIFF
FROZEN WATER
FRUIT MARKET

FRUITY VOICE
FULL ACCOUNT
FULL ADDRESS
FULL APOLOGY
FULL AS AN EGG
FULL BROTHER
FULL CONSENT
FULL DETAILS
FULL ENQUIRY
FULL FLAVOUR
FULL GENERAL
FULL MEASURE
FULL OF BEANS
FULL OF FIGHT
FULL OF GRACE
FULL OF HOLES
FULL OF IDEAS
FULL OF MIRTH
FULL OF PRIDE
FULL REGALIA
FULL SERVICE
FULL SUPPORT
FULL-TIME JOB
FULLY BOOKED
FULLY RIGGED
FUN AND GAMES
FUNERAL HYMN
FUNERAL PACE
FUNERAL PILE
FUNERAL PYRE
FUNERAL SONG
FUNNY AFFAIR
FUNNY PERSON
FURIOUS PACE
FUTURE HOPES
FUTURE PLANS
FUTURE STATE
FUTURE TENSE

G – 11

GAIN CONTROL
GAIN IN VALUE
GAIN THE LEAD
GALA EVENING
GALE WARNING
GALLERY SEAT
GALLEY PROOF
GALLEY SLAVE
GALLON OF OIL
GAMBLING DEN
GAME CHICKEN
GAME LICENCE
GAME OF BOWLS
GAME OF CARDS
GAME OF CHESS

GAME OF SKILL	GET INTO A ROW	GLASS OF BEER
GAME OF WHIST	GET INTO A RUT	GLASS OF MILK
GAME RESERVE	GET INTO DEBT	GLASS OF PORT
GAMES MASTER	GET ONE'S GOAT	GLASS OF WINE
GAMING HOUSE	GET ONE'S WISH	GLASS VESSEL
GAMING TABLE	GET ON WITH IT	GLASSY STARE
GAMMON STEAK	GET OUT OF BED	GLEAM OF HOPE
GANG ROBBERY	GET SUNBURNT	GLEEFUL MOOD
GANG WARFARE	GET THE FACTS	GLEEFUL NEWS
GARDEN CHAIR	GET THE KNACK	GLEE SINGERS
GARDEN FENCE	GET THE POINT	GLENN HODDLE
GARDEN PARTY	GET THE TASTE	GLIB SPEAKER
GARDEN TOOLS	GETTING WARM	GLIDER PILOT
GARRICK CLUB	GETTING WELL	GLIDING CLUB
GARY LINEKER	GET TOGETHER	GLYNIS JOHNS
GATHER ROSES	GET TO THE TOP	GLORIOUS DAY
GATHER ROUND	GET UNDER WAY	GLORIOUS FUN
GATHER SPEED	GET WELL SOON	GLORIOUS ROW
GAY BACHELOR	GET WISE TO IT	GLOSSY PAINT
GAY DECEIVER	GHASTLY MESS	GNAWING PAIN
GAY LOTHARIO	GHASTLY PALE	GO-AHEAD SIGN
GAY NINETIES	GHOST WRITER	GO ALL THE WAY
GEFILTE FISH	GIANT KILLER	GO BACKWARDS
GENERAL IDEA	GIANT OF A MAN	GO BY DEFAULT
GENERAL LEVY	GIFT OF MONEY	GO BY THE BOOK
GENERAL POST	GIFT VOUCHER	GOD OF THE SEA
GENERAL RATE	GILDED YOUTH	GOG AND MAGOG
GENERAL VIEW	GILD THE LILY	GO GREAT GUNS
GENERIC NAME	GILD THE PILL	GOING STEADY
GENEROUS ACT	GIN AND LEMON	GOING STRONG
GENE THERAPY	GIN AND TONIC	GO IN PURSUIT
GENETIC CODE	GINGER GROUP	GO INTO EXILE
GENEVA CROSS	GIRLS' SCHOOL	GO INTO ORBIT
GENGHIS KHAN	GIRL STUDENT	GOLD BULLION
GENTLE BIRTH	GIVE AND TAKE	GOLD COINAGE
GENTLE SLOPE	GIVE AN ORDER	GOLD DEPOSIT
GENTLE TOUCH	GIVE A REASON	GOLDEN APPLE
GENTLE VOICE	GIVE A RULING	GOLDEN ARROW
GENUINE CASE	GIVE IT A MISS	GOLDEN BOUGH
GEORGE BROWN	GIVE IT A NAME	GOLDEN BROWN
GEORGE CROSS	GIVE IT A REST	GOLDEN DREAM
GEORGE ELIOT	GIVE LESSONS	GOLDEN EAGLE
GEORGE MEDAL	GIVEN PERIOD	GOLDEN GATES
GEORGE ROBEY	GIVEN THE TIP	GOLDEN GOOSE
GERMAN MONEY	GIVE OFFENCE	GOLDEN OLDIE
GERM CARRIER	GIVE QUARTER	GOLDEN SANDS
GERM WARFARE	GIVE SUPPORT	GOLDEN SYRUP
GET A BAD NAME	GIVE THE SACK	GOLDEN TOUCH
GET A DIVORCE	GIVE THE WORD	GOLD FILLING
GET A MENTION	GIVE TROUBLE	GOLD RESERVE
GET AN ENCORE	GIVE WARNING	GOLF TROLLEY
GET A RECEIPT	GLAD TIDINGS	GO LIKE A BOMB
GET CRACKING	GLAMOUR GIRL	GONE FOR EVER
GET DOWN TO IT	GLANCE ASIDE	GONE FOR GOOD
GET EVEN WITH	GLANCE TO LEG	GONE TO EARTH
GET IN THE WAY	GLASS HOUSES	GONE TO GLORY

GONE TO LUNCH
GONE TO WASTE
GOOD ACCOUNT
GOOD ACTRESS
GOOD ADDRESS
GOOD AND EVIL
GOOD AS A PLAY
GOOD AT HEART
GOOD BARGAIN
GOOD BEARING
GOOD BEATING
GOOD CITIZEN
GOOD COMPANY
GOOD CONDUCT
GOOD COUNSEL
GOOD DEFENCE
GOOD DICTION
GOOD EVENING
GOOD EXAMPLE
GOOD FEEDING
GOOD FEELING
GOOD FICTION
GOOD FORTUNE
GOOD FRIENDS
GOOD GRAMMAR
GOOD GROUNDS
GOOD HARMONY
GOOD HARVEST
GOOD HEARING
GOOD HEAVENS
GOOD HUNTING
GOOD HUSBAND
GOOD INNINGS
GOOD IN PARTS
GOOD MANAGER
GOOD MANNERS
GOOD MEASURE
GOOD MORNING
GOOD OFFICES
GOOD OLD DAYS
GOOD OLD TIME
GOOD OPENING
GOOD OPINION
GOOD QUALITY
GOOD READING
GOOD SCHOLAR
GOOD SEND OFF
GOOD SERVANT
GOOD SERVICE
GOOD SOCIETY
GOOD SOLDIER
GOOD SPENDER
GOOD SPIRITS
GOOD SWIMMER
GOOD TEMPLAR
GOOD THEATRE

GOOD TIDINGS
GOOD WEATHER
GOOD WORKMAN
GOOD WRITE-UP
GO ON A PICNIC
GO ONE BETTER
GO ON FOR EVER
GO ON HOLIDAY
GO ON THE DOLE
GO OUT TO WORK
GO OVER THERE
GORDIAN KNOT
GORDON GECKO
GORDON RIOTS
GORGON'S HEAD
GOSPEL TRUTH
GO THE ROUNDS
GOTHIC STYLE
GO THROUGH IT
GO TO BED LATE
GO TO HALIFAX
GO TO JERICHO
GO TO PARTIES
GO TO THE DOGS
GO TO THE FAIR
GO TO THE MOON
GO TO THE WALL
GO TO THE WARS
GOT UP TO KILL
GO UP IN SMOKE
GRAHAM GOOCH
GRAIN OF GOLD
GRAIN OF SALT
GRAIN OF SAND
GRAND CANYON
GRAND CIRCLE
GRAND FELLOW
GRAND FINALE
GRAND MANNER
GRAND MASTER
GRAND OLD MAN
GRAND REVIEW
GRAND VIZIER
GRANITE CITY
GRANT ACCESS
GRANT ASYLUM
GRANT A TRUCE
GRAPHIC ARTS
GRAVE ACCENT
GRAVE AFFAIR
GRAVE CHARGE
GRAVE CRISIS
GRAVE DOUBTS
GRAVE MATTER
GRAVEN IMAGE
GRAVE SPEECH

GREASE PAINT
GREASY SPOON
GREAT AMOUNT
GREAT BEAUTY
GREAT BURDEN
GREAT CAESAR
GREAT CHANCE
GREAT CHANGE
GREAT CIRCLE
GREAT DAMAGE
GREAT DANCER
GREAT DANGER
GREAT DARING
GREAT DETAIL
GREAT DIVIDE
GREAT DOINGS
GREAT EFFORT
GREATER GOOD
GREATER PART
GREAT FAVOUR
GREAT FRIEND
GREAT HEALER
GREAT HEIGHT
GREAT HONOUR
GREAT IMPORT
GREAT NEPHEW
GREAT NUMBER
GREAT PLAGUE
GREAT PLAYER
GREAT REGRET
GREAT RELIEF
GREAT SCHISM
GREAT SNAKES
GREAT SORROW
GREAT STRAIN
GREAT STRESS
GREAT TALKER
GREAT THINGS
GREAT UNPAID
GREAT WEALTH
GREAT WEIGHT
GRECIAN BEND
GRECIAN KNOT
GRECIAN NOSE
GREED IS GOOD
GREEK CHURCH
GREEK COMEDY
GREEK LEGEND
GREEK STATUE
GREEN BERETS
GREEN BOTTLE
GREEN CHEESE
GREEN FIELDS
GREEN GABLES
GREEN GINGER
GREEN PEPPER

GREEN RIBBON
GREER GARSON
GREGORY PECK
GRESHAM'S LAW
GRETNA GREEN
GRILLED CHOP
GRILLED FISH
GRILLED SOLE
GRIM COURAGE
GRIM OUTLOOK
GRIM PASTIME
GRIND TO BITS
GRIP OF STEEL
GRIZZLY BEAR
GROCER'S SHOP
GROOMING SET
GROSS AMOUNT
GROSS INCOME
GROSS PROFIT
GROSS RETURN
GROSS WEIGHT
GROUND FLOOR
GROUND FROST
GROUND GLASS
GROUND LEVEL
GROUND SPEED
GROUND STAFF
GROUND SWELL
GROUND TO AIR
GROUP OF FIVE
GROUP OF FOUR
GROUP OF NINE
GROUP THEORY
GROUSE MOORS
GROWING GIRL
GROW SHORTER
GROW SMALLER
GROW UPWARDS
GROW YOUNGER
GUAVA CHEESE
GUERILLA WAR
GUEST ARTIST
GUIDING HAND
GUIDING STAR
GUILTY PARTY
GUILTY WOMAN
GULF OF GENOA
GUMMED LABEL
GUSTAV HOLST
GUTTER PRESS

H – 11

HACKNEY WICK
HAGGARD LOOK
HAIR TRIMMER

HAIRPIN BEND
HALCYON DAYS
HALF A BOTTLE
HALF A DOLLAR
HALF A GALLON
HALF A GUINEA
HALF A LEAGUE
HALF A LENGTH
HALF A MINUTE
HALF A MOMENT
HALF AND HALF
HALF AN OUNCE
HALF A SECOND
HALF BROTHER
HALF HOLIDAY
HALF THE TIME
HALTING GAIT
HAMMER DRILL
HAMMER IT OUT
HAMMER THROW
HAM OMELETTE
HAMPTON WICK
HAM SANDWICH
HAND AND FOOT
HAND GRENADE
HAND IN GLOVE
HAND OF CARDS
HAND OF DEATH
HANDSOME BOY
HANDSOME MAN
HANDSOME SUM
HANDSOME TIP
HANDS ON HIPS
HAND TO MOUTH
HANG-DOG LOOK
HANGING BILL
HANG IN THERE
HANG ONESELF
HANG THE HEAD
HANG UP TO DRY
HANKER AFTER
HAPPY CHANCE
HAPPY COUPLE
HAPPY DREAMS
HAPPY ENDING
HAPPY FAMILY
HAPPY MEDIUM
HAPPY VALLEY
HARBOUR A SPY
HARBOUR DUES
HARD AND FAST
HARD AS NAILS
HARD AS STEEL
HARD BARGAIN
HARD CONTEST
HARD DRINKER

HARD DRIVING
HARD MEASURE
HARD PRESSED
HARD PUT TO IT
HARD SURFACE
HARD TO CATCH
HARD TO GRASP
HARDY ANNUAL
HARE KRISHNA
HARICOT BEAN
HAROLD LLOYD
HARRIS TWEED
HARRY LAUDER
HARRY TRUMAN
HARVEST HOME
HARVEST MOON
HARVEST TIME
HARVEY SMITH
HASTY GLANCE
HASTY TEMPER
HATCHET FACE
HATEFUL TASK
HAUNT OF VICE
HAVANA CIGAR
HAVE A CHOICE
HAVE A FRIGHT
HAVE-A-GO HERO
HAVE A HAIR-DO
HAVE A LIKING
HAVE AND HOLD
HAVE AN EYE ON
HAVE AN EYE TO
HAVE ANOTHER
HAVE A PICNIC
HAVE A POLICY
HAVE A SECRET
HAVE A SHOWER
HAVE A SNOOZE
HAVE A SQUINT
HAVE A STROKE
HAVE A THEORY
HAVE A THIRST
HAVE COMPANY
HAVE COURAGE
HAVE IN STORE
HAVE NO DOUBT
HAVEN OF REST
HAVE NO MERCY
HAVE NO VOICE
HAVE ONE'S DAY
HAVE ONE'S SAY
HAVE ONE'S WAY
HAVE REGRETS
HAVE THE URGE
HAVE THE VOTE
HAVE TROUBLE

HAYLEY MILLS	HEROIC VERSE	HOARD WEALTH
HEAD AND TAIL	HERO WORSHIP	HOARSE COUGH
HEAD CLEANER	HERRING GULL	HOARSE LAUGH
HEAD TEACHER	HERRING POND	HOARSE VOICE
HEAD THE LIST	HIDDEN FIRES	HOBBLE SKIRT
HEALING GIFT	HIDDEN MERIT	HOCKEY MATCH
HEAL THE SICK	HIDDEN PANEL	HOCKEY STICK
HEALTHY FEAR	HIDE AND SEEK	HOLD CLASSES
HEALTHY MIND	HIDING PLACE	HOLD IN CHECK
HEAPED PLATE	HIGH ACCOUNT	HOLD IN LEASH
HEAPS OF TIME	HIGH CALLING	HOLD IN TRUST
HEAR NOTHING	HIGH CEILING	HOLD ONE'S JAW
HEART ATTACK	HIGH CIRCLES	HOLD ONE'S OWN
HEAR THE CALL	HIGH COMMAND	HOLD ON TIGHT
HEART OF GOLD	HIGH CONTENT	HOLD OUT HOPE
HEART'S BLOOD	HIGH COURAGE	HOLD THE BABY
HEARTS OF OAK	HIGH DENSITY	HOLD THE FORT
HEARTY CHEER	HIGH DUDGEON	HOLD THE LEAD
HEARTY EATER	HIGHER CLASS	HOLD THE LINE
HEARTY LAUGH	HIGHER FARES	HOLD THE ROAD
HEARTY SMACK	HIGHER LEVEL	HOLD TO SCORN
HEAT BARRIER	HIGHER POWER	HOLIDAY CAMP
HEATED WORDS	HIGHER WAGES	HOLIDAY HOME
HEAVE A BRICK	HIGH FEATHER	HOLIDAY MOOD
HEAVY AS LEAD	HIGH FINANCE	HOLIDAY SNAP
HEAVY BOMBER	HIGH HOLBORN	HOLIDAY TASK
HEAVY BURDEN	HIGH MOTIVES	HOLIDAY TIME
HEAVY EATING	HIGH OLD TIME	HOLIDAY WEAR
HEAVY FATHER	HIGH OPINION	HOLLAND PARK
HEAVY HITTER	HIGH QUALITY	HOLLAND'S GIN
HEAVY HUMOUR	HIGH RESOLVE	HOLLOW LAUGH
HEAVY OBJECT	HIGH SHERIFF	HOLLOW SOUND
HEAVY SHOWER	HIGH SOCIETY	HOLLOW TOOTH
HEAVY SMOKER	HIGH SPIRITS	HOLLOW TRUCE
HEAVY WEIGHT	HIGH STATION	HOLLOW TRUTH
HECTIC FLUSH	HIGH TENSION	HOLLOW VOICE
HEDDA GABLER	HIGH TRAGEDY	HOLY TRINITY
HELD CAPTIVE	HIGH TREASON	HOLY UNCTION
HELD HOSTAGE	HIGH VOLTAGE	HOLY WEDLOCK
HELD IN CHECK	HIGHWAY CODE	HOME AFFAIRS
HELD IN TRUST	HIGH-WIRE ACT	HOME AND AWAY
HELEN JACOBS	HIGH WYCOMBE	HOME BANKING
HELEN KELLER	HILL AND DALE	HOME CIRCUIT
HELEN OF TROY	HILL COUNTRY	HOME COOKING
HELL ON EARTH	HILTON HOTEL	HOME COUNTRY
HELL'S ANGELS	HINDLE WAKES	HOME FOR GOOD
HELPING HAND	HIP AND THIGH	HOME-MADE JAM
HENRIK IBSEN	HIP AND HAWS	HOME ON LEAVE
HENRY COOPER	HIS EMINENCE	HOME SERVICE
HENRY COTTON	HIS HIGHNESS	HOME STRETCH
HENRY ESMOND	HIS LORDSHIP	HOMO SAPIENS
HENRY IRVING	HISTORY BOOK	HONEST DOUBT
HERALDIC ART	HITHER GREEN	HONEST INJUN
HERD OF GOATS	HITLER YOUTH	HONEST MONEY
HER HIGHNESS	HIT THE TRAIL	HONEST PENNY
HER LADYSHIP	H.M.S. PINAFORE	HONEST TRUTH

HONEST WOMAN
HONITON LACE
HONOUR A BILL
HONOUR BOUND
HONOURED SIR
HONOURS EASY
HONOURS EVEN
HONOURS LIST
HOOP EARRING
HOORAY HENRY
HOPE AND PRAY
HOPE DIAMOND
HOPEFUL SIGN
HORNED VIPER
HORNETS' NEST
HORROR COMIC
HORS D'OEUVRE
HORSE DEALER
HORSE DOCTOR
HORSE GUARDS
HORSE MARINE
HORSE PISTOL
HORSE RACING
HORSE'S MOUTH
HOSPITAL BED
HOSTILE ARMY
HOSTILE VOTE
HOT AS PEPPER
HOT CHESTNUT
HOT-CROSS BUN
HOT-DOG STAND
HOTEL ANNEXE
HOTEL KEEPER
HOTEL LOUNGE
HOTEL PORTER
HOT-WATER TAP
HOUND'S TOOTH
HOURLY VIGIL
HOUR OF TRIAL
HOURS OF WORK
HOUSE ARREST
HOUSE HUNTER
HOUSE MARTIN
HOUSE MASTER
HOUSE MOTHER
HOUSE NUMBER
HOUSE OF CALL
HOUSE OF KEYS
HOUSE OF REST
HOUSE OF YORK
HOUSE ON FIRE
HOVER AROUND
HOWLING WIND
HUDSON RIVER
HUGE EXPENSE
HUGE SUCCESS

HUGHIE GREEN
HUG THE COAST
HUG THE SHORE
HUMAN DYNAMO
HUMAN EFFORT
HUMAN FAMILY
HUMAN NATURE
HUMAN RIGHTS
HUMAN SHIELD
HUMBLE BIRTH
HUMBLE HEART
HUMBLE STOCK
HUMMING BIRD
HUMS AND HAWS
HUNDRED DAYS
HUNGER MARCH
HUNK OF BREAD
HUNT BIG GAME
HUNTER'S MOON
HUNT FOR A JOB
HUNTING CROP
HUNTING HORN
HUNTING PACK
HUNTING PINK
HUNTING SONG
HUNT IN PAIRS
HUNT THE HARE
HURRIED MEAL
HUSBAND TO BE
HUSHED TONES
HUSH-HUSH JOB

I – 11

IAIN MACLEOD
IDEAL SCHEME
IDES OF MARCH
IDLE DISPLAY
IDLE THOUGHT
IF YOU PLEASE
IGNEOUS ROCK
IGNITION KEY
IGNORANT MAN
I HAVE A DREAM
ILE DE FRANCE
I'LL BE HANGED!
ILLICIT LOVE
iL PENSEROSO
IL TROVATORE
IMPOSE A DUTY
IMPROPER USE
IN A BAD STATE
IN A FEW WORDS
IN A FLAT SPIN
IN A GOOD MOOD
IN AGREEMENT

IN A HAYSTACK
IN ALL EVENTS
IN A LOW VOICE
IN A MINORITY
IN AND AROUND
INANE REMARK
IN AN INSTANT
IN A NUTSHELL
IN A QUANDARY
IN A REAL MESS
IN A SMALL WAY
IN AT THE KILL
IN AUTHORITY
IN BAD REPAIR
IN CAPTIVITY
IN CHARACTER
IN COLD BLOOD
IN COLLISION
IN COLLUSION
IN COMMITTEE
IN CONDITION
IN CONFUSION
INCUR LOSSES
IN DAYS OF OLD
IN DEEP WATER
IN DETENTION
INDEX FINGER
INDEX NUMBER
INDEX SEARCH
INDIAN BRAVE
INDIAN CHIEF
INDIAN CURRY
INDIAN OCEAN
INDIAN SQUAW
INDIAN TRIBE
INDIA OFFICE
INDIA RUBBER
INDIRECT TAX
INDOOR GAMES
IN DREAMLAND
IN DUE COURSE
IN DUE SEASON
IN DUPLICATE
IN DUTY BOUND
IN ECSTASIES
IN EVERY PORT
IN EXISTENCE
IN FACSIMILE
IN FINE STYLE
IN FOR A PENNY
IN FOR A POUND
IN FOR A STORM
IN FORMATION
INFRA-RED RAY
IN FULL BLAST
IN FULL BLOOM

IN FULL SPATE
IN FULL SWING
IN GOOD FAITH
IN GOOD HANDS
IN GOOD HEART
IN GOOD ODOUR
IN GOOD SHAPE
IN GOOD TASTE
IN GOOD VOICE
IN GRATITUDE
IN GREAT FORM
IN HYSTERICS
IN IGNORANCE
INITIAL MOVE
INJURED BACK
INJURED LOOK
INK-BLOT TEST
IN LOW RELIEF
IN MINIATURE
INMOST BEING
IN MY OPINION
INNER CIRCLE
INNER MARGIN
INNER PLANET
INNER TEMPLE
INNOCENT MAN
IN NO RESPECT
INNS OF COURT
IN ONE'S HEART
IN ONE'S POWER
IN ONE'S PRIME
IN ONE'S SHELL
IN ONE'S SLEEP
IN ONE'S TEENS
IN OPEN COURT
IN OPERATION
IN PANTOMIME
IN PRINCIPLE
IN PROFUSION
IN PURGATORY
IN READINESS
IN REBELLION
IN REPERTORY
IN RESIDENCE
IN SAFE HANDS
IN SECLUSION
INSECT WORLD
IN SHORTHAND
INSIDE RIGHT
INSIDE STORY
INSIDE TRACK
INSTANT CURE
INTENSE COLD
INTENSE HEAT
IN THAT PLACE
IN THE CELLAR

IN THE CENTRE
IN THE CHARTS
IN THE CHORUS
IN THE CHURCH
IN THE CINEMA
IN THE CIRCLE
IN THE CLOUDS
IN THE CORNER
IN THE CRADLE
IN THE DEPTHS
IN THE DESERT
IN THE FAMILY
IN THE FIELDS
IN THE FINISH
IN THE FOREST
IN THE FRIDGE
IN THE FUTURE
IN THE GARAGE
IN THE GARDEN
IN THE GROOVE
IN THE GROUND
IN THE GUARDS
IN THE GUTTER
IN THE JUNGLE
IN THE LOCK-UP
IN THE MAKING
IN THE MARGIN
IN THE MARKET
IN THE MIDDLE
IN THE MIRROR
IN THE MORGUE
IN THE NAME OF
IN THE OFFICE
IN THE OFFING
IN THE PAPERS
IN THE PLURAL
IN THE PULPIT
IN THE PURPLE
IN THE SADDLE
IN THE SEASON
IN THE SECRET
IN THE SPRING
IN THE STALLS
IN THE STOCKS
IN THE STREET
IN THE STUDIO
IN THE THROES
IN THE VALLEY
IN THE WAKE OF
IN THE WINDOW
IN THE WINTER
IN THE ZENITH
IN THIS PLACE
INTO THE BLUE
INTO THE WIND
INTO THIN AIR

IN TWO SHAKES
INVALID DIET
INVERT SUGAR
IN WHICH CASE
IONIC COLUMN
IRISH BROGUE
IRISH GUARDS
IRISH SETTER
IRMA LA DOUCE
IRON CURTAIN
IRON FILINGS
IRON FOUNDRY
IRON PYRITES
IRON RATIONS
IRONY OF FATE
ISAAC NEWTON
ISAAC PITMAN
ISLE OF ARRAN
ISLE OF CAPRI
ISLE OF WIGHT
ISSUE SHARES
ITALIA CONTI
ITALIAN ALPS
ITALIAN WINE
ITCHING PALM
IT'S A FAIR COP
IT STRIKES ME
IVOR NOVELLO
IVORY CASTLE
IZAAK WALTON

J – 11

JACK AND JILL
JACK DEMPSEY
JACK HAWKINS
JACK HULBERT
JACK JACKSON
JACK JOHNSON
JACK OF CLUBS
JAFFA ORANGE
JAMBOREE BAG
JAMES BRIDIE
JAMES CAGNEY
JAMESON RAID
JAM SANDWICH
JAM TOMORROW
JANE SEYMOUR
JAPANESE ART
JARRING NOTE
JARROW MARCH
JAUNTING CAR
JAWS OF DEATH
JAZZ SESSION
JEALOUS WIFE
JEAN BOROTRA

JEAN COCTEAU
JEAN SIMMONS
JELLIED EELS
JEREMY IRONS
JET AIRCRAFT
JIMMY PORTER
JINGLE BELLS
JOAN COLLINS
JODRELL BANK
JOHN GIELGUD
JOHN HALIFAX
JOHN MCENROE
JOHN OF GAUNT
JOHN O' GROATS
JOHN O' LONDON
JOHN OSBORNE
JOIE DE VIVRE
JOINT ACTION
JOINT APPEAL
JOINT EFFORT
JOIN THE ARMY
JOIN THE NAVY
JOINT OF BEEF
JOINT OF LAMB
JOINT OF PORK
JOINT OF VEAL
JOINT TENANT
JOKING APART
JOLLY HUNGRY
JOSEPH'S COAT
JOURNEY'S END
JUBILEE YEAR
JUDGMENT DAY
JUDY GARLAND
JUGULAR VEIN
JUKE-BOX JURY
JUMPING BEAN
JUMPING JACK
JUNE WEDDING
JUNGLE FEVER
JUNGLE GREEN
JUNGLE JUICE
JUNIPER TREE
JURY SERVICE
JUST A CHANCE
JUST A LITTLE
JUST A MINUTE
JUST A MOMENT
JUST A SECOND
JUST DESERTS
JUST FOR ONCE
JUST IMAGINE
JUST MARRIED
JUST PERFECT
JUST THE SAME
JUST THE TIME

JUST VISIBLE
JUST WILLIAM

K – 11

KEEN BARGAIN
KEEN CONTEST
KEEN HEARING
KEEN STUDENT
KEEP ABREAST
KEEP AN EYE ON
KEEP A RECORD
KEEP A SECRET
KEEP COMPANY
KEEP COUNSEL
KEEP IN CHECK
KEEP IN SIGHT
KEEP IN STOCK
KEEP IN STORE
KEEP IN TOUCH
KEEP IT GOING
KEEP ONE'S JOB
KEEP OUT OF IT
KEEP RIGHT ON
KEEP SMILING
KEEP THE CASH
KEEP TRACK OF
KEEP WAITING
KELLOGG PACT
KEMPTON PARK
KENNETH MORE
KENSAL GREEN
KENTISH TOWN
KEY INDUSTRY
KEY POSITION
KEY QUESTION
KHAKI SHORTS
KICK AGAINST
KICK UP A DUST
KICK UP A FUSS
KIDNEY BEANS
KILKENNY CAT
KILLER WHALE
KILLING PACE
KILL ONESELF
KIND FRIENDS
KIND GESTURE
KINDRED SOUL
KIND REGARDS
KIND THOUGHT
KIND WELCOME
KING CHARLES
KINGDOM COME
KING EMPEROR
KING OF BIRDS
KING OF CLUBS

KING OF KINGS
KING OF SWING
KING PENGUIN
KING RICHARD
KING'S BISHOP
KING'S BOUNTY
KING'S COLOUR
KING'S FLIGHT
KING'S KNIGHT
KING SOLOMON
KING'S RANSOM
KING WILLIAM
KIRK DOUGLAS
KISSING GAME
KISSING GATE
KISS ME, HARDY
KISS OF DEATH
KISS OF JUDAS
KISS OF PEACE
KISS THE BOOK
KISS THE DUST
KITCHEN FIRE
KITCHEN HAND
KITCHEN MAID
KITCHEN ROLL
KITCHEN SINK
KITCHEN UNIT
KNEELER SEAT
KNEE SUPPORT
KNIGHT'S MOVE
KNIGHT'S PAWN
KNIT THE BROW
KNITTING BEE
KNOCK AROUND
KNOCK IT BACK
KNOCK ON WOOD
KNOTTY POINT
KNOW A LITTLE
KNOW BY HEART
KNOW BY SIGHT
KNOWING LOOK
KNOW ONE'S JOB
KNOW ONE'S WAY
KNOW THE FORM
KNOW THYSELF
KNOW TOO MUCH
KNUCKLE DOWN
KUALA LUMPUR

L – 11

LABOUR FORCE
LABOUR PARTY
LABRADOR DOG
LACK COURAGE
LACK OF DRIVE

LACK OF FAITH
LACK OF FLAIR
LACK OF MONEY
LACK OF POWER
LACK OF SCOPE
LACK OF SENSE
LACK OF SHAPE
LACK OF SLEEP
LACK OF TASTE
LACK SPARKLE
LADIES FIRST
LADIES' NIGHT
LA DOLCE VITA
LADY ALMONER
LADY BARNETT
LADY MACBETH
LADY MACDUFF
LADY'S FINGER
LADY TEACHER
LAKE LUCERNE
LAKE ONTARIO
LAKE SUCCESS
LAMBETH WALK
LANDING GEAR
LAND MEASURE
LAND OF ROSES
LANKY FIGURE
LANTERN JAWS
LAPIS LAZULI
LAP OF LUXURY
LAPSE OF TIME
LARGE AMOUNT
LARGE AS LIFE
LARGE BRANDY
LARGE CIRCLE
LARGE FAMILY
LARGE INCOME
LARGE NUMBER
LARGE PROFIT
LARGE SALARY
LARGE SCOTCH
LARGE SCREEN
LARGE SHERRY
LARGE SUPPLY
LARGE VESSEL
LARGE VOLUME
LARGE WHISKY
LASH OF A WHIP
LAST ADDRESS
LAST ARRIVAL
LAST ATTEMPT
LAST BASTION
LAST CENTURY
LAST CHAPTER
LAST EDITION
LAST EVENING

LAST FOR EVER
LAST HONOURS
LAST INNINGS
LAST JANUARY
LAST JOURNEY
LAST OF EIGHT
LAST OF SEVEN
LAST OF THREE
LAST OUTPOST
LAST QUARTER
LAST TO LEAVE
LAST TRIBUTE
LAST TUESDAY
LAST VESTIGE
LATCHKEY KID
LATE ARRIVAL
LATE AT NIGHT
LATE BOOKING
LATE EDITION
LATE EVENING
LATE FOR WORK
LATE HARVEST
LATE HUSBAND
LATE STARTER
LATEST CRAZE
LATEST ISSUE
LATEST MODEL
LATEST SCORE
LATEST SHADE
LATEST STYLE
LATEST THING
LATIN CHURCH
LATIN LESSON
LATIN MASTER
LATIN PRIMER
LAUGHING GAS
LAUNDRY BILL
LAUNDRY MAID
LAUREL CROWN
LAW AND ORDER
LAWFUL ORDER
LAW MERCHANT
LAW OF NATURE
LAW OF THE SEA
LAY ABOUT ONE
LAY-FLAT HOSE
LAY IN AMBUSH
LAY IN A STOCK
LAY OUT MONEY
LAY PREACHER
LAY THE CLOTH
LAY THE GHOST
LAY THE TABLE
LAZY HOLIDAY
LEADEN HOURS
LEADING CASE

LEADING EDGE
LEADING LADY
LEADING NOTE
LEADING PART
LEADING RÔLE
LEADING WREN
LEAGUE MATCH
LEAN AGAINST
LEAN AS A RAKE
LEAN FORWARD
LEAN TOWARDS
LEARN A HABIT
LEARN A TRADE
LEARN TO HATE
LEARN TO LOVE
LEARN TO PLAY
LEARN TO READ
LEARN TO RIDE
LEARN TO WALK
LEARN WISDOM
LEATHER BELT
LEATHER COAT
LEATHER LANE
LEATHER SOLE
LEAVE A SPACE
LEAVE A TRAIL
LEAVE BEHIND
LEAVE FALLOW
LEAVE IT OPEN
LEAVE IT TO ME
LEAVE NO HOPE
LEAVE SCHOOL
LEAVE UNDONE
LEAVE UNSAID
LE CORBUSIER
LECTURE HALL
LECTURE TOUR
LEDGER CLERK
LEFT HANGING
LEFT LUGGAGE
LEFT OUTSIDE
LEGAL ACTION
LEGAL ADVICE
LEGAL BATTLE
LEGAL ENTITY
LEGAL JARGON
LEGAL REMEDY
LEGAL RULING
LEGAL TENDER
LEG OF MUTTON
LEISURE TIME
LEMON BARLEY
LEMON SQUASH
LEMON YELLOW
LEND SUPPORT
LEON TROTSKY

LESLIE CARON
LESS AND LESS
LESSER BREED
LESSON EIGHT
LESSON SEVEN
LESSON THREE
LESS TROUBLE
LET A MAN DOWN
LET IN THE SUN
LET OFF STEAM
LEVEL FLIGHT
LEVEL TEMPER
LIBEL ACTION
LIBERAL ARTS
LIBERAL VIEW
LIBERTY BOAT
LIBERTY HALL
LIBERTY SHIP
LIBRARY BOOK
LIBRARY LIST
LICK OF PAINT
LICK THE DUST
LIE AT ANCHOR
LIE DETECTOR
LIE END TO END
LIE IN AMBUSH
LIE IN PRISON
LIE ON VELVET
LIE PARALLEL
LIFE CHANCES
LIFE HISTORY
LIFE OF BLISS
LIFE OF CRIME
LIFE OR DEATH
LIFE PARTNER
LIFE PEERAGE
LIFE SAVINGS
LIFT A FINGER
LIFT THE ROOF
LIFT THE VEIL
LIGHT A MATCH
LIGHT BOMBER
LIGHT BREEZE
LIGHT COLOUR
LIGHT COMEDY
LIGHT DUTIES
LIGHTER FUEL
LIGHTER VEIN
LIGHT OF FOOT
LIGHT RELIEF
LIGHT REMARK
LIGHT THE GAS
LIGHT THE WAY
LIGHT VESSEL
LIGHT WEIGHT
LIGHT YELLOW

LIKE A MASTER
LIKE AN ARROW
LIKE AN IDIOT
LIKE A PARROT
LIKE A STATUE
LIKE A STREAK
LIKE A TROJAN
LIKE FOR LIKE
LIKE IT OR NOT
LIKELY STORY
LIKE THE IDEA
LIKE THE WIND
LILAC DOMINO
LILLI PALMER
LILY LANGTRY
LILI MARLENE
LIMITED TIME
LIMPID STYLE
LINCOLN CITY
LINCOLN'S INN
LINE DRAWING
LINEN BASKET
LINEN DRAPER
LINE OF MARCH
LINE OF SIGHT
LION RAMPANT
LISLE THREAD
LIST OF ITEMS
LIST OF NAMES
LITERARY MAN
LITERARY SET
LITMUS PAPER
LITTLE ANGEL
LITTLE DEVIL
LITTLE KNOWN
LITTLE SPACE
LITTLE THING
LITTLE TO SAY
LITTLE WHILE
LITTLE WOMAN
LITTLE WOMEN
LITTLE VALUE
LIVE FOR EVER
LIVE IN DREAD
LIVE IN PEACE
LIVE IN STYLE
LIVELONG DAY
LIVELY DANCE
LIVELY PARTY
LIVELY PITCH
LIVE ON BOARD
LIVE THEATRE
LIVE THROUGH
LIVING BEING
LIVING DEATH
LIVING IMAGE

LIVING IN SIN
LIVING PROOF
LIVING SPACE
LIVING THING
LIZARD POINT
LLOYD GEORGE
LOAD OF STRAW
LOAD OF TRIPE
LOAF OF BREAD
LO AND BEHOLD
LOAN OF MONEY
LOCAL BRANCH
LOCAL COLOUR
LOCAL CUSTOM
LOCAL GOSSIP
LOCAL OPTION
LOCAL TALENT
LOCK THE DOOR
LOCUM TENENS
LOGICAL MIND
LOGICAL STEP
LOLLIPOP MAN
LONDON CRIES
LONDON DOCKS
LONDON PRIDE
LONDON STAGE
LONDON STONE
LONG ACCOUNT
LONG CLOTHES
LONG DROUGHT
LONG HOLIDAY
LONG INNINGS
LONG JOURNEY
LONG, LONG AGO
LONG MEASURE
LONG SERVICE
LONG SESSION
LONG STRETCH
LONG STRIDES
LONG TIME AGO
LONG WEEK-END
LOOK A FRIGHT
LOOK ASKANCE
LOOK DAGGERS
LOOK FOOLISH
LOOK FOR DIGS
LOOK FORWARD
LOOK FOR WORK
LOOK GHASTLY
LOOK LIKE NEW
LOOK-OUT POST
LOOK OUTSIDE
LOOK PLEASED
LOOK THE PART
LOOK THROUGH
LOOK VOLUMES

LOOP THE LOOP
LOOSE CANNON
LOOSE CHANGE
LOOSE COVERS
LOOSE LIVING
LOOSE MORALS
LOOSE THREAD
LORD BALDWIN
LORD BOOTHBY
LORD PROVOST
LORD RUSSELL
LORDS' DEBATE
LORD'S PRAYER
LORD'S SUPPER
LORRY DRIVER
LOSE A CHANCE
LOSE CONTROL
LOSE COURAGE
LOSE FRIENDS
LOSE ONE'S ALL
LOSE ONESELF
LOSE ONE'S WAY
LOSE SIGHT OF
LOSE THE GAME
LOSE THE LEAD
LOSE THE RACE
LOSE THE TOSS
LOSE THE VOTE
LOSS OF BLOOD
LOSS OF FAITH
LOSS OF MONEY
LOSS OF NERVE
LOSS OF SIGHT
LOSS OF SOUND
LOSS OF SMELL
LOSS OF TOUCH
LOSS OF VALUE
LOSS OF VOICE
LOST HORIZON
LOST TO SHAME
LOST TO SIGHT
LOST WEEK-END
LOTS AND LOTS
LOTS OF MONEY
LOUD AND LONG
LOUD PROTEST
LOUD SPEAKER
LOUIS QUINZE
LOUIS TREIZE
LOUNGE ABOUT
LOVE AND HATE
LOVE FIFTEEN
LOVE IS BLIND
LOVELY MONEY
LOVELY NIGHT
LOVELY SIGHT

LOVE OF MONEY
LOVE OF ORDER
LOVE OF TRUTH
LOVE OR MONEY
LOVE PHILTRE
LOVING WORDS
LOW ALTITUDE
LOW COMEDIAN
LOWER ANIMAL
LOWER SCHOOL
LOW ESTIMATE
LOW FOREHEAD
LOW LATITUDE
LOW POSITION
LOW PRESSURE
LOW RAINFALL
LOW STANDARD
LOYAL FRIEND
L-SHAPED ROOM
LUCID MOMENT
LUCILLE BALL
LUCKY BEGGAR
LUCKY CHANCE
LUCKY ESCAPE
LUCKY FELLOW
LUCKY MASCOT
LUCKY MOMENT
LUCKY NUMBER
LUCKY RASCAL
LUCKY STREAK
LUCKY STRIKE
LUCKY STROKE
LUCKY WINNER
LUDGATE HILL
LUGGAGE RACK
LULL TO SLEEP
LUMP OF SUGAR
LUNCHEON CAR
LUNDY ISLAND
LUXURY FOODS
LUXURY GOODS
LUXURY HOTEL
LUXURY PRICE
LYRIC POETRY

M – 11

MACASSAR OIL
MACHINE CODE
MACHINE HAND
MACHINE SHOP
MACHINE TOOL
MACKEREL SKY
MADE A KNIGHT
MADE A MEMBER
MADE IN ITALY

MADE IN JAPAN
MADE IN SPAIN
MADEIRA CAKE
MADEIRA WINE
MADE OF MONEY
MADE OF STRAW
MADE TO ORDER
MADE WELCOME
MADONNA LILY
MADRAS CURRY
MAD SCRAMBLE
MAD WITH RAGE
MAGIC CARPET
MAGIC CIRCLE
MAGIC MIRROR
MAGIC MOMENT
MAGIC POTION
MAGIC RECIPE
MAGIC REMEDY
MAGIC SQUARE
MAGINOT LINE
MAGNUM BONUM
MAILING LIST
MAIL SERVICE
MAIN ELEMENT
MAIN FEATURE
MAIN MEANING
MAIN PROBLEM
MAIN PURPOSE
MAIN STATION
MAJOR CRISIS
MAJOR PLANET
MAKE A CHANGE
MAKE A CHOICE
MAKE A CORNER
MAKE A DETOUR
MAKE A FOOL OF
MAKE A LIVING
MAKE AND MEND
MAKE AN ENTRY
MAKE AN ERROR
MAKE AN OFFER
MAKE A PACKET
MAKE A PROFIT
MAKE A RECORD
MAKE A REMARK
MAKE A REPORT
MAKE A SEARCH
MAKE A SIGNAL
MAKE A SPEECH
MAKE A SPLASH
MAKE BELIEVE
MAKE CERTAIN
MAKE CHANGES
MAKE CONTACT
MAKE DEMANDS

MAKE ENEMIES
MAKE EXCUSES
MAKE FRIENDS
MAKE HEADWAY
MAKE HISTORY
MAKE INROADS
MAKE IT CLEAR
MAKE IT PLAIN
MAKE IT STICK
MAKE LIGHTER
MAKE LIGHT OF
MAKE MUCH ADO
MAKE NO NOISE
MAKE NO SOUND
MAKE OBVIOUS
MAKE ONE'S BED
MAKE ONE'S BOW
MAKE ONE'S WAY
MAKE OR BREAK
MAKE SMALLER
MAKES NO ODDS
MAKE SPORT OF
MAKE THE FIRE
MAKE THE PACE
MAKE TROUBLE
MAKE WELCOME
MAKE WHOOPEE
MALACCA CANE
MALAY STATES
MALE DESCENT
MALMSEY WINE
MALT VINEGAR
MAN AND WOMAN
MAN AT THE TOP
MAN BITES DOG
MANFRED MANN
MAN FROM MARS
MANICURE SET
MAN IN CHARGE
MAN IN OFFICE
MANLY FIGURE
MANLY SPIRIT
MAN OF ACTION
MAN OF GENIUS
MAN OF HONOUR
MAN OF METTLE
MAN OF MUSCLE
MAN OF PRAYER
MAN OF RENOWN
MAN OF REPUTE
MAN ON THE JOB
MAN PROPOSES
MANSARD ROOF
MAN THE PUMPS
MAN THE WALLS
MAP OF EUROPE

MAP OF FRANCE
MAP OF GREECE
MAP OF LONDON
MAP OF NORWAY
MAP OF SWEDEN
MARBLE HALLS
MARCH IN STEP
MARCH OF TIME
MARIA CALLAS
MARIE STOPES
MARINE CORPS
MARINE STORE
MARITIME LAW
MARKED CARDS
MARKET OVERT
MARKET PLACE
MARKET PRICE
MARKET RASEN
MARKET TREND
MARKET VALUE
MARKET WOMAN
MARK MY WORDS
MARK OF ZORRO
MARK THE SPOT
MARRIAGE TIE
MARRIED LIFE
MARRIED NAME
MARRON GLACÉ
MARRYING MAN
MARSHAL FOCH
MARSHAL TITO
MARSTON MOOR
MARTIAL ARTS
MARTIAL RACE
MARTIN'S BANK
MASONIC HALL
MASSED BANDS
MASS EMOTION
MASSIVE ROCK
MASS MEETING
MATE IN THREE
MATERIAL AID
MATINÉE IDOL
MATT SURFACE
MATURE YEARS
MAUNDY MONEY
MAX BEERBOHM
MAX BYGRAVES
MAY THE FIFTH
MAY THE FIRST
MAY THE NINTH
MAY THE SIXTH
MAY THE TENTH
ME AND MY GIRL
MEANING LOOK
MEAN MACHINE

MEAN NOTHING
MEASURE TIME
MEAT EXTRACT
MEDAL RIBBON
MEDICAL BOOK
MEDICAL CARE
MEDICAL CASE
MEDICAL TEST
MEDICAL WARD
MEDICINE HAT
MEDICINE MAN
MEDIUM BUILD
MEEK AND MILD
MEET HALFWAY
MEET ONE'S END
MEET THE BILL
MEGATON BOMB
MELODY MAKER
MELTING MOOD
MELT IN TEARS
MEMBERS ONLY
MEMORIAL DAY
MENAI STRAIT
MEN AND WOMEN
MENDIP HILLS
MENTAL ERROR
MENTAL GRASP
MENTAL IMAGE
MENTAL LAPSE
MENTALLY ILL
MENTAL POWER
MENTAL SHOCK
MENTAL STATE
MERE FEELING
MERE NOTHING
MERLE OBERON
MERRY ANDREW
MERSEY DOCKS
MERSEY SOUND
MERVYN JOHNS
METAL POLISH
METHOD ACTOR
MEWS COTTAGE
MEXICAN WAVE
MICKEY MOUSE
MIDDLE CLASS
MIDDLE POINT
MIDDLE STUMP
MIDDLE WATCH
MIDLAND BANK
MIDLAND TOWN
MIDNIGHT OIL
MIDNIGHT SUN
MIGHT AS WELL
MILD CLIMATE
MILD FLUTTER

MILD REPROOF
MILD WEATHER
MILE A MINUTE
MILE END ROAD
MILITARY AID
MILITARY LAW
MILITARY MAN
MILKING TIME
MILK PUDDING
MINCING LANE
MIND MAPPING
MIND THE BABY
MIND THE STEP
MINERAL VEIN
MINIMUM WAGE
MINOR DETAIL
MINOR INJURY
MINOR MATTER
MINOR PLANET
MINSTREL BOY
MINT FLAVOUR
MINT OF MONEY
MINUTE STEAK
MINUTE WALTZ
MIRACLE DRUG
MIRACLE PLAY
MISERY INDEX
MISS A CHANCE
MISS A SITTER
MISSED CATCH
MISS ENGLAND
MISSING HEIR
MISSING LINK
MISS NOTHING
MISS ONE'S WAY
MISS THE BOAT
MISS THE MARK
MISS THE POST
MISTER RIGHT
MIXED SCHOOL
MOB HYSTERIA
MOBILE PHONE
MOB VIOLENCE
MOCKING BIRD
MOCK MODESTY
MODERN BLOCK
MODERN DANCE
MODERN DRESS
MODERN HOUSE
MODERN IDEAS
MODERN IDIOM
MODERN LATIN
MODERN MUSIC
MODERN NOVEL
MODERN STYLE
MODERN TIMES

MODERN TREND
MODERN USAGE
MODERN YOUTH
MODEST HOPES
MODEST MEANS
MOIRA LISTER
MOLLY MALONE
MONDAY NIGHT
MONEY FOR JAM
MONEY MARKET
MONEY MATTER
MONEY SPIDER
MONEY SUPPLY
MONEY'S WORTH
MONEY TO BURN
MONKEY ABOUT
MONTE CRISTO
MONTHLY RENT
MONTH'S LEAVE
MONTY PYTHON
MOON GODDESS
MOON LANDING
MOP ONE'S BROW
MORAL APATHY
MORAL DEFECT
MORAL EFFECT
MORAL IMPACT
MORE AND MORE
MORE THAN ONE
MORNING CALL
MORNING COAT
MORNING POST
MORNING STAR
MORRIS DANCE
MORTAL AGONY
MORTAL ENEMY
MORTALLY ILL
MORTAL PERIL
MORTAL WOUND
MORTISE LOCK
MOSAIC FLOOR
MOSELLE WINE
MOSES BASKET
MOSQUITO NET
MOTHER CAREY
MOTHER EARTH
MOTHER GOOSE
MOTHER'S HELP
MOTHER'S MILK
MOTHER'S RUIN
MOTION STUDY
MOTIVE FORCE
MOTIVE POWER
MOTLEY CROWD
MOTOR LAUNCH
MOTOR RACING

MOTOR TRIALS
MOULIN ROUGE
MOUNT A HORSE
MOUNTAIN AIR
MOUNTAIN ASH
MOUNTAIN DEW
MOUNTAIN TOP
MOUNT ARARAT
MOUNT VERNON
MOUSE DRIVER
MOUTH HONOUR
MOVABLE TYPE
MOVE FORWARD
MOVE QUICKLY
MOVE TO ANGER
MOVE TO TEARS
MOVE TOWARDS
MOVING FORCE
MOVING SCENE
MOVING STORY
MOVING WORDS
MOW THE GRASS
MRS MALAPROP
MRS THATCHER
MUCH MARRIED
MUCH OBLIGED
MUCH THE SAME
MUCH TROUBLE
MUCH WENLOCK
MUFFLED DRUM
MUHAMMAD ALI
MUM'S THE WORD
MURDER TRIAL
MURKY DEPTHS
MUSCOVY DUCK
MUSEUM PIECE
MUSICAL NOTE
MUSICAL SHOW
MUSICAL TRIO
MUSICAL WORK
MUSIC CENTRE
MUSIC CRITIC
MUSIC LESSON
MUSIC MASTER
MUSTARD BATH
MUSTARD SEED
MUSWELL HILL
MUTT AND JEFF
MUTTON CURRY
MUTUAL TERMS
MYSTERY BOAT
MYSTERY PLAY
MYSTERY SHIP
MYSTERY TOUR
MYSTERY TRIP
MYSTIC RITES

N – 11

	NET RECEIPTS	NINE HUNDRED
	NEUTRAL TINT	NINE MINUTES
NAGGING PAIN	NEUTRAL ZONE	NINE OF CLUBS
NAGGING WIFE	NEUTRON BOMB	NINE PER CENT
NAIL VARNISH	NEUTRON STAR	NINE SQUARED
NAME NO NAMES	NEVER BEFORE	NINETY MILES
NARROW GAUGE	NEVER ENDING	NINETY TIMES
NARROW SHAVE	NEVER FORGET	NINETY YEARS
NARROW TRAIL	NEVER ON TIME	NINE WICKETS
NASAL ACCENT	NEVER SAY DIE	NINTH LETTER
NASTY PEOPLE	NEW AGE MUSIC	NINTH OF JULY
NASTY TEMPER	NEW APPROACH	NINTH OF JUNE
NASTY TUMBLE	NEW ATLANTIS	NINTH STOREY
NATIVE CHIEF	NEW-BORN BABE	NINTH VOLUME
NATIVE DRESS	NEW-BORN BABY	NIP IN THE AIR
NATIVE HEATH	NEW BRIGHTON	NIP IN THE BUD
NATIVE STATE	NEWGATE GAOL	NIP OF BRANDY
NATIVE TRIBE	NEW HEBRIDES	NIP OF WHISKY
NAT KING COLE	NEW POTATOES	NO ADDITIVES
NATURAL BENT	NEW PROSPECT	NO ADMISSION
NATURAL GIFT	NEWS CAPTION	NO AUTHORITY
NATURAL LIFE	NEWS IN BRIEF	NOBBY CLARKE
NATURE LOVER	NEWS SUMMARY	NOBLE EFFORT
NATURE STUDY	NEWTON ABBOT	NOBLE FAMILY
NAUGHTY GIRL	NEW TO THE JOB	NOBLE FIGURE
NAUGHTY WORD	NEW YEAR'S DAY	NOBLE NATURE
NAVAL BATTLE	NEW YEAR'S EVE	NOBLE SAVAGE
NAVAL RATING	NEW YORK CITY	NOBLE STRAIN
NAVAL STORES	NEW YORK METS	NOBODY'S FOOL
NAVEL ORANGE	NEXT CENTURY	NO CIRCULARS
NAZI GERMANY	NEXT CHAPTER	NOD ONE'S HEAD
NEAR AND DEAR	NEXT IN ORDER	NOEL EDMONDS
NEAR FAILURE	NEXT JANUARY	NO EXCEPTION
NEARLY READY	NEXT OCTOBER	NO GENTLEMAN
NEARLY THERE	NEXT STATION	NOGGIN OF ALE
NEAR ONE'S END	NEXT TUESDAY	NO GREAT LOSS
NEAR PERFECT	NICAM STEREO	NO HOPE AT ALL
NEAR THE BONE	NICE AND EVEN	NO ILLUSIONS
NEAR THE EDGE	NICE MANNERS	NOISE ABROAD
NEAR THE MARK	NICE PICTURE	NOMADIC RACE
NEAR THE WIND	NIGHT AND DAY	NOM DE GUERRE
NEAT AND TIDY	NIGHT ATTIRE	NOMINAL HEAD
NEAT AND TRIM	NIGHT CURFEW	NOMINAL LIST
NECK AND CROP	NIGHT EDITOR	NOMINAL RATE
NECK AND NECK	NIGHT FLIGHT	NOMINAL RENT
NEEDLE MATCH	NIGHT FLYING	NONE SO BLIND
NEEDLE POINT	NIGHT PATROL	NONE THE LESS
NEIL KINNOCK	NIGHT PORTER	NONE TOO WARM
NELSON TOUCH	NIGHT SCHOOL	NO, NO, NANETTE
NE PLUS ULTRA	NIGHT SISTER	NON-STICK PAN
NERVE CENTRE	NIGHT WORKER	NON-STICK WOK
NETBALL TEAM	NINE DEGREES	NON-STOP SHOW
NET CURTAINS	NINE DOLLARS	NO OBJECTION
NETHER LIMBS	NINE FATHOMS	NO QUESTIONS
NETHER WORLD	NINE GALLONS	NORFOLK SUIT
NET PRACTICE	NINE GUINEAS	NO RIGHT TURN

O – 11

NORMAL SIGHT		OLD POTATOES
NORMAL STATE		OLD TRAFFORD
NORMAN STYLE	OAK-APPLE DAY	OLD WAR-HORSE
NORTH AFRICA	OBITER DICTA	OLIVE BRANCH
NORTH BORNEO	OBLIQUE LINE	OLIVER LODGE
NORTH DAKOTA	OBTUSE ANGLE	OLIVER TWIST
NORTH ISLAND	OCEAN TRAVEL	OMAR KHAYYAM
NORTH LONDON	ODDLY ENOUGH	OMNIBUS BOOK
NORTH RIDING	ODDS AGAINST	ON ALL POINTS
NORTH SEA OIL	ODDS AND ENDS	ON AN AVERAGE
NO SCORE DRAW	OFFER ADVICE	ON A PEDESTAL
NOSE FOR NEWS	OFFER A PRICE	ON A PITTANCE
NOSEY PARKER	OFFER NO HOPE	ON AUTHORITY
NOT A BIT OF IT	OFFICE BLOCK	ON BOARD SHIP
NOT ALL THERE	OFFICE CLOCK	ON BOTH SIDES
NOT A RED CENT	OFFICE HOURS	ONCE OR TWICE
NOT FAR WRONG	OFFICE PARTY	ONCE REMOVED
NOTHING LEFT	OFFICE STAFF	ONE AND A HALF
NOTHING LIKE	OFFICE STOOL	ON EASY TERMS
NOTHING MUCH	OFFICE SWEEP	ONE ELEVENTH
NOTHING TO DO	OFF ONE'S BEAT	ONE GOOD TURN
NOTHING TO IT	OFF ONE'S FEED	ONE IN THE EYE
NOTICE BOARD	OFF ONE'S FOOD	ONE IN TWELVE
NOT MUCH GOOD	OFF ONE'S HEAD	ONE-MAN REVUE
NOT-OUT SCORE	OFF-PEAK CALL	ONE MAN'S MEAT
NO-TRUMP HAND	OFF-SIDE RULE	ONE MEAT BALL
NOT SPEAKING	OFF THE BOOZE	ONE'S BETTERS
NOT THE THING	OFF THE COAST	ONE'S HOSTESS
NOTTING HILL	OFF THE GREEN	ONE SPOONFUL
NOTTS COUNTY	OFF THE LEASH	ONE'S VERY OWN
NOTTS FOREST	OFF THE POINT	ONE SYLLABLE
NOT UP-TO-DATE	OFF THE RAILS	ONE THOUSAND
NOT UP TO MUCH	OFF THE SCENT	ON EVERY SIDE
NOT VERY MANY	OFF THE STAGE	ON GOOD TERMS
NOT VERY MUCH	OFF THE TRACK	ON HORSEBACK
NOT VERY WELL	OF GOOD STOCK	ONION SELLER
NOT YOUR TYPE	OF ILL REPUTE	ONLY THE BEST
NO VACANCIES	OFF LATE YEARS	ON NO ACCOUNT
NOW AND AGAIN	OF NO ACCOUNT	ON ONE'S GUARD
NOWHERE NEAR	OIL AND WATER	ON ONE'S HANDS
NOWHERE TO GO	OIL OF CLOVES	ON ONE'S KNEES
NUCLEAR BOMB	OIL PAINTING	ON ONE'S PLATE
NULL AND VOID	OIL REFINERY	ON ONE'S RIGHT
NUMBER EIGHT	OLD AND TRIED	ON POINT DUTY
NUMBER PLATE	OLD BLUE EYES	ON PRINCIPLE
NUMBER SEVEN	OLD CUSTOMER	ON PROBATION
NUMBERS GAME	OLDER SISTER	ON THE AGENDA
NUMBER THREE	OLD FAITHFUL	ON THE ATTACK
NUPTIAL VOWS	OLD GREY MARE	ON THE BOARDS
NURSE CAVELL	OLD KENT ROAD	ON THE BOTTLE
NURSERY GAME	OLD KING COLE	ON THE BRIDGE
NURSERY MAID	OLD MAN RIVER	ON THE CARPET
NURSERY TALE	OLD MEMORIES	ON THE COMMON
NURSING HOME	OLD OAK CHEST	ON THE CORNER
	OLD OFFENDER	ON THE COURSE
	OLD OLD STORY	ON THE DANUBE

ON THE FIDDLE
ON THE FRINGE
ON THE GROUND
ON THE INSIDE
ON THE MARKET
ON THE MORROW
ON THE PARISH
ON THE RAZZLE
ON THE RECORD
ON THE SCALES
ON THE SCREEN
ON THE SQUARE
ON THE STAIRS
ON THE STOCKS
ON THE SWINGS
ON THE TARGET
ON THE THAMES
ON THE THRONE
ON THE WAGGON
ON THE WAY OUT
ON TWO WHEELS
ONUS OF PROOF
ONWARD MARCH
ON WEDNESDAY
OPAQUE GLASS
OPEN ACCOUNT
OPEN-AIR LIFE
OPEN-AIR TYPE
OPEN AND SHUT
OPEN CIRCUIT
OPEN COUNTRY
OPENING MOVE
OPENING TIME
OPEN MEETING
OPEN OUTWARD
OPEN QUARREL
OPEN RUPTURE
OPEN SCANDAL
OPEN THE BALL
OPEN THE CASE
OPEN THE DOOR
OPEN THE EYES
OPEN THE GATE
OPEN THE SAFE
OPEN THIS END
OPEN TO DOUBT
OPEN TO ERROR
OPEN TO OFFER
OPEN VERDICT
OPEN WARFARE
OPERA BOUFFE
OPERA SINGER
OPINION POLL
OPIUM ADDICT
OPIUM SMOKER
OPPOSITE SEX

OPPOSITE WAY
ORANGE DRINK
ORANGE GROVE
ORANGE JUICE
ORCHID HOUSE
ORDER DINNER
ORDERLY DUTY
ORDERLY ROOM
ORDER TO VIEW
ORDINARY MAN
ORDNANCE MAP
ORGANIC LIFE
ORIEL WINDOW
ORIENTAL ART
ORIGINAL SIN
ORNATE STYLE
ORPHAN CHILD
ORSON WELLES
ORTHODOX JEW
OSTRICH FARM
OTHER PEOPLE
OUT AND ABOUT
OUT COURTING
OUTDOOR GAME
OUTDOOR LIFE
OUTER CIRCLE
OUTER OFFICE
OUTER TEMPLE
OUT FOR A DUCK
OUT FOR BLOOD
OUT FOR KICKS
OUT OF ACTION
OUT OF BOUNDS
OUT OF BREATH
OUT OF DANGER
OUT OF FAVOUR
OUT OF HUMOUR
OUT OF OFFICE
OUT OF PETROL
OUT OF POCKET
OUT OF REPAIR
OUT OF SCHOOL
OUT OF SEASON
OUT OF THE ARK
OUT OF THE BAG
OUT OF THE CUP
OUT OF THE SKY
OUT OF THE SUN
OUT OF THE WAY
OUT ON STRIKE
OUTRIGHT WIN
OUTSIDE EDGE
OUTSIDE HELP
OUTSIDE LEFT
OUTSIDE WORK
OUTWARD SELF

OUTWARD SHOW
OVER AGAINST
OVER AND OVER
OVER ANXIOUS
OVERCAST SKY
OVER SHE GOES
OVER THE EDGE
OVER THE HILL
OVER THE LINE
OVER THE MARK
OVER THE MOON
OVER THE ODDS
OVER THE ROAD
OVER THE SIDE
OVER THE WALL
OVERTIME PAY
OWNER DRIVER
OWN FREE WILL
OXFORD COACH
OXFORD GROUP
OXFORD SHOES
OXFORD UNION
OYSTER SHELL

P – 11

PABLO CASALS
PACE THE DECK
PACKAGE DEAL
PACKED HOUSE
PACKED LUNCH
PACKET OF TEN
PACK OF CARDS
PACK OF FOOLS
PACK UP AND GO
PAGAN PEOPLE
PAGE HEADING
PAID SERVANT
PAID TRIBUTE
PAIL OF WATER
PAINFUL TASK
PAINTED LADY
PAINTED SHIP
PAINTED VEIL
PAINT IN OILS
PAIR BONDING
PAIR OF BOOTS
PAIR OF CLOGS
PAIR OF CUFFS
PAIR OF DUCKS
PAIR OF FIVES
PAIR OF FOURS
PAIR OF HANDS
PAIR OF HORNS
PAIR OF JACKS
PAIR OF KINGS

PAIR OF LACES
PAIR OF NINES
PAIR OF PANTS
PAIR OF PUMPS
PAIR OF SHOES
PAIR OF SIXES
PAIR OF SOCKS
PAIR OF SPATS
PAIR OF SPURS
PAIR OF STAYS
PAIR OF STEPS
PAIR OF TONGS
PALACE GUARD
PALAIS GLIDE
PALE AS DEATH
PAMPAS GRASS
PANAMA CANAL
PANCAKE RACE
PANDIT NEHRU
PANDORA'S BOX
PANEL DOCTOR
PANE OF GLASS
PANIC BUTTON
PAPER PROFIT
PAPIER MÂCHÉ
PARAFFIN OIL
PARISH CLERK
PARISH VICAR
PARK AND RIDE
PARLOUR GAME
PARLOUR MAID
PARSNIP WINE
PARSON'S NOSE
PART COMPANY
PART FRIENDS
PARTING GIFT
PARTING SHOT
PART PAYMENT
PART-TIME JOB
PARTY LEADER
PARTY MEMBER
PARTY SLOGAN
PARTY SPIRIT
PARTY SYSTEM
PAS DE CALAIS
PASS A REMARK
PASSING RICH
PASSING SHOW ·
PASSING WHIM
PASSING WORD
PASSING PLAY
PASSION WEEK
PASSIVE ROLE
PASS THE BALL
PASS THE BUCK
PASS THE PORT

PASS THE SALT
PASS THE TEST
PASS THE TIME
PASS THIS WAY
PASS THROUGH
PAST AND GONE
PASTEL SHADE
PAST HISTORY
PAST THE POST
PATH TO GLORY
PAT OF BUTTER
PATROL PLANE
PATRON OF ART
PATRON SAINT
PATTERN SHOP
PAUL ROBESON
PAX VOBISCUM
PAY A FORFEIT
PAY AND A HALF
PAY A PENALTY
PAY A PREMIUM
PAY BY CHEQUE
PAY CASH DOWN
PAY INCREASE
PAYING GUEST
PAY INTEREST
PAY ON DEMAND
PAY ON THE DOT
PAY THE COSTS
PAY THE DEVIL
PAY THE PIPER
PAY THE PRICE
PAY THE SCORE
PAY THE TABLE
PAY UP OR ELSE!
PEACEFUL END
PEACE OF MIND
PEACE PLEDGE
PEACE SPEECH
PEACE TREATY
PEACH BRANDY
PEACOCK BLUE
PEAL OF BELLS
PEARL BAILEY
PEARL BARLEY
PEARL BUTTON
PEARL HARBOR
PEARLY GATES
PEARLY QUEEN
PEBBLE BEACH
PEBBLY BEACH
PELTING RAIN
PENAL COLONY
PENAL REFORM
PENAL SYSTEM
PENALTY AREA

PENALTY GOAL
PENALTY KICK
PENALTY LINE
PENALTY SPOT
PEN AND PAPER
PENNY POINTS
PENSION FUND
PENSIVE MOOD
PERFECT CASE
PERFECT CURE
PERFECT FOOL
PERFECT LADY
PERFECT TRIM
PERIOD DRESS
PERIOD HOUSE
PERIOD PIECE
PERSIAN GULF
PERSIAN LAMB
PERSONAL LAW
PET AVERSION
PETER DAWSON
PETER GRIMES
PETER O'TOOLE
PETER RABBIT
PETER'S PENCE
PETER WIMSEY
PETE SAMPRAS
PETROL FUMES
PETTY TYRANT
PETULA CLARK
PEWTER PLATE
PHANTOM SHIP
PHIL COLLINS
PHOENIX PARK
PHONE NUMBER
PHOTO FINISH
PIANO LESSON
PIANO PLAYER
PICK A WINNER
PICKET FENCE
PICK FLOWERS
PICK HOLES IN
PICK ONE'S WAY
PICK POCKETS
PICK THE BEST
PICK THE LOCK
PICK UP SPEED
PICNIC PARTY
PICTURE BOOK
PICTURE DISC
PIECE OF CAKE
PIECE OF LAND
PIECE OF LUCK
PIECE OF NEWS
PIE IN THE SKY
PIERCED EARS

PIGEON'S MILK	PLAY THE LEAD	PORT OF SPAIN
PILE OF CHIPS	PLEAD GUILTY	PORT STANLEY
PILE OF MONEY	PLEASANT DAY	PORT THE HELM
PILLION RIDE	PLEASURE MAD	POSTAGE FREE
PILLION SEAT	PLENTY TO EAT	POSTAGE PAID
PILLOW FIGHT	PLOT A COURSE	POST A LETTER
PILOT ENGINE	PLUMB WICKET	POSTAL ORDER
PILOT SCHEME	PLUM PUDDING	POSTAL UNION
PILOT VESSEL	PLUS OR MINUS	POSTERN GATE
PILSEN LAGER	PLYMOUTH HOE	POTATO CHIPS
PILTDOWN MAN	POCKET GUIDE	POTATO CRISP
PINCH OF SALT	POCKET MONEY	POTATO SALAD
PINT MEASURE	POCKET VENUS	POT OF COFFEE
PINT OF CIDER	POETIC STYLE	POTS AND PANS
PINT OF LAGER	POETS' CORNER	POTS OF MONEY
PINT OF STOUT	POINT A MORAL	POTTED PLANT
PINT TANKARD	POINTED CLUE	POTTER ABOUT
PIPE CLEANER	POINT OF SALE	POTTER'S CLAY
PIPE OF PEACE	POINT OF TIME	POT THE BLACK
PIPE ON BOARD	POINT OF VIEW	POTTING SHED
PIPE TOBACCO	POINT THE WAY	POULTRY FARM
PIRATE RADIO	POISON DWARF	POURING RAIN
PIRATE VIDEO	POKER PLAYER	POVERTY TRAP
PITHY REMARK	POKER SCHOOL	POWER OF GOOD
PITHY SAYING	POKE THE FIRE	POWER SUPPLY
PIZZA CUTTER	POLAR CIRCLE	PRACTICE RUN
PLACE OF CALL	POLAR LIGHTS	PRACTISE LAW
PLACE OF REST	POLAR REGION	PRAED STREET
PLAIN ANSWER	POLE VAULTER	PRAIRIE FIRE
PLAIN FIGURE	POLICE COURT	PRAIRIE WOLF
PLAIN LIVING	POLICE FORCE	PRANCE ABOUT
PLAIN PEOPLE	POLICE STATE	PRAY FOR RAIN
PLAIN SPEECH	POLO SWEATER	PRECISE TIME
PLAIN STUPID	PONY AND TRAP	PREMIUM BOND
PLASTER CAST	PONY EXPRESS	PRESENT ARMS
PLASTIC BOMB	POOLS COUPON	PRESENT TIME
PLATE ARMOUR	POOR CALIBRE	PRESS A CLAIM
PLAY AGAINST	POOR COMPANY	PRESSED BEEF
PLAYBOY TYPE	POOR HARVEST	PRESS NOTICE
PLAY CHICKEN	POOR LOOK-OUT	PRESS OFFICE
PLAY COWBOYS	POOR OLD SOUL	PRESS ONWARD
PLAY CRICKET	POOR OPINION	PRESS TICKET
PLAYER PIANO	POOR OUTLOOK	PRETTY AWFUL
PLAY FOR LOVE	POOR QUALITY	PRETTY DANCE
PLAY FOR TIME	POOR SOLDIER	PRETTY PENNY
PLAY FORWARD	POOR SWIMMER	PRETTY POLLY
PLAYING CARD	POOR VINTAGE	PRETTY SCENE
PLAY MARBLES	POPULAR HERO	PRETTY SMART
PLAY ON WORDS	POPULAR NAME	PRE-WAR PRICE
PLAY PONTOON	POPULAR PLAY	PREY TO FEARS
PLAY THE BALL	POPULAR SONG	PRICE OF FAME
PLAY THE FOOL	POPULAR TUNE	PRICE TICKET
PLAY THE GAME	POPULAR WILL	PRICKLY HEAT
PLAY THE HARP	PORK BUTCHER	PRICKLY PEAR
PLAY THE HERO	PORTLAND BAY	PRIDE AND JOY
PLAY THE HOST	PORT OF ENTRY	PRIDE OF RANK

PRIEST'S HOLE
PRIME FACTOR
PRIME NUMBER
PRIME OF LIFE
PRIMROSE DAY
PRIMUS STOVE
PRINCE HARRY
PRINCESS BEA
PRINCESS IDA
PRINTED PAGE
PRINTED WORD
PRINTER'S INK
PRINTER'S PIE
PRINTING INK
PRISON BREAK
PRISON GATES
PRISON GUARD
PRISON HOUSE
PRISON WALLS
PRIVATE BANK
PRIVATE BILL
PRIVATE HELL
PRIVATE LIFE
PRIVATE LINE
PRIVATE MASS
PRIVATE PATH
PRIVATE ROAD
PRIVATE ROOM
PRIVATE SALE
PRIVATE TALK
PRIVATE VIEW
PRIVATE WARD
PRIVET HEDGE
PRIZE CATTLE
PROBATE DUTY
PROBE DEEPLY
PROBLEM PLAY
PRODIGAL SON
PROM CONCERT
PROMISE WELL
PROMPT REPLY
PROOF READER
PROOF SPIRIT
PROPER PLACE
PROPER PRIDE
PROPER SENSE
PROPERTY TAX
PROS AND CONS
PROSE POETRY
PROTEIN DIET
PROUD FATHER
PROVE GUILTY
PRUSSIC ACID
PUBLIC ALARM
PUBLIC BATHS
PUBLIC ENEMY

PUBLIC FUNDS
PUBLIC HOUSE
PUBLIC IMAGE
PUBLIC MONEY
PUBLIC PURSE
PUBLIC TASTE
PUBLIC WORKS
PUBLIC WRONG
PUDDING FACE
PUDDING LANE
PUFF AND BLOW
PUFF OF SMOKE
PULL ASUNDER
PULL ONE'S LEG
PULL STRINGS
PULL THROUGH
PULL UP SHORT
PULP FICTION
PUMICE STONE
PUMPING IRON
PUPPET STATE
PURCHASE TAX
PURE ALCOHOL
PURE ENGLISH
PURE FICTION
PURE IN HEART
PURE MOTIVES
PURE SCIENCE
PURL OR PLAIN
PURPLE HEART
PURPLE PATCH
PURSE OF GOLD
PUSH AND PULL
PUSH FORWARD
PUSH THROUGH
PUSS IN BOOTS
PUT A SPOKE IN
PUT IN A CLAIM
PUT IN CHARGE
PUT IN DANGER
PUT IN LIGHTS
PUT IN MOTION
PUT IN OFFICE
PUT IN PRISON
PUT IN THE WAY
PUT INTO CODE
PUT INTO TYPE
PUT IT MILDLY
PUT ON A SPURT
PUT ON A STUNT
PUT ONE'S CASE
PUT ON PAROLE
PUT ON RECORD
PUT ON THE MAP
PUT ON WEIGHT
PUT OUT TO SEA

PUT STRAIGHT
PUT THE LID ON
PUT TO FLIGHT
PUT TOGETHER
PUT TO RANSOM
PUT TO RIGHTS
PUTT THE SHOT
PUT UP A BLACK
PUT UP A BLUFF
PUT-UP AFFAIR
PUT UP A FIGHT
PUT WISE TO IT
PUZZLE IT OUT
PYJAMA PARTY

Q – 11

QUACK DOCTOR
QUACK REMEDY
QUALITY TIME
QUANTUM LEAP
QUART BOTTLE
QUARTER DECK
QUARTER LEFT
QUARTER MILE
QUART OF BEER
QUARTO PAPER
QUARTZ WATCH
QUEEN MOTHER
QUEEN SALOTE
QUEEN'S AWARD
QUEEN'S BENCH
QUEEN'S COURT
QUEEN'S GUIDE
QUEEN'S SCOUT
QUEER PERSON
QUEER STREET
QUICK ANSWER
QUICK FREEZE
QUICK GLANCE
QUICK GROWTH
QUICK PROFIT
QUICK RETURN
QUICK TEMPER
QUICK TONGUE
QUICK WORKER
QUIET DREAMS
QUIETEN DOWN
QUIET PLEASE!
QUITE AT HOME
QUITE ENOUGH
QUITE LIKELY
QUIT THE RING
QUOTA SYSTEM
QUOTED PRICE

R – 11

	RAPID GROWTH	RED TRIANGLE
	RAPID MOTION	REDUCED FARE
RABBIT PUNCH	RAPID SPEECH	REDUCED RATE
RABBIT'S FOOT	RARE EXAMPLE	REDUCE SPEED
RACE HISTORY	RARE QUALITY	REFINED GOLD
RACE MEETING	RASH PROMISE	REFLEX LIGHT
RACE PROBLEM	RATTLE ALONG	REFUGEE CAMP
RACIAL PRIDE	RAW MATERIAL	REFUSE A GIFT
RACING EIGHT	REACH BOTTOM	REFUSE TO ACT
RACING MODEL	REACH SAFETY	REFUSE TO MIX
RACING SLANG	REACH THE END	REFUSE TO PAY
RACING WORLD	REACH THE TOP	REGATTA WEEK
RACING YACHT	READ A SPEECH	REGENCY BUCK
RACK AND RUIN	READING DESK	REGENT'S PARK
RACY FLAVOUR	READING GAOL	REGULAR ARMY
RADAR SCREEN	READING LAMP	REGULAR HERO
RADIANT HEAT	READING LIST	REGULAR LIFE
RADIANT RING	READING ROOM	REGULAR VERB
RADIATE LOVE	READ THE WILL	REGULAR WORK
RADICAL CHIC	READ THROUGH	RELEASE DATE
RADICAL CURE	READY ACCESS	RELIEF FORCE
RADICAL IDEA	READY ANSWER	RELIEF PARTY
RADICAL SIGN	READY ENOUGH	REMAIN ALOOF
RADIO BEACON	READY FOR BED	REMAIN AWAKE
RADIO DOCTOR	READY FOR USE	REMNANT SALE
RADIO SIGNAL	READY RETORT	REMOTE CAUSE
RAGGED ROBIN	READY TO DROP	RENEW A LEASE
RAGTIME ARMY	READY TO HAND	RENEWED HOPE
RAGTIME BAND	READY TONGUE	RENTAL VALUE
RAILWAY ARCH	READY TO WEAR	RENT ASUNDER
RAILWAY LINE	READY WORKER	RENT CONTROL
RAINBOW'S END	REAM OF PAPER	REPORT STAGE
RAIN OF BLOWS	REAP A PROFIT	REQUEST ITEM
RAIN OR SHINE	REAPING HOOK	REQUEST NOTE
RAINY SEASON	REAR ADMIRAL	REQUEST STOP
RAISE A CHEER	REBECCA WEST	REQUIEM MASS
RAISE A LAUGH	REBEL ATTACK	RESCUE FORCE
RAISE A STORM	REBEL LEADER	RESCUE PARTY
RAISED VOICE	RECEIPT BOOK	RESCUE SQUAD
RAISE MORALE	RECEIVE NEWS	RESERVE FUND
RAISE ON HIGH	RECENT ISSUE	RESERVE TEAM
RAISE PRICES	RECENT TIMES	REST ASSURED
RAISE THE BID	RECORD ALBUM	REST CONTENT
RAISE THE HEM	RECORD CROWD	REST IN PEACE
RAISON D'ÊTRE	RECORD ENTRY	RETAIL PRICE
RAJIV GANDHI	RECORD SCORE	RETAIL TRADE
RALLY AROUND	RECORD TOKEN	RETIRED LIFE
RALLYING CRY	RED AND BLACK	RETIRED LIST
RAMBLER ROSE	RED AND GREEN	RETIRE TO BED
RANGING SHOT	RED AND WHITE	RETIRING AGE
RANK AND FILE	RED BURGUNDY	RETURN A BLOW
RANSOM MONEY	RED-HOT COALS	RETURN FIGHT
RANT AND RAVE	RED-HOT POKER	RETURN MATCH
RAPID CHANGE	RED MAHOGANY	RETURN VISIT
RAPID EFFECT	RED, RED ROBIN	REVERSE GEAR
RAPID GLANCE	RED SQUIRREL	REVERSE SIDE

REVISED COPY	ROAD HAULAGE	ROUGH SKETCH
REX HARRISON	ROAD MANAGER	ROUGH TONGUE
RHODE ISLAND	ROAD REPAIRS	ROUND CHEEKS
RHUBARB TART	ROADSIDE INN	ROUND FIGURE
RHYMED VERSE	ROAD SURFACE	ROUND LETTER
RICE AND PEAS	ROAD SWEEPER	ROUND NUMBER
RICE PUDDING	ROAD TRAFFIC	ROUND OBJECT
RICH HARVEST	ROARING FIRE	ROUND OF BEEF
RICH HUSBAND	ROAR OF ANGER	ROUND OF FIRE
RICH IN IDEAS	ROASTING HOT	ROUND OF GOLF
RIDE A TANDEM	ROAST MUTTON	ROUSING SONG
RIDE SHOTGUN	ROAST POTATO	ROW OF HOUSES
RIDING BOOTS	ROAST TURKEY	ROW OF MEDALS
RIDING HABIT	ROBBER BARON	ROWS AND ROWS
RIGGED TRIAL	ROBE OF STATE	ROWTON HOUSE
RIGHT AMOUNT	ROBERT BRUCE	ROYAL ASSENT
RIGHT ANSWER	ROBERT BURNS	ROYAL CIRCLE
RIGHT AS RAIN	ROBERT CLIVE	ROYAL FAMILY
RIGHT A WRONG	ROBERT DONAT	ROYAL MARINE
RIGHT INSIDE	ROCK AND ROLL	ROYAL OCTAVO
RIGHT MOMENT	ROCK CONCERT	ROYAL PALACE
RIGHT NUMBER	ROCKET RANGE	ROYAL PARDON
RIGHT PEOPLE	ROCK THE BOAT	ROYAL PURPLE
RIGHT SIDE UP	ROCK TO SLEEP	ROYAL SALUTE
RIGHTS OF MAN	ROD IN PICKLE	RUBBER GLOVE
RIGHT TO VOTE	ROES ON TOAST	RUBBER HEELS
RIGHT WINGER	ROLLER BLIND	RUBBER PLANT
RIGHT YOU ARE	ROLLER BOOTS	RUBBER SOLES
RIGOR MORTIS	ROLLER DISCO	RUBBER STAMP
RINGING TONE	ROLLER TOWEL	RUBBER TORCH
RING OF ROSES	ROLLING GAIT	RUBBISH DUMP
RING OF STEEL	ROLLING HOME	RUBBISH HEAP
RING OF TRUTH	ROLLING ROAD	RUB TOGETHER
RING THE BELL	ROLL INTO ONE	RUBY WEDDING
RIOT OF SOUND	ROLL OF DRUMS	RUDDY CHEEKS
RISE AGAINST	ROLL OF PAPER	RUDE GESTURE
RISE AND FALL	ROLL THE LAWN	RUGBY LEAGUE
RISE IN PRICE	ROLL-TOP DESK	RUGBY SCHOOL
RISE TO A PEAK	ROMAN CANDLE	RUGBY TACKLE
RISE TO POWER	ROMAN CHURCH	RUGGER FIELD
RISE TO SPEAK	ROMAN EMPIRE	RUGGER MATCH
RISING COSTS	ROMANTIC ART	RUGGER PITCH
RISING SALES	ROMNEY MARSH	RUGGER SCRUM
RITUAL DANCE	ROOKERY NOOK	RUINED HOUSE
RIVER DANUBE	ROOM SERVICE	RUIN ONESELF
RIVER GANGES	ROSES ARE RED	RULE OF FORCE
RIVER JORDAN	ROSY OUTLOOK	RULE OF MIGHT
RIVER LAUNCH	ROSY PICTURE	RULE OF THREE
RIVER MEDWAY	ROTARY AIRER	RULE OF THUMB
RIVER MERSEY	ROTARY PRESS	RULING CLASS
RIVER OF LAVA	ROTARY VALVE	RULING PARTY
RIVER PATROL	ROTTEN APPLE	RULING POWER
RIVER POLICE	ROUGE ET NOIR	RULING PRICE
RIVER SEVERN	ROUGH GROUND	RUM CUSTOMER
RIVER THAMES	ROUGH MANNER	RUMMAGE SALE
RIVER TRAVEL	ROUGH SCHEME	RUMOUR HAS IT

RUN A MAN DOWN
RUN AN ERRAND
RUN FOR COVER
RUN FOR MAYOR
RUN INTO DEBT
RUN INTO FORM
RUN INTO PORT
RUN MESSAGES
RUNNER BEANS
RUNNING AMOK
RUNNING BACK
RUNNING BEAR
RUNNING COLD
RUNNING COST
RUNNING DOWN
RUNNING FIRE
RUNNING JUMP
RUNNING KNOT
RUNNING OVER
RUNNING RIOT
RUNNING SHOT
RUNNING WILD
RUN PARALLEL
RUN SMOOTHLY
RUN STRAIGHT
RUN TOGETHER
RUN UP A SCORE
RUSH FORWARD
RUSH THROUGH
RUSSIAN BATH
RUSSIAN EGGS

S – 11

SABRINA FAIR
SACK OF FLOUR
SACRED HEART
SACRED MUSIC
SACRED TRUST
SAD FAREWELL
SADLY MISSED
SAD TO RELATE
SAFE AND SURE
SAFE AND WELL
SAFE BREAKER
SAFE COMPANY
SAFE CONDUCT
SAFE CUSTODY
SAFE DEPOSIT
SAFE JOURNEY
SAFE KEEPING
SAFE LANDING
SAFE RETREAT
SAFETY CATCH
SAFETY FIRST
SAFETY GLASS

SAFETY MATCH
SAFETY RAZOR
SAFETY STRAP
SAFETY VALVE
SAFFRON CAKE
SAGO PUDDING
SAILING BOAT
SAILING CLUB
SAILING DATE
SAILING SHIP
SAILING TIME
SAILOR'S HOME
SAILOR'S KNOT
SAINT GEORGE
SAINT HELENA
SAINT HELIER
SALMON STEAK
SALMON TROUT
SAL VOLATILE
SAME FOOTING
SAME MEANING
SAME OLD GAME
SAME PATTERN
SAMUEL PEPYS
SANCHO PANZA
SANDOWN PARK
SANDS OF TIME
SANDWICH BAG
SANDWICH BAR
SANDWICH BOX
SAN FAIRY ANN
SAPPHIRE SEA
SATANIC HOST
SATIN FINISH
SATIN STITCH
SAUCEPAN LID
SAUDI ARABIA
SAUSAGE MEAT
SAUSAGE ROLL
SAVAGE BEAST
SAVAGE BRUTE
SAVAGE SCENE
SAVAGE TRIBE
SAVE NOTHING
SAVE ONESELF
SAVE THE MARK
SAVING GRACE
SAVINGS BANK
SAVOIR FAIRE
SAVOURY DISH
SCALDED MILK
SCALE FILTER
SCARED STIFF
SCENT BOTTLE
SCENT DANGER
SCENTED SOAP

SCILLY ISLES
SCHOOL BADGE
SCHOOL BOARD
SCHOOL HOURS
SCHOOL HOUSE
SCHOOL OF ART
SCHOOL TREAT
SCORE A POINT
SCORE FREELY
SCORE SLOWLY
SCOTCH BROTH
SCOTS ACCENT
SCOTS GUARDS
SCOUT AROUND
SCOUT MASTER
SCRAP DEALER
SCRAPE ALONG
SCRAPPY MEAL
SCRATCH CREW
SCRATCH RACE
SCRATCH SIDE
SCRATCH TEAM
SCRATCHY PEN
SCREEN SAVER
SCUBA DIVING
SCUD MISSILE
SEA ELEPHANT
SEA FRONTAGE
SEAM BOWLING
SEAN CONNERY
SEARCH PARTY
SEASIDE TOWN
SEAT OF KINGS
SEAT OF POWER
SEAT ONESELF
SECOND CHILD
SECOND CLASS
SECOND EVENT
SECOND FLOOR
SECOND FRONT
SECOND GRADE
SECOND GREEN
SECOND HOUSE
SECOND JOINT
SECOND MONTH
SECOND OF MAY
SECOND PARTY
SECOND PLACE
SECOND PRIZE
SECOND ROUND
SECOND SHIFT
SECOND SIGHT
SECONDS LATE
SECOND STAGE
SECOND TEETH
SECOND VERSE

SECOND WORLD	SERIOUS VIEW	SHAM ILLNESS
SECOND YOUTH	SERVANT GIRL	SHANKS'S PONY
SECRET AGENT	SERVE A FAULT	SHARON STONE
SECRET ENEMY	SERVE NOTICE	SHARP ANSWER
SECRET HAUNT	SERVICE FLAT	SHARP ATTACK
SECRET PLACE	SERVICE ROAD	SHARP CORNER
SECURED LOAN	SERVICE ROOM	SHARP LESSON
SECURE GRASP	SERVING TIME	SHARP REBUFF
SEE A DENTIST	SET AN AMBUSH	SHARP TEMPER
SEE DAYLIGHT	SET AND MATCH	SHARP TONGUE
SEED OF DOUBT	SET A PROBLEM	SHARP TWINGE
SEE EYE TO EYE	SET AT NAUGHT	SHAVEN CROWN
SEE FAIR PLAY	SET IN MOTION	SHAVING SOAP
SEEK A WAY OUT	SET MOVEMENT	SHEAF OF CORN
SEE NEXT WEEK	SET OF CHAIRS	SHED THE LOAD
SEE STRAIGHT	SET OF STAMPS	SHEEP FARMER
SEE THE LIGHT	SET ONE RIGHT	SHEER LUNACY
SEE THE POINT	SET QUESTION	SHEER MURDER
SEE THE TRUTH	SET STANDARD	SHEET ANCHOR
SEE THE WORLD	SET STRAIGHT	SHEET COPPER
SEETHING MOB	SET THE ALARM	SHELL JACKET
SELF CONTROL	SET THE FIELD	SHERMAN TANK
SELF-MADE MAN	SET THE SCENE	SHERRY GLASS
SELF SERVICE	SETTING FREE	SHERRY PARTY
SELL AT A LOSS	SETTLING DAY	SHIFT WORKER
SELLING LINE	SET TO RIGHTS	SHINING HOUR
SELLING RACE	SET UP A CLAIM	SHIP OF STATE
SELL THE PASS	SET UP IN TYPE	SHIP'S COURSE
SELL TICKETS	SEVEN AND ONE	SHIP'S DOCTOR
SENATE HOUSE	SEVEN AND SIX	SHIP'S MASTER
SEND A LETTER	SEVEN AND TEN	SHIP'S PAPERS
SEND AN ORDER	SEVEN AND TWO	SHIP'S PURSER
SEND A SIGNAL	SEVEN DWARFS	SHIP'S STOKER
SEND FOR A CAB	SEVEN HEARTS	SHOAL OF FISH
SEND FOR HELP	SEVEN MONTHS	SHOCK HORROR
SEND PACKING	SEVEN NINTHS	SHOCK OF HAIR
SEND TO SLEEP	SEVEN O'CLOCK	SHOCK TROOPS
SENILE DECAY	SEVEN OUNCES	SHODDY GOODS
SENIOR PUPIL	SEVEN POINTS	SHOE CABINET
SENSE OF DUTY	SEVEN POUNDS	SHOE LEATHER
SENSE OF LOSS	SEVEN SPADES	SHOOTING BOX
SENSE OF PAIN	SEVEN TENTHS	SHOOTING WAR
SENSIBLE BOY	SEVENTH HOLE	SHOOT TO KILL
SENSIBLE MAN	SEVENTH PART	SHOP COUNTER
SENT HAYWIRE	SEVENTH RACE	SHOP DOORWAY
SENT PACKING	SEVENTH TIME	SHOP FOR SALE
SERIAL STORY	SEVEN TO FOUR	SHOPPING BAG
SERIOUS BOOK	SEVERE FROST	SHOP STEWARD
SERIOUS LOOK	SEVERE SHOCK	SHORT AND FAT
SERIOUS LOSS	SEVERE STYLE	SHORT ANSWER
SERIOUS MIND	SEWING CLASS	SHORTEN SAIL
SERIOUS MOOD	SEXTON BLAKE	SHORTEST BOY
SERIOUS PLAY	SHABBY TRICK	SHORTEST DAY
SERIOUS STEP	SHAGGY BEARD	SHORTEST MAN
SERIOUS TALK	SHALLOW DISH	SHORTEST WAY
SERIOUS VEIN	SHALLOW MIND	SHORT JACKET

SHORT LESSON
SHORT LETTER
SHORT MEMORY
SHORT NOTICE
SHORT OF CASH
SHORT OF FOOD
SHORT OF TIME
SHORT OF WORK
SHORT PERIOD
SHORT SHRIFT
SHORT SPEECH
SHORT STROLL
SHORT SUPPLY
SHORT TEMPER
SHORT VOYAGE
SHORT WAY OFF
SHORT WEIGHT
SHOT THROUGH
SHOULDER BAG
SHOUT FOR JOY
SHOUT HURRAH
SHOW A PROFIT
SHOW COURAGE
SHOW FEELING
SHOW NO FIGHT
SHOW NO MERCY
SHOW OF FORCE
SHOW OF HANDS
SHOW ONE'S AGE
SHOW ONESELF
SHOW PROMISE
SHOW PROWESS
SHOW RESPECT
SHOW RESULTS
SHOW THE FLAG
SHOW UP AGAIN
SHOW WILLING
SHREWD GUESS
SHRILL SOUND
SHRILL VOICE
SHUN COMPANY
SHUT THE DOOR
SHUT THE GATE
SIAMESE TWIN
SICK AT HEART
SICK BENEFIT
SICKLY SMILE
SICK TO DEATH
SIDE AGAINST
SIDE OF BACON
SIDE TURNING
SIEGE OF TROY
SIERRA LEONE
SIGNAL CORPS
SIGNAL LIGHT
SIGNS OF WEAR

SILAS MARNER
SILENT MIRTH
SILENT NIGHT
SILICON CHIP
SILLY ANSWER
SILLY DONKEY
SILLY DUFFER
SILLY PERSON
SILLY REMARK
SILLY SEASON
SILVER BIRCH
SILVER GHOST
SILVER MEDAL
SILVER MONEY
SILVER PAPER
SILVER PLATE
SILVER SPOON
SILVERY MOON
SILVERY TONE
SIMNEL BREAD
SIMPLE HEART
SIMPLE SIMON
SIMPLE SOUND
SIMPLE STYLE
SIMPLE TASTE
SIMPLE TRUTH
SIMPLON PASS
SIMPLY AWFUL
SINEWS OF WAR
SINGING BIRD
SINGING FOOL
SINGLE BERTH
SINGLE ENTRY
SINGLE HEART
SINGLE PIECE
SINGLE STATE
SINGLE TRACK
SINGLE VOICE
SINGLE WOMAN
SINKING FAST
SINKING FUND
SINKING SHIP
SINK THE BOAT
SIP OF BRANDY
SIR JOHN HUNT
SIR LANCELOT
SISTER SHIPS
SISTER SUSIE
SIT-DOWN MEAL
SITTING BULL
SITTING DOWN
SITTING DUCK
SITTING ROOM
SITTING SHOT
SIX AND A HALF
SIX COUNTIES

SIX DIAMONDS
SIX FEET TALL
SIX FURLONGS
SIX NO-TRUMPS
SIX OF HEARTS
SIX OF SPADES
SIX OF TRUMPS
SIXPENNY TIP
SIX SEVENTHS
SIXTH LETTER
SIXTH OF JULY
SIXTH OF JUNE
SIX THOUSAND
SIXTH STOREY
SIXTH VOLUME
SKATING RINK
SKEIN OF WOOL
SKELETON KEY
SKETCHY MEAL
SKI BINDING
SKILLED WORK
SKIMMED MILK
SKIM THROUGH
SKIN AND BONE
SKIN DISEASE
SKIN MASSAGE
SKYE TERRIER
SLAB OF STONE
SLACK MARKET
SLACK SEASON
SLADE SCHOOL
SLAM DANCING
SLAM THE DOOR
SLASH POCKET
SLATE PENCIL
SLAVE LABOUR
SLAVE MARKET
SLAVE TO DUTY
SLEEP DOUBLE
SLEEPING BAG
SLEEPING CAR
SLEEPING DOG
SLEIGH BELLS
SLENDER HOPE
SLICED BREAD
SLICE OF CAKE
SLICE OF LUCK
SLICE OF MEAT
SLIDE GUITAR
SLIDING DOOR
SLIDING ROOF
SLIDING SEAT
SLIGHT DOUBT
SLIGHT PAUSE
SLIPPED DISC
SLIPPER BATH

SLIP OF A GIRL
SLIP OF PAPER
SLIP THROUGH
SLOPING DESK
SLOPING EDGE
SLOPING FACE
SLOPING ROOF
SLOPING TYPE
SLOPPY SMILE
SLOT MACHINE
SLOUCH ALONG
SLOW AND SURE
SLOW BOWLING
SLOW BUT SURE
SLOW DECLINE
SLOW DEGREES
SLOW FOXTROT
SLOW PROCESS
SLOW STARTER
SLOW TO ANGER
SLOW TO LEARN
SLUM DWELLER
SMALL AMOUNT
SMALL BITTER
SMALL CHANCE
SMALL CHANGE
SMALL CHARGE
SMALL CIRCLE
SMALL FAMILY
SMALL FARMER
SMALL INCOME
SMALL LETTER
SMALL MATTER
SMALL NUMBER
SMALL PROFIT
SMALL SALARY
SMALL SCOTCH
SMALL SHERRY
SMALL VESSEL
SMALL WHISKY
SMART DEVICE
SMART PEOPLE
SMART PERSON
SMART RETORT
SMART SAYING
SMART TALKER
SMELL DANGER
SMILE PLEASE
SMOKE A CIGAR
SMOKED GLASS
SMOKED TROUT
SMOKE SCREEN
SMOKE SIGNAL
SMOKING ROOM
SMOOTH AS ICE
SMOOTH WATER

SNAKE POISON
SNAKES ALIVE!
SNAP OUT OF IT
SNATCH A KISS
SNATCH SQUAD
SNOWED UNDER
SNOW LEOPARD
SOB BITTERLY
SOBER COLOUR
SOBER PERSON
SOCCER MATCH
SOCIAL CLASS
SOCIAL GROUP
SOCIAL PARTY
SOCIAL ROUND
SOCIAL SCALE
SOCIAL WHIRL
SOCIETY LADY
SOCIETY NEWS
SOCIETY PAGE
SOCKET BOARD
SODA AND MILK
SO FAR, SO GOOD
SOFT AND RIPE
SOFT OUTLINE
SOILED GOODS
SOILED LINEN
SOIL EROSION
SOLAR CORONA
SOLAR PLEXUS
SOLAR SYSTEM
SOLD FOR A PUP
SOLDIER KING
SOLDIER'S KIT
SOLDIER'S PAY
SOLE AND HEEL
SOLE COMFORT
SOLEMN MUSIC
SOLEMN TRUTH
SOLE SUPPORT
SOLID FIGURE
SOLID GROUND
SOLID MATTER
SOLID SILVER
SOLITARY MAN
SOLWAY FIRTH
SOMEONE ELSE
SOME TIME AGO
SONG CONTEST
SONG OF SONGS
SONG RECITAL
SONNY LISTON
SOPHIA LOREN
SORDID STORY
SORELY TRIED
SORE PRESSED

SORE SUBJECT
SORRY FIGURE
SORRY PLIGHT
SOUND ADVICE
SOUND ASLEEP
SOUND CREDIT
SOUND IN MIND
SOUND PLAYER
SOUND POLICY
SOUND REASON
SOUP KITCHEN
SOUTH AFRICA
SOUTH BY EAST
SOUTH BY WEST
SOUTH DAKOTA
SOUTH EALING
SOUTH HARROW
SOUTH LONDON
SOUTH MOLTON
SOUTH RIDING
SOVIET UNION
SPACE FLIGHT
SPACE OF TIME
SPACE TRAVEL
SPADE GUINEA
SPANISH GOLD
SPANISH MAIN
SPANISH TOWN
SPANISH WINE
SPARE A PENNY
SPARE THE ROD
SPARK OF LIFE
SPARTAN FARE
SPARTAN LIFE
SPATE OF NEWS
SPEAK FIRMLY
SPEAK FREELY
SPEAK FRENCH
SPEAK GERMAN
SPEAK NO EVIL
SPEAK OPENLY
SPEAK POLISH
SPEAK SLOWLY
SPEAK SOFTLY
SPECIAL CASE
SPECIAL DIET
SPECIAL DUTY
SPECIAL GIFT
SPECIAL JURY
SPECIAL LINE
SPECIAL NOTE
SPECK OF DUST
SPEED MANIAC
SPEED RECORD
SPEED TRIALS
SPELL DANGER

SPELLING BEE	STAND AT EASE	STEP THIS WAY
SPELL OF DUTY	STAND IN FEAR	STERILE LAND
SPELL OF WORK	STAND IN LINE	STERN REBUKE
SPEND FREELY	STAND IN NEED	STEWED FRUIT
SPICE OF LIFE	STAND OR FALL	STEWED PEARS
SPIKED SHOES	STAND SQUARE	STICK IN A RUT
SPINNING TOP	STAND TO GAIN	STICK OF ROCK
SPIRIT LEVEL	STAND TO LOSE	STICKY LABEL
SPLIT SECOND	STAR CHAMBER	STICKY PAPER
SPOILS OF WAR	STARCHY FOOD	STICKY STUFF
SPOILT CHILD	STAR CLUSTER	STIFF BREEZE
SPOIL THE FUN	STAR OF DAVID	STIFF COLOUR
SPORTING DOG	STAR OF INDIA	STIFLE A YAWN
SPORTING GUN	STAR QUALITY	STILL HOPING
SPORTING MAN	STARRY NIGHT	STILL TO COME
SPORTS ARENA	STAR STUDDED	STILL TONGUE
SPORTS MODEL	START A FIGHT	STILL WATERS
SPORTS SHIRT	START AFRESH	STILL WITH IT
SPORTS WATCH	STARTER HOME	STIR A FINGER
SPOTTED DICK	STARTER'S GUN	STIR ONE'S TEA
SPOT THE BALL	START SAVING	STIRRUP PUMP
SPREAD GLOOM	STATE A CLAIM	STIR THE FIRE
SPRING A LEAK	STATED TERMS	ST JOHN'S WOOD
SPRING APART	STATELY HOME	ST MARGARET'S
SPRING A TRAP	STATE OF FLUX	STOCK ANSWER
SPRING FEVER	STATE OF MIND	STOCK EXCUSE
SPRING ONION	STATE PRISON	STOCK IN HAND
SPRING VALVE	STATE SCHOOL	STOCK LETTER
SPRING WATER	STATE SECRET	STOCK MARKET
SPROUT WINGS	STATUTE BOOK	STOCK PHRASE
SPRUCE GOOSE	STATUTE MILE	STOLE A MARCH
SPY IN THE CAB	ST AUGUSTINE	STOLEN FRUIT
SPY THRILLER	STAY INDOORS	STOLEN GOODS
SQUARE DANCE	STAY IN SIGHT	STONE QUARRY
SQUARE WORLD	STAY NEUTRAL	STONE'S THROW
SQUASH COURT	STAY OUTSIDE	STONY GROUND
SQUEEZE PLAY	STAY THE PACE	STOP A BULLET
SQUIRE'S LADY	STAY TOO LONG	STOP BURNING
STACK OF COAL	ST DAVID'S DAY	STOP OUTSIDE
STACK OF WORK	STEADY FLAME	STOP PAYMENT
STAFF OF LIFE	STEADY LIGHT	STOP SMOKING
STAGE EFFECT	STEADY PULSE	STOP TALKING
STAGE FRIGHT	STEADY TREND	STOP TEASING
STAGE MAKE-UP	STEAL A MARCH	STOP THE FLOW
STAGE PLAYER	STEAM COOKER	STOP TO THINK
STAGE STRUCK	STEAMED FISH	STOP WORKING
STAIR CARPET	STEAM ENGINE	STORE OF NUTS
STAKE A CLAIM	STEAMING HOT	STORM CENTRE
STALK ABROAD	STEAM LAUNCH	STORM CLOUDS
STALKY AND CO.	STEEL GIRDER	STORM SIGNAL
STAMP DEALER	STEEL HELMET	STORM TROOPS
STAND A DRINK	ST ELMO'S FIRE	STORMY NIGHT
STAND AGHAST	STEM THE TIDE	STORMY SCENE
STANDARD ONE	STEM TO STERN	STORY WRITER
STAND A ROUND	STEP FORWARD	STOUT CORTEZ
STAND AROUND	STEP OUTSIDE	STOUT EFFORT

STOUT FELLOW
STRAIGHT BAT
STRAIGHT HIT
STRAIGHT MAN
STRAIGHT OFF
STRAIGHT OUT
STRAIGHT RUN
STRAIGHT SET
STRAIGHT TIP
STRAIGHT WIN
STRANGE LAND
STRAY BULLET
STRAY REMARK
STREAM FORTH
STREET CRIES
STREET LEVEL
STREET OF INK
STREET SCENE
STRICT ORDER
STRICT TEMPO
STRICT TRUTH
STRIDE ALONG
STRIKE A BLOW
STRIKE A NOTE
STRIKE A POSE
STRIKE BLIND
STRIKE LUCKY
STRING ALONG
STRING BEANS
STRING MUSIC
STRIP OF LAND
STRIVE AFTER
STRONG DRINK
STRONG FAITH
STRONG LIGHT
STRONG POINT
STRONG PULSE
STRONG SMELL
STRONG TASTE
STRONG VIEWS
STRONG VOICE
STRONG WORDS
STUB ONE'S TOE
STUD EARRING
STUDENT BODY
STUDENT DAYS
STUDENTS' RAG
STUDIO COUCH
STUFFED BIRD
STUFFED FOWL
STUFF IT AWAY
STUMBLE OVER
STUMBLE UPON
STUMP ORATOR
STUNT FLYING
STURDY FRAME

STURDY LIMBS
ST VALENTINE
SUAVE MANNER
SUBLIME LIFE
SUCH AND SUCH
SUDDEN BREAK
SUDDEN DEATH
SUDDEN SHOCK
SUE FOR LIBEL
SUE FOR PEACE
SUET PUDDING
SUFFER A BLOW
SUFFER A LOSS
SUICIDE CLUB
SUICIDE NOTE
SUICIDE PACT
SUIT OF CARDS
SUMMER DRESS
SUMMIT LEVEL
SUMMIT TALKS
SUM OF THINGS
SUNDAY HOURS
SUNDAY JOINT
SUNDAY LUNCH
SUNDAY NIGHT
SUNDAY PAPER
SUNDAY TIMES
SUNDRY ITEMS
SUNK IN GLOOM
SUNNY SIDE UP
SUNSET STRIP
SUPERIOR AIR
SUPPER PARTY
SUPPER TABLE
SUPPORT LIFE
SUPPLY DEPOT
SUPREME GOOD
SURE FOOTING
SURFACE AREA
SURFACE MAIL
SURPLUS CASH
SURREY HILLS
SUSSEX DOWNS
SWALLOW DIVE
SWANEE RIVER
SWANSEA TOWN
SWARM OF ANTS
SWARM OF BEES
SWEAR AN OATH
SWEAR ON OATH
SWEATER GIRL
SWEDISH BATH
SWEENEY TODD
SWEET AND LOW
SWEET AS A NUT
SWEET DREAMS

SWEET NATURE
SWEET PICKLE
SWEET POTATO
SWEET SHERRY
SWEET TEMPER
SWEET THINGS
SWELLED HEAD
SWIFT GLANCE
SWIFT OF FOOT
SWISS CANTON
SWISS CHALET
SWISS CHEESE
SWISS GUARDS
SWISS RESORT
SWIVEL CHAIR
SWOLLEN HEAD
SWORD IN HAND
SWORD THRUST
SYDNEY SMITH
SYRUP OF FIGS

T – 11

TABLE FOR TWO
TABLE TENNIS
TACTICAL WAR
TAINTED GOLD
TAINTED LOVE
TAKE A CENSUS
TAKE A CHANCE
TAKE A CORNER
TAKE A COURSE
TAKE A CRUISE
TAKE A DEGREE
TAKE A GANDER
TAKE A HEADER
TAKE A LETTER
TAKE AN OFFER
TAKE A NUMBER
TAKE A PLEDGE
TAKE A POWDER
TAKE A STROLL
TAKE A TICKET
TAKE A TUMBLE
TAKE A WICKET
TAKE BY FORCE
TAKE BY STORM
TAKE CAPTIVE
TAKE CHANCES
TAKE COMFORT
TAKE COMMAND
TAKE COUNSEL
TAKE COURAGE
TAKE LESSONS
TAKE LIGHTLY
TAKE NO RISKS

TAKE OFFENCE	TAX AND SPEND	TERM OF YEARS
TAKE ON BOARD	TAX INCREASE	TERSE SPEECH
TAKE ONE'S CUE	TEA AND CAKES	TEST CRICKET
TAKE ON TRUST	TEA AND TOAST	TESTING TIME
TAKE ON WATER	TEA CANISTER	TEST OF SKILL
TAKE-OVER BID	TEACHER'S PET	THAMES BASIN
TAKE POT-LUCK	TEACH SCHOOL	THANK HEAVEN!
TAKE SHELTER	TEACH TO READ	THAT IS TO SAY
TAKE STOCK OF	TEACH TO RIDE	THAT'S THE WAY
TAKE THE BAIT	TEACH TO SWIM	THAT'S TORN IT
TAKE THE CAKE	TEA FOR THREE	THE ALMIGHTY
TAKE THE HELM	TEA INTERVAL	THE ALPHABET
TAKE THE HINT	TEAM CAPTAIN	THE ATLANTIC
TAKE THE LEAD	TEA MERCHANT	THEATRE BILL
TAKE THE LIFT	TEAM OF MULES	THEATRE CLUB
TAKE THE OATH	TEAM SUPPORT	THEATRE LAND
TAKE THE VEIL	TEAR ASUNDER	THEATRE SEAT
TAKE THOUGHT	TEARS OF PITY	THEATRE SHOW
TAKE TIME OFF	TEARS OF RAGE	THE AVENGERS
TAKE TO COURT	TEA STRAINER	THE BARBICAN
TAKE TO DRINK	TEA WITH MILK	THE BASTILLE
TAKE TO HEART	TEDIOUS TASK	THE BEREAVED
TAKE TOO MUCH	TEDIOUS WORK	THE BEST PART
TAKE TROUBLE	TEEMING RAIN	THE BIG APPLE
TAKE UMBRAGE	TEEN-AGE CLUB	THE BIG HOUSE
TAKE UP A CASE	TEETH ON EDGE	THE BISMARCK
TAKE WARNING	TELEGRAM BOY	THE BITER BIT
TALENT MONEY	TELL AGAINST	THE BLUE LAMP
TALENT SCOUT	TELL NO TALES	THE BOAT RACE
TALKING BIRD	TELL THE TALE	THE CANARIES
TALKING BOOK	TELL THE TIME	THE CENOTAPH
TALKING DOLL	TEMPLE BELLS	THE CHAMPION
TALKING HEAD	TEMPUS FUGIT	THE CHEVIOTS
TALKING SHOP	TEN AND A HALF	THE CLASSICS
TALK OUT TIME	TENDER HEART	THE COLONIES
TALK RUBBISH	TENDER MERCY	THE CONQUEST
TALK TOO MUCH	TENDER STEAK	THE CREATION
TALK TREASON	TENDER YEARS	THE CRUEL SEA
TALK TWADDLE	TEND THE SICK	THE CRUSADES
TALL AND SLIM	TENNIS COURT	THE DAY AFTER
TALLEST GIRL	TENNIS DRESS	THE EIGHTIES
TAMMANY HALL	TENNIS ELBOW	THE ELEMENTS
TAM O'SHANTER	TENNIS MATCH	THE FAITHFUL
TANK WARFARE	TEN OF HEARTS	THE FINE ARTS
TAPE COUNTER	TEN OF SPADES	THE FIRST TWO
TAPE MACHINE	TEN OF TRUMPS	THE FUGITIVE
TAP ONE'S FEET	TEN OR ELEVEN	THE GAME IS UP
TAP ONE'S FOOT	TENSE MOMENT	THE GREATEST
TAP THE WIRES	TENS MACHINE	THE GREAT WAR
TARRY AWHILE	TENTH LETTER	THE GREEN MAN
TARTAN PLAID	TENTH OF JULY	THE GOLD RUSH
TARTAN SHIRT	TENTH OF JUNE	THE GOOD BOOK
TARTAN SKIRT	TEN THOUSAND	THE HAVE-NOTS
TARTAN SOCKS	TENTH STOREY	THE HEBRIDES
TASTY MORSEL	TENTH VOLUME	THE HIGH SEAS
TATE GALLERY	TERM OF ABUSE	THE HOLY CITY

THE HOLY LAND	THE SIMPSONS	THIS CENTURY
THE HUNT IS UP	THE SKIN GAME	THIS DAY WEEK
THE HUSTINGS	THE SORBONNE	THIS ENGLAND
THE INFINITE	THESPIAN ART	THIS INSTANT
THE INKSPOTS	THE SQUEAKER	THIS MORNING
THE INNER MAN	THE SUPREMES	THIS TUESDAY
THE INNOCENT	THE TAJ MAHAL	THOMAS HARDY
THE INTERIOR	THE TALISMAN	THRASH IT OUT
THE JUNGFRAU	THE THIRD MAN	THREAD BEADS
THE KATTEGAT	THE THIRTIES	THREAT OF WAR
THE KING AND I	THE TROUBLES	THREE A PENNY
THE LAST GASP	THE TWENTIES	THREE CHEERS
THE LAST PAGE	THE TREASURY	THREE COPIES
THE LAST POST	THE UNIVERSE	THREE DECKER
THE LAST WORD	THE VERY FACT	THREE EIGHTS
THE LIBERALS	THE VERY SAME	THREE FIFTHS
THE LION KING	THE VERY SPOT	THREE GRACES
THE LISTENER	THE WALL GAME	THREE HEARTS
THE LOVED ONE	THE WAXWORKS	THREE KNAVES
THE LOWLANDS	THE WELL-TO-DO	THREE MONTHS
THE LUDDITES	THE WHOLE HOG	THREE O'CLOCK
THE MAJORITY	THE WHOLE LOT	THREE OR FOUR
THE MARATHON	THE WILD DUCK	THREE OUNCES
THE MIDLANDS	THE WOOLSACK	THREE POINTS
THE MILKY WAY	THICK SPEECH	THREE POUNDS
THE MIND'S EYE	THICK STRING	THREE QUARTS
THE MINISTRY	THIEF OF TIME	THREE QUEENS
THE MINORITY	THIN AS A LATH	THREE SEVENS
THE MOHICANS	THIN AS A RAKE	THREE SPADES
THE MONUMENT	THINKING CAP	THREE TENTHS
THE MOUNTIES	THINK IT OVER	THREE THREES
THE NAKED EYE	THINK MUCH OF	THREE TRICKS
THE NEAR EAST	THINK WELL OF	THREE WHEELS
THE NEW WORLD	THIN RED LINE	THREE WISHES
THE NINETIES	THIRD CHOICE	THREE VERSES
THE OBSERVER	THIRD COURSE	THRESH ABOUT
THE OCCIDENT	THIRD DEGREE	THROUGH ROAD
THE OLD FOLKS	THIRD ESTATE	THROUGH TRIP
THE OLD GUARD	THIRD FINGER	THROW A LIGHT
THE OLD WORLD	THIRD LEAGUE	THROW A PARTY
THE ONCE-OVER	THIRD LESSON	THROW A PUNCH
THE OPEN ROAD	THIRD LETTER	THROW STONES
THE OTHER DAY	THIRD OF JULY	THRUST ASIDE
THE OTHER MAN	THIRD OF JUNE	THUMPING LIE
THE OTHER ONE	THIRD PERSON	TICKLED PINK
THE OTHER WAY	THIRD SEASON	TICKLE TROUT
THE PANTHEON	THIRD STOREY	TICKLISH JOB
THE PENNINES	THIRD STROKE	TIDAL WATERS
THE PENTAGON	THIRD VOLUME	TIDE ONE OVER
THE PROPHETS	THIRST AFTER	TIED COTTAGE
THE PYRAMIDS	THIRSTY WORK	TIED IN A KNOT
THE PYRENEES	THIRTY FORTY	TIES OF BLOOD
THE QUEEN VIC	THIRTY MILES	TIGHT CORNER
THE REVEREND	THIRTY TIMES	TILL THE SOIL
THERMAL UNIT	THIRTY YEARS	TIMBER TRADE
THE SERVICES	THIS AND THAT	TIME AND TIDE

TIME CAPSULE	TOPICAL NEWS	TREAD WARILY
TIME ELEMENT	TOP SERGEANT	TREE DWELLER
TIME IS MONEY	TOP TO BOTTOM	TREE SURGERY
TIME MACHINE	TORCH SINGER	TRENCH FEVER
TIME OF NIGHT	TORPEDO BOAT	TRENT BRIDGE
TIMES CHANGE	TORPEDO TUBE	TRIAL BY JURY
TIMES SQUARE	TOSS AND TURN	TRIAL FLIGHT
TIME TO GET UP	TOTAL AMOUNT	TRIAL PERIOD
TIME TO LEAVE	TOTAL CHANGE	TRIAL STAKES
TIME TO SPARE	TOTAL DEFEAT	TRICK RIDING
TIME TO START	TOTAL NUMBER	TRICKY DICKY
TIME TO THINK	TOTAL OUTPUT	TRIED BY JURY
TIME TO WASTE	TO THE BOTTOM	TRIM THE HAIR
TINKER'S CUSS	TO THE LETTER	TRIM THE LAMP
TINKER'S DAMN	TO THE MINUTE	TRIM THE WICK
TINNED BEANS	TO THE RESCUE	TRINITY HALL
TINNED FRUIT	TO THE TUNE OF	TRINITY TERM
TINNED GOODS	TO THE UTMOST	TRIPLE CROWN
TINNED MUSIC	TOTTER ABOUT	TRIPLE EVENT
TINNED PEARS	TOUCH BOTTOM	TRIP LIGHTLY
TIN OF POLISH	TOUCH GROUND	TRITE REMARK
TIN OF SALMON	TOUCH SCREEN	TRIUMPH OVER
TIN PAN ALLEY	TOUCH TYPING	TRIVIAL LOSS
TIN SOLDIERS	TOUCH TYPIST	TROJAN HORSE
TIP THE SCALE	TOUGH AS TEAK	TROLLEY JACK
TIRED OF LIFE	TOUR DE FORCE	TROPICAL KIT
TISSUE PAPER	TOUSLED HAIR	TROPICAL SEA
TITLE HOLDER	TOUT DE SUITE	TROPICAL SUN
TOAST MASTER	TOUT LE MONDE	TROUBLE FREE
TOBACCO DUTY	TOWER BRIDGE	TROUBLE SPOT
TOBACCO ROAD	TOWER OF PISA	TROUT STREAM
TOBOGGAN RUN	TOWN AND GOWN	TRUCK DRIVER
TODDLE ALONG	TOWN COUNCIL	TRUDGE ALONG
TOFFEE APPLE	TOWN DWELLER	TRUE ACCOUNT
TOILET BRUSH	TRACY ISLAND	TRUE COLOURS
TOILET WATER	TRADE SECRET	TRUE EQUINOX
TOKEN OF LOVE	TRADING POST	TRUE PICTURE
TOLL THE BELL	TRAFFIC LANE	TRUE READING
TOM AND JERRY	TRAGIC EVENT	TRUE TO SCALE
TOMATO JUICE	TRAGIC IRONY	TRULY SPOKEN
TOMATO SAUCE	TRAGIC SCENE	TRUMPET CALL
TOMMY ATKINS	TRAIL BEHIND	TRUNDLE DOWN
TOMMY COOPER	TRAIL BLAZER	TRUST TO LUCK
TOMMY DORSEY	TRAIL DRIVER	TRUSTY STEED
TOMMY STEELE	TRAIL OF DUST	TRUSTY SWORD
TOMMY TUCKER	TRAIL OF SAND	TRUTH TO TELL
TONE CONTROL	TRAINED BAND	TRYING TIMES
TONE OF VOICE	TRAIN STRIKE	TRY ONE'S BEST
TON OF BRICKS	TRAMPLE DOWN	TRY ONE'S HAND
TO NO PURPOSE	TRANSFER FEE	TRY ONE'S LUCK
TONS AND TONS	TRAVEL ABOUT	TRY TO BE FAIR
TONS OF MONEY	TRAVEL AGENT	TRY TO PLEASE
TONY HANCOCK	TRAVEL ALONG	TRY, TRY AGAIN
TOO FAMILIAR	TRAVEL LIGHT	TUBE STATION
TOO MUCH ROOM	TREACLE TART	TUDOR PERIOD
TOP-BACK ROOM	TREAD SOFTLY	TUESDAY WEEK

TUFT OF GRASS
TUITION FEES
TURIN SHROUD
TURKISH BATH
TURN AGAINST
TURN CRIMSON
TURN HOSTILE
TURN OF SPEED
TURN OUT WELL
TURN THE PAGE
TURN THE TIDE
TURN TO ASHES
TURN TO STONE
TURN TRAITOR
TURN UPWARDS
TWEED JACKET
TWELFTH HOLE
TWELFTH HOUR
TWELFTH PART
TWELVE DOZEN
TWELVE GROSS
TWELVE HOURS
TWELVE MILES
TWELVE PARTS
TWELVE SCORE
TWELVE TIMES
TWELVE WEEKS
TWELVE YEARS
TWENTY MILES
TWENTY TIMES
TWENTY TO ONE
TWENTY WEEKS
TWICE A MONTH
TWICE AS MUCH
TWICE AS NICE
TWICE ELEVEN
TWICE THE MAN
TWICE TWELVE
TWICE WEEKLY
TWICE YEARLY
TWIN BROTHER
TWIN PARADOX
TWIN SISTERS
TWIST AROUND
TWIST THE ARM
TWO AND A HALF
TWO DIAMONDS
TWO EXTREMES
TWO-FEET TALL
TWO-FOOT RULE
TWO FURLONGS
TWO HUSBANDS
TWO NO-TRUMPS
TWO OF A TRADE
TWO OF SPADES
TWO OF TRUMPS

TWO'S COMPANY
TWO SEVENTHS
TWO THOUSAND
TYPE A LETTER
TYPICAL CASE
TYPING ERROR
TYPING SPEED
TYPISTS' POOL
TYROLEAN HAT

U – 11

UGLY RUFFIAN
UGLY SISTERS
UGLY THOUGHT
UGLY WEATHER
ULTIMATE END
ULTIMA THULE
ULTRA VIOLET
UMBRELLA MAN
UNABLE TO PAY
UNBROKEN RUN
UNCALLED FOR
UNDER A CLOUD
UNDER A CURSE
UNDER ARREST
UNDER A SPELL
UNDER CANVAS
UNDER DURESS
UNDER NOTICE
UNDER ORDERS
UNDER PAROLE
UNDER REPAIR
UNDER REVIEW
UNDER STRAIN
UNDER STRESS
UNDER THE MAT
UNDER THE SEA
UNDER THE SUN
UNDER WEIGHT
UNDYING LOVE
UNEASY TRUCE
UNFAIR MEANS
UNFAIR PRICE
UNFIT FOR USE
UNFOLD A TALE
UNHOLY NOISE
UNIFORM HEAT
UNIFORM SIZE
UNION LEADER
UNITED FRONT
UNITED PRESS
UNIT OF SOUND
UNLAWFUL ACT
UNLICKED CUB
UNLUCKY STAR

UNPAID LEAVE
UNSHED TEARS
UNSOUND MIND
UNTIMELY END
UNUSUAL NAME
UP AGAINST IT
UP AND COMING
UP FOR THE CUP
UP FOR THE DAY
UPHILL CLIMB
UPHILL FIGHT
UP ON A CHARGE
UPPER CIRCLE
UPPER SCHOOL
UPPER STOREY
UPRIGHT POST
UPS AND DOWNS
UP THE REBELS!
UP THE STAIRS
UP THE STREET
UP THE THAMES
UP TO SCRATCH
UP TO THE EARS
UP TO THE EYES
UP TO THE HILT
UP TO THE MARK
UP TO THE NECK
UPWARD TREND
URBAN LEGEND
URBAN SPRAWL
USELESS WORD
USE ONE'S EARS
USE ONE'S HEAD
USE ONE'S LOAF
USE ONE'S WITS
USE THE KNIFE
USE THE 'PHONE
USE THE PRESS
USE VIOLENCE
USUAL CUSTOM
UTMOST SPEED
UTTER BUNKUM
UTTER COWARD
UTTER DEFEAT
UTTER MISERY

V – 11

VACANT HOUSE
VACANT STARE
VACUUM BRAKE
VACUUM FLASK
VAGRANCY ACT
VAIN ATTEMPT
VAL DOONICAN
VALE OF TEARS

VALID REASON
VALLEY FORGE
VANITY TABLE
VAPOUR TRAIL
VARIETY SHOW
VAST ACREAGE
VAST EXPANSE
VAST EXPENSE
VATICAN CITY
VAULTED ROOF
VELVET GLOVE
VELVET TREAD
VENETIAN RED
VENICE BEACH
VENN DIAGRAM
VENUS DI MILO
VERY PLEASED
VERY SPECIAL
VERY STRANGE
VERY WELL OFF
VERY WORRIED
VESTA TILLEY
V FOR VICTORY
VICAR OF BRAY
VICTORIA DAY
VICTORY ROLL
VICTORY SIGN
VIDEO CAMERA
VIDEO SIGNAL
VIENNA WOODS
VILLAGE FÉTE
VILLAGE HALL
VILLAGE LIFE
VILLAGE POND
VILLAGE PUMP
VILLAGE SHOP
VILLAGE TALK
VILLAGE TEAM
VINTAGE PORT
VINTAGE WINE
VINTAGE YEAR
VIOLENT BLOW
VIOLENT RAGE
VIRGIN BIRTH
VIRGIN QUEEN
VIRILE STYLE
VISITING DAY
VITAL ENERGY
VITAMIN PILL
VIVID COLOUR
VIVID YELLOW
VIVIEN LEIGH
VIV RICHARDS
VOCAL CHORDS
VOCAL EFFORT
VOCAL NUMBER

VOCAL ORGANS
VOCAL TALENT
VOICE OF DOOM
VOID OF SENSE
VOLATILE OIL
VOLATILE WIT
VOLCANIC ASH
VOLUME THREE
VOTE AGAINST
VOTE BY PROXY
VOTE LIBERAL
VOTE TO ORDER
VOTING PAPER

W – 11

WADDLE ALONG
WADE THROUGH
WAG ONE'S HEAD
WAGON WHEELS
WAILING WALL
WAIT A MINUTE
WAIT A MOMENT
WAIT A SECOND
WAIT AT TABLE
WAITING GAME
WAITING LIST
WAITING ROOM
WAKE THE DEAD
WAKE UP EARLY
WAKING DREAM
WAKING HOURS
WALK IN FRONT
WALKING BASS
WALKING PACE
WALKING RACE
WALKING TOUR
WALK OFF WITH
WALK OUT WITH
WALK QUICKLY
WALK TOWARDS
WALK UPRIGHT
WALL BRACKET
WALL OF DEATH
WALL OF FLAME
WALL OF SOUND
WALLOW IN MUD
WALTER MITTY
WALTER SCOTT
WALT WHITMAN
WANDER ABOUT
WANDER ALONG
WANING LIGHT
WANT OF FAITH
WAR AND PEACE
WAR CRIMINAL

WARD OF COURT
WARD ORDERLY
WARM AS TOAST
WARM CLIMATE
WARM CLOTHES
WARM COUNTRY
WAR MEASURES
WAR MEMORIAL
WAR MINISTER
WARM WEATHER
WARM WELCOME
WAR NEUROSES
WARNING LOOK
WARNING NOTE
WARNING SHOT
WARNING SIGN
WAR OF NERVES
WARP AND WEFT
WARP AND WOOF
WASHING SOAP
WASHING SODA
WASTE GROUND
WASTE NO TIME
WASTE OF TIME
WATCHFUL EYE
WATCH POCKET
WATCH POINTS
WATER BABIES
WATER COLOUR
WATERED SILK
WATER FILTER
WATERLOO CUP
WATER OF LIFE
WATER PISTOL
WATER SKIING
WATER SPORTS
WATER SUPPLY
WATER TRAVEL
WATER VAPOUR
WATERY GRAVE
WAVE GOODBYE
WEAK AS WATER
WEAKEST LINK
WEAK LOOKING
WEAK SERVICE
WEAK STOMACH
WEALD OF KENT
WEAR AND TEAR
WEARY WILLIE
WEASEL WORDS
WEATHER SHIP
WEATHER SIDE
WEAVE A SPELL
WEAVE SPELLS
WEB OF DECEIT
WEDDED BLISS

WEDDING CAKE
WEDDING CARD
WEDDING HYMN
WEDDING RING
WEDDING VOWS
WEEKLY PAPER
WEEK'S NOTICE
WEIGH ANCHOR
WEIRD SISTER
WELCOME GIFT
WELCOME HOME
WELCOME SIGN
WELFARE WORK
WELL AND GOOD
WELL CONTENT
WELL GROOMED
WELL IN FRONT
WELL MATCHED
WELL OUT OF IT
WELL-READ MAN
WELL-TO-DO MAN
WELL WORTH IT
WELL WRITTEN
WELSH ACCENT
WELSH BORDER
WELSH COLLIE
WELSH GUARDS
WELSH LEGEND
WELSH RABBIT
WELSH WIZARD
WEND ONE'S WAY
WENT FLAT OUT
WEST AFRICAN
WEST BY NORTH
WEST BY SOUTH
WEST CENTRAL
WEST COUNTRY
WESTERN ROLE
WESTERN ROLL
WESTERN WALL
WEST GERMANY
WET ONE'S LIPS
WE WUZ ROBBED
WHACKING LIE
WHAT A RELIEF!
WHAT HAVE YOU
WHAT'S MY LINE?
WHAT YOU WILL
WHEEL OF LIFE
WHEEL WRENCH
WHEN PIGS FLY
WHIPPING BOY
WHISTLE AWAY
WHISTLE STOP
WHITE AS MILK
WHITE AS SNOW

WHITE BISHOP
WHITE CASTLE
WHITE CIRCLE
WHITE CLIFFS
WHITE COFFEE
WHITE COLLAR
WHITE COTTON
WHITE ENSIGN
WHITE FRIARS
WHITE HORSES
WHITE KNIGHT
WHITE PEPPER
WHITE POWDER
WHITE RABBIT
WHITE RIBBON
WHITE RUSSIA
WHITE SQUARE
WHITE TO MOVE
WHITE TO PLAY
WHITSUN WEEK
WHITTLE AWAY
WHITTLE DOWN
WHO GOES HOME?
WHOLE NUMBER
WICKED FAIRY
WICKED UNCLE
WICKED WITCH
WICKED WORLD
WICKER CHAIR
WIDEN THE GAP
WIDE READING
WIDE VARIETY
WIDOW'S CRUSE
WIDOW'S WEEDS
WIELD THE BAT
WIGHTMAN CUP
WILD COUNTRY
WILD DELIGHT
WILD FLOWERS
WILFUL WASTE
WILLIAM PEAR
WILLIAM PENN
WILLIAM PITT
WILLIAM TELL
WILLING HAND
WILLING HELP
WILL OF ALLAH
WILL SCARLET
WIN A FORTUNE
WINDING ROAD
WIND ONE'S WAY
WINDY CORNER
WINE AND DINE
WINE HARVEST
WINE VINEGAR
WINGED HORSE

WINGED WORDS
WING FORWARD
WING ONE'S WAY
WINK OF SLEEP
WINNING CARD
WINNING GAME
WINNING GOAL
WINNING HAND
WINNING LEAD
WINNING LINE
WINNING MOVE
WINNING POST
WINNING SHOT
WINNING SIDE
WINNING TEAM
WINNING TOSS
WINNING WAYS
WIN ON POINTS
WIN OUTRIGHT
WINSOME WAYS
WINSON GREEN
WINTER SLEEP
WINTER WHEAT
WIN THE FIGHT
WIN THE MATCH
WIN THE POOLS
WIN THE TITLE
WIN THE TRICK
WINTRY SMILE
WIPE THE EYES
WIRELESS SET
WISDOM TOOTH
WISE AS AN OWL
WISE AS SOLON
WISE COUNSEL
WISE OLD BIRD
WISHING WELL
WITCH DOCTOR
WITCHES' BREW
WITCH'S SPELL
WITH ABANDON
WITH HONOURS
WITHIN AN ACE
WITHIN DOORS
WITHIN RANGE
WITHIN REACH
WITHIN SIGHT
WITH KNOBS ON
WITH MEANING
WITHOUT BIAS
WITHOUT FAIL
WITHOUT HOPE
WITHOUT LOSS
WITHOUT PEER
WITHOUT PITY
WITH RESERVE

WITH RESPECT
WITH THE TIDE
WITH THE WIND
WITTY REMARK
WITTY RETORT
WITTY SPEECH
WIZARD PRANG
WOBURN ABBEY
WOLF WHISTLE
WOMAN DOCTOR
WOMAN DRIVER
WOMAN'S WORLD
WOMEN POLICE
WOMEN'S GUILD
WOOD ALCOHOL
WOODEN FRAME
WOODEN HORSE
WOODEN SPOON
WOOL SHEARER
WORD FOR WORD
WORD OF MOUTH
WORD PERFECT
WORD PICTURE
WORDS FAIL ME!
WORK AGAINST
WORK AND PLAY
WORK AS A TEAM
WORKING LIFE
WORKING WEEK
WORKOUT TAPE
WORKS OUTING
WORK TO DEATH
WORK WONDERS
WORLD BEATER
WORLD CRUISE
WORLD EVENTS
WORLDLY WISE
WORLD RECORD
WORLDS APART
WORLD TO COME
WORLD-WAR ONE
WORLD-WAR TWO
WORM ONE'S WAY
WORRIED LOOK
WORSE TO COME
WORTH SEEING
WORTHY CAUSE
WRAPPED LOAF
WRESTLE WITH
WRETCHED MAN
WRINGING WET
WRITE A LYRIC
WRITE A NOVEL
WRITE A STORY
WRITE IT DOWN
WRITE POETRY

WRITING DESK
WRITING ROOM
WRITTEN WORD
WRONG ANSWER
WRONG CHANGE
WRONG COURSE
WRONG MOMENT
WRONG NUMBER
WRONG PERSON
WRONG TICKET
WROUGHT IRON

Y – 11

YACHTING CAP
YACHT RACING
YARD MEASURE
YEAR AND A DAY
YEAR OF GRACE
YEARS GONE BY
YEARS TO COME
YELLOW FEVER
YELLOW METAL
YELLOW OCHRE
YELLOW PAINT
YELLOW PERIL
YELLOW PRESS
YELLOW RIVER
YELLOW SANDS
YELLOW SPOTS
YIELD A POINT
YOGIC FLYING
YOLK OF AN EGG
YORK MINSTER
YOU AND YOURS
YOU DIRTY RAT
YOUNG AND OLD
YOUNGEST BOY
YOUNGEST SON
YOUNG MONKEY
YOUNG PEOPLE
YOUNG PERSON
YOUNG RASCAL
YOUR MAJESTY
YOUR OPINION
YOURS ALWAYS
YOUR VERSION
YOUR VERY OWN
YOUR WORSHIP
YOUTH CENTRE
YOUTH HOSTEL
YOUTH LEADER

Z – 11

ZIP FASTENER

ZONE THERAPY

A – 12

ABBEY THEATRE
ABILITY TO MIX
ABJECT SPIRIT
ABLATIVE CASE
ABOUT AVERAGE
ABOVE AVERAGE
ABOVE THE LINE
ABRUPT MANNER
ABSOLUTE COLD
ABSOLUTE FACT
ABSOLUTE FOOL
ABSOLUTE RULE
ABSOLUTE ZERO
ABSTRACT IDEA
ABSTRACT NOUN
ABSTRACT TERM
ABSURD MANNER
ABUSE THE MIND
ACADEMY AWARD
ACCEPT ADVICE
ACCEPT DEFEAT
ACCEPT IN TOTO
ACCEPT OFFICE
ACCIDENT SPOT
ACE IN THE HOLE
ACHILLES' HEEL
ACROSS THE SKY
ACROSS THE WAY
ACT FOOLISHLY
ACT IN CONCERT
ACTION REPLAY
ACTION SCHOOL
ACTIVE MEMBER
ACT LIKE A FOOL
ACT LIKE MAGIC
ACT OF CHARITY
ACT OF COURAGE
ACT OF TREASON
ACT OF WORSHIP
ACT OF IMPULSE
ACTOR MANAGER
ACTORS' STUDIO
ADAGIO DANCER
ADD A FEW WORDS
ADDER'S TONGUE
ADDITION SIGN
ADD TO THE LIST
ADELINA PATTI
ADHESIVE TAPE
ADJUTANT BIRD
ADMIT NOTHING
ADMIT ONE'S AGE

ADMITTED FACT
ADMITTED FREE
ADOPTED CHILD
ADVANCED IDEA
ADVANCE GUARD
ADVANCE PARTY
AERATED WATER
AERIAL SURVEY
AESOP'S FABLES
AFFECTED AIRS
AFFINITY CARD
A FINE ROMANCE
AFRICAN QUEEN
AFTERNOON NAP
AFTERNOON TEA
AFTER SUNDOWN
AFTER THE BALL
AFTER THE FACT
AFTER THE RAIN
AGE OF CONSENT
AGREED RESULT
AGREE TO TERMS
AIM AT THE MOON
AIR COMMODORE
AIR-FORCE BLUE
AIR OF MYSTERY
AIR OF TRIUMPH
AIR ONE'S VIEWS
AIR PASSENGER
AIR PERSONNEL
AIR-SEA RESCUE
AIR TRANSPORT
AIR TRAVELLER
ALADDIN'S CAVE
ALADDIN'S LAMP
ALAN MELVILLE
ALAS AND ALACK!
ALBERT BRIDGE
ALBERT FINNEY
ALBERT SQUARE
ALDOUS HUXLEY
ALDWYCH FARCE
ALEC GUINNESS
ALEXANDRA DAY
ALFRESCO MEAL
ALGERIAN WINE
ALICE SPRINGS
ALIEN ELEMENT
ALIGN ONESELF
ALL AND SUNDRY
ALL ATTENTION
ALL BY ONESELF
ALLIED FORCES
ALLIED TROOPS
ALL IN THE GAME
ALL IN THE MIND

ALL IS NOT LOST
ALL MOONSHINE
ALL MY OWN WORK
ALL NIGHT LONG
ALL OF A DITHER
ALL OF A QUIVER
ALL OF A SUDDEN
ALL OF THE TIME
ALL ON ONE SIDE
ALL ON ONE'S OWN
ALL OR NOTHING
ALLOTTED SPAN
ALLOTTED TASK
ALLOW TO STAND
ALL SAINTS' DAY
ALL STEAMED UP
ALL SYSTEMS GO
ALL THE BETTER
ALL THE FAMILY
ALL THE OTHERS
ALL TO PLAY FOR
ALL TO THE GOOD
ALMOND TOFFEE
A LONG TIME AGO
ALPACA JACKET
ALPHA TO OMEGA
ALPINE FLOWER
ALPINE GARDEN
ALTER THE CASE
AMATEUR ACTOR
AMATEUR BOXER
AMATEUR NIGHT
AMATEUR STAGE
AMBER GAMBLER
AMERICAN FLAG
AMERICAN NAVY
A MILE A MINUTE
AMONG FRIENDS
AMOROUS DITTY
AMUSE ONESELF
ANCHOVY PASTE
ANCHOVY SAUCE
ANCIENT HOUSE
ANCIENT ROMAN
ANCIENT RUINS
ANCIENT TIMES
ANCIENT WORLD
ANEURIN BEVAN
ANGELIC SMILE
ANGEL OF DEATH
ANGEL OF MERCY
ANGELS OF MONS
ANGORA RABBIT
ANGRY SILENCE
ANIMAL DOCTOR
ANIMAL RIGHTS

ANKLE SUPPORT
ANNA KARENINA
ANNE HATHAWAY
ANNE OF CLEVES
ANNUAL AFFAIR
ANNUAL BUDGET
ANNUAL DINNER
ANNUAL OUTING
ANNUAL REPORT
ANNUAL RETURN
ANOTHER GUESS
ANOTHER STORY
ANOTHER THING
ANY QUESTIONS
ANYTHING GOES
APOSTLE SPOON
APPEAL TO ARMS
APPLE BLOSSOM
APPLE FRITTER
APPLE HARVEST
APPLE OF SODOM
APPLE ORCHARD
APPLY FOR A JOB
APPLY FOR BAIL
APPLY ONESELF
APPLY THE MIND
APPROACH ROAD
APPROACH SHOT
APPROVED LIST
APRIL IN PARIS
APRIL SHOWERS
APRON STRINGS
APTITUDE TEST
APT QUOTATION
AQUATIC PLANT
AQUATIC SPORT
AQUILINE NOSE
ARCH CRIMINAL
ARCH OF HEAVEN
ARCH ONE'S BACK
ARCTIC CIRCLE
ARCTIC REGION
ARCTIC WINTER
ARDENT SPIRIT
ARGUE THE CASE
ARGUE THE TOSS
ARMED ROBBERY
ARMISTICE DAY
ARMY CHAPLAIN
ARMY EXERCISE
ARMY GRATUITY
ARMY PAY CORPS
ARMY QUARTERS
ARNOLD PALMER
ARNOLD WESKER
ARRANGE A DATE

ARRESTER GEAR
ARRIVE ON TIME
ART CRITICISM
ARTERIAL ROAD
ARTESIAN WELL
ARTFUL DODGER
ARTHUR MILLER
ARTISTIC WORK
ARTIST'S MODEL
ARTIST'S PROOF
ART OF DEFENCE
ART OF HEALING
ART TREASURES
ASBESTOS SUIT
AS BLACK AS INK
AS BUSY AS A BEE
ASCENSION DAY
AS CLEAR AS DAY
AS CLEAR AS MUD
ASCOT GOLD CUP
AS GOOD AS DEAD
AS GOOD AS EVER
AS GOOD AS GOLD
ASHES TO ASHES
ASH WEDNESDAY
ASK A QUESTION
ASK FOR ADVICE
ASK FOR CREDIT
ASK ME ANOTHER
ASK NO FAVOURS
ASK QUESTIONS
AS LIGHT AS AIR
AS MUCH AS EVER
ASSEMBLY HALL
ASSEMBLY LINE
ASSEMBLY ROOM
ASSUMED TITLE
AS SURE AS EGGS
AS SURE AS FATE
AS SWEET AS PIE
AS UNDERSTOOD
AT A LATER DATE
AT ALL HAZARDS
AT ARM'S LENGTH
AT CLOSE GRIPS
AT DEATH'S DOOR
AT FIRST SIGHT
AT FULL GALLOP
AT FULL LENGTH
ATHLETE'S FOOT
ATLANTIC CITY
ATOMIC ENERGY
ATOMIC NUMBER
ATOMIC THEORY
ATOMIC WEIGHT
AT SECOND-HAND

AT SOME LENGTH
ATTAR OF ROSES
ATTEND CHURCH
AT THE LAUNDRY
AT THE SEASIDE
AT THE STATION
AT THE THEATRE
AT THE WEIGH-IN
AT WHICH PLACE
AUCTION ROOMS
AULD LANG SYNE
AUSTIN FRIARS
AUTUMN CROCUS
AUTUMN LEAVES
AVERAGE CHILD
AVERAGE SPEED
AVERAGE WOMAN
AWAIT PAYMENT
AWAKE THE DEAD
AWAY DULL CARE!
AWAY FROM HOME
AWFUL SILENCE
AWKWARD SQUAD
AZTEC TWO-STEP

B – 12

BABY CARRIAGE
BABY LISTENER
BABY SNATCHER
BACHELOR FLAT
BACHELOR GIRL
BACK AND FORTH
BACK AND FRONT
BACK ENTRANCE
BACKING STORE
BACK OF BEYOND
BACK-ROOM BOYS
BACK THE FIELD
BACK TO BASICS
BACK TO MOTHER
BACK TO NATURE
BACK TO NORMAL
BACKWARD STEP
BACON AND EGGS
BAD BEGINNING
BAD BEHAVIOUR
BAD CHARACTER
BAD CONDUCTOR
BAD DIGESTION
BAD ELOCUTION
BADGE OF MERIT
BAD HALFPENNY
BAD HOUSEWIFE
BAD INFLUENCE
BADLY BEHAVED

BADLY DAMAGED
BADLY WOUNDED
BAD NEIGHBOUR
BAD OF ITS KIND
BAD QUALITIES
BAD REPORTING
BAD TREATMENT
BAG OF TOFFEES
BAILEY BRIDGE
BAKED CUSTARD
BAKEWELL TART
BAKING POWDER
BALANCED DIET
BALANCED MIND
BALANCE SHEET
BALANCE WHEEL
BALANCING ACT
BALCONY SCENE
BALKAN STATES
BALLAD SINGER
BALL AND CHAIN
BALL BEARINGS
BALLET DANCER
BALLET MASTER
BALLET SCHOOL
BALL OF STRING
BALL OF THREAD
BALL-POINT PEN
BALM OF GILEAD
BALTIC STATES
BAMBOO SHOOTS
BANBURY CROSS
BAND OF HEROES
BAND TOGETHER
BANG IN THE EYE
BANG ONE'S HEAD
BANKER'S DRAFT
BANKER'S ORDER
BANKING HOURS
BANK INTEREST
BARBARY COAST
BARBARY SHEEP
BARBER'S CHAIR
BARCLAYS BANK
BARE CUPBOARD
BAREFACED LIE
BARE MAJORITY
BARE ONE'S HEAD
BARGAIN PRICE
BARKING CREEK
BARNABY RUDGE
BARNACLE BILL
BARNES BRIDGE
BARNES COMMON
BARNYARD FOWL
BAROQUE STYLE

BARRED WINDOW
BARREL OF BEER
BARS AND BOLTS
BASEBALL TEAM
BASEMENT FLAT
BASIC ENGLISH
BASK IN THE SUN
BASS CLARINET
BATCH OF BREAD
BATHING BEACH
BATTERING RAM
BATTING ORDER
BATTLE OF LIFE
BATTLE OF WITS
BAY AT THE MOON
BAYONET DRILL
BEACH PYJAMAS
BEAMING SMILE
BEANS ON TOAST
BEARDED WOMAN
BEAR DOWN UPON
BEARD THE LION
BEARD TRIMMER
BEARER CHEQUE
BEAR THE BLAME
BEAR THE BRUNT
BEAT A RETREAT
BEATEN HOLLOW
BEATING HEART
BEAT THE CLOCK
BEAT THE COUNT
BEAUTY OF MIND
BECHER'S BROOK
BECOME PUBLIC
BECOME SILENT
BED OF NETTLES
BED-TIME STORY
BEEF MOUNTAIN
BEEF SANDWICH
BEEF SAUSAGES
BEFORE CHRIST
BEFORE DINNER
BEFORE SUPPER
BEFORE THE WAR
BEG FOR CRUMBS
BEGGAR'S OPERA
BEHIND THE BAR
BELCHER CHAIN
BELGIAN CONGO
BELOVED ENEMY
BELOW AVERAGE
BELOW THE BELT
BELOW THE KNEE
BELOW THE LINE
BELOW THE MARK
BENARES BRASS

BEND BACKWARD
BEND SINISTER
BEND THE ELBOW
BEND THE RULES
BENEFIT MATCH
BENEFIT NIGHT
BENIGN MANNER
BENNY GOODMAN
BE OFF WITH YOU!
BEREFT OF LIFE
BERING STRAIT
BERTRAM MILLS
BESETTING SIN
BESIDE THE SEA
BEST OF THE LOT
BEST ONE CAN DO
BETHNAL GREEN
BET ON THE SIDE
BETRAY A TRUST
BETTER CHOICE
BETTER THINGS
BETTING HOUSE
BETWEEN MEALS
BETWEEN TIMES
BEVERLY HILLS
BEXHILL ON SEA
BEYOND A DOUBT
BEYOND BELIEF
BEYOND BOUNDS
BEYOND REASON
BEYOND RECALL
BEYOND REPAIR
BEYOND THE LAW
BIB AND TUCKER
BIBLE SOCIETY
BIBLE THUMPER
BICYCLE CHAIN
BICYCLE THIEF
BIDE ONE'S TIME
BIG AND LITTLE
BIG HINDRANCE
BIG OFFENSIVE
BILLIARD BALL
BILLIARD HALL
BILLIARD REST
BILLIARD ROOM
BILL OF HEALTH
BILL OF LADING
BILL OF RIGHTS
BILLYCOCK HAT
BINARY NUMBER
BIRDCAGE WALK
BIRD'S-EYE VIEW
BIRD WATCHING
BIRTH CONTROL
BIRTHDAY CAKE

BIRTHDAY CARD
BIRTHDAY GIFT
BIRTHDAY SUIT
BISHOP'S APRON
BISHOP'S MITRE
BITE ONE'S LIPS
BITE THE THUMB
BIT OF AN UPSET
BIT OF SCANDAL
BIT OF TROUBLE
BITTERLY COLD
BITTER MEMORY
BITTER ORANGE
BITTER STRIFE
BITTER TONGUE
BLACK AND BLUE
BLACK AND TANS
BLACK AS NIGHT
BLACK AS PITCH
BLACK CLOTHES
BLACK COUNTRY
BLACK DESPAIR
BLACK ECONOMY
BLACK LOOK-OUT
BLACK OR WHITE
BLACK OUTLOOK
BLACK PANTHER
BLACK PUDDING
BLADE OF GRASS
BLARNEY STONE
BLASTED HEATH
BLAST FURNACE
BLAZE OF GLORY
BLAZE OF LIGHT
BLEACHED HAIR
BLEAK OUTLOOK
BLEED TO DEATH
BLESSED STATE
BLIND BARGAIN
BLIND IMPULSE
BLITHE SPIRIT
BLOATER PASTE
BLOCK LETTERS
BLOCK OF FLATS
BLOCK OF STONE
BLONDE HAIRED
BLOOD AND IRON
BLOOD AND SAND
BLOOD BROTHER
BLOOD DISEASE
BLOODY SUNDAY
BLOOM OF YOUTH
BLOSSOM FORTH
BLOW A WHISTLE
BLOWN SKY-HIGH
BLOW OFF STEAM

BLOW ONE'S MIND
BLOW TO PIECES
BLUE AS THE SKY
BLUE-BLACK INK
BLUE STOCKING
BLUE WITH COLD
BLUFF KING HAL
BOARD MEETING
BOARD OF TRADE
BOB MONKHOUSE
BOB UP AND DOWN
BODY BUILDING
BODY OF TROOPS
BODY SNATCHER
BOHEMIAN GIRL
BOILED SWEETS
BOILING POINT
BOILING WATER
BOIL WITH RAGE
BOLT ONE'S FOOD
BOMB DISPOSAL
BOMBER HARRIS
BOMBER JACKET
BONFIRE NIGHT
BONNY WEE LASS
BOOK A PASSAGE
BOOK A SLEEPER
BOOKING CLERK
BOOK LEARNING
BOOK OF PSALMS
BOOK OF STAMPS
BOOK OF WISDOM
BORDER BALLAD
BORED TO DEATH
BORED TO TEARS
BORIS KARLOFF
BORN IN A TRUNK
BORN OPTIMIST
BORROW A FIVER
BORROW A POUND
BORROWED TIME
BOSOM FRIENDS
BOTH ENDS MEET
BOTH TOGETHER
BOTTLE BLONDE
BOTTLED CIDER
BOTTLED FRUIT
BOTTLED WATER
BOTTLE OF BEER
BOTTLE OF HOCK
BOTTLE OF MILK
BOTTLE OF PORT
BOTTLE OF WINE
BOTTLE OPENER
BOTTLE WARMER
BOTTOM DOLLAR

BOTTOM DRAWER
BOTTOM WEIGHT
BOULTER'S LOCK
BOUNCING BABY
BOUNDARY LINE
BOUND EDITION
BOW AND SCRAPE
BOWLING ALLEY
BOWLING GREEN
BOXING GLOVES
BOX OF MATCHES
BOX ON THE EARS
BOY ARTIFICER
BOY MEETS GIRL
BRACE OF BIRDS
BRACE ONESELF
BRAIN SCANNER
BRAIN SURGEON
BRAIN SURGERY
BRAIN WASHING
BRAISED STEAK
BRAMBLE JELLY
BRANCH MEMBER
BRANCH OFFICE
BRANDED GOODS
BRANDING IRON
BRANDY BOTTLE
BRANDY BUTTER
BRASS SECTION
BRAVE AS A LION
BRAVE ATTEMPT
BRAVE WARRIOR
BREAD AND MILK
BREAD AND WINE
BREAD PUDDING
BREAK A RECORD
BREAK CONTACT
BREAKFAST CUP
BREAK NO BONES
BREAK RECORDS
BREAK SURFACE
BREAK THE BANK
BREAK THE NEWS
BREAK THE RULE
BREAK THE SEAL
BREAK THROUGH
BREAST POCKET
BREAST STROKE
BREATHE AGAIN
BREATH OF LIFE
BREECHES BUOY
BREEZY MANNER
BRICK BY BRICK
BRIDGE LESSON
BRIDGE PLAYER
BRIDGE THE GAP

BRIEF OUTLINE
BRIEF SUMMARY
BRIGADE MAJOR
BRIGHT COLOUR
BRIGHT LIGHTS
BRIGHTON ROCK
BRIGHT PERIOD
BRIGHT PURPLE
BRIGHT YELLOW
BRILLIANT WIT
BRING A CHARGE
BRING COMFORT
BRING FORWARD
BRING THROUGH
BRING TO A HEAD
BRING TO AN END
BRING TO LIGHT
BRING TO TERMS
BRING TO TRIAL
BRISTOL BOARD
BRISTOL CREAM
BRITISH ISLES
BRITISH LIONS
BROAD OUTLINE
BROAD OUTLOOK
BROKEN ACCENT
BROKEN GROUND
BROKEN THREAD
BROKEN VOYAGE
BROKEN WINDOW
BROOK NO DELAY
BROUGHT FORTH
BROWN AND MILD
BROWN WINDSOR
BRUCE FORSYTH
BRUIN THE BEAR
BRUSH AGAINST
BRUSH AND COMB
BRUSSELS LACE
BUCKING HORSE
BUDDHIST MONK
BUDDING ACTOR
BUDDING YOUTH
BUDGET SPEECH
BUGLE-CALL RAG
BUILD A BRIDGE
BUILDER'S MATE
BUILDING LAND
BUILDING PLOT
BUILDING SITE
BUILT-IN FLASH
BUILT OF STONE
BUILT ON A ROCK
BULBOUS PLANT
BULLDOG BREED
BULL ELEPHANT

BUNCH OF ROSES
BUNDLE OF RAGS
BUNSEN BURNER
BURGLAR ALARM
BURIAL GROUND
BURMA CHEROOT
BURNHAM SCALE
BURNING FEVER
BURNING GLASS
BURNING SHAME
BURNING TORCH
BURNT ALMONDS
BURNT FINGERS
BURNT TO ASHES
BURN WITH LOVE
BURST OF ANGER
BURST OF SOUND
BURST OF SPEED
BURY ONE'S HEAD
BUS CONDUCTOR
BUSINESS CARD
BUSINESS DEAL
BUSINESS LIFE
BUSINESS TRIP
BUSTER KEATON
BUTCHER'S SHOP
BUTTERED ROLL
BUTTERFLY NET
BUYER'S MARKET
BY A LONG CHALK
BY COMPARISON
BY EASY STAGES
BY FAR THE BEST
BY PERSUASION
BY THE SEASIDE
BY THE WAYSIDE
BY WAY OF A JOKE

C – 12

CABBAGE PATCH
CABIN CRUISER
CABINET MAKER
CABIN STEWARD
CABLE RAILWAY
CABLE'S LENGTH
CAFÉ CHANTANT
CAIRN TERRIER
CAKED WITH MUD
CALABASH PIPE
CALAMITY JANE
CALENDAR YEAR
CALL A MEETING
CALL FOR ORDER
CALL INTO PLAY
CALL IT SQUARE

CALL OF THE SEA
CALL THE BANNS
CALL TO PRAYER
CALL TO THE BAR
CALYPSO MUSIC
CAMERA OUTFIT
CAMP FOLLOWER
CANARY YELLOW
CANDID CAMERA
CANDID CRITIC
CANDID FRIEND
CANDLE GREASE
CANNON FODDER
CANNON STREET
CANON COLLINS
CANVEY ISLAND
CAPABLE HANDS
CAPE PROVINCE
CAPITAL ASSET
CAPITAL CRIME
CAPITAL GAINS
CAPITAL GOODS
CAPTAIN BLOOD
CAPTAIN SCOTT
CARAFE OF WINE
CARAWAY SEEDS
CARBOLIC ACID
CARBOLIC SOAP
CARBON DATING
CARBON FIBRES
CARDBOARD BOX
CARDINAL'S HAT
CAREFREE MIND
CAREFUL STUDY
CARELESS TALK
CARIBBEAN SEA
CARNEGIE HALL
CARNIVAL TIME
CARNIVAL WEEK
CARPET KNIGHT
CARRIAGE PAID
CARRY A REPORT
CARRY FORWARD
CARRY ONE'S BAT
CARRY THROUGH
CARTE BLANCHE
CARVING KNIFE
CASE OF MURDER
CASE OF SCOTCH
CASE OF WHISKY
CASE THE JOINT
CASE TO ANSWER
CASH AND CARRY
CASH CUSTOMER
CASH ON DEMAND
CASH REGISTER

CASSETTE DECK
CASSETTE TAPE
CAST AWAY FEAR
CAST-IRON CASE
CAST ONE'S VOTE
CAST THE BLAME
CASUAL GLANCE
CASUAL LABOUR
CASUAL MANNER
CASUAL REMARK
CASUALTY LIST
CASUALTY WARD
CASUAL WORKER
CAT AND FIDDLE
CATCH A TARTAR
CATCH BENDING
CATCH NAPPING
CATCH SIGHT OF
CATCH THE POST
CATCH THE TUBE
CAT'S WHISKERS
CATTLE DEALER
CATTLE MARKET
CAUSE CÉLÈBRE
CAUSE OF DELAY
CAUSE OFFENCE
CAUSE TROUBLE
CAUTION MONEY
CAUTIOUS MOVE
CAUTIOUS TYPE
CAVALRY HORSE
CAVALRY TWILL
CAVEAT EMPTOR
CEASE TO EXIST
CEILING PRICE
CEMENT A UNION
CENTURIES OLD
CERTAIN DEATH
CERTAIN ISSUE
CERTAINLY NOT
CERTAIN PLACE
C'EST LA GUERRE
CHAISE LONGUE
CHALLENGE CUP
CHAMBER MUSIC
CHAMPAGNE CUP
CHANCE REMARK
CHANCERY LANE
CHANGE COLOUR
CHANGE COURSE
CHANGE HORSES
CHANGE OF DIET
CHANGE OF FACE
CHANGE OF LUCK
CHANGE OF MIND
CHANGE OF MOOD

CHANGE PLACES
CHANGE TRAINS
CHANGING ROOM
CHAOTIC STATE
CHAPTER HOUSE
CHAPTER THREE
CHARING CROSS
CHARITY MATCH
CHARLES ATLAS
CHARLES BOYER
CHARLES PEACE
CHARLES READE
CHARLES'S WAIN
CHARLEY'S AUNT
CHARLIE BROWN
CHARLIE DRAKE
CHARNEL HOUSE
CHARTER PARTY
CHARTER PLANE
CHASE SHADOWS
CHEAP-DAY FARE
CHEAP EDITION
CHEAP SUCCESS
CHEAP TWISTER
CHEAT AT CARDS
CHECK THE TILL
CHEDDAR GORGE
CHEEK TO CHEEK
CHEEKY MONKEY
CHEERFUL FIRE
CHEERFUL MOOD
CHEERY MANNER
CHEESE STRAWS
CHELSEA CHINA
CHEMICAL FUEL
CHEMICAL TEST
CHEMISTRY SET
CHEMIST'S SHOP
CHERISH HOPES
CHERRY BRANDY
CHESHIRE HOME
CHESS OPENING
CHESS PROBLEM
CHESTNUT TREE
CHEVAL MIRROR
CHEVIOT HILLS
CHICAGO BEARS
CHICKEN CURRY
CHICKEN LIVER
CHIEF CASHIER
CHIEF JUSTICE
CHIEF MOURNER
CHIEF OFFICER
CHIEF OF STAFF
CHIEF SKIPPER
CHIEF STEWARD

CHIEF SUSPECT
CHIEF WITNESS
CHILDE HAROLD
CHILDISH WAYS
CHILD BENEFIT
CHILD PRODIGY
CHILDREN'S TOY
CHILD SUPPORT
CHILD WELFARE
CHILLI PEPPER
CHILLY MANNER
CHIMNEY SWEEP
CHINA CABINET
CHINESE WHITE
CHOCOLATE BAR
CHOCOLATE BOX
CHOCOLATE EGG
CHOICE MORSEL
CHOOSE FREELY
CHOP AND CHIPS
CHOSEN CAREER
CHOSEN PEOPLE
CHRISTIAN ERA
CHRISTMAS BOX
CHRISTMAS DAY
CHRISTMAS EVE
CHROME YELLOW
CHUBBY CHEEKS
CHURCH BAZAAR
CHURCH LIVING
CHURCH MEMBER
CHURCH OF ROME
CHURCH PARADE
CHURCH SCHOOL
CIGARETTE ASH
CIGARETTE END
CIGARETTE TIN
CINEMA SCREEN
CINEMA STUDIO
CINEMA VERITE
CIRCLE AROUND
CIRCUIT COURT
CIRCUIT JUDGE
CIRCULAR TOUR
CITIZENS' BAND
CITY ALDERMAN
CITY BOUNDARY
CITY MERCHANT
CITY OF LONDON
CIVIC WELCOME
CIVIL DEFENCE
CIVILIAN LIFE
CIVILIZED MAN
CIVIL LIBERTY
CIVIL SERVANT
CIVIL SERVICE

CLADDAGH RING
CLAIM A REWARD
CLAIM DAMAGES
CLAP THE HANDS
CLASH OF STEEL
CLASH OF VIEWS
CLASPED HANDS
CLASSICAL AGE
CLASSICAL ART
CLASSIC STYLE
CLASS WARFARE
CLEAN LICENCE
CLEAR AS A BELL
CLEAR OUTLINE
CLEAR PASSAGE
CLEAR THE PATH
CLEAR THE ROAD
CLEAR THE ROOM
CLEAR THOUGHT
CLEAR WARNING
CLEAR WEATHER
CLENCHED FIST
CLERICAL GARB
CLERICAL GREY
CLERICAL WORK
CLERK OF WORKS
CLEVER MANNER
CLEVER SPEECH
CLEVER STROKE
CLIFFORD'S INN
CLIFF RAILWAY
CLIFF RICHARD
CLIMB TO POWER
CLINGING VINE
CLING LIKE IVY
CLINK GLASSES
CLIPPED HEDGE
CLIP THE WINGS
CLIVE OF INDIA
CLOCK WATCHER
CLOCKWORK TOY
CLOSE BARGAIN
CLOSE CONTACT
CLOSE CONTEST
CLOSED CIRCLE
CLOSED DRAWER
CLOSE HARMONY
CLOSE TEXTURE
CLOSE THE DOOR
CLOSE THE EYES
CLOSE THE GATE
CLOSE TO DEATH
CLOSING PRICE
CLOSING WORDS
CLOTHES BRUSH
CLOTHES HORSE

CLOTHES SENSE
CLOTHING CLUB
CLOTTED CREAM
CLOUD EFFECTS
CLOUDLESS SKY
CLOUD OF SMOKE
CLOUD OF STEAM
CLUB OFFICIAL
CLUB SANDWICH
CLUB TOGETHER
CLUMP OF TREES
CLUTCH OF EGGS
COACH AND FOUR
COACH AND PAIR
COACHING DAYS
COACH STATION
COAL INDUSTRY
COAL MERCHANT
COAL SHORTAGE
COARSE FABRIC
COARSE MANNER
COASTAL TRADE
COAST TO COAST
COAT AND SKIRT
COCONUT GROVE
CODE NAPOLEON
CODE OF HONOUR
COILED SPRING
COLD AS MARBLE
COLD COMPRESS
COLD SHOULDER
COLD-WATER TAP
COLIN COWDREY
COLLAR AND TIE
COLLECT TAXES
COLOGNE WATER
COLONEL BLIMP
COLONEL BOGEY
COLONIAL LIFE
COLOURED BIRD
COLOUR SCHEME
COMBAT TROOPS
COMB ONE'S HAIR
COME A CROPPER
COME AND GET IT
COME DOWN A PEG
COME IN SECOND
COME IN TO LAND
COME INTO LINE
COME INTO PLAY
COME INTO VIEW
COME IN USEFUL
COME IT STRONG
COME OUT ON TOP
COME OVER HERE
COME TO A CLOSE

COME TO A POINT
COME TOGETHER
COME TO NAUGHT
COME TO NO GOOD
COME TO NO HARM
COME TO PIECES
COME TO THE END
COME UP FOR AIR
COME UPSTAIRS
COME UP TRUMPS
COMIC SECTION
COMING EVENTS
COMMANDO RAID
COMMANDO UNIT
COMMIT A CRIME
COMMIT BIGAMY
COMMIT MURDER
COMMITTEE MAN
COMMON ACCENT
COMMON AS DIRT
COMMON CENTRE
COMMON FACTOR
COMMON FRIEND
COMMON GENDER
COMMON GOSSIP
COMMON GROUND
COMMON HATRED
COMMON LAWYER
COMMON MARKET
COMMON ORIGIN
COMMON PEOPLE
COMMON PERSON
COMMON PRAYER
COMMON PRISON
COMMON SAYING
COMMON SPEECH
COMMUNAL FARM
COMMUTER BELT
COMPANIES ACT
COMPANION WAY
COMPARE NOTES
COMPASS POINT
COMPLETE LIST
COMPOSE MUSIC
COMPOS MENTIS
COMPOUND TIME
COMPUTER GAME
CONCEITED PUP
CONCERT GRAND
CONCERT PARTY
CONCERT PITCH
CONCRETE FACT
CONCRETE PATH
CONCRETE POST
CONDEMNED MAN
CONFUSED MIND

CONIC SECTION
CONSOLE TABLE
CONSUMER UNIT
CONTENTED MAN
CONTOUR LINES
CONTROL LINES
CONTROL PANEL
CONTROL TOWER
CONVEX MIRROR
CONVEYOR BELT
CONVICTED MAN
COOKERY CLASS
COOKING APPLE
COOK THE BOOKS
COOK UP A STORY
COOL CUSTOMER
COOLING AGENT
COOLING PLANT
COOL JUDGMENT
COOL THOUSAND
COPIOUS NOTES
COPPER KETTLE
COPYRIGHT ACT
CORDIAL SMILE
CORDLESS IRON
CORE SUBJECTS
CORNET PLAYER
CORN EXCHANGE
CORN IN ISRAEL
CORNISH CREAM
CORNISH PASTY
CORN MERCHANT
CORN ON THE COB
CORONER'S JURY
CORRECT DRESS
CORRECT STYLE
CORRECT THING
COSSACK DANCE
COST ACCOUNTS
COST OF LIVING
COST OF UPKEEP
COST THE EARTH
COSTUME PIECE
COTTAGE PIANO
COTTON GLOVES
COTTON THREAD
COUGH MIXTURE
COULD BE WORSE
COUNCIL HOUSE
COUNCIL OF WAR
COUNT DRACULA
COUNTER CLAIM
COUNTRY DANCE
COUNTRY HOUSE
COUNTRY MOUSE
COUNT THE COST

COUNT THE DAYS
COUNT THE RISK
COUNT UP TO TEN
COUNTY ANTRIM
COUNTY FAMILY
COUNTY SCHOOL
COUPE JACQUES
COURSE OF DUTY
COURSE OF LIFE
COURSE OF LOVE
COURSE OF TIME
COURSE OF WORK
COURSE RECORD
COURTEOUS ACT
COURTESY CALL
COURT MARTIAL
COURT OFFICER
COURT PLASTER
COURT SUMMONS
COUSIN GERMAN
COVENT GARDEN
COVENTRY CITY
COVERED COURT
COVERED DRAIN
COVERED WAGON
COVERT ACTION
COVER THE COST
COVER THE LOSS
CRACK A BOTTLE
CRACK COCAINE
CRACKED VOICE
CRACKING PACE
CRACKING SHOW
CRACK-POT IDEA
CRACK THE WHIP
CRAFTY FELLOW
CRAMPED STYLE
CRASHING BORE
CRASH LANDING
CRAVEN SPIRIT
CREAM CRACKER
CREAM SHAMPOO
CREATE A SCENE
CREATIVE MIND
CREATIVE MOOD
CREATIVE URGE
CREATIVE WORK
CREDIT RATING
CREDIT TITLES
CRÊPE DE CHINE
CRÊPE SUZETTE
CRESCENT MOON
CRICKET EXTRA
CRICKET MATCH
CRICKET PITCH
CRICKET SCORE

CRICKET STUMP
CRIMINAL CASE
CRIMINAL CODE
CRIMINAL SUIT
CRIMINAL TYPE
CRIPPLING TAX
CRITICAL TIME
CROMWELL ROAD
CROSSED LINES
CROSSED WIRES
CROSS OF DAVID
CROSS SECTION
CROSS THE LINE
CROSS THE ROAD
CROSSWORD FAN
CROWD CONTROL
CROWNED HEADS
CROWN WITNESS
CRUDE MANNERS
CRUDE METHODS
CRUISE AROUND
CRUSHING BLOW
CRUST OF BREAD
CRY LIKE A BABY
CRY OF DESPAIR
CRY ONE'S WARES
CRYPTIC SMILE
CRYSTAL CLEAR
CRYSTAL GLASS
CUBIC CONTENT
CULINARY HERB
CULLODEN MOOR
CULTURE SHOCK
CUP AND SAUCER
CUPBOARD LOVE
CUP FINALISTS
CURDS AND WHEY
CURIOUS SIGHT
CURIOUS SOUND
CURIOUS THING
CURLING TONGS
CURL OF THE LIP
CURL UP AND DIE
CURRANT BREAD
CURRENCY NOTE
CURRENCY SWAP
CURRENT CRAZE
CURRENT ISSUE
CURRENT MONTH
CURRENT OF AIR
CURRENT PRICE
CURRENT TIMES
CURRENT TREND
CURRENT YIELD
CURRY AND RICE
CURVE INWARDS

CUSHION COVER
CUSHION OF AIR
CUSTOM DUTIES
CUSTOMS UNION
CUT AND THRUST
CUT FOR TRUMPS
CUT OFF THE GAS
CUT OF ONE'S JIB
CUT ONE'S NAILS
CUT ONE'S TEETH
CUT THE CACKLE
CUTTING TEETH
CUTTING WORDS
CUT TO RIBBONS
CUT TO THE BONE
CYNICAL SMILE
CZAR OF RUSSIA

D – 12

DAGGERS DRAWN
DAILY EXPRESS
DAILY ROUTINE
DAILY SERVICE
DAINTY HABITS
DAINTY PALATE
DAIRY FARMING
DAIRY PRODUCE
DALAMATIAN DOG
DAMAGED GOODS
DAME MYRA HESS
DANCE HOSTESS
DANCE OF DEATH
DANCE ROUTINE
DANCE SESSION
DANGEROUS AGE
DANGEROUS JOB
DANGEROUS MAN
DANGER SIGNAL
DANISH BUTTER
DANISH PASTRY
DANSE MACABRE
DARBY AND JOAN
DARKENED MIND
DARK THOUGHTS
DASH TO PIECES
DAVID GARRICK
DAVID KOSSOFF
DAYLIGHT RAID
DAY OF LEISURE
DAY OF WORSHIP
DAYTONA BEACH
DEAD AS MUTTON
DEAD LANGUAGE
DEADLY COMBAT
DEADLY POISON

DEADLY SECRET
DEADLY WEAPON
DEAD MAN'S HAND
DEAD-SEA FRUIT
DEAD STRAIGHT
DEAFENING ROW
DEAF TO REASON
DEAL THE CARDS
DEAR DEPARTED
DEAREST HEART
. DEAR OLD THING
DEARTH OF FOOD
DEATH CHAMBER
DEATH PENALTY
DEATH WARRANT
DEBATING HALL
DEBIT BALANCE
DEBT OF HONOUR
DECIDING VOTE
DECIMAL POINT
DEEP FEELINGS
DEEP INTEREST
DEEP-LAID PLOT
DEEP MOURNING
DEEP-SEA DIVER
DEEP THOUGHTS
DEFENCE BONDS
DEFENCE MEDAL
DEFINITE TIME
DEJECTED LOOK
DELICATE HINT
DELIVERY DATE
DELIVERY NOTE
DEMAND RANSOM
DEMON FOR WORK
DENIS COMPTON
DEN OF THIEVES
DEPUTY LEADER
DESCENT OF MAN
DESERT ISLAND
DESERT SHIELD
DESERVE A RISE
DESIGN CENTRE
DESIGNER DRUG
DESK CALENDAR
DESPATCH CASE
DESPERATE BID
DESPERATE DAN
DESPERATE MAN
DESSERT KNIFE
DESSERT SPOON
DETACHED MIND
DETACHED VIEW
DETAILED PLAN
DEVIL MAY CARE
DEVIL OF A MESS

DEVIL OF A TIME
DEVIL'S ISLAND
DEVIL'S TATTOO
DEVIL WORSHIP
DEVIOUS MEANS
DEVIOUS PATHS
DEVOID OF FEAR
DEVON VIOLETS
DIAGONAL LINE
DIALLING TONE
DIAMOND CLASP
DIAMOND TIARA
DIANA'S TEMPLE
DICTATE TERMS
DIE IN HARNESS
DIE IN ONE'S BED
DIESEL ENGINE
DIFFICULT AGE
DIFFICULT JOB
DIFFICULT SUM
DIFFUSED HEAT
DIG IN THE RIBS
DIGITAL CLOCK
DIGITAL TUNER
DIGITAL WATCH
DIG ONESELF IN
DIG ONE'S GRAVE
DIG UP THE PAST
DINING SALOON
DIN IN THE EARS
DIRECT ACCESS
DIRECT ACTION
DIRECT COURSE
DIRECT METHOD
DIRECT OBJECT
DIRECT SPEECH
DIRE DISTRESS
DIRTY DANCING
DIRTY WEATHER
DISASTER AREA
DISCOVERY BAY
DISHONEST ACT
DISPATCH CASE
DISPENSE WITH
DISTRICT BANK
DISTRICT LINE
DIVE FOR COVER
DIVIDE BY FIVE
DIVIDE BY FOUR
DIVIDE BY NINE
DIVIDED SKIRT
DIVIDING LINE
DIVIDING WALL
DIVINE COMEDY
DIVINE NATURE
DIVINE RIGHTS

DIVISION BELL
DIVISION SIGN
DIVORCE COURT
DIZZY FEELING
DIZZY HEIGHTS
DO A HAND'S TURN
DO AS ONE'S TOLD
DO AS OTHERS DO
DO AS ROME DOES
DOCK LABOURER
DOCTOR FOSTER
DOCTOR JEKYLL
DOCTOR WATSON
DOG IN A MANGER
DO IT YOURSELF
DOMBEY AND SON
DOMESDAY BOOK
DOMESTIC HELP
DOMINANT FACT
DOMINO THEORY
DONALD WOLFIT
DONEGAL TWEED
DONKEY ENGINE
DONKEY'S YEARS
DO NO MAN WRONG
DO NOT DISTURB
DO ONE A FAVOUR
DO ONE'S UTMOST
DOPPLER SHIFT
DORIS LESSING
DORMER WINDOW
DOROTHY TUTIN
DORSET SQUARE
DOSE OF PHYSIC
DO THE HONOURS
DO THE NEEDFUL
DO THE WASHING
DOUBLE BARREL
DOUBLE BRANDY
DOUBLE ELEVEN
DOUBLE FLOWER
DOUBLE SCOTCH
DOUBLES MATCH
DOUBLE THE BID
DOUBLE TWELVE
DOUBLE TWENTY
DOUBLE VISION
DOUBLE WHAMMY
DOUBLE WHISKY
DOUGHTY DEEDS
DOWN PLATFORM
DOWNRIGHT LIE
DOWN THE AISLE
DOWN THE DRAIN
DOWN THE FIELD
DOWN THE HATCH

DOWN THE RIVER
DOWN THE SPOUT
DOWN THE YEARS
DOWNWARD BEND
DOWNWARD PATH
DOZEN OYSTERS
DRAGGING FEET
DRAG ONE'S FEET
DRAGON'S BLOOD
DRAGON'S TEETH
DRAMATIC FORM
DRAMATIC POEM
DRAMATIC POET
DRAPERY STORE
DRAUGHT CIDER
DRAUGHT HORSE
DRAUGHT STOUT
DRAW A MEANING
DRAW A PENSION
DRAW A PICTURE
DRAWING PAPER
DRAW INTEREST
DRAWN TO SCALE
DRAW THE BLIND
DRAW THE MORAL
DRAW THE SWORD
DRAW THE TEETH
DRAW TO A CLOSE
DRAW TOGETHER
DREADFUL BORE
DREADFUL PAIN
DREAD SUMMONS
DREAM FACTORY
DREAM OF YOUTH
DRESDEN CHINA
DRESS CLOTHES
DRESSED IN RED
DRESSING CASE
DRESSING DOWN
DRESSING GOWN
DRESSING ROOM
DRESS THE PART
DRESS UNIFORM
DRINK HEAVILY
DRINKING BOUT
DRINKING CLUB
DRINKING ORGY
DRINKING SONG
DRINKING TIME
DRINK OF WATER
DRIVE FORWARD
DRIVE THROUGH
DRIVE TO DRINK
DRIVING FORCE
DRIVING RANGE
DROP A CLANGER

DROP A CURTSEY
DROP A BRANDY
DROP OF SCOTCH
DROP OF WHISKY
DROPPED CATCH
DROP THE PILOT
DROWN ONESELF
DRUNK AS A LORD
DRUNKEN BRAWL
DUCKING STOOL
DUCK ONE'S HEAD
DUCK'S DISEASE
DUE DEFERENCE
DULL MONOTONY
DUMB CHARADES
DUMB CREATURE
DUM-DUM BULLET
DUNMOW FLITCH
DUPLICATE KEY
DURING THE DAY
DURING THE WAR
DUST AND ASHES
DUTCH AUCTION
DUTCH COMFORT
DUTCH COURAGE
DUTCH GUILDER
DYERS' COMPANY
DYNAMIC FORCE

E – 12

EALING COMEDY
EALING COMMON
EAR AND THROAT
EARLY CLOSING
EARLY EDITION
EARLY ENGLISH
EARLY MORNING
EARLY WARNING
EARNED INCOME
EARNEST MONEY
EARN ONE'S KEEP
EASE ONE'S MIND
EASILY SOLVED
EAST CHINA SEA
EASTER BONNET
EASTER ISLAND
EASTERLY GALE
EASTER MONDAY
EASTERN FRONT
EASTER PARADE
EASTER RISING
EASTER SUNDAY
EASY ON THE EYE
EASY PAYMENTS
EASY SOLUTION

EASY TO PLEASE
EAT HUMBLE-PIE
EATING HABITS
EAT ONE'S WORDS
EAT SPARINGLY
EAU DE COLOGNE
ECONOMY DRIVE
EDGAR WALLACE
EDGE OF BEYOND
EDIBLE FUNGUS
EDITH SITWELL
EDWARD GIBBON
EEL-PIE ISLAND
EFFORT OF WILL
EGGS AND BACON
EGYPTIAN GODS
EIGHT DEGREES
EIGHT DOLLARS
EIGHT FATHOMS
EIGHT GALLONS
EIGHT GUINEAS
EIGHTH LETTER
EIGHTH OF JULY
EIGHTH OF JUNE
EIGHTH STOREY
EIGHT HUNDRED
EIGHTH VOLUME
EIGHT MINUTES
EIGHT OF CLUBS
EIGHT PER CENT
EIGHT SQUARED
EIGHT WICKETS
ELBOW ONE'S WAY
ELDER BROTHER
ELDEST SISTER
ELECTION DATE
ELECTION YEAR
ELECTRIC BELL
ELECTRIC BLUE
ELECTRIC BULB
ELECTRIC FIRE
ELECTRIC HARE
ELECTRIC HORN
ELECTRIC IRON
ELECTRIC LAMP
ELECTRIC OVEN
ELECTRIC PLUG
ELECTRIC WIRE
ELEGANT LINES
ELEVEN MONTHS
ELEVEN O'CLOCK
ELEVEN OUNCES
ELEVEN POINTS
ELEVENTH HOLE
ELEVENTH HOUR
ELGIN MARBLES

ELIXIR OF LIFE
ELVIS PRESLEY
ELY CATHEDRAL
EMERALD GREEN
EMPEROR WALTZ
EMPTY FEELING
EMPTY STOMACH
EMPTY VESSELS
END IN FAILURE
ENDLESS CHAIN
ENDLESS WORRY
END OF CHAPTER
END OF THE LINE
END OF THE ROAD
END OF THE WEEK
END OF THE YEAR
ENDURING FAME
ENDURING LOVE
ENFIELD RIFLE
ENGAGED IN WAR
ENGINE DRIVER
ENGLISH MONEY
ENGLISH VERSE
ENJOY ONESELF
ENORMOUS MEAL
ENQUIRE AFTER
ENQUIRY AGENT
ENRICO CARUSO
ENTERIC FEVER
ENTRANCE FREE
ENTRANCE HALL
EPPING FOREST
EQUAL CONTEST
EQUAL THE BEST
ERIC ROBINSON
ERMINE COLLAR
ERUDITE STYLE
ESCAPE CLAUSE
ESCAPE NOTICE
ESCORT VESSEL
ESSAYS OF ELIA
ESSENTIAL OIL
ESTEEM HIGHLY
ETERNAL YOUTH
ETERNITY RING
ETON WALL-GAME
EUGENE O'NEILL
EUROPEAN CITY
EVENING CLASS
EVENING DRESS
EVENING PAPER
EVEN TEMPERED
EVE OF THE POLL
EVER AND AGAIN
EVER-OPEN DOOR
EVER SO LITTLE

EVERYBODY OUT
EVERY FEW DAYS
EVERY MAN JACK
EVERY MORNING
EVERY QUARTER
EVERY SO OFTEN
EVERY TUESDAY
EVIL SPEAKING
EVIL THOUGHTS
EVOKE THE PAST
EXACT ACCOUNT
EXACTLY RIGHT
EXACT MEANING
EXACT SCIENCE
EXALTED STYLE
EXCEL ONESELF
EXCESS PROFIT
EXCESS WEIGHT
EXCHANGE RATE
EXCITING BOOK
EXCITING NEWS
EXCITING PLAY
EXERCISE BOOK
EXERT ONESELF
EXHAUST VALVE
EXPANSE OF SEA
EXPANSE OF SKY
EXPERT ADVICE
EXPERT SYSTEM
EXPLODED IDEA
EXPORT MARKET
EXPOSED NERVE
EXPRESS GRIEF
EXPRESS SPEED
EXPRESS TRAIN
EX-SERVICE MAN
EXTEND CREDIT
EXTENDED PLAY
EXTERIOR WALL
EXTRACTOR FAN
EXTRA EDITION
EXTRA SPECIAL
EXTREMES MEET
EXTREME VIEWS
EXTREME YOUTH
EYE FOR BEAUTY
EYE FOR COLOUR
EYE OF A NEEDLE
EYES OF THE LAW
EYE ON THE BALL

F – 12

FABLED ANIMAL
FABULOUS SIZE
FACE BOTH WAYS

FACE DISGRACE
FACE THE ENEMY
FACE THE FACTS
FACE THE FRONT
FACE THE ISSUE
FACE THE MUSIC
FACE THE TRUTH
FACT AND FANCY
FAERIE QUEENE
FAILING LIGHT
FAILING SIGHT
FAIL IN HEALTH
FAIL TO APPEAR
FAIL TO FINISH
FAINT ATTEMPT
FAIR DECISION
FAIR EXCHANGE
FAIR PROSPECT
FAIR QUESTION
FAIR TO MEDIUM
FAIT ACCOMPLI
FAITHFUL COPY
FALKLANDS WAR
FALL BACK UPON
FALL BY THE WAY
FALLEN ARCHES
FALL HEADLONG
FALL IN BATTLE
FALLING SALES
FALLING TEARS
FALL IN PRICE
FALL INTO LINE
FALL INTO RUIN
FALL OF FRANCE
FALL TO PIECES
FALSE ACCOUNT
FALSE ADDRESS
FALSE COLOURS
FALSE ECONOMY
FALSE HORIZON
FALSE MODESTY
FALSE PICTURE
FALSE PROPHET
FALSE VERDICT
FALSE WITNESS
FALSE WORSHIP
FAMILIAR FACE
FAMILIAR RING
FAMILY AFFAIR
FAMILY CIRCLE
FAMILY CREDIT
FAMILY DOCTOR
FAMILY FRIEND
FAMILY JEWELS
FAMILY LAWYER
FAMILY MATTER

FAMINE RELIEF
FANCY ONESELF
FAN THE EMBERS
FAN THE FLAMES
FAR DIFFERENT
FARE THEE WELL
FAREWELL SONG
FARMHOUSE TEA
FARMING STOCK
FARM LABOURER
FAROE ISLANDS
FARTHING WOOD
FASCIST PARTY
FASHION HOUSE
FASHION MODEL
FASHION PLATE
FAST AND LOOSE
FAST THINKING
FATAL BLUNDER
FATAL DISEASE
FATAL MISTAKE
FATHER AND SON
FATHER FIGURE
FATHER THAMES
FATIGUE PARTY
FAT LOT OF GOOD
FAT OF THE LAND
FATUOUS SMILE
FAULTY SWITCH
FAWLTY TOWERS
FEAR EXPOSURE
FEAR THE WORST
FEAT OF MEMORY
FEATURE STORY
FEDERAL AGENT
FEDERAL COURT
FEDERAL STATE
FEDERAL UNION
FEEBLE ATTACK
FEEBLE EFFORT
FEEBLE EXCUSE
FEEBLE SPEECH
FEED THE BRUTE
FEEL DOUBTFUL
FEEL GRATEFUL
FEEL HELPLESS
FEEL HOMESICK
FEEL ONE'S FEET
FEEL STRONGLY
FEEL SUPERIOR
FEEL SYMPATHY
FEEL THE PANGS
FEEL THE PINCH
FEET FOREMOST
FELL HEADLONG
FELLOW MEMBER

FERTILE BRAIN
FESTIVAL HALL
FESTIVE BOARD
FEUDAL SYSTEM
FEUDAL TENURE
FEVERISH COLD
FIELDING SIDE
FIELD KITCHEN
FIELD MARSHAL
FIELD OFFICER
FIELD OF STUDY
FIELD OF WHEAT
FIERCE ATTACK
FIERCE HATRED
FIERCE TEMPER
FIERY FURNACE
FIFTEEN FORTY
FIFTEEN MILES
FIFTH CENTURY
FIFTH OF APRIL
FIFTH OF MARCH
FIFTY DOLLARS
FIFTY GUINEAS
FIFTY PER CENT
FIGHT AGAINST
FIGHTER PILOT
FIGHTER PLANE
FIGHTING COCK
FIGHTING TALK
FIGHTING TRIM
FIGHT ONE'S WAY
FIGURE SKATER
FILING SYSTEM
FILL A VACANCY
FILM DIRECTOR
FILM FESTIVAL
FILM INDUSTRY
FILM MAGAZINE
FILM PREMIERE
FILM PRODUCER
FINAL ACCOUNT
FINAL ATTEMPT
FINAL CURTAIN
FINAL EDITION
FINAL EPISODE
FINAL OPINION
FINAL OUTCOME
FINAL PAYMENT
FINAL PROCESS
FINAL VICTORY
FINAL WARNING
FINANCIAL AID
FIND A FORMULA
FIND A HUSBAND
FIND AN OUTLET
FIND NO FAVOUR

FIND ONE'S FEET
FIND ONE'S LEGS
FIND PLEASURE
FIND THE CAUSE
FIND THE MONEY
FIND THE PLACE
FINE AND DANDY
FINE AND LARGE
FINE FEATHERS
FINE FEATURES
FINE GOINGS-ON
FINE PROSPECT
FINER FEELING
FINE SPECIMEN
FINISHED WORK
FINISH SECOND
FINISH THE JOB
FINSBURY PARK
FIRE AND SWORD
FIRE AND WATER
FIRE AT RANDOM
FIREMAN'S LIFT
FIRE OF LONDON
FIRE PRACTICE
FIRESIDE CHAT
FIRESIDE TALK
FIRE SURROUND
FIRM DECISION
FIRM FOOTHOLD
FIRMLY ROOTED
FIRM MEASURES
FIRM PRESSURE
FIRM PROPOSAL
FIRST-AID POST
FIRST AND LAST
FIRST ARRIVAL
FIRST ATTEMPT
FIRST CENTURY
FIRST CHAPTER
FIRST EDITION
FIRST FOOTING
FIRST INNINGS
FIRST OF APRIL
FIRST OFFENCE
FIRST OFFICER
FIRST OF MARCH
FIRST PAYMENT
FIRST QUARTER
FIRST READING
FIRST REFUSAL
FIRST RESERVE
FIRST SEA-LORD
FIRST SERVICE
FIRST SESSION
FIRST THOUGHT
FIRST TIME OUT

FIRST TO LEAVE
FIRST TURNING
FIRST-YEAR MAN
FIRTH OF CLYDE
FIRTH OF FORTH
FISH AND CHIPS
FISH FOR TROUT
FISHING FLEET
FISHING SMACK
FISHING SPEAR
FIT AND PROPER
FIT AS A FIDDLE
FITFUL BREEZE
FIT OF MADNESS
FITTED CARPET
FIVE AND A HALF
FIVE AND EIGHT
FIVE AND SEVEN
FIVE AND THREE
FIVE-DAY MATCH
FIVE DIAMONDS
FIVE FEET TALL
FIVE FURLONGS
FIVE-LINE WHIP
FIVE NO-TRUMPS
FIVE OF HEARTS
FIVE OF SPADES
FIVE OF TRUMPS
FIVE SEVENTHS
FIVE THOUSAND
FIVE-YEAR PLAN
FIXED CAPITAL
FIXED PAYMENT
FIXED PURPOSE
FIXED ROUTINE
FLAGON OF WINE
FLAMING HEART
FLASHING EYES
FLASH OF LIGHT
FLEECY CLOUDS
FLEET OF SHIPS
FLEET OF TAXIS
FLIGHT NUMBER
FLIGHT OF TIME
FLIMSY EXCUSE
FLOATING DEBT
FLOATING DOCK
FLOATING FUND
FLOATING MINE
FLOATING VOTE
FLOCK OF BIRDS
FLOCK OF GEESE
FLOCK OF GOATS
FLOCK OF SHEEP
FLODDEN FIELD
FLOOD BARRIER

FLOOD OF TEARS
FLOOD OF WATER
FLOOD OF WORDS
FLOOR SERVICE
FLOUNCE ABOUT
FLOWERED SILK
FLOWER GARDEN
FLOWER MARKET
FLOWER PEOPLE
FLOWER-POT MEN
FLOWER SELLER
FLOWERY STYLE
FLOWERY LOCKS
FLOWING WATER
FLUENT FRENCH
FLUID MEASURE
FLURRY OF SNOW
FLUSH FITTING
FLUSH OF YOUTH
FLUTED COLUMN
FLY AWAY PETER
FLYING BEETLE
FLYING CARPET
FLYING CIRCUS
FLYING COLUMN
FLYING DOCTOR
FLYING GROUND
FLYING PICKET
FLYING SAUCER
FLYING TACKLE
FLY INTO A RAGE
FOAM MATTRESS
FOGGY WEATHER
FOLDING BUGGY
FOLDING CHAIR
FOLDING DOORS
FOLDING STOOL
FOLD ONE'S ARMS
FOLLOW ADVICE
FOLLOW MY LEAD
FOLLOW THE SEA
FOND OF A GLASS
FOOD ADDITIVE
FOOD AND DRINK
FOOD SHORTAGE
FOOD SUPPLIES
FOOT AND MOUTH
FOOTBALL CLUB
FOOTBALL POOL
FOOTBALL TEAM
FOOTPLATE MAN
FOOT REGIMENT
FOR A LIFETIME
FOR AMUSEMENT
FOR A RAINY DAY
FORCE AN ENTRY

FORCE AN ISSUE
FORCED GAIETY
FORCED LABOUR
FORCE MAJEURE
FORCE OF HABIT
FORCE ONE'S WAY
FORCE THE PACE
FOREIGN AGENT
FOREIGN LANDS
FOREIGN MONEY
FOREIGN PARTS
FOREIGN STAMP
FOREIGN TRADE
FOREST OF DEAN
FOREST RANGER
FOREVER AMBER
FOR GALLANTRY
FORGE A CHEQUE
FORGE ONE'S WAY
FORK OUT MONEY
FORMAL GARDEN
FORMAL SPEECH
FORMER FRIEND
FOR PITY'S SAKE
FOR THE BETTER
FOR THE MOMENT
FOR THE RECORD
FORTY FIFTEEN
FORTY PER CENT
FORTY THIEVES
FORWARD DRIVE
FORWARD MARCH
FORWARD PUPIL
FOSTER FATHER
FOSTER MOTHER
FOSTER PARENT
FOSTER SISTER
FOUL LANGUAGE
FOUND MISSING
FOUND WANTING
FOUR AND A HALF
FOUR DIAMONDS
FOUR FEATHERS
FOUR FEET TALL
FOUR FREEDOMS
FOUR FURLONGS
FOUR HORSEMEN
FOUR NO-TRUMPS
FOUR OF HEARTS
FOUR OF SPADES
FOUR OF TRUMPS
FOURPENNY ONE
FOUR QUARTERS
FOUR SEVENTHS
FOURTEEN DAYS
FOURTH ESTATE

FOURTH FINGER
FOURTH LEAGUE
FOURTH LETTER
FOURTH OF JULY
FOURTH OF JUNE
FOUR THOUSAND
FOURTH SEASON
FOURTH STOREY
FOURTH VOLUME
FOX AND HOUNDS
FRACTURED ARM
FRACTURED LEG
FRAGRANT WEED
FRANCIS BACON
FRANCIS DRAKE
FRANK SINATRA
FRANTIC HASTE
FRAYED NERVES
FREE AS THE AIR
FREE DELIVERY
FREE FROM CARE
FREE FROM DEBT
FREE FROM PAIN
FREE FROM RAIN
FREE FROM VICE
FREE FROM WANT
FREE MOVEMENT
FREE OF CHARGE
FREE QUARTERS
FREE THINKING
FREE TO CHOOSE
FREEZING COLD
FREIGHT TRAIN
FRENCH ACCENT
FRENCH CUSTOM
FRENCH GUINEA
FRENCH LESSON
FRENCH LETTER
FRENCH MASTER
FRENCH PASTRY
FRENCH POLISH
FRENCH POODLE
FRENCH WINDOW
FRENZIED RAGE
FRESH ADVANCE
FRESH AS PAINT
FRESH CHAPTER
FRESH COURAGE
FRESH FLOWERS
FRESH HERRING
FRESH OUTLOOK
FREUDIAN SLIP
FRIAR'S BALSAM
FRICTION FEED
FRIDAY'S CHILD
FRIEND INDEED

FRIEND IN NEED
FRIENDLY CHAT
FRIENDLY FACE
FRIENDLY FIRE
FRIENDLY HAND
FRIENDLY WORD
FRIGHTEN AWAY
FROMAGE FRAIS
FROM ALL SIDES
FROM DAY TO DAY
FROM END TO END
FROM THE FIRST
FROM THE NORTH
FROM THE SOUTH
FROM THE START
FROM TOP TO TOE
FRONT AND BACK
FRONTIER ZONE
FRONT PARLOUR
FROSTED GLASS
FROZEN ASSETS
FRUIT MACHINE
FUEL MERCHANT
FULHAM PALACE
FUEL CAPACITY
FULL COVERAGE
FULL DAYLIGHT
FULLER'S EARTH
FULL MATURITY
FULL OF ACTION
FULL OF ENERGY
FULL OF HORROR
FULL OF SORROW
FULL OF SPIRIT
FULL PRESSURE
FULLY DRESSED
FULLY ENGAGED
FULLY SECURED
FUME WITH RAGE
FUND OF HUMOUR
FUNERAL MARCH
FUNERAL RITES
FUNNY FEELING
FUN OF THE FAIR
FUR-LINED COAT
FURNITURE VAN
FURNIVAL'S INN
FURTHER DELAY
FURTHER PLANS
FUTILE EFFORT
FUTURE EVENTS

G – 12

GAIN A FOOTING
GAIN A HEARING

GAIN A VICTORY
GAIN CURRENCY
GAIN ONE'S ENDS
GAIN PRESTIGE
GAIN STRENGTH
GALA OCCASION
GALLON OF BEER
GALLON OF MILK
GAMBLING DEBT
GAMBLING GAME
GAMBLING HELL
GAME AND MATCH
GAME OF CHANCE
GAME OF TENNIS
GAME PRESERVE
GAMING TABLES
GAMMA COUNTER
GAMMON RASHER
GARBLED STORY
GARDEN OF EDEN
GARDEN ROLLER
GARDEN SUBURB
GARDEN TROWEL
GARRISON TOWN
GARTER STITCH
GAS POISONING
GATE BRACELET
GATE-LEG TABLE
GENDER BENDER
GENERAL ALARM
GENERAL ALERT
GENERAL BOOTH
GENERAL GRANT
GENERAL ISSUE
GENERAL SMUTS
GENERAL STAFF
GENERAL STALL
GENERAL SYNOD
GENERAL TERMS
GENERAL TREND
GENERAL USAGE
GENERAL VOICE
GENERAL WOLFE
GENITIVE CASE
GENTLE BREEZE
GENTLEMAN JIM
GENTLE NATURE
GENTLE READER
GENTLE REBUKE
GENTLY DOES IT!
GEORGE BORROW
GEORGE ORWELL
GEORGE ROMNEY
GERMAN LESSON
GERMAN SCHOOL
GERMAN SILVER

GERM OF AN IDEA	GIVE PLEASURE	GOLD RESERVE
GET CLEAN AWAY	GIVE SECURITY	GOLD STANDARD
GET CLEAR AWAY	GIVE THE ALARM	GOLF CHAMPION
GET INTO A MESS	GIVE THE FACTS	GOLF UMBRELLA
GET NO SUPPORT	GIVE THE ORDER	GONE IN A FLASH
GET ONE'S CARDS	GIVE UP EATING	GONE TO GROUND
GET ONE'S EYE IN	GIVE UP OFFICE	GOOD AND READY
GET OUT OF HAND	GIVE UP TRYING	GOOD APPETITE
GET PLASTERED	GLADSTONE BAG	GOOD ARGUMENT
GET PROMOTION	GLANCING BLOW	GOOD BREEDING
GET TECHNICAL	GLARING ERROR	GOOD BUSINESS
GET THE CREDIT	GLASS FACTORY	GOOD CLEAN FUN
GET THE NEEDLE	GLASS OF STOUT	GOOD CROSSING
GET THE STITCH	GLASS OF WATER	GOOD DAY'S WORK
GET THE WIND UP	GLASS SLIPPER	GOOD DELIVERY
GET WELL-OILED	GLASS STOPPER	GOOD EYESIGHT
GIANT DESPAIR	GLASS TANKARD	GOOD FEATURES
GIANT'S STRIDE	GLASS TOO MUCH	GOOD FOR TRADE
GIDDY FEELING	GLASS TUMBLER	GOOD GRACIOUS
GIDDY HEIGHTS	GLEAM OF LIGHT	GOOD JUDGMENT
GIFT OF THE GAB	GLOBE THEATRE	GOOD LIKENESS
GIN AND FRENCH	GLOOMY ASPECT	GOOD LINGUIST
GIN AND ORANGE	GLORIOUS MESS	GOOD LISTENER
GINGER BRANDY	GLORIOUS TIME	GOOD MATERIAL
GINGER ROGERS	GLORIOUS VIEW	GOOD OLD TIMES
GINGHAM FROCK	GLOWING TERMS	GOOD PHYSIQUE
GIPSY CARAVAN	GLUE SNIFFING	GOOD POSITION
GIRLS AND BOYS	GO AND EAT COKE	GOOD PRACTICE
GIVE A CONCERT	GO BACK IN TIME	GOOD PROGRESS
GIVE A LECTURE	GO BACK TO WORK	GOOD QUARTERS
GIVE AN ENCORE	GO BY THE BOARD	GOOD QUESTION
GIVE A PRESENT	GOD BE WITH YOU	GOOD RECOVERY
GIVE A RECEIPT	GO DOWNSTAIRS	GOOD RIDDANCE
GIVE A SUMMARY	GO FIFTY-FIFTY	GOOD ROUND SUM
GIVE AUDIENCE	GO FOR A BURTON	GOOD SHEPHERD
GIVE EVIDENCE	GO FOR A CRUISE	GOOD SHOOTING
GIVE FIRST-AID	GO FOR A STROLL	GOOD SMACKING
GIVE HIM SOCKS	GO FOR A VOYAGE	GOOD SPANKING
GIVE IN CHARGE	GO FOR NOTHING	GOODS STATION
GIVE IT A TWIST	GO HOT AND COLD	GOOD TEMPLARS
GIVE IT THE GUN	GOING BEGGING	GOOD THINKING
GIVE JUDGMENT	GOING CONCERN	GOOD THRILLER
GIVEN A CHANCE	GO INTO DETAIL	GOOD-TIME GIRL
GIVEN A PARDON	GO INTO HIDING	GOOD WATCH-DOG
GIVEN THE BIRD	GOLAN HEIGHTS	GOODWIN SANDS
GIVEN THE BOOT	GOLD BRACELET	GOODWOOD PARK
GIVEN THE CANE	GOLDEN FLEECE	GO ON ALL FOURS
GIVEN THE PUSH	GOLDEN GLOVES	GO ON AN ERRAND
GIVEN THE SACK	GOLDEN NUMBER	GO ON AS BEFORE
GIVEN THE SLIP	GOLDEN REMEDY	GO ONE'S OWN WAY
GIVEN THE VOTE	GOLDEN SQUARE	GO ON THE SPREE
GIVE ONE A LIFT	GOLDEN SUNSET	GO ON THE STAGE
GIVE ONE'S BEST	GOLDERS GREEN	GOOSE PIMPLES
GIVE ONE'S LIFE	GOLDFISH BOWL	GO OVER THE TOP
GIVE ONE'S VOTE	GOLDFISH POND	GORGEOUS TIME
GIVE ONE'S WORD	GOLD MERCHANT	GO-SLOW POLICY

GO-SLOW STRIKE
GOSSIP COLUMN
GOSSIP WRITER
GO SWIMMINGLY
GO THE SAME WAY
GOTHIC SCRIPT
GO TO A WEDDING
GO TO EXTREMES
GO TO HOSPITAL
GO TO ONE'S HEAD
GO TO THE DEVIL
GO TO THE FRONT
GO TO THE OPERA
GO TO THE POLLS
GO TO THE RACES
GO UP IN FLAMES
GO WITH A SWING
GRACE DARLING
GRACEFUL EXIT
GRACIE FIELDS
GRACIOUS LADY
GRAHAM GREENE
GRAIN HARVEST
GRAIN OF SENSE
GRAIN OF TRUTH
GRAND CENTRAL
GRAND DUCHESS
GRAND FEELING
GRAND GUIGNOL
GRAND LARCENY
GRANDMA MOSES
GRAND MISTAKE
GRAND OPENING
GRAND SEND-OFF
GRANNY ANNEXE
GRAPE HARVEST
GRASS WIDOWER
GRATED CHEESE
GRATING LAUGH
GRATING VOICE
GRAVE MISTAKE
GRAVE OFFENCE
GRAVE SCANDAL
GREAT BRAVERY
GREAT BRITAIN
GREAT CAR RACE
GREAT COMFORT
GREAT COMPANY
GREAT EASTERN
GREAT EXPENSE
GREAT FORTUNE
GREAT FRIENDS
GREAT MALVERN
GREAT PAINTER
GREAT RESPECT
GREAT SECRECY

GREAT SOLDIER
GREAT SUCCESS
GREAT TRAGEDY
GREAT TRIUMPH
GREAT URGENCY
GREAT VARIETY
GREAT VICTORY
GRECIAN STYLE
GREEK PROFILE
GREEK SCHOLAR
GREEK THEATRE
GREEK TRAGEDY
GREEK VERSION
GREEN FINGERS
GREEN GODDESS
GREEN HOWARDS
GREEN IN MY EYE
GREEN WITH AGE
GREY EMINENCE
GREY SQUIRREL
GRIEVOUS PAIN
GRILLED BACON
GRILLED STEAK
GRILLED TROUT
GRIM BUSINESS
GRIM LAUGHTER
GRIND ONE'S AXE
GRIPPING TALE
GRIT THE TEETH
GROCERY CHAIN
GROCERY STORE
GROPE ONE'S WAY
GROSS BLUNDER
GROSS NEGLECT
GROSS RETURNS
GROSS TONNAGE
GROUND GINGER
GROUND TO DUST
GROUP CAPTAIN
GROUP OF EIGHT
GROUP OF SEVEN
GROUP OF THREE
GROUP THERAPY
GROUSE SEASON
GROW ANIMATED
GROWING CHILD
GROWING PAINS
GROWING THING
GROW POTATOES
GROW RADISHES
GROW TOGETHER
GRUDGING HAND
GUARD AGAINST
GUARDED REPLY
GUERRILLA WAR
GUESSING GAME

GUIDING LIGHT
GUILT COMPLEX
GUILTY PERSON
GUILTY SECRET
GUITAR PLAYER
GUITAR STRING
GULF OF MEXICO
GUNSHOT WOUND
GUY MANNERING
GUYS AND DOLLS
GUY'S HOSPITAL
GYPSY ROSE LEE

H – 12

HABEAS CORPUS
HABIT FORMING
HABITUAL LIAR
HACKING COUGH
HACK AND SLASH
HACK TO PIECES
HADRIAN'S WALL
HAIR MATTRESS
HAIR OF THE DOG
HAIR RESTORER
HAIR'S BREADTH
HALF DISTANCE
HALF MEASURES
HALF MOURNING
HALF OF BITTER
HALF-SEAS OVER
HALF-WAY HOUSE
HALLEY'S COMET
HALL OF MEMORY
HALTING PLACE
HAM AND TONGUE
HAMBURG STEAK
HAMMER HORROR
HAMPTON COURT
HANDEL'S LARGO
HANDFUL OF MEN
HANDICAP RACE
HAND OVER FIST
HAND OVER HAND
HANDS AND FEET
HAND'S BREADTH
HANGING JUDGE
HANGMAN'S ROPE
HANG ONE'S HEAD
HANG TOGETHER
HANS ANDERSEN
HAPPY AS A KING
HAPPY AS A LARK
HAPPY HOLIDAY
HAPPY LANDING
HAPPY NEW YEAR
HAPPY OUTCOME

HAPPY RELEASE	HAVE THE POWER	HEDGE SPARROW
HAPPY RETURNS	HAZARD A GUESS	HEDGE TRIMMER
HAPPY THOUGHT	HAZARD LIGHTS	HEIGHT OF FAME
HAPPY WARRIOR	HEAD FOREMOST	HEINOUS CRIME
HARBOUR LIGHT	HEAD GARDENER	HEIR APPARENT
HARD CURRENCY	HEAD IN THE AIR	HELD IN COMMON
HARD DRINKING	HEADLINE NEWS	HELD TO RANSOM
HARD FEELINGS	HEAD MISTRESS	HELEN SHAPIRO
HARD MATTRESS	HEAD OF CATTLE	HELL LET LOOSE
HARD MEASURES	HEAD OUT TO SEA	HELL OF A NOISE
HARD QUESTION	HEAD SHRINKER	HELP YOURSELF
HARD ROCK CAFE	HEADS OR TAILS	HENRY PURCELL
HARD SHOULDER	HEAD THE QUEUE	HERBAL REMEDY
HARD STRUGGLE	HEADY MIXTURE	HERD INSTINCT
HARD SWEARING	HEADY PERFUME	HERD OF CATTLE
HARD THINKING	HEALING CREAM	HERD TOGETHER
HARD THOUGHTS	HEALING POWER	HERE AND THERE
HARD TO COME BY	HEALING TOUCH	HEROIC POETRY
HARD TO FATHOM	HEALTH CENTRE	HERO OF THE DAY
HARD TO HANDLE	HEALTH RESORT	HERO'S WELCOME
HARD TO PLEASE	HEALTHY STATE	HEWERS OF WOOD
HARD TRAINING	HEAP OF STONES	HIDDEN DANGER
HARE AND HOUND	HEAPS OF MONEY	HIDDEN DEPTHS
HARICOT BEANS	HEAR A PIN DROP	HIDDEN MENACE
HARLEY STREET	HEAR IN CAMERA	HIDDEN TALENT
HARMLESS DRUG	HEART AND HAND	HIDDEN WEALTH
HAROLD PINTER	HEART AND SOUL	HIDE ONE'S FACE
HAROLD WILSON	HEART DISEASE	HIDE ONE'S HEAD
HARRY ENFIELD	HEART FAILURE	HIDEOUS CRIME
HARRY SECOMBE	HEAR THE TRUTH	HIDEOUS NOISE
HARVEST MOUSE	HEART OF FLINT	HIDE THE TRUTH
HARVEST QUEEN	HEART OF STONE	HIGH ALTITUDE
HASTY PUDDING	HEART'S DESIRE	HIGH BUILDING
HASTY RETREAT	HEART SURGERY	HIGH DIVIDEND
HATTON GARDEN	HEART TO HEART	HIGHER DEGREE
HAUNTED HOUSE	HEART TROUBLE	HIGHER ORDERS
HAUTE COUTURE	HEARTY ASSENT	HIGH ESTIMATE
HAVE A FLUTTER	HEATING AGENT	HIGHEST POINT
HAVE A NICE DAY	HEAT OF BATTLE	HIGHEST SCORE
HAVE A PURPOSE	HEAT OF THE DAY	HIGH FIDELITY
HAVE A RELAPSE	HEAT OF THE SUN	HIGHGATE HILL
HAVE A VACANCY	HEAVE IN SIGHT	HIGH INTEREST
HAVE FEELINGS	HEAVEN FORBID!	HIGH IN THE AIR
HAVE NO ANSWER	HEAVENLY BODY	HIGHLAND CLAN
HAVE NO CHOICE	HEAVENLY CITY	HIGHLAND REEL
HAVE NO DOUBTS	HEAVENLY HOST	HIGH LATITUDE
HAVE NO OPTION	HEAVENS ABOVE!	HIGHLY AMUSED
HAVE ONE'S WILL	HEAVY AT HEART	HIGHLY STRUNG
HAVE PATIENCE	HEAVY BIDDING	HIGHLY VALUED
HAVE PRIORITY	HEAVY BRIGADE	HIGH MOUNTAIN
HAVE SCRUPLES	HEAVY DRINKER	HIGH OFFICIAL
HAVE THE FACTS	HEAVY PENALTY	HIGH POSITION
HAVE THE FLOOR	HEAVY SLEEPER	HIGH PRESSURE
HAVE THE KNACK	HEAVY TRAFFIC	HIGH RAINFALL
HAVE THE LAUGH	HEAVY VEHICLE	HIGH STANDARD
HAVE THE MEANS	HEAVY WEATHER	HIGH STANDING

HIGH VELOCITY
HILLY COUNTRY
HIP-HIP HURRAH!
HIRED SERVANT
HIRE PURCHASE
HIS REVERENCE
HIT A BOUNDARY
HITCHING POST
HIT ON THE HEAD
HIT THE BOTTLE
HIT THE STUMPS
HIT THE TARGET
HOARY WITH AGE
HOCKEY PLAYER
HOCKEY STICKS
HOIST THE FLAG
HOIST THE SAIL
HOLD A MEETING
HOLD DOWN A JOB
HOLD IN COMMON
HOLD IN ESTEEM
HOLD IN HORROR
HOLD IN PLEDGE
HOLD ONE'S LEAD
HOLD OUT A HAND
HOLD OUT HOPES
HOLD THE CARDS
HOLD THE FIELD
HOLD THE REINS
HOLD THE STAGE
HOLD TOGETHER
HOLD TO RANSOM
HOLIDAY HAUNT
HOLIDAY MONEY
HOLLAND HOUSE
HOLLOW CHEEKS
HOLLOW SPHERE
HOLLOW SQUARE
HOLLOW THREAT
HOLLOW VESSEL
HOLY ALLIANCE
HOLY MACKEREL
HOLY OF HOLIES
HOME COMFORTS
HOME COUNTIES
HOME FROM HOME
HOME INDUSTRY
HOMELY PERSON
HOME-MADE CAKE
HOME PRODUCTS
HOME SHOPPING
HOMING PIGEON
HONEST FELLOW
HONEST LABOUR
HONEST LIVING
HONEYED WORDS

HONORARY RANK
HONOUR BRIGHT
HONOURED NAME
HONOURS OF WAR
HOODED TERROR
HOOKS AND EYES
HOPE AND GLORY
HOPE DEFERRED
HOPELESS CASE
HOPELESS LOSS
HOPELESS MESS
HOPELESS TASK
HORN OF PLENTY
HORRIBLE BORE
HORS DE COMBAT
HORSE AND CART
HORSE AND TRAP
HORSE BLANKET
HORSE DEALING
HORSE MARINES
HORSE SOLDIER
HORSE TRADING
HORSE TRAINER
HOSPITAL CASE
HOSPITAL SHIP
HOSPITAL WARD
HOSTILE CROWD
HOSTILE FORCE
HOSTILE PRESS
HOT AND STRONG
HOTBED OF VICE
HOT CHESTNUTS
HOT CHOCOLATE
HOT CROSS-BUNS
HOTEL OMNIBUS
HOT FAVOURITE
HOT GOSPELLER
HOT-WATER PIPE
HOUND TO DEATH
HOURLY CHIMES
HOUR OF DANGER
HOUR OF THE DAY
HOUSE AND HOME
HOUSE BREAKER
HOUSE COLOURS
HOUSE FOR SALE
HOUSEHOLD GOD
HOUSE OF CARDS
HOUSE OF LORDS
HOUSE OF PEERS
HOUSE OF TUDOR
HOUSE OF USHER
HOUSE PAINTER
HOUSE SITTING
HOUSE SPARROW
HOUSE SURGEON

HOUSE TO HOUSE
HOUSE WARMING
HOUSEY HOUSEY
HUMAN AFFAIRS
HUMANE KILLER
HUMAN ELEMENT
HUMAN FAILING
HUMAN FRAILTY
HUMAN REMAINS
HUMAN SPECIES
HUMBER BRIDGE
HUMBLE ORIGIN
HUMBLE PERSON
HUMMING SOUND
HUMOROUS VEIN
HUMPTY DUMPTY
HUNDRED A YEAR
HUNDRED LINES
HUNDRED MILES
HUNDRED TO ONE
HUNDRED YARDS
HUNDRED YEARS
HUNGER STRIKE
HUNK OF CHEESE
HUNTING FIELD
HUNTING LODGE
HUNTING SPEAR
HUNTSMAN'S CRY
HURL DEFIANCE
HURRIED VISIT
HURT FEELINGS
HYDRAULIC RAM
HYDROGEN BOMB
HYMN OF PRAISE

I – 12

ICE-CREAM SODA
ICY RECEPTION
IDEAL HUSBAND
IDENTITY CARD
IDENTITY DISC
IDLE THOUGHTS
IF THE CAP FITS
IGNEOUS ROCKS
ILLEGAL ENTRY
ILLICIT GAINS
ILLICIT MEANS
ILLICIT STILL
ILL-TIMED JEST
IMMORTAL FAME
IMMORTAL NAME
IMMORTAL POET
IMMORTAL SOUL
IMPERIAL PINT
IMPERIAL RULE

IMPLIED TRUTH
IMPROPER WORD
IN A BAD TEMPER
IN A COLD SWEAT
IN A DEAD FAINT
IN A GOOD LIGHT
IN ALL HONESTY
IN A LOUD VOICE
IN AN ACCIDENT
IN AN ARMCHAIR
IN APPEARANCE
IN A SHORT TIME
IN ATTENDANCE
IN AT THE DEATH
IN CASE OF NEED
INCHCAPE ROCK
INCHES TALLER
INCLUDE ME OUT
INCOMING TIDE
IN CONCLUSION
IN CONFERENCE
IN CONFIDENCE
INCREASED PAY
IN DEEP WATERS
INDELIBLE INK
INDIAN MILLET
INDIAN MUTINY
INDIAN SUMMER
IN DIFFICULTY
INDIRECT HINT
INDOOR AERIAL
INDOOR SPORTS
IN EMPLOYMENT
INFANT IN ARMS
INFANTRY UNIT
INFANT SCHOOL
INFERIOR RANK
IN FINE FETTLE
INFINITE TIME
INFRA-RED LAMP
INFRA-RED RAYS
IN FULL FLIGHT
IN GOOD HEALTH
IN GOOD REPAIR
IN GOOD SUPPLY
IN HIGH FAVOUR
IN HIGH RELIEF
IN HOLY ORDERS
IN HOT PURSUIT
INITIAL STAGE
INJURED PARTY
INJURED PRIDE
IN LEAGUE WITH
IN LIKE MANNER
IN LOVE AND WAR
IN LOW SPIRITS

IN MODERATION
IN NEED OF HELP
INNER CABINET
INNER SANCTUM
IN NO FIT STATE
IN OCCUPATION
IN ONE RESPECT
IN ONE'S FAVOUR
IN ONE'S HEYDAY
IN ONE'S OLD AGE
IN ONE'S SENSES
IN ONE'S STRIDE
IN OPPOSITION
IN OTHER WORDS
IN OUR OPINION
IN PARTICULAR
IN POOR HEALTH
IN POSSESSION
IN PROCESSION
IN PROPORTION
IN QUARANTINE
IN RECORD TIME
IN RETIREMENT
IN RETROSPECT
INSANE ASYLUM
INSECURE HOLD
IN SETTLEMENT
IN SILHOUETTE
IN SINGLE FILE
IN SLOW MOTION
IN SUBJECTION
IN SUCCESSION
INTEGRAL PART
INTEREST FREE
INTEREST RATE
INTERIOR WALL
IN TERMS OF LAW
IN THE BALANCE
IN THE BALCONY
IN THE BEDROOM
IN THE CABINET
IN THE CAPITAL
IN THE COUNTRY
IN THE CRYSTAL
IN THE DAYTIME
IN THE DEEP END
IN THE EVENING
IN THE EXTREME
IN THE FASHION
IN THE GALLERY
IN THE HONOURS
IN THE INTERIM
IN THE KITCHEN
IN THE LIBRARY
IN THE LONG RUN
IN THE MORNING

IN THE NURSERY
IN THE OLD DAYS
IN THE OPEN AIR
IN THE PADDOCK
IN THE PARLOUR
IN THE PEERAGE
IN THE PICTURE
IN THE PRESENT
IN THE RUNNING
IN THE SHADOWS
IN THE SUBURBS
IN THE THEATRE
IN THE TROPICS
IN THE VERY ACT
IN THE VILLAGE
IN THE YEAR ONE
IN TRIPLICATE
IN UNDERTONES
IN UTMOST NEED
INVALID CHAIR
INVERSE ORDER
INVERSE RATIO
INVERTED SNOB
INVERTED TURN
INVISIBLE INK
INVISIBLE MAN
INVOICE CLERK
IRISH COLLEEN
IRISH TERRIER
IRISH WHISKEY
IRON AND STEEL
IRONING BOARD
IRVING BERLIN
ISLAND OF CUBA
ISLE OF CYPRUS
ISLE OF THANET
ISOLATED CASE
ISSUE A THREAT
ITALIAN MONEY
IT ALL DEPENDS
IT'S AN ILL WIND
IT'S A PLEASURE

J – 12

JACK CHARLTON
JACKET POTATO
JACK IN OFFICE
JACK NICKLAUS
JACK OF HEARTS
JACK OF SPADES
JACK OF TRUMPS
JACK ROBINSON
JACK SHEPPARD
JACOB'S LADDER
JADE NECKLACE

JAMES BOSWELL
JAMES HERRIOT
JAMES STEWART
JAMES THURBER
JANETTE SCOTT
JANUARY SALES
JASPER CONRAN
JAUNDICED EYE
JAZZ FESTIVAL
JEAN METCALFE
JE NE SAIS QUOI
JERMYN STREET
JESUS SANDALS
JIG-SAW PUZZLE
JIMMY CONNORS
JIMMY DURANTE
JIMMY EDWARDS
JIM THE PENMAN
JOAN CRAWFORD
JOG THE MEMORY
JOHN CLEMENTS
JOHNNY MATHIS
JOHN TRAVOLTA
JOIN IN THE FUN
JOIN ONE'S SHIP
JOINT ACCOUNT
JOINT CONCERN
JOINT CUSTODY
JOIN THE CHOIR
JOIN THE DANCE
JOIN THE ENEMY
JOIN THE PARTY
JOIN THE QUEUE
JOIN THE RANKS
JOINT HOLDING
JOIN TOGETHER
JOINT TENANCY
JOINT TRUSTEE
JOKING MATTER
JOLLY JACK TAR
JOLLY SWAGMAN
JONATHAN WILD
JORDAN ALMOND
JOSEPH CONRAD
JOSEPH COTTON
JOSEPH STALIN
JUDGE AND JURY
JUDGMENT SEAT
JULIAN HUXLEY
JULIA ROBERTS
JULIE ANDREWS
JULIENNE SOUP
JULIE WALTERS
JULIUS CAESAR
JULY THE FIFTH
JULY THE FIRST

JULY THE NINTH
JULY THE SIXTH
JULY THE TENTH
JULY THE THIRD
JUMP THE QUEUE
JUMP THE RAILS
JUNE THE FIFTH
JUNE THE FIRST
JUNE THE NINTH
JUNE THE SIXTH
JUNE THE TENTH
JUNE THE THIRD
JUNIOR SCHOOL
JUNIOR TYPIST
JURASSIC PARK
JUST AS YOU SAY
JUST FOR SPITE
JUST THE THING
JUST THIS ONCE
JUVENILE LEAD

K – 12

KEEN APPETITE
KEEN AS A RAZOR
KEEN INTEREST
KEEN PLEASURE
KEEP ACCOUNTS
KEEP A LOOK-OUT
KEEP A PROMISE
KEEP CHEERFUL
KEEP-FIT CLASS
KEEP GOOD TIME
KEEP GUESSING
KEEP IN PRISON
KEEP IN PURDAH
KEEP IN REPAIR
KEEP ONE'S COOL
KEEP ONE'S FEET
KEEP ONE'S HEAD
KEEP ONE'S SEAT
KEEP ONE'S WORD
KEEP ON TRYING
KEEP PRISONER
KEEP THE BOOKS
KEEP THE FAITH
KEEP THE PEACE
KEEP THE SCORE
KEEP TOGETHER
KEEP UP-TO-DATE
KENNETH HORNE
KEPT ON A LEASH
KETTLE OF FISH
KEVIN COSTNER
KEY OF THE DOOR
KEY SIGNATURE

KEYSTONE COPS
KEY TO THE SAFE
KHAKI UNIFORM
KILL BY INCHES
KILL OUTRIGHT
KINDLING WOOD
KING AND QUEEN
KING OF BEASTS
KING OF FRANCE
KING OF HEARTS
KING OF SPADES
KING OF TRUMPS
KING'S COLLEGE
KING'S COUNSEL
KING'S ENGLISH
KING'S HIGHWAY
KINGSLEY AMIS
KING'S PROCTOR
KITCHEN CHAIR
KITCHEN RANGE
KITCHEN SCALE
KITCHEN STOVE
KITCHEN TABLE
KNACKER'S YARD
KNAVE OF CLUBS
KNEE BREECHES
KNIFE AND FORK
KNIFE GRINDER
KNIGHT ERRANT
KNIGHTLY DEED
KNIT A SWEATER
KNIT ONE'S BROW
KNIT THE BROWS
KNIT TOGETHER
KNOCK AGAINST
KNOCKING COPY
KNOCK OFF WORK
KNOCK-OUT BLOW
KNOW FOR A FACT
KNOW FULL WELL
KNOW NO BETTER
KNOW NO BOUNDS
KNOW ONE'S DUTY
KNOW THE DRILL
KNOW THE FACTS
KNOW THE ROPES
KNOW THE SCORE
KNOW THE TRUTH
KNOW THE WORST
KNOW WHAT TO DO
KNUCKLE UNDER
KNUR AND SPELL
KRISS KRINGLE

L – 12

LABOURED JOKE
LABOUR IN VAIN
LABOUR LEADER
LABOUR MARKET
LABOUR OFFICE
LABOUR OF LOVE
LABOUR POLICY
LACE CURTAINS
LACKING MONEY
LACKING POINT
LACKING POISE
LACKING PROOF
LACKING SENSE
LACK INTEREST
LACK OF BRAINS
LACK OF FINISH
LACK OF POLISH
LACK OF PROFIT
LACK OF REASON
LACK OF SPIRIT
LACK OF WISDOM
LACROSSE TEAM
LADDER OF FAME
LADY HAMILTON
LADY JANE GREY
LADY MARGARET
LADY MAYORESS
LADY NICOTINE
LADY'S BICYCLE
LADY SUPERIOR
LAGER AND LIME
LAISSEZ FAIRE
LAKE DISTRICT
LAKE MAGGIORE
LAKE MICHIGAN
LAKE SUPERIOR
LAKE VICTORIA
LAKE WINNIPEG
LALIQUE GLASS
LAMBENT LIGHT
LAMB SANDWICH
LANDED ESTATE
LANDED GENTRY
LANDING CRAFT
LANDING PARTY
LANDING PLACE
LANDING STRIP
LAND OF DREAMS
LAND OF PLENTY
LAND SURVEYOR
LAND TRANSFER
LANTERN SLIDE
LAP OF THE GODS
LARGE ACCOUNT

LARGE EXPANSE
LARGE HELPING
LARGE PORTION
LARGE SECTION
LARGE VARIETY
LASER PRINTER
LASER SURGERY
LASH THE WAVES
LAST BUT THREE
LAST DELIVERY
LAST ELECTION
LAST FRONTIER
LASTING PEACE
LAST JUDGMENT
LAST RESOURCE
LAST SATURDAY
LAST SYLLABLE
LAST THURSDAY
LAST TO ARRIVE
LATE IN THE DAY
LATE LAMENTED
LATE MARRIAGE
LATENT ENERGY
LATENT TALENT
LATEST REPORT
LATIN AMERICA
LATIN GRAMMAR
LATIN QUARTER
LATIN TEACHER
LAUGH OUT LOUD
LAUGH TO SCORN
LAUNCHING PAD
LAUNCH WINDOW
LAUREL WREATH
LAVENDER HILL
LAVISH PRAISE
LAW OF ENGLAND
LAW OF GRAVITY
LAW OF THE LAND
LAWS OF MOTION
LAWYER'S BRIEF
LAY A FINGER ON
LAY DOWN A PLAN
LAYER ON LAYER
LAY IT ON THICK
LEADED LIGHTS
LEADER WRITER
LEADING ACTOR
LEADING LIGHT
LEAD IN PRAYER
LEAD THE DANCE
LEAD THE FIELD
LEANING TOWER
LEAP IN THE AIR
LEARN A LESSON
LEARN BY HEART

LEARNED JUDGE
LEARN TO DRIVE
LEARN TO RELAX
LEARN TO WRITE
LEATHER GOODS
LEATHER STRAP
LEAVE A LEGACY
LEAVE IT ALONE
LEAVE NO DOUBT
LEAVE NO TRACE
LEAVE NO WISER
LEAVE OFF WORK
LEAVE THE ARMY
LEAVE THE NAVY
LEAVE THE NEST
LEAVE THE ROOM
LED ONE A DANCE
LED TO BELIEVE
LEFT AND RIGHT
LEFT-HAND BEND
LEFT-HAND SIDE
LEFT-HAND TURN
LEFT IN THE AIR
LEFT NO CHOICE
LEFT SHOULDER
LEFT STANDING
LEFT TO CHANCE
LEGAL ADVISER
LEGAL CUSTODY
LEGAL DEFENCE
LEGAL FICTION
LEGAL JOURNAL
LEGAL OPINION
LEGAL PROCESS
LEGAL VERDICT
LEGS TOGETHER
LEG TO STAND ON
LEISURE HOURS
LEMON PUDDING
LENGTH OF TIME
LESSON ELEVEN
LESSON TWELVE
LESS THAN COST
LETHAL WEAPON
LET ONESELF GO
LET OUT ON HIRE
LETTER OPENER
LETTER WRITER
LET THINGS RIP
LET WELL ALONE
LEVEL PEGGING
LEVEL STRETCH
LEWIS CARROLL
LEYTON ORIENT
LIBERAL DONOR
LIBERAL PARTY

LIBERAL SHARE
LIBERTY HORSE
LIBYAN DESERT
LICENSING ACT
LICENSING LAW
LICK ONE'S LIPS
LIE OF THE LAND
LIE PROSTRATE
LIFE AND DEATH
LIFE IMMORTAL
LIFE INSTINCT
LIFE INTEREST
LIFE IN THE RAW
LIFE OF LUXURY
LIFE SENTENCE
LIFT ONE'S HAND
LIFT THE ELBOW
LIGHT A CANDLE
LIGHT AND AIRY
LIGHT AND DARK
LIGHT BRIGADE
LIGHT CAVALRY
LIGHT CRUISER
LIGHT DRAGOON
LIGHTED TORCH
LIGHT FINGERS
LIGHT FITTING
LIGHTNING ROD
LIGHT OF HEART
LIGHT RAILWAY
LIGHT READING
LIGHT SLEEPER
LIGHT THE LAMP
LIGHT TRAFFIC
LIGHT VEHICLE
LIKE HOT CAKES
LIKE OLD BOOTS
LIKE SARDINES
LIKE THE DEVIL
LIKE UNTO LIKE
LIKE WILDFIRE
LILY OF LAGUNA
LIMB FROM LIMB
LIMB OF THE LAW
LIMITED MEANS
LIMITED OVERS
LIMITED SCOPE
LIMITED SCORE
LIMITED SPACE
LINCOLN GREEN
LINE OF ACTION
LINE OF BATTLE
LINE OF FLIGHT
LINE REGIMENT
LINE UPON LINE
LINGUA FRANCA

LINK TOGETHER
LIQUEUR GLASS
LIQUID ASSETS
LIQUID MAKE-UP
LIST OF VOTERS
LITERAL ERROR
LITERAL TRUTH
LITERARY AIMS
LITERARY CLUB
LITERARY FAME
LITERARY HACK
LITERARY LION
LITERARY PAGE
LITERARY STAR
LITERARY WORK
LITTER BASKET
LITTLE CHANCE
LITTLE CHANGE
LITTLE DEMAND
LITTLE DORRIT
LITTLE ENOUGH
LITTLE FINGER
LITTLE HITLER
LITTLE MONKEY
LITTLE PEOPLE
LITTLE SISTER
LITTLE SQUIRT
LITTLE TERROR
LITTLE THANKS
LITTLE THINGS
LITTLE TIN GOD
LITTLE WONDER
LIVE AND LEARN
LIVE FOR KICKS
LIVE FOR TODAY
LIVE IN A DREAM
LIVE IN CLOVER
LIVE IN LUXURY
LIVELY DEBATE
LIVE ON CREDIT
LIVE ONE'S LIFE
LIVER SAUSAGE
LIVERY STABLE
LIVE TOGETHER
LIVING MATTER
LIVING MEMORY
LIVING TISSUE
LOADED WEAPON
LOAD SHEDDING
LOBSTER PATTY
LOBSTER SALAD
LOCAL AFFAIRS
LOCAL DIALECT
LOCAL FEELING
LOCALISED WAR
LOCK-UP GARAGE

LODGING HOUSE
LOGICAL ERROR
LOGICAL ORDER
LOLLIPOP LADY
LONDON BRIDGE
LONDON EDITOR
LONDON LIGHTS
LONDON SEASON
LONG ANCESTRY
LONG AND OFTEN
LONG CORRIDOR
LONG DISTANCE
LONG DIVISION
LONG DRAWN-OUT
LONGEST NIGHT
LONG EXPECTED
LONG FAREWELL
LONG-FELT WANT
LONG FOR PEACE
LONG-LIFE MILK
LONG SENTENCE
LONG STANDING
LONG-TERM LOAN
LONG-TERM VIEW
LONG TROUSERS
LONG VACATION
LONG WAY ROUND
LONSDALE BELT
LOOK BOTH WAYS
LOOK DOWNCAST
LOOK DOWN UPON
LOOK ONE'S BEST
LOOK PECULIAR
LOOK PLEASANT
LOOK SHEEPISH
LOOK SIDEWAYS
LOOK SUPERIOR
LOOSE CLOTHES
LOOSE CONDUCT
LOOSE GARMENT
LORD ADVOCATE
LORD ALMIGHTY
LORD LEIGHTON
LORD MACAULAY
LORD OF APPEAL
LORD TENNYSON
LORETTA YOUNG
LOSE BUSINESS
LOSE INTEREST
LOSE MOMENTUM
LOSE ONE'S FORM
LOSE ONE'S GRIP
LOSE ONE'S HAIR
LOSE ONE'S HEAD
LOSE ONE'S LIFE
LOSE ONE'S SEAT

LOSE ONE'S WIFE
LOSE ONE'S WITS
LOSE PATIENCE
LOSE PRESTIGE
LOSE STRENGTH
LOSE THE ASHES
LOSE THE MATCH
LOSE THE SCENT
LOSING BATTLE
LOSING HAZARD
LOSING TICKET
LOSS OF CUSTOM
LOSS OF ENERGY
LOSS OF HEALTH
LOSS OF HONOUR
LOSS OF MEMORY
LOSS OF MORALE
LOSS OF PROFIT
LOSS OF REASON
LOSS OF SPEECH
LOSS OF VISION
LOSS OF WEIGHT
LOST AND FOUND
LOST ELECTION
LOST FOR A WORD
LOST FOR WORDS
LOST IN WONDER
LOST PROPERTY
LOTUS BLOSSOM
LOUD AND CLEAR
LOUD APPLAUSE
LOUD LAUGHTER
LOUIS GOLDING
LOUIS PASTEUR
LOUNGE LIZARD
LOVE INTEREST
LOVELY FIGURE
LOVELY JUBBLY
LOVE OF NATURE
LOVING COUPLE
LOW CHURCHMAN
LOW CONDITION
LOW COUNTRIES
LOW-DOWN TRICK
LOWER ANIMALS
LOWER BRACKET
LOWER CHAMBER
LOWER CLASSES
LOWER ONESELF
LOWER REGIONS
LOWER THE FLAG
LOWEST BIDDER
LOWEST DEPTHS
LOW FREQUENCY
LOW VALUATION
LOW WATER MARK

LOYAL CITIZEN
LOYAL SUBJECT
LOYAL SUPPORT
LUCIFER MATCH
LUCKY AT CARDS
LUCKY VENTURE
LUGGAGE LABEL
LULWORTH COVE
LUMBER JACKET
LUMP TOGETHER
LUSH PASTURES
LUST FOR POWER
LUXURIOUS BED
LUXURY CRUISE
LYRIC THEATRE

M – 12

MACHINE TOOLS
MACK THE KNIFE
MAD AS A HATTER
MADDING CROWD
MADE IN FRANCE
MADE IN HEAVEN
MAGAZINE RACK
MAGIC FORMULA
MAGIC LANTERN
MAGNETIC FISH
MAGNETIC MINE
MAGNETIC POLE
MAGNETIC TAPE
MAIDEN FLIGHT
MAIDEN SPEECH
MAIDEN STAKES
MAIDEN VOYAGE
MAID OF HONOUR
MAIN BUSINESS
MAIN DRAINAGE
MAIN ENTRANCE
MAIN INDUSTRY
MAIN QUESTION
MAINS ADAPTOR
MAIN SEQUENCE
MAÎTRE D'HÔTEL
MAJOR BARBARA
MAJOR EDITION
MAJOR GENERAL
MAJORITY RULE
MAJORITY VOTE
MAJOR PREMISE
MAJOR PROPHET
MAJOR TRAGEDY
MAKE A BARGAIN
MAKE A BEE-LINE
MAKE A BEQUEST
MAKE A BONFIRE

MAKE ABSOLUTE
MAKE A CENTURY
MAKE A CIRCUIT
MAKE A CURTSEY
MAKE A DEAD SET
MAKE ADVANCES
MAKE A FAUX PAS
MAKE A FORTUNE
MAKE A GESTURE
MAKE A GET-AWAY
MAKE A HUNDRED
MAKE A LANDING
MAKE A LONG ARM
MAKE A MISTAKE
MAKE AN APPEAL
MAKE AN ARREST
MAKE AN EFFORT
MAKE AN ESCAPE
MAKE A NEW WILL
MAKE A PRESENT
MAKE A PROMISE
MAKE A PROTEST
MAKE A REQUEST
MAKE BAD BLOOD
MAKE BANKRUPT
MAKE ENDS MEET
MAKE IT SNAPPY
MAKE MISCHIEF
MAKE NO PROFIT
MAKE ONE'S EXIT
MAKE ONE SIT UP
MAKE ONE'S MARK
MAKE ONE'S PILE
MAKE ONE'S WILL
MAKE OUT A CASE
MAKE PROGRESS
MAKE SPEECHES
MAKE THE GRADE
MAKE-UP ARTIST
MAKE UP LEEWAY
MALAY STRAITS
MALE STRIPPER
MALTESE CROSS
MALVERN HILLS
MAN ABOUT TOWN
MAN AT THE HELM
MANDARIN DUCK
MANGO CHUTNEY
MANILLA PAPER
MAN IN THE DOCK
MAN IN THE MOON
MAN-MADE FIBRE
MAN OF DESTINY
MAN OF FASHION
MAN OF FORTUNE
MAN OF HIS WORD

MAN OF LEISURE
MAN OF LETTERS
MAN OF MYSTERY
MAN OF SCIENCE
MAN OF THE HOUR
MAN ON THE MOON
MAN ON THE SPOT
MAN OVERBOARD
MANSION HOUSE
MAN THE BREACH
MAN-TO-MAN TALK
MANUAL LABOUR
MANUAL WORKER
MANY A LONG DAY
MANY RESPECTS
MANY YEARS AGO
MAP OF AUSTRIA
MAP OF BELGIUM
MAP OF DENMARK
MAP OF ENGLAND
MAP OF GERMANY
MAP OF HOLLAND
MAP OF IRELAND
MARATHON RACE
MARCHING SONG
MARGINAL LAND
MARGINAL NOTE
MARGINAL SEAT
MARIE CELESTE
MARIE CORELLI
MARIE TEMPEST
MARIE THERESA
MARINE ANIMAL
MARINE ENGINE
MARINE GROWTH
MARINE PARADE
MARINE STORES
MARITIME ALPS
MARIUS GORING
MARKED MANNER
MARKET GARDEN
MARKET SQUARE
MARKET STREET
MARKET TRENDS
MARK OF ESTEEM
MARK OF GENIUS
MARK THE CARDS
MARK THE SCORE
MARLEY'S GHOST
MARLON BRANDO
MARMALADE CAT
MARRIAGE KNOT
MARRIAGE RATE
MARRIAGE TIES
MARRIAGE VOWS
MARRIED BLISS

MARRIED WOMAN
MARRY BY PROXY
MARRY IN HASTE
MARSHALL PLAN
MARTIAL MUSIC
MARTIN LUTHER
MARX BROTHERS
MARY OF ARGYLL
MARY PICKFORD
MASONIC LODGE
MASSED CHOIRS
MASSES OF FOOD
MASS HYSTERIA
MASS MOVEMENT
MASS MURDERER
MASS OF NERVES
MASTER AND MAN
MASTER CUTLER
MASTER GUNNER
MASTER OF ARTS
MASTER SPIRIT
MASTER STROKE
MASTER TAILOR
MATCHING PAIR
MATERIAL GAIN
MATERNAL LOVE
MATERNITY PAY
MATING SEASON
MATTER IN HAND
MATTER OF FACT
MAXIMUM BREAK
MAXIMUM PRICE
MAXIMUM SPEED
MAYPOLE DANCE
MAY THE EIGHTH
MAY THE FOURTH
MAY THE SECOND
MEAN BUSINESS
MEAN MISCHIEF
MEANS TO AN END
MEASURED MILE
MEAT AND DRINK
MEAT SANDWICH
MEDALLION MAN
MEDICAL BOARD
MEDICAL CHECK
MEDICAL STAFF
MEDICINE BALL
MEDIUM HEIGHT
MEDIUM SHERRY
MEET BY CHANCE
MEETING HOUSE
MEETING PLACE
MEETING POINT
MEET IN SECRET
MEET ONE'S FATE

MEET THE PLANE
MEET THE TRAIN
MELTED BUTTER
MELTED CHEESE
MELTING POINT
MELT THE HEART
MEMORIAL HALL
MEND ONE'S WAYS
MEN OF HARLECH
MENTAL EFFORT
MENTAL ENERGY
MENTAL HEALTH
MENTAL STRAIN
MENTAL STRESS
MERCHANT BANK
MERCHANT NAVY
MERCHANT SHIP
MERCY KILLING
MERE FLEA-BITE
MERE PITTANCE
MERRY MONARCH
MERRY OLD SOUL
MERSEY TUNNEL
MESSENGER BOY
METAL FATIGUE
METEOR SHOWER
METHOD ACTING
METRICAL UNIT
METRIC SYSTEM
MEZZO SOPRANO
MICHAEL ASPEL
MICHAEL CAINE
MICHAEL PALIN
MIDDLE AND LEG
MIDDLE COURSE
MIDDLE FINGER
MIDDLE TEMPLE
MIDDLE WICKET
MIDNIGHT BLUE
MIDNIGHT HOUR
MIDNIGHT MASS
MIDNIGHT SWIM
MIDSUMMER DAY
MIGHT AND MAIN
MIGHT IS RIGHT
MIGHTY EFFORT
MIGHTY HUNTER
MILES PER HOUR
MILE UPON MILE
MILFORD HAVEN
MILITARY BAND
MILITARY BASE
MILITARY BODY
MILITARY CAMP
MILITARY DUTY
MILITARY LIFE

MILITARY PACE
MILITARY RANK
MILITARY TYPE
MILITARY UNIT
MILK AND A DASH
MILK AND HONEY
MILK AND SUGAR
MILK AND WATER
MILKING STOOL
MILK SHORTAGE
MILLION YEARS
MILTON KEYNES
MINCE MATTERS
MINCING STEPS
MIND HOW YOU GO!
MIND YOUR HEAD!
MIND YOUR STEP!
MINERAL SALTS
MINERAL WATER
MINERAL WORLD
MINERS STRIKE
MINIATURE DOG
MINING EXPERT
MINING RIGHTS
MINOR AILMENT
MINORITY RULE
MINORITY VOTE
MINOR PREMISE
MINOR PROPHET
MINOR SET-BACK
MINOR TRAGEDY
MINSTREL SHOW
MISPLACED WIT
MISSED CHANCE
MISSING PIECE
MISS THE PLANE
MISS THE POINT
MISS THE TRAIN
MISS UNIVERSE
MISTAKEN IDEA
MISTRESS FORD
MIXED BATHING
MIXED COMPANY
MIXED DOUBLES
MIXED FARMING
MIXED MOTIVES
MIXED PICKLES
MIX IN SOCIETY
MOATED GRANGE
MOBILE COLUMN
MODEL HUSBAND
MODEL PATIENT
MODEL RAILWAY
MODE OF LIVING
MODERATE RENT
MODERN SCHOOL

MODEST INCOME
MODEST PERSON
MODUS VIVENDI
MOIRA SHEARER
MOLL FLANDERS
MOMENT OF TIME
MONASTIC LIFE
MONASTIC VOWS
MONDAY'S CHILD
MONETARY HELP
MONETARY UNIT
MONEYED CLASS
MONEY MATTERS
MONEY TO SPARE
MONKEY GLANDS
MONKEY JACKET
MONKEY PUZZLE
MONKEY TRICKS
MONTH BY MONTH
MONTHLY VISIT
MONTH'S NOTICE
MOOR OF VENICE
MOOT QUESTION
MOP AND BUCKET
MORAL CONDUCT
MORAL COURAGE
MORALITY PLAY
MORALLY BOUND
MORAL SCIENCE
MORAL STAMINA
MORAL SUPPORT
MORAL VICTORY
MORE'S THE PITY
MORE THAN EVER
MORE THAN ONCE
MORMON CHURCH
MORNING AFTER
MORNING DRESS
MORNING GLORY
MORNING PAPER
MORRIS DANCER
MORTAL COMBAT
MORTAL TERROR
MORTAR ATTACK
MORTE D'ARTHUR
MORTGAGE DEED
MOSQUITO BITE
MOST EXCITING
MOST GRACIOUS
MOST OF THE DAY
MOST REVEREND
MOTE IN THE EYE
MOTHER AND SON
MOTHER CHURCH
MOTHER GRUNDY
MOTHERLY LOVE

MOTHER NATURE
MOTHER OF MINE
MOTHERS' UNION
MOTHER TERESA
MOTHER TONGUE
MOTOR BICYCLE
MOTOR CRUISER
MOTORING CLUB
MOTOR LICENCE
MOTOR SCOOTER
MOTOR VEHICLE
MOUNTAIN BIKE
MOUNTAIN GOAT
MOUNTAIN LAKE
MOUNTAIN PASS
MOUNTAIN PEAK
MOUNTAIN TARN
MOUNT A LADDER
MOUNT EVEREST
MOUNT OF VENUS
MOUNT OLYMPUS
MOUNT PEGASUS
MOURA LYMPANY
MOUSTACHE CUP
MOUTH TO MOUTH
MOVABLE FEAST
MOVED TO TEARS
MOVE SIDEWAYS
MOVING APPEAL
MOVING FINGER
MOVING SPEECH
MOVING SPIRIT
MOVING TARGET
MUCH IMPROVED
MUCH IN DEMAND
MUCH MISTAKEN
MUD IN YOUR EYE
MUFFLED DRUMS
MUFFLED TONES
MUFFLED VOICE
MUGGY WEATHER
MULBERRY BUSH
MULBERRY TREE
MULTIPLE SHOP
MULTIPLE STAR
MUNICH CRISIS
MUNICIPAL LAW
MURDER CHARGE
MURDER VICTIM
MURDER WEAPON
MURIEL PAVLOW
MUSCATEL WINE
MUSHROOM SOUP
MUSICAL PIECE
MUSICAL SCALE
MUSICAL SCORE

MUSICAL SOUND
MUSICAL VOICE
MUSIC AT NIGHT
MUSIC LICENCE
MUSIC TEACHER
MUTED STRINGS
MUTTON CUTLET
MUTUAL FRIEND
MUTUAL HATRED
MUTUAL PROFIT
MUTUAL REGARD
MY BLUE HEAVEN
MY DEAR FELLOW
MY DEAR WATSON
MY GOOD FRIEND
MY LITTLE PONY
MYSTERY STORY

N – 12

NAIL POLISHER
NAIL SCISSORS
NAKED REALITY
NAME IN LIGHTS
NARROW DEFEAT
NARROW ESCAPE
NARROW GROOVE
NARROW MARGIN
NARROW SQUEAK
NARROW STREET
NARROW THE GAP
NARROW TUNNEL
NATIONAL BANK
NATIONAL DEBT
NATIONAL DISH
NATIONAL FLAG
NATIONAL GAME
NATIONAL GRID
NATIONAL HERO
NATIONAL PARK
NATIONAL POLL
NATIONAL ROAD
NATIONAL STUD
NATION IN ARMS
NATIVE CUSTOM
NATIVE TONGUE
NATIVE TROOPS
NATIVITY PLAY
NATURAL BREAK
NATURAL CHARM
NATURAL CHILD
NATURAL COVER
NATURAL DEATH
NATURAL ENEMY
NATURAL FIBRE
NATURAL ORDER

NATURAL PRIDE
NATURAL SCALE
NATURAL STATE
NAUGHTY CHILD
NAUTICAL FLAG
NAUTICAL LIFE
NAUTICAL MILE
NAUTICAL ROLL
NAVAL ATTACHÉ
NAVAL BRIGADE
NAVAL COLLEGE
NAVAL COMMAND
NAVAL OFFICER
NAVAL RESERVE
NAVAL SERVICE
NAVAL STATION
NAVAL TACTICS
NAVAL UNIFORM
NAVAL WARFARE
NEAR DISTANCE
NEAR RELATION
NEAR RELATIVE
NEAR THE COAST
NEAR THE SHORE
NEAR THE TRUTH
NECKING PARTY
NECK OF MUTTON
NEEDLESS RISK
NEGATIVE POLE
NEGATIVE SIGN
NEGATIVE VOTE
NEON LIGHTING
NERVE ONESELF
NERVOUS STATE
NERVOUS WRECK
NEST OF TABLES
NEUTER GENDER
NEUTRAL POWER
NEUTRAL STATE
NEVER DESPAIR
NEVER GO WRONG
NEVER THE SAME
NEVER TOO LATE
NEVER YOU MIND!
NEW AMSTERDAM
NEW BRUNSWICK
NEW DEPARTURE
NEW ENGLANDER
NEW HAMPSHIRE
NEW INVENTION
NEW JERUSALEM
NEWLY MARRIED
NEW PARAGRAPH
NEWS BULLETIN
NEWS OF THE DAY
NEW STATESMAN

NEW TECHNIQUE
NEW TESTAMENT
NEW YORK STATE
NEW ZEALANDER
NEXT ELECTION
NEXT QUESTION
NEXT SATURDAY
NEXT THURSDAY
NIAGARA FALLS
NICE AND HANDY
NICE AND SWEET
NICE AND TIGHT
NICE BUSINESS
NICELY PLACED
NICE ONE CYRIL
NICE QUESTION
NICKEL SILVER
NIGEL MANSELL
NIGEL PATRICK
NIGGLING PAIN
NIGHT CLASSES
NIGHT CLOTHES
NIGHT DRIVING
NIGHT FIGHTER
NIGHT NURSERY
NIGHT OF BLISS
NIGHT PROWLER
NINE AND A HALF
NINE AND EIGHT
NINE AND SEVEN
NINE AND THREE
NINE OF HEARTS
NINE OF SPADES
NINE OF TRUMPS
NINE OUT OF TEN
NINE THOUSAND
NINJA TURTLES
NINTH CENTURY
NINTH OF APRIL
NINTH OF MARCH
NITROUS OXIDE
NO ADMITTANCE
NO BED OF ROSES
NOBLE BEARING
NOBLE DESCENT
NOBLE EDIFICE
NOBLE GESTURE
NOBLE MANNERS
NOBODY'S CHILD
NOBODY'S FAULT
NO-CLAIM BONUS
NO COMPARISON
NO CONFIDENCE
NO DIFFERENCE
NO DOUBT AT ALL
NO EARTHLY USE

NO END OF MONEY
NO FIXED ABODE
NO FLIES ON HIM
NO IMPORTANCE
NOLENS VOLENS
NOMINAL POWER
NOMINAL PRICE
NOMINAL RULER
NOMINAL VALUE
NONE THE WISER
NONE THE WORSE
NONE WHATEVER
NON-STOP REVUE
NON-STOP TRAIN
NO PREFERENCE
NORMAN WISDOM
NORTH AMERICA
NORTH BRITAIN
NORTH COUNTRY
NORTHERN LINE
NORTH GERMANY
NORTH SHIELDS
NORTH TO SOUTH
NOTABLE POINT
NOTARY PUBLIC
NOT A STITCH ON
NOTHING AMISS
NOTHING AT ALL
NOTHING DOING
NOTHING FOR IT
NOTHING KNOWN
NOTHING TO ADD
NOTHING TO EAT
NOTHING TO PAY
NOTHING TO SAY
NOTICE TO QUIT
NO TIME TO LOSE
NOT IN KEEPING
NOT IN THE MOOD
NOT WORTH A RAP
NOUVEAU RICHE
NOVEMBER DAYS
NUCLEAR POWER
NUDIST COLONY
NUMBER ELEVEN
NUMBER-ONE MAN
NUMBER ONE SON
NUMBER, PLEASE
NUMBER TWELVE
NUMBER TWENTY
NUMB WITH COLD
NURSERY CLASS
NURSERY RHYME
NURSERY SLOPE
NURSERY STORY
NURSING STAFF

NUT CHOCOLATE
NUTMEG GRATER
NUTS AND BOLTS

O – 12

OBITER DICTUM
OBJECT LESSON
OBJECT OF PITY
OBLIQUE ANGLE
OBSTACLE RACE
OCCULT POWERS
OCEANS OF TIME
OCEAN TRAFFIC
OCTANE NUMBER
ODDS AND EVENS
ODD SENSATION
ODDS-ON CHANCE
OF EVIL REPUTE
OFFER A CHOICE
OFFER A REWARD
OFFER FOR SALE
OFFERTORY BOX
OFF HIS OWN BAT
OFF HIS ROCKER
OFFICER CADET
OFFICERS' MESS
OFFICIAL COPY
OFFICIAL DUTY
OFFICIAL FORM
OFFICIAL LIST
OFFICIAL VIEW
OFF LIKE A SHOT
OFF ONE'S CHUMP
OFF ONE'S GUARD
OFF ONE'S HANDS
OFFSHORE FUND
OFF THE COURSE
OFF THE RECORD
OFF THE SCREEN
OF GREAT WORTH
OF MICE AND MEN
OIL OF JUNIPER
OIL OF VITRIOL
OIL THE WHEELS
OKLAHOMA CITY
OLD AS HISTORY
OLD BATTLE-AXE
OLDER BROTHER
OLD FAVOURITE
OLD FOLKS' HOME
OLD FOR HIS AGE
OLD GENTLEMAN
OLD HARROVIAN
OLD HUNDREDTH
OLD MAN'S BEARD
OLD MORTALITY

OLD PRETENDER
OLD SCHOOL TIE
OLD SHOULDERS
OLD TESTAMENT
OLD-TIME DANCE
OLD-TIME WALTZ
OLD WIVES' TALE
OLYMPIC GAMES
OLYMPIC MEDAL
OMINOUS CLOUD
OMISSION MARK
OMIT NO DETAIL
ON A GOOD THING
ON A LEVEL WITH
ON AN EVEN KEEL
ON A STRETCHER
ONCE AND AGAIN
ONCE IN A WHILE
ONCE TOO OFTEN
ON COMMISSION
ONE AND TWENTY
ONE-DAY STRIKE
ONE FELL SWOOP
ONE FOR HIS NOB
ONE FOR THE POT
ONE-HORSE SHOW
ONE-HORSE TOWN
ONE JUMP AHEAD
ONE-LEGGED MAN
ONE LONG DREAM
ONE MOVE AHEAD
ONE OF THE BEST
ONE OF THE GANG
ONE OF THE LADS
ON EQUAL TERMS
ONE'S FAIR NAME
ONE-SIDED VIEW
ONE-TRACK MIND
ONE-WAY STREET
ON FIRM GROUND
ON FOUR WHEELS
ONLY DAUGHTER
ON ONE'S HONOUR
ON ONE'S METTLE
ON ONE'S UPPERS
ON REFLECTION
ON SAFE GROUND
ON SENTRY DUTY
ON SUFFERANCE
ON TELEVISION
ON THE AVERAGE
ON THE CEILING
ON THE COUNCIL
ON THE COUNTER
ON THE DECLINE
ON THE DEFENCE

ON THE FAIRWAY
ON THE FAR SIDE
ON THE HORIZON
ON THE LEE-SIDE
ON THE LOOK-OUT
ON THE OFF-SIDE
ON THE ONE HAND
ON THE OUTSIDE
ON THE PAY-ROLL
ON THE QUI VIVE
ON THE RAMPAGE
ON THE REBOUND
ON THE RETREAT
ON THE SURFACE
ON THE TERRACE
ON THE TOP RUNG
ON THE TOW-PATH
ON THE UP-AND-UP
ON THE UPGRADE
ON THE WARPATH
ON THE WAY DOWN
ON WITH THE JOB
OPEN ALL NIGHT
OPEN CARRIAGE
OPEN CHAMPION
OPEN CONFLICT
OPENING NIGHT
OPENING SCENE
OPENING WORDS
OPEN MARRIAGE
OPEN ONE'S EYES
OPEN OUTWARDS
OPEN QUESTION
OPEN SANDWICH
OPEN TO ATTACK
OPEN TO CHANCE
OPEN TO CHOICE
OPERA COMIQUE
OPERA GLASSES
OPERATIC ARIA
OPERATIC STAR
OPIUM TRAFFIC
OPPOSING SIDE
OPPOSING TEAM
OPPOSITE CAMP
OPPOSITE ENDS
OPPOSITE SIDE
OPTICAL FIBRE
OPTICAL GLASS
ORANGE PIPPIN
ORANGE SQUASH
ORDEAL BY FIRE
ORDER IN COURT
ORDER OF MERIT
ORDINARY FARE
ORGAN BUILDER

ORGAN GRINDER
ORGAN OF SIGHT
ORGAN RECITAL
ORIEL COLLEGE
ORIGINAL COPY
ORIGINAL COST
ORIGINAL IDEA
ORIGINAL PLAN
OSBORNE HOUSE
OTHER EXTREME
OUNCE OF FLESH
OUNCE OF SENSE
OUNCE OF SNUFF
OUR ANCESTORS
OUTDATED WORD
OUTDOOR GAMES
OUTDOOR SPORT
OUTDOOR STAFF
OUTER GARMENT
OUT FIRST BALL
OUT FOR A SPREE
OUT FOR SCALPS
OUTGOING SHIP
OUTGOING TIDE
OUT IN THE COLD
OUT IN THE OPEN
OUT OF BALANCE
OUT OF COMPANY
OUT OF CONCEIT
OUT OF CONTEXT
OUT OF CONTROL
OUT OF EARSHOT
OUT OF FASHION
OUT OF HARMONY
OUT OF HARNESS
OUT OF HEARING
OUT OF KEEPING
OUT OF ONE'S WAY
OUT OF SERVICE
OUT OF SPIRITS
OUT OF THE BLUE
OUT OF THE RACE
OUT OF THE ROAD
OUT OF THE ROOM
OUT OF THE WIND
OUT OF THE WOOD
OUT OF TROUBLE
OUT OF UNIFORM
OUTRIGHT GIFT
OUTSIDE COURT
OUTSIDE PRICE
OUTSIDE RIGHT
OUTWARD BOUND
OUTWARD SIGNS
OVER AND ABOVE
OVERDO THINGS

OVERNIGHT BAG
OVER ONE'S HEAD
OVER THE COALS
OVER THE HILLS
OVER THE LIMIT
OVER THE VERGE
OVER THE WATER
OVER THE WAVES
OVER THE WORST
OVER THE YEARS
OWE OBEDIENCE
OXFORD ACCENT
OXFORD CIRCUS
OXFORD STREET

P – 12

PABLO PICASSO
PACIFIC OCEAN
PACKAGE COUNT
PACKET OF PINS
PACK OF HOUNDS
PACK OF WOLVES
PACK ONE'S BAGS
PADDLING POOL
PAGE OF HONOUR
PAID-UP MEMBER
PAINFUL SIGHT
PAINTED IMAGE
PAINTED OCEAN
PAINTED WOMAN
PAINTING BOOK
PAINT THE LILY
PAINT THE WALL
PAIR OF BRACES
PAIR OF EIGHTS
PAIR OF GLOVES
PAIR OF HORSES
PAIR OF KNAVES
PAIR OF PLIERS
PAIR OF QUEENS
PAIR OF SCALES
PAIR OF SEVENS
PAIR OF SHEARS
PAIR OF SHORTS
PAIR OF SKATES
PAIR OF SLACKS
PAIR OF THREES
PAIR OF TIGHTS
PAIR OF TRUNKS
PAISLEY SCARF
PAISLEY SHAWL
PALE AS A GHOST
PALETTE KNIFE
PALMERS GREEN
PAPER PATTERN

PAPER THE ROOM
PAPER THE WALL
PAPER WEDDING
PARADE GROUND
PARADISE LOST
PARAFFIN LAMP
PARALLEL BARS
PARISH CHURCH
PARISH PRIEST
PARISH RELIEF
PARISH SCHOOL
PARKING METER
PARKING PLACE
PARKING SPACE
PARLOUR TRICK
PARLOUS STATE
PARMA VIOLETS
PARQUET FLOOR
PARSLEY SAUCE
PART EXCHANGE
PARTHIAN SHOT
PARTIAL TRUTH
PARTING GUEST
PARTING WORDS
PART OF SPEECH
PART OF THE ACT
PART OF THE WAY
PART ONE'S HAIR
PART-TIME WORK
PARTY IN POWER
PARTY MANNERS
PASSAGE MONEY
PASSING FANCY
PASSING PHASE
PASSION FRUIT
PASSIVE VOICE
PASS JUDGMENT
PASS SENTENCE
PASS THE CRUET
PASS THE SAUCE
PAST MIDNIGHT
PAST ONE'S BEST
PASTORAL POEM
PATENT OFFICE
PATENT REMEDY
PATENT RIGHTS
PATERNAL LOVE
PATERNAL ROOF
PATIENT AS JOB
PAT ON THE BACK
PAT ON THE HEAD
PATRICK MOORE
PATROL LEADER
PATTERN MAKER
PAUPER'S GRAVE
PAW THE GROUND

PAY A DIVIDEND
PAY AS YOU EARN
PAY AS YOU WEAR
PAY ATTENTION
PAY DIVIDENDS
PAY IN ADVANCE
PAYING-IN BOOK
PAYING-IN SLIP
PAY ONE'S DEBTS
PAY ONE'S SHARE
PAY ON THE NAIL
PEACE ON EARTH
PEACE STUDIES
PEACH BLOSSOM
PEACOCK'S TAIL
PEAK DISTRICT
PEANUT BUTTER
PEARL FISHING
PEASE PUDDING
PEDAL PUSHERS
PEDIGREE HERD
PEEL ME A GRAPE
PELT WITH RAIN
PEN AND PENCIL
PENCIL SKETCH
PENNY FOR THEM
PENNY WHISTLE
PEOPLE'S PARTY
PEPPER'S GHOST
PERFECT FIFTH
PERFECT IMAGE
PERFECT MATCH
PERFECT ORDER
PERFECT PEACE
PERFECT SIGHT
PERFECT STYLE
PERFECT TENSE
PERFECT WRECK
PERMANENT JOB
PERMANENT WAY
PERMIT TO LAND
PERSONA GRATA
PERSONAL CALL
PERSONAL GAIN
PERSONAL HI-FI
PERSONAL LOAN
PERSONAL NOTE
PERSON OF NOTE
PETER CUSHING
PETER SELLERS
PETER USTINOV
PET GRIEVANCE
PETROL ENGINE
PETROL RATION
PETTING PARTY
PETTY DETAILS

PETTY LARCENY
PETTY OFFICER
PETTY TREASON
PHARAOH'S TOMB
PHONE CHARGES
PHYSICAL PAIN
PIANO RECITAL
PICK A QUARREL
PICKED TROOPS
PICKLED ONION
PICK OUT A TUNE
PICK TO PIECES
PICNIC BASKET
PICNIC HAMPER
PICTORIAL ART
PICTURE FRAME
PICTURE HOUSE
PICTURE PAPER
PICTURE STORY
PIECE BY PIECE
PIECE OF BREAD
PIECE OF CHALK
PIECE OF MUSIC
PIECE OF PAPER
PIERCED HEART
PIERCING LOOK
PIERCING NOTE
PIG'S TROTTERS
PILE UP A SCORE
PILLAR-BOX RED
PILLAR OF SALT
PILLAR TO POST
PILLION RIDER
PILOT OFFICER
PINCH OF SNUFF
PING-PONG BALL
PINK AND WHITE
PINK ELEPHANT
PINK FOR A GIRL
PINK TRIANGLE
PIN ONE'S FAITH
PIN ONE'S HOPES
PINT OF BITTER
PINT OF WALLOP
PIONEER CORPS
PITCH AND TOSS
PIZZA PARLOUR
PLACE AN ORDER
PLACE BETTING
PLACE IN ORDER
PLACE OF BIRTH
PLACE OF EXILE
PLAIN AND PURL
PLAIN CLOTHES
PLAIN COOKING
PLAIN DEALING

PLAIN ENGLISH
PLAIN SAILING
PLAINTIVE CRY
PLAIN WRAPPER
PLANE SPOTTER
PLAN OF ACTION
PLAN OF ATTACK
PLANT ONESELF
PLASTER SAINT
PLASTIC MONEY
PLATES OF MEAT
PLATFORM SHOE
PLATFORM SOLE
PLATINUM RING
PLATONIC LOVE
PLAY A BLINDER
PLAY CHARADES
PLAY DOMINOES
PLAY DRAUGHTS
PLAY FOOTBALL
PLAY FOR A DRAW
PLAY FORFEITS
PLAY FOR MONEY
PLAY HARDBALL
PLAYING CARDS
PLAYING FIELD
PLAY LEAP-FROG
PLAY OLD HARRY
PLAY ONE FALSE
PLAY ONE'S PART
PLAY OPPOSITE
PLAY ROULETTE
PLAY SKITTLES
PLAY THE BANJO
PLAY THE CLOWN
PLAY THE DEUCE
PLAY THE DEVIL
PLAY THE FIELD
PLAY THE HALLS
PLAY THE ORGAN
PLAY THE PIANO
PLAY WITH FIRE
PLEAD POVERTY
PLEA FOR MERCY
PLEA FOR PEACE
PLEA OF GUILTY
PLEASANT NEWS
PLEASANT TIME
PLEASANT TRIP
PLEASANT WEEK
PLEASURE BOAT
PLEASURE TRIP
PLEATED DRESS
PLEATED SKIRT
PLENTY IN HAND
PLENTY OF GUTS

PLENTY OF ROOM
PLENTY OF ROPE
PLENTY OF TIME
PLIGHTED WORD
PLIMSOLL LINE
PLIMSOLL MARK
PLOUGHED LAND
PLOUGH MONDAY
PLUCK A PIGEON
PLUMBER'S MATE
PLUS AND MINUS
PLYMOUTH ROCK
POETIC FRENZY
POET LAUREATE
POINT AT ISSUE
POINT BY POINT
POINT OF ISSUE
POINT OF ORDER
POINTS SYSTEM
POINT TO POINT
POISONED DART
POKE IN THE EYE
POKER SESSION
POLAR REGIONS
POLE POSITION
POLES ASUNDER
POLICE ACTION
POLICE CORDON
POLICE ESCORT
POLICE MATTER
POLICE PATROL
POLICE PERMIT
POLITE PHRASE
POLITICAL MAP
POLITICAL SET
POLLING BOOTH
POLYTHENE BAG
PONS ASINORUM
POOL OF LABOUR
POOL OF LONDON
POOR ARGUMENT
POOR CREATURE
POOR DELIVERY
POOR FEATURES
POOR IN SPIRIT
POOR LINGUIST
POOR PHYSIQUE
POOR PROSPECT
POOR RELATION
POOR RELATIVE
POOR SPECIMEN
POPULAR BRAND
POPULAR FANCY
POPULAR FRONT
POPULAR MUSIC
POPULAR NOVEL

POPULAR PRESS
POPULAR PRICE
POPULAR SPORT
PORGY AND BESS
PORK AND BEANS
PORK SAUSAGES
PORT ADELAIDE
PORT AND LEMON
PORTER'S LODGE
PORTLAND BILL
PORTLAND BOWL
PORTLAND VASE
PORTLY FIGURE
PORT OF LONDON
PORT SUNLIGHT
POSE A PROBLEM
POSITIVE POLE
POSITIVE SIGN
POSSIBLE NEED
POSTAGE STAMP
POSTED ABROAD
POST MERIDIAN
POST OF HONOUR
POST-WAR WORLD
POTATO CRISPS
POTATO FAMINE
POTTER'S WHEEL
POULTRY HOUSE
POUND FOOLISH
POUND OF FLESH
POUND OF SUGAR
POUND THE BEAT
POUR WITH RAIN
POUTER PIGEON
POWDER MONKEY
POWER OF SIGHT
POWER RANGERS
POWER SHARING
POWER STATION
POWERS THAT BE
PRACTICE GAME
PRACTISED EYE
PRAY FOR MERCY
PRAY FOR PEACE
PRECIOUS BANE
PRECIOUS LAMB
PREEN ONESELF
PREMIUM BONDS
PREMIUM OFFER
PREPARE A CASE
PREPARE A MEAL
PREPARED TEXT
PRESENT TENSE
PRESS COUNCIL
PRESS CUTTING
PRESSED STEEL

PRESS FORWARD
PRESS GALLERY
PRESS HAND-OUT
PRESSING NEED
PRESS OFFICER
PRESS ONWARDS
PRESS THE BELL
PRESSURE PUMP
PRETTY ACTIVE
PRETTY PICKLE
PRETTY SPEECH
PRETTY USEFUL
PRICE CONTROL
PRICE OF MONEY
PRICKLY PLANT
PRIDE OF LIONS
PRIDE OF PLACE
PRIDE ONESELF
PRIMAL SCREAM
PRIME SUSPECT
PRIMITIVE ART
PRIMITIVE MAN
PRIMO CARNERA
PRIMROSE HILL
PRIMROSE PATH
PRINCE ALBERT
PRINCE EDWARD
PRINCE GEORGE
PRINCE PHILIP
PRINCE REGENT
PRINCE RUPERT
PRINCESS ANNE
PRINCE'S TRUST
PRINCIPAL BOY
PRINTED SHEET
PRINTER'S COPY
PRISON RECORD
PRISON REFORM
PRISON WARDEN
PRISON WARDER
PRIVATE BEACH
PRIVATE CLASS
PRIVATE FIGHT
PRIVATE HOTEL
PRIVATE HOUSE
PRIVATE LIVES
PRIVATE MEANS
PRIVATE PARTY
PRIVATE TUTOR
PRIVATE VISIT
PRIVATE WORLD
PRIVATE WRONG
PRIVY COUNCIL
PRIZE EDITION
PROBATE COURT
PROBLEM CHILD

PROFIT MARGIN
PROFIT MOTIVE
PROMISED LAND
PROMISE TO PAY
PROMPT ACTION
PROMPT ANSWER
PROMPT CORNER
PROOF OF GUILT
PROPER COURSE
PROPER PERSON
PROPERTY DEAL
PROPHET OF WOE
PROTEST MARCH
PROTOTYPE CAR
PROUD AS PUNCH
PROUD PRESTON
PROVEN GUILTY
PROVE THE RULE
PROVIDE LUNCH
PRUNING KNIFE
PRUSSIAN BLUE
PSYCHIC FORCE
PUBLIC AFFAIR
PUBLIC APATHY
PUBLIC DEMAND
PUBLIC FIGURE
PUBLIC HEALTH
PUBLIC NOTICE
PUBLIC OFFICE
PUBLIC ORATOR
PUBLIC OUTCRY
PUBLIC POLICY
PUBLIC SCHOOL
PUBLIC SPEECH
PUBLIC SPIRIT
PUDDING BASIN
PUFFING BILLY
PUFFIN ISLAND
PULL A FAST ONE
PULLING POWER
PULL-OUT AIRER
PULL THE WIRES
PULL TOGETHER
PULL TO PIECES
PULP MAGAZINE
PUNCH AND JUDY
PUPIL TEACHER
PURE NONSENSE
PURL AND PLAIN
PURSE THE LIPS
PURSUE A THEME
PURSUIT PLANE
PUSH ONE'S LUCK
PUT AN END TO IT
PUT A QUESTION
PUT A SOCK IN IT

PUT A STOP TO IT
PUT IN ITALICS
PUT IN SPLINTS
PUT IN THE DOCK
PUT INTO FORCE
PUT INTO RHYME
PUT INTO SHAPE
PUT INTO WORDS
PUT IN WRITING
PUT IT BLUNTLY
PUTNEY BRIDGE
PUTNEY COMMON
PUT ONE ACROSS
PUT ONE'S OAR IN
PUT ON ONE SIDE
PUT ON THE LIST
PUT ON THE RACK
PUT OUT OF GEAR
PUT THE BOOT IN
PUT THE CAT OUT
PUT THE WIND UP
PUTTING GREEN
PUT TO AUCTION
PUT TO GOOD USE
PUT TO THE RACK
PUT TO THE TEST
PUT TO THE VOTE
PUT TO TORTURE
PUT UP FOR SALE

Q – 12

QUARTER FINAL
QUARTER RIGHT
QUARTER TO ONE
QUARTER TO SIX
QUARTER TO TEN
QUARTER TO TWO
QUART MEASURE
QUEEN CONSORT
QUEEN OF CLUBS
QUEEN OF SHEBA
QUEEN OF TONGA
QUEEN'S BISHOP
QUEEN'S BOUNTY
QUEEN'S COLOUR
QUEEN'S FLIGHT
QUEEN'S GAMBIT
QUEEN'S KNIGHT
QUEEN'S SPEECH
QUEEN TITANIA
QUEER FEELING
QUESTION MARK
QUESTION TIME
QUEUE JUMPING
QUICK JOURNEY

QUICK RETURNS
QUIET WEDDING
QUIET WEEK-END
QUITE CERTAIN
QUITE CORRECT
QUITE IN ORDER
QUIT ONE'S POST
QUIT THE SCENE
QUIT THE STAGE
QUOTE THE ODDS

R – 12

RABBIT WARREN
RACE OF GIANTS
RACIAL HATRED
RACING DRIVER
RACING JARGON
RACING SEASON
RACING STABLE
RADAR STATION
RADIANT SMILE
RADICAL ERROR
RADIO AMATEUR
RADIO LICENCE
RADIO MESSAGE
RADIO NETWORK
RADIO STATION
RAFFLE TICKET
RAGING TEMPER
RAGLAN SLEEVE
RAGS AND BONES
RAGS TO RICHES
RAIDING PARTY
RAILWAY HOTEL
RAILWAY LINES
RAILWAY TRAIN
RAILWAY TRUCK
RAINBOW TROUT
RAINY CLIMATE
RAINY WEATHER
RAISE A FAMILY
RAISED VOICES
RAISE ONE'S HAT
RAISE THE ANTE
RAISE THE DEAD
RAISE THE DUST
RAISE THE FARE
RAISE THE RENT
RAISE THE ROOF
RAISE THE WIND
RAKE TOGETHER
RAMBLING ROSE
RANDOM EFFORT
RANDOM NUMBER
RANDOM SAMPLE

RANK OUTSIDER
RAPID DECLINE
RAPID SPEAKER
RAPID STRIDES
RAPID TRANSIT
RAPIER THRUST
RASPBERRY JAM
RASPING VOICE
RATABLE VALUE
RATHER LITTLE
RATHER POORLY
RAVEN TRESSES
RAY ELLINGTON
RAY OF COMFORT
REACH FORWARD
REACT AGAINST
REACT SHARPLY
READ AND WRITE
READING GLASS
READ ONE'S HAND
READ ONE'S PALM
READ THE CARDS
READ THE SIGNS
READ THE STARS
READY CONSENT
READY FOR WEAR
READY-MIX CAKE
READY TO BURST
READY TO LEARN
READY TO LEAVE
READY TO START
REALM OF PLUTO
REAL PRESENCE
REAL PROPERTY
REAL SECURITY
REAR ENTRANCE
REAR ONE'S HEAD
RECALL TO LIFE
RECALL TO MIND
RECEIVING END
RECEIVING SET
RECENT EVENTS
RECITE POETRY
RECORD OFFICE
RECORD OUTPUT
RECORD PLAYER
RED AND YELLOW
RED CORPUSCLE
RED FOR DANGER
RED IN THE FACE
RED-LETTER DAY
RED STOCKINGS
REDUCED FARES
REDUCED PRICE
REDUCED SPEED
REDUCE IN RANK

REDUCE TO PULP
REDUCE TO SIZE
RED WITH ANGER
REEFER JACKET
REEL OF COTTON
REFINED SUGAR
REFINED TASTE
REFLEX ACTION
REFORM SCHOOL
REFUSE CREDIT
REFUSE OFFICE
REFUSE TO MEET
REFUSE TO MOVE
REFUSE TO PLAY
REFUSE TO SIGN
REFUSE TO VOTE
REFUSE TO WORK
REGAL BEARING
REGENCY HOUSE
REGENCY STYLE
REGENT'S CANAL
REGENT STREET
REGIONAL NEWS
REGULAR BRICK
REGULAR DEMON
REGULAR HABIT
REGULAR HOURS
REGULAR MEALS
REGULAR ORDER
REIGN SUPREME
REITH LECTURE
RELAY STATION
RELEVANT FACT
RELIEF WORKER
RELIGIOUS WAR
REMAIN AT HOME
REMAIN BEHIND
REMAIN SEATED
REMAIN SILENT
REMAIN SINGLE
REMOTE CHANCE
REMOTE FUTURE
REMOTE OBJECT
REMOVE BODILY
REMOVE ERRORS
RENDER THANKS
REND THE SKIES
RENÉE HOUSTON
RENT A CARAVAN
RENT A COTTAGE
RENT TRIBUNAL
REPAIR OUTFIT
REPEAT ACTION
REPORTED CASE
REPTILE HOUSE
REPUTED OWNER

RESCUE WORKER	RINGING LAUGH	ROMANTIC FOOL
RESEARCH TEAM	RINGING SOUND	ROMANTIC GIRL
RESEARCH WORK	RINGING TONES	ROMANTIC IDEA
RESERVED LIST	RING IN THE NEW	RONALD COLMAN
RESERVED SEAT	RINGSIDE SEAT	RONALD REAGAN
RESERVE PRICE	RIO DE JANEIRO	RONALD SHINER
RESERVE STOCK	RIOT OF COLOUR	ROOM AT THE TOP
RESIDE ABROAD	RIPE TOMATOES	ROOM FOR DOUBT
RESORT TO ARMS	RIPPLE EFFECT	ROOM THIRTEEN
RESPONSE TIME	RIP VAN WINKLE	ROOM TO EXPAND
RESTING ACTOR	RISE AND SHINE	ROPE OF ONIONS
RESTING PLACE	RISE IN REVOLT	ROPE OF PEARLS
REST OF THE DAY	RISE TO THE FLY	ROSE AND CROWN
REST ONE'S CASE	RISE TO THE TOP	ROSE-HIP SYRUP
REST ONE'S EYES	RISING GROUND	ROSE OF TRALEE
RESTORE ORDER	RISING PRICES	ROSE TO THE TOP
RETAIL DEALER	RISK ONE'S LIFE	ROSETTA STONE
RETAINING FEE	RISK ONE'S NECK	ROSY PROSPECT
RETURN A VISIT	RIVAL COMPANY	ROTARY ACTION
RETURN OF POST	RIVER OF BLOOD	ROTTEN BRANCH
RETURN TICKET	RIVER SHANNON	ROUGH COUNTRY
RETURN TO BASE	RIVER STEAMER	ROUGH DIAMOND
RETURN TO PORT	RIVER TRAFFIC	ROUGH DRAWING
RETURN VOYAGE	ROAD ACCIDENT	ROUGH JUSTICE
REVERSE ORDER	ROAD JUNCTION	ROUGH MANNERS
REVERT TO TYPE	ROADSIDE CAFÉ	ROUGH PASSAGE
REVOLVER SHOT	ROAR FOR MERCY	ROUGH PICTURE
RHESUS MONKEY	ROARING TRADE	ROUGH SURFACE
RHYMING SLANG	ROAR WITH PAIN	ROUGH TEXTURE
RICHARD CONTE	ROAR WITH RAGE	ROUGH WEATHER
RICHMOND HILL	ROAST CHICKEN	ROUND BY ROUND
RICHMOND PARK	ROASTED ALIVE	ROUND FIGURES
RICH RELATION	ROBE OF HONOUR	ROUND OF CALLS
RICH RELATIVE	ROBERT BEATTY	ROUND OF TOAST
RICHTER SCALE	ROBERT GRAVES	ROUND THE BACK
RIDE AT ANCHOR	ROBERT MORLEY	ROUND THE BEND
RIDE BARE-BACK	ROBERT NEWTON	ROUND THE CAPE
RIDE FOR A FALL	ROBERT TAYLOR	ROUND THE EDGE
RIDE FULL TILT	ROBOT DANCING	ROUND THE FIRE
RIDER HAGGARD	ROBUST HEALTH	ROUND THE MOON
RIDE THE STORM	ROCKING HORSE	ROUND THE TOWN
RIDE TO HOUNDS	ROGATION DAYS	ROUSE ONESELF
RIDING LESSON	ROGATION WEEK	ROUSING CHEER
RIDING MASTER	ROLLER SKATES	ROUTINE CHECK
RIDING SCHOOL	ROLLING STOCK	ROVING REPORT
RIDING STABLE	ROLLING STONE	ROW OF BUTTONS
RIFLE BRIGADE	ROLL OF HONOUR	ROYAL ACADEMY
RIGHT AND LEFT	ROLL ONE'S EYES	ROYAL ARSENAL
RIGHTFUL HEIR	ROMAN EMPEROR	ROYAL BANQUET
RIGHT-HAND MAN	ROMAN FIGURES	ROYAL CHARTER
RIGHT OF ENTRY	ROMAN HISTORY	ROYAL CIRCLES
RIGHT OR WRONG	ROMAN HOLIDAY	ROYAL COMMAND
RIGHT OUTSIDE	ROMAN LETTERS	ROYAL CONSENT
RIGHT QUALITY	ROMAN NUMBERS	ROYAL DYNASTY
RIGHT THROUGH	ROMAN REMAINS	ROYAL HUNT CAP
RIG THE MARKET	ROMAN SOLDIER	ROYAL MARINES

ROYAL SOCIETY
ROYAL WARRANT
ROYAL WEDDING
ROYAL WELCOME
RUBBER BULLET
RUBBER CHEQUE
RUBBER DINGHY
RUBBER GLOVES
RUB ONE'S HANDS
RUB SHOULDERS
RUDE REMINDER
RUGBY COLOURS
RUGGER GROUND
RUGGER PLAYER
RUINED CASTLE
RUINOUS FOLLY
RULE OF TERROR
RULE THE ROOST
RUMOURS OF WAR
RUN-AWAY HORSE
RUN-AWAY MATCH
RUN AWAY TO SEA
RUN-AWAY TRAIN
RUN FOR OFFICE
RUN FOR SAFETY
RUN LIKE A DEER
RUN LIKE A HARE
RUNNING COSTS
RUNNING FIGHT
RUNNING FLUSH
RUNNING TITLE
RUNNING TRACK
RUNNING WATER
RUN OF BAD LUCK
RUN OF THE MILL
RUN ON THE BANK
RUPERT BROOKE
RUSH HEADLONG
RUSHING WATER
RUSSIAN BOOTS
RUSSIAN DANCE
RUSSIAN NOVEL
RUSSIAN SALAD
RUSSIAN VODKA
RUSTIC BRIDGE

S – 12

SACRED NUMBER
SACRED PLEDGE
SADDLE OF LAMB
SADLER'S WELLS
SAD SPECTACLE
SAFE AND SOUND
SAFE AS HOUSES
SAFE CROSSING

SAFE DISTANCE
SAFETY DEVICE
SAFETY FACTOR
SAGE AND ONION
SAHARA DESERT
SAILING BARGE
SAINT BERNARD
SAINT PANCRAS
SAINT PATRICK
SAINT SWITHIN
SALE OR RETURN
SALES FIGURES
SALES MANAGER
SALIENT ANGLE
SALIENT POINT
SALOON PRICES
SALTED ALMOND
SALTED BUTTER
SALT LAKE CITY
SALUTING BASE
SALVADOR DALI
SALVAGE CORPS
SALVAGE MONEY
SAMPLE BOTTLE
SAMUEL BUTLER
SAN FRANCISCO
SAN SEBASTIAN
SAPPHIRE RING
SARACEN'S HEAD
SARDONIC GRIN
SATAN'S PALACE
SATURDAY CLUB
SAUCE TARTARE
SAVAGE ATTACK
SAVAGE TEMPER
SAVE ONE'S FACE
SAVE ONE'S LIFE
SAVE ONE'S NECK
SAVE ONE'S SKIN
SAVE OUR SOULS
SAVING CLAUSE
SAVING FACTOR
SAVINGS STAMP
SAVOY CABBAGE
SAY A FEW WORDS
SAY A GOOD WORD
SAY A MOUTHFUL
SAY ONE'S PIECE
SAY SOMETHING
SCALE DRAWING
SCALLOP SHELL
SCARLET FEVER
SCARLET WOMAN
SCENE OF CHAOS
SCENE STEALER
SCENTED PAPER

SCEPTRED ISLE
SCHOLAR GIPSY
SCHOOL BLAZER
SCHOOL FRIEND
SCHOOL MATRON
SCHOOL OUTING
SCHOOL REPORT
SCHOOL SPORTS
SCOOP THE POOL
SCORCHING HOT
SCORE A SINGLE
SCORE THROUGH
SCOTCH BONNET
SCOTCH HUMOUR
SCOTCH WHISKY
SCOTLAND YARD
SCOTTISH PEER
SCOTTISH REEL
SCOUT'S HONOUR
SCRAMBLED EGG
SCRAP OF PAPER
SCRIPT WRITER
SCROLL OF FAME
SCULLERY MAID
SEAFARING MAN
SEAL A BARGAIN
SEALED ORDERS
SEAL OF OFFICE
SEALSKIN COAT
SEA OF GALILEE
SEA OF MARMARA
SEA OF TROUBLE
SEARCH IN VAIN
SEASONAL WIND
SEASON TICKET
SEAT OF HONOUR
SEBASTIAN COE
SECLUDED SPOT
SECOND CHANCE
SECOND CHOICE
SECOND COMING
SECOND COURSE
SECOND COUSIN
SECOND DANIEL
SECOND DEGREE
SECOND ELEVEN
SECOND FIDDLE
SECOND FINGER
SECOND GLANCE
SECOND LEAGUE
SECOND LESSON
SECOND LETTER
SECOND NATURE
SECOND OF JULY
SECOND OF JUNE
SECOND PERSON

SECOND RUBBER
SECOND SEASON
SECOND SERIES
SECOND STOREY
SECOND STRING
SECOND TO NONE
SECOND VIOLIN
SECOND VOLUME
SECRET BALLOT
SECRET DRAWER
SECRET ERRAND
SECRET PAPERS
SECRET POLICE
SECRET TREATY
SECRET WEAPON
SECURE FUTURE
SECURE OLD AGE
SECURITY LEAK
SECURITY RISK
SEE AT A GLANCE
SEEDED PLAYER
SEED MERCHANT
SEEDS OF DECAY
SEEDS OF DOUBT
SEE IN THE DARK
SEE IT THROUGH
SEEK A FORMULA
SEEK A FORTUNE
SEEK AN EFFECT
SEEK A QUARREL
SEEK GUIDANCE
SEESAW MOTION
SEE THE SIGHTS
SEETHING MASS
SELL FOR A SONG
SELLING PLATE
SELLING PRICE
SELL ON CREDIT
SELL ONE'S SOUL
SELL THE DUMMY
SEND A MESSAGE
SEND TO PRISON
SENIOR BRANCH
SENIOR MASTER
SENIOR MEMBER
SENIOR PURSER
SENIOR SCHOOL
SENSE OF GUILT
SENSE OF SHAME
SENSE OF SIGHT
SENSE OF SMELL
SENSE OF TASTE
SENSE OF TOUCH
SENSE OF WRONG
SENSIBLE GIRL
SENSITIVE EAR

SENT TO BLAZES
SENT TO SCHOOL
SEPARATE WAYS
SERENE NATURE
SERENE TEMPER
SERIAL KILLER
SERIAL NUMBER
SERIAL RIGHTS
SERIOUSLY ILL
SERIOUS MONEY
SERIOUS MUSIC
SERIOUS OFFER
SERIOUS RIVAL
SERIOUS WOUND
SERRIED RANKS
SERVANT CLASS
SERVANTS' HALL
SERVE AT TABLE
SERVE ITS TURN
SERVICE CHIEF
SERVICE DEPOT
SERVICE DRESS
SERVICE OF GOD
SERVICE RIFLE
SERVING HATCH
SET AN EXAMPLE
SET A STANDARD
SET AT LIBERTY
SET BY THE EARS
SET OF LANCERS
SET ONE AT EASE
SET ONE'S TEETH
SET PROGRAMME
SETTLE A SCORE
SETTLE IN TOWN
SETTLE THE DAY
SEVEN COURSES
SEVEN DEGREES
SEVEN DOLLARS
SEVEN EIGHTHS
SEVEN FATHOMS
SEVEN GALLONS
SEVEN GUINEAS
SEVEN HUNDRED
SEVEN LEAGUES
SEVEN MINUTES
SEVEN OCTAVES
SEVEN OF CLUBS
SEVEN OR EIGHT
SEVEN PER CENT
SEVEN SISTERS
SEVEN SQUARED
SEVENTH FLOOR
SEVENTH GREEN
SEVENTH OF MAY
SEVENTH PLACE

SEVENTH ROUND
SEVENTY MILES
SEVENTY TIMES
SEVENTY YEARS
SEVEN VIRTUES
SEVEN WICKETS
SEVEN WISE MEN
SEVEN WONDERS
SEVERAL TIMES
SEVERE ATTACK
SEVERE CRITIC
SEVERE MASTER
SEVERE STRAIN
SEVERE WINTER
SEVERN BRIDGE
SEVERN TUNNEL
SEWING BASKET
SEWING CIRCLE
SEW ON A BUTTON
SHADE OF DOUBT
SHADOW BOXING
SHADY RETREAT
SHAFT OF LIGHT
SHAH OF PERSIA
SHAKE THE HEAD
SHALLOW GRAVE
SHALLOW WATER
SHAMELESS LIE
SHARE CAPITAL
SHARE THE LOAD
SHARE THE LOOT
SHARP LOOK-OUT
SHARP OUTLINE
SHARP REPROOF
SHAVING BRUSH
SHAVING STICK
SHEEPISH GRIN
SHEEPISH LOOK
SHEEP'S TONGUE
SHEER TORTURE
SHEET OF FLAME
SHEET OF GLASS
SHEET OF PAPER
SHEET OF WATER
SHEIK OF ARABY
SHELLING PEAS
SHEPHERD'S PIE
SHERRY TRIFLE
SHETLAND PONY
SHINING LIGHT
SHINING WHITE
SHIPPING LANE
SHIPPING LINE
SHIP'S BISCUIT
SHIP'S CAPTAIN
SHIP'S COMPANY

SHIP'S COMPASS
SHIP'S STEWARD
SHIRLEY EATON
SHIRT SLEEVES
SHIVERING FIT
SHOCKING COLD
SHOCKING PINK
SHOCK TACTICS
SHOCK THERAPY
SHOE REPAIRER
SHOE-SHINE BOY
SHOOTER'S HILL
SHOOTING PAIN
SHOOTING STAR
SHOOT ONESELF
SHOOT THE MOON
SHOPPING LIST
SHORE TO SHORE
SHORN OF GLORY
SHORT ACCOUNT
SHORT CIRCUIT
SHORT COMMONS
SHORTER HOURS
SHORTEST GIRL
SHORT EXTRACT
SHORT JOURNEY
SHORTLY AFTER
SHORT MEASURE
SHORT OF FUNDS
SHORT OF MONEY
SHORT OF SPACE
SHORT OF STAFF
SHORT OF WORDS
SHORT PASSAGE
SHORT ROMANCE
SHORT SESSION
SHORT SUMMARY
SHORT TENANCY
SHORT TIME AGO
SHORT VERSION
SHOT AND SHELL
SHOT IN THE ARM
SHOT ONE'S BOLT
SHOT TO PIECES
SHOULDER ARMS
SHOULDER PADS
SHOUT FOR HELP
SHOUT THE ODDS
SHOVE HA'PENNY
SHOW APTITUDE
SHOW BUSINESS
SHOWER OF RAIN
SHOWER SCREEN
SHOW INTEREST
SHOWN THE DOOR
SHOW OF REASON

SHOW ONE ROUND
SHOW ONE'S FACE
SHOW ONE'S HAND
SHOW PRUDENCE
SHRIMPING NET
SHUFFLE ALONG
SHUT OFF STEAM
SHUT ONE'S EYES
SHUTTER SPEED
SHUT YOUR TRAP!
SIAMESE TWINS
SICK AND TIRED
SICK BUILDING
SICK OF TRYING
SIDE ENTRANCE
SIDE MOVEMENT
SIDE OF MUTTON
SIDNEY STREET
SIEGE OF PARIS
SIERRA NEVADA
SIGH OF RELIEF
SIGHTING SHOT
SIGMUND FREUD
SIGNAL DEFEAT
SIGNAL REWARD
SIGN LANGUAGE
SIGN OF DANGER
SIGN ONE'S NAME
SILENT LETTER
SILENT PRAYER
SILK STOCKING
SILLY SUFFOLK
SILVER DOLLAR
SILVER LINING
SILVER SALVER
SILVER SCREEN
SILVER STREAK
SILVER TEA-POT
SILVER THREAD
SIMON TEMPLAR
SIMPLE ANSWER
SIMPLE ATTIRE
SIMPLE BEAUTY
SIMPLE DEVICE
SIMPLE EFFORT
SIMPLE MATTER
SIMPLE PERSON
SIMPLE REMEDY
SINGING VOICE
SING IN UNISON
SINGLE COMBAT
SINGLE HANDED
SINGLE NUMBER
SINGLE PERSON
SINGLES CHART
SINGLE SCOTCH

SINGLES MATCH
SINGLE TICKET
SINGLE WHISKY
SINISTER MOVE
SIR HENRY WOOD
SIR JOHN MOORE
SIR PETER HALL
SIR TOBY BELCH
SIT AT THE BACK
SIT IN COUNCIL
SIX FEET UNDER
SIX OF THE BEST
SIXTEEN MILES
SIXTH CENTURY
SIXTH OF APRIL
SIXTH OF MARCH
SIXTY MINUTES
SIXTY PER CENT
SIXTY SECONDS
SKEIN OF GEESE
SKELETON CREW
SKIFFLE GROUP
SKIN AND BONES
SKIN GRAFTING
SKITTLE ALLEY
SKYE BOAT-SONG
SLACKEN SPEED
SLAP IN THE EYE
SLAVE TO DRINK
SLAVE TRAFFIC
SLEAZE FACTOR
SLEEPING DOGS
SLEEPING LION
SLEEPING PILL
SLEEP SOUNDLY
SLEEP SWEETLY
SLENDER HOPES
SLENDER MEANS
SLENDER PURSE
SLENDER WAIST
SLICE OF BREAD
SLICE OF LEMON
SLICE OF TOAST
SLICE THE BALL
SLIDING PANEL
SLIDING SCALE
SLIGHT CHANCE
SLIGHT CHANGE
SLIGHT DAMAGE
SLIGHT FIGURE
SLIGHT INJURY
SLIGHTLY DEAF
SLIMMING DIET
SLIMMING PILL
SLIP AND SLIDE
SLIP OF A THING

SLIP OF THE PEN
SLIP THE CABLE
SLIP UP ON A JOB
SLITHER ALONG
SLOANE RANGER
SLOANE SQUARE
SLOANE STREET
SLOPING SIDES
SLOW MOVEMENT
SLOW OF SPEECH
SLOW PROGRESS
SLOW PUNCTURE
SLUM PROPERTY
SMALL ACCOUNT
SMALL COMFORT
SMALL FORTUNE
SMALL HELPING
SMALL HOLDING
SMALL LETTERS
SMALL MEASURE
SMALL MERCIES
SMALL PORTION
SMALL PURPOSE
SMALL SAVINGS
SMALL WRITING
SMART CLOTHES
SMART DEALING
SMART OFFICER
SMART SERVANT
SMART TURN-OUT
SMASH AND GRAB
SMASHING BLOW
SMEAR TACTICS
SMELL SWEETLY
SMILE SWEETLY
SMOKE A LITTLE
SMOKED SALMON
SMOKED TONGUE
SMOKER'S COUGH
SMOKER'S HEART
SMOKE TOO MUCH
SMOOTH TEMPER
SMOOTH THE WAY
SMOOTH TONGUE
SNACK COUNTER
SNAKE CHARMER
SNAP AND SNARL
SNAP DECISION
SNAP JUDGMENT
SNEAK PREVIEW
SNOW CRYSTALS
SOAP AND WATER
SOBER THOUGHT
SOCIAL CENTRE
SOCIAL CIRCLE
SOCIAL CREDIT

SOCIAL MISFIT
SOCIAL SEASON
SOCIAL STATUS
SOCIAL SURVEY
SOCIAL UNREST
SOCIAL WORKER
SOCIETY WOMAN
SOCK IN THE EYE
SODA FOUNTAIN
SOFT AS BUTTER
SOFT AS VELVET
SOFT CURRENCY
SOFT HANDLING
SOFTLY SOFTLY
SOFT NOTHINGS
SOLAR ECLIPSE
SOLDERING GUN
SOLEMN THREAT
SOLE SURVIVOR
SOLID CITIZEN
SOLITARY LIFE
SOLITARY WALK
SOLOMON'S SEAL
SOLVENT ABUSE
SOMETHING NEW
SOMETHING OLD
SOME TIME BACK
SON ET LUMIÈRE
SONG AND DANCE
SONG OF A SHIRT
SONG OF PRAISE
SONIC BARRIER
SON OF THE SOIL
SONS OF BELIAL
SOPRANO VOICE
SOPWITH CAMEL
SORE DISTRESS
SORRY OUTCOME
SOUL OF HONOUR
SOUND AND FURY
SOUND AS A BELL
SOUND BACKING
SOUND BARRIER
SOUND EFFECTS
SOUND OF MUSIC
SOUND SLEEPER
SOUND TACTICS
SOUP OF THE DAY
SOUTH AFRICAN
SOUTH AMERICA
SOUTHEND PIER
SOUTHERN AREA
SOUTH PACIFIC
SOUTH SHIELDS
SOVIET RUSSIA
SPACE FICTION

SPACE SHUTTLE
SPACE STATION
SPACE TO BUILD
SPADE AND FORK
SPANISH DANCE
SPANISH MONEY
SPANISH ONION
SPANISH TANGO
SPANKING PACE
SPARE A COPPER
SPARE BEDROOM
SPARE NO PAINS
SPARE-TIME JOB
SPARKING PLUG
SPARKLING WIT
SPARTAN BREED
SPATE OF WORDS
SPEAK CLEARLY
SPEAK ENGLISH
SPEAKER STAND
SPEAKING PART
SPEAKING TUBE
SPEAK ITALIAN
SPEAK PLAINLY
SPEAK RAPIDLY
SPEAK RUSSIAN
SPEAK SPANISH
SPEAK VOLUMES
SPEAR CARRIER
SPECIAL AGENT
SPECIAL CHARM
SPECIAL ISSUE
SPECIAL NURSE
SPECIAL OFFER
SPECIAL POINT
SPECIAL PRICE
SPECIAL TERMS
SPECIAL TRAIN
SPECIAL TREAT
SPECIFIC HEAT
SPECIMEN COPY
SPECIMEN PAGE
SPEECH DEFECT
SPEED OF LIGHT
SPEED OF SOUND
SPEEDY ANSWER
SPELL CHECKER
SPELLING GAME
SPENCER TRACY
SPEND A PACKET
SPICK AND SPAN
SPIDER AND FLY
SPIKE THE GUNS
SPILL THE MILK
SPILL THE SALT
SPINAL COLUMN

SPIN LIKE A TOP
SPIN THE WHEEL
SPIRIT OF EVIL
SPLENDID TIME
SPLIT THE ATOM
SPLIT THE VOTE
SPOILED CHILD
SPORTING LIFE
SPORTING NEWS
SPORT OF KINGS
SPORT ONE'S OAK
SPORTS EDITOR
SPORTS GROUND
SPORTS JACKET
SPORTS MASTER
SPORTS REPORT
SPORTS TROPHY
SPOT AND PLAIN
SPOT OF BOTHER
SPOT OF WHISKY
SPREAD ABROAD
SPREAD CANVAS
SPRING BUDGET
SPRING GREENS
SPRING ONIONS
SPRING SEASON
SPRING TO MIND
SPURN AN OFFER
SPY SATELLITE
SQUARE NUMBER
STACK OF CHIPS
STACK OF STRAW
STACK THE DECK
STAFF CAPTAIN
STAFF COLLEGE
STAFF OFFICER
STAFF PROBLEM
STAGE A STRIKE
STAGE BY STAGE
STAGE EFFECTS
STAGE MANAGER
STAGE VILLAIN
STAGE WHISPER
STAINED GLASS
STALL FOR TIME
STAMP AUCTION
STAMP MACHINE
STAMP OF TRUTH
STAND ABASHED
STAND ACCUSED
STAND A CHANCE
STAND AGAINST
STAND AND WAIT
STANDARD LAMP
STANDARD RATE
STANDARD ROSE

STANDARD SIZE
STANDARD TIME
STANDARD WORK
STAND BETWEEN
STAND IN FRONT
STANDING ARMY
STANDING JOKE
STANDING ONLY
STANDING ROOM
ST ANDREW'S DAY
STAND THE PACE
STAND THE TEST
STAND-UP FIGHT
STAND UPRIGHT
STAND WAITING
STANLEY BLACK
ST ANNE'S ON SEA
STARK MADNESS
STARK REALITY
STARLIT NIGHT
STAR MATERIAL
STARRING ROLE
STARTING GATE
STARTING POST
START PACKING
START TALKING
START TO CHEER
START TOO LATE
START TOO SOON
STARVE A FEVER
STATE CONTROL
STATED PERIOD
STATE FUNERAL
STATE LIBRARY
STATE LOTTERY
STATE OF BLISS
STATE OF GRACE
STATE OF PEACE
STATE OF SIEGE
STATE PENSION
STATE SCHOLAR
STATE SUBSIDY
STATION HOTEL
STATION WAGON
STATUE OF EROS
STATUS SYMBOL
STAYING POWER
STAY ONE'S HAND
STAY THE NIGHT
STAY TO DINNER
STAY TO THE END
ST BERNARD DOG
STEADY DEMAND
STEADY INCOME
STEAK TARTARE
STEAL THE SHOW

STEALTHY STEP
STEAM CLEANER
STEAM TURBINE
STEAM WHISTLE
STEERING GEAR
STEFAN EDBERG
STEP AEROBICS
STEP BACKWARD
STEP ON THE GAS
STERLING AREA
STERN REALITY
STEWED APPLES
STEWED PRUNES
ST GEORGE'S DAY
STICK NO BILLS
STICK OF BOMBS
STICK OF CHALK
STICK OR TWIST
STICK TO PROSE
STICKY TOFFEE
STICKY WICKET
STIFF PENALTY
STILETTO HEEL
STINGING BLOW
STINGING PAIN
STIRRING GAME
STIRRING NEWS
STIRRING TALE
STIR THE BLOOD
STIR UP STRIFE
STITCH IN TIME
ST JAMES'S PARK
ST LOUIS BLUES
ST MARYLEBONE
STOCK COMPANY
STOCK EXAMPLE
STOCKING FEET
STOCK IN TRADE
STOKE THE FIRE
STOLEN KISSES
STONE OF SCONE
STONE TO DEATH
STOOD THE TEST
STOOGE AROUND
STOP AND START
STOP DRINKING
STOP FIGHTING
STOP-GO POLICY
STOP LAUGHING
STOP ONE'S EARS
STOP THE CLOCK
STOP THE FIGHT
STOP THE NIGHT
STOP WORRYING
STORAGE SPACE
STORM BREWING

STORM OF ABUSE	STRIKE A LIGHT	SUGAR REFINER
STORM TROOPER	STRIKE A MATCH	SUGAR THE PILL
STORM WARNING	STRIKE BOTTOM	SUICIDAL IDEA
STORMY CAREER	STRIKE IT RICH	SUITE OF ROOMS
STORMY DEBATE	STRIKE ME DEAD!	SUIT OF ARMOUR
STORMY PETREL	STRIKE ME PINK!	SUIT YOURSELF
STORMY TEMPER	STRIKE TERROR	SULTAN'S HAREM
STOUT AND MILD	STRIKE THE EYE	SULTAN'S WIVES
STOUT OF HEART	STRIKE WEAPON	SUMMARY COURT
STOVEPIPE HAT	STRING OF LIES	SUMMER MONTHS
ST PETERSBURG	STRIP CARTOON	SUMMER RESORT
STRAIGHT AWAY	STRIP OF PAPER	SUMMER SCHOOL
STRAIGHT BACK	STRIP OF WATER	SUMMER SEASON
STRAIGHT DEAL	STRIVE IN VAIN	SUNDAY DINNER
STRAIGHT DOWN	STROKE OF LUCK	SUNDAY'S CHILD
STRAIGHT DROP	STROKE OF WORK	SUNDAY SCHOOL
STRAIGHTEN UP	STROKE THE CAT	SUNKEN CHEEKS
STRAIGHT FACE	STROKE THE DOG	SUNKEN GARDEN
STRAIGHT HAIR	STRONG-ARM MAN	SUNNY WEATHER
STRAIGHT HOME	STRONG AS AN OX	SUNSHINE ROOF
STRAIGHT LEFT	STRONG COLOUR	SUN-TAN LOTION
STRAIGHT LINE	STRONG DEMAND	SUPERB FIGURE
STRAIGHT NOSE	STRONG DENIAL	SUPERB FINISH
STRAIGHT PART	STRONG DESIRE	SUPERIOR AIRS
STRAIGHT PLAY	STRONGLY MADE	SUPERIOR RANK
STRAIGHT ROAD	STRONG NERVES	SUPERIOR TYPE
STRAIGHT SETS	STRONG THIRST	SUPPORT A WIFE
STRAIGHT SHOT	STRONG WHISKY	SUPREME BEING
STRAIGHT TALK	STRUGGLE HARD	SUPREME COURT
STRAIN A POINT	STUDENT OF LAW	SUPREME ISSUE
STRAIT JACKET	STUDY CLOSELY	SUPREME POWER
STRAND OF HAIR	STUFFED HEART	SURE TO PLEASE
STRANGE FACES	STUFFED OLIVE	SURGE FORWARD
STRANGE PLACE	STUFFED SHIRT	SURGERY HOURS
STRANGE TO SAY	STUFF ONESELF	SURGICAL CASE
STRANGE WOMAN	STUMBLE ALONG	SURGICAL WARD
STRAPPING LAD	STUMP ORATORY	SURPLUS FLESH
STREAK OF LUCK	STUNNING BLOW	SURPLUS GOODS
STREAKY BACON	STUPID ANSWER	SURPLUS STOCK
STREAM OF CARS	STUPID FELLOW	SURPRISE MOVE
STREET ARTIST	STYGIAN SHORE	SUSAN HAYWARD
STREET CORNER	STYLING TONGS	SUSTAIN A LOSS
STREET MARKET	SUBDUED LIGHT	SWALLOW WHOLE
STREETS AHEAD	SUBMARINE PEN	SWARM OF FLIES
STREET SELLER	SUBTLE CHANGE	SWARM OF GNATS
STREET SINGER	SUCCESS STORY	SWARM UP A ROPE
STREET TRADER	SUCK AN ORANGE	SWAY TO AND FRO
STREET URCHIN	SUDDEN ATTACK	SWEAR FALSELY
STREET VENDOR	SUDDEN CHANGE	SWEDISH DRILL
STRETCH NYLON	SUDDEN MOTION	SWEEP THE DECK
STRETCH TIGHT	SUDDEN STRAIN	SWEEP THROUGH
STRICTLY TRUE	SUDDEN TWITCH	SWEET ADELINE
STRICT ORDERS	SUFFER DEFEAT	SWEET AND SOUR
STRIFE AND WOE	SUFFOLK PUNCH	SWEET AS HONEY
STRIKE A CHORD	SUGAR CONTENT	SWEET AS SUGAR
STRIKE ACTION	SUGAR IS SWEET	SWEET CONTENT

SWEET MARTINI
SWEET PICKLES
SWEET REVENGE
SWEET SIXTEEN
SWEET SUCCESS
SWEET THOUGHT
SWEET VIOLETS
SWEET WILLIAM
SWIFT CURRENT
SWIFT TO ANGER
SWIMMING BATH
SWIMMING CLUB
SWIMMING GALA
SWIMMING POOL
SWIM UP-STREAM
SWING THE LEAD
SWISS COTTAGE
SWOLLEN RIVER
SWORD OF STATE
SWORN ENEMIES
SYCAMORE TREE
SYDNEY BRIDGE
SYDNEY CARTON
SYSTEM FOLDER

T – 12

TABLE A MOTION
TABLE MANNERS
TABLET OF SOAP
TAIL OF THE EYE
TAILORED SUIT
TAILOR'S DUMMY
TAILOR'S GOOSE
TAILS YOU LOSE!
TAINTED GOODS
TAINTED MONEY
TAKE A BEATING
TAKE A HOLIDAY
TAKE A LIBERTY
TAKE A LOOK-SEE
TAKE A PENALTY
TAKE A POT-SHOT
TAKE A PRIDE IN
TAKE A READING
TAKEAWAY FOOD
TAKEAWAY MEAL
TAKE DELIVERY
TAKE DOWN A PEG
TAKE EXERCISE
TAKE FOR A RIDE
TAKE GOOD CARE
TAKE IT FROM ME
TAKE MEASURES
TAKE MY ADVICE
TAKE NO DENIAL

TAKE NO NOTICE
TAKE ON A PILOT
TAKE ONE'S EASE
TAKE ONE'S HOOK
TAKE ONE'S NAME
TAKE ONE'S PICK
TAKE ONE'S TIME
TAKE ONE'S TURN
TAKE ONE'S WORD
TAKE PLEASURE
TAKE PRISONER
TAKE THE BLAME
TAKE THE CHAIR
TAKE THE COUNT
TAKE THE FIELD
TAKE THE FLOOR
TAKE THE MICKY
TAKE THE POINT
TAKE THE PRIZE
TAKE THE REINS
TAKE THE STAGE
TAKE THE STAND
TAKE THE TRICK
TAKE TO FLIGHT
TAKE TO PIECES
TAKE TO THE AIR
TAKE UP A STAND
TAKE UP OFFICE
TALCUM POWDER
TALE OF A SHIRT
TALK AT LENGTH
TALK AT RANDOM
TALK BUSINESS
TALKING POINT
TALK NONSENSE
TALK OF ANGELS
TALK POLITICS
TALK STRAIGHT
TALK TO NOBODY
TALLEST WOMAN
TALLOW CANDLE
TANGLED SKEIN
TANKARD OF ALE
TANK REGIMENT
TAP AT THE DOOR
TAPE RECORDER
TAP ON THE HEAD
TAP THE BARREL
TARIFF REFORM
TASTE OF HONEY
TASTES DIFFER
TAX COLLECTOR
TAX INSPECTOR
TEACH SKATING
TEAM OF HORSES
TEARING HURRY

TEAR ONE'S HAIR
TEARS OF GRIEF
TEAR TO PIECES
TEAR TO SHREDS
TEA WITH LEMON
TEEM WITH RAIN
TEEN-AGE DREAM
TEEN-AGE YEARS
TEENY-BOPPERS
TEETHING RING
TELEGRAPH BOY
TELEPHONE BOX
TELL A WHOPPER
TELL EVERYONE
TELL FORTUNES
TELL ME A STORY
TELL-TALE SIGN
TELL THE TRUTH
TELL THE WORLD
TEMPLE OF FAME
TEMPORARY JOB
TEMPT FORTUNE
TEMPTING BAIT
TENANT FARMER
TEN-GALLON HAT
TENNIS LESSON
TENNIS PLAYER
TENNIS RACKET
TEN-POUND NOTE
TEN SHILLINGS
TENTH CENTURY
TENTH OF APRIL
TENTH OF MARCH
TERMINAL HOME
TERM OF OFFICE
TERRACED ROOF
TERRIBLE TIME
TESSA ACCOUNT
TEST-TUBE BABY
TET OFFENSIVE
TEXAS RANGERS
THAMES DITTON
THAMES TUNNEL
THAMES VALLEY
THATCHED ROOF
THE ACROPOLIS
THE ADMIRALTY
THE ALCHEMIST
THE ALL-BLACKS
THE ANTARCTIC
THE ANTIPODES
THE APPLE-CART
THE ARCADIANS
THE ARGENTINE
THE ARGONAUTS
THEATRE OF WAR

THEATRE QUEUE	THE MORSE CODE	THIRD CENTURY
THEATRE ROYAL	THE MOUSETRAP	THIRD CHANNEL
THEATRE USHER	THEN AND THERE	THIRD CHAPTER
THEATRE WORLD	THE NEW FOREST	THIRD EDITION
THE BACHELORS	THE NORTH-EAST	THIRD OF APRIL
THE BEES' KNEES	THE NORTH-WEST	THIRD OFFICER
THE BIG DIPPER	THE OLD BAILEY	THIRD OF MARCH
THE BITTER END	THE OLD ONE-TWO	THIRD QUARTER
THE BLUE ANGEL	THE OLD SCHOOL	THIRD READING
THE BOSPHORUS	THE OTHER SIDE	THIRTEEN DAYS
THE BOY FRIEND	THE OUTSKIRTS	THIS ABOVE ALL
THE CATACOMBS	THE PALLADIUM	THIS SATURDAY
THE CATECHISM	THE PARTHENON	THIS THURSDAY
THE CHILTERNS	THE PIPER'S SON	THIS VERY ROOM
THE COMMON MAN	THE POLONAISE	THOMAS ARNOLD
THE CONQUEROR	THE POTTERIES	THOMAS EDISON
THE CONTINENT	THE PROVINCES	THOMAS WOLSEY
THE COTSWOLDS	THE REAL THING	THOSE AGAINST
THE CRUSADERS	THERE AND BACK	THREAD OF LIFE
THE DARK BLUES	THERE AND THEN	THREAT OF RAIN
THE DAY BEFORE	THE REICHSTAG	THREE-ACT PLAY
THE DEEP SOUTH	THE REMAINDER	THREE AT A TIME
THE DEFENDERS	THERE'S THE RUB	THREE BY THREE
THE DEVIL'S OWN	THERMOS FLASK	THREE COLOURS
THE DIE IS CAST	THE SAME THING	THREE COURSES
THE DOLOMITES	THE SEAMY SIDE	THREE-DAY WEEK
THE DONE THING	THE SEVEN SEAS	THREE DEGREES
THE DOVER ROAD	THE SEVENTIES	THREE DOLLARS
THE FALKLANDS	THE SOUTH-EAST	THREE EIGHTHS
THE FALL OF MAN	THE SOUTH-WEST	THREE FATHOMS
THE FAVOURITE	THE SPECTATOR	THREE FIGURES
THE FIVE TOWNS	THE STORY GOES	THREE GALLONS
THE FOLLOWING	THE THING TO DO	THREE GUESSES
THE FOUR WINDS	THE TRUTH GAME	THREE GUINEAS
THE GENTLE SEX	THE UPPER HAND	THREE HUNDRED
THE GRAMPIANS	THE VERY DEVIL	THREE LENGTHS
THE GUILDHALL	THE VERY IMAGE	THREE MILLION
THE HAPPY MEAN	THE VERY PLACE	THREE MINUTES
THE HAYMARKET	THE VERY THING	THREE OCTAVES
THE HEREAFTER	THE WEAKER SEX	THREE OF A KIND
THE HERMITAGE	THE WHOLE TIME	THREE OF CLUBS
THE HIGHLANDS	THE WILL TO WIN	THREE PER CENT
THE HIMALAYAS	THE WOMENFOLK	THREE-PLY WOOD
THE IMMORTALS	THE WORM TURNS	THREE-PLY WOOL
THE IRONSIDES	THE WORST OF IT	THREE RASHERS
THE IVY LEAGUE	THE YOUNG IDEA	THREE'S A CROWD
THE KNOWLEDGE	THICK AND FAST	THREE SISTERS
THE LAST DITCH	THICK AND THIN	THREE SQUARED
THE LAST LAUGH	THICK GLASSES	THREE STOOGES
THE LAST STRAW	THIEVES' SLANG	THREE STRIPES
THE LAST TRUMP	THIN AS A WAFER	THREE STROKES
THE LIMELIGHT	THIN DISGUISE	THREE UNITIES
THE LISTENERS	THINGS CHANGE	THREE WICKETS
THE LOST CHORD	THINGS TO COME	THREE WISE MEN
THE MAD HATTER	THINK ABOUT IT	THREE WITCHES
THE MAYFLOWER	THIN MATERIAL	THROATY LAUGH

THROTTLE DOWN
THROUGH COACH
THROUGH TRAIN
THROW A GLANCE
THROW A SWITCH
THROW A WOBBLY
THYROID GLAND
TICKET HOLDER
TICKET OFFICE
TICKET POCKET
TIDE OF EVENTS
TIE ONE'S HANDS
TIGHT AS A LORD
TIGHT BANDAGE
TIGHT SQUEEZE
TILL ALL HOURS
TILL DOOMSDAY
TILL NEXT TIME
TILTING MATCH
TIMBERED ROOF
TIME AND AGAIN
TIME AND A HALF
TIME AND MONEY
TIME AND PLACE
TIME AND SPACE
TIME EXPOSURE
TIME FOR LUNCH
TIMELY ADVICE
TIME SCHEDULE
TIME TO FINISH
TIME TO GO HOME
TIME WILL TELL
TINKER'S CURSE
TINNED SALMON
TINTERN ABBEY
TIP THE SCALES
TIP THE WINNER
TIRED OF IT ALL
TIRED TO DEATH
TISSUE OF LIES
TITLED PEOPLE
TITLED PERSON
TITTLE TATTLE
TO ALL INTENTS
TOASTING FORK
TOBACCO JUICE
TOBACCO PLANT
TOBACCO POUCH
TOBACCO SMOKE
TOBACCO STAIN
TO ERR IS HUMAN
TOKEN GESTURE
TOKEN PAYMENT
TOMATO CATSUP
TOM COURTENAY
TOMMY HANDLEY

TOMMY TRINDER
TONE DIALLING
TONGUE OF LAND
TOO HOT TO HOLD
TOOK A DIM VIEW
TOOLS OF TRADE
TOO MANY COOKS
TO ONE'S CREDIT
TOOTH AND CLAW
TOOTH AND NAIL
TOOT ONE'S HORN
TOPLESS DRESS
TOP OF THE BILL
TOP OF THE FORM
TOP OF THE HILL
TOP OF THE MILK
TOP OF THE POLL
TOP OF THE POPS
TOP OF THE TREE
TOREADOR SONG
TORN TO SHREDS
TORY MAJORITY
TORY MINORITY
TOSS A PANCAKE
TOSS FOR SIDES
TOSS ONE'S HEAD
TOSS THE CABER
TOTAL ECLIPSE
TO THE GALLOWS
TO THE LAST MAN
TOTTER AROUND
TOUCH OF FROST
TOUCH ONE'S CAP
TOUCHY PERSON
TOUGH AS NAILS
TOUGH AS STEEL
TOUR DE FRANCE
TOURIST CLASS
TOURIST TRADE
TOUR OPERATOR
TOUT ENSEMBLE
TOWERING RAGE
TOWER OF BABEL
TOWN PLANNING
TOWN SURVEYOR
TRACER BULLET
TRACING PAPER
TRADE FIGURES
TRADE JOURNAL
TRADE RETURNS
TRADE SURPLUS
TRADING HOUSE
TRADING STAMP
TRAFFIC LIGHT
TRAFFIC RULES
TRAFFORD PARK

TRAGIC ENDING
TRAGIC LOVERS
TRAILING EDGE
TRAINED NURSE
TRAINED VOICE
TRAINING SHIP
TRAIN JOURNEY
TRAIN OF IDEAS
TRAIN ROBBERY
TRAIN SERVICE
TRAIN SPOTTER
TRAIN THE MIND
TRAITOR'S GATE
TRAMP STEAMER
TRANQUIL MIND
TRAPPIST MONK
TRAVEL ABROAD
TRAVEL AGENCY
TRAVEL AROUND
TRAVEL BUREAU
TRAVEL BY LAND
TRAVEL BY RAIL
TRAVEL BY TUBE
TRAVEL KETTLE
TREAD LIGHTLY
TREASURE HUNT
TREASURY BILL
TREASURY NOTE
TREAT IN STORE
TREAT LIGHTLY
TREAT ROUGHLY
TREATY OF ROME
TREBLE CHANCE
TRENCHANT WIT
TRENCH MORTAR
TRESPASS UPON
TRESTLE TABLE
TREVOR HOWARD
TRIAL BALANCE
TRIAL IN COURT
TRIBAL CUSTOM
TRIBAL SYSTEM
TRICK CYCLIST
TRICK OR TREAT
TRIED IN COURT
TRIFLING TALK
TRIGGER HAPPY
TRIM THE SAILS
TRINITY HOUSE
TRIPE DRESSER
TRIVIAL ROUND
TROMBONE SOLO
TROOP CARRIER
TROPHY HUNTER
TROPICAL BIRD
TROPICAL FISH

TROPICAL HEAT
TROPICAL MOON
TROPICAL SUIT
TROPICAL WIND
TROTTING PACE
TROUBLE AHEAD
TROUBLED MIND
TROUSER PRESS
TROUT FISHING
TRUE BELIEVER
TRUE FEELINGS
TRUE TO NATURE
TRUE TO THE END
TRUMPET BLAST
TRUNDLE ALONG
TRUSS OF STRAW
TRUST COMPANY
TRUSTEE STOCK
TRUSTY FRIEND
TRUTH WILL OUT
TRYING PERSON
TRY ONE'S SKILL
TSAR OF RUSSIA
TUBELESS TYRE
TUESDAY NIGHT
TUGBOAT ANNIE
TUNES OF GLORY
TUNNEL OF LOVE
TURKISH TOWEL
TURN A DEAF EAR
TURNED-UP NOSE
TURNHAM GREEN
TURNING POINT
TURN INTO CASH
TURN OF EVENTS
TURN OF PHRASE
TURN OF SPEECH
TURN ONE'S BACK
TURN ONE'S HEAD
TURN ON THE GAS
TURN ON THE TAP
TURN THE PAGES
TURN THE SCALE
TURN THE SCREW
TURN THE TAP ON
TURN UP TRUMPS
TWELFTH GREEN
TWELFTH NIGHT
TWELFTH OF MAY
TWELFTH PLACE
TWELFTH ROUND
TWELVE MONTHS
TWELVE O'CLOCK
TWELVE OUNCES
TWELVES POINTS
TWELVE POUNDS

TWELVE TRICKS
TWENTY POINTS
TWENTY POUNDS
TWICE AS HEAVY
TWICE AS QUICK
TWICE MONTHLY
TWICE NIGHTLY
TWICE REMOVED
TWICE THE SIZE
TWIN BROTHERS
TWIN CHILDREN
TWINGE OF PAIN
TWIST AND BUST
TWIST AND TURN
TWIST ONE'S ARM
TWO AND ELEVEN
TWO IN THE BUSH
TWO-SEATER CAR
TWO SHILLINGS
TWO-SPEED GEAR
TWO SYLLABLES
TWO-WAY STREET
TYPHOID FEVER
TYPING LESSON
TYPIST'S ERROR
TYRE PRESSURE

U – 12

UGLY CUSTOMER
UGLY DUCKLING
UMBRELLA BIRD
UMPTEEN TIMES
UNABLE TO COPE
UNABLE TO HELP
UNABLE TO MOVE
UNBROKEN LINE
UNCERTAIN JOY
UNCUT DIAMOND
UNDER A BUSHEL
UNDER A LADDER
UNDER AND OVER
UNDER A STRAIN
UNDER CONTROL
UNDER ENQUIRY
UNDER HATCHES
UNDER LICENCE
UNDER ONE ROOF
UNDER ONE'S HAT
UNDER PROTEST
UNDER SHERIFF
UNDER TENSION
UNDER THE HEEL
UNDER THE LASH
UNDER THE ROSE
UNDER THE SKIN

UNDER THE WING
UNEVEN CHANCE
UNFAIR CHOICE
UNFIT FOR WORK
UNHAPPY TIMES
UNIFORM SPEED
UNION MEETING
UNITED ACTION
UNITED EFFORT
UNITED STATES
UNIT OF ENERGY
UNIT OF LENGTH
UNKINDEST CUT
UNKNOWN THING
UNLUCKY PATCH
UNMARRIED MAN
UNPAID LABOUR
UNPAID WORKER
UNTIE THE KNOT
UNTIMELY JEST
UNTOLD WEALTH
UNUSUAL TWIST
UNWORTHY PART
UNWRITTEN LAW
UP FOR AUCTION
UP IN A BALLOON
UP IN THE HILLS
UP ONE'S SLEEVE
UP ONE'S STREET
UPON MY HONOUR
UPPER CHAMBER
UPPER CIRCLES
UPPER CLASSES
UPPER REGIONS
UPRIGHT GRAND
UPRIGHT PIANO
UPSTAIRS ROOM
UP THE CHIMNEY
UP TO MISCHIEF
UP TO ONE'S EYES
UP TO ONE'S NECK
UP TO STANDARD
UP TO STRENGTH
UP TO THE NINES
UP TO THE WAIST
UPWARD GLANCE
UPWARD MOTION
UPWARD STROKE
UP WITH THE SUN
URBAN RENEWAL
URGENT DEMAND
URGENT MATTER
USEFUL ADVICE
USE OF KITCHEN
USE ONE'S BRAIN
USE ONE'S HANDS

UTMOST EXTENT
UTTER FAILURE
UTTER POVERTY
UTTER RUBBISH
UTTER SILENCE
UTTER THREATS

V – 12

VACANT OFFICE
VALE OF SORROW
VALET SERVICE
VALIANT HEART
VALUED ADVICE
VALUED FRIEND
VANDYKE BEARD
VANITY MIRROR
VANTAGE POINT
VARIABLE GEAR
VARIETY HOUSE
VARIETY STAGE
VARIOUS TYPES
VARSITY MATCH
VAST QUANTITY
VEGETABLE DYE
VEGETABLE OIL
VEILED THREAT
VENETIAN LACE
VENI, VIDI, VICI
VENTURE FORTH
VENTURE SCOUT
VENTURE TO SAY
VERBAL ATTACK
VERNAL SEASON
VERTICAL LINE
VERY REVEREND
VERY TOUCHING
VESTED RIGHTS
VIALS OF WRATH
VICE-LIKE GRIP
VICTIM OF FATE
VICTORIA LINE
VICTORIAN AGE
VICTORIAN ERA
VICTORIA PLUM
VICTORIA WOOD
VICTORY AT SEA
VICTORY BONDS
VICTORY MARCH
VICTORY MEDAL
VIDEO JUKEBOX
VILLAGE GREEN
VILLAGE IDIOT
VIM AND VIGOUR
VINCENT PRICE
VIN ORDINAIRE

VIOLENT DEATH
VIOLENT STORM
VIOLENT UPSET
VIOLIN PLAYER
VIOLIN STRING
VIRGIN FOREST
VIRGINIA MAYO
VIRGINIA REEL
VIRULENT TONE
VISIBLE MEANS
VISIT FRIENDS
VISITING CARD
VISITING TEAM
VISITING TIME
VISITORS' BOOK
VISIT THE SICK
VITAL CONCERN
VIVE LA FRANCE
VIVID PICTURE
VOCATIVE CASE
VODKA AND LIME
VOLCANIC ROCK
VOLGA BOATMAN
VOLUME OF FIRE
VOODOO DOCTOR
VOODOO PRIEST
VOTE IN FAVOUR
VOTE OF THANKS
VOW OF SILENCE
VULGAR TASTES

W – 12

WAGE INCREASE
WAG OF THE HEAD
WAG THE FINGER
WAITING WOMAN
WAIT ONE'S TURN
WALK GINGERLY
WALKING MATCH
WALK ON STILTS
WALK ON TIPTOE
WALK SIDEWAYS
WALK STRAIGHT
WALK THE EARTH
WALK THE PLANK
WALK TOGETHER
WALK WITH EASE
WALLED GARDEN
WANDERING JEW
WAND OF OFFICE
WANTED PERSON
WARLIKE TRIBE
WARM THE BLOOD
WARM THE HEART
WARNING LIGHT

WARNING SOUND
WARNING VOICE
WAR TO END WARS
WASH AND DRY UP
WASHED ASHORE
WASH ONE'S FACE
WASH ONE'S HAIR
WASTED EFFORT
WASTED LABOUR
WASTE NOTHING
WASTE NO WORDS
WASTE OF MONEY
WASTE PRODUCT
WATCH AND PRAY
WATCH AND WAIT
WATCH CLOSELY
WATCH REPAIRS
WATER BISCUIT
WATER COLOURS
WATER DIVINER
WATER HYDRANT
WATERING CART
WATER SPANIEL
WAVE FAREWELL
WAXWORKS SHOW
WAYS AND MEANS
WAYWARD CHILD
WEAK APPROACH
WEAK ARGUMENT
WEAKER VESSEL
WEAKEST POINT
WEAK SOLUTION
WEALTHY WIDOW
WEAPONS OF WAR
WEAR BLINKERS
WEAR MOURNING
WEAR THE CLOTH
WEAR THE CROWN
WEATHER CHART
WEATHER GAUGE
WEATHER GLASS
WEB OF CUNNING
WEDDED COUPLE
WEDDING BELLS
WEDDING DRESS
WEDDING FEAST
WEDDING GROUP
WEDDING GUEST
WEDDING MARCH
WEDDING RITES
WEDGWOOD BLUE
WEEK-END LEAVE
WEEK-END PARTY
WEEKLY COLUMN
WEEKLY MARKET
WEEKLY REPORT

WEEKLY SALARY
WEEP WITH RAGE
WEIGH HEAVILY
WEIGH ONESELF
WEIGHTED MEAN
WEIGHT FOR AGE
WEIRD SISTERS
WELCOME EVENT
WELCOME GUEST
WELCOME SIGHT
WELD TOGETHER
WELFARE STATE
WELL ADVANCED
WELL AND TRULY
WELL DESERVED
WELL DISPOSED
WELL IN POCKET
WELL-MADE SUIT
WELL REPORTED
WELL TAILORED
WELL-TIMED ACT
WELSH COSTUME
WELSH DRESSER
WELSH RAREBIT
WEST BROMWICH
WEST-END STAGE
WESTERLY WIND
WESTERN FRONT
WESTERN ISLES
WESTERN UNION
WESTERN WORLD
WEST VIRGINIA
WET TO THE SKIN
WHALE OF A TIME
WHAT'S COOKING?
WHAT'S THE GAME?
WHAT'S THE ODDS?
WHAT THE DEUCE?
WHEN AND WHERE?
WHERE AND WHEN?
WHETHER OR NOT
WHET THE KNIFE
WHICH IS WHICH?
WHIFF OF SMOKE
WHILE YOU WAIT
WHIPPED CREAM
WHIPPING POST
WHIP SCORPION
WHIPSNADE ZOO
WHISKY GALORE
WHISTLE FOR IT
WHITE CABBAGE
WHITE FEATHER
WHITE HEATHER
WHITE OF AN EGG
WHITE RUSSIAN

WHITE WEDDING
WHITHER BOUND?
WHO DARES WINS
WHO GOES THERE?
WICKED TYRANT
WICKER BASKET
WICKET KEEPER
WIDE CURRENCY
WIDELY SPACED
WIDE RECEIVER
WIDOW TWANKEY
WILBUR WRIGHT
WILD APPLAUSE
WILD CREATURE
WILD HYACINTH
WILD LAUGHTER
WILD-WEST SHOW
WILFUL DAMAGE
WILFUL MURDER
WILLIAM BLAKE
WILLIAM BOOTH
WILLIAM RUFUS
WILLING HANDS
WILLING HEART
WILLING HORSE
WILLING PARTY
WILLING SLAVE
WILLING VOTER
WILL OF HEAVEN
WILL O' THE WISP
WILTON CARPET
WIN BY A LENGTH
WINDING TRAIL
WINDMILL GIRL
WIND OF CHANGE
WINDOW SCREEN
WINDSOR CHAIR
WIND THE CLOCK
WINDY WEATHER
WINE AND WOMEN
WINE IMPORTER
WINE MERCHANT
WINGED INSECT
WIN HANDS DOWN
WIN IN A CANTER
WINNING HORSE
WINNING SCORE
WINNING SMILE
WIN ONE'S SPURS
WINSOME SMILE
WINTER ABROAD
WINTER GARDEN
WINTER RESORT
WINTER SEASON
WINTER SPORTS
WIN THE BATTLE

WIN THE RUBBER
WIPE ONE'S EYES
WIPE ONE'S FEET
WIPE THE FLOOR
WISE DECISION
WIT AND WISDOM
WITCHING HOUR
WITCH OF ENDOR
WITH ALL HASTE
WITH ALL SPEED
WITH AN ACCENT
WITH A PURPOSE
WITH IMPUNITY
WITHIN BOUNDS
WITHIN LIMITS
WITHIN RADIUS
WITHIN REASON
WITH INTEREST
WITHIN THE LAW
WITH ONE VOICE
WITH OPEN ARMS
WITH OPEN EYES
WITHOUT A BEAN
WITHOUT A CARE
WITHOUT A CENT
WITHOUT A HOPE
WITHOUT A WORD
WITHOUT CAUSE
WITHOUT DELAY
WITHOUT DOUBT
WITHOUT FAULT
WITHOUT LIMIT
WITHOUT PRICE
WITHOUT STINT
WITHOUT SUGAR
WITH PLEASURE
WITH THIS RING
WOMAN IN WHITE
WOMAN'S HONOUR
WOMAN STUDENT
WOMAN TO WOMAN
WOMEN'S RIGHTS
WON BY A STREET
WON IN A CANTER
WOODEN BUCKET
WOOD SHAVINGS
WOOLLEN SOCKS
WOOL MERCHANT
WORD IN SEASON
WORD IN THE EAR
WORD OF ADVICE
WORD OF HONOUR
WORDS OF CHEER
WORDY WARFARE
WORKABLE PLAN
WORK FOR PEACE

WORKING CLASS
WORKING HOURS
WORKING MODEL
WORKING ORDER
WORKING PARTY
WORKING WIVES
WORKING WOMAN
WORK MIRACLES
WORK OFF STEAM
WORK ONE'S WILL
WORK OVERTIME
WORKS CANTEEN
WORKS COUNCIL
WORKS MANAGER
WORK TOGETHER
WORLDLY GOODS
WORLD OF SPORT
WORLD OF TODAY
WORLD SERVICE
WORM'S EYE VIEW
WORRIED FROWN
WORRYING TIME
WORRY TO DEATH
WORSE FOR WEAR
WORTH A PACKET
WORTH NOTHING
WORTHY OF NOTE
WOULD YOU MIND?

WOUNDED PRIDE
WRACK AND RUIN
WRETCHED DIGS
WRIST SUPPORT
WRISTWATCH TV
WRITE A CHEQUE
WRITE A LETTER
WRITE AN ESSAY
WRITE A REPORT
WRITE A SONNET
WRITER'S CRAMP
WRITHE IN PAIN
WRITING PAPER
WRITING TABLE
WRITTEN MUSIC
WRITTEN ORDER
WRITTEN REPLY
WRITTEN TERMS
WRONG ADDRESS
WRONG MEANING
WRONG SIDE OUT
WRONG SOCIETY
WRONG TURNING
WRONG VERDICT

Y – 12

YACHTING CLUB

YANKEE DOODLE
YARD AND A HALF
YEARLY SALARY
YEARS OF STUDY
YELLOW BASKET
YELLOW COLOUR
YELLOW FLOWER
YELLOW JERSEY
YELLOW RIBBON
YELLOW STREAK
YELL WITH PAIN
YOUNG AT HEART
YOUNG ENGLAND
YOUNGEST GIRL
YOUNG HOPEFUL
YOUNG IN HEART
YOUNG WOODLEY
YOUR EMINENCE
YOUR HIGHNESS
YOUR LADYSHIP
YOUR LORDSHIP
YOUR OWN FAULT
YOURS IN HASTE

Z – 12

ZACHARY SCOTT
ZIGZAG COURSE

A – 13

ABERDEEN ANGUS
ABIDE BY THE LAW
ABJECT APOLOGY
ABJECT POVERTY
ABJECT SLAVERY
ABOUT ONE'S EARS
ABOVE ONE'S HEAD
ABOVE REPROACH
ABOVE SEA-LEVEL
ABOVE STRENGTH
ABRAHAM'S BOSOM
ABRUPT DESCENT
ABSENCE OF MIND
ABSENT FRIENDS
ABSOLUTE POWER
ABSOLUTE PROOF
ABSOLUTE RULER
ABSOLUTE TRUST
ABSTRACT TERMS
ABUSIVE SPEECH
ABYSSINIAN CAT
ACADEMIC DRESS
ACADEMIC TITLE
ACCEPT AN OFFER
ACCEPTED TRUTH
ACCEPT PAYMENT
ACCIDENT PRONE
ACCORDION BAND
ACCOUNTS CLERK
ACCUSED PERSON
ACCUSE FALSELY
ACE OF DIAMONDS
ACHES AND PAINS
ACQUIRED SKILL
ACQUIRED TASTE
ACQUIT ONESELF
ACROSS AND DOWN
ACROSS COUNTRY
ACROSS THE ROAD
ACT AS CHAIRMAN
ACT FOR THE BEST
ACTING CAPTAIN
ACTING MANAGER
ACTION PAINTER
ACTION PICTURE
ACTIVE PARTNER
ACTIVE SERVICE
ACTIVE VOLCANO
ACT LIKE A CHARM
ACT LIKE A TONIC
ACT OF COURTESY
ACT OF HUMANITY
ACT OF KINDNESS
ACT OF VIOLENCE

ACUTE DISTRESS
ADAM FIREPLACE
ADDED PLEASURE
ADDED STRENGTH
ADDING MACHINE
ADEQUATE CAUSE
A DEUCE OF A MESS
ADIPOSE TISSUE
ADJUST THE TYPE
ADMIRAL NELSON
ADMIRALTY ARCH
ADMISSION CARD
ADMISSION FREE
ADMITTED GUILT
ADVANCED LEVEL
ADVANCED PUPIL
ADVANCE NOTICE
ADVENTURE GAME
ADVISE AGAINST
ADVISORY BOARD
AERIAL RAILWAY
AERIAL TORPEDO
AERIAL WARFARE
AFFECTED STYLE
AFFECTED VOICE
AFFORDING HOPE
AFRAID TO SPEAK
AFTER A FASHION
AFTER MIDNIGHT
AFTERNOON POST
AFTERNOON REST
AFTER THE EVENT
AFTER THE STORM
AGAIN AND AGAIN
AGAINST THE LAW
AGE OF AQUARIUS
AGE OF CHIVALRY
AGREE TO DIFFER
AIR A GRIEVANCE
AIR COMPRESSOR
AIR FORCE CROSS
AIR OF APPROVAL
AIR ON A G STRING
AIR OPERATIONS
AIRPORT LOUNGE
AIR RAID WARDEN
AIRS AND GRACES
ALEXANDER POPE
ALEXANDRA PARK
ALFRED DREYFUS
ALICE BLUE GOWN
ALL CHANGE HERE
ALL-DAY SESSION
ALLEGED MOTIVE
ALLEGED REASON
ALL FOR NOTHING

ALL FOR THE BEST
ALL FOR THE GOOD
ALL HALLOWS' EVE
ALLIED ADVANCE
ALLIED LANDING
ALLIGATOR PEAR
ALLIGATOR SKIN
ALL IN A FLUSTER
ALL IN GOOD TIME
ALL IN ONE PIECE
ALL-IN WRESTLER
ALL IS FORGIVEN
ALL OF A TREMBLE
ALL OF A TWITTER
ALL THE ANSWERS
ALL THE WINNERS
ALL-TIME RECORD
ALLUVIAL PLAIN
ALMOND BLOSSOM
ALONG THE COAST
A LONG WAY AFTER
A LONG WAY AHEAD
ALPHA AND OMEGA
ALPINE CLIMBER
ALTER THE RULES
ALTOGETHER BAD
ALWAYS ON THE GO
AMATEUR BOXING
AMATEUR GOLFER
AMATEUR PLAYER
AMATEUR SLEUTH
AMATEUR STATUS
AMATEUR TALENT
AMERICAN CLOTH
AMERICAN DREAM
AMERICAN EAGLE
AMERICAN NEGRO
AMERICAN ORGAN
AMERICAN SLANG
AMOROUS GLANCE
AMUSEMENT PARK
ANATOLE FRANCE
ANCESTRAL HALL
ANCESTRAL HOME
ANCIENT BRITON
ANCIENT GREECE
ANCIENT GRUDGE
ANCIENT LIGHTS
ANCIENT WISDOM
ANDREW JACKSON
ANGELIC VOICES
ANGEL PAVEMENT
ANGRY YOUNG MAN
ANGUISH OF MIND
ANGULAR FIGURE
ANIMAL KINGDOM

ANIMAL RESERVE
ANIMAL SPIRITS
ANIMAL TRAINER
ANIMATED SMILE
ANITA BROOKNER
ANNOTATED TEXT
ANNUAL ECLIPSE
ANNUAL FIXTURE
ANNUAL HOLIDAY
ANNUAL MEETING
ANNUAL PAYMENT
ANNUAL PREMIUM
ANOINT WITH OIL
ANONYMOUS GIFT
ANOTHER CHANCE
ANOTHER MATTER
ANOTHER PLEASE
ANSWER THE BELL
ANSWER THE HELM
ANTHONY NEWLEY
ANTHONY QUAYLE
ANTHROPOID APE
ANTIQUE DEALER
ANTONY ADVERSE
ANXIOUS MOMENT
ANYBODY'S GUESS
APPEAL FOR HELP
APPEALING LOOK
APPEAR IN COURT
APPLE DUMPLING
APPLE FRITTERS
APPLE OF THE EYE
APPLE-PIE ORDER
APPLE TURNOVER
APPLY FOR A LOAN
APPLY FOR LEAVE
APPLY PRESSURE
APPLY THE BRAKE
APPLY THE MATCH
APOLLO THEATRE
APOSTLES' CREED
APPOINTED TIME
APRICOT BRANDY
APRIL FOOL'S DAY
APRIL THE FIFTH
APRIL THE FIRST
APRIL THE NINTH
APRIL THE SIXTH
APRIL THE TENTH
APRIL THE THIRD
ARABIAN DESERT
ARABIAN NIGHTS
ARC DE TRIOMPHE
ARCHIE ANDREWS
ARCTIC REGIONS
ARDENT ADMIRER

ARDENT SPIRITS
ARGUE THE POINT
ARMAMENTS RACE
ARMED CONFLICT
ARMS AND THE MAN
ARMS PROGRAMME
ARMY COMMANDER
ARMY ESTIMATES
ARMY EXERCISES
ARMY PAY-OFFICE
ARNOLD BENNETT
AROUND THE TOWN
ARRANGE A MATCH
ARREARS OF WORK
ART COLLECTION
ART DEPARTMENT
ART EXHIBITION
ARTHUR ENGLISH
ARTICLED CLERK
ARTICLES OF WAR
ARTIFICIAL ARM
ARTIFICIAL FLY
ARTIFICIAL LEG
ARTILLERY FIRE
ARTISTIC VALUE
ARTISTS' COLONY
ARTISTS' RIFLES
ASTIST'S STUDIO
ART OF SPEAKING
ARTS AND CRAFTS
AS BLIND AS A BAT
AS BOLD AS BRASS
AS DARK AS NIGHT
AS DARK AS PITCH
AS FAR AS IT GOES
AS FULL AS AN EGG
AS GOOD AS A PLAY
AS HARD AS NAILS
ASHDOWN FOREST
AS HEAVY AS LEAD
ASK A POLICEMAN
ASK FOR NOTHING
ASK FOR TROUBLE
ASK PERMISSION
AS LARGE AS LIFE
AS LIKELY AS NOT
AS LONG AS MY ARM
AS PALE AS DEATH
ASPARAGUS TIPS
AS RIGHT AS RAIN
ASSEMBLY ROOMS
ASSERT ONESELF
ASSUME AN ALIAS
ASSUME COMMAND
AS SURE AS CAN BE
AS SWEET AS A NUT

AS THIN AS A LATH
A STITCH IN TIME
AS TRUE AS STEEL
AS WARM AS TOAST
AS WEAK AS WATER
ATALANTA'S RACE
AT AN ADVANTAGE
AT A STANDSTILL
AT FULL STRETCH
AT GREAT LENGTH
ATHLETE'S HEART
ATHLETIC COACH
ATLANTIC LINER
ATLANTIC OCEAN
AT LOGGERHEADS
ATOMIC FISSION
ATOMIC REACTOR
ATOMIC WARFARE
ATOMIC WARHEAD
AT ONE'S LEISURE
AT ONE'S OWN RISK
AT ONE'S WITS' END
AT RIGHT-ANGLES
AT SHORT NOTICE
ATTEND COLLEGE
AT THE CONTROLS
AT THE DENTIST'S
AT THE LAST GASP
AT THE RINGSIDE
AT THE SAME TIME
AT THE WAXWORKS
ATTORNEY AT LAW
ATTRACT NOTICE
AT YOUR SERVICE
AUCTION BRIDGE
AUDIO CASSETTE
AUDITORY NERVE
AUDREY HEPBURN
AUGEAN STABLES
AUTHENTIC WORK
AUTOMATIC LIFT
AUTOMATIC LOCK
AUTUMN COLOURS
AUXILIARY VERB
AVENGING ANGEL
AVENUE OF TREES
AVERAGE AMOUNT
AVERAGE FIGURE
AVERAGE HEIGHT
AVERAGE PERSON
AVERAGE WEIGHT
AVERT ONE'S EYES
AVOID THE ISSUE
AWAY FROM IT ALL
AWKWARD PERSON

B – 13

BABBLING BROOK	BARE-FACED LIAR
BACHELOR OF LAW	BARE ONE'S TEETH
BACK-HAND DRIVE	BARGAIN HUNTER
BACK IN HARNESS	BARK AT THE MOON
BACK IN THE FOLD	BARK ONE'S SHINS
BACK OF THE HAND	BAR OF THE HOUSE
BACK OF THE HEAD	BARRISTER'S WIG
BACK OF THE NECK	BARTERED BRIDE
BACK ONE'S FANCY	BASHFUL MANNER
BACK THE WINNER	BASIC INSTINCT
BACK TO THE LAND	BASQUE COUNTRY
BACK TO THE WALL	BASSO PROFUNDO
BACKWARD CHILD	BATHED IN TEARS
BACON SANDWICH	BATHING BEAUTY
BAD COMPLEXION	BATHING TRUNKS
BAD CONNECTION	BATTER PUDDING
BAD CONSCIENCE	BATTERSEA PARK
BADGE OF OFFICE	BATTERY BACKUP
BAD IMPRESSION	BATTERY OF GUNS
BADLY HAMMERED	BATTLE CRUISER
BADLY REPORTED	BATTLE HONOURS
BAD MANAGEMENT	BATTLE OF WORDS
BAD REPUTATION	BAYONET CHARGE
BAD UPBRINGING	BAYSWATER ROAD
BAG AND BAGGAGE	BEANS AND BACON
BAGGY TROUSERS	BEAR THE BURDEN
BALANCE IN HAND	BEAST OF BELSEN
BALD ADMISSION	BEAST OF BURDEN
BALD STATEMENT	BEAT ALL COMERS
BALL AND SOCKET	BEATLES' RECORD
BALLET DANCING	BEAT ONE HOLLOW
BALLOON ASCENT	BEAT THE BOUNDS
BALLY NUISANCE	BEAT THE RECORD
BAMBOO CURTAIN	BEAUFORT SCALE
BAND OF OUTLAWS	BEAUTIFUL FACE
BAND OF ROBBERS	BEAUTIFUL VIEW
BANG ON THE HEAD	BEAUTY CONTEST
BANKER'S CREDIT	BEAUTY CULTURE
BANK MESSENGER	BEAUTY PARLOUR
BANK OF ENGLAND	BECOME A MARTYR
BANK OF IRELAND	BECOME A MEMBER
BANK OVERDRAFT	BECOME A NEW MAN
BANKRUPT STOCK	BECOME ENGAGED
BANKS AND BRAES	BECOME EXTINCT
BANK STATEMENT	BECOME FRIENDS
BAPTISMAL NAME	BE CONSPICUOUS
BAPTISM OF FIRE	BEDSIDE MANNER
BAPTIST CHURCH	BEETLING BROWS
BARBARA MULLEN	BEFORE THE DAWN
BARBECUE PARTY	BEFORE THE FACT
BARBER SURGEON	BEFORE THE MAST
BARCELONA NUTS	BEFORE THE WIND
BARE-BACK RIDER	BEG FOR FAVOURS
BARE EXISTENCE	BEGGING LETTER
	BEGINNER'S LUCK
	BEGIN TO WEAKEN

BEG PERMISSION
BEHAVE ONESELF
BEHIND THE LINE
BEHIND THE VEIL
BE IN DISFAVOUR
BE IN THE SADDLE
BELATED EFFORT
BELISHA BEACON
BELLES LETTRES
BELONGING TO ME
BELONGING TO US
BELOVED OBJECT
BELOW FREEZING
BELOW SEA-LEVEL
BELOW STANDARD
BELOW STRENGTH
BE MY VALENTINE
BEND BACKWARDS
BEND IN THE ROAD
BENEATH NOTICE
BENEATH THE SUN
BENIGN NEGLECT
BE OF GOOD CHEER
BE OF GOOD HEART
BERNARD BRADEN
BERTIE WOOSTER
BESIDE ONESELF
BESIDE THE MARK
BESSEMER STEEL
BEST BEHAVIOUR
BEST END OF NECK
BESTIR ONESELF
BEST OF A BAD JOB
BEST OF FRIENDS
BEST OF ITS KIND
BEST OF MOTIVES
BEST THING TO DO
BETTER ONESELF
BETTER OR WORSE
BEYOND ALL HELP
BEYOND COMPARE
BEYOND CONTROL
BEYOND DISPUTE
BEYOND MEASURE
BEYOND ONE'S KEN
BEYOND THE PALE
BEYOND THE VEIL
BICYCLE RACING
BID FOR FREEDOM
BIG-GAME HUNTER
BIG WHITE CHIEF
BILLIARD TABLE
BIRD IN THE HAND
BIRD OF ILL OMEN
BIRD OF PASSAGE
BIRD ON THE WING

BIRD SANCTUARY
BIRD'S-NEST SOUP
BIRDS OF THE AIR
BIRMINGHAM SIX
BIRTHDAY PARTY
BIRTHDAY TREAT
BISCUIT BARREL
BITE ONE'S NAILS
BITE ONE'S THUMB
BITING SARCASM
BIT OF A MYSTERY
BIT OF NONSENSE
BITS AND PIECES
BITTER DRAUGHT
BITTER FLAVOUR
BITTER QUARREL
BITTER REMORSE
BLACK AND WHITE
BLACK AS A SWEEP
BLACK DIAMONDS
BLACKPOOL ROCK
BLANKET FINISH
BLANKET OF SNOW
BLANKET STITCH
BLANKETY BLANK
BLAZE OF COLOUR
BLAZE THE TRAIL
BLAZING TEMPER
BLEEDING HEART
BLESS THE BRIDE
BLIGHTED HOPES
BLINDING LIGHT
BLINDING STORM
BLIND IN ONE EYE
BLINDMAN'S BUFF
BLISSFUL STATE
BLOCK CAPITALS
BLOOD BROTHERS
BLOOD PRESSURE
BLOOD RELATION
BLOODSHOT EYES
BLOODY ASSIZES
BLOTTING PAPER
BLOW GREAT GUNS
BLUE IN THE FACE
BLUNT QUESTION
BLUSH FOR SHAME
BLUSHING BRIDE
BOARDING HOUSE
BOARDING PARTY
BOBBY CHARLTON
BOB'S YOUR UNCLE
BODY CORPORATE
BODY OF OPINION
BOHEMIAN GLASS
BOLSHOI BALLET

BOMBER COMMAND
BONY STRUCTURE
BOOKING OFFICE
BOOK OF GENESIS
BOOK OF THE FILM
BOOK OF THE PLAY
BOOK OF THE YEAR
BOOK OF TICKETS
BOOK ONE'S BERTH
BOOMING MARKET
BOON COMPANION
BOOSTER ROCKET
BOOT AND SADDLE
BORDER BALLADS
BORDER COUNTRY
BORN IN WEDLOCK
BORN ORGANISER
BORN YESTERDAY
BORROWED MONEY
BORSTAL SYSTEM
BOSTON TERRIER
BOSTON TWO-STEP
BOTTLED SWEEETS
BOTTLE OF SCENT
BOTTLE OF STOUT
BOTTLE OF WATER
BOTTOMLESS PIT
BOUGHT AND SOLD
BOUNDARY FENCE
BOUNDARY STONE
BOUNDLESS DEEP
BOWLER'S WICKET
BOWLING CREASE
BOW TO THE STORM
BOX OF BISCUITS
BOX OF CRACKERS
BOX THE COMPASS
BRACE OF SHAKES
BRANCH LIBRARY
BRANCH MEETING
BRANCH OFFICE
BRANDY AND SODA
BRASS BEDSTEAD
BRASS FARTHING
BRAVE NEW WORLD
BREACH OF FAITH
BREACH OF TRUST
BREAD AND HONEY
BREAD AND WATER
BREAD OF HEAVEN
BREAD POULTICE
BREAD SHORTAGE
BREADTH OF MIND
BREADTH OF VIEW
BREAK A JOURNEY
BREAK A PROMISE

BREAKDOWN GANG
BREAKERS AHEAD
BREAKFAST DISH
BREAKFAST FOOD
BREAKFAST TIME
BREAKING POINT
BREAK INTO A RUN
BREAK INTO SONG
BREAK IT GENTLY
BREAK OFF SHORT
BREAK ONE'S BACK
BREAK ONE'S DUCK
BREAK ONE'S FAST
BREAK ONE'S WORD
BREAK THE PEACE
BREAK THE RULES
BREAK THE SPELL
BREAK TO PIECES
BREAST THE TAPE
BREATHE FREELY
BREATHING ROOM
BREATHING TUBE
BRED IN THE BONE
BRIDE AND GROOM
BRIDGE BUILDER
BRIDGE OF BOATS
BRIDGE OF SIGHS
BRIDGE PROBLEM
BRIEF INTERVAL
BRIGHTON BEACH
BRIGHTON BELLE
BRIGHTON RACES
BRILLIANT IDEA
BRILLIANT MIND
BRING AN ACTION
BRING INTO LINE
BRING NTO PLAY
BRING TO A CLOSE
BRING TOGETHER
BRING UP TO DATE
BRISKET OF BEEF
BRISK MOVEMENT
BRISTOL ROVERS
BRITISH COLONY
BRITISH CONSUL
BRITISH EMPIRE
BRITISH GUIANA
BRITISH LEGION
BRITISH MUSEUM
BRITISH PUBLIC
BROAD DAYLIGHT
BROKEN ENGLISH
BROKEN PROMISE
BROKEN ROMANCE
BROKEN SILENCE
BROOK NO DENIAL

BROTHERLY LOVE
BROUGHT TO BOOK
BROWN AS A BERRY
BROWNIE POINTS
BRUSH ONE'S HAIR
BRUSQUE MANNER
BRUTE STRENGTH
BUBONIC PLAGUE
BUCKET OF WATER
BUDDING AUTHOR
BUDDING GENIUS
BUDGET SURPLUS
BUFF ORPINGTON
BUILDING BLOCK
BULLS AND BEARS
BUMPER HARVEST
BUNCH OF GRAPES
BURDEN OF GUILT
BURDEN OF POWER
BURDEN OF PROOF
BURIAL CUSTOMS
BURIAL SERVICE
BURKE'S PEERAGE
BURLESQUE SHOW
BURNING DESIRE
BURNING THIRST
BURN ONE'S BOATS
BURN ONE'S MONEY
BURN TO A CINDER
BURNT OFFERING
BURN WITH ANGER
BURSTING POINT
BURST OF ENERGY
BURST THE BONDS
BURTON ON TRENT
BUSH TELEGRAPH
BUSINESS CYCLE
BUSINESS HOURS
BUSINESS HOUSE
BUSINESS LUNCH
BUSINESS TERMS
BUSINESS WOMAN
BUSINESS WORLD
BUTLER'S PANTRY
BUTTERED TOAST
BUTTERFLY KISS
BUTTON YOUR LIP
BY ALL ACCOUNTS
BY APPOINTMENT
BY ARRANGEMENT
BY CANDLELIGHT
BY INSTALMENTS
BYPASS SURGERY
BY THE ROADSIDE
BY UNDERGROUND
BY WORD OF MOUTH

C – 13

CABINET MEMBER
CALCULATED LIE
CALENDAR MONTH
CALL FOR TRUMPS
CALL INTERCEPT
CALL INTO BEING
CALL OF THE WILD
CALL ONE'S BLUFF
CALL SCREENING
CALL THE POLICE
CALL TO ACCOUNT
CALL TO WITNESS
CAMBRIDGE BLUE
CAMCORDER TAPE
CAMEL-HAIR COAT
CAMERA OBSCURA
CAMPAIGN MEDAL
CAMPING GROUND
CANARY ISLANDS
CANDID OPINION
CANNIBAL TRIBE
CAPACITY CROWD
CAPACITY HOUSE
CAPE CANAVERAL
CAPED CRUSADER
CAPITAL CHARGE
CAPITAL FELLOW
CAPITAL LETTER
CAPITAL MURDER
CAP OF DARKNESS
CAPTAIN CUTTLE
CAPTAIN KETTLE
CAPTAIN'S TABLE
CARAFE OF WATER
CARBON DIOXIDE
CARDBOARD CITY
CARDINAL POINT
CAREER OF CRIME
CAREFUL DRIVER
CARNABY STREET
CARNEGIE TRUST
CARNIVAL QUEEN
CARPET BOMBING
CARPET CLEANER
CARPET SWEEPER
CARRIAGE CLOCK
CARRIER PIGEON
CARRY THE BLAME
CARRY THE TORCH
CARRY TO EXCESS
CARTRiDGE CASE
CARVE ONE'S NAME
CARVE THE JOINT
CASH DISPENSER

CASH IN ADVANCE
CASH IN THE BANK
CASHMERE SHAWL
CASH ON THE NAIL
CASSE NOISETTE
CASSEROLE DISH
CAST IN ONE'S LOT
CAST-IRON ALIBI
CASTLE IN SPAIN
CASUAL CLOTHES
CASUAL MEETING
CASUAL VISITOR
CATALOGUE SHOP
CAT-AND-DOG LIFE
CATCH A GLIMPSE
CATCH AT STRAWS
CATCH UNAWARES
CATERING CORPS
CATHEDRAL CITY
CATHEDRAL TOWN
CATHERINE PARR
CATHOLIC FAITH
CAT O' NINE TAILS
CATTLE BREEDER
CATTLE FARMING
CAUGHT BENDING
CAUGHT IN A TRAP
CAUGHT NAPPING
CAUSE A FLUTTER
CAUSE FOR ALARM
CAUSE OF INJURY
CAUSTIC REMARK
CAVALRY CHARGE
CAVALRY SCHOOL
CAVALRY TROOPS
CAYENNE PEPPER
CELEBRATED MAN
CELESTIAL BODY
CELESTIAL CITY
CELESTIAL POLE
CELLULAR RADIO
CEMENT MIXTURE
CENTRAL AFRICA
CENTRAL EUROPE
CENTRAL FIGURE
CENTRAL LONDON
CENTRAL OFFICE
CENTRE FORWARD
CENTRE OF TRADE
CERTAIN EXTENT
CERTAIN PERSON
CERTIFIED MILK
CHAIN OF EVENTS
CHAIN OF OFFICE
CHAIN REACTION
CHALLENGE FATE

CHAMP AT THE BIT
CHAMPION BOXER
CHANCE MEETING
CHANCE ONE'S ARM
CHANGE A CHEQUE
CHANGED PERSON
CHANGE OF FRONT
CHANGE OF HEART
CHANGE OF PLACE
CHANGE OF SCENE
CHANGE OF VENUE
CHANGING ROOMS
CHANGING VOICE
CHANNEL BRIDGE
CHANNEL TUNNEL
CHARACTER PART
CHARGE ACCOUNT
CHARGE TOO MUCH
CHARITY BAZAAR
CHARLES DARWIN
CHARLES WESLEY
CHARLOT'S REVUE
CHARM BRACELET
CHARMED CIRCLE
CHARM OF MANNER
CHARTER FLIGHT
CHASE ONE'S TAIL
CHAUVINIST PIG
CHEAP AND NASTY
CHECK THE SPEED
CHEDDAR CHEESE
CHEERFUL GIVER
CHEERFUL SIGHT
CHEESE AND WINE
CHEESE BISCUIT
CHEF DE CUISINE
CHELSEA BRIDGE
CHELTENHAM SPA
CHEMICAL AGENT
CHERISH AN IDEA
CHERRY BLOSSOM
CHERRY ORCHARD
CHESS CHAMPION
CHEST EXPANDER
CHESTNUT BROWN
CHESTNUT HORSE
CHICKEN FARMER
CHIEF ARMOURER
CHIEF ENGINEER
CHIEF OF POLICE
CHIEFTAIN TANK
CHILDHOOD DAYS
CHILDISH PRANK
CHILD OF NATURE
CHILDREN'S BOOK
CHILDREN'S GAME

CHILDREN'S HOME	CLEMENT ATTLEE
CHILDREN'S HOUR	CLENCHED TEETH
CHILLY WELCOME	CLERICAL BLACK
CHILTERN HILLS	CLERICAL DRESS
CHIMNEY CORNER	CLERICAL ERROR
CHIMNEY-POT HAT	CLERICAL STAFF
CHINA SYNDROME	CLIFFS OF DOVER
CHINESE PUZZLE	CLIMBING IRONS
CHOCOLATE DROP	CLIMBING PLANT
CHOICE OF WORDS	CLIMBING SHRUB
CHOIR PRACTICE	CLIMB LIKE A CAT
CHOP AND CHANGE	CLINCH THE DEAL
CHOPPING BLOCK	CLING TOGETHER
CHORAL CONCERT	CLIP ONE'S WINGS
CHORAL SERVICE	CLIP ONE'S WORDS
CHORAL SOCIETY	CLIPPED SPEECH
CHORUS OF ABUSE	CLOSED CHAPTER
CHRIS CHATAWAY	CLOSED CIRCUIT
CHRISTIAN NAME	CLOSE FIGHTING
CHRISTMAS CAKE	CLOSELY ALLIED
CHRISTMAS CARD	CLOSE ONE'S EYES
CHRISTMAS FAIR	CLOSE PRISONER
CHRISTMAS GIFT	CLOSE QUARTERS
CHRISTMAS TREE	CLOSE RELATIVE
CHURCHILL TANK	CLOSE SECURITY
CHURCH OFFICER	CLOSE THE RANKS
CHURCH SERVICE	CLOSE TOGETHER
CHURCH STEEPLE	CLOSE TO NATURE
CHURCH WEDDING	CLOSING SEASON
CIGARETTE CARD	CLOSING SPEECH
CIGARETTE CASE	CLOSING STAGES
CIGARETTE GIRL	CLOTHES BASKET
CIRCLE OF LIGHT	CLOTHING TRADE
CIRCUS MANAGER	CLOUD THE ISSUE
CITY OF THE DEAD	COARSE FISHING
CIVIL AVIATION	COASTAL RESORT
CIVIL ENGINEER	COASTAL WATERS
CIVILIAN DRESS	COAST DOWNHILL
CIVIL MARRIAGE	COBBLED STREET
CIVIL QUESTION	COCKER SPANIEL
CLAIM THE CROWN	COCKNEY ACCENT
CLAPHAM COMMON	COCK OF THE WALK
CLAP OF THUNDER	COCKTAIL DRESS
CLAP ONE'S HANDS	COCKTAIL PARTY
CLAP ON THE BACK	COCKTAIL STICK
CLARENCE HOUSE	CODE OF CONDUCT
CLASSIC REMARK	COFFEE ESSENCE
CLASS STRUGGLE	COFFEE GROUNDS
CLEAN THE SLATE	COFFEE PLANTER
CLEARANCE SALE	COLD AS CHARITY
CLEARING HOUSE	COLD COLLATION
CLEAR SPEAKING	COLD IN THE HEAD
CLEAR THE COURT	COLD RECEPTION
CLEAR THE DECKS	COLD-WATER CURE
CLEAR THE TABLE	COLLECTION BOX
CLEAR THINKING	COLLECT STAMPS

COLLEGE OF ARMS
COLONIAL HOUSE
COLONIAL STYLE
COLOUR DECODER
COLOURED CHALK
COLOURED SLIDE
COLOURED VINYL
COLOURED WATER
COLOUR MONITOR
COLOUR PROBLEM
COLUMN OF ROUTE
COLUMN OF SMOKE
COMBINED FORCE
COMBINE FORCES
COME ALONGSIDE
COME AWAY EMPTY
COME BACK AGAIN
COME DOWN HEADS
COME DOWN TAILS
COMEDY ACTRESS
COMEDY THEATRE
COME IN CONTACT
COME INTO BEING
COME INTO FORCE
COME INTO MONEY
COME INTO SIGHT
COME OUT EASILY
COME OVER QUEER
COME TO A BAD END
COME TO A CLIMAX
COME TO A CRISIS
COME TO NOTHING
COME TO ONESELF
COME TO THE BALL
COME TO THE FAIR
COME TO THE FORE
COME UNDER FIRE
COME UNINVITED
COME UP FOR MORE
COME UP SMILING
COMING SHORTLY
COMMERCIAL ART
COMMERCIAL LAW
COMMIT A FELONY
COMMIT AN ERROR
COMMIT ONESELF
COMMIT PERJURY
COMMIT SUICIDE
COMMITTEE ROOM
COMMIT TO PAPER
COMMON ASSAULT
COMMON CARRIER
COMMON CONSENT
COMMON FEATURE
COMMON GROUNDS
COMMON HONESTY

COMMON MEASURE
COMMON MISTAKE
COMMON PATTERN
COMMON PURPOSE
COMMON SOLDIER
COMMUNION WINE
COMMUNIST BLOC
COMMUNITY CARE
COMPACT CAMERA
COMPANY LAWYER
COMPANY MERGER
COMPANY REPORT
COMPASS NEEDLE
COMPLAINT BOOK
COMPLETE WORKS
COMPLEX NUMBER
COMPLEX SYSTEM
COMPONENT PART
COMPOSING ROOM
COMPRESSED AIR
COMPUTER CRIME
COMPUTER MODEL
COMPUTER VIRUS
COMRADE IN ARMS
CONCEDE A POINT
CONCEPTUAL ART
CONCERT ARTIST
CONCRETE MIXER
CONCRETE OFFER
CONDEMNED CELL
CONDEMNED FORM
CONDENSED MILK
CONDUCTED TOUR
CONFIDENCE MAN
CONFINED PLACE
CONFINED SPACE
CONFINED TO BED
CONFIRMED CASE
CONFIRMED LIAR
CONGRESS MEDAL
CONGRESS PARTY
CONISTON WATER
CONNECTING ROD
CONSCRIPT ARMY
CONSTANT LOSER
CONSTANT NYMPH
CONSUL GENERAL
CONSUMER GOODS
CONTACT LENSES
CONTENTED MIND
CONTENT TO REST
CONTINUITY MAN
CONTRITE HEART
CONTROL CENTRE
CONTROL PRICES
CONVECTOR OVEN

CONVENT SCHOOL
COOKERY LESSON
COOKING MEDIUM
COOKING SHERRY
COOK ONE'S GOOSE
COOLING BREEZE
COOL ONE'S HEELS
COOL RECEPTION
COPPER COINAGE
COPYCAT MURDER
CORAL NECKLACE
CORDLESS DRILL
CORDLESS PHONE
CORONATION CUP
CORONER'S COURT
CORPORATE BODY
CORPS DE BALLET
CORPUS CHRISTI
CORPUS DELICTI
CORRECT ACCENT
CORRECT ANSWER
CORRECT SPEECH
CORRIDOR TRAIN
COSTA DEL CRIME
COSTLY FAILURE
COSTLY VENTURE
COTSWOLD HILLS
COTSWOLD STONE
COTTAGE CHEESE
COTTON PLANTER
COULD BE BETTER
COULEUR DE ROSE
COUNCIL ESTATE
COUNCIL SCHOOL
COUNTING HOUSE
COUNTRY COUSIN
COUNTRY CUSTOM
COUNTRY SQUIRE
COUNT THE HOURS
COUNTY BOROUGH
COUNTY COUNCIL
COUNTY CRICKET
COURSE BETTING
COURSE OF STUDY
COURT CIRCULAR
COURT DISASTER
COURTESY TITLE
COURT INTRIGUE
COURT OF APPEAL
COURT OF RECORD
COURT REPORTER
COVERED MARKET
COWARD AT HEART
CRABBED OLD AGE
CRACK REGIMENT
CRAFTSMAN'S JOB

CRAVEN COTTAGE
CRAZY LIKE A FOX
CRAZY PAVEMENT
CREAM OF TARTAR
CREATE A RUMPUS
CREATE A VACUUM
CREATE DISCORD
CREATE TROUBLE
CREDIT ACCOUNT
CREDIT BALANCE
CREDIT COMPANY
CREDIT SQUEEZE
CREEPING JENNY
CRÊME DE MENTHE
CREOLE EARRING
CRIBBAGE BOARD
CRICKET ELEVEN
CRICKET GROUND
CRICKET SEASON
CRICKET UMPIRE
CRICK ONE'S NECK
CRIME REPORTER
CRIMINAL CLASS
CRIMINAL COURT
CRIMINAL ERROR
CRIMINAL TRIAL
CRIMINAL WORLD
CRIPPLING BLOW
CRITICAL ANGLE
CRITICALLY ILL
CRITICAL POWER
CRITICAL STAGE
CROCHET NEEDLE
CROIX DE GUERRE
CROQUET MALLET
CROSSED CHEQUE
CROSSED IN LOVE
CROSS EXAMINED
CROSS ONE'S MIND
CROSS ONE'S PALM
CROSS ONE'S PATH
CROSS PURPOSES
CROSS THE FLOOR
CROSS THE OCEAN
CROWDED CANVAS
CROWDED STREET
CROWD OF PEOPLE
CROWD TOGETHER
CROWN COLONIES
CROWNING GLORY
CROWNING MERCY
CROWN OF THORNS
CROWN PRINCESS
CROWN PROPERTY
CRUCIAL MOMENT
CRUCIAL PERIOD

CRUDE ESTIMATE
CRUISE MISSILE
CRUISING SPEED
CRUSHING REPLY
CRUSH TO PIECES
CRY BLUE MURDER
CRY FOR NOTHING
CRY FOR THE MOON
CRY LIKE A CHILD
CRY OF DERISION
CRYPTIC REMARK
CRYSTAL GAZING
CRYSTAL PALACE
CS GAS CANISTER
CUBIC CAPACITY
CUBIC CONTENTS
CUBIC ZIRCONIA
CUCUMBER FRAME
CUDDLE UP CLOSE
CULTIVATED MAN
CUNNING FELLOW
CUP THAT CHEERS
CURIOSITY SHOP
CURIOUS DESIGN
CURIOUS EFFECT
CURIOUS TO KNOW
CURRENT ASSETS
CURRENT BELIEF
CURRENT EVENTS
CURRENT NUMBER
CURRENT REPORT
CURRENT RUMOUR
CURRENT SERIES
CURSE AND SWEAR
CURSORY GLANCE
CURTAIN OF FIRE
CURTAIN RAISER
CUT DOWN TO SIZE
CUT OFF A CORNER
CUT ONE'S LOSSES
CUT ONE'S THROAT
CUT THE PAINTER
CUTTING REMARK
CUTTING RETORT
CUT TO THE QUICK
CYCLE OF EVENTS
CYCLE OF THE SUN
CYRIL FLETCHER

D – 13

DADDY AND MUMMY
DADDY-LONG-LEGS
DAILY DELIVERY
DAILY PRACTICE
DAILY PURSUITS

DALLAS COWBOYS
DAME CLARA BUTT
DAME COMMANDER
DAMP THE ARDOUR
DANCE THE POLKA
DANCE THE TANGO
DANCE WITH RAGE
DANCING LESSON
DANCING MASTER
DANCING SCHOOL
DANDELION WINE
DANDIE DINMONT
DANGEROUS BEND
DANGEROUS DRUG
DANGEROUS GAME
DANGEROUS LEAK
DANTE'S INFERNO
DARE-DEVIL TYPE
DARING ATTEMPT
DARK CONTINENT
DARKEST AFRICA
DARNING NEEDLE
DASH ONE'S HOPES
DATA RETRIEVAL
DAUGHTER OF EVE
DAUNTLESS HERO
DAWN OF A NEW ERA
DAY OF JUDGMENT
DAY OF MOURNING
DAYS AND NIGHTS
DAYS OF THE WEEK
DAY TO REMEMBER
DAZZLING SMILE
DEAD AND BURIED
DEAD AS THE DODO
DEAD CERTAINTY
DEAD-LETTER BOX
DEADLY SILENCE
DEAD MAN'S CHEST
DEAD MAN'S SHOES
DEAD RECKONING
DEARLY BELOVED
DEATH AND GLORY
DEATH-BED SCENE
DEATH BY INCHES
DEATH REGISTER
DEATH SENTENCE
DEATH STRUGGLE
DEBATING POINT
DEBT COLLECTOR
DEBTORS' PRISON
DECIDE AGAINST
DECIDUOUS TREE
DECIMAL SYSTEM
DECLINE OF LIFE
DECORATIVE ART

DEDICATED LIFE	DEVILISH FUNNY
DEED OF RELEASE	DEVIL'S KITCHEN
DEEP ANTIPATHY	DEVIL'S OWN LUCK
DEEP BREATHING	DEVIOUS MANNER
DEEP GRATITUDE	DEVOID OF SENSE
DEEP IN THOUGHT	DEVOID OF TRUTH
DEEPLY TOUCHED	DEVOUT ADMIRER
DEEP-SEA DIVING	DIAGONAL LINES
DEFEND ONESELF	DIAL THE POLICE
DEFINITE PROOF	DIAMOND BROOCH
DEFRAY THE COST	DIAMOND CUTTER
DEFY AUTHORITY	DIAMOND SCULLS
DEGREE OF SKILL	DIATONIC SCALE
DEIGN TO NOTICE	DICE WITH DEATH
DELAYED ACTION	DIE AT ONE'S POST
DELIBERATE LIE	DIE FLEDERMAUS
DELICATE CHILD	DIEGO MARADONA
DELICATE POINT	DIE OF EXPOSURE
DELICATE SHADE	DIE OF LAUGHING
DELICATE STAGE	DIFFERENT KIND
DELICATE TOUCH	DIFFERENT TUNE
DELIGHT THE EAR	DIFFERENT VIEW
DELPHIC ORACLE	DIFFICULT CASE
DELUDE ONESELF	DIFFICULT TASK
DE LUXE EDITION	DIFFUSED LIGHT
DEMAND JUSTICE	DIGESTIVE PILL
DEMAND PAYMENT	DIG FOR VICTORY
DEMERARA SUGAR	DIG IN ONE'S TOES
DEMON PATIENCE	DIGNIFIED EXIT
DEN OF INIQUITY	DIG FOR VICTORY
DENTAL SURGEON	DIG ONE'S TOES IN
DENTAL SURGERY	DING-DONG FIGHT
DENTIST'S CHAIR	DINNER AT EIGHT
DENTIST'S DRILL	DINNER SERVICE
DENY THE CHARGE	DIONNE WARWICK
DEPARTED GLORY	DIPLOMATIC BAG
DEPRESSED AREA	DIRECT CONTACT
DEPRIVE OF LIFE	DIRECT CURRENT
DEPTH OF WINTER	DIRECT DESCENT
DEPUTY PREMIER	DIRECTION POST
DEPUTY SHERIFF	DIRE NECESSITY
DESERT WARFARE	DISASTER MOVIE
DESERVE NOTICE	DISCOUNT HOUSE
DESERVING CASE	DISMAL FAILURE
DESERVING POOR	DISOBEY ORDERS
DESIGNER LABEL	DISPATCH RIDER
DESIRED EFFECT	DISPUTED POINT
DESIRED OBJECT	DISTANT COUSIN
DESOLATE SCENE	DISTANT FUTURE
DESPATCH CLERK	DISTANT OBJECT
DESPATCH RIDER	DISTRICT COURT
DESPERATE MOVE	DISTRICT NURSE
DESPERATE RUSH	DISTURBED MIND
DETACHED HOUSE	DIVIDE AND RULE
DETECTIVE WORK	DIVIDE BY EIGHT
DEUCE OF HEARTS	DIVIDE BY SEVEN

DIVIDE BY THREE
DIVIDED WE FALL
DIVINE JUSTICE
DIVINE SERVICE
DIVISION LOBBY
DIVISION THREE
DIVORCE DECREE
DO AS YOU PLEASE
DOCTOR FAUSTUS
DOCTOR JOHNSON
DOCTOR KILDARE
DOCTOR OF MUSIC
DOCTOR'S ORDERS
DOCTOR THE WINE
DODGE IN AND OUT
DODGE THE ISSUE
DOG'S BREAKFAST
DOLL'S HOSPITAL
DOLPHIN SQUARE
DOME OF ST PAUL'S
DOMESTIC BLISS
DONE FOR EFFECT
DON'T BELIEVE IT
DON'T FENCE ME IN
DON'T MENTION IT
DO ONESELF WELL
DOOMSDAY CLOCK
DOOR TO SUCCESS
DORMITORY AREA
DORMITORY TOWN
DOROTHY LAMOUR
DOROTHY SAYERS
DOTING HUSBAND
DOTS AND DASHES
DOUBLE BASSOON
DOUBLE DEALING
DOUBLE FIFTEEN
DOUBLE FIGURES
DOUBLE HARNESS
DOUBLE HELPING
DOUBLE MEANING
DOUBLE OR QUITS
DOUBLE PORTION
DOUBLE SIXTEEN
DOUBLE TROUBLE
DOUBLE WEDDING
DOUBTFUL POINT
DOUBTFUL REPLY
DOWNING STREET
DOWN ON THE FARM
DOWNRIGHT LIAR
DOWN THE COURSE
DOWN THE STAIRS
DOWN THE STRAND
DOWN THE STREET
DOWN THE THAMES

DOWN TO BEDROCK
DOWNWARD CURVE
DOWNWARD SLOPE
DOWNWARD TREND
DRAB EXISTENCE
DRAGOON GUARDS
DRAINING BOARD
DRAIN THE DREGS
DRAMA FESTIVAL
DRAMATIC SCENE
DRASTIC REMEDY
DRAW A PARALLEL
DRAW ATTENTION
DRAW A VEIL OVER
DRAWING MASTER
DRAWN FROM LIFE
DRAW ONE'S SCREW
DRAW ONE'S SWORD
DRAW THE BLINDS
DREADED MOMENT
DREADFUL SIGHT
DREADFUL STORY
DREADFUL VOICE
DREAM SEQUENCE
DREARY OUTLOOK
DRENCHING RAIN
DRESS DESIGNER
DRESSED TO KILL
DRESSING TABLE
DRESS MATERIAL
DRESS OPTIONAL
DRIBS AND DRABS
DRILL SERGEANT
DRINKING GLASS
DRINKING PARTY
DRINKING STRAW
DRINKING WATER
DRINK ONE'S FILL
DRINK TO EXCESS
DRIVE A BARGAIN
DRIVE HEADLONG
DRIVE-IN CINEMA
DRIVEN TO DRINK
DRIVE WITH CARE
DRIVING LESSON
DRIVING MIRROR
DRIVING SCHOOL
DROP OF QUININE
DROP ONE'S GUARD
DROP ONE'S VOICE
DROPPED STITCH
DR STRANGELOVE
DRUM-HEAD COURT
DRUNKEN SAILOR
DRUNKEN STUPOR
DRYING MACHINE

DUAL OWNERSHIP
DUBIOUS MANNER
DUCHESS OF KENT
DUCHESS OF YORK
DUELLING SWORD
DUE REFLECTION
DUKE ELLINGTON
DUKE OF BEDFORD
DUKE OF NORFOLK
DUKE OF WINDSOR
DULL AND DREARY
DULLING EFFECT
DUMB INSOLENCE
DUODENAL ULCER
DURING REPAIRS
DUSTING POWDER
DUSTIN HOFFMAN
DWELLING HOUSE
DYED IN THE WOOL
DYNAMIC ENERGY

E – 13

EACH-WAY DOUBLE
EACH-WAY TREBLE
EAGER TO PLEASE
EAMONN ANDREWS
EARL OF WARWICK
EARLY DECISION
EARN A DIVIDEND
EARNEST DESIRE
EARTHLY THINGS
EASE THE BURDEN
EASILY AROUSED
EASILY MANAGED
EASILY PLEASED
EASTERN BAZAAR
EASTERN CHURCH
EAST GRINSTEAD
EAT LIKE A HORSE
EAT WITH RELISH
ECLIPSE STAKES
ECONOMIC VALUE
EDGAR ALLAN POE
EDIFYING STORY
EDINBURGH ROCK
EDITION DE LUXE
EDITORIAL DESK
EDITOR IN CHIEF
EDMUND SPENSER
EDWARDIAN DAYS
EFFACE ONESELF
EGGSHELL CHINA
EGYPTIAN MUMMY
EIGHT AND A HALF
EIGHT-DAY CLOCK

EIGHTEEN CARAT
EIGHTEEN HOLES
EIGHTEEN MILES
EIGHT FURLONGS
EIGHTH CENTURY
EIGHTH OF APRIL
EIGHTH OF MARCH
EIGHT OF HEARTS
EIGHT OF SPADES
EIGHT OF TRUMPS
EIGHTSOME REEL
EIGHT THOUSAND
EIGHT TO THE BAR
EIGHTY PER CENT
EJECTION ORDER
ELABORATE MEAL
ELECTION AGENT
ELECTION FEVER
ELECTION NIGHT
ELECTORAL ROLL
ELECTRIC CABLE
ELECTRIC CHAIR
ELECTRIC CLOCK
ELECTRIC DRILL
ELECTRIC FENCE
ELECTRIC KNIFE
ELECTRIC LIGHT
ELECTRIC METER
ELECTRIC MIXER
ELECTRIC MOTOR
ELECTRIC ORGAN
ELECTRIC PIANO
ELECTRIC POWER
ELECTRIC RAZOR
ELECTRIC SHOCK
ELECTRIC STORM
ELECTRIC STOVE
ELECTRIC TORCH
ELECTRIC TRAIN
ELECTRONIC TOY
ELEMENT OF RISK
ELEPHANT'S TUSK
ELEVEN GUINEAS
ELEVEN MINUTES
ELEVEN PER CENT
ELEVENTH GREEN
ELEVENTH OF MAY
ELEVENTH PLACE
ELEVENTH ROUND
ELUSIVE PERSON
ELY CULBERTSON
ELYSIAN FIELDS
EMERGENCY CALL
EMERGENCY EXIT
EMERGENCY STOP
EMERGENCY WARD

EMINENTLY FAIR
EMOTIONAL LIFE
EMPIRE BUILDER
EMPTY PROMISES
EMULSION PAINT
END OF DISASTER
ENDLESS EFFORT
END OF THE MONTH
END OF THE STORY
END OF THE WORLD
END UP IN PRISON
ENDURANCE TEST
ENDURE FOR EVER
ENEMY AIRCRAFT
ENFORCE THE LAW
ENGAGED COUPLE
ENGAGED SIGNAL
ENGAGING SMILE
ENGINE FAILURE
ENGINE TROUBLE
ENGLISH GARDEN
ENGLISH LESSON
ENGLISH MASTER
ENGLISH SETTER
ENJOY IMMUNITY
ENJOY IMPUNITY
ENLARGED HEART
ENORMOUS SALES
ENOUGH'S ENOUGH
ENQUIRING MIND
ENTER A PROTEST
ENTER THE LISTS
ENTRANCE MONEY
EQUABLE TEMPER
EQUAL DIVISION
EQUAL QUANTITY
ERECT A BARRIER
ERIC LINKLATER
ERNEST MARPLES
ERRAND OF MERCY
ESCAPE ME NEVER
ESCORT CARRIER
ESPRIT DE CORPS
ESSENTIAL PART
ESTIMATED COST
ESTIMATED TIME
ETON AND HARROW
EUCALYPTUS OIL
EUROPEAN UNION
EUSTON STATION
EVADE THE ISSUE
EVASION OF DUTY
EVASIVE ACTION
EVASIVE ANSWER
EVENING PRAYER
EVENING STROLL

EVEN THINGS OUT
EVERGREEN TREE
EVERY FEW HOURS
EVERY FEW YEARS
EVERY OTHER DAY
EVERY SATURDAY
EVERY THURSDAY
EVIL INFLUENCE
EXACT LIKENESS
EXALTED PERSON
EXCELLENT SHOT
EXCESS BAGGAGE
EXCESSIVE ZEAL
EXCESS LUGGAGE
EXCESS PROFITS
EXCHANGE BLOWS
EXCHANGE CARDS
EXCHANGE IDEAS
EXCHANGE SHOTS
EXCHANGE VALUE
EXCHANGE VIEWS
EXCHANGE WORDS
EXCHEQUER BOND
EXCISE OFFICER
EXCITING MATCH
EXCITING SCENE
EXCLUSIVE CLUB
EXCURSION RATE
EXCUSE-ME DANCE
EXCUSE ONESELF
EXECUTIVE BODY
EXEMPLI GRATIA
EXERCISE A PULL
EXERCISE CYCLE
EXERCISE POWER
EXERCISE WHEEL
EXERT PRESSURE
EXORBITANT FEE
EXPECTANT HEIR
EXPECTED THING
EXPECT TOO MUCH
EXPENSIVE ITEM
EXPENSIVE LINE
EXPERT OPINION
EXPERT TUITION
EXPERT WITNESS
EXPLOSION SHOT
EXPOSED TO VIEW
EXPRESS DESIRE
EXPRESS LETTER
EXPRESS REGRET
EXTENSION LEAD
EXTENSIVE VIEW
EXTERIOR ANGLE
EXTINCT ANIMAL
EXTRACT A TOOTH

EXTRACT OF BEEF
EXTREME HATRED
EXTREMELY NICE
EXTREME OLD AGE
EYEBROW PENCIL
EYELASH CURLER
EYELESS IN GAZA
EYES LIKE A HAWK
EYES LIKE STARS
EYE TO BUSINESS

F – 13

FABIAN SOCIETY
FABULOUS BEAST
FABULOUS STORY
FACE DOWNWARDS
FACED WITH RUIN
FACE HEAVY ODDS
FACIAL MASSAGE
FACT OR FICTION
FACTORY HOOTER
FACULTY MEMBER
FACULTY OF ARTS
FAEROE ISLANDS
FAILING HEALTH
FAIL MISERABLY
FAIL TO CONNECT
FAINT WITH FEAR
FAIR AND SQUARE
FAIR APPRAISAL
FAIR CONDITION
FAIRLY CERTAIN
FAIRLY CONTENT
FAIRLY WELL OFF
FAIRLY WRITTEN
FAIR RECEPTION
FAIR TREATMENT
FAIRY PRINCESS
FAKE JEWELLERY
FALL FROM GRACE
FALLING LEAVES
FALLING PRICES
FALLING VALUES
FALL INTO A RAGE
FALL INTO A TRAP
FALL INTO ERROR
FALL INTO PLACE
FALL OF JERICHO
FALL OUT OF LOVE
FALL OVERBOARD
FALL PROSTRATE
FALSE CLAIMANT
FALSE EVIDENCE
FALSE OPTIMISM
FALSE POSITION

FALSE TEACHING
FALSETTO VOICE
FAMILIAR FACES
FAMILIAR SIGHT
FAMILIAR STYLE
FAMILIAR TERMS
FAMILIAR VOICE
FAMILY BUTCHER
FAMILY CONCERN
FAMILY FAILING
FAMILY MATTERS
FAMILY PRAYERS
FAMILY QUARREL
FAMILY REUNION
FAMILY WELFARE
FAR-AWAY PLACES
FAREWELL PARTY
FARM BUILDING
FARTHEST POINT
FASCIST REGIME
FASHION PARADE
FASHION VICTIM
FATAL ACCIDENT
FATAL CASUALTY
FATAL DECISION
FAT CONTROLLER
FATHER NEPTUNE
FATHER WILLIAM
FAVOURITE TUNE
FAVOUR ONE SIDE
FEAR OF HEIGHTS
FEAR OF THE DARK
FEAST OF REASON
FEAST ONE'S EYES
FEATHER DUSTER
FEATHER PILLOW
FEATHER STITCH
FEATURE EDITOR
FED AND WATERED
FEDERAL STATES
FED TO THE TEETH
FEEBLE ATTEMPT
FEEBLE GESTURE
FEEDING BOTTLE
FEED THE FLAMES
FEEL EXHAUSTED
FEEL MORTIFIED
FEEL NO EMOTION
FEEL ONE'S PULSE
FEIGN SICKNESS
FELLOW CITIZEN
FELLOW FEELING
FELLOW SOLDIER
FEMALE WARRIOR
FEMININE CHARM
FEMININE LOGIC

FEMININE WILES
FENCING LESSON
FENCING MASTER
FENCING SCHOOL
FERTILE GROUND
FERTILE REGION
FERTILITY DRUG
FERVENT DESIRE
FESTIVE SEASON
FESTIVE SPIRIT
FETCH AND CARRY
FEVER HOSPITAL
FEVERISH HASTE
FEVERISH STATE
FICTION WRITER
FIDDLERS THREE
FIELD DRESSING
FIELD HOSPITAL
FIELD OF ACTION
FIELD OF BATTLE
FIELD OF HONOUR
FIELD OF VISION
FIFTEEN ROUNDS
FIFTEEN THIRTY
FIFTEENTH HOLE
FIFTH DIVIDEND
FIFTH OF AUGUST
FIFTH REPUBLIC
FIFTH SYMPHONY
FIFTY THOUSAND
FIGHTER PATROL
FIGHTING DRUNK
FIGHT PROMOTER
FIGURE OF EIGHT
FIGURE SKATING
FILING CABINET
FILLET OF STEAK
FILL ONE'S GLASS
FILM PROJECTOR
FILTER THROUGH
FINAL DECISION
FINAL DIVIDEND
FINAL ESTIMATE
FINAL JUDGMENT
FINAL MOVEMENT
FINAL SOLUTION
FINANCIAL NEWS
FINANCIAL PAGE
FINANCIAL RUIN
FINANCIAL YEAR
FIND A FOOTHOLD
FIND A LOOP-HOLE
FIND A SOLUTION
FIND ONE'S LEVEL
FINE ONE'S MATCH
FIND SALVATION

FIND THE NEEDLE
FIND THE REMEDY
FINE CHARACTER
FINE GENTLEMAN
FINER FEELINGS
FINE SELECTION
FINE SITUATION
FINE TOOTH-COMB
FINGER OF SCORN
FINISHING POST
FINISH THE RACE
FINNAN HADDOCK
FINNEGAN'S WAKE
FIRE A QUESTION
FIRE INSURANCE
FIREWORK PARTY
FIRM FAVOURITE
FIRM HANDSHAKE
FIRM PRINCIPLE
FIRM TREATMENT
FIRST-AID CLASS
FIRST BIRTHDAY
FIRST DELIVERY
FIRST DIVIDEND
FIRST DIVISION
FIRST LANGUAGE
FIRST OF AUGUST
FIRST OFFENDER
FIRST OF THE FEW
FIRST QUESTION
FIRST SYMPHONY
FIRST THOUGHTS
FIRST TO ARRIVE
FIRST WORLD WAR
FISHING RIGHTS
FISHING SEASON
FISHING TACKLE
FISHY BUSINESS
FIT FOR NOTHING
FIT FOR THE GODS
FITFUL SLUMBER
FIT LIKE A GLOVE
FIT OF COUGHING
FIT OF LAUGHTER
FIT OF THE BLUES
FIT OF THE SULKS
FITS AND STARTS
FIVE-O'CLOCK TEA
FIVE-POUND NOTE
FIVE YEAR DIARY
FIXED DOMICILE
FIXED INTERVAL
FLANDERS POPPY
FLANK MOVEMENT
FLASHING SMILE
FLASH IN THE PAN

FLASH OF GENIUS
FLAT OF THE HAND
FLEA IN ONE'S EAR
FLEMISH SCHOOL
FLESH AND BLOOD
FLICKER OF HOPE
FLIGHT OF FANCY
FLIGHT OF STEPS
FLIRTY FISHING
FLITCH OF BACON
FLOAT A COMPANY
FLOATING VOTER
FLOCK TOGETHER
FLOODS OF TEARS
FLORA AND FAUNA
FLORAL PATTERN
FLORAL TRIBUTE
FLOUR AND WATER
FLOWERING TREE
FLOWER OF YOUTH
FLOWERY SPEECH
FLOW LIKE WATER
FLOW OF SPIRITS
FLOW OF TRAFFIC
FLUSHED CHEEKS
FLYING COLOURS
FLYING MACHINE
FLYING OFFICER
FLYING TRAPEZE
FLY THE COUNTRY
FOLD ONE'S HANDS
FOLIES BERGÈRE
FOLLOWING WIND
FOLLOW ROUTINE
FOLLOW THAT CAR
FOLLOW THE BAND
FOLLOW THE FLAG
FOLLOW THE HERD
FOLLOW THE HUNT
FOLLOW THE ROAD
FOLLOW THROUGH
FOND OF COMFORT
FOND OF DISPLAY
FONDUE EVENING
FOOD AND WARMTH
FOOD FOR FISHES
FOOD OF THE GODS
FOOD POISONING
FOOD PROCESSOR
FOOLISH ACTION
FOOLISH FELLOW
FOOLISH PERSON
FOOLISH VIRGIN
FOOLSCAP PAPER
FOOL'S PARADISE
FOOTBALL FIELD

FOOTBALL MATCH
FOOTBALL PITCH
FOOTBALL POOLS
FOR AND AGAINST
FORBIDDEN GAME
FORBIDDEN TREE
FORCE A PASSAGE
FORCED LANDING
FORCED SAVINGS
FORCE ONE'S HAND
FORCE THE ISSUE
FORCIBLE ENTRY
FOREHAND DRIVE
FOREIGN ACCENT
FOREIGN EDITOR
FOREIGN FIELDS
FOREIGN LEGION
FOREIGN MARKET
FOREIGN OFFICE
FOREIGN ORIGIN
FOREIGN POLICY
FOREIGN SHORES
FOREIGN TONGUE
FOREIGN TRAVEL
FOREST OF ARDEN
FOREST OF MASTS
FORGET ONESELF
FOR GOOD AND ALL
FORGOTTEN ARMY
FORK LIGHTNING
FORMAL PROTEST
FORMAL REQUEST
FORM AN OPINION
FOR MERCY'S SAKE
FORMER STUDENT
FORM OF ADDRESS
FORM OF WORSHIP
FOR THE PRESENT
FORTIFIED POST
FORTIFIED TOWN
FORTIFIED WINE
FORTUNE HUNTER
FORTUNES OF WAR
FORTUNE'S WHEEL
FORTUNE TELLER
FORTY-HOUR WEEK
FORTY THOUSAND
FOSTER BROTHER
FOUNDED ON FACT
FOUNDER MEMBER
FOUNT OF HONOUR
FOUNT OF WISDOM
FOUR AND TWENTY
FOUR-POSTER BED
FOUR SYLLABLES
FOURTEEN MILES

FOURTH CENTURY
FOURTH OF APRIL
FOURTH OFFICER
FOURTH OF MARCH
FOWLS OF THE AIR
FRAGRANT SMELL
FRAME A PICTURE
FRANKIE HOWERD
FRANTIC APPEAL
FRATERNITY PIN
FREAK OF NATURE
FREE ADMISSION
FREE AS THE WIND
FREE FROM BLAME
FREE FROM ERROR
FREE FROM FAULT
FREE FROM GUILE
FREE FROM GUILT
FREEHOLD HOUSE
FREE-RANGE EGGS
FREE RENDERING
FREE TO CONFESS
FREE-TRADE AREA
FREEZE TO DEATH
FREEZING AGENT
FREEZING POINT
FREIGHT CHARGE
FRENCH ACADEMY
FRENCH CRICKET
FRENCH CUISINE
FRENCH GRAMMAR
FRENCH MUSTARD
FRENCH PERFUME
FRENCH TEACHER
FRENCH WINDOWS
FREQUENCY BAND
FRESH-AIR FIEND
FRESH APPROACH
FRESH AS A DAISY
FRESH EVIDENCE
FRESH OUTBREAK
FRICTION MATCH
FRIDAY EVENING
FRIDAY MORNING
FRIED POTATOES
FRIED TOMATOES
FRIEND AT COURT
FRIEND IN COURT
FRIENDLY MATCH
FRIENDLY TERMS
FRIENDLY TOUCH
FRIEND'S FRIEND
FRIGHTFUL TIME
FRINGE BENEFIT
FRINGE THEATRE
FRITZ KREISLER

FROM A DISTANCE
FROM ONE'S HEART
FROM THE BOTTOM
FROM THE CRADLE
FROM THE OUTSET
FRONTAL ATTACK
FRONT ENTRANCE
FRONTIER GUARD
FRONT-PAGE NEWS
FRONT POSITION
FROSTY WEATHER
FROSTY WELCOME
FROZEN BALANCE
FROZEN TO DEATH
FRUIT AND CREAM
FRUITLESS TASK
FRUIT MERCHANT
FRYING TONIGHT
FULL ASSURANCE
FULL IN THE FACE
FULL OF COURAGE
FULL OF MEANING
FULL OF PROMISE
FULL OF REGRETS
FULL OF THE NEWS
FULL OWNERSHIP
FULL PROGRAMME
FULL TO THE BRIM
FULL TREATMENT
FULLY EQUIPPED
FULLY LICENSED
FULLY OCCUPIED
FULLY RESTORED
FUMBLE THE BALL
FUME WITH ANGER
FUNERAL SERMON
FUNNY BUSINESS
FUNNY PECULIAR
FUR AND FEATHER
FURIOUS TEMPER
FURNISHED FLAT
FURNISHED ROOM
FURTHER NOTICE
FURTHEST POINT
FUSS AND BOTHER
FUTILE ATTEMPT
FUTILE PURSUIT
FUTURE HUSBAND
FUTURE OUTLOOK
FUTURE PERFECT
FUTURES MARKET

G – 13

GADARENE SWINE
GAGGLE OF GEESE

GAIETY THEATRE
GAIN ADMISSION
GAIN SUPREMACY
GALE-FORCE WIND
GALLANT MEMBER
GAMES MISTRESS
GAME TO THE LAST
GANG OF THIEVES
GANGWAY PLEASE
GARBLED REPORT
GARDENING CLUB
GARDEN OF WEEDS
GARDEN PRODUCE
GARDEN SYRINGE
GARLIC SAUSAGE
GASP FOR BREATH
GATHER FLOWERS
GEIGER COUNTER
GENERAL CUSTER
GENERAL DEALER
GENERAL EXODUS
GENERAL FRANCO
GENERAL GORDON
GENERAL MARKET
GENERAL PARDON
GENERAL PUBLIC
GENERAL READER
GENERAL STORES
GENERAL STRIKE
GENERAL SURVEY
GENERATION GAP
GENEROUS GIVER
GENEROUS OFFER
GENEROUS SHARE
GENEROUS TERMS
GENIUS WILL OUT
GENTLE AS A LAMB
GENTLE BEARING
GENTLE MANNERS
GENTLE REPROOF
GENUINE REGARD
GEOMETRIC MEAN
GEORGE FOREMAN
GEORGE GISSING
GEORGIAN HOUSE
GERMAN MEASLES
GERMAN SAUSAGE
GET AT THE FACTS
GET AT THE TRUTH
GET AWAY WITH IT
GET IN ON THE ACT
GET IT STRAIGHT
GET IT TOGETHER
GET OFF LIGHTLY
GET ONE'S HAND IN
GET ONE'S OWN WAY

GET ON TOGETHER
GET OUT OF SIGHT
GET THE GIGGLES
GET THE MESSAGE
GET THERE FIRST
GETTING ON A BIT
GETTING STONED
GET TO ONE'S FEET
GET TO WINDWARD
GIACONDA SMILE
GIFT OF TONGUES
GIN AND BITTERS
GIN AND ITALIAN
GIORGIO ARMANI
GIPSY'S WARNING
GIRTON COLLEGE
GIUSEPPE VERDI
GIVE A DOG A BONE
GIVE A FIRM DATE
GIVE AN ACCOUNT
GIVE AN EXAMPLE
GIVE AN OPINION
GIVE-AWAY PRICE
GIVE COMMUNION
GIVE IT A CHANCE
GIVE A NEW LOOK
GIVEN IN CHARGE
GIVE NO QUARTER
GIVE NO TROUBLE
GIVEN THE STRAP
GIVEN THE WORKS
GIVEN TO EXCESS
GIVE ONESELF UP
GIVE ONE THE LIE
GIVE ONE THE PIP
GIVE THE SIGNAL
GIVE UP ALL HOPE
GIVE UP SMOKING
GIVE UP THE IDEA
GIVE UTTERANCE
GLACIAL PERIOD
GLAD OF A CHANCE
GLASS AND CHINA
GLASS MOUNTAIN
GLASS OF SHERRY
GLASS OF WHISKY
GLASS WITH CARE
GLASSY SURFACE
GLEAM OF HUMOUR
GLIMMER OF HOPE
GLOATING SMILE
GLOBAL VILLAGE
GLOBAL WARMING
GLOOMY OUTLOOK
GLOOMY PICTURE
GLORIA SWANSON

GLORIOUS DEVON
GLORIOUS MUSIC
GLORIOUS REIGN
GLORIOUS YEARS
GLOWING CHEEKS
GLOWING EMBERS
GLOWING REPORT
GLOW WITH PRIDE
GNASH THE TEETH
GO AS YOU PLEASE
GODDESS OF LOVE
GOD OF LAUGHTER
GO FOR A JOURNEY
GOING FOR A SONG
GOING STRAIGHT
GO INTO A TRANCE
GO INTO DETAILS
GOLD AND SILVER
GOLDEN HAMSTER
GOLDEN JUBILEE
GOLDEN TRESSES
GOLDEN WEDDING
GOLD MEDALLIST
GO LIKE THE WIND
GONE TO THE DOGS
GOOD ACOUSTICS
GOOD AFTERNOON
GOOD AND PROPER
GOOD AT FIGURES
GOOD BEGINNING
GOOD BEHAVIOUR
GOOD BREAKFAST
GOOD CHARACTER
GOOD CONDITION
GOOD CONDUCTOR
GOOD DIGESTION
GOOD FOR A LAUGH
GOOD GROUNDING
GOOD HOUSEWIFE
GOOD HUSBANDRY
GOOD INFLUENCE
GOOD NEIGHBOUR
GOOD NEWS BIBLE
GOOD PROSPECTS
GOOD QUEEN BESS
GOOD RECEPTION
GOOD SAMARITAN
GOOD SELECTION
GOOD SPORTSMAN
GOOD TALKING-TO
GOOD THRASHING
GOOD WALLOPING
GOODWOOD RACES
GOODY TWO-SHOES
GO OFF ONE'S HEAD
GO ON THE PARISH

GORDON BENNETT
GO THE DISTANCE
GO THE WHOLE HOG
GO TO THE BOTTOM
GO TO THE CINEMA
GO TO THE CIRCUS
GO TO THE MOVIES
GO TO THE OFFICE
GO TO THE RESCUE
GO UNDERGROUND
GOVERNING BODY
GO WITH THE TIDE
GRADUAL CHANGE
GRAIN OF POWDER
GRAMMAR SCHOOL
GRAND ALLIANCE
GRAND ENTRANCE
GRAND FUNCTION
GRAND JUNCTION
GRAND NATIONAL
GRAND STRATEGY
GRANT A DIVORCE
GRANT A REQUEST
GRANT IMMUNITY
GRAPES OF WRATH
GRAPHITE SHAFT
GRAPPLING IRON
GRASP AT A STRAW
GRASP OF DETAIL
GRATEFUL HEART
GRATE ON THE EAR
GRAVE DECISION
GRAVE THOUGHTS
GREASE THE PALM
GREAT DISTANCE
GREATER LONDON
GREAT IN NUMBER
GREAT INTEREST
GREAT KINDNESS
GREATLY MISSED
GREAT MAJORITY
GREAT OCCASION
GREAT PATIENCE
GREAT PLEASURE
GREAT QUANTITY
GREAT SALT LAKE
GREAT STRENGTH
GREAT THOUGHTS
GREAT UNWASHED
GREAT WEST ROAD
GREAT WHITE WAY
GREAT YARMOUTH
GREEK ALPHABET
GREEK LANGUAGE
GREEN CURRENCY
GREEN FRACTURE

GREENHOUSE GAS
GREEN PASTURES
GREENWICH TIME
GREEN WITH ENVY
GREENWOOD TREE
GREETINGS CARD
GREYHOUND RACE
GRILLED CUTLET
GRIN AND BEAR IT
GRIND INTO DUST
GRIND THE TEETH
GRIND TO POWDER
GRIP LIKE A VICE
GRIPPING STORY
GRIT ONE'S TEETH
GROANING BOARD
GROAN INWARDLY
GROSS RECEIPTS
GROUND CONTROL
GROUP ACTIVITY
GROW BEAUTIFUL
GROW DESPERATE
GROW DOWNWARDS
GRUELLING HEAT
GRUELLING PACE
GRUELLING RACE
GRUELLING TIME
GRUYÈRE CHEESE
GUARDED REMARK
GUARDIAN ANGEL
GUARD OF HONOUR
GUARDS' OFFICER
GUERRILLA BAND
GUEST OF HONOUR
GUIDED MISSILE
GUILDFORD FOUR
GUILTY FEELING
GUNNERY SCHOOL
GUNPOWDER PLOT
GUSHING LETTER
GUTTERAL VOICE
GUY THE GORILLA
GYPSY'S WARNING

H – 13

HACKING JACKET
HAILE SELASSIE
HAIL OF BULLETS
HAIR OF THE HEAD
HALE AND HEARTY
HALF THE BATTLE
HALF THE NUMBER
HALF-TIME SCORE
HALIFAX BOMBER

HALL OF JUSTICE
HALL OF MIRRORS
HALLOWED PLACE
HALTING SPEECH
HALVE THE MATCH
HAMILTON HOUSE
HANDLE ROUGHLY
HAND OF BANANAS
HAND OUT ADVICE
HANDSOME OFFER
HANDSOME STYLE
HANDSOME THING
HANG BY A THREAD
HANGING BASKET
HANGING GARDEN
HANGING MATTER
HANG ONE'S HAT UP
HANG UP ONE'S HAT
HANNEN SWAFFER
HANOVER SQUARE
HAPPILY IN LOVE
HAPPY ACCIDENT
HAPPY BIRTHDAY
HAPPY FAMILIES
HAPPY MARRIAGE
HAPPY MEMORIES
HAPPY WANDERER
HARBOUR LIGHTS
HARBOUR MASTER
HARD-BOILED EGG
HARDEN ONESELF
HARD-LUCK STORY
HARD NECESSITY
HARD OF HEARING
HARD TO BELIEVE
HARD TO IMAGINE
HARD TO SATISFY
HARD TO SWALLOW
HARDWARE STORE
HARE AND HOUNDS
HARMONIC SCALE
HARROWING TALE
HARROWING TIME
HARRY THE HORSE
HARSH CONTRAST
HARSH DECISION
HARSH SENTENCE
HARVEST SUNDAY
HARVEST SUPPER
HASTEN ONE'S END
HASTY DECISION
HATEFUL OBJECT
HATFIELD HOUSE
HATTER'S CASTLE
HAVE A BAD NIGHT
HAVE A BREATHER

HAVE A GOOD MIND
HAVE A GOOD TALK
HAVE A GOOD TIME
HAVE A MANICURE
HAVE AN ADDRESS
HAVE A TOOTH OUT
HAVE A WALK-OVER
HAVE DELUSIONS
HAVE HALF A MIND
HAVE HYSTERICS
HAVELOCK ELLIS
HAVEN OF REFUGE
HAVE NO REGRETS
HAVE NO SECRETS
HAVE NO TROUBLE
HAVE ONE'S FLING
HAVE ONE'S WHACK
HAVE THE ANSWER
HAVE THE HONOUR
HAVE THE OPTION
HAVE THE WIND UP
HAYLING ISLAND
HAYWARDS HEATH
HEADLONG SPEED
HEAD OF THE FORM
HEAD OF THE POLL
HEAD OVER HEELS
HEADS TOGETHER
HEALING SPIRIT
HEAL THE BREACH
HEALTH OFFICER
HEALTH SERVICE
HEALTH VISITOR
HEALTHY COLOUR
HEAPS OF PEOPLE
HEAR BOTH SIDES
HEARD IN CAMERA
HEARTH AND HOME
HEART OF HEARTS
HEART OF MARBLE
HEART'S CONTENT
HEARTY DISLIKE
HEARTY WELCOME
HEATED DISPUTE
HEATED QUARREL
HEATH ROBINSON
HEAT TREATMENT
HEAVEN HELP HIM!
HEAVENLY CHOIR
HEAVENLY TWINS
HEAVEN ON EARTH
HEAVILY LOADED
HEAVY DOWNPOUR
HEAVY EXPENSES
HEAVY HYDROGEN
HEAVY INDUSTRY

HEAVY MATERIAL
HEAVY SENTENCE
HEIGHT OF FOLLY
HELD FOR RANSOM
HELL UPON EARTH
HELPFUL ADVICE
HENLEY REGATTA
HENRY FIELDING
HENRY THE FIFTH
HENRY THE FIRST
HENRY THE SIXTH
HENRY THE THIRD
HERALDIC SWORD
HERCULEAN TASK
HERCULE POIROT
HER EXCELLENCY
HEROIC COUPLET
HEW OUT A CAREER
HIDDEN MEANING
HIDDEN RESERVE
HIGH AND MIGHTY
HIGH BIRTH-RATE
HIGH CHARACTER
HIGH CHURCHMAN
HIGH COLOURING
HIGH ENDEAVOUR
HIGHER BRACKET
HIGHEST BIDDER
HIGH EXPLOSIVE
HIGH FREQUENCY
HIGHLAND CHIEF
HIGHLAND DANCE
HIGHLAND DRESS
HIGHLAND FLING
HIGHLAND GAMES
HIGHLY PLEASED
HIGH VALUATION
HIGH-WATER MARK
HIGHWAY PATROL
HIGHWAY ROBBER
HIKING HOLIDAY
HILAIRE BELLOC
HINDU RELIGION
HIRED ASSASSIN
HIS EXCELLENCY
HISTORIC SCENE
HISTORIC TENSE
HISTORY IS BUNK
HISTORY LESSON
HISTORY MASTER
HISTRIONIC ART
HITLER DIARIES
HIT THE JACKPOT
HIT THE UPRIGHT
HOBSON'S CHOICE
HOLD AN INQUEST

HOLD AN INQUIRY
HOLD AN OPINION
HOLD IN BONDAGE
HOLD IN RESPECT
HOLD ONE GUILTY
HOLD ONE'S PEACE
HOLD THAT TIGER!
HOLD THE RECORD
HOLD THE RUDDER
HOLD THE SCALES
HOLD THE STAKES
HOLE AND CORNER
HOLE IN THE ROAD
HOLIDAY CHALET
HOLIDAY COURSE
HOLIDAY RESORT
HOLIDAY SEASON
HOLIDAY SPIRIT
HOLLOW FEELING
HOLLOW MOCKERY
HOLLOW VICTORY
HOLLYWOOD BOWL
HOLY COMMUNION
HOLY INNOCENTS
HOLY MATRIMONY
HOME ECONOMICS
HOME FOR THE DAY
HOME INTERESTS
HOME-MADE BREAD
HOME PROGRAMME
HOMERIC BATTLE
HOME SECRETARY
HOME SWEET HOME
HOMEWARD BOUND
HONEST ATTEMPT
HONEST DEALING
HONEYDEW MELON
HONOR BLACKMAN
HONOURABLE MAN
HONOUR AND OBEY
HONOURED GUEST
HONOURS DEGREE
HOOK OF HOLLAND
HOPE AND BELIEF
HOPELESS STATE
HORACE WALPOLE
HORATIO NELSON
HORRIBLE NOISE
HORRIBLE CRIME
HORRIBLE SIGHT
HORSE AND GROOM
HORSE CHESTNUT
HORSESHOE BEND
HOSPITAL NURSE
HOSPITAL TRAIN
HOSTILE ATTACK

HOSTILE CRITIC
HOSTILE MANNER
HOST OF FRIENDS
HOT-HOUSE PLANT
HOT ON THE SCENT
HOT ON THE TRAIL
HOUR AFTER HOUR
HOURLY SERVICE
HOUR OF TRIUMPH
HOURS AND HOURS
HOUSEHOLD GODS
HOUSEHOLD HINT
HOUSEHOLD LOAF
HOUSEHOLD WORD
HOUSE MAGAZINE
HOUSE OF BRICKS
HOUSE OF ORANGE
HOUSE OF PRAYER
HOUSE OF REFUGE
HOUSE ON WHEELS
HOUSE PROPERTY
HOUSING ESTATE
HUB OF INDUSTRY
HUGH GAITSKELL
HUMAN ACTIVITY
HUMAN CREATURE
HUMAN DOCUMENT
HUMAN SOCIETY
HUMAN INTEREST
HUMAN PROGRESS
HUMAN TRIANGLE
HUMAN WEAKNESS
HUMBLE ADMIRER
HUMBLE APOLOGY
HUMBLE OPINION
HUMBLE REQUEST
HUMBLE SERVANT
HUMBLE STATION
HUMPBACK WHALE
HUNDRED AND ONE
HUNDRED POUNDS
HUNGER MARCHER
HUNGER STRIKER
HUNGRY FORTIES
HUNTING SEASON
HURRICANE LAMP
HURRIED GLANCE
HURRIED SPEECH
HURT ONE'S PRIDE
HYDRAULIC JACK
HYDRAULIC LIFT

I – 13

IAN CARMICHAEL

ICE-CREAM WAFER	IN FINE FEATHER
IDEALLY SUITED	INFINITE SPACE
IDENTICAL TWIN	INFLATED IDEAS
IF YOU DON'T MIND!	INFLATED PRICE
ILL MANAGEMENT	IN FOR A STRETCH
IMAGINARY LINE	INFORM AGAINST
IMITATION WARE	INFORMAL DRESS
IMPENDING DOOM	INFORMAL PARTY
IMPERIAL CROWN	IN FORMER TIMES
IMPERIAL EAGLE	IN FULL FEATHER
IMPERIAL GUARD	IN FULL MEASURE
IMPERIAL TOKAY	IN FULL RETREAT
IMPLICIT FAITH	IN GREAT DEMAND
IMPORTANT POST	INGRID BERGMAN
IMPUDENT ROGUE	IN HIGH FEATHER
IMPULSE BUYING	IN HONOUR BOUND
IN A CLEFT STICK	IN IMAGINATION
IN A GENERAL WAY	INITIAL LETTER
IN A GOOD TEMPER	INITIAL OUTLAY
IN ALL FAIRNESS	INITIAL STAGES
IN ALL RESPECTS	INITIATION FEE
IN ALL WEATHERS	INK ERADICATOR
IN AN AMBULANCE	INKJET PRINTER
IN AN EMERGENCY	INLAND REVENUE
IN AN UNDERTONE	IN LIQUIDATION
IN A SORRY STATE	IN MORTAL PERIL
IN A STILL VOICE	INNATE ABILITY
IN A STRANGE WAY	INNER CONFLICT
IN AT THE FINISH	INNER HEBRIDES
INBORN ABILITY	INNOCENT PARTY
INCENSE BURNER	IN ONE'S ELEMENT
IN CIRCULATION	IN ONE SENTENCE
INCLINED PLANE	IN ONE'S OWN NAME
IN COLD STORAGE	IN PARTNERSHIP
INCOME BRACKET	IN PERSPECTIVE
INCOMES POLICY	IN POINT OF FACT
INCOME SUPPORT	IN PREPARATION
INCOME-TAX FORM	IN QUEER STREET
IN COMPETITION	INQUIRING MIND
IN CONFINEMENT	INQUIRY OFFICE
IN CONSEQUENCE	IN SAFE KEEPING
IN CONVULSIONS	IN SELF-DEFENCE
INCREASED WAGE	INSERT A NOTICE
INCREASE OF PAY	IN SHORT SUPPLY
INCUR A PENALTY	INSIDE FORWARD
IN DEAD EARNEST	IN SIGHT OF LAND
INDECENT HASTE	IN SO MANY WORDS
IN DESPERATION	IN SOME MEASURE
INDIAN CHUTNEY	INSPECTION PIT
INDIRECT ROUTE	INSPIRED GUESS
IN DIRE TROUBLE	INSPIRED WORDS
INDOOR SERVANT	INSTANT CAMERA
IN EVERY DETAIL	INSTANT COFFEE
INFANT BAPTISM	INSULAR HABITS
INFANT PRODIGY	INSURANCE CARD
INFERIOR GOODS	INSURANCE RISK

INSURED PERSON
INTENSIVE CARE
INTEREST RATES
INTERIM PERIOD
INTERIM REPORT
INTERVAL MUSIC
IN THE ABSTRACT
IN THE AIR FORCE
IN THE AUDIENCE
IN THE BASEMENT
IN THE BUSINESS
IN THE CORRIDOR
IN THE DARKNESS
IN THE DAYLIGHT
IN THE DISTANCE
IN THE DISTRICT
IN THE DOG-HOUSE
IN THE DOLDRUMS
IN THE FAST LANE
IN THE FOUNTAIN
IN THE GLOAMING
IN THE INTERIOR
IN THE INTERVAL
IN THE LION'S DEN
IN THE MAJORITY
IN THE MEANTIME
IN THE MIND'S EYE
IN THE MINORITY
IN THE NEGATIVE
IN THE ORIGINAL
IN THE PAVILION
IN THE SAME BOAT
IN THE SAME CAMP
IN THE SERVICES
IN THE SINGULAR
IN THE STIRRUPS
IN THE STRAIGHT
IN THE SUNSHINE
IN THE TREASURY
IN THE TRENCHES
IN THE TWILIGHT
IN THE USUAL WAY
IN THE VANGUARD
IN THE VICINITY
IN THE WRONG BOX
INTIMATE REVUE
INTIMATE STYLE
INTIMATE TERMS
IN TIMES OF YORE
INTO THE BREACH
IN TOWN TONIGHT
IN TREPIDATION
IN VARIOUS WAYS
INVERNESS CAPE
INVERTED ORDER
INVERTED PLEAT

IN VINO VERITAS
INVITE TENDERS
INVOLVED STYLE
IRISH BAGPIPES
IRISH LANGUAGE
IRISH REGIMENT
IRREGULAR VERB
ISLE OF SHEPPEY
ISLES OF GREECE
ISOBEL BARNETT
ISOLATION WARD
ISSUE A COMMAND
ISSUE A SUMMONS
ISSUED CAPITAL
ITALIAN LESSON
IT'S NOT CRICKET
IVORY CHESSMAN

J – 13

JACK THE RIPPER
JACOBEAN STYLE
JAUNDICED VIEW
JEFFREY ARCHER
JEKYLL AND HYDE
JENNIFER JONES
JET PROPULSION
JEWELLER'S SHOP
JOAN GREENWOOD
JOB'S COMFORTER
JOG ONE'S MEMORY
JOHANN STRAUSS
JOHN CONSTABLE
JOHN MASEFIELD
JOIN THE ANGELS
JOIN THE FORCES
JOINT PARTNERS
JOLLY GOOD CHAP
JONATHAN SWIFT
JORDAN ALMONDS
JOSEPH ADDISON
JOYCE GRENFELL
JUDAS ISCARIOT
JUDGE ADVOCATE
JUDGE JEFFREYS
JUDICIAL COURT
JULIA LOCKWOOD
JULY THE EIGHTH
JULY THE FOURTH
JULY THE SECOND
JUMP AT AN OFFER
JUMPING SEASON
JUMP OVERBOARD
JUMP THE COURSE
JUNE THE EIGHTH
JUNE THE FOURTH

JUNE THE SECOND
JUNGLE WARFARE
JUNIOR COUNSEL
JUNIOR PARTNER
JUNIOR SERVICE
JUST A FEW LINES
JUST AS YOU LIKE
JUST PUBLISHED
JUST SO STORIES
JUVENILE COURT

K – 13

KAISER WILHELM
KEEN AS MUSTARD
KEEP AN ACCOUNT
KEEP GOOD HOURS
KEEP IN CUSTODY
KEEP IN THE DARK
KEEP LATE HOURS
KEEP ONE'S END UP
KEEP ONE'S EYE IN
KEEP ONE'S HAT ON
KEEP ONE'S PLACE
KEEP ON THE BEAM
KEEP OPEN HOUSE
KEEP THE CHANGE
KEEP TO ONESELF
KEEP TO THE LEFT
KEEP UP THE PACE
KEEP YOUR SEATS
KENTUCKY DERBY
KEPT IN REVERSE
KEPT IN THE DARK
KEPT ON THE TROT
KEYBOARD STAND
KEY TO A MYSTERY
KICK ONE'S HEELS
KICK THE BUCKET
KICK UP A SHINDY
KIDNEY MACHINE
KILLING FIELDS
KILL THE RUMOUR
KINDRED SPIRIT
KING OF DENMARK
KING OF ENGLAND
KING'S BIRTHDAY
KING'S CHAMPION
KING'S EVIDENCE
KING'S RHAPSODY
KISS AND CUDDLE
KISS AND MAKE UP
KISSING COUSIN
KISS IN THE RING
KISS THE GROUND
KITCHEN GARDEN

KITCHEN SCALES
KIT INSPECTION
KNAVE OF HEARTS
KNAVE OF SPADES
KNAVE OF TRUMPS
KNAVISH TRICKS
KNEW IN ADVANCE
KNIT ONE'S BROWS
KNOCK-DOWN BLOW
KNOCK FOR KNOCK
KNOCK-OUT DROPS
KNOCK SIDEWAYS
KNOCK SPOTS OFF
KNOTTY PROBLEM
KNOW BACKWARDS
KNOWING FELLOW
KNOWING PERSON
KNOW ONE'S PLACE
KNOW WHAT'S WHAT

L – 13

LA BELLE FRANCE
LABOUR TROUBLE
LABOUR VICTORY
LABURNUM GROVE
LACE INSERTION
LACK OF CANDOUR
LACK OF CAUTION
LACK OF FEELING
LACK OF HARMONY
LACK OF MEANING
LACK OF RESPECT
LACK OF WARNING
LADIES' GALLERY
LADS AND LASSES
LADY BOUNTIFUL
LADY COMPANION
LADY IN WAITING
LADY OF LEISURE
LADY OF QUALITY
LADY OF SHALOTT
LADY OF THE LAKE
LADY OF THE LAMP
LADY PRINCIPAL
LAKE CONSTANCE
LAKE ULLSWATER
LAMBETH BRIDGE
LAMBETH PALACE
LAMBING SEASON
LANCE PERCIVAL
LANDING GROUND
LAND IN THE SOUP
LAND-LOCKED SEA
LAND OF PROMISE
LAND OF THE FREE

LAND OF THE MOON
LANE OF TRAFFIC
LAPSE OF MEMORY
LAPSUS LINGUAE
LARGE AND SMALL
LARGE AUDIENCE
LARGE MAJORITY
LARGE MINORITY
LARGE PRACTICE
LARGE QUANTITY
LARGE-SCALE MAP
LAST CHRISTMAS
LAST EXTREMITY
LAST HANDSHAKE
LAST OF THE LINE
LAST WEDNESDAY
LATE AFTERNOON
LATE BREAKFAST
LATE FOR DINNER
LATE FOR SCHOOL
LATE-NIGHT NEWS
LATENT ABILITY
LATEST FASHION
LATIN AMERICA
LATIN LANGUAGE
LATTICE WINDOW
LAUGH AT DANGER
LAUGHING HYENA
LAUGHING STOCK
LAUGHING WATER
LAUGH OUTRIGHT
LAUNCHING SITE
LAUNDRY BASKET
LAVENDER WATER
LAW COMMISSION
LAWFUL WEDLOCK
LAW OF AVERAGES
LAW OF CONTRACT
LAY BY THE HEELS
LAY DOWN THE LAW
LAYETTE BASKET
LAY IN THE GRAVE
LEAD A DOG'S LIFE
LEAD BY THE HAND
LEAD BY THE NOSE
LEADING DANCER
LEADING SEAMAN
LEADING STOKER
LEAD ONE A DANCE
LEAD ONE STRAY
LEAD POISONING
LEAGUE CRICKET
LEAGUE OF PEACE
LEAMINGTON SPA
LEAN BACKWARDS
LEAP IN THE DARK

LEARNED FRIEND
LEARNER DRIVER
LEARNING CURVE
LEARN THE ROPES
LEARN THE TRUTH
LEATHER GLOVES
LEATHER JACKET
LEAVE A FORTUNE
LEAVE A MESSAGE
LEAVE HALF-DONE
LEAVE HOSPITAL
LEAVE IN THE AIR
LEAVE NO CHOICE
LEAVE NO OPTION
LEAVE ONE'S CARD
LEAVE STANDING
LEAVE THE STAGE
LEAVE TO APPEAL
LED TO THE ALTAR
LEFT AT THE POST
LEFT-HAND DRIVE
LEFT-HAND SCREW
LEFT TO ONESELF
LEGAL CURRENCY
LEGAL DOCUMENT
LEGAL EVIDENCE
LEGAL GUARDIAN
LEGAL LANGUAGE
LEGAL POSITION
LEGAL SENTENCE
LEISURE CENTRE
LEMON MERINGUE
LEMON SQUEEZER
LEOPARD'S SPOTS
LES MISERABLES
LESTER PIGGOTT
LET GO THE REINS
LETHAL CHAMBER
LET IN DAYLIGHT
LET OUT A SECRET
LETTER PERFECT
LETTERS OF FIRE
LETTERS OF GOLD
LETTERS PATENT
LET THINGS SLIP
LEVEL CROSSING
LIABLE TO ERROR
LIBERAL LEADER
LIBERAL MINDED
LIBERAL POLICY
LIBRARY TICKET
LICENCE HOLDER
LICENCE TO KILL
LICENSED TRADE
LICENSING LAWS
LICK INTO SHAPE

LICK ONE'S CHOPS
LIE ON ONE'S BACK
LIFE ASSURANCE
LIFEBOAT DRILL
LIFE HEREAFTER
LIFE INSURANCE
LIFELONG ENEMY
LIFELONG HABIT
LIFE OF LEISURE
LIFETIME'S WORK
LIFT ATTENDANT
LIGHT AND SHADE
LIGHT AS A FAIRY
LIGHT COMEDIAN
LIGHT-FINGERED
LIGHT INDUSTRY
LIGHT INFANTRY
LIGHTNING MOVE
LIGHT OF MY EYES!
LIGHT OF MY LIFE!
LIGHT OF NATURE
LIGHT SENTENCE
LIGHT THE STOVE
LIGHT TRAINING
LIKE A BAD PENNY
LIKE CLOCKWORK
LIKE GRIM DEATH
LIKE LIGHTNING
LIKE MEETS LIKE
LIKE ONE O'CLOCK
LIMITED AMOUNT
LIMITED APPEAL
LIMITED CHOICE
LIMITED NUMBER
LIMITED PERIOD
LIMITED SEASON
LIMITED SUPPLY
LIMP HANDSHAKE
LINEAR MEASURE
LINEN CUPBOARD
LINE OF ADVANCE
LINE OF CONDUCT
LINE OF COUNTRY
LINE OF DEFENCE
LINE OF RETREAT
LINE OF THOUGHT
LINGERING LOOK
LINGERING NOTE
LIQUEUR BRANDY
LIQUEUR WHISKY
LIQUID CRYSTAL
LIQUID MEASURE
LIQUID SHAMPOO
LISTENING POST
LIST OF RUNNERS
LITERARY AGENT

LITERARY STYLE
LITERARY THEFT
LITERARY WORKS
LITERARY WORLD
LITTLE AND GOOD
LITTLE BIG HORN
LITTLE BOY BLUE
LITTLE BUT GOOD
LITTLE COMFORT
LITTLE RED BOOK
LITTLE SIR ECHO
LITTLE THEATRE
LITTLE TO SPARE
LITTLE TROUBLE
LIVE BROADCAST
LIVE CARTRIDGE
LIVE FOR THE DAY
LIVE IN COMFORT
LIVE IN HARMONY
LIVE IN HISTORY
LIVE IN POVERTY
LIVE IN SQUALOR
LIVE IN THE PAST
LIVE LIKE A LORD
LIVEN THINGS UP
LIVE ON NOTHING
LIVE PROGRAMME
LIVER AND BACON
LIVE RECORDING
LIVERY COMPANY
LIVERY SERVANT
LIVID WITH RAGE
LIVING THEATRE
LOAD OF RUBBISH
LOAD OF TROUBLE
LOCAL CURRENCY
LOCAL LANDMARK
LOCAL PREACHER
LODGE AN APPEAL
LOFTY AMBITION
LOFTY CONTEMPT
LOFTY THOUGHTS
LOGICAL ACTION
LOGICAL RESULT
LOMBARD STREET
LONDON SPECIAL
LONE-STAR STATE
LONG CASE CLOCK
LONG HOT SUMMER
LONG PARAGRAPH
LONG TIME NO SEE!
LONG WAY BEHIND
LONG WAY TO FALL
LONNIE DONEGAN
LOOK DANGEROUS
LOOK DIFFERENT

LOOK IMPORTANT
LOOK IN THE FACE
LOOK OVER THERE
LOOK SURPRISED
LOOK UP AND DOWN
LOOSE THINKING
LORD AND MASTER
LORD KITCHENER
LORDLY GESTURE
LORD MAYOR'S DAY
LORD PRESIDENT
LORD PRIVY SEAL
LORD PROTECTOR
LORDS TEMPORAL
LOSE COHERENCE
LOSE HANDS DOWN
LOSE ONE'S FAITH
LOSE ONE'S HEART
LOSE ONE'S LOOKS
LOSE ONE'S MONEY
LOSE ONE'S NERVE
LOSE ONE'S PLACE
LOSE ONE'S SHIRT
LOSE ONE'S SIGHT
LOSE ONE'S STAKE
LOSE ONE'S VOICE
LOSE THE BATTLE
LOSE THE RUBBER
LOSE THE THREAD
LOSS OF BALANCE
LOSS OF CONTROL
LOSS OF FORTUNE
LOSS OF FREEDOM
LOST IN THOUGHT
LOST IN TRANSIT
LOTS OF FRIENDS
LOTTERY TICKET
LOTUS POSITION
LOUD EXPLOSION
LOUIS QUATORZE
LOVE AND KISSES
LOVE OF COUNTRY
LOVE OF THE GAME
LOVE ONE'S ENEMY
LOVE ON THE DOLE
LOVING GESTURE
LOWER AND LOWER
LOWER ONE'S FLAG
LOWER REGISTER
LOWER THE LIGHT
LOWER THE PRICE
LOWLAND SCOTCH
LOW VISIBILITY
LOYAL DEVOTION
LOYALIST CAUSE
LUCID ARGUMENT

LUCID INTERVAL
LUCK OF THE DRAW
LUCK OF THE GAME
LUCKY SIXPENCE
LUCKY TALISMAN
LUCRATIVE DEAL
LUDGATE CIRCUS
LUKEWARM WATER
LUMINOUS PAINT
LUNATIC ASYLUM
LUNATIC FRINGE
LUNCHEON PARTY
LUNCHEON TABLE
LUXURIOUS FOOD
LUXURY HOLIDAY
LYCEUM THEATRE
LYRICAL POETRY
LYRICAL PRAISE

M – 13

MACHINE MINDER
MADAME TUSSAUD
MAD COW DISEASE
MADE IN ENGLAND
MADE IN GERMANY
MADE IN IRELAND
MAD ENTERPRISE
MADE THE WEIGHT
MADE TO MEASURE
MADISON SQUARE
MAGAZINE RIFLE
MAGAZINE STORY
MAGIC MUSHROOM
MAGNETIC FIELD
MAGNETIC NORTH
MAGNETIC POLES
MAGNETIC STORM
MAIDEN CENTURY
MAID OF ALL WORK
MADE OF ORLEANS
MAIDS OF HONOUR
MAIMED FOR LIFE
MAIN CHARACTER
MAJOR DISASTER
MAJOR INCIDENT
MAJOR INTERVAL
MAKE A COMEBACK
MAKE A CONQUEST
MAKE A CROSSING
MAKE A DECISION
MAKE A GOOD WIFE
MAKE ALLOWANCE
MAKE A LONG NOSE
MAKE A MESS OF IT
MAKE AN ATTEMPT

MAKE AN OPENING
MAKE A PROPOSAL
MAKE DO AND MEND
MAKE ECONOMIES
MAKE INQUIRIES
MAKE MINCEMEAT
MAKE MINE MUSIC
MAKE NO DEMANDS
MAKE NO MISTAKE
MAKE OBEISANCE
MAKE ONE'S DEBUT
MAKE ONE'S PEACE
MAKE ONE'S POINT
MAKE OVERTURES
MAKE PROVISION
MAKE REDUNDANT
MAKE SHORT WORK
MAKE THE ASCENT
MAKE THE EFFORT
MAKE THE FUR FLY
MAKE THINGS HUM
MALADIE DU PAYS
MALTESE FALCON
MANAGING CLERK
MAN AT THE WHEEL
MANDELBROT SET
MAN OF BREEDING
MAN OF BUSINESS
MAN OF DECISION
MAN OF EMINENCE
MAN OF FEW WORDS
MAN OF LEARNING
MAN OF PROPERTY
MAN OF THE WORLD
MANSFIELD PARK
MAP OF SCOTLAND
MAP OF THE WORLD
MARCH OF EVENTS
MARCH THE FIFTH
MARCH THE FIRST
MARCH THE NINTH
MARCH THE SIXTH
MARCH THE TENTH
MARCH THE THIRD
MARGARET SMITH
MARGIN OF ERROR
MARGIN OF PROOF
MARGOT FONTEYN
MARILYN MONROE
MARINE COMPASS
MARINE OFFICER
MARITIME TRADE
MARKET DRAYTON
MARKET ECONOMY
MARK OF RESPECT
MARRIAGE BANNS

MARRIAGE BELLS
MARRIAGE FEAST
MARRIAGE LINES
MARRIAGE RITES
MARRIED COUPLE
MARRY A FORTUNE
MARTELLO TOWER
MARTIAL SPIRIT
MARY MAGDALENE
MASS EXECUTION
MASS FORMATION
MASTER BUILDER
MASTER MARINER
MASTER'S TICKET
MATCH-BOX LABEL
MATCH ONE'S WITS
MATERIAL ISSUE
MATERIAL POINT
MATERIAL SENSE
MATERNITY WARD
MATINÉE JACKET
MATTHEW ARNOLD
MATURE THOUGHT
MAXIMUM AMOUNT
MAXIMUM CHARGE
MAXIMUM GROWTH
MAXIMUM POINTS
MAY THE SEVENTH
MAY THE TWELFTH
MEALS ON WHEELS
MEANS OF ACCESS
MEANS OF ASCENT
MEANS OF ESCAPE
MEANS OF SAFETY
MEASURED TREAD
MEASURE OF LAND
MEASURE SWORDS
MEASURING TAPE
MEAT AND TWO VEG
MECHANICAL AID
MECHANICAL MAN
MEDAL OF HONOUR
MEDICAL ADVICE
MEDICAL SCHOOL
MEDICINAL BATH
MEDICINE CHEST
MEDICINE GLASS
MEDIUM QUALITY
MEET ONE'S MAKER
MEET ONE'S MATCH
MELTON MOWBRAY
MEMORIAL STONE
MEND A PUNCTURE
MENTAL BALANCE
MENTAL CALIBRE
MENTAL CRUELTY

MENTAL DISEASE
MENTAL FATIGUE
MENTAL HYGIENE
MENTAL ILLNESS
MENTALLY ALERT
MENTALLY BLIND
MENTALLY SOUND
MENTAL PATIENT
MENTAL PICTURE
MENTAL PROCESS
MENTAL RESERVE
MENTAL THERAPY
MENTAL TORMENT
MENTAL TORTURE
MENTAL TROUBLE
MERCANTILE LAW
MERCENARY ARMY
MERCI BEAUCOUP
MERE BAGATELLE
MERE EXISTENCE
MERMAID TAVERN
MERRIE ENGLAND
MERTHYR TYDFIL
MERTON COLLEGE
MESS OF POTTAGE
MESSY BUSINESS
METAL DETECTOR
METALLIC SOUND
METAL MERCHANT
METRIC MEASURE
MIAMI DOLPHINS
MICHAELMAS DAY
MICK THE MILLER
MICROWAVE OVEN
MIDDLE-AGED MAN
MIDDLE CLASSES
MIDDLE ENGLISH
MIDLAND ACCENT
MIDLAND COUNTY
MIDLIFE CRISIS
MIDSUMMER'S DAY
MIGRANT WORKER
MILD AND BITTER
MILD EXPLETIVE
MILE AFTER MILE
MILES AND MILES
MILITARY CLOAK
MILITARY CROSS
MILITARY DRESS
MILITARY FORCE
MILITARY MARCH
MILITARY MEDAL
MILITARY MUSIC
MILITARY STAFF
MILITARY STORE
MILK CHOCOLATE

MILLING THRONG
MIND OF ONE'S OWN
MINERAL SPRING
MINIMUM AMOUNT
MINIMUM CHARGE
MINISTER OF WAR
MINOR COUNTIES
MINOR INCIDENT
MINOR INTERVAL
MINT CONDITION
MINUS QUANTITY
MIRACLE WORKER
MISCHIEF AFOOT
MISSING PERSON
MISSPENT YOUTH
MISS PINKERTON
MISS THE TARGET
MIXED BLESSING
MIXED FEELINGS
MIXED FOURSOME
MIXED MARRIAGE
MIXED METAPHOR
MOANING MINNIE
MOBILE CANTEEN
MOBILE LIBRARY
MOBILE WARFARE
MODELLING CLAY
MODE OF ADDRESS
MODERATE MEANS
MODERATE PRICE
MODERATE SKILL
MODERATE SPEED
MODERN COSTUME
MODERN ENGLISH
MODERN FASHION
MODERN HISTORY
MODERN METHODS
MODERN OUTLOOK
MODERN PAINTER
MODERN SETTING
MODERN SOCIETY
MODERN WARFARE
MODEST DEMANDS
MODEST FORTUNE
MODEST REQUEST
MODUS OPERANDI
MOMENT OF TRUTH
MONASTIC ORDER
MONDAY EVENING
MONDAY MORNING
MONETARY UNION
MONETARY VALUE
MONEY IN THE BAG
MONEY TROUBLES
MONOTONOUS JOB
MONTHLY REPORT

MONTHLY SALARY
MOONLESS NIGHT
MOONLIGHT FLIT
MORAL CONFLICT
MORAL MAJORITY
MORAL PRESSURE
MORAL STRENGTH
MORAL TRAINING
MORAL WEAKNESS
MORBID CRAVING
MORE THAN A JOKE
MORNING COFFEE
MORNING PRAYER
MORTALITY RATE
MORTAL REMAINS
MOST DESIRABLE
MOST EXCELLENT
MOTH-BALL FLEET
MOTHER COUNTRY
MOTHER HUBBARD
MOTHER OF PEARL
MOTHER SHIPTON
MOTION PICTURE
MOTOR MECHANIC
MOUNTAIN CHAIN
MOUNTAIN RANGE
MOUNTAIN SHEEP
MOUNTAIN SLOPE
MOUNTAIN TRAIL
MOUNTED POLICE
MOUNTED TROOPS
MOUNTING ANGER
MOUNT OF OLIVES
MOUNT PLEASANT
MOUNT RUSHMORE
MOVE IN SOCIETY
MOVE MOUNTAINS
MOVING ACCOUNT
MOVING PICTURE
MOWING MACHINE
MUCH REGRETTED
MUDDLE THROUGH
MULTIPLE STORE
MULTIPLY BY SIX
MULTIPLY BY TEN
MULTIPLY BY TWO
MULTUM IN PARVO
MUMMY AND DADDY
MUNICIPAL BANK
MUNICIPAL PARK
MURAL PAINTING
MURDER MYSTERY
MURDER WILL OUT
MUSE OF DANCING
MUSE OF HISTORY
MUSHROOM CLOUD

MUSICAL CHAIRS
MUSICAL COMEDY
MUSICAL STRESS
MUSICAL FESTIVAL
MUSIC-HALL JOKE
MUSIC-HALL STAR
MUSIC-HALL TURN
MUSIC MISTRESS
MUSTARD PICKLE
MUSTARD YELLOW
MUTUAL BENEFIT
MUTUAL CONSENT
MUTUAL DISLIKE
MUTUAL FRIENDS
MUTUAL RESPECT
MY HUSBAND AND I
MYSTERY OF LIFE
MYSTERY WRITER
MYTHICAL BEING

N – 13

NAGGING TONGUE
NAME ONE'S PRICE
NAPOLEON CLOCK
NARRATIVE POEM
NARROW OUTLOOK
NARROW PASSAGE
NARROW VICTORY
NASTY BUSINESS
NATIONAL DANCE
NATIONAL DRESS
NATIONAL DRINK
NATIONAL FRONT
NATIONAL GUARD
NATIONAL PRIDE
NATIONAL SPORT
NATIONAL TRUST
NATIONAL UNITY
NATIVE COSTUME
NATIVE QUARTER
NATURAL BEAUTY
NATURAL CAUSES
NATURAL COLOUR
NATURAL COURSE
NATURAL HAZARD
NATURAL SYSTEM
NATURAL TALENT
NATURAL WEALTH
NATURE RESERVE
NATURE WORSHIP
NAVAL BARRACKS
NAVAL EXPLOITS
NAVAL HOSPITAL
NEAPOLITAN ICE
NEAR NEIGHBOUR

NEAR ONE'S HEART	NOBODY ON EARTH
NEAR THE GROUND	NO BONES BROKEN
NEAR THE WICKET	NO EXPECTATION
NEAT AS A NEW PIN	NO EXTRA CHARGE
NECESSARY EVIL	NO GREAT SHAKES
NECK OR NOTHING	NO HIDING PLACE
NEEDLESS TO SAY	NO HOLDS BARRED
NEGATIVE REPLY	NOMINAL CHARGE
NELLIE WALLACE	NOMINATION DAY
NELSON MANDELA	NONSENSE RHYME
NELSON'S COLUMN	NONSENSE VERSE
NERVE HOSPITAL	NON-STOP TALKER
NERVES OF STEEL	NO OIL PAINTING
NERVOUS ENERGY	NOOK AND CRANNY
NERVOUS SYSTEM	NORFOLK BROADS
NERVOUS TWITCH	NORFOLK JACKET
NESTING SEASON	NORMAL SERVICE
NEST OF HORNETS	NORMAN ENGLISH
NETHER REGIONS	NORMAN VAUGHAN
NEURAL NETWORK	NORTH AMERICAN
NEUTRAL COLOUR	NORTH AND SOUTH
NEUTRAL CORNER	NORTH ATLANTIC
NEUTRAL GROUND	NORTH CAROLINA
NEVER LOOK BACK	NORTH-EAST WIND
NEVER ON SUNDAY	NOTABLE SPEECH
NEW BOND STREET	NOTE OF CENSURE
NEW EXPERIMENT	NOTE OF TRIUMPH
NEW FOUNDATION	NOTE OF WARNING
NEWGATE PRISON	NOT GOOD ENOUGH
NEW IMPRESSION	NOTHING LIKE IT
NEW REGULATION	NOTHING TO COME
NEW RESOLUTION	NOTHING TO GAIN
NEW SOUTH WALES	NOTHING TO GO ON
NEWSPAPER FILE	NOTHING TO LOSE
NEWSPAPER RACK	NOT IMPOSSIBLE
NEW WORLD ORDER	NOT IN LUCK'S WAY
NEW YORK GIANTS	NOT IN THE LEAST
NEXT BEST THING	NOT LONG TO WAIT
NEXT CHRISTMAS	NOT MY CUP OF TEA
NEXT GENTLEMAN	NOT NEGOTIABLE
NEXT ON THE LIST	NOT ON YOUR LIFE
NEXT TO NOTHING	NO TURNING BACK
NEXT WEDNESDAY	NOW AND FOREVER
NICE AND TENDER	NUCLEAR ENERGY
NICKEL COINAGE	NUCLEAR FAMILY
NIGHTLY VISITS	NUCLEAR FUSION
NIGHT MUST FALL	NUCLEAR WEAPON
NIGHT OF TERROR	NUCLEAR WINTER
NIGHT WATCHMAN	NUISANCE VALUE
NIMBLE FINGERS	NUMBER ENGAGED
NINETEEN MILES	NUMBERS RACKET
NINETY PER CENT	NUMERICAL LIST
NINTH OF AUGUST	NURSERY GARDEN
NINTH SYMPHONY	NURSERY SCHOOL
NO ALTERNATIVE	NURSERY SLOPES
NOBLE AMBITION	NURSING SISTER

O – 13

OBEY AN IMPULSE
OBJECTIVE CASE
OBJECT OF MIRTH
OBJECT OF PRIDE
OBJECT OF SCORN
OBLIGE A FRIEND
OBSCURE MOTIVE
OBSERVER CORPS
OCCUPY THE MIND
OCEANS OF MONEY
OFF AT A TANGENT
OFFER AN EXCUSE
OFF-HAND MANNER
OFFICE CLEANER
OFFICE MANAGER
OFFICE OF WORKS
OFFICE ROUTINE
OFFICIAL REPLY
OFF ONE'S OWN BAT
OFF ONE'S ROCKER
OFF-SEASON RATE
OFF THE DEEP END
OFF THE FAIRWAY
OFF THE SUBJECT
OF LITTLE WORTH
OIL AND VINEGAR
OLD-AGE PENSION
OLD AS THE HILLS
OLD-BOY NETWORK
OLD CAMPAIGNER
OLD-CLOTHES MAN
OLD CROCKS' RACE
OLDER AND WISER
OLDER THAN TIME
OLD FATHER TIME
OLD FOUNDATION
OLD IN THE TOOTH
OLD TRADITIONS
OLD WIVES' TALES
OLYMPIC RECORD
OMNIBUS VOLUME
ON A BROOMSTICK
ON A GRAND SCALE
ON A LARGE SCALE
ON A SHOE-STRING
ON A SMALL SCALE
ON BENDED KNEES
ONCE AND FOR ALL
ONCE UPON A TIME
ONE AND THE SAME
ONE DAY CRICKET
ONE FOR THE ROAD
ONE IN A HUNDRED
ONE IN A MILLION

ONE-NIGHT STAND
ONE OF THE CROWD
ONE OR THE OTHER
ONE'S PROSPECTS
ONE'S RELATIVES
ONE-WAY TRAFFIC
ONE WICKET DOWN
ON HER BEAM ENDS
ON ITS LAST LEGS
ONLY EXCEPTION
ON ONE'S OWN FEET
ON PAIN OF DEATH
ON TENTER-HOOKS
ON THE CONTRARY
ON THE DOOR-STEP
ON THE FACE OF IT
ON THE FIRST LAP
ON THE FRONTIER
ON THE HIGH SEAS
ON THE INCREASE
ON THE LEFT SIDE
ON THE LONG SIDE
ON THE NEAR-SIDE
ON THE PAVEMENT
ON THE PLATFORM
ON THE PREMISES
ON THE ROOF-TOPS
ON THE SAFE SIDE
ON THE SCAFFOLD
ON THE SCROUNGE
ON THE SICK LIST
ON THE STRENGTH
ON THE WIRELESS
ON WINGS OF SONG
OPEN A CAMPAIGN
OPEN-AIR MARKET
OPEN AN ACCOUNT
OPEN CONSONANT
OPENED IN ERROR
OPEN HOSTILITY
OPENING GAMBIT
OPENING SPEECH
OPEN ONE'S HEART
OPEN ONE'S MOUTH
OPEN ONE'S PURSE
OPEN REBELLION
OPEN THE DEBATE
OPEN THE DRAWER
OPEN THE WINDOW
OPERATION ROOM
OPERATIVE WORD
OPPOSITE CAMPS
OPPOSITE POLES
OPPOSITE SIDES
OPPOSITE VIEWS
OPTICAL DEVICE

ORANGE BITTERS
ORANGE BLOSSOM
ORANGE FLAVOUR
ORB AND SCEPTRE
ORBITAL SANDER
ORDEAL BY WATER
ORDER A RETREAT
ORDERLY MANNER
ORDER OF BATTLE
ORDER OF THE DAY
ORDINAL NUMBER
ORDINARY SHARE
ORDINARY STOCK
ORDNANCE CORPS
ORGANIC CHANGE
ORGANIC MATTER
ORGAN OF SPEECH
ORGAN OF VISION
ORIENT EXPRESS
ORIGINAL MODEL
ORKNEY ISLANDS
OSBERT SITWELL
OTHER WAY ROUND
OTTOMAN EMPIRE
OUT AT THE ELBOW
OUTBOARD MOTOR
OUTBREAK OF WAR
OUTDOOR RELIEF
OUTDOOR SPORTS
OUTER DARKNESS
OUTER HEBRIDES
OUT FOR THRILLS
OUT-HEROD HEROD
OUT LIKE A LIGHT
OUT OF BUSINESS
OUT-OF-DATE IDEA
OUT OF HARM'S WAY
OUT OF INTEREST
OUT OF KINDNESS
OUT OF MISCHIEF
OUT OF MOURNING
OUT OF ONE'S HEAD
OUT OF ONE'S MIND
OUT OF PATIENCE
OUT OF POSITION
OUT OF PRACTICE
OUT OF SYMPATHY
OUT OF TRAINING
OUT ON ONE'S FEET
OUTSIDE CHANCE
OUTSIDE THE LAW
OVER-ALL LENGTH
OVERHEAD CABLE
OVERHEAD WIRES
OVERLAND ROUTE
OVERLAND TRAIN

OVERNIGHT CASE
OVERSEAS TRADE
OVER THE BORDER
OVER THE STICKS
OVER THE WICKET
OVER TWENTY-ONE
OWNER OCCUPIER
OXFORD COLLEGE
OXFORD ENGLISH
OZONE FRIENDLY
OZONE SICKNESS

P – 13

PACE UP AND DOWN
PACIFIC ISLAND
PACKET OF SEEDS
PACK OF THIEVES
PAC-MAN DEFENCE
PAGAN FESTIVAL
PAGAN LOVE SONG
PAGE THREE GIRL
PAID BY THE HOUR
PAIN IN THE NECK
PAINT A PICTURE
PAINT ONE'S FACE
PAIR OF BELLOWS
PAIR OF GARTERS
PAIR OF GLASSES
PAIR OF KIPPERS
PAIR OF PINCERS
PAIR OF PYJAMAS
PAIR OF SANDALS
PALACE THEATRE
PALAIS DE DANSE
PALE AS A CORPSE
PALE IMITATION
PALE WITH ANGER
PAMELA FRANKAU
PANDA CROSSING
PANELLED WALLS
PANEL OF JUDGES
PANG OF REMORSE
PANGS OF HUNGER
PANIC MEASURES
PANTOMINE DAME
PAPER-BACK BOOK
PAPER CLIPPING
PAPER CURRENCY
PAPER SHORTAGE
PAPER THE WALLS
PARACHUTE JUMP
PARAFFIN STOVE
PARALLEL LINES
PAR EXCELLENCE
PARIS AND HELEN

PARIS CREATION
PARIS FASHIONS
PARISH COUNCIL
PARK ATTENDANT
PARKINSON'S LAW
PAR OF EXCHANGE
PARROT FASHION
PART AND PARCEL
PARTIAL CHANGE
PARTIAL EXCUSE
PARTLY COVERED
PART OF HISTORY
PART OF THE PLAN
PART OF THE TIME
PARTY OFFICIAL
PARTY POLITICS
PASSAGE OF ARMS
PASSAGE OF TIME
PASS AND REPASS
PASS AN OPINION
PASSENGER LIST
PASSENGER SHIP
PASSING GLANCE
PASSING REMARK
PASSION FLOWER
PASSION SUNDAY
PASS THE BUTTER
PASS THE PEPPER
PASS UNNOTICED
PAST BEHAVIOUR
PAST ENDURANCE
PAST ONE'S PRIME
PATENT LEATHER
PATENT PENDING
PATENT SWINDLE
PATHETIC SIGHT
PATIENCE OF JOB
PATRICK SWAYZE
PATRIOTIC SONG
PAUL GASCOIGNE
PAUL McCARTNEY
PAVED WITH GOLD
PAWN IN THE GAME
PAX BRITANNICA
PAY BY THE PIECE
PAY LIP-SERVICE
PAYMENT IN KIND
PAYMENT IN LIEU
PAY THE PENALTY
PEACE AND QUIET
PEACE DIVIDEND
PEACE OFFERING
PEAK OF SUCCESS
PEAL OF THUNDER
PEARL NECKLACE
PEBBLE GLASSES

PECULIAR SMELL
PECUNIARY LOSS
PEGGY ASHCROFT
PENALTY CLAUSE
PENCIL DRAWING
PENDULUM CLOCK
PENINSULAR WAR
PENNY DREADFUL
PENNY FARTHING
PENSION SCHEME
PEOPLE AT LARGE
PEPPER AND SALT
PERCUSSION CAP
PERFECT CIRCLE
PERFECT FOURTH
PERFECT FRIGHT
PERFECT NUMBER
PERFECT RYHTHM
PERFECT SCREAM
PERFECT SQUARE
PERFECT TIMING
PERFECT WICKET
PERFORM A STUNT
PERIOD COSTUME
PERISHING COLD
PERKIN WARBECK
PERMANENT HOME
PERMANENT PASS
PERMANENT POST
PERMANENT WAVE
PERSIAN CARPET
PERSIAN GARDEN
PERSIAN MARKET
PERSONAL ABUSE
PERSONAL ALARM
PERSONAL CHARM
PERSONAL CLAIM
PERSONAL GUEST
PERSONAL PRIDE
PERSONAL STYLE
PERSONAL TOUCH
PETER CAVANAGH
PETER THE GREAT
PETIT DÉJEUNER
PETROL LIGHTER
PETROL STATION
PETTICOAT LANE
PETTY OFFICIAL
PETTY SESSIONS
PEWTER TANKARD
PHANTOM FIGURE
PHILIP MARLOWE
PHYSICAL FORCE
PHYSICAL JERKS
PHYSICALLY FIT
PHYSICAL POWER

PHYSICAL WRECK
PHYSICS MASTER
PIANO CONCERTO
PIANO EXERCISE
PICK AND CHOOSE
PICK AND SHOVEL
PICKLED WALNUT
PICK OF THE POPS
PICK ONE'S WORDS
PICK THE WINNER
PICK UP A LIVING
PICTS AND SCOTS
PICTURE PALACE
PIDGIN ENGLISH
PIECE OF ADVICE
PIECE OF STRING
PIECES OF EIGHT
PIECE TOGETHER
PIG AND WHISTLE
PIGEON FANCIER
PILE OF RUBBISH
PILOT'S LICENCE
PILTDOWN SKULL
PING-PONG TABLE
PINK ELEPHANTS
PINKY AND PERKY
PIN-STRIPE SUIT
PIONEER SPIRIT
PIOUS THOUGHTS
PIPE OF TOBACCO
PISTACHIO NUTS
PISTOLS FOR TWO
PITCH DARKNESS
PITCHED BATTLE
PITCH ONE'S TENT
PITH AND MARROW
PLACE END TO END
PLACE IN THE SUN
PLACE OF HONOUR
PLACE OF REFUGE
PLACE ON RECORD
PLAIN ENVELOPE
PLAIN FEATURES
PLAIN LANGUAGE
PLAIN QUESTION
PLAIN SPEAKING
PLAQUE REMOVER
PLASTIC BULLET
PLAUSIBLE TALE
PLAY A LONE HAND
PLAY FOR SAFETY
PLAY HARD TO GET
PLAYING TRICKS
PLAY ONE'S CARDS
PLAY THE DESPOT
PLAY THE FIDDLE

PLAY THE GUITAR
PLAY THE MARKET
PLAY THE MARTYR
PLAY THE TYRANT
PLAY THE VIOLIN
PLAY THE WANTON
PLAY UPON WORDS
PLEAD FOR MERCY
PLEAD INNOCENT
PLEAD THE CAUSE
PLEA OF ABSENCE
PLEASED TO COME
PLEASE ONESELF
PLEDGE ONESELF
PLENTIFUL FARE
PLENTY OF MONEY
PLENTY TO SPARE
PLOUGH A FURROW
PLOUGHED FIELD
PLOUGH THE LAND
PLUCKED PIGEON
PLUMB NONSENSE
PLYMOUTH SOUND
PNEUMATIC TYRE
POCKET BOROUGH
POCKET EDITION
POETICAL WORKS
POETIC JUSTICE
POETIC LICENCE
POETRY READING
POINTED REMARK
POINTED SAYING
POINT FOR POINT
POINT IN COMMON
POINT IN FAVOUR
POINT OF HONOUR
POINT OF THE JAW
POISONED ARROW
POISON THE MIND
POLAR EXPLORER
POLICEMAN'S LOT
POLICE MESSAGE
POLICE OFFICER
POLICE STATION
POLICE TACTICS
POLICE WHISTLE
POLISHED ACTOR
POLISHED STYLE
POLITE FICTION
POLITE FORMULA
POLITE REFUSAL
POLITE SOCIETY
POLITE WELCOME
POLITICAL BLOC
POLITICAL NEWS
POLITICAL UNIT

POLITICAL VIEW
POMERANIAN DOG
PONTIUS PILATE
PONTOON BRIDGE
POOL RESOURCES
POOR BUT HONEST
POOR CONDITION
POOR IN QUALITY
POORLY DRESSED
POOR PERFORMER
POOR PROSPECTS
POOR RECEPTION
POPPING CREASE
POPULAR BALLAD
POPULAR CHOICE
POPULAR DECREE
POPULAR DEMAND
POPULAR ESTEEM
POPULAR FIGURE
POPULAR PEOPLE
POPULAR PRICES
POPULAR RESORT
POPULAR SINGER
POPULATED AREA
PORTABLE RADIO
PORT ELIZABETH
PORTLAND STONE
POSE A QUESTION
POSITIVE PROOF
POSTAL ADDRESS
POSTAL SERVICE
POSTED MISSING
POSTER COLOURS
POSTE RESTANTE
POSTMAN'S KNOCK
POST-OFFICE RED
POST-WAR CREDIT
POTTED SHRIMPS
POULTRY FARMER
POUND OF APPLES
POUND OF BUTTER
POUND STERLING
POUR OUT THE TEA
POWDER AND SHOT
POWDER COMPACT
POWDER SHAMPOO
POWER AND GLORY
POWER DRESSING
POWERFUL VOICE
POWER OF SPEECH
POWER OF THE LAW
POWER POLITICS
PRACTICAL JOKE
PRACTICAL MIND
PRACTICAL TEST
PRACTICE MATCH

PRACTICE ROUND
PRACTISED HAND
PRACTISED LIAR
PRAIRIE OYSTER
PRAISE THE LORD
PRAWN COCKTAIL
PRAYER MEETING
PRAYING MANTIS
PRECIOUS METAL
PRECIOUS STONE
PRECIOUS WORDS
PRECISE MOMENT
PRECISION TOOL
PREFER A CHARGE
PREMIER LEAGUE
PREPARE A DRINK
PREPARE FOR WAR
PRESENT EVENTS
PRESENT MOMENT
PRESS CAMPAIGN
PRESS CUTTINGS
PRESSED FLOWER
PRESSED TONGUE
PRESS EXCHANGE
PRESS FASTENER
PRESSING CLAIM
PRESS ONE'S SUIT
PRESS THE FLESH
PRESSURE GAUGE
PRESSURE GROUP
PRETTY PICTURE
PREY ON THE MIND
PRICE INCREASE
PRIM AND PROPER
PRIMARY COLOUR
PRIMARY SCHOOL
PRIME MINISTER
PRIMEVAL CHAOS
PRIMITIVE FORM
PRINCE CHARLES
PRINCE CONSORT
PRINCE OF PEACE
PRINCE OF WALES
PRINCESS DIANA
PRINCESS DRESS
PRINCESS ROYAL
PRINCE'S STREET
PRINCE WILLIAM
PRINCIPAL FOOD
PRINCIPAL PART
PRINCIPAL TOWN
PRINTED LETTER
PRINTED MATTER
PRINTER'S DEVIL
PRINTER'S ERROR
PRINTING PRESS

PRINTING WORKS	PUBLIC OUTRAGE
PRISONER OF WAR	PUBLIC PROTEST
PRISONER'S BASE	PUBLIC RECORDS
PRISON VISITOR	PUBLIC SCANDAL
PRIVATE AFFAIR	PUBLIC SERVANT
PRIVATE INCOME	PUBLIC SERVICE
PRIVATE LESSON	PUBLIC SPEAKER
PRIVATE LETTER	PUBLIC TRUSTEE
PRIVATE MATTER	PUBLIC UTILITY
PRIVATE MEMBER	PUBLIC VEHICLE
PRIVATE OFFICE	PUBLIC WARNING
PRIVATE PERSON	PUBLIC WORSHIP
PRIVATE REASON	PUBLISHED WORK
PRIVATE SCHOOL	PULITZER PRIZE
PRIVATE SOURCE	PULL A LONG FACE
PRIZE SPECIMEN	PULL INTO SHAPE
PROBABLE CAUSE	PULL NO PUNCHES
PROBABLE ERROR	PULSE DIALLING
PROCESSED FOOD	PUNCTURED TYRE
PROCESS OF TIME	PUNISHING WORK
PRODUCER GOODS	PUPPET THEATRE
PROFANE PERSON	PURCHASE MONEY
PROFIT AND LOSS	PURCHASE PRICE
PROFIT SHARING	PURE AND SIMPLE
PROFOUND SLEEP	PURE IN THOUGHT
PROFUMO AFFAIR	PURE MISCHANCE
PROFUSE THANKS	PURE PREJUDICE
PROGRESS CHART	PURPLE AND GOLD
PROLONGED NOTE	PURPLE EMPEROR
PROMENADE DECK	PURPLE HEATHER
PROMISING IDEA	PURPLE PASSAGE
PROMPT PAYMENT	PURSE ONE'S LIPS
PROMPT SERVICE	PURSER'S OFFICE
PROOF POSITIVE	PUSH-BUTTON WAR
PROPER CHARLEY	PUSHED FOR TIME
PROPERTY OWNER	PUSH TO THE WALL
PROPOSE A TOAST	PUT IN FOR A RISE
PROSAIC PERSON	PUT IN JEOPARDY
PROSPEROUS MAN	PUT IN THE KITTY
PROVE ONE'S CASE	PUT IN THE SHADE
PROVIDE AN HEIR	PUT IN THE WRONG
PROVING GROUND	PUT ONE'S BACK UP
PUBLIC ADDRESS	PUT ONESELF OUT
PUBLIC AFFAIRS	PUT ONE'S FEET UP
PUBLIC ANALYST	PUT ONE'S HAIR UP
PUBLIC COMMENT	PUT ON PRESSURE
PUBLIC COMPANY	PUT ON THE BRAKE
PUBLIC GALLERY	PUT ON THE LIGHT
PUBLIC HANGING	PUT ON THE SCREW
PUBLIC HIGHWAY	PUT ON THE STAGE
PUBLIC HOLIDAY	PUT OUT A FEELER
PUBLIC INQUIRY	PUT OUT FEELERS
PUBLIC LECTURE	PUT OUT OF COURT
PUBLIC LIBRARY	PUT OUT OF JOINT
PUBLIC MEETING	PUT OUT OF SIGHT
PUBLIC OPINION	PUT OUT TO GRASS

PUT PEN TO PAPER
PUT THE BRAKE ON
PUT THE CAP ON IT
PUT THE LID ON IT
PUT TO THE BLUSH
PUT TO THE PROOF
PUT TO THE SWORD
PUT UP THE BANNS
PUT UP THE MONEY
PUT UP THE PRICE

Q – 13

QUADRUPLE TIME
QUALITY OF LIFE
QUALITY STREET
QUANTUM THEORY
QUARTER BOTTLE
QUARTERLY RENT
QUARTER TO FIVE
QUARTER TO FOUR
QUARTER TO NINE
QUARTZ CRYSTAL
QUEEN CAROLINE
QUEEN OF HEARTS
QUEEN OF SPADES
QUEEN OF THE MAY
QUEEN OF TRUMPS
QUEEN'S COLLEGE
QUEEN'S COUNSEL
QUEEN'S ENGLISH
QUEEN'S HIGHWAY
QUEEN'S PROCTOR
QUEEN VICTORIA
QUEER CUSTOMER
QUEER GOINGS-ON
QUEER THE PITCH
QUICK AS A FLASH
QUICK MOVEMENT
QUICK RECOVERY
QUICK-SET HEDGE
QUICK THINKING
QUICK TURNOVER
QUIET AS A MOUSE
QUITE POSITIVE
QUITE POSSIBLE
QUITE THE THING
QUIZ PROGRAMME
QUOTATION MARK

R – 13

RACE PREJUDICE
RACING CIRCUIT
RACING TIPSTER
RACING TRAINER

RACK ONE'S BRAIN
RADIANT ENERGY
RADIATION BELT
RADICAL CHANGE
RADICAL REFORM
RADIO OPERATOR
RADIO RECEIVER
RAG-AND-BONE MAN
RAGING TEMPEST
RAGING TORRENT
RAID THE LARDER
RAILWAY BRIDGE
RAILWAY ENGINE
RAILWAY SHARES
RAILWAY SIDING
RAILWAY SIGNAL
RAILWAY SYSTEM
RAILWAY TICKET
RAILWAY TUNNEL
RAISE A BARRIER
RAISE CHICKENS
RAISED GLASSES
RAISE ONE'S EYES
RAISE ONE'S HAND
RAISE THE ALARM
RAISE THE FUNDS
RAISE THE MONEY
RAISE THE PRICE
RAISE THE SIEGE
RAISE THE TEMPO
RAISE THE VOICE
RAKE'S PROGRESS
RAKE UP THE PAST
RALLYING POINT
RALPH WIGHTMAN
RANGE OF CHOICE
RANGE OF COLOUR
RAPE OF THE LOCK
RAPID PROGRESS
RAPID TURNOVER
RAPT ATTENTION
RASH BEHAVIOUR
RASHER OF BACON
RASH STATEMENT
RASPBERRY CANE
RATEABLE VALUE
RATE COLLECTOR
RATE FOR THE JOB
RATES AND TAXES
RATIONAL DRESS
RAVAGES OF TIME
RAVENOUS BEAST
RAVING LUNATIC
RAYMOND BAXTER
RAYMOND MASSEY
RAY OF SUNSHINE

REACH A NEW HIGH
REACH A VERDICT
REACH MATURITY
REACH ONE'S GOAL
REACH THE LIMIT
REACT IN FAVOUR
READER'S DIGEST
READ FOR THE BAR
READING MATTER
READING PUBLIC
READ THE FUTURE
READ THE LESSON
READY-MADE SUIT
READY RECKONER
READY RESPONSE
READY, STEADY, GO!
READY TO ATTACK
READY TO POUNCE
READY TO SPRING
REAL-LIFE STORY
REALMS OF FANCY
REAP THE FRUITS
REAP THE REWARD
RECEIPT IN FULL
RECEIVE NOTICE
RECEIVE ORDERS
RECENT ARRIVAL
RECEPTION DESK
RECEPTION ROOM
RECEPTIVE MIND
RECKLESS SPEED
RECKLESS YOUTH
RECLAIMED LAND
RECORD ATTEMPT
RECORD BREAKER
RECORD COUNTER
RECORDED MUSIC
RECORD ROUND-UP
RECORD SESSION
RED AS A LOBSTER
RED-CROSS NURSE
REDEEM A PLEDGE
RED RAG TO A BULL
RED RIDING HOOD
RED SEALING-WAX
RED SKY AT NIGHT
REDUCE TO ASHES
REDUCE TO SCALE
REDUCE TO TEARS
REDUCING AGENT
REDUCING PILLS
REFERENCE BOOK
REFER TO DRAWER
REFINED ACCENT
REFINED PALATE
REFLECTOR FIRE

REFUSE A CHANCE
REFUSE AN OFFER
REFUSE PAYMENT
REFUSE THE BAIT
REFUSE TO SPEAK
REGAIN COMMAND
REGAIN CONTROL
REGAIN THE LEAD
REGENCY STRIPE
REGRET THE LOSS
REGULAR FORCES
REGULAR HABITS
REGULAR INCOME
REGULAR PEOPLE
REGULAR READER
REGULAR SALARY
REGULAR STAGES
REGULAR TROOPS
REGULAR VISITS
REHEARSAL ROOM
REIGNING QUEEN
REIGN OF TERROR
REJECTION SLIP
RELATIVE MERIT
RELATIVE PROOF
RELATIVE VALUE
RELATIVE WORTH
RELAXED THROAT
RELEASE ON BAIL
REMAIN AT PEACE
REMAIN HOPEFUL
REMAIN NEUTRAL
REMAIN PASSIVE
REMAIN THE SAME
REMAIN UPRIGHT
REMAIN VISIBLE
REMARKABLE BOY
REMARKABLE MAN
REMITTANCE MAN
REMOTE CONTROL
REMOTE SENSING
REMOTE VILLAGE
REMOVE ONE'S HAT
RENEWED ENERGY
RENEW ONE'S VOWS
RENT COLLECTOR
RENT IN ADVANCE
REPEAT A SIGNAL
REPEAT ONESELF
REPEL AN ATTACK
REPETITIVE JOB
REPLY BY RETURN
REPORT FOR DUTY
REPUBLICAN ERA
RESERVED TABLE
RESERVE ELEVEN

RESIGN ONESELF
RESPECT THE LAW
RESTAURANT CAR
RESTIVE NATURE
RESTLESS NIGHT
REST ONE'S BONES
RESTORE TO LIFE
REST SATISFIED
RETAIL TRADING
RETAINING WALL
RETARDED BRAIN
RETARDED CHILD
RETIRED PEOPLE
RETROUSSÉ NOSE
RETURN A FAVOUR
RETURN A PROFIT
RETURN JOURNEY
RETURN SERVICE
RETURN TO EARTH
REVENUE CUTTER
REVERSE MOTION
REVOLT AGAINST
REVOLVING DOOR
REWARD OFFERED
REYNARD THE FOX
RHODES SCHOLAR
RHONDDA VALLEY
RHYMED COUPLET
RIBSTON PIPPIN
RICEYMAN STEPS
RICHARD BRIERS
RICHARD BURTON
RICHARD HANNAY
RICHARD HEARNE
RICHARD TAUBER
RICHARD WAGNER
RICH AS CROESUS
RICHMOND GREEN
RICH OFFERINGS
RIDE A TRICYCLE
RIDE POST-HASTE
RIDE ROUGH-SHOD
RIDE THE WINNER
RIFLE PRACTICE
RIFT IN THE LUTE
RIGHT AND WRONG
RIGHT APPROACH
RIGHT AT THE END
RIGHT DECISION
RIGHT-DOWN LIAR
RIGHTFUL OWNER
RIGHTFUL SHARE
RIGHT-HAND BEND
RIGHT-HAND SIDE
RIGHT-HAND TURN
RIGHT OF ACCESS

RIGHT OF APPEAL
RIGHT OF CHOICE
RIGHT OF SEARCH
RIGHT ON THE DOT
RIGHT OPPOSITE
RIGHT REVEREND
RIGHT SHOULDER
RIGHT TO STRIKE
RIGHT TO THE END
RIGHT TO THE TOP
RIGHT UP TO DATE
RING OUT THE OLD
RIOT OF EMOTION
RIOTOUS LIVING
RISE IN DISGUST
RISE OF THE TIDE
RISE TO THE BAIT
RISING SPIRITS
RISK ONE'S MONEY
RISKY BUSINESS
RITUAL KILLING
RIVAL BUSINESS
RIVER CROSSING
RIVERSIDE WALK
ROAD DIVERSION
ROAD TO SUCCESS
ROAD TRANSPORT
ROAST CHESTNUT
ROAST POTATOES
ROBBINS REPORT
ROBERT BRIDGES
ROBERT MITCHUM
ROBERT REDFORD
ROBERTSON HARE
ROBERT SOUTHEY
ROCKET WARFARE
ROCK THE CRADLE
ROGUE ELEPHANT
ROGUES' GALLERY
ROLL AND BUTTER
ROLLED INTO ONE
ROLLER COASTER
ROLLING IN CASH
ROLLING STONES
ROLL IN THE DUST
ROLL-ON ROLL-OFF
ROMAN ALPHABET
ROMAN CATHOLIC
ROMAN NUMERALS
ROMANTIC NOVEL
ROMANTIC SCENE
ROMANTIC STORY
ROMNEY MARSHES
RONALD CHESNEY
ROOM TO BREATHE
ROOM WITH A VIEW

ROOT AND BRANCH
ROOTED DISLIKE
ROOT OF ALL EVIL
ROOT VEGETABLE
ROPE AND PULLEY
RORSCHACH TEST
ROTATE THE CROP
ROTTEN BOROUGH
ROUGH AND READY
ROUGH CROSSING
ROUGH CUSTOMER
ROUGH ESTIMATE
ROUGH EXTERIOR
ROUGH HANDLING
ROUGH QUARTERS
ROULETTE TABLE
ROULETTE WHEEL
ROUND-ABOUT WAY
ROUND AND ABOUT
ROUND AND ROUND
ROUNDLY ABUSED
ROUND OF DRINKS
ROUND OF GAIETY
ROUND OF VISITS
ROUND THE BLOCK
ROUND THE CLOCK
ROUND THE EARTH
ROUND THE HOUSE
ROUND THE TABLE
ROUND THE WAIST
ROUND THE WORLD
ROUSING CHEERS
ROUSING CHORUS
ROUSING SERMON
ROUTINE DUTIES
ROUTINE MATTER
ROWAN ATKINSON
ROYAL AERO CLUB
ROYAL AIR FORCE
ROYAL EXCHANGE
ROYAL FUNCTION
ROYAL HIGHNESS
ROYAL HOSPITAL
ROYAL MARRIAGE
ROYAL OCCASION
ROYAL STANDARD
RUBBER PLANTER
RUB OF THE GREEN
RUDE AWAKENING
RUGBY FOOTBALL
RUGGED COUNTRY
RUINED FOR LIFE
RUINOUS CHARGE
RULE BRITANNIA
RULE OF THE ROAD
RULING CLASSES

RULING PASSION
RUN FOR SHELTER
RUN IN THE BLOOD
RUN INTO DANGER
RUN LIKE BLAZES
RUNNING BATTLE
RUNNING BUFFET
RUNNING STREAM
RUN OF THE GREEN
RUN OF THE HOUSE
RUN ON SMOOTHLY
RUN ON THE ROCKS
RUN OUT OF FUNDS
RUN OUT OF MONEY
RUN OUT OF STEAM
RUN OUT OF WORDS
RUN THINGS FINE
RURAL DISTRICT
RURAL INDUSTRY
RUSHING STREAM
RUSH INTO PRINT
RUSSELL SQUARE
RUSSIAN BALLET
RUSSIAN LESSON

S – 13

SACRED EDIFICE
SADDAM HUSSEIN
SAFE ANCHORAGE
SAFETY CURTAIN
SAFETY GLASSES
SAFETY GOGGLES
SAFETY HARNESS
SAFETY MEASURE
SAFFRON WALDEN
SAGE AND ONIONS
SAILING MASTER
SAILING ORDERS
SAILING VESSEL
SAINT AUGUSTUS
SAINT LAWRENCE
SAINT NICHOLAS
SALAD DRESSING
SALARIED CLASS
SALE BY AUCTION
SALMAN RUSHDIE
SALMON FISHING
SALT AND PEPPER
SALT-WATER FISH
SALUTE THE FLAG
SALVATION ARMY
SAMUEL JOHNSON
SAND IN THE EYES
SANDWICH MAKER
SARATOGA TRUNK

SATANIC VERSES
SATELLITE DISH
SATELLITE TOWN
SATURDAY NIGHT
SAUCE PIQUANTE
SAUTÉ POTATOES
SAVE ONE'S BACON
SAY BO TO A GOOSE
SCALDING TEARS
SCARCITY VALUE
SCARED TO DEATH
SCARLET RUNNER
SCARLETT O'HARA
SCENE OF STRIFE
SCENIC RAILWAY
SCHOOL EDITION
SCHOOL HOLIDAY
SCHOOL OF MUSIC
SCHOOL PREFECT
SCHOOL UNIFORM
SCIENCE MASTER
SCIENCE MUSEUM
SCIENTIFIC AGE
SCILLY ISLANDS
SCORCHED EARTH
SCORE A CENTURY
SCORE A SUCCESS
SCORING STROKE
SCOTCH AND SODA
SCOTCH TERRIER
SCRAMBLED EGGS
SCRAPE A LIVING
SCRAPE THROUGH
SCRAP MERCHANT
SCRATCH PLAYER
SCRATCH RUNNER
SCREEN VERSION
SCRIBBLED NOTE
SCRIPT WRITING
SEALED VERDICT
SEAL OF SECRECY
SEA OF TROUBLES
SEA OPERATIONS
SEARCHING LOOK
SEARCH WARRANT
SEASIDE RESORT
SEAT OF JUSTICE
SECOND ATTEMPT
SECOND CENTURY
SECOND CHAMBER
SECOND CHAPTER
SECOND EDITION
SECOND FEATURE
SECOND-HAND CAR
SECOND HELPING
SECOND HUSBAND

SECOND INNINGS
SECOND OF APRIL
SECOND OFFENCE
SECOND OFFICER
SECOND OF MARCH
SECOND OPINION
SECOND QUARTER
SECOND READING
SECOND SERVICE
SECOND TURNING
SECRET ARRIVAL
SECRETARY BIRD
SECRET FORMULA
SECRET INQUIRY
SECRET MEETING
SECRET PASSAGE
SECRET PROCESS
SECRET SERVICE
SECRET SESSION
SECRET SOCIETY
SECRET THOUGHT
SECRET WRITING
SECURE FOOTING
SECURITY ALARM
SECURITY ALERT
SECURITY CHECK
SECURITY LIGHT
SEDENTARY LIFE
SEE FOR ONESELF
SEE HOW THEY RUN
SEEK ADVENTURE
SEEK A SOLUTION
SEEMLY CONDUCT
SEE ONE THROUGH
SEE THINGS DONE
SEIZE THE CROWN
SELECT CIRCLES
SELECT COMPANY
SELECTION LIST
SELFISH MOTIVE
SELL AT A PROFIT
SELL BY AUCTION
SELLER'S MARKET
SEMPER FIDELIS
SEND A POSTCARD
SEND A REMINDER
SEND A TELEGRAM
SEND TO JERICHO
SENIOR CITIZEN
SENIOR PARTNER
SENIOR SERVICE
SENSELESS TALK
SENSE OF DANGER
SENSE OF HUMOUR
SENSE OF INJURY
SENSE OF RELIEF

SENSE OF TIMING	SHADES OF NIGHT
SENSE OF VALUES	SHADOW CABINET
SENSIBLE CHILD	SHADOW FACTORY
SENSIBLE WOMAN	SHADOW OF DEATH
SEPARATE COVER	SHADOW OF DOUBT
SEPARATE ROOMS	SHADY BUSINESS
SEPTEMBER MORN	SHAKE ONE'S FIST
SEPTEMBER TIDE	SHAKE ONE'S HEAD
SERGEANT MAJOR	SHAKE WITH COLD
SERGEANTS' MESS	SHAKE WITH FEAR
SERIOUS CHARGE	SHALLOW STREAM
SERIOUS DAMAGE	SHALLOW VESSEL
SERIOUS DANGER	SHAME THE DEVIL
SERIOUS DEFEAT	SHAMPOO AND SET
SERIOUS INJURY	SHAPELY FIGURE
SERIOUS MATTER	SHARE EXPENSES
SERIOUS PERSON	SHARE THE BLAME
SERPENT'S TOOTH	SHARP AS A KNIFE
SERVE A PURPOSE	SHARP AS A RAZOR
SERVE AS A MODEL	SHARP FEATURES
SERVE ONE RIGHT	SHARP PRACTICE
SERVE ONE'S TIME	SHARP'S THE WORD
SERVE ONE'S TURN	SHAVING SALOON
SERVE THE DEVIL	SHED LIGHT UPON
SERVE UP DINNER	SHEEP AND GOATS
SERVICE CHARGE	SHEEPSKIN COAT
SERVIETTE RING	SHEER NONSENSE
SET A NEW RECORD	SHELTERED LIFE
SET AT DEFIANCE	SHELTERED SIDE
SET AT VARIANCE	SHELTERED SPOT
SET ONE'S SIGHTS	SHEPHERD'S BUSH
SET THE FASHION	SHEPTON MALLET
SETTING LOTION	SHERATON TABLE
SETTLEMENT DAY	SHERIFF'S POSSE
SEVEN AND A HALF	SHERRY COBBLER
SEVEN DIAMONDS	SHETLAND ISLES
SEVEN FURLONGS	SHIFTING SANDS
SEVEN NO-TRUMPS	SHIFTING SCENE
SEVEN OF HEARTS	SHIFT THE BLAME
SEVEN OF SPADES	SHIFT THE SCENE
SEVEN OF TRUMPS	SHILLING PIECE
SEVEN SLEEPERS	SHILLING STAMP
SEVENTH HEAVEN	SHINING ARMOUR
SEVENTH LETTER	SHINING KNIGHT
SEVENTH OF JULY	SHIP IN A BOTTLE
SEVENTH OF JUNE	SHIP OF THE LINE
SEVEN THOUSAND	SHIPPING AGENT
SEVENTH STOREY	SHIPPING CLERK
SEVENTH VOLUME	SHIPPING ORDER
SEVEN-YEAR ITCH	SHIP'S CHANDLER
SEVEN YEARS OLD	SHIP'S CORPORAL
SEVEN YEARS' WAR	SHIP'S REGISTER
SEVERE ILLNESS	SHIRLEY BASSEY
SEVERE WEATHER	SHIRLEY TEMPLE
SEVILLE ORANGE	SHOCK ABSORBER
SEWING MACHINE	SHOCKING STATE

SHOOTING BRAKE
SHOOTING MATCH
SHOOTING PAINS
SHOOTING PARTY
SHOOTING RANGE
SHOOT STRAIGHT
SHOOT THE WORKS
SHOP ASSISTANT
SHOP DETECTIVE
SHOPPING SPREE
SHORT AND SWEET
SHORT DISTANCE
SHORTEST NIGHT
SHORTEST ROUTE
SHORTEST WOMAN
SHORTHAND NOTE
SHORTLY BEFORE
SHORT OF BREATH
SHORT OF CHANGE
SHORT OF SPEECH
SHORT OF TALENT
SHORT SENTENCE
SHORT SYNOPSIS
SHORT-TERM LOAN
SHORT TROUSERS
SHORT VACATION
SHOT IN THE BACK
SHOT IN THE DARK
SHOULDER STRAP
SHOUTING MATCH
SHOW ANIMOSITY
SHOW DEFERENCE
SHOWER CURTAIN
SHOW FORESIGHT
SHOW NO REMORSE
SHOW NO RESPECT
SHOW ONE'S CARDS
SHOW ONE'S PACES
SHOW ONE'S TEETH
SHOW RESTRAINT
SHREDDED WHEAT
SHROPSHIRE LAD
SHROVE TUESDAY
SHUT YOUR MOUTH
SICK AS A PARROT
SICK OF WAITING
SICK UNTO DEATH
SIDE ELEVATION
SIEGFRIED LINE
SIGNAL EXAMPLE
SIGNAL FAILURE
SIGNAL SUCCESS
SIGNAL VICTORY
SIGNATURE TUNE
SIGNED ARTICLE
SIGNIFY ASSENT

SIGNIFY LITTLE
SIGN OF EMOTION
SIGN OF FATIGUE
SIGN OF SUCCESS
SIGN THE PLEDGE
SILENT CONSENT
SILENT PARTNER
SILENT PROTEST
SILENT SERVICE
SILICON VALLEY
SILK STOCKINGS
SILLY QUESTION
SILLY SYMPHONY
SILVER AND GOLD
SILVER COINAGE
SILVER JUBILEE
SILVER PLATTER
SILVER TANKARD
SILVER THIMBLE
SILVER THREADS
SILVER WEDDING
SIMON STYLITES
SIMPLE PROBLEM
SIMPLE REQUEST
SIMPLY FURIOUS
SIMPLY KILLING
SINCERELY FELT
SINGING MASTER
SING IN HARMONY
SINGLE ARTICLE
SINGLE PURPOSE
SINGLE THOUGHT
SINGLETON LEAD
SING LIKE A BIRD
SING LIKE A LARK
SING ME TO SLEEP
SING-SONG VOICE
SING THE CHORUS
SIR DON BRADMAN
SIRLOIN OF BEEF
SIR ROBERT PEEL
SISTER OF MERCY
SISTINE CHAPEL
SIT-DOWN STRIKE
SIT IN CONCLAVE
SIT IN JUDGMENT
SIT IN THE FRONT
SIT ON ONE'S TAIL
SIT ON THE FENCE
SIT ON THE FLOOR
SITTING PRETTY
SITTING TARGET
SITTING TENANT
SIX O'CLOCK NEWS
SIX OF DIAMONDS
SIXTEEN OUNCES

SIXTEENTH HOLE
SIXTH OF AUGUST
SIXTH SYMPHONY
SIXTY THOUSAND
SKELETON STAFF
SKETCHES BY BOZ
SKIING HOLIDAY
SKILLED LABOUR
SKILLED WORKER
SKINFUL OF WINE
SKIN TREATMENT
SKITTLES MATCH
SLANDER ACTION
SLANGING MATCH
SLAP AND TICKLE
SLAP IN THE FACE
SLAP ON THE BACK
SLEEPING PILLS
SLEEP LIKE A LOG
SLEEP LIKE A TOP
SLEIGHT OF HAND
SLENDER CHANCE
SLENDER INCOME
SLICK OPERATOR
SLIGHTLY BUILT
SLIGHT QUARREL
SLING ONE'S HOOK
SLIP INTO PLACE
SLIPPERY SLOPE
SLIP THE COLLAR
SLOPING GROUND
SLOW AND STEADY
SLUM CLEARANCE
SMACK ONE'S LIPS
SMALL ADDITION
SMALL BUSINESS
SMALL CAPITALS
SMALL DIVIDEND
SMALL INVESTOR
SMALL MAJORITY
SMALL OFFERING
SMALL POTATOES
SMALL PRACTICE
SMALL QUANTITY
SMART TROUSERS
SMASH TO PIECES
SMEAR CAMPAIGN
SMELLING SALTS
SMITH AND JONES
SMOKED HADDOCK
SMOKED SAUSAGE
SMOKE-FREE ZONE
SMOKELESS FUEL
SMOKELESS ZONE
SMOKER'S THROAT
SMOKING JACKET

SMOOTH AS GLASS
SMOOTHING IRON
SMOOTH JOURNEY
SMOOTH MANNERS
SMOOTH PASSAGE
SMOOTH SAILING
SMOOTH SURFACE
SMOOTH TEXTURE
SMUGGLED GOODS
SNOOKER PLAYER
SNOWBALL FIGHT
SOAP-BOX ORATOR
SOARING PRICES
SOBER AS A JUDGE
SOBER ESTIMATE
SOBER THOUGHTS
SOCIAL CHAPTER
SOCIAL CIRCLES
SOCIAL CLIMBER
SOCIAL DEMANDS
SOCIAL EVENING
SOCIAL MACHINE
SOCIAL OUTCAST
SOCIAL PROBLEM
SOCIAL REALISM
SOCIAL REUNION
SOCIAL SCIENCE
SOCIAL SERVICE
SOCIAL SUCCESS
SOCIAL WELFARE
SOCIETY COLUMN
SOCIETY GOSSIP
SOCIETY PEOPLE
SOFTEN THE BLOW
SOFT IN THE HEAD
SOFTWARE HOUSE
SOIL ONE'S HANDS
SOLDERING IRON
SOLDIERS THREE
SOLDIER'S TUNIC
SOLEMN PROMISE
SOLEMN SILENCE
SOLEMN WARNING
SOLE OWNERSHIP
SOLICIT ORDERS
SOLITAIRE RING
SOLOMON GRUNDY
SOLVE A PROBLEM
SOME OF THE TIME
SOME OTHER TIME
SOMERSET HOUSE
SOMETHING DONE
SOMETHING ELSE
SOMETHING LIKE
SOMETHING NICE
SOMETHING OVER

SOMETHING TO DO
SOME TIME LATER
SOMEWHERE ELSE
SONG OF SOLOMON
SONG OF THE FLEA
SONG OF TRIUMPH
SON OF A SEA COOK
SONS AND LOVERS
SOONER OR LATER
SOONEST MENDED
SOON FORGOTTEN
SOOTHING MUSIC
SOOTHING SYRUP
SOOTHING TOUCH
SOOTHING WORDS
SOP TO CERBERUS
SORRY BUSINESS
SORTING OFFICE
SORT THINGS OUT
SOUND A FANFARE
SOUND ARGUMENT
SOUND CURRENCY
SOUND DETECTOR
SOUND DOCTRINE
SOUNDING BOARD
SOUNDING BRASS
SOUND JUDGMENT
SOUND MATERIAL
SOUND ONE'S HORN
SOUND THE ALARM
SOURCE OF LIGHT
SOURCE OF POWER
SOURCE OF PRIDE
SOUR SUBSTANCE
SOUSED HERRING
SOUTH CAROLINA
SOUTH CHINA SEA
SOUTH-EAST WIND
SOUTHERN CROSS
SOUTHERN STATE
SOUTH OF FRANCE
SPACE INVADERS
SPACE RESEARCH
SPANISH ARMADA
SPANISH GUITAR
SPANISH LESSON
SPANISH ONIONS
SPARE A THOUGHT
SPARE NO EFFORT
SPARKLING WINE
SPARK OF GENIUS
SPARTAN REGIME
SPEAK AT LENGTH
SPEAKER'S NOTES
SPEAKING CLOCK
SPEAKING TERMS

SPEAKING VOICE
SPEAK ONE'S MIND
SPEAK THE TRUTH
SPECIAL BRANCH
SPECIAL FAVOUR
SPECIAL FRIEND
SPECIAL NUMBER
SPECIAL PRAYER
SPECIAL SCHOOL
SPECIFIED DOSE
SPECK OF COLOUR
SPECTACLE CASE
SPEECH THERAPY
SPEED MERCHANT
SPEEDWAY TRACK
SPELL DISASTER
SPEND A FORTUNE
SPENDING MONEY
SPENDING POWER
SPENDING SPREE
SPIKE MILLIGAN
SPIKE ONE'S GUNS
SPILL THE BEANS
SPINNING JENNY
SPINNING WHEEL
SPIN THE COIN
SPIRITED REPLY
SPIRIT OF YOUTH
SPIRITUAL LIFE
SPIRITUAL PEER
SPIRITUAL SELF
SPIRITUAL SONG
SPIRIT WRITING
SPIT AND POLISH
SPITEFUL WOMAN
SPITTING IMAGE
SPLINTER GROUP
SPLINTER PARTY
SPLIT DECISION
SPLITTING HEAD
SPOILT DARLING
SPOIL THE CHILD
SPORTING EVENT
SPORTING GOODS
SPORTING OFFER
SPORTING PRESS
SPORTING PRINT
SPORTING RIFLE
SPORTING WORLD
SPORTS EDITION
SPORTS STADIUM
SPOT OF TROUBLE
SPOT THE WINNER
SPRAINED ANKLE
SPREAD A RUMOUR
SPREAD THE LOAD

SPREAD THE NEWS
SPRING BALANCE
SPRING BLOSSOM
SPRING CHICKEN
SPRING FLOWERS
SPRING MADNESS
SPRING MEETING
SPRING THE TRAP
SPRING THROUGH
SPY OUT THE LAND
SQUARE BASHING
SQUARE MEASURE
SQUASH RACKETS
SQUASH RACQUET
SQUIRE OF DAMES
STAB IN THE BACK
STACK THE CARDS
STAFF ENTRANCE
STAFF OF OFFICE
STAFF PROBLEMS
STAFF SERGEANT
STAGGERING SUM
STAKE ONE'S LIFE
STALKING HORSE
STAMP OF GENIUS
STAND AND FIGHT
STAND AND STARE
STANDARD BREAD
STANDARD GAUGE
STANDARD MODEL
STANDARD PRICE
STANDARD USAGE
STANDING ORDER
STANDING START
STAND IN THE WAY
STAND ON TIPTOE
STAND OPPOSITE
STAND OUT A MILE
STAND PREPARED
STAND TOGETHER
STAND TO REASON
STANLEY LUPINO
STAR AND GARTER
STARBOARD BEAM
STARBOARD SIDE
STAR OF THE SHOW
STAR PERFORMER
START A QUARREL
STARTING POINT
STARTING PRICE
START LAUGHING
STARTLING NEWS
STAR TREATMENT
START THINKING
START TO FINISH
START TOGETHER

STATE BOUNDARY
STATE CARRIAGE
STATE CRIMINAL
STATE FUNCTION
STATE MONOPOLY
STATE OCCASION
STATE OF FRENZY
STATE OF NATURE
STATE OF REASON
STATE OF UNREST
STATE ONE'S CASE
STATE PRISONER
STATE RELIGION
STATIC WARFARE
STATION IN LIFE
STATION MASTER
STATUTORY MILE
STAY OVERNIGHT
STAY THE COURSE
STAY UNMARRIED
ST BARTHOLOMEW
ST BERNARD PASS
ST CRISPIN'S DAY
STEADY ADVANCE
STEADY AS A ROCK
STEAK AND CHIPS
STEAL A MARCH ON
STEEL INDUSTRY
STEERAGE CLASS
STEERING WHEEL
STEP OUT OF LINE
STEPTOE AND SON
STERLING WORTH
STERN MEASURES
STEVE DONOGHUE
STICKING POINT
STICK IN THE MUD
STICK LIKE GLUE
STICK OF CELERY
STICK OUT A MILE
STICK TOGETHER
STICKY PROBLEM
STIFF AND STARK
STIFF AS A BOARD
STIFF AS A POKER
STIFF SENTENCE
STIFF UPPER-LIP
STILETTO HEELS
STILL LEMONADE
STILTON CHEESE
STIR IN THE WIND
STIRRING MUSIC
STIRRING TIMES
STIR THE EMBERS
STIR UP TROUBLE
STOCK EXCHANGE

STOCK QUESTION
STOLEN ARTICLE
STOLE THE TARTS
STOMACH POWDER
STONE THE CROWS!
STOP AT NOTHING
STOP BREATHING
STOPPING PLACE
STOPPING TRAIN
STOP-PRESS NEWS
STORMIN' NORMAN
STORMY MEETING
STORMY PASSAGE
STORMY SESSION
STORMY WEATHER
ST PATRICK'S DAY
ST PAUL'S SCHOOL
STRAIGHT ACTOR
STRAIGHT AHEAD
STRAIGHT ANGLE
STRAIGHT DRAMA
STRAIGHT DRIVE
STRAIGHTEN OUT
STRAIGHT FIGHT
STRAIGHT FLUSH
STRAIGHT RIGHT
STRAIN AT A GNAT
STRAIN ONESELF
STRAIN THE EYES
STRAIT OF DOVER
STRANGE DEVICE
STRANGE GROUND
STRANGE MANNER
STRAPPING GIRL
STRAWBERRY BED
STRAWBERRY ICE
STRAWBERRY JAM
STRAWBERRY TEA
STRAW MATTRESS
STRAY CUSTOMER
STRAY FROM HOME
STREAK OF LIGHT
STREAMING COLD
STREAM OF BLOOD
STREAM OF LIGHT
STREAM OF TEARS
STREAM OF WATER
STREET BETTING
STREET CLOTHES
STRESS THE FACT
STRETCH A POINT
STRETCHER CASE
STRETCH OF LAND
STRETCH OF ROAD
STRICT INQUIRY
STRICTLY LEGAL

STRICT PARENTS
STRIKE IT LUCKY
STRIKE THE BALL
STRIKE THE FLAG
STRIKE THE HOUR
STRIKE UP A TUNE
STRIKING CLOCK
STRIKING FORCE
STRING OF BEADS
STRING OF NAMES
STRING OF OATHS
STRING QUARTET
STRIP LIGHTING
STRONG AS A LION
STRONG BACKING
STRONG CURRENT
STRONG DEFENCE
STRONG DISLIKE
STRONG EMOTION
STRONG FEELING
STRONG GROUNDS
STRONG PROTEST
STRONG REQUEST
STRONG STOMACH
STRONG SUPPORT
STRONG SWIMMER
STRUGGLE ALONG
ST SWITHIN'S DAY
STUDENT GUITAR
STUDENT PRINCE
STUDY ALL SIDES
STUDY MEDICINE
STUDY THE FACTS
STUDY THE PLANS
STUDY THE STARS
STUFFED MARROW
STUFFED OLIVES
STUFFED TURKEY
STUMBLE ACROSS
STUNG TO ACTION
STUNTED GROWTH
ST VITUS'S DANCE
SUBJECT MATTER
SUBJECT TO DUTY
SUB-MACHINE GUN
SUBMARINE BASE
SUBMARINE CREW
SUBMIT A REPORT
SUBURBAN HOUSE
SUBURBAN VILLA
SUCCESSFUL MAN
SUCCESS SYMBOL
SUCK ONE'S THUMB
SUDDEN DISLIKE
SUDDEN IMPULSE
SUDDEN THOUGHT

SUE FOR DAMAGES
SUE FOR DIVORCE
SUFFER A STROKE
SUFFER DAMAGES
SUFFERING CATS!
SUFFER TORMENT
SUGAR AND SPICE
SUGARED ALMOND
SUGARLESS DIET
SUGAR REFINERY
SUGGESTION BOX
SUICIDAL MANIA
SUITABLE MATCH
SUIT OF CLOTHES
SULPHURIC ACID
SULTAN'S PALACE
SUMMER HOLIDAY
SUMMER MADNESS
SUMMER SESSION
SUMMER VISITOR
SUMMIT MEETING
SUNBURN LOTION
SUNDAY CLOSING
SUNDAY CLOTHES
SUNDAY EVENING
SUNDAY MORNING
SUNDAY SERVICE
SUN-DRIED BRICK
SUNK IN DESPAIR
SUPERIOR BEING
SUPERIOR COURT
SUPERIOR FORCE
SUPREME SOVIET
SURE OF ONESELF
SURE OF SUCCESS
SURFACE RAIDER
SURGEON'S KNIFE
SURGICAL KNIFE
SURPLUS ENERGY
SURPRISE PARTY
SURPRISE VISIT
SURROUND SOUND
SURTAX BRACKET
SUSPECT A TRICK
SUSPENDER BELT
SUSTAINED NOTE
SWANEE WHISTLE
SWAP AND CHANGE
SWAY IN THE WIND
SWEATED LABOUR
SWEEPING CLAIM
SWEEPING GAINS
SWEEP THE BOARD
SWEEP THE FLOOR
SWEET CHESTNUT
SWEET LAVENDER

SWEET NOTHING
SWEET SURPRISE
SWEET THOUGHTS
SWEET TO THE EAR
SWELLING SAILS
SWELL THE RANKS
SWELTERING SUN
SWIM LIKE A FISH
SWIMMING MATCH
SWING ONE'S ARMS
SWORN EVIDENCE
SYDNEY HARBOUR
SYMPHONIC POEM

T – 13

TABLEAU VIVANT
TABLE DELICACY
TABLE MOUNTAIN
TAKE A BACK SEAT
TAKE A BREATHER
TAKE ADVANTAGE
TAKE A FIRM HOLD
TAKE A HIGH TONE
TAKE A LONG TIME
TAKE AN AVERAGE
TAKE A SHORT CUT
TAKE A SNAPSHOT
TAKE BY THE HAND
TAKE DICTATION
TAKE EXCEPTION
TAKE FOR GOSPEL
TAKE GREAT CARE
TAKE IN BAD PART
TAKE IN LODGERS
TAKE IN WASHING
TAKE IT IN TURNS
TAKE IT TO COURT
TAKE IT TO HEART
TAKE LIBERTIES
TAKEN AT RANDOM
TAKEN DOWN A PEG
TAKEN FOR A RIDE
TAKE NO CHANCES
TAKE NO REFUSAL
TAKEN PRISONER
TAKEN UNAWARES
TAKE OFF WEIGHT
TAKE ONE'S FANCY
TAKE ONE'S LEAVE
TAKE ONE'S PLACE
TAKE ONE'S PULSE
TAKE ONE'S STAND
TAKE OUT TRUMPS
TAKE SANCTUARY
TAKE SERIOUSLY

TAKE SHORTHAND
TAKE SOUNDINGS
TAKE THE CREDIT
TAKE THE DAY OFF
TAKE THE MICKEY
TAKE THE PLEDGE
TAKE THE PLUNGE
TAKE THE SALUTE
TAKE THE STRAIN
TAKE THE TILLER
TAKE THE WATERS
TAKE TO ONE'S BED
TAKE TO THE ROAD
TALENT CONTEST
TALENT SPOTTER
TALK FOR EFFECT
TALK GIBBERISH
TALKING PARROT
TALK IN RIDDLES
TALK LIKE A FOOL
TALK OF THE TOWN
TALK OUT OF TURN
TALK PRIVATELY
TALK TO ONESELF
TANGIBLE ASSET
TANKARD OF BEER
TANKARD OF MILD
TAN THE HIDE OFF
TAPE RECORDING
TAP ONE'S CLARET
TAR AND FEATHER
TASTE FOR MUSIC
TAUGHT A LESSON
TAURUS THE BULL
TAWNY COLOURED
TAXABLE INCOME
TAX CONCESSION
TAX ONE'S MEMORY
TEACHING STAFF
TEACH SWIMMING
TEAM OF EXPERTS
TEA PLANTATION
TEAR OFF A STRIP
TEARS OF SORROW
TEAR TO RIBBONS
TEAR UP THE ROAD
TECHNICAL TERM
TELEGRAPH LINE
TELEGRAPH POLE
TELEGRAPH POST
TELEGRAPH WIRE
TELEPHONE BILL
TELEPHONE BOOK
TELEPHONE CALL
TELEPHONE LINE
TELEPHOTO LENS

TELEVISION AGE
TELEVISION FAN
TELEVISION SET
TELL A GOOD TALE
TELL A GOOD YARN
TELL AN UNTRUTH
TELL AT A GLANCE
TELLING EFFECT
TELL ME ANOTHER
TELL ONE'S BEADS
TEMPERATE ZONE
TEMPER THE WIND
TEMPLE OF DIANA
TEMPORAL POWER
TEMPORARY HOME
TEMPORARY LEAD
TEMPORARY LOAN
TEMPORARY RANK
TEMPORARY STOP
TEMPTING OFFER
TEMPT THE DEVIL
TENANT FOR LIFE
TEN CIGARETTES
TENDER FEELING
TENDER MERCIES
TENDER PASSION
TEN-DOLLAR BILL
TENEMENT HOUSE
TENNIS RACQUET
TEN OF DIAMONDS
TENOR CLARINET
TENPIN BOWLING
TENTH OF AUGUST
TEPID RESPONSE
TERMINAL POINT
TERRIBLE CHILD
TERRIBLE HAVOC
TERRIBLE TWINS
TERRIFIC STORM
TERRORIST ARMY
TERRORIST BAND
TEST-BAN TREATY
TEST CRICKETER
TEST MARKETING
THAMES BARRIER
THANE OF CAWDOR
THANK GOODNESS!
THANKLESS TASK
THAT'S ALL FOLKS
THE ABDICATION
THEATRE CRITIC
THEATRE SISTER
THEATRE TICKET
THE BARBARIANS
THE BEST OF LUCK
THE BEST PEOPLE

THE BIG BAD WOLF	THE SOUTH DOWNS
THE BLUE DANUBE	THE SPOKEN WORD
THE CHALLENGER	THE THREE BEARS
THE CHARLESTON	THE TIME IS RIPE
THE COLLECTION	THE TWO RONNIES
THE COMMON HERD	THE UNDERWORLD
THE DEEPEST DYE	THE UNEMPLOYED
THE DEUCE TO PAY	THE UNEXPECTED
THE DEVIL TO PAY	THE UNFORESEEN
THE DIRECT ROAD	THE VANQUISHED
THE DOLL'S HOUSE	THE VIGILANTES
THE EISTEDDFOD	THE WATER-WAGON
THE EMBANKMENT	THE WHITE HOUSE
THE FIRST TRAIN	THE WHOLE TRUTH
THE FIRST WATER	THE WHOLE WORLD
THE FOOTLIGHTS	THE WILDERNESS
THE GIDDY LIMIT	THE WILL TO LIVE
THE GOLDEN RULE	THE WINSLOW BOY
THE GONDOLIERS	THE WIZARD OF OZ
THE GOVERNMENT	THICK WITH DUST
THE GUILLOTINE	THIEF OF BAGDAD
THE HONOURABLE	THING OF BEAUTY
THE INS AND OUTS	THINK BETTER OF
THE ISRAELITES	THINK LITTLE OF
THE JOY STRINGS	THINK STRAIGHT
THE KERRY DANCE	THINK THE WORST
THE LAST SUPPER	THIRD DIVIDEND
THE LAW IS AN ASS	THIRD DIVISION
THE LIBERATION	THIRD ENGINEER
THE LIGHT BLUES	THIRD OF AUGUST
THE MAGIC FLUTE	THIRD SYMPHONY
THE MAIN CHANCE	THIRTEEN HOURS
THE MATTERHORN	THIRTEEN MILES
THE MERRY WIDOW	THIRTEEN TIMES
THE METROPOLIS	THIRTEEN WEEKS
THE MILLENNIUM	THIRTEEN YEARS
THE MOODY BLUES	THIRTY FIFTEEN
THE NOES HAVE IT	THIRTY GUINEAS
THE NORTH DOWNS	THIRTY MINUTES
THE OLD BRIGADE	THIRTY-ONE DAYS
THE OLD COUNTRY	THIRTY PER CENT
THE OPPOSITION	THIRTY SECONDS
THE OTHER WOMAN	THIS LITTLE PIG
THE OTHER WORLD	THIS WEDNESDAY
THE QUAKER GIRL	THOMAS À BECKET
THE RESISTANCE	THOMAS BEECHAM
THE RIGHT STUFF	THOMAS CARLYLE
THE ROUNDHEADS	THORNY PROBLEM
THE SAME ANSWER	THORNY SUBJECT
THE SCOTS GREYS	THOROUGH ROGUE
THE SECOND-RATE	THOSE IN FAVOUR
THE SERPENTINE	THOUGHT POLICE
THE SHALLOW END	THOUSAND MILES
THE SIMPLE LIFE	THOUSAND YEARS
THE SMALL HOURS	THREAD A NEEDLE
THE SNOW MAIDEN	THREAD ONE'S WAY

THREE AND A HALF	TO A HIGH DEGREE
THREE BAGS FULL	TOASTED CHEESE
THREE-DAY MATCH	TO BE CONTINUED
THREE DIAMONDS	TO BE OR NOT TO BE
THREE FEET TALL	TOGETHER AGAIN
THREE-FOOT RULE	TOKEN OF ESTEEM
THREE FURLONGS	TOLL OF THE ROAD
THREE-LINE WHIP	TOMATO KETCHUP
THREE NO-TRUMPS	TOMORROW NIGHT
THREE OF HEARTS	TOMORROW WE DIE
THREE OF SPADES	TONGUE IN CHEEK
THREE OF TRUMPS	TONGUE OF FLAME
THREE QUARTERS	TONGUE TWISTER
THREE SEVENTHS	TONGUE WAGGING
THREE THOUSAND	TOO GOOD BY HALF
THRICE BLESSED	TOO GOOD TO LAST
THROES OF AGONY	TOO LITTLE ROOM
THROUGH A STRAW	TOO MANY CHIEFS
THROW A LIGHT ON	TOO MUCH PEPPER
THROWAWAY LINE	TOOTING COMMON
THROW IN THE AIR	TOO WEAK TO RISE
THUMB ONE'S NOSE	TOP OF THE CLASS
THUMP THE TABLE	TOP OF THE SCALE
THURSDAY NIGHT	TOP OF THE TABLE
TICHBORNE CASE	TOP-SECRET FILE
TICKET MACHINE	TORE OFF A STRIP
TICKET OF LEAVE	TORRENT OF RAIN
TICKETS PLEASE	TO SOME PURPOSE
TIDAL MOVEMENT	TOSTI'S 'GOODBYE'
TIDE OF AFFAIRS	TOTAL DARKNESS
TIED UP IN KNOTS	TO THE BACKBONE
TIE WITH STRING	TOUCHING SCENE
TILT AT THE RING	TOUCH OF COLOUR
TILT THE SCALES	TOUCH OF GARLIC
TIME AFTER TIME	TOUCH OF GENIUS
TIME AND MOTION	TOUCH OF NATURE
TIME FOR DINNER	TOUCH OF THE SUN
TIME FOR SUPPER	TOUCH ONE'S TOES
TIMELY RETREAT	TOUCH ON THE RAW
TIMELY WARNING	TOUCH THE HEART
TIME MARCHES ON	TOUGH CUSTOMER
TIME OF ARRIVAL	TOURIST AGENCY
TIME OUT OF MIND	TOURIST CENTRE
TIMES OF STRESS	TOURIST SEASON
TIME TO REFLECT	TOURIST TICKET
TIMID AS A MOUSE	TOURIST TROPHY
TIMON OF ATHENS	TOUR OF BRITAIN
TINNED PEACHES	TOUT FOR CUSTOM
TIN OF SARDINES	TOWER OF LONDON
TIP-AND-RUN RAID	TOWN AND AROUND
TIP ONE THE WINK	TOY WITH AN IDEA
TIPPED THE WINK	TRACTOR DRIVER
TIRED OF LIVING	TRADE DISCOUNT
TIRESOME CHORE	TRADE ENTRANCE
TITLE OF HONOUR	TRADE MAGAZINE
TOAD IN THE HOLE	TRADE UNIONIST

TRADING CENTRE
TRADING ESTATE
TRADING VESSEL
TRAFFIC ISLAND
TRAFFIC LIGHTS
TRAFFIC SIGNAL
TRAFFIC WARDEN
TRAIL ONE'S COAT
TRAINED SINGER
TRAINING SHOES
TRAIN OF CAMELS
TRAIN OF EVENTS
TRAIN SPOTTING
TRAIN TERMINUS
TRAITOR'S DEATH
TRAM CONDUCTOR
TRANQUIL SCENE
TRANSISTOR SET
TRANSPORT CAFÉ
TRAPEZE ARTIST
TRAVEL BY TRAIN
TRAVELLER'S JOY
TRAVEL LIGHTLY
TREACLE TOFFEE
TREAD THE STAGE
TREASURE CHEST
TREASURE HOUSE
TREASURE TRAIL
TREASURE TROVE
TREASURY BENCH
TREASURY BILLS
TREASURY BONDS
TREAT LIKE DIRT
TREAT WITH CARE
TREE OF LIBERTY
TREMENDOUS JOB
TRENCH WARFARE
TREND OF EVENTS
TRIAL AND ERROR
TRIAL MARRIAGE
TRIBAL WARFARE
TRICK QUESTION
TRICKY PROBLEM
TRIFLING ERROR
TRIGGER FINGER
TRILLING SOUND
TRINITY CHURCH
TRIUMPHAL ARCH
TRIVIAL MATTER
TROPICAL FRUIT
TROPICAL PLANT
TROPICAL STORM
TROTTING RACES
TROUSER BUTTON
TRUE CRITERION
TRUE STATEMENT

TRUE TO HIS SALT
TRUE TO ONESELF
TRUE TO THE LAST
TRUE UNTO DEATH
TRULY GRATEFUL
TRULY GREAT MAN
TRUMPET PLAYER
TRUST ACCOUNTS
TRUST TO CHANCE
TRUSTY SERVANT
TRYING JOURNEY
TRYSTING PLACE
TRYSTING POINT
TUBE OF MUSTARD
TUESDAY'S CHILD
TUNNEL THROUGH
TURKISH COFFEE
TURN A BLIND EYE
TURN CLOCKWISE
TURN DOWNWARDS
TURNED TO STONE
TURNING WICKET
TURN INSIDE OUT
TURN INTO MONEY
TURN OFF THE GAS
TURN OFF THE TAP
TURN OF THE CARD
TURN OF THE TIDE
TURN ON THE HEAT
TURN THE CORNER
TURN THE HEAT ON
TURN THE TABLES
TURN TO ACCOUNT
TURN TO THE LEFT
TURQUOISE BLUE
TWEED TROUSERS
TWELFTH LETTER
TWELFTH OF JULY
TWELFTH OF JUNE
TWELVE DOLLARS
TWELVE GOOD MEN
TWELVE GUINEAS
TWELVE MINUTES
TWELVE PER CENT
TWELVE SQUARED
TWENTY DOLLARS
TWENTY GUINEAS
TWENTY MINUTES
TWENTY-ONE DAYS
TWENTY PER CENT
TWICE-TOLD TALE
TWILIGHT SLEEP
TWINKLING EYES
TWINKLING FEET
TWINKLING STAR
TWIST AND SHAKE

TWIST AND TWIRL
TWISTED NATURE
TWIST THE WORDS
TWO-EDGED SWORD
TWO-LETTER WORD
TWO-MASTED SHIP
TWO OF DIAMONDS
TWOS AND THREES
TWO-TIERED CAKE
TWO-WAY STRETCH
TWO-WAY TRAFFIC

U – 13

UGLY SITUATION
ULTERIOR PLANS
ULTIMATE CAUSE
UMBILICAL CORD
UMBRELLA STAND
UNABLE TO PLEAD
UNANIMOUS VOTE
UNARMED COMBAT
UNATTACHED MAN
UNBOLT THE DOOR
UNBOUNDED LOVE
UNBROKEN FRONT
UNBROKEN HORSE
UNCROWNED KING
UNDATED CHEQUE
UNDECLARED WAR
UNDER CONTRACT
UNDER-COVER MAN
UNDER MILK WOOD
UNDER ONE'S NOSE
UNDER ONE'S SKIN
UNDER ONE'S WING
UNDER PRESSURE
UNDER SENTENCE
UNDER STRENGTH
UNDER THE KNIFE
UNDER THE TABLE
UNDER THE THUMB
UNDER TRAINING
UNDER TWO FLAGS
UNDUE PRESSURE
UNEASY FEELING
UNEVEN CONTEST
UNEVEN SURFACE
UNFAIR PICTURE
UNFAIR VERDICT
UNFRIENDLY ACT
UNFURL THE FLAG
UNGUARDED HOUR
UNHAPPY REMARK
UNIFORM WEIGHT
UNIONIST PARTY

UNION JACK CLUB
UNITED IN DEATH
UNITED KINGDOM
UNITED NATIONS
UNITED WE STAND
UNIT OF CURRENT
UNIVERSAL AUNT
UNIVERSAL BUTT
UNIVERSITY RAG
UNKIND THOUGHT
UNKNOWN ORIGIN
UNKNOWN PERSON
UNLAWFUL ENTRY
UNLOCK THE DOOR
UNLUCKY CHOICE
UNLUCKY COLOUR
UNLUCKY IN LOVE
UNLUCKY NUMBER
UNLUCKY PERSON
UNPAID SERVANT
UNSECURED DEBT
UNSECURED LOAN
UNSEEN DANGERS
UNSKILLED WORK
UNSOCIAL HOURS
UNSOLVED CRIME
UNTIMELY DEATH
UNTOLD NUMBERS
UNVEIL A STATUE
UNWANTED CHILD
UNWORTHY CAUSE
UP AT CAMBRIDGE
UP BOYS AND AT 'EM
UP IN THE CLOUDS
UP IN THE SADDLE
UPPER REGISTER
UPRIGHT FELLOW
UPRIGHT FIGURE
UPRIGHT PERSON
UP THE MOUNTAIN
UP TO HIS TRICKS
UP TO SOMETHING
UP TO THE ELBOWS
UP TO THE MINUTE
UPTURNED GLASS
UP WITH THE DAWN
UP WITH THE LARK
URBAN DISTRICT
USEFUL PURPOSE
USEFUL STAND-BY
USE OF BATHROOM
USE ONE'S BRAINS
USUAL CHANNELS
USUAL QUESTION
UTTER CONTEMPT
UTTER DEVOTION

UTTER NONSENSE

V – 13

VACUUM CLEANER
VALENTINE CARD
VALENTINE'S DAY
VALE OF EVESHAM
VALIANT EFFORT
VALID ARGUMENT
VALID CONTRACT
VALLEY OF DEATH
VALUE ADDED TAX
VALUE FOR MONEY
VALUE ONE'S LIFE
VALUE RECEIVED
VAN ALLEN BELTS
VANTAGE GROUND
VARIABLE SPEED
VARIABLE WINDS
VARICOSE VEINS
VARIETY ARTIST
VARNISHING DAY
VAUDEVILLE ACT
VAULTING HORSE
VAULT OF HEAVEN
VEAL AND HAM PIE
VEER TO THE LEFT
VEGETABLE DIET
VEGETABLE DISH
VEGETABLE LIFE
VEGETABLE SOUP
VENERABLE BEDE
VENETIAN BLIND
VENETIAN GLASS
VENOMOUS SNAKE
VERBAL QUIBBLE
VERNAL EQUINOX
VERSATILE MIND
VERTICAL PLANE
VERY DIFFERENT
VESSEL OF WRATH
VETERAN TROOPS
VEXED IN SPIRIT
VEXED QUESTION
VICIOUS CIRCLE
VICIOUS GOSSIP
VICTOR HERBERT
VICTORIA CROSS
VICTORIA FALLS
VICTORIAN DAYS
VICTORY PARADE
VIDEO CASSETTE
VIDEO RECORDER
VIENNESE GLASS
VIENNESE WALTZ

VILLAGE BEAUTY
VILLAGE CHURCH
VILLAGE GOSSIP
VILLAGE SCHOOL
VILLAGE SMITHY
VILLAGE SQUIRE
VILLAGE STREET
VINEGARY SMILE
VIOLATE THE LAW
VIOLENT ATTACK
VIOLENT CHANGE
VIOLENT EFFORT
VIOLENT NATURE
VIOLENT SPEECH
VIOLENT TEMPER
VIOLIN RECITAL
VIRGINIA STOCK
VIRGINIA WATER
VIRGINIA WOOLF
VIRGIN ISLANDS
VIRTUAL MEMORY
VIRULENT ABUSE
VISIBLE EFFECT
VISITING HOURS
VISITING TERMS
VISUAL DISPLAY
VITAL QUESTION
VITAMIN TABLET
VOICE OF REASON
VOICE TRAINING
VOID OF FEELING
VOLLEY OF ABUSE
VOLUME CONTROL
VOLUME OF SMOKE
VOLUNTARY ARMY
VOLUNTARY GIFT
VOLUNTARY WORK
VOLUNTEER ARMY
VOTED A FAILURE
VOTE OF CENSURE
VOTES FOR WOMEN
VULGAR DISPLAY

W – 13

WAG ONE'S FINGER
WAIT FOR ORDERS
WAIT PATIENTLY
WALK BACKWARDS
WALKING-ON PART
WALKING THE DOG
WALK INTO A TRAP
WALK THE BOARDS
WALK UP AND DOWN
WALLOW IN MONEY
WALLS HAVE EARS

WALTER PIDGEON
WALTER RALEIGH
WANDERING MIND
WANTED ON BOARD
WANT OF COURAGE
WANT OF THOUGHT
WAR DEPARTMENT
WARDOUR STREET
WARLIKE HABITS
WARLIKE MANNER
WARLIKE PEOPLE
WARM RECEPTION
WARNING NOTICE
WARNING SIGNAL
WAR TO THE DEATH
WAR TO THE KNIFE
WASHING POWDER
WASH ONE'S HANDS
WASH THE DISHES
WASPISH NATURE
WASTE OF BREATH
WATCH AND CHAIN
WATCH EXPENSES
WATCHING BRIEF
WATCH ONE'S STEP
WATCH THE BIRDY
WATCH THE CLOCK
WATERING PLACE
WATER SHORTAGE
WATER SOFTENER
WATLING STREET
WAVE OF FEELING
WAVE OF THE HAND
WAY OF ALL FLESH
WAY OF THE CROSS
WAY OF THE WORLD
WAY OF THINKING
WAYSIDE TAVERN
WAY TO THE STARS
WEAK AS A KITTEN
WEAK CHARACTER
WEAK IN THE HEAD
WEAK ON HIS PINS
WEATHER BUREAU
WEATHER EXPERT
WEATHER REPORT
WEB OF INTRIGUE
WEDGWOOD CHINA
WEDNESDAY WEEK
WEED THE GARDEN
WEEK AFTER NEXT
WEEK AFTER WEEK
WEEK IN, WEEK OUT
WEEKLY ACCOUNT
WEEKLY PAYMENT
WEEK OF SUNDAYS

WEEKS AND WEEKS
WEEPING WILLOW
WEIGH THINGS UP
WEIGHTY MATTER
WELCOME RELIEF
WELFARE CENTRE
WELFARE WORKER
WELL-AIMED SHOT
WELL BROUGHT UP
WELL-KNIT FRAME
WELL PRESERVED
WELL-SPENT LIFE
WELL THOUGHT OF
WELL TO THE FORE
WELL TURNED OUT
WELSH REGIMENT
WE NEVER CLOSED
WENT LIKE A BOMB
WENT TO THE DOGS
WESTERLY WINDS
WESTERN CHURCH
WESTERN DESERT
WESTERN EUROPE
WESTERN POWERS
WEST HAM UNITED
WEST OF ENGLAND
WEST SIDE STORY
WHAT A SCORCHER
WHAT DO YOU KNOW?
WHATEVER YOU DO
WHIRLING ROUND
WHISKY AND SODA
WHISPER SOFTLY
WHITE AS A GHOST
WHITE AS A SHEET
WHITE AS MARBLE
WHITE ELEPHANT
WHITE FLANNELS
WHITE HORSE INN
WHITE OF THE EYE
WHITE SAPPHIRE
WHOLE OF THE DAY
WHOLESOME FOOD
WHOOPING COUGH
WIDE ANGLE LENS
WIDE INTERESTS
WIDE KNOWLEDGE
WIDE OF THE MARK
WIDE PUBLICITY
WIDOW'S PENSION
WIELD THE BATON
WILD AND WOOLLY
WILD-CAT STRIKE
WILDEST DREAMS
WILFUL SILENCE
WILLIAM CAXTON

WILLIAM COWPER
WILLIAM MORRIS
WILLIAM WALTON
WILLING HELPER
WILLING WORKER
WILL OF ONE'S OWN
WILLOW PATTERN
WILLOWY FIGURE
WIMPOLE STREET
WINDING COURSE
WINDING STAIRS
WINDOW CLEANER
WINDOW DRESSER
WINDOW SHOPPER
WINDSOR CASTLE
WINED AND DINED
WIN FIRST PRIZE
WING COMMANDER
WINGED MONSTER
WINGED VICTORY
WINNIE THE POOH
WINNING COUPON
WINNING DOUBLE
WINNING HAZARD
WINNING NUMBER
WINNING STREAK
WINNING STROKE
WINNING TICKET
WINNING TREBLE
WINTER GARDENS
WINTER HOLIDAY
WINTER SESSION
WINTER VISITOR
WINTER WEATHER
WIN THE JACKPOT
WINTRY WEATHER
WIPE OFF THE MAP
WIPE ONE'S HANDS
WIRED FOR SOUND
WIRELESS WAVES
WISE AS SOLOMON
WISH OTHERWISE
WITH A BAD GRACE
WITH A FLOURISH
WITH A HIGH HAND
WITH AUTHORITY
WITH BOTH HANDS
WITH CERTAINTY
WITHERING LOOK
WITHIN EARSHOT
WITHIN HEARING
WITHIN MEASURE
WITH ONE ACCORD
WITHOUT A DOUBT
WITHOUT A HITCH
WITHOUT A RIVAL

WITHOUT CHARGE
WITHOUT MALICE
WITHOUT NOTICE
WITHOUT NUMBER
WITHOUT REASON
WITHOUT REGARD
WITHOUT REMARK
WITHOUT WARMTH
WITHOUT WEIGHT
WITH RESTRAINT
WITH THE LID OFF
WITH THE STREAM
WOLF AT THE DOOR
WOLF IN THE FOLD
WONDERFUL NEWS
WOOD ENGRAVING
WOOLLEN GLOVES
WORD BLINDNESS
WORD IN ONE'S EAR
WORD OF COMFORT
WORD OF COMMAND
WORD OF WARNING
WORD PROCESSOR
WORDS AND MUSIC
WORDS OF WISDOM
WORD TO THE WISE
WORDY ARGUMENT
WORK LIKE MAGIC
WORKMEN'S TRAIN
WORK OF FICTION
WORK ONE'S WAY UP
WORK THE ORACLE
WORK UP A LATHER
WORK WITH A WILL
WORLD CHAMPION
WORLDLY WISDOM
WORLD OF NATURE
WORLD PREMIÈRE
WORLD-WIDE FAME
WORM ONE'S WAY IN
WORN TO A SHADOW
WORSE AND WORSE
WORSE THAN EVER
WORST POSSIBLE
WORTH A FORTUNE
WORTH A MILLION
WORTHLESS JUNK
WORTH MILLIONS
WORTH ONE'S SALT
WORTH VISITING
WOW AND FLUTTER
WRAPPING PAPER
WRITE AT LENGTH
WRITE IN PENCIL
WRITE ONE'S NAME
WRITHE IN AGONY

WRITTEN ANSWER
WRITTEN MATTER
WRITTEN PERMIT
WRITTEN SPEECH
WRONG APPROACH
WRONG DECISION
WRONG TENDENCY

X – 13

X-RAY APPARATUS

Y – 13

YABBA DABBA DOO
YARDS AND YARDS
YEAR AFTER YEAR
YEAR IN, YEAR OUT
YEHUDI MENUHIN
YELLOW BUNTING
YELLOW WAGTAIL
YELLOW WITH AGE
YEOMAN SERVICE
YORKSHIRE POST
YOUNG CHILDREN
YOUNGER SISTER
YOUNGEST CHILD
YOUNG HOOLIGAN
YOUR NUMBER'S UP
YOUTH MOVEMENT

Z – 13

ZEBRA CROSSING
ZOO TELEVISION

A – 14

A BOOK AT BEDTIME
ABOVE CRITICISM
ABOVE SUSPICION
ABOVE THE GROUND
A BOW AT A VENTURE
ABRAHAM LINCOLN
ABRUPT ENTRANCE
ABSOLUTE DECREE
ABSOLUTE MASTER
ABSOLUTE PIFFLE
ABSTRACT DESIGN
ABSTRACT NUMBER
ABUSE ONE'S POWER
ACADEMIC DEGREE
ACADEMIC MANNER
ACCESSIBLE SPOT
ACCIDENT POLICY
ACCORDING TO LAW

ACCORDION PLEAT
ACCUSATIVE CASE
ACCUSING FINGER
ACHIEVE ONE'S AIM
ACHIEVE VICTORY
ACHILLES TENDON
ACROSS THE OCEAN
ACROSS THE RIVER
ACT ACCORDINGLY
ACT AS A LANDMARK
ACT AS GUARANTOR
ACT IMMEDIATELY
ACT IN GOOD FAITH
ACTION FOR LIBEL
ACTION PAINTING
ACTION STATIONS
ACTIVE INTEREST
ACTIVE STRENGTH
ACT THE BUSYBODY
ADDRESS THE BALL
ADDRESS UNKNOWN
ADD TO ONE'S GRIEF
ADELPHI TERRACE
ADELPHI THEATRE
ADEQUATE AMOUNT
ADEQUATE INCOME
ADEQUATE REASON
ADJUST THE HANDS
ADMIRALTY CHART
ADMIRALTY HOUSE
ADMIT THE CHARGE
ADOPTION PAPERS
ADULT EDUCATION
ADVANCE BOOKING
ADVANCING YEARS
ADVENTURE STORY
ADVERSE BALANCE
AERIAL PING-PONG
AEROBIC WEIGHTS
AESTHETIC SENSE
AESTHETIC TASTE
AFFAIRE DE COEUR
AFFAIR OF HONOUR
AFFAIRS OF STATE
AFFECTED MANNER
AFFECTED SPEECH
AFFILIATED BODY
AFTER BREAKFAST
AFTER CHRISTMAS
AFTER-DINNER NAP
AFTER LIGHTS-OUT
AFTER THE DELUGE
AGAINST ALL ODDS
AGAINST THE ODDS
AGAINST THE TIDE
AGAINST THE WIND

AGATHA CHRISTIE
AGE OF IGNORANCE
AGE OF INNOCENCE
AGREE IN MEANING
AIM AT THE TARGET
AIRBORNE FORCES
AIRBORNE TROOPS
AIRING CUPBOARD
AIR OF GRIEVANCE
AIR ONE'S OPINION
AIR PHOTOGRAPHY
AIR RAID SHELTER
AIR RAID WARNING
AIR VICE-MARSHAL
ALBERT EINSTEIN
ALBERT MEMORIAL
ALCOCK AND BROWN
ALCOHOLIC DRINK
ALDWYCH THEATRE
ALEXANDER DUMAS
ALFRED TENNYSON
ALFRED THE GREAT
ALL GUNS BLAZING
ALL HANDS ON DECK
ALLIED LANDINGS
ALL IN A DAY'S WORK
ALL-IN WRESTLING
ALL KINDS OF WAYS
ALLOTTED SPHERE
ALL OVER THE SHOP
ALL-ROUND PLAYER
ALL THE KING'S MEN
ALL WELL AND GOOD
ALMIGHTY DOLLAR
ALPES MARITIMES
ALSACE LORRAINE
AMATEUR COMPANY
AMERICAN ACCENT
AMERICAN INDIAN
AMERICAN LEGION
AMERICAN PATROL
AMERICAN SCHOOL
AMERICAN TROOPS
AMMUNITION DUMP
AMONGST FRIENDS
ANCIENT BRITAIN
ANCIENT HISTORY
ANCIENT LINEAGE
ANCIENT MARINER
ANDAMAN ISLANDS
ANDREW CARNEGIE
ANGINA PECTORIS
ANGLICAN CHURCH
ANIMAL CRACKERS
ANNUAL TURNOVER
ANNUS MIRABILIS

ANONYMOUS DONOR
ANOTHER OPINION
ANOTHER VERSION
ANSWER ONE'S NAME
ANTARCTIC OCEAN
ANTHONY HOPKINS
ANY SUGGESTIONS?
ANYTHING TO COME
APARTMENT HOUSE
APARTMENT TO LET
APPEAL FOR FUNDS
APPEAL FOR MERCY
APPEAL TO REASON
APPEAR IN PUBLIC
APPLE CHARLOTTE
APPLE OF DISCORD
APPLE OF ONE'S EYE
APPLES AND PEARS
APPLIED PHYSICS
APPLIED SCIENCE
APPLY THE BRAKES
APPROVED SCHOOL
APRIL THE EIGHTH
APRIL THE FOURTH
APRIL THE SECOND
ARABIC NUMERALS
ARBITER OF TASTE
ARMCHAIR CRITIC
ARMS OF MORPHEUS
ARMY CADET FORCE
ARMY MANOEUVRES
AROUND THE WORLD
ARRANT NONSENSE
ARROGANT MANNER
ART FOR ART'S SAKE
ARTFUL CUSTOMER
ARTICLE OF FAITH
ARTIFICIAL HAND
ARTIFICIAL LAKE
ARTIFICIAL LIMB
ARTIFICIAL POND
ARTIFICIAL SILK
ARTISTIC EFFECT
ARTISTIC EFFORT
ART OF REASONING
AS A GENERAL RULE
AS BLACK AS NIGHT
AS BRAVE AS A LION
ASCENDING ORDER
ASCENDING SCALE
AS DEAD AS MUTTON
AS DRUNK AS A LORD
AS FAST AS YOU CAN
AS FIT AS A FIDDLE
AS FRESH AS PAINT
AS GOOD AS A FEAST

AS GREEN AS GRASS
AS HARD AS A STONE
ASK FORGIVENESS
AS MAD AS A HATTER
AS PALE AS A GHOST
A PLACE IN THE SUN
AS PLAIN AS PLAIN
AS SAFE AS HOUSES
ASSENTING PARTY
ASSET STRIPPING
AS SMART AS PAINT
ASSOCIATION CUP
AS SOFT AS BUTTER
AS SOFT AS VELVET
AS SOUND AS A BELL
AS SWEET AS SUGAR
ASTERIX THE GAUL
AS THE CASE MAY BE
AS THE CROW FLIES
AS TIGHT AS A DRUM
AT DAGGERS DRAWN
ATHLETIC GROUND
ATHLETIC SPORTS
ATLANTIC FLIGHT
ATLANTIC ROLLER
ATLAS MOUNTAINS
AT ONE FELL SWOOP
AT ONE'S DISPOSAL
A TOWN LIKE ALICE
ATTACKING FIELD
ATTACK OF NERVES
ATTEMPT TOO MUCH
AT THE RIGHT TIME
AT THE THRESHOLD
AT THIS JUNCTURE
ATTITUDE OF MIND
AUF WIEDERSEHEN
AUGUST THE FIFTH
AUGUST THE FIRST
AUGUST THE NINTH
AUGUST THE SIXTH
AUGUST THE TENTH
AUGUST THE THIRD
AUGUSTUS CAESAR
AURORA BOREALIS
AUSTRALIA HOUSE
AUSTRALIAN BUSH
AUSTRALIAN WINE
AUTO CORD REWIND
AUTOGRAPH ALBUM
AUTOMATIC PILOT
AUTOMATIC RIFLE
AUTOMOBILE CLUB
AVERAGE ABILITY
AVIATION SPIRIT
AVOID A DECISION

AVOID BLOODSHED
AWKWARD SILENCE

B – 14

BABES IN THE WOOD
BACHELOR OF ARTS
BACK AT THE RANCH
BACK-SEAT DRIVER
BACKS TO THE WALL
BACKWARD GLANCE
BACONIAN THEORY
BAD CIRCULATION
BAD FOR BUSINESS
BAD HANDWRITING
BAD HOUSEKEEPER
BADMINTON COURT
BAD VENTILATION
BAGATELLE TABLE
BALANCED BUDGET
BALANCE OF POWER
BALANCE OF TRADE
BALANCING TRICK
BALL AT ONE'S FEET
BALLET MISTRESS
BALLIOL COLLEGE
BALL OF THE THUMB
BALLOON BARRAGE
BALLPARK FIGURE
BALMORAL CASTLE
BALTIC EXCHANGE
BANANA FRITTERS
BANANA REPUBLIC
BANDED TOGETHER
BAND OF BROTHERS
BAND OF PILGRIMS
BANE OF ONE'S LIFE
BANGERS AND MASH
BANKING ACCOUNT
BANK OF SCOTLAND
BANNER HEADLINE
BANQUETING HALL
BARBIZON SCHOOL
BARE-BACK RIDING
BARE ESSENTIALS
BAREFOOT DOCTOR
BARELY POSSIBLE
BARGAIN COUNTER
BARKIS IS WILLIN'
BAR OF CHOCOLATE
BARRAGE BALLOON
BAR THE ENTRANCE
BASIC SUBSTANCE
BASKETBALL RING
BASKETBALL TEAM
BATHING COSTUME

BATHING MACHINE
BATHROOM HEATER
BATHROOM SCALES
BATTERY CHARGER
BATTING AVERAGE
BATTLE OF NASEBY
BATTLE STATIONS
BAYEUX TAPESTRY
BEACH INSPECTOR
BE-ALL AND END-ALL
BEAM ME UP SCOTTY
BEAR ALLEGIANCE
BEAT GENERATION
BEAT ONE'S BRAINS
BEAT ONE'S BREAST
BEAT THE BIG DRUM
BEAT TO A FRAZZLE
BEAUTIFUL VOICE
BEAUTIFUL WOMAN
BECOME A CITIZEN
BECOME AIRBORNE
BECOME A PATIENT
BECOME CHAMPION
BEDROOM SLIPPER
BEDSIDE READING
BED-SITTING ROOM
BEFORE AND AFTER
BEFORE AND SINCE
BEFORE DAYLIGHT
BEFORE MIDNIGHT
BEFORE ONE'S EYES
BEFORE ONE'S TIME
BEFORE THE JUDGE
BEG FORGIVENESS
BEG THE QUESTION
BEHIND ONE'S BACK
BEHIND SCHEDULE
BEHIND THE CLOCK
BEHIND THE TIMES
BEHIND THE WHEEL
BELGRAVE SQUARE
BELIEVE IT OR NOT
BELLE OF NEW YORK
BELLE OF THE BALL
BELOW THE GROUND
BENCH OF BISHOPS
BENEATH ACCOUNT
BENEFIT SOCIETY
BENEVOLENT FUND
BEREFT OF REASON
BERKELEY SQUARE
BERLIN QUESTION
BESEECHING LOOK
BESIDE THE POINT
BEST DRESSED MAN
BEST INTENTIONS

BEST LEG FORWARD
BEST OF THE BUNCH
BETSEY TROTWOOD
BETTER FEELINGS
BETTER THAN EVER
BETTER THAN MOST
BETTER THOUGHTS
BETWEEN FRIENDS
BETWEEN THE EYES
BEWARE OF THE DOG
BEYOND ALL DOUBT
BEYOND HUMAN AID
BEYOND REPROACH
BEYOND THE GRAVE
BEYOND THE LIMIT
BID GOOD MORNING
BIFOCAL GLASSES
BIG-GAME HUNTING
BIGGEST PORTION
BIJOU RESIDENCE
BILLIARD MARKER
BILLIARD PLAYER
BILLIARD SALOON
BILL OF EXCHANGE
BINARY NOTATION
BIRD OF PARADISE
BIRTH OF A NATION
BISHOP AUCKLAND
BITE ONE'S TONGUE
BIT OF A COME-DOWN
BIT OF A NUISANCE
BITTER FEELINGS
BITTER MEMORIES
BITTER STRUGGLE
BITTER THOUGHTS
BITUMINOUS COAL
BLACK AS THUNDER
BLACK-EYED SUSIE
BLACK IN THE FACE
BLACKPOOL TOWER
BLACK STOCKINGS
BLACK CARTRIDGE
BLASTING POWDER
BLAZING INFERNO
BLEACHING AGENT
BLENHEIM ORANGE
BLENHEIM PALACE
BLESS THIS HOUSE
BLIND IGNORANCE
BLIND REASONING
BLOCK AND TACKLE
BLOCK OF OFFICES
BLOOD POISONING
BLOUSE AND SKIRT
BLOW EVERYTHING
BLOW HOT AND COLD

BLOWING BUBBLES
BLOW SMOKE-RINGS
BLOW THE EXPENSE
BLOW THE MAN DOWN
BLUE-COAT SCHOOL
BLUE SPECTACLES
BLUNT STATEMENT
BOA CONSTRICTOR
BOARDING SCHOOL
BOARD OF CONTROL
BOARD OF INQUIRY
BOARD RESIDENCE
BODILY MOVEMENT
BODILY STRENGTH
BODILY WEAKNESS
BODY OF EVIDENCE
BODY OF SOLDIERS
BOILED POTATOES
BOLD EXPERIMENT
BOLOGNESE SAUCE
BONNIE AND CLYDE
BONNIE SCOTLAND
BOOK DEPARTMENT
BOOK OF NONSENSE
BOOK OF PROVERBS
BOOK OF THE MONTH
BOOK PRODUCTION
BOOMING ECONOMY
BOON COMPANIONS
BORDERLINE CASE
BORDER MINSTREL
BORDER REGIMENT
BORDER SKIRMISH
BOROUGH COUNCIL
BORROWED PLUMES
BOSTON CRACKERS
BOSTON TEA PARTY
BOTTLE OF BRANDY
BOTTLE OF BUBBLY
BOTTLE OF CLARET
BOTTLE OF SCOTCH
BOTTLE OF SWEETS
BOTTLE OF WHISKY
BOTTOM OF THE BAG
BOTTOM OF THE SEA
BOUGHT FOR A SONG
BOUT OF SICKNESS
BOWLING AVERAGE
BOWL OF CHERRIES
BOXER REBELLION
BOYS WILL BE BOYS
BRACING CLIMATE
BRADSHAW'S GUIDE
BRAHMS AND LISZT
BRAND AWARENESS
BREACH OF ORDERS

BREAD AND BUTTER
BREAD AND CHEESE
BREAD AND SCRAPE
BREADFRUIT TREE
BREAKFAST IN BED
BREAKFAST TABLE
BREAKNECK SPEED
BREAK NEW GROUND
BREAK ONE'S HEART
BREAK THE CORDON
BREAK THE RECORD
BREAK THE THREAD
BREAST THE WAVES
BREATHE HEAVILY
BREATHE REVENGE
BREATHING SPACE
BREATH OF SEA AIR
BREATH OF SPRING
BREEDER REACTOR
BREEDING GROUND
BREWERS' COMPANY
BRIEF ENCOUNTER
BRIEF INTERLUDE
BRIGHT AND EARLY
BRIGHT AS SILVER
BRIGHT PROSPECT
BRIGHT'S DISEASE
BRIGITTE BARDOT
BRIMFUL OF IDEAS
BRING GOOD CHEER
BRING IN A PROFIT
BRING INTO BEING
BRING INTO FOCUS
BRING TO ACCOUNT
BRING TO JUSTICE
BRING TO THE BOIL
BRING TO THE FORE
BRING UP THE REAR
BRISTOL CHANNEL
BRISTOL FASHION
BRITANNIA METAL
BRITISH BULLDOG
BRITISH COUNCIL
BRITISH DISEASE
BRITISH EMBASSY
BRITISH LIBRARY
BRITISH SUBJECT
BRITTLE AS GLASS
BROAD IN THE BEAM
BROAD SHOULDERS
BROADWAY MELODY
BROKEN CONTRACT
BROKEN MARRIAGE
BROKE THE WICKET
BROKE TO THE WIDE
BRONCHIAL TUBES

BROOKLYN BRIDGE
BROOK NO REFUSAL
BROTHER OFFICER
BROTHERS IN ARMS
BROUGHT TO LIGHT
BRUSH ONE'S TEETH
BRUSSELS CARPET
BUBBLEGUM MUSIC
BUBBLING STREAM
BUCKET AND SPADE
BUILDING BRICKS
BULIMIA NERVOSA
BULLDOG COURAGE
BULLET-PROOF CAR
BUMP OF LOCALITY
BUNCH OF BANANAS
BUNCH OF FLOWERS
BUNDLE OF NERVES
BURIED TREASURE
BURN AT THE STAKE
BURNHAM BEECHES
BURNISHED BRASS
BURNT SACRIFICE
BURNT TO A CINDER
BURST INTO FLAME
BURST INTO TEARS
BURST ONE'S BONDS
BURST THE BUBBLE
BURY ONE'S TALENT
BURY THE HATCHET
BUS CONDUCTRESS
BUSINESS CAREER
BUSINESS LETTER
BUSINESS MATTER
BUSINESS ON HAND
BUSINESS TYCOON
BUSMAN'S HOLIDAY
BUTTER MOUNTAIN
BUTTONS AND BOWS
BUY A PIG IN A POKE
BY A LONG STRETCH
BY PRESCRIPTION
BY THE SAME TOKEN

C – 14

CABBAGE LETTUCE
CABINET MEETING
CABINET PUDDING
CAGE ME A PEACOCK
CALAMINE LOTION
CALCIUM CARBIDE
CALCULATED ODDS
CALCULATED RISK
CALF'S-FOOT JELLY
CALLED TO THE BAR

CALL FOR A REPORT
CALLING ALL CARS
CALL IN QUESTION
CALL OFF ALL BETS
CALL OFF THE DOGS
CALM REFLECTION
CAMBRIDGE COACH
CAMP COMMANDANT
CAMPHORATED OIL
CAMPING HOLIDAY
CANADIAN POLICE
CANNED LAUGHTER
CANNING FACTORY
CANTEEN CULTURE
CANTERBURY BELL
CANTERBURY LAMB
CAPABLE OF PROOF
CAPE OF GOOD HOPE
CAPITAL OFFENCE
CAPITAL OF ITALY
CAPITAL OF SPAIN
CAPTAIN BOYCOTT
CAPTAIN SCARLET
CAPTIVE BALLOON
CARAVAN HOLIDAY
CARBON MONOXIDE
CARDEW ROBINSON
CARDIAC DISEASE
CARDINAL NEWMAN
CARDINAL NUMBER
CARDINAL POINTS
CARDINAL VIRTUE
CARDINAL WOLSEY
CAREFUL THOUGHT
CAR IMMOBILISER
CARMELITE ORDER
CARPET SLIPPERS
CARRIAGE RETURN
CARRY ONE'S POINT
CARTRIDGE PAPER
CASEMENT WINDOW
CASH ON DELIVERY
CAST ASPERSIONS
CAST INTO PRISON
CAST-IRON EXCUSE
CASTLE IN THE AIR
CASTLES IN SPAIN
CAST SHEEP'S EYES
CASUAL LABOURER
CASUAL OBSERVER
CAT AND MOUSE ACT
CATCH ONE'S DEATH
CATCH RED-HANDED
CATCH THE BREATH
CATHEDRAL CLOSE
CATHERINE BOYLE

CATHERINE WHEEL
CATHODE-RAY TUBE
CAT ON HOT BRICKS
CAT OUT OF THE BAG
CAUGHT IN A STORM
CAUGHT IN THE ACT
CAUGHT ON THE HOP
CAUGHT STEALING
CAUGHT UNAWARES
CAULIFLOWER EAR
CAUSE AND EFFECT
CAUSE A STOPPAGE
CAUSE CONFUSION
CAUSE FOR REGRET
CAUTIONARY TALE
CAVALRY OFFICER
CELESTIAL BLISS
CELESTIAL GLOBE
CENTRAL AMERICA
CENTRAL CASTING
CENTRAL HEATING
CENTRAL STATION
CERAMIC PLANTER
CERTAIN VICTORY
CHAINED TO A DESK
CHAIN OF COMMAND
CHAIN OF THOUGHT
CHAIR THE WINNER
CHALK AND CHEESE
CHALLENGE ROUND
CHALLENGER TANK
CHAMPAGNE GLASS
CHAMPAGNE LUNCH
CHAMPION GOLFER
CHAMPION JOCKEY
CHANCERY OFFICE
CHANGE OF BELIEF
CHANGE OF COURSE
CHANGE ONE'S LUCK
CHANGE ONE'S MIND
CHANGE ONE'S NAME
CHANGE ONE'S TUNE
CHANGE ONE'S WAYS
CHANGE PARTNERS
CHANGE THE ORDER
CHANGE THE VENUE
CHANNEL ISLANDS
CHANNEL STEAMER
CHANNEL SURFING
CHANNEL SWIMMER
CHAPTER HEADING
CHARACTER ACTOR
CHARACTER STUDY
CHARCOAL BURNER
CHARGE THE EARTH
CHARITABLE DEED

CHARITABLE GIFT
CHARITY MEETING
CHARLES CHAPLIN
CHARLES DICKENS
CHARLES GARVICE
CHARLIE CHESTER
CHARLOTTE RUSSE
CHARLTON HESTON
CHARMING FELLOW
CHARMING MANNER
CHARRED REMAINS
CHASE ME CHARLIE
CHASE THE DRAGON
CHEAP EXCURSION
CHECKING SYSTEM
CHEER TO THE ECHO
CHEESE SANDWICH
CHEMICAL CHANGE
CHEMICAL ENERGY
CHEMISTRY CLASS
CHESHIRE CHEESE
CHESTNUT SUNDAE
CHEST OF DRAWERS
CHEST PROTECTOR
CHEWING TOBACCO
CHICKEN IN ASPIC
CHIEF CONSTABLE
CHIEF EXECUTIVE
CHIEF INSPECTOR
CHILD ALLOWANCE
CHILD OF FORTUNE
CHILDREN'S NURSE
CHILDREN'S PARTY
CHILDREN'S STORY
CHINESE CRACKER
CHINESE LANTERN
CHINESE LAUNDRY
CHINESE TORTURE
CHINLESS WONDER
CHIPPING BARNET
CHIPPING NORTON
CHOCOLATE CREAM
CHOCOLATE WAFER
CHOPPED PARSLEY
CHRISTMAS BONUS
CHRISTMAS CAROL
CHRISTMAS CHEER
CHRISTMAS DAISY
CHRISTMAS PARTY
CHRISTOPHER FRY
CHROMATIC SCALE
CHRONIC INVALID
CHUCK OVERBOARD
CHUCK UP ONE'S JOB
CHURCH ASSEMBLY
CHURCH DOCTRINE

CHURCH MILITANT
CHURCH PROPERTY
CIGARETTE PAPER
CIRCLE THE EARTH
CIRCUIT BREAKER
CIRCULAR COURSE
CIRCULAR LETTER
CIRCULAR TICKET
CITY MAGISTRATE
CIVILIZED WORLD
CIVIL LIBERTIES
CLAIM ATTENTION
CLAIM THE REWARD
CLAP INTO PRISON
CLARENDON PRESS
CLASH OF CYMBALS
CLASS CONSCIOUS
CLASSICAL LATIN
CLASSICAL MUSIC
CLASSICAL TASTE
CLASSIC EXAMPLE
CLASSIC QUALITY
CLASSICS MASTER
CLASS PREJUDICE
CLEAN AS A NEW PIN
CLEAN ONE'S TEETH
CLEANSING CREAM
CLEAN THE SILVER
CLEAR AS CRYSTAL
CLEAR STATEMENT
CLEAR THE GROUND
CLEAR THE THROAT
CLEMENT WEATHER
CLERICAL COLLAR
CLERICAL DUTIES
CLERICAL WORKER
CLICK ONE'S HEELS
CLIMB A MOUNTAIN
CLIMBING PRICES
CLOAK AND DAGGER
CLOCKWORK TRAIN
CLOISTERED LIFE
CLOSE AN ACCOUNT
CLOSE ATTENTION
CLOSELY GUARDED
CLOSE ONE'S MOUTH
CLOSE PROXIMITY
CLOSE THE WINDOW
CLOSE TO THE WIND
CLOTHING COUPON
CLOUD FORMATION
CLOUT ON THE HEAD
CLUB MEMBERSHIP
CLUBS ARE TRUMPS
CLUSTER OF STARS
CLUTCH AT STRAWS

COACH AND HORSES
COALING STATION
COARSE LANGUAGE
COASTAL BATTERY
COASTAL COMMAND
COASTAL EROSION
COCK OF THE NORTH
COCKTAIL SHAKER
COFFEE STRAINER
COHERENT MANNER
COIN OF THE REALM
COLLAR ATTACHED
COLLECTED POEMS
COLLECTIVE FARM
COLLECTIVE NOUN
COLLECT ONESELF
COLLECTOR'S ITEM
COLLEGE PUDDING
COLLEGE STUDENT
COLONIAL OFFICE
COLONIAL SYSTEM
COLORADO BEETLE
COLOUR QUESTION
COLOUR SERGEANT
COMBINED EFFORT
COME BACK TO ERIN
COME DOWNSTAIRS
COMEDY OF ERRORS
COME FACE TO FACE
COME FROM BEHIND
COME FULL CIRCLE
COME-HITHER LOOK
COME INTO FAVOUR
COME ON THE SCENE
COME ROUND AGAIN
COME SECOND BEST
COME TO A DEAD-END
COME TO THE FRONT
COME TO THE POINT
COMFORTABLY OFF
COMIC INTERLUDE
COMING OF ARTHUR
COMING-OUT PARTY
COMMANDING LEAD
COMMAND OF WORDS
COMMAND RESPECT
COMMAND SILENCE
COMMAND SUPPORT
COMMERCIAL ROOM
COMMIT A FAUX PAS
COMMIT FOR TRIAL
COMMIT HARA-KIRI
COMMITTEE STAGE
COMMIT TO MEMORY
COMMIT TO PRISON
COMMON ANCESTOR

COMMON COURTESY
COMMON CURRENCY
COMMON ENTRANCE
COMMON FRONTIER
COMMON HUMANITY
COMMON INFORMER
COMMON INTEREST
COMMON MULTIPLE
COMMON NUISANCE
COMMON OR GARDEN
COMMON PARLANCE
COMMON PRACTICE
COMMON PROPERTY
COMMON SERJEANT
COMMUNION BREAD
COMMUNION TABLE
COMMUNIST PARTY
COMMUNITY CHEST
COMPANION PIECE
COMPANY MANNERS
COMPANY MATTERS
COMPANY MEETING
COMPANY OFFICER
COMPASS BEARING
COMPASS READING
COMPLEAT ANGLER
COMPLETE ANSWER
COMPLETE CHANGE
COMPLETE FIASCO
COMPONENT PARTS
COMPOSED MANNER
COMPOSE ONESELF
COMPUTER DATING
COMPUTER HACKER
COMPULSORY LOAN
COMRADES IN ARMS
CONCEALED DRIVE
CONCERT PIANIST
CONCRETE JUNGLE
CONDEMN TO DEATH
CONDUCT A SEARCH
CONFER A BENEFIT
CONFERENCE ROOM
CONFIRMED ENEMY
CONFIRMED HABIT
CONIFEROUS TREE
CONJUGAL RIGHTS
CONJURING TRICK
CONQUERING HERO
CONSIGN TO EARTH
CONSTANT READER
CONSTANT STRAIN
CONSTANT SUPPLY
CONSULTING ROOM
CONSUMER DEMAND
CONTAIN ONESELF

CONTINUITY GIRL
CONTRACT BRIDGE
CONTRARY ADVICE
CONTROLLED RENT
CONTROL ONESELF
CONVERSION LOAN
CONVEY A MEANING
COOKING UTENSIL
COPPER SULPHATE
COPS AND ROBBERS
COPYHOLD ESTATE
CORDIAL WELCOME
CORNFLOWER BLUE
CORNISH RIVIERA
CORONARY BYPASS
CORPORATION TAX
CORRUGATED IRON
COSMETIC MIRROR
COTTON EXCHANGE
COTTON INDUSTRY
COUNCIL CHAMBER
COUNCIL MEETING
COUNCIL OF STATE
COUNTLESS TIMES
COUNT ONE'S BEADS
COUNT ONE'S MONEY
COUNTRY BUMPKIN
COUNTRY COTTAGE
COUNTRY RETREAT
COUNTY PALATINE
COURSE OF ACTION
COURSE OF EVENTS
COURTING COUPLE
COURT OF INQUIRY
COURT OF JUSTICE
COURT PROCEDURE
COVERED WITH ICE
COVERING LETTER
CRACK OF THE WHIP
CRADLE SNATCHER
CRAMP ONE'S STYLE
CRANBERRY SAUCE
CRASH ONE'S GEARS
CRASS IGNORANCE
CRASS STUPIDITY
CREAM OF SOCIETY
CREATE AN EFFECT
CREATE AN UPROAR
CREATE A SCANDAL
CREATIVE ARTIST
CREATIVE GENIUS
CREATIVE WORKER
CREATIVE WRITER
CREDIBILITY GAP
CREDIT CUSTOMER
CREDIT TRANSFER

CRÈME DE LA CRÈME
CREST OF THE WAVE
CRICKET FIXTURE
CRICKET RESULTS
CRIME DETECTION
CRIME DOESN'T PAY
CRIME OF PASSION
CRIME PASSIONEL
CRIMINAL CHARGE
CRIMINAL LAWYER
CRIMINAL RECORD
CRINOLINE DRESS
CRITICAL MOMENT
CRITICAL PERIOD
CROCODILE TEARS
CROOK THE FINGER
CROSSED FINGERS
CROSS ONE'S HEART
CROSS REFERENCE
CROSS THE BORDER
CROSS THE BRIDGE
CROSS THE STREET
CROWN AND ANCHOR
CROWNING STROKE
CROWN OF THE HEAD
CROWN OF THE ROAD
CRUMBLING POWER
CRUMB OF COMFORT
CRUSHING DEFEAT
CRUSHING REMARK
CRUSHING RETORT
CRY ONE'S EYES OUT
CULTIVATED LAND
CULTIVATED MIND
CULTURAL CENTRE
CULTURE VULTURE
CUP FINAL TICKET
CUP OF HAPPINESS
CURB ONE'S TEMPER
CURDLE THE BLOOD
CURIOUS MIXTURE
CURRANT PUDDING
CURRENT ACCOUNT
CURRENT AFFAIRS
CURRENT EDITION
CURRENT FASHION
CURRENT OPINION
CURRIED CHICKEN
CURTAIN LECTURE
CURTAIN OF SMOKE
CUSTOM AND USAGE
CUSTOMS BARRIER
CUSTOMS OFFICER
CUT A FINE FIGURE
CUT A POOR FIGURE
CUT FOR PARTNERS

CUTLERS' COMPANY
CUT OFF ONE'S NOSE
CUT OFF THE JOINT
CUT-THROAT PRICE
CUT-THROAT RAZOR
CUTTING CONTEST

D – 14

DAILY ENDEAVOUR
DAILY HAPPENING
DAILY NEWSPAPER
DAILY TELEGRAPH
DAILY TRAVELLER
DAMAGING REPORT
DAME EDITH EVANS
DAME ELLEN TERRY
DANCE PROGRAMME
DANCING ACADEMY
DANCING DERVISH
DANCING LICENCE
DANCING PARTNER
DANGEROUSLY ILL
DARING YOUNG MAN
DARK COMPLEXION
DARKEN ONE'S DOOR
DAVID TOMLINSON
DAVID WHITFIELD
DAY IN AND DAY OUT
DAYLIGHT SAVING
DAY OF ATONEMENT
DAY OF RECKONING
DAY OF THE JACKAL
DAZZLING BEAUTY
DEAD MAN'S HANDLE
DEAD SEA SCROLLS
DEAD TO THE WORLD
DEAL A DEATH BLOW
DEAN AND CHAPTER
DEAR AT THE PRICE
DEAR JOHN LETTER
DEATH BY BURNING
DEATHLY SILENCE
DEBASED COINAGE
DEBATABLE POINT
DEBIT AND CREDIT
DECEIVE ONESELF
DECENT INTERVAL
DECENTLY HOUSED
DECIDING FACTOR
DECIMAL COINAGE
DECISIVE FACTOR
DECLINE AND FALL
DECLINE IN VALUE
DECLINE TO STAND
DECLINING YEARS

DECREE ABSOLUTE
DEEP DEPRESSION
DEEPLY AFFECTED
DEEPLY OFFENDED
DEEP REFLECTION
DEEP-SEA FISHING
DEFEAT THE ENEMY
DEFENCE COUNSEL
DEFENCE IN DEPTH
DEFENCE MEASURE
DEFENCE WITNESS
DEFERRED SHARES
DEFINITE FIGURE
DEFRAY EXPENSES
DEGREES OF FROST
DELAYING ACTION
DELICATE HEALTH
DELICIOUS TASTE
DELIVER A SERMON
DELIVER A SPEECH
DEMAND A HEARING
DEMAND A RE-COUNT
DEMAND ENTRANCE
DEMAND SECURITY
DENTAL PRACTICE
DEPARTED SPIRIT
DEPART FROM LIFE
DEPARTING GUEST
DEPOSIT ACCOUNT
DEPRESSED CLASS
DEPRESSING NEWS
DEPRIVED PERSON
DEPTH OF FEELING
DEPTHS OF MISERY
DEPUTY CHAIRMAN
DERBY FAVOURITE
DERELICT VESSEL
DEROGATORY TERM
DESERT ONE'S POST
DESIRABLE THING
DESPATCH BY MAIL
DESPERATE STATE
DETACHED MANNER
DETAILED REPORT
DETECTIVE NOVEL
DETECTIVE STORY
DETENTION ORDER
DEVELOP THE MIND
DEVIL INCARNATE
DEVIL OF A TEMPER
DEVIL'S ADVOCATE
DEVIL'S DISCIPLE
DEVIL'S TRIANGLE
DEVOTED ADMIRER
DEVOTED HUSBAND
DEVOTION TO DUTY

DIAMOND JUBILEE
DIAMOND WEDDING
DIARY OF A NOBODY
DICTATE A LETTER
DICTATION SPEED
DICTIONARY WORD
DIE IN ONE'S SHOES
DIEU ET MON DROIT
DIFFERENT ANGLE
DIFFICULT CATCH
DIFFICULT CLIMB
DIG IN ONE'S HEELS
DIGITAL MAPPING
DIGNIFIED STYLE
DIG ONE'S SPURS IN
DIMINUTIVE SIZE
DING-DONG BATTLE
DINNER AND DANCE
DINNER IS SERVED
DIPLOMATIC BODY
DIPLOMATIC MOVE
DIRECT APPROACH
DIRECT EVIDENCE
DIRECT OPPOSITE
DIRECT QUESTION
DIRECT TAXATION
DISABLED PERSON
DISCHARGED A DEBT
DISCORDANT NOTE
DISCOUNT BROKER
DISGUISED VOICE
DISORDERED MIND
DISTILLED WATER
DISTORTED IMAGE
DISTRESSED AREA
DISTRESS SIGNAL
DISTURBED NIGHT
DISTURBED SLEEP
DIVIDE BY ELEVEN
DIVIDE BY TWELVE
DIVIDED LOYALTY
DIVIDE THE HOUSE
DIVISION OF WORK
DIVORCED PERSON
DOCTOR BARNARDO
DOCTORS' COMMONS
DOCTOR'S DILEMMA
DOCTOR'S MANDATE
DODGE THE COLUMN
DOG IN THE MANGER
DOLL'S FURNITURE
DOMESTIC ANIMAL
DOMESTIC DRUDGE
DOMESTIC POLICY
DOMINION STATUS
DONALD CAMPBELL

DONKEY SERENADE
DO ONESELF PROUD
DOROTHY PERKINS
DOSE OF MEDICINE
DOT AND CARRY ONE
DOUBLE EIGHTEEN
DOUBLE ENTENDRE
DOUBLE EXPOSURE
DOUBLE FOURTEEN
DOUBLE NEGATIVE
DOUBLE NINETEEN
DOUBLE STANDARD
DOUBLE STOPPING
DOUBLET AND HOSE
DOUBLE THIRTEEN
DOUBTFUL FUTURE
DOUBTFUL ORIGIN
DOUBTFUL TEMPER
DOUBTING THOMAS
DOUGHTY WARRIOR
DOWAGER DUCHESS
DOWN IN THE DUMPS
DOWN IN THE MOUTH
DOWN IN THE WORLD
DOWN LAMBETH WAY
DOWN MEMORY LANE
DOWN ON ONE'S LUCK
DOWNSTAIRS ROOM
DOWN THE CHIMNEY
DOWNWARD MOTION
DOWNWARD STROKE
DOZENS OF PEOPLE
DRAIN ONE'S GLASS
DRAMATIC CRITIC
DRAMATIC EFFECT
DRAMATIC FINISH
DRAPERS' COMPANY
DRAWERS OF WATER
DRAW FIRST BLOOD
DRAW THE CURTAIN
DRAW THE LONG-BOW
DRAW THE RATIONS
DREAMING SPIRES
DREGS OF SOCIETY
DRESSED IN BLACK
DRESSED OVER ALL
DRESS FOR DINNER
DRESS REHEARSAL
DRINKING HABITS
DRINKING TROUGH
DRINKING VESSEL
DRINK LIKE A FISH
DRIVE CAREFULLY
DRIVE TO DESPAIR
DRIVE TO THE WALL
DRIVING LICENCE

DROP FROM THE SKY
DROP IN THE OCEAN
DROP OFF TO SLEEP
DROP THE SUBJECT
DROWNED IN TEARS
DUBIOUS COMPANY
DUBLIN BAY PRAWN
DUCKS AND DRAKES
DUELLING PISTOL
DUEL TO THE DEATH
DUKE OF BURGUNDY
DUKE OF CLARENCE
DUKE OF CORNWALL
DUPLICATE SHEET
DURATION OF LIFE
DURING THE NIGHT
DUTY-FREE DRINKS
DWELL ON THE PAST
DYING FOR A DRINK

E – 14

EACH FOR HIMSELF
EARL OF HAREWOOD
EARLY BREAKFAST
EARLY VICTORIAN
EARN ONE'S LIVING
EARTH SATELLITE
EAR TO THE GROUND
EASE OF HANDLING
EASTER HOLIDAYS
EASTER OFFERING
EASTER VACATION
EASY COME, EASY GO
EASY CONSCIENCE
EASY IN ONE'S MIND
EAT ONE'S HEAD OFF
ECONOMIC CRISIS
ECONOMY OF WORDS
EDITORIAL CHAIR
EDITORIAL STAFF
EDUCATE THE MIND
EDUCATIONAL TOY
EDWARDIAN HOUSE
EFFICIENCY TEST
EIGHTEEN AND SIX
EIGHTEENTH HOLE
EIGHTH OF AUGUST
EIGHTH SYMPHONY
EIGHTY THOUSAND
ELABORATE STYLE
ELDERBERRY WINE
ELDER STATESMAN
ELDEST DAUGHTER
ELECTION RESULT
ELECTRICAL UNIT

ELECTRIC CHARGE
ELECTRICAL COOKER
ELECTRIC GUITAR
ELECTRIC HEATER
ELECTRICITY CUT
ELECTRIC KETTLE
ELECTRIC SHAVER
ELECTRIC WASHER
ELECTRONIC MAIL
ELEMENTARY RULE
ELEMENT OF DOUBT
ELEMENT OF TRUTH
ELEPHANT'S TRUNK
ELEVEN OR TWELVE
ELEVENTH LETTER
ELEVENTH OF JULY
ELEVENTH OF JUNE
ELEVEN THOUSAND
ELICIT THE TRUTH
ELIZABETHAN AGE
ELIZABETHAN ERA
ELIZA DOOLITTLE
ELLA FITZGERALD
ELOCUTION CLASS
ELOQUENT TONGUE
EMINENT SOLDIER
EMINENT SPEAKER
EMOTIONAL WRECK
EMPEROR OF JAPAN
EMPHATICAL DENIAL
EMPIRE LOYALIST
EMPTY OF MEANING
EMPTY PLEASURES
ENCLOSE A CHEQUE
ENDEARING SMILE
ENDLESS PROBLEM
ENDLESS TROUBLE
END OF ALL THINGS
END OF THE MATTER
END OF THE STREET
ENDS OF THE EARTH
ENDURE TO THE END
ENEMY OF FREEDOM
ENEMY OF MANKIND
ENEMY TERRITORY
ENFANT TERRIBLE
ENGAGED IN TRADE
ENGAGEMENT RING
ENGAGE THE ENEMY
ENGAGING MANNER
ENGLISH BY BIRTH
ENGLISH CHANNEL
ENGLISH GRAMMAR
ENGLISH HISTORY
ENGLISH MUSTARD
ENGLISH TEACHER

ENIGMATIC SMILE
ENJOY ILL HEALTH
ENLARGE THE MIND
ENLIGHTENED AGE
ENORMOUS NUMBER
ENTERTAIN A HOPE
ENTER THE CHURCH
ENTRECOTE STEAK
EQUABLE CLIMATE
EQUALLY DIVIDED
EQUAL THE RECORD
ERRATIC CONDUCT
ESCAPED CONVICT
ESPRESSO COFFEE
ESTUARY ENGLISH
ETHEREAL BEAUTY
EUCALYPTUS TREE
EVADE DETECTION
EVAPORATED MILK
EVENING CLOTHES
EVENING SERVICE
EVERGREEN PLANT
EVERGREEN SHRUB
EVERY BIT AS MUCH
EVERY INCH A KING
EVERY SECOND DAY
EVERYTHING GOES
EVIDENCE ON OATH
EVIL REPUTATION
EXACTING MASTER
EXCEED THE LIMIT
EXCELLENT MARKS
EXCHANGE OF VOWS
EXCHANGE VISITS
EXCITABLE STATE
EXCURSION TRAIN
EXCUSE MY FRENCH
EXECUTION BLOCK
EXECUTIVE SUITE
EXERT AUTHORITY
EXHIBIT FEELING
EXPANSIVE SMILE
EXPENSE ACCOUNT
EXPLAIN ONESELF
EXPLODED BELIEF
EXPORT MERCHANT
EXPOSE TO DANGER
EXPRESS COMMAND
EXPRESS ONESELF
EXPRESS PURPOSE
EXPRESS REGRETS
EXPURGATED BOOK
EXQUISITE TASTE
EXTENDED CREDIT
EXTENDED FAMILY
EXTENSIVE FIELD

EXTENSIVE SALES
EXTINCT VOLCANO
EXTREME DISLIKE
EXTREME PENALTY
EXTREME POVERTY
EXTREME UNCTION
EYE FOR BUSINESS

F – 14

FABULOUS WEALTH
FABULOUS WRITER
FACE OF THE GLOBE
FACE UP TO THINGS
FACIAL SOLARIUM
FACT AND FICTION
FACTORY CHIMNEY
FACTS OF THE CASE
FAIL IN ONE'S DUTY
FAIL TO INTEREST
FAIR COMPARISON
FAIR COMPLEXION
FAIR TO MIDDLING
FAIR TO MODERATE
FAIRY GODMOTHER
FAITHFUL FRIEND
FAITHFUL REPORT
FAITHFUL SPOUSE
FALL DOWNSTAIRS
FALL INTO DISUSE
FALL ON EVIL DAYS
FALL ON ONE'S FEET
FALSE COLOURING
FALSE EYELASHES
FALSELY ACCUSED
FALSE MOUSTACHE
FALSE PRETENCES
FALSE REASONING
FALSE STATEMENT
FALTERING STEPS
FALTERING VOICE
FAME AND FORTUNE
FAMILIAR MANNER
FAMILIAR SPIRIT
FAMILY BUSINESS
FAMILY HEIRLOOM
FAMILY LIKENESS
FAMILY PORTRAIT
FAMILY RETAINER
FAMILY SKELETON
FANCY-DRESS BALL
FAREWELL SPEECH
FAREWELL TO ARMS
FAR-FLUNG EMPIRE
FARMING SUBSIDY
FAST AND FURIOUS

FATALLY WOUNDED
FATHER SUPERIOR
FAT-STOCK PRICES
FATUOUS ATTEMPT
FAVOURABLE WIND
FAVOURED PERSON
FAVOURITE PIECE
FEARLESS HITTER
FEAST OF STEPHEN
FEAT OF STRENGTH
FEATURE PICTURE
FEATURES EDITOR
FEDERAL COUNCIL
FEDERAL RESERVE
FEEL THE BENEFIT
FEEL THE DRAUGHT
FELLOW COMMONER
FELLOW CREATURE
FEMININE APPEAL
FEMININE GENDER
FEMME DE CHAMBRE
FEND FOR ONESELF
FEVERISH DESIRE
FICTITIOUS NAME
FIELD AMBULANCE
FIELD ARTILLERY
FIELD OF INQUIRY
FIELD TELEGRAPH
FIFTEEN PER CENT
FIFTEENTH GREEN
FIFTEENTH OF MAY
FIFTEENTH ROUND
FIFTH AMENDMENT
FIFTH COLUMNIST
FIFTH OF JANUARY
FIFTH OF OCTOBER
FIGHTER COMMAND
FIGHTING CHANCE
FIGHTING SPIRIT
FIGHT TO A FINISH
FIGURE OF SPEECH
FILLETED PLAICE
FILLING STATION
FILL THE VACANCY
FILL UP THE RANKS
FILL WITH DISMAY
FILTHY LANGUAGE
FINAL INTENTION
FINAL RECKONING
FINANCIAL TIMES
FINANCIAL WORRY
FIND A PUBLISHER
FINDERS, KEEPERS
FIND THE MEANING
FINGER IN THE PIE
FINGERS AND TOES

FINGER'S BREADTH
FINIAN'S RAINBOW
FINISHING TOUCH
FINISH STRONGLY
FINITE QUANTITY
FIRE A BROADSIDE
FIRE DEPARTMENT
FIREMAN'S HELMET
FIREMAN'S LADDER
FIRE PROTECTION
FIRM CONVICTION
FIRM FOUNDATION
FIRM GOVERNMENT
FIRM IMPRESSION
FIRM MANAGEMENT
FIRM OPPOSITION
FIRST AND SECOND
FIRST-BORN CHILD
FIRST CHRISTMAS
FIRST-CLASS FARE
FIRST-CLASS IDEA
FIRST-CLASS SHOT
FIRST CONDITION
FIRST-FLOOR FLAT
FIRST INTENTION
FIRST MAGNITUDE
FIRST OF JANUARY
FIRST OF OCTOBER
FIRST ON THE LIST
FIRST PRINCIPLE
FIRST-RATE ACTOR
FIRST SECRETARY
FIRST TIME LUCKY
FIRST TIME ROUND
FIRST VIOLINIST
FISHERMAN'S YARN
FISHING LICENCE
FISHING VILLAGE
FISH OUT OF WATER
FIT OF GIDDINESS
FIT THE OCCASION
FIVE-BARRED GATE
FIVE-DOLLAR BILL
FIVE OF DIAMONDS
FIXED ALLOWANCE
FLAG LIEUTENANT
FLAG OF DISTRESS
FLASHING STREAM
FLAT AS A PANCAKE
FLAT ON ONE'S BACK
FLAT ON ONE'S FACE
FLATTER ONESELF
FLEE THE COUNTRY
FLEETING GLANCE
FLIGHT OF STAIRS
FLIGHT RECORDER

FLIGHT SERGEANT
FLIPPANT SPEECH
FLOATING BRIDGE
FLOATING KIDNEY
FLOATING PALACE
FLOCK OF PIGEONS
FLOG A DEAD HORSE
FLOOD WITH LIGHT
FLOWERING PLANT
FLOWERING SHRUB
FLUSH OF TRIUMPH
FLUSH WITH ANGER
FLUSH WITH MONEY
FLY FOR ONE'S LIFE
FLYING BEDSTEAD
FLYING BUTTRESS
FLYING DUTCHMAN
FLYING FORTRESS
FLYING SCOTSMAN
FLYING SQUIRREL
FLY INTO A TEMPER
FLY TO THE RESCUE
FLY-WEIGHT TITLE
FOAM AT THE MOUTH
FOLD UP ONE'S TENT
FOLLOW A CALLING
FOLLOW A PATTERN
FOLLOW MY LEADER
FOLLOW ONE'S NOSE
FOLLOW THE CROWD
FOLLOW THE SCENT
FOLLOW THE TRAIL
FOOD CONTROLLER
FOOD FOR THE GODS
FOOD FOR THE MIND
FOOD FOR THOUGHT
FOOD PRODUCTION
FOOTBALL COUPON
FOOTBALL GROUND
FOOTBALL LEAGUE
FOOTBALL PLAYER
FOOTBALL SEASON
FOR ALL THE WORLD
FORBIDDEN FRUIT
FORBID THE BANNS
FORCED MARRIAGE
FORCE OF GRAVITY
FORCIBLE DEMAND
FOREIGN AFFAIRS
FOREIGN CAPITAL
FOREIGN COUNTRY
FOREIGN SERVICE
FOREIGN STATION
FOR EVER AND A DAY
FOR EVER AND EVER
FOR HEAVEN'S SAKE!

FOR LOVE OR MONEY
FORMAL APPROACH
FORMAL OCCASION
FORMAL SANCTION
FORM AN ESTIMATE
FORMATIVE YEARS
FORMIDABLE TASK
FOR THE DURATION
FOR THE HIGH JUMP
FOR THE LAST TIME
FOR THE LIFE OF ME
FOR THE MOST PART
FORTUNATE EVENT
FOR WANT OF A NAIL
FOSTER DAUGHTER
FOUNDER'S SHARES
FOUR-DOOR SALOON
FOUR-LEAF CLOVER
FOUR-LETTER WORD
FOUR-MASTED SHIP
FOUR-MILE RADIUS
FOUR-MINUTE MILE
FOUR OF DIAMONDS
FOURPENNY STAMP
FOURTEEN OUNCES
FOURTEEN POUNDS
FOURTEENTH HOLE
FOURTH DIVIDEND
FOURTH DIVISION
FOURTH OF AUGUST
FOURTH SYMPHONY
FRACTIONAL PART
FRAGRANT MEMORY
FRAIL STRUCTURE
FRANK STATEMENT
FRED FLINTSTONE
FREEDOM FROM WAR
FREE ENTERPRISE
FREE FROM DANGER
FREEMASONS' HALL
FREE OF INTEREST
FREEZING MANNER
FRENCH CANADIAN
FRENCH DRESSING
FRENCH LANGUAGE
FRENCH POLISHER
FRENCH VERMOUTH
FRESHWATER FISH
FREUDIAN SCHOOL
FRIENDLY ACTION
FRIENDLY CRITIC
FRIENDLY DEBATE
FRIENDLY NATION
FRIGHTFUL SIGHT
FROM BAD TO WORSE
FROM BANK TO BANK

FROM EAST TO WEST
FROM HAND TO HAND
FROM HEAD TO FOOT
FROM SIDE TO SIDE
FROM THE CONTEXT
FROM TIME TO TIME
FROM WALL TO WALL
FRONT ELEVATION
FRONT-PAGE STORY
FROTH AND BUBBLE
FROZEN SHOULDER
FULFIL A PROMISE
FULHAM BROADWAY
FULL COMPLEMENT
FULL DIRECTIONS
FULL EMPLOYMENT
FULL MEMBERSHIP
FULL OF INTEREST
FULL OF MISCHIEF
FULL OF NONSENSE
FULL OF VITALITY
FULL-SCALE MODEL
FULL SETTLEMENT
FULL SPEED AHEAD
FULL STEAM AHEAD
FULL TO CAPACITY
FULLY CONSCIOUS
FULLY DEVELOPED
FULLY FASHIONED
FULLY FURNISHED
FUNERAL ORATION
FUNERAL PARLOUR
FUNNY PROGRAMME
FUR-LINED GLOVES
FURNISHED HOUSE
FURNISH SUPPORT
FURNITURE STORE
FURTHER DETAILS
FURTHER OUTLOOK

G – 14

GAIN ADMITTANCE
GAIN CONFIDENCE
GAIN EXPERIENCE
GAIN POSSESSION
GAINS AND LOSSES
GAIN THE MASTERY
GAIN THE VICTORY
GALLANT COMPANY
GALLANT SOLDIER
GALLOPING MAJOR
GALVANIZED IRON
GAMBLING CHANCE
GAME OF DRAUGHTS
GAME OF SKITTLES

GARBLED VERSION
GARGANTUAN MEAL
GARLAND OF ROSES
GATHERING STORM
GATHER MOMENTUM
GATHER STRENGTH
GATHER TOGETHER
GATWICK AIRPORT
GENERAL AMNESTY
GENERAL BENEFIT
GENERAL CONSENT
GENERAL COUNCIL
GENERAL MANAGER
GENERAL MEETING
GENERAL OFFICER
GENERAL OUTLINE
GENERAL OUTLOOK
GENERAL POVERTY
GENERAL RELEASE
GENERAL ROUTINE
GENERAL SERVANT
GENERAL SERVICE
GENERAL SURGEON
GENERAL SURGERY
GENERAL WARRANT
GENEROUS AMOUNT
GENEROUS NATURE
GENEROUS PRAISE
GENEROUS SPIRIT
GENIE OF THE LAMP
GENTLE BREEDING
GENTLE HANDLING
GENTLEMAN CROOK
GENTLEMAN'S CODE
GENTLEMAN USHER
GENTLE REMINDER
GENUINE ARTICLE
GENUINE EXAMPLE
GENUINE RESPECT
GEORGE BRADSHAW
GEORGE GERSHWIN
GEORGE HARRISON
GEORGE MEREDITH
GEORGE MITCHELL
GEORGES SIMENON
GERMAN LANGUAGE
GET AN EXTENSION
GET INTO TROUBLE
GET IT IN THE NECK
GET OFF SCOT-FREE
GET ONE'S DESERTS
GET ONE'S FEET WET
GET ONE'S OWN BACK
GET OUT OF THE WAY
GET THE BEST OF IT
GET THE BETTER OF

GET THE BREEZE UP
GET THE HANG OF IT
GET THE WHIP-HAND
GHASTLY MISTAKE
GHOST OF A CHANCE
GIANT REFRESHED
GIANT'S CAUSEWAY
GIFTED COMPOSER
GILBERT HARDING
GIMCRACK STAKES
GINGERBREAD MAN
GIRD UP THE LOINS
GIRL IN A MILLION
GIVE A MAN HIS DUE
GIVE AN INSTANCE
GIVE ASSISTANCE
GIVE ASSURANCES
GIVE FULL CREDIT
GIVE GENEROUSLY
GIVE IN MARRIAGE
GIVE IT A THOUGHT
GIVEN A REPRIEVE
GIVE ONE A ROCKET
GIVE ONE HIS HEAD
GIVE ONE'S ASSENT
GIVE ONE THE BIRD
GIVE ONE THE PUSH
GIVE ONE THE SLIP
GIVE PERMISSION
GIVE THE GLAD EYE
GIVE TO THE WORLD
GIVE UP DRINKING
GIVE UP ONE'S SEAT
GIVE UP THE GHOST
GLAMOROUS NIGHT
GLARING MISTAKE
GLASGOW RANGERS
GLEAMING ARMOUR
GLOBE ARTICHOKE
GLOOMY FORECAST
GLOOMY PROSPECT
GLORIOUS MUDDLE
GLORIOUS SUNSET
GLOSSY MAGAZINE
GLOWING ACCOUNT
GLOWING COLOURS
GLOW WITH HEALTH
GLUTTON FOR FOOD
GLUTTON FOR WORK
GNASH ONE'S TEETH
GNOMES OF ZURICH
GO DOWN FIGHTING
GOD SAVE THE KING!
GOD'S OWN COUNTRY
GOING! GOING! GONE!
GOING GREAT GUNS

GOING TO THE DOGS
GO INTO HOSPITAL
GO INTO MOURNING
GO INTO RAPTURES
GOLDEN PHEASANT
GOLDEN TREASURY
GOLSMITHS' HALL
GOLF TOURNAMENT
GO LIKE HOT CAKES
GONE BY THE BOARD
GONE FOR A BURTON
GOOD BACKGROUND
GOOD-BYE MR CHIPS
GOOD COMPANIONS
GOOD COMPLEXION
GOOD CONSCIENCE
GOOD DISCIPLINE
GOOD FELLOWSHIP
GOOD FOR NOTHING
GOOD FOR THE SOUL
GOOD FOUNDATION
GOOD IMPRESSION
GOOD INTENTIONS
GOOD INVESTMENT
GOOD LITERATURE
GOOD MANAGEMENT
GOOD NEIGHBOURS
GOOD REPUTATION
GOOD RESOLUTION
GOODS IN TRANSIT
GOOD TIME-KEEPER
GOOD UPBRINGING
GO OFF LIKE A BOMB
GO OFF THE HANDLE
GOOSEBERRY BUSH
GOOSEBERRY FOOL
GO OUT OF ONE'S WAY
GORDON RICHARDS
GO TO ANY LENGTHS
GO TO CONFESSION
GO TO THE COUNTRY
GO TO THE SEASIDE
GO TO THE THEATRE
GO UP IN THE WORLD
GOVERNMENT LOAN
GOVERNMENT POST
GOVERNMENT WHIP
GO WEST, YOUNG MAN
GO WITH THE TIMES
GRACE AND FAVOUR
GRACIOUS LIVING
GRADUAL DECLINE
GRADUATED SCALE
GRAIN OF COMFORT
GRAIN OF MUSTARD
GRAND COMMITTEE

GRAND CONDITION
GRANDSTAND VIEW
GRAPHIC ACCOUNT
GRAPHIC DRAWING
GRAPHITE DRIVER
GRASP THE NETTLE
GRAVE ADMISSION
GRAVE SITUATION
GRAVE STATEMENT
GRAVE SUSPICION
GRAVEYARD COUGH
GRAVEYARD SHIFT
GREASE ONE'S PALM
GREAT BED OF WARE
GREAT IGNORANCE
GREAT INJUSTICE
GREAT IN STATURE
GREAT NORTH ROAD
GREAT RECEPTION
GREAT SACRIFICE
GREAT SCOUNDREL
GREAT STATESMAN
GREAT VARIATION
GRECIAN PROFILE
GREEN CROSS CODE
GREENHAM COMMON
GREEN LABELLING
GREEN LINE COACH
GREEN VEGETABLE
GRENADIER GUARD
GREYHOUND DERBY
GREYHOUND TRACK
GRIND ONE'S TEETH
GRIST TO THE MILL
GROCERS' COMPANY
GROPE IN THE DARK
GROSS INJUSTICE
GROSVENOR HOUSE
GROUND LANDLORD
GROUNDLESS FEAR
GROUSE SHOOTING
GROWING ANXIETY
GROW UP TOGETHER
GROW VEGETABLES
GRUB STREET HACK
GRUDGING PRAISE
GUARDIAN ANGELS
GUERRILLA CHIEF
GUERRILLA FORCE
GUESS THE ANSWER
GUEST CELEBRITY
GUIDED BY REASON
GUILTY OF MURDER
GUN EMPLACEMENT
GURKHA REGIMENT
GUTTURAL ACCENT

GUTTURAL SPEECH

H – 14

HACKNEY MARSHES
HALF-DAY HOLIDAY
HALF-MOON STREET
HALF-SPOKEN WORD
HALLÉ ORCHESTRA
HALLOWEEN PARTY
HALT FOR A MOMENT
HAMMER AND TONGS
HAMPSTEAD HEATH
HAND EMBROIDERY
HANDLE TENDERLY
HANDLE WITH CARE
HAND ON THE TORCH
HANDS-OFF POLICY
HANDSOME MARGIN
HANDSOME PROFIT
HANGING GARDENS
HANG OUT A SIGNAL
HANG THE EXPENSE
HANNIBAL LECTER
HAPPILY MARRIED
HAPPY CHILDHOOD
HAPPY CHRISTMAS
HARBOUR REVENGE
HARD DISCIPLINE
HARDENED SINNER
HARDLY ANYTHING
HARDLY CREDIBLE
HARD NUT TO CRACK
HARD TASKMASTER
HARD TO CONVINCE
HARD TO DESCRIBE
HARRIER JUMP-JET
HARRY BELAFONTE
HARSH TREATMENT
HAUNTING MELODY
HAVE A GOOD NIGHT
HAVE A SUSPICION
HAVE COMPASSION
HAVE CONFIDENCE
HAVE IT BOTH WAYS
HAVE MISGIVINGS
HAVE NO SCRUPLES
HAVE ONE'S DOUBTS
HAVE ONE'S OWN WAY
HAVE THE COURAGE
HAVE THE KNOW-HOW
HEAD ABOVE WATER
HEADACHE POWDER
HEAD FOR FIGURES
HEAD FOR HEIGHTS
HEADLONG FLIGHT

HEAD OF THE HOUSE
HEAD OF THE RIVER
HEAD OF THE TABLE
HEALTH-FOOD SHOP
HEALTHY OUTLOOK
HEALTHY RESPECT
HEART CONDITION
HEART OF ENGLAND
HEARTS AND MINDS
HEARTY APPETITE
HEARTY APPROVAL
HEARTY LAUGHTER
HEATED ARGUMENT
HEATHER MIXTURE
HEAVEN AND EARTH
HEAVIER THAN AIR
HEAVY ARTILLERY
HEAVY TRANSPORT
HEAVY WITH SLEEP
HEEL OF ACHILLES
HEIGHT OF GENIUS
HEIGHT OF SUMMER
HEIR TO A FORTUNE
HELD IN CONTEMPT
HELL-FIRE CORNER
HELL FOR LEATHER
HELL HATH NO FURY
HELPLESS VICTIM
HELP ONE ANOTHER
HEMEL HEMPSTEAD
HENLEY ON THAMES
HENRY KISSINGER
HENRY THE EIGHTH
HENRY THE FOURTH
HENRY THE SECOND
HERALDIC COLOUR
HERALDIC DEVICE
HERALDIC SHIELD
HERALD'S COLLEGE
HERBAL MEDICINE
HERBERT SPENCER
HEREFORD CASTLE
HERO AND LEANDER
HIDDEN TREASURE
HIGH AS A STEEPLE
HIGH CASUALTIES
HIGH CHANCELLOR
HIGH COMMISSION
HIGH COURT JUDGE
HIGH IN THE SCALE
HIGHLAND CATTLE
HIGH-LEVEL TALKS
HIGHLY EDUCATED
HIGHLY ESTEEMED
HIGHLY ORIGINAL
HIGHLY POLISHED

HIGHLY POSSIBLE
HIGHLY SEASONED
HIGH PERCENTAGE
HIGH SPEED TRAIN
HIGHWAY ROBBERY
HIP MEASUREMENT
HISTORICAL PLAY
HISTORICAL WORK
HISTORIC MOMENT
HISTORY TEACHER
HIT OVER THE HEAD
HIVE OF ACTIVITY
HIVE OF INDUSTRY
HOBNAILED BOOTS
HOLD AN ARGUMENT
HOLD AN ELECTION
HOLD EVERYTHING
HOLD IN ABEYANCE
HOLD IN CONTEMPT
HOLDING COMPANY
HOLDING PATTERN
HOLDING QUALITY
HOLD IN SUSPENSE
HOLD ONE'S BREATH
HOLD ONE'S GROUND
HOLD ONE'S HEAD UP
HOLD ONE'S HORSES
HOLD ONE'S TONGUE
HOLD UP ONE'S HEAD
HOLIDAY TRAFFIC
HOLIDAY WITH PAY
HOLIER THAN THOU
HOLLOWAY PRISON
HOLLOW LAUGHTER
HOLLOW PRETENCE
HOME DEPARTMENT
HOMELESS PERSON
HOME ON THE RANGE
HOMES FOR HEROES
HONEYMOON HOTEL
HONKY-TONK PIANO
HONORARY DEGREE
HONORARY FELLOW
HONORARY MEMBER
HONORARY STATUS
HONOUR AND GLORY
HOPE AND BELIEVE
HOPE FOR THE BEST
HOPELESS MISFIT
HOP, SKIP AND JUMP
HORIZONTAL BARS
HORIZONTAL LINE
HORSE AND HOUNDS
HORSE ARTILLERY
HORSE OF THE YEAR
HOSPITAL ANNEXE

HOSPITAL MATRON
HOSPITAL SUNDAY
HOSTILE COUNTRY
HOSTILE VERDICT
HOSTILE WITNESS
HOT-AIR MERCHANT
HOT AND BOTHERED
HOTEL DETECTIVE
HOTLY CONTESTED
HOT ON ONE'S HEELS
HOT ON ONE'S TRAIL
HOT-WATER BOTTLE
HOT-WATER SUPPLY
HOT-WATER SYSTEM
HOUSE DECORATOR
HOUSE DETECTIVE
HOUSEHOLD GOODS
HOUSEHOLD LINEN
HOUSEHOLD STAFF
HOUSEMAID'S KNEE
HOUSE OF COMMONS
HOUSE OF HANOVER
HOUSE OF ONE'S OWN
HOUSE OF THE LORD
HOUSE OF WINDSOR
HOUSE OF WORSHIP
HOUSE PHYSICIAN
HOUSING PROBLEM
HOUSING PROJECT
HOWLING DERVISH
HOWLING SUCCESS
HOW THE LAND LIES
HUMAN ENDEAVOUR
HUMAN RELATIONS
HUMAN SACRIFICE
HUMAN SUFFERING
HUMBLE DWELLING
HUMBLE PETITION
HUMPBACK BRIDGE
HUMPHREY BOGART
HUNDRED DOLLARS
HUNDRED GUINEAS
HUNDRED PER CENT
HUNG PARLIAMENT
HUNT HIGH AND LOW
HUNT THE SLIPPER
HUNT THE THIMBLE
HURT EXPRESSION
HUSBAND AND WIFE
HYDE PARK CORNER
HYDE PARK ORATOR
HYDRAULIC POWER
HYDRAULIC PRESS
HYPHENATED WORD
HYPNOTIC TRANCE

1 – 14

ICE-CREAM CORNET
ICE-CREAM SUNDAE
IDEAL COMPANION
IDENTICAL TWINS
IDENTITY PARADE
IGNOMINIOUS END
IGNORANT MASSES
IGNORANT PERSON
ILLEGAL TRAFFIC
ILL-GOTTEN GAINS
ILL-TIMED REMARK
IMAGINARY POINT
IMMEDIATE REPLY
IMMEMORIAL ELMS
IMMINENT DANGER
IMMORAL CONDUCT
IMMOVABLE FEAST
IMPART MOMENTUM
IMPENDING STORM
IMPERATIVE MOOD
IMPERFECT RHYME
IMPERFECT TENSE
IMPERIAL BALLET
IMPERIAL GALLEON
IMPERIAL PURPLE
IMPERIAL WEIGHT
IMPLACABLE MOOD
IMPLIED CONSENT
IMPORTANT EVENT
IMPOSING FIGURE
IMPOSSIBLE TASK
IMPROPER PERSON
IMPROVE MATTERS
IMPROVE ONESELF
IMPUDENT CHARGE
IMPUDENT SPEECH
IMPURE THOUGHTS
IN A LITTLE WHILE
IN ALL INNOCENCE
IN A MORTAL HURRY
IN ANCIENT TIMES
IN ANOTHER CLASS
IN ANTICIPATION
IN A STATE OF FLUX
INCENDIARY BOMB
IN CERTAIN CASES
INCLINE ONE'S EAR
INCLUSIVE TERMS
INCOMING TENANT
IN COURSE OF TIME
INCREASED FARES
INCREASED SPEED
IN DEEP MOURNING
INDEFINITE TIME

INDEPENDENT AIR
INDIAN ELEPHANT
INDICATIVE MOOD
IN DIFFICULTIES
INDIRECT EFFECT
INDIRECT METHOD
INDIRECT OBJECT
INDIRECT SPEECH
INDUSTRIAL AREA
INDUSTRIAL ARTS
INERTIA SELLING
IN EVERY QUARTER
IN EVERY RESPECT
INEXORABLE FATE
INFERIOR NATURE
INFERIOR STATUS
INFINITE NUMBER
INFORMAL SPEECH
INFRINGE THE LAW
INGRAINED HABIT
INHERITANCE TAX
INITIAL ATTEMPT
INITIAL EXPENSE
INITIATIVE TEST
INJURED HUSBAND
INLAND WATERWAY
IN LOCO PARENTIS
INMOST THOUGHS
INNER CITY RIOTS
INNER EARPHONES
INNERMOST BEING
INNER SANCTUARY
INNINGS VICTORY
INNOCENT ABROAD
INNOCENT REMARK
INNOCENT VICTIM
INNS OF CHANCERY
IN ONE'S BORN DAYS
IN ONE'S MIND'S EYE
IN ONE'S OWN LIGHT
IN ONE'S OWN RIGHT
IN ORDER OF MERIT
IN RELATIONSHIP
IN ROUND NUMBERS
INSIDE POSITION
INSIDER DEALING
IN SOUTH AMERICA
INSPECTION LAMP
INSPIRE RESPECT
INSTANT DISLIKE
INSULATED CABLE
INSULTING WORDS
INSULT TO INJURY
INSURANCE AGENT
INSURANCE CLAIM
INTEGRATED CHIP

INTENSE DISLIKE
INTENSE FEELING
INTENSE LONGING
INTENSIVE STUDY
INTERESTED LOOK
INTERNAL STRIFE
INTERNMENT CAMP
INTERVAL OF TIME
IN THE AFTERNOON
IN THE AGGREGATE
IN THE ASCENDANT
IN THE BEGINNING
IN THE FIRM'S TIME
IN THE FOREFRONT
IN THE HEADLINES
IN THE LIMELIGHT
IN THE MEANWHILE
IN THE MOONLIGHT
IN THE MOUNTAINS
IN THE NEWSPAPER
IN THE NEXT WORLD
IN THE ORCHESTRA
IN THE PROVINCES
IN THE PUBLIC EYE
IN THE SAME CLASS
IN THE THICK OF IT
INTIMATE CIRCLE
INTIMATE FRIEND
INTO A COCKED HAT
INTO THE BARGAIN
INTRINSIC VALUE
INTRINSIC WORTH
INTRODUCE A BILL
INVARIABLE RULE
INVENT AN EXCUSE
INVERTED COMMAS
INVETERATE LIAR
INVINCIBLE ARMY
INVITE A QUARREL
INVITE RIDICULE
IRISH FREE STATE
IRISH PEASANTRY
IRONS IN THE FIRE
IRREGULAR UNION
ISLAND IN THE SUN
ISLAND PARADISE
IT'S A SMALL WORLD

J – 14

JACK OF DIAMONDS
JACOBITE RISING
JAYNE MANSFIELD
JEALOUS HUSBAND
JESSIE MATTHEWS
JIMMINY CRICKET

JOAN SUTHERLAND
JOBS FOR THE BOYS
JOHN BARLEYCORN
JOHN BROWN'S BODY
JOHN DRINKWATER
JOHN GALSWORTHY
JOHN LOGIE BAIRD
JOHN THE BAPTIST
JOIN IN MARRIAGE
JOINT COMMITTEE
JOIN THE COLOURS
JOIN THE RAT-RACE
JOINT LIABILITY
JOINT OWNERSHIP
JOINT-STOCK BANK
JOSHUA REYNOLDS
JUDE THE OBSCURE
JUDICIAL MANNER
JUDICIAL MURDER
JUDICIAL NOTICE
JUICE EXTRACTOR
JULIAN CALENDAR
JULY THE SEVENTH
JULY THE TWELFTH
JUMPING CRACKER
JUNE THE SEVENTH
JUNE THE TWELFTH
JUNIOR REPORTER
JUPITER PLUVIUS

K – 14

KARAOKE MACHINE
KEEP A GOOD TABLE
KEEP A TIGHT REIN
KEEP EARLY HOURS
KEEP IN SUSPENSE
KEEP IN THE SHADE
KEEP ONE'S CHIN UP
KEEP ONE'S FIGURE
KEEP ONE'S HAIR ON
KEEP ONE'S HAND IN
KEEP ONE'S SENSES
KEEP ONE'S TEMPER
KEEP OUT OF SIGHT
KEEP STRAIGHT ON
KEEP THE COLD OUT
KEEP THE RIGHT
KEEP TO THE RULES
KEEP UNDER COVER
KEEP WELL IN HAND
KENNETH BRANAGH
KENSINGTON GORE
KEPT IN HIS PLACE
KEYHOLE SURGERY
KEYSTONE COMEDY

KIDNEY AND BACON
KIDNEY POTATOES
KILLED IN ACTION
KINDLY INTEREST
KING AND COUNTRY
KING ARTHUR'S MEN
KING OF DIAMONDS
KING'S MESSENGER
KITCHEN CABINET
KITCHEN DRESSER
KITCHEN UTENSIL
KNIGHT IN ARMOUR
KNIGHTS OF MALTA
KNITTING NEEDLE
KNIVES AND FORKS
KNOCK-ABOUT TURN
KNOCK AT THE DOOR
KNOCK-DOWN PRICE
KNOCK INTO SHAPE
KNOCK KNOCK JOKE
KNOCK ON THE DOOR
KNOCK ON THE HEAD
KNOW A MOVE OR TWO
KNOW BY INSTINCT
KNOW FOR CERTAIN
KNOWLEDGE OF LAW
KNOWN CHARACTER
KNOW ONE'S ONIONS
KNOW WHEN TO STOP

L – 14

LABOUR EXCHANGE
LABOUR MAJORITY
LABOUR MINORITY
LABOUR MOVEMENT
LABOUR THE POINT
LACK OF EVIDENCE
LACK OF FRICTION
LACK OF INTEREST
LACK OF JUDGMENT
LACK OF PRACTICE
LACK OF STRENGTH
LACK OF SYMPATHY
LACK OF TRAINING
LACRIMA CHRISTI
LADY CHATTERLEY
LADY OF THE HOUSE
LADY OF THE MANOR
LADY WINDERMERE
LAID BY THE HEELS
LAID ON THE SHELF
LAKE WINDERMERE
LAME CONCLUSION
LANCASTER HOUSE
LAND COMMISSION

LANDED INTEREST
LANDED PROPERTY
LAND OF NO RETURN
LAND ON ONE'S FEET
LANGUAGE MASTER
LANTERN LECTURE
LAPTOP COMPUTER
LARGE INTESTINE
LARGE OVERDRAFT
LARGER THAN LIFE
LASSIES AND LADS
LAST APPEARANCE
LAST CONNECTION
LAST GENERATION
LASTING BENEFIT
LASTING QUALITY
LASTING SUCCESS
LAST INSTALMENT
LAST IN THE QUEUE
LATE NIGHT FINAL
LATEST BULLETIN
LATH AND PLASTER
LATTER-DAY SAINT
LAUGHING MATTER
LAUNCH AN ATTACK
LAUNCHING STAGE
LAUREL AND HARDY
LAURENCE HARVEY
LAURENCE STERNE
LAW ENFORCEMENT
LAWFUL OCCASION
LAW OF THE JUNGLE
LAY DOWN A CELLAR
LAY ON TRANSPORT
LEADING ACTRESS
LEADING ARTICLE
LEADING CITIZEN
LEADING COUNSEL
LEADING STRINGS
LEAD THE FASHION
LEAD TO THE ALTAR
LEAGUE FOOTBALL
LEAN-BURN ENGINE
LEAPS AND BOUNDS
LEARNED COUNSEL
LEARNED SOCIETY
LEASEHOLD HOUSE
LEAVE A LOOPHOLE
LEAVE DESTITUTE
LEAVE NO ADDRESS
LEAVE OF ABSENCE
LEAVE SENSELESS
LEAVE THE GROUND
LEAVE WELL ALONE
LEDA AND THE SWAN
LEEWARD ISLANDS

LEFT HIGH AND DRY
LEFT IN THE LURCH
LEFT SPEECHLESS
LEFT UNFINISHED
LEGAL AUTHORITY
LEGAL CHICANERY
LEGAL ETIQUETTE
LEGAL FORMALITY
LEGAL LIABILITY
LEGALLY BINDING
LEGAL OWNERSHIP
LEGAL PROCEDURE
LEGION OF HONOUR
LEMONADE POWDER
LEMONADE SHANDY
LENDING LIBRARY
LEND ME YOUR EARS
LESLIE MITCHELL
LET DOWN LIGHTLY
LET DOWN THE SIDE
LET OR HINDRANCE
LETTER OF ADVICE
LETTER OF CREDIT
LETTER OF THE LAW
LET THE SIDE DOWN
LET THINGS SLIDE
LETTRE DE CACHET
LIAISON OFFICER
LIBERAL HELPING
LIBRARY EDITION
LICK ONE'S WOUNDS
LICK THE PLATTER
LIFE EXPECTANCY
LIFELONG FRIEND
LIFE OF PLEASURE
LIFE WITH FATHER
LIFT UP ONE'S HEAD
LIGHT AND BITTER
LIGHT ARTILLERY
LIGHT BREAKFAST
LIGHTEN THE LOAD
LIGHTER THAN AIR
LIGHT FANTASTIC
LIGHTING-UP TIME
LIGHTNING FLASH
LIGHTNING SPEED
LIGHT PROGRAMME
LIGHTS OF LONDON
LIGHT TRANSPORT
LIKE A BOMBSHELL
LIKE A MILLSTONE
LILY-WHITE HANDS
LIMITED COMPANY
LIMITED EDITION
LIMITING FACTOR
LINEAR EQUATION

LINE OF APPROACH
LINE OF BUSINESS
LINGERING DEATH
LINK IN THE CHAIN
LION OF THE NORTH
LISLE STOCKINGS
LISTED BUILDING
LISTEN TO REASON
LIST OF CONTENTS
LITERAL ACCOUNT
LITERAL MEANING
LITERARY CRITIC
LITERARY DIGEST
LITERARY EDITOR
LITERARY OUTPUT
LITHIUM BATTERY
LITTLE AND OFTEN
LITTLE BROWN JUG
LITTLE BY LITTLE
LITTLE CHILDREN
LITTLE CORPORAL
LITTLE DISTANCE
LITTLE IN COMMON
LITTLE INTEREST
LITTLE LEARNING
LITTLE PITCHERS
LITTLE PROGRESS
LITTLE RESPONSE
LITTLE STRANGER
LIVE A CLEAN LIFE
LIVE AMMUNITION
LIVE AND LET LIVE
LIVE ON ONE'S WITS
LIVER AND ONIONS
LIVE TO A HUNDRED
LIVING LANGUAGE
LIVING QUARTERS
LIVING REMINDER
LIVING STANDARD
LIVING TOGETHER
LLOYD'S REGISTER
LOADED QUESTION
LOAD ON ONE'S MIND
LOAD WITH CHAINS
LOCAL AUTHORITY
LOCAL NEWSPAPER
LOFTY AMBITIONS
LOGICAL CONDUCT
LOGICAL PROCESS
LOGIC OPERATION
LONDONDERRY AIR
LONDON HOSPITAL
LONDON MARATHON
LONDON REGIMENT
LONDON RHAPSODY
LONDON SCOTTISH

LONDON TERMINUS
LONG ENGAGEMENT
LONGHAND WRITER
LONG IN THE TOOTH
LONG JOHN SILVER
LONG-LOST FRIEND
LONG PARLIAMENT
LONG-TERM POLICY
LOOK FOR TROUBLE
LOOK IN THE GLASS
LOOK ON ALL SIDES
LOOK PROSPEROUS
LOOK TO THE FRONT
LOOSE BEHAVIOUR
LOOSE RENDERING
LORD CHANCELLOR
LORD LIEUTENANT
LORD MAYOR'S SHOW
LORD OF CREATION
LORD OF THE FLIES
LORD OF THE ISLES
LORD OF THE MANOR
LORD OF THE RINGS
LORD PALMERSTON
LORDS AND LADIES
LORDS SPIRITUAL
LORD'S TAVERNERS
LOSE CONFIDENCE
LOSE ONE'S MEMORY
LOSE ONE'S REASON
LOSE ONE'S TEMPER
LOSE ONE'S TICKET
LOSE ONE'S TONGUE
LOSS OF APPETITE
LOSS OF INTEREST
LOSS OF PRESTIGE
LOSS OF STRENGTH
LOST GENERATION
LOST TO THE WORLD
LOT TO ANSWER FOR
LOUIS ARMSTRONG
LOVE IN A COTTAGE
LOVE IN IDLENESS
LOVELY TO LOOK AT
LOVE OF PLEASURE
LOVING KINDNESS
LOWER ONE'S VOICE
LOW TEMPERATURE
LOYAL SUPPORTER
LUBRICATING OIL
LUCK OF THE DEVIL
LUCK OF THE IRISH
LUCREZIA BORGIA
LUNATIC AT LARGE
LUNCHEON BASKET
LUNCH-TIME SCORE

LYON KING OF ARMS
LYTTON STRACHEY

M – 14

MACARONI CHEESE
MACHINE-GUN POST
MADAM BUTTERFLY
MADAM POMPADOUR
MADE FOR THE PART
MAGNETIC NEEDLE
MAGNOLIA STREET
MAIL VAN ROBBERY
MAIN ATTRACTION
MAIN INGREDIENT
MAINTENANCE MAN
MAJOR OPERATION
MAJOR ROAD AHEAD
MAKE A BEGINING
MAKE A BIG SPLASH
MAKE A BOLT FOR IT
MAKE A COMPLAINT
MAKE A DISCOVERY
MAKE A GOOD GUESS
MAKE A GOOD SCORE
MAKE A GOOD START
MAKE ALLOWANCES
MAKE AN ENTRANCE
MAKE AN ESTIMATE
MAKE A NIGHT OF IT
MAKE A REFERENCE
MAKE A STATEMENT
MAKE DELIVERIES
MAKE EXCEPTIONS
MAKE FEW DEMANDS
MAKE FOR THE DOOR
MAKE NO PROGRESS
MAKE PROVISIONS
MAKE REPARATION
MAKE RINGS ROUND
MAKE SACRIFICES
MAKE THE RUNNING
MAKE THINGS EASY
MAKE UP A QUARREL
MAKE UP ONE'S MIND
MALCOLM SARGENT
MALE VOICE CHOIR
MANAGING EDITOR
MAN AND SUPERMAN
MANCHESTER CITY
MANDARIN ORANGE
MAN-EATING SHARK
MAN IN THE STREET
MAN OF CHARACTER
MAN OF INFLUENCE
MAN OF MANY PARTS

MAN OF SUBSTANCE	MEERSCHAUM PIPE
MAN OF THE MOMENT	MELT IN THE MOUTH
MAN OF THE PEOPLE	MEMBER OF THE BAR
MAN ON HORSEBACK	MEMBERSHIP CARD
MAN'S BEST FRIEND	MENDICANT ORDER
MAN THE DEFENCES	MEN IN GREY SUITS
MANUAL LABOURER	MENTAL ATTITUDE
MAPPIN TERRACES	MENTAL CAPACITY
MARATHON RUNNER	MENTAL CONFLICT
MARCHING ORDERS	MENTAL DISORDER
MARCH THE EIGHTH	MENTAL EXERCISE
MARCH THE FOURTH	MENTAL HOSPITAL
MARCH THE SECOND	MENTAL SICKNESS
MARCUS ANTONIUS	MENTAL STIMULUS
MARCUS AURELIUS	MENTAL STRUGGLE
MARGIN OF ERROR	MENTAL WEAKNESS
MARGIN OF PROFIT	MERCHANT BANKER
MARGIN OF SAFETY	MERCHANT PRINCE
MARINE ENGINEER	MERCHANT SEAMAN
MARITIME NATION	MERCHANT TAILOR
MARKED TENDENCY	MERCHANT VESSEL
MARKET GARDENER	MERMAID THEATRE
MARKETING BOARD	MERRY AND BRIGHT
MARKET RESEARCH	MERRY CHRISTMAS
MARK OF APPROVAL	METEORIC SHOWER
MARK OF THE BEAST	MEZZANINE FLOR
MARK OUT A COURSE	MICHAEL BENTINE
MARRIAGE BROKER	MICHAEL FARADAY
MARRIAGE BUREAU	MICHAEL JACKSON
MARRIAGE MARKET	MICHAELMAS TERM
MARSUPIAL POUCH	MICHAEL WILDING
MASHED POTATOES	MIDDLE DISTANCE
MASS PRODUCTION	MIDDLE OF THE DAY
MASTERMAN READY	MIDDLE REGISTER
MASTER OF HOUNDS	MIDNIGHT REVELS
MATCH FOR ANYONE	MIDSHIPMAN EASY
MATERIAL WEALTH	MIDSUMMER NIGHT
MATERNITY LEAVE	MILD PUNISHMENT
MATRON OF HONOUR	MILITARY ATTACK
MATTER OF CHOICE	MILITARY CAREER
MATTER OF COURSE	MILITARY ESCORT
MATTER OF RECORD	MILITARY GENIUS
MATTER OF REGRET	MILITARY PARADE
MATTERS OF STATE	MILITARY POLICE
MAUNDY THURSDAY	MILITARY SCHOOL
MAY THE ELEVENTH	MILITARY SPIRIT
MEANS OF SUPPORT	MILITARY TATTOO
MECHANISED ARMY	MILK OF MAGNESIA
MEDICAL ADVISER	MILLENNIUM FUND
MEDICAL COLLEGE	MILLION DOLLARS
MEDICAL HISTORY	MILL ON THE FLOSS
MEDICAL OFFICER	MIND OVER MATTER
MEDICAL SCIENCE	MINERAL DEPOSIT
MEDICAL STUDENT	MINERAL KINGDOM
MEDICINAL VALUE	MINESTRONE SOUP
MEDICINE BOTTLE	MINING ENGINEER

MINISTRY OF FOOD
MINOR OPERATION
MISSIONARY WORK
MISTER MICAWBER
MISTLETOE BOUGH
MNEMONIC DEVICE
MOBILE FEATURES
MOCK TURTLE SOUP
MODEL AEROPLANE
MODEL BEHAVIOUR
MODEL HOUSEHOLD
MODERATE DEGREE
MODERATE HEALTH
MODERATE HEIGHT
MODERATE INCOME
MODERATE WEIGHT
MODERN BUILDING
MODERN LANGUAGE
MODS AND ROCKERS
MOLECULAR CLOCK
MONEY IN THE BANK
MONKEY BUSINESS
MONOTONOUS LIFE
MONROE DOCTRINE
MONSTROUS CRIME
MONTHLY ACCOUNT
MONTHLY PAYMENT
MONTH OF SUNDAYS
MONUMENTAL WORK
MOONLIGHT NIGHT
MORAL BLACKMAIL
MORAL CERTAINTY
MORAL CHARACTER
MORAL COWARDICE
MORAL IGNORANCE
MORAL NECESSITY
MORAL PRINCIPLE
MORAL TURPITUDE
MORE THAN A MATCH
MORE THAN ENOUGH
MORE TO THE POINT
MORNING SERVICE
MOROCCO LEATHER
MOST HONOURABLE
MOST OF THE NIGHT
MOTHER AND CHILD
MOTHER'S DARLING
MOTHERS' MEETING
MOTHER SUPERIOR
MOTLEY ASSEMBLY
MOTOR AMBULANCE
MOTOR TRANSPORT
MOUNTAIN RESORT
MOUNTING DANGER
MOUNT THE THRONE
MOVE TO LAUGHTER

MOVING PAVEMENT
MUCH IN EVIDENCE
MUCH-MARRIED MAN
MULTIPLY BY FIVE
MULTIPLY BY FOUR
MULTIPLY BY NINE
MUNITIONS OF WAR
MURDER MOST FOUL
MUSCULAR ENERGY
MUSEUM SPECIMEN
MUSHROOM GROWTH
MUSHROOM SUBURB
MUSICAL ABILITY
MUSICAL EVENING
MUSICAL GLASSES
MUSICAL MOMENTS
MUSICAL PRODIGY
MUSICAL QUALITY
MUSIC PUBLISHER
MUSTARD PLASTER
MUTE ADMIRATION
MUTUAL GOODWILL
MUTUAL SYMPATHY
MUZZLE VELOCITY
MY LADY NICOTINE

N – 14

NADINE GORDIMER
NAME AND ADDRESS
NAMELESS TERROR
NAME YOUR POISON
NAMING CEREMONY
NANSEN PASSPORT
NAPOLEON BRANDY
NAPOLEONIC CODE
NAPOLEONIC WARS
NARRATIVE VERSE
NARROW INTERVAL
NARROW MAJORITY
NASTY BIT OF WORK
NATIONAL ANTHEM
NATIONAL CREDIT
NATIONAL CRISIS
NATIONAL DEVICE
NATIONAL EMBLEM
NATIONAL FIGURE
NATIONAL HEALTH
NATIONAL INCOME
NATIONAL SPIRIT
NATIONAL STATUS
NATIONAL WEALTH
NATIONAL WINNER
NATION-WIDE HUNT
NATIVE COMPOUND
NATIVE LANGUAGE

NATIVE QUARTERS
NATURAL HARBOUR
NATURAL HISTORY
NATURAL IMPULSE
NATURAL PROCESS
NATURAL SCIENCE
NATURAL YOGHURT
NAUGHTY BUT NICE
NAVAL ARCHITECT
NAVAL EXERCISES
NAVAL OPERATION
NAVIGABLE RIVER
NEANDERTHAL MAN
NEAR NEIGHBOURS
NEAR THE KNUCKLE
NEAT AS A BANDBOX
NEEDLES AND PINS
NE'ER CAST A CLOUT
NEGATIVE ACTION
NEGATIVE ANSWER
NEGATIVE EQUITY
NEGATIVE RESULT
NEGRO SPIRITUAL
NERVOUS TENSION
NETHER GARMENTS
NEUTRAL COUNTRY
NEVER-NEVER LAND
NEVER SATISFIED
NEW CONSIGNMENT
NEW-FANGLED IDEA
NEW LAMPS FOR OLD
NEW LEASE OF LIFE
NEWS OF THE WORLD
NEWSPAPER WORLD
NEXT BEST FRIEND
NEXT GENERATION
NICE DIFFERENCE
NICELY BALANCED
NICE PERCEPTION
NIGGER MINSTREL
NIGHT BLINDNESS
NIGHT-CLUB QUEEN
NIL DESPERANDUM
NINE DAYS' WONDER
NINE MEN'S MORRIS
NINE O'CLOCK NEWS
NINE OF DIAMONDS
NINETEENTH HOLE
NINETEEN TWENTY
NINETY THOUSANDS
NINTH OF JANUARY
NINTH OF OCTOBER
NIPPED IN THE BUD
NOBLESSE OBLIGE
NOBODY'S DARLING
NO END OF A FELLOW

NO FIXED ADDRESS
NO HALF MEASURES
NOISE ABATEMENT
NOISE POLLUTION
NOISE REDUCTION
NO JOKING MATTER
NOMINAL CAPITAL
NOMINAL DAMAGES
NOMINATIVE CASE
NORMAL SOLUTION
NORMAN CONQUEST
NO ROOM AT THE INN
NO ROOM FOR DOUBT
NORTH AUSTRALIA
NORTHERN ACCENT
NORTHERN LIGHTS
NORTH OF ENGLAND
NORTH OF THE WASH
NORTHWARD BOUND
NOSE OUT OF JOINT
NO STOMACH FOR IT
NOTHING DAUNTED
NOTHING TO OFFER
NOTHING TO SPARE
NOTHING VENTURE
NO THOROUGHFARE
NO TROUBLE AT ALL
NOT THE FULL QUID
NOUN OF ASSEMBLY
NOVEL SITUATION
NO VISIBLE MEANS
NO-WIN SITUATION
NUCLEAR FALLOUT
NUCLEAR FISSION
NUCLEAR PHYSICS
NUCLEAR REACTOR
NUCLEAR WARFARE
NUMBER CRUNCHER
NUMBER THIRTEEN
NUMERICAL ORDER
NURSING SERVICE
NUTS AND RAISINS
NYLON STOCKINGS

O – 14

OBITUARY NOTICE
OBJECT OF TERROR
OBSCURE PROBLEM
OBSERVATION CAR
OCCASIONAL SHOT
OCCUPYING FORCE
OCEAN GREYHOUND
OCTAVIUS CAESAR
ODER–NEISSE LINE
OEDIPUS COMPLEX

OFFER AN OPINION
OFFICE BUILDING
OFFICE OF PROFIT
OFFICER OF STATE
OFFICERS AND MEN
OFFICIAL CENSUS
OFFICIAL NOTICE
OFFICIAL REPORT
OFFICIAL SECRET
OFFICIAL SOURCE
OFFICIAL STRIKE
OFF LIKE A STREAK
OFF-PISTE SKIING
OFFSET PRINTING
OFF THE PREMISES
OFF WITH THE HEAD
OF HUMAN BONDAGE
OLD BOYS' REUNION
OLD CLOTHES SHOP
OLD FOLKS AT HOME
OLD MAN OF THE SEA
OLD MOTHER RILEY
OLD PEOPLE'S HOME
OLD-TIME DANCING
OLD-WORLD GARDEN
OLIVER CROMWELL
OMNIBUS EDITION
ON A HEROIC SCALE
ON A HIGHER PLANE
ONE AND A QUARTER
ONE-ARMED BANDIT
ONE CLAIM TO FAME
ONE CROWDED HOUR
ONE FINE MORNING
ONE IN A THOUSAND
ONE-MAN BUSINESS
ONE NIGHT OF LOVE
ONE OF THE FAMILY
ONE OF THE PEOPLE
ONE OF THESE DAYS
ONE THAT GOT AWAY
ONLY TOO PLEASED
ON ONE CONDITION
ON ONE'S BEAM-ENDS
ON ONE'S DEATH-BED
ON ONE'S HIND LEGS
ON ONE'S LAST LEGS
ON ONE'S OWN TERMS
ON PLEASURE BENT
ON PUBLIC GROUND
ON SHORT RATIONS
ON SUBSCRIPTION
ON THE BAND-WAGON
ON THE CONTINENT
ON THE DEBIT SIDE
ON THE DEFENSIVE

ON THE DOWNGRADE
ON THE HOME FRONT
ON THE LARGE SIZE
ON THE OFF CHANCE
ON THE OFFENSIVE
ON THE OTHER HAND
ON THE OTHER SIDE
ON THE OUTSKIRTS
ON THE PROMENADE
ON THE RIGHT SIDE
ON THE SHADY SIDE
ON THE SHORT LIST
ON THE SHORT SIDE
ON THE SMALL SIDE
ON THE SUNNY SIDE
ON THE TELEPHONE
ON THE THRESHOLD
ON THE TIGHT SIDE
ON THE TOUCH-LINE
ON THE WRONG FOOT
ON THE WRONG SIDE
ONTO A GOOD THING
ON WITH THE DANCE
OPEN-AIR CONCERT
OPEN-AIR SERVICE
OPEN-AIR SPEAKER
OPEN-AIR THEATRE
OPEN-CAST MINING
OPEN CONFESSION
OPEN DISCUSSION
OPEN-DOOR POLICY
OPENING BATSMAN
OPEN PARLIAMENT
OPEN THE BIDDING
OPEN THE INNINGS
OPEN THE SLUICES
OPEN TO ARGUMENT
OPEN TO QUESTION
OPEN TOURNAMENT
OPEN UNIVERSITY
OPERATING TABLE
OPERATIONS ROOM
OPPOSITE NUMBER
OPPOSITION WHIP
ORCHESTRA STALL
ORDER IN ADVANCE
ORDER IN COUNCIL
ORDERLY CONDUCT
ORDERLY OFFICER
ORDER OF THE BATH
ORDER OF THE BOOT
ORDINARY SEAMAN
ORDINARY SHARES
ORDNANCE SURVEY
ORGANIC DISEASE
ORGANIC FARMING

ORGANISED GAMES
ORNAMENTAL POND
ORNAMENTAL TREE
ORTHODOX CHURCH
OSCILLATING FAN
OSTRICH FEATHER
OTHER FISH TO FRY
OUNCE OF TOBACCO
OUT-AND-OUT ROGUE
OUTDOOR MEETING
OUTDOOR SERVANT
OUT OF THE CLOSET
OUT FOR THE COUNT
OUTGOING TENANT
OUT OF CHARACTER
OUT OF CONDITION
OUT OF CURIOSITY
OUT OF ONE'S DEPTH
OUT OF ONE'S SHELL
OUT OF THE COMMON
OUT OF THE GUTTER
OUT OF THIS WORLD
OUTSIDE ONE'S KEN
OUTSIDE OPINION
OVERCOME BY FEAR
OVERDUE ACCOUNT
OVER THE COUNTER
OVER THE RAINBOW
OXFORD MOVEMENT
OXYGEN CYLINDER

P – 14

PACKAGE HOLIDAY
PACKAGE PROGRAM
PACKET OF CRISPS
PACKET OF TWENTY
PACKING STATION
PACK OF NONSENSE
PACK ONE'S TRUNKS
PAGES OF HISTORY
PAINT AND POWDER
PAINT A PORTRAIT
PAIR OF BREECHES
PAIR OF CALIPERS
PAIR OF CLIPPERS
PAIR OF CRUTCHES
PAIR OF SCISSORS
PAIR OF SLIPPERS
PAIR OF SPEAKERS
PAIR OF TROUSERS
PAIR OF TWEEZERS
PALM OF ONE'S HAND
PANCAKE LANDING
PANCAKE TUESDAY
PANGS OF REMORSE

PANTOMIME QUEEN
PANZER DIVISION
PARADISE FOR TWO
PARALLEL COURSE
PARCHMENT PAPER
PARDON MY FRENCH
PARISH MAGAZINE
PARISH REGISTER
PARKING PROBLEM
PARLIAMENT HILL
PARMESAN CHEESE
PAROXYSM OF RAGE
PARTIAL CONSENT
PARTIAL ECLIPSE
PARTIAL SUCCESS
PARTING PRESENT
PARTISAN SPIRIT
PARTNER IN CRIME
PARTY MACHINERY
PARTY PROGRAMME
PASS DOWN THE CAR
PASSENGER PLANE
PASSENGER TRAIN
PASSING THOUGHT
PASSIONATE PLEA
PASSIVE SMOKING
PASS THE MUSTARD
PAST AND PRESENT
PAST EXPERIENCE
PASTORAL LETTER
PAST PARTICIPLE
PAST REDEMPTION
PATCHWORK QUILT
PATÉ DE FOIS GRAS
PATENT MEDICINE
PATERNOSTER ROW
PATRIOT MISSILE
PAUSE FOR A WHILE
PAUSE FOR BREATH
PAVEMENT ARTIST
PAVING MATERIAL
PAYABLE AT SIGHT
PAY A COMPLIMENT
PAY NO ATTENTION
PEACE AND PLENTY
PEACEFUL ENDING
PEACE IN OUR TIME
PEAL OF LAUGHTER
PEARLS OF WISDOM
PECULIAR PEOPLE
PECULIAR PERSON
PEDIGREE CATTLE
PEER OF THE REALM
PEG-TOP TROUSERS
PENAL SERVITUDE
PENCIL AND PAPER

PENNY FOR THE GUY
PENNY IN THE SLOT
PENSIONABLE AGE
PEPPERCORN RENT
PERCUSSION BAND
PERFECT DARLING
PERFECT EXAMPLE
PERFECT SETTING
PERFECT SILENCE
PERFORMANCE ART
PERFORMING BEAR
PERFORMING FLEA
PERFORMING SEAL
PERPETUAL BLISS
PERPETUAL WORRY
PERSONAL APPEAL
PERSONAL COLUMN
PERSONAL ESTATE
PERSONAL ESTEEM
PERSONAL FACTOR
PERSONAL FAVOUR
PERSONAL LETTER
PERSONAL MATTER
PERSONAL REMARK
PERSONAL STEREO
PERSON IN CHARGE
PERSON OF REPUTE
PERSONS UNKNOWN
PERSON TO PERSON
PERTINENT REPLY
PETER PRINCIPLE
PETER THE HERMIT
PETROLEUM JELLY
PETROL SHORTAGE
PETTY GRIEVANCE
PHOTOGRAPH WELL
PHRASE AND FABLE
PHYSICAL BEAUTY
PHYSICAL ENERGY
PICCADILLY LINE
PICKLED CABBAGE
PICKLED HERRING
PICK OF THE BUNCH
PICK UP A FEW TIPS
PICK UP STRENGTH
PICKWICK PAPERS
PICTURE GALLERY
PICTURE OF GLOOM
PICTURE WRITING
PIERCE THE HEART
PIERCING GLANCE
PIETRO ANNIGONI
PILE ON THE AGONY
PILGRIM FATHERS
PILLAR OF THE LAW
PILLAR OF WISDOM

PILOTLESS PLANE
PINCER MOVEMENT
PINCH AND SCRAPE
PINEAPPLE JUICE
PINNACLE OF FAME
PINS AND NEEDLES
PIT BULL TERRIER
PITCH OVERBOARD
PLACE IN HISTORY
PLACE OF ONE'S OWN
PLACE OF WORSHIP
PLAGUE OF LONDON
PLAICE AND CHIPS
PLAIN AND SIMPLE
PLAIN CHOCOLATE
PLAIN STATEMENT
PLANCK CONSTANT
PLANETARY ORBIT
PLANNED ECONOMY
PLANNING BLIGHT
PLANNING OFFICE
PLAN OF CAMPAIGN
PLANTATION SONG
PLASTER OF PARIS
PLASTIC SURGEON
PLASTIC SURGERY
PLATE TECTONICS
PLATFORM ORATOR
PLATFORM TICKET
PLATINUM BLONDE
PLAUSIBLE ROGUE
PLAY AT SOLDIERS
PLAY FOR ENGLAND
PLAY GOOSEBERRY
PLAY IT AGAIN SAM
PLAY THE TRAITOR
PLAY THE VILLAIN
PLAY TO THE CROWD
PLEAD IGNORANCE
PLEAD NOT GUILTY
PLEAD ONE'S CAUSE
PLEASANT DREAMS
PLEASANT MANNER
PLEASANT PEOPLE
PLEASED AS PUNCH
PLEASE TURN OVER
PLEASURE CRUISE
PLEASURE GROUND
PLEASURE LAUNCH
PLEASURE SEEKER
PLEDGE ONE'S WORD
PLOT ONE'S COURSE
PLOUGHING MATCH
PLOUGH THE WAVES
PLUCK UP COURAGE
PLUMB THE DEPTHS

PLUNGED IN GRIEF
PLUNGE INTO DEBT
PNEUMATIC BRAKE
PNEUMATIC DRILL
POCKET AN INSULT
POET AND PEASANT
POETRY IN MOTION
POINT OF CONTACT
POINT OUT THE WAY
POINT WELL TAKEN
POISED TO STRIKE
POISONOUS PLANT
POKE ONE'S NOSE IN
POLARIZED GLASS
POLICEMAN'S BEAT
POLICE SERGEANT
POLISH CORRIDOR
POLISH OFF A MEAL
POLITICAL AGENT
POLITICAL EXILE
POLITICAL PARTY
POLITICAL SPIRIT
POLLING STATION
PONTEFRACT CAKE
POOR MAN'S FRIEND
POOR MAN'S LAWYER
POOR VISIBILITY
POOR VOCABULARY
POPPA PICCOLINO
POP THE QUESTION
POPULAR CONCERT
POPULAR EDITION
POPULAR OPINION
POPULAR REQUEST
POPULAR SCIENCE
POPULAR VERDICT
PORTLAND CEMENT
PORTRAIT ARTIST
POSITIVE ACTION
POSITIVE CHARGE
POSITIVE COLOUR
POSITIVE DEGREE
POSITIVE MENACE
POSSESSIVE CASE
POSSESSIVE LOVE
POSTAL DELIVERY
POSTAL DISTRICT
POSTHUMOUS FAME
POST-WAR CREDITS
POWDER AND PAINT
POWDER MAGAZINE
POWDER ONE'S NOSE
POWERFUL SPEECH
PRACTICAL JOKER
PRACTISE DECEIT
PRECIOUS LITTLE

PRE-NATAL CLINIC
PREPARE A BUDGET
PREPARED SPEECH
PREPARE ONESELF
PRESCRIBED TEXT
PRESENCE OF MIND
PRESENT A CHEQUE
PRESENT ADDRESS
PRESENT COMPANY
PRESERVED FRUIT
PRESIDENT ELECT
PRESIDING JUDGE
PRESSED FOR TIME
PRESS FOR ACTION
PRESSING DANGER
PRESSING DUTIES
PRESS SECRETARY
PRESS THE BUTTON
PRESSURE COOKER
PRESSURE OF WORK
PRESUMED GUILTY
PREVAILING WIND
PREY ON ONE'S MIND
PRICE OF SILENCE
PRICE REDUCTION
PRICKLY FEELING
PRIMA BALLERINA
PRIMARY MEANING
PRIME CONDITION
PRIMEVAL FOREST
PRIMITIVE TRIBE
PRIMORDIAL SOUP
PRIMROSE LEAGUE
PRIMROSE YELLOW
PRINCE CHARMING
PRINCE OF ORANGE
PRINCE OF ROGUES
PRISON CHAPLAIN
PRISON GOVERNOR
PRISON SENTENCE
PRIVATE ADDRESS
PRIVATE CITIZEN
PRIVATE COMPANY
PRIVATE HEARING
PRIVATE OPINION
PRIVATE SOCIETY
PRIVATE SOLDIER
PRIVATE TEACHER
PRIVATE TUITION
PRIZE-GIVING DAY
PROBABLE WINNER
PRO BONO PUBLICO
PRODUCE RESULTS
PRODUCTION LINE
PROFITABLE DEAL
PROFITLESS TASK

PROFOUND EFFECT
PROFOUND SECRET
PROGRAMME MUSIC
PROGRESS OF TIME
PROGRESS REPORT
PROHIBITION ERA
PROLIFIC WRITER
PROMISING PUPIL
PROMISING START
PROMISSORY NOTE
PROMPT DECISION
PROMPT DELIVERY
PROOF OF POSTING
PROPER FRACTION
PROPOSE A MOTION
PROPOSED ACTION
PROSCENIUM ARCH
PROSPEROUS YEAR
PROTECTED STATE
PROTEST AGAINST
PROTEST MEETING
PROTEST TOO MUCH
PROVE EXPENSIVE
PROVEN INNOCENT
PROVE ONE'S POINT
PROVIDE HEATING
PROVOST MARSHAL
PSYCHEDELIC ART
PSYCHIC HEALING
PUBLIC APPLAUSE
PUBLIC DISGRACE
PUBLIC ENTRANCE
PUBLIC EXPOSURE
PUBLIC FOOTPATH
PUBLIC INTEREST
PUBLICITY AGENT
PUBLIC NUISANCE
PUBLIC PROPERTY
PUBLIC SPIRITED
PUBLISHER'S NOTE
PULL ONE'S WEIGHT
PULL THE STRINGS
PULL THE TRIGGER
PUMPING STATION
PUNCH ON THE HEAD
PUNCH ON THE NOSE
PUNITIVE ACTION
PURE CONJECTURE
PURSUIT OF POWER
PUSHED FOR MONEY
PUSH OUT THE BOAT
PUSH THE BOAT OUT
PUT IN A BAD LIGHT
PUT IN A GOOD WORD
PUT IN ONE'S PLACE
PUT IN THE MIDDLE

PUT IN THE STOCKS
PUT IT IN WRITING
PUT IT TO THE VOTE
PUT NEW LIFE INTO
PUT OFF THE SCENT
PUT ON A BOLD FACE
PUT ON A PEDESTAL
PUT ONE'S SPOKE IN
PUT ON THE AGENDA
PUT ON THE MARKET
PUT ON THE SCALES
PUT OUT OF ACTION
PUT OUT THE LIGHT
PUT THE CLOCKS ON
PUT THE HELM DOWN
PUT THE KETTLE ON
PUT THE KIBOSH ON
PUT THE QUESTION
PUT THINGS RIGHT
PUT UNDER ARREST
PUT UP A GOOD SHOW
PUT UP A STRUGGLE
PYRAMID SELLING
PYRRHIC VICTORY

Q – 14

QUALITY OF MERCY
QUARTER OF A YARD
QUARTER PAST ONE
QUARTER PAST SIX
QUARTER PAST TEN
QUARTER PAST TWO
QUARTER TO EIGHT
QUARTER TO SEVEN
QUARTER TO THREE
QUARTZ MOVEMENT
QUEEN ANNE HOUSE
QUEEN ANNE'S GATE
QUEEN ANNE STYLE
QUEEN CHARLOTTE
QUEEN ELIZABETH
QUEEN OF ENGLAND
QUEEN'S BIRTHDAY
QUEEN'S EVIDENCE
QUEEN'S PLEASURE
QUEEN'S SHILLING
QUEEN'S SUBJECT
QUEER IN THE HEAD
QUEER ONE'S PITCH
QUEER SITUATION
QUESTION MASTER
QUESTION OF TIME
QUICK AS THOUGHT
QUICK-FIRING GUN
QUICK LOOK ROUND

QUICK ON THE DRAW
QUICK VENGEANCE
QUITE A STRANGER
QUITE DIFFERENT
QUIVER AND SHAKE
QUIVER WITH RAGE
QUOTATION MARKS
QWERTY KEYBOARD

R – 14

RACING CALENDAR
RACKED WITH PAIN
RADICAL OUTLOOK
RADIO ANNOUNCER
RADIO ASTRONOMY
RADIO FREQUENCY
RADIO PROGRAMME
RADIO TELEGRAPH
RADIO TELEPHONE
RADIO TELESCOPE
RADIO THERAPIST
RAGS AND TATTERS
RAILWAY COMPANY
RAILWAY CUTTING
RAILWAY JOURNEY
RAILWAY SLEEPER
RAILWAY STATION
RAILWAY VIADUCT
RAILWAY WARRANT
RAIN IN TORRENTS
RAISE A MEMORIAL
RAISE A QUESTION
RAISED EYEBROWS
RAISED PLATFORM
RAISE ONE'S GLASS
RAISE ONE'S HOPES
RAISE ONE'S VOICE
RAISE THE SIGHTS
RAKE IN THE MONEY
RAKE OUT THE FIRE
RANGE OF MEANING
RAPID PROMOTION
RAPT EXPRESSION
RARE ATMOSPHERE
RARE OCCURRENCE
RASH ASSUMPTION
RATE OF EXCHANGE
RATE OF INTEREST
RATE OF PROGRESS
RATTLE THE SABRE
RAVENOUS HUNGER
REACH A DECISION
REACH AGREEMENT
REACH FOR THE SKY
REACH THE DEPTHS

REACH THE ZENITH
READING GLASSES
READ MEN'S HEARTS
READ-ONLY MEMORY
READ THE MINUTES
READ THE RIOT ACT
REALITY THERAPY
REALLY AND TRULY
REAPING MACHINE
REAP THE BENEFIT
REAP THE HARVEST
REAR-VIEW MIRROR
REAR-VIEW WINDOW
REASONABLE TIME
RECEIVE A LEGACY
RECEIVE A LETTER
RECEIVE QUARTER
RECEIVING ORDER
RECEPTION CLERK
RECKLESS DRIVER
RECKLESS GAMBLE
RECORDING ANGEL
RECORD TURNOVER
RECOVER ONESELF
RECREATION ROOM
RED ARMY FACTION
REDUCE IN NUMBER
REDUCE TO POWDER
REED INSTRUMENT
REFECTORY TABLE
REFINED SOCIETY
REFLECTED GLORY
REFLECTED IMAGE
REFLECTIVE MOOD
REFORMED CHURCH
REFRESHMENT BAR
REFRESH ONESELF
REFUGEE PROBLEM
REFUSE A HEARING
REFUSE DISPOSAL
REGAL SPLENDOUR
REGIMENTAL BAND
REGISTERED MAIL
REGISTERED POST
REGISTER OFFICE
REGULAR BEDTIME
REGULAR SERVICE
REGULAR SOLDIER
REGULATION SIZE
REIGNING BEAUTY
REIGNING FAMILY
RELATIVE CLAUSE
RELATIVE DATING
RELATIVE VALUES
RELIC OF THE PAST
RELIEVING FORCE

RELIGIOUS FAITH
RELIGIOUS HOUSE
RELIGIOUS MANIA
RELIGIOUS ORDER
RELIGIOUS RITES
RELIGIOUS TRACT
REMAINS OF A MEAL
REMARKABLE GIRL
REMEMBRANCE DAY
REMOTE ANCESTOR
REMOVE FRICTION
RENDER A SERVICE
RENEW ONE'S YOUTH
RENEW THE ATTACK
REPAIRING LEASE
REPEATING RIFLE
REPEATING WATCH
REPORTED SPEECH
REPORT PROGRESS
REPRESS THE NEWS
REPUBLICAN VOTE
REPULSIVE FORCE
RESEARCH WORKER
RESERVE ACCOUNT
RESIDENT ABROAD
RESISTANCE COIL
RESISTANCE UNIT
RESPECT ONESELF
RESPONSIBLE MAN
RESTLESS NATURE
REST ON ONE'S OARS
RESTORE HARMONY
RESTORE TO POWER
RESTRICTED AREA
RETAILER OF NEWS
RETAINING FORCE
RETROGRADE STEP
RETURN A VERDICT
RETURN TO HEALTH
RETURN TO NORMAL
RETURN TO SENDER
REVENGE IS SWEET
REVENGE ONESELF
REVENUE OFFICER
REVERSIBLE COAT
REVERT TO NORMAL
REVISED EDITION
REVISED VERSION
REVOLVING DOORS
REVOLVING STAGE
RHAPSODY IN BLUE
RHEUMATIC FEVER
RHINOCEROS HIDE
RHODE ISLAND RED
RHYME NOR REASON
RHYMING COUPLET

RICHARD BRANSON
RICHARD MURDOCH
RICHARD STRAUSS
RICH IN VITAMINS
RICHMOND BRIDGE
RICH VOCABULARY
RIDE A COCK-HORSE
RIDE SIDE-SADDLE
RIDING BREECHES
RIGHT ABOUT FACE
RIGHT ABOUT TURN
RIGHT AND PROPER
RIGHT AS A TRIVET
RIGHT DIRECTION
RIGHT FIRST TIME
RIGHT FROM WRONG
RIGHT-HAND DRIVE
RING IN ONE'S EARS
RING THE CHANGES
RIPE EXPERIENCE
RISE IN THE WORLD
RISE TO ONE'S FEET
RISK EVERYTHING
RITUAL PRACTICE
ROAD TO THE ISLES
ROAD TRAFFIC ACT
ROARING FORTIES
ROARING SUCCESS
ROAR OF LAUGHTER
ROBERT BROWNING
ROBERT CUMMINGS
ROBERT HELPMANN
ROBERT THE BRUCE
ROBIN REDBREAST
ROBINSON CRUSOE
ROCKY MOUNTAINS
RODENT OPERATOR
ROD FOR ONE'S BACK
ROD, POLE OR PERCH
ROGER BANNISTER
ROLL A CIGARETTE
ROLLED UMBRELLA
ROLLING COUNTRY
ROLLING EXPANSE
ROLLING IN MONEY
ROMANTIC AFFAIR
ROMANTIC COMEDY
ROMEO AND JULIET
ROOF OF THE MOUTH
ROOF OF THE WORLD
ROOM FOR DISPUTE
ROSES ALL THE WAY
ROSES OF PICARDY
ROUGH AND TUMBLE
ROUGH TREATMENT
ROUND SHOULDERS

ROUND THE CORNER
ROUND THE HOUSES
ROUND THE WICKET
ROUSE CURIOSITY
ROUTE NATIONALE
ROVING REPORTER
ROW OVER NOTHING
ROYAL ARTILLERY
ROYAL AUTHORITY
ROYAL ENCLOSURE
ROYAL ENGINEERS
ROYAL FUSILIERS
ROYAL HOUSEHOLD
ROYAL RECEPTION
ROYAL RESIDENCE
ROYAL ST GEORGE'S
ROYAL TANK CORPS
RUBBER OF BRIDGE
RUB THE WRONG WAY
RUDYARD KIPLING
RUGGED FEATURES
RUINOUS EXPENSE
RULE ABSOLUTELY
RULE OUT OF ORDER
RULES OF CRICKET
RULES OF THE GAME
RUMP PARLIAMENT
RUNAWAY VICTORY
RUN FOR DEAR LIFE
RUN FOR ONE'S LIFE
RUN INTO TROUBLE
RUN LIKE A RABBIT
RUN LIKE THE WIND
RUNNING ACCOUNT
RUNNING REMARKS
RUNNING REPAIRS
RUN OF THE MARKET
RUN OUT OF PETROL
RUN THE GAUNTLET
RUN UP AN ACCOUNT
RUN WITH THE HARE
RUN WITH THE PACK
RUSH-HOUR TRAVEL
RUSH INTO THINGS
RUSH ONE'S FENCES
RUSSIAN LEATHER
RUSTLE OF SPRING

S – 14

SACK OF POTATOES
SACRED PRECINCT
SACRED WRITINGS
SADDER AND WISER
SADDLE OF MUTTON
SAFETY MEASURES

SAGE REFLECTION
SALES PROMOTION
SALIENT FEATURE
SALINE SOLUTION
SALISBURY PLAIN
SALT OF THE EARTH
SALUTARY LESSON
SAMUEL PICKWICK
SAMUEL PLIMSOLL
SARAH BERNHARDT
SARTOR RESARTUS
SATANIC MAJESTY
SATELLITE STATE
SATURDAY'S CHILD
SAUSAGE AND MASH
SAVELOY SAUSAGE
SAVE ONE'S BREATH
SAVINGS ACCOUNT
SAY GOOD MORNING
SAYING AND DOING
SAY ONE'S PRAYERS
SCALE OF CHARGES
SCALP TREATMENT
SCATTER THE SEED
SCENARIO WRITER
SCHEME OF THINGS
SCHOLASTIC POST
SCHOOL BUILDING
SCHOOL GOVERNOR
SCHOOL HOLIDAYS
SCHOOL MAGAZINE
SCHOOL OF WHALES
SCIENCE FICTION
SCIENTIFIC GAME
SCOBIE BREASLEY
SCORE A BULL'S EYE
SCOTCH AND WATER
SCOTCH THE SNAKE
SCOTCH WOODCOCK
SCOTS FUSILIERS
SCOTTISH CHURCH
SCOTTISH LEAGUE
SCOTTISH OFFICE
SCRAPE TOGETHER
SCATCH A LIVING
SCREAMING FARCE
SCROLL OF HONOUR
SCRUBBING BRUSH
SCRUPULOUS CARE
SCUM OF THE EARTH
SEA-GOING VESSEL
SEALED ENVELOPE
SEAL OF APPROVAL
SEARCH FOR TRUTH
SEASIDE HOLIDAY
SEASONABLE GIFT

SEASONABLE TIME
SEASONED TIMBER
SEAT IN THE LORDS
SEAT OF LEARNING
SEAT ON THE BENCH
SEAT ON THE BOARD
SECLUDED CORNER
SECOND DIVIDEND
SECOND DIVISION
SECOND ENGINEER
SECOND-HAND BOOK
SECOND-HAND SHOP
SECOND INTERVAL
SECOND MARRIAGE
SECOND OF AUGUST
SECOND-RATE MIND
SECOND SYMPHONY
SECOND THOUGHTS
SECOND WORLD WAR
SECRET INTRIGUE
SECURE A VICTORY
SECURE FOOTHOLD
SECURE POSITION
SECURITY POLICE
SEE JUSTICE DONE
SEE WHAT HAPPENS
SEIDLITZ POWDER
SEIZE THE CHANCE
SELECTION BOARD
SELF-SERVICE BAR
SEMI-FINAL MATCH
SEMI-FINAL ROUND
SEND A MESSENGER
SEND IN ONE'S CARD
SEND ONE PACKING
SEND TO THE STAKE
SENIOR REGIMENT
SENIOR WRANGLER
SENSELESS ORDER
SENSE OF BALANCE
SENSE OF DECENCY
SENSE OF HEARING
SENSE OF LOYALTY
SENSE OF PURPOSE
SENSITIVE PAPER
SENSITIVE PLANT
SENTIMENTAL BOY
SENT TO COVENTRY
SEPARATE TABLES
SERENE HIGHNESS
SERIES OF EVENTS
SERIOUS ATTEMPT
SERIOUS ILLNESS
SERIOUS MISTAKE
SERIOUS OFFENCE
SERIOUS STUDENT

SERIOUS SUBJECT
SERIOUS THOUGHT
SERIOUS TROUBLE
SERVANT PROBLEM
SERVE A SENTENCE
SERVES ONE RIGHT
SERVICE STATION
SET A BAD EXAMPLE
SET ARRANGEMENT
SET OF GOLF-CLUBS
SET THINGS RIGHT
SETTLE ACCOUNTS
SETTLE A QUARREL
SETTLED PURPOSE
SETTLED WEATHER
SETTLE ONE'S HASH
SEVEN AGES OF MAN
SEVENTEEN MILES
SEVENTH CENTURY
SEVENTH OF APRIL
SEVENTH OF MARCH
SEVENTY PER CENT
SEVERE SENTENCE
SEXUAL POLITICS
SHADOW MINISTER
SHADOW OF A DOUBT
SHADY CHARACTER
SHAGGY-DOG STORY
SHAKE BEFORE USE
SHAKE LIKE A LEAF
SHAKE OF THE HEAD
SHAKE THE BOTTLE
SHAKE UP AND DOWN
SHALLOW PRETEXT
SHANNON AIRPORT
SHARE OWNERSHIP
SHARE THE SPOILS
SHARK REPELLENT
SHARP AS A NEEDLE
SHARP ENCOUNTER
SHARPEN THE WITS
SHARP REJOINDER
SHARPS AND FLATS
SHATTERING BLOW
SHEEPDOG TRIALS
SHEEP'S CLOTHING
SHEET LIGHTNING
SHEFFIELD PLATE
SHEFFIELD STEEL
SHEPHERD MARKET
SHEPHERD'S CROOK
SHEPHERD'S PURSE
SHERLOCK HOLMES
SHERWOOD FOREST
SHILLING A POUND
SHINING EXAMPLE

SHIP IN DISTRESS	SIMPLE FRACTURE
SHIPPING CENTRE	SIMPLE INTEREST
SHIPPING OFFICE	SIMPLE SENTENCE
SHIP'S CARPENTER	SIMPLE SOLUTION
SHIVER AND SHAKE	SIMPLY FABULOUS
SHOCKED SILENCE	SIMPLY STARVING
SHOCKING TEMPER	SINCERE APOLOGY
SHOCK TREATMENT	SINGLE CURRENCY
SHOOTING RIGHTS	SINGLE INSTANCE
SHOOTING SEASON	SINGULAR NUMBER
SHOOTING TROPHY	SINKING FEELING
SHOOT THE RAPIDS	SINK LIKE A STONE
SHOPPING ARCADE	SINK OF INIQUITY
SHOPPING BASKET	SINS OF OMISSION
SHOPPING CENTRE	SINS OF THE FLESH
SHORT AND STOCKY	SIR ADRIAN BOULT
SHORTHAND SPEED	SIR EDWARD ELGAR
SHORT OF CAPITAL	SIR HENRY IRVING
SHORT PARAGRAPH	SIR HUGH WALPOLE
SHORT STATEMENT	SIR ISAAC NEWTON
SHOT-GUN WEDDING	SIR ISAAC PITMAN
SHOULDER OF LAMB	SIR JAMES BARRIE
SHOULDER OF VEAL	SIR JOHN GIELGUD
SHOW A BOLD FRONT	SIR WALTER SCOTT
SHOW COMPASSION	SIT-DOWN PROTEST
SHOW MODERATION	SIT ON THE GROUND
SHOW OF STRENGTH	SIT ON THE THRONE
SHOW OF SYMPATHY	SIXES AND SEVENS
SHOW ONE'S TICKET	SIX FEET OF EARTH
SHOW ONE THE DOOR	SIXTEEN PER CENT
SHOW RELUCTANCE	SIXTEENTH GREEN
SHOW REPENTANCE	SIXTEENTH OF MAY
SHREWD OBSERVER	SIXTH OF JANUARY
SHRIMP COCKTAIL	SIXTH OF OCTOBER
SHUTTLE SERVICE	SIX WICKETS DOWN
SICKENING SIGHT	SKATE ON THIN ICE
SIEGE OF LUCKNOW	SKILLED WORKMAN
SIGH WITH RELIEF	SKIRTING HEATER
SIGMUND ROMBERG	SKITTLES PLAYER
SIGNALS OFFICER	SLASHING ATTACK
SIGN OF GOOD LUCK	SLAVE OF FASHION
SIGN OF STRENGTH	SLAVE OF THE LAMP
SIGN OF THE CROSS	SLAVE TO FASHION
SIGN OF THE TIMES	SLEEPING BEAUTY
SIGN OF WEAKNESS	SLEEPING TABLET
SILENCE IN COURT	SLEEPLESS NIGHT
SILENCE REIGNED	SLEEP LIKE A BABY
SILENT MAJORITY	SLEEP OF THE JUST
SILENT REPROACH	SLEEPY SICKNESS
SILKS AND SATINS	SLIP ONE'S MEMORY
SILVANA MANGANO	SLOW-MOTION FILM
SILVER BRACELET	SLOW PROCESSION
SILVER STANDARD	SLUGS AND SNAILS
SIMPLE ADDITION	SLUM POPULATION
SIMPLE EQUATION	SMALL-BORE RIFLE
SIMPLE FRACTION	SMALL INTESTINE

SMALL OF THE BACK
SMALL REDUCTION
SMALL-TIME CROOK
SMART INVENTION
SMASHING DEFEAT
SMELL OF BURNING
SMILING THROUGH
SMOKE-ROOM STORY
SMOKING CONCERT
SMOOTH AS MARBLE
SMOOTH AS VELVET
SMOOTH CROSSING
SMOOTH ONE'S PATH
SNATCH A VERDICT
SNIP OFF THE ENDS
SOBERLY DRESSED
SOCIAL ACTIVITY
SOCIAL CLIMBING
SOCIAL CONTRACT
SOCIAL DEMOCRAT
SOCIAL INFERIOR
SOCIAL MOBILITY
SOCIAL PLANNING
SOCIAL POSITION
SOCIAL REGISTER
SOCIAL SECURITY
SOCIAL STANDING
SOCIAL SUPERIOR
SOCIETY ISLANDS
SOCIETY WEDDING
SODIUM CHLORIDE
SOFT FURNISHING
SOFT-SHOE DANCER
SOLDIER'S CHORUS
SOLE BONNE FEMME
SOLED AND HEELED
SOLEMN ENTREATY
SOLEMNLY AFFIRM
SOLEMN OCCASION
SOLE POSSESSION
SOLE PROPRIETOR
SOLID SUBSTANCE
SOLOMON ISLANDS
SOLVE THE RIDDLE
SOME DAY OR OTHER
SOMETHING EXTRA
SOMETHING FISHY
SOMETHING TO SAY
SOMEHWERE ABOUT
SO MUCH THE WORSE
SONG OF THE SHIRT
SONGS OF SOLOMON
SORE AFFLICTION
SOUND CHARACTER
SOUND EDUCATION
SOUND PRINCIPLE

SOUND REASONING
SOUND RECORDING
SOUND THE CHARGE
SOURCE OF DANGER
SOUR EXPRESSION
SOUSED MACKEREL
SOUTH AUSTRALIA
SOUTHERN ACCENT
SOUTHERN ASPECT
SOUTHERN REGION
SOUTHERN STATES
SOUTH OF ENGLAND
SOUTH SEA BUBBLE
SOVEREIGN POWER
SOVEREIGN STATE
SPACE PROGRAMME
SPACE TRAVELLER
SPARE NO EXPENSE
SPARING OF WORDS
SPEAKERS' CORNER
SPEAK ESPERANTO
SPEAK IN EARNEST
SPEAK IN RIDDLES
SPEAK OUT OF TURN
SPEAK THE TONGUE
SPECIAL DAMAGES
SPECIAL EDITION
SPECIAL EFFECTS
SPECIAL FEATURE
SPECIAL LICENCE
SPECIAL MENTION
SPECIAL MISSION
SPECIAL REQUEST
SPECIAL SERVICE
SPECIAL TROUBLE
SPECIAL VERDICT
SPECIFIC ANSWER
SPECIFIC OBJECT
SPECIFIC REMEDY
SPEECH TRAINING
SPEED OF THOUGHT
SPEED THE PLOUGH
SPEEDWAY RACING
SPEEDY RECOVERY
SPELLING LESSON
SPENT CARTRIDGE
SPINNING MOTION
SPIRITED ATTACK
SPIRIT OF THE AGE
SPIRIT OF THE LAW
SPIRITS OF SALTS
SPIRITUAL NEEDS
SPIRITUAL POWER
SPLENDID CHANCE
SPLIT ONE'S SIDES
SPOIL FOR A FIGHT

SPOIL THE EFFECT
SPOIL THE MARKET
SPOKEN LANGUAGE
SPOKEN LIKE A MAN
SPORTING CHANCE
SPORTING FINISH
SPORTS PAVILION
SPORTS REPORTER
SPRAY OF FLOWERS
SPREAD MISCHIEF
SPRIG OF HEATHER
SPRINGHEEL JACK
SPRING IN THE AIR
SPRING MATTRESS
SQUADRON LEADER
SQUARE ACCOUNTS
SQUARE BRACKETS
SQUASH RACKETS
STAGE A COMEBACK
STAGE CARPENTER
STAGE DIRECTION
STAGGERED HOURS
STAGGERING BLOW
STAINLESS STEEL
STAKE ONE'S CLAIM
STAMFORD BRIDGE
STAMP COLLECTOR
STAMPING GROUND
STANDARD WEIGHT
STAND CONDEMNED
STAND CONVICTED
STAND CORRECTED
STANDING CUSTOM
STANDING ORDERS
STAND IN THE DOCK
ST ANDREW'S CROSS
STANDS TO REASON
STAND THE RACKET
STAND THE STRAIN
STANLEY BALDWIN
STAPLE INDUSTRY
STAR ATTRACTION
STARBOARD WATCH
STARE IN THE FACE
STARTER'S ORDERS
STARTING HANDLE
STARTING PISTOL
START SOMETHING
START TO QUARREL
STARVATION DIET
STARVATION WAGE
STATE DOCUMENTS
STATE OF AFFAIRS
STATE OF DENMARK
STATE OWNERSHIP
STATIONERS' HALL

STAY-AT-HOME TYPE
STAY ON THE SHELF
ST CLEMENT DANES
STEADY INCREASE
STEADY PROGRESS
STEAK AND KIDNEY
STEAK AND ONIONS
STEEL ENGRAVING
STEEL ONE'S HEART
STEEPED IN CRIME
STEERING COLUMN
STEM THE CURRENT
STEPHEN LEACOCK
STEPHEN SPENDER
STEP ON THE JUICE
STEP UP THE SPEED
STERLING SILVER
STEWART GRANGER
ST GEORGE'S CROSS
STICK AT NOTHING
STICK OF RHUBARB
STICKS OUT A MILE
STICK UP A NOTICE
STIFF AS A RAMROD
STILL-LIFE STUDY
STINGING NETTLE
STING IN THE TAIL
STIRLING CASTLE
STIR ONE'S STUMPS
STIRRING SPEECH
ST JAMES'S PALACE
ST JAMES'S STREET
STOCK-CAR RACING
STOCK CHARACTER
STOCKINGED FEET
STOCKTON ON TEES
STOKE NEWINGTON
STOKE THE BOILER
STOLEN PROPERTY
STOMACH TROUBLE
STONE-COLD SOBER
STOOP TO CONQUER
STORAGE BATTERY
STORE DETECTIVE
STORM IN A TEA-CUP
STORMY EXCHANGE
STRADDLE A HORSE
STRAIGHT ANSWER
STRAIGHT AS A DIE
STRAIGHT COMEDY
STRAIN AT THE BIT
STRAINED MUSCLE
STRAIN ONE'S EYES
STRAIN THE TRUTH
STRAITS OF DOVER
STRAND OF COTTON

STRANGE BUT TRUE
STRANGE DESTINY
STRANGE FEELING
STRANGE REQUEST
STRATEGIC SKILL
STRAWBERRY FAIR
STRAWBERRY HILL
STRAWBERRY MARK
STRAWBERRY ROAN
STRAW IN THE WIND
STREAK OF HUMOUR
STREAMLINED CAR
STREET FIGHTING
STREET LIGHTING
STREET MUSICIAN
STRENGTH OF MIND
STRENGTH OF WILL
STRETCH OF WATER
STRICTLY HONEST
STRICT TRAINING
STRIKE A BALANCE
STRIKE A BARGAIN
STRIKE A NEW NOTE
STRIKE ONE'S FLAG
STRIKE WITH FEAR
STRIKING EFFECT
STRING OF HORSES
STRING OF ONIONS
STRING OF PEARLS
STRING TOGETHER
STRIP FOR ACTION
STIP-TEASE SHOW
STRIVE FOR GLORY
STROKE OF GENIUS
STROKE OF THE PEN
STRONG ARGUMENT
STRONG AS A HORSE
STRONG FEELINGS
STRONG IN THE ARM
STRONG LANGUAGE
STRONGLY WORDED
STRONG MEASURES
STRONG POSITION
STRONG RIGHT ARM
STRONG SOLUTION
STUBBORN FELLOW
STUDIO AUDIENCE
STUDIO PORTRAIT
STUMBLING BLOCK
STUPID QUESTION
STYLISH FASHION
SUBMERGED TENTH
SUBMIT TO DEFEAT
SUBSTANTIAL SUM
SUCCESSFUL PLAY
SUDDEN DOWNPOUR

SUDDEN MOVEMENT
SUDDEN PROGRESS
SUGAR-PLUM FAIRY
SUITABLE TENANT
SUMMARY JUSTICE
SUMMER HOLIDAYS
SUMMER VACATION
SUMPTUOUS FEAST
SUNK IN OBLIVION
SUPERIOR PERSON
SUPPORT A FAMILY
SUPPORTERS' CLUB
SUPPORTING CAST
SUPPORTING FILM
SUPPORTING PART
SUPPORTING ROLE
SUPREME COMMAND
SUPREME CONTROL
SUPREME COUNCIL
SURFACE TENSION
SURGICAL SPIRIT
SURPRISE ATTACK
SURPRISE PACKET
SURRENDER VALUE
SUSPEND PAYMENT
SUSPICIOUS MIND
SUZANNE LENGLEN
SWAGGER CLOTHES
SWALLOW THE BAIT
SWALLOW THE PILL
SWARM OF INSECTS
SWARTHY SKINNED
SWEAR TO SECRECY
SWEEPING ACTION
SWEEPING GLANCE
SWEEPING REMARK
SWEEP THE BOARDS
SWEET AND TWENTY
SWEET SEVENTEEN
SWEETS OF OFFICE
SWEET SUBSTANCE
SWEET SURRENDER
SWELL WITH PRIDE
SWELTERING HEAT
SWIFT AS AN ARROW
SWIMMING LESSON
SWIMMING TRUNKS
SWIM THE CHANNEL
SWORD SWALLOWER
SWORN STATEMENT
SWORN TO SECRECY
SYBIL THORNDIKE

T – 14

TABLE OF WEIGHTS

TACTICAL VOTING
TACTICAL WEAPON
TAILOR-MADE SUIT
TAKE AN INTEREST
TAKE A RISE OUT OF
TAKE BY SURPRISE
TAKE FIRST PRIZE
TAKE FOR GRANTED
TAKE IN GOOD PART
TAKE IN MARRIAGE
TAKE IT FROM HERE
TAKE NO INTEREST
TAKE ONE'S CHANCE
TAKE ONE'S CHOICE
TAKE ONESELF OFF
TAKE ONE'S FENCES
TAKE ONE'S HAT OFF
TAKE OUT A PATENT
TAKE OUT A POLICY
TAKE POSSESSION
TAKE PRECEDENCE
TAKE THE BISCUIT
TAKE THE EDGE OFF
TAKE THE GILT OFF
TAKE THE LIBERTY
TAKE THE TROUBLE
TAKE THINGS EASY
TAKE TO THE BOATS
TAKE TO THE HILLS
TAKE TO THE WATER
TAKE TO THE WOODS
TAKE UP AN OPTION
TAKE UP THE SLACK
TALK IN A WHISPER
TALKING PICTURE
TALK OF THE DEVIL
TANGIBLE OBJECT
TANGLED THREADS
TANNED BY THE SUN
TAPIOCA PUDDING
TAP OUT A MESSAGE
TARGET PRACTICE
TARPAULIN SHEET
TARTAN TROUSERS
TASTE OF THE WHIP
TAXED TO THE HILT
TEA AND BISCUITS
TEA AND SYMPATHY
TEAR OFF THE MASK
TECHNICAL HITCH
TECHNICAL SKILL
TEETH OF THE WIND
TELEGRAPH WIRES
TELEPHONE KIOSK
TELEPHONE SHELF
TELEPHONE WIRES

TELESCOPIC LENS
TELESCOPIC VIEW
TELEVISION MAST
TELEVISION PLAY
TELEVISION STAR
TELL A TALL STORY
TELL EVERYTHING
TEMPLE OF APOLLO
TEMPORARY ABODE
TEMPORARY LEASE
TEMPORARY VISIT
TEN AND A QUARTER
TEN AND SIXPENCE
TEN AND TENPENCE
TEN AND TWOPENCE
TENDER FEELINGS
TEN-MINUTE ALIBI
TENSE SITUATION
TENTH OF JANUARY
TENTH OF OCTOBER
TERM OF CONTEMPT
TERMS OF THE WILL
TERRIBLE ORDEAL
TERRIBLE WRENCH
TESTIFY AGAINST
TEST OF STRENGTH
THANKLESS CHILD
THANKS A MILLION
THANKS VERY MUCH
THAT CERTAIN AGE
THAT'S THE TICKET
THE ARMED FORCES
THEATRICAL STAR
THE AUTHORITIES
THE BEE'S WEDDING
THE BEST CIRCLES
THE BLACK FOREST
THE BLACK PRINCE
THE CAT'S PYJAMAS
THE CESAREWITCH
THE COMMON TOUCH
THE CORINTHIANS
THE CRUCIFIXION
THE DARDENELLES
THE END OF THE DAY
THE ETERNAL CITY
THE EXACT AMOUNT
THE EXTREMITIES
THE FIRST CUCKOO
THE FIRST PERSON
THE FLINTSTONES
THE FORSYTE SAGA
THE FOUR JUST MEN
THE GOLDEN BOUGH
THE GOOD OLD DAYS
THE GRAND MANNER

THE GRAND OLD MAN	THIRTEEN OUNCES
THE GREAT DIVIDE	THIRTEENTH HOLE
THE HIGHWAY CODE	THIRTEEN TRICKS
THE INQUISITION	THIRTIETH OF MAY
THEIR MAJESTIES	THIRTY THOUSAND
THE JUNGLE BOOKS	THIRTY YEARS' WAR
THE LILAC DOMINO	THIS HAPPY BREED
THE LORD'S PRAYER	THIS IS YOUR LIFE
THE LOTUS-EATERS	THOMAS SHERATON
THE MINSTREL BOY	THORN IN THE SIDE
THE NELSON TOUCH	THOROUGH SEARCH
THE NETHERLANDS	THOUGHTFUL MOOD
THE OLD GREY MARE	THOUSAND AND ONE
THE OLD OAK CHEST	THOUSAND POUNDS
THE PHILLIPINES	THREADING BEADS
THE PLANEMAKERS	THREAD TOGETHER
THE PLANETARIUM	THREATEN DANGER
THE POLICE FORCE	THREE BLIND MICE
THE POLYTECHNIC	THREE-BOTTLE MAN
THE QUEEN MOTHER	THREE-CARD TRICK
THE REFORMATION	THREE MEN IN A TUB
THE RENAISSANCE	THREE-MILE LIMIT
THE RESTORATION	THREE-PIECE SUIT
THE SEVEN DWARFS	THREE SHILLINGS
THE SHINING HOUR	THREE-SPEED GEAR
THE SINGING FOOL	THREE SYLLABLES
THE SIX COUNTIES	THRILLER WRITER
THE STAR CHAMBER	THROAT PASTILLE
THE THIRD DEGREE	THROATY CHUCKLE
THE TIME MACHINE	THROUGH THE AGES
THE UNCONSCIOUS	THROUGH THE MILL
THE UNDERGROUND	THROUGH THE NOSE
THE UNDERSIGNED	THROUGH THE POST
THE VICAR OF BRAY	THROUGH THE TOWN
THE WATER BABIES	THROW IN ONE'S LOT
THE WHEREWITHAL	THROW LIGHT UPON
THE WINTER'S TALE	THROW OF THE DICE
THE WORST IS OVER	THROW OVERBOARD
THICK AS THIEVES	THROW THE HAMMER
THICK OF THE FRAY	THROW TO THE DOGS
THIEVES' KITCHEN	THURSDAY ISLAND
THIEVING MAGPIE	THURSDAY'S CHILD
THINK CAREFULLY	TICKLED TO DEATH
THINK OF ANOTHER	TICKLISH MATTER
THINK OF A NUMBER	TIMBER MERCHANT
THINK OF THE PAST	TIME FOR THOUGHT
THINK THINGS OUT	TIME IMMEMORIAL
THIRD DIMENSION	TIMELY REMINDER
THIRD-FLOOR BACK	TIME OF ONE'S LIFE
THIRD OF JANUARY	TIME WITHOUT END
THIRD OF OCTOBER	TIN OF PILCHARDS
THIRD-PARTY RISK	TIP OF THE TONGUE
THIRD PROGRAMME	TIRELESS WORKER
THIRD TIME LUCKY	TOAD OF TOAD HALL
THIRST FOR BLOOD	TO A GREAT EXTENT
THIRTEEN MONTHS	TO A LARGE DEGREE

TO A LARGE EXTENT
TOASTED TEA-CAKE
TOAST OF THE TOWN
TOBACCO AUCTION
TOBACCO LICENCE
TOBACCO PLANTER
TOIL AND TROUBLE
TOKEN OF RESPECT
TONTONS MACOUTE
TOOTH FOR A TOOTH
TOP-HAT AND TAILS
TOPICAL SUBJECT
TOPLESS BATHING
TOP OF ONE'S VOICE
TOP OF THE CHARTS
TOP OF THE LADDER
TOP OF THE LEAGUE
TORRENTIAL RAIN
TORRENT OF ABUSE
TORTURE CHAMBER
TORTURED BY FEAR
TORVILL AND DEAN
TOTAL ABSTAINER
TOTAL IGNORANCE
TOTAL IMMERSION
TO THE BITTER END
TO THE END OF TIME
TOUCH A SOFT SPOT
TOUGH AS LEATHER
TOURING COMPANY
TOURING THE COUNTRY
TOWN AND COUNTRY
TOWN COUNCILLOR
TRACKED VEHICLE
TRACTION ENGINE
TRADE REFERENCE
TRADING STATION
TRAFFIC CONTROL
TRAFFIC DENSITY
TRAFFIC PROBLEM
TRAINED SOLDIER
TRAINING GROUND
TRAINING SCHOOL
TRAIN OF THOUGHT
TRANSFER BY DEED
TRANSITIVE VERB
TRANSPORT HOUSE
TRANSPORT PLANE
TRAVEL BROCHURE
TRAVELLER'S REST
TRAVELLER'S TALE
TRAVELLING TIME
TRAVEL THE WORLD
TREACLE PUDDING
TREAD THE BOARDS
TREAD UNDERFOOT

TREASURE ISLAND
TREMBLE TO THINK
TREMBLING HANDS
TREMBLING VOICE
TRIANGULAR DUEL
TRICKLE OF BLOOD
TRICKLE OF WATER
TRICK OF FORTUNE
TRICKY BUSINESS
TRICKY QUESTION
TRIDENT MISSILE
TRIED FOR MURDER
TRIFLING AMOUNT
TRIFLING CHARGE
TRIFLING MATTER
TRIFLING REMARK
TRINITY COLLEGE
TRIPE AND ONIONS
TRIPLE ALLIANCE
TRISTRAM SHANDY
TRIUMPHAL CROWN
TRIVIAL PURSUIT
TROOP MOVEMENTS
TROOP THE COLOUR
TROPIC OF CANCER
TROUBLE BREWING
TROUBLED WATERS
TROUBLE IN STORE
TROUPE OF ACTORS
TROUSERS POCKET
TRUE CONFESSION
TRUMPED-UP STORY
TRUNDLE THEM OUT
TRY AND TRY AGAIN
TRY ONE'S FORTUNE
TRY ONE'S HARDEST
TUESDAY EVENING
TUESDAY MORNING
TUMBLER OF WATER
TUNBRIDGE WELLS
TURF ACCOUNTANT
TURKISH DELIGHT
TURKISH TOBACCO
TURN AT THE WHEEL
TURN DOWN THE BED
TURN DOWN THE GAS
TURN EVERY STONE
TURN OFF THE HEAT
TURN OF THE SCREW
TURN OF THE WHEEL
TURN ON ONE'S HEEL
TURN ON THE LIGHT
TURN OUT TO GRASS
TURN RIGHT ROUND
TURN TOPSYTURVY
TURN TO THE RIGHT

TURN UP ONE'S NOSE
TURN UPSIDE DOWN
TWELFTH CENTURY
TWELFTH OF APRIL
TWELFTH OF MARCH
TWELVE AND A HALF
TWELVE APOSTLES
TWELVE THOUSAND
TWENTIETH OF MAY
TWENTY THOUSAND
TWICE THE WEIGHT
TWIST OF TOBACCO
TWISTS AND TURNS
TWITTER OF BIRDS
TWO AND A QUARTER
TWO-HANDED SWORD
TWO-HEADED EAGLE
TWO WICKETS DOWN
TYPICAL EXAMPLE

U – 14

ULTERIOR MOTIVE
ULTERIOR OBJECT
ULTIMATE RESULT
ULTRA-VIOLET RAY
UNABLE TO CHOOSE
UNACCOUNTED FOR
UNBALANCED MIND
UNBOSOM ONSELF
UNBROKEN SPIRIT
UNCIVILIZED MAN
UNCLE TOM'S CABIN
UNDER A HANDICAP
UNDER AN EMBARGO
UNDER CROSS-FIRE
UNDER DETENTION
UNDERGO REPAIRS
UNDER GUARANTEE
UNDER ONE'S THUMB
UNDER RESTRAINT
UNDER SUSPICION
UNDER THE BONNET
UNDER THE CARPET
UNDER THE DOCTOR
UNDER THE GROUND
UNDER THE HAMMER
UNDER THE HARROW
UNDER TREATMENT
UNDER TWENTY-ONE
UNDRESS UNIFORM
UNDUE INFLUENCE
UNEARNED INCOME
UNEASY PROGRESS
UNFAMILIAR WORD
UNIFORM PATTERN

UNINVITED GUEST
UNIQUE OCCASION
UNITED SERVICES
UNIVERSAL AGENT
UNIVERSAL AUNTS
UNIVERSAL JOINT
UNIVERSAL PEACE
UNIVERSITY TERM
UNIVERSITY TOWN
UNIVERSITY VOTE
UNKNOWN COUNTRY
UNKNOWN ELEMENT
UNKNOWN SOLDIER
UNKNOWN WARRIOR
UNLEADED PETROL
UNLIMITED SCOPE
UNLIMITED SPACE
UNMARRIED WOMAN
UNOCCUPIED FLAT
UNPLEASANT DUTY
UNPLOUGHED LAND
UNREQUITED LOVE
UNSALTED BUTTER
UNSETTLING NEWS
UNSUITABLE TIME
UNTER DEN LINDEN
UPWARDLY MOBILE
UPWARD MOBILITY
UNWELCOME GUEST
UPHILL STRUGGLE
UPON REFLECTION
UPRIGHT POSTURE
URBAN GUERRILLA
USUAL SIGNATURE
USURP THE THRONE

V – 14

VACATE ONE'S SEAT
VAGRANCY CHARGE
VAGUE SUSPICION
VAIN AS A PEACOCK
VALET DE CHAMBRE
VALID OBJECTION
VALSE DES FLEURS
VANILLA FLAVOUR
VANISHING CREAM
VANISHING POINT
VANISHING TRICK
VARIABLE TEMPER
VARIETY THEATRE
VARIOUS COLOURS
VARIOUS REASONS
VARNISH REMOVER
VARYING SUCCESS
VAST DIFFERENCE

VAST EXPERIENCE
VATICAN COUNCIL
VAUDEVILLE SHOW
VEER TO THE RIGHT
VEGETABLE CURRY
VEGETABLE FIBRE
VEGETABLE SALAD
VEGETABLE WORLD
VEGETARIAN DIET
VEGETARIAN DISH
VEGETARIAN MEAL
VENDING MACHINE
VENERABLE BEARD
VENERABLE RUINS
VENETIAN CARPET
VENETIAN SCHOOL
VENETIAN WINDOW
VENTURE CAPITAL
VENUS AND ADONIS
VERBAL ARGUMENT
VERBAL CONTRACT
VERBAL EVIDENCE
VERBATIM REPORT
VERIFY THE FACTS
VERSATILE ACTOR
VERTICAL FLIGHT
VESTED INTEREST
VETERAN SERVICE
VICTIM OF CHANGE
VICTORIA PALACE
VICTORIA REGINA
VIETNAM VETERAN
VIEW WITH FAVOUR
VINCENT VAN GOGH
VIOLENT QUARREL
VIOLENT TEMPEST
VIOLETS ARE BLUE
VIOLIN CONCERTO
VIRTUAL REALITY
VISIBLE EXPORTS
VISIBLE HORIZON
VITAL PRINCIPLE
VOICE AN OPINION
VOICE OF AMERICA
VOLATILE LIQUID
VOLUNTEER CORPS
VOTING STRENGTH
VULGAR FRACTION
VULGAR LANGUAGE
VULGAR PARLANCE
VULNERABLE SPOT

W – 14

WAG A FOREFINGER
WAGGING TONGUES

WAIFS AND STRAYS
WAIT TILL THE END
WAKE WITH A START
WALKING HOLIDAY
WALKING LIBRARY
WALK INTO A PUNCH
WALK INTO DANGER
WALLOW IN LUXURY
WALLS OF JERICHO
WALPURGIS NIGHT
WALTER DE LA MARE
WALTZ COTILLION
WANTED BY THE LAW
WANT FOR NOTHING
WANT OF ALACRITY
WANT OF PRACTICE
WANT OF SYMMETRY
WARD IN CHANCERY
WARD OF THE COURT
WARDROBE DEALER
WAREHOUSE PARTY
WARM FRIENDSHIP
WARM TO ONE'S WORK
WARNER BROTHERS
WARNING EXAMPLE
WAR OF ATTRITION
WAR OF EXPANSION
WARRANT OFFICER
WARREN HASTINGS
WARSAW CONCERTO
WARS OF THE ROSES
WARWICK DEEPING
WASH AND BRUSH-UP
WASH DIRTY LINEN
WASHING MACHINE
WASHINGTON POST
WASTE ONE'S WORDS
WATCH CAREFULLY
WATCH COMMITTEE
WATCH THE BIRDIE
WATER FILTER JUG
WATERLOO BRIDGE
WATER ON THE KNEE
WATER THE GARDEN
WATER THE HORSES
WATER THE WICKET
WAVE OF VIOLENCE
WAVERLEY NOVELS
WEAK AT THE KNEES
WE ARE NOT AMUSED
WEARING APPAREL
WEATHER BALLOON
WEATHER OUTLOOK
WEATHER PROPHET
WEATHER STATION
WEDDING MORNING

WEDDING PRESENT
WEDDING SERVICE
WEDNESDAY NIGHT
WEEK-END VISITOR
WEEKLY MAGAZINE
WEEK'S GOOD CAUSE
WEIGH ONE'S WORDS
WEIGHTY PROBLEM
WELFARE OFFICER
WELL ACQUAINTED
WELL-CHOSEN WORD
WELL-EARNED REST
WELLINGTON BOOT
WELL-READ PERSON
WELL-WORN PHRASE
WELL WORTH WHILE
WELSH MOUNTAINS
WEMBLEY STADIUM
WENT WITH A SWING
WESTERN GERMANY
WEST HARTLEPOOL
WET ONE'S WHISTLE
WHAT DO YOU THINK?
WHAT IN THE WORLD?
WHAT OF THE CLOCK?
WHAT OF THE NIGHT?
WHAT'S THE DAMAGE?
WHAT'S THE MATTER?
WHAT THE DICKENS!
WHEELED TRAFFIC
WHEEL OF FORTUNE
WHICH WAY TO TURN
WHIGS AND TORIES
WHITE CHRISTMAS
WHITE CORPUSCLE
WHITEHALL FARCE
WHITE IN THE FACE
WHITE MAN'S GRAVE
WHITER THAN SNOW
WHITNEY HOUSTON
WHITSUN HOLIDAY
WHOLE-MEAL BREAD
WHOLESALE PRICE
WIDDICOMBE FAIR
WIDELY BELIEVED
WIDEN THE BREACH
WIDE OF THE TRUTH
WIDE-OPEN SPACES
WIDE VOCABULARY
WIELD THE WILLOW
WIFE IN NAME ONLY
WILD ACCUSATION
WILD ENTHUSIASM
WILD EXCITEMENT
WILD-GOOSE CHASE
WILFRED PICKLES

WILLIAM AND MARY
WILLIAM HOGARTH
WILLING AND ABLE
WIN BY A KNOCK-OUT
WIND INSTRUMENT
WINDOW CURTAINS
WINDOW DRESSING
WINDOW ENVELOPE
WINDOW SHOPPING
WIND UP A COMPANY
WINE BY THE GLASS
WINNER TAKES ALL
WIN SECOND PRIZE
WINTER CLOTHING
WINTER PLANTING
WINTER QUARTERS
WINTER WOOLLIES
WISE AS A SERPENT
WITH A GOOD GRACE
WITH ALL MY HEART
WITH A VENGEANCE
WITHHOLD ASSENT
WITHOUT BLEMISH
WITHOUT CEASING
WITHOUT CONTEXT
WITHOUT MEASURE
WITHOUT PURPOSE
WITHOUT REMORSE
WITHOUT RESERVE
WITHOUT RESPECT
WITHOUT STRINGS
WITHOUT WARNING
WITH PERMISSION
WITH THE COLOURS
WITH THE CURRENT
WOMAN OF FASHION
WOMEN'S LAND ARMY
WOMEN'S MOVEMENT
WOMEN'S QUARTERS
WOMEN'S SUFFRAGE
WONDERFUL SIGHT
WONDERFUL WORLD
WOOLLEN SWEATER
WOOLLY THINKING
WORCESTER SAUCE
WORKING CAPITAL
WORKING CLOTHES
WORKING FOREMAN
WORKING HOLIDAY
WORK IN PROGRESS
WORK LIKE A CHARM
WORK LIKE A HORSE
WORK LIKE A NAVVY
WORK LIKE BLAZES
WORK ONE'S TICKET
WORK TO SCHEDULE

WORLDLY AFFAIRS
WORLD OF FASHION
WORLD OF MEANING
WORLD OF ONE'S OWN
WORLD OF REALITY
WORLD SITUATION
WORMWOOD SCRUBS
WORN TO A FRAZZLE
WORTH A BOB OR TWO
WORTH IMITATING
WORTH ONE'S WHILE
WORTHY CHAMPION
WORTHY OF ESTEEM
WORTHY OF PRAISE
WORTHY OF REMARK
WRAPPED IN GLOOM
WRATH OF THE GODS
WREAK VENGEANCE
WRESTLING MATCH
WRIGHT BROTHERS
WRING ONE'S HANDS
WRITTEN APOLOGY
WRITTEN CONSENT
WRITTEN IN VERSE
WRITTEN MESSAGE
WRONG DIRECTION
WRONGFUL ARREST

Y – 14

YACHTING CENTRE
YELLOWISH BROWN
YELLOW JAUNDICE
YELLOW SAPPHIRE
YORKSHIRE DALES
YORKSHIRE MOORS
YOUNG AND TENDER
YOUNGER BROTHER
YOUNGEST SISTER
YOUNG LOCHINVAR
YOUNG MAN'S FANCY
YOUNG PRETENDER
YOUNG SHOULDERS
YOU'RE TELLING ME!
YOUR EXCELLENCY
YOURS SINCERELY
YOU SHOULD WORRY!

A – 15

ABANDON ONE'S POST
ABERDEEN TERRIER
ABERFAN DISASTER
ABLAZE WITH LIGHT
ABODE OF WARRIORS
ABOVE EVERYTHING

ABOVE THE AVERAGE
ABOVE THE SURFACE
ABOVE THE WEATHER
ABRIDGED VERSION
ABRUPT DEPARTURE
ABSOLUTE MINIMUM
ABSOLUTE MONARCH
ABSTRACT PAINTER
ABSTRACT SCIENCE
ABUNDANCE OF FOOD
ABUSE OF LANGUAGES
ACADEMIC CIRCLES
ACCEPT A PROPOSAL
ACCEPTED MEANING
ACCEPTED PAIRING
ACCEPTED VERSION
ACCIDENTAL DEATH
ACCIDENT OF BIRTH
ACCORDING TO PLAN
ACCOUNT RENDERED
ACCREDITED AGENT
A CHRISTMAS CAROL
ACID BATH MURDERS
ACQUISITIVE MIND
ACROSS THE STREET
ACTIVE SUPPORTER
ACT OF AGGRESSION
ACT OF DEDICATION
ACT OF FRIENDSHIP
ACT OF PARLIAMENT
ACT OF PROVIDENCE
ACT OF SETTLEMENT
ACT THE GIDDY GOAT
ADDED ATTRACTION
ADDISON'S DISEASE
ADD TO ONE'S INCHES
ADHESIVE PLASTER
ADJUTANT GENERAL
ADMIT EVERYTHING
ADOPTION SOCIETY
A DROP IN THE OCEAN
ADVANCED BOOKING
ADVANCED IN YEARS
ADVANCED STUDENT
ADVANCED STUDIES
ADVANCED THINKER
ADVERTISING SITE
AEROPLANE TRIALS
AFFLUENT SOCIETY
AFRAID OF COMPANY
AFER MY OWN HEART
AFTERNOON SIESTA
AGAINST ONE'S WILL
AGAINST THE CLOCK
AGAINST THE GRAIN
AGAINST THE RULES

AGE OF AUTOMATION
AGE OF DISCRETION
AGING POPULATION
AGREE BEFOREHAND
AGREE ON A VERDICT
AGREE TO DISAGREE
AHEAD OF SCHEDULE
AIDER AND ABETTER
AIMLESS ACTIVITY
AIR CHIEF MARSHAL
AIR CONDITIONING
AIRCRAFT CARRIER
AIREDALE TERRIER
AIR FORCE OFFICER
AIR FORCE RESERVE
AIR MINISTRY ROOF
AIR OF DETACHMENT
ALBERT CHEVALIER
ALDERSHOT TATTOO
ALEXANDRA PALACE
ALFRED HITCHCOCK
ALIMENTARY CANAL
A LITTLE LEARNING
ALIVE AND KICKING
ALL ALONG THE LINE
ALL FOUR QUARTERS
ALL MANNER OF WAYS
ALL-NIGHT SESSION
ALL-NIGHT SITTING
ALLOTMENT HOLDER
ALL OVER THE PLACE
ALL PASSION SPENT
ALL PULL TOGETHER
ALL-ROUND ABILITY
ALL-ROUND ATHLETE
ALL THE TRIMMINGS
ALL THE WORLD OVER
ALL THE YEAR ROUND
ALONE IN THE WORLD
ALTERNATIVE PLAN
ALTERNATIVE VOTE
AMATEUR CHAMPION
AMATEUR FOOTBALL
AMBIGUOUS SAYING
AMBITIOUS SCHEME
AMBULANCE CHASER
AMBULANCE DRIVER
AMERICAN EMBASSY
AMERICAN IN PARIS
AMMUNITION BOOTS
AMUSEMENT ARCADE
ANABOLIC STEROID
ANCIENT LANGUAGE
ANCIENT MONUMENT
ANCIENT PEDIGREE
ANDERSON SHELTER

ANDROMEDA STRAIN
AND SO SAY ALL OF US
ANGULAR VELOCITY
ANIMAL MAGNETISM
ANIMATED CARTOON
ANIMATED GESTURE
ANNIE GET YOUR GUN
ANNIVERSARY DATE
ANNOUNCE ONESELF
ANNUS HORRIBILUS
ANONYMOUS LETTER
ANOREXIA NERVOSA
ANOTHER CUP OF TEA
ANOTHER FINE MESS
ANTARCTIC CIRCLE
ANTE-NATAL CLINIC
ANTE POST BETTING
ANTHONY TROLLOPE
ANTI-AIRCRAFT GUN
ANTIQUE MERCHANT
ANTI RED-EYE FLASH
ANXIETY NEUROSIS
ANXIOUS TO PLEASE
ANYONE FOR TENNIS
ANY PORT IN A STORM
APPEALING GLANCE
APPEALING MANNER
APPLICATION FORM
APPLIED RESEARCH
APPLY THE CLOSURE
APPROACH MANHOOD
APPROXIMATE COST
APRIL THE SEVENTH
APRIL THE TWELFTH
ARMED NEUTRALITY
ARMED TO THE TEETH
AROUND THE CORNER
ARRIVAL PLATFORM
ARTICLE FOR SALE
ARTICLES OF FAITH
ARTIFICIAL FIBRE
ARTIFICIAL LIGHT
ARTIFICIAL SMILE
ARTIFICIAL STONE
ARTIFICIAL TEETH
ART OF MANAGEMENT
AS A MATTER OF FACT
AS AN ALTERNATIVE
ASCEND THE THRONE
ASCENSION ISLAND
AS FAR AS POSSIBLE
AS FAR AS YOU CAN GO
AS FRESH AS A DAISY
AS GENTLE AS A LAMB
AS GOOD AS ONE GETS
AS HARD AS GRANITE

ASHMOLEAN MUSEUM
AS KEEN AS MUSTARD
ASK FOR ONE'S CARDS
AS LIKE AS TWO PEAS
AS LONG AS YOU LIKE
AS NEAT AS A NEW PIN
AS OLD AS THE HILLS
AS QUIET AS A MOUSE
AS RICH AS CROESUS
ASSISTANT MASTER
ASSISTED PASSAGE
ASSOCIATED IDEAS
ASSORTED TOFFEES
AS STIFF AS A POKER
ASSUME A DISGUISE
AS THE SAYING GOES
ASTRAL INFLUENCE
ASTRONOMER ROYAL
A STUDY IN SCARLET
AS WHITE AS A SHEET
AT A DISADVANTAGE
AT A LOSS FOR WORDS
AT CLOSE QUARTERS
AT CROSS PURPOSES
ATLANTIC CHARTER
ATOMIC SUMARINE
ATTEMPTED MURDER
AT THE CROSS-ROADS
AT THE DROP OF A HAT
ATTORNEY GENERAL
AT TRINITY CHURCH
AUGUST THE EIGHTH
AUGUST THE FOURTH
AUGUST THE SECOND
AUSTERITY BUDGET
AUTOGRAPH HUNTER
AUTOMATIC CHANGE
AUTOMATIC PISTOL
AUTUMNAL EQUINOX
AUXILIARY FORCES
AUXILIARY TROOPS
AVERAGE SPECIMEN
AVERSION THERAPY
AWKWARD CUSTOMER
AWKWARD POSITION
AWKWARD QUESTION

B – 15

BABY-FACED NELSON
BACHELOR OF MUSIC
BACHELOR'S BUTTON
BACKGROUND MUSIC
BACK OF THE BEYOND
BACKSTAGE NERVES
BACK TO SQUARE ONE
BACK TO THE FUTURE

BACKWARD PEOPLES
BALACLAVA HELMET
BALANCE OF TERROR
BALANCE THE BOOKS
BALLROOM DANCING
BANKRUPTCY COURT
BANKS OF THE CLYDE
BANNER HEADLINES
BANNS OF MARRIAGE
BARBARA CARTLAND
BARBARA STANWYCK
BARBER OF SEVILLE
BARE POSSIBILITY
BARE SUBSISTENCE
BARGAIN BASEMENT
BARNUM AND BAILEY
BARON MUNCHAUSEN
BARRISTER'S CLERK
BARROW IN FURNESS
BARTHOLOMEW FAIR
BASIC INGREDIENT
BATCH OF RECRUITS
BATS IN THE BELFRY
BATTERSEA BRIDGE
BATTLE OF BRITAIN
BATTLE OF FLOWERS
BATTLE OF JUTLAND
BATTLE OF THE NILE
BAYONET PRACTICE
BEAST OF THE FIELD
BEATEN ON THE POST
BEAUTIFUL FIGURE
BEAUTY TREATMENT
BEAUTY UNADORNED
BECOME ENAMOURED
BECOME INVISIBLE
BED AND BREAKFAST
BEE IN ONE'S BONNET
BEER AND SKITTLES
BEFORE BREAKFAST
BEFORE THE FINISH
BEGINNERS, PLEASE
BEGINNING AND END
BEGIN THE BEGUINE
BEHAVE NATURALLY
BEHIND THE SCENES
BEHIND THE STUMPS
BELLOW LIKE A BULL
BELONG TO THE PAST
BELOW THE AVERAGE
BELOW THE HORIZON
BELOW THE SURFACE
BENEATH CONTEMPT
BENEFIT OF CLERGY
BENITO MUSSOLINI
BENJAMIN BRITTEN

BERMUDA TRIANGLE
BERNE CONVENTION
BERNESE OBERLAND
BERTRAND RUSSELL
BESSEMER PROCESS
BEST FOOT FORWARD
BEST OF ALL WORLDS
BET ON A CERTAINTY
BETRAY THE SECRET
BETTER AND BETTER
BETTER RELATIONS
BETWEEN THE LINES
BETWEEN TWO FIRES
BETWEEN YOU AND ME
BEVERIDGE REPORT
BEVERLEY NICHOLS
BEVERLEY SISTERS
BEWARE OF THE BULL
BEYOND ALL BOUNDS
BEYOND CRITICISM
BEYOND ONE'S DEPTH
BEYOND ONE'S GRASP
BEYOND ONE'S MEANS
BEYOND ONE'S PRIME
BEYOND ONE'S REACH
BEYOND THE FRINGE
BIGGER AND BETTER
BIGGER AND BIGGER
BILLIARDS PLAYER
BINDING CONTRACT
BIOLOGICAL CLOCK
BIRDS OF A FEATHER
BIRTHDAY HONOURS
BIRTHDAY PRESENT
BIRTH OF THE BLUES
BITE ONE'S HEAD OFF
BLACK AS MIDNIGHT
BLACK AS THE DEVIL
BLACKBURN ROVERS
BLACK-COAT WORKER
BLACKMAIL LETTER
BLACKWALL TUNNEL
BLACKWATER FEVER
BLEACHING POWDER
BLISSFULLY HAPPY
BLOOD AND THUNDER
BLOOMSBURY GROUP
BLOW HOT; BLOW COLD
BLOW TO ONE'S PRIDE
BLUES IN THE NIGHT
BLUNT INSTRUMENT
BLUSHING HONOURS
BOARD AND LODGING
BOARDING OFFICER
BODLEIAN LIBRARY
BODY-LINE BOWLING

BODY OF KNOWLEDGE
BODY TEMPERATURE
BOLD IMAGINATION
BOLTED AND BARRED
BOLT FROM THE BLUE
BONDED WAREHOUSE
BOOKMAKER'S CLERK
BOOK OF REFERENCE
BORN IN THE PURPLE
BORROWING POWERS
BOTANICAL GARDEN
BOTTLE OF PERFUME
BOTTLE OF VINEGAR
BOTTOMLESS PURSE
BOTTOM OF THE FORM
BOTTOM OF THE HILL
BOTTOM OF THE POLL
BOTTOM THE WEAVER
BOWL AT THE STUMPS
BOWLED BY A YORKER
BOWLING ANALYSIS
BOW-STREET RUNNER
BOX OF CHOCOLATES
BRASS INSTRUMENT
BRAVE ALL HAZARDS
BREACH OF PROMISE
BREAD OF IDLENESS
BREAKFAST CEREAL
BREAKING OF BREAD
BREAK ON THE WHEEL
BREAK THE BAD NEWS
BREAK THE SILENCE
BREAST OF CHICKEN
BREATHE ONE'S LAST
BREATHLESS HURRY
BREATH OF SCANDAL
BRICKS AND MORTAR
BRIDES IN THE BATH
BRIDGE OF THE NOSE
BRIGADE OF GUARDS
BRIGADIER GERARD
BRIGHT AND BREEZY
BRIGHT AS A BUTTON
BRIGHT AS A NEW PIN
BRIGHTON AND HOVE
BRIGHT PROSPECTS
BRIGHT YOUNGSTER
BRILLIANT SUNSET
BRING IN A VERDICT
BRING IN NEW BLOOD
BRING TO FRUITION
BRISTLE WITH RAGE
BRITISH COLUMBIA
BRITISH HONDURAS
BRITISH PASSPORT
BRITISH RAILWAYS

BROAD-BRIMMED HAT
BROADEN ONE'S MIND
BROADLY SPEAKING
BRONZE MEDALLIST
BROTHEL CREEPERS
BROTHER JONATHAN
BROTHER OFFICERS
BROWN AS MAHOGANY
BRUSSELS SPROUTS
BUBBLE AND SQUEAK
BUDDING CHAMPION
BUDGET ESTIMATES
BUILDING SOCIETY
BULLDOG DRUMMOND
BULLET-PROOF VEST
BULL'S-EYE LANTERN
BUMP OF KNOWLEDGE
BURIAL OF THE DEAD
BURLINGTON HOUSE
BURNHAM ON CROUCH
BURNING QUESTION
BURN ONE'S BRIDGES
BURN ONE'S FINGERS
BURNT AT THE STAKE
BURNT TO A FRAZZLE
BURST AT THE SEAMS
BURST INTO FLAMES
BURST INTO FLOWER
BURST OF APPLAUSE
BURST OF LAUGHTER
BUSINESS ADDRESS
BUSINESS AFFAIRS
BUSINESS AS USUAL
BUSINESS CIRCLES
BUSINESS COLLEGE
BUSINESS CONTACT
BUSINESS FOOTING
BUSINESS MANAGER
BUSINESS MEETING
BUSINESS METHODS
BUSINESS ROUTINE
BUSINESS VENTURE
BUTTERFLY COLLAR
BUTTERFLY EFFECT
BUTTERFLY STROKE
BUTTON MUSHROOMS
BY FITS AND STARTS
BY HOOK OR BY CROOK
BY THE SHORT HAIRS
BYZANTINE EMPIRE
BYZANTINE SCHOOL

C – 15

CABINET MINISTER
CABLE TELEVISION
CALCiUM CHLORIDE

CALCULATING MIND
CALEDONIAN CANAL
CALL AN AMBULANCE
CALL ATTENTION TO
CALL IN THE DOCTOR
CALL IN THE POLICE
CALL NO MAN MASTER
CALL TO SURRENDER
CALM AS A MILL-POND
CAMBERWELL GREEN
CAMBRIDGE CIRCUS
CAMEMBERT CHEESE
CAMERA-READY COPY
CAME TO THE THRONE
CANADIAN PACIFIC
CANDLEWICK COVER
CANTERBURY BELLS
CANTERBURY TALES
CAPABILITY BROWN
CAPITAL GAINS TAX
CAPITAL OF FRANCE
CAPITAL OF NORWAY
CAPITAL OF SWEDEN
CAPITAL SENTENCE
CAPTIVE AUDIENCE
CARDIFF ARMS PARK
CARDINAL NUMBERS
CARDINAL VIRTUES
CARDS ON THE TABLE
CARELESS DRIVING
CARELESS RAPTURE
CARES OF THE WORLD
CARPENTER'S BENCH
CARRIAGE AND PAIR
CARRIAGE FORWARD
CARRY CONVICTION
CARRY OUT ONE'S BAT
CARRY THE CAN BACK
CASEMENT DIARIES
CASH IN ONE'S CHIPS
CASH TRANSACTION
CASTING DIRECTOR
CASTLES IN THE AIR
CAST OF THOUSANDS
CASTOR AND POLLUX
CASUAL REFERENCE
CASUALTY STATION
CAT AND THE FIDDLE
CATCH AS CATCH CAN
CATCH BY THE HEELS
CATCH ONE NAPPING
CATCH ONE'S BREATH
CATERING OFFICER
CATHEDRAL SQUARE
CAUGHT AMIDSHIPS
CAUGHT AND BOWLED

CAUGHT RED-HANDED
CAUSE A SENSATION
CAVALRY REGIMENT
CEASELESS ENERGY
CEDARS OF LEBANON
CELESTIAL SPHERE
CELLULAR NETWORK
CELLULOID COLLAR
CELLULOID EMPIRE
CENTRAL POSITION
CENTRE OF GRAVITY
CERTAIN EVIDENCE
CERTAIN QUANTITY
CERTIFIED INSANE
CHAMPAGNE BOTTLE
CHAMPAGNE SUPPER
CHANCE DISCOVERY
CHANCE ENCOUNTER
CHANCE OF SUCCESS
CHANGE DIRECTION
CHANGE OF ADDRESS
CHANGE OF CLIMATE
CHANGE OF CLOTHES
CHANGE OF COSTUME
CHANGE OF FORTUNE
CHANGE OF OPINION
CHANGE OF PURPOSE
CHANGE OF SCENERY
CHANGE OF TACTICS
CHANGE ONE'S IDEAS
CHANNEL CROSSING
CHANTREY BEQUEST
CHAPTER AND VERSE
CHARACTER SKETCH
CHARCOAL DRAWING
CHARGE TOO LITTLE
CHARITABLE CAUSE
CHARLES KINGSLEY
CHARLES LAUGHTON
CHARLES THE FIRST
CHARLOTTE BRONTË
CHATSWORTH HOUSE
CHEAP AT THE PRICE
CHEAP RESTAURANT
CHEAT THE GALLOWS
CHECK ONE'S COURSE
CHECK THE RECORDS
CHEERFUL CONSENT
CHEERFUL OLD SOUL
CHELSEA ARTS BALL
CHELSEA BARRACKS
CHEMICAL FORMULA
CHEMICAL PROCESS
CHEMICAL WARFARE
CHEQUERED CAREER
CHERCHEZ LA FEMME

CHESS TOURNAMENT
CHICKEN MARYLAND
CHICKEN SANDWICH
CHIEF MAGISTRATE
CHILDHOOD FRIEND
CHILDISH ATTEMPT
CHILD PSYCHOLOGY
CHILDREN'S ANNUAL
CHILDREN'S CORNER
CHILLED WITH FEAR
CHILLY RECEPTION
CHINESE TAKEAWAY
CHINESE WHISPERS
CHIPPED POTATOES
CHOCOLATE ÉCLAIR
CHOCOLATE FINGER
CHOCOLATE SUNDAE
CHOICE OF COLOURS
CHOICE OF WEAPONS
CHOOSE ONE'S WORDS
CHRISTIE MURDERS
CHRISTMAS ANNUAL
CHRISTMAS DINNER
CHRISTMAS ISLAND
CHRISTMAS SEASON
CHRISTMAS SPIRIT
CHRISTOPHER WREN
CHRIST'S HOSPITAL
CHURCH OF ENGLAND
CIGARETTE COUPON
CIGARETTE HOLDER
CINDERELLA DANCE
CIRCLE OF FRIENDS
CIRCUIT TRAINING
CITIZENS' CHARTER
CITY AND SUBURBAN
CITY CORPORATION
CIVILIAN CLOTHES
CLAIMS OF SOCIETY
CLAIM THE VICTORY
CLAPHAM JUNCTION
CLASHING COLOURS
CLASH OF OPINIONS
CLASSICAL BALLET
CLASSICAL GUITAR
CLASSICAL WRITER
CLASSIC FEATURES
CLASSICS SCHOLAR
CLEAN AS A WHISTLE
CLEANING UTENSIL
CLEAN THE WINDOWS
CLEAR AS DAYLIGHT
CLEAR CONSCIENCE
CLEAR IN ONE'S MIND
CLEAR ONE'S THROAT
CLEAR REFLECTION

CLENCH ONE'S FISTS
CLENCH ONE'S TEETH
CLERK OF THE COURT
CLERK OF THE HOUSE
CLERK OF THE WORKS
CLEVER DECEPTION
CLIFF MICHELMORE
CLING LIKE IVY
CLINICAL LECTURE
CLINICAL SURGERY
CLOAK-ROOM TICKET
CLOSE AS AN OYSTER
CLOSE COMPANIONS
CLOSE FRIENDSHIP
CLOSER AND CLOSER
CLOSE TO THE SHORE
CLOSING-DOWN SALE
CLOTHING COUPONS
CLOUD-CUCKOO LAND
COACHING STATION
COCKPIT OF EUROPE
COCKTAIL CABINET
CODE OF BEHAVIOUR
COLD AS CHRISTMAS
COLD COMFORT FARM
COLDSTREAM GUARD
COLERIDGE TAYLOR
COLLAPSIBLE BOAT
COLLECT EVIDENCE
COLLECTING POINT
COLLECTION PLATE
COLLECT MATERIAL
COLLECT ONE'S WITS
COLLECTOR'S PIECE
COLLIERY MANAGER
COLLISION COURSE
COLORADO SPRINGS
COLOUR BLINDNESS
COLOURFUL BORDER
COLOURING MATTER
COLOURLESS FLUID
COLOUR PREJUDICE
COMBINATION LOCK
COME DOWN TO EARTH
COME HOME TO ROOST
COME IN LIKE A LION
COME INTO CONTACT
COME INTO ONE'S OWN
COME INTO THE OPEN
COME OUT ON STRIKE
COME THE RAW PRAWN
COME TO A DEAD STOP
COME TO A DECISION
COME TO A FULL STOP
COME TO ATTENTION
COME TO THE RESCUE

COME TO THINK OF IT
COME UP TO SCRATCH
COMFORTABLE SEAT
COMFORTING WORDS
COMMANDING VOICE
COMMERCIAL HOTEL
COMMERCIAL VALUE
COMMISSION AGENT
COMMIT AN OFFENCE
COMMIT TO WRITING
COMMON AGREEMENT
COMMON COMPLAINT
COMMON KNOWLEDGE
COMMON OWNERSHIP
COMMUNAL FEEDING
COMMUNAL KITCHEN
COMMUNITY CENTRE
COMMUNITY CHARGE
COMPACT CASSETTE
COMPANION IN ARMS
COMPANION LADDER
COMPANION VOLUME
COMPANY DIRECTOR
COMPANY PROMOTER
COMPLETE ABANDON
COMPLETE CONTROL
COMPLETE DEBACLE
COMPLETE EDITION
COMPLETE FAILURE
COMPLETE SWINDLE
COMPLETE VICTORY
COMPLETE WASH-OUT
COMPLEX SENTENCE
COMPOUND A FELONY
COMPULSORY GAMES
CONCERTED ACTION
CONCERTED EFFORT
CONCERT PLATFORM
CONCLUSIVE PROOF
CONDITIONAL MOOD
CONDITION POWDER
CONFERENCE TABLE
CONFESS THE TRUTH
CONFIDENCE TRICK
CONFUSE THE ISSUE
CONGENITAL IDIOT
CONSCIENCE MONEY
CONSCIOUS HUMOUR
CONSENTING PARTY
CONSIDERABLE SUM
CONSIGNMENT NOTE
CONSOLATION RACE
CONSTANT ANXIETY
CONSTANT CHATTER
CONSULAR SERVICE
CONSUMMATE SKILL

CONTACT MAGAZINE
CONTEMPT OF COURT
CONTINENTAL TIME
CONTROLLED PRICE
CONVECTOR HEATER
CONVENIENCE FOOD
CONVENIENT PLACE
CONVERSION TABLE
CONVERTIBLE BOND
CONVIVIAL PERSON
COOKING UTENSILS
COOK THE ACCOUNTS
COOL AS A CUCUMBER
COOLWALL TOASTER
CORDIAL GREETING
CORDLESS CLEANER
CORNER THE MARKET
CORONATION COACH
CORONATION ROBES
CORONATION STONE
CORONER'S INQUEST
CORONER'S VERDICT
CORPORATE RAIDER
CORRECTED PROOFS
CORRECT ESTIMATE
CORRUGATED PAPER
COTTAGE BY THE SEA
COTTAGE HOSPITAL
COTTAGE INDUSTRY
COUNCIL OF ELDERS
COUNCIL OF EUROPE
COUNSEL'S OPINION
COUNTERFEIT COIN
COUNTER IRRITANT
COUNT FOR NOTHING
COUNT ONE'S CHANGE
COUNTRY OF ORIGIN
COUNT THE MINUTES
COUNT THE TAKINGS
COUNTY CRICKETER
COURT DRESSMAKER
COURT OF JUDGMENT
COVER MUCH GROUND
COVER ONE'S TRACKS
CRADLE OF THE DEEP
CRAMPED QUARTERS
CRAZY MIXED-UP KID
CREAMED POTATOES
CREASE RESISTANT
CREATE AN OPENING
CREATE A NUISANCE
CREATE A STOPPAGE
CREATIVE WRITING
CREATURE COMFORT
CREATURE FEATURE
CREATURE OF HABIT

CREDULOUS PERSON
CREEPING BARRAGE
CREMORNE GARDENS
CRICKET PAVILION
CRIMINAL AT LARGE
CRIMINAL CLASSES
CRIMINAL LUNATIC
CRIMINAL NEGLECT
CRIMINAL OFFENCE
CRIPPLED FOR LIFE
CRITICAL OPINION
CROOKED SIXPENCE
CROSS-COUNTRY RUN
CROSSING THE LINE
CROSS THE CHANNEL
CROSS THE RUBICON
CROSSWORD PUZZLE
CROWD PSYCHOLOGY
CRUCIAL QUESTION
CRUSADING SPIRIT
CRUSHING VICTORY
CRUX OF THE MATTER
CUCKOO IN THE NEST
CUDGEL ONE'S BRAIN
CULLINAN DIAMOND
CULTIVATE A HABIT
CULTIVATED PEARL
CULTIVATED TASTE
CUP OF BITTERNESS
CURRENT EXPENSES
CURSE OF SCOTLAND
CURTAIN MATERIAL
CUSTOMS OFFICIAL
CUT AND COME AGAIN
CUT A SORRY FIGURE
CUT DOWN EXPENSES
CUT OFF AT THE PASS
CUT ONESELF LOOSE
CYLINDER CLEANER

D – 15

DAILY OCCURRENCE
DAME EDNA EVERAGE
DAME NELLIE MELBA
DAMNING EVIDENCE
DAMON AND PYTHIAS
DAMPENED SPIRITS
DANCE ATTENDANCE
DANCE OF THE HOURS
DANCING MISTRESS
DANGEROUS CORNER
DANGEROUS PERSON
DANGEROUS VOYAGE
DANGEROUS WEAPON
DASH TO THE GROUND

DATA COMPRESSION
DAVID AND GOLIATH
DAVY JONES' LOCKER
DAYLIGHT ROBBERY
DAY OF ABSTINENCE
DAY OF LIBERATION
DEAD AS A DOORNAIL
DEAD ON THE TARGET
DEAFENING CHEERS
DEAF TO ALL ADVICE
DEAL DESTRUCTION
DEAR LITTLE THING
DEATH BY DROWNING
DEATH ON THE ROADS
DEBT OF GRATITUDE
DECEIVED HUSBAND
DECIMAL FRACTION
DECISIVE VICTORY
DECLARED MISSING
DECLARE ONE'S LOVE
DECREE OF NULLITY
DEFECTIVE MEMORY
DEFECTIVE VISION
DEFENCE MINISTER
DEFENSIVE BATTLE
DEFENSIVE WEAPON
DEFERRED PAYMENT
DEFINITE ARTICLE
DELAYED REACTION
DELAYING TACTICS
DELICATE BALANCE
DELIRIUM TREMENS
DELIVERED BY HAND
DELIVER JUDGMENT
DELIVER THE GOODS
DEMAND AND SUPPLY
DEMAND ATTENTION
DEMENTIA PRAECOX
DEMOCRATIC PARTY
DEMOLITION SQUAD
DENIAL OF JUSTICE
DENTAL TREATMENT
DEPARTMENT STORE
DEPARTURE LOUNGE
DEPTHS OF DESPAIR
DESCENDING ORDER
DESCRIBE A CIRCLE
DESERTED VILLAGE
DESIGNER CLOTHES
DESIGNER STUBBLE
DESIGN FOR LIVING
DESIGNING FEMALE
DESIRABLE OBJECT
DESOLATE COUNTRY
DESPERATE PLIGHT
DESPERATE REMEDY

DETACHED OPINION
DETAILED ACCOUNT
DETENTION CENTRE
DETERRENT EFFECT
DEVALUE THE POUND
DEVELOPMENT AREA
DEVILLED KIDNEYS
DEVIL'S COMPANION
DEVIL'S PUNCH BOWL
DEVONSHIRE CREAM
DEVONSHIRE HOUSE
DIAMOND MERCHANT
DIAMOND NECKLACE
DIAMOND SMUGGLER
DICKIE HENDERSON
DICKIE VALENTINE
DICK WHITTINGTON
DIE IN THE ATTEMPT
DIE WITH LAUGHTER
DIFFERENT TASTES
DIFFICULT CHOICE
DIFFICULT MATTER
DIFFICULT PERSON
DIFFIDENT MANNER
DIG ONE'S OWN GRAVE
DINING-ROOM TABLE
DIPLOMATIC AGENT
DIPLOMATIC CORPS
DIPLOMATIC STAFF
DIRECT INFLUENCE
DIRECT INPUTTING
DIRECTION FINDER
DIRECTOR GENERAL
DIRT-TRACK RACING
DISAPPEARING ACT
DISARMAMENT PLAN
DISCARDED CUSTOM
DISCHARGE PAPERS
DISCLOSING AGENT
DISGUISE ONESELF
DISLOCATED ELBOW
DISORDERED BRAIN
DISORDERLY HOUSE
DISPENSE CHARITY
DISPENSE JUSTICE
DISPLACED PERSON
DISPOSABLE GOODS
DISPUTE THE FACTS
DISTANT LIKENESS
DISTANT PROSPECT
DISTANT RELATIVE
DISTINCTIVE NOTE
DISTORT THE TRUTH
DISTRESSING NEWS
DISTRESS WARRANT
DISTRICT OFFICER

DISTRICT RAILWAY
DISTRICT VISITOR
DISTURB THE PEACE
DIVIDEND WARRANT
DIVINE MESSENGER
DIVINITY STUDENT
DO A ROARING TRADE
DO AS THE ROMANS DO
DOCTOR OF SCIENCE
DOCUMENTARY FILM
DOG WITH TWO TAILS
DO-IT-YOURSELF FAN
DO-IT-YOURSELF KIT
DOLLAR RESOURCES
DOLLARS AND CENTS
DOMESTIC AFFAIRS
DOMESTIC ECONOMY
DOMESTIC OFFICES
DOMESTIC PROBLEM
DOMESTIC SCIENCE
DOMESTIC SERVANT
DOMESTIC SERVICE
DONE IN COLD BLOOD
DO ONE'S LEVEL BEST
DORA COPPERFIELD
DORCHESTER HOTEL
DORMITORY SUBURB
DO THE CHARLESTON
DO THE CIVIL THING
DO THE IMPOSSIBLE
DO THE RIGHT THING
DO THE WRONG THING
DO THINGS IN STYLE
DOUBLE ADVANTAGE
DOUBLE INDEMNITY
DOUBLE OR NOTHING
DOUBLE-QUICK TIME
DOUBLE SEVENTEEN
DOUBLE THE STAKES
DOUBLE WHITE LINE
DOUBLE YOUR MONEY
DOUBTFUL STARTER
DOWN IN THE DEPTHS
DOWN IN THE FOREST
DOWN IN THE VALLEY
DOWN THE MOUNTAIN
DOWN THE STRAIGHT
DOWN TO THE GROUND
DOZENS AND DOZENS
DRAIN TO THE DREGS
DRAMATIC GESTURE
DRAMATIC SETTING
DRAMATIC SOCIETY
DRASTIC MEASURES
DRAW A COMPARISON
DRAW A DEEP BREATH

DRAW AN INFERENCE
DRAW A RED HERRING
DRAW CONCLUSIONS
DRAW IN ONE'S HORNS
DRAW INSPIRATION
DRAW ONE'S PENSION
DRAW THE CURTAINS
DREAMER OF DREAMS
DRESSING STATION
DRILLING MACHINE
DRILL INSTRUCTOR
DRINK ONE'S HEALTH
DRINK ON THE HOUSE
DRIVEN TO THE WALL
DRIVE RECKLESSLY
DROOPING SPIRITS
DROP IN THE BUCKET
DROP OF GOOD STUFF
DROP OVER THE SIDE
DRUG ON THE MARKET
DRUM AND FIFE BAND
DRUMHEAD SERVICE
DUAL CARRIAGE-WAY
DUAL PERSONALITY
DUBIOUS BLESSING
DUBLIN BAY PRAWNS
DUCHY OF CORNWALL
DUELLING PISTOLS
DUKE OF EDINBURGH
DUKE OF LANCASTER
DUSTPAN AND BRUSH
DUTCH ELM DISEASE

E – 15

EAGER FOR THE FRAY
EARLY-CLOSING DAY
EARLY-MORNING TEA
EARNING CAPACITY
EARTHLY PARADISE
EASTERN COUNTIES
EASTERN QUESTION
EASY-PACED WICKET
EAT YOUR HEART OUT
EBENEZER SCROOGE
ECLIPSE OF THE SUN
ECONOMIC WARFARE
EDINBURGH CASTLE
EDITORIAL COLUMN
EDITOR'S DECISION
EDMUND HOCKRIDGE
EDWARD THE FOURTH
EDWARD THE SECOND
EGG-AND-SPOON RACE
EIGHTEEN HUNDRED
EIGHTEEN PER CENT

EIGHTEENTH GREEN
EIGHTEENTH OF MAY
EIGHTH OF JANUARY
EIGHTH OF OCTOBER
EIGHT O'CLOCK NEWS
EIGHT OF DIAMONDS
ELABORATE DESIGN
ELABORATE DETAIL
ELECTION ADDRESS
ELECTION RESULTS
ELECTORAL DEFEAT
ELECTORAL SYSTEM
ELECTRICAL FAULT
ELECTRIC BATTERY
ELECTRIC BLANKET
ELECTRIC CIRCUIT
ELECTRIC CURRENT
ELECTRIC FURNACE
ELECTRICITY BILL
ELECTRIC MACHINE
ELECTRIC RAILWAY
ELECTRIC TOASTER
ELECTRONIC BRAIN
ELECTRONIC DRUMS
ELECTRONIC TIMER
ELEVATED RAILWAY
ELEVENTH CENTURY
ELEVENTH OF APRIL
ELEVENTH OF MARCH
ELIZABETH TAYLOR
ELOCUTION LESSON
EMERALD BRACELET
EMERALD NECKLACE
EMERGENCY POWERS
EMERGENCY RATION
EMOTIONAL RELIEF
ENCASED IN ARMOUR
ENDEAVOUR TO HELP
ENDLESS ARGUMENT
ENDLESS ATTEMPTS
END OF ONE'S TETHER
END OF THE CENTURY
END OF THE CHAPTER
END OF THE JOURNEY
ENDOWMENT POLICY
ENEMY OF PROGRESS
ENERGETIC PERSON
ENGAGEMENT DIARY
ENGINEER A STRIKE
ENGLAND AND WALES
ENGLISH CIVIL WAR
ENGLISH LANGUAGE
ENGLISHMAN'S HOME
ENJOY GOOD HEALTH
ENJOY POOR HEALTH
ENTENTE CORDIALE

ENTER PARLIAMENT
EPICUREAN TASTES
EPSOM RACECOURSE
EQUESTRIAN SKILL
ERNEST HEMINGWAY
ERRONEOUS BELIEF
ERROR CORRECTION
ERROR OF JUDGMENT
ERROR OF OMISSION
ESCAPED PRISONER
ESCAPE MECHANISM
ESPOUSE THE CAUSE
ESSENTIAL CLAUSE
ESTABLISH A CLAIM
ETERNAL TRIANGLE
ETHNIC CLEANSING
ETON BOATING-SONG
EVENING STANDARD
EVEN MONEY CHANCE
EVERLASTING FAME
EVERY MOTHER'S SON
EVERY NOW AND THEN
EVERYONE'S FRIEND
EVIDENCE IN COURT
EXAGGERATED IDEA
EXALTED POSITION
EXAMINATION HALL
EXCELLENT CHANCE
EXCELLENT REASON
EXCELLENT RESULT
EXCEPTIONAL WORD
EXCESSIVE CHARGE
EXCESSIVE WEIGHT
EXCHANGE AND MART
EXCHANGE CONTROL
EXCHANGE GLANCES
EXCHANGE LETTERS
EXCHANGE OF VIEWS
EXCHANGE SIGNALS
EXCLAMATION MARK
EXCLUSIVE REPORT
EXCLUSIVE RIGHTS
EXCURSION TICKET
EXERCISE CONTROL
EXERCISE THE MIND
EXERCISE THE VETO
EXHAUSTION POINT
EXORBITANT PRICE
EXPANDING BULLET
EXPECT OTHERWISE
EXPENSE NO OBJECT
EXPENSIVE TASTES
EXPERT KNOWLEDGE
EXPLODE WITH RAGE
EXPLOSIVE CHARGE
EXPLOSIVE DEVICE

EXPORT AND IMPORT
EXPOSED POSITION
EXPOSED TO DANGER
EXPRESS CONTEMPT
EXPRESS DELIVERY
EXPRESSIVE SMILE
EXQUISITE CHOICE
EXTENDING MIRROR
EXTENSION OF TIME
EXTORTIONATE FEE
EXTREME KINDNESS
EXTREME MEASURES
EXTREME PATIENCE
EYEBROW TWEEZERS

F – 15

FACE LIKE A FIDDLE
FACE THE OTHER WAY
FACE THE PROSPECT
FACT OF THE MATTER
FACTS AND FIGURES
FADED REPUTATION
FAIR MAID OF PERTH
FAIR MEANS OR FOUL
FAIR WEAR AND TEAR
FAITHFUL ACCOUNT
FAITHFUL PROMISE
FAITHFUL SERVANT
FALKLAND ISLANDS
FALKLANDS FACTOR
FALL ON HARD TIMES
FALL TO THE GROUND
FALSE ACCUSATION
FALSE APPEARANCE
FALSE CONCEPTION
FALSE IMPRESSION
FALSE REPUTATION
FAMILY ALLOWANCE
FAMILY GATHERING
FAMILY LOYALTIES
FAMILY SOLICITOR
FAMOUS LAST WORDS
FANCY-DRESS DANCE
FANCY-DRESS PARTY
FANNY BY GASLIGHT
FAN-TAILED PIGEON
FAREWELL ADDRESS
FAR FROM THE TRUTH
FARMING ACCOUNTS
FARTHING DAMAGES
FASHIONABLE AREA
FASTER THAN SOUND
FATAL ATTRACTION
FATHER AND MOTHER
FATHER CHRISTMAS

FATHER CONFESSOR
FATHERLESS CHILD
FAVOURABLE ISSUE
FAVOURABLE REPLY
FAVOURABLE START
FAVOURABLE TERMS
FEAR FOR ONE'S LIFE
FEAST FOR THE GODS
FEATHERED FRIEND
FEATHER ONE'S NEST
FEDERAL REPUBLIC
FEEBLE IMITATION
FEEL COMFORTABLE
FEEL IN ONE'S BONES
FEET ON THE GROUND
FELLOWSHIP HOUSE
FELLOW TRAVELLER
FEMININE PRONOUN
FENCED ENCLOSURE
FENCHURCH STREET
FESTIVAL GARDENS
FESTIVE OCCASION
FIELD OF ACTIVITY
FIELD PUNISHMENT
FIFTEEN AND A HALF
FIFTEENTH LETTER
FIFTEENTH OF JULY
FIFTEENTH OF JUNE
FIFTEEN THOUSAND
FIFTH OF DECEMBER
FIFTH OF FEBRUARY
FIFTH OF NOVEMBER
FIFTY-PENCE PIECE
FIGHT FOR FREEDOM
FIGHT LIKE DEVILS
FIGHT TO THE DEATH
FIGURATIVE SENSE
FILL IN THE CRACKS
FILTH AND SQUALOR
FINANCE MINISTER
FINANCIAL CRISIS
FINANCIAL WIZARD
FINDING'S KEEPING
FINE OPPORTUNITY
FINISHED PRODUCT
FINISHING SCHOOL
FINISHING STROKE
FIREWORK DISPLAY
FIRST-AID STATION
FIRST APPEARANCE
FIRST BEGININGS
FIRST-CLASS HOTEL
FIRST-CLASS MATCH
FIRST-CLASS STAMP
FIRST-FLOOR FRONT
FIRST IMPORTANCE

FIRST IMPRESSION
FIRST INSTALMENT
FIRST INTENTIONS
FIRST IN THE FIELD
FIRST IN THE QUEUE
FIRST LIEUTENANT
FIRST OCCURRENCE
FIRST OF DECEMBER
FIRST OF FEBRUARY
FIRST OF NOVEMBER
FIRST PORT OF CALL
FIRST PRINCIPLES
FIRST-RATE ACTING
FIRST WICKET DOWN
FISH AND CHIP SHOP
FISHING INDUSTRY
FISHMONGERS' HALL
FIT OF GENEROSITY
FIT OF THE VAPOURS
FIVE AND A QUARTER
FIVE WICKETS DOWN
FIXED IMPRESSION
FLAGGING SPIRITS
FLAMBOROUGH HEAD
FLAMING NUISANCE
FLANDERS POPPIES
FLANNEL TROUSERS
FLAWLESS DIAMOND
FLAWLESS MANNERS
FLEETING GLIMPSE
FLEET OPERATIONS
FLEMISH LANGUAGE
FLICK OF THE WRIST
FLIGHT SIMULATOR
FLING INTO PRISON
FLIRT WITH THE LAW
FLOATING CAPITAL
FLOOR OF THE HOUSE
FLOURISHING TIME
FLOWER OF THE ARMY
FLY INTO A PASSION
FLY OFF THE HANDLE
FOLLOW PRECEDENT
FOLLOW THE HOUNDS
FOLLOW THE PLOUGH
FOND OF THE BOTTLE
FOOL OF THE FAMILY
FOOTBALL RESULTS
FOOT OF THE LADDER
FOR ALL ONE'S WORTH
FOR A YEAR AND A DAY
FORBIDDEN GROUND
FORCE AN ENTRANCE
FORCE THE BIDDING
FORCIBLE FEEDING
FOREIGN CURRENCY

FOREIGN EXCHANGE
FOREIGN LANGUAGE
FOREIGN MINISTER
FORENSIC CHEMIST
FORFEIT ONE'S BAIL
FORGED SIGNATURE
FORGET ONE'S PIECE
FORGIVING NATURE
FOR GOODNESS' SAKE!
FORGOTTEN CUSTOM
FORKED LIGHTNING
FORM A GOVERNMENT
FORMAL AGREEMENT
FORMAL COMPLAINT
FORMAL STATEMENT
FOR MANY A LONG DAY
FOR OLD TIMES' SAKE
FOR THE FIRST TIME
FOR THE THIRD TIME
FOR THE TIME BEING
FORTY-EIGHT HOURS
FORTY-NINTH STATE
FORWARDING AGENT
FORWARD MOVEMENT
FOR WHAT IT'S WORTH
FOSTER AN OPINION
FOUNDATION CREAM
FOUNDATION STONE
FOUNTAIN OF YOUTH
FOUR AND A QUARTER
FOURTEEN PER CENT
FOURTEENTH GREEN
FOURTEENTH OF MAY
FOURTH DIMENSION
FOURTH OF JANUARY
FOURTH OF OCTOBER
FOUR WICKETS DOWN
FRAGRANT PERFUME
FRANCIS OF ASSISI
FRANCO-GERMAN WAR
FRANKLY SPEAKING
FREDERICK DELIUS
FREE ASSOCIATION
FREEDOM FROM FEAR
FREEDOM FROM WANT
FREEDOM OF ACCESS
FREEDOM OF ACTION
FREEDOM OF CHOICE
FREEDOM OF SPEECH
FREEDOM OF THE AIR
FREE FROM SLAVERY
FREEHAND DRAWING
FREELANCE WRITER
FREE OF INCOME TAX
FREE TRANSLATION
FREEZE ONE'S BLOOD

FREEZING MIXTURE
FRENCH BREAKFAST
FRENCH DICTATION
FRENCH GRAND PRIX
FRENCH PEASANTRY
FRENCH SUBTITLES
FRENZIED EFFORTS
FREQUENT VISITOR
FRESH COMPLEXION
FRICASSEE OF VEAL
FRICTIONAL FORCE
FRIDAY AFTERNOON
FRIENDLY FEELING
FRIENDLY FOOTING
FRIENDLY GESTURE
FRIENDLY ISLANDS
FRIENDLY RIVALRY
FRIENDLY SOCIETY
FRIGHTENED CHILD
FROG IN THE THROAT
FROM ALL QUARTERS
FROM FIRST TO LAST
FROM HAND TO MOUTH
FROM LEFT TO RIGHT
FROM OBSERVATION
FROM STEM TO STERN
FROM THE ROOF-TOPS
FROM TOP TO BOTTOM
FRONT-LINE TROOPS
FROTH AT THE MOUTH
FRUITFUL SESSION
FRUITLESS SEARCH
FRUITS OF VICTORY
FUEL TO THE FLAMES
FULL-BOTTOMED WIG
FULL-DRESS DEBATE
FULL EXPLANATION
FULL OF INCIDENTS
FULL OF SURPRISES
FULL SPEED ASTERN
FULLY GUARANTEED
FUND OF KNOWLEDGE
FUNERAL CEREMONY
FUNERAL DIRECTOR
FURNISH EVIDENCE
FURNITURE POLISH
FUTURE EXISTENCE
FUTURE REFERENCE

G – 15

GAIN A REPUTATION
GAIN INFORMATION
GAIN ONE'S FREEDOM
GALA PERFORMANCE
GALL AND WORMWOOD

GAME FOR ANYTHING
GAME, SET AND MATCH
GARDEN OF ENGLAND
GARGANTUAN FEAST
GATE-LEGGED TABLE
GATHERING CLOUDS
GATHERING STICKS
GENERAL ASSEMBLY
GENERAL DE GAULLE
GENERAL DELIVERY
GENERAL ELECTION
GENERAL FACTOTUM
GENERAL HOSPITAL
GENERAL INTEREST
GENERAL LAUGHTER
GENERAL OVERHAUL
GENERAL PRACTICE
GENERATING PLANT
GENEROUS HELPING
GENEROUS MEASURE
GENETIC ENGINEER
GENTLEMAN FARMER
GEOFFREY CHAUCER
GEOGRAPHY LESSON
GEORGE THE FOURTH
GET CONFIDENTIAL
GET DOWN TO THE JOB
GET INTO HOT WATER
GET INTO MISCHIEF
GET ONE'S MONKEY UP
GET ON ONE'S NERVES
GET ON SWIMMINGLY
GET ON WITH THE JOB
GET OUT OF THE ROAD
GET OUT OF TROUBLE
GET THE ADVANTAGE
GET THE UPPER HAND
GET THE WORST OF IT
GET UP TO MISCHIEF
GET YOUR SKATES ON
GHOSTS OF THE PAST
GIFT FROM THE GODS
GIN AND ANGOSTURA
GIRD UP ONE'S LOINS
GIRLISH LAUGHTER
GIST OF THE MATTER
GIVE A LEATHERING
GIVE FULL DETAILS
GIVE IN THE MIDDLE
GIVE ONE A BAD TIME
GIVE ONE'S CONSENT
GIVE ONESELF AIRS
GIVE ONESELF AWAY
GIVE ONE THE WORKS
GIVE PARTICULARS
GIVE THE ALL-CLEAR

GIVE THE GAME AWAY
GIVE THE PASSWORD
GIVE THE SHOW AWAY
GIVE UP THE SPONGE
GLITTERING PRIZE
GLOBE ARTICHOKES
GLOOMY COMPANION
GLORIOUS HOLIDAY
GLORIOUSLY DRUNK
GLORIOUS TWELFTH
GLORIOUS VICTORY
GLUT ON THE MARKET
GO A LONG WAY ROUND
GO BY UNDERGROUND
GODDESS OF WISDOM
GOD-FORSAKEN HOLE
GOD SAVE THE QUEEN
GO IN FOR LUXURIES
GO INTO ECSTASIES
GOLDEN HANDCUFFS
GOLDEN HANDSHAKE
GOLDEN PARACHUTE
GOLDEN RETRIEVER
GOLDEN SOVEREIGN
GONE WITH THE WIND
GOOD CIRCULATION
GOOD CITIZENSHIP
GOOD CONNECTIONS
GOOD DAY'S JOURNEY
GOOD ENOUGH TO EAT
GOOD HANDWRITING
GOOD HOUSEKEEPER
GOODNESS OF HEART
GOOD RESOLUTIONS
GOOD VENTILATION
GO OFF AT A TANGENT
GO OFF THE DEEP END
GO OUT OF BUSINESS
GO OVER THE GROUND
GORGEOUS WEATHER
GO THE LONGEST WAY
GO THROUGH WITH IT
GO TO MUCH TROUBLE
GO TO THE SCAFFOLD
GO TO WORK ON AN EGG
GOVERNMENT GRANT
GOVERNMENT HOUSE
GOVERNOR GENERAL
GO WITHOUT SAYING
GO WITH THE STREAM
GRACE BEFORE MEAT
GRACEFUL GESTURE
GRADUAL PROGRESS
GRAMOPHONE MUSIC
GRAND INQUISITOR
GRANDIOSE MANNER

GRAND UNION CANAL
GRANT ABSOLUTION
GRANULATED SUGAR
GRAPEFRUIT JUICE
GRAVE MISGIVINGS
GREASE THE WHEELS
GREAT ASSISTANCE
GREAT DEPRESSION
GREATEST RESPECT
GREAT EXCITEMENT
GREAT EXHIBITION
GREAT IMPORTANCE
GREATLY ESTEEMED
GREATLY INDEBTED
GREATLY SUPERIOR
GREAT MISFORTUNE
GREAT POPULARITY
GREEK MEETS GREEK
GREEK RESTAURANT
GREEN CHARTREUSE
GREENHOUSE GASES
GREENHOUSE PLANT
GREEN REVOLUTION
GRENADIER GUARDS
GREYHOUND RACING
GRIEVOUS MISTAKE
GRILLED SAUSAGES
GRILLED TOMATOES
GRIST FOR THE MILL
GROCERY BUSINESS
GROSS NEGLIGENCE
GROSVENOR SQUARE
GROUND-FLOOR FLAT
GROUND-NUT SCHEME
GROW INDIFFERENT
GUARDED LANGUAGE
GUESS ONE'S WEIGHT
GUEST APPEARANCE
GUILTY BEHAVIOUR
GUILTY BUT INSANE
GUNNER'S DAUGHTER
GUNNERY PRACTICE
GUY DE MAUPASSANT

H – 15

HACKNEY CARRIAGE
HACKNEYED PHRASE
HACKNEYED SAYING
HAGUE CONVENTION
HAIL AND FAREWELL
HAILING DISTANCE
HALF AS MUCH AGAIN
HALF-TERM HOLIDAY
HALF THE DISTANCE
HALIBUT-LIVER OIL

HAMMER AND SICKLE
HANDFUL OF SILVER
HANDSOME APOLOGY
HANDSOME FORTUNE
HANDSOME PRESENT
HANDS-ON TRAINING
HAND-TO-HAND FIGHT
HANGED BY THE NECK
HANGING ORNAMENT
HANGING SHOE RACK
HANG OUT THE FLAGS
HANG UP A STOCKING
HANSEL AND GRETEL
HAPPY AS A SANDBOY
HAPPY IN ONE'S WORK
HARBOUR FEELINGS
HARBOUR OF REFUGE
HARD AND FAST RULE
HARDEN ONE'S HEART
HARDNESS OF HEART
HARE AND TORTOISE
HARMLESS LUNATIC
HAROLD MACMILLAN
HARP ON ONE STRING
HARROW ON THE HILL
HARVEST FESTIVAL
HAUL DOWN THE FLAG
HAUNCH OF VENISON
HAUNTING REFRAIN
HAVE A BONE TO PICK
HAVE AN INTERVIEW
HAVE A SWEET TOOTH
HAVE ONE'S REVENGE
HAVE THE BEST OF IT
HAVE THE LAST WORD
HAVE THE PLEASURE
HAVE THE WHIP-HAND
HAVE WHAT IT TAKES
HAZARD AN OPINION
HEAD IN THE CLOUDS
HEAD OF THE FAMILY
HEAD OF THE SCHOOL
HEAD-ON COLLISION
HEADPHONE SOCKET
HEALING OINTMENT
HEALTH AND WEALTH
HEALTH AUTHORITY
HEALTH INSURANCE
HEALTH SCREENING
HEALTHY APPETITE
HEALTHY EXERCISE
HEAP COALS OF FIRE
HEARSAY EVIDENCE
HEARTBREAK HOUSE
HEARTLESS MANNER
HEARTS ARE TRUMPS

HEART TRANSPLANT
HEARTY BREAKFAST
HEARTY GREETINGS
HEATHROW AIRPORT
HEAT OF THE MOMENT
HEAVEN BE PRAISED
HEAVY CASUALTIES
HEAVY PUNISHMENT
HEIGHT OF FASHION
HEIR PRESUMPTIVE
HEIR TO THE THRONE
HELLO HELLO HELLO
HENRY THE SEVENTH
HERBACEOUS PLANT
HERBERT MORRISON
HEREDITARY TITLE
HEREWARD THE WAKE
HERMIONE GINGOLD
HEROIC QUALITIES
HERRING INDUSTRY
HESITATION WALTZ
HIDE UNDERGROUND
HIGHER AND HIGHER
HIGHER CRITICISM
HIGHER EDUCATION
HIGHLAND COSTUME
HIGHLY COMMENDED
HIGHLY CONNECTED
HIGHLY DANGEROUS
HIGHLY DELIGHTED
HIGHLY EFFICIENT
HIGHLY QUALIFIED
HIGH TEMPERATURE
HINGE AND BRACKET
HIPPOCRATIC OATH
HIS MASTER'S VOICE
HISTORICAL NOVEL
HISTORIC PRESENT
HIT-AND-RUN DRIVER
HIT BELOW THE BELT
HIT THE HEADLINES
HIT THE HIGH SPOTS
HOLD ONE TO RANSOM
HOLD OUT ONE'S HAND
HOLD THE BEST HAND
HOLD UP YOUR HANDS
HOLE IN THE CORNER
HOLE IN THE GROUND
HOLES AND CORNERS
HOLIDAY BY THE SEA
HOLY ROMAN EMPIRE
HOME CONSUMPTION
HOMERIC LAUGHTER
HOMEWARD JOURNEY
HOME WITH THE MILK
HOMICIDAL MANIAC

HONEYMOON COUPLE
HONEYSUCKLE ROSE
HONOURS OF BATTLE
HOPE AGAINST HOPE
HOPELESS FAILURE
HORIZONTAL PLANE
HORNS OF A DILEMMA
HORRIBLE WEATHER
HORSE-SHOE MAGNET
HOSPICE MOVEMENT
HOSPITAL ALMONER
HOSPITAL GROUNDS
HOSPITAL SURGEON
HOSTILE EVIDENCE
HOTEL PROPRIETOR
HOT FROM THE PRESS
HOURS OF BUSINESS
HOURS OF IDLENESS
HOUSEHOLD CHORES
HOUSEHOLD DRUDGE
HOUSEHOLD TROOPS
HOUSING MINISTER
HOUSING SHORTAGE
HOVER ON THE BRINK
HOW GOES THE ENEMY?
HUCKLEBERRY FINN
HUDDLED TOGETHER
HUMAN EXPERIENCE
HUMANLY POSSIBLE
HUMANLY SPEAKING
HUMID ATMOSPHERE
HUNDRED THOUSAND
HUNDRED YEARS WAR
HUNGER AND THIRST
HUNGRY AS A HUNTER
HUSH-HUSH SUBJECT

I – 15

ICE-CREAM PARLOUR
ICE-CREAM SELLERS
ICE HOCKEY PLAYER
IDEAL SUGGESTION
IDLEWILD AIRPORT
ILLUSTRATED WORK
ILLUSTRIOUS PAST
IMITATION PEARLS
IMMACULATE STYLE
IMMEDIATE ACTION
IMMERSED IN STUDY
IMMERSION HEATER
IMMORTAL DREAMER
IMMOVABLE OBJECT
IMPENDING DANGER
IMPERIAL COLLEGE
IMPERIAL MEASURE

IMPLORING GLANCE
IMPORTANT MATTER
IMPORTANT PERSON
IMPOSSIBLE STORY
IMPRESSIVE SCENE
IMPROBABLE STORY
IMPROVED VERSION
IMPROVE IN HEALTH
IMPROVE ON NATURE
IMPULSIVE NATURE
IN A LESSER DEGREE
IN ALL CONSCIENCE
IN ALL DIRECTIONS
IN ALL LIKELIHOOD
INANIMATE MATTER
IN APPLE-PIE ORDER
IN A STRAIGHT LINE
INAUGURAL SPEECH
IN BLACK AND WHITE
INCIDENTAL MUSIC
INCLINE ONE'S HEAD
INCLUSIVE CHARGE
INCOME-TAX DEMAND
INCOME-TAX REBATE
INCOME-TAX RELIEF
INCOME-TAX RETURN
IN CONSIDERATION
INCREASED DEMAND
INDELIBLE PENCIL
INDEPENDENCE DAY
INDIAN ROPE-TRICK
INDIA-RUBBER BALL
INDIA-RUBBER BAND
INDIRECT CURRENT
INDIVIDUAL STYLE
INDOOR FIREWORKS
INDULGENT PARENT
INDUSTRIAL PLANT
IN EXTREME DANGER
INFAMOUS CONDUCT
INFANT MORTALITY
INFANTRY SOLDIER
INFERIOR ARTICLE
INFERIOR NUMBERS
INFERIOR QUALITY
INFERIOR VERSION
INFERNAL MACHINE
INFERNAL REGIONS
INFIRM OF PURPOSE
INFORMATION DESK
INFORMATION ROOM
INFORMED OPINION
IN FULL AGREEMENT
INGENIOUS DEVICE
INGENIOUS EXCUSE
INIQUITOUS PRICE

INITIAL EXPENSES
INJURED INNOCENT
IN JUXTAPOSITION
INNINGS DECLARED
INNOCENTS ABROAD
IN ONE'S RIGHT MIND
INORDINATE PRIDE
INORGANIC MATTER
IN SEARCH OF TRUTH
INSECURE FOOTING
IN SHARP CONTRAST
INSPECTION LIGHT
INSPECTOR FRENCH
INSTANT RESPONSE
INSTRUMENT BOARD
INSTRUMENT PANEL
INSUPARABLE ODDS
INSURANCE BROKER
INSURANCE OFFICE
INSURANCE POLICY
INTELLIGENT FOLK
INTELLIGENT TALK
INTERESTED PARTY
INTERIM DIVIDEND
INTERNAL AFFAIRS
IN THE ACCUSATIVE
IN THE ALTOGETHER
IN THE BACKGROUND
IN THE FIRST PLACE
IN THE FOREGROUND
IN THE LABORATORY
IN THE LAST RESORT
IN THE LIGHT OF DAY
IN THE LION'S MOUTH
IN THE MANNER BORN
IN THE MELTING-POT
IN THE MIDDLE EAST
IN THE NEAR FUTURE
IN THE NICK OF TIME
IN THE RIGHT PLACE
IN THE SAME BREATH
IN THE SHOP-WINDOW
IN THE SMALL HOURS
IN THE VERNACULAR
IN THE WILDERNESS
IN THE WITNESS-BOX
IN THE WRONG PLACE
INVALID CARRIAGE
INVENTIVE GENIUS
INVESTMENT TRUST
INVEST WITH POWER
INVISIBLE EXPORT
INVISIBLE IMPORT
INVITATION WALTZ
INVITED AUDIENCE
IRISH SWEEPSTAKE

IRREGULAR TROOPS
IRREPARABLE HARM
IRREPARABLE LOSS
ISLAND CONTINENT
ISSUE A CHALLENGE
ITALIAN VERMOUTH
IT'S THAT MAN AGAIN
IVAN THE TERRIBLE

J – 15

JACK OF ALL TRADES
JAM AND JERUSALEM
JANUARY THE FIFTH
JANUARY THE FIRST
JANUARY THE NINTH
JANUARY THE SIXTH
JANUARY THE TENTH
JANUARY THE THIRD
JERRY-BUILT HOUSE
JEWEL IN THE CROWN
JOBBING GARDENER
JOCKEY FOR PLACES
JOIN IN THE CHORUS
JOINT GOVERNMENT
JOIN THE MAJORITY
JOINT OPERATIONS
JOINT POSSESSION
JOLLY GOOD FELLOW
JUDGE FOR ONESELF
JUDGMENT OF PARIS
JUDGMENT SUMMONS
JUICE OF THE GRAPE
JULY THE ELEVENTH
JUMPING-OFF PLACE
JUNE THE ELEVENTH
JUNIOR BARRISTER
JUPITER SYMPHONY
JUST ABOUT ENOUGH

K – 15

KAMIKAZE PRICING
KATHLEEN FERRIER
KEEN COMPETITION
KEENLY CONTESTED
KEEP AT A DISTANCE
KEEP BRITAIN TIDY
KEEPER OF THE KEYS
KEEP IN CAPTIVITY
KEEP IN IGNORANCE
KEEP NOTHING BACK
KEEP OFF THE GRASS
KEEP ONE GUESSING
KEEP ONE'S BALANCE
KEEP ONE'S COUNSEL

KEEP ONE'S PROMISE
KEEP ONE'S SHIRT ON
KEEP ON THE COURSE
KEEP OUT OF THE WAY
KEEP THE DOOR OPEN
KEEP THINGS GOING
KEEP TO THE MIDDLE
KEEP UNDER ARREST
KENNETH McKELLAR
KERB-SIDE PARKING
KEY TO THE MYSTERY
KICK UP ONE'S HEELS
KID-GLOVE METHODS
KIDNEYS AND BACON
KINDLE OF KITTENS
KINDNESS OF HEART
KINGDOM OF HEAVEN
KING OF HOLLYWOOD
KING OF THE BEASTS
KING OF THE CASTLE
KING OF THE FOREST
KING OF THE JUNGLE
KITTEN ON THE KEYS
KNAVE OF DIAMONDS
KNEE-JERK LIBERAL
KNIGHT COMMANDER
KNIGHT OF THE BATH
KNIGHT OF THE ROAD
KNIGHTS TEMPLARS
KNITTING MACHINE
KNITTING PATTERN
KNOW A THING OR TWO
KNOW ONE'S OWN MIND

L – 15

LABOUR CANDIDATE
LABOUR RELATIONS
LABOUR SUPPORTER
LACK OF EDUCATION
LACK OF KNOWLEDGE
LACK OF WILL POWER
LADDER OF SUCCESS
LADIES' COMPANION
LADIES IN WAITING
LAKE WOBEGON DAYS
LAND OF MY FATHERS
LAND OF THE LIVING
LANDSCAPE ARTIST
LANGUAGE BARRIER
LANGUAGE PROBLEM
LANGUAGE TEACHER
LARGE PERCENTAGE
LARGE POPULATION
LAST BUT NOT LEAST
LASTING MOMUMENT

LAST PERFORMANCE
LATERAL THINKING
LATEST INVENTION
LATEST QUOTATION
LAUGH AND GROW FAT
LAUGHING JACKASS
LAUGH LIKE A DRAIN
LAUGH LIKE A HYENA
LAUGH OUT OF COURT
LAUGHTER IN COURT
LAURENCE OLIVIER
LAVENDER HILL MOB
LAY DOWN ONE'S ARMS
LAY DOWN ONE'S LIFE
LEAD A DOUBLE LIFE
LEAD A MERRY DANCE
LEADER OF FASHION
LEADER OF SOCIETY
LEADER OF THE BAND
LEADING BUSINESS
LEADING NOVELIST
LEADING QUESTION
LEADING THE FIELD
LEAGUE OF NATIONS
LEAP OVER THE MOON
LEARN ONE'S LESSON
LEATHER INDUSTRY
LEAVE FOOTPRINTS
LEAVE IN SUSPENSE
LEAVE IN THE LURCH
LEAVE IT TO CHANCE
LEAVE NOTHING OUT
LEAVE THE COUNTRY
LEAVE UNFINISHED
LEE HARVEY OSWALD
LEGAL DEPARTMENT
LEGAL PROFESSION
LEGAL SEPARATION
LEGAL SETTLEMENT
LEG BEFORE WICKET
LEGISLATIVE BODY
LEGITIMATE CLAIM
LEGITIMATE DRAMA
LEGITIMATE STAGE
LEGUMINOUS PLANT
LEICESTER SQUARE
LEIGHTON BUZZARD
LEISURED CLASSES
LEMON CHEESE-CAKE
LENGTH OF SERVICE
LENGTHY ARGUMENT
LENGTHY BUSINESS
LENIENT SENTENCE
LEONARDO DA VINCI
LESSEN THE STRAIN
LESS THAN THE DUST

LET DOWN ONE'S HAIR
LET ONE'S HAIR DOWN
LETTER OF REQUEST
LET THERE BE LIGHT!
LETTRES DE CACHET
LEVERAGED BUY-OUT
LIBERAL DEMOCRAT
LIBERAL MAJORITY
LIBERAL MINORITY
LICENCE ENDORSED
LICK AND A PROMISE
LICK ONE'S FINGERS
LIE IN ONE'S THROAT
LIE LIKE A TROOPER
LIFE-BOAT STATION
LIFT THE RECEIVER
LIFT UP ONE'S VOICE
LIFT UP YOUR HEART
LIGHT AS A FEATHER
LIGHT LITERATURE
LIGHT MACHINE-GUN
LIGHTNING SKETCH
LIGHTNING STRIKE
LIGHT OF THE WORLD
LIGHT PUNISHMENT
LIKE A DROWNED RAT
LIKE A DUTCH UNCLE
LIKE A HOUSE AFIRE
LIKE QUICKSILVER
LILY OF THE VALLEY
LINCOLN HANDICAP
LINCOLN MEMORIAL
LINE OF DIRECTION
LINE ONE'S POCKETS
LINFORD CHRISTIE
LINK WITH THE PAST
LIQUID RESOURCES
LIST TO STARBOARD
LITERARY CIRCLES
LITERARY FORGERY
LITERARY OUTLINE
LITERARY SUBJECT
LITTLE BLACK BOOK
LITTLE ENGLANDER
LITTLE GENTLEMAN
LITTLE KNOWLEDGE
LITTLE MISS FIX-IT
LITTLE OR NOTHING
LITTLE WOODEN HUT
LIVE DANGEROUSLY
LIVE IN A SMALL WAY
LIVE IN SECLUSION
LIVE LIKE A PAUPER
LIVERPOOL STREET
LIVING TESTIMONY
LOADED WITH MONEY

LOAD OFF ONE'S MIND
LOAVES AND FISHES
LOCAL GOVERNMENT
LOCAL INHABITANT
LOCH NESS MONSTER
LOCKED AND BOLTED
LODGE A COMPLAINT
LOGICAL ARGUMENT
LOGICAL SEQUENCE
LONDON TRANSPORT
LONDON WEIGHTING
LONG ARM OF THE LAW
LONGEST WAY ROUND
LONG LIVE THE KING!
LONG-TERM SOLDIER
LONG-WINDED STORY
LOOK BACK IN ANGER
LOOK FOR A WELCOME
LOOK FOR SYMPATHY
LOOK THE OTHER WAY
LOOK TO THE FUTURE
LORD CHAMBERLAIN
LORD HIGH ADMIRAL
LORD HIGH STEWARD
LORD MAYOR'S COACH
LORD PETER WIMSEY
LORDS AND COMMONS
LORDS OF CREATION
LOSE COUNTENANCE
LOSE ONE'S BALANCE
LOSE ONE'S FOOTING
LOSE ONE'S HUSBAND
LOSE ONE'S STRIPES
LOSE ON THE SWINGS
LOSE THE ELECTION
LOST OPPORTUNITY
LOVE AND MARRIAGE
LOVE ME, LOVE MY DOG
LOVE OF ADVENTURE
LOVER AND HIS LASS
LOWER ONE'S SIGHTS
LOW LIGHT WARNING
LOW SUBSCRIPTION
LUKEWARM SUPPORT
LUMINANCE SIGNAL
LUMP IN THE THROAT
LUNCHEON SAUSAGE
LUNCHEON VOUCHER
LUTON GIRLS' CHOIR
LUXURIANT GROWTH

M – 15

MAD AS A MARCH HARE
MAGAZINE ARTICLE
MAGAZINE SECTION

MAGIC INSTRUMENT	MARRIED QUARTERS
MAGNETIC COMPASS	MARSHALLING YARD
MAGNIFYING GLASS	MARY'S LITTLE LAMB
MAGNIFYING POWER	MASCULINE GENDER
MAIN CLAIM TO FAME	MASQUERADE DRESS
MAIN LINE STATION	MASS INFORMATION
MAJESTY OF THE LAW	MASS OBSERVATION
MAJORITY VERDICT	MASTER CARPENTER
MAKE A COLLECTION	MASTER CRAFTSMAN
MAKE A CONFESSION	MASTER OF SCIENCE
MAKE A FRESH START	MATERIAL BENEFIT
MAKE ALTERATIONS	MATERIAL CULTURE
MAKE AN ASSERTION	MATERIAL SUCCESS
MAKE AN EXCEPTION	MATERIAL WITNESS
MAKE APPLICATION	MATERNAL FEELING
MAKE A PREDICTION	MATTER OF OPINION
MAKE A RESOLUTION	MAXIMUM PRESSURE
MAKE A SUGGESTION	MAY THE FIFTEENTH
MAKE COMPARISONS	MAY THE SIXTEENTH
MAKE CONCESSIONS	MAY THE THIRTIETH
MAKE CORRECTIONS	MAY THE TWENTIETH
MAKE ONE'S FORTUNE	MEANS OF APPROACH
MAKE REPARATIONS	MEAN WHAT ONE SAYS
MAKE RESTITUTION	MEASURE OF LENGTH
MAKE SHORT WORK OF	MECHANICAL MEANS
MAKE THE BEST OF IT	MECHANICAL POWER
MAKE THE MOST OF IT	MEMBER OF SOCIETY
MAKE THINGS CLEAR	MEMBER OF THE CAST
MAKE THINGS WORSE	MEMORIAL SERVICE
MALE SUPERIORITY	MENTAL AGITATION
MALIGNANT GROWTH	MENTAL BREAKDOWN
MALIGN INFLUENCE	MENTAL DEFECTIVE
MALVERN FESTIVAL	MENTAL FACULTIES
MANIC DEPRESSION	MENTAL TELEPATHY
MANILLA ENVELOPE	MENTAL TREATMENT
MAN IN POSSESSION	MERCENARY TROOPS
MANNEQUIN PARADE	MERCHANT SERVICE
MAN OF EXPERIENCE	MERE COINCIDENCE
MANY-HEADED BEAST	MERRY AS A CRICKET
MARCH OF PROGRESS	MERRY MONTH OF MAY
MARCH THE SEVENTH	MESSAGE RECEIVED
MARCH THE TWELFTH	METHOD OF WORKING
MARGINAL COMMENT	MEXICAN HAIRLESS
MARIE ANTOINETTE	MICHAEL FLANDERS
MARINE INSURANCE	MICHAEL HOLLIDAY
MARINER'S COMPASS	MICHAELMAS DAISY
MARK OF AUTHORITY	MICHAELMAS GOOSE
MARK THE OCCASION	MICHAEL REDGRAVE
MARLENE DIETRICH	MIDDLE-AGE SPREAD
MARRIAGEABLE AGE	MIDDLE OF THE ROAD
MARRIAGE ADVISER	MIDDLE OF THE ROOM
MARRIAGE BY PROXY	MIDLAND COUNTIES
MARRIAGE LICENCE	MIDNIGHT MATINEE
MARRIAGE PARTNER	MILITARY ACADEMY
MARRIAGE PORTION	MILITARY BEARING
MARRIAGE SERVICE	MILITARY COLLEGE

MILITARY COLOURS
MILITARY FUNERAL
MILITARY HISTORY
MILITARY HONOURS
MILITARY MISSION
MILITARY SERVICE
MILITARY STATION
MILITARY TACTICS
MILITARY TRIBUNE
MILITARY TWO-STEP
MILITATE AGAINST
MILLICENT MARTIN
MILLIONAIRE'S ROW
MIND ONE'S MANNERS
MIND THE WET PAINT
MINIATURE POODLE
MINISTER OF POWER
MINISTER OF STATE
MINISTER OF WORKS
MINISTRY OF POWER
MINISTRY OF STATE
MINISTRY OF WORKS
MIRROR OF FASHION
MISERABLE SINNER
MISS ONE'S FOOTING
MISTRESS QUICKLY
MIXTURE AS BEFORE
MODEL OF INDUSTRY
MODE OF BEHAVIOUR
MODERATE DEMANDS
MODERATE DRINKER
MODERATE SUCCESS
MODEST BEHAVIOUR
MOLOTOV COCKTAIL
MOMENT OF MADNESS
MONASTERY GARDEN
MONDAY AFTERNOON
MONEY FOR NOTHING
MONEY FOR OLD ROPE
MONEY MAKES MONEY
MONTE CARLO RALLY
MONTH AFTER MONTH
MONTHLY MAGAZINE
MONTHLY PAYMENTS
MONTHS AND MONTHS
MONTHS OF THE YEAR
MONUMENTAL MASON
MOON AND SIXPENCE
MOONLIGHT SONATA
MORAL INJUNCTION
MORAL OBLIGATION
MORAL PHILOSOPHY
MORAL REARMAMENT
MORAL STANDPOINT
MORBID CURIOSITY
MORE THAN WELCOME

MORRISON SHELTER
MOST INTERESTING
MOST RESPECTABLE
MOTHER AND FATHER
MOTHERING SUNDAY
MOTHERLESS CHILD
MOTIVATING FORCE
MOTLEY GATHERING
MOTORING OFFENCE
MOTORWAY MADNESS
MOUNTAIN OF FLESH
MOUNTAINOUS AREA
MOUNTAIN RAILWAY
MOUNTAIN TORRENT
MOUTH OF THE RIVER
MOVING SPECTACLE
MOVING STAIRCASE
MUCH OF A MUCHNESS
MUCH SOUGHT AFTER
MULBERRY HARBOUR
MULTIPLY BY EIGHT
MULTIPLY BY SEVEN
MULTIPLY BY THREE
MUNICH AGREEMENT
MURAL DECORATION
MURDEROUS WEAPON
MUSICAL DIRECTOR
MUSICAL FESTIVAL
MUSICAL INTERVAL
MUSIC-HALL ARTIST
MUSIC HATH CHARMS
MUSTARD AND CRESS
MUSTER UP COURAGE
MUTUAL AFFECTION
MUTUAL AGREEMENT
MUTUAL HOSTILITY
MUTUAL INSURANCE
MUTUAL SUSPICION
MY LEARNED FRIEND
MYTHOLOGICAL AGE

N – 15

NATIONAL COLOURS
NATIONAL COSTUME
NATIONAL DEFENCE
NATIONAL GALLERY
NATIONAL HOLIDAY
NATIONAL LIBERAL
NATIONAL LIBRARY
NATIONAL LOTTERY
NATIONAL SAVINGS
NATIONAL SERVICE
NATIONAL SOCIETY
NATIONAL THEATRE
NATURAL APTITUDE

NATURAL CAPACITY
NATURAL INSTINCT
NAUGHTY NINETIES
NAVAL ENGAGEMENT
NAVAL OPERATIONS
NAVAL TOURNAMENT
NAVIGATION LIGHT
NEARER AND NEARER
NEAREST RELATIVE
NEAT AS NINEPENCE
NEAT BUT NOT GAUDY
NEAT HANDWRITING
NEAT PIECE OF WORK
NECK-AND-NECK RACE
NECTAR OF THE GODS
NEEDLE AND COTTON
NEEDLE AND THREAD
NEGATIVE REQUEST
NEGLECT ONE'S DUTY
NEGOTIABLE BONDS
NERVOUS DISORDER
NEVER A CROSS WORD
NEVER-ENDING TASK
NEW ACQUAINTANCE
NEW AGE TRAVELLER
NEWCASTLE ON TYNE
NEWCASTLE UNITED
NEW ENGLISH BIBLE
NEWFOUNDLAND DOG
NEWGATE CALENDAR
NEWS COMMENTATOR
NEW SCOTLAND YARD
NEWS FROM NOWHERE
NEWSPAPER REPORT
NEWSPAPER SELLER
NIBBLE AT THE BAIT
NICE DISTINCTION
NICE LITTLE THING
NIGHT AFTER NIGHT
NIGHT ON THE TILES
NIGHT STARVATION
NINE AND A QUARTER
NINE AND SIXPENCE
NINE AND TENPENCE
NINE AND TWOPENCE
NINETEEN AND FIVE
NINETEEN AND FOUR
NINETEEN AND NINE
NINETEEN PER CENT
NINETEENTH OF MAY
NINE WICKETS DOWN
NINTH OF DECEMBER
NINTH OF FEBRUARY
NINTH OF NOVEMBER
NOBEL PEACE PRIZE
NOBLE SENTIMENTS

NOBODY'S BUSINESS
NO CONCERN OF MINE
NO DISTANCE AT ALL
NOISY NEIGHBOURS
NOMINATION PAPER
NON COMPOS MENTIS
NONE BUT THE BRAVE
NO PRESERVATIVES
NORFOLK DUMPLING
NORMAL BEHAVIOUR
NORMAL PROCEDURE
NORTHERN IRELAND
NORTH OF THE RIVER
NORTH OF THE TWEED
NO STONE UNTURNED
NOT A LIVING THING
NOTHING IN COMMON
NOT IN MY BACKYARD
NOT IN THE RUNNING
NOT OUT OF THE WOOD
NOT STRONG ENOUGH
NOTTING HILL GATE
NOUVELLE CUISINE
NOVEL EXPERIENCE
NUCLEAR DISARMER
NUCLEAR REACTION
NUFFIELD COLLEGE
NUREMBERG TRIALS
NURSE A GRIEVANCE
NURSE AN AMBITION
NURSERY HANDICAP
NUTCRACKER SUITE

O – 15

OBEDIENT SERVANT
OBEY REGULATIONS
OBJECT OF CHARITY
OBJECT OF DISLIKE
OBJECT OF WORSHIP
OBLIQUE QUESTION
OBSERVATION POST
OCCASIONAL TABLE
OCCUPYING TENANT
OCTOBER THE FIFTH
OCTOBER THE FIRST
OCTOBER THE NINTH
OCTOBER THE SIXTH
OCTOBER THE TENTH
OCTOBER THE THIRD
ODDS-ON FAVOURITE
ODOUR OF SANCTITY
OFFENSIVE MANNER
OFFENSIVE REMARK
OFFENSIVE WEAPON
OFFER IN EXCHANGE

OFFICER IN CHARGE
OFFICER MATERIAL
OFFICER OF THE DAY
OFFICIAL INQUIRY
OFFICIAL JOURNAL
OFFICIOUS PERSON
OFF TO A FINE START
OFF TO A GOOD START
OF THE FIRST WATER
OLD ACQUAINTANCE
OLD-AGE PENSIONER
OLD AS METHUSELAH
OLD CONTEMPTIBLE
OLDER GENERATION
OLD FATHER THAMES
OLIVER GOLDSMITH
OMNIA VINCIT AMOR
ON ACTIVE SERVICE
ONCE IN A BLUE MOON
ONCE IN A LIFETIME
ON-COURSE BETTING
ONE AFTER ANOTHER
ONE MAN WENT TO MOW
ONE OF THE COMPANY
ONE OVER THE EIGHT
ONE STAGE AT A TIME
ONE THING AT A TIME
ONE WAY OR ANOTHER
ON HANDS AND KNEES
ON ONE'S HIGH HORSE
ON SPEAKING TERMS
ON THE BORDERLINE
ON THE BRADEN BEAT
ON THE BRIGHT SIDE
ON THE CREDIT SIDE
ON THE DOTTED LINE
ON THE RIGHT LINES
ON THE RIGHT SCENT
ON THE RIGHT TRACK
ON THE ROAD TO RUIN
ON THE WATER-WAGON
ON THE WRONG LINES
ON THE WRONG SCENT
ON THE WRONG TRACK
ON TOP OF THE WORLD
ON VISITING TERMS
ON WITH THE MOTLEY
OPEN-AND-SHUT CASE
OPEN COMPETITION
OPEN HOSTILITIES
OPENING CEREMONY
OPENING SENTENCE
OPEN SCHOLARSHIP
OPEN THE QUESTION
OPEN THE THROTTLE
OPEN TO CRITICISM

OPEN TO OBJECTION
OPEN TO SUSPICION
OPEN TO THE PUBLIC
OPPORTUNE MOMENT
OPPORTUNE REMARK
OPPOSING COUNSEL
OPPOSITE EXTREME
OPPOSITE MEANING
OPPOSITE PARTIES
OPPOSITION BENCH
OPPOSITION PARTY
OPTICAL ILLUSION
ORAL EXAMINATION
ORANGE FREE STATE
ORANGE MARMALADE
ORCHESTRAL MUSIC
ORCHESTRA STALLS
ORDERLY CORPORAL
ORDERLY SERGEANT
ORDNANCE OFFICER
ORGANISED LABOUR
ORIENTAL SCHOLAR
ORIGINAL MEANING
ORIGIN OF SPECIES
ORNAMENTAL PLANT
OUNCE OF PRACTICE
OUR MUTUAL FRIEND
OUTDOOR CLOTHING
OUTDOOR EXERCISE
OUT OF COMMISSION
OUT OF EMPLOYMENT
OUT OF HIS ELEMENT
OUT OF ONE'S SENSES
OUT OF PROPORTION
OUT OF THE COUNTRY
OUT OF THE PICTURE
OUT OF THE RUNNING
OUT-OF-THE-WAY SPOT
OUTRIGHT SCANDAL
OUTSIDE INTEREST
OUTSTANDING DEBT
OVER AND DONE WITH
OVERCOME BY GRIEF
OVERFLOW MEETING
OVERHEAD CHARGES
OVERHEAD RAILWAY
OVERSTEP THE MARK
OVER THE BASE-LINE

P – 15

PADDINGTON GREEN
PAINT THE TOWN RED
PAIR OF CALLIPERS
PAIR OF COMPASSES
PAIR OF DUMB-BELLS

PAIR OF STOCKINGS
PALACE OF SOVIETS
PALAEOLITHIC AGE
PARACHUTE TROOPS
PARAGON OF VIRTUE
PARENTAL CONSENT
PARENTAL CONTROL
PARKHURST PRISON
PARTIAL LIKENESS
PARTNERS IN CRIME
PARTY CONFERENCE
PASS ALONG PLEASE
PASS A RESOLUTION
PASS AWAY THE TIME
PASSIVE INTEREST
PASSIVE RESISTER
PASSPORT CONTROL
PASS ROUND THE HAT
PASS THE HAT ROUND
PASS WITH HONOURS
PASTEURIZED MILK
PATCH UP A QUARREL
PATENTLY OBVIOUS
PATERNAL FEELING
PATRICK CAMPBELL
PATRON OF THE ARTS
PATTERN OF VIRTUE
PAUSE FOR A MOMENT
PAWNBROKER'S SIGN
PAYABLE ON DEMAND
PAY COMPENSATION
PAY OFF OLD SCORES
PAY ONE'S RESPECTS
PEACE AT ANY PRICE
PEACE CONFERENCE
PEACE WITH HONOUR
PEACHES AND CREAM
PECULIAR FLAVOUR
PELICAN CROSSING
PENAL SETTLEMENT
PENCIL SHARPENER
PENNY IN THE POUND
PEOPLE IN GENERAL
PEOPLE OF FASHION
PEOPLE OF QUALITY
PER ARDUA AD ASTRA
PERCENTAGE BASIS
PEREGRINE FALCON
PERFECT CREATURE
PERFECT INTERVAL
PERFECT LIKENESS
PERFECTLY HONEST
PERFECT NONSENSE
PERFECT NUISANCE
PERFECT STRANGER
PERFECT TREASURE

PERFORMING FLEAS
PERFUME ATOMISER
PERILOUS VENTURE
PERIOD FURNITURE
PERISHABLE GOODS
PERMANENT RECORD
PERPETUAL MOTION
PERSHING MISSILE
PERSONAL ACCOUNT
PERSONAL AFFRONT
PERSONAL BENEFIT
PERSONAL EFFECTS
PERSONALITY CULT
PERSONAL OPINION
PERSONAL PRONOUN
PERSONAL REASONS
PERSONAL SERVICE
PERSONA NON GRATA
PERTINENT REMARK
PESTLE AND MORTAR
PETER AND THE WOLF
PETER THE PAINTER
PETITION OF RIGHT
PETRIFIED FOREST
PETROL RATIONING
PHOTOGRAPH ALBUM
PHYSICAL CRAVING
PHYSICAL CULTURE
PHYSICAL FATIGUE
PHYSICAL SCIENCE
PICK UP THE PIECES
PICK UP THE THREAD
PICTURE OF HEALTH
PICTURE OF MISERY
PICTURE POSTCARD
PIECE OF EVIDENCE
PIECE OF GOOD NEWS
PIECE OF NONSENSE
PIECE OF ONE'S MIND
PILLAR OF SOCIETY
PINCHED WITH COLD
PINK OF CONDITION
PIOUS SENTIMENTS
PIPPED AT THE POST
PIT OF THE STOMACH
PLACE OF BUSINESS
PLAGUE OF LOCUSTS
PLAIN-CLOTHES MAN
PLANETARY SYSTEM
PLANNING OFFICER
PLAY A DOUBLE GAME
PLAY A LOSING GAME
PLAY CAT AND MOUSE
PLAYERS' ENTRANCE
PLAY FIRST FIDDLE
PLAY HIDE-AND-SEEK

PLAY ONE'S OWN HAND
PLAY THE BAGPIPES
PLAY THE INFORMER
PLAY THE PARASITE
PLAYTHING OF FATE
PLAY TIDDLYWINKS
PLEASANT EVENING
PLEASANT FLAVOUR
PLEASURE GARDENS
PLEASURE GROUNDS
PLEASURE STEAMER
PLIGHT ONE'S TROTH
PLOUGHMAN'S LUNCH
PLOUGH THE FIELDS
PLUM IN ONE'S MOUTH
PLYMOUTH BROTHER
PLYMOUTH HARBOUR
POCKET ONE'S PRIDE
POCKET TELESCOPE
POETICAL JUSTICE
POINT-BLANK RANGE
POINTED REMINDER
POINTLESS REMARK
POINT OF NO RETURN
POLAR EXPEDITION
POLICE CONSTABLE
POLICE INSPECTOR
POLICE RADAR TRAP
POLISHED MANNERS
POLITICAL ASYLUM
POLITICAL CAREER
POLITICAL EVENTS
POLITICAL OFFICE
POLITICAL RIGHTS
POLITICAL SPEECH
POLITICAL THEORY
POLITICAL WEAPON
POLITICAL WRITER
POLYSTYRENE TILE
POMP AND CEREMONY
POOR CIRCULATION
POOR CONSOLATION
POOR VENTILATION
POPEYE THE SAILOR
POPULAR LANGUAGE
PORTMANTEAU WORD
PORTRAIT GALLERY
PORTRAIT OF A LADY
PORTRAIT PAINTER
POSITION OF POWER
POSITION OF TRUST
POSITIVE ELEMENT
POST-DATED CHEQUE
POST-OFFICE GUIDE
POTENTIAL DANGER
POTENTIAL ENERGY

POWER OF ATTORNEY
POWER OF JUDGMENT
POWER OF RECOVERY
POWER OF THE PRESS
PRACTICAL RESULT
PRACTISE SORCERY
PRAIRIE SCHOONER
PRAYER FOR THE DAY
PREACH THE GOSPEL
PREACH TO THE WISE
PRECARIOUS STATE
PREFECT OF POLICE
PREFERENCE SHARE
PREFERRED SHARES
PRELIMINARY HEAT
PRELIMINARY STEP
PREMEDITATED ACT
PRE-PAID TELEGRAM
PREPARED TO FIGHT
PRESERVED GINGER
PRESERVING SUGAR
PRESIDENT MARCOS
PRESIDENT REAGAN
PRESS CONFERENCE
PRESSED FOR FUNDS
PRESSED FOR MONEY
PRESSED FOR SPACE
PRESS FOR PAYMENT
PRESS THE TRIGGER
PRESTON NORTH END
PRETTY MUCH ALIKE
PREVAILING TASTE
PREVAILING WINDS
PREVIOUS OFFENCE
PRICE ON ONE'S HEAD
PRICE REGULATION
PRICK ONE'S EARS UP
PRICK UP ONE'S EARS
PRIMARY ELECTION
PRIMITIVE COLOUR
PRINCE OF DENMARK
PRINCESS EUGENIE
PRINCESS OF WALES
PRINCIPAL CLAUSE
PRINCIPAL PERSON
PRIOR CONDITIONS
PRIOR ENGAGEMENT
PRISONER OF STATE
PRISONER OF ZENDA
PRISONER'S FRIEND
PRIVATE CARRIAGE
PRIVATE CHANNELS
PRIVATE DEVOTION
PRIVATE HOSPITAL
PRIVATE LANGUAGE
PRIVATE PRACTICE

PRIVATE PROPERTY
PRIVATE QUARTERS
PRIVATE TEACHING
PRIVILEGED CLASS
PRIVY COUNCILLOR
PROBABLE STARTER
PROCESSED CHEESE
PRODIGAL'S RETURN
PROFESSED BELIEF
PROFESSIONAL AIR
PROFESSIONAL FEE
PROFESSIONAL MAN
PROFOUND THINKER
PROFOUND THOUGHT
PROGRAMME PARADE
PROGRAMME SELLER
PROHIBITION DAYS
PROHIBITION ZONE
PROLONG THE AGONY
PRONOUNCE GUILTY
PROOF OF PURCHASE
PROPERLY DRESSED
PROPER TREATMENT
PROPOSE MARRIAGE
PROSPECTIVE WIFE
PROUD AS A PEACOCK
PROVE ACCEPTABLE
PROVIDE THE MEANS
PROVINCIAL PAPER
PRUNES AND PRISMS
PUBLIC CHARACTER
PUBLIC DECEPTION
PUBLIC EDUCATION
PUBLIC ENCLOSURE
PUBLIC EXECUTION
PUBLIC KNOWLEDGE
PUBLIC MANIFESTO
PUBLIC OWNERSHIP
PUBLIC RELATIONS
PUBLIC-SCHOOL BOY
PUBLIC TRANSPORT
PUBLISH THE BANNS
PULL FOR THE SHORE
PULL ONE'S PUNCHES
PULL OUT THE STOPS
PULL-UP FOR CARMEN
PULL UP ONE'S SOCKS
PUMP UP THE VOLUME
PUNCTUATION MARK
PURCHASING POWER
PURE COINCIDENCE
PURELY AND SIMPLY
PURE MATHEMATICS
PURR WITH CONTENT
PURSUE AN INQUIRY
PURSUE THE MATTER

PUSS IN THE CORNER
PUT AN END TO IT ALL
PUT BACK THE CLOCK
PUT IN A WORD OR TWO
PUT IN POSSESSION
PUT IN QUARANTINE
PUT IN THE PICTURE
PUT INTO PRACTICE
PUT IT ANOTHER WAY
PUT IT ON THE SHELF
PUT ONE'S FOOT DOWN
PUT ONE'S FOOT IN IT
PUT ONE'S NAME DOWN
PUT ON ONE'S ARMOUR
PUT THE CLOCK BACK
PUT THE MOCKERS ON
PUTTING IT MILDLY
PUT UP A GOOD FIGHT
PUT UP FOR AUCTION

Q – 15

QUALIFIED PERSON
QUARTERLY REVIEW
QUARTER OF AN HOUR
QUARTER OF A POUND
QUARTER PAST FIVE
QUARTER PAST FOUR
QUARTER PAST NINE
QUARTER SESSIONS
QUARTER TO ELEVEN
QUARTER TO TWELVE
QUEEN OF DIAMONDS
QUEEN OF THE SOUTH
QUEEN'S MESSENGER
QUICKEN THE PULSE
QUICK OFF THE MARK
QUICK SUCCESSION
QUIET AS THE GRAVE
QUIET RESENTMENT
QUITE A CHARACTER
QUITE DELIGHTFUL
QUITE THE REVERSE
QUOTE FROM MEMORY

R – 15

RACE AGAINST TIME
RACIAL TOLERANCE
RACING CERTAINTY
RACKING HEADACHE
RADIO-ACTIVE ZONE
RADIO ALARM CLOCK
RADIO ASTRONOMER
RADIO JOURNALISM
RAILWAY ACCIDENT

RAILWAY CARRIAGE
RAILWAY JUNCTION
RAILWAY TERMINUS
RAINBOW ALLIANCE
RAIN CATS AND DOGS
RAIN STOPPED PLAY
RAISE A HUE AND CRY
RAISE OBJECTIONS
RAISE ONE'S SIGHTS
RAISE THE CURTAIN
RAISE THE SUBJECT
RAISE VEGETABLES
RALPH RICHARDSON
RAMSAY MACDONALD
RAPID SUCCESSION
RATTLING SUCCESS
RAZE TO THE GROUND
REACH FOR THE MOON
REACH PERFECTION
REACH ROCK-BOTTOM
READY AND WILLING
READY-BUILT HOUSE
READY FOR THE FRAY
READY-MADE EXCUSE
REARGUARD ACTION
REASONABLE DOUBT
REASONABLE OFFER
REASONABLE TERMS
RECENT DISCOVERY
RECEPTION CENTRE
RECKLESS EXPENSE
RECKLESS SPENDER
RECORDING STUDIO
RECOVER LOST TIME
RECOVER ONE'S MIND
RECOVER THE ASHES
RECRUITING DRIVE
RED-CURRANT JELLY
REDS UNDER THE BED
REDUCE TO NOTHING
REDUCE TO POVERTY
REDUCE TO SILENCE
RED, WHITE AND BLUE
REFILL ONE'S GLASS
REFLECTED VISION
REFRESHER COURSE
REFRESHMENT ROOM
REFRESHMENT TENT
REFUSE COLLECTOR
REGIMENTAL BADGE
REGIMENTAL MARCH
REGIMENTAL STAFF
REGIMENT OF WOMEN
REGISTRATION FEE
REGULAR CUSTOMER
REGULAR EXERCISE

REGULAR FEATURES
REGULAR PRACTICE
REGULATION DRESS
REGULATION SPEED
REIGNING MONARCH
RELATIVE DENSITY
RELATIVELY QUIET
RELATIVE PRONOUN
RELAXING CLIMATE
RELEASE ONE'S HOLD
RELIABLE QUALITY
RELIABLE SERVICE
RELIGIOUS BELIEF
RELIGIOUS MANIAC
REMARKABLE CHILD
REMARKABLE SIGHT
REMARKABLE VOICE
REMARKABLE WOMAN
REMEMBER NOTHING
REMOVE ALL TRACES
REMOVE MOUNTAINS
REMOVE THE TRACES
RENDER AN ACCOUNT
RENDER NECESSARY
RENT RESTRICTION
RE-OPEN OLD WOUNDS
REPAIRING CLAUSE
REPAIR THE DAMAGE
REPENT AT LEISURE
REPUBLICAN PARTY
REPULSE AN ATTACK
RESEARCH CHEMIST
RESERVE OF ENERGY
RESERVE STRENGTH
RESIDENTIAL AREA
RESIDENT SURGEON
RESTORATION FUND
RESTORATION PLAY
RESTORE TO HEALTH
RESTORE TO REASON
RESTORE TO SANITY
RESTRAINING HAND
RESTRICT IMPORTS
RESURRECTION DAY
RETORT COURTEOUS
RETURN IN TRIUMPH
RETURN TO SERVICE
RETURN TO THE PAST
REVERSION TO TYPE
RICHARD DIMBLEBY
RICHARD THE THIRD
RICHLY FURNISHED
RIDE A BROOMSTICK
RIDE A HOBBY-HORSE
RIDE OUT THE STORM
RIGHT DOWN THE CAR

RIGHT HONOURABLE
RIGHT OFF THE REEL
RIGHT OF PURCHASE
RIGHTS AND WRONGS
RIGHT TO THE POINT
RIGHT WAVELENGTH
RIGID DISCIPLINE
RILLINGTON PLACE
RINGING APPLAUSE
RIOTOUS ASSEMBLY
RIPE FOR MISCHIEF
RISE FROM THE DEAD
RISE WITH THE LARK
RITUAL FIRE-DANCE
ROARING TWENTIES
ROARS OF LAUGHTER
ROBBED OF FREEDOM
ROBIN GOODFELLOW
ROB WITH VIOLENCE
ROCK-BOTTOM PRICE
ROCK OF GIBRALTAR
ROGER DE COVERLEY
ROGET'S THESAURUS
ROLL OF WALLPAPER
ROLY-POLY PUDDING
ROMULUS AND REMUS
ROOM TEMPERATURE
ROOM TO SWING A CAT
ROOTED OBJECTION
ROOTED TO THE SPOT
ROOT OF THE MATTER
ROSS AND CROMARTY
ROTATION OF CROPS
ROTTEN AT THE CORE
ROTTEN TO THE CORE
ROUGHLY SPEAKING
ROUNDABOUT ROUTE
ROUND OF APPLAUSE
ROUND OF PLEASURE
ROYAL ALBERT HALL
ROYAL AND ANCIENT
ROYAL COMMISSION
ROYAL OPERA HOUSE
ROYAL TOURNAMENT
RUBBER TRUNCHEON
RUDDY COMPLEXION
RUDE FOREFATHERS
RUFFLED FEATHERS
RUFFLED FEELINGS
RUIN ONE'S CHANCES
RULES OF FOOTBALL
RUN A TEMPERATURE
RUN-AWAY MARRIAGE
RUN FOR ONE'S MONEY
RUN FOR PRESIDENT
RUN LIKE WILD-FIRE

RURAL POPULATION
RUSSIAN LANGUAGE
RUSSIAN ROULETTE

S – 15

SAFETY IN NUMBERS
SAIL INTO THE WIND
SAIL NEAR THE WIND
SAILOR'S HORNPIPE
SAINT GEORGE'S DAY
SAINT MARLYEBONE
SALES RESISTANCE
SALLY IN OUR ALLEY
SALMON AND SHRIMP
SAMSON AGONISTES
SANDWICH ISLANDS
SARATOGA SPRINGS
SARDINE SANDWICH
SARDINES ON TOAST
SATURATION POINT
SATURDAY EVENING
SATURDAY MORNING
SAUSAGE AND CHIPS
SAUSAGES AND MASH
SAVAGE CRITICISM
SAVE APPEARANCES
SAVE THE CHILDREN
SAVINGS MOVEMENT
SAVOURY OMELETTE
SAY THE MAGIC WORD
SAY WITH EMPHASIS
SCALENE TRIANGLE
SCALES OF JUSTICE
SCALE THE HEIGHTS
SCENE OF THE CRIME
SCHEDULED FLIGHT
SCHNEIDER TROPHY
SCHOLASTIC AGENT
SCHOOLBOY HOWLER
SCHOOL INSPECTOR
SCHOOL OF DANCING
SCHOOL OF THOUGHT
SCIENTIFIC BOXER
SCIENTIFIC WORLD
SCOTTISH TERRIER
SCOTTISH THISTLE
SCRAPE THE BARREL
SCRATCH OF THE PEN
SCRATCHING ONE'S HEAD
SCRIBBLING BLOCK
SCRIMP AND SCRAPE
SCRIPTURE LESSON
SCRUFF OF THE NECK
SEA ISLAND COTTON
SEARCHING GLANCE

SEARCH ONE'S HEART
SEASIDE LANDLADY
SEATING CAPACITY
SEAWORTHY VESSEL
SECONDARY COLOUR
SECONDARY MATTER
SECONDARY MODERN
SECONDARY SCHOOL
SECOND-BEST THING
SECOND CHILDHOOD
SECOND FAVOURITE
SECOND-HAND GOODS
SECOND IN COMMAND
SECOND INTENTION
SECOND OF JANUARY
SECOND OF OCTOBER
SECOND-RATE HOTEL
SECOND TIME ROUND
SECRET ANIMOSITY
SECRET COURTSHIP
SECRET INFLUENCE
SECRET POLICEMAN
SECRET STAIRCASE
SECURITY BLANKET
SECURITY COUNCIL
SECURITY MEASURE
SECURITY OFFICER
SEEDS OF MISTRUST
SEEK A COMPROMISE
SEEK INFORMATION
SEEK ONE'S FORTUNE
SEE NAPLES AND DIE
SEE ONE'S WAY CLEAR
SEE THE FUNNY SIDE
SEE WHAT YOU CAN DO
SELECT COMMITTEE
SELF-EDUCATED MAN
SELF-IMPOSED TASK
SELF-SERVICE SHOP
SELL INTO SLAVERY
SELL ONE'S COUNTRY
SEMOLINA PUDDING
SEND AN ULTIMATUM
SEND IN THE CLOWNS
SEND ROUND THE HAT
SEND THE CAP ROUND
SEND TO THE BOTTOM
SENIOR BARRISTER
SENIORES PRIORES
SENSATIONAL NEWS
SENSATION MONGER
SENSE OF DISTANCE
SENSE OF PLEASURE
SENSE OF SECURITY
SENSITIVE MARKET
SENSITIVE NATURE

SENSUAL PLEASURE
SENTENCE OF DEATH
SENTENCE TO DEATH
SENTIMENTAL GIRL
SEPARATION ORDER
SERIOUS ACCIDENT
SERIOUS LANGUAGE
SERIOUS QUESTION
SERMONS IN STONES
SERVANT QUESTION
SERVED WITH A WRIT
SERVE TWO MASTERS
SERVICE INCLUDED
SERVICE REVOLVER
SESAME AND LILIES
SET A GOOD EXAMPLE
SET A LOW STANDARD
SET OF FALSE TEETH
SET OF QUADRILLES
SETTLE AN ACCOUNT
SETTLE OLD SCORES
SETTLE THE MATTER
SET UP IN BUSINESS
SEVE BALLESTEROS
SEVEN DEADLY SINS
SEVEN OF DIAMONDS
SEVENPENNY STAMP
SEVENTEEN AND SIX
SEVENTEEN AND TWO
SEVENTEENTH HOLE
SEVENTH OF AUGUST
SEVENTH SYMPHONY
SEVEN TIMES SEVEN
SEVENTY THOUSAND
SEVERE THRASHING
SHABBY GENTILITY
SHABBY TREATMENT
SHADY REPUTATION
SHAKE LIKE A JELLY
SHAKEN TO THE CORE
SHALLOW ARGUMENT
SHARPEN ONE'S WITS
SHARP IMPRESSION
SHEATHE THE SWORD
SHEEPSKIN JACKET
SHEER PERFECTION
SHEFFIELD UNITED
SHERBET FOUNTAIN
SHETLAND ISLANDS
SHIFT FOR ONESELF
SHIFT ONE'S GROUND
SHIP OF THE DESERT
SHIPPING COMPANY
SHIPPING MAGNATE
SHIP'S COMPLEMENT
SHIVER ME TIMBERS

SHOCKING SCANDAL
SHOCKING WEATHER
SHOOTING GALLERY
SHOPPING TROLLEY
SHORTHAND TYPIST
SHORTHAND WRITER
SHORT OF PRACTICE
SHORT SHARP SHOCK
SHORT-TERM POLICY
SHOTGUN MARRIAGE
SHOT IN THE LOCKER
SHOUT OF LAUGHTER
SHOW DISCOURTESY
SHOW FAVOURITISM
SHOW INGRATITUDE
SHOW ONE'S COLOURS
SHOW TO ADVANTAGE
SHRED OF EVIDENCE
SHRINKING VIOLET
SHUFFLE THE CARDS
SICKNESS BENEFIT
SIEGE OF MAFEKING
SIGHT FOR THE GODS
SIGHT-SEEING TOUR
SIGN OF THE ZODIAC
SIGN THE REGISTER
SILENCE IS GOLDEN
SILENT AS THE TOMB
SILVER MEDALLIST
SIMPLE PLEASURES
SIMPLY AND SOLELY
SINCE THE YEAR DOT
SING ANOTHER SONG
SING ANOTHER TUNE
SINGLE USE CAMERA
SINK ONE'S CAPITAL
SINK TO ONE'S KNEES
SINK TO THE BOTTOM
SIN OF COMMISSION
SIR EDWARD GERMAN
SIR FRANCIS DRAKE
SIR JOHN FALSTAFF
SISTER OF CHARITY
SITUATION COMEDY
SITUATION VACANT
SITUATION WANTED
SIXTEEN AND A HALF
SIXTEENTH LETTER
SIXTEENTH OF JULY
SIXTEENTH OF JUNE
SIXTEEN THOUSAND
SIXTH OF DECEMBER
SIXTH OF FEBRUARY
SIXTH OF NOVEMBER
SKELETON SERVICE
SKIM THE ROOF-TOPS

SKIN OF ONE'S TEETH
SKIP OUT OF THE WAY
SLAB OF CHOCOLATE
SLACKEN ONE'S PACE
SLAKE ONE'S THIRST
SLANG EXPRESSION
SLAPSTICK COMEDY
SLEEPING DRAUGHT
SLEEPING PARTNER
SLEEVELESS DRESS
SLIGHT VARIATION
SLINGS AND ARROWS
SLIP OF THE TONGUE
SLIPPERY AS AN EEL
SLIPPERY SURFACE
SLOUGH OF DESPOND
SLOW BOAT TO CHINA
SLOW IN THE UPTAKE
SLOWLY AND SURELY
SLOWLY BUT SURELY
SMALL PERCENTAGE
SMELTING FURNACE
SMOKE A CIGARETTE
SMOKY ATMOSPHERE
SNAKE IN THE GRASS
SNAP ONE'S FINGERS
SNAP ONE'S NOSE OFF
SOAKED TO THE SKIN
SOARING AMBITION
SOARING THOUGHTS
SOBERING THOUGHT
SOB ONE'S HEART OUT
SOCIAL DEMOCRATS
SOCIAL GATHERING
SOCIAL INSURANCE
SOCIAL OSTRACISM
SOCIAL SECRETARY
SODA-WATER SYPHON
SODIUM CARBONATE
SOFT-NOSED BULLET
SOFT-SHOE SHUFFLE
SOLD INTO SLAVERY
SOLICITOR'S CLERK
SOLID FOUNDATION
SOLO PERFORMANCE
SOMEBODY OR OTHER
SOME CONSOLATION
SOMERSET MAUGHAM
SOMETHING IN HAND
SOMETHING ROTTEN
SOMETHING TO COME
SOMETHING TO GO ON
SOME TIME OR OTHER
SOMEWHERE AROUND
SO MUCH THE BETTER
SORRY FOR ONESELF

SOUND EXPRESSION
SOUND INVESTMENT
SOUND OF BOW BELLS
SOUND THE KEYNOTE
SOUND THE RETREAT
SOURCE OF TROUBLE
SOUTH AFRICAN WAR
SOUTHERN RAILWAY
SOUTH KENSINGTON
SOUTH OF THE RIVER
SOUTH OF THE TWEED
SOUTH SEA ISLANDS
SOVEREIGN REMEDY
SOW ONE'S WILD OATS
SPADES ARE TRUMPS
SPANISH BURGUNDY
SPANISH CHESTNUT
SPANISH CIVIL WAR
SPANISH LANGUAGE
SPARRING PARTNER
SPEAKER BRACKETS
SPEAK FOR ONESELF
SPEAK IN A WHISPER
SPEAK OF THE DEVIL
SPECIAL DELIVERY
SPECIAL OCCASION
SPECIAL PLEADING
SPECIFIC GRAVITY
SPEED-BOAT RACING
SPEEDY VENGEANCE
SPELLING MISTAKE
SPEND SPEND SPEND
SPINAL COMPLAINT
SPIRAL STAIRCASE
SPIRITED DISPLAY
SPIRIT OF ST LOUIS
SPLASH ONE'S MONEY
SPLENDID VICTORY
SPLENDID WEATHER
SPLIT INFINITIVE
SPOIL EVERYTHING
SPOIL ONE'S RECORD
SPOILS OF VICTORY
SPORTING CONDUCT
SPORTING FIXTURE
SPORTING GESTURE
SPORTS ANNOUNCER
SPORTS EQUIPMENT
SPOT ADVERTISING
SPOTLESSLY CLEAN
SPRAY OF DIAMONDS
SPREAD ONE'S WINGS
SPREAD THE GOSPEL
SPRING A SURPRISE
SPRINGER SPANIEL
SPUR OF THE MOMENT

SQUARE THE CIRCLE
SQUATTER'S RIGHTS
SQUATTING RIGHTS
SQUEEZED TO DEATH
STABLE COMPANION
STAGE DIRECTIONS
STAGE-DOOR JOHNNY
STAKE EVERYTHING
STAMP COLLECTING
STAMP COLLECTION
STAMP OF APPROVAL
STAND AND DELIVER
STANDARD EDITION
STANDARD ENGLISH
STANDARD PRODUCT
STAND BARE-HEADED
STAND IN FULL VIEW
STANDING OVATION
STAND IN THE LIGHT
STAND IN THE QUEUE
STAND NO NONSENSE
STAND ON CEREMONY
STAND ONE'S GROUND
STAND ON ONE'S HEAD
STAND ON ONE'S TOES
STAND STOCK-STILL
STANLEY HOLLOWAY
STANLEY MATTHEWS
STARK, STARING MAD
STAR OF BETHLEHEM
STARS AND STRIPES
START AN ARGUMENT
STARVED WITH COLD
STATE APARTMENTS
STATE ASSISTANCE
STATE DEPARTMENT
STATE ENTERPRISE
STATELESS PERSON
STATEMENT OF FACT
STATEMENT ON OATH
STATE OF COLLAPSE
STATE OF CONFLICT
STATE OF DISORDER
STATE OF EQUALITY
STATE OF SOBRIETY
STATION APPROACH
STATUE OF LIBERTY
STAY OF EXECUTION
STAY UNDERGROUND
STAY WHERE YOU ARE
STEALER OF HEARTS
STEAL THE THUNDER
STEAM STERILISER
STENTORIAN VOICE
STEVEN SPIELBERG
STICKING PLASTER

STICK LIKE A LEECH	STRINGS ATTACHED
STICK OF DYNAMITE	STRIVE FOR EFFECT
STICKS AND STONES	STROLLING PLAYER
STICK THE SPURS IN	STRONG INFLUENCE
STICK TO ONE'S GUNS	STRONG OBJECTION
STICK TO ONE'S LAST	STRONG, SILENT MAN
STICK TO THE FACTS	STRONG SITUATION
STICK TO THE POINT	STRONG WILL-POWER
STICK TO THE RULES	STRUGGLE FOR LIFE
STICK TO THE TRUTH	STRUGGLE THROUGH
STICKY SITUATION	STUBBORN AS A MULE
STILL AS THE GRAVE	STUNT ONE'S GROWTH
STILL OF THE NIGHT	ST VALENTINE'S DAY
STILL, SMALL VOICE	STYGIAN DARKNESS
STIR THE PORRIDGE	SUBJUNCTIVE MOOD
STIR UP THE EMBERS	SUBMARINE CHASER
ST MARTIN'S SUMMER	SUBMIT A QUESTION
ST MICHAEL'S MOUNT	SUBSTANTIAL MEAL
STOCKBROKER BELT	SUBURBAN STATION
STOCKS AND SHARES	SUCCESS ALL ROUND
STOCKTAKING SALE	SUCH SWEET SORROW
STOMACH DISORDER	SUDDEN DEPARTURE
STOOD UP STRAIGHT	SUFFER IN SILENCE
STOP ME AND BUY ONE!	SUGAR PLANTATION
STOPPED THE FIGHT	SUITABLE PARTNER
STOP THE BLEEDING	SUITED TO THE PART
STOP WHERE YOU ARE	SUIT THE OCCASION
STORM OF APPLAUSE	SUM AND SUBSTANCE
STRAIGHT ACTRESS	SUMMER LIGHTNING
STRAIGHT BOURBON	SUMMER RESIDENCE
STRAIGHT DEALING	SUMMON UP COURAGE
STRAIGHT IN FRONT	SUNDAY AFTERNOON
STRAIGHT STRETCH	SUNDAY NEWSPAPER
STRAIN ONE'S LUNGS	SUNDAY TELEGRAPH
STRAIN THE NERVES	SUN, MOON AND STARS
STRANGE GOINGS-ON	SUNRISE INDUSTRY
STRANGE TO RELATE	SUNSET BOULEVARD
STRAPPING FELLOW	SUPERIOR NUMBERS
STRATFORD ON AVON	SUPERIOR OFFICER
STRAWS IN THE WIND	SUPERIOR QUALITY
STREAM OF THOUGHT	SUPERSONIC SPEED
STREAM OF TRAFFIC	SUPPLY AND DEMAND
STREET DIRECTORY	SUPREME CONTEMPT
STRENUOUS EFFORT	SURE OF ONE'S FACTS
STRESS AND STRAIN	SURPRISE IN STORE
STRETCHER BEARER	SURPRISE VISITOR
STRETCH ONE'S LEGS	SURPRISING THING
STRICKEN IN YEARS	SURROGATE MOTHER
STRICTLY NEUTRAL	SUSPECTED PERSON
STRICTLY PRIVATE	SUSPECT FOUL PLAY
STRIKE A BAD PATCH	SUSPEND SENTENCE
STRIKE AN AVERAGE	SUSPENSE ACCOUNT
STRIKE A RICH VEIN	SUSTAINED ACTION
STRIKE UP THE BAND	SUSTAINED EFFORT
STRIKING SUCCESS	SUSTAIN INJURIES
STRING ORCHESTRA	SWALLOW AN INSULT

SWALLOW-TAIL COAT
SWEAR ALLEGIANCE
SWEAR ON THE BIBLE
SWEAT OF ONE'S BROW
SWEEPING CHANGES
SWEEPING REFORMS
SWEEPING SUCCESS
SWEEPING VICTORY
SWEEP THE CHIMNEY
SWEET FANNY ADAMS
SWEET SIMPLICITY
SWEET TO THE TASTE
SWIM FOR THE SHORE
SWIMMING COSTUME
SWIM WITH THE TIDE
SWINGING SIXTIES
SWORD OF DAMOCLES
SYDNEY WOODERSON
SYLVIA PANKHURST
SYMBOL OF JUSTICE
SYMPHONY CONCERT
SYNTHETIC RUBBER
SYSTEMATIC STUDY

T – 15

TABLEAUX VIVANTS
TABLE DECORATION
TABLE OF CONTENTS
TABLES AND CHAIRS
TAILOR AND CUTTER
TAKE A COLLECTION
TAKE A DEEP BREATH
TAKE A FLYING LEAP
TAKE A PHOTOGRAPH
TAKE A RESOLUTION
TAKE A SECOND LOOK
TAKE A STRONG LINE
TAKE FRENCH LEAVE
TAKE INTO ACCOUNT
TAKE INTO CUSTODY
TAKE IT LYING DOWN
TAKE IT ON THE CHIN
TAKE IT OR LEAVE IT
TAKEN AT THE FLOOD
TAKE ONE'S COAT OFF
TAKE ONE'S MEASURE
TAKE PRECAUTIONS
TAKES TWO TO TANGO
TAKE THE BLOOM OFF
TAKE THE CHILL OFF
TAKE THE LONG VIEW
TAKE THE SEA ROUTE
TAKE THE SHILLING
TAKE TO ONE'S HEELS
TAKE TO THE BOTTLE

TAKE UP THE THREAD
TALE OF TWO CITIES
TALES OF HOFFMANN
TALKS ABOUT TALKS
TANGERINE ORANGE
TANKARD OF BITTER
TAPERED TROUSERS
TASTE OF THE STRAP
TATTENHAM CORNER
TATTERED AND TORN
TEAR ONE'S CLOTHES
TEAR ONESELF AWAY
TEARS OF LAUGHTER
TECHNICAL SCHOOL
TELEGRAPH OFFICE
TELEPHONE NUMBER
TELEPHONE SYSTEM
TELESCOPIC SIGHT
TELEVISION TABLE
TELL IT NOT IN GATH
TELL ONE'S FORTUNE
TEMPERANCE HOTEL
TEMPORARY RELIEF
TEMPT PROVIDENCE
TENACIOUS MEMORY
TEN COMMANDMENTS
TENSE ATMOSPHERE
TENTH OF DECEMBER
TENTH OF FEBRUARY
TENTH OF NOVEMBER
TERENCE RATTIGAN
TERM OF REFERENCE
TERRIBLE TRAGEDY
TERRIBLE WEATHER
TERRIFIC SERVICE
TERRITORIAL ARMY
TEST OF ENDURANCE
THANKSGIVING DAY
THATCHED COTTAGE
THE AMOROUS PRAWN
THE ANCIENT WORLD
THE ARTFUL DODGER
THEATRE WORKSHOP
THE BACK OF BEYOND
THE BARON KNIGHTS
THE BEGGAR'S OPERA
THE BLACK COUNTRY
THE BOHEMIAN GIRL
THE CAT'S WHISKERS
THE CAT AND FIDDLE
THE CHIPPENDALES
THE COAST IS CLEAR
THE COMMON MARKET
THE COMMON PEOPLE
THE COMMONWEALTH
THE COST OF LIVING

THE DANCING YEARS
THE DEMON ALCOHOL
THE DESCENT OF MAN
THE DEVIL YOU KNOW
THE ELEVENTH HOUR
THE EMPEROR JONES
THE END OF THE ROAD
THE FIRST SWALLOW
THE FOUR FEATHERS
THE FOURTH ESTATE
THE FOURTH OF JULY
THE GARDEN OF EDEN
THE GOLDEN FLEECE
THE GROUP OF SEVEN
THE HAPPY WARRIOR
THE HOUSE OF USHER
THE INVISIBLE MAN
THEIR FINEST HOUR
THE KING'S ENGLISH
THE LAP OF THE GODS
THE LAST MINSTREL
THE LATE-LAMENTED
THE LONDON SEASON
THE LONG VACATION
THE LOW COUNTRIES
THE MAN IN THE MOON
THE MARSEILLAISE
THE MERRY MONARCH
THE MORNING AFTER
THE NAME'S THE SAME
THE OLD PRETENDER
THE PLOT THICKENS
THE POTTER'S WHEEL
THE POWERS THAT BE
THE PRETTY THINGS
THE PRIMROSE PATH
THE PRIVY COUNCIL
THE PROMISED LAND
THE QUEEN OF SHEBA
THE ROYAL SOCIETY
THE SHOW MUST GO ON
THE SKY'S THE LIMIT
THE SOUND OF MUSIC
THE SUBCONSCIOUS
THE SUN NEVER SETS
THE SUPERNATURAL
THE THANKSGIVING
THE THREE ESTATES
THE TIME WILL COME
THE UNTOUCHABLES
THE VERY REVEREND
THE WOMAN IN WHITE
THE WORLD AT LARGE
THE WORSE FOR WEAR
THIEF IN THE NIGHT
THINK BETTER OF IT

THINK THINGS OVER
THINLY SCATTERED
THIN ON THE GROUND
THIRD OF DECEMBER
THIRD OF FEBRUARY
THIRD OF NOVEMBER
THIRTEEN AT TABLE
THIRTEEN MINUTES
THIRTEEN OF A SUIT
THIRTEEN PER CENT
THIRTEENTH GREEN
THIRTEENTH OF MAY
THIRTIETH OF JULY
THIRTIETH OF JUNE
THIRTY-NINE STEPS
THIS YEAR OF GRACE
THORN IN ONE'S SIDE
THORN IN THE FLESH
THOUSAND GUINEAS
THREATENING LOOK
THREE BRASS BALLS
THREE-LEGGED RACE
THREE-LETTER WORD
THREE LITTLE PIGS
THREE-MASTED SHIP
THREE MEN IN A BOAT
THREE MILE ISLAND
THREE MUSKETEERS
THREE OF DIAMONDS
THREEPENNY OPERA
THREE-PIECE SUITE
THREE-TIERED CAKE
THREE TIMES THREE
THRILLED WITH JOY
THRILLING CLIMAX
THROUGH CARRIAGE
THROUGH THE NIGHT
THROUGH THE YEARS
THROWAWAY REMARK
THROW IN ONE'S HAND
THROW IN THE TOWEL
THROW OFF THE YOKE
THROW OUT A FEELER
THROW TO THE WINDS
THUMBNAIL SKETCH
THURSDAY EVENING
THURSDAY MORNING
TICKET COLLECTOR
TICKET INSPECTOR
TICKLE ONE'S FANCY
TICKLE THE PALATE
TICKLISH PROBLEM
TIED HAND AND FOOT
TIES OF AFFECTION
TIGHTEN ONE'S BELT
TIGHTEN ONE'S GRIP

TIGHT-ROPE WALKER
TILLER OF THE SOIL
TILL WE MEET AGAIN
TIME OF DEPARTURE
TIME ON ONE'S HANDS
TIP OF ONE'S TONGUE
TIPPED CIGARETTE
TITANIC STRENGTH
TITUS ANDRONICUS
TO A LESSER DEGREE
TOE THE PARTY LINE
TO HAVE AND TO HOLD
TO LITTLE PURPOSE
TOMATOES ON TOAST
TOM, DICK AND HARRY
TOMORROW EVENING
TOMORROW MORNING
TOM, THE PIPER'S SON
TONSORIAL ARTIST
TOO CLEVER BY HALF
TOO FULL FOR WORDS
TOO GOOD TO BE TRUE
TOOK THE LONG VIEW
TOOLS OF THE TRADE
TOOTHSOME MORSEL
TOPICAL ALLUSION
TOPICAL INTEREST
TOPLESS WAITRESS
TOP-LEVEL MEETING
TOP OF THE MORNING
TOSSING THE CABER
TOTAL ABSTINENCE
TOTAL CASUALTIES
TO THE FULL EXTENT
TO THE MANNER BORN
TOUCH ROCK-BOTTOM
TOUGH ASSIGNMENT
TOUGH NUT TO CRACK
TOURIST INDUSTRY
TOWERING PASSION
TOWER OF STRENGTH
TRADE COMMISSION
TRADE DELEGATION
TRADE SUPPLEMENT
TRADITIONAL FARE
TRADITIONAL JAZZ
TRAFALGAR SQUARE
TRAFFIC MOVEMENT
TRAIN CONNECTION
TRAINING COLLEGE
TRAIN OF THOUGHT
TRANSFER A PLAYER
TRANSISTOR RADIO
TRANSPORT SYSTEM
TRAVEL INCOGNITO
TRAVEL IN COMFORT

TRAVELLER'S TALES
TRAVELLING CLOCK
TRAVELLING CRANE
TRAVEL ORGANISER
TRAVEL STEAM IRON
TREASURED MEMORY
TREATED LIKE DIRT
TREATY OF LOCARNO
TREE OF KNOWLEDGE
TREMBLE WITH FEAR
TREMBLING POPLAR
TREND OF THE TIMES
TRESPASS AGAINST
TRIAL OF STRENGTH
TRICK OF THE TRADE
TRICKY SITUATION
TRIUMPHANT SMILE
TROOP OF SOLDIERS
TROUBLE-FREE MIND
TRUE TO THE LETTER
TRUMPED-UP CHARGE
TRY ANYTHING ONCE
TRY ONE'S PATIENCE
TRY ONE'S STRENGTH
TURN A SOMERSAULT
TURN A WILLING EAR
TURN FOR THE WORSE
TURN IN ONE'S GRAVE
TURN OFF THE LIGHT
TURN OUT A FAILURE
TURN OUT THE GUARD
TURN OUT THE LIGHT
TURN THE LIGHT OFF
TURN UP THE VOLUME
TWELFTH OF AUGUST
TWELVE DISCIPLES
TWELVE-MILE LIMIT
TWELVE-TONE MUSIC
TWENTIETH LETTER
TWENTIETH OF JULY
TWENTIETH OF JUNE
TWENTY-FOUR HOURS
TWENTY-ONE AND SIX
TWENTY QUESTIONS
TWIST OF THE WRIST
TWO-FISTED ATTACK
TWO OF EVERYTHING
TWO-SLICE TOASTER
TWO-STROKE ENGINE

U – 15

ULTRA-VIOLET RAYS
UMPIRE'S DECISION
UNANIMOUS CHOICE
UNBRIDLED TONGUE

UNCIVILIZED RACE
UNDENIABLE TRUTH
UNDER A FALSE NAME
UNDERARM BOWLING
UNDER CLOSE GUARD
UNDER COMPLEMENT
UNDER COMPULSION
UNDER CORRECTION
UNDER-COVER AGENT
UNDER DISCIPLINE
UNDER DISCUSSION
UNDER LOCK AND KEY
UNDER OBLIGATION
UNDER ONE'S BREATH
UNDER-SEA WARFARE
UNDER THE COUNTER
UNDER THE SURFACE
UNDER THE WEATHER
UNDERWATER CRAFT
UNDESERVING CASE
UNEMPLOYMENT PAY
UNEQUAL STRUGGLE
UNEXPECTED EVENT
UNEXPECTED VISIT
UNFAIR ADVANTAGE
UNFAIR DISMISSAL
UNFAIR TREATMENT
UNFEELING PERSON
UNFINISHED STATE
UNFOUNDED REPORT
UNFROCKED PRIEST
UNFURNISHED FLAT
UNFURNISHED ROOM
UNGUARDED MINUTE
UNGUARDED MOMENT
UNGUARDED REMARK
UNHAPPY MEMORIES
UNION IS STRENGTH
UNITED PROVINCES
UNIVERSAL REMEDY
UNIVERSITY GRANT
UNKIND CRITICISM
UNKNOWN QUANTITY
UNLEAVENED BREAD
UNLUCKY THIRTEEN
UNMARRIED MOTHER
UNPAID SECRETARY
UNPUBLISHED WORK
UNSKILLED LABOUR
UNSOLVED MYSTERY
UNTOUCHED BY HAND
UNTROUBLED SLEEP
UNTRUE STATEMENT
UNVARNISHED TALE
UP BEFORE THE BEAK
UP GUARDS AND AT 'EM!

UPHOLSTERY BRUSH
UPRIGHT CARRIAGE
UPRIGHT POSITION
UP THE GARDEN PATH
UP TO THE EYEBROWS
URBAN POPULATION
UTTER A FALSEHOOD
UTTER STARVATION

V – 15

VACCINATION MARK
VAIN EXPECTATION
VANCOUVER ISLAND
VANILLA ICE-CREAM
VARSITY BOAT-RACE
VAST IMPROVEMENT
VAUGHAN WILLIAMS
VAUXHALL GARDENS
VEGETABLE GARDEN
VEGETABLE MARKET
VEGETABLE MARROW
VENERABLE PRIEST
VENGEANCE IS MINE
VERBAL AGREEMENT
VERBAL CRITICISM
VETO THE PROPOSAL
VICHY GOVERNMENT
VICTORIA STATION
VICTORY IN THE AIR
VIOLATE THE TERMS
VIOLENT CONTRAST
VIOLENT EXERCISE
VIOLENT OUTBURST
VIOLENT REACTION
VIOLENT STRUGGLE
VIRGINIA CREEPER
VIRGINIA TOBACCO
VIRGIN TERRITORY
VISIBLE DISTANCE
VISION OF DELIGHT
VITAL STATISTICS
VOICE PRODUCTION
VOLLEY OF THUNDER
VOLUNTARY SCHOOL
VULNERABLE POINT

W – 15

WADDLE LIKE A DUCK
WAISTCOAT POCKET
WAITING FOR GODOT
WALKING DISTANCE
WALK INTO TROUBLE
WALK WITH PURPOSE
WALL OF MOUNTAINS

WALL STREET CRASH	WHOLESALE DEALER
WALRUS MOUSTACHE	WHOLESALE MURDER
WALTZING MATILDA	WHOM THE GODS LOVE
WANDERING WILLIE	WIELD THE SCEPTRE
WANTED FOR MURDER	WIENER SCHNITZEL
WAR PREPARATIONS	WIFE AND CHILDREN
WASHED OVERBOARD	WILD IMAGINATON
WASTE NOT, WANT NOT	WILL AND BEQUEATH
WASTE ONE'S BREATH	WILLIAM CONGREVE
WATCH ON THE RHINE	WILLIAM OF ORANGE
WATCH WITH MOTHER	WILLIAM THE FIRST
WATERLOO STATION	WILLIAM THE THIRD
WATER ON THE BRAIN	WILLING TO PLEASE
WATER RESISTANCE	WILL SHAKESPEARE
WATERTIGHT ALIBI	WIMBLEDON COMMON
WEALTH OF NATIONS	WIN BY A SHORT HEAD
WEAR THE BREECHES	WINCHESTER RIFLE
WEAR THE TROUSERS	WINDMILL THEATRE
WEATHER FORECAST	WINDSCREEN WIPER
WEATHER THE STORM	WINDWARD ISLANDS
WEDDING CEREMONY	WINE BY THE BARREL
WEDNESDAY'S CHILD	WINES AND SPIRITS
WEEK-END SHOPPING	WINNING POSITION
WEEKLY NEWSPAPER	WINNING SEQUENCE
WE HAVE NO BANANAS	WINTER SPORTSMAN
WEIGHING MACHINE	WIN THE LAST ROUND
WEIGHT OF NUMBERS	WIRELESS LICENCE
WEIGHT OF OPINION	WIRELESS MESSAGE
WEIGHTY ARGUMENT	WIRELESS STATION
WELCOME STRANGER	WISDOM OF SOLOMON
WELLINGTON BOOTS	WISE MEN OF GOTHAM
WELL-MEANING TYPE	WISHFUL THINKING
WELL REPRESENTED	WISH YOU WERE HERE
WENT LIKE THE WIND	WITCHES' CAULDRON
WESTERN ALLIANCE	WITH A DIFFERENCE
WESTMINSTER BANK	WITH A LITTLE LUCK
WESTMINSTER HALL	WITH COMPLIMENTS
WET AND DRY SHAVER	WITHERING GLANCE
WET THE BABY'S HEAD	WITHHOLD PAYMENT
WHATEVER HAPPENS	WITHIN EASY REACH
WHAT'S THE VERDICT?	WITHIN ONE'S GRASP
WHERE THERE'S LIFE	WITHOUT AN EFFORT
WHET THE APPETITE	WITHOUT A PURPOSE
WHIFF OF FRESH AIR	WITHOUT A SCRATCH
WHILE THERE'S LIFE	WITHOUT CEREMONY
WHIRLING DERVISH	WITHOUT INCIDENT
WHISPER TOGETHER	WITHOUT INTEREST
WHISTLE AND FLUTE	WITHOUT PARALLEL
WHISTLE-STOP TOUR	WITHOUT THINKING
WHISTLING KETTLE	WOMAN OF FEW WORDS
WHITED SEPULCHRE	WOMAN OF THE WORLD
WHITEHALL PALACE	WOMAN'S INTUITION
WHITE MAN'S BURDEN	WOMAN'S PRIVILEGE
WHITER THAN WHITE	WOMEN'S INSTITUTE
WHITES OF THE EYES	WOODCUTTERS' BALL
WHITSUN VACATION	WOODEN PARTITION

WOODY WOODPECKER
WOOLLEN INDUSTRY
WOOLWICH ARSENAL
WORK AGAINST TIME
WORKERS' PLAYTIME
WORKING MAJORITY
WORKING-MAN'S CLUB
WORK LIKE A NIGGER
WORK LIKE A TROJAN
WORK OF REFERENCE
WORK ONE'S PASSAGE
WORK UNDERGROUND
WORLD GOVERNMENT
WORLD OF COMMERCE
WORLD OF LEARNING
WORLD WITHOUT END
WORTHY ADVERSARY
WOUNDED FEELINGS
WRETCHED WEATHER
WRINKLED WITH AGE
WRITING MATERIAL
WRITTEN CONTRACT
WRITTEN EVIDENCE
WRITTEN LANGUAGE
WRONG ASSUMPTION
WRONG IMPRESSION
WRONG WAVE-LENGTH

WROUGHT-IRON GATE

X – 15

XMAS DECORATIONS

Y – 15

YELLOWSTONE PARK
YELL WITH DELIGHT
YEOMEN OF ENGLAND
YESTERDAY'S PAPER
YIELD GRACEFULLY
YIELD TO PRESSURE
YORKSHIRE RELISH
YOU NEVER CAN TELL
YOUNG AND HEALTHY
YOUNGER DAUGHTER
YOUNGEST BROTHER
YOURS FAITHFULLY
YOURS OBEDIENTLY
YOUTH-CLUB LEADER

Z – 15

ZAPATA MOUSTACHE
ZIEGFELD FOLLIES

WORDS

A – 3	AXE	CAN	DOG	FAN
	AYE	CAP	DOH	FAR
ABC		CAR	DON	FAT
ACE		CAT	DOT	FAY
ACT	B – 3	CAW	DRY	FEB
ADA	BAA	CHA	DUB	FED
ADD	BAD	CID	DUD	FEE
ADO	BAG	COB	DUE	FEN
AFT	BAH	COD	DUG	FEW
AGA	BAN	COG	DUN	FEY
AGE	BAR	COL	DUO	FEZ
AGO	BAT	CON	DYE	FIB
AHA	BAY	COO		FIE
AID	BBC	COP	E – 3	FIG
AIL	BED	COS		FIN
AIM	BEE	COT	EAR	FIR
AIN	BEG	COW	EAT	FIT
AIR	BEN	COX	EAU	FIX
AIT	BET	COY	EBB	FLU
ALB	BEY	CRY	EEL	FLY
ALE	BIB	CUB	E'EN	FOB
ALL	BID	CUD	E'ER	FOE
ALP	BIG	CUE	EFT	FOG
ALT	BIN	CUP	EGG	FOP
AMP	BIS	CUR	EGO	FOR
ANA	BIT	CUT	EKE	FOX
AND	BOA	CWT	ELF	FRO
ANN	BOB		ELI	FRY
ANT	BOG		ELK	FUG
ANY	BOO	D – 3	ELL	FUN
APE	BOW		ELM	FUR
APT	BOX	DAB	ELY	
ARC	BOY	DAD	EMU	G – 3
ARE	BOZ	DAM	END	
ARK	BRA	DAN	EON	GAB
ARM	BUD	DAW	ERA	GAD
ART	BUG	DAY	ERE	GAG
ASH	BUM	DEB	ERG	GAL
ASK	BUN	DEE	ERR	GAP
ASP	BUS	DEF	ESS	GAR
ASS	BUT	DEN	ETC	GAS
ATE	BUY	DEW	EVE	GAT
AUK	BYE	DIB	EWE	GAY
AVA		DID	EYE	GEE
AVE		DIE		GEM
AWA	C – 3	DIG		GEN
AWE	CAB	DIM	F – 3	GET
AWL	CAD	DIN		GIB
AWN	CAM	DIP	FAD	GIE
		DOE	FAG	

GIG	ILK	LAX	**N – 3**	OWE
GIN	ILL	LAY		OWL
GNU	IMP	LBW	NAB	OWN
GOB	INK	LEA	NAG	
GOD	INN	LED	NAP	**P – 3**
GOG	ION	LEE	NAY	
GOT	I.O.U.	LEG	NCO	PAD
GUM	IRE	LEI	NEB	PAH
GUN	IRK	LEO	NÉE	PAL
GUT	ISM	LET	NEO	PAM
GUY	ITS	LEW	NET	PAN
GYM	IVY	LEX	NEW	PAP
GYP		LIB	NIB	PAR
		LID	NIL	PAS
	J – 3	LIE	NIP	PAT
H – 3		LIP	NIT	PAW
	JAB	LIT	NIX	PAX
HAD	JAG	LOB	NOB	PAY
HAG	JAM	LOG	NOD	PEA
HAH	JAP	LOO	NOG	PEG
HAM	JAR	LOP	NOR	PEN
HAP	JAW	LOT	NOT	PEP
HAS	JAY	LOW	NOW	PER
HAT	JET	LSD	NUB	PET
HAW	JEW	LUD	NUN	PEW
HAY	JIB	LUG	NUT	PIE
HEM	JIG	LYE	NYE	PIG
HEN	JOB			PIN
HEP	JOE			PIP
HER	JOG	**M – 3**	**O – 3**	PIT
HEW	JOT			PLY
HEY	JOY	MAB	OAF	POD
HID	JUG	MAC	OAK	POE
HIE	JUT	MAD	OAR	POM
HIM		MAN	OAT	POP
HIP		MAP	OBI	POT
HIS	**K – 3**	MAR	OCH	POW
HIT		MAT	ODD	PRO
HOB	KAY	MAW	ODE	PRY
HOD	KEG	MAX	O'ER	PUB
HOE	KEN	MAY	OFF	PUG
HOG	KEY	MEN	OFT	PUN
HOP	KID	MET	OHM	PUP
HOT	KIM	MEW	OHO	PUS
HOW	KIN	MID	OIL	PUT
HUB	KIP	MIX	OLD	PYX
HUE	KIT	MOA	ONE	
HUG	KOI	MOB	OOF	
HUM		MOO	OPE	
HUN	**L – 3**	MOP	OPT	**R – 3**
HUT		MOT	ORB	
	LAC	MOW	ORC	RAG
	LAD	MRS	ORE	RAJ
	LAG	MUD	ORT	RAM
I – 3	LAM	MUG	OUR	RAN
	LAP	MUM	OUT	RAP
IAN	LAR		OVA	RAS
ICE	LAW			RAT
ICY				

RAW	SIS	TOM	WHO	ADZE
RAY	SIT	TON	WHY	AEON
RED	SIX	TOO	WIG	AFAR
REF	SKI	TOP	WIN	AFRO
REP	SKY	TOR	WIT	AGED
RET	SLY	TOT	WOE	AGOG
REV	SOB	TOW	WOK	AGUE
REX	SOD	TOY	WON	AHEM
RIB	SOL	TRY	WOO	AHOY
RID	SON	TUB	WOW	AIDA
RIG	SOP	TUG	WRY	AIDE
RIM	SOS	TUN	WYE	AIRY
RIO	SOT	TUP		AJAR
RIP	SOU	TUT	**Y – 3**	AKIN
ROB	SOW	TWA		ALAR
ROC	SOX	TWO	YAH	ALAS
ROD	SOY		YAK	ALEE
ROE	SPA	**U – 3**	YAM	ALGA
ROM	SPY		YAP	ALLY
RON	STY	UGH	YAW	ALMA
ROT	SUB	ULT	YEA	ALMS
ROW	SUE	UNA	YEN	ALOE
ROY	SUM	UNO	YEP	ALPS
RUB	SUN	URE	YES	ALSO
RUE	SUP	URN	YET	ALTO
RUG		USE	YEW	ALUM
RUM		UVA	YOB	AMBO
RUN	**T – 3**		YON	AMEN
RUT	TAB		YOU	AMID
RYE	TAG	**V – 3**		AMMO
	TAJ			AMOK
	TAN	V.A.D.	**Z – 3**	AMYL
S – 3	TAP	VAN		ANEW
	TAR	VAT	ZAP	ANIL
SAC	TAT	VET	ZED	ANNA
SAD	TAU	VEX	ZIP	ANON
SAG	TAW	VIA	ZIT	ANTE
SAL	TAX	VIE	ZOO	ANTI
SAM	TEA	VIM		APED
SAP	TEC	VIZ	**A – 4**	APEX
SAT	TED	VOW		APSE
SAW	TEE		ABBE	AQUA
SAX	TEG	**W – 3**	ABED	ARAB
SAY	TEN		ABET	ARCH
SEA	THE	WAD	ABLE	AREA
SEC	THO'	WAG	ABLY	ARIA
SEE	THY	WAN	ABUT	ARID
SEN	TIC	WAR	ACER	ARIL
SET	TIE	WAS	ACHE	ARMS
SEW	TIN	WAT	ACHY	ARMY
SEX	TIP	WAX	ACID	ARTS
SHE	TIS	WAY	ACME	ARTY
SHY	TIT	WEB	ACNE	ARUM
SIC	TOD	WED	ACOL	ASHY
SIN	TOE	WEE	ACRE	ASIA
SIP	TOG	WEN	ADAM	ASTI
SIR		WET	ADIT	

ATOM	BATH	BODY	BURY	CHUG
ATOP	BAUD	BOER	BUSH	CHUM
AULD	BAWD	BOGY	BUSS	CITE
AUNT	BAWL	BOIL	BUST	CITY
AURA	BAYS	BOKO	BUSY	CLAD
AUTO	BEAD	BOLD	BUTT	CLAM
AVER	BEAK	BOLE	BUZZ	CLAN
AVID	BEAM	BOLL	BYRE	CLAP
AVON	BEAN	BOLT	BYTE	CLAW
AVOW	BEAR	BOMB		CLAY
AWAY	BEAT	BOND		CLEF
AWED	BEAU	BONE	C – 4	CLIO
AWRY	BECK	BONY		CLIP
AXED	BEDE	BOOB	CADE	CLOD
AXEL	BEEF	BOOK	CADI	CLOG
AXIL	BEEN	BOOM	CAFÉ	CLOT
AXIS	BEER	BOON	CAGE	CLOY
AXLE	BEET	BOOR	CAIN	CLUB
AYAH	BELL	BOOT	CAKE	CLUE
	BELT	BORE	CAKY	COAL
	BEND	BORN	CALF	COAT
B – 4	BENT	BOSH	CALL	COAX
	BERG	BOSS	CALM	COCA
BAAL	BEST	BOTH	CAME	COCK
BAAS	BETA	BOUT	CAMP	COCO
BABA	BEVY	BOWL	CANE	CODA
BABE	BIAS	BOWS	CANT	CODE
BABU	BIDE	BRAD	CAPE	COIF
BABY	BIER	BRAE	CARD	COIL
BACK	BIFF	BRAG	CARE	COIN
BADE	BIKE	BRAN	CARL	COIR
BAIL	BILE	BRAT	CARP	COKE
BAIT	BILK	BRAW	CART	COLD
BAKE	BILL	BRAY	CASE	COLE
BALD	BIND	BRED	CASH	COLT
BALE	BINE	BREN	CASK	COMA
BALK	BING	BRER	CAST	COMB
BALL	BIRD	BREW	CAVE	COME
BALM	BISH	BRIE	CAVY	CONE
BAND	BISK	BRIG	CEDE	CONK
BANE	BITE	BRIM	CELL	CONS
BANG	BLAB	BRIO	CELT	CONY
BANK	BLAG	BROW	CENT	COOK
BANT	BLED	BUCK	CERE	COOL
BARB	BLEW	BUDE	CERT	COON
BARD	BLIP	BUFF	CHAP	COOP
BARE	BLOB	BUHL	CHAR	COOT
BARK	BLOC	BULB	CHAT	COPE
BARM	BLOT	BULK	CHEF	COPT
BARN	BLOW	BULL	CHEW	COPY
BART	BLUB	BUMP	CHIC	CORD
BASE	BLUE	BUNG	CHIN	CORE
BASH	BLUR	BUNK	CHIP	CORK
BASK	BOAR	BUOY	CHIT	CORM
BASS	BOAT	BURN	CHOP	CORN
BAST	BODE	BURR	CHOW	COSH
BATE			CHUB	

COST	DATE	DOFF	DUSE	ETON
COSY	DAUB	DOGE	DUSK	ETUI
COTE	DAVY	DOLE	DUST	EVEN
COUP	DAWN	DOLL	DUTY	EVER
COVE	DAZE	DOLT	DYAD	EVIL
COWL	D-DAY	DOME	DYAK	EWER
CRAB	DEAD	DONE	DYED	EXAM
CRAG	DEAF	DOOM	DYER	EXIT
CRAM	DEAL	DOOR	DYKE	EXON
CRAN	DEAN	DOPE	DYNE	EYED
CRAW	DEAR	DORA		EYOT
CREE	DEBT	DORY		EYRE
CREW	DECK	DOSE	**E – 4**	EYRY
CRIB	DEED	DOSH		
CROP	DEEM	DOSS	EACH	
CROW	DEEP	DOTE	EARL	**F – 4**
CRUD	DEER	DOTH	EARN	
CRUX	DEFT	DOUR	EASE	FACE
CUBE	DEFY	DOVE	EAST	FACT
CUFF	DELE	DOWN	EASY	FADE
CULL	DELL	DOZE	EBON	FAIL
CULM	DEMO	DOZY	ECHO	FAIN
CULT	DEMY	DRAB	ECHT	FAIR
CURB	DENE	DRAG	ECRU	FAKE
CURD	DENT	DRAM	EDAM	FALL
CURE	DENY	DRAT	EDDA	FAME
CURL	DERV	DRAW	EDDY	FANG
CURT	DESK	DRAY	EDEN	FARE
CUSP	DEWY	DREE	EDGE	FARM
CUTE	DHAL	DREW	EDGY	FARO
CYAN	DHOW	DREY	EDIT	FASH
CYST	DIAL	DRIP	EGAD	FAST
CZAR	DICE	DROP	EIRE	FATE
	DICK	DRUB	ELAN	FAUN
	DIDO	DRUG	ELIA	FAWN
D – 4	DIED	DRUM	ELMO	FEAR
	DIET	DUAL	ELSE	FEAT
DACE	DIGS	DUCE	ELUL	FEED
DADA	DIKE	DUCK	EMIR	FEEL
DADO	DILL	DUCT	EMIT	FEET
DAFT	DIME	DUDE	EMMY	FELL
DAGO	DINE	DUDS	ENOW	FELT
DAIL	DING	DUEL	ENSA	FEND
DAIS	DINT	DUET	ENVY	FERN
DALE	DIRE	DUFF	EPEE	FETE
DALI	DIRK	DUKE	EPIC	FEUD
DAME	DIRT	DUKW	EPOS	FIAT
DAMN	DISC	DULL	ERGO	FIFE
DAMP	DISH	DULY	ERIC	FILE
DANE	DISK	DUMA	ERIN	FILL
DANK	DISS	DUMB	ERNE	FILM
DARE	DIVA	DUMP	EROS	FIND
DARK	DIVE	DUNE	ERSE	FINE
DARN	DOCK	DUNG	ERST	FINN
DART	DODO	DUNK	ESPY	FIRE
DASH	DOER	DUPE	ETCH	FIRM
DATA			ETNA	FISH

FIST	FURL	GNAT	HAME	HOBO
FIVE	FURY	GNAW	HAND	HOCK
FIZZ	FUSE	GOAD	HANG	HOED
FLAG	FUSS	GOAL	HANK	HOLD
FLAK	FUZZ	GOAT	HARD	HOLE
FLAM		GOBI	HARE	HOLM
FLAN		GODS	HARK	HOLT
FLAP	G – 4	GOLD	HARM	HOLY
FLAT	GAEL	GOLF	HARP	HOME
FLAW	GAFF	GONE	HART	HOMY
FLAX	GAGE	GONG	HASH	HONE
FLAY	GAIN	GONK	HASP	HONK
FLEA	GAIT	GOOD	HATE	HOOD
FLED	GALA	GOOF	HATH	HOOF
FLEE	GALE	GORE	HAUL	HOOK
FLEW	GALL	GORY	HAVE	HOOP
FLEX	GAME	GOSH	HAWK	HOOT
FLIP	GAMP	GOTH	HAZE	HOPE
FLIT	GANG	GOUT	HAZY	HOPS
FLOE	GAOL	GOWN	HEAD	HORN
FLOG	GAPE	GRAB	HEAL	HOSE
FLOP	GARB	GRAF	HEAP	HOST
FLOW	GASH	GRAM	HEAR	HOUR
FLUE	GASP	GRAY	HEAT	HOVE
FLUX	GATE	GREW	HEBE	HOWL
FOAL	GAUD	GREY	HEED	HUED
FOAM	GAUL	GRID	HEEL	HUFF
FOIL	GAVE	GRIM	HEIR	HUGE
FOLD	GAWK	GRIN	HELD	HULA
FOLK	GAZE	GRIP	HELL	HULK
FOND	GEAR	GRIT	HELM	HULL
FONT	GENT	GROG	HELP	HUMP
FOOD	GERM	GROT	HEMP	HUNG
FOOL	GEUM	GROW	HERB	HUNK
FOOT	GIBE	GRUB	HERD	HUNT
FORD	GIFT	GULF	HERE	HURL
FORE	GILD	GULL	HERN	HURT
FORK	GILL	GULP	HERO	HUSH
FORM	GILT	GURU	HERR	HUSK
FORT	GIMP	GUSH	HERS	HYMN
FOUL	GIRD	GUST	HEWN	HYPE
FOUR	GIRL	GYVE	HICK	HYPO
FOWL	GIRO		HIDE	
FOXY	GIRT		HIED	
FRAU	GIST	H – 4	HIGH	I – 4
FRAY	GIVE	HACK	HIKE	IBEX
FREE	GLAD	HAFT	HILL	IBIS
FRET	GLEE	HA-HA	HILT	ICED
FROG	GLEN	HAIL	HIND	ICON
FROM	GLIB	HAIR	HINT	IDEA
FUEL	GLIM	HAKE	HIRE	IDES
FULL	GLOW	HALE	HISS	IDLE
FUME	GLUE	HALF	HIST	IDLY
FUMY	GLUM	HALL	HIVE	IDOL
FUND	GLUT	HALO	HOAR	IFFY
FUNK	G-MAN	HALT	HOAX	IMAM

IMPI	KEEN	LARD	LINO	M – 4
INCA	KEEP	LARK	LINT	
INCH	KELP	LASH	LION	MACE
INKY	KEMP	LASS	LIRA	MADE
INTO	KENT	LAST	LIRE	MAGI
IOTA	KEPI	LATE	LISP	MAID
IRAN	KEPT	LATH	LIST	MAIL
IRIS	KERB	LAUD	LIVE	MAIM
IRON	KHAN	LAVA	LOAD	MAIN
ISIS	KICK	LAVE	LOAF	MAKE
ISLE	KILL	LAWN	LOAM	MALE
ITCH	KILN	LAZE	LOAN	MALL
ITEM	KILO	LAZY	LOBE	MALT
	KILT	LEAD	LOCH	MAMA
	KIND	LEAF	LOCK	MANE
J – 4	KINE	LEAK	LODE	MANX
	KING	LEAL	LOFT	MANY
JACK	KINK	LEAN	LOGO	MARE
JADE	KIRK	LEAP	LOIN	MARK
JAIL	KISS	LEAR	LOLL	MARL
JAMB	KITE	LEDA	LONE	MARS
JANE	KITH	LEEK	LONG	MART
JAPE	KIWI	LEER	LOOK	MASH
JAZZ	KNAP	LEES	LOOM	MASK
JEAN	KNEE	LEET	LOON	MASS
JEEP	KNEW	LEFT	LOOP	MAST
JEER	KNIT	LEND	LOOS	MATE
JEHU	KNOB	LENO	LOOT	MAUD
JERK	KNOT	LENS	LOPE	MAUL
JEST	KNOW	LENT	LORD	MAZE
JIFF	KNUR	LESS	LORE	MEAD
JILL	KRIS	LEST	LORN	MEAL
JILT	KUDU	LETT	LORY	MEAN
JINX	KURD	LEVY	LOSE	MEAT
JIVE	KYLE	LEWD	LOSS	MEED
JOCK		LIAR	LOST	MEEK
JOEY		LICE	LOTH	MEET
JOHN	L – 4	LICK	LOUD	MELT
JOKE		LIDO	LOUR	MEMO
JOLT	LACE	LIED	LOUT	MEND
JOSS	LACK	LIEF	LOVE	MENU
JOVE	LADE	LIEN	LUCK	MERE
JOWL	LADY	LIEU	LUDO	MESH
JUDO	LAIC	LIFE	LUFF	MESS
JUDY	LAID	LIFT	LUGE	METE
JU-JU	LAIN	LIKE	LULL	MEWS
JUMP	LAIR	LILT	LUMP	MICA
JUNE	LAKE	LILY	LUNG	MICE
JUNK	LAMA	LIMB	LURE	MIEN
JUNO	LAMB	LIME	LURK	MIKE
JURY	LAME	LIMN	LUSH	MILD
JUST	LAMP	LIMP	LUST	MILE
	LANA	LIMY	LUTE	MILK
	LAND	LINE	LYNX	MILL
K – 4	LANE	LING	LYON	MIME
KALE	LANK	LING	LYRE	MIND
KEEL	LAPP	LINK		

MINE	NARK	OGPU	PARR	PLOT
MING	NAVE	OGRE	PART	PLOY
MINI	NAVY	OILY	PASS	PLUG
MINK	NAZE	OKAY	PAST	PLUM
MINT	NAZI	OLIO	PATE	PLUS
MINX	NEAP	OMAR	PATH	POEM
MIRE	NEAR	OMEN	PAUL	POET
MIRY	NEAT	OMIT	PAVE	POKE
MISS	NECK	ONCE	PAWL	POKY
MIST	NEED	ONER	PAWN	POLE
MITE	NEEP	ONLY	PAYE	POLL
MITT	NE'ER	ONUS	PEAK	POLO
MOAN	NEON	ONYX	PEAL	POMP
MOAT	NERO	OOZE	PEAR	POND
MOCK	NESS	OPAL	PEAT	PONY
MODE	NEST	OPEN	PECK	POOH
MODS	NETT	OPUS	PEEK	POOL
MOKE	NEWS	ORAL	PEEL	POOP
MOLE	NEWT	ORFE	PEEP	POOR
MOLL	NEXT	ORGY	PEER	POPE
MONK	NIBS	OTIC	PEKE	PORE
MOOD	NICE	OUCH	PELF	PORK
MOON	NICK	OURS	PELT	PORT
MOOR	NIGH	OUSE	PENT	POSE
MOOT	NINE	OUST	PEON	POSH
MOPE	NISI	OVAL	PERI	POST
MOPS	NODE	OVEN	PERK	POSY
MORE	NOEL	OVER	PERM	POUR
MORN	NOLL	OVUM	PERT	POUT
MOSS	NONE	OWED	PESO	PRAM
MOST	NOOK	OXEN	PEST	PRAY
MOTE	NOON	OYES	PHEW	PREP
MOTH	NORM	OYEZ	PHIZ	PREY
MOUE	NOSE		PHUT	PRIG
MOVE	NOSY	**P – 4**	PICA	PRIM
MOWN	NOTE		PICE	PROA
MUCH	NOUN	PACE	PICK	PROD
MUCK	NOUS	PACK	PICT	PROM
MUFF	NOVA	PACT	PIED	PROP
MULE	NOWT	PAGE	PIER	PROS
MULL	NUDE	PAID	PIKE	PROW
MURK	NULL	PAIL	PILE	PROX
MUSE	NUMB	PAIN	PILL	PUCE
MUSH		PAIR	PINE	PUCK
MUSK		PALE	PING	PUFF
MUST	**O – 4**	PALI	PINK	PULL
MUTE		PALL	PINT	PULP
MUTT	OAKS	PALM	PIPE	PUMA
MYTH	OAST	PANE	PISH	PUMP
	OATH	PANG	PITH	PUNK
	OBEY	PANT	PITY	PUNT
N – 4	OBIT	PAPA	PLAN	PUNY
	OBOE	PARA	PLAY	PUPA
NAIL	ODDS	PARD	PLEA	PURE
NAME	ODIN	PARE	PLOD	PURL
NAPE	OGEE	PARK	PLOP	PURR
NARD	OGLE			

PUSH	REST	RULE	SECT	SKIN
PUSS	RHEA	RUMP	SEED	SKIP
PUTT	RICE	RUNE	SEEK	SKIT
PYRE	RICH	RUNG	SEEM	SKUA
	RICK	RUNT	SEEN	SKYE
Q – 4	RIDE	RUSE	SEEP	SLAB
	RIFE	RUSH	SEER	SLAG
QUAD	RIFF	RUSK	SELF	SLAM
QUAY	RIFT	RUSS	SELL	SLAP
QUID	RIGA	RUST	SEMI	SLAT
QUIN	RILE	RUTH	SEND	SLAV
QUIP	RILL	RYOT	SENT	SLAY
QUIT	RIME		SEPT	SLED
QUIZ	RIND		SERB	SLEW
QUOD	RING	**S – 4**	SERE	SLID
	RINK		SERF	SLIM
R – 4	RIOT	SACK	SETT	SLIP
	RIPE	SAFE	SEWN	SLIT
RACE	RISE	SAGA	SHAD	SLOE
RACK	RISK	SAGE	SHAG	SLOG
RACY	RITE	SAGO	SHAH	SLOP
RAFT	RIVE	SAID	SHAM	SLOT
RAGE	ROAD	SAIL	SHAW	SLOW
RAID	ROAM	SAKE	SHED	SLUG
RAIL	ROAN	SAKI	SHEW	SLUM
RAIN	ROAR	SALE	SHIM	SLUR
RAKE	ROBE	SALT	SHIN	SLUT
RALE	ROCK	SAME	SHIP	SMEE
RAMP	RODE	SAND	SHOD	SMEW
RAND	ROLE	SANE	SHOE	SMOG
RANI	ROLL	SANG	SHOO	SMUG
RANK	ROME	SANK	SHOP	SMUT
RANT	ROMP	SANS	SHOT	SNAG
RAPE	ROOD	SARD	SHOW	SNAP
RAPT	ROOF	SARI	SHUN	SNIP
RARE	ROOK	SARK	SHUT	SNOB
RASH	ROOM	SASH	SICK	SNOW
RASP	ROOT	SATE	SIDE	SNUB
RATE	ROPE	SAUL	SIFT	SNUG
RAVE	ROPY	SAVE	SIGH	SOAK
RAZE	ROSE	SAWN	SIGN	SOAP
READ	ROSS	SAXE	SIKH	SOAR
REAL	ROSY	SCAB	SILK	SOCK
REAM	ROTA	SCAM	SILL	SODA
REAP	ROTE	SCAN	SILO	SOFA
REAR	ROUE	SCAR	SILT	SOFT
REDE	ROUP	SCAT	SINE	SOHO
REED	ROUT	SCOT	SING	SOIL
REEF	ROVE	SCOW	SINK	SOKE
REEK	RUBY	SCUD	SIRE	SOLA
REEL	RUCK	SCUM	SITE	SOLD
REIN	RUDD	SCUT	SIZE	SOLE
REIS	RUDE	SEAL	SKEP	SOLO
RELY	RUED	SEAM	SKEW	SOME
REND	RUFF	SEAN	SKID	SONG
RENT	RUIN	SEAR	SKIM	SOON
		SEAT		

SOOT	SWAN	THAW	TOUT	**V – 4**
SORE	SWAP	THEE	TOWN	
SORT	SWAT	THEM	TRAM	VAIN
SO-SO	SWAY	THEN	TRAP	VALE
SOUL	SWIG	THEY	TRAY	VAMP
SOUP	SWIM	THIN	TREE	VANE
SOUR	SWOP	THIS	TREK	VARY
SOWN	SWOT	THOR	TRET	VASE
SOYA	SWUM	THOU	TREY	VAST
SPAM	SYCE	THRO	TRIM	VEAL
SPAN		THUD	TRIO	VEER
SPAR	**T – 4**	THUG	TRIP	VEIL
SPAT		THUS	TROD	VEIN
SPEC	TACK	TICK	TROT	VEND
SPED	TACO	TIDE	TROY	VENT
SPIN	TACT	TIDY	TRUE	VERB
SPIT	TAEL	TIED	TRUG	VERT
SPIV	TAFT	TIER	TSAR	VERY
SPOT	TAIL	TIFF	TUBA	VEST
SPRY	TAKE	TIKE	TUBE	VETO
SPUD	TALC	TILE	TUCK	VICE
SPUN	TALE	TILL	TUFT	VIDE
SPUR	TALK	TILT	TUNA	VIED
STAB	TALL	TIME	TUNE	VIEW
STAG	TAME	TINE	TURF	VILE
STAR	TAMP	TING	TURK	VINE
STAY	TANG	TINT	TURN	VIOL
STEM	TANK	TINY	TUSH	VISA
STEN	TAPE	TIRE	TUSK	VIVA
STEP	TARA	TOAD	TUTU	VIVE
STET	TARE	TOBY	'TWAS	VOCE
STEW	TARN	TO-DO	TWIG	VOID
STIR	TARO	TOED	TWIN	VOLE
STOP	TART	TOFF	TWIT	VOLT
STOW	TASK	TOFU	TYKE	VOTE
STUB	TASS	TOGA	TYNE	
STUD	TA-TA	TOGS	TYPE	**W – 4**
STUN	TATE	TOIL	TYRE	
STYE	TAUT	TOLD	TYRO	WADE
STYX	TAXI	TOLL		WADI
SUCH	TEAK	TOMB		WAFT
SUCK	TEAL	TOME	**U – 4**	WAGE
SUDS	TEAM	TONE		WAIF
SUED	TEAR	TONY	UGLY	WAIL
SUET	TEAT	TOOK	ULNA	WAIN
SUEZ	TEED	TOOL	UNCO	WAIT
SUIT	TEEM	TOOT	UNDO	WAKE
SULK	TELL	TOPE	UNIT	WALE
SUMP	TEND	TORE	UNTO	WALK
SUNG	TENT	TORN	UPAS	WALL
SUNK	TERM	TORT	UPON	WALT
SURE	TERN	TORY	URDU	WAND
SURF	TEST	TOSH	URGE	WANE
SWAB	THAI	TOSS	URSA	WANT
SWAG	THAN	TOTE	USED	WARD
SWAM	THAT	TOUR	USER	WARE

WARM	WIRY	**Z – 4**	ADOPT	ALOUD
WARN	WISE		ADORE	ALPHA
WARP	WISH	ZANY	ADORN	ALTAR
WART	WISP	ZEAL	ADSUM	ALTER
WARY	WITH	ZEBU	ADULT	AMASS
WASH	WOAD	ZERO	AEGIS	AMAZE
WASP	WOLD	ZEST	AERIE	AMBER
WATT	WOLF	ZETA	AESOP	AMBIT
WAVE	WOMB	ZEUS	AFFIX	AMBLE
WAVY	WONT	ZINC	AFIRE	AMEER
WAXY	WOOD	ZING	AFOOT	AMEND
WEAK	WOOF	ZION	AFTER	AMISS
WEAL	WOOL	ZONE	AGAIN	AMITY
WEAN	WORD	ZOOM	AGAPE	AMONG
WEAR	WORE	ZULU	AGATE	AMOUR
WEED	WORK		AGAVE	AMPLE
WEEK	WORM	**A – 5**	AGENT	AMPLY
WEEP	WORN		AGILE	AMUCK
WEFT	WORT	ABACK	AGLEY	AMUSE
WEIR	WOVE	ABAFT	AGLOW	ANENT
WELD	WRAP	ABASE	AGONE	ANGEL
WELL	WREN	ABASH	AGONY	ANGER
WELT	WRIT	ABATE	AGREE	ANGLE
WEND		ABBEY	AHEAD	ANGRY
WENT	**X – 4**	ABBOT	AHEAP	ANISE
WEPT		ABEAM	AIDED	ANKLE
WERE	XMAS	ABELE	AILED	ANNEX
WERT	X-RAY	ABEND	AIMED	ANNOY
WEST		ABHOR	AIRED	ANNUL
WHAT	**Y – 4**	ABIDE	AISLE	ANODE
WHEN		ABIES	AITCH	ANONA
WHET	YANK	ABLER	AKELE	ANTIC
WHEW	YARD	ABODE	ALACK	ANVIL
WHEY	YARN	ABOIL	ALARM	ANZAC
WHIG	YAWL	ABORT	ALBUM	AORTA
WHIM	YAWN	ABOUT	ALDER	APACE
WHIN	YAWS	ABOVE	ALERT	APART
WHIP	YEAH	ABRIM	ALGAE	APHIS
WHIT	YEAR	ABUSE	ALGOL	APING
WHOA	YELL	ABYSS	ALIAS	APISH
WHOM	YELP	ACHED	ALIBI	APORT
WICK	YETI	ACRID	ALIEN	APPAL
WIDE	YOGA	ACTED	ALIGN	APPLE
WIFE	YOGI	ACTON	ALIKE	APPLY
WILD	YO-HO	ACTOR	ALIVE	APRIL
WILE	YOKE	ACUTE	ALLAH	APRON
WILL	YOLK	ADAGE	ALLAY	APTLY
WILT	YOMP	ADAPT	ALLEY	ARABY
WILY	YORE	ADDED	ALL-IN	ARECA
WIMP	YOUR	ADDER	ALLOT	ARENA
WIND	YOWL	ADDLE	ALLOW	ARGON
WINE	YO-YO	ADEPT	ALLOY	ARGOT
WING	YULE	ADIEU	ALOFT	ARGUE
WINK		ADMIT	ALONE	ARGUS
WIPE		ADMIX	ALONG	ARIEL
WIRE		ADOBE	ALOOF	ARIES

ARISE	AZTEC	BEEFY	BLAZE	BOSON
ARMED	AZURE	BEERY	BLEAK	BOSSY
AROMA		BEFIT	BLEAR	BOSUN
AROSE		BEFOG	BLEAT	BOTCH
ARRAS	**B – 5**	BEGAD	BLEED	BOUGH
ARRAY	BABEL	BEGAN	BLEND	BOULE
ARROW	BACCY	BEGAT	BLESS	BOUND
ARSON	BACON	BEGET	BLEST	BOWED
ARYAN	BADGE	BEGIN	BLIMP	BOWEL
ASCOT	BADLY	BEGOT	BLIND	BOWER
ASDIC	BAGGY	BEGUM	BLINK	BOWIE
ASHEN	BAIRN	BEGUN	BLISS	BOWLS
ASHES	BAIZE	BEIGE	BLOCK	BOXED
ASHET	BAKED	BEING	BLOKE	BOXER
ASIAN	BAKER	BELAY	BLOND	BOYER
ASIDE	BALED	BELCH	BLOOD	BRACE
ASKED	BALER	BELIE	BLOOM	BRACT
ASKEW	BALMY	BELLE	BLOWN	BRAID
ASPEN	BALSA	BELOW	BLOWY	BRAIN
ASPIC	BAMBI	BENCH	BLUED	BRAKE
ASSAY	BANAL	BERET	BLUER	BRAND
ASSES	BANDY	BERRY	BLUES	BRASH
ASSET	BANJO	BERTH	BLUEY	BRASS
ASTER	BANNS	BERYL	BLUFF	BRAVE
ASTIR	BANTU	BESET	BLUNT	BRAVO
ASTON	BARED	BESOM	BLURB	BRAWL
ATILT	BARGE	BESOT	BLURT	BRAWN
ATLAS	BARMY	BETEL	BLUSH	BRAZE
ATOLL	BARON	BETTY	BOARD	BREAD
ATONE	BARRY	BEVEL	BOAST	BREAK
ATTAR	BASAL	BHANG	BOBBY	BREAM
ATTIC	BASED	BIBLE	BOCHE	BREED
AUDIO	BASIC	BIDDY	BODED	BREVE
AUDIT	BASIL	BIDET	BODGE	BRIAR
AUGER	BASIN	BIGHT	BOGEY	BRIBE
AUGHT	BASIS	BIGOT	BOGGY	BRICK
AUGUR	BASSO	BIJOU	BOGIE	BRIDE
AUNTY	BASTE	BILGE	BOGUS	BRIEF
AURAL	BATCH	BILLY	BOHEA	BRIER
AVAIL	BATED	BIMBO	BOLAS	BRILL
AVAST	BATHE	BINGE	BONED	BRINE
AVENS	BATON	BINGO	BONES	BRING
AVERT	BATTY	BIPED	BONNE	BRINK
AVIAN	BAULK	BIRCH	BONUS	BRINY
AVION	BAWDY	BIRTH	BOOBY	BRISK
AVOID	BAYED	BISON	BOOED	BROAD
AWAIT	BEACH	BITCH	BOOST	BROCK
AWAKE	BEADS	BITER	BOOTH	BROIL
AWARD	BEADY	BLACK	BOOTS	BROKE
AWARE	BE-ALL	BLADE	BOOTY	BRONX
AWASH	BEANO	BLAME	BORAX	BROOD
AWFUL	BEARD	BLAND	BORED	BROOK
AWING	BEAST	BLANK	BORER	BROOM
AWOKE	BEBOP	BARE	BORNE	BROSE
AXIAL	BEDEW	BLASE	BORON	BROTH
AXIOM	BEECH	BLAST	BOSOM	BROWN

BRUIN	CANAL	CHESS	CLIFF	COURT
BRUNT	CANDY	CHEST	CLIMB	COVER
BRUSH	CANED	CHICK	CLIME	COVET
BRUTE	CANNA	CHIDE	CLING	COVEY
BUDDY	CANNY	CHIEF	CLINK	COWED
BUDGE	CANOE	CHILD	CLOAK	COWER
BUFFS	CANON	CHILI	CLOCK	COYLY
BUGGY	CANTO	CHILL	CLOSE	COYPU
BUGLE	CAPER	CHIME	CLOTH	COZEN
BUILD	CAPON	CHINA	CLOUD	CRACK
BUILT	CARAT	CHINE	CLOUT	CRAFT
BULGE	CARED	CHINK	CLOVE	CRAIG
BULGY	CARET	CHIPS	CLOWN	CRAKE
BULKY	CARGO	CHIRP	CLUCK	CRAMP
BULLY	CARIB	CHIVE	CLUMP	CRANE
BUMPY	CAROB	CHOCK	CLUNG	CRANK
BUNCE	CAROL	CHOIR	CLUNK	CRASH
BUNCH	CARRY	CHOKE	CLUNY	CRASS
BUNNY	CARTE	CHOPS	COACH	CRATE
BUNTY	CARVE	CHORD	COAST	CRAVE
BURGH	CASED	CHORE	COATI	CRAWL
BURKE	CASTE	CHOSE	COBRA	CRAZE
BURLY	CATCH	CHUCK	COCKY	CRAZY
BURNT	CATER	CHUMP	COCOA	CREAK
BURRO	CATTY	CHUNK	CODED	CREAM
BURST	CAULK	CHURL	CODEX	CREDO
BUSBY	CAUSE	CHURN	COLIC	CREED
BUSES	CAVIL	CHUTE	COLIN	CREEK
BUSHY	CAWED	CIDER	COLON	CREEL
BUTTS	CD-ROM	CIGAR	COMET	CREEP
BUTTY	CEASE	CINCH	COMIC	CREPE
BUXOM	CEDAR	CIRCA	COMMA	CREPT
BUYER	CEDED	CIRCE	COMPO	CRESS
BWANA	CELLO	CISSY	CONCH	CREST
BY-LAW	CERES	CITED	CONEY	CREWE
BYWAY	CHAFE	CIVET	CONGA	CRICK
	CHAFF	CIVIC	CONGE	CRIED
	CHAIN	CIVIL	CONGO	CRIER
C – 5	CHAIR	CIVVY	CONIC	CRIES
CABAL	CHALK	CLACK	COOED	CRIME
CABBY	CHAMP	CLAIM	COOMB	CRIMP
CABER	CHANT	CLAMP	CO-OPT	CRISP
CABIN	CHAOS	CLAMS	COPAL	CROAK
CABLE	CHAPS	CLANG	COPED	CROCK
CACAO	CHARD	CLANK	COPER	CROFT
CACHE	CHARM	CLARE	COPRA	CRONE
CADDY	CHART	CLASH	COPSE	CRONY
CADET	CHARY	CLASP	CORAL	CROOK
CADGE	CHASE	CLASS	CORGI	CROON
CADRE	CHASM	CLEAN	CORNY	CRORE
CAGED	CHEAP	CLEAR	CORPS	CROSS
CAGEY	CHEAT	CLEAT	COSTS	CROUP
CAIRN	CHECK	CLEEK	COUGH	CROWD
CAKED	CHEEK	CLEFT	COULD	CROWN
CAMEL	CHEEP	CLERK	COUNT	CRUDE
CAMEO	CHEER	CLICK	COUPE	CRUEL

CRUET	DEFER	DOLCE	DRUID	ELEMI
CRUMB	DEIFY	DOLED	DRUNK	ELEVE
CRUMP	DEIGN	DOLLY	DRUPE	ELFIN
CRUSE	DEITY	DOMED	DRYAD	ELGIN
CRUSH	DEKKO	DONAH	DRYER	ELIDE
CRUST	DELAY	DONAT	DRYLY	ELITE
CRYPT	DELFT	DONNA	DUCAL	ELOPE
CUBAN	DELTA	DONOR	DUCAT	ELUDE
CUBED	DELVE	DOPED	DUCHY	ELVER
CUBIC	DEMOB	DORIC	DULLY	EMBED
CUBIT	DEMON	DORMY	DUMMY	EMBER
CUPID	DEMUR	DOSED	DUMPS	EMEER
CURED	DENIM	DOTED	DUMPY	EMEND
CURER	DENSE	DOTTY	DUNCE	EMERY
CURIE	DEPOT	DOUBT	DUPED	EMMET
CURIO	DEPTH	DOUGH	DUSKY	EMPTY
CURLY	DERBY	DOUSE	DUSTY	ENACT
CURRY	DETER	DOVER	DUTCH	ENDED
CURSE	DEUCE	DOWDY	DUVET	END-ON
CURVE	DEVIL	DOWEL	DWARF	ENDOR
CUSHY	DHOBI	DOWER	DWELL	ENDOW
CUTER	DHOTI	DOWNY	DWELT	ENEMY
CUTTY	DIANA	DOWRY	DYING	ENJOY
CYCLE	DIARY	DOYEN		ENNUI
CYDER	DIBIT	DOZED		ENROL
CYNIC	DICED	DOZEN	E – 5	ENSUE
CZECH	DICKY	DRAFT	EAGER	ENTER
	DICTA	DRAIN	EAGLE	ENTRY
	DIGIT	DRAKE	EAGRE	ENVOI
D – 5	DIMLY	DRAMA	EARED	ENVOY
	DINAR	DRANK	EARLY	EPHOD
DADDY	DINED	DRAPE	EARTH	EPOCH
DAILY	DINER	DRAWL	EASED	EPOXY
DAIRY	DINGO	DRAWN	EASEL	EPSOM
DAISY	DINGY	DREAD	EATEN	EQUAL
DALAI	DINKY	DREAM	EAVES	EQUIP
DALLY	DIODE	DREAR	EBBED	ERASE
DAMON	DIRGE	DREGS	EBONY	ERATO
DANCE	DIRTY	DRESS	ECLAT	ERECT
DANDY	DISCO	DRIED	EDGED	ERICA
DARBY	DITCH	DRIER	EDICT	ERODE
DARED	DITTO	DRIFT	EDIFY	ERRED
DATED	DITTY	DRILL	EDUCE	ERROR
DATUM	DIVAN	DRILY	EERIE	ERUPT
DAUNT	DIVED	DRINK	EGGED	ESSAY
DAVIT	DIVER	DRIVE	EGRET	ESTER
DAZED	DIVES	DROIT	EIDER	ESTOP
DEALT	DIVOT	DROLL	EIGHT	ETHER
DEATH	DIXIE	DROME	EJECT	ETHIC
DEBAR	DODGE	DRONE	EKING	ETHOS
DEBIT	DODGY	DROOL	ELAND	ETHYL
DEBUG	DOGGO	DROOP	ELATE	ETUDE
DEBUT	DOGGY	DROPS	ELBOW	EVADE
DECAY	DOGMA	DROSS	ELDER	EVENS
DECOR	DOILY	DROVE	ELECT	EVENT
DECOY	DOING	DROWN	ELEGY	EVERT
DECRY				

EVERY	FETED	FLOSS	FROZE	GIBUS
EVICT	FEVER	FLOUR	FRUIT	GIDDY
EVOKE	FEWER	FLOUT	FRUMP	GIGOT
EXACT	FIBRE	FLOWN	FRYER	GIPSY
EXALT	FICHU	FLUFF	FUDGE	GIRTH
EXCEL	FIELD	FLUID	FUGUE	GISMO
EXEAT	FIEND	FLUKE	FULLY	GIVEN
EXERT	FIERY	FLUKY	FUNGI	GIVER
EXILE	FIFTH	FLUNG	FUNKY	GIVES
EXIST	FIFTY	FLUSH	FUNNY	GIZMO
EXPEL	FIGHT	FLUTE	FURRY	GLACÉ
EXTOL	FILCH	FLYER	FURZE	GLADE
EXTRA	FILED	FOAMY	FUSED	GLAND
EXUDE	FILLY	FOCAL	FUSEE	GLARE
EXULT	FILMY	FOCUS	FUSIL	GLASS
EYING	FILTH	FOGEY	FUSSY	GLAZE
EYRE	FINAL	FOGGY	FUSTY	GLEAM
	FINCH	FOIST	FUTON	GLEAN
	FINED	FOLIO	FUZZY	GLEBE
F – 5	FINER	FOLLY		GLIDE
	FINIS	FORAY		GLINT
FABLE	FIORD	FORBY	**G – 5**	GLITZ
FACED	FIRED	FORCE		GLOAT
FACET	FIRST	FORGE	GABLE	GLOBE
FADDY	FIRTH	FORGO	GAFFE	GLOOM
FAGIN	FISHY	FORME	GAILY	GLORY
FAINT	FITCH	FORTE	GALOP	GLOSS
FAIRY	FITLY	FORTH	GAMED	GLOVE
FAITH	FIVER	FORTY	GAMIN	GLUED
FAKED	FIVES	FORUM	GAMMA	GLUEY
FAKIR	FIXED	FOSSE	GAMUT	GLUON
FALSE	FJORD	FOUND	GAPED	GNARL
FAMED	FLAIL	FOUNT	GARTH	GNASH
FANCY	FLAIR	FOXED	GASSY	GNOME
FARAD	FLAKE	FOYER	GATED	GODLY
FARED	FLAKY	FRAIL	GAUDY	GOING
FARCE	FLAME	FRAME	GAUGE	GOLLY
FATAL	FLANK	FRANCE	GAUNT	GONER
FATED	FLARE	FRANK	GAUZE	GOODS
FATES	FLASH	FRAUD	GAUZY	GOODY
FATLY	FLASK	FREAK	GAVEL	GOOSE
FATTY	FLECK	FREED	GAWKY	GORED
FATWA	FLEET	FREER	GAYER	GORGE
FAULT	FLESH	FRESH	GAZED	GORSE
FAUNA	FLICK	FRIAR	GECKO	GOUDA
FAUST	FLIER	FRIED	GEESE	GOUGE
FEAST	FLIES	FRILL	GELID	GOURD
FED-UP	FLING	FRISK	GENET	GOUTY
FEIGN	FLINT	FRITZ	GENIE	GRACE
FEINT	FLIRT	FRIZZ	GENOA	GRADE
FELIX	FLOAT	FROCK	GENRE	GRAFT
FELON	FLOCK	FROND	GENUS	GRAIL
FEMUR	FLONG	FRONT	GET-UP	GRAIN
FENCE	FLOOD	FROST	GHOST	GRAND
FERNY	FLOOR	FROTH	GHOUL	GRANT
FERRY	FLORA	FROWN	GIANT	GRAPE
FETCH			GIBED	

GRAPH	GYPSY	HINDI	I – 5	IXION
GRASP	GYVES	HINDU		
GRASS		HINGE	ICENI	J – 5
GRATE		HINNY	ICHOR	
GRAVE	H – 5	HINNY	ICIER	JABOT
GRAVY	HABIT	HIPPO	ICILY	JADED
GRAZE	HADES	HIRED	ICING	JAMES
GREAT	HADJI	HIRER	IDEAL	JAMMY
GREBE	HAIRY	HITCH	IDIOM	JAPAN
GREED	HALLO	HIVED	IDIOT	JAUNT
GREEK	HALMA	HIVES	IDLED	JAWED
GREEN	HALON	HOARD	IDLER	JEANS
GREET	HALVE	HOARY	IDRIS	JELLY
GREYS	HANDY	HOBBY	IDYLL	JEMMY
GRIEF	HANKY	HOCUS	IGLOO	JENNY
GRILL	HAPLY	HODGE	ILIAD	JERKY
GRIME	HAPPY	HOIST	ILIUM	JERRY
GRIMY	HARDY	HOLLY	IMAGE	JETTY
GRIND	HARED	HOMER	IMAGO	JEWEL
GRIPE	HAREM	HONED	IMBUE	JEWRY
GRIST	HARRY	HONEY	IMPEL	JIBED
GRITS	HARSH	HOOCH	IMPLY	JIFFY
GROWN	HASTE	HOOEY	INANE	JIMMY
GROAT	HASTY	HOPED	INAPT	JINGO
GROCK	HATCH	HOPPY	INCOG	JINKS
GROIN	HATED	HORDE	INCUR	JOINT
GROOM	HAULM	HORNY	INDEX	JOIST
GROPE	HAUNT	HORSE	INEPT	JOKED
GROSS	HAVEN	HORSY	INERT	JOKER
GROUP	HAVER	HOTEL	INFER	JOLLY
GROUT	HAVOC	HOTLY	INFIX	JONAH
GROVE	HAWSE	HOUND	INGLE	JOULE
GROWL	HAZEL	HOURI	INGOT	JOUST
GROWN	HEADS	HOUSE	INKED	JUDAS
GRUEL	HEADY	HOVEL	IN-LAW	JUDGE
GRUFF	HEARD	HOVER	INLAY	JUICE
GRUNT	HEART	HOWDY	INLET	JUICY
GUANO	HEATH	HUBBY	INNER	JULEP
GUARD	HEDGE	HUFFY	INPUT	JUMBO
GUAVA	HEFTY	HULLO	INSET	JUMPY
GUESS	HEIGH	HUMAN	INTER	JUNTA
GUEST	HELIX	HUMID	INURE	JUROR
GUIDE	HELLO	HUMPH	IONIC	
GUILD	HELOT	HUMUS	IRAQI	
GUILE	HE-MAN	HUNCH	IRATE	K – 5
GUISE	HENCE	HUNKS	IRENE	KAPOK
GULAG	HENNA	HURRY	IRISH	KAPUT
GULCH	HENRY	HUSKY	IRKED	KARMA
GULES	HEROD	HUSSY	IRONS	KAYAK
GULLY	HERON	HUTCH	IRONY	KEDGE
GUNNY	HERTZ	HYDRA	ISLAM	KEEPS
GUSTO	HEWED	HYDRO	ISLET	KETCH
GUSTY	HEWER	HYENA	ISSUE	KEYED
GUTTA	HIKED	HYRAX	ITCHY	KHAKI
GUTTY	HIKER	HYTHE	IVIED	KIDDY
GUYED	HILLY		IVORY	KINGS

KINKY	LAUGH	LIVID	M – 5	MEATH
KIOSK	LAURA	LLAMA		MEATY
KITTY	LAVED	LLANO	MACAW	MECCA
KLOOF	LAXLY	LOACH	MACHO	MEDAL
KNACK	LAY-BY	LOAMY	MACON	MEDIA
KNARL	LAYER	LOATH	MADAM	MEDOC
KNAVE	LAZED	LOBBY	MADGE	MELEE
KNEAD	LEACH	LOCAL	MADLY	MELON
KNEED	LEAFY	LOCUM	MAFIA	MERCY
KNEEL	LEANT	LODGE	MAGIC	MERGE
KNELL	LEARN	LOFTY	MAGOG	MERIT
KNELT	LEASE	LOGAN	MAHDI	MERLE
KNIFE	LEASH	LOGIC	MAIZE	MERRY
KNOCK	LEAST	LOLLY	MAJOR	MESON
KNOLL	LEAVE	LOOFA	MAKER	MESSY
KNOUT	LEDGE	LOONY	MALAY	METAL
KNOWN	LEECH	LOOPY	MALTY	METED
KNURL	LEERY	LOOSE	MAMBA	METER
KOALA	LEGAL	LOPED	MAMMA	METRE
KOPIE	LEGER	LORDS	MAMMY	MEWED
KORAN	LEGGY	LORIS	MANED	MEZZO
KRAAL	LEMON	LORRY	MANET	MIAOW
KRAIT	LEMUR	LOSER	MANGE	MICKY
KRONE	LENTO	LOTTO	MANGO	MIDAS
KUDOS	LEPER	LOTUS	MANGY	MIDDY
KUKRI	LETHE	LOUGH	MANIA	MIDGE
KULAK	LET-UP	LOUIS	MANLY	MID-ON
KVASS	LEVEE	LOUSE	MANNA	MIDST
	LEVEL	LOUSY	MANOR	MIGHT
	LEVER	LOVAT	MANSE	MILCH
L – 5	LEWIS	LOVED	MAORI	MILER
	LIANA	LOVER	MAPLE	MILKY
LABEL	LIBEL	LOWER	MARCH	MIMED
LACED	LIBRA	LOWLY	MARGE	MIMIC
LADEN	LICIT	LOYAL	MARRY	MINCE
LADLE	LIEGE	LUCID	MARSH	MINED
LAGER	LIFER	LUCKY	MASAI	MINER
LAIRD	LIGHT	LUCRE	MASER	MINIM
LAITY	LIKED	LUGER	MASHY	MINOR
LAKER	LIKEN	LUMPY	MASON	MINUS
LAMED	LILAC	LUNAR	MASSA	MIRTH
LANCE	LIMBO	LUNCH	MASSE	MISER
LANKY	LIMIT	LUNGE	MATCH	MISSY
LAPEL	LINED	LUPIN	MATED	MISTY
LAPSE	LINEN	LURCH	MATER	MITRE
LARCH	LINER	LURED	MATEY	MIXED
LARDY	LINGO	LURID	MATIN	MIXER
LARGE	LINKS	LUSTY	MAUVE	MIX-UP
LARGO	LISLE	LYCEE	MAVIS	MOCHA
LARRY	LISTS	LYING	MAWKY	MODEL
LARVA	LITHE	LYMPH	MAXIM	MODEM
LASSO	LITHO	LYNCH	MAYBE	MODUS
LATCH	LITRE	LYRIC	MAYOR	MOGUL
LATER	LIVED		MEALY	MOIRE
LATEX	LIVEN		MEANS	MOIST
LATHE	LIVER		MEANT	MOLAR
LATIN				

MOLLY	MYRRH	NOHOW	OOZED	PALSY
MOLTO		NOISE	OPERA	PANDA
MONDE	**N – 5**	NOISY	OPINE	PANED
MONEY		NOMAD	OPIUM	PANEL
MONTE	NABOB	NONCE	OPTED	PANIC
MONTH	NACRE	NONET	OPTIC	PANSY
MOOCH	NADIR	NOOSE	ORANG	PANTS
MOODY	NAIAD	NORMA	ORATE	PAPAL
MOOED	NAIVE	NORSE	ORBED	PAPAW
MOONY	NAKED	NORTH	ORBIT	PAPER
MOOSE	NAMED	NOSED	ORDER	PAPPY
MOPED	NANNY	NOSEY	OREAD	PARCH
MORAL	NAPOO	NOTCH	ORGAN	PARED
MORAY	NAPPY	NOTED	ORIEL	PARKA
MORON	NASAL	NOVEL	ORION	PARKY
MORSE	NASTY	NOYAU	ORLON	PARRY
MOSES	NATAL	NUDGE	ORLOP	PARSE
MOSSY	NATTY	NURSE	ORMER	PARTS
MOTEL	NAVAL	NUTTY	ORRIS	PARTY
MOTET	NAVEL	NYLON	OSCAR	PASHA
MOTIF	NAVVY		OSIER	PASSE
MOTOR	NAWAB	**O – 5**	OTHER	PASTE
MOTTO	NAZIS		OTTER	PASTY
MOULD	NEDDY	OAKEN	OUGHT	PATCH
MOULT	NEEDS	OAKUM	OUIJA	PATEN
MOUND	NEEDY	OARED	OUNCE	PATER
MOUNT	NEGRO	OASIS	OUSEL	PATIO
MOURN	NEGUS	OATEN	OUTDO	PATLY
MOUSE	NEIGH	OBEAH	OUTER	PATSY
MOUSY	NERVE	OBESE	OUTRE	PATTY
MOUTH	NERVY	OCCUR	OVATE	PAUSE
MOVED	NEVER	OCEAN	OVERT	PAVAN
MOVER	NEWEL	OCHRE	OVINE	PAVED
MOVIE	NEWLY	OCTET	OVOID	PAWED
MOWED	NEWSY	ODDLY	OVULE	PAWKY
MOWER	NEXUS	ODEON	OWING	PAYEE
MUCKY	NICER	ODIUM	OWLET	PAYER
MUCUS	NICHE	ODOUR	OWNED	PEACE
MUDDY	NIECE	OFFAL	OWNER	PEACH
MUFTI	NIFTY	OFFER	OX-EYE	PEAKY
MUGGY	NIGHT	OFLAG	OXIDE	PEARL
MULCH	NIHIL	OFTEN	OXLIP	PEASE
MULCT	NIMBY	OGIVE	OZONE	PEATY
MUMMY	NINNY	OGLED		PECAN
MUMPS	NINON	OILED		PEDAL
MUNCH	NINTH	OKAPI	**P – 5**	PEGGY
MURAL	NIOBE	OLDEN		PEKOE
MURKY	NIPPY	OLDER	PACED	PENAL
MUSED	NITRE	OLEIC	PACER	PENCE
MUSHY	NIZAM	OLIVE	PADDY	PENNY
MUSIC	NOBBY	OMAHA	PADRE	PEONY
MUSTY	NOBEL	OMBRE	PAEAN	PERCH
MUTED	NOBLE	OMEGA	PAGAN	PERDU
MUZZY	NOBLY	ONION	PAGED	PERIL
MYNAH	NODAL	ONSET	PAINT	PERKY
MYOPE	NODDY	OOMPH	PALED	PERRY
			PALMY	

PESKY	PODGY	PRUDE	QUORN	REEDY
PETAL	POESY	PRUNE	QUOTA	REEVE
PETER	POILU	PSEUD	QUOTE	REFER
PETIT	POINT	PSALM	QUOTH	REFIT
PEWIT	POISE	PUFFY		REFIX
PHASE	POKED	PUKKA		REGAL
PHIAL	POKER	PULED	R – 5	REICH
PHLOX	POLAR	PULPY	RABBI	REIGN
PHONE	POLIO	PULSE	RABID	REINS
PHOTO	POLKA	PUNCH	RACED	RELAX
PIANO	POLLY	PUNIC	RACER	RELAY
PICEL	POPPY	PUPIL	RADAR	RELET
PICOT	PORCH	PUPPY	RADII	RELIC
PIECE	PORED	PUREE	RADIO	RELIT
PIETY	PORKY	PURER	RADIX	REMIT
PIGMY	POSED	PURGE	RAGED	RENAL
PILAU	POSER	PURSE	RAGGA	RENEW
PILAW	POSSE	PUSSY	RAINY	RENTE
PILED	POTTO	PUTTY	RAISE	REPAY
PILOT	POTTY	PUT-UP	RAJAH	REPEL
PINED	POUCH	PYGMY	RAKED	REPLY
PINKY	POULT	PYLON	RALLY	REPOT
PINNY	POUND	PYRUS	RANCH	RERUN
PIN-UP	POWER		RANDY	RESET
PIOUS	PRANG		RANEE	RESIN
PIPED	PRANK	Q – 5	RANGE	RESOW
PIPER	PRATE	QUACK	RANGY	RETCH
PIPIT	PRAWN	QUADS	RAPID	RETRY
PIQUE	PREEN	QUAFF	RARER	REVEL
PITCH	PRESS	QUAIL	RASED	REVUE
PITHY	PRICE	QUAKE	RATED	RHEUM
PIVOT	PRICK	QUAKY	RATEL	RHINE
PIXEL	PRIDE	QUALM	RATIO	RHINO
PIXIE	PRIED	QUANT	RATTY	RHOMB
PIZZA	PRIMA	QUARK	RAVED	RHYME
PLACE	PRIME	QUART	RAVEL	RIANT
PLAID	PRIMO	QUASH	RAVEN	RIBES
PLAIN	PRINK	QUASI	RAWLY	RIDER
PLAIT	PRINT	QUEEN	RAYON	RIDGE
PLANE	PRIOR	QUEER	RAZED	RIFLE
PLANK	PRISE	QUELL	RAZOR	RIGHT
PLANT	PRISM	QUERY	REACH	RIGID
PLATE	PRIVY	QUEST	REACT	RIGOR
PLATO	PRIZE	QUEUE	READY	RILED
PLAZA	PROBE	QUICK	REALM	RIMED
PLEAD	PROEM	QUIET	RE-ARM	RINSE
PLEAT	PRONE	QUIFF	REBEL	RIPEN
PLEBS	PRONG	QUILL	REBID	RIPER
PLIED	PROOF	QUILT	REBUS	RIPON
PLUCK	PROPS	QUINS	REBUT	RISEN
PLUMB	PROSE	QUIRE	RECCE	RISER
PLUME	PROSY	QUIRK	RECTO	RISKY
PLUMP	PROUD	QUIET	RECUR	RIVAL
PLUSH	PROVE	QUITS	REDAN	RIVEN
POACH	PROWL	QUOIN	REDLY	RIVER
PODGE	PROXY	QUOIT	RE-DYE	RIVET

ROACH	SAINT	SCORN	SHARK	SISAL
ROAST	SAITH	SCOTS	SHARP	SISSY
ROBED	SALAD	SCOUR	SHAVE	SIXTH
ROBIN	SALIC	SCOUT	SHAWL	SIXTY
ROBOT	SALIX	SCOWL	SHEAF	SIZED
ROCKY	SALLY	SCRAG	SHEAR	SKATE
RODEO	SALMI	SCRAM	SHEEN	SKEAN
ROGER	SALON	SCRAP	SHEEP	SKEIN
ROGUE	SALSA	SCREE	SHEER	SKIED
ROMAN	SALTS	SCREW	SHEET	SKIER
ROMEO	SALTY	SCRIM	SHEIK	SKIFF
RONDO	SALVE	SCRIP	SHELF	SKILL
ROOMY	SALVO	SCRUB	SHELL	SKIMP
ROOST	SAMBA	SCRUM	SHEWN	SKINK
ROPED	SAMMY	SCUBA	SHIED	SKIRL
ROSIN	SANDY	SCUFF	SHIFT	SKIRT
ROTOR	SANER	SCULL	SHINE	SKIVE
ROUGE	SAPID	SCURF	SHINY	SKULK
ROUGH	SAPOR	SEAMY	SHIRE	SKULL
ROUND	SAPPY	SEDAN	SHIRK	SKUNK
ROUSE	SATAN	SEDGE	SHIRT	SLACK
ROUTE	SATED	SEEDY	SHOAL	SLADE
ROVED	SATIN	SEGUE	SHOCK	SLAIN
ROVER	SATYR	SEINE	SHONE	SLAKE
ROWAN	SAUCE	SEIZE	SHOOK	SLANG
ROWDY	SAUCY	SENNA	SHOOT	SLANT
ROWED	SAUNA	SENSE	SHORE	SLASH
ROWEL	SAUTÉ	SEPAL	SHORN	SLATE
ROWER	SAVED	SEPIA	SHORT	SLATY
ROYAL	SAVER	SEPOY	SHOUT	SLAVE
RUCHE	SAVOY	SERAI	SHOVE	SLEEK
RUDDY	SAVVY	SERGE	SHOWN	SLEEP
RUDER	SAWED	SERIF	SHOWY	SLEET
RUGBY	SAXON	SERUM	SHRED	SLEPT
RUING	SAY-SO	SERVE	SHREW	SLICE
RULED	SCALA	SETAE	SHRUB	SLICK
RULER	SCALD	SET-TO	SHRUG	SLIDE
RUMBA	SCALE	SET-UP	SHUCK	SLIME
RUMMY	SCALP	SEVEN	SHUNT	SLIMY
RUNIC	SCALY	SEVER	SHYLY	SLING
RUN-IN	SCAMP	SEWER	SIBYL	SLINK
RUNNY	SCANT	SHACK	SIDED	SLOOP
RUPEE	SCARE	SHADE	SIDLE	SLOPE
RURAL	SCARF	SHADY	SIEGE	SLOSH
RUSTY	SCARP	SHAFT	SIEVE	SLOTH
RUTTY	SCENA	SHAKE	SIGHT	SLUMP
	SCENE	SHAKO	SIGMA	SLUNG
	SCENT	SHAKY	SILKY	SLUNK
S – 5	SCION	SHALE	SILLY	SLUSH
	SCOFF	SHALL	SINCE	SLYLY
SABLE	SCOLD	SHALT	SINEW	SMACK
SABOT	SCONE	SHAME	SINGE	SMALL
SABRE	SCOOP	SHANK	SINGS	SMART
SADLY	SCOOT	SHAPE	SINUS	SMASH
SAFER	SCOPE	SHARD	SIOUX	SMEAR
SAGAN	SCORE	SHARE	SIRED	SMELL
SAHIB			SIREN	

SMELT	SOWED	SQUAT	STORE	SWIFT
SMILE	SOWER	SQUAW	STORK	SWILL
SMIRK	SPACE	SQUIB	STORM	SWINE
SMITE	SPADE	SQUID	STORY	SWING
SMITH	SPAHI	STACK	STOUP	SWIPE
SMOCK	SPAKE	STAFF	STOUR	SWIRL
SMOKE	SPANK	STAGE	STOUT	SWISH
SMOKY	SPARE	STAGY	STOVE	SWISS
SMOTE	SPARK	STAID	STRAD	SWOON
SNACK	SPASM	STAIN	STRAP	SWOOP
SNAIL	SPATE	STAIR	STRAW	SWORD
SNAKE	SPAWN	STAKE	STRAY	SWORE
SNAKY	SPEAK	STALE	STREW	SWORN
SNARE	SPEAR	STALK	STRIP	SWUNG
SNARL	SPECK	STALL	STROP	SYLPH
SNATH	SPECS	STAMP	STRUM	SYNOD
SNEAD	SPEED	STAND	STRUT	SYRUP
SNEAK	SPELL	STANK	STUCK	
SNEER	SPELT	STARE	STUDY	
SNICK	SPEND	STARK	STUFF	T – 5
SNIDE	SPERM	START	STUMP	TABBY
SNIFF	SPICE	STASH	STUNG	TABLE
SNIPE	SPICK	STATE	STUNK	TABOO
SNOEK	SPICY	STAVE	STUNT	TACIT
SNOOD	SPIED	STEAD	STYLE	TACKY
SNOOP	SPIKE	STEAK	STYLO	TAFFY
SNORE	SPIKY	STEAL	SUAVE	TAILS
SNORT	SPILL	STEAM	SUEDE	TAINT
SNOUT	SPILT	STEED	SUETY	TAKEN
SNOWY	SPINE	STEEL	SUGAR	TAKER
SNUFF	SPINY	STEEP	SUING	TALES
SOAPY	SPIRE	STEER	SUITE	TALLY
SOBER	SPITE	STEIN	SULKS	TALON
SOGGY	SPLAY	STERN	SULKY	TAMED
SOLAR	SPLIT	STICK	SULLY	TAMER
SOLDO	SPODE	STIFF	SUNNY	TAMIL
SOLED	SPOIL	STILE	SUN-UP	TAMMY
SOL-FA	SPOKE	STILL	SUPER	TANGO
SOLID	SPOOF	STILT	SURER	TANGY
SOLUS	SPOOK	STING	SURGE	TANSY
SOLVE	SPOOL	STINK	SURLY	TAPAS
SONAR	SPOON	STINT	SWAIN	TAPED
SONIC	SPOOR	STOAT	SWALE	TAPER
SONNY	SPORE	STOCK	SWAMP	TAPIR
SOOTH	SPORT	STOEP	SWANK	TARDY
SOOTY	SPOUT	STOIC	SWARD	TAROT
SOPPY	SPRAT	STOKE	SWARF	TARRY
SORBO	SPRAY	STOLE	SWARM	TASTE
SORER	SPREE	STOMA	SWATS	TATTY
SORRY	SPRIG	STOMP	SWEAR	TAUNT
SOUGH	SPRIT	STONE	SWEAT	TAWNY
SOUND	SPUME	STONY	SWEDE	TAXED
SOUPY	SPURN	STOOD	SWEEP	TEACH
SOUSE	SPURT	STOOK	SWEET	TEASE
SOUTH	SQUAB	STOOL	SWELL	TEDDY
SOWAR	SQUAD	STOOP	SWEPT	TEENS

TEENY	TILER	TREAT	TWIST	UTTER
TEETH	TILTH	TREED	TWITE	UVULA
TEHEE	TIMED	TREND	TWIXT	
TELEX	TIMID	TRESS	TYING	**V – 5**
TEMPO	TIMON	TREWS	TYPED	
TEMPT	TINED	TRIAL		VAGUE
TENCH	TINGE	TRIBE		VALET
TENET	TINNY	TRICE	**U – 5**	VALID
TENON	TIPSY	TRICK		VALSE
TENOR	TIRED	TRIED	U-BOAT	VALUE
TENSE	TITAN	TRIER	UDDER	VALVE
TENTH	TITHE	TRILL	UHLAN	VANED
TEPEE	TITLE	TRIPE	UKASE	VAPID
TEPID	TIZZY	TRITE	ULCER	VASTY
TEPOR	TOADY	TROLL	ULNAR	VAULT
TERRA	TOAST	TRONC	ULTRA	VAUNT
TERRY	TODAY	TROOP	UMBEL	VEGAN
TERSE	TODDY	TROTH	UMBER	VELDT
TESLA	TOKAY	TROUT	UMBRA	VENAL
TESTY	TOKEN	TROVE	UNAPT	VENOM
THANE	TOMMY	TRUCE	UNARM	VENUE
THANK	TONAL	TRUCK	UNBAR	VENUS
THEFT	TONED	TRUER	UNBID	VERGE
THEIR	TONGA	TRULY	UNCLE	VERSE
THEME	TONIC	TRUMP	UNCUT	VERSO
THERE	TONNE	TRUNK	UNDER	VERST
THERM	TOOTH	TRUSS	UNDID	VERVE
THESE	TOPAZ	TRUST	UNDUE	VESPA
THETA	TOPEE	TRUTH	UNFED	VESTA
THICK	TOPER	TRY-ON	UNFIT	VETCH
THIEF	TOPIC	TRYST	UNFIX	VEXED
THIGH	TOQUE	TUBBY	UNIFY	VIAND
THINE	TORCH	TUBED	UNION	VIBES
THING	TORSO	TUBER	UNITE	VICAR
THINK	TOTAL	TUDOR	UNITY	VIDEO
THIRD	TOTEM	TULIP	UNLED	VIGIL
THOLE	TOTED	TULLE	UNLET	VILER
THONG	TOUCH	TUNED	UNMAN	VILLA
THORN	TOUGH	TUNER	UNPEG	VIOLA
THOSE	TOWED	TUNIS	UNPEN	VIPER
THREE	TOWEL	TUNNY	UNPIN	VIRGO
THREW	TOWER	TURFY	UNSET	VIRTU
THROB	TOWNY	TURPS	UNTIE	VIRUS
THROE	TOXIC	TUTOR	UNTIL	VISIT
THROW	TOXIN	TUTTI	UNWED	VISOR
THUMB	TOYED	TWAIN	UP-END	VISTA
THUMP	TRACE	TWANG	UPPER	VITAL
THYME	TRACK	TWEAK	UPSET	VIVAT
TIARA	TRACT	TWEED	URBAN	VIVID
TIBET	TRADE	TWEEN	URGED	VIZOR
TIBIA	TRAIL	TWERP	URIAL	VOCAL
TIDAL	TRAIN	TWICE	USAGE	VODKA
TIDED	TRAMP	TWILL	USHER	VOGUE
TIGER	TRASH	TWINE	USING	VOICE
TIGHT	TRAWL	TWINS	USUAL	VOILE
TILED	TREAD	TWIRL	USURP	VOMIT
			USURY	

VOTED	WATER	WHIRL	WIVES	X – 5
VOTER	WAVED	WHISK	WODEN	
VOUCH	WAVER	WHIST	WOMAN	XEBEC
VOWED	WAXED	WHITE	WOMEN	X-RAYS
VOWEL	WAXEN	WHIZZ	WOODY	
VYING	WEALD	WHOLE	WOOED	Y – 5
	WEARY	WHOOP	WOOER	
	WEAVE	WHORL	WORDY	YACHT
W – 5	WEDGE	WHOSE	WORLD	YAHOO
	WEEDS	WHOSO	WORMY	YAWED
WADED	WEEDY	WIDEN	WORRY	YEARN
WADER	WEEPY	WIDER	WORSE	YEAST
WAFER	WEIGH	WIDOW	WORST	YIELD
WAGED	WEIRD	WIDTH	WORTH	YOBBO
WAGER	WELSH	WIELD	WOULD	YODEL
WAGES	WENCH	WIGHT	WOUND	YOKED
WAGON	WHACK	WILLY	WOVEN	YOKEL
WAIST	WHALE	WINCE	WRACK	YOUNG
WAITS	WHANG	WINCH	WRATH	YOURS
WAIVE	WHARF	WINDY	WREAK	YOUTH
WAKEN	WHEAT	WINED	WRECK	YUCCA
WALLY	WHEEL	WIPED	WREST	YUPPY
WALTZ	WHELK	WIPER	WRING	
WANED	WHELP	WIRED	WRIST	Z – 5
WANLY	WHERE	WISER	WRITE	
WARES	WHICH	WISPY	WRONG	ZEBRA
WASHY	WHIFF	WITCH	WROTE	ZEBUS
WASTE	WHILE	WITHY	WRUNG	ZINCO
WATCH	WHINE	WITTY	WRYLY	ZONAL
				ZONED

A – 6

	ADRIFT	ALLURE	ARCADY
	ADROIT	ALMOND	ARCHED
ABACUS	ADVENT	ALMOST	ARCHER
ABASED	ADVERT	ALPACA	ARCHLY
ABATED	ADVICE	ALPINE	ARCING
ABBESS	ADVISE	ALPINI	ARCTIC
ABDUCT	AENEID	ALUMNA	ARDENT
ABIDED	AERATE	ALUMNI	ARDOUR
ABJECT	AERIAL	ALWAYS	ARGALI
ABJURE	AERTEX	AMAZED	ARGENT
ABLAZE	AFFAIR	AMAZON	ARGOSY
ABLEST	AFFECT	AMBLED	ARGUED
ABLOOM	AFFIRM	AMBLER	ARIGHT
ABOARD	AFFORD	AMBUSH	ARISEN
ABOUND	AFFRAY	AMOEBA	ARMADA
ABRADE	AFGHAN	AMORAL	ARMIES
ABROAD	AFLAME	AMOUNT	ARMING
ABRUPT	AFLOAT	AMPERE	ARMLET
ABSENT	AFRAID	AMPLER	ARMOUR
ABSORB	AFRESH	AMULET	ARMPIT
ABSURD	AGARIC	AMUSED	ARNICA
ABUSED	AGEING	ANCHOR	AROUND
ABVOLT	AGENCY	ANCONA	AROUSE
ABWATT	AGENDA	ANGINA	ARRACK
ACACIA	AGHAST	ANGLED	ARRANT
ACCEDE	AGNATE	ANGLER	ARREAR
ACCENT	AGOING	ANGOLA	ARREST
ACCEPT	AGOUTI	ANGORA	ARRIVE
ACCESS	AGREED	ANIMAL	ARTERY
ACCORD	AIDING	ANIMUS	ARTFUL
ACCOST	AIKIDO	ANKLET	ARTIST
ACCRUE	AILING	ANNALS	ASCEND
ACETIC	AIMING	ANNEAL	ASCENT
ACHING	AIRBAG	ANNEXE	ASHAKE
ACIDIC	AIR-BED	ANNUAL	ASHLAR
ACK-ACK	AIRBUS	ANOINT	ASHORE
ACQUIT	AIR-GUN	ANONYM	ASH-PAN
ACROSS	AIRILY	ANSWER	ASH-PIT
ACTING	AIRING	ANTHEM	ASKANT
ACTION	AIRMAN	ANTHER	ASKARI
ACTIVE	AIR-SAC	ANTLER	ASKING
ACTUAL	AIRWAY	ANYHOW	ASLANT
ACUITY	AKIMBO	ANYWAY	ASLEEP
ACUMEN	ALARUM	APACHE	ASPECT
ADAGIO	ALBEIT	APATHY	ASPIRE
ADDICT	ALBERT	APIARY	ASSAIL
ADDING	ALBINO	APIECE	ASSENT
ADDLED	ALBION	APLOMB	ASSERT
ADDUCE	ALCOVE	APPEAL	ASSESS
ADHERE	ALIGHT	APPEAR	ASSIGN
ADJOIN	ALKALI	APPEND	ASSIST
ADJURE	ALLEGE	ARABIC	ASSIZE
ADJUST	ALLIED	ARABIS	ASSORT
ADMIRE	ALLIES	ARABLE	ASSUME
ADONIS	ALL-OUT	ARBOUR	ASSURE
ADORED	ALLUDE	ARCADE	ASTERN

ASTHMA	BAGGED	BARREL	BEDECK
ASTRAL	BAGMAN	BARREN	BEDLAM
ASTRAY	BAGNIO	BARROW	BEETLE
ASTUTE	BAILED	BARSAC	BEFALL
ASYLUM	BAILEY	BARTER	BEFORE
ATHENE	BAILIE	BARTON	BEFOUL
AT-HOME	BAITED	BARYON	BEGGAR
ATKINS	BAKERY	BASALT	BEGGED
ATOMIC	BAKING	BASELY	BEGONE
ATONED	BALAAM	BASHED	BEHALF
ATTACH	BALDER	BASING	BEHAVE
ATTACK	BALDLY	BASKED	BEHEAD
ATTAIN	BALEEN	BASKET	BEHELD
ATTEND	BALING	BASQUE	BEHEST
ATTEST	BALKAN	BASSET	BEHIND
ATTIRE	BALKED	BASTED	BEHOLD
ATTUNE	BALLAD	BATEAU	BELDAM
AUBURN	BALLET	BATHED	BELFRY
AUGURY	BALLOT	BATHER	BELIAL
AUGUST	BALSAM	BATHOS	BELIED
AUNTIE	BALTIC	BATMAN	BELIEF
AURIST	BAMBOO	BATTED	BELLOW
AURORA	BANANA	BATTEN	BELONG
AUSSIE	BANDED	BATTER	BELTED
AUSTER	BANDIT	BATTLE	BEMOAN
AUSTIN	BANGED	BAUBLE	BEMUSE
AUTHOR	BANGLE	BAWBEE	BENDER
AUTUMN	BANISH	BAWLED	BENGAL
AVAUNT	BANKED	BAWLEY	BENIGN
AVENGE	BANKER	BAXTER	BENNET
AVENUE	BANNED	BAYARD	BENUMB
AVERSE	BANNER	BAYEUX	BENZOL
AVIARY	BANTAM	BAYING	BERATE
AVIDLY	BANTER	BAZAAR	BERBER
AVOCET	BANYAN	BEACHY	BEREFT
AVOWAL	BANZAI	BEACON	BERLIN
AVOWED	BAOBAB	BEADED	BERTHA
AWAKEN	BARBED	BEADLE	BESIDE
AWEIGH	BARBEL	BEAGLE	BESTED
AWHEEL	BARBER	BEAKER	BESTIR
AWHILE	BARDIC	BEAMED	BESTOW
AWNING	BARELY	BEARER	BETAKE
AYE-AYE	BAREST	BEATEN	BETHEL
AZALEA	BARGED	BEATER	BETIDE
	BARGEE	BEAUNE	BETONY
	BARING	BEAUTY	BETRAY
B – 6	BARIUM	BEAVER	BETTED
	BARKED	BECALM	BETTER
BAAING	BARKER	BECAME	BETTOR
BABBLE	BARKIS	BECKET	BEWAIL
BABOON	BARLEY	BECKON	BEWARE
BACKED	BARMAN	BECOME	BEYOND
BACKER	BARNEY	BEDAUB	BIASED
BACKUP	BARONY	BED-BUG	BIBBER
BADGER	BARQUE	BEDDED	BICEPS
BAFFLE	BARRED	BEDDER	BICKER
BAGFUL			

BIDDER	BOFFIN	BRAHMA	BUFFER
BIDDING	BOGGLE	BRAINY	BUFFET
BIFFED	BOG-OAK	BRAISE	BUGLER
BIGAMY	BOILED	BRAKED	BULGAR
BIG-END	BOILER	BRANCH	BULGED
BIGGER	BOLDER	BRANDY	BULKED
BIG-WIG	BOLDLY	BRASSY	BULLET
BIKING	BOLERO	BRAVED	BUMPED
BILKED	BOLTED	BRAVER	BUMPER
BILKER	BOMBED	BRAWNY	BUNDLE
BILLED	BON-BON	BRAZED	BUNGED
BILLET	BONDED	BRAZEN	BUNGLE
BILLIE	BONING	BREACH	BUNION
BILLOW	BONNET	BREAST	BUNKED
BINARY	BONNIE	BREATH	BUNKER
BINDER	BOODLE	BREECH	BUNKUM
BIONIC	BOOHOO	BREEKS	BUNSEN
BIRDIE	BOOING	BREEZE	BUNTER
BISECT	BOOKED	BREEZY	BUOYED
BISHOP	BOOKIE	BRETON	BURBLE
BISLEY	BOOMED	BREVET	BURDEN
BISTRO	BOOTED	BREWED	BUREAU
BITING	BOOTEE	BREWER	BURGEE
BITTEN	BO-PEEP	BRIBED	BURGLE
BITTER	BORAGE	BRIDAL	BURIAL
BLAMED	BORDER	BRIDGE	BURIED
BLANCH	BOREAS	BRIDLE	BURMAN
BLARED	BORING	BRIGHT	BURNED
BLAZED	BORROW	BRITON	BURNER
BLAZER	BORZOI	BROACH	BURNET
BLEACH	BOSCHE	BROADS	BURRED
BLEARY	BOSSED	BROGAN	BURROW
BLENNY	BOSTON	BROGUE	BURSAR
BLIGHT	BOTANY	BROKEN	BURTON
BLITHE	BOTHER	BROKER	BUSHEL
BLONDE	BOTHIE	BROLLY	BUSIED
BLOODY	BOTTLE	BRONCO	BUSILY
BLOTCH	BOTTOM	BRONZE	BUSKER
BLOTTO	BOUFFE	BROOCH	BUSMEN
BLOUSE	BOUGHT	BROODY	BUSTED
BLOWED	BOUNCE	BROUGH	BUSTER
BLOWER	BOUNTY	BROWSE	BUSTLE
BLOWZY	BOURSE	BRUISE	BUTANE
BLUEST	BOVINE	BRUNCH	BUTLER
BLUING	BOWERY	BRUTAL	BUTTED
BLUISH	BOWING	BRUTUS	BUTTER
BOATER	BOWLED	BRYONY	BUTTON
BOBBED	BOWLER	BUBBLE	BUYING
BOBBIN	BOWMAN	BUBBLY	BUZZED
BOBBLE	BOW-SAW	BUCKED	BUZZER
BODEGA	BOW-TIE	BUCKET	BYE-BYE
BODGER	BOW-WOW	BUCKLE	BYGONE
BODICE	BOXING	BUDDED	BYPASS
BODILY	BOYISH	BUDDHA	BY-PLAY
BODING	BRACED	BUDGET	BY-ROAD
BODKIN	BRACER	BUFFED	BYWORD

C – 6	CAPFUL	CEDING	CHORAL
	CAPPED	CELERY	CHORUS
CABLED	CAPTOR	CELLAR	CHOSEN
CABMAN	CARAFE	CELTIC	CHOUGH
CACHED	CARBON	CEMENT	CHROME
CACHET	CARBOY	CENSER	CHUBBY
CACHOU	CARDED	CENSOR	CHUKKA
CACKLE	CAREEN	CENSUS	CHUMMY
CACTUS	CAREER	CENTRE	CHURCH
CADDIE	CARESS	CEREAL	CICADA
CADDIS	CARFAX	CERISE	CICELY
CADGED	CARIES	CHAFED	CICERO
CADGER	CARMAN	CHAFER	CINDER
CAESAR	CARMEN	CHAISE	CINEMA
CAGING	CARNAL	CHALET	CINQUE
CAHOOT	CARNET	CHALKY	CIPHER
CAIMAN	CARPED	CHANCE	CIRCLE
CAIQUE	CARPEL	CHANCY	CIRCUS
CAJOLE	CARPET	CHANGE	CIRRUS
CAKING	CARROT	CHANTY	CITING
CALICO	CARTED	CHAPEL	CITRIC
CALIPH	CARTEL	CHAPPY	CITRON
CALLER	CARTER	CHARGE	CITRUS
CALLOW	CARTON	CHARON	CIVICS
CALMED	CARVED	CHASED	CLAMMY
CALMLY	CASHED	CHASER	CLARET
CALVED	CASHEW	CHASSE	CLASSY
CAMBER	CASING	CHASTE	CLAUSE
CAMERA	CASINO	CHATTY	CLAWED
CAMLET	CASKET	CHEEKY	CLAYEY
CAMPED	CASSIA	CHEERY	CLEAVE
CAMPER	CASTLE	CHEESE	CLENCH
CAMPUS	CASTOR	CHEESY	CLERGY
CANAPE	CASUAL	CHEQUE	CLERIC
CANARD	CATCHY	CHERRY	CLEVER
CANARY	CATGUT	CHERUB	CLEVIS
CANCAN	CATHAY	CHESTY	CLICHE
CANCEL	CATKIN	CHEVAL	CLIENT
CANCER	CATNIP	CHEWED	CLIMAX
CANDID	CATSUP	CHILDE	CLINCH
CANDLE	CATTLE	CHILLI	CLINIC
CANINE	CAUCUS	CHILLY	CLIQUE
CANING	CAUDAL	CHIMED	CLOCHE
CANKER	CAUGHT	CHINTZ	CLOSED
CANNED	CAUSED	CHIPPY	CLOSER
CANNON	CAVEAT	CHIRPY	CLOSET
CANNOT	CAVERN	CHISEL	CLOTHE
CANOPY	CAVIAR	CHITTY	CLOUDY
CANTAB	CAVIES	CHOICE	CLOVEN
CANTED	CAVING	CHOKED	CLOVER
CANTER	CAVITY	CHOKER	CLOYED
CANTON	CAVORT	CHOLER	CLUMSY
CANTOR	CAXTON	CHOOSE	CLUTCH
CANUCK	CAYMAN	CHOOSY	COARSE
CANVAS	CAYUSE	CHOPIN	COATED
CANYON	CEASED	CHOPPY	COATEE

COAXED	CONKED	COUPON	CUDDLE
COAXER	CONKER	COURSE	CUDGEL
COBALT	CONSUL	COUSIN	CULLED
COBBLE	CONTRA	COVERT	CUPFUL
COBNUT	CONVEX	COWARD	CUPOLA
COBURG	CONVEY	COWBOY	CUPPED
COBWEB	CONVOY	COWING	CUP-TIE
COCKED	COOEED	COWLED	CURACY
COCKER	COOING	COW-MAN	CURARE
COCKLE	COOKED	COWRIE	CURATE
COCOON	COOKER	COYOTE	CURBED
CODDED	COOKIE	CRABBY	CURDLE
CODGER	COOLED	CRADLE	CURFEW
CODIFY	COOLER	CRAFTY	CURING
CODING	COOLIE	CRAGGY	CURLED
CODLIN	COOLLY	CRAMBO	CURLER
COERCE	COOPED	CRANED	CURLEW
COEVAL	COOPER	CRANKY	CURSED
COFFEE	COPECK	CRANNY	CURSOR
COFFER	COPIED	CRATED	CURTLY
COFFIN	COPIER	CRATER	CURTSY
COGENT	COPING	CRAVAT	CURVED
COGNAC	COPPED	CRAVED	CUSTOM
CO-HEIR	COPPER	CRAVEN	CUTEST
COHERE	COPTIC	CRAYON	CUTLER
COHORT	COQUET	CRAZED	CUTLET
COILED	CORBEL	CREAMY	CUT-OFF
COINED	CORDED	CREASE	CUT-OUT
COINER	CORDON	CREATE	CUTTER
COKING	CORKED	CRECHE	CUTTLE
COLDER	CORKER	CREDIT	CYBORG
COLDLY	CORNEA	CREEPY	CYCLED
COLLIE	CORNED	CREOLE	CYGNET
COLLOP	CORNER	CRESTA	CYMBAL
COLONY	CORNET	CRETIN	CYMRIC
COLOUR	CORONA	CREWEL	CYPHER
COLUMN	CORPSE	CRIKEY	CYPRUS
COMBAT	CORPUS	CRINGE	
COMBED	CORRAL	CRISES	
COMBER	CORSET	CRISIS	D – 6
COMEDY	CORTES	CRISPY	
COMELY	COSHED	CRITIC	DABBED
COMFIT	COSIER	CROCUS	DABBLE
COMING	COSILY	CROTCH	DACOIT
COMMIT	COSINE	CROUCH	DAFTLY
COMMON	COSMIC	CROWED	DAGGER
COMPEL	COSMID	CRUDER	DAHLIA
COMPLY	COSMOS	CRUISE	DAINTY
CONCHY	COSSET	CRUMBY	DAMAGE
CONCUR	COSTER	CRUNCH	DAMASK
CONNED	COSTLY	CRUSTY	DAMMED
CONDOR	COTTAR	CRUTCH	DAMNED
CONFAB	COTTER	CRYING	DAMPED
CONFER	COTTON	CUBISM	DAMPEN
CONGEE	COUGAR	CUBIST	DAMPER
CONGER	COUPLE	CUCKOO	DAMPLY
			DAMSEL

DAMSON	DEDUCE	DESIST	DISBUD
DANCED	DEDUCT	DESPOT	DISCUS
DANCER	DEEMED	DETACH	DISHED
DANDER	DEEPEN	DETAIL	DISMAL
DANDLE	DEEPER	DETAIN	DISMAY
DANGER	DEEPLY	DETECT	DISOWN
DANGLE	DEFACE	DETEST	DISPEL
DANIEL	DEFAME	DETOUR	DISTIL
DANISH	DEFEAT	DETUNE	DISUSE
DAPHNE	DEFECT	DEUCED	DITHER
DAPPER	DEFEND	DEVICE	DIVERS
DAPPLE	DEFIED	DEVISE	DIVERT
DARING	DEFILE	DEVOID	DIVEST
DARKEN	DEFINE	DEVOTE	DIVIDE
DARKER	DEFORM	DEVOUR	DIVINE
DARKLY	DEFRAY	DEVOUT	DIVING
DARNED	DEFTLY	DEWLAP	DOBBIN
DARNEL	DEFUSE	DEXTER	DOCILE
DARNER	DEGREE	DIADEM	DOCKED
DARTED	DE-ICER	DIAPER	DOCKER
DASHED	DEJECT	DIATOM	DOCKET
DATING	DELETE	DIBBED	DOCTOR
DATIVE	DELUDE	DIBBER	DODDER
DAUBED	DELUGE	DIBBLE	DODGED
DAVITS	DEMAND	DICING	DODGER
DAWDLE	DEMEAN	DICKER	DOFFED
DAWNED	DEMISE	DICKEY	DOG-FOX
DAY-BED	DEMODE	DICTUM	DOGGED
DAY-FLY	DEMOTE	DIDDLE	DOINGS
DAZING	DEMURE	DIESEL	DOLING
DAZZLE	DENIAL	DIETED	DOLLAR
DEACON	DENIED	DIFFER	DOLLED
DEADEN	DENIER	DIGEST	DOLLOP
DEADLY	DENOTE	DIGGER	DOLMEN
DEAFEN	DENSER	DIK-DIK	DOLOUR
DEAFLY	DENTAL	DIKING	DOMAIN
DEALER	DENUDE	DILATE	DOMINO
DEARER	DEODAR	DILUTE	DONATE
DEARIE	DEPART	DIMITY	DONGLE
DEARLY	DEPEND	DIMMED	DONJON
DEARTH	DEPICT	DIMMER	DONKEY
DEBASE	DEPLOY	DIMPLE	DOODLE
DEBATE	DEPORT	DIMPLY	DOOMED
DEBRIS	DEPOSE	DINGHY	DOPING
DEBTOR	DEPUTE	DINGLE	DORCAS
DEBUNK	DEPUTY	DINING	DORIAN
DECADE	DERAIL	DINKUM	DORMER
DECAMP	DERATE	DINNED	DORSAL
DECANT	DERIDE	DINNER	DOSAGE
DECEIT	DERIVE	DIPOLE	DOTAGE
DECENT	DERMAL	DIPPED	DOTARD
DECIDE	DERMIS	DIPPER	DOTING
DECKED	DESCRY	DIRECT	DOTTED
DECKLE	DESERT	DIREST	DOTTLE
DECODE	DESIGN	DISARM	DOUANE
DECREE	DESIRE	DISBAR	DOUBLE

DOUCHE	DURING	ELOPED	EOCENE
DOUGHY	DUSTER	ELUDED	EOLITH
DOURLY	DUYKER	ELVISH	EQUATE
DOUSED	DYEING	ELYSEE	EQUINE
DOWNED	DYNAMO	EMBALM	EQUITY
DOWSED	DYNAST	EMBARK	ERASED
DOWSER		EMBLEM	ERASER
DOYLEY		EMBODY	EREBUS
DOZING	**E – 6**	EMBOSS	ERENOW
DRACHM	EAGLET	EMBRYO	ERMINE
DRAGON	EAR-CAP	EMERGE	ERODED
DRAPED	EARFUL	EMETIC	EROTIC
DRAPER	EARNED	EMIGRE	ERRAND
DRAWER	EARTHY	EMPIRE	ERRANT
DREAMT	EARWIG	EMPLOY	ERRATA
DREAMY	EASIER	ENABLE	ERRING
DREARY	EASILY	ENAMEL	ERSATZ
DREDGE	EASING	ENCAGE	ESCAPE
DRENCH	EASTER	ENCAMP	ESCHEW
DRESSY	EATING	ENCASE	ESCORT
DRIEST	EBBING	ENCASH	ESCUDO
DRIVEL	ECARTE	ENCORE	ESKIMO
DRIVEN	ECHOED	END-ALL	ESPIAL
DRIVER	ECLAIR	ENDEAR	ESPIED
DRONED	ECZEMA	ENDING	ESPRIT
DROPSY	EDDIED	ENDIVE	ESSENE
DROVER	EDGING	ENDURE	ESTATE
DROWSY	EDIBLE	ENERGY	ESTEEM
DRUDGE	EDITED	ENFOLD	ETCHED
DRY-BOB	EDITOR	ENGAGE	ETCHER
DRY-FLY	EDUCED	ENGINE	ETHICS
DRYING	EERILY	ENGULF	ETHNIC
DRYISH	EFFACE	ENIGMA	EUCHRE
DRY-ROT	EFFECT	ENJOIN	EUCLID
DUBBED	EFFETE	ENLACE	EULOGY
DUBBIN	EFFIGY	ENLIST	EUNUCH
DUCKED	EFFLUX	ENMESH	EUREKA
DUENNA	EFFORT	ENMITY	EUSTON
DUFFEL	EGG-CUP	ENNEAD	EVADED
DUFFER	EGGING	ENOUGH	EVENER
DUFFLE	EGG-NOG	ENRAGE	EVENLY
DUGONG	EGOISM	ENRICH	EVILLY
DUGOUT	EGOIST	ENROBE	EVINCE
DUIKER	EGRESS	ENSIGN	EVOLVE
DULCET	EIFFEL	ENSUED	EXCEED
DULLED	EIGHTH	ENSURE	EXCEPT
DULLER	EIGHTY	ENTAIL	EXCESS
DUMBLY	EITHER	ENTICE	EXCISE
DUMDUM	ELAINE	ENTIRE	EXCITE
DUMPED	ELAPSE	ENTITY	EXCUSE
DUNLIN	ELATED	ENTOMB	EXEMPT
DUNNED	ELDEST	ENTRAP	EXEUNT
DUPING	ELEVEN	ENTREE	EXHALE
DURBAR	ELFISH	ENVIED	EXHORT
DURESS	ELICIT	ENWRAP	EXHUME
DURHAM	ELIXIR	ENZYME	EXILED

EXODUS	FARROW	FIERCE	FLEDGE
EXOTIC	FASCIA	FIGARO	FLEECE
EXPAND	FASTED	FIGURE	FLEECY
EXPECT	FASTEN	FILIAL	FLESHY
EXPEND	FASTER	FILING	FLEXED
EXPERT	FATHER	FILLED	FLEXOR
EXPIRE	FATHOM	FILLER	FLICKS
EXPIRY	FATTED	FILLET	FLIGHT
EXPORT	FATTEN	FILLIP	FLIMSY
EXPOSE	FATTER	FILMED	FLINCH
EXTANT	FAUCET	FILTER	FLINTY
EXTEND	FAULTY	FILTHY	FLITCH
EXTENT	FAVOUR	FINALE	FLOPPY
EXTORT	FAWNED	FINDER	FLORAL
EXUDED	FEALTY	FINELY	FLORET
EYEFUL	FEARED	FINERY	FLORID
EYEING	FEDORA	FINEST	FLORIN
EYELET	FEEBLE	FINGER	FLOSSY
EYELID	FEEBLY	FINIAL	FLOURY
	FEEDER	FINING	FLOWER
	FEELER	FINISH	FLUENT
F – 6	FELINE	FINITE	FLUFFY
	FELLAH	FINNAN	FLUKED
FABIAN	FELLED	FINNED	FLUNKY
FABLED	FELLER	FIRING	FLURRY
FABRIC	FELLOE	FIRKIN	FLUTED
FACADE	FELLOW	FIRMED	FLUXED
FACIAL	FELONY	FIRMLY	FLYING
FACILE	FELTED	FISCAL	FLY-NET
FACING	FEMALE	FISHED	FOALED
FACTOR	FENCED	FISHER	FOAMED
FADING	FENCER	FISHES	FOBBED
FAERIE	FENDED	FISTED	FO'C'SLE
FAG-END	FENDER	FISTIC	FODDER
FAGGED	FENIAN	FITFUL	FOEMAN
FAGGOT	FENNEL	FITTED	FOETID
FAILED	FERRER	FITTER	FOGGED
FAIRER	FERRET	FIXING	FOIBLE
FAIRLY	FERVID	FIXITY	FOILED
FAKING	FESCUE	FIZZED	FOKKER
FALCON	FESTAL	FIZZER	FOLDED
FALLAL	FESTER	FIZZLE	FOLDER
FALLEN	FETISH	FLABBY	FOLLOW
FALLOW	FETTER	FLAGON	FOMENT
FALSER	FETTLE	FLAKED	FONDER
FALTER	FEUDAL	FLAMED	FONDLE
FAMILY	FEWEST	FLANGE	FONDLY
FAMINE	FIACRE	FLANKS	FOODIE
FAMISH	FIANCÉ	FLARED	FOOLED
FAMOUS	FIASCO	FLASHY	FOOTED
FANGED	FIBBED	FLATLY	FOOTER
FANNED	FIBBER	FLATTY	FOOTLE
FAN-TAN	FIBULA	FLAUNT	FOOZLE
FARINA	FICKLE	FLAVIN	FORAGE
FARING	FIDDLE	FLAXEN	FORBID
FARMED	FIDGET	FLAYED	FORBYE
FARMER			

FORCED	FUMBLE	GARDEN	GILLIE
FORDED	FUNDED	GARGLE	GILPIN
FOREGO	FUNGUS	GARISH	GIMBAL
FOREST	FUNKED	GARLIC	GIMLET
FORGED	FUNNEL	GARNER	GINGER
FORGER	FURIES	GARNET	GIRDED
FORGET	FURLED	GARRET	GIRDER
FORGOT	FURORE	GARTER	GIRDLE
FORKED	FURROW	GAS-BAG	GITANA
FORMAL	FUSING	GASCON	GIVING
FORMAT	FUSION	GASHED	GLADLY
FORMED	FUSSED	GASKET	GLANCE
FORMER	FUTILE	GAS-MAN	GLARED
FORMIC	FUTURE	GASPED	GLASSY
FOSSIL		GASPER	GLAZED
FOSTER		GASSED	GLAZER
FOUGHT	G – 6	GATEAU	GLIBLY
FOULED		GATHER	GLIDED
FOULLY	GABBLE	GATING	GLIDER
FOURTH	GABLED	GAUCHE	GLITCH
FOWLER	GADDED	GAUCHO	GLOBAL
FOXILY	GADFLY	GAUGED	GLOOMY
FOXING	GADGET	GAYEST	GLORIA
FRACAS	GAELIC	GAZEBO	GLOSSY
FRAMED	GAFFED	GAZING	GLOVED
FRAPPÉ	GAFFER	GAZUMP	GLOVER
FRAYED	GAGGED	GEARED	GLOWED
FREELY	GAGGLE	GEEZER	GLOWER
FREEZE	GAIETY	GEIGER	GLUING
FRENCH	GAINED	GEISHA	GLUMLY
FRENZY	GAITER	GEMINI	GLYTCH
FRESCO	GALAXY	GENDER	GNAWED
FRIARY	GALLEY	GENERA	GNOMON
FRIDAY	GALLIC	GENEVA	GOADED
FRIDGE	GALLON	GENIAL	GOATEE
FRIEND	GALLOP	GENIUS	GO-BANG
FRIEZE	GALLUP	GENTLE	GOBBET
FRIGHT	GALOOT	GENTLY	GOBBLE
FRIGID	GALORE	GENTRY	GOBLET
FRINGE	GALOSH	GEORGE	GOBLIN
FRISKY	GAMBIT	GERMAN	GO-CART
FROGGY	GAMBLE	GERUND	GO-DOWN
FROLIC	GAMBOL	GEW-GAW	GODSON
FROSTY	GAMELY	GEYSER	GODWIT
FROTHY	GAMING	GHARRY	GOFFER
FROWSY	GAMMER	GHETTO	GOGGLE
FROZEN	GAMMON	GIBBER	GOITRE
FRUGAL	GANDER	GIBBET	GOLDEN
FRUITY	GANGER	GIBBON	GOLFER
FRUMPY	GANNET	GIBING	GONGED
FUDDLE	GANTRY	GIBLET	GOODLY
FUDGED	GAOLED	GIFTED	GOOGLY
FULFIL	GAOLER	GIGGLE	GOPHER
FULHAM	GAPING	GIGOLO	GORGED
FULLER	GARAGE	GILDED	GORGET
FULMAR	GARBLE	GILDER	GORGIO
	GARCON		

GORGON	GRUDGE	HANGED	HECTOR
GORING	GRUMPY	HANGER	HEDGED
GOSHEN	GRUNDY	HANKER	HEEDED
GOSPEL	GRUNGE	HANSEL	HEE-HAW
GOSSIP	GUFFAW	HANSOM	HEELED
GOTCHA	GUIDED	HAPPEN	HEIFER
GOTHIC	GUIDER	HARASS	HEIGHT
GOUGED	GUIDON	HARDEN	HELIUM
GOVERN	GUILTY	HARDER	HELMET
GOWNED	GUINEA	HARDLY	HELPED
GRACED	GUITAR	HARD-UP	HELPER
GRACES	GULLED	HARING	HEMMED
GRADED	GULLET	HARKED	HEMPEN
GRAINS	GULLEY	HARKEN	HERALD
GRAMME	GULPED	HARLOT	HERBAL
GRANGE	GUMMED	HARMED	HERDED
GRANNY	GUN-MAN	HARPED	HEREAT
GRASSY	GUN-MEN	HARRIS	HEREBY
GRATER	GUNNEL	HARROW	HEREIN
GRATIS	GUNNER	HASTEN	HEREOF
GRAVEL	GUN-SHY	HAT-BOX	HEREON
GRAVEN	GURGLE	HATING	HERESY
GRAVER	GURKHA	HAT-PEG	HERETO
GRAVES	GURNET	HAT-PIN	HERMES
GRAZED	GUSHED	HATRED	HERMIT
GREASE	GUSHER	HATTED	HERNIA
GREASY	GUSSET	HATTER	HEROIC
GREATS	GUTTED	HAULED	HEROIN
GREECE	GUTTER	HAUNCH	HERPES
GREEDY	GUZZLE	HAVANA	HERREN
GREENS	GYBING	HAVING	HETMAN
GRETNA	GYPSUM	HAWHAW	HEWING
GRIEVE	GYRATE	HAWKED	HEYDAY
GRILLE		HAWKER	HIATUS
GRILSE		HAWSER	HICCUP
GRIMED	**H – 6**	HAYBOX	HIDDEN
GRIMLY	HACKED	HAZARD	HIDING
GRINGO	HACKER	HAZILY	HIEING
GRIPED	HACKLE	HEADED	HIGHER
GRIPPE	HADRON	HEADER	HIGHLY
GRISLY	HAGGIS	HEALED	HIKING
GRITTY	HAGGLE	HEALER	HILARY
GROATS	HAILED	HEALTH	HINDER
GROCER	HALLOA	HEAPED	HINDOO
GROGGY	HALLOW	HEARER	HINGED
GROOVE	HALOED	HEARSE	HINTED
GROPED	HALTED	HEARTH	HIPPED
GROTTO	HALTER	HEARTY	HIRING
GROTTY	HALVED	HEATED	HISSED
GROUND	HAMLET	HEATER	HITHER
GROUSE	HAMMAM	HEAVED	HITTER
GROVEL	HAMMER	HEAVEN	HOARSE
GROWER	HAMPER	HEBREW	HOAXED
GROWTH	HANDED	HECATE	HOAXER
GROYNE	HANDLE	HECKLE	HOBBLE
GRUBBY	HANGAR	HECTIC	HOBNOB

HOCKEY	HUMBUG	IMPOSE	INSURE
HOEING	HUMMED	IMPOST	INTACT
HOGGET	HUMOUR	IMPUGN	INTAKE
HOLDER	HUMPED	IMPURE	INTEND
HOLD-UP	HUNGER	IMPUTE	INTENT
HOLIER	HUNGRY	INBORN	INTERN
HOLILY	HUNTED	INBRED	INTONE
HOLLOW	HUNTER	INCHED	INURED
HOMAGE	HURDLE	INCISE	INVADE
HOMELY	HURLED	INCITE	INVENT
HOMILY	HURRAH	INCOME	INVERT
HOMING	HURTLE	INDEED	INVEST
HONEST	HUSHED	INDENT	INVITE
HONING	HUSKED	INDIAN	INVOKE
HONKED	HUSSAR	INDICT	INWARD
HONOUR	HUSSIF	INDIGO	IODINE
HOODED	HUSTLE	INDITE	IONIAN
HOODIE	HUTTED	INDOOR	IRITIS
HOODOO	HYBRID	INDUCE	IRKING
HOOFED	HYMNAL	INDUCT	IRONED
HOOKAH	HYPHEN	INFAMY	IRONER
HOOKED	HYSSOP	INFANT	IRONIC
HOOKER		INFECT	ISABEL
HOOPED	I – 6	INFEST	ISLAND
HOOPER		INFIRM	ISOBAR
HOOP-LA	IAMBIC	INFLOW	ISRAEL
HOOPOE	IBERIA	INFLUX	ISSUED
HOOTED	IBIDEM	INFORM	ISSUER
HOOTER	ICARUS	INFUSE	ITALIC
HOPING	ICE-AGE	INHALE	ITCHED
HOPPED	ICE-AXE	INHERE	ITSELF
HOPPER	ICE-CAP	INJECT	
HORNED	ICE-MAN	INJURE	
HORNER	ICE-SAW	INJURY	J – 6
HORNET	ICICLE	INK-BAG	JABBED
HORRID	ICIEST	INKING	JABBER
HORROR	IDIOCY	INK-POT	JACKAL
HOSIER	IDLING	INK-SAC	JACKED
HOSTEL	IGNITE	INLAID	JACKET
HOTBED	IGNORE	INLAND	JAGGED
HOT-DOG	IGUANA	INMATE	JAGUAR
HOT-POT	ILLUDE	INMOST	JAILED
HOTTER	ILLUME	INNATE	JAILER
HOURLY	IMBIBE	INROAD	JAMMED
HOUSED	IMBUED	INRUSH	JANGLE
HOWDAH	IMMUNE	INSANE	JARGON
HOWLED	IMMURE	INSECT	JARRED
HOWLER	IMPACT	INSERT	JASPER
HOYDEN	IMPAIR	INSIDE	JAUNTY
HUBBUB	IMPALA	INSIST	JAWING
HUDDLE	IMPALE	INSOLE	JAZZED
HUFFED	IMPART	INSPAN	JEERED
HUGELY	IMPEDE	INSTAL	JENNET
HUMANE	IMPEND	INSTEP	JERBOA
HUMBLE	IMPISH	INSTIL	JERKED
HUMBLY	IMPORT	INSULT	JERKIN

JERSEY	K – 6	KUMMEL	LAUNCH
JESTED			LAUREL
JESTER	KAFFIR		LAVING
JESUIT	KAISER	L – 6	LAVISH
JETSAM	KANAKA	LAAGER	LAWFUL
JEWESS	KAOLIN	LABIAL	LAWYER
JEWISH	KEELED	LABOUR	LAXITY
JIBBED	KEENED	LACING	LAYING
JIGGED	KEENER	LACKED	LAYMAN
JIGGLE	KEENLY	LACKEY	LAY-OUT
JIG-SAW	KEEPER	LACTIC	LAZIER
JILTED	KENNEL	LADDER	LAZILY
JINGLE	KERNEL	LADDIE	LAZING
JITTER	KERSEY	LADING	LAZULI
JOBBER	KETTLE	LADLED	LEADED
JOB-LOT	KEY-MEN	LAGGED	LEADEN
JOCKEY	KEYPAD	LAGOON	LEADER
JOCOSE	KIBOSH	LAID-UP	LEAD-IN
JOCUND	KICKED	LAMBED	LEAFED
JOGGED	KICKER	LAMELY	LEAGUE
JOGGER	KIDDED	LAMENT	LEAKED
JOHNNY	KIDDER	LAMINA	LEANED
JOINED	KIDNAP	LAMING	LEANER
JOINER	KIDNEY	LAMMAS	LEAN-TO
JOKING	KILLED	LAMMED	LEAPED
JOLTED	KILLER	LANCED	LEASED
JORDAN	KILROY	LANCER	LEAVEN
JOSEPH	KILTED	LANCET	LEAVER
JOSSER	KILTIE	LANDAU	LEDGER
JOSTLE	KIMONO	LANDED	LEERED
JOTTED	KINDER	LAPDOG	LEEWAY
JOVIAL	KINDLE	LAPFUL	LEGACY
JOYFUL	KINDLY	LAPPED	LEGATE
JOYOUS	KINEMA	LAPSED	LEGATO
JUDAIC	KINGLY	LAPTOP	LEG-BYE
JUDGED	KINKED	LARDED	LEGEND
JUGFUL	KIPPER	LARDER	LEGGED
JUGGED	KIRSCH	LARGER	LEGION
JUGGLE	KIRTLE	LARIAT	LEGIST
JUJUBE	KISMET	LARRUP	LEGUME
JULIAN	KISSED	LARVAE	LENDER
JUMBLE	KISSER	LARVAL	LENGTH
JUMPED	KITBAG	LARYNX	LENTEN
JUMPER	KITSCH	LASCAR	LENTIL
JUNGLE	KITTEN	LASHED	LEPTON
JUNIOR	KLAXON	LASSIE	LESION
JUNIUS	KLUDGE	LASTED	LESSEE
JUNKER	KNIFED	LASTLY	LESSEN
JUNKET	KNIGHT	LATEEN	LESSER
JURIST	KNOBBY	LATELY	LESSON
JUSTER	KNOTTY	LATENT	LESSOR
JUSTLY	KOODOO	LATEST	LETHAL
JUTTED	KOREAN	LATHER	LET-OFF
	KOSHER	LATTER	LETTER
	KOWTOW	LAUDED	LEVANT
	KULTUR	LAUDER	LEVITE

LEVITY	LOATHE	LUNGED	MANUAL
LEWDLY	LOBATE	LUPINE	MANURE
LEYDEN	LOBBED	LURING	MAOIST
LIABLE	LOCALE	LURKED	MAPPED
LIAISE	LOCATE	LUSTED	MAQUIS
LIBYAN	LOCKED	LUSTRE	MARAUD
LICHEN	LOCKER	LUTINE	MARBLE
LICKED	LOCKET	LUXURY	MARCEL
LIDDED	LOCK-UP	LYCEUM	MARGIN
LIEDER	LOCUST		MARIAN
LIFTED	LODGED		MARINE
LIFTER	LODGER	M – 6	MARKED
LIGNUM	LOFTED		MARKER
LIKELY	LOGGED	MACRON	MARKET
LIKING	LOGGIA	MADCAP	MARMOT
LIMBED	LOG-HUT	MADDEN	MAROON
LIMBER	LOGMAN	MADDER	MARQUE
LIMING	LOITER	MADMAN	MARRED
LIMPED	LOLLED	MADRAS	MARRON
LIMPET	LOLLOP	MAENAD	MARROW
LIMPID	LONELY	MAGGOT	MARSHY
LINAGE	LONGER	MAGNET	MARTEN
LINDEN	LOOFAH	MAGNUM	MARTIN
LINEAL	LOOKED	MAGPIE	MARTYR
LINEAR	LOOKER	MAGYAR	MARVEL
LINE-UP	LOOMED	MAHOUT	MASCOT
LINGER	LOOPED	MAIDEN	MASHED
LINING	LOOPER	MAIGRE	MASHER
LINKED	LOOSEN	MAILED	MASHIE
LINNET	LOOTED	MAIMED	MASKED
LINTEL	LOOTER	MAINLY	MASKER
LIONEL	LOPING	MAKE-UP	MASQUE
LIPPED	LOPPED	MAKING	MASSED
LIQUID	LOPPER	MALADY	MASSIF
LIQUOR	LORDED	MALAGA	MASTED
LISBON	LORDLY	MALICE	MASTER
LISPED	LOSING	MALIGN	MASTIC
LISSOM	LOTION	MALLET	MATING
LISTED	LOUDER	MALLOW	MATINS
LISTEN	LOUDLY	MALTED	MATRIX
LISTER	LOUNGE	MAMMAL	MATRON
LITANY	LOUVRE	MAMMON	MATTED
LITCHI	LOVELY	MANAGE	MATTER
LITMUS	LOVING	MANANA	MATURE
LITTER	LOWEST	MANCHU	MAULED
LITTLE	LOWING	MANEGE	MAUNDY
LIVELY	LUBBER	MANFUL	MAUSER
LIVERY	LUFFED	MANGER	MAY-BUG
LIVING	LUGGED	MANGLE	MAYDAY
LIZARD	LUGGER	MANIAC	MAYFLY
LLOYD'S	LULLED	MANIOC	MAYHAP
LOADED	LUMBAR	MANNED	MAYHEM
LOADER	LUMBER	MANNER	MEADOW
LOAFED	LUMPED	MANTEL	MEAGRE
LOAFER	LUNACY	MANTIS	MEALIE
LOANED	LUNATE	MANTLE	MEANLY
		MANTUA	

MEASLY	MID-RIB	MOATED	MOUNTY
MEDDLE	MIDWAY	MOBBED	MOUSER
MEDIAL	MIGHTY	MOBCAP	MOUSSE
MEDIAN	MIGNON	MOBILE	MOUTHY
MEDICO	MIKADO	MOB-LAW	MOVIES
MEDIUM	MILADY	MOCKED	MOVING
MEDLAR	MILDEN	MOCKER	MOWING
MEDLEY	MILDER	MODENA	MUCKED
MEDUSA	MILDEW	MODERN	MUCKER
MEEKER	MILDLY	MODEST	MUCKLE
MEEKLY	MILIEU	MODIFY	MUCOUS
MEETLY	MILKED	MODISH	MUDDLE
MEGILP	MILKEN	MODULE	MUD-PIE
MEGOHM	MILKER	MOHAIR	MUFFED
MEGRIM	MILLED	MOHAWK	MUFFIN
MELLOW	MILLER	MOIETY	MUFFLE
MELODY	MILLET	MOLOCH	MUGGED
MELTED	MILORD	MOLEST	MUGGER
MELTER	MIMING	MOLTEN	MULISH
MELTON	MIMOSA	MOMENT	MULLED
MEMBER	MINCED	MONDAY	MULLET
MEMOIR	MINCER	MONGOL	MUMBLE
MEMORY	MINDED	MONIES	MUMMER
MENACE	MINDER	MONIED	MURDER
MENAGE	MINGLE	MONKEY	MURMUR
MENDED	MINIFY	MONODY	MURPHY
MENDER	MINING	MOOING	MUSCAT
MENIAL	MINION	MOONED	MUSCLE
MENTAL	MINNIE	MOONER	MUSEUM
MENTOR	MINNOW	MOOTED	MUSING
MERCER	MINOAN	MOOTER	MUSKET
MERELY	MINTED	MOPING	MUSLIM
MERGED	MINUET	MOPISH	MUSLIN
MERGER	MINUTE	MOPPED	MUSSED
MERINO	MIRAGE	MOPPET	MUSSEL
MERLIN	MIRING	MORALE	MUSTER
MERMAN	MIRROR	MORASS	MUTATE
MESHED	MISCUE	MORBID	MUTELY
MESSED	MISERE	MORGUE	MUTING
METEOR	MISERY	MORMON	MUTINY
METHOD	MISFIT	MOROSE	MUTISM
METHYL	MISHAP	MORRIS	MUTTER
METIER	MISLAY	MORROW	MUTTON
METING	MISLED	MORSEL	MUTUAL
METRIC	MISSAL	MORTAL	MUZZLE
METTLE	MISSED	MORTAR	MYOPIA
MEWING	MISSEL	MOSAIC	MYOPIC
MIASMA	MISSIS	MOSLEM	MYRIAD
MICKLE	MISTER	MOSQUE	MYRTLE
MICRON	MISUSE	MOSTLY	MYSELF
MID-AIR	MITRAL	MOTHER	MYSTIC
MIDDAY	MITRED	MOTION	
MIDDEN	MITTEN	MOTIVE	
MIDDLE	MIXING	MOTLEY	N – 6
MIDGET	MIZZEN	MOTTLE	NAGGED
MID-OFF	MOANED	MOULDY	NAGGER

NAILED
NAILER
NAMELY
NAMING
NAPALM
NAPERY
NAPKIN
NAPPED
NARROW
NATANT
NATION
NATIVE
NATTER
NATURE
NAUGHT
NAUSEA
NEAPED
NEARBY
NEARER
NEARLY
NEATLY
NEBULA
NECKED
NECTAR
NEED-BE
NEEDED
NEEDER
NEEDLE
NEEDLY
NEGATE
NEPHEW
NEREID
NERVED
NESTED
NESTLE
NESTOR
NETHER
NETTED
NETTLE
NEUTER
NEWISH
NEWTON
NIBBED
NIBBLE
NICELY
NICENE
NICEST
NICETY
NICHED
NICKED
NICKEL
NICKER
NIGGER
NIGGLE
NIMBLE
NIMBLY

NIMBUS
NIMROD
NINETY
NIPPED
NIPPER
NIPPLE
NITRIC
NITWIT
NO-BALL
NOBBLE
NOBLER
NOBODY
NODDED
NODDER
NODDLE
NODOSE
NODULE
NOGGIN
NONAGE
NONARY
NON-COM
NON-EGO
NOODLE
NOOSED
NORDIC
NORMAL
NORMAN
NORROY
NO-SIDE
NOSING
NOTARY
NOTICE
NOTIFY
NOTING
NOTION
NOUGAT
NOUGHT
NOVENA
NOVICE
NOWAYS
NOWISE
NOZZLE
NUANCE
NUBIAN
NUBILE
NUCLEI
NUDELY
NUDGED
NUDISM
NUDIST
NUDITY
NUGGET
NUMBED
NUMBER
NUNCIO
NURSED

NURSER
NUTANT
NUTMEG
NUT-OIL
NUTRIA
NUZZLE
NYBBLE

O – 6

OAFISH
OARAGE
OARING
OBELUS
OBERON
OBEYED
OBEYER
OBITER
OBJECT
OBLATE
OBLIGE
OBLONG
OBOIST
OBSESS
OBTAIN
OBTUSE
OBVERT
OCCULT
OCCUPY
OCELOT
O'CLOCK
OCTANE
OCTANT
OCTAVE
OCTAVO
OCULAR
ODDITY
ODIOUS
OEDEMA
OFFEND
OFFICE
OFFING
OFFISH
OFFSET
OGLING
OGRESS
OILCAN
OIL-GAS
OILING
OILMAN
OIL-NUT
OLDEST
OLDISH
OLIVER
OLIVET
OMELET

OMENED
OMNIUM
ONAGER
ONCOST
ONE-MAN
ONE-WAY
ONFLOW
ONIONY
ON-LINE
ONRUSH
ONWARD
OODLES
OOLITE
OOZING
OPAQUE
OPENED
OPENER
OPENLY
OPIATE
OPINED
OPPOSE
OPPUGN
OPTICS
OPTIME
OPTING
OPTION
ORACLE
ORALLY
ORANGE
ORATED
ORATOR
ORCHID
ORDAIN
ORDEAL
ORDURE
ORGASM
ORGIES
ORIENT
ORIGAN
ORIGIN
ORIOLE
ORISON
ORMULU
ORNATE
ORPHAN
ORPHIC
OSIRIS
OSMIUM
OSPREY
OSSIFY
OSTEND
OSTLER
OTIOSE
OUSTED
OUTBID
OUTCRY

OUTDID	PANADA	PATRON	PENNED
OUTFIT	PANAMA	PATTED	PENNON
OUTFLY	PANDER	PATTEN	PENTAD
OUTING	PANDIT	PATTER	PENT-UP
OUTLAW	PANFUL	PAUNCH	PENULT
OUTLAY	PANNED	PAUPER	PENURY
OUTLET	PANTED	PAUSED	PEOPLE
OUTPUT	PANTER	PAUSER	PEPPER
OUTRUN	PANTRY	PAVAGE	PEPSIN
OUTSET	PANZER	PAVANE	PEPTIC
OUTWIT	PAPACY	PAVING	PERIOD
OVALLY	PAPERY	PAWING	PERISH
OVERDO	PAPISH	PAWNED	PERKED
OWLERY	PAPISM	PAWNEE	PERMIT
OWLISH	PAPIST	PAWNER	PERSON
OWNING	PAPUAN	PAWPAW	PERTLY
OXALIC	PARADE	PAY-DAY	PERUKE
OX-EYED	PARCEL	PAYING	PERUSE
OXFORD	PARDON	PAY-OFF	PESETA
OXLIKE	PAREIL	PAYOLA	PESTER
OXTAIL	PARENT	PEACHY	PESTLE
OXYGEN	PARGET	PEAHEN	PETARD
OYSTER	PARIAH	PEAKED	PETITE
	PARING	PEALED	PETREL
	PARISH	PEANUT	PETROL
P – 6	PARITY	PEA-POD	PETTED
	PARKED	PEARLY	PEWTER
PACIFY	PARKER	PEBBLE	PHAROS
PACING	PARKIN	PEBBLY	PHENOL
PACKED	PARLEY	PECKED	PHLEGM
PACKER	PARODY	PECKER	PHOBIA
PACKET	PAROLE	PECTEN	PHOEBE
PADDED	PARROT	PECTIC	PHONED
PADDER	PARSED	PECTIN	PHONEY
PADDLE	PARSEE	PEDALO	PHONIC
PADUAN	PARSON	PEDANT	PHOTON
PAGING	PARTED	PEDATE	PHRASE
PAGODA	PARTER	PEDDLE	PHYSIC
PAINED	PARTLY	PEDLAR	PIAZZA
PAIRED	PASCAL	PEELED	PICKED
PALACE	PASSED	PEELER	PICKER
PALATE	PASSEE	PEEPED	PICKET
PALELY	PASSER	PEEPER	PICKLE
PALING	PASSIM	PEERER	PICKUP
PALISH	PASTED	PEEVED	PICNIC
PALLAS	PASTEL	PEEWIT	PICRIC
PALLED	PASTIL	PEGGED	PIDGIN
PALLET	PASTOR	PEG-LEG	PIECED
PALLID	PASTRY	PEGTOP	PIECER
PALLOR	PATCHY	PELLET	PIEDOG
PALMAR	PATENT	PELMET	PIEMAN
PALMED	PATHIC	PELOTA	PIERCE
PALMER	PATHOS	PELVIC	PIFFLE
PALTER	PATINA	PELVIS	PIGEON
PALTRY	PATOIS	PENCIL	PIGNUT
PAMPAS	PATROL	PENMAN	PIG-STY
PAMPER			

PILAFF	PLEACH	POPERY	PRETOR
PILFER	PLEASE	POPGUN	PRETTY
PILING	PLEDGE	POPISH	PRE-WAR
PILLAR	PLEIAD	POPLAR	PREYED
PILLAU	PLENTY	POPLIN	PREYER
PILLED	PLENUM	POPPED	PRICED
PILLOW	PLEURA	POPPER	PRIDED
PILULE	PLEXUS	POPPET	PRIEST
PIMPLE	PLIANT	PORING	PRIMAL
PIMPLY	PLIERS	PORKER	PRIMER
PINCER	PLIGHT	PORKET	PRIMLY
PINDAR	PLINTH	POROUS	PRIMUS
PINEAL	PLOUGH	PORTAL	PRINCE
PINGED	PLOVER	PORTER	PRIORY
PINING	PLUCKY	PORTLY	PRISED
PINION	PLUG-IN	POSEUR	PRISMY
PINKED	PLUMED	POSING	PRISON
PINNED	PLUMPY	POSSET	PRIVET
PIPING	PLUNGE	POSSUM	PRIZED
PIPKIN	PLURAL	POSTAL	PROFIT
PIPPED	PLUSHY	POSTED	PROLIX
PIPPIN	PLYERS	POSTER	PROMPT
PIQUED	PLYING	POTASH	PRONTO
PIQUET	POCKED	POTATO	PROPEL
PIRACY	POCKET	POTBOY	PROPER
PIRATE	PODDED	POTEEN	PROSED
PISCES	PODIUM	POTENT	PROSER
PISTIL	POETIC	POTHER	PROSIT
PISTOL	POETRY	POTION	PROTON
PISTON	POGROM	POT-LID	PROVED
PITCHY	POISED	POTMAN	PROVEN
PITIED	POISER	POTTED	PROVER
PITIER	POISON	POTTER	PRUNED
PITMAN	POKING	POUDRE	PRUNER
PITSAW	POLICE	POUFFE	PRYING
PITTED	POLICY	POUNCE	PSEUDO
PLACED	POLING	POURED	PSYCHE
PLACER	POLISH	POURER	PUBLIC
PLACET	POLITE	POUTED	PUCKER
PLACID	POLITY	POUTER	PUDDLE
PLAGUE	POLLED	POWDER	PUFFED
PLAGUY	POLLEN	POW-WOW	PUFFIN
PLAICE	POLLUX	PRAISE	PUG-DOG
PLAINT	POLONY	PRANCE	PUISNE
PLANED	POMACE	PRATED	PUKKHA
PLANER	POMADE	PRATER	PULING
PLANET	POMMEL	PRAYED	PULLED
PLAQUE	POMONA	PRAYER	PULLER
PLASHY	POM-POM	PREACH	PULLET
PLASMA	POMPON	PRECIS	PULLEY
PLATAN	PONDER	PREFAB	PULPED
PLATED	POODLE	PREFER	PULPIT
PLATEN	POOLED	PREFIX	PULQUE
PLATER	POOPED	PREPAY	PULSAR
PLAYED	POORER	PRESET	PULSED
PLAYER	POORLY	PRESTO	PUMICE

PUMMEL	QUASAR	RAMIFY	REARED
PUMPED	QUAVER	RAMMED	REARER
PUMPER	QUAYED	RAMMER	REASON
PUNCHY	QUEASY	RAMPED	REAVOW
PUNDIT	QUENCH	RAMROD	REBATE
PUNIER	QUEUED	RANCHO	REBECK
PUNISH	QUINCE	RANCID	REBIND
PUNNET	QUINSY	RANDOM	REBOIL
PUNTED	QUINZE	RANGED	REBORN
PUNTER	QUIRED	RANGER	REBUFF
PUPPED	QUIRKY	RANKER	REBUKE
PUPPET	QUIVER	RANKLE	REBURY
PURDAH	QUORUM	RANKLY	RECALL
PURELY	QUOTED	RANSOM	RECANT
PUREST		RANTED	RECAST
PURGED	**R – 6**	RANTER	RECEDE
PURGER		RAPHIA	RECENT
PURIFY	RABBIN	RAPIER	RECESS
PURISM	RABBIT	RAPINE	RECIPE
PURIST	RABBLE	RAPING	RECITE
PURITY	RABIES	RAPPED	RECKED
PURLED	RACIAL	RAPPER	RECKON
PURLER	RACILY	RAREFY	RECOAL
PURPLE	RACING	RARELY	RECOCT
PURRED	RACISM	RAREST	RECOIL
PURSED	RACKED	RARITY	RECOIN
PURSER	RACKER	RASCAL	RECORD
PURSUE	RACKET	RASHER	RECOUP
PURVEY	RACOON	RASHLY	RECTOR
PUSHED	RADIAL	RASING	RECUSE
PUSHER	RADIAN	RASPED	REDACT
PUTRID	RADISH	RASPER	REDCAP
PUTSCH	RADIUM	RASTER	REDDEN
PUTTED	RADIUS	RASURE	REDEEM
PUTTEE	RAFFIA	RATHER	RED-EYE
PUTTER	RAFFLE	RATIFY	RED-GUM
PUZZLE	RAFTER	RATING	RED-HOT
PYEDOG	RAGGED	RATION	REDIAL
PYEMIA	RAGING	RATTAN	RED-OAK
PYEMIC	RAGLAN	RAT-TAT	REDRAW
PYOSIS	RAGMAN	RATTED	REDUCE
PYRENE	RAGOUT	RATTER	REDUIT
PYRITE	RAG-TAG	RATTLE	RE-DYED
PYTHON	RAIDED	RAVAGE	RE-ECHO
	RAIDER	RAVINE	REEDED
	RAILED	RAVING	REEFED
Q – 6	RAILER	RAVISH	REEFER
	RAINED	RAWISH	REEKED
QUAGGA	RAISED	RAZING	REELED
QUAGGY	RAISER	READER	REELER
QUAINT	RAISIN	REALLY	REFILL
QUAKED	RAJPUT	REALTY	REFINE
QUAKER	RAKERY	REAMED	REFLEX
QUANGO	RAKING	REAMER	REFLOW
QUARRY	RAKISH	REAPED	REFLUX
QUARTO	RAMBLE	REAPER	REFOLD
QUARTZ			

REFOOT	RENTAL	REVERS	RISING
REFORM	RENTED	REVERT	RISKED
REFUEL	RENTER	REVIEW	RISKER
REFUGE	RENTES	REVILE	RISQUE
REFUND	RE-OPEN	REVIVE	RITUAL
REFUSE	REPACK	REVOKE	RIVAGE
REFUTE	REPAID	REVOLT	RIVING
REGAIN	REPAIR	REVVED	ROADIE
REGALE	REPASS	REWARD	ROAMED
REGARD	REPAST	REWOOD	ROAMER
REGENT	REPEAL	REWORD	ROARED
REGGAE	REPEAT	RHESUS	ROARER
REGILD	REPENT	RHEUMY	ROBBED
REGIME	REPINE	RHYMED	ROBBER
REGINA	REPLAY	RHYMER	ROBING
REGION	REPORT	RHYTHM	ROBUST
REGIUS	REPOSE	RIALTO	ROCKED
REGIVE	REPPED	RIBALD	ROCKER
REGLOW	REPUGN	RIBAND	ROCKET
REGNAL	REPUTE	RIBBED	ROCOCO
REGNUM	REREAD	RIBBON	RODENT
REGRET	RESAIL	RICHER	ROILED
REHANG	RESALE	RICHES	ROLAND
REHASH	RESCUE	RICHLY	ROLLED
REHEAR	RESEAT	RICKED	ROLLER
REHEAT	RESECT	RIDDEN	ROMAIC
REINED	RESELL	RIDDLE	ROMANY
REJECT	RESEND	RIDGED	ROMIST
REJOIN	RESENT	RIDING	ROMPED
RELAID	RESHIP	RIFFLE	ROMPER
RELATE	RESIDE	RIFLED	RONDEL
RELENT	RESIGN	RIFLER	ROOFED
RELICT	RESINY	RIFTED	ROOFER
RELIED	RESIST	RIGGED	ROOKED
RELIEF	RESOLD	RIGGER	ROOKER
RELIER	RESORB	RIGOUR	ROOKIE
RELISH	RESORT	RIG-OUT	ROOMED
RELIVE	RESOWN	RILING	ROOMER
RELOAD	RESTED	RILLED	ROOTED
RELUME	RESULT	RILLET	ROOTER
REMADE	RESUME	RIMMED	ROOTLE
REMAIN	RETAIL	RIMMED	ROPERY
REMAKE	RETAIN	RINDED	ROPING
REMAND	RETAKE	RINGER	ROSARY
REMARK	RETARD	RINSED	ROSERY
REMAST	RETINA	RINSER	ROSIED
REMEDY	RETIRE	RIOTED	ROSIER
REMIND	RETOLD	RIOTER	ROSILY
REMISE	RETOOK	RIPELY	ROSINY
REMISS	RETORT	RIPEST	ROSTER
REMOTE	RETRIM	RIP-OFF	ROTARY
REMOVE	RETYRE	RIPPED	ROTATE
RENAME	REUTER	RIPPER	ROT-GUT
RENDER	REVAMP	RIPPLE	ROTTED
RENNET	REVEAL	RIPPLY	ROTTEN
RENOWN	REVERE	RIPSAW	ROTTER

ROTUND	SADDEN	SAUCER	SEA-COB
ROUBLE	SADDLE	SAVAGE	SEA-COW
ROUGED	SADISM	SAVANT	SEA-DOG
ROUMAN	SAFARI	SAVING	SEA-FOX
ROUSED	SAFELY	SAVORY	SEA-GOD
ROUSER	SAFEST	SAVOUR	SEA-HOG
ROUTED	SAFETY	SAVVEY	SEALED
ROUTER	SAGELY	SAW-FLY	SEALER
ROVING	SAGEST	SAWING	SEAMAN
ROWING	SAGGED	SAW-PIT	SEAMED
RUBATO	SAHARA	SAW-SET	SEAMER
RUBBED	SAILED	SAWYER	SEA-MEW
RUBBER	SAILER	SAXONY	SEANCE
RUBBLE	SAILOR	SAYING	SEARCH
RUBBLY	SALAAM	SCABBY	SEARED
RUBIED	SALAME	SCALED	SEASON
RUBRIC	SALARY	SCALER	SEATED
RUCKLE	SALINE	SCALES	SEA-WAY
RUDDER	SALIVA	SCAMPI	SECANT
RUDELY	SALLOW	SCANTY	SECEDE
RUDEST	SALMON	SCARAB	SECOND
RUEFUL	SALOON	SCARCE	SECRET
RUFFED	SALTED	SCARED	SECTOR
RUFFLE	SALTER	SCATHE	SECUND
RUFOUS	SALTLY	SCATTY	SECURE
RUGATE	SALUKI	SCENIC	SEDATE
RUGGED	SALUTE	SCHEME	SEDUCE
RUGGER	SALVED	SCHISM	SEEDED
RUGOSE	SALVER	SCHOOL	SEEDER
RUINED	SALVIA	SCILLA	SEEING
RUINER	SAMELY	SCONCE	SEEKER
RULING	SAMIAN	SCORCH	SEEMED
RUMBLE	SAMITE	SCORED	SEEMER
RUMOUR	SAMLET	SCORER	SEEMLY
RUMPLE	SAMOAN	SCOTCH	SEEPED
RUMPUS	SAMOSA	SCOTIA	SEE-SAW
RUNLET	SAMPAN	SCRAPE	SEETHE
RUNNEL	SAMPLE	SCRAWL	SEISED
RUNNER	SANDAL	SCREAM	SEISIN
RUNWAY	SANDED	SCREED	SEIZED
RUSHED	SANELY	SCREEN	SEIZIN
RUSHER	SANEST	SCREWY	SIEZOR
RUSSET	SANIFY	SCRIBE	SELDOM
RUSSIA	SANITY	SCRIMP	SELECT
RUSTED	SAPPED	SCRIPT	SELENE
RUSTIC	SAPPER	SCROLL	SELLER
RUSTLE	SAPPHO	SCRUFF	SELVES
RUTTED	SARONG	SCULPT	SENATE
	SASHES	SCUMMY	SENDER
	SATEEN	SCURFY	SENILE
S – 6	SATING	SCURRY	SENIOR
	SATINY	SCURVY	SENORA
SABLED	SATIRE	SCUTUM	SENSED
SACHET	SATRAP	SCYLLA	SENSOR
SACKED	SATURN	SCYTHE	SENTRY
SACKER	SAUCED	SEACAT	SEPSIS
SACRED			

SEPTET	SHIFTY	SILKEN	SLEAZY
SEPTIC	SHIMMY	SILLER	SLEDGE
SEPTUM	SHINDY	SILTED	SLEEPY
SEQUEL	SHINER	SILVAN	SLEETY
SEQUIN	SHINTO	SILVER	SLEEVE
SERAPH	SHIRES	SIMIAL	SLEIGH
SEREIN	SHIRTY	SIMIAN	SLEUTH
SERENE	SHIVER	SIMILE	SLEWED
SERIAL	SHOALY	SIMMER	SLICED
SERIES	SHODDY	SIMNEL	SLICER
SERMON	SHOOED	SIMONY	SLIDER
SEROUS	SHOPPY	SIMPER	SLIGHT
SERVED	SHORED	SIMPLE	SLINKY
SERVER	SHORER	SIMPLY	SLIPPY
SESAME	SHORTS	SINEWY	SLITHY
SESTET	SHOULD	SINFUL	SLIVER
SET-OFF	SHOVED	SINGED	SLOGAN
SETOSE	SHOVEL	SINGER	SLOPED
SET-OUT	SHOVER	SINGLE	SLOPPY
SETTEE	SHOWER	SINGLY	SLOUCH
SETTER	SHRANK	SINKER	SLOUGH
SETTLE	SHREWD	SINNER	SLOVAK
SEVERE	SHRIEK	SIPHON	SLOVEN
SÈVRES	SHRIFT	SIPPED	SLOWER
SEWAGE	SHRIKE	SIPPER	SLOWLY
SEWING	SHRILL	SIPPET	SLUDGE
SEXISM	SHRIMP	SIRDAR	SLUDGY
SEXIST	SHRINE	SIRING	SLUICE
SEXTAN	SHRINK	SIRIUS	SLUING
SEXTET	SHRIVE	SIRRAH	SLUMPY
SEXTON	SHROUD	SISKIN	SLURRY
SEXUAL	SHROVE	SISTER	SLUSHY
SHABBY	SHRUNK	SITCOM	SLYEST
SHADED	SHUCKS	SITTER	SMALLS
SHADES	SHYING	SIZING	SMARMY
SHADOW	SICKER	SIZZLE	SMARTY
SHAGGY	SICKEN	SKATED	SMEARY
SHAKEN	SICKLE	SKATER	SMELLY
SHAKER	SICKLY	SKERRY	SMILAX
SHAMED	SIDING	SKETCH	SMILED
SHANTY	SIDLED	SKEWER	SMILER
SHAPED	SIENNA	SKILLY	SMIRCH
SHAPER	SIERRA	SKIMPY	SMITER
SHARED	SIESTA	SKINNY	SMITHY
SHARER	SIFTED	SKYISH	SMOKED
SHAVED	SIFTER	SLABBY	SMOKER
SHAVER	SIGHED	SLAKED	SMOOTH
SHEARS	SIGHER	SLANGY	SMOUCH
SHEATH	SIGNAL	SLAP-UP	SMUDGE
SHEIKH	SIGNED	SLATED	SMUDGY
SHEKEL	SIGNER	SLATER	SMUGLY
SHELLY	SIGNET	SLAVED	SMUTCH
SHELVE	SIGNOR	SLAVER	SMUTTY
SHELVY	SILAGE	SLAVEY	SNAGGY
SHERRY	SILENT	SLAVIC	SNAKED
SHIELD	SILICA	SLAYER	SNAPPY

SNARED	SORELY	SPOUSE	STAYER
SNARER	SOREST	SPRAIN	STAY-IN
SNATCH	SORREL	SPRANG	STEADY
SNEEZE	SORROW	SPRAWL	STEAMY
SNIFFY	SORTED	SPREAD	STEELY
SNIPER	SORTER	SPRENT	STENCH
SNIPPY	SORTIE	SPRING	STEPPE
SNITCH	SOUGHT	SPRINT	STEREO
SNIVEL	SOURCE	SPRITE	STEWED
SNOBBY	SOURER	SPROUT	STICKY
SNOOZE	SOURLY	SPRUCE	STIFLE
SNORED	SOUSED	SPRUNG	STIGMA
SNORER	SOVIET	SPRYER	STILLY
SNOTTY	SOWING	SPUNKY	STINGO
SNOUTY	SOZZLE	SPURGE	STINGY
SNOWED	SPACED	SPURRY	STITCH
SNUBBY	SPACER	SPYING	STOCKY
SNUDGE	SPADED	SPYISM	STODGE
SNUFFY	SPADIX	SQUALL	STODGY
SNUGLY	SPARED	SQUARE	STOKED
SOAKED	SPARER	SQUASH	STOKER
SOAKER	SPARES	SQUAWK	STOLEN
SOAPED	SPARKS	SQUEAK	STOLID
SOARED	SPARRY	SQUEAL	STONED
SOBBED	SPARSE	SQUILL	STONER
SOCAGE	SPAVIN	SQUINT	STOOGE
SOCCER	SPECIE	SQUIRE	STOP-GO
SOCIAL	SPECKY	SQUIRM	STORED
SOCKED	SPEECH	SQUIRT	STORER
SOCKET	SPEEDY	STABLE	STORES
SODDEN	SPENCE	STABLY	STOREY
SODIUM	SPHERE	STAGED	STORMY
SO-EVER	SPHINX	STAGER	STOVED
SOFISM	SPICED	STAGEY	STOVER
SOFTEN	SPIDER	STAKED	STOWED
SOFTER	SPIGOT	STALAG	STOWER
SOFTLY	SPIKED	STALER	STRAFE
SOILED	SPINAL	STALKY	STRAIN
SOIREE	SPINED	STAMEN	STRAIT
SOLACE	SPINET	STANCE	STRAKE
SOLDER	SPINNY	STANCH	STRAND
SOLELY	SPIRAL	STANZA	STRASS
SOLEMN	SPIRED	STAPLE	STRATA
SO-LONG	SPIRIT	STARCH	STRAWY
SOLVED	SPITED	STARED	STREAK
SOLVER	SPLASH	STARER	STREAM
SOMBRE	SPLEEN	STARRY	STREET
SONANT	SPLICE	STARVE	STRESS
SONATA	SPLIFF	STATED	STREWN
SONNET	SPLINE	STATER	STRIAE
SOONER	SPOKEN	STATIC	STRICT
SOOTHE	SPONGE	STATUE	STRIDE
SOPPED	SPONGY	STATUS	STRiFE
SOPPER	SPOOKY	STAVED	STRIKE
SORBET	SPOONY	STAVES	STRING
SORDID	SPOTTY	STAYED	STRIPE

STRIVE	SUNDAE	T – 6	TARTAN
STROBE	SUNDAY		TARTAR
STRODE	SUNDER	TABARD	TARTLY
STROKE	SUNDEW	TABBED	TASKED
STROLL	SUN-DOG	TABLED	TASKER
STRONG	SUNDRY	TABLET	TASSEL
STROVE	SUN-GOD	TABOUR	TASTED
STRUCK	SUN-HAT	TACKED	TASTER
STRUNG	SUNKEN	TACKER	TATLER
STUBBY	SUNLIT	TACKLE	TATTED
STUCCO	SUNNED	TACTIC	TATTER
STUDIO	SUNSET	TAGGED	TATTLE
STUFFY	SUN-TAN	TAGGER	TATTOO
STUMER	SUPERB	TAG-RAG	TAUGHT
STUMPS	SUPINE	TAILED	TAURUS
STUMPY	SUPPED	TAILOR	TAUTEN
STUPID	SUPPER	TAKE-IN	TAUTER
STUPOR	SUPPLE	TAKING	TAVERN
STURDY	SUPPLY	TALBOT	TAWDRY
STYLAR	SURELY	TALCKY	TAWING
STYLED	SUREST	TALENT	TAXIED
STYLET	SURETY	TALKED	TAXING
STYLUS	SURGED	TALKER	TCHICK
STYMIE	SURREY	TALLER	TEA-CUP
STYRAX	SURTAX	TALLOW	TEAMED
SUABLE	SURVEY	TALMUD	TEA-POT
SUBDUE	SUTLER	TAMELY	TEARER
SUBITO	SUTTEE	TAMEST	TEASED
SUBLET	SUTURE	TAMPED	TEASEL
SUBMIT	SVELTE	TAMPER	TEASER
SUBORN	SWAMPY	TAMPON	TEA-SET
SUBTIL	SWANKY	TAM-TAM	TEA-URN
SUBTLE	SWARDY	TANDEM	TECHNO
SUBTLY	SWARMY	TANGED	TEDIUM
SUBURB	SWATCH	TANGLE	TEEING
SUBWAY	SWATHE	TANGLY	TEEMED
SUCKED	SWAYED	TANKED	TEETER
SUCKER	SWEATY	TANKER	TEETHE
SUCKLE	SWERVE	TANNED	TELLER
SUDDEN	SWINGE	TANNER	TEMPER
SUEING	SWIPED	TANNIC	TEMPLE
SUFFER	SWIPES	TANNIN	TENACE
SUFFIX	SWITCH	TANNOY	TENANT
SUGARY	SWIVEL	TAOISM	TENDED
SUITED	SYLVAN	TAOIST	TENDER
SUITOR	SYMBOL	TAPING	TENDON
SUIVEZ	SYNDIC	TAPPED	TENNER
SULKED	SYNTAX	TAPPER	TENNIS
SULLEN	SYPHON	TAPPET	TENSER
SULTAN	SYRIAC	TARGET	TENSED
SULTRY	SYRIAN	TARIFF	TENTED
SUMMED	SYRINX	TARMAC	TENTER
SUMMER	SYRUPY	TARPON	TENURE
SUMMIT	SYSTEM	TARSAL	TENUTO
SUMMON		TARSIA	TEPEFY
SUNBOW		TARSUS	TERCET

TERMED	TICKLY	TOFFEE	TOYING
TERMLY	TIC-TAC	TOGGED	TOYISH
TERROR	TIDIED	TOGGLE	TOY-MAN
TESTED	TIDIER	TOILED	TRACED
TESTER	TIDILY	TOILER	TRACER
TETCHY	TIEING	TOILET	TRADED
TETHER	TIE-PIN	TOLEDO	TRADER
TETRAD	TIERCE	TOLLED	TRAGIC
TEUTON	TIE-WIG	TOLLER	TRANCE
THALER	TIFFIN	TOMATO	TRAPES
THALIA	TIGHTS	TOMBED	TRAPPY
THANKS	TILERY	TOMBOY	TRASHY
THATCH	TILING	TOM-CAT	TRAUMA
THAWED	TILLED	TOMTIT	TRAVEL
THEBAN	TILLER	TOMTOM	TREATY
THEIRS	TILTED	TONGUE	TREBLE
THEISM	TILTER	TONING	TREMOR
THEIST	TIMBAL	TONISH	TRENCH
THENAR	TIMBER	TONSIL	TRENDY
THENCE	TIMBRE	TOOLED	TREPAN
THEORY	TIMELY	TOOTED	TREPID
THESIS	TIMING	TOOTER	TRIBAL
THETIS	TIMIST	TOOTHY	TRICAR
THEWED	TINDER	TOOTLE	TRICKY
THIEVE	TINGED	TOO-TOO	TRICOT
THINLY	TINGLE	TOP-DOG	TRIFID
THIRST	TINIER	TOP-HAT	TRIFLE
THIRTY	TINKER	TOPMAN	TRILBY
THORNY	TINKLE	TOPPED	TRIMLY
THORPE	TINMAN	TOPPER	TRINAL
THOUGH	TINNED	TOPPLE	TRIODE
THRALL	TINNER	TORERO	TRIPLE
THRASH	TIN-POT	TORPID	TRIPLY
THREAD	TINSEL	TORPOR	TRIPOD
THREAT	TINTED	TORQUE	TRIPOS
THRESH	TINTER	TORRID	TRISTE
THRICE	TIP-CAT	TOSSED	TRITON
THRIFT	TIP-OFF	TOSSER	TRIUNE
THRILL	TIPPED	TOSS-UP	TRIVET
THRIVE	TIPPET	TOTING	TROIKA
THROAT	TIPPLE	TOTTED	TROJAN
THRONE	TIPTOE	TOTTER	TROLLY
THRONG	TIPTOP	TOUCAN	TROPHY
THROVE	TIRADE	TOUCHY	TROPIC
THROWN	TIRING	TOUPEE	TROPPO
THRUSH	TISANE	TOURED	TROUGH
THRUST	TISSUE	TOUSLE	TROUPE
THWACK	TITBIT	TOUTED	TROWEL
THWART	TITHED	TOUTER	TRUANT
THYMOL	TITLED	TOWAGE	TRUDGE
THYMUS	TITTER	TOWARD	TRUEST
TIBIAL	TITTUP	TOWERY	TRUISM
TICKED	TOCSIN	TOWING	TRUSTY
TICKER	TODDLE	TOWSER	TRYING
TICKET	TOE-CAP	TOY-BOX	TRY-OUT
TICKLE	TOEING	TOY-BOY	TSETSE

T-SHIRT	TYPING	UNGLUE	UNSHOD
TUBAGE	TYPIST	UNGOWN	UNSHOT
TUBBED	TYRANT	UNGUAL	UNSHUT
TUBING	TYRIAN	UNHAND	UNSOLD
TUCKED		UNHANG	UNSOWN
TUCKER	**U – 6**	UNHASP	UNSPIN
TUFFET		UNHEWN	UNSTOP
TUFTED	UBIETY	UNHOLY	UNSUNG
TUGGED	UGLIER	UNHOOK	UNSURE
TUGGER	UGLIFY	UNHUNG	UNTACK
TUMBLE	UGLILY	UNHURT	UNTAME
TUMOUR	ULLAGE	UNIPED	UNTIDY
TUMULI	ULSTER	UNIQUE	UNTIED
TUMULT	ULTIMO	UNISEX	UNTOLD
TUNDRA	UMBRAL	UNISON	UNTORN
TUNE-IN	UMLAUT	UNITED	UNTROD
TUNING	UMPIRE	UNITER	UNTRUE
TUNNED	UNABLE	UNJUST	UNTUCK
TUNNEL	UNAWED	UNKEPT	UNTUNE
TUPPED	UNBEND	UNKIND	UNUSED
TURBAN	UNBENT	UNKNOT	UNVEIL
TURBID	UNBIND	UNLACE	UNWARY
TURBOT	UNBOLT	UNLAID	UNWELL
TUREEN	UNBORN	UNLASH	UNWEPT
TURFED	UNBRED	UNLENT	UNWIND
TURGID	UNCAGE	UNLESS	UNWIRE
TURKEY	UNCASE	UNLIKE	UNWISE
TURNED	UNCATE	UNLOAD	UNWORN
TURNER	UNCIAL	UNLOCK	UNWRAP
TURNIP	UNCLAD	UNMADE	UNYOKE
TURN-ON	UNCLOG	UNMAKE	UPBEAR
TURN-UP	UNCOIL	UNMASK	UPCAST
TURRET	UNCORD	UNOWED	UPDATE
TURTLE	UNCORK	UNPACK	UPHILL
TUSCAN	UNCURL	UNPAID	UPHOLD
TUSKED	UNDATE	UNPICK	UPKEEP
TUSKER	UNDIES	UNPROP	UPLAND
TUSSLE	UNDINE	UNREAD	UPLEAN
TU-WHIT	UNDOCK	UNREAL	UPLIFT
TU-WHOO	UNDOER	UNREST	UP-LINE
TUXEDO	UNDONE	UNRIPE	UPMOST
TWEENY	UNDULY	UNROBE	UPPING
TWELVE	UNEASE	UNROLL	UPPISH
TWENTY	UNEASY	UNROOF	UPRISE
TWIGGY	UNEVEN	UNROOT	UPROAR
TWINED	UNFAIR	UNROPE	UPROOT
TWINER	UNFEED	UNRULY	UPRUSH
TWINGE	UNFELT	UNSAFE	UPSHOT
TWITCH	UNFOLD	UNSAID	UPSIDE
TWO-PLY	UNFREE	UNSEAL	UPTAKE
TWOULD	UNFURL	UNSEAM	UPTURN
TWO-WAY	UNGEAR	UNSEAT	UPWARD
TYBURN	UNGILD	UNSEEN	URAEUS
TYCOON	UNGILT	UNSENT	URANIA
TYPHUS	UNGIRD	UNSEWN	URANIC
TYPIFY	UNGIRT	UNSHED	URANUS

URBANE	VENDOR	VISUAL	WANTED
URCHIN	VENDUE	VITALS	WANTER
URGENT	VENEER	VIVACE	WANTON
URGING	VENERY	VIVIFY	WARBLE
URSINE	VENIAL	VIZARD	WAR-CRY
USABLE	VENITE	VOICED	WARDED
USANCE	VENTED	VOIDED	WARDEN
USEFUL	VERBAL	VOIDER	WARDER
USURER	VERGED	VOLANT	WARIER
UTERUS	VERGER	VOLLEY	WARILY
UTMOST	VERIFY	VOLUME	WARMER
UTOPIA	VERILY	VOODOO	WARMLY
UVULAR	VERITY	VORTEX	WARMTH
	VERMIN	VOTARY	WARNED
V – 6	VERNAL	VOTING	WARPED
	VERSED	VOTIVE	WARREN
VACANT	VERSER	VOWING	WASHED
VACATE	VERSUS	VOYAGE	WASHER
VACUUM	VERTEX	VULCAN	WASH-UP
VAGARY	VERVET	VULGAR	WASTED
VAGUER	VESPER		WASTER
VAINER	VESSEL		WATERY
VAINLY	VESTAL	**W – 6**	WATTLE
VALISE	VESTED		WAVING
VALLEY	VESTRY	WADDED	WAX-END
VALLUM	VETOED	WADDLE	WAXIER
VALOUR	VETTED	WADING	WAXING
VALUED	VEXING	WAFERY	WAYLAY
VALUER	VIABLE	WAFFLE	WEAKEN
VALVED	VIANDS	WAFTED	WEAKER
VAMPED	VICTIM	WAFTER	WEAKLY
VAMPER	VICTOR	WAGGED	WEAKON
VANDAL	VICUNA	WAGGLE	WEALTH
VANISH	VIEWED	WAGGON	WEANED
VANITY	VIEWER	WAGING	WEAPON
VAN-MAN	VIGOUR	WAILED	WEARER
VAPOUR	VIKING	WAILER	WEASEL
VARIED	VILELY	WAITED	WEAVER
VARIER	VILEST	WAITER	WEAZEN
VARLET	VILIFY	WAIVED	WEBBED
VASSAL	VINERY	WAIVER	WEB-EYE
VASTER	VINOUS	WAKING	WEDDED
VASTLY	VINTED	WALKED	WEDGED
VAULTY	VINTRY	WALKER	WEEDED
VECTOR	VIOLET	WALLAH	WEEDER
VEERED	VIOLIN	WALLED	WEEKLY
VEILED	VIRAGO	WALLER	WEEPER
VEINED	VIRGIN	WALLET	WEEPIE
VELCRO	VIRILE	WALLOP	WEEVER
VELLUM	VIROUS	WALLOW	WEEVIL
VELOCE	VIRTUE	WALNUT	WEIGHT
VELOUR	VISAGE	WALRUS	WEIRDO
VELVET	VISCID	WAMBLE	WELDED
VENDED	VISHNU	WAMPUM	WELDER
VENDEE	VIZIER	WANDER	WELKIN
VENDER	VISION	WANGLE	WELLED
		WANING	

WELTED	WIND-UP	Y – 6	ABASING
WELTER	WINGED		ABATING
WENDED	WINGER	YAMMER	ABDOMEN
• WET-BOB	WINKED	YANKED	ABETTED
WETHER	WINKER	YANKEE	ABETTER
WETTER	WINKLE	YAPPED	ABIDING
WHALER	WINNER	YAPPER	ABIGAIL
WHEEZE	WINNOW	YARDIE	ABILITY
WHEEZY	WINTRY	YARNED	ABJURED
WHENCE	WIPING	YARROW	ABJURER
WHERRY	WIRING	YAWING	ABOLISH
WHILED	WIZARD	YAWLED	ABRADED
WHILES	WISDOM	YAWNED	ABREAST
WHILOM	WISELY	YCLEPT	ABRIDGE
WHILST	WISEST	YEANED	ABROACH
WHIMSY	WISHED	YEARLY	ABSCESS
WHINED	WISHER	YEASTY	ABSCOND
WHINER	WISTLY	YELLED	ABSENCE
WHINGE	WITHAL	YELLOW	ABSINTH
WHINNY	WITHER	YELPED	ABSOLVE
WHIPPY	WITHIN	YELPER	ABSTAIN
WHISKY	WITH-IT	YEOMAN	ABUSING
WHITEN	WITTED	YES-MAN	ABUSIVE
WHITER	WOBBLE	YESTER	ABUTTAL
WHITES	WOBBLY	YOGISM	ABUTTED
WHOLLY	WOEFUL	YOICKS	ABYSMAL
WHOMSO	WOLVES	YOKING	ABYSSAL
WICKED	WOMBAT	YOLKED	ACADEMY
WICKER	WONDER	YONDER	ACCEDED
WICKET	WONTED	YORKER	ACCLAIM
WIDELY	WOODED	YOWLED	ACCOUNT
WIDEST	WOODEN	YUPPIE	ACCRETE
WIDGET	WOOFER		ACCRUED
WIELDY	WOOING	Z – 6	ACCUSED
WIFELY	WOOLLY		ACCUSER
WIGEON	WORDED	ZAPPER	ACETATE
WIGGED	WORKED	ZEALOT	ACETIFY
WIGGLE	WORKER	ZENANA	ACETONE
WIGWAM	WORMED	ZENITH	ACHATES
WILDER	WORSEN	ZEPHYR	ACHERON
WILDLY	WORTHY	ZIG-ZAG	ACHIEVE
WILFUL	WOUNDY	ZILLAH	ACIDIFY
WILIER	WRAITH	ZINNIA	ACIDITY
WILILY	WREATH	ZIPPED	ACK-EMMA
WILLED	WRENCH	ZIRCON	ACOLYTE
WILLER	WRETCH	ZITHER	ACONITE
WILLOW	WRIGHT	ZODIAC	ACQUIRE
WILTED	WRITER	ZOMBIE	ACREAGE
WIMPLE	WRITHE	ZONATE	ACROBAT
WINCED	WYVERN	ZONKED	ACTABLE
WINCER			ACTRESS
WINCEY	X – 6	A – 7	ACTUARY
WINDED			ACTUATE
WINDER	XANADU	ABALONE	ACUSHLA
WINDLE	XERXES	ABANDON	ACUTELY
WINDOW	X-RAYED	ABASHED	ADAMANT

ADAPTED	AIMLESS	AMALGAM	ANILINE
ADAPTER	AIR-BASE	AMASSED	ANILITY
ADDENDA	AIR-BATH	AMATEUR	ANIMATE
ADDRESS	AIR-CELL	AMATIVE	ANIMISM
ADDUCED	AIR-HOLE	AMATORY	ANIMIST
ADDUCER	AIRLESS	AMAZING	ANISEED
ADELPHI	AIRLIFT	AMBAGES	ANNATES
ADENOID	AIRLINE	AMBIENT	ANNEXED
ADHERED	AIRLOCK	AMBLING	ANNOYED
ADHERER	AIR-MAIL	AMENDED	ANNUITY
ADIPOSE	AIRMISS	AMENITY	ANNULAR
ADJOURN	AIRPORT	AMERCED	ANNULET
ADJUDGE	AIR-PUMP	AMIABLE	ANODYNE
ADJUNCT	AIR-RAID	AMIABLY	ANOMALY
ADJURED	AIR SHIP	AMMETER	ANOSMIA
ADJURER	AIR-TRAP	AMMONAL	ANOTHER
ADMIRAL	AIRWAYS	AMMONIA	ANTACID
ADMIRED	ALADDIN	AMNESIA	ANT-BEAR
ADMIRER	A-LA-MODE	AMNESTY	ANTENNA
ADONAIS	A-LA-MORT	AMONGST	ANT-HILL
ADOPTED	ALARMED	AMORIST	ANTHONY
ADORING	ALASKAN	AMOROUS	ANTHRAX
ADORNED	ALBUMEN	AMPHORA	ANTIQUE
ADRENAL	ALCALDE	AMPLEST	ANTI-RED
ADULATE	ALCHEMY	AMPLIFY	ANTI-LIKE
ADVANCE	ALCOHOL	AMPOULE	ANT-LION
ADVERSE	ALEMBIC	AMPULLA	ANTONYM
ADVISED	ALENGTH	AMUSING	ANXIETY
ADVISOR	ALERTLY	AMUSIVE	ANXIOUS
AEOLIAN	ALFALFA	AMYLOID	ANYBODY
AERATED	ALGEBRA	ANAEMIA	ANYWISE
AERATOR	ALIDADE	ANAEMIC	APANAGE
AEROBUS	ALIGNED	ANAGRAM	APELIKE
AEROSOL	ALIMENT	ANALOGY	APHASIA
AFFABLE	ALIMONY	ANALYSE	APHONIA
AFFABLY	ALIQUOT	ANALYST	APISHLY
AFFINED	ALLAYED	ANARCHY	APOCOPE
AFFIXED	ALLEGED	ANATOMY	APOGEAN
AFFLICT	ALLEGRO	ANCHOVY	APOLOGY
AFFRONT	ALLERGY	ANCIENT	APOSTLE
AFRICAN	ALLOWED	ANDANTE	APPAREL
AGAINST	ALLOYED	ANDIRON	APPEASE
AGELESS	ALLUDED	ANDROID	APPLAUD
AGELONG	ALLURED	ANEMONE	APPLIED
AGENDUM	ALLUVIA	ANEROID	APPOINT
AGGRESS	ALLYING	ANEURIN	APPRISE
AGILELY	ALMANAC	ANGELIC	APPRIZE
AGILITY	ALMONER	ANGELUS	APPROVE
AGITATE	ALMONRY	ANGERED	APRICOT
AGITATO	ALMSMAN	ANGEVIN	APRONED
AGNOMEN	ALREADY	ANGLICE	APROPOS
AGONIZE	ALSATIA	ANGLING	APSIDAL
AGROUND	ALTERED	ANGRILY	APTNESS
AIDLESS	ALTHAEA	ANGUINE	AQUARIA
AILERON	ALUMNUS	ANGUISH	AQUATIC
AILMENT	ALYSSUM	ANGULAR	AQUEOUS

ARABIAN	ASQUINT	AVERAGE	BAMBINO
ARABIST	ASSAGAI	AVERRED	BANBURY
ARACHIS	ASSAULT	AVERTED	BANDAGE
ARAMAIC	ASSAYED	AVIATOR	BANDANA
ARBITER	ASSAYER	AVIDITY	BANDBOX
ARBUTUS	ASSEGAI	AVOCADO	BANDEAU
ARCADED	ASSUAGE	AVOIDED	BANDIED
ARCADIA	ASSUMED	AVOWING	BANDING
ARCANUM	ASSURED	AWAITED	BAND-SAW
ARCHAIC	ASSURER	AWAKING	BANEFUL
ARCHERY	ASTATIC	AWARDED	BANGING
ARCHING	ASTOUND	AWAYDAY	BANKING
ARCHIVE	ASTRIDE	AWESOME	BANNING
ARCHWAY	ASUNDER	AWFULLY	BANNOCK
ARC-LAMP	ATAVISM	AWKWARD	BANQUET
ARDENCY	ATELIER	AWNLESS	BANSHEE
ARDUOUS	ATHEISM	AXIALLY	BANTING
ARENOSE	ATHEIST	AXLE-BOX	BAPTISM
ARIDITY	ATHIRST	AXLE-PIN	BAPTIST
ARIGHTS	ATHLETE	AXOLOTL	BAPTIZE
ARIPPLE	ATHWART		BARBARY
ARISING	ATOMIST		BARBATE
ARMHOLE	ATOMIZE	**B – 7**	BARDISM
ARMIGER	ATONING	BABBLED	BARGAIN
ARMLESS	ATROPHY	BABBLER	BARGING
ARMOIRE	ATTABOY	BABYISH	BARKING
ARMOURY	ATTACHE	BABYISM	BARMAID
AROUSAL	ATTEMPT	BABYLON	BARMIER
AROUSED	ATTIRED	BACCHIC	BARNABY
ARRAIGN	ATTRACT	BACCHUS	BARNOWL
ARRANGE	ATTUNED	BACILLI	BARONET
ARRAYED	AUBERGE	BACKEND	BAROQUE
ARRIVAL	AUCTION	BACKING	BARRACK
ARSENAL	AUDIBLE	BACKLOG	BARRAGE
ARSENIC	AUDIBLY	BADNESS	BARRIER
ARTICLE	AUDITED	BAFFLED	BARRING
ARTISAN	AUDITOR	BAFFLER	BASENJI
ARTISTE	AUGMENT	BAGGAGE	BASHFUL
ARTLESS	AUGURED	BAGGING	BASHING
ASCETIC	AURALLY	BAGPIPE	BASILIC
ASCRIBE	AUREATE	BAILAGE	BASKING
ASEPSIS	AUREOLA	BAILIFF	BASSOON
ASEPTIC	AUREOLE	BAILING	BASTARD
ASEXUAL	AURICLE	BAITING	BASTING
ASHAMED	AUROCHS	BALANCE	BASTION
ASHIVER	AUSTERE	BALCONY	BATH-BUN
ASHTRAY	AUSTRAL	BALDEST	BATHING
ASIATIC	AUTOBUS	BALDISH	BATSMAN
ASININE	AUTOCAR	BALDRIC	BATTELS
ASKANCE	AUTOCUE	BALEFUL	BATTERY
ASPERSE	AUTONYM	BALKING	BATTING
ASPHALT	AUTOPSY	BALLAST	BATTLED
ASPIRED	AVAILED	BALLBOY	BATTLER
ASPIRIN	AVARICE	BALLOON	BAULKED
ASPRAWL	AVENGED	BALMILY	BAUXITE
ASPROUT	AVENGER	BALMING	BAWDILY

BAWLING	BELLHOP	BIASING	BLENDED
BAYONET	BELLIED	BIAXIAL	BLENDER
BAY-TREE	BELLING	BICYCLE	BLESSED
BAYWOOD	BELLMAN	BIDDING	BLETHER
BEACHED	BELLOWS	BIFOCAL	BLIGHTY
BEADING	BELOVED	BIGGEST	BLINDED
BEAMING	BELTING	BIGGISH	BLINDER
BEARDED	BELYING	BIGOTED	BLINDLY
BEARING	BEMAZED	BIGOTRY	BLINKED
BEARISH	BEMIRED	BILGING	BLISTER
BEAR-PIT	BEMUSED	BILIOUS	BLOATED
BEASTLY	BENCHER	BILKING	BLOATER
BEATIFY	BENDING	BILLING	BLOCKED
BEATING	BENEATH	BILLION	BLONDIN
BECAUSE	BENEFIT	BILLOWY	BLOODED
BECLOUD	BENGALI	BILTONG	BLOOMED
BEDDING	BENISON	BINDING	BLOOMER
BEDEVIL	BENZENE	BIOCHIP	BLOSSOM
BEDEWED	BENZOIN	BIOLOGY	BLOTCHY
BED-GOWN	BEPAINT	BIOTICS	BLOTTED
BED-MATE	BEQUEST	BIPEDAL	BLOTTER
BEDOUIN	BERATED	BIPLANE	BLOWFLY
BEDPOST	BEREAVE	BIRCHED	BLOW-GUN
BED-REST	BERHYME	BIRDMAN	BLOWING
BEDROCK	BERRIED	BIRETTA	BLOW-OUT
BEDROOM	BERSERK	BIRYANI	BLOWZED
BEDSIDE	BERTHED	BISCUIT	BLUBBER
BEDSORE	BESEECH	BISMUTH	BLUCHER
BED-TICK	BESHAME	BITTERN	BLUE-CAP
BEDTIME	BESHONE	BITUMEN	BLUEING
BEDWARF	BESHREW	BIVALVE	BLUFFED
BEEF-TEA	BESIDES	BIVOUAC	BLUFFER
BEEHIVE	BESIEGE	BIZARRE	BLUFFLY
BEE-LINE	BESMEAR	BLABBED	BLUNDER
BEE-MOTH	BESMOKE	BLABBER	BLUNGER
BEESWAX	BESPEAK	BLACKED	BLUNTED
BEETLED	BESPOKE	BLACKEN	BLUNTER
BEGGARY	BESTIAL	BLACKER	BLUNTLY
BEGGING	BESTILL	BLACKLY	BLURRED
BEGLOOM	BESTING	BLADDER	BLURTED
BEGONIA	BEST-MAN	BLAMING	BLUSHED
BEGORED	BESTREW	BLANDLY	BLUSTER
BEGRIME	BETAKEN	BLANKET	BOARDED
BEGUILE	BETHINK	BLANKLY	BOARDER
BEGUINE	BETHUMB	BLARING	BOARISH
BEHAVED	BETHUMP	BLARNEY	BOASTED
BEHOVED	BETIDED	BLASTED	BOASTER
BEJEWEL	BETIMES	BLASTER	BOAT-CAR
BEKNOWN	BETITLE	BLATANT	BOAT-FLY
BELACED	BETOKEN	BLATHER	BOATFUL
BELATED	BETROTH	BLATTER	BOATING
BELAYED	BETTING	BLAZING	BOATMAN
BELCHED	BETWEEN	BLEAKER	BOBADIL
BELCHER	BETWIXT	BLEAKLY	BOBBING
BELGIAN	BEWITCH	BLEATED	BOBBISH
BELIEVE	BEZIQUE	BLEMISH	BOB-SLED

BOB-STAY	BOX-CALF	BRISKER	BULLACE
BOBTAIL	BOX-COAT	BRISKET	BULL-DOG
BODEFUL	BOX-IRON	BRISKLY	BULLIED
BOGGLED	BOX-KITE	BRISTLE	BULLING
BOILING	BOX-WOOD	BRISTLY	BULLION
BOLDEST	BOYCOTT	BRISTOL	BULLOCK
BOLLARD	BOYHOOD	BRITISH	BULL-PUP
BOLLING	BRACING	BRITTLE	BULRUSH
BOLOGNA	BRACKEN	BROADEN	BULWARK
BOLSTER	BRACKET	BROADER	BUMMALO
BOLTING	BRAGGED	BROADLY	BUMPING
BOMBARD	BRAIDED	BROCADE	BUMPKIN
BOMBAST	BRAILLE	BROILED	BUNCHED
BOMBING	BRAINED	BROILER	BUNDLED
BONANZA	BRAISED	BROKAGE	BUNGLED
BONDAGE	BRAKING	BROKING	BUNGLER
BONDING	BRAMBLE	BROMIDE	BUNKING
BONDMAN	BRAMBLY	BRONZED	BUNTING
BONFIRE	BRANCHY	BROODED	BUOYAGE
BONNILY	BRANDED	BROOKED	BUOYANT
BOOKING	BRASSIE	BROTHER	BUOYING
BOOKISH	BRAVADO	BROUGHT	BURDOCK
BOOKLET	BRAVELY	BROWNED	BURETTE
BOOKMAN	BRAVERY	BROWNER	BURGEON
BOOMING	BRAVEST	BROWNIE	BURGESS
BOORISH	BRAVING	BROWSED	BURGHAL
BOOSTED	BRAVURA	BRUISED	BURGHER
BOOSTER	BRAWLED	BRUISER	BURGLAR
BOOT-LEG	BRAWLER	BRUMOUS	BURGLED
BOOZING	BRAYING	BRUSHED	BURLIER
BORACIC	BRAZIER	BRUSQUE	BURLING
BOREDOM	BRAZING	BRUTIFY	BURMESE
BOROUGH	BREADTH	BRUTISH	BURNING
BORSTAL	BREAKER	BRUTISM	BURNISH
BOSOMED	BREATHE	BUBBLED	BURNOUS
BOSSING	BREEDER	BUBONIC	BURRING
BOSWELL	BREVITY	BUCKING	BURSARY
BOTANIC	BREWERY	BUCKISH	BURTHEN
BOTCHED	BREWING	BUCKISM	BURYING
BOTCHER	BRIBERY	BUCKLED	BUSH-CAT
BOTTLED	BRIBING	BUCKLER	BUSHIDO
BOTTLER	BRICKED	BUCKRAM	BUSHMAN
BOUDOIR	BRIDGED	BUCKSAW	BUSKING
BOULDER	BRIDLED	BUCOLIC	BUS-STOP
BOULTER	BRIDLER	BUDDING	BUSTARD
BOUNCED	BRIEFED	BUDGING	BUSTLED
BOUNCER	BRIEFER	BUDLESS	BUSTLER
BOUNDED	BRIEFLY	BUFFALO	BUSYING
BOUNDEN	BRIGADE	BUFFING	BUTCHER
BOUNDER	BRIGAND	BUFFOON	BUTLERY
BOUQUET	BRIMFUL	BUGBEAR	BUTMENT
BOURBON	BRIMMED	BUILT-UP	BUTT-END
BOWLESS	BRIMMER	BULBOUS	BUTTERY
BOWLINE	BRINDLE	BULGING	BUTTING
BOWLING	BRINISH	BULKIER	BUTTOCK
BOWSHOT	BRIOCHE	BULKING	BUTTONS

BUXOMLY	CAMELOT	CARRIED	CENTRAL
BUYABLE	CAMORRA	CARRIER	CENTRED
BUZZARD	CAMPHOR	CARRION	CENTURY
BUZZING	CAMPING	CARROTY	CERAMIC
BUZZ-SAW	CAMPION	CARTAGE	CERTAIN
BY-AND-BY	CANDIED	CARTING	CERTIFY
BYRONIC	CANDOUR	CARTOON	CESSION
	CANASTA	CARVING	CESSPIT
	CANNERY	CASCADE	CHABLIS
C – 7	CANNING	CASCARA	CHAFFED
	CANTATA	CASE-LAW	CHAFFER
CABARET	CANTEEN	CASEMAN	CHAFING
CABBAGE	CANTING	CASHIER	CHAGRIN
CABBALA	CANVASS	CASHING	CHAINED
CAB-FARE	CAPABLE	CASSAVA	CHAIRED
CABINED	CAPABLY	CASSOCK	CHALDEE
CABINET	CAP-A-PIE	CASTING	CHALICE
CABLING	CAPELIN	CASTLED	CHALLIS
CABOOSE	CAPERED	CAST-OFF	CHAMBER
CAB-RANK	CAPERER	CASUIST	CHAMOIS
CA'CANNY	CAPITAL	CATALAN	CHAMPED
CACKLED	CAPITAN	CATARRH	CHANCED
CACKLER	CAPITOL	CATCALL	CHANCEL
CADDISH	CAPORAL	CATCHER	CHANGED
CADENCE	CAPPING	CATCHUP	CHANGER
CADENCY	CAPRICE	CATERAN	CHANNEL
CADENZA	CAPRINE	CATERED	CHANTED
CADGING	CAPROIC	CATERER	CHANTER
CAESURA	CAPSIZE	CAT-EYED	CHANTRY
CAFFEIN	CAPSTAN	CATFISH	CHAOTIC
CAITIFF	CAPSULE	CATHEAD	CHAPLET
CAJOLED	CAPTAIN	CATHODE	CHAPMAN
CAJOLER	CAPTION	CAT-LIKE	CHAPPED
CALCIFY	CAPTIVE	CATMINT	CHAPTER
CALCINE	CAPTURE	CAT'S-EYE	CHARADE
CALCIUM	CAPULET	CAT'S-PAW	CHARGED
CALDRON	CARAMEL	CATTISH	CHARGER
CALENDS	CARAVAN	CAUDATE	CHARILY
CALIBAN	CARAVEL	CAULKED	CHARING
CALIBRE	CARAWAY	CAUSING	CHARIOT
CALIPER	CARBIDE	CAUSTIC	CHARITY
CALKING	CARBINE	CAUTION	CHARLEY
CALL-BOY	CARCASE	CAVALRY	CHARMED
CALLING	CARDIAC	CAVE-MAN	CHARMER
CALLOUS	CARDING	CAVIARE	CHARNEL
CALMING	CARDOON	CAYENNE	CHARRED
CALOMEL	CAREFUL	CEASING	CHARTED
CALORIC	CARIBOU	CEDARED	CHARTER
CALORIE	CARIOUS	CEDILLA	CHASING
CALTROP	CARKING	CEILING	CHASSIS
CALUMET	CARLINE	CELLIST	CHASTEN
CALUMNY	CARMINE	CENSING	CHATEAU
CALVARY	CARNAGE	CENSURE	CHATTED
CALVING	CAROTID	CENTAUR	CHATTEL
CALYPSO	CAROUSE	CENTAVO	CHATTER
CAMBIUM	CARPING	CENTIME	CHEAPEN
CAMBRIC			

CHEAPER	CHORTLE	CLEARER	COATING
CHEAPLY	CHOWDER	CLEARLY	COAXIAL
CHEATED	CHRONIC	CLEAVED	COAXING
CHEATER	CHUCKED	CLEAVER	COBBING
CHECKED	CHUCKLE	CLEMENT	COBBLED
CHECKER	CHUMMED	CLEMMED	COBBLER
CHEDDAR	CHURCHY	CLICKED	COCAINE
CHEEKED	CHURNED	CLIMATE	COCKADE
CHEEPED	CHURRED	CLIMBED	COCKEYE
CHEERED	CINDERY	CLIMBER	COCKING
CHEERIO	CIRCEAN	CLINKED	COCKLED
CHEETAH	CIRCLED	CLIPPED	COCKLER
CHELSEA	CIRCLET	CLIPPER	COCKNEY
CHEMISE	CIRCUIT	CLIPPIE	COCKPIT
CHEMIST	CISTERN	CLOAKED	COCONUT
CHEQUER	CITABLE	CLOBBER	COCOTTE
CHERISH	CITADEL	CLOCKED	CODDING
CHEROOT	CITIZEN	CLOCKER	CODDLED
CHERVIL	CITRATE	CLOGGED	CODEINE
CHESTED	CITRINE	CLOGGER	CODFISH
CHEVIOT	CIVILLY	CLONING	CODICIL
CHEVRON	CIVVIES	CLOSELY	CODLING
CHEWING	CLACKED	CLOSEST	COERCED
CHIANTI	CLAIMED	CLOSE-UP	COEXIST
CHICANE	CLAIMER	CLOSING	COGENCY
CHICKEN	CLAMANT	CLOSURE	COGNATE
CHICORY	CLAMBER	CLOTHED	COHABIT
CHIDING	CLAMMED	CLOTTED	COHERED
CHIEFLY	CLAMOUR	CLOUDED	COHERER
CHIFFON	CLAMPED	CLOUTED	COiFFED
CHIGNON	CLAMPER	CLOWNED	COILING
CHILEAN	CLANGED	CLUBBED	COINAGE
CHILIAD	CLANKED	CLUBBER	COINING
CHILLED	CLAP-NET	CLUB-LAW	COJUROR
CHILLER	CLAPPED	CLUB-MAN	COLDEST
CHIMNEY	CLAPPER	CLUCKED	COLDISH
CHINDIT	CLARIFY	CLUMBER	COLICKY
CHINESE	CLARION	CLUMPED	COLITIS
CHINKED	CLARITY	CLUSTER	COLLATE
CHIP-HAT	CLASHED	CLUTTER	COLLECT
CHIPPED	CLASPED	COACHED	COLLEEN
CHIPPER	CLASPER	COACTED	COLLEGE
CHIRPED	CLASSED	COAGENT	COLLIDE
CHIRPER	CLASSIC	COAL-BED	COLLIER
CHIRRED	CLATTER	COAL-BOX	COLLOID
CHIRRUP	CLAVIER	COAL-GAS	COLLUDE
CHITTER	CLAWING	COALING	COLONEL
CHLORAL	CLAYING	COALMAN	COLOURS
CHLORIC	CLAYISH	COAL-PIT	COLTISH
CHOIRED	CLAY-PIT	COAL-TAR	COMBINE
CHOKING	CLEANED	COAL-TIT	COMBING
CHOLERA	CLEANER	COARSEN	COMFORT
CHOOSER	CLEANLY	COARSER	COMICAL
CHOPPED	CLEANSE	COASTAL	COMMAND
CHOPPER	CLEAN-UP	COASTED	COMMEND
CHORALE	CLEARED	COASTER	COMMENT

COMMERE	CONNATE	CORK-LEG	COWLIKE
COMMODE	CONNECT	CORN-COB	COWLING
COMMONS	CONNING	CORNEAL	COWSLIP
COMMUNE	CONNIVE	CORNICE	COXCOMB
COMMUTE	CONNOTE	CORNISH	COYNESS
COMPACT	CONQUER	COROLLA	COZENED
COMPANY	CONSENT	CORONER	COZENER
COMPARE	CONSIGN	CORONET	CRABBED
COMPART	CONSIST	CORRECT	CRACKED
COMPASS	CONSOLE	CORRODE	CRACKER
COMPEER	CONSOLS	CORRUPT	CRACKLE
COMPERE	CONSORT	CORSAGE	CRADLED
COMPETE	CONSULT	CORSAIR	CRAGGED
COMPILE	CONSUME	CORSLET	CRAKING
COMPLEX	CONTACT	CORTEGE	CRAMMED
COMPORT	CONTAIN	CORVINE	CRAMMER
COMPOSE	CONTEMN	COSHING	CRAMPED
COMPOST	CONTEND	COSIEST	CRAMPON
COMPOTE	CONTENT	COSSACK	CRANAGE
COMPUTE	CONTEST	COSTARD	CRANIAL
COMRADE	CONTEXT	COSTING	CRANING
CONCAVE	CONTORT	COSTIVE	CRANIUM
CONCEAL	CONTOUR	COSTUME	CRANKED
CONCEDE	CONTRAS	COTERIE	CRANKLE
CONCEIT	CONTROL	COTTAGE	CRASHED
CONCEPT	CONTUSE	COTTONY	CRASHER
CONCERN	CONVENE	COUCHED	CRATING
CONCERT	CONVENT	COUGHED	CRAUNCH
CONCISE	CONVERT	COULDST	CRAVING
CONCOCT	CONVICT	COULOMB	CRAWLED
CONCORD	CONVOKE	COUNCIL	CRAWLER
CONCUSS	COOKERY	COUNSEL	CRAZIER
CONDEMN	COOKING	COUNTED	CRAZILY
CONDIGN	COOLEST	COUNTER	CRAZING
CONDOLE	COOLING	COUNTRY	CREAKED
CONDONE	COOLISH	COUPLED	CREAMED
CONDUCE	COOPING	COUPLER	CREASED
CONDUCT	CO-OPTED	COUPLET	CREATED
CONDUIT	CO-PILOT	COURAGE	CREATOR
CONFECT	COPIOUS	COURANT	CREEPER
CONFESS	COPPERY	COURIER	CREMATE
CONFEST	COPPICE	COURSED	CREMONA
CONFIDE	COPPING	COURSER	CRENATE
CONFINE	COPYING	COURTED	CREOSOL
CONFIRM	COPYIST	COURTER	CRESSET
CONFLUX	CORACLE	COURTLY	CRESTED
CONFORM	CORBEAU	COUTEAU	CREVICE
CONFUSE	CORBEIL	COUVADE	CRIBBED
CONFUTE	CORDAGE	COVERED	CRICKED
CONGEAL	CORDATE	COVETED	CRICKET
CONGEST	CORDIAL	COWBANE	CRIMPED
CONICAL	CORDING	COW-CALF	CRIMPER
CONIFER	CORDITE	COWERED	CRIMSON
CONJOIN	CORINTH	COWHERD	CRINGED
CONJURE	CORKAGE	COWHIDE	CRINGER
CONJURY	CORKING	COWLICK	CRINKLE

CRINOID	CUCKOLD	CYPRESS	DEALING
CRIPPLE	CUDDLED	CYPRIAN	DEANERY
CRISPED	CUE-BALL	CYPRIOT	DEAREST
CRISPER	CUFFING	CZARISM	DEATHLY
CRISPIN	CUIRASS		DEBACLE
CRISPLY	CUISINE	**D – 7**	DEBASED
CROAKED	CULLING		DEBASER
CROAKER	CULPRIT	DABBING	DEBATED
CROCHET	CULTURE	DABBLED	DEBATER
CROCKED	CULVERT	DABBLER	DEBAUCH
CROCKET	CUMULUS	DABSTER	DEBITED
CROESUS	CUNEATE	DAFTEST	DEBOUCH
CROFTER	CUNNING	DAGGLED	DECADAL
CROODLE	CUPPING	DAISIED	DECAGON
CROOKED	CUPRITE	DALLIED	DECANAL
CROONED	CURABLE	DALLIER	DECAPOD
CROONER	CURACAO	DAMAGED	DECAYED
CROPFUL	CURATOR	DAMMING	DECAYER
CROPPED	CURBING	DAMNIFY	DECEASE
CROPPER	CURDING	DAMNING	DECEIVE
CROQUET	CURDLED	DAMOSEL	DECENCY
CROSSED	CURE-ALL	DAMPING	DECIBEL
CROSSLY	CURETTE	DAMPISH	DECIDED
CROWBAR	CURIOUS	DANCING	DECIDER
CROWDED	CURLING	DANDIFY	DECIMAL
CROWING	CURRANT	DANDLED	DECKING
CROWNED	CURRENT	DANELAW	DECKLED
CRUCIAL	CURRIED	DANGLED	DECLAIM
CRUCIFY	CURRIER	DANGLER	DECLARE
CRUDELY	CURRISH	DANKISH	DECLINE
CRUDEST	CURSING	DANTEAN	DECODED
CRUDITY	CURSIVE	DAPPLED	DECODER
CRUELTY	CURSORY	DARKEST	DECORUM
CRUISED	CURTAIL	DARKISH	DECOYED
CRUISER	CURTAIN	DARLING	DECREED
CRUMBED	CURTANA	DARNING	DECRIAL
CRUMBLE	CURTEST	DARTING	DECRIED
CRUMBLY	CURTSEY	DASHING	DECRIER
CRUMPED	CURVATE	DASHPOT	DECROWN
CRUMPET	CURVING	DASTARD	DEDUCED
CRUMPLE	CUSHION	DATABLE	DEEDING
CRUPPER	CUSSING	DAUBING	DEEMING
CRUSADE	CUSTARD	DAUNTED	DEEPEST
CRUSADO	CUSTODY	DAUPHIN	DEEP-SEA
CRUSHED	CUSTOMS	DAWDLED	DEFACED
CRUSHER	CUT-AWAY	DAWDLER	DEFACER
CRUSTED	CUTICLE	DAWNING	DEFAMED
CRY-BABY	CUTLASS	DAY-BOOK	DEFAMER
CRYPTIC	CUTLERY	DAY-STAR	DEFAULT
CRYSTAL	CUTTING	DAYTIME	DEFENCE
CUBBING	CUT-WORM	DAYWORK	DEFIANT
CUBBISH	CYCLING	DAZZLED	DEFICIT
CUBICAL	CYCLIST	DEAD-END	DEFILED
CUBICLE	CYCLONE	DEAD-EYE	DEFILER
CUBITAL	CYCLOPS	DEADISH	DEFINED
CUBITED	CYNICAL	DEAD-SET	DEFINER

DEFLATE	DERIDED	DIE-HARD	DISPONE
DEFLECT	DERIDER	DIETARY	DISPORT
DEFRAUD	DERIVED	DIETING	DISPOSE
DEFUNCT	DERRICK	DIFFUSE	DISPUTE
DEFYING	DERVISH	DIGGING	DISRATE
DEGLAZE	DESCENT	DIGITAL	DISROBE
DEGRADE	DESCEND	DIGNIFY	DISROOT
DE-ICING	DESCANT	DIGNITY	DISRUPT
DEIFIED	DESERVE	DIGRESS	DISSECT
DEIFORM	DESIRED	DILATED	DISSENT
DEIGNED	DESIRER	DILATER	DISTAFF
DEISTIC	DESKTOP	DILEMMA	DISTANT
DELAYED	DESPAIR	DILUENT	DISTEND
DELAYER	DESPISE	DILUTED	DISTICH
DELETED	DESPITE	DILUTER	DISTORT
DELIGHT	DESPOIL	DIMETER	DISTURB
DELILAH	DESPOND	DIMMING	DISUSED
DELIMIT	DESSERT	DIMMISH	DITCHED
DELIVER	DESTINE	DIMNESS	DITCHER
DELOUSE	DESTINY	DIMPLED	DITHERY
DELPHIC	DESTROY	DINGING	DIURNAL
DELTAIC	DETERGE	DINNING	DIVERGE
DELUDED	DETINUE	DIOCESE	DIVERSE
DELUDER	DETRACT	DIORAMA	DIVIDED
DELUGED	DETRAIN	DIOXIDE	DIVIDER
DELVING	DETRUDE	DIPLOMA	DIVINER
DEMERIT	DEVALUE	DIPOLAR	DIVISOR
DEMESNE	DEVELOP	DIPPING	DIVORCE
DEMIGOD	DEVIATE	DIPTERA	DIVULGE
DEMISED	DEVILRY	DIREFUL	DIZZIED
DEMODED	DEVIOUS	DIRTIED	DIZZIER
DEMONIC	DEVISED	DIRTIER	DIZZILY
DEMONRY	DEVISEE	DIRTILY	DOCKAGE
DENIZEN	DEVISER	DISABLE	DOCKING
DENOTED	DEVISOR	DISAVOW	DODGERY
DENSELY	DEVOLVE	DISBAND	DODGING
DENSEST	DEVOTED	DISCARD	DOESKIN
DENSITY	DEVOTEE	DISCERN	DOFFING
DENTING	DEW-DROP	DISCOID	DOG-BANE
DENTIST	DEW-FALL	DISCORD	DOGCART
DENTOID	DEWLESS	DISCOUS	DOG-DAYS
DENTURE	DEXTRAL	DISCUSS	DOGFISH
DENUDED	DIABOLO	DISDAIN	DOGGING
DENYING	DIAGRAM	DISEASE	DOGGISH
DEPLETE	DIALECT	DISEUSE	DOGHEAD
DEPLORE	DIALLED	DISGUST	DOG-HOLE
DEPLUME	DIAMOND	DISHFUL	DOGLIKE
DEPOSAL	DIARCHY	DISHING	DOG-NAIL
DEPOSED	DIARIST	DISJOIN	DOGROSE
DEPOSIT	DIBBLED	DISLIKE	DOG'S-EAR
DEPRAVE	DICE-BOX	DISMAST	DOG-STAR
DEPRESS	DICKENS	DISMISS	DOLEFUL
DEPRIVE	DICTATE	DISOBEY	DOLLIED
DEPUTED	DICTION	DISPARK	DOLPHIN
DERANGE	DIDDLED	DISPART	DOLTISH
DERATED	DIDDLER	DISPLAY	DOMINIE

DONATOR	DREDGED	DUELLER	EARTHLY
DONNING	DREDGER	DUENESS	EASEFUL
DONNISH	DRESDEN	DUFFING	EASIEST
DONSHIP	DRESSED	DUKEDOM	EAST-END
DOOMING	DRESSER	DULCIFY	EASTERN
DOORMAT	DRIBBLE	DULLARD	EASTING
DOORWAY	DRIBLET	DULLEST	EATABLE
DORMANT	DRIFTED	DULLING	EBB-TIDE
DORMICE	DRIFTER	DULLISH	EBONISE
DOSSIER	DRILLED	DUMPING	EBONITE
DOTTIER	DRINKER	DUMPISH	EBRIOUS
DOTTING	DRIPPED	DUNCIAD	ECHELON
DOUBLED	DRIVING	DUNGEON	ECHOING
DOUBLET	DRIZZLE	DUNNAGE	ECLIPSE
DOUBTED	DRIZZLY	DUNNING	ECLOGUE
DOUBTER	DROLLED	DUNNISH	ECOLOGY
DOUCEUR	DRONING	DUNNOCK	ECONOMY
DOUCHED	DRONISH	DUPABLE	ECSTASY
DOUGHTY	DROOLED	DURABLE	EDDYING
DOUREST	DROOPED	DURABLY	EDENTAL
DOUSING	DROPLET	DURANCE	EDIFICE
DOUTING	DROP-NET	DUSKIER	EDIFIED
DOVECOT	DROPPED	DUSKILY	EDIFIER
DOWABLE	DROPPER	DUSKISH	EDITING
DOWAGER	DROUGHT	DUSTBIN	EDITION
DOWDILY	DROWNED	DUSTIER	EDUCATE
DOWERED	DROWNER	DUSTING	EDUCING
DOWNING	DROWSED	DUSTMAN	EFFACED
DOWSING	DRUBBED	DUSTPAN	EFFECTS
DRABBER	DRUBBER	DUTEOUS	EFFENDI
DRACHMA	DRUDGED	DUTIFUL	EGALITY
DRACULA	DRUDGER	DWARFED	EGG-COSY
DRAFTED	DRUGGED	DWELLED	EGG-FLIP
DRAGGED	DRUGGER	DWELLER	EGOTISE
DRAGGLE	DRUGGET	DWINDLE	EGOTISM
DRAG-MAN	DRUIDIC	DYNAMIC	EGOTIST
DRAG-NET	DRUMMED	DYNASTY	EJECTED
DRAGOON	DRUMMER		EJECTOR
DRAINED	DRUNKEN		ELAPSED
DRAINER	DRYDOCK	E – 7	ELASTIC
DRAPERY	DRY-EYED		ELATING
DRAPING	DRY-FOOT	EAGERLY	ELATION
DRAPPIE	DRYNESS	EANLING	ELBOWED
DRASTIC	DRY-SHOD	EARACHE	ELDERLY
DRATTED	DUALISM	EAR-DROP	ELECTED
DRAUGHT	DUALIST	EAR-DRUM	ELECTOR
DRAWBAR	DUALITY	EAR-HOLE	ELECTRO
DRAWING	DUBBING	EARLDOM	ELEGANT
DRAWLED	DUBIETY	EARLESS	ELEGIAC
DRAWLER	DUBIOUS	EARLIER	ELEGISE
DRAW-NET	DUCALLY	EARMARK	ELEGIST
DRAYAGE	DUCHESS	EARNEST	ELEMENT
DRAYMAN	DUCKING	EARNING	ELEVATE
DREADED	DUCTILE	EARRING	ELEVENS
DREAMED	DUDGEON	EARSHOT	ELF-LOCK
DREAMER	DUELLED	EARTHED	ELIDING
		EARTHEN	

ELISION	ENDORSE	ENVIRON	EVASION
ELLIPSE	ENDOWED	ENVYING	EVASIVE
ELOPING	ENDOWER	EPAULET	EVENING
ELUDING	ENDUING	EPERGNE	EVERTED
ELUSION	ENDURED	EPICARP	EVICTED
ELUSIVE	ENDURER	EPICURE	EVICTOR
ELUSORY	ENDWAYS	EPIGRAM	EVIDENT
ELYSIAN	ENDWISE	EPISODE	EVIL-EYE
ELYSIUM	ENERGIC	EPISTLE	EVINCED
EMANATE	ENFORCE	EPITAPH	EVOKING
EMBARGO	ENFRAME	EPITHET	EVOLVED
EMBASSY	ENGAGED	EPITOME	EWE-LAMB
EMBLAZE	ENGAGER	EPOCHAL	EXACTED
EMBOSOM	ENGINED	EQUABLE	EXACTER
EMBOWER	ENGLISH	EQUABLY	EXACTLY
EMBOXED	ENGORGE	EQUALLY	EXACTOR
EMBRACE	ENGRAFT	EQUATED	EXALTED
EMBROIL	ENGRAIN	EQUATOR	EXAMINE
EMBROWN	ENGRAVE	EQUERRY	EXAMPLE
EMENDED	ENGROSS	EQUINOX	EXCERPT
EMERALD	ENGUARD	ERASING	EXCISED
EMERGED	ENHANCE	ERASURE	EXCITED
EMINENT	ENJOYED	ERECTED	EXCITER
EMITTED	ENLACED	ERECTER	EXCLAIM
EMOTION	ENLARGE	ERECTLY	EXCLUDE
EMOTIVE	ENLIVEN	ERELONG	EXCUSED
EMPALED	ENNOBLE	EREMITE	EXECUTE
EMPANEL	ENOUNCE	ERMINED	EXEMPLA
EMPEROR	ENQUIRE	ERODENT	EXERTED
EMPIRIC	ENQUIRY	ERODING	EXHALED
EMPLANE	ENRAGED	EROSION	EXHAUST
EMPOWER	ENROBED	EROSIVE	EXHIBIT
EMPRESS	ENSLAVE	ERRATIC	EXHUMED
EMPTIED	ENSNARE	ERRATUM	EXIGENT
EMPTIER	ENSTAMP	ERUDITE	EXILING
EMULATE	ENSUING	ERUPTED	EXISTED
EMULOUS	ENSURED	ESCAPED	EXPANSE
ENABLED	ENTAMED	ESCAPER	EX-PARTE
ENACTED	ENTENTE	ESCHEAT	EXPENSE
ENCAGED	ENTERED	ESPARTO	EXPIATE
ENCASED	ENTERIC	ESPOUSE	EXPIRED
ENCAVED	ENTHRAL	ESPYING	EXPLAIN
ENCHAIN	ENTHUSE	ESQUIRE	EXPLODE
ENCHANT	ENTICED	ESSAYED	EXPLOIT
ENCLASP	ENTICER	ESSENCE	EXPLORE
ENCLAVE	ENTITLE	ESTUARY	EXPOSED
ENCLOSE	ENTRAIN	ETCHING	EXPOSER
ENCLOUD	ENTRANT	ETERNAL	EXPOUND
ENCODER	ENTREAT	ETHICAL	EXPRESS
ENCORED	ENTRUST	ETONIAN	EXPUNGE
ENCRUST	ENTWINE	EUGENIC	EXTINCT
ENDEMIC	ENTWIST	EUPHONY	EXTRACT
ENDIRON	ENURING	EUTERPE	EXTREME
ENDLESS	ENVELOP	EVACUEE	EXTRUDE
ENDLONG	ENVENOM	EVADING	EXUDING
ENDMOST	ENVIOUS	EVANGEL	EXULTED

EYEBALL	FASCIST	FEWNESS	FISSURE
EYE-BOLT	FASHING	FIANCEE	FITMENT
EYEBROW	FASHION	FIBBING	FITNESS
EYEHOLE	FAST-DAY	FIBROID	FITTING
EYELASH	FASTEST	FIBROUS	FIXABLE
EYELESS	FASTING	FIBSTER	FIXEDLY
EYESHOT	FATALLY	FIBULAR	FIXTURE
EYESORE	FATEFUL	FICTILE	FIZZING
EYEWASH	FAT-HEAD	FICTION	FIZZLED
	FATIGUE	FICTIVE	FLACCID
F – 7	FATNESS	FIDDLED	FLAG-DAY
	FATTEST	FIDDLER	FLAGGED
FACETED	FATTISH	FIDGETY	FLAKING
FACTION	FATUITY	FIELDED	FLAMING
FACTORY	FATUOUS	FIELDER	FLANEUR
FACTUAL	FAULTED	FIERCER	FLANGED
FACULTY	FAUVISM	FIERILY	FLANKED
FADDISH	FAWNING	FIFTEEN	FLANKER
FADDIST	FEARFUL	FIFTHLY	FLANNEL
FADE-OUT	FEARING	FIGHTER	FLAPPED
FAGGING	FEASTED	FIG-LEAF	FLAPPER
FAIENCE	FEASTER	FIGMENT	FLARING
FAILING	FEATHER	FIG-TREE	FLASHED
FAILURE	FEATURE	FIGURAL	FLASHER
FAINTED	FEBRILE	FIGURED	FLATLET
FAINTER	FEDERAL	FIGWORT	FLATTEN
FAINTLY	FEEDING	FILBERT	FLATTER
FAIREST	FEELING	FILCHED	FLAVOUR
FAIRING	FEE-TAIL	FILCHER	FLAWING
FAIRISH	FEIGNED	FILINGS	FLAYING
FAIRWAY	FEINTED	FILLING	FLECKED
FALLACY	FELLING	FILM-FAN	FLECKER
FALLING	FELONRY	FILMING	FLEDGED
FALSELY	FELSPAR	FINABLE	FLEECED
FALSEST	FELTING	FINALLY	FLEECER
FALSIFY	FELUCCA	FINANCE	FLEEING
FALSITY	FEMORAL	FINDING	FLEETED
FANATIC	FENCING	FINESSE	FLEETER
FANCIED	FENDING	FINICAL	FLEETLY
FANFARE	FEOFFEE	FINICKY	FLEMING
FAN-MAIL	FERMENT	FINLESS	FLEMISH
FANNING	FERMION	FINNISH	FLESHED
FANTAIL	FERNERY	FIREARM	FLESHER
FANTAST	FERN-OWL	FIREBAR	FLESHLY
FANTASY	FERRATE	FIRE-BOX	FLEURET
FANZINE	FERRIED	FIREDOG	FLEXILE
FAR-AWAY	FERROUS	FIREFLY	FLEXING
FARCEUR	FERRULE	FIREMAN	FLEXION
FARCING	FERTILE	FIREPAN	FLEXURE
FARMERY	FERVENT	FIRSTLY	FLICKED
FARMING	FERVOUR	FISHERY	FLICKER
FARMOST	FESTIVE	FISHILY	FLIGHTY
FARRAGO	FESTOON	FISHING	FLIPPED
FARRIER	FETCHED	FISH-OIL	FLIPPER
FARTHER	FETLOCK	FISSILE	FLIRTED
FASCISM	FEVERED	FISSION	FLITTED

FLITTER	FONDANT	FOULING	FROTHED
FLIVVER	FONDEST	FOUNDED	FROWARD
FLOATED	FONDLED	FOUNDER	FROWNED
FLOATER	FONDLER	FOUNDRY	FRUITED
FLOCKED	FOOLERY	FOWLING	FRUITER
FLOGGED	FOOLING	FOX-HUNT	FUCHSIA
FLOODED	FOOLISH	FOXLIKE	FUDDLED
FLOORED	FOOTBOY	FOXTAIL	FUDDLER
FLOORER	FOOTING	FOXTROT	FUDGING
FLOPPED	FOOTLED	FRACTAL	FUEHRER
FLORIST	FOOTMAN	FRAGILE	FUELLED
FLOTAGE	FOOTPAD	FRAILLY	FULCRUM
FLOTANT	FOOT-ROT	FRAILTY	FULGENT
FLOTSAM	FOOTSPA	FRAME-UP	FULLEST
FLOUNCE	FOOTWAY	FRAMING	FULL-PAY
FLOURED	FOPPERY	FRANKED	FULSOME
FLOUTED	FOPPISH	FRANKLY	FUMBLED
FLOUTER	FORAGED	FRANTIC	FUMBLER
FLOWERY	FORAGER	FRAUGHT	FUNDING
FLOWING	FORAYED	FRAYING	FUNERAL
FLUENCY	FORBADE	FRAZZLE	FUNGOID
FLUFFED	FORBEAR	FREAKED	FUNGOUS
FLUKILY	FORBORE	FRECKLE	FUNKING
FLUKING	FORCEPS	FRECKLY	FUNNILY
FLUMMOX	FORCING	FREEDOM	FUNNING
FLUNKEY	FORDING	FREEING	FURBISH
FLUSHED	FORDONE	FREEMAN	FURCATE
FLUSTER	FOREARM	FREESIA	FURIOSO
FLUTING	FOREIGN	FREEZER	FURIOUS
FLUTIST	FORELEG	FREIGHT	FURLING
FLUTTER	FOREMAN	FRESHEN	FURLONG
FLUVIAL	FORERAN	FRESHER	FURNACE
FLY-AWAY	FORERUN	FRESHET	FURNISH
FLY-BOOK	FORESAW	FRESHLY	FURRIER
FLY-FLAP	FORESEE	FRETFUL	FURRING
FLY-HALF	FORETOP	FRETSAW	FURTHER
FLYLEAF	FOREVER	FRETTED	FURTIVE
FLYOVER	FORFEIT	FRIABLE	FUSIBLE
FLY-PAST	FORFEND	FRIEZED	FUSSIER
FLY-TRAP	FORGAVE	FRIGATE	FUSSILY
FOALING	FORGERY	FRILLED	FUSSING
FOAMING	FORGING	FRINGED	FUSS-POT
FOBBING	FORGIVE	FRISIAN	FUSTIAN
FOCUSED	FORGONE	FRISKED	FUSTIER
FOE-LIKE	FORKING	FRISKER	FUZZIER
FOG-BANK	FORLORN	FRITTED	FUZZLED
FOGGIER	FORMATE	FRITTER	
FOGGILY	FORMING	FRIZZED	
FOGGING	FORMULA	FRIZZLE	G – 7
FOG-HORN	FORSAKE	FROCKED	
FOILING	FORSOOK	FROGGED	GABBING
FOISTED	FORTIFY	FROGMAN	GABBLED
FOLDING	FORTUNE	FRONDED	GABBLER
FOLIAGE	FORWARD	FRONTAL	GADDING
FOLIATE	FORWENT	FRONTED	GADDISH
FOLLIES	FOULARD	FROSTED	GAEKWAR
			GAFFING

GAGGING	GAUNTLY	GLADDER	GODLILY
GAINFUL	GAUNTRY	GLAD-EYE	GODSEND
GAINING	GAVOTTE	GLAMOUR	GODSHIP
GAINSAY	GAYNESS	GLANCED	GODWARD
GALATEA	GAYSOME	GLARING	GOGGLED
GALILEE	GAZELLE	GLASSES	GOGGLES
GALILEO	GAZETTE	GLAZIER	GOITRED
GALLANT	GEARING	GLAZING	GOLFING
GALLEON	GELDING	GLEAMED	GOLIATH
GALLERY	GELIDLY	GLEANED	GONDOLA
GALLING	GEMMING	GLEANER	GONGING
GALLOWS	GENERAL	GLEEFUL	GOOD-BYE
GALUMPH	GENERIC	GLIDING	GOOD-DAY
GAMBIST	GENESIS	GLIMMER	GOODISH
GAMBLED	GENETIC	GLIMPSE	GOODMAN
GAMBLER	GENITAL	GLINTED	GOOSERY
GAMBOGE	GENOESE	GLISTEN	GORDIAN
GAMEFUL	GENTEEL	GLISTER	GORGING
GAME-LEG	GENTIAN	GLITTER	GORILLA
GANGING	GENTILE	GLOATED	GORMAND
GANGLIA	GENTLER	GLOBATE	GORSEDD
GANGWAY	GENUINE	GLOBING	GOSLING
GAPPING	GEOLOGY	GLOBOID	GOSSIPY
GARAGED	GEORDIE	GLOBOSE	GOUACHE
GARBAGE	GERMANE	GLOBULE	GOUGING
GARBLED	GESTAPO	GLOOMED	GOULASH
GARFISH	GESTURE	GLORIED	GOURMET
GARGLED	GETABLE	GLORIFY	GOUTILY
GARLAND	GET-AWAY	GLOSSED	GRABBED
GARMENT	GETTING	GLOSSER	GRABBER
GARNISH	GHASTLY	GLOTTIC	GRABBLE
GAROTTE	GHERKIN	GLOTTIS	GRACING
GARPIKE	GHILLIE	GLOWING	GRADATE
GAS-BUOY	GHOSTLY	GLUCOSE	GRADELY
GAS-COAL	GIBLETS	GLUE-POT	GRADING
GAS-COKE	GIDDILY	GLUMMER	GRADUAL
GASEITY	GIFTING	GLUTTED	GRAFTED
GASEOUS	GIGGLED	GLUTTON	GRAFTER
GAS-FIRE	GIGGLER	GNARLED	GRAINED
GASHING	GILDING	GNARRED	GRAINER
GAS-LIME	GIMBALS	GNASHED	GRAMMAR
GAS-MAIN	GIMMICK	GNAWING	GRAMPUS
GAS-MASK	GIN-FIZZ	GNOSTIC	GRANARY
GAS-OVEN	GINGERY	GOADING	GRANDAD
GASPING	GINGHAM	GO-AHEAD	GRANDAM
GAS-PIPE	GIN-SHOP	GOATISH	GRANDEE
GAS-RING	GIRAFFE	GOBBLED	GRANDER
GASSING	GIRDING	GOBBLER	GRANDLY
GASTRIC	GIRDLED	GOBELIN	GRANDMA
GATEMAN	GIRDLER	GODDESS	GRANGER
GATEWAY	GIRLISH	GODETIA	GRANITE
GATLING	GIRTHED	GODHEAD	GRANTED
GAUDERY	GIZZARD	GODHOOD	GRANTEE
GAUDILY	GLACIAL	GODLESS	GRANTER
GAUGING	GLACIER	GODLIER	GRANTOR
GAULISH	GLADDEN	GODLIKE	GRANULE

GRAPERY
GRAPHIC
GRAPNEL
GRAPPLE
GRASPED
GRASPER
GRASSED
GRATIFY
GRATING
GRAVELY
GRAVEST
GRAVIED
GRAVITY
GRAVLAX
GRAVURE
GRAZIER
GRAZING
GREASED
GREASER
GREATER
GREATLY
GRECIAN
GRECISM
GRECIZE
GREENER
GREENLY
GREETED
GREMLIN
GRENADE
GREY-HEN
GREYISH
GREYLAG
GRIDDED
GRIDDLE
GRIEVED
GRIFFIN
GRIFFON
GRILLED
GRIMACE
GRIMING
GRIMMER
GRINDER
GRINNED
GRIPING
GRIPPED
GRIPPER
GRISTLE
GRISTLY
GRITTED
GRIZZLE
GRIZZLY
GROANED
GROCERY
GROMMET
GROOMED
GROOVED

GROPING
GROSSER
GROSSLY
GROUNDS
GROUPED
GROUPER
GROUSED
GROUSER
GROUTED
GROWING
GROWLED
GROWLER
GROWN-UP
GRUBBED
GRUBBER
GRUDGED
GRUDGER
GRUFFER
GRUFFLY
GRUMBLE
GRUNTED
GRUNTER
GRUYERE
GUARDED
GUDGEON
GUELDER
GUERDON
GUESSED
GUESSER
GUICHET
GUIDAGE
GUIDING
GUILDER
GUILDRY
GUIPURE
GULLERY
GULLIED
GULLING
GUMBOIL
GUMBOOT
GUMDROP
GUMMING
GUM-TREE
GUNBOAT
GUN-DECK
GUN-FIRE
GUNNERY
GUNNING
GUNROOM
GUNSHOT
GUN-SITE
GUNWALE
GURGLED
GURNARD
GUSHING
GUSTILY

GUTTING
GUZZLED
GUZZLER
GYMNAST
GYRATED

H – 7

HABITAT
HABITED
HABITUE
HACKBUT
HACKING
HACKLED
HACKNEY
HACK-SAW
HADDOCK
HAFTING
HAGGARD
HAGGISH
HAGGLED
HAGGLER
HAILING
HAIRCUT
HAIR-OIL
HAIRPIN
HALBERD
HALCYON
HALF-PAY
HALFWAY
HALF-WIT
HALIBUT
HALOGEN
HALTING
HALVING
HALYARD
HAMBURG
HAMMOCK
HAMSTER
HAMULAR
HANDBAG
HANDFUL
HANDIER
HANDILY
HANDING
HANDLED
HANDLER
HANDSAW
HANGDOG
HANGING
HANGMAN
HANG-NET
HANSARD
HAPLESS
HAP'ORTH
HAPPIER

HAPPILY
HARBOUR
HARDEST
HARDIER
HARDILY
HARDISH
HARD-PAN
HARDSET
HARD-WON
HAREING
HARELIP
HARICOT
HARKING
HARMFUL
HARMING
HARMONY
HARNESS
HARPING
HARPIST
HARPOON
HARRIED
HARRIER
HARSHER
HARSHLY
HARVEST
HASHING
HASHISH
HASSOCK
HASTIER
HASTILY
HASTING
HATABLE
HATCHER
HATCHET
HATEFUL
HATLESS
HAT-RACK
HAUBERK
HAUGHTY
HAULAGE
HAULIER
HAULING
HAUNTED
HAUNTER
HAUTBOY
HAUTEUR
HAWKBIT
HAWKING
HAWK-OWL
HAY-BAND
HAYCOCK
HAYFORK
HAY-LOFT
HAYRICK
HAYSEED
HAYWARD

HAYWIRE	HERBOUS	HOLSTER	HUMANLY
HAZIEST	HERDING	HOMERIC	HUMBLED
HEADILY	HERETIC	HONESTY	HUMBLER
HEADING	HERITOR	HONEYED	HUMDRUM
HEADMAN	HEROINE	HONITON	HUMERUS
HEADWAY	HEROISM	HONKING	HUMIDLY
HEALING	HEROIZE	HOODING	HUMMING
HEALTHY	HERONRY	HOODLUM	HUMMOCK
HEAPING	HERRING	HOOFING	HUMULUS
HEARING	HERSELF	HOOKING	HUNCHED
HEARKEN	HESSIAN	HOOPING	HUNDRED
HEARSAY	HEXAGON	HOOTING	HUNTING
HEARTED	HEXAPOD	HOPEFUL	HURDLED
HEARTEN	HICKORY	HOPKILN	HURDLER
HEATHEN	HIDALGO	HOPLITE	HURLING
HEATING	HIDEOUS	HOPPING	HURRIED
HEAVE-TO	HIDE-OUT	HOP-POLE	HURRIER
HEAVIER	HIGGLED	HOP-VINE	HURTFUL
HEAVILY	HIGGLER	HORIZON	HURTLED
HEAVING	HIGHDAY	HORMONE	HUSBAND
HEBRAIC	HIGHEST	HORNBAR	HUSHABY
HECKLED	HIGH-HAT	HORNING	HUSHING
HECKLER	HIGHWAY	HORNISH	HUSKING
HECTARE	HILLIER	HORN-OWL	HUSTLED
HEDGING	HILLMAN	HORRIFY	HUSTLER
HEDONIC	HILLOCK	HOSANNA	HUTMENT
HEEDFUL	HILLTOP	HOSIERY	HYDRANT
HEEDING	HIMSELF	HOSPICE	HYDRATE
HEELING	HINNIED	HOSTAGE	HYGIENE
HEELTAP	HINTING	HOSTESS	HYMNIST
HEFTIER	HIPPING	HOSTILE	HYMNODY
HEFTILY	HIRABLE	HOSTLER	
HEIGH-HO	HIRCINE	HOTFOOT	
HEINOUS	HIRSUTE	HOTNESS	**I – 7**
HEIRDOM	HISSING	HOTSPUR	
HEIRESS	HISTORY	HOTTEST	IBERIAN
HELICAL	HITCHED	HOTTING	ICEBERG
HELICON	HITTING	HOT-WALL	ICEBOAT
HELIPAD	HITTITE	HOUNDED	ICE-FLOE
HELL-CAT	HOARDED	HOUSAGE	ICEPACK
HELLENE	HOARDER	HOUSING	ICE-RINK
HELLISH	HOAXING	HOVERED	ICHABOD
HELPFUL	HOBBLED	HOVERER	ICINESS
HELPING	HOBNAIL	HOWBEIT	IDEALLY
HEMLOCK	HOGGING	HOWDY-DO	IDIOTIC
HEMMING	HOGGISH	HOWEVER	IDOLISE
HENBANE	HOGWASH	HOWLING	IDYLLIC
HEN-COOP	HOGSWEED	HUDDLED	IGNEOUS
HENNAED	HOISTED	HUDDLER	IGNITED
HENNERY	HOISTER	HUELESS	IGNITER
HENPECK	HOLDALL	HUFFILY	IGNOBLE
HENWIFE	HOLDING	HUFFING	IGNOBLY
HEPATIC	HOLIDAY	HUFFISH	IGNORED
HERBAGE	HOLIEST	HUGGING	ILL-BRED
HERBARY	HOLLAND	HULKING	ILLEGAL
HERBIST	HOLM-OAK	HULLING	ILL-FAME
			ILLICIT

ILLNESS	INCURVE	INSULAR	JACK-TAR
ILL-TIME	INDEXED	INSULIN	JACOBIN
ILLUMED	INDITED	INSURED	JACUZZI
ILL-USED	INDOORS	INSURER	JADEDLY
ILL-WILL	INDRAWN	INTEGER	JAGGING
IMAGERY	INDUCED	INTENSE	JAILING
IMAGINE	INDULGE	INTERIM	JAMMING
IMAGING	INEPTLY	INTONED	JANGLED
IMBIBED	INERTIA	INTRUDE	JANITOR
IMBIBER	INERTLY	INTRUST	JANKERS
IMBRUED	INEXACT	INTWINE	JANUARY
IMBUING	INFANCY	INURING	JARRING
IMITATE	INFANTA	INVADED	JASMINE
IMMENSE	INFANTE	INVADER	JAVELIN
IMMERSE	INFERNO	INVALID	JAWBONE
IMMORAL	INFIDEL	INVEIGH	JAZZING
IMMURED	INFIELD	INVERSE	JEALOUS
IMPALED	INFIXED	INVIOUS	JEERING
IMPASSE	INFLAME	INVITED	JEHOVAH
IMPEACH	INFLATE	INVITER	JELLIED
IMPEDED	INFLECT	INVOICE	JELLIFY
IMPERIL	INFLICT	INVOKED	JERICHO
IMPETUS	INFUSED	INVOKER	JERKING
IMPIETY	INFUSER	INVOLVE	JESTFUL
IMPINGE	INGENUE	INWARDS	JESTING
IMPIOUS	INGOING	INWOVEN	JETFOIL
IMPLANT	INGRATE	IODISED	JETTIED
IMPLIED	INGRESS	IONISED	JETTING
IMPLORE	INHABIT	IONISER	JEZEBEL
IMPOSED	INHALED	IRACUND	JIBBING
IMPOSER	INHALER	IRANIAN	JIB-BOOM
IMPOUND	INHERED	IRIDIUM	JIGGING
IMPRESS	INHERIT	IRKSOME	JIGGLED
IMPREST	INHIBIT	IRONING	JILTING
IMPRINT	INHUMAN	ISHMAEL	JIM-CROW
IMPROVE	INITIAL	ISLAMIC	JINGLED
IMPULSE	INJURED	ISOLATE	JITTERS
IMPUTED	INJURER	ISOTOPE	JITTERY
IMPUTER	INKHORN	ISSUING	JOBBERY
INANELY	INKLING	ISTHMUS	JOBBING
INANITY	INKWELL	ITALIAN	JOBLESS
INAPTLY	INLACED	ITALICS	JOCULAR
INBEING	INLAYER	ITCHING	JOGGING
INBOARD	INNINGS	ITEMISE	JOGGLED
INBOUND	INQUEST	ITERATE	JOGTROT
INBREAK	INQUIRE	IVORIED	JOINDER
INBREED	INQUIRY	IVY-BUSH	JOINERY
INCENSE	INSHORE		JOINING
INCHING	INSIDER		JOINTED
INCISED	INSIGHT	J – 7	JOINTER
INCISOR	INSIPID		JOINTLY
INCITED	INSPECT	JABBING	JOISTED
INCLINE	INSPIRE	JACINTH	JOLLIER
INCLUDE	INSTALL	JACKASS	JOLLIFY
INCOMER	INSTANT	JACKDAW	JOLLILY
INCUBUS	INSTEAD	JACKING	JOLLITY
		JACKPOT	

JOLTING	KHEDIVE	LACONIC	LAUNDRY
JONQUIL	KIBBUTZ	LACQUER	LAW-BOOK
JOSTLED	KICKING	LACTATE	LAWLESS
JOTTING	KICK-OFF	LACTOSE	LAW-LORD
JOUNCED	KIDDING	LADLING	LAW-SUIT
JOURNAL	KILLING	LADY-DAY	LAXNESS
JOURNEY	KILLJOY	LAGGARD	LAYERED
JOUSTED	KILN-DRY	LAGGING	LAYETTE
JOYLESS	KILOBIT	LAKELET	LAYLAND
JOY-RIDE	KINDEST	LAMBADA	LAZIEST
JUBILEE	KINDLED	LAMBENT	LAZY-BED
JUDAISM	KINDRED	LAMBING	LEACHED
JUDAIST	KINETIC	LAMBKIN	LEADING
JUDAISE	KINGCUP	LAMINAR	LEAFAGE
JUDGING	KINGDOM	LAMMING	LEAFING
JUGGING	KINGPIN	LAMP-LIT	LEAFLET
JUGGINS	KINKING	LAMPOON	LEAGUED
JUGGLED	KINLESS	LAMPREY	LEAGUER
JUGGLER	KINSHIP	LANCERS	LEAKAGE
JUGULAR	KINSMAN	LANCING	LEAKING
JUICIER	KIRTLED	LANDING	LEANDER
JU-JITSU	KISSING	LANDTAG	LEANEST
JUKE-BOX	KITCHEN	LAND-TAX	LEANING
JUMBLED	KNACKER	LANGUID	LEAPING
JUMBLER	KNAPPED	LANGUOR	LEARNED
JUMPING	KNAPPER	LANKIER	LEARNER
JUNIPER	KNARLED	LANOLIN	LEASHED
JUNKMAN	KNAVERY	LANTERN	LEASING
JUPITER	KNAVISH	LANYARD	LEATHER
JURY-BOX	KNEADED	LAPPING	LEAVING
JURYMAN	KNEECAP	LAPPISH	LECTERN
JUSSIVE	KNEE-PAN	LAPSING	LECTION
JUSTICE	KNIFING	LAPWING	LECTURE
JUSTIFY	KNITTED	LARCENY	LEEMOST
JUTTING	KNITTER	LARDING	LEERILY
JUVENAL	KNOBBED	LARGELY	LEERING
	KNOBBLY	LARGEST	LEE-SIDE
K – 7	KNOCKED	LARGISH	LEE-TIDE
	KNOCKER	LARKING	LEEWARD
KALIMBA	KNOCK-ON	LASAGNE	LEGALLY
KAMERAD	KNOTTED	LASHING	LEGATEE
KARAOKE	KNOUTED	LASHKAR	LEGGING
KATYDID	KNOW-ALL	LASSOED	LEGIBLE
KEENEST	KNOWING	LASTING	LEGIBLY
KEENING	KNUCKLE	LATAKIA	LEG-IRON
KEEPING	KNURLED	LATCHED	LEGLESS
KENTISH	KCUMISS	LATCHET	LEG-PULL
KESTREL	KREMLIN	LATENCY	LEISURE
KETCHUP	KRISHNA	LATERAL	LEMMING
KEYBOLT	KRYPTON	LATERAN	LENDING
KEYED-UP	KURSAAL	LATHING	LENGTHY
KEYHOLE		LATTICE	LENIENT
KEYNOTE	**L – 7**	LATVIAN	LENTOID
KEY-RING		LAUDING	LEONINE
KEYWORD	LABIATE	LAUGHED	LEOPARD
KHAMSIN	LACKING	LAUNDER	LEOTARD

LEPROSY	LIONISM	LONGING	LUMPISH
LEPROUS	LIONISE	LONGISH	LUNATIC
LESBIAN	LIPPING	LONG-LEG	LUNCHED
LET-DOWN	LIQUATE	LONG-RUN	LUNETTE
LETTING	LIQUEFY	LOOKING	LUNGING
LETTISH	LIQUEUR	LOOKOUT	LURCHED
LETTUCE	LISPING	LOOMING	LURCHER
LEUCOMA	LISSOME	LOOPING	LURKING
LEVELLY	LISTING	LOOSELY	LUSHING
LEVERED	LITERAL	LOOSING	LUSTFUL
LEVERET	LITHELY	LOOTING	LUSTIER
LEVYING	LITHIUM	LOPPING	LUSTILY
LEXICAL	LITHOID	LORDING	LUSTING
LEXICON	LITOTES	LORELEI	LYCHNIS
LIAISON	LITURGY	LORINER	LYDDITE
LIBERAL	LIVABLE	LOSABLE	LYING-IN
LIBERTY	LIVENED	LOTTERY	LYINGLY
LIBRARY	LIVE-OAK	LOTTING	LYNCHED
LICENCE	LIVERED	LOUDEST	LYRICAL
LICENSE	LOADING	LOUNGED	
LICITLY	LOAFING	LOUNGER	
LICKING	LOAMING	LOURING	M – 7
LIDLESS	LOANING	LOUSILY	
LIE-ABED	LOATHED	LOUTISH	MACABRE
LIFTING	LOATHER	LOVABLE	MACADAM
LIFTOFF	LOATHLY	LOW-BORN	MACAQUE
LIGATED	LOBBIED	LOW-BRED	MACHETE
LIGHTED	LOBBING	LOWDOWN	MACHINE
LIGHTEN	LOBELIA	LOWERED	MADDEST
LIGHTER	LOBSTER	LOW-GEAR	MADDING
LIGHTLY	LOBULAR	LOWLAND	MADEIRA
LIGNIFY	LOCALLY	LOW-LIFE	MADNESS
LIGNITE	LOCATED	LOWLILY	MADONNA
LIGNOSE	LOCKAGE	LOWNESS	MAESTRO
LIKABLE	LOCKING	LOW-TIDE	MAGENTA
LIKENED	LOCKJAW	LOYALLY	MAGGOTY
LILY-PAD	LOCK-OUT	LOYALTY	MAGICAL
LIMBATE	LODGING	LOZENGE	MAGINOT
LIMBING	LOFTIER	LUCENCY	MAGNATE
LIME-PIT	LOFTILY	LUCERNE	MAGNETO
LIMINAL	LOFTING	LUCIDLY	MAGNIFY
LIMITED	LOG-BOOK	LUCIFER	MAHATMA
LIMITER	LOGGING	LUCKIER	MAHJONG
LIMNING	LOGICAL	LUCKILY	MAIL-BAG
LIMPING	LOGLINE	LUFFING	MAILING
LINCTUS	LOG-REEL	LUGGAGE	MAIL-VAN
LINEAGE	LOG-ROLL	LUGGING	MAIMING
LINEATE	LOG-SHIP	LUGMARK	MAINOUR
LINEMAN	LOGWOOD	LUGSAIL	MAINTOP
LINGUAL	LOLLARD	LUGWORM	MAJESTY
LINKAGE	LOLLING	LULLABY	MALACCA
LINKBOY	LOMBARD	LULLING	MALAISE
LINKING	LONG-AGO	LUMBAGO	MALARIA
LINSEED	LONGBOW	LUMINAL	MALAYAN
LION-CUB	LONGEST	LUMPIER	MALISON
LIONESS	LONG-HOP	LUMPING	MALLARD
			MALLING

MALMSEY	MARSALA	MEDICAL	MILLING
MALTESE	MARSHAL	MEETING	MILLION
MALTING	MARTIAL	MEGABIT	MIMESIS
MALTMAN	MARTIAN	MEISSEN	MIMETIC
MAMMARY	MARTINI	MELANGE	MIMICAL
MAMMOTH	MARTLET	MELODIC	MIMICRY
MANACLE	MARXIAN	MELTING	MINARET
MANAGED	MARXISM	MEMENTO	MINCING
MANAGER	MARXIST	MENACED	MINDFUL
MANAKIN	MASHING	MENACER	MINDING
MANATEE	MASH-TUB	MENDING	MINERAL
MANCHET	MASKING	MENFOLK	MINERVA
MANDATE	MASONIC	MENTHOL	MINGLED
MANDREL	MASONRY	MENTION	MINGLER
MANDRIL	MASSAGE	MERCERY	MINIBUS
MANGLED	MASSEUR	MERCURY	MINIKIN
MANGLER	MASSING	MERGING	MINIMAL
MANGOLD	MASSIVE	MERITED	MINIMUM
MANHOLE	MASTERY	MERLING	MINIMUS
MANHOOD	MASTIFF	MERMAID	MINSTER
MAN-HOUR	MASTING	MERRIER	MINTING
MAN-HUNT	MASTOID	MERRILY	MINUTED
MANIKIN	MATADOR	MESEEMS	MIOCENE
MANILLA	MATCHED	MESHING	MIRACLE
MANITOU	MATCHET	MESSAGE	MISCALL
MANKIND	METALOT	MESSIAH	MISCAST
MANLESS	MATINEE	MESSING	MISCITE
MANLIKE	MATTING	METHANE	MISCUED
MAN-MADE	MATTOCK	METONIC	MISDATE
MANNING	MATURED	METTLED	MISDEAL
MANNISH	MAUDLIN	MEWLING	MISDEED
MAN-ROPE	MAULING	MEXICAN	MISDEEM
MANSARD	MAUNDER	MAISMAL	MISDOER
MANSION	MAWKISH	MIAUING	MISDONE
MANTLED	MAXIMAL	MIAULED	MISERLY
MANTLET	MAXIMUM	MICROBE	MISFALL
MANTRAP	MAYFAIR	MICROHM	MISFIRE
MANURED	MAY-LILY	MIDLAND	MISFORM
MANX-CAT	MAY-MORN	MID-LIFE	MISGAVE
MAPPING	MAYORAL	MIDMOST	MISGIVE
MAPPIST	MAYPOLE	MIDRIFF	MISHEAR
MARABOU	MAY-TIME	MIDWIFE	MISJOIN
MARBLED	MAY-WEED	MIGRANT	MISLAID
MARCHED	MAZURKA	MIGRATE	MISLEAD
MARCHER	MEADOWY	MIDLEST	MISLIKE
MARINER	MEANDER	MILDEWY	MISNAME
MARITAL	MEANEST	MILEAGE	MISRATE
MARKING	MEANING	MILFOIL	MISREAD
MARLINE	MEASLED	MILIARY	MISRULE
MARLING	MEASLES	MILITIA	MISSAID
MARLPIT	MEASURE	MILKILY	MISSEEM
MARQUEE	MEAT-TEA	MILKING	MISSEND
MARQUIS	MECHLING	MILKMAN	MISSENT
MARRIED	MEDDLED	MILKSOP	MISSILE
MARRING	MEDDLER	MILL-DAM	MISSING
MARROWY	MEDIATE	MILLIER	MISSION

MISSIVE	MOOTING	MUMMING	NEBULAR
MISTAKE	MOPPING	MUMPING	NECKING
MISTRELL	MORALLY	MUMPISH	NECKLET
MISTERM	MORDANT	MUNCHED	NECKTIE
MISTFUL	MORELLO	MUNCHER	NEEDFUL
MISTILY	MORNING	MUNDANE	NEEDIER
MISTIME	MOROCCO	MURKIER	NEEDILY
MISTRAL	MORPHIA	MURKILY	NEEDING
MISTUNE	MORTISE	MURRAIN	NEEDLED
MISUSED	MORTIFY	MUSCLED	NEGATED
MITHRAS	MOSELLE	MUSETTE	NEGLECT
MIXABLE	MOTORED	MUSHING	NEGLIGE
MIXEDLY	MOTTLED	MUSICAL	NEGRESS
MIXTURE	MOULDED	MUSK-RAT	NEGROID
MIZZLED	MOULDER	MUSTANG	NEIGHED
MOANFUL	MOULTED	MUSTARD	NEITHER
MOANING	MOUNDED	MUSTILY	NEMESIS
MOBBING	MOUNTED	MUTABLE	NEOLOGY
MOBBISH	MOUNTER	MUTABLY	NEPOTIC
MOBSMAN	MOURNED	MUTANDA	NEPTUNE
MOCKERY	MOURNER	MUTTONY	NERVING
MOCKING	MOUSING	MUZZILY	NERVOUS
MOCK-SUN	MOUTHED	MUZZLED	NEST-EGG
MODALLY	MOUTHER	MYNHEER	NESTING
MODESTY	MOVABLE	MYSTERY	NESTLED
MODICUM	MOVABLY	MYSTIFY	NESTLER
MODISTE	MUCKING		NETBALL
MODULAR	MUD-BATH		NET-CORD
MODULUS	MUD-CART	**N – 7**	NETTING
MOHICAN	MUDDIED		NETTLED
MOIDORE	MUDDIER	NABBING	NETTLER
MOILING	MUDDILY	NAGGING	NETWORK
MOISTEN	MUDDING	NAILERY	NEURINE
MOLE-RAT	MUDDLED	NAILING	NEUROSE
MOLLIFY	MUDFISH	NAIVELY	NEUTRAL
MOLLUSC	MUD-FLAT	NAIVETE	NEUTRON
MONARCH	MUD-HOLE	NAKEDLY	NEW-BORN
MONEYED	MUDLARK	NAMABLE	NEWGATE
MONGREL	MUEZZIN	NANKEEN	NEW-MADE
MONIKER	MUFFING	NAPHTHA	NEWNESS
MONITOR	MUFFLED	NAPLESS	NEWSBOY
MONKISH	MUFFLER	NAPPING	NEWSMAN
MONOCLE	MUGGING	NARRATE	NIAGARA
MONSOON	MUGGINS	NARWHAL	NIBBLED
MONSTER	MUGGISH	NASALLY	NIBBLER
MONTHLY	MUGWUMP	NASCENT	NIBLICK
MOOCHED	MULATTO	NASTIER	NICKING
MOODILY	MULCHED	NASTILY	NIGELLA
MOONIES	MULCTED	NATTIER	NIGGARD
MOONING	MULLING	NATTILY	NIGGLED
MOONISH	MULLION	NATURAL	NIGGLER
MOONLIT	MUMBLED	NATURED	NIGHTIE
MOORAGE	MUMBLER	NAUGHTY	NIGHTLY
MOOR-HEN	MUMMERY	NAZIISM	NIMBLER
MOORING	MUMMIED	NEAREST	NINE-PIN
MOORISH	MUMMIFY	NEATEST	NINTHLY
		NEBULAE	

NIPPERS	NUPTIAL	OFFHAND	ORIFICE
NIPPIER	NURSERY	OFFICER	ORIGAMI
NIPPIES	NURSING	OFF-LINE	OROLOGY
NIPPING	NURTURE	OFFSIDE	ORPHEAN
NIRVANA	NUTTING	OGREISH	ORPHEUS
NITRATE	NUT-TREE	OILCAKE	ORTOLAN
NITROUS	NUZZLED	OILSHOP	OSCULAR
NOBBLED		OILSKIN	OSMANLI
NOBBLER		OIL-WELL	OSTEOID
NOBLEST	O – 7	OLDNESS	OSTRICH
NO-CLAIM		OLDSTER	OTTOMAN
NODATED	OAFLIKE	OLD-TIME	OUTSELF
NODDING	OAK-LEAF	OLYMPIA	OUSTING
NODULAR	OAKLING	OLYMPIC	OUTBACK
NODULED	OARFISH	OLYMPUS	OUTBRAG
NOGGING	OARLOCK	OMINOUS	OUTCAST
NOISILY	OARSMAN	OMITTED	OUTCOME
NOISING	OATCAKE	OMNIBUS	OUTCROP
NOISOME	OATMEAL	OMNIFIC	OUTDARE
NOMADIC	OBELISK	ONE-EYED	OUTDONE
NOMINAL	OBESITY	ONEFOLD	OUTDOOR
NOMINEE	OBEYING	ONENESS	OUTFACE
NON-ACID	OBLIGED	ONERARY	OUTFALL
NONAGON	OBLIGEE	ONEROUS	OUTFLOW
NONPLUS	OBLIGER	ONESELF	OUTGOER
NONSTOP	OBLIGOR	ONE STEP	OUTGROW
NONSUCH	OBLIQUE	ONGOING	OUTHAUL
NON-SUIT	OBLOQUY	ONWARDS	OUTLAND
NOONDAY	OBSCENE	OPACITY	OUTLAST
NORFOLK	OBSCURE	OPALINE	OUTLEAP
NORWICH	OBSERVE	OPALISE	OUTLIER
NOSEBAG	OBTRUDE	OPEN-AIR	OUTLINE
NOSEGAY	OBVERSE	OPENING	OUTLIVE
NOSTRIL	OBVIATE	OPERATE	OUTLOOK
NOSTRUM	OBVIOUS	OPINING	OUTMOST
NOTABLE	OCARINA	OPINION	OUTMOVE
NOTABLY	OCCIPUT	OPOSSUM	OUTPLACE
NOTANDA	OCCLUDE	OPPIDAN	OUTPLAY
NOTCHED	OCEANIA	OPPOSED	OUTPOST
NOTEDLY	OCEANIC	OPPOSER	OUTPOUR
NOTHING	OCTAGON	OPPRESS	OUTRAGE
NOTICED	OCTAVUS	OPTICAL	OUTRIDE
NOURISH	OCTETTE	OPTIMUM	OUTRODE
NOVELTY	OCTOBER	OPULENT	OUTSAIL
NOWHERE	OCTOPOD	ORATING	OUTSELL
NOXIOUS	OCTOPUS	ORATION	OUTSIDE
NUCLEAR	OCTUPLE	ORATORY	OUTSIZE
NUCLEUS	OCULIST	ORBITAL	OUTSOLD
NUDGING	ODDMENT	ORCHARD	OUTSPAN
NULLIFY	ODDNESS	ORDERED	OUTSTAY
NULLITY	ODORANT	ORDERER	OUTTALK
NUMBERS	ODOROUS	ORDERLY	OUTVOTE
NUMBING	ODYSSEY	ORDINAL	OUTWALK
NUMERAL	OEDIPUS	ORDINEE	OUTWARD
NUNNERY	OFFENCE	OREADES	OUTWEAR
NUNNISH	OFFERED	ORGANIC	OUTWORK
	OFFERER		

OUTWORN	PAIRING	PARSING	PECCANT
OVARIAN	PALADIN	PARSLEY	PECCAVI
OVATION	PALATAL	PARSNIP	PECKING
OVERACT	PALAVER	PARTAKE	PECKISH
OVERALL	PALETOT	PARTIAL	PECTATE
OVERATE	PALETTE	PARTING	PECTINE
OVERAWE	PALFREY	PARTNER	PEDDLED
OVERBID	PALLING	PARVENU	PEDDLER
OVERBUY	PALMARY	PASCHAL	PEDICEL
OVERDID	PALMATE	PASSAGE	PEDICLE
OVERDUE	PALMERY	PASSING	PEELING
OVEREAT	PALMING	PASSION	PEEPING
OVERFAR	PALMIST	PASSIVE	PEERAGE
OVERJOY	PALM-OIL	PASSKEY	PEERESS
OVERLAP	PALPATE	PASSMAN	PEERING
OVERLAY	PALSIED	PASTERN	PEEVISH
OVERLIE	PANACEA	PASTIME	PEGASUS
OVERMAN	PANACHE	PASTING	PEGGING
OVERPAY	PANCAKE	PASTURE	PELAGIC
OVERPLY	PANDEAN	PATBALL	PELICAN
OVERRAN	PANDORA	PATCHED	PELISSE
OVERRUN	PANICKY	PATCHER	PELTING
OVERSEA	PANNAGE	PATELLA	PENALLY
OVERSEE	PANNIER	PATHWAY	PENALTY
OVERSET	PANNING	PATIENT	PENANCE
OVERSEW	PANOPLY	PATNESS	PENATES
OVERTAX	PAN-PIPE	PATRIOT	PENDANT
OVERTLY	PANSIED	PATTERN	PENDENT
OVERTOP	PANTHER	PATTING	PENGUIN
OVIDIAN	PANTIES	PAUCITY	PEN-NAME
OVOIDAL	PANTILE	PAULINE	PENNANT
OVOLOGY	PANTING	PAUNCHY	PENNIED
OWL-LIKE	PAPALLY	PAUSING	PENNING
OXIDATE	PAPERED	PAVLOVA	PENSION
OXIDISE	PAPERER	PAWNING	PENSIVE
OXONIAN	PAPILLA	PAYABLE	PENTODE
	PAPOOSE	PAY-BILL	PEOPLED
P – 7	PAPRIKA	PAY-BOOK	PEPPERY
	PAPULAR	PAY-DIRT	PEPSINE
PACIFIC	PAPYRUS	PAY-LIST	PEPTICS
PACKAGE	PARABLE	PAYLOAD	PEPTONE
PACK-ICE	PARADED	PAYMENT	PERCEPT
PACKING	PARADOX	PAY-ROLL	PERCHED
PACKMAN	PARAGON	PEACHED	PERCHER
PADDING	PARAPET	PEACHER	PERCUSS
PADDLED	PARASOL	PEACOCK	PERDURE
PADDLER	PARBOIL	PEAFOWL	PERFECT
PADDOCK	PARCHED	PEAKING	PERFIDY
PADLOCK	PARESIS	PEAKISH	PERFORM
PADRONE	PARETIC	PEALING	PERFUME
PAGEANT	PARKING	PEARLED	PERFUSE
PAILFUL	PARLOUR	PEASANT	PERGOLA
PAINFUL	PARLOUS	PEA-SOUP	PERHAPS
PAINING	PARODIC	PEATBOG	PERIAPT
PAINTED	PARQUET	PEAT-HAG	PERIDOT
PAINTER	PARRIED	PEBBLED	PERIQUE

PERIWIG	PICTISH	PIQUANT	PLEASER
PERJURE	PICTURE	PIQUING	PLEATED
PERJURY	PIEBALD	PIRATED	PLEDGED
PERKIER	PIECING	PIROGUE	PLEDGEE
PERKILY	PIERAGE	PISCARY	PLEDGER
PERKING	PIERCED	PITAPAT	PLENARY
PERMUTE	PIERCER	PITCHED	PLENISH
PERPLEX	PIERROT	PITCHER	PLENIST
PERRIER	PIFFLED	PITCOAL	PLEROMA
PERSEUS	PIG-EYED	PITEOUS	PLEURAL
PERSIAN	PIGGERY	PITFALL	PLEXURE
PERSIST	PIGGING	PIT-HEAD	PLIABLE
PERSONA	PIGGISH	PITHILY	PLIABLY
PERSPEX	PIG-IRON	PITIFUL	PLIANCY
PERTAIN	PIG-LEAD	PITTING	PLIMSOL
PERTURB	PIGMENT	PITYING	PLODDED
PERUSAL	PIGSKIN	PIVOTAL	PLODDER
PERUSED	PIGTAIL	PIVOTED	PLOPPED
PERUSER	PIGWASH	PLACARD	PLOTTED
PERVADE	PIKELET	PLACATE	PLOTTER
PERVERT	PIKEMAN	PLACEBO	PLUCKED
PESTLED	PILEATE	PLACING	PLUCKER
PETERED	PILGRIM	PLACKET	PLUGGER
PETRIFY	PILLAGE	PLAFOND	PLUGGED
PETROUS	PILLBOX	PLAGUED	PLUMAGE
PETTILY	PILLING	PLAGUER	PLUMBED
PETTING	PILLION	PLAINER	PLUMBER
PETTISH	PILLORY	PLAINLY	PLUMING
PETUNIA	PILLOWY	PLAITED	PLUMMET
PEW-RENT	PILOTED	PLAITER	PLUMPED
PFENNIG	PIMENTO	PLANARY	PLUMPER
PHAETON	PIMPLED	PLANING	PLUMPLY
PHALANX	PINBALL	PLANISH	PLUNDER
PHANTOM	PINCERS	PLANKED	PLUNGED
PHARAOH	PINCHED	PLANNED	PLUNGER
PHARYNX	PINCHER	PLANNER	PLUVIAL
PHILTRE	PINDOWN	PLANTAR	PLUVIUS
PHINEAS	PINFOLD	PLANTED	PLYWOOD
PHOEBUS	PINGING	PLANTER	POACHED
PHOENIX	PINGUID	PLASHED	POACHER
PHONATE	PINGUIN	PLASTER	POETESS
PHONICS	PINHOLE	PLASTIC	POINTED
PHOTISM	PINK-EYE	PLATEAU	POINTER
PHRASED	PINKING	PLATING	POISING
PHRENIC	PINKISH	PLATOON	POLE-AXE
PHYSICS	PINNACE	PLATTED	POLECAT
PIANIST	PINNATE	PLATTER	POLEMIC
PIANOLA	PINNING	PLAUDIT	POLENTA
PIASTRE	PINT-POT	PLAY-BOX	POLICED
PIBROCH	PIONEER	PLAYBOY	POLITER
PICADOR	PIOUSLY	PLAY-DAY	POLITIC
PICCOLO	PIP-EMMA	PLAYFUL	POLLACK
PICKAXE	PIPERIC	PLAYING	POLLARD
PICKING	PIPETTE	PLEADED	POLL-AXE
PICKLED	PIPLESS	PLEADER	POLLING
PICQUET	PIPPING	PLEASED	POLL-MAN

POLL-TAX	POUNCED	PREVIEW	PROPHET
POLLUTE	POUNDED	PREYING	PROPOSE
POLYGON	POUNDER	PRICING	PROPPED
POLYPUS	POURING	PRICKED	PROSAIC
POMFRET	POUTING	PRICKER	PROSIFY
POMMARD	POVERTY	PRICKLE	PROSILY
POMPOUS	POWDERY	PRICKLY	PROSING
PONIARD	POWERED	PRIDIAN	PROSODY
PONTIFF	PRAETOR	PRIDING	PROSPER
PONTOON	PRAIRIE	PRIMACY	PROTEAN
POOH-BAH	PRAISED	PRIMAGE	PROTECT
POOLING	PRAISER	PRIMARY	PROTEGE
POOPING	PRALINE	PRIMATE	PROTEIN
POOREST	PRANCED	PRIMELY	PROTEST
POOR-LAW	PRANGED	PRIMING	PROTEUS
POPCORN	PRANKED	PRIMULA	PROUDER
POPEDOM	PRATIES	PRINKED	PROUDLY
POP-EYED	PRATING	PRINTED	PROVERB
POPPIED	PRATTLE	PRINTER	PROVIDE
POPPING	PRAYING	PRISING	PROVINE
POPPLED	PREACHY	PRITHEE	PROVING
POP-SHOP	PREBEND	PRIVACY	PROVISO
POPULAR	PRECEDE	PRIVATE	PROVOKE
PORCINE	PRECEPT	PRIVILY	PROVOST
PORK-PIE	PRECISE	PRIVITY	PROWESS
PORT-BAR	PREDATE	PRIZING	PROWLED
PORTEND	PREDICT	PROBANG	PROWLER
PORTENT	PREDOOM	PROBATE	PROXIMO
PORTICO	PREEMPT	PROBING	PRUDENT
PORTIFY	PREENED	PROBITY	PRUDERY
PORTING	PREFACE	PROBLEM	PRUDISH
PORTION	PREFECT	PROCEED	PRUNING
PORTRAY	PRELACY	PROCESS	PRUSSIC
POSSESS	PRELATE	PROCTOR	PRYTHEE
POSTAGE	PRELECT	PROCURE	PSALTER
POST-BAG	PRELUDE	PRODDED	PSYCHIC
POST-BOY	PREMIER	PRODDER	PUBERTY
POST-DAY	PREMISE	PRODIGY	PUBLISH
POSTERN	PREMISS	PRODUCE	PUCKISH
POSTING	PREMIUM	PRODUCT	PUDDING
POSTMAN	PREPAID	PROFANE	PUDDLED
POSTURE	PREPARE	PROFESS	PUDDLER
POST-WAR	PREPPIE	PROFFER	PUDDOCK
POTABLE	PREQUEL	PROFILE	PUERILE
POTENCY	PRESAGE	PROFUSE	PUFFING
POT-HERB	PRESENT	PROGENY	PUFFIER
POT-HOLE	PRESIDE	PROGRAM	PUFFILY
POT-HOOK	PRESOAK	PROJECT	PUGMILL
POT-LUCK	PRESSED	PROLATE	PUG-NOSE
POT-SHOT	PRESSER	PROLONG	PULLING
POTTAGE	PRESUME	PROMISE	PULLMAN
POTTERY	PRETEND	PROMOTE	PULL-OUT
POTTING	PRETEXT	PRONELY	PULPING
POUCHED	PRETZEL	PRONGED	PULPOUS
POULARD	PREVAIL	PRONOUN	PULSATE
POULTRY	PREVENT	PROOFED	PULSING

PUMPAGE	QUARREL	RADIANT	RATATAT
PUMPING	QUARTAN	RADIATE	RATCHED
PUMPKIN	QUARTER	RADICAL	RATCHET
PUNCHED	QUARTET	RADICLE	RATTING
PUNCHER	QUASHED	RADIOED	RATTLED
PUNCTUM	QUASSIA	RAFFISH	RATTLER
PUNGENT	QUAVERY	RAFFLED	RAT-TRAP
PUNNING	QUEENED	RAFFLER	RAUCOUS
PUNSTER	QUEENLY	RAGEFUL	RAUNCHY
PUNTING	QUEERER	RAG-FAIR	RAVAGED
PURGING	QUEERLY	RAGGING	RAVINED
PURITAN	QUELLED	RAGTIME	RAVIOLI
PURLIEU	QUELLER	RAGWEED	RAWHIDE
PURLING	QUEROUS	RAGWORT	RAWNESS
PURLOIN	QUERIED	RAIDING	RAYLESS
PURPLED	QUERIST	RAIL-CAR	REACHED
PURPORT	QUESTED	RAILING	REACHER
PURPOSE	QUESTER	RAILWAY	REACTED
PURRING	QUESTOR	RAIMENT	REACTOR
PURSING	QUIBBLE	RAINBOW	READIED
PURSUED	QUICKEN	RAINING	READIER
PURSUER	QUICKER	RAISING	READIES
PURSUIT	QUICKIE	RAKE-OFF	READILY
PURVIEW	QUICKLY	RALLIED	READING
PUSHFUL	QUIESCE	RAMADAN	READMIT
PUSHING	QUIETED	RAMBLED	READOPT
PUSTULE	QUIETEN	RAMBLER	READORN
PUTREFY	QUIETER	RAMEKIN	READOUT
PUTTIED	QUIETLY	RAMEOUS	REAGENT
PUTTING	QUIETUS	RAMLINE	REALISE
PUZZLED	QUILLED	RAMMING	REALISM
PUZZLER	QUILTED	RAMPAGE	REALIST
PYGMEAN	QUILTER	RAMPANT	REALITY
PYJAMAS	QUINARY	RAMPART	REALLOT
PYRAMID	QUINATE	RAMPING	REALTOR
PYRETIC	QUININE	RAMPION	RE-ANNEX
PYREXIA	QUINTET	RANCHED	REAPING
PYRITES	QUIPPED	RANCHER	REAPPLY
PYRITIC	QUITTAL	RANCOUR	REARGUE
PYROSIS	QUITTED	RANGERS	REARING
PYROTIC	QUITTER	RANGING	REARISE
PYRRHIC	QUI-VIVE	RANKEST	REARMED
PYTHIAD	QUIXOTE	RANKING	RE-AROSE
PYTHIAN	QUIZZED	RANKLED	REAWAKE
	QUIZZER	RANSACK	REBATED
	QUONDAM	RANTING	REBIRTH
Q – 7	QUOTING	RAPHAEL	REBLOOM
		RAPIDLY	REBORED
QUACKED		RAPPING	REBOUND
QUAFFED	**R – 7**	RAPPORT	REBUILD
QUAFFER		RAPTURE	REBUILT
QUAILED	RABIDLY	RAREBIT	REBUKED
QUAKING	RACCOON	RASHEST	REBUKER
QUALIFY	RACKETY	RASPING	RECEDED
QUALITY	RACKING	RATABLE	RECEIPT
QUANTIC	RACQUET	RATAFIA	RECEIVE
QUANTUM	RADDLED		

RECHEAT	RE-FOUND	REMOVER	RE-SPOKE
RECITAL	REFRACT	RENAMED	RESPOND
RECITED	REFRAIN	RENDING	RESTAMP
RECITER	REFRAME	RENEWAL	RESTATE
RECKING	REFRESH	RENEWED	REST-DAY
RECLAIM	REFUGEE	RENT-DAY	RESTFUL
RECLAME	REFUSAL	RENTIER	RESTING
RECLASP	REFUSED	RENTING	RESTIVE
RECLINE	REFUSER	REORDER	RESTOCK
RECLOSE	REFUTED	REPAINT	RESTORE
RECLUSE	REFUTER	REPAPER	RESUMED
RECOUNT	REGALED	REPINED	RESURGE
RECOVER	REGALIA	REPINER	RETAKEN
RECROSS	REGALLY	REPLACE	RETINUE
RECRUIT	REGATTA	REPLANT	RETIRAL
RECTIFY	REGENCY	REPLETE	RETIRED
RECTORY	REGIMEN	REPLEVY	RETOUCH
RECURVE	REGNANT	REPLICA	RETRACE
RECYCLE	REGORGE	REPLIED	RETRACT
REDCOAT	REGREET	REPLIER	RETREAD
REDDEST	REGRESS	REPOINT	RETREAT
REDDISH	REGULAR	REPOSAL	RETRIAL
RED-EYED	REGULUS	REPOSED	RETRIED
RED-FISH	REHOUSE	REPOSER	RETYPED
REDHEAD	REIGNED	REPRESS	REUNIFY
REDNECK	REINING	REPRINT	REUNION
REDNESS	REINTER	REPRISE	REUNITE
REDOUBT	REISSUE	REPROOF	REURGED
REDOUND	REJOICE	REPROVE	REVALUE
REDPOLL	REJOINT	REPRUNE	REVELRY
REDRAFT	REJUDGE	REPTILE	REVENGE
REDRAWN	RELABEL	REPULSE	REVENUE
REDRESS	RELAPSE	REPUTED	REVERED
REDSKIN	RELATED	REQUEST	REVERIE
RED-TAPE	RELATER	REQUIEM	REVERSE
REDUCED	RELATOR	REQUIRE	REVERSI
REDUCER	RELAXED	REQUITE	REVILED
REDWING	RELAYED	REREDOS	REVILER
REDWOOD	RELEASE	RESCIND	REVISAL
REEKING	RELIANT	RE-SCORE	REVISED
RE-ELECT	RELIEVE	RESCUED	REVISER
REELING	RELIGHT	RESCUER	REVISIT
RE-ENACT	RELIVED	RESEIZE	REVIVAL
RE-ENDOW	RELUMED	RESERVE	REVIVED
RE-ENJOY	RELYING	RESHAPE	REVIVER
RE-ENTER	REMAINS	RESIDED	REVOKED
RE-ENTRY	REMARRY	RESIDER	REVOLVE
RE-EQUIP	REMBLAI	RESIDUE	REVVING
RE-ERECT	REMNANT	RESOLVE	REWRITE
REEVING	REMODEL	RESOUND	REWROTE
REFEREE	REMORSE	RESPECT	REYNARD
REFINED	REMOTER	RE-SPELL	RHEMISH
REFINER	REMOULD	RE-SPELT	RHENISH
REFLECT	REMOUNT	RESPIRE	RHODIAN
REFLOAT	REMOVAL	RESPITE	RHOMBUS
REFORGE	REMOVED	RESPLIT	RHUBARB

RHYMING	RODLIKE	ROYALTY	SALIENT
RHYMIST	ROEBUCK	RUB-A-DUB	SALLIED
RIBBING	ROGUERY	RUBBING	SALLOWY
RIBLESS	ROGUISH	RUBBISH	SALSIFY
RIBSTON	ROILING	RUB-DOWN	SALT-BOX
RICHEST	ROISTER	RUBICON	SALTIER
RICKETS	ROLLICK	RUCHING	SALTING
RICKETY	ROLLING	RUCKING	SALTIRE
RIDDING	ROMANCE	RUCKLED	SALTISH
RIDDLED	ROMANIC	RUCTION	SALT-PAN
RIDDLER	ROMAUNT	RUDDIER	SALT-PIT
RIFLING	ROMPERS	RUDDILY	SALUTED
RIFTING	ROMPING	RUFFIAN	SALVAGE
RIGGING	ROMPISH	RUFFING	SALVING
RIGHTED	RONDEAU	RUFFLED	SAMOVAR
RIGHTEN	ROOFING	RUNNING	SAMOYED
RIGHTER	ROOKERY	RUINOUS	SAMPLED
RIGHTLY	ROOKING	RUMBLED	SAMPLER
RIGIDLY	ROOMAGE	RUMBLER	SAMURAI
RIMLESS	ROOMFUL	RUMMAGE	SANCTUM
RIMMING	ROOMIER	RUMNESS	SANCTUS
RINDING	ROOMILY	RUMPLED	SANDBAG
RINGING	ROOMING	RUNAWAY	SAND-BOX
RINGLET	ROOSTED	RUNNING	SANDBOY
RINSING	ROOSTER	RUNTIME	SAND-EEL
RIOTING	ROOTING	RUPTURE	SAND-FLY
RIOTOUS	ROPEWAY	RURALLY	SAND-PIT
RIPCORD	ROSEATE	RUSHING	SAPHEAD
RIPOSTE	ROSE-BAY	RUSH-MAT	SAPIENT
RIPPING	ROSE-BOX	RUSSETY	SAPLESS
RIPPLED	ROSE-BUD	RUSSIAN	SAPLING
RISIBLE	ROSETTE	RUSTIER	SAPPHIC
RISIBLY	ROSIEST	RUSTILY	SAPPING
RISKIER	ROSTRUM	RUSTING	SAPWOOD
RISKING	ROTATED	RUSTLED	SARACEN
RISOTTO	ROTATOR	RUSTLER	SARCASM
RISSOLE	ROTTING		SARCOMA
RIVALRY	ROTUNDA		SATANIC
RIVETED	ROUGHED	**S – 7**	SATCHEL
RIVETER	ROUGHEN		SATIATE
RIVIERA	ROUGHER	SABBATH	SATIETY
RIVULET	ROUGHLY	SACKAGE	SATINET
ROAD-HOG	ROULADE	SACKBUT	SATIRIC
ROADMAN	ROULEAU	SACKFUL	SATISFY
ROAD-MAP	ROUNDED	SACKING	SAUCIER
ROADWAY	ROUNDEL	SACRIST	SAUCILY
ROAMING	ROUNDER	SADDEST	SAUCING
ROARING	ROUNDLY	SADDLED	SAUNTER
ROASTED	ROUND-UP	SADDLER	SAURIAN
ROASTER	ROUSING	SAD-EYED	SAUSAGE
ROBBERY	ROUTING	SADIRON	SAVAGED
ROBBING	ROUTINE	SADNESS	SAVANNA
ROCKERY	ROWDIER	SAFFRON	SAVE-ALL
ROCKIER	ROWDILY	SAGGING	SAVELOY
ROCKILY	ROWLOCK	SAILING	SAVINGS
ROCKING	ROYALLY	SAINTED	SAVIOUR
		SAINTLY	

SAVOURY	SCORNED	SEA-HARE	SEGMENT
SAWDUST	SCORNER	SEA-HAWK	SEIZING
SAWFISH	SCORPIO	SEA-KALE	SEIZURE
SAWMILL	SCOURED	SEA-KING	SELF-FED
SAW-WORT	SCOURER	SEA-LARK	SELFISH
SAXHORN	SCOURGE	SEA-LEGS	SELLING
SCABIES	SCOWLED	SEALERY	SELTZER
SCABRID	SCRAGGY	SEA-LILY	SELVAGE
SCALDED	SCRAPED	SEA-LINE	SEMATIC
SCALENE	SCRAPER	SEALING	SEMI-GOD
SCALING	SCRAPPY	SEA-LION	SEMINAL
SCALLOP	SCRATCH	SEA-MARK	SEMITIC
SCALPED	SCRAWLY	SEA-MILE	SEMIPED
SCALPEL	SCRAWNY	SEAMING	SEMITIC
SCALPER	SCREECH	SEA-MOSS	SENATOR
SCAMPED	SCREEVE	SEA-PIKE	SENDING
SCAMPER	SCREWED	SEA-PORT	SEND-OFF
SCANDAL	SCREWER	SEARING	SENEGAL
SCANNED	SCRIBAL	SEA-RISK	SENSING
SCANNER	SCRIBED	SEA-ROOM	SENSORY
SCANTLE	SCRIBER	SEA-SALT	SENSUAL
SCANTLY	SCROOGE	SEASICK	SEPTATE
SCAPULA	SCRUBBY	SEASIDE	SEQUENT
SCARCER	SCRUFFY	SEA-SLUG	SEQUOIA
SCARFED	SCRUMPY	SEATING	SERBIAN
SCARIFY	SCRUNCH	SEA-VIEW	SERENER
SCARING	SCRUPLE	SEA-WALL	SERFAGE
SCARLET	SCUDDED	SEAWARD	SERFDOM
SCARPED	SCUFFLE	SEAWEED	SERIATE
SCARPER	SCULLED	SEA-WIFE	SERINGA
SCARRED	SCULLER	SEA-WING	SERIOUS
SCATHED	SCUPPER	SEA-WOLF	SERPENT
SCATTER	SCUTATE	SEA-WORM	SERRATE
SCAUPER	SCUTTLE	SECEDED	SERRIED
SCENERY	SCYTHED	SECEDER	SERVANT
SCENTED	SEA-BANK	SECLUDE	SERVIAN
SCEPTIC	SEA-BEAR	SECONDO	SERVICE
SCEPTRE	SEA-BEET	SECRECY	SERVILE
SCHEMED	SEA-BIRD	SECRETE	SERVING
SCHEMER	SEA-BOAT	SECTILE	SESSION
SCHERZO	SEA-CALF	SECTION	SET-BACK
SCHOLAR	SEA-CARD	SECULAR	SET-DOWN
SCHOLIA	SEA-COAL	SECURED	SETTING
SCIATIC	SEA-COCK	SECURER	SETTLED
SCIENCE	SEA-COOK	SEDUCED	SETTLER
SCISSOR	SEA-CROW	SEDUCER	SEVENTH
SCOFFED	SEA-DACE	SEEABLE	SEVENTY
SCOFFER	SEA-FIRE	SEEDBED	SEVERAL
SCOLDED	SEA-FISH	SEEDILY	SEVERED
SCOLLOP	SEA-FOAM	SEEDING	SEVERER
SCOOPED	SEA-FOLK	SEED-LAC	SEXLESS
SCOOPER	SEAFOOD	SEED-OIL	SEXTAIN
SCOOTED	SEA-FOWL	SEEKING	SEXTANT
SCOOTER	SEA-GATE	SEEMING	SEXTILE
SCORIFY	SEA-GIRT	SEEPAGE	SHACKLE
SCORING	SEA-GULL	SEETHED	SHADIER

SHADILY	SHIRRED	SIFTING	SKIMMER
SHADING	SHIVERY	SIGHING	SKIMPED
SHADOWY	SHOALED	SIGHTED	SKINFUL
SHAFTED	SHOCKED	SIGHTER	SKINNED
SHAGGED	SHOCKER	SIGHTLY	SKINNER
SHAKILY	SHOEING	SIGNIFY	SKIPPED
SHAKING	SHOE-TIE	SIGNING	SKIPPER
SHALLOP	SHOOING	SIGNORA	SKIPPET
SHALLOT	SHOOTER	SIGNORY	SKIRLED
SHALLOW	SHOP-BOY	SILENCE	SKIRTED
SHAMBLE	SHOPMAN	SILENUS	SKIRTER
SHAMING	SHOPPED	SILICIC	SKITTER
SHAMMED	SHOPPER	SILICON	SKITTLE
SHAMMER	SHORING	SILK-HAT	SKIVING
SHAMPOO	SHORTED	SILKIER	SKULKED
SHAPELY	SHORTEN	SILKILY	SKY-BLUE
SHAPING	SHORTER	SILK-MAN	SKY-HIGH
SHARING	SHOTGUN	SILLIER	SKYLARK
SHARPEN	SHOTTED	SILLILY	SKYLINE
SHARPER	SHOUTED	SILTING	SKYSAIL
SHARPLY	SHOUTER	SILVERN	SKYWARD
SHATTER	SHOVING	SILVERY	SLABBED
SHAVIAN	SHOW-BOX	SIMILAR	SLABBER
SHAVING	SHOWERY	SIMPLER	SLACKED
SHEAFED	SHOWILY	SINCERE	SLACKEN
SHEARER	SHOWING	SINEWED	SLACKER
SHEATHE	SHOWMAN	SINGING	SLACKLY
SHEAVED	SHREDDY	SINGLED	SLAKING
SHEBEEN	SHRILLY	SINGLET	SLAMMED
SHEDDER	SHRINED	SINKING	SLAMMER
SHEERED	SHRIVEL	SINLESS	SLANDER
SHEETED	SHRIVEN	SINNING	SLANGED
SHELLAC	SHROUDS	SINUATE	SLANTED
SHELLED	SHRUBBY	SINUOUS	SLANTLY
SHELLER	SHUDDER	SIPPING	SLAPPED
SHELTER	SHUFFLE	SIRGANG	SLASHED
SHELTIE	SHUNNED	SIRLOIN	SLASHER
SHELVED	SHUNNER	SIROCCO	SLATING
SHERBET	SHUNTED	SISTINE	SLAVERY
SHERIFF	SHUNTER	SITTING	SLAVING
SHEWING	SHUT-EYE	SITUATE	SLAVISH
SHIFTED	SHUTTER	SIXFOLD	SLAYING
SHIFTER	SHUTTLE	SIXTEEN	SLEDDED
SHIKARI	SHYLOCK	SIXTHLY	SLEDGED
SHIMMER	SHYNESS	SIZABLE	SLEEKED
SHINGLE	SHYSTER	SIZZLED	SLEEKER
SHINGLY	SIAMESE	SKATING	SLEEKLY
SHINING	SIBLING	SKEPFUL	SLEEPER
SHIP-BOY	SICK-BAY	SKEPTIC	SLEETED
SHIPFUL	SICK-BED	SKETCHY	SLEIGHT
SHIP-MAN	SICKEST	SKIDDED	SLENDER
SHIPPED	SICKISH	SKIFFLE	SLICING
SHIPPER	SIDEARM	SKILFUL	SLICKER
SHIP-WAY	SIDECAR	SKILLED	SLIDDER
SHIRKED	SIDLING	SKILLET	SLIDING
SHIRKER	SIFFLED	SKIMMED	SLIMILY

SLIMMER	SNAGGED	SOFTEST	SPANKER
SLINGER	SNAGGER	SOFTISH	SPANNED
SLIPPED	SNAKING	SOIGNEE	SPANNER
SLIPPER	SNAKISH	SOILING	SPARELY
SLIPWAY	SNAPPED	SOJOURN	SPARING
SLITHER	SNAPPER	SOLACED	SPARKED
SLITTED	SNARING	SOLDIER	SPARKLE
SLITTER	SNARLED	SOLICIT	SPARRED
SLOBBER	SNATCHY	SOLIDLY	SPARROW
SLOE-GIN	SNEAKED	SOLIDUS	SPARTAN
SLOGGED	SNEAKER	SOLOIST	SPASTIC
SLOGGER	SNEERED	SOLOMON	SPATIAL
SLOPING	SNEERER	SOLUBLE	SPATTER
SLOPPED	SNEEZED	SOLVENT	SPATULA
SLOTTED	SNICKED	SOLVING	SPAWNED
SLOUCHY	SNICKER	SOMATIC	SPAWNER
SLOWEST	SNIFFED	SOMEHOW	SPEAKER
SLOWING	SNIFFLE	SOMEONE	SPEARED
SLUBBER	SNIFTED	SONGFUL	SPEARER
SLUDGER	SNIFTER	SONSHIP	SPECIAL
SLUGGED	SNIGGER	SOOTHED	SPECIES
SLUICED	SNIGGLE	SOOTHER	SPECIFY
SLUMBER	SNIPING	SOOTING	SPECKED
SLUMMER	SNIPPED	SOPHISM	SPECKLE
SLUMPED	SNIPPER	SOPHIST	SPECTRA
SLURRED	SNIPPET	SOPPING	SPECTRE
SLYNESS	SNOOKER	SOPRANO	SPEEDED
SMACKED	SNOOPED	SORCERY	SPEEDER
SMACKER	SNOOPER	SORDINE	SPEED-UP
SMARTED	SNOOZED	SORITES	SPELLED
SMARTEN	SNOOZER	SORORAL	SPELLER
SMARTER	SNORING	SOROSIS	SPELTER
SMARTLY	SNORTED	SORRILY	SPENCER
SMASHED	SNORTER	SORTING	SPENDER
SMASHER	SNOUTED	SOTTISH	SPEWING
SMASH-UP	SNOW-ICE	SOUFFLÉ	SPHERAL
SMATTER	SNOWILY	SOULFUL	SPHERED
SMEARED	SNOWMAN	SOUNDLY	SPHERIC
SMELLED	SNUBBED	SOUNDED	SPICERY
SMELLER	SNUBBER	SOUNDER	SPICILY
SMELTED	SNUFFED	SOUPÇON	SPICING
SMELTER	SNUFFER	SOUREST	SPIDERY
SMICKER	SNUFFLE	SOURING	SPIKING
SMILING	SNUGGLE	SOURISH	SPILLED
SMIRKED	SOAKAGE	SOUSING	SPILLER
SMITING	SOAKING	SOUTANE	SPINACH
SMITTEN	SO-AND-SO	SOUTHER	SPINATE
SMOKIER	SOAPBOX	SOU'WEST	SPINDLE
SMOKILY	SOAPING	SOZZLED	SPINDLY
SMOKING	SOARING	SPACIAL	SPINNER
SMOOTHE	SOBBING	SPACING	SPINNEY
SMOTHER	SOBERED	SPANGLE	SPIRANT
SMUDGED	SOBERLY	SPANGLY	SPIRING
SMUDGER	SOCIETY	SPANIEL	SPIRTED
SMUGGLE	SOCKEYE	SPANISH	SPITING
SNAFFLE	SOCKING	SPANKED	SPITTED

SPITTER	SQUEEZE	STEALER	STONILY
SPITTLE	SQUELCH	STEALTH	STONING
SPLASHY	SQUIFFY	STEAMED	STOOGED
SPLAYED	SQUIRED	STEAMER	STOOKED
SPLEENY	STABBED	STEELED	STOOPED
SPLENIC	STABBER	STEEPED	STOOPER
SPLICED	STABLED	STEEPEN	STOPGAP
SPLODGE	STACKED	STEEPER	STOPPED
SPLODGY	STACKER	STEEPLE	STOPPER
SPLOTCH	STADIUM	STEEPLY	STORAGE
SPOILED	STAFFED	STEERED	STORIED
SPOILER	STAGERY	STEERER	STORING
SPONDEE	STAGGER	STELLAR	STORMED
SPONGED	STAGING	STEMLET	STORMER
SPONGER	STAIDLY	STEMMED	STOUTER
SPONSAL	STAINED	STENCIL	STOUTLY
SPONSON	STAINER	STENTOR	STOWAGE
SPONSOR	STAITHE	STEPNEY	STOWING
SPOOFED	STAKING	STEPPED	STRANGE
SPOOLED	STATELY	STEPPER	STRATUM
SPOONED	STALEST	STEPSON	STRATUS
SPORRAN	STALKED	STERILE	STRAYED
SPORTED	STALKER	STERNAL	STRAYER
SPORTER	STALLED	STERNER	STREAKY
SPOTTED	STAMINA	STERNLY	STREAMY
SPOTTER	STAMMER	STERNUM	STRETCH
SPOUSAL	STAMPED	STETSON	STREWED
SPOUTED	STAMPER	STEWARD	STRIATE
SPOUTER	STAND-BY	STEWING	STRIKER
SPRAYED	STANDER	STEWPAN	STRINGY
SPRAYEY	STAND-TO	STEWPOT	STRIPED
SPRIGGY	STAND-UP	STICKER	STRIVEN
SPRIGHT	STAPLED	STICKLE	STRIVER
SPRINGE	STAPLER	STICK-UP	STROKED
SPRINGY	STARCHY	STIFFEN	STROKER
SPRUCED	STARDOM	STIFFER	STROPHE
SPUMING	STARING	STIFFLY	STUBBED
SPUN-OUT	STARKLY	STIFLED	STUBBLE
SPURNED	STARLIT	STILLED	STUBBLY
SPURNER	STARRED	STILLER	STUCK-UP
SPURRED	STARTED	STILTED	STUDDED
SPURREY	STARTER	STILTON	STUDENT
SPURTED	STARTLE	STIMULI	STUDIED
SPURTLE	STARVED	STINGER	STUFFED
SPUR-WAY	STATANT	STINKER	STUFFER
SPUTNIK	STATELY	STINTED	STUMBLE
SPUTTER	STATICS	STINTER	STUMPED
SPY-BOAT	STATING	STIPEND	STUMPER
SPYHOLE	STATION	STIPPLE	STUNNED
SQUABBY	STATIST	STIRRED	STUNNER
SQUALID	STATUED	STIRRER	STUNTED
SQUALLY	STATURE	STIRRUP	STUPEFY
SQUALOR	STATUTE	STOCKED	STUTTER
SQUARED	STAUNCH	STOICAL	STYGIAN
SQUASHY	STAVING	STOKING	STYLING
SQUATTY	STAYING	STOMACH	STYLISE

STYLISH	SULKING	SWADDLE	SYNESIS
STYLIST	SULLAGE	SWAGGER	SYNODAL
STYLITE	SULLENS	SWAGMAN	SYNONYM
STYLOID	SULLIED	SWAHILI	SYRINGE
STYMIED	SULPHUR	SWALING	
SUASION	SULTANA	SWALLOW	
SUASIVE	SUMLESS	SWAMPED	T – 7
SUASORY	SUMMARY	SWANKED	
SUAVELY	SUMMERY	SWAPPED	TABASCO
SUAVITY	SUMMING	SWARDED	TABINET
SUBACID	SUMMONS	SWARMED	TABLEAU
SUBBING	SUMPTER	SWARTHY	TABLING
SUBDEAN	SUN-BATH	SWASHED	TABLOID
SUBDUAL	SUNBEAM	SWASHER	TABOOED
SUBDUCT	SUN-BEAT	SWATTED	TABULAR
SUBDUED	SUN-BIRD	SWATTER	TACITLY
SUBDUER	SUNBURN	SWAYING	TACKING
SUBEDIT	SUN-DIAL	SWEALED	TACKLED
SUBFUSC	SUNDOWN	SWEARER	TACTFUL
SUB-HEAD	SUNFISH	SWEATED	TACTICS
SUBJECT	SUNLESS	SWEATER	TACTILE
SUBJOIN	SUNNING	SWEDISH	TACTION
SUBLATE	SUNRISE	SWEEPER	TACTUAL
SUBLIME	SUNSPOT	SWEETEN	TADPOLE
SUBRENT	SUNWARD	SWEETER	TAFFETA
SUBSALT	SUNWISE	SWEETLY	TAGGING
SUBSIDE	SUPPING	SWELLED	TAIL-END
SUBSIDY	SUPPLED	SWELTER	TAILING
SUBSIGN	SUPPORT	SWELTRY	TAINTED
SUBSIST	SUPPOSE	SWERVED	TAKE-OFF
SUBSOIL	SUPREME	SWERVER	TAKINGS
SUBSUME	SURCOAT	SWIFTER	TALIPED
SUBTEND	SURDITY	SWIFTLY	TALIPES
SUBTILE	SURFACE	SWIGGED	TALKIES
SUBTLER	SURFEIT	SWILLED	TALKING
SUBTYPE	SURGENT	SWILLER	TALLBOY
SUBURBS	SURGEON	SWIMMER	TALLEST
SUBVENE	SURGERY	SWINDLE	TALLIED
SUBVERT	SURGING	SWINERY	TALLIER
SUCCEED	SURLIER	SWINGED	TALLISH
SUCCESS	SURLILY	SWINGER	TALLOWY
SUCCOUR	SURLOIN	SWINISH	TALLY-HO
SUCCUMB	SURMISE	SWIPING	TALONED
SUCKING	SURNAME	SWIRLED	TAMABLE
SUCKLED	SURPASS	SWISHED	TAMBOUR
SUCKLER	SURPLUS	SWISHER	TANGLED
SUCROSE	SURTOUT	SWIZZLE	TANGENT
SUCTION	SURVIVE	SWOLLEN	TANGLED
SUFFICE	SUSPECT	SWOONED	TANGOED
SUFFUSE	SUSPEND	SWOOPED	TANKAGE
SUGARED	SUSPIRE	SWOPPED	TANKARD
SUGGEST	SUSTAIN	SWOTTED	TANNAGE
SUICIDE	SUTURAL	SYLPHID	TANNATE
SUITING	SUTURED	SYMPTOM	TANNERY
SULKIER	SWABBED	SYNAXIS	TANNING
SULKILY	SWABBER	SYNCOPE	TANTRUM
			TAPERED

TAPIOCA	TEMPTED	THICKER	TIMPANI
TAPPING	TEMPTER	THICKET	TIMPANO
TAPROOM	TENABLE	THICKLY	TINDERY
TAPROOT	TENANCY	THIEVED	TINFOIL
TAPSTER	TENDING	THIMBLE	TINGING
TARDIER	TENDRIL	THINKER	TINGLED
TARDILY	TENFOLD	THINNED	TINIEST
TARNISH	TENSELY	THINNER	TINKING
TARRIED	TENSEST	THIRDLY	TINKLED
TARRIER	TENSILE	THIRSTY	TINKLER
TARRING	TENSION	THISTLE	TIN-MINE
TARTISH	TENSITY	THISTLY	TINNING
TARTLET	TENTHLY	THITHER	TIN-TACK
TASKING	TENT-PEG	THOLING	TINTAGE
TASTIER	TENUITY	THOUGHT	TINTING
TASTILY	TENUOUS	THREADY	TINTYPE
TASTING	TERMING	THRIFTY	TINWARE
TATTERY	TERMINI	THRIVED	TIP-CART
TATTING	TERMITE	THRIVEN	TIPPING
TATTLED	TERNARY	THRIVER	TIPPLED
TATTLER	TERNATE	THROATY	TIPPLER
TAUNTED	TERRACE	THRONAL	TIPSILY
TAUNTER	TERRAIN	THRONED	TIPSTER
TAURINE	TERRENE	THROUGH	TIPTOED
TAUTEST	TERRIER	THROWER	TISSUED
TAXABLE	TERRIFY	THUMBED	TITANIA
TAX-FREE	TERRINE	THUMPED	TITANIC
TAXI-CAB	TERSELY	THUMPER	TITHING
TAXYING	TERTIAN	THUNDER	TITLARK
TEACAKE	TESTACY	THYROID	TITLING
TEACHER	TESTATE	THYSELF	TITMICE
TEA-COSY	TESTIER	TIARAED	TITULAR
TEA-GOWN	TESTIFY	TIBETAN	TOADIED
TEA-LEAF	TESTILY	TICKING	TOASTED
TEAMING	TESTING	TICKLED	TOASTER
TEARFUL	TETANUS	TICKLER	TOBACCO
TEARING	TEXTILE	TIDDLER	TOBYMAN
TEA-ROSE	TEXTUAL	TIDE-WAY	TOCCATA
TEASING	TEXTURE	TIDIEST	TODDLED
TEA-TIME	THALIAN	TIDINGS	TODDLER
TEA-TREE	THANAGE	TIE-BEAM	TOE-NAIL
TECHNIC	THANKED	TIERCEL	TOGGERY
TEDDING	THAWING	TIGHTEN	TOILFUL
TEDIOUS	THEATRE	TIGHTER	TOILING
TEEMFUL	THEOREM	TIGHTLY	TOLLAGE
TEEMING	THERAPY	TIGRESS	TOLL-BAR
TEENAGE	THEREAT	TIGRISH	TOLLING
TEETHER	THEREBY	TILBURY	TOLLMAN
TEKTITE	THEREIN	TILLAGE	TOMBOLA
TELERGY	THEREOF	TILLING	TOMFOOL
TELLING	THEREON	TILTING	TOMPION
TEMPERA	THERETO	TIMBREL	TONGUED
TEMPEST	THERMAL	TIME-LAG	TONIGHT
TEMPLAR	THERMOS	TIMEOUS	TONNAGE
TEMPLED	THESEUS	TIMIDLY	TONNEAU
TEMPLET	THICKEN	TIMOTHY	TONSURE

TONTINE	TRACING	TRICKLE	TRUSSED
TOOLING	TRACKED	TRICKLY	TRUSTED
TOOTHED	TRACKER	TRICKSY	TRUSTEE
TOOTING	TRACTOR	TRICORN	TRUSTER
TOOTLED	TRADING	TRIDENT	TRY-SAIL
TOPARCH	TRADUCE	TRIFFID	TRYSTED
TOP-BOOT	TRAFFIC	TRIFLED	TSARINA
TOPCOAT	TRAGEDY	TRIFLER	TSARIST
TOP-HOLE	TRAILED	TRIFORM	T-SQUARE
TOPIARY	TRAILER	TRIGAMY	TUBBING
TOPICAL	TRAINED	TRIGGER	TUBBISH
TOPKNOT	TRAINEE	TRILLED	TUBULAR
TOPLESS	TRAINER	TRILOGY	TUCKING
TOPMAST	TRAIPSE	TRIMMED	TUCK-OUT
TOPMOST	TRAITOR	TRIMMER	TUESDAY
TOPPING	TRAJECT	TRINARY	TUFTING
TOPPLED	TRAMCAR	TRINGLE	TUGBOAT
TOPSAIL	TRAMMEL	TRINITY	TUGGING
TOPSIDE	TRAMPED	TRINKET	TUITION
TOPSMAN	TRAMPER	TRINKLE	TUMBLED
TOPSOIL	TRAMPLE	TRIOLET	TUMBLER
TORCHON	TRAMWAY	TRIPLED	TUMBREL
TORMENT	TRANCED	TRIPLET	TUMIDLY
TORNADO	TRANSIT	TRIPOLI	TUMULAR
TORPEDO	TRANSOM	TRIPPED	TUMULUS
TORRENT	TRANTER	TRIPPER	TUNABLE
TORSION	TRAPEZE	TRIREME	TUNABLY
TORTURE	TRAPPED	TRISECT	TUNEFUL
TORYISM	TRAPPER	TRITELY	TUNNAGE
TOSSILY	TRASHED	TRIUMPH	TUNNERY
TOSSING	TRAVAIL	TRIVIAL	TURBINE
TOSSPOT	TRAWLED	TROCHEE	TURFING
TOTALLY	TRAWLER	TRODDEN	TURGENT
TOTTERY	TREACLE	TROLLED	TURGITE
TOUCHED	TREACLY	TROLLER	TURKISH
TOUCHER	TREADER	TROLLEY	TURMOIL
TOUGHEN	TREADLE	TROLLOP	TURNCAP
TOUGHLY	TREASON	TROOPED	TURNERY
TOURING	TREATED	TROOPER	TURNING
TOURISM	TREATER	TROPICS	TURNKEY
TOURIST	TREBLED	TROTTED	TURN-OFF
TOURNEY	TREEING	TROTTER	TURN-OUT
TOUSING	TREFOIL	TROUBLE	TUSSLED
TOUSLED	TREKKED	TROUNCE	TUSSOCK
TOUTING	TREKKER	TROUPER	TUSSORE
TOWARDS	TRELLIS	TROWING	TUTELAR
TOWBOAT	TREMBLE	TRUANCY	TUTORED
TOWERED	TREMBLY	TRUCKED	TWADDLE
TOWLINE	TREMOLO	TRUCKER	TWANGED
TOWNISH	TRESTLE	TRUCKLE	TWANGLE
TOW-PATH	TRIABLE	TRUDGED	TWANKED
TOW-ROPE	TRIBUNE	TRUFFLE	TWEAKED
TOYSHOP	TRIBUTE	TRUMPED	TWEEDLE
TOYSOME	TRICEPS	TRUMPET	TWEENIE
TRACERY	TRICKED	TRUNCAL	TWEETER
TRACHEA	TRICKER	TRUNDLE	TWELFTH

TWIDDLE	UNCARED	UNHOUSE	UNSLING
TWIGGED	UNCASED	UNICITY	UNSLUNG
TWINGED	UNCEDED	UNICORN	UNSOLID
TWINING	UNCHAIN	UNIDEAL	UNSOUND
TWINKLE	UNCHARY	UNIFIED	UNSPELL
TWINNED	UNCINAL	UNIFIER	UNSPENT
TWIRLED	UNCIVIL	UNIFORM	UNSPIED
TWIRLER	UNCLASP	UNITARY	UNSPIKE
TWISTED	UNCLEAN	UNITING	UNSPILT
TWISTER	UNCLEAR	UNJOINT	UNSPLIT
TWITTED	UNCLOAK	UNKEMPT	UNSPOIL
TWITTER	UNCLOSE	UNKNOWN	UNSTACK
TWOFOLD	UNCLOUD	UNLACED	UNSTAID
TWONESS	UNCOUTH	UNLADEN	UNSTEEL
TWOSOME	UNCOVER	UNLATCH	UNSTICK
TWO-STEP	UNCROSS	UNLEARN	UNSTUCK
TYNWALD	UNCROWN	UNLEASH	UNSWEET
TYPHOID	UNCTION	UNLIMED	UNSWEPT
TYPHOON	UNDATED	UNLINED	UNSWORN
TYPHOUS	UNDEIFY	UNLIVED	UNTAKEN
TYPICAL	UNDERDO	UNLOOSE	UNTAMED
TYRANNY	UNDERGO	UNLOVED	UNTAXED
TZARINA	UNDOING	UNLUCKY	UNTHINK
	UNDRAPE	UNMANLY	UNTILED
	UNDRAWN	UNMARRY	UNTIRED
U – 7	UNDRESS	UNMEANT	UNTRIED
	UNDRIED	UNMEWED	UNTRULY
UKULELE	UNDYING	UNMIXED	UNTRUSS
ULULATE	UNEARTH	UNMOIST	UNTRUTH
ULYSSES	UNEATEN	UNMORAL	UNTUNED
UMBERED	UNEQUAL	UNMOULD	UNTWINE
UMBRAGE	UNEXACT	UNMOVED	UNTWIST
UMBROSE	UNFADED	UNNAMED	UNTYING
UMPIRED	UNFAITH	UNNERVE	UNURGED
UMPTEEN	UNFILED	UNNOTED	UNUSUAL
UNACTED	UNFITLY	UNOILED	UNVEXED
UNAGING	UNFIXED	UNOWNED	UNVOWED
UNAIDED	UNFOUND	UNPAVED	UNWAGED
UNAIRED	UNFROCK	UNPERCH	UNWEARY
UNAPTLY	UNFUSED	UNPLAIT	UNWEAVE
UNARMED	UNGIVEN	UNPLUMB	UNWIRED
UNASKED	UNGLUED	UNQUIET	UNWOOED
UNAWARE	UNGODLY	UNRAKED	UNWOUND
UNBAKED	UNGUENT	UNRAVEL	UNWOVEN
UNBEGUN	UNHANDY	UNREADY	UNWRUNG
UNBLIND	UNHAPPY	UNREEVE	UNYOKED
UNBLOCK	UNHARDY	UNRIVET	UNZONED
UNBLOWN	UNHASTY	UNROBED	UPBORNE
UNBOSOM	UNHEARD	UNROYAL	UPBRAID
UNBOUND	UNHEEDY	UNRULED	UPDATED
UNBOWED	UNHINGE	UNSATED	UPENDED
UNBRACE	UNHIRED	UNSCREW	UPFRONT
UNBRAID	UNHITCH	UNSEXED	UPGRADE
UNBUILT	UNHIVED	UNSHORN	UPHEAVE
UNBURNT	UNHOPED	UNSHOWN	UPLYING
UNCAGED	UNHORSE	UNSIZED	UPRAISE
UNCANNY			

UPRIGHT	VAPOURY	VICEROY	WADDLER
UPRISEN	VARIANT	VICIOUS	WAFERED
UPSTAGE	VARIATE	VICTORY	WAFTING
UPSTART	VARIETY	VICTUAL	WAGERED
UPSURGE	VARIOUS	VIEWING	WAGGERY
UPSWEEP	VARMINT	VILLAGE	WAGGING
UPTIGHT	VARNISH	VILLAIN	WAGGISH
UP-TRAIN	VARSITY	VILLEIN	WAGGLED
UPWARDS	VARYING	VINEGAR	WAGONER
URALITE	VASTEST	VINTAGE	WAGTAIL
URANITE	VATICAN	VINTNER	WAILING
URANIUM	VAULTED	VIOLATE	WAISTED
URGENCY	VAULTER	VIOLENT	WAITING
USELESS	VAUNTED	VIOLIST	WAIVING
USHERED	VEERING	VIRGATE	WAKEFUL
USUALLY	VEHICLE	VIRTUAL	WAKENED
USURPED	VEILING	VISAGED	WAKENER
USURPER	VEINING	VIS-A-VIS	WALKING
UTENSIL	VEINOUS	VISCOUS	WALLABY
UTILISE	VELLUMY	VISIBLE	WALL-EYE
UTILITY	VELOURS	VISIBLY	WALLING
UTOPIAN	VELVETY	VISITED	WALLOON
UTTERED	VENALLY	VISITOR	WALTZED
UTTERER	VENDING	VISORED	WALTZER
UTTERLY	VENISON	VITALLY	WANGLED
UXORIAL	VENOMED	VITAMIN	WANNABE
	VENTAGE	VITIATE	WANNESS
	VENTAIL	VITRIFY	WANNISH
V – 7	VENTING	VITRINE	WANTAGE
VACANCY	VENT-PEG	VITRIOL	WARBLED
VACATED	VENTRAL	VIVIDLY	WARBLER
VACATOR	VENTURE	VIXENLY	WARDING
VACCINE	VERANDA	VOCABLE	WAREFUL
VACUITY	VERBENA	VOCALLY	WARFARE
VACUOLE	VERBOSE	VOICING	WARHOOP
VACUOUS	VERDANT	VOIDING	WARIEST
VAGRANT	VERDICT	VOLCANO	WARLIKE
VAGUELY	VERDURE	VOLTAGE	WARLOCK
VAGUEST	VERGING	VOLTAIC	WAR-LORD
VAINEST	VERIEST	VOLUBLE	WARMEST
VALANCE	VERONAL	VOLUBLY	WARMING
VALIANT	VERSIFY	VOLUTED	WARNING
VALIDLY	VERSING	VOTABLE	WARPATH
VALUING	VERSION	VOUCHED	WARPING
VALVATE	VERTIGO	VOUCHEE	WARRANT
VAMOOSE	VERVAIN	VOUCHER	WARRING
VAMPING	VESICLE	VOYAGED	WARRIOR
VAMPIRE	VESTIGE	VOYAGER	WARSHIP
VANDYKE	VESTING	VULGATE	WAR-SONG
VANESSA	VESTRAL	VULPINE	WART-HOG
VANILLA	VETERAN	VULTURE	WAR-WORN
VANNING	VETOING		WASHING
VANTAGE	VIADUCT		WASH-OUT
VANWARD	VIBRANT	W – 7	WASH-POT
VAPIDLY	VIBRATE	WADDING	WASH-TUB
VAPOURS	VIBRATO	WADDLED	WASP-FLY

WASPISH	WELCOME	WHISKER	WIREMAN
WASSAIL	WELDING	WHISKEY	WIRE-WAY
WASTAGE	WELFARE	WHISPER	WISHFUL
WASTING	WELLING	WHISTLE	WISTFUL
WASTREL	WELL-MET	WHITELY	WITCHED
WATCHED	WELL-OFF	WHITEST	WITHERS
WATCHER	WELL-SET	WHITHER	WITHOUT
WATCHET	WELL-WON	WHITING	WITLESS
WATERED	WELSHED	WHITISH	WITLING
WATERER	WELSHER	WHITLOW	WITNESS
WATTLED	WELTING	WHITSUN	WITTIER
WAVELET	WENDING	WHITTLE	WITTILY
WAVERED	WESTERN	WHIZZED	WIZENED
WAVERER	WESTING	WHIZZER	WOBBLED
WAXBILL	WETDOCK	WHOEVER	WOBBLER
WAXDOLL	WETNESS	WHOOPEE	WOESOME
WAX-MOTH	WETTEST	WHOOPED	WOLF-CUB
WAX-PALM	WETTING	WHOOPER	WOLF-DOG
WAX-TREE	WETTISH	WHOPPED	WOLFISH
WAXWING	WHACKED	WHOPPER	WOLF-NET
WAXWORK	WHACKER	WHORLED	WOLFRAM
WAY-BILL	WHALING	WIDENED	WOMANLY
WAYMARK	WHARFED	WIDENER	WOOD-ANT
WAYSIDE	WHARVES	WIDGEON	WOODCUT
WAYWARD	WHATNOT	WIDOWED	WOODMAN
WAYWISE	WHEATEN	WIDOWER	WOOLLEN
WAYWORN	WHEEDLE	WIELDED	WOOLMAN
WEAKEST	WHEELED	WIELDER	WOOMERA
WEALDEN	WHEELER	WIGGERY	WORDILY
WEALTHY	WHEEZED	WIGGING	WORDING
WEANING	WHELPED	WIGGLED	WORDISH
WEARIED	WHEREAS	WIGGLER	WORK-BAG
WEARIER	WHEREAT	WIGLESS	WORK-BOX
WEARILY	WHEREBY	WILDCAT	WORKDAY
WEARING	WHEREIN	WILDEST	WORKING
WEARISH	WHEREOF	WILDING	WORKMAN
WEATHER	WHEREON	WILDISH	WORKOUT
WEAVING	WHERESO	WILIEST	WORK-SHY
WEBBING	WHERETO	WILLING	WORLDLY
WEB-FOOT	WHETHER	WILLOWY	WORMING
WEBSTER	WHETTED	WILTING	WORN-OUT
WEB-TOED	WHETTER	WIMPLED	WORRIED
WEDDING	WHIFFED	WINCHED	WORRIER
WEDGING	WHIFFLE	WINDAGE	WORSHIP
WEDLOCK	WHILING	WINDBAG	WORSTED
WEEDING	WHIMPER	WINDIER	WOTTING
WEEKDAY	WHIMSEY	WINDILY	WOULD-BE
WEEK-END	WHINING	WINDING	WOULDST
WEENING	WHIPPED	WINDROW	WOUNDED
WEEPING	WHIPPER	WINDSOR	WOUNDER
WEFTAGE	WHIPPET	WINE-BAG	WRANGLE
WEIGHED	WHIP-SAW	WINGING	WRAPPED
WEIGHER	WHIP-TOP	WINGLET	WRAPPER
WEIGHTY	WHIRLED	WINKING	WREAKED
WEIRDER	WHIRRED	WINNING	WREAKER
WEIRDLY	WHIRLER	WINSOME	WREATHE

WREATHY	ZEALOUS	ABSORBED	ADENOIDS
WRECKED	ZEOLITE	ABSTRACT	ADEPTION
WRECKER	ZESTFUL	ABSTRUSE	ADEQUACY
WRESTED	ZESTING	ABSURDLY	ADEQUATE
WRESTER	ZINCOID	ABUNDANT	ADHERENT
WRESTLE	ZIONISM	ABUSABLE	ADHERING
WRICKED	ZIONIST	ABUTMENT	ADHESION
WRIGGLE	ZIPPING	ABUTTING	ADHESIVE
WRIGGLY	ZONALLY	ACADEMIC	ADJACENT
WRINGER	ZONULAR	ACANTHUS	ADJOINED
WRINKLE	ZOOIDAL	ACCEDING	ADJUDGED
WRINKLY	ZOOLITE	ACCENTED	ADJURING
WRITHED	ZOOLOGY	ACCEPTED	ADJUSTER
WRITING	ZOOMING	ACCEPTER	ADJUTANT
WRITTEN		ACCEPTOR	ADMIRING
WRONGED	**A – 8**	ACCIDENT	ADMITTED
WRONGER		ACCOLADE	ADMIXING
WRONGLY	ABASHING	ACCORDED	ADMONISH
WROUGHT	ABATABLE	ACCOSTED	ADOPTING
WRYNECK	ABATTOIR	ACCOUTRE	ADOPTION
WRYNESS	ABDICANT	ACCREDIT	ADOPTIVE
WYCH-ELM	ABDICATE	ACCRUING	ADORABLE
	ABDUCTED	ACCURACY	ADORABLY
	ABDUCTOR	ACCURATE	ADORNING
X – 7	ABERDEEN	ACCURSED	ADROITLY
X-RAYING	ABERRANT	ACCUSANT	ADSCRIPT
	ABERRATE	ACCUSING	ADULATED
	ABETMENT	ACCUSTOM	ADULATOR
Y – 7	ABETTING	ACERBATE	ADVANCED
	ABEYANCE	ACERBITY	ADVERTED
YANKING	ABHORRED	ACESCENT	ADVISING
YAPPING	ABHORRER	ACHIEVED	ADVISORY
YARDAGE	ABJECTLY	ACIDNESS	ADVOCACY
YARD-ARM	ABJURING	ACIDOSIS	ADVOCATE
YARDING	ABLATION	ACONITIC	ADVOWSON
YARD-MAN	ABLATIVE	ACORN–CUP	AERATING
YARNING	ABLENESS	ACOUSTIC	AERATION
YASHMAK	ABLUTION	ACQUAINT	AERIALLY
YAWNING	ABNEGATE	ACQUIRED	AERIFIED
YEARNED	ABNORMAL	ACRIDITY	AERIFORM
YELLING	ABORTING	ACRIMONY	AEROBICS
YELLOWY	ABORTION	ACROSTIC	AERONAUT
YELPING	ABORTIVE	ACTINISM	AEROSTAT
YEW-TREE	ABRADING	ACTIVATE	AESTHETE
YIDDISH	ABRASION	ACTIVELY	AFFECTED
YIELDED	ABRASIVE	ACTIVITY	AFFIANCE
YOGHURT	ABRIDGED	ACTUALLY	AFFINITY
YOMPING	ABROGATE	ACTUATED	AFFIRMED
YORKIST	ABSENTED	ACTUATOR	AFFIRMER
YOUNGER	ABSENTEE	ADAPTING	AFFIXING
YOWLING	ABSENTLY	ADAPTIVE	AFFLATUS
YULE-LOG	ABSINTHE	ADDENDUM	AFFLUENT
	ABSOLUTE	ADDICTED	AFFORDED
Z – 7	ABSOLVED	ADDITION	AFFOREST
ZANYISM	ABSOLVER	ADDUCING	AFFRIGHT
ZEALFUL	ABSONANT	ADDUCTOR	AGAR-AGAR

AGEDNESS	ALLEGING	ANALOGUE	ANYTHING
AGGRIEVE	ALLEGORY	ANALYSED	ANYWHERE
AGITATED	ALLELUIA	ANALYSER	APERIENT
AGITATOR	ALLERGEN	ANALYSIS	APERITIF
AGITPROP	ALLERGIC	ANALYTIC	APERTURE
AGLIMMER	ALLEYWAY	ANARCHIC	APHIDIAN
AGNATION	ALL-FIRED	ANATHEMA	APHORISM
AGNOSTIC	ALL-FOURS	ANATOMIC	APHORIST
AGONISED	ALLIANCE	ANCESTOR	APIARIST
AGRARIAN	ALLOCATE	ANCESTRY	APICALLY
AGREEING	ALLOTTED	ANCHORED	APOLLYON
AGRIMONY	ALLOWING	ANCHORET	APOLOGIA
AGRONOMY	ALLOYING	ANDERSON	APOPLEXY
AIRGRETTE	ALLSPICE	ANECDOTE	APOSTASY
AIRBORNE	ALLUDING	ANEURISM	APOSTATE
AIR-BRAKE	ALLURING	ANGELICA	APPALLED
AIR-BRICK	ALLUSION	ANGERING	APPARENT
AIRCRAFT	ALLUSIVE	ANGLICAN	APPEALED
AIREDALE	ALLUSORY	ANGRIEST	APPEARED
AIRFIELD	ALLUVIAL	ANGSTROM	APPEASED
AIR-GRAPH	ALLUVION	ANIMATED	APPEASER
AIRINESS	ALLUVIUM	ANIMATOR	APPENDED
AIR-LINER	ALMIGHTY	ANISETTE	APPENDIX
AIR-PILOT	ALPHABET	ANNALIST	APPETITE
AIRPLANE	ALPINIST	ANNAMITE	APPLAUSE
AIR-POWER	ALSATIAN	ANNEALED	APPLE-PIE
AIRSCREW	ALTERING	ANNELIDA	APPLIQUE
AIR-SHAFT	ALTHOUGH	ANNEXING	APPLYING
AIR-SPACE	ALTITUDE	ANNOTATE	APPOSITE
AIRSTRIP	ALTRUISM	ANNOUNCE	APPRAISE
AIRTIGHT	ALTRUIST	ANNOYING	APPRISED
ALACRITY	AMARANTH	ANNUALLY	APPRIZED
ALARM-GUN	AMASSING	ANNULATE	APPROACH
ALARMING	AMAZEDLY	ANNULLED	APPROVAL
ALARMIST	AMBITION	ANODISED	APPROVED
ALBACORE	AMBROSIA	ANOINTED	APPROVER
ALBANIAN	AMBULANT	ANSERINE	APRES-SKI
ALBINISM	AMBULATE	ANSWERED	APTEROUS
ALDEHYDE	AMBUSHED	ANT-EATER	APTITUDE
ALDERMAN	AMENABLE	ANTECEDE	AQUARIUM
ALEATORY	AMENABLY	ANTEDATE	AQUARIUS
ALEHOUSE	AMENDING	ANTELOPE	AQUATINT
ALFRESCO	AMERICAN	ANTENNAE	AQUEDUCT
ALGERIAN	AMETHYST	ANTENNAL	AQUIFORM
ALGORISM	AMICABLE	ANTERIOR	AQUILINE
ALHAMBRA	AMICABLY	ANTEROOM	ARACHNID
ALICANTE	AMMONIAC	ANTIBODY	ARBITRAL
ALIENATE	AMMONITE	ANTIDOTE	ARBOREAL
ALIENISM	AMORTISE	ANTIMONY	ARBOURED
ALIENIST	AMOUNTED	ANTI-NAZI	ARCADIAN
ALIGHTED	AMPHIBIA	ANTIPHON	ARCHAISM
ALIGNING	AMPUTATE	ANTIPOLE	ARCHDUKE
ALKALINE	AMUSABLE	ANTIPOPE	ARCHIVES
ALKALOID	ANABASIS	ANTI-TANK	ARCHNESS
ALLAYING	ANACONDA	ANTITYPE	ARCTURUS
ALL-CLEAR	ANAGLYPH	ANTLERED	ARDENTLY

ARGONAUT
ARGUABLE
ARGUFIED
ARGUMENT
ARIDNESS
ARMAMENT
ARMATURE
ARMCHAIR
ARMORIAL
ARMOURED
ARMOURER
AROMATIC
AROUSING
ARPEGGIO
ARQUEBUS
ARRANGED
ARRANTLY
ARRAYING
ARRESTED
ARRIVING
ARROGANT
ARROGATE
ARSONIST
ARTERIAL
ARTESIAN
ARTFULLY
ARTICLED
ARTIFICE
ARTISTIC
ARTISTRY
ASBESTOS
ASCENDED
ASCIDIUM
ASCORBIC
ASCRIBED
ASH-STAND
ASPERITY
ASPERSED
ASPHODEL
ASPHYXIA
APSIRANT
ASPIRATE
ASPIRING
ASSAILED
ASSASSIN
ASSAYING
ASSEMBLE
ASSENTED
ASSERTED
ASSESSED
ASSESSOR
ASSIGNED
ASSIGNEE
ASSIGNOR
ASSISTED
ASSONANT

ASSORTED
ASSUAGED
ASSUMING
ASSURING
ASSYRIAN
ASTERISK
ASTEROID
ASTONISH
ASTRAGAL
ASTUTELY
ATABRINE
ATHELING
ATHENIAN
ATHLETIC
ATLANTIC
ATLANTIS
ATOMISED
ATOMISER
ATONABLE
ATREMBLE
ATROCITY
ATROPINE
ATTACHED
ATTACKED
ATTACKER
ATTAINED
ATTENDED
ATTESTED
ATTICISIM
ATTIRING
ATTITUDE
ATTORNEY
ATTUNING
AUDACITY
AUDiENCE
AUDITING
AUDITION
AUDITORY
AUGURING
AUGUSTAN
AUGUSTLY
AURICULA
AURIFORM
AUSTRIAN
AUTARCHY
AUTOCRAT
AUTO-DA-FE
AUTO-DYNE
AUTOGIRO
AUTOMATA
AUTONOMY
AUTUMNAL
AVAILING
AVENGING
AVERAGED
AVERRING

AVERSELY
AVERSION
AVIATION
AVIFAUNA
AVIONICS
AVOIDING
AVOWABLE
AVOWABLY
AVOWEDLY
AWAITING
AWAKENED
AWARDING
AXLE-TREE

B – 8

BABBLING
BABY-FACE
BABY-FARM
BABYHOOD
BACCARAT
BACCHANT
BACHELOR
BACKBITE
BACKBONE
BACKCHAT
BACK-DOOR
BACKDROP
BACKFIRE
BACKHAND
BACKLASH
BACK-ROOM
BACKSIDE
BACK-STEP
BACKWARD
BACKWASH
BACONIAN
BACTERIA
BACTRIAN
BADGERED
BADINAGE
BAFFLING
BAGUETTE
BAKELITE
BALANCED
BALANCER
BALDNESS
BALLCOCK
BALLISTA
BALLOTED
BALLROOM
BALLYHOO
BALLYRAG
BALMORAL
BALUSTER
BANALITY

BANDAGED
BANDANNA
BANDEAUX
BANDITTI
BANDSMAN
BANDYING
BANISHED
BANISTER
BANJOIST
BANK-BILL
BANK-BOOK
BANKNOTE
BANK-RATE
BANKRUPT
BANNERET
BANNEROL
BANTERED
BANTERER
BANTLING
BAPTISED
BARATHEA
BARBARIC
BARBECUE
BARBERRY
BARBETTE
BARBICAN
BARDLING
BAREBACK
BAREFOOT
BARGEMAN
BARITONE
BARNABAS
BARNACLE
BARN-DOOR
BARNYARD
BAROLOGY
BARONAGE
BARONESS
BARONIAL
BAROUCHE
BARRACKS
BARRATOR
BARRATRY
BARRENLY
BARTERED
BARTERER
BARYTONE
BASALTIC
BASEBALL
BASELESS
BASELINE
BASEMENT
BASENESS
BASILICA
BASILISK
BASKETRY

BASS-DRUM	BEFOOLED	BESTIARY	BIRTHDOM
BASS-HORN	BEFOULED	BESTOWAL	BISECTED
BASSINET	BEFRIEND	BESTOWED	BISECTOR
BASS-TUBA	BEGGARED	BESTREWN	BISEXUAL
BASS-VIOL	BEGGARLY	BESTRIDE	BISTABLE
BASTARDY	BEGINNER	BESTRODE	BITINGLY
BASTILLE	BEGOTTEN	BETAKING	BITTERLY
BATAVIAN	BEGRIMED	BETA-RAYS	BI-WEEKLY
BATHROOM	BEGRUDGE	BETEL-NUT	BLABBING
BATSWING	BEGUILED	BETIDING	BLACKCAP
BATTENED	BEHAVING	BETRAYAL	BLACKFLY
BATTERED	BEHEADED	BETRAYED	BLACK-GUM
BATTLING	BEHEMOTH	BETRAYER	BLACKING
BAULKING	BEHOLDEN	BETTERED	BLACKISH
BAVARIAN	BEHOLDER	BEVELLED	BLACKLEG
BEACHING	BEHOVING	BEVERAGE	BLACKOUT
BEAD-WORK	BELABOUR	BEWAILED	BLAMABLE
BEAMLESS	BELAYING	BEWARING	BLAMABLY
BEARABLE	BELCHING	BEWIGGED	BLAMEFUL
BEARABLY	BELIEVED	BEWILDER	BLANCHED
BEARDING	BELIEVER	BIBLICAL	BLANDEST
BEARINGS	BELITTLE	BIBULOUS	BLANDISH
BEARLIKE	BELLBIND	BICAUDAL	BLANKEST
BEARSKIN	BELL-BIRD	BICKERED	BLANKING
BEATIFIC	BELL-BUOY	BICOLOUR	BLASTING
BEAUTIFY	BELLOWED	BICYCLED	BLATANCY
BEAVERED	BELL-PULL	BIDDABLE	BLAZONED
BECALMED	BELL-ROPE	BIENNIAL	BLEACHED
BECHAMEL	BELL-TENT	BIGAMIST	BLEAKEST
BECHANCE	BELLWORT	BIGAMOUS	BLEAKISH
BECKONED	BELLYFUL	BIG-BONED	BLEATING
BECOMING	BELLYING	BIGNONIA	BLEEDING
BEDAUBED	BELONGED	BILBERRY	BLENCHED
BED-CHAIR	BEMOANED	BILL-BOOK	BLENDING
BEDECKED	BENCHING	BILLETED	BLENHEIM
BEDEWING	BENDABLE	BILLHEAD	BLESSING
BEDIMMED	BENEDICK	BILLHOOK	BLIGHTED
BED-LINEN	BENEDICT	BILLIARD	BLIGHTER
BEDMAKER	BENEFICE	BILLY-BOY	BLIMPERY
BEDPLATE	BENIGNLY	BILLY-CAN	BLINDAGE
BED-QUILT	BENJAMIN	BINDWEED	BLINDEST
BED-STAFF	BENUMBED	BINNACLE	BLINDING
BEDSTEAD	BEQUEATH	BINOMIAL	BLINDMAN
BEDSTRAW	BERATING	BIOGRAPH	BLINKERS
BEDTABLE	BERBERRY	BIOMETRY	BLINKING
BEE-BREAD	BEREAVED	BIOSCOPE	BLISSFUL
BEE-EATER	BERGAMOT	BIRCHING	BLISTERY
BEEFIEST	BERI-BERI	BIRDBATH	BLITHELY
BEER-PUMP	BERRYING	BIRDCAGE	BLITHEST
BEERSHOP	BESIEGED	BIRDCALL	BLITZING
BEESWING	BESIEGER	BIRDLIKE	BLIZZARD
BEETLING	BESMIRCH	BIRD-LIME	BLOATING
BEETROOT	BESOTTED	BIRDSEED	BLOCKADE
BEFITTED	BESOUGHT	BIRD'S-EYE	BLOCKING
BEFLOWER	BESPOKEN	BIRD-SONG	BLOOD-HOT
BEFOGGED	BESSEMER	BIRTHDAY	BLOODIED

BLOODILY	BONHOMIE	BRAIN-PAN	BROOKLET
BLOODING	BONIFACE	BRAISING	BROUGHAM
BLOOD-RED	BONNETED	BRAKEMAN	BROWBEAT
BLOOMERS	BONSPIEL	BRAKE-VAN	BROWLESS
BLOOMING	BOOBYISH	BRAMBLED	BROWNING
BLOSSOMY	BOOBYISM	BRANCHED	BROWNISH
BLOTCHED	BOOHOOED	BRANDIED	BROWNOUT
BLOTTING	BOOKCASE	BRANDING	BROWSING
BLOWBALL	BOOK-CLUB	BRANDISH	BRUISING
BLOW-HOLE	BOOK-DEBT	BRAND-NEW	BRUNETTE
BLOW-PIPE	BOOKLAND	BRASSARD	BRUSHING
BLUDGEON	BOOKLESS	BRASS-HAT	BRUSSELS
BLUE-BACK	BOOKMARK	BRASSICA	BRYOLOGY
BLUEBELL	BOOK-NAME	BRAWLING	BUBBLING
BLUEBIRD	BOOK-POST	BRAZENED	BUCKBEAN
BLUEBOOK	BOOKSHOP	BRAZENLY	BUCKETED
BLUECOAT	BOOKWORM	BREACHED	BUCKHORN
BLUE-EYED	BOOSTING	BREAKAGE	BUCKJUMP
BLUEFISH	BOOT-HOOK	BREAKING	BUCKLING
BLUENESS	BOOTJACK	BREASTED	BUCKSHEE
BLUENOSE	BOOTLACE	BREATHED	BUCK-SHOT
BLUFFEST	BOOT-LAST	BREATHER	BUCKSKIN
BLUFFING	BOOTLESS	BREECHED	BUDDHISM
BLUISHLY	BOOT-TREE	BREECHES	BUDDHIST
BLUNTING	BORDEAUX	BREEDING	BUDGETED
BLUNTISH	BORDERED	BRETHREN	BUFFETED
BLURRING	BORDERER	BREVIARY	BUILDING
BLURTING	BORECOLE	BREWSTER	BULKHEAD
BLUSHFUL	BORROWED	BRIBABLE	BULKIEST
BLUSHING	BORROWER	BRICKBAT	BULL-CALF
BLUSTERY	BOTANIST	BRICKING	BULLDOZE
BOARDING	BOTCHERY	BRICK-RED	BULLETIN
BOASTFUL	BOTCHING	BRICK-TEA	BULLFROG
BOASTING	BOTHERED	BRIDGING	BULLHEAD
BOAT-HOOK	BOTTLING	BRIDLING	BULLRING
BOATRACE	BOTTOMED	BRIEFING	BULL'S-EYE
BOBBINET	BOTTOMRY	BRIGHTEN	BULLYING
BOBOLINK	BOTULISM	BRIGHTLY	BULLYRAG
BODLEIAN	BOUFFANT	BRIMLESS	BUMMAREE
BODYLINE	BOUILLON	BRIMMING	BUNCHING
BOG-BERRY	BOUNCING	BRINDLED	BUNDLING
BOG-EARTH	BOUNDARY	BRINE-PAN	BUNGALOW
BOGEYISM	BOUNDING	BRINE-PIT	BUNG-HOLE
BOGEYMAN	BOWINGLY	BRINGING	BUNGLING
BOGGLING	BOWSPRIT	BRISLING	BUNKERED
BOG-WHORT	BOX-PLEAT	BRISTLED	BUOYANCY
BOHEMIAN	BOYISHLY	BROACHED	BURBERRY
BOLDNESS	BRACELET	BROADEST	BURDENED
BOLTHOLE	BRACKISH	BROADISH	BURGLARY
BOLT-ROPE	BRADBURY	BROCADED	BURGLING
BOMB-FREE	BRADSHAW	BROCCOLI	BURGUNDY
BONA-FIDE	BRAGGART	BROCHURE	BURROWED
BONDMAID	BRAGGING	BROILING	BURSTING
BONDSMAN	BRAIDING	BROKENLY	BUSH-BABY
BONE-IDLE	BRAIN-FAG	BROODING	BUSHBUCK
BONELESS	BRAINING	BROOKING	BUSHVELD

BUSINESS
BUSYBODY
BUSYNESS
BUTCHERY
BUTTERED
BUTTONED
BUTTRESS
BUZZWORD
BYPASSED
BYRONISM
BY-STREET

C – 8

CABIN-BOY
CABOODLE
CABOTAGE
CABRIOLE
CABSTAND
CACHALOT
CACKLING
CADENCED
CADILLAC
CAERLEON
CAFFEINE
CAJOLERY
CAJOLING
CAKEHOLE
CAKESHOP
CAKEWALK
CALABASH
CALAMINE
CALAMITY
CALCINED
CALCULUS
CALENDAR
CALENDER
CALF-LOVE
CALFSKIN
CALIBRED
CALIPASH
CALIPERS
CALL-BIRD
CALLIOPE
CALL-NOTE
CALL-OVER
CALMNESS
CAMBERED
CAMBRIAN
CAMELLIA
CAMISOLE
CAMOMILE
CAMPAIGN
CAMP-FIRE
CAMSHAFT
CAM-WHEEL

CANADIAN
CANAILLE
CANALISE
CANASTER
CANDIDLY
CANDYING
CANE-MILL
CANISTER
CANKERED
CANNIBAL
CANNONED
CANOEIST
CANONISE
CANOODLE
CANOPIED
CANTERED
CANTICLE
CAPACITY
CAPERING
CAPITANO
CAPITATE
CAPRIOLE
CAPSICUM
CAPSULAR
CAPTIOUS
CAPTURED
CAPUCHIN
CAPYBARA
CARAPACE
CARBOLIC
CARBONIC
CARBURET
CARDAMOM
CARD-CASE
CARDIGAN
CARDINAL
CAREENED
CAREERED
CAREFREE
CARELESS
CARESSED
CAREWORN
CARILLON
CARINATE
CARNIVAL
CAROLINE
CAROLLED
CAROUSAL
CAROUSED
CARPETED
CARRIAGE
CARRIOLE
CARRYING
CART-LOAD
CARYATID
CASCADED

CASE-BOOK
CASEMATE
CASEMENT
CASE-SHOT
CASHMERE
CASKETED
CASSETTE
CASTANET
CASTAWAY
CAST-IRON
CASTLING
CASTRATE
CASUALLY
CASUALTY
CATACOMB
CATALYST
CATAPULT
CATARACT
CATCHFLY
CATCHING
CATEGORY
CATERING
CATHEDRA
CATHOLIC
CATILINE
CATONIAN
CAT'S-FOOT
CAT'S-MEAT
CAT'S-TAIL
CAULDRON
CAULKING
CAUSALLY
CAUSERIE
CAUSEUSE
CAUSEWAY
CAUTIOUS
CAVALIER
CAVATINA
CAVE-BEAR
CAVERNED
CAVILLED
CAVORTED
CELERIAC
CELERITY
CELIBACY
CELIBATE
CELLARER
CELLARET
CELLULAR
CEMENTED
CEMETERY
CENOTAPH
CENSORED
CENSURED
CENTAURY
CENTRING

CEPHALIC
CERAMICS
CERASTES
CERBERUS
CEREBRAL
CEREBRUM
CEREMENT
CEREMONY
CERULEAN
CERVICAL
CESAREAN
CESSPOOL
CETACEAN
CHAFFING
CHAINING
CHAIR-BED
CHAIRING
CHAIRMAN
CHALDRON
CHALICED
CHALKING
CHALK-PIT
CHAMPING
CHAMPION
CHANCERY
CHANCING
CHANDLER
CHANGING
CHANTING
CHAPBOOK
CHAPELRY
CHAPERON
CHAPITER
CHAPLAIN
CHAPPING
CHARCOAL
CHARGING
CHARLOCK
CHARMING
CHARRING
CHARTING
CHARTISM
CHARTIST
CHASSEUR
CHASTELY
CHASTISE
CHASTITY
CHASUBLE
CHATLINE
CHATTLES
CHATTING
CHAUFFER
CHEATING
CHECKERS
CHECKING
CHECK-OUT

CHEEKING	CHURLISH	CLICKING	COBBLING
CHEEPING	CHURNING	CLIMATIC	COBWEBBY
CHEERFUL	CHUTZPAH	CLIMBING	COCKADED
CHEERILY	CICATRIX	CLINCHED	COCKATOO
CHEERING	CICERONE	CLINGING	COCK-CROW
CHEMICAL	CIDER-CUP	CLINICAL	COCKEREL
CHENILLE	CINCHONA	CLINKING	COCK-EYED
CHERUBIC	CINNABAR	CLIPPERS	COCKLING
CHERUBIM	CINNAMON	CLIPPING	COCKSPUR
CHESHIRE	CIPHERED	CLIQUISH	COCKSURE
CHESSMAN	CIRCLING	CLOAKING	COCKTAIL
CHESTING	CIRCULAR	CLOCKING	CODDLING
CHESTNUT	CITATION	CLODDISH	CODIFIED
CHEVYING	CITY-BRED	CLOGGING	CO-EDITOR
CHIASMUS	CIVET-CAT	CLOISTER	COERCING
CHICANED	CIVILIAN	CLOSE-CUT	COERCION
CHICK-PEA	CIVILITY	CLOSETED	COERCIVE
CHILDBED	CIVILISE	CLOTHIER	COFFERED
CHILDISH	CLACKING	CLOTHING	COFFINED
CHILDREN	CLAIMANT	CLOTTING	COGENTLY
CHILIASM	CLAIMING	CLOUDILY	COGITATE
CHILIAST	CLAMBAKE	CLOUDING	COGNOMEN
CHILLIER	CLAMPING	CLOUDLET	COG-WHEEL
CHILLING	CLANGING	CLOUTING	COHERENT
CHILTERN	CLANGOUR	CLOWNERY	COHERING
CHIMAERA	CLANKING	CLOWNING	COHESION
CHIMERIC	CLANNISH	CLOWNISH	COHESIVE
CHINAMAN	CLANSHIP	CLUBBING	COIFFEUR
CHIN-CHIN	CLANSMAN	CLUBBISH	COIFFING
CHINKING	CLAPPING	CLUB-FOOT	COIFFURE
CHIPMUNK	CLAPTRAP	CLUBLAND	COINCIDE
CHIPPERY	CLARENCE	CLUB-MOSS	COINLESS
CHIPPING	CLARINET	CLUB-ROOM	COLANDER
CHIRPING	CLASHING	CLUB-ROOT	COLDNESS
CHIRRING	CLASPING	CLUB-RUSH	COLE-SLAW
CHIT-CHAT	CLASSIER	CLUCKING	COLEWORT
CHIVALRY	CLASSIFY	CLUELESS	COLISEUM
CHLORATE	CLASSING	CLUMPING	COLLAPSE
CHLORIDE	CLASSMAN	CLUMSIER	COLLARED
CHLORINE	CLASS-WAR	CLUMSILY	COLLARET
CHLOROUS	CLAVICLE	CLUTCHED	COLLATED
CHOICELY	CLAYMORE	CLUTCHED	COLLATOR
CHOIRBOY	CLEANING	COACH-BOX	COLLEGER
CHOLERIC	CLEANSED	COACHDOG	COLLIDED
CHOOSING	CLEANSER	COACHFUL	COLLIERY
CHOPPING	CLEAR-CUT	COACHING	COLLOQUY
CHOP-SUEY	CLEAREST	COACHMAN	COLLUDED
CHORALLY	CLEARING	COACTIVE	COLONIAL
CHORTLED	CLEAVAGE	CO-AGENCY	COLONISE
CHORUSED	CLEAVING	COALESCE	COLONIST
CHOW-CHOW	CLEMATIS	COAL-HOLE	COLLOSSAL
CHRISTEN	CLEMENCY	COAL-MINE	COLOSSUS
CHROMIUM	CLENCHED	COAL-SHIP	COLOURED
CHUCKING	CLERICAL	COARSELY	COLUMNAR
CHUCKLED	CLEVERER	COARSEST	COLUMNED
CHUMP-END	CLEVERLY	COASTING	COMATOSE

COMBINED	CONQUEST	COSINESS	CREAMERY
COME-BACK	CONSERVE	COSMETIC	CREAMING
COMEDIAN	CONSIDER	COSSETED	CREASING
COMMANDO	CONSOLED	COSTLIER	CREATING
COMMENCE	CONSOMME	COST-PLUS	CREATION
COMMERCE	CONSPIRE	COSTUMED	CREATIVE
COMMONER	CONSTANT	CO-TENANT	CREATURE
COMMONLY	CONSTRUE	COTSWOLD	CREDENCE
COMMUNAL	CONSULAR	COTTAGER	CREDIBLE
COMMUNED	CONSUMED	COTTONED	CREDIBLY
COMMUTED	CONSUMER	COUCHANT	CREDITED
COMMUTER	CONTANGO	COUCHING	CREDITOR
COMPARED	CONTEMPT	COUGHING	CREEPING
COMPETED	CONTENTS	COUNTESS	CREMATED
COMPILED	CONTINUE	COUNTING	CREOSOTE
COMPILER	CONTRACT	COUPLING	CRESCENT
COMPLAIN	CONTRARY	COURSING	CRESTING
COMPLETE	CONTRAST	COURTESY	CRETONNE
COMPLIED	CONTRITE	COURTIER	CREVASSE
COMPOSED	CONTRIVE	COURTING	CRIBBAGE
COMPOSER	CONTUSED	COUSINLY	CRIBBING
COMPOUND	CONVENED	COVENANT	CRIMINAL
COMPRESS	CONVENER	COVENTRY	CRIMPING
COMPRISE	CONVERGE	COVERAGE	CRINGING
COMPUTED	CONVERSE	COVERING	CRINKLED
COMPUTER	CONVEXLY	COVERLET	CRIPPLED
CONCEDED	CONVEYED	COVERTLY	CRITERIA
CONCEIVE	CONVEYOR	COVETING	CRITICAL
CONCERTO	CONVINCE	COVETOUS	CRITIQUE
CONCLAVE	CONVOKED	COWARDLY	CROAKING
CONCLUDE	CONVOYED	COWERING	CROCKERY
CONCOURS	CONVULSE	COWHOUSE	CROCKING
CONCRETE	COOEEING	CO-WORKER	CROMLECH
CONDENSE	COOK-SHOP	COXSWAIN	CROOKING
CONDOLED	COOLNESS	CRABBING	CROONING
CONDONED	COOPERED	CRACKING	CROPPING
CONDUCED	CO-OPTING	CRACK-JAW	CROSSBAR
CONFETTI	CO-OPTION	CRACKLED	CROSSBOW
CONFIDED	COPPERED	CRACKNEL	CROSSCUT
CONFINED	COPULATE	CRACKPOT	CROSSING
CONFLICT	COPY-BOOK	CRADLING	CROTCHED
CONFOUND	COPYHOLD	CRAFTIER	CROTCHET
CONFRERE	COQUETRY	CRAFTILY	CROUCHED
CONFRONT	COQUETTE	CRAMMING	CROUPIER
CONFUSED	CORDUROY	CRAMPING	CROWDING
CONFUTED	CORDWAIN	CRANE-FLY	CROWFOOT
CONGRESS	CORN-BEEF	CRANKING	CROWNING
CONGREVE	CORNEOUS	CRANNIED	CRUCIBLE
CONJOINT	CORNERED	CRASHING	CRUCIFIX
CONJUGAL	CORPORAL	CRAVENLY	CRUISING
CONJUNCT	CORRIDOR	CRAWFISH	CRUMBLED
CONJURED	CORRODED	CRAWLING	CRUMPLED
CONJURER	CORSELET	CRAYFISH	CRUNCHED
CONJUROR	CORSICAN	CRAYONED	CRUSADED
CONNIVED	CORUNDUM	CRAZIEST	CRUSADER
CONNOTED	CORVETTE	CREAKING	CRUSHING

CRUSTILY
CRUTCHED
CRYONICS
CUBIFORM
CUCUMBER
CUDDLING
CUL-DE-SAC
CULINARY
CULPABLE
CULPABLY
CULTURED
CUVERIN
CUMBRIAN
CUPBOARD
CUPIDITY
CUPREOUS
CURATIVE
CURATORY
CURBLESS
CURDLING
CURELESS
CURRENCY
CURRICLE
CURRYING
CURSEDLY
CURTNESS
CURTSIED
CUSPIDOR
CUSTOMER
CUT-GLASS
CUTHBERT
CUTPURSE
CUT-WATER
CYCLAMEN
CYCLE-CAR
CYCLICAL
CYCLONIC
CYLINDER
CYNICISM
CYNOSURE
CZARITZA

D – 8

DABBLING
DABCHICK
DAEDALUS
DAFFODIL
DAFTNESS
DAINTILY
DAIRYING
DAIRYMAN
DALESMAN
DALLYING
DALMATIA
DAMAGING

DAMNABLE
DAMOCLES
DAMPENED
DAMPNESS
DANDIEST
DANDLING
DANDRUFF
DANDYISH
DANDYISM
DANGLING
DANSEUSE
DAPPLING
DARINGLY
DARKENED
DARKLING
DARKNESS
DARK-ROOM
DATA-BANK
DATABASE
DATALESS
DATE-LINE
DATE-PALM
DATE-PLUM
DAUGHTER
DAUNTING
DAUPHINE
DAWDLING
DAYBREAK
DAYDREAM
DAYLIGHT
DAY-TO-DAY
DAZZLING
DEAD-BEAT
DEADENED
DEAD-HEAD
DEAD HEAT
DEADLIER
DEADLINE
DEADLOCK
DEADNESS
DEAD WOOD
DEAFENED
DEAFNESS
DEANSHIP
DEARNESS
DEATH-BED
DEBARRED
DEBASING
DEBATING
DEBILITY
DEBITING
DEBONAIR
DEBUNKED
DEBUTANT
DECADENT
DECAMPED

DECANTED
DECANTER
DECAYING
DECEASED
DECEIVED
DECEIVER
DECEMBER
DECENTLY
DECIDING
DECIMATE
DECIPHER
DECISION
DECISIVE
DECK-HAND
DECLARED
DECLASSE
DECLINED
DECODING
DECORATE
DECOROUS
DECOYING
DECREASE
DECREPIT
DECRYING
DEDICATE
DEDUCING
DEDUCTED
DEEDPOLL
DEEMSTER
DEEPENED
DEEP-LAID
DEERSKIN
DEFACING
DEFAMING
DEFEATED
DEFENDED
DEFENDER
DEFERRED
DEFIANCE
DEFILING
DEFINING
DEFINITE
DEFLATED
DEFOREST
DEFORMED
DEFRAYAL
DEFRAYED
DEFTNESS
DEGRADED
DEIFYING
DEIGNING
DEJECTED
DEJEUNER
DELAYING
DELECTUS
DELEGACY

DELEGATE
DELETING
DELETION
DELICACY
DELICATE
DELIRIUM
DELIVERY
DELOUSED
DELPHIAN
DELUDING
DELUGING
DELUSION
DELUSIVE
DEMAGOGY
DEMANDED
DEMARCHE
DEMEANED
DEMENTED
DEMENTIA
DEMERARA
DEMIJOHN
DEMISING
DEMOBBED
DEMOCRAT
DEMOLISH
DEMONIAC
DEMONISM
DEMPSTER
DEMURELY
DEMURRED
DENARIUS
DENATURE
DENIABLE
DENOTING
DENOUNCE
DENUDING
DEPARTED
DEPENDED
DEPICTED
DEPILATE
DEPLETED
DEPLORED
DEPLOYED
DEPONENT
DEPORTED
DEPORTEE
DEPOSING
DEPRAVED
DEPRIVED
DEPUTING
DEPUTISE
DERAILED
DERANGED
DERATING
DERELICT
DERIDING

DERISION
DERISIVE
DERISORY
DERIVING
DEROGATE
DESCRIBE
DESCRIED
DESERTED
DESERTER
DESERVED
DESIGNED
DESIGNER
DESIRING
DESIROUS
DESISTED
DESOLATE
DESPATCH
DESPISED
DESPOTIC
DESTINED
DETACHED
DETAILED
DETAINED
DETECTED
DETECTOR
DETERRED
DETESTED
DETHRONE
DETONATE
DETRITUS
DEUCEDLY
DEVALUED
DEVIATED
DEVILISH
DEVILISM
DEVILLED
DEVISING
DEVOLVED
DEVONIAN
DEVOTING
DEVOTION
DEVOURED
DEVOUTLY
DEWBERRY
DEWINESS
DEXTROSE
DEXTROUS
DIABETES
DIABETIC
DIABOLIC
DIAGNOSE
DIAGONAL
DIALLING
DIALOGUE
DIAMETER
DIANTHUS

DIAPASON
DIASTASE
DIASTOLE
DIATOMIC
DIATONIC
DIATRIBE
DIBBLING
DICKERED
DICTATED
DICTATOR
DIDACTIC
DIDDLING
DIETETIC
DIFFERED
DIFFRACT
DIFFUSED
DIFFUSER
DIGESTED
DIGGINGS
DIGITATE
DIHEDRAL
DILATING
DILATION
DILATORY
DILIGENT
DILUTING
DILUTION
DILUVIAL
DIMINISH
DIMPLING
DINER-OUT
DING-DONG
DINGIEST
DINORNIS
DINOSAUR
DIOCESAN
DIORAMIC
DIPLEXER
DIPLOMAT
DIRECTED
DIRECTLY
DIRECTOR
DIRTIEST
DIRTYING
DISABLED
DISABUSE
DISAGREE
DISALLOW
DISARMED
DISARRAY
DISASTER
DISBURSE
DISCIPLE
DISCLAIM
DISCLOSE
DISCOUNT

DISCOVER
DISCREET
DISEASED
DISGORGE
DISGRACE
DISGUISE
DISHEVEL
DISINTER
DISJOINT
DISKETTE
DISLIKED
DISLODGE
DISLOYAL
DISMALLY
DISMAYED
DISMOUNT
DISORDER
DISOWNED
DISPATCH
DISPENSE
DISPERSE
DISPIRIT
DISPLACE
DISPOSAL
DISPOSED
DISPROOF
DISPROVE
DISPUTED
DISQUIET
DISROBED
DISSOLVE
DISSUADE
DISTANCE
DISTASTE
DISTINCT
DISTRACT
DISTRAIN
DISTRAIT
DISTRESS
DISTRICT
DISTRUST
DISUNION
DISUNITE
DISUNITY
DITCHING
DITHERED
DITTY-BAG
DITTY-BOX
DIVE-BOMB
DIVERGED
DIVERTED
DIVESTED
DIVIDEND
DIVIDING
DIVINELY
DIVINITY

DIVISION
DIVORCED
DIVORCEE
DIVULGED
DIZZYING
DOCILITY
DOCKYARD
DOCTORED
DOCTRINE
DOCUMENT
DODDERED
DODDERER
DOGBERRY
DOG-EARED
DOGESHIP
DOG-FACED
DOGGEDLY
DOGGEREL
DOGHOUSE
DOG-LATIN
DOGMATIC
DOG'S-BODY
DOG'S-MEAT
DOG'S-NOSE
DOG-TIRED
DOG-TOOTH
DOG-WATCH
DOLDRUMS
DOLLED-UP
DOLOMITE
DOLOROSO
DOLORUS
DOMELIKE
DOMESDAY
DOMESTIC
DOMICILE
DOMINANT
DOMINATE
DOMINEER
DOMINION
DOMINOES
DONATING
DONATION
DOOMSDAY
DOORBELL
DOORKNOB
DOORLESS
DOORNAIL
DOORPOST
DOORSTEP
DORMANCY
DORMOUSE
DORSALLY
DOTARDLY
DOTINGLY
DOTTEREL

DOUBLETS
DOUBLING
DOUBLOON
DOUBTFUL
DOUBTING
DOUCHING
DOUGHBOY
DOUGHNUT
DOUM-PALM
DOURNESS
DOVECOTE
DOVE-EYED
DOVELIKE
DOVETAIL
DOWDYISH
DOWDYISM
DOWELLED
DOWEL-PIN
DOWERING
DOWNCAST
DOWNCOME
DOWNFALL
DOWNHILL
DOWNLAND
DOWN-LINE
DOWNLINK
DOWNPOUR
DOWNWARD
DOXOLOGY
DOZINESS
DRAFTING
DRAGGING
DRAGGLED
DRAG-HOOK
DRAG-HUNT
DRAGOMAN
DRAINAGE
DRAINING
DRAMATIC
DRAM-SHOP
DRAUGHTS
DRAUGHTY
DRAWABLE
DRAWBACK
DRAWBOLT
DRAW-GEAR
DRAWLING
DRAW-LINK
DRAW-WELL
DREADFUL
DREADING
DREAMFUL
DREAMILY
DREAMING
DREARILY
DREDGING

DRENCHED
DRESSING
DRIBBLED
DRIBBLET
DRIFT-ICE
DRIFTING
DRIFT-NET
DRIFT-WAY
DRILLING
DRINKING
DRIPPING
DRIVABLE
DRIZZLED
DROLLERY
DROOLING
DROOPING
DROP-GOAL
DROPPING
DROPSIED
DROPWORT
DROUGHTY
DROWNING
DROWSILY
DROWSING
DRUBBING
DRUDGERY
DRUDGING
DRUGGING
DRUGGIST
DRUIDISM
DRUMFIRE
DRUMFISH
DRUMHEAD
DRUMMING
DRUNKARD
DRY-CLEAN
DRY-GOODS
DRY-NURSE
DRY-PLATE
DRY-POINT
DRYSTONE
DUCHESSE
DUCKBILL
DUCK-HAWK
DUCKLING
DUCK-MOLE
DUCK'S-EGG
DUCK-SHOT
DUCKWEED
DUELLING
DUELLIST
DUETTING
DUETTIST
DUKELING
DUKERIES
DUKESHIP

DULCIMER
DULL-EYED
DULLNESS
DUMB-BELL
DUMBNESS
DUMB-SHOW
DUMPLING
DUNGAREE
DUNG-CART
DUNG-FORK
DUNGHILL
DUODENAL
DUODENUM
DUOLOGUE
DURATION
DUST-CART
DUST-COAT
DUST-HOLE
DUTCHMAN
DUTIABLE
DUTY-FREE
DUTY-PAID
DWARFING
DWARFISH
DWELLING
DWINDLED
DYE-HOUSE
DYESTUFF
DYNAMICS
DYNAMISM
DYNAMIST
DYNAMITE
DYNASTIC
DYSLEXIA

E – 8

EAGLE-OWL
EARPHONE
EARPIECE
EARTHING
EARTH-NUT
EASEMENT
EASINESS
EASTERLY
EASTWARD
EAU-DE-VIE
EBENEZER
EBONISED
ECLECTIC
ECLIPSED
ECLIPTIC
ECONOMIC
ECSTATIC
EDENTATA
EDENTATE

EDGE-TOOL
EDGEWAYS
EDGEWISE
EDGINESS
EDIFYING
EDITRESS
EDUCABLE
EDUCATED
EDUCATOR
EDUCIBLE
EDUCTION
EEL-GRASS
EEL-SPEAR
EERINESS
EFFACING
EFFECTED
EFFICACY
EFFLUENT
EFFLUVIA
EFFUSING
EFFUSION
EFFUSIVE
EGG-PLANT
EGGSHELL
EGG-SLICE
EGG-SPOON
EGG-TOOTH
EGG-WHISK
EGOISTIC
EGYPTIAN
EIGHTEEN
EIGHTHLY
EJECTING
EJECTION
EJECTIVE
ELAPSING
ELATEDLY
ELBOWING
ELDORADO
ELDRITCH
ELECTING
ELECTION
ELECTIVE
ELECTRIC
ELECTRON
ELEGANCE
ELEGANCY
ELEGIAST
ELEGISED
ELEPHANT
ELEVATED
ELEVATOR
ELEVENTH
ELF-CHILD
ELICITED
ELIGIBLE

ELIGIBLY	ENCAMPED	ENTICING	ESSAYIST
ELLIPSIS	ENCASHED	ENTIRELY	ESTEEMED
ELLIPTIC	ENCASING	ENTIRETY	ESTIMATE
ELONGATE	ENCIRCLE	ENTITLED	ESTRANGE
ELOQUENT	ENCLOSED	ENTOMBED	ESURIENT
ELSEWISE	ENCOMIUM	ENTR'ACTE	ETCETERA
ELVISHLY	ENCORING	ENTRAILS	ETERNITY
EMACIATE	ENCROACH	ENTRANCE	ETHEREAL
EMANATED	ENCUMBER	ENTREATY	ETHNICAL
EMBALMED	ENCYCLIC	ENTRENCH	ETRUSCAN
EMBALMER	ENDANGER	ENTWINED	EUGENICS
EMBANKED	ENDEARED	ENVELOPE	EULOGISE
EMBARKED	ENDORSED	ENVIABLE	EULOGIST
EMBATTLE	ENDOWING	ENVIABLY	EUPHONIC
EMBEDDED	ENDURING	ENVIRONS	EURASIAN
EMBEZZLE	ENERGISE	ENVISAGE	EUROPEAN
EMBITTER	ENERVATE	EOLITHIC	EUROSTAR
EMBLAZON	ENFACING	EPHEMERA	EVACUATE
EMBODIED	ENFEEBLE	EPICERIE	EVADABLE
EMBOLDEN	ENFILADE	EPICYCLE	EVENNESS
EMBOLISM	ENFOLDED	EPIDEMIC	EVENSONG
EMBOSSED	ENFORCED	EPIGRAPH	EVENTFUL
EMBRACED	ENGAGING	EPILEPSY	EVENTIDE
EMBUSSED	ENGENDER	EPILOGUE	EVENTUAL
EMENDING	ENGINEER	EPIPHANY	EVERMORE
EMERGENT	ENGRAVED	EPISODIC	EVERSION
EMERGING	ENGRAVER	EQUALISE	EVERTING
EMERITUS	ENGULFED	EQUALITY	EVERYDAY
EMERSION	ENHANCED	EQUALLED	EVERYONE
EMIGRANT	ENJOINED	EQUATING	EVICTING
EMIGRATE	ENJOYING	EQUATION	EVICTION
EMINENCE	ENLACING	EQUIPAGE	EVIDENCE
EMISSARY	ENLARGED	EQUIPPED	EVILDOER
EMISSION	ENLARGER	ERASABLE	EVINCING
EMISSIVE	ENLISTED	ERECTING	EVOLVING
EMITTING	ENMESHED	ERECTION	EXACTING
EMPHASIS	ENNOBLED	EREWHILE	EXACTION
EMPHATIC	ENORMITY	ERUPTING	EXALTING
EMPLANED	ENORMOUS	ERUPTION	EXAMINED
EMPLOYED	ENOUNCED	ERUPTIVE	EXAMINEE
EMPLOYEE	ENQUIRED	ESCALADE	EXAMINER
EMPLOYER	ENQUIRER	ESCALLOP	EXCAVATE
EMPORIUM	ENRAGING	ESCAPADE	EXCEEDED
EMPTYING	ENRICHED	ESCAPING	EXCEPTED
EMPURPLE	ENROLLED	ESCAPISM	EXCHANGE
EMPYREAN	ENSCONCE	ESCAPIST	EXCISING
EMULATED	ENSHRINE	ESCHEWED	EXCISION
EMULATOR	ENSHROUD	ESCORTED	EXCITING
EMULSIFY	ENSLAVED	ESCULENT	EXCLUDED
EMULSINE	ENSNARED	ESOTERIC	EXCUSING
EMULSION	ENSURING	ESPALIER	EXECRATE
EMULSIVE	ENTAILED	ESPECIAL	EXECUTED
ENABLING	ENTANGLE	ESPOUSAL	EXECUTOR
ENACTING	ENTERING	ESPOUSED	EXEMPLAR
ENACTION	ENTHRONE	ESSAYING	EXEMPTED
ENACTIVE	ENTHUSED	ESSAYISH	EXEQUIES

EXERCISE	FAILSAFE	FEATURED	FILTHIER
EXERTING	FAINTEST	FEBRUARY	FILTHILY
EXERTION	FAINTING	FECKLESS	FILTRATE
EXHALING	FAINTISH	FEDERATE	FINALIST
EXHORTED	FAIRNESS	FEEBLISH	FINALITY
EXHUMING	FAITHFUL	FEEDBACK	FINANCED
EXIGENCY	FALCONER	FEED-PIPE	FINDABLE
EXISTENT	FALCONET	FEIGNING	FINENESS
EX-LIBRIS	FALCONRY	FEINTING	FINE-SPUN
EXORCISE	FALDERAL	FELICITY	FINESSED
EXORCISM	FALLIBLE	FELLSIDE	FINGERED
EXPANDED	FALLOWED	FELO-DE-SE	FINISHED
EXPECTED	FALSETTO	FEMININE	FINISHER
EXPEDITE	FALTERED	FEMINISE	FIREBACK
EXPENDED	FAMILIAR	FEMINISM	FIRE-BALL
EXPERTLY	FAMISHED	FEMINIST	FIRE-BOMB
EXPIATED	FAMOUSLY	FENCIBLE	FIRECLAY
EXPIRING	FANCIFUL	FEROCITY	FIREDAMP
EXPLICIT	FANCYING	FERRETED	FIRE-HOSE
EXPLODED	FANDANGO	FERRYING	FIRELOCK
EXPLORED	FANGLESS	FERRYMAN	FIRE-PLUG
EXPLORER	FANLIGHT	FERVENCY	FIRESHIP
EXPONENT	FANTASIA	FERVIDLY	FIRESIDE
EXPORTED	FARCICAL	FESTALLY	FIRE-STEP
EXPORTER	FAREWELL	FESTERED	FIREWOOD
EXPOSING	FAR-FLUNG	FESTIVAL	FIRMNESS
EXPOSURE	FARINOSE	FETCHING	FIRMWARE
EXPUNGED	FARMYARD	FETTERED	FISHABLE
EXTENDED	FARRIERY	FEUDALLY	FISH-BALL
EXTENSOR	FARROWED	FEVERFEW	FISH-CAKE
EXTERIOR	FARTHEST	FEVERING	FISH-GLUE
EXTERNAL	FARTHING	FEVERISH	FISH-HAWK
EXTOLLED	FASCISTA	FEVEROUS	FISH-HOOK
EXTORTED	FASCISTI	FIBROSIS	FISH-MEAL
EXTRUDED	FASTBACK	FIDDLING	FISH-POND
EXULTANT	FASTENED	FIDELITY	FISH-SKIN
EXULTING	FASTNESS	FIDGETED	FISH-TAIL
EYEGLASS	FATALISM	FIELD-DAY	FISHWIFE
EYE-PIECE	FATALIST	FIELD-GUN	FISSURED
EYE-TEETH	FATALITY	FIELDING	FITFULLY
EYE-TOOTH	FATHERED	FIENDISH	FIVEFOLD
EYE-WATER	FATHERLY	FIERCELY	FIXATION
	FATHOMED	FIERCEST	FIXATIVE
F – 8	FATIGUED	FIFTIETH	FIZZLING
	FATTENED	FIGHTING	FLABBILY
FABULOUS	FAUBOURG	FIGURANT	FLAGGING
FACE-ACHE	FAULTILY	FIGURINE	FLAGRANT
FACELESS	FAULTING	FIGURING	FLAG-SHIP
FACE-LIFT	FAUTEUIL	FILAMENT	FLAMBEAU
FACIALLY	FAVOURED	FILCHING	FLAMINGO
FACILELY	FEARLESS	FILIALLY	FLANKING
FACILITY	FEARSOME	FILIGREE	FLAP-JACK
FACTIOUS	FEASIBLE	FILLETED	FLAPPING
FACTOTUM	FEASIBLY	FILMGOER	FLASHILY
FADELESS	FEASTING	FILM-STAR	FLASHING
FADINGLY	FEATHERY	FILTERED	FLATFISH

FLATFOOT	FLUENTLY	FORBORNE	FOUNDING
FLAT-IRON	FLUFFING	FORCEDLY	FOUNTAIN
FLATNESS	FLUIDITY	FORCEFUL	FOURFOLD
FLAT-RACE	FLUMMERY	FORCIBLY	FOURSOME
FLATTERY	FLUORIDE	FORDABLE	FOURTEEN
FLATTEST	FLUORINE	FOREBEAR	FOURTHLY
FLATTISH	FLURRIED	FOREBODE	FOXGLOVE
FLATWORM	FLUSHING	FORECAST	FOXHOUND
FLAUNTED	FLUSTERY	FOREDECK	FOXINESS
FLAUTIST	FLYBLOWN	FOREDONE	FRACTION
FLAWLESS	FLY-MAKER	FOREDOOM	FRACTURE
FLAX-LILY	FLY-PAPER	FOREFOOT	FRAGMENT
FLAX-SEED	FLYSHEET	FOREGONE	FRAGRANT
FLEABANE	FLYWHEEL	FOREHAND	FRAILISH
FLEA-BITE	FOAMLESS	FOREHEAD	FRAME-SAW
FLECKING	FOCUSING	FORELAND	FRANKING
FLEECING	FOG-BOUND	FORELOCK	FRANKISH
FLEETEST	FOGGIEST	FOREMAST	FRANKLIN
FLEETING	FOLDEROL	FOREMOST	FRAULEIN
FLETCHER	FOLDLESS	FORENAME	FREAKISH
FLEXIBLE	FOLIAGED	FORENOON	FRECKLED
FLEXIBLY	FOLIATED	FORENSIC	FREEBORN
FLICKING	FOLKLAND	FOREPART	FREED-MAN
FLIGHTED	FOLKLORE	FOREPEAK	FREEHAND
FLIMFLAM	FOLK-SONG	FORESAID	FREEHOLD
FLIMSIES	FOLK-TALE	FORESAIL	FREE-LOVE
FLIMSILY	FOLLICLE	FORESEEN	FREENESS
FLINCHED	FOLLOWED	FORESHIP	FREE-PORT
FLINGING	FOLLOWER	FORESHOW	FREE-SHOT
FLIP-FLAP	FOMENTED	FORESTAY	FREE-WILL
FLIP-FLOP	FONDLING	FORESTER	FREEZING
FLIPPANT	FONDNESS	FORESTRY	FRENZIED
FLIPPING	FOODLESS	FORETELL	FREQUENT
FLIRTING	FOOLSCAP	FORETOLD	FRETTING
FLITTING	FOOTBALL	FOREWARN	FRETWORK
FLOATING	FOOT-BATH	FOREWORD	FREUDIAN
FLOCK-BED	FOOTFALL	FORGIVEN	FRICTION
FLOCKING	FOOTGEAR	FORGOING	FRIENDLY
FLOGGING	FOOTHILL	FORMALIN	FRIESIAN
FLOODING	FOOTHOLD	FORMALLY	FRIGHTEN
FLOODLIT	FOOTLESS	FORMERLY	FRIGIDLY
FLOORING	FOOTLING	FORMLESS	FRILLING
FLOPPILY	FOOTMARK	FORMULAE	FRINGING
FLOPPING	FOOTNOTE	FORSAKEN	FRIPPERY
FLORALLY	FOOTPATH	FORSOOTH	FRISKILY
FLORENCE	FOOT-RACE	FORSWEAR	FRISKING
FLORIDLY	FOOT-ROPE	FORSWORE	FRIZZLED
FLOTILLA	FOOTRULE	FORSWORN	FROCKING
FLOUNCED	FOOTSLOG	FORTIETH	FRONTAGE
FLOUNDER	FOOTSORE	FORTRESS	FRONTIER
FLOURING	FOOTSTEP	FORTUITY	FRONTING
FLOURING	FOOTWEAR	FORWARDS	FROSTILY
FLOURISH	FOOTWORN	FOSTERED	FROSTING
FLOUTING	FOOZLING	FOUGASSE	FROTHILY
FLOWERED	FORAGING	FOULNESS	FROTHING
FLOWERET	FORAYING	FOUL PLAY	FROU-FROU

FROWNING	GAMEPLAN	GIGGLING	GOLDFISH
FRUCTIFY	GAMESTER	GIG-LAMPS	GOLD-FOIL
FRUGALLY	GANGLION	GILT-EDGE	GOLD-LACE
FRUIT-BUD	GANGRENE	GIMCRACK	GOLD-LEAF
FRUIT-FLY	GANGSTER	GINGERLY	GOLDLESS
FRUITFUL	GANYMEDE	GIN-SLING	GOLD-MINE
FRUITING	GAOLBIRD	GIRDLING	GOLD-SIZE
FRUITION	GAPINGLY	GIRLHOOD	GOLF-BALL
FRUITLET	GARBLING	GIVE-AWAY	GOLF-CLUB
FRUMPISH	GARDENED	GLADDEST	GOLGOTHA
FUDDLING	GARDENER	GLADIOLI	GOLLIWOG
FUELLING	GARDENIA	GLADNESS	GONENESS
FUGITIVE	GAREFOWL	GLADSOME	GOODLIER
FULL-BACK	GARGANEY	GLANCING	GOODNESS
FULL-FACE	GARGLING	GLASNOST	GOODWIFE
FULLNESS	GARGOYLE	GLASSFUL	GOODWILL
FULL-STOP	GARISHLY	GLASSILY	GOOGLIES
FUMBLING	GARNERED	GLAUCOMA	GOOSE-EGG
FUMELESS	GARRETED	GLAUCOUS	GORGEOUS
FUMIGANT	GARRISON	GLEAMING	GOSSAMER
FUMIGATE	GARROTTE	GLEANING	GOSSIPED
FUNCTION	GARTERED	GLIBNESS	GOURMAND
FUNDABLE	GASIFIED	GLIMPSED	GOVERNED
FUNDLESS	GASLIGHT	GLINTING	GOVERNOR
FUNEREAL	GAS-METER	GLISSADE	GOWNSMAN
FUNK-HOLE	GAS-MOTOR	GLOAMING	GRABBING
FURBELOW	GASOLINE	GLOATING	GRACEFUL
FURLOUGH	GAS-STOVE	GLOBULAR	GRACIOUS
FURROWED	GAS-TIGHT	GLOBULIN	GRADATED
FURTHEST	GATELESS	GLOOMILY	GRADIENT
FUSELAGE	GATEPOST	GLORIOUS	GRADUATE
FUSILIER	GATHERED	GLORYING	GRAFTING
FUTILELY	GAUNTLET	GLOSSARY	GRAINING
FUTILITY	GAZETTED	GLOSSILY	GRANDDAD
FUTURISM	GEARCASE	GLOSSING	GRANDEST
FUTURIST	GELATINE	GLOWERED	GRANDEUR
FUTURITY	GENDARME	GLOW-WORM	GRANDSON
	GENERATE	GLOXINIA	GRANTING
	GENEROUS	GLUMMEST	GRANULAR
G – 8	GENETICS	GLUMNESS	GRAPHICS
GABBLING	GENIALLY	GLUTTING	GRAPHITE
GABLE-END	GENITIVE	GLUTTONY	GRAPPLED
GADABOUT	GENOCIDE	GNASHING	GRASPING
GADZOOKS	GEOMETRY	GOAL-LINE	GRASSING
GAINSAID	GEORGIAN	GOATHERD	GRATEFUL
GAITERED	GERANIUM	GOAT-MOTH	GRATUITY
GALACTIC	GERMANIC	GOATSKIN	GRAVAMEN
GALILEAN	GESTURED	GOAT'S-RUE	GRAVELLY
GALLIPOT	GHOSTING	GOBBLING	GRAVITON
GALLOPED	GHOULISH	GODCHILD	GRAYLING
GALLOWAY	GIANTESS	GODSPEED	GREASILY
GALVANIC	GIBBERED	GOFFERED	GREASING
GAMBLING	GIBINGLY	GOGGLING	GREATEST
GAMECOCK	GIDDIEST	GOINGS-ON	GREEDILY
GAME-LAWS	GIGABYTE	GOLD-DUST	GREENERY
GAMENESS	GIGANTIC	GOLDENLY	GREEN-FLY

GREENING	GUTTURAL	HANGER-ON	HEADLONG
GREENISH	GUZZLING	HANGNAIL	HEAD-REST
GREEN-TEA	GYMKHANA	HANDOVER	HEADSHIP
GREETING	GYRATING	HANKERED	HEAD-WIND
GREYNESS	GYRATION	HAPPENED	HEAD-WORK
GRID-BIAS	GYRATORY	HAPPIEST	HEARABLE
GRIDIRON		HARA-KIRI	HEARTILY
GRIDLOCK		HARANGUE	HEATHERY
GRIEVOUS	H – 8	HARASSED	HEATHROW
GRILLING	HABITUAL	HARDBAKE	HEAT-SPOT
GRIMACED	HACIENDA	HARDBALL	HEAT-WAVE
GRIMALDI	HAGGLING	HARDCORE	HEAVENLY
GRIMMEST	HAIRLESS	HARDENED	HEAVIEST
GRIMNESS	HAIRLINE	HARDIEST	HECKLING
GRINDING	HALF-BACK	HARDNESS	HECTORED
GRINNING	HALF-BOOT	HARDSHIP	HEDGEHOG
GRIPPING	HALF-BRED	HARDTACK	HEDGE-HOP
GRISELDA	HALF-COCK	HARDWARE	HEDGEROW
GRITTING	HALF-DEAD	HARDWOOD	HEEDLESS
GRIZZLED	HALF-DONE	HAREBELL	HEELBALL
GROANING	HALF-FACE	HARMLESS	HEFTIEST
GROG-SHOP	HALF-MAST	HARMONIC	HEIGHTEN
GROOMING	HALF-MOON	HARRIDAN	HEIRLESS
GROOVING	HALF-NOTE	HARROWED	HEIRLOOM
GROSBEAK	HALF-PAST	HARRYING	HELLENIC
GROUNDED	HALF-SEAS	HASTENED	HELL-FIRE
GROUNDER	HALF-TIME	HASTINGS	HELMETED
GROUPING	HALF-TINT	HATBRUSH	HELMLESS
GROUSING	HALF-TONE	HATCHERY	HELMSMAN
GROUTING	HALL-MARK	HATCHING	HELPLESS
GROWABLE	HALLOOED	HATCHWAY	HELPLINE
GROWLING	HALLOWED	HATSTAND	HELPMATE
GRUBBIER	HALTERED	HAT-TRICK	HELPMEET
GRUBBING	HAMMERED	HAUNTING	HELVETIA
GRUDGING	HAMPERED	HAUSFRAU	HEMP-SEED
GRUESOME	HANDBALL	HAWAIIAN	HENCHMAN
GRUMBLED	HANDBELL	HAWFINCH	HEN-HOUSE
GRUMBLER	HANDBILL	HAWK-EYED	HEN-ROOST
GUARDIAN	HANDBOOK	HAWK-MOTH	HEPTAGON
GUARDING	HANDCART	HAWTHORN	HEPTARCH
GUERNSEY	HANDCUFF	HAY-FEVER	HERALDED
GUIDABLE	HANDGRIP	HAYFIELD	HERALDIC
GUIDANCE	HANDHOLD	HAYMAKER	HERALDRY
GUILEFUL	HANDICAP	HAYSTACK	HERCULES
GUILTILY	HANDLINE	HAZARDED	HERD-BOOK
GULF-WEED	HANDLING	HAZEL-NUT	HERDSMAN
GULLIBLE	HANDLOOM	HAZINESS	HEREDITY
GULLIVER	HANDMADE	HEADACHE	HEREUNTO
GUMPTION	HANDMAID	HEADACHY	HEREUPON
GUM-RESIN	HANDMILL	HEADBAND	HEREWITH
GUN-LAYER	HAND-PICK	HEAD-BOOM	HERITAGE
GUNMETAL	HANDPOST	HEADGEAR	HERMETIC
GUNSMITH	HANDRAIL	HEADIEST	HESITANT
GUNSTOCK	HANDSOME	HEADLAND	HESITATE
GURGLING	HAND-WORK	HEADLESS	HESPERUS
GUTTERED	HANDYMAN	HEADLINE	HIAWATHA

HIBERNIA
HIBISCUS
HICCOUGH
HICCUPED
HIGHBALL
HIGHBORN
HIGHBRED
HIGHBROW
HIGHLAND
HIGH-LIFE
HIGHNESS
HIGH-ROAD
HIGH-SPOT
HIGH-TIDE
HI-JACKED
HI-JACKER
HILARITY
HILL-FOLK
HILL-FORT
HILLOCKY
HILLSIDE
HINDERED
HINDMOST
HINDUISM
HIP-JOINT
HIRELING
HISTORIC
HITCHING
HITHERTO
HOARDING
HOARSELY
HOBBLING
HOCKTIDE
HOGMANAY
HOGSHEAD
HOISTING
HOLDFAST
HOLINESS
HOLLANDS
HOLLOWED
HOLLOWLY
HOLOGRAM
HOLYROOD
HOMEBORN
HOMEBRED
HOME-FARM
HOMELAND
HOMELESS
HOMELIKE
HOME-MADE
HOMESICK
HOMESPUN
HOMEWARD
HOMICIDE
HONESTLY
HONEY-BEE

HONEYDEW
HONEY-POT
HONORARY
HONOURED
HOODWINK
HOOFLESS
HOOF-MARK
HOOKWORM
HOOLIGAN
HOOP-IRON
HOPELESS
HOPINGLY
HORNBEAM
HORNBILL
HORNLESS
HORNPIPE
HOROLOGY
HORRIBLE
HORRIBLY
HORRIDLY
HORRIFIC
HORSE-BOX
HORSE-BOY
HORSE-CAR
HORSE-FLY
HORSEMAN
HOSE-PIPE
HOSE-REEL
HOSPITAL
HOSTELRY
HOTCHPOT
HOTELIER
HOTHOUSE
HOT-PLATE
HOT-PRESS
HOUNDING
HOUR-HAND
HOUSEBOY
HOUSE-DOG
HOUSE-FLY
HOUSE-TAX
HOVERING
HOWITZER
HUCKSTER
HUDDLING
HUDIBRAS
HUGENESS
HUGUENOT
HUMANELY
HUMANISE
HUMANISM
HUMANIST
HUMANITY
HUMBLING
HUMIDIFY
HUMIDITY

HUMILITY
HUMMOCKY
HUMORIST
HUMOROUS
HUMOURED
HUMPBACK
HUNGERED
HUNGRILY
HUNTRESS
HUNTSMAN
HURDLING
HURRYING
HURTLING
HUSHED-UP
HUSH-HUSH
HUSKIEST
HUSTINGS
HUSTLING
HYACINTH
HYDRATED
HYDROGEN
HYGIENIC
HYMN-BOOK
HYPERION
HYPHENED
HYPNOSIS
HYPNOTIC
HYSTERIA

I – 8

ICE-BOUND
ICE-CREAM
ICE-FIELD
ICE-HOUSE
ICE-PLANT
ICE-WATER
ICE-YACHT
IDEALISE
IDEALISM
IDEALIST
IDEALITY
IDENTIFY
IDENTITY
IDEOLOGY
IDLENESS
IDOLATER
IDOLATRY
IDOLISED
IGNITING
IGNITION
IGNOMINY
IGNORANT
IGNORING
ILL-BLOOD
ILL-FATED

ILL-TIMED
ILL-TREAT
ILLUDING
ILLUMINE
ILLUSION
ILLUSIVE
ILLUSORY
IMAGINED
IMBECILE
IMBIBING
IMITABLE
IMITATED
IMITATOR
IMMANENT
IMMATURE
IMMERSED
IMMINENT
IMMINGLE
IMMOBILE
IMMODEST
IMMOLATE
IMMORTAL
IMMUNISE
IMMUNITY
IMPACTED
IMPAIRED
IMPALING
IMPARITY
IMPARTED
IMPEDING
IMPELLED
IMPELLER
IMPENDED
IMPERIAL
IMPETIGO
IMPINGED
IMPISHLY
IMPLICIT
IMPLORED
IMPLYING
IMPOLITE
IMPORTED
IMPORTER
IMPOSING
IMPOSTOR
IMPOTENT
IMPRISON
IMPROPER
IMPROVED
IMPROVER
IMPUDENT
IMPUGNED
IMPUNITY
IMPURELY
IMPURITY
IMPUTING

INACTION	INFUSING	INTERPOL	JACKAROO
INACTIVE	INFUSION	INTERRED	JACKBOOT
INASMUCH	INFUSIVE	INTERVAL	JACKETED
INCENSED	INHALANT	INTIFADA	JACOBEAN
INCEPTOR	INHALING	INTIMACY	JACOBITE
INCHOATE	INHERENT	INTIMATE	JACQUARD
INCIDENT	INHERING	INTONING	JAGGEDLY
INCISELY	INHESION	INTREPID	JAILBIRD
INCISING	INIMICAL	INTRIGUE	JAMBOREE
INCISION	INIQUITY	INTRUDER	JANGLING
INCISIVE	INITIATE	INUNDATE	JAPANESE
INCISORY	INJECTED	INVADING	JAPANNED
INCITING	INJECTOR	INVASION	JAPONICA
INCLINED	INJURING	INVASIVE	JAUNDICE
INCLUDED	INKINESS	INVEIGLE	JAUNTIER
INCOMING	INK-MAKER	INVENTED	JAUNTILY
INCREASE	INKSTAND	INVENTOR	JAUNTING
INCUBATE	INLAYING	INVERTER	JAVANESE
INCURRED	INNATELY	INVESTED	JEALOUSY
INCURVED	INNOCENT	INVESTOR	JEANETTE
INDEBTED	INNOVATE	INVITING	JEJUNELY
INDECENT	INNUENDO	INVOICED	JELLYBAG
INDENTED	INQUIRED	INVOKING	JEOPARDY
INDEXING	INQUIRER	INVOLVED	JEREMIAD
INDIAMAN	INSANELY	INWARDLY	JEREMIAH
INDICATE	INSANITY	IODISING	JEROBOAM
INDICTED	INSCRIBE	IOLANTHE	JERRICAN
INDIGENT	INSECURE	IREFULLY	JEST-BOOK
INDIRECT	INSERTED	IRISHISM	JET-BLACK
INDITING	INSIGNIA	IRONBARK	JETPLANE
INDOLENT	INSISTED	IRONCLAD	JETTISON
INDUCING	INSOLENT	IRON-GREY	JEWELLED
INDUCTED	INSOMNIA	IRONICAL	JEWELLER
INDULGED	INSOMUCH	IRONSIDE	JEWISHLY
INDUSTRY	INSPIRED	IRONWARE	JEW'S-HARP
INEDIBLE	INSPIRER	IRONWOOD	JIGGERED
INEQUITY	INSPIRIT	IRONWORK	JIGGLING
INEXPERT	INSTANCE	IRRIGATE	JIGMAKER
INFAMOUS	INSTINCT	IRRITANT	JINGLING
INFANTRY	INSTRUCT	IRRITATE	JINGOISM
INFECTED	INSULATE	ISABELLE	JOBSHARE
INFERIOR	INSULTED	ISLAMISM	JOCKEYED
INFERNAL	INSURING	ISLAMITE	JOCOSELY
INFERRED	INTAGLIO	ISLANDED	JOCOSITY
INFESTED	INTEGRAL	ISLANDER	JOCUNDLY
INFINITE	INTENDED	ISOBARIC	JODHPURS
INFINITY	INTENTLY	ISOLATED	JOGGLING
INFIRMLY	INTERACT	ISOLATOR	JOHANNES
INFLAMED	INTERCOM	ISOTHERM	JOINTING
INFLATED	INTEREST	ISSUABLE	JOINTURE
INFLATOR	INTERIOR	ISTHMIAN	JOKINGLY
INFORMAL	INTERLAY	ITERATED	JOLLIEST
INFORMED	INTERMIX		JONATHAN
INFORMER	INTERNAL	**J – 8**	JONGLEUR
INFRA-RED	INTERNED		JOSTLING
INFRINGE	INTERNEE	JABBERED	JOUNCING

JOUSTING
JOVIALLY
JOYFULLY
JOYOUSLY
JOYSTICK
JUBILANT
JUDGMENT
JUDICIAL
JUGGLERY
JUGGLING
JUGOSLAV
JULIENNE
JUMBLING
JUNCTION
JUNCTURE
JUNKETED
JUSTNESS
JUVENILE

K – 8

KAMIKAZE
KANGAROO
KEDGEREE
KEEL-HAUL
KEENNESS
KEEPSAKE
KERCHIEF
KEROSENE
KEYBOARD
KEY-MONEY
KEYSTONE
KICKABLE
KICKSHAW
KID-GLOVE
KILOGRAM
KILOWATT
KINDLIER
KINDLING
KINDNESS
KING-CRAB
KINGLIKE
KINGPOST
KINGSHIP
KINKAJOU
KINSFOLK
KIPPERED
KISS-CURL
KITEMARK
KNAPPING
KNAPSACK
KNAPWEED
KNEADING
KNEE-DEEP
KNEE-HIGH
KNEELING

KNICKERS
KNIGHTED
KNIGHTLY
KNITTING
KNITWEAR
KNOCKING
KNOCK-OUT
KNOTLESS
KNOTTIER
KNOTTING
KNOUTING
KNOWABLE
KNUCKLED
KOHINOOR
KOHLRABI
KOTOWING

L – 8

LABELLED
LABOURED
LABOURER
LABURNUM
LACERATE
LACEWING
LACK-A-DAY
LACKEYED
LACROSSE
LADDERED
LADLEFUL
LADYBIRD
LADYLIKE
LADY-LOVE
LADYSHIP
LAKELAND
LAMBENCY
LAMB-LIKE
LAMBSKIN
LAMENESS
LAMENTED
LAMINATE
LAMPLESS
LAMPPOST
LAND-CRAB
LANDFALL
LAND-GIRL
LANDLADY
LANDLESS
LANDLORD
LANDMARK
LANDRAIL
LANDSLIP
LANDSMAN
LANDWARD
LANDWEHR
LAND-WIND

LANGUAGE
LANGUISH
LANKIEST
LAPELLED
LAPIDARY
LAP-JOINT
LARBOARD
LARGESSE
LARKSPUR
LARRIKIN
LARRUPED
LASSOING
LATCHKEY
LATENESS
LATENTLY
LATHERED
LATHWORK
LATINISE
LATINISM
LATINIST
LATINITY
LATITUDE
LATTERLY
LATTICED
LAUDABLE
LAUDABLY
LAUDANUM
LAUGHING
LAUGHTER
LAUNCHED
LAUREATE
LAVA-LIKE
LAVATORY
LAVENDER
LAVISHED
LAVISHLY
LAWFULLY
LAWGIVER
LAWMAKER
LAWYERLY
LAXATIVE
LAYERING
LAZINESS
LEACHING
LEADSMAN
LEAFLESS
LEANNESS
LEAP-FROG
LEAP-YEAR
LEARNING
LEASABLE
LEASHING
LEATHERY
LEAVENED
LEAVINGS
LEBANESE

LECTURED
LECTURER
LEE-BOARD
LEE-SHORE
LEFTHAND
LEFTWARD
LEFT-WING
LEGALISE
LEGALISM
LEGALIST
LEGALITY
LEGATION
LEG-BREAK
LEMONADE
LENGTHEN
LENIENCE
LENIENCY
LENT-LILY
LESSENED
LETHARGY
LETTERED
LEVELLED
LEVELLER
LEVERAGE
LEVERING
LEVIABLE
LEVITATE
LEWDNESS
LEWISITE
LIBATION
LIBELLED
LIBERATE
LIBERIAN
LIBRETTO
LICENSED
LICENSEE
LIEGEMAN
LIFEBELT
LIFEBOAT
LIFEBUOY
LIFELESS
LIFELIKE
LIFELINE
LIFELONG
LIFE-PEER
LIFE-RAFT
LIFE-SIZE
LIFETIME
LIFE-WORK
LIFTABLE
LIGAMENT
LIGATURE
LIGHTING
LIGHTISH
LIGHT-PEN
LIKEABLE

LIKENESS	LOCALITY	LUBBERLY	MAJORITY
LIKENING	LOCATING	LUCIDITY	MAKEOVER
LIKEWISE	LOCATION	LUCKIEST	MALAPROP
LILLIPUT	LOCK-GATE	LUCKLESS	MALARIAL
LIME-FREE	LOCKSMAN	LUCKY-DIP	MAL-DE-MER
LIME-KILN	LOCUTION	LUKEWARM	MALIGNED
LIMERICK	LODESTAR	LUMBERED	MALINGER
LIME-TREE	LODGINGS	LUMINARY	MALODOUR
LIME-WASH	LODGMENT	LUMINOUS	MALT-KILN
LIMITING	LOG-CABIN	LUMPFISH	MALT-MILL
LINCHPIN	LOG-CANOE	LUNCHEON	MALTREAT
LINEALLY	LOITERED	LUNCHING	MALTSTER
LINEARLY	LOITERER	LUNG-FISH	MALT-WORM
LINESMAN	LOLLIPOP	LURCHING	MANACLED
LINGERED	LOLLOPED	LUSCIOUS	MAN-CHILD
LINGERIE	LONDONER	LUSTIEST	MAN-EATER
LINGUIST	LONESOME	LUSTROUS	MAN-HATER
LINIMENT	LONGBOAT	LUTHERAN	MAN-HOURS
LINNAEUS	LONGHAND	LYCH-GATE	MAN-OF-WAR
LINOLEUM	LONG-LEGS	LYNCHING	MANPOWER
LINOTYPE	LONG-SHIP	LYNCH-LAW	MANDAMUS
LIONISED	LONG-SLIP	LYNX-EYED	MANDARIN
LIPSTICK	LONGSTOP	LYRE-BIRD	MANDATOR
LIPSYNCH	LONG-TERM	LYRICISM	MANDIBLE
LIQUIDLY	LONGWAYS		MANDOLIN
LIQUORED	LONGWISE	**M – 8**	MANDRAKE
LISTENED	LONICERA		MANDRILL
LISTENER	LOOKER-ON	MACARONI	MANELESS
LISTEN-IN	LOOPHOLE	MACAROON	MANFULLY
LISTERIA	LOOP-LINE	MACERATE	MANGLING
LISTLESS	LOOSE-BOX	MACHINED	MANGROVE
LITERACY	LOOSENED	MACKEREL	MANIACAL
LITERARY	LOPSIDED	MADDENED	MANICURE
LITERATE	LORD-LIKE	MADELINE	MANIFEST
LITERATI	LORDLING	MADHOUSE	MANIFOLD
LITIGANT	LORD'S-DAY	MADRIGAL	MANNERLY
LITIGATE	LORDSHIP	MAGAZINE	MANORIAL
LITTERED	LORIKEET	MAGICIAN	MANTILLA
LITTLE-GO	LOSINGLY	MAGNESIA	MANTLING
LITTORAL	LOTHARIO	MAGNETIC	MANUALLY
LIVE-AXLE	LOUDNESS	MAGNOLIA	MANURING
LIVE-BAIT	LOUNGING	MAHARAJA	MARATHON
LIVELONG	LOVEBIRD	MAHOGANY	MARAUDER
LIVENING	LOVE-KNOT	MAIDENLY	MARBLING
LIVE-RAIL	LOVELACE	MAIL-BOAT	MARCHING
LIVERIED	LOVELESS	MAIL-CART	MARGINAL
LIVERISH	LOVE-LIFE	MAIL-CLAD	MARGRAVE
LIVEWIRE	LOVELILY	MAIN-DECK	MARIGOLD
LOADLINE	LOVELOCK	MAINLAND	MARINADE
LOANABLE	LOVELORN	MAINMAST	MARINATE
LOATHING	LOVE-NEST	MAINSAIL	MARITIME
LOBBYING	LOVESICK	MAINSTAY	MARJORAM
LOBBYIST	LOVESOME	MAINTAIN	MARKEDLY
LOBOTOMY	LOVINGLY	MAINYARD	MARKETED
LOCALISE	LOWERING	MAJESTIC	MARKSMAN
LOCALISM	LOYALIST	MAJOLICA	MARMOSET

MAROCAIN	MEGALITH	MILTONIC	MISUSING
MAROONED	MEGASTAR	MIMICKED	MITIGATE
MARQUESS	MELLOWED	MINATORY	MITTENED
MARQUISE	MELLOWLY	MINCE-PIE	MIZZLING
MARRIAGE	MELODEON	MINDLESS	MNEMONIC
MARRYING	MELODISE	MINGLING	MOBILITY
MARSH-GAS	MELODIST	MINIMISE	MOBILIZE
MARSH-HEN	MELTDOWN	MINISTER	MOCCASIN
MARSH-TIT	MEMBERED	MINISTRY	MOCKABLE
MARTELLO	MEMBRANE	MINORITY	MODELLED
MARTINET	MEMORIAL	MINOTAUR	MODELLER
MARTYRED	MEMORISE	MINSTREL	MODERATE
MARZIPAN	MEM-SAHIB	MINUTELY	MODERATO
MASSACRE	MENACING	MINUTEST	MODESTLY
MASSAGED	MENDABLE	MINUTIAE	MODIFIED
MASSEUSE	MENTALLY	MINUTING	MODIFIER
MASTERED	MERCHANT	MIRRORED	MODISHLY
MASTERLY	MERCIFUL	MIRTHFUL	MODULATE
MAST-HEAD	MERICARP	MISAPPLY	MOISTURE
MASTLESS	MERIDIAN	MISCARRY	MOLASSES
MASTODON	MERINGUE	MISCHIEF	MOLE-CAST
MATCHBOX	MERITING	MISCOUNT	MOLEHILL
MATCHING	MERRIEST	MISCUING	MOLESKIN
MATERIAL	MESSMATE	MISDATED	MOLECULE
MATERIEL	MESS-ROOM	MISDEALT	MOLESTED
MATERNAL	MESSUAGE	MISDOING	MOLLUSCA
MATHILDA	METALLED	MISDRAWN	MOMENTUM
MATRONLY	METALLIC	MISERERE	MONARCHY
MATTERED	METAPHOR	MISFIRED	MONASTIC
MATTRESS	METEORIC	MISGUIDE	MONDAINE
MATURELY	METERAGE	MISHEARD	MONETARY
MATURING	METHINKS	MISHMASH	MONEYBOX
MATURITY	METHODIC	MISJUDGE	MONGOOSE
MAVERICK	METRICAL	MISNAMED	MONITORY
MAY-QUEEN	MICRODOT	MISNOMER	MONKEYED
MAYORESS	MIDDLING	MISOGAMY	MONKFISH
MAZINESS	MIDNIGHT	MISOGYNY	MONKHOOD
MEAGRELY	MIDSHIPS	MISPLACE	MONOCLED
MEALTIME	MIGHTILY	MISPRINT	MONOGAMY
MEAL-WORM	MIGRAINE	MISQUOTE	MONOGRAM
MEANNESS	MIGRATED	MISRULED	MONOKINI
MEANTIME	MIGRATOR	MISSHAPE	MONOLITH
MEASURED	MILANESE	MISSPELL	MONOPOLY
MEAT-SAFE	MILDEWED	MISSPELT	MONORAIL
MECHANIC	MILDNESS	MISSPEND	MONOTONE
MEDDLING	MILE-POST	MISSPENT	MONOTONY
MEDIATED	MILITANT	MISSTATE	MONOTYPE
MEDIATOR	MILITARY	MISTAKEN	MONOXIDE
MEDICATE	MILKMAID	MISTEACH	MONSIEUR
MEDICINE	MILKWEED	MISTIMED	MONUMENT
MEDIEVAL	MILL-HAND	MISTITLE	MOOCHING
MEDIOCRE	MILLIARD	MISTRESS	MOONBEAM
MEDITATE	MILLIBAR	MISTRIAL	MOONCALF
MEEKNESS	MILLINER	MISTRUST	MOONFACE
MEETNESS	MILLPOND	MISTUNED	MOONFISH
MEGABYTE	MILLRACE	MISUSAGE	MOONLESS

MOONWALK	MUCK-HEAP	**N – 8**	NETTLING
MOORCOCK	MUCK-RAKE		NEURITIS
MOORFOWL	MUDDLING	NACREOUS	NEUROSIS
MOORLAND	MUDDYING	NAIL-FILE	NEUROTIC
MOOT-HALL	MUDGUARD	NAINSOOK	NEUTRINO
MOOTABLE	MUFFLING	NAMELESS	NEWCOMER
MOQUETTE	MULBERRY	NAMESAKE	NEWSHAWK
MORALIST	MULCHING	NAPOLEON	NEWSPEAK
MORALITY	MULCTING	NARCISSI	NEWS-REEL
MORALIZE	MULE-DEER	NARCOSIS	NEWS-ROOM
MORATORY	MULETEER	NARCOTIC	NIBBLING
MORAVIAN	MULISHLY	NARGHILE	NIBELUNG
MORBIDLY	MULTIPLE	NARRATED	NICENESS
MOREOVER	MULTIPLY	NARRATOR	NICKNAME
MORIBUND	MUMBLING	NARROWED	NICOTINE
MOROCCAN	MUNCHIES	NARROWER	NIGGLING
MOROSELY	MUNCHING	NARROWLY	NIGHTCAP
MORPHEAN	MUNCHKIN	NATATION	NIGHTJAR
MORPHEUS	MUNIMENT	NATATORY	NIGHTMAN
MORPHINE	MUNITION	NATIONAL	NIGHT-OWL
MORTALLY	MURALLED	NATIVELY	NIHILISM
MORTARED	MURDERED	NATIVITY	NIHILIST
MORTGAGE	MURDERER	NATTERED	NIHILITY
MORTISED	MURIATED	NATTIEST	NINEFOLD
MORTUARY	MURMURED	NATURISM	NINEPINS
MOSQUITO	MUSCATEL	NATURIST	NINETEEN
MOSS-CLAD	MUSCULAR	NAUSEATE	NITRATED
MOSS-ROSE	MUSHROOM	NAUSEOUS	NITROGEN
MOTHERED	MUSICIAN	NAUTICAL	NOBBLING
MOTHERLY	MUSINGLY	NAUTILUS	NOBILITY
MOTIONED	MUSK-BALL	NAVIGATE	NOBLEMAN
MOTIVATE	MUSK-DEER	NAVY BLUE	NOBLESSE
MOTOR-BUS	MUSK-PEAR	NAZARENE	NOCTURNE
MOTOR-CAR	MUSK-PLUM	NAZARITE	NOISETTE
MOTORING	MUSK-ROSE	NAZIFIED	NOMADISM
MOTORIST	MUSKETRY	NEARNESS	NOMINATE
MOTORMAN	MUSQUASH	NEARSIDE	NON-CLAIM
MOTORWAY	MUSTERED	NEATHERD	NON-ELECT
MOTTLING	MUTATION	NEATNESS	NONJUROR
MOUFFLON	MUTENESS	NEBULOUS	NON-MORAL
MOULDING	MUTILATE	NECKBAND	NON-PARTY
MOULTING	MUTINEER	NECKBEEF	NON-RIGID
MOUNDING	MUTINIED	NECKLACE	NON-STICK
MOUNTAIN	MUTINOUS	NEEDLESS	NON-TOXIC
MOUNTIES	MUTTERED	NEEDLING	NON-UNION
MOUNTING	MUTUALLY	NEGATING	NONESUCH
MOURNFUL	MUZZLING	NEGATION	NONSENSE
MOURNING	MYCELIUM	NEGATIVE	NOONTIDE
MOUSE-EAR	MYCOLOGY	NEGLIGEE	NORMALCY
MOUTHFUL	MYOSOTIS	NEGROISM	NORMALLY
MOUTHING	MYRMIDON	NEIGHING	NORSEMAN
MOVELESS	MYSTICAL	NEO-LATIN	NORTHERN
MOVEMENT	MYTHICAL	NEOPHYTE	NORTHING
MOVINGLY		NEPALESE	NORTHMAN
MUCHNESS		NEPOTISM	NOSEDIVE
MUCILAGE		NESTLING	NOSERING

NOSEBAND	OBTAINED	ONE-HORSE	OUTFLING
NOSELESS	OBTRUDED	ONE-SIDED	OUTFLOWN
NOTANDUM	OBTUSELY	ONLOOKER	OUTFLUSH
NOTATION	OBVIATED	OOLOGIST	OUTGOING
NOTCHING	OCCASION	OPEN-EYED	OUTGROWN
NOTEBOOK	OCCIDENT	OPEN-WORK	OUTHOUSE
NOTELESS	OCCLUDED	OPENCAST	OUTLAWED
NOTICING	OCCULTLY	OPENNESS	OUTLAWRY
NOTIFIED	OCCUPANT	OPERA-HAT	OUTLEAPT
NOTIONAL	OCCUPIED	OPERATED	OUTLEARN
NOVELIST	OCCUPIER	OPERATIC	OUTLINED
NOVEMBER	OCCURRED	OPERATOR	OUTLIVED
NOWADAYS	OCHREOUS	OPERETTA	OUTLYING
NUDENESS	OCTOROON	OPIUM-DEN	OUTMARCH
NUGATORY	OCTUPLET	OPPONENT	OUTPACED
NUISANCE	OCULARLY	OPPOSING	OUTPOWER
NUMBERED	ODIOUSLY	OPPOSITE	OUTRAGED
NUMBNESS	ODOMETER	OPTICIAN	OUTRANGE
NUMERARY	OERLIKON	OPTIMISM	OUTREACH
NUMERATE	OFF-BREAK	OPTIMIST	OUTRIDER
NUMEROUS	OFF-PISTE	OPTIONAL	OUTRIGHT
NUMSKULL	OFFPRINT	OPULENCE	OUTSHINE
NUPTIALS	OFFSHOOT	ORACULAR	OUTSHONE
NURSLING	OFF-SHORE	ORANGERY	OUTSIDER
NURTURED	OFF-STAGE	ORATORIO	OUTSLEEP
NUT-BROWN	OFFENDED	ORCADIAN	OUTSLEPT
NUTHATCH	OFFENDER	ORDAINED	OUTSLIDE
NUTMEGGY	OFFERING	ORDERING	OUTSMART
NUTRIENT	OFFICIAL	ORDINARY	OUTSPEAK
NUTSHELL	OFTTIMES	ORDNANCE	OUTSPENT
NUZZLING	OHMMETER	ORGANDIE	OUTSPOKE
	OILCLOTH	ORGANISM	OUTSTAND
	OILFIELD	ORGANIST	OUTSTARE
O – 8	OIL-GLAND	ORGANISE	OUTSTOOD
	OIL-PAPER	ORIENTAL	OUTSTRIP
OAK-APPLE	OIL-PRESS	ORIENTED	OUTSWEAR
OBDURACY	OILSKINS	ORIGINAL	OUTVALUE
OBDURATE	OILINESS	ORNAMENT	OUTVENOM
OBEDIENT	OILSTONE	ORNATELY	OUTVOTED
OBEISANT	OINTMENT	ORPHANED	OUTWARDS
OBITUARY	OLD-TIMER	ORTHODOX	OUTWEIGH
OBJECTED	OLD-WORLD	OSCULANT	OVEN-BIRD
OBJECTOR	OLEANDER	OSCULATE	OVERALLS
OBLATION	OLEASTER	OSSIFIED	OVERARCH
OBLATORY	OLIPHANT	OTOSCOPE	OVERAWED
OBLIGANT	OLIVE-OIL	OUTBOARD	OVERBEAR
OBLIGATE	OLYMPIAD	OUTBOUND	OVERBOIL
OBLIGATO	OLYMPIAN	OUTBREAK	OVERBOLD
OBLIGING	OLYMPICS	OUTBURST	OVERBUSY
OBLIVION	OMELETTE	OUTCLASS	OVERCAME
OBSCURED	OMISSION	OUTDOING	OVERCAST
OBSERVED	OMISSIVE	OUTDOORS	OVERCOAT
OBSERVER	OMITTING	OUTFACED	OVERCOLD
OBSESSED	OMPHALOS	OUTFIELD	OVERCOME
OBSOLETE	ONCE-OVER	OUTFLANK	OVERDONE
OBSTACLE	ONCOMING	OUTFLASH	OVERDOSE
OBSTRUCT			

OVERDRAW
OVERDREW
OVERFAST
OVERFEED
OVERFILL
OVERFISH
OVERFLOW
OVERFOLD
OVERFOND
OVERFULL
OVERGIVE
OVERGROW
OVERHAND
OVERHANG
OVERHAUL
OVERHEAD
OVERHEAR
OVERHEAT
OVERJUMP
OVERKIND
OVERLAID
OVERLAIN
OVERLAND
OVERLEAF
OVERLEAP
OVERLOAD
OVERLOCK
OVERLONG
OVERLOOK
OVERLORD
OVERMUCH
OVERNEAT
OVERNICE
OVERPAID
OVERPASS
OVERRAKE
OVERRATE
OVERRIDE
OVERRIPE
OVERRULE
OVERSEAS
OVERSEEN
OVERSEER
OVERSELL
OVERSEWN
OVERSHOE
OVERSHOT
OVERSIDE
OVERSIZE
OVERSLIP
OVERSOLD
OVERSTAY
OVERSTEP
OVERTAKE
OVERTASK
OVERTIME

OVERTONE
OVERTURE
OVERTURN
OVERWASH
OVERWEAR
OVERWIND
OVERWORK
OVERWORN
OXIDIZED
OX-PECKER
OX-TONGUED

P – 8

PACIFIED
PACIFIER
PACIFISM
PACIFIST
PACK-LOAD
PACK-MULE
PACKETED
PADDLING
PAGANISE
PAGANISH
PAGANISM
PAGINATE
PAINLESS
PAINTING
PAKISTAN
PALATIAL
PALATINE
PALE-EYED
PALE-FACE
PALENESS
PALIMONY
PALISADE
PALL-MALL
PALLIATE
PALLIDLY
PALM-TREE
PALPABLE
PALPABLY
PAMPERED
PAMPHLET
PANCAKED
PANCREAS
PANDERED
PANELLED
PANGOLIN
PANICKED
PANORAMA
PANTHEON
PANTSUIT
PAPERING
PARABOLA
PARABOLE

PARADING
PARADISE
PARAFFIN
PARAKEET
PARALLAX
PARALLEL
PARALYSE
PARAMOUR
PARNAOIA
PARASITE
PARAVANE
PARCHING
PARDONED
PARENTAL
PARGETED
PARGETER
PARISIAN
PARLANCE
PARLEYED
PARMESAN
PARODIED
PARODIST
PAROXYSM
PARRYING
PARTAKEN
PARTERRE
PARTHIAN
PARTICLE
PARTISAN
PART-SONG
PASSABLE
PASSABLY
PASSBOOK
PASSER-BY
PASSOVER
PASSPORT
PASSWORD
PASTICHE
PASTILLE
PASTORAL
PASTURED
PATCHING
PATENTED
PATENTEE
PATENTOR
PATERNAL
PATHETIC
PATHLESS
PATIENCE
PATTERED
PATTYPAN
PAVEMENT
PAVILION
PAWNSHOP
PAY-CLERK
PAYPHONE

PAY-SHEET
PEACEFUL
PEACHING
PEA-GREEN
PEARMAIN
PEASECOD
PEAT-MOOR
PEATMOSS
PECTORAL
PECULIAR
PEDAGOGY
PEDALLED
PEDANTIC
PEDANTRY
PEDDLERY
PEDDLING
PEDESTAL
PEDICURE
PEDIGREE
PEDIMENT
PEEP-HOLE
PEEP-SHOW
PEERLESS
PEIGNOIR
PEKINESE
PELLAGRA
PELL-MELL
PELLUCID
PEMMICAN
PENALISE
PENCHANT
PENDULUM
PENELOPE
PENITENT
PENKNIFE
PENN'ORTH
PENOLOGY
PENT-ROOF
PENTAGON
PENWIPER
PENWOMAN
PEOPLING
PEPPERED
PERCEIVE
PERCHING
PERFORCE
PERFUMED
PERIANTH
PERICARP
PERILOUS
PERIODIC
PERISHED
PERJURED
PERMEATE
PERMUTED
PERORATE

PEROXIDE	PINCHERS	PLAYBOOK	POLEMICS
PERSONAL	PINCHING	PLAYGOER	POLICING
PERSPIRE	PINE-CLAD	PLAYMATE	POLISHED
PERSUADE	PINE-CONE	PLAYSOME	POLITELY
PERTNESS	PINE-WOOD	PLAYTIME	POLITICS
PERUSING	PING-PONG	PLEACHED	POLLUTED
PERUVIAN	PININGLY	PLEADING	POLONIUM
PERVADED	PINIONED	PLEASANT	POLTROON
PERVERSE	PINK-EYED	PLEASING	POLYGAMY
PESTERED	PIN-MAKER	PLEASURE	POLYGLOT
PESTLING	PIN-MONEY	PLEATING	POLYGRAM
PETERING	PINNACLE	PLEBEIAN	POMANDER
PETERMAN	PINPOINT	PLECTRUM	POMPEIAN
PETITION	PIPE-CASE	PLEDGING	PONDERED
PETRONEL	PIPECLAY	PLEIADES	POND-LILY
PETULANT	PIPE-FISH	PLETHORA	POND-WEED
PHALANGE	PIPE-LINE	PLEURISY	PONTIFEX
PHANTASM	PIPE-RACK	PLIANTLY	PONTIFIC
PHANTASY	PIPE-WORK	PLIGHTED	PONY-SKIN
PHARISEE	PIQUANCY	PLIOCENE	POOH-POOH
PHARMACY	PIRATING	PLODDING	POOLROOM
PHEASANT	PISCATOR	PLOPPING	POOR-LAWS
PHILOMEL	PISTOLET	PLOTTING	POORNESS
PHONE-BOX	PITCHING	PLOUGHED	POOR-RATE
PHONETIC	PITIABLE	PLUCKILY	POPELING
PHOSGENE	PITIABLY	PLUCKING	POPINJAY
PHOSPHOR	PITILESS	PLUGGING	POPISHLY
PHOTOFIT	PITTANCE	PLUG-UGLY	POPULACE
PHRASING	PIVOT-MAN	PLUMBAGO	POPULATE
PHRYGIAN	PIVOTING	PLUMB-BOB	POPULOUS
PHTHISIS	PIXY-RING	PLUMBING	POROSITY
PHYSICAL	PLACATED	PLUM-CAKE	PORPHYRY
PHYSIQUE	PLACEMAN	PLUM-DUFF	PORPOISE
PIANETTE	PLACIDLY	PLUMELET	PORRIDGE
PICAROON	PLAGIARY	PLUMPEST	PORTABLE
PICKETED	PLAGUILY	PLUMPING	PORTHOLE
PICKLING	PLAGUING	PLUNGING	PORTIERE
PICKLOCK	PLAITING	PLURALLY	PORTLAND
PICK-ME-UP	PLANGENT	PLUTARCH	PORTRAIT
PICKWICK	PLANKING	PLUTONIC	POSEIDON
PICTURED	PLANKTON	PLUVIOUS	POSINGLY
PIERCING	PLANLESS	POACHING	POSITION
PIFFLING	PLANNING	POCHETTE	POSITIVE
PIG-FACED	PLANTAIN	POCKETED	POSSIBLE
PIKEHEAD	PLANTING	POCKMARK	POSSIBLY
PILASTER	PLANTLET	POETICAL	POSTABLE
PILCHARD	PLASHING	POETIZED	POSTCARD
PILFERED	PLATEFUL	POIGNANT	POST-DATE
PILLAGED	PLATFORM	POIGNARD	POST-FREE
PILLARED	PLATINIC	POINTING	POST-HORN
PILLOWED	PLATINUM	POISONED	POSTICHE
PILOTAGE	PLATONIC	POISONER	POSTMARK
PILOTING	PLATTING	POLARITY	POST-PAID
PIN-WHEEL	PLATYPUS	POLARIZE	POSTPONE
PINAFORE	PLAYABLE	POLE-JUMP	POST-TIME
PINCE-NEZ	PLAYBILL	POLE-STAR	POSTURED

POTATION	PRESTIGE	PROPHECY	PURBLIND
POTENTLY	PRE-STUDY	PROPHESY	PURCHASE
POTHERED	PRESUMED	PROPOSAL	PURENESS
POT-HOUSE	PRETENCE	PROPOSED	PURIFIED
POT-PLANT	PRETTIFY	PROPOSER	PURPLING
POTSHERD	PRETTILY	PROPOUND	PURPLISH
POT-STICK	PREVIOUS	PROPPING	PURPOSED
POT-STILL	PRICKING	PROROGUE	PURSEFUL
POTTERED	PRICKLED	PROSEMAN	PURSE-NET
POUCHING	PRIDEFUL	PROSPECT	PURSLANE
POULTICE	PRIESTLY	PROTEGEE	PURSUANT
POUNCING	PRIGGERY	PROTOCOL	PURSUING
POUNDAGE	PRIGGISH	PROTOZOA	PURVEYED
POUNDING	PRIMATES	PROTRACT	PURVEYOR
POWDERED	PRIMEVAL	PROTRUDE	PUSHBALL
POWERFUL	PRIMNESS	PROVABLE	PUSHBIKE
POWWOWED	PRIMROSE	PROVABLY	PUSS-MOTH
PRACTICE	PRINCELY	PROVIDED	PUSS-TAIL
PRACTISE	PRINCEPS	PROVINCE	PUSSY-CAT
PRAISING	PRINCESS	PROVOKED	PUTTYING
PRANCING	PRINTING	PROWLING	PUZZLING
PRANDIAL	PRINTOUT	PRUDENCE	PYRIFORM
PRANGING	PRIORESS	PRUNELLA	PYROXENE
PRATTLED	PRIORITY	PRUSSIAN	
PREACHED	PRISONER	PRYINGLY	
PREACHER	PRISTINE	PSALMIST	**Q – 8**
PREAMBLE	PRIZEMAN	PSALMODY	
PRECEDED	PROBABLE	PSALTERY	QUACKERY
PRECINCT	PROBABLY	PTOMAINE	QUACKING
PRECIOUS	PROCEEDS	PUBLICAN	QUACKISH
PRECLUDE	PROCLAIM	PUBLICLY	QUADRANT
PREDATED	PROCURED	PUCKERED	QUADRATE
PRE-ELECT	PRODDING	PUDDLING	QUADRIGA
PREENING	PRODIGAL	PUFF-BALL	QUADROON
PRE-ENTRY	PRODUCED	PUFF-PUFF	QUAFFING
PRE-EXIST	PRODUCER	PUG-FACED	QUAGMIRE
PREFACED	PROFANED	PUGILISM	QUAILING
PREFIXED	PROFILED	PUGILIST	QUAINTER
PREGNANT	PROFITED	PUISSANT	QUAINTLY
PREJUDGE	PROFOUND	PULINGLY	QUAKERLY
PRELUDED	PROGRESS	PULLOVER	QUANDARY
PREMIERE	PROHIBIT	PULSATOR	QUANTITY
PREMISED	PROLAPSE	PUMP-ROOM	QUARRIED
PREMISES	PROLIFIC	PUNCHEON	QUARTERN
PRENATAL	PROLIXLY	PUNCHING	QUARTERS
PRENTICE	PROLOGUE	PUNCTUAL	QUASHING
PREPARED	PROMISED	PUNCTURE	QUATORZE
PRESAGED	PROMOTED	PUNGENCY	QUATRAIN
PRESCIND	PROMOTER	PUNINESS	QUAVERED
PRESENCE	PROMPTED	PUNISHED	QUEASILY
PRESERVE	PROMPTER	PUNITIVE	QUEEN-BEE
PRESIDED	PROMPTLY	PUNITORY	QUEENING
PRESS-BOX	PRONG-HOE	PUPATION	QUEEREST
PRESSING	PROOFING	PUPPETRY	QUEERING
PRESSMAN	PROPERLY	PUPPYISH	QUEERISH
PRESSURE	PROPERTY	PUPPYISM	QUELLING
			QUENCHED

QUENCHER	RAINDROP	REAR-RANK	REDIRECT
QUERYING	RAINFALL	RE-ARMING	RE-DIVIDE
QUESTFUL	RAINLESS	REARMOST	RED-NOSED
QUESTING	RAKEHELL	REARWARD	REDOLENT
QUESTION	RAKISHLY	RE-ASCEND	REDOUBLE
QUEUEING	RALLYING	RE-ASCENT	REDSHANK
QUIBBLED	RAMADHAN	REASONED	REDSHIFT
QUICKEST	RAMBLING	RE-ASSERT	REDUCING
QUICKSET	RAMIFIED	RE-ASSESS	RE-DYEING
QUIDNUNC	RAMPAGED	RE-ASSIGN	RE-ECHOED
QUIETEST	RAMPANCY	REASSURE	REED-MACE
QUIETUDE	RAM'S-HORN	RE-ATTACH	REED-STOP
QUILLING	RANCHERO	RE-ATTAIN	REEF-KNOT
QUILL-PEN	RANCHING	REBATING	REELABLE
QUILTING	RANCHMAN	REBELLED	RE-EMBARK
QUIPPING	RANCIDLY	RE-BOILED	RE-EMBODY
QUIRKING	RANDOMLY	REBUFFED	RE-EMERGE
QUISLING	RANKLING	REBUKING	RE-ENLIST
QUITRENT	RANKNESS	REBURIED	RE-EXPORT
QUITTING	RANSOMED	REBUTTAL	REFASTEN
QUIXOTIC	RAPACITY	REBUTTED	REFERRED
QUIXOTRY	RAPE-SEED	RECALLED	REFILLED
QUIZZERY	RAPIDITY	RECANTED	REFINERY
QUIZZING	RAREFIED	RECEDING	REFINING
QUOTABLE	RARENESS	RECEIVED	REFITTED
QUOTIENT	RASCALLY	RECEIVER	REFLEXED
	RASHNESS	RECENTLY	REFORGED
	RATAPLAN	RECESSED	REFORMED
R – 8	RATEABLE	RECHARGE	REFORMER
	RATE-BOOK	RECISION	REFRAMED
RABBETED	RATIFIED	RECITING	REFUNDED
RABELAIS	RATIONAL	RECKLESS	REFUSING
RABIDITY	RATIONED	RECKONED	REFUTING
RACECARD	RATS-BANE	RECLINED	REGAINED
RACEGOER	RAT'S-TAIL	RECLOSED	REGALING
RACINESS	RATTLING	RECLOTHE	REGALITY
RACK-RENT	RAVAGING	RECOILED	REGARDED
RACKETED	RAVELLED	RECOINED	RE-GATHER
RADIALLY	RAVENING	RE-COLOUR	REGICIDE
RADIANCE	RAVENOUS	RE-COMMIT	REGILDED
RADIATED	RAVINGLY	RE-CONVEY	REGIMENT
RADIATOR	RAVISHED	RECORDED	REGIONAL
RADIOING	RAW-BONED	RECORDER	REGISTER
RAFFLING	RE-ABSORB	RECOUPED	REGISTRY
RAFTERED	RE-ACCUSE	RECOURSE	REGNANCY
RAFTSMAN	REACHING	RECOVERY	RE-GROUND
RAG-PAPER	REACTION	RECREANT	REGROWTH
RAG-WHEEL	REACTIVE	RECREATE	REGULATE
RAGGEDLY	READABLE	RECURRED	RE-HANDLE
RAGINGLY	READABLY	RECURVED	REHASHED
RAGSTONE	RE-ADJUST	REDBRICK	REHEARSE
RAILHEAD	READY-MIX	RED-FACED	RE-HEATED
RAILLERY	RE-AFFIRM	RED-SHIRT	RE-HOUSED
RAILROAD	REALIZED	REDDENED	REIGNING
RAINBAND	REALNESS	REDEEMED	RE-IGNITE
RAINBIRD	RE-APPEAR	REDEEMER	RE-IMPORT
RAINCOAT			

473

REIMPOSE	RENT-FREE	RESISTED	REVISING
REINDEER	RENT-ROLL	RE-SOLDER	REVISION
RE-INFECT	RE-NUMBER	RESOLUTE	REVIVIFY
RE-INFUSE	RE-OBTAIN	RESOLVED	REVIVING
RE-INSERT	RE-OCCUPY	RESONANT	REVOKING
RE-INSURE	RE-OPENED	RE-SORTED	REVOLTED
RE-INVEST	RE-OPPOSE	RESOURCE	REVOLVED
REISSUED	RE-ORDAIN	RESOWING	REVOLVER
REJECTED	REPAIRED	RESPIRED	REWARDED
REJOICED	REPAIRER	RESPONSE	RE-WORDED
REJOINER	REPARTEE	RE-STATED	RHAPSODY
RE-JUDGED	REPASSED	REST-CURE	RHEOSTAT
REKINDLE	REPAYING	RESTLESS	RHETORIC
RELANDED	REPEALED	RESTORED	RHOMBOID
RELAPSED	REPEATED	RESTORER	RHYTHMIC
RELATING	REPEATER	RESTRAIN	RIBALDRY
RELATION	REPELLED	RESTRICT	RIBBONED
RELAXING	REPENTED	RE-STRIKE	RICHNESS
RELAYING	REPINING	RESULTED	RICKSHAW
RELEASED	REPLACED	RESUMING	RICOCHET
RELEGATE	RE-PLEDGE	RE-SUMMON	RIDDANCE
RELEVANT	REPLYING	RETAILED	RIDDLING
RELIABLE	RE-POLISH	RETAILER	RIDEABLE
RELIABLY	REPORTED	RETAINED	RIDICULE
RELIANCE	REPORTER	RETAINER	RIFENESS
RELIEVED	REPOSING	RETAKING	RIFF-RAFF
RELIGION	RE-POTTED	RETARDED	RIFLEMAN
RELISHED	REPRIEVE	RETICENT	RIGADOON
RE-LIVING	REPRISAL	RETICULE	RIGHTFUL
RE-LOADED	REPROACH	RETIRING	RIGHTING
REMAINED	REPROVAL	RETORTED	RIGIDITY
REMAKING	REPROVED	RE-TOSSED	RIGOROUS
REMANENT	RE-PRUNED	RETRACED	RING-BARK
RE-MANNED	REPTILIA	RETRENCH	RING-BOLT
REMARKED	REPUBLIC	RETRIEVE	RINGBONE
REMARQUE	REPUGNED	RETROACT	RING-DOVE
REMEDIAL	REPULSED	RE-TRYING	RINGWORM
REMEDIED	RE-PURIFY	RETURNED	RIPARIAN
REMEMBER	REPUTING	RETURNER	RIPENESS
REMINDED	REQUIRED	RE-UNITED	RIPPLING
REMINDER	REQUITAL	REVALUED	RISKIEST
REMISSLY	REQUITED	REVAMPED	RITUALLY
REMITTAL	RE-ROOFED	REVEALED	RIVALLED
REMITTED	RE-SCORED	REVEILLE	RIVER-BED
RE-MODIFY	RESCRIPT	REVELLED	RIVER-GOD
REMOTELY	RESCUING	REVELLER	RIVER-HOG
REMOVING	RESEARCH	REVENGED	RIVER-MAN
RENAMING	RESEATED	REVEREND	RIVETING
RENDERED	RESEMBLE	REVERENT	ROAD-BLOCK
RENEGADE	RESENTED	REVERING	ROADLESS
RENEWING	RESERVED	REVERSAL	ROADSIDE
RENOUNCE	RESETTLE	REVERSED	ROADSTER
RENOVATE	RESIDENT	RE-VETTED	ROASTING
RENOWNED	RESIDUAL	REVIEWED	ROBOTICS
RENTABLE	RESIDUUM	REVIEWER	ROBUSTLY
RENT-A-MOB	RESIGNED	REVILING	ROCK-ALUM

ROCK-CAKE	ROUGHING	SADDENED	SAND-HILL
ROCK-DOVE	ROUGHISH	SADDLERY	SAND-IRON
ROCKETED	ROULETTE	SADDLING	SAND-REED
ROCKLESS	ROUND-ARM	SADDUCEE	SAND-REEL
ROCK-ROSE	ROUNDERS	SADFACED	SAND-ROLL
ROCK-SALT	ROUNDING	SAGACITY	SAND-SHOT
ROCK-WORK	ROUNDISH	SAGAMORE	SAND-STAR
ROGATION	ROUNDLET	SAGENESS	SAND-TRAP
ROLL-CALL	ROUND-TOP	SAGO-PALM	SAND-WASP
ROLY-POLY	ROUTEING	SAILABLE	SANDWICH
ROMANCED	ROVINGLY	SAIL-BOAT	SANDWORM
ROMANCER	ROWDYISH	SAILLESS	SANDWORT
ROMANISE	ROWDYISM	SAIL-LOFT	SANENESS
ROMANISH	ROWELLED	SAIL-PLAN	SANGUINE
ROMANIST	ROYALISM	SAIL-ROOM	SANITARY
ROMANTIC	ROYALIST	SAIL-YARD	SANSKRIT
ROOD-BEAM	RUBBISHY	SAINFOIN	SAPIDITY
ROOD-LOFT	RUBICUND	SALACITY	SAPIENCE
ROOD-TREE	RUCKSACK	SALAD-OIL	SAPPHIRE
ROOFLESS	RUDENESS	SALADING	SARABAND
ROOF-TREE	RUDIMENT	SALARIED	SARATOGA
ROOSTING	RUEFULLY	SALEABLE	SARDONIC
ROOT-BEER	RUFFLING	SALEABLY	SARDONYX
ROOT-CROP	RUGGEDLY	SALE-ROOM	SARGASSO
ROOT-HAIR	RUINABLE	SALESMAN	SARSENET
ROOTLESS	RUINATED	SALE-WORK	SASH-CORD
ROPE-WALK	RULELESS	SALIENCE	SATANISM
ROPE-YARN	RULINGLY	SALIFIED	SATANITY
ROPINESS	RUMANIAN	SALINITY	SATIABLE
ROSARIAN	RUMBLING	SALLYING	SATIATED
ROSARIUM	RUMINANT	SALMONET	SATIRIST
ROSE-BUSH	RUMINATE	SALOPIAN	SATIRIZE
ROSE-GALL	RUMMAGED	SALT-BUSH	SATURATE
ROSE-HUED	RUMOURED	SALTLESS	SATURDAY
ROSE-KNOT	RUMPLING	SALT-LICK	SAUCEBOX
ROSEMARY	RUNABOUT	SALT-MINE	SAUCEPAN
ROSE-PINK	RUNAGATE	SALTNESS	SAUTERNE
ROSE-ROOT	RUNNER-UP	SALT-WELL	SAVAGELY
ROSE-TREE	RURALISE	SALT-WORT	SAVAGERY
ROSETTED	RURALISM	SALUTARY	SAVAGING
ROSEWOOD	RURALIST	SALUTING	SAVANNAH
ROSE-WORM	RURALITY	SALVABLE	SAVEABLE
ROSINESS	RUSHLIKE	SALVAGED	SAVINGLY
ROSINING	RUSTLESS	SAMENESS	SAVOURED
ROSIN-OIL	RUSTLING	SAMPHIRE	SAVOYARD
ROTARIAN	RUTHLESS	SAMPLING	SAWBONES
ROTATING	RYE-GRASS	SANCTIFY	SAW-FRAME
ROTATION		SANCTION	SAW-GRASS
ROTATIVE		SANCTITY	SAW-HORSE
ROTATORY	**S – 8**	SANDBANK	SAW-TABLE
ROT-GRASS		SANDBATH	SCABBARD
ROTIFERA	SABOTAGE	SAND-BIRD	SCABIOSA
ROTTENLY	SABOTEUR	SAND-CRAB	SCABIOUS
ROUGHAGE	SACKLESS	SAND-DUNE	SCABROUS
ROUGH-DRY	SACK-RACE	SAND-FISH	SCAFFOLD
ROUGH-HEW	SACREDLY	SAND-FLEA	SCALABLE
	SACRISTY		

SCALDING	SCRATCHY	SEAMSTER	SELF-HELP
SCALPING	SCRAWLED	SEA-NYMPH	SELFLESS
SCAMPING	SCREAMED	SEA-PERCH	SELF-LIKE
SCAMPISH	SCREAMER	SEAPLANE	SELF-LOVE
SCANNING	SCREECHY	SEA-PLANT	SELF-MADE
SCANSION	SCREENED	SEA-PURSE	SELF-PITY
SCANTIES	SCREEVER	SEARCHED	SELFSAME
SCANTILY	SCREWING	SEARCHER	SELF-WILL
SCAPULAR	SCRIBBLE	SEA-ROVER	SELLABLE
SCARCELY	SCRIBING	SEASCAPE	SELVEDGE
SCARCITY	SCRIMPED	SEA-SHELL	SEMANTIC
SCARFING	SCRIMPLY	SEA-SHORE	SEMESTER
SCARF-PIN	SCROFULA	SEA-SHRUB	SEMI-NUDE
SCARLESS	SCROUNGE	SEA-SNAIL	SEMINARY
SCARRING	SCRUB-OAK	SEA-SNAKE	SEMINOLE
SCATHING	SCRUBBED	SEASONED	SEMITISM
SCAVENGE	SCRUBBER	SEA-TROUT	SEMITONE
SCENARIO	SCRUPLED	SEA-WATER	SEMOLINA
SCENE-MAN	SCRUTINY	SEA-WOMAN	SEMPSTER
SCENT-BAG	SCUDDING	SEA-WRACK	SENILITY
SCENT-BOX	SCUFFLED	SECATEUR	SENNIGHT
SCEPTRED	SCULLERY	SECEDING	SENORITA
SCHEDULE	SCULLING	SECLUDED	SENSEFUL
SCHEMING	SCULLION	SECONDED	SENSIBLE
SCHILLER	SCULPTOR	SECONDLY	SENSIBLY
SCHMALTZ	SCUMBLED	SECRETED	SENSUOUS
SCHNAPPS	SCURRIED	SECRETLY	SENTENCE
SCHOOLED	SCURRIES	SECURELY	SENTIENT
SCHOONER	SCURVILY	SECURING	SENTINEL
SCIATICA	SCUTTLED	SECURITY	SENTRY-GO
SCIMITAR	SCYTHIAN	SEDATELY	SEPARATE
SCISSORS	SEA-ACORN	SEDATIVE	SEPTUPLE
SCOFFING	SEA-ADDER	SEDIMENT	SEQUENCE
SCOLDING	SEA-BEAST	SEDITION	SERAGLIO
SCOOP-NET	SEABOARD	SEDUCING	SERAPHIC
SCOOPING	SEABORNE	SEDULITY	SERAPHIM
SCOOTING	SEA-BREAM	SEDULOUS	SERENADE
SCORCHED	SEACOAST	SEED-CAKE	SERENATA
SCORCHER	SEA-CRAFT	SEED-COAT	SERENELY
SCORNFUL	SEA-DEVIL	SEED-CORN	SERENEST
SCORNING	SEA-EAGLE	SEED-GALL	SERENITY
SCORPION	SEAFARER	SEED-LEAF	SERGEANT
SCOTCHED	SEA-FIGHT	SEEDLESS	SERIALLY
SCOT-FREE	SEA-FRONT	SEEDLING	SERIATIM
SCOTSMAN	SEA-FROTH	SEED-PLOT	SERJEANT
SCOTTISH	SEAGOING	SEEDSMAN	SERRATED
SCOURGED	SEA-GREEN	SEEDTIME	SERVITOR
SCOURING	SEA-HEATH	SEESAWED	SET-PIECE
SCOUTING	SEA-HOLLY	SEETHING	SETTLING
SCOWLING	SEA-HORSE	SIEDLITZ	SEVERELY
SCRABBLE	SEA-HOUND	SEIGNEUR	SEVERING
SCRAGGED	SEA-LEVEL	SEIGNIOR	SEVERITY
SCRAGGLY	SEALSKIN	SEIZABLE	SEWERAGE
SCRAMBLE	SEAMANLY	SELECTED	SEWER-GAS
SCRAPING	SEAMIEST	SELECTOR	SEXTUPLE
SCRAPPED	SEAMLESS	SELF-HEAL	SEXUALLY

SFORZATO	SHIVERED	SIDE-DRUM	SIZZLING
SHABBIER	SHOCKING	SIDELINE	SKEAN-DHU
SHABBILY	SHOEBILL	SIDELING	SKELETAL
SHACKING	SHOEHORN	SIDE-LOCK	SKELETON
SHACKLED	SHOELACE	SIDELONG	SKETCHED
SHADDOCK	SHOELESS	SIDE-NOTE	SKEWBALD
SHADIEST	SHOOTING	SIDEREAL	SKEWERED
SHADOWED	SHOP-BELL	SIDE-SHOW	SKIDDING
SHAFTING	SHOP-GIRL	SIDE-SLIP	SKIM-MILK
SHAGREEN	SHOPPING	SIDESMAN	SKIMMING
SHAMBLES	SHOPWORN	SIDE-STEP	SKIMPING
SHAMEFUL	SHORTAGE	SIDE-VIEW	SKIN-DEEP
SHAMMING	SHORT-CUT	SIDEWALK	SKINHEAD
SHAMROCK	SHORT-LEG	SIDEWAYS	SKINLESS
SHANGHAI	SHORT-RIB	SIFFLEUR	SKINNING
SHANKING	SHOT-HOLE	SIFFLING	SKIPJACK
SHARP-CUT	SHOT-SILK	SIGHTING	SKIPPING
SHARPING	SHOULDER	SIGNABLE	SKIRLING
SHARP-SET	SHOUTING	SIGNALLY	SKIRMISH
SHEARING	SHOW-BILL	SIGNIEUR	SKIRTING
SHEATHED	SHOW-CARD	SIGNLESS	SKITTISH
SHEAVING	SHOW-CASE	SIGNPOST	SKITTLES
SHEDDING	SHOW-DOWN	SILENCED	SKULKING
SHEEP-DIP	SHOWERED	SILENCER	SKULL-CAP
SHEEPDOG	SHOW-ROOM	SILENTLY	SKUNKISH
SHEEPFLY	SHOW-YARD	SILICATE	SKYLIGHT
SHEEPISH	SHRAPNEL	SILKWORM	SKY-PILOT
SHEEP-PEN	SHREDDED	SILLABUB	SKYSCAPE
SHEEP-RUN	SHREWDLY	SILURIAN	SLABBING
SHEERING	SHREWISH	SILVANUS	SLACKING
SHEER-LEG	SHRIEKED	SIMMERED	SLAMMING
SHEETING	SHRILLED	SIMPERED	SLANGILY
SHELDUCK	SHRIMPED	SIMPLIFY	SLANGING
SHELLING	SHRIMPER	SIMULANT	SLANTING
SHELVING	SHRINKER	SIMULATE	SLAP-BANG
SHEPHERD	SHROUDED	SINCIPUT	SLAPDASH
SHERATON	SHRUGGED	SINECURE	SLAPJACK
SHIELDED	SHUCKING	SINFULLY	SLAPPING
SHIFTILY	SHUFFLED	SINGABLE	SLASHING
SHIFTING	SHUNNING	SINGEING	SLATE-AXE
SHILLING	SHUNTING	SINGLING	SLATTERN
SHIMMING	SHUT-DOWN	SING-SING	SLAVERED
SHIN-BONE	SHUTTING	SINGSONG	SLAVONIC
SHINGLED	SIBERIAN	SINGULAR	SLEDGING
SHINGLES	SIBILANT	SINISTER	SLEEPILY
SHINNING	SIBILATE	SINK-HOLE	SLEEPING
SHIPLESS	SICILIAN	SIPHONAL	SLEETING
SHIPLOAD	SICKENED	SIPHONIC	SLIDABLE
SHIPMATE	SICKLILY	SIPHONED	SLIGHTLY
SHIPMENT	SICK-LIST	SISTERLY	SLIMMING
SHIPPING	SICKNESS	SISYPHUS	SLIMNESS
SHIP-WORM	SICK-ROOM	SITUATED	SLINGING
SHIPYARD	SIDE-ARMS	SIXPENCE	SLINKING
SHIREMAN	SIDE-BEAM	SIXTIETH	SLIP-KNOT
SHIRKING	SIDE-COMB	SIZEABLE	SLIPPERY
SHIRTING	SIDE-DISH	SIZINESS	SLIPPING

SLIPSHOD	SNATCHED	SOFT-SOAP	SOUTHERN
SLITHERY	SNATCHER	SOFTWARE	SOUTHPAW
SLITTING	SNEAKING	SOFT-WOOD	SOUVENIR
SLIVERED	SNEERING	SOILLESS	SOZZLING
SLOGGING	SNEEZING	SOIL-PIPE	SPACELAB
SLOP-BOWL	SNICKING	SOLACING	SPACIOUS
SLOP-PAIL	SNIFFING	SOLARIUM	SPADILLE
SLOPPING	SNIPPETY	SOLATIUM	SPALPEEN
SLOTHFUL	SNIPPING	SOLDERED	SPANDREL
SLOTTING	SNIP-SNAP	SOLDIERY	SPANGLED
SLOUCHED	SNIVELLY	SOLECISE	SPANKING
SLOUGHED	SNOBBERY	SOLECISM	SPANLESS
SLOVENLY	SNOBBISH	SOLECIST	SPANNING
SLOWNESS	SNOOPING	SOLEMNLY	SPAN-ROOF
SLOW-WORM	SNOOZING	SOLENESS	SPARERIB
SLUGGARD	SNORTING	SOLENOID	SPARKING
SLUGGING	SNOWBALL	SOLIDIFY	SPARKLER
SLUGGISH	SNOWBIRD	SOLIDITY	SPARKLET
SLUICING	SNOWBOOT	SOLITARY	SPARRING
SLUMMING	SNOWDROP	SOLITUDE	SPARSELY
SLUMPING	SNOWFALL	SOLSTICE	SPAVINED
SLURRING	SNOWLESS	SOLUTION	SPAWNING
SLUTTISH	SNOWLIKE	SOLVABLE	SPEAKING
SLYBOOTS	SNOWLINE	SOLVENCY	SPEARING
SMACKING	SNOW-SLED	SOMBRERO	SPEARMAN
SMALL-ALE	SNOWSHOE	SOMEBODY	SPECIFIC
SMALLEST	SNUBBING	SOMERSET	SPECIMEN
SMALLISH	SNUBBISH	SOMESUCH	SPECIOUS
SMALLPOX	SNUB-NOSE	SOMETIME	SPECKING
SMARTING	SNUFFBOX	SOMEWHAT	SPECKLED
SMASHING	SNUFFERS	SOMNIFIC	SPECTRAL
SMEARING	SNUFFLED	SONATINA	SPECTRUM
SMELLING	SNUGGERY	SONG-BIRD	SPEEDIER
SMELTING	SNUGGING	SONG-BOOK	SPEEDILY
SMIRCHED	SNUGGLED	SONGLESS	SPEEDING
SMIRKING	SNUGNESS	SONGSTER	SPEEDWAY
SMOCKING	SOAPBALL	SON-IN-LAW	SPELLING
SMOKABLE	SOAPSUDS	SONORITY	SPEND-ALL
SMOKE-BOX	SOAP-TEST	SONOROUS	SPENDING
SMOKE-DRY	SOAP-TREE	SOOTHING	SPERM-OIL
SMOOTHED	SOAPWORT	SORBONNE	SPHAGNUM
SMOOTHLY	SOB-STUFF	SORCERER	SPHERICS
SMORZATO	SOBRANJE	SORDIDLY	SPHEROID
SMOTHERY	SOBRIETY	SOREHEAD	SPHERULE
SMOULDER	SO-CALLED	SORENESS	SPICCATO
SMUDGING	SOCIABLE	SORORITY	SPICE-BOX
SMUGGLED	SOCIABLY	SORROWED	SPIFFING
SMUGGLER	SOCIALLY	SORTABLE	SPIKELET
SMUGNESS	SOCKETED	SOUCHONG	SPILLING
SNACK-BAR	SOCKLESS	SOUGHING	SPILLWAY
SNAFFLED	SOCRATES	SOULLESS	SPINDLED
SNAGGING	SODDENED	SOUNDING	SPINNING
SNAPPING	SOFTENED	SOUPED-UP	SPINSTER
SNAPPISH	SOFT-EYED	SOUR-EYED	SPIRACLE
SNAPSHOT	SOFTLING	SOURNESS	SPIRALLY
SNARLING	SOFTNESS	SOURPUSS	SPIRITED

SPITEFUL	SQUARELY	STARRING	STONE-PIT
SPITFIRE	SQUARING	STARTING	STOOKING
SPITTING	SQUARISH	STARTLED	STOOPING
SPITTOON	SQUASHED	STARVING	STOPCOCK
SPLASHED	SQUATTED	STARWEED	STOPPAGE
SPLATTER	SQUATTER	STARWORT	STOPPING
SPLAYING	SQUAWKED	STATUARY	STORABLE
SPLENDID	SQUAWMAN	STATURED	STORMING
SPLICING	SQUEAKED	STAY-BOLT	STOWAWAY
SPLINTER	SQUEAKER	STAY-LACE	STRADDLE
SPLITTER	SQUEALED	STAYSAIL	STRAGGLE
SPLOTCHY	SQUEEGEE	STEADIED	STRAIGHT
SPLUTTER	SQUEEZED	STEADILY	STRAINED
SPOILING	SQUEEZER	STEADING	STRAINER
SPOLIATE	SQUIBBED	STEALING	STRAITEN
SPONGING	SQUIGGLE	STEALTHY	STRANDED
SPOOFING	SQUINTED	STEAMING	STRANGER
SPOOKISH	SQUIREEN	STEAM-TUG	STRANGLE
SPOONFUL	SQUIRING	STEELING	STRAPPED
SPOONILY	SQUIRMED	STEEL-PEN	STRATEGY
SPOONING	SQUIRREL	STEEPING	STRATIFY
SPORADIC	SQUIRTED	STEEPLED	STRAYING
SPORTFUL	STABBING	STEERAGE	STREAKED
SPORTING	STABLING	STEERING	STREAKER
SPORTIVE	STACCATO	STEINBOK	STREAMED
SPOTLESS	STACKING	STELLATE	STREAMER
SPOTTING	STAFFING	STEMLESS	STRENGTH
SPOUTING	STAGGERS	STEMMING	STRESSED
SPRAGGED	STAGHORN	STEPPING	STRETCHY
SPRAINED	STAGNANT	STERLING	STREWING
SPRAWLED	STAGNATE	STERNWAY	STRICKEN
SPRAYING	STAINING	STICKING	STRICTLY
SPREADER	STAIR-ROD	STICKLER	STRIDENT
SPRIGGED	STAIRWAY	STIFFISH	STRIDING
SPRINGER	STALKING	STIFLING	STRIKING
SPRINKLE	STALL-FED	STIGMATA	STRINGED
SPRINTED	STALLING	STILETTO	STRIPING
SPRINTER	STALLION	STILLING	STRIPPED
SPROCKET	STALWART	STIMULUS	STRIPPER
SPRUCELY	STAMENED	STINGILY	STROKING
SPRUCIFY	STAMPEDE	STINGING	STROLLED
SPRUCING	STAMPING	STING-RAY	STROLLER
SPUN-YARN	STANDARD	STINKPOT	STRONGLY
SPUR-GALL	STANDING	STINTING	STROPPED
SPUR-GEAR	STANDISH	STIPPLED	STRUGGLE
SPURIOUS	STAND-OFF	STIRRING	STRUMMED
SPURLESS	STAND-PAT	STITCHED	STRUMPET
SPURNING	STANHOPE	STOCKADE	STRUTTED
SPURRING	STAPLING	STOCKIER	STRUTTER
SPURTING	STARCHED	STOCKILY	STUBBING
SPYGLASS	STARDUST	STOCKING	STUBBLED
SPY-MONEY	STARFISH	STOCKIST	STUBBORN
SQUABBLE	STARGAZE	STOCKMAN	STUCCOED
SQUADRON	STARLESS	STOCKPOT	STUD-BOLT
SQUALLED	STAR-LIKE	STOICISM	STUD-BOOK
SQUANDER	STARLING	STOLIDLY	STUDDING

STUD-FARM	SUNBURST	SWEET-BAY	TALENTED
STUDIOUS	SUNDERED	SWEETING	TALISMAN
STUDWORK	SUN-DRIED	SWEETISH	TALKABLE
STUDYING	SUNDRIES	SWEET-OIL	TALLNESS
STUFFING	SUNLIGHT	SWEET-PEA	TALLYING
STULTIFY	SUN-PROOF	SWEET-SOP	TALLYMAN
STUMBLED	SUNSHADE	SWELLING	TAMARIND
STUMPING	SUNSHINE	SWERVING	TAMARISK
STUNNING	SUNSHINY	SWIFTEST	TAMEABLE
STUNTING	SUPERBLY	SWIGGING	TAMELESS
STUNTMAN	SUPERHET	SWILLING	TAMENESS
STUPIDLY	SUPERIOR	SWIMMING	TAMPERED
STURDILY	SUPERMAN	SWINDLED	TANGIBLE
STURGEON	SUPERTAX	SWINDLER	TANGIBLY
SUBAGENT	SUPINELY	SWINGING	TANGLING
SUBDUING	SUPPLANT	SWIRLING	TANNABLE
SUBGENUS	SUPPLIED	SWISHING	TANTALUS
SUBGRADE	SUPPLIER	SWITCHED	TAPERING
SUBGROUP	SUPPOSED	SWOONING	TAPESTRY
SUBHUMAN	SUPPRESS	SWOOPING	TAPEWORM
SUB-LEASE	SURCEASE	SWOPPING	TARBOOSH
SUBMERGE	SURENESS	SWORD-ARM	TARRAGON
SUBORDER	SURETIES	SWORD-CUT	TARRYING
SUBORNED	SURF-BOAT	SWOTTING	TARTARIC
SUBPOENA	SURFACED	SYBARITE	TARTNESS
SUB-POLAR	SURGICAL	SYCAMORE	TASTABLE
SUBSERVE	SURMISED	SYLLABIC	TASTE-BUD
SUBSIDED	SURMOUNT	SYLLABLE	TASTEFUL
SUBTITLE	SURNAMED	SYLLABUS	TATTERED
SUBTLETY	SURPLICE	SYMBOLIC	TATTLING
SUBTRACT	SURPRISE	SYMMETRY	TATTOOED
SUBURBAN	SURROUND	SYMPATHY	TAUNTING
SUBURBIA	SURVEYED	SYMPHONY	TAUTENED
SUCCINCT	SURVEYOR	SYNDROME	TAUTNESS
SUCHLIKE	SURVIVAL	SYNOPSIS	TAVERNER
SUCKLING	SURVIVED	SYSTEMIC	TAWDRILY
SUDDENLY	SURVIVOR		TAXATION
SUFFERED	SUSPENSE		TEA-CADDY
SUFFERER	SWABBING	T – 8	TEA-CHEST
SUFFICED	SWADDLED		TEACHING
SUFFIXED	SWAMPING	TABBY-CAT	TEA-CLOTH
SUFFRAGE	SWAMP-OAK	TABLEAUX	TEA-HOUSE
SUFFUSED	SWAN-LIKE	TABLEFUL	TEAMSTER
SUGARING	SWAN-NECK	TABOOING	TEAMWORK
SUICIDAL	SWANNERY	TABULATE	TEA-PARTY
SUITABLE	SWANKING	TACITURN	TEA-PLANT
SUITABLY	SWAPPING	TACKLING	TEASPOON
SUITCASE	SWARMING	TACTICAL	TEA-TABLE
SULLENLY	SWASTIKA	TACTLESS	TEARDROP
SULLYING	SWATHING	TAFFRAIL	TEAR-DUCT
SULPHATE	SWATTING	TAIL-BOOM	TEARLESS
SULPHIDE	SWEARING	TAILLESS	TEENAGER
SULPHITE	SWEATILY	TAILORED	TEETHING
SULPHURY	SWEATING	TAIL-RACE	TEETOTAL
SUMMONED	SWEEPING	TAIL-ROPE	TEETOTUM
SUNBURNT	SWEEP-NET	TAINTING	TEHEEING
		TAKINGLY	

TELEGRAM	THINKING	TIME-BILL	TOREADOR
TELETEXT	THINNESS	TIME-BOOK	TORPIDLY
TELETHON	THINNING	TIME-CARD	TORTILLA
TELEVISE	THINNISH	TIME-FUSE	TORTOISE
TELLTALE	THINNEST	TIMELESS	TORTUOUS
TEMERITY	THIRSTED	TIME-WORK	TORTURED
TEMPERED	THIRTEEN	TIMEWORN	TORTURER
TEMPLATE	THOLE-PIN	TIMIDITY	TOTALISE
TEMPORAL	THORACIC	TIMOROUS	TOTALITY
TEMPTING	THOROUGH	TINCTURE	TOTTERED
TENACITY	THOUSAND	TINGLING	TOUCHILY
TENANTED	THRALDOM	TINKERED	TOUCHING
TENANTRY	THRASHED	TINKLING	TOUGHEST
TENDENCY	THREADED	TINPLATE	TOUGHISH
TENDERED	THREATEN	TINSELLY	TOUSLING
TENDERLY	THREE-PLY	TINSMITH	TOWERING
TENEMENT	THRESHED	TINSTONE	TOWN HALL
TENON-SAW	THRESHER	TINTLESS	TOWNLESS
TENTACLE	THRILLED	TIPPLING	TOWNSHIP
TERMINAL	THRILLER	TIPSTAFF	TOWNSMAN
TERMINUS	THRIVING	TIRELESS	TOWN-TALK
TERMLESS	THROBBED	TIRESOME	TOXAEMIA
TERRACED	THRONGED	TITANIUM	TOXICANT
TERRAPIN	THROSTLE	TITIVATE	TOXICITY
TERRIBLE	THROTTLE	TITMOUSE	TOYISHLY
TERRIBLY	THROWING	TITTERED	TRACHEAL
TERRIFIC	THRUMMED	TITULARY	TRACHEAN
TERTIARY	THUDDING	TOADFLAX	TRACKAGE
TESTABLE	THUGGERY	TOADYING	TRACKING
TESTATOR	THUMBING	TOADYISH	TRACKMAN
TEST-CASE	THUMB-POT	TOADYISM	TRACKWAY
TEST-TUBE	THUMPING	TOBOGGAN	TRACTILE
TETCHILY	THUNDERY	TODDLING	TRACTION
TETHERED	THURSDAY	TOGETHER	TRACTIVE
TETRAGON	THWACKED	TOILSOME	TRACTORY
TETRARCH	THWARTED	TOILWORN	TRADUCED
TEUTONIC	TICK-BEAN	TOLBOOTH	TRAGICAL
TEXTBOOK	TICKETED	TOLERANT	TRAILING
THAILAND	TICKLING	TOLERATE	TRAIL-NET
THALLIUM	TICKLISH	TOLL-GATE	TRAINING
THANKFUL	TICK-TICK	TOM-NODDY	TRAIN-OIL
THANKING	TICK-TOCK	TOMAHAWK	TRAIPSED
THATCHED	TIDEGATE	TOMBLESS	TRAMPING
THATCHER	TIDELESS	TOMMY-BAR	TRAMPLED
THEMATIC	TIDE-LOCK	TOMMY-GUN	TRAMROAD
THEOLOGY	TIDEMARK	TOMMY-ROT	TRANCING
THEORISE	TIDEMILL	TOMORROW	TRANQUIL
THEORIST	TIDES-MAN	TONALITY	TRANSACT
THESPIAN	TIDINESS	TONELESS	TRANSEPT
THICKEST	TIGER-CAT	TONSURED	TRANSFER
THICKISH	TIGERISH	TOOTHFUL	TRANSFIX
THICKSET	TIGHTWAD	TOOTLING	TRANSHIP
THIEVERY	TILLABLE	TOP-DRESS	TRANSMIT
THIEVING	TILT-YARD	TOP-HEAVY	TRAPBALL
THIEVISH	TIMBERED	TOP-NOTCH	TRAPDOOR
THINGAMY	TIME-BALL	TOPPLING	TRAPPING

TRAPPIST	TROTTING	TWANGING	UNBLAMED
TRASHILY	TROUBLED	TWEAKING	UNBLOODY
TRAVERSE	TROUNCED	TWEEZERS	UNBOILED
TRAVESTY	TROUSERS	TWIDDLED	UNBOLTED
TRAWLING	TROUTLET	TWIDDLER	UNBOOTED
TREACLED	TRUANTLY	TWIGGING	UNBOUGHT
TREADING	TRUCKAGE	TWILIGHT	UNBRACED
TREADLED	TRUCKING	TWILLING	UNBRIDLE
TREASURE	TRUDGEON	TWIN-BORN	UNBROKEN
TREASURY	TRUDGING	TWINKLED	UNBUCKLE
TREATING	TRUE-BLUE	TWIRLING	UNBUDDED
TREATISE	TRUE-BORN	TWISTING	UNBUOYED
TREBLING	TRUE-BRED	TWITCHED	UNBURDEN
TRECENTO	TRUE-LOVE	TWITCHER	UNBURIED
TREE-CRAB	TRUENESS	TWITTING	UNBURNED
TREE-DOVE	TRUMPERY	TWOCCING	UNBUTTON
TREE-FERN	TRUMPING	TWO-EDGED	UNCAGING
TREE FROG	TRUNCATE	TWO-FACED	UNCALLED
TREELESS	TRUNDLED	TWOPENCE	UNCAPPED
TREENAIL	TRUNKFUL	TWOPENNY	UNCASING
TREKKING	TRUNNION	TWO-SIDED	UNCAUGHT
TREMBLED	TRUSSING	TWO-SPEED	UNCHASTE
TREMBLER	TRUSTFUL	TYMPANIC	UNCHEWED
TRENCHED	TRUSTILY	TYPANUM	UNCLENCH
TRENCHER	TRUSTING	TYPE-HIGH	UNCLOSED
TRENDING	TRUTHFUL	TYPIFIED	UNCLOTHE
TRESPASS	TRYSTING	TYROLEAN	UNCLOUDY
TRIALITY	TSARITSA	TYROLESE	UNCOATED
TRIANGLE	TUBERCLE	TYRRANIC	UNCOCKED
TRIARCHY	TUBEROSE		UNCOILED
TRIASSIC	TUBEROUS	**U – 8**	UNCOINED
TRIAXIAL	TUCKSHOP		UNCOMBED
TRIBUNAL	TUG-OF-WAR	UBIQUITY	UNCOMELY
TRICKERY	TUMBLING	UDOMETER	UNCOMMON
TRICKILY	TUNELESS	UGLINESS	UNCOOKED
TRICKING	TUNGSTEN	ULTERIOR	UNCORKED
TRICKLED	TUNING-IN	ULTIMATA	UNCOSTLY
TRICYCLE	TURBANED	ULTIMATE	UNCOUPLE
TRIFLING	TURBIDLY	ULULATED	UNCTUOUS
TRILLING	TURF-CLAD	UMBRELLA	UNCURBED
TRILLION	TURGIDLY	UNABASED	UNCURLED
TRIMMING	TURKOMAN	UNABATED	UNDAMPED
TRIMNESS	TURMERIC	UNAFRAID	UNDEFIED
TRIPLANE	TURNCOAT	UNAMAZED	UNDENTED
TRIPLETS	TURNCOCK	UNAMUSED	UNDERACT
TRIPLING	TURNDOWN	UNATONED	UNDERAGE
TRIPPING	TURNOVER	UNAVOWED	UNDERARM
TRIPTYCH	TURNPIKE	UNAWARES	UNDERBID
TRIUMVIR	TURNSPIT	UNBACKED	UNDERCUT
TRIVALVE	TURRETED	UNBARBED	UNDER-DOG
TROLLING	TUSSOCKY	UNBARRED	UNDERFED
TROLLOPY	TUTELAGE	UNBATHED	UNDERLAY
TROMBONE	TUTELARY	UNBEATEN	UNDERLET
TROOPING	TUTORAGE	UNBELIEF	UNDERLIE
TROPHIES	TUTORIAL	UNBIASED	UNDER-LIP
TROPICAL	TUTORING	UNBIDDEN	UNDERPAY

UNDERPIN	UNHORSED	UNPRICED	UNTHROWN
UNDERTOW	UNHOUSED	UNPROVED	UNTIDILY
UNDEVOUT	UNICYCLE	UNPRUNED	UNTILLED
UNDIMMED	UNIFYING	UNRAISED	UNTIMELY
UNDIPPED	UNIMBUED	UNREASON	UNTINGED
UNDIVINE	UNIONISM	UNREELED	UNTIRING
UNDOCKED	UNIONIST	UNROBING	UNTOWARD
UNDOUBLE	UNIQUELY	UNROLLED	UNTRACED
UNDRAPED	UNITEDLY	UNROOFED	UNTUCKED
UNDREAMT	UNIVALVE	UNROUTED	UNTURFED
UNDULANT	UNIVERSE	UNRUFFLE	UNTURNED
UNDULATE	UNIVOCAL	UNSADDLE	UNTWINED
UNDULOUS	UNJOINED	UNSAFELY	UNVALUED
UNEARNED	UNJOYFUL	UNSALTED	UNVARIED
UNEASILY	UNJOYOUS	UNSEALED	UNVEILED
UNENDING	UNJUDGED	UNSEATED	UNVENTED
UNERRING	UNJUSTLY	UNSEEDED	UNVERSED
UNEVENLY	UNKINDLY	UNSEEING	UNVOICED
UNFADING	UNKINGLY	UNSEEMLY	UNWANTED
UNFAIRLY	UNLACING	UNSETTLE	UNWARILY
UNFASTEN	UNLARDED	UNSHADED	UNWARMED
UNFENCED	UNLASHED	UNSHAKEN	UNWARNED
UNFILLED	UNLAWFUL	UNSHAVED	UNWASHED
UNFIXING	UNLEARNT	UNSHAVEN	UNWEDDED
UNFOLDED	UNLIKELY	UNSLAKED	UNWEEDED
UNFORCED	UNLOADED	UNSMOKED	UNWIELDY
UNFORMED	UNLOCKED	UNSOCIAL	UNWISELY
UNFOUGHT	UNLOOSED	UNSOILED	UNWONTED
UNFRAMED	UNLOVELY	UNSOLDER	UNWORTHY
UNFROZEN	UNLOVING	UNSOLVED	UNYOKING
UNFURLED	UNMAKING	UNSORTED	UPHEAVAL
UNGAINLY	UNMANNED	UNSOUGHT	UPLIFTED
UNGENTLE	UNMAPPED	UNSPARED	UP-MARKET
UNGENTLY	UNMARKED	UNSPEEDY	UPRAISED
UNGIFTED	UNMARRED	UNSPIKED	UPRISING
UNGILDED	UNMASKED	UNSPOILT	UPROOTED
UNGIRDED	UNMELTED	UNSPOKEN	UPSTAIRS
UNGIVING	UNMILKED	UNSTABLE	UPSTREAM
UNGLAZED	UNMILLED	UNSTATED	UPSTROKE
UNGLOVED	UNMOCKED	UNSTEADY	UPTHRUST
UNGLUING	UNMODISH	UNSTITCH	UPTURNED
UNGROUND	UNMOORED	UNSTRUNG	UPWARDLY
UNGUIDED	UNMOVING	UNSUITED	URBANITY
UNGULATA	UNNERVED	UNSURELY	URBANISE
UNGULATE	UNOPENED	UNSWAYED	URGENTLY
UNGUMMED	UNPACKED	UNTACKED	URSIFORM
UNHANDED	UNPAIRED	UNTANGLE	URSULINE
UNHANGED	UNPEELED	UNTANNED	USEFULLY
UNHARMED	UNPEGGED	UNTAPPED	USHERING
UNHASPED	UNPENNED	UNTASTED	USURIOUS
UNHEATED	UNPICKED	UNTAUGHT	USURPING
UNHEDGED	UNPINNED	UNTENDED	UTILIZED
UNHEEDED	UNPLACED	UNTESTED	UTTERING
UNHEROIC	UNPOISED	UNTETHER	UXORIOUS
UNHINGED	UNPOSTED	UNTHAWED	
UNHOOKED	UNPRETTY	UNTHREAD	

V – 8

VACATING
VACATION
VAGABOND
VAGRANCY
VAINNESS
VALANCED
VALENCIA
VALERIAN
VALETING
VALHALLA
VALIDATE
VALIDITY
VALOROUS
VALUABLE
VAMOOSED
VANADIUM
VANGUARD
VANISHED
VANQUISH
VAPIDITY
VAPORIZE
VAPOROUS
VARIABLE
VARIABLY
VARIANCE
VARICOSE
VASCULAR
VASELINE
VASTNESS
VAULTING
VAUNTING
VEGANISM
VEGETATE
VEHEMENT
VELOCITY
VENALITY
VENDETTA
VENDIBLE
VENDIBLY
VENEERED
VENERATE
VENETIAN
VENGEFUL
VENOMOUS
VENT-HOLE
VENT-PLUG
VENTURED
VERACITY
VERANDAH
VERBALLY
VERBATIM
VERBIAGE
VERDANCY
VERDERER

VERIFIED
VERMOUTH
VERONESE
VERONICA
VERTEBRA
VERTICAL
VESTMENT
VESUVIAN
VEXATION
VEXINGLY
VIBRATED
VIBRATOR
VIBURNUM
VICARAGE
VICINITY
VICTORIA
VICTUALS
VIEWABLE
VIEWDATA
VIEWLESS
VIGILANT
VIGNETTE
VIGOROSO
VIGOROUS
VILENESS
VILIFIED
VILLAGER
VILLAINY
VINE-CLAD
VINE-GALL
VINEGARY
VINEYARD
VIOLABLE
VIOLATOR
VIOLENCE
VIPERINE
VIPERISH
VIPEROUS
VIRGINAL
VIRGINIA
VIRILITY
VIRTUOSO
VIRTUOUS
VIRULENT
VISCERAL
VISCOUNT
VISIGOTH
VISITANT
VISITING
VITALITY
VITALISE
VITIATED
VITREOUS
VIVACITY
VIVARIUM
VIVA-VOCE

VIVIFIED
VIVISECT
VIXENISH
VOCALIST
VOCALITY
VOCALIZE
VOCATION
VOCATIVE
VOGUEING
VOIDABLE
VOLATILE
VOLCANIC
VOLITION
VOLLEYED
VOLPLANE
VOMITING
VORACITY
VOTARESS
VOUCHING
VOYAGEUR
VULGARLY

W – 8

WADDLING
WAFERING
WAGELESS
WAGERING
WAGGLING
WAGGONER
WAGONFUL
WAGON-LIT
WAINSCOT
WAITRESS
WAKENING
WALKABLE
WALK-OVER
WALLAROO
WALL-EYED
WALLOPED
WALLOWED
WALTZING
WANDERER
WANGLING
WANTONLY
WARBLING
WAR-DANCE
WARDMOTE
WARDRESS
WARDROBE
WARDROOM
WARDSHIP
WAR-HORSE
WARINESS
WARMNESS
WARPAINT

WAR-PLANE
WARRANTY
WAR-WEARY
WAR-WHOOP
WASHABLE
WASHAWAY
WASHBALL
WASHBOWL
WASP-BITE
WASTEFUL
WATCHDOG
WATCHFUL
WATCHING
WATCH-KEY
WATCHMAN
WATERCAN
WATER-HEN
WATER-ICE
WATERING
WATERMAN
WATER-RAM
WATER-RAT
WATER-TAP
WATERWAY
WATT-HOUR
WATTLING
WAVEBAND
WAVELESS
WAVELIKE
WAVERING
WAVINESS
WAXCLOTH
WAXLIGHT
WAX-PAPER
WAXWORKS
WAYFARER
WAYGOOSE
WAYLEAVE
WEAKENED
WEAK-EYED
WEAKLING
WEAKNESS
WEARABLE
WEARYING
WEED-HOOK
WEEDLESS
WEIGHING
WEIGHTED
WELCOMED
WELDABLE
WELL-BORN
WELL-BRED
WELLDOER
WELL-HEAD
WELL-HOLE
WELL-KNIT

WELLNIGH	WIGGLING	WOODWORK	YEARNING
WELL-READ	WIGMAKER	WOODWORM	YELLOWED
WELLSIAN	WILDFIRE	WOOD-WREN	YEOMANLY
WELL-TO-DO	WILDFOWL	WOOINGLY	YEOMANRY
WELL-WORN	WILDNESS	WOOLSACK	YIELDING
WELSHING	WILFULLY	WOOLWORK	YODELLED
WELSHMAN	WILINESS	WORDBOOK	YOKELESS
WEREWOLF	WILLOWED	WORDLESS	YOUNGEST
WESLEYAN	WINCHMAN	WORKABLE	YOUNGISH
WESTERLY	WINDFALL	WORKADAY	YOURSELF
WESTWARD	WINDLASS	WORKGIRL	YOUTHFUL
WET-NURSE	WINDLESS	WORKMATE	YUGOSLAV
WHACKING	WINDMILL	WORKROOM	YULETIDE
WHALEMAN	WINDOWED	WORKSHOP	
WHALE-OIL	WINDPIPE	WORMCAST	
WHANGHEE	WIND-PUMP	WORMGEAR	Z – 8
WHANGING	WINDWARD	WORM-HOLE	ZEPPELIN
WHARFAGE	WINE-CASK	WORMLIKE	
WHARFING	WINELESS	WORMWOOD	
WHATEVER	WINESKIN	WORRYING	A – 9
WHEATEAR	WING-CASE	WORSENED	ABANDONED
WHEEDLED	WINGLESS	WORSTING	ABASEMENT
WHEELING	WINNOWED	WORTHILY	ABASHMENT
WHEEZILY	WINTERED	WOUNDING	ABATEMENT
WHEEZING	WINTERLY	WRACKING	ABDICATED
WHELPING	WIRELESS	WRANGLED	ABDOMINAL
WHENEVER	WIRE-WORM	WRANGLER	ABDUCTING
WHEREVER	WIRINESS	WRAPPING	ABDUCTION
WHETTING	WISEACRE	WRATHFUL	ABHORRENT
WHIMBREL	WISHBONE	WREAKING	ABHORRING
WHINCHAT	WISTARIA	WREATHED	ABIDINGLY
WHINNIED	WITHDRAW	WRECKAGE	ABJECTION
WHIPCORD	WITHDREW	WRECKING	ABNEGATED
WHIPHAND	WITHERED	WRENCHED	ABOLITION
WHIPLASH	WITHHELD	WRESTING	ABOMINATE
WHIPPING	WITHHOLD	WRESTLED	ABOUNDING
WHIRLING	WIZARDLY	WRESTLER	ABRIDGING
WHIRRING	WIZARDRY	WRETCHED	ABROGATED
WHISKING	WOEFULLY	WRIGGLED	ABSCINDED
WHISTLED	WOLF-FISH	WRINGING	ABSCONDED
WHITE-HOT	WOLF-SKIN	WRINKLED	ABSENTING
WHITENED	WOMANISH	WRINKLIE	ABSOLVING
WHITTLED	WONDERED	WRISTLET	ABSORBENT
WHIZZING	WONDROUS	WRITHING	ABSORBING
WHODUNIT	WOOD-ACID	WRONGFUL	ABSTAINER
WHOOPING	WOODBINE	WRONGING	ABSTINENT
WHOPPING	WOODCOCK		ABSURDITY
WICKEDLY	WODDLAND		ABUNDANCE
WIDE-EYED	WOODLARK	X – 8	ABUSIVELY
WIDENESS	WOODLESS	XYLONITE	ACCENTING
WIDENING	WOOD-LICE		ACCEPTING
WIDOWING	WOODMOTE	Y – 8	ACCESSION
WIELDING	WOOD-PULP		ACCESSORY
WIFEHOOD	WOOD-SHED	YACHTING	ACCLIVITY
WIFELESS	WOODSMAN	YEAR-BOOK	ACCOMPANY
WIFELIKE	WOOD-VINE	YEARLING	ACCORDING

ACCORDION	ADULATORY	AGREEMENT	ALTO-VIOLA
ACCOUNTED	ADULTERER	AGRONOMIC	ALUMINIUM
ACCRETION	ADULTNESS	AIMLESSLY	AMARYLLIS
ACCRETIVE	ADUMBRATE	AIR-ENGINE	AMASSABLE
ACCUSABLE	ADVANCING	AIR-FILTER	AMAZEMENT
ACETYLENE	ADVANTAGE	AIR-FUNNEL	AMAZINGLY
ACHIEVING	ADVENTIST	AIR-INTAKE	AMAZONIAN
ACIDIFIED	ADVENTURE	AIR-JACKET	AMBERGRIS
ACIDIFIER	ADVERBIAL	AIR-POCKET	AMBIGUITY
ACIDULATE	ADVERSARY	AIR-VESSEL	AMBIGUOUS
ACIDULOUS	ADVERSELY	AIRWORTHY	AMBITIOUS
ACOUSTICS	ADVERSITY	AITCHBONE	AMBLINGLY
ACQUIESCE	ADVERTENT	ALABASTER	AMBROSIAL
ACQUIRING	ADVERTING	ALARM-BELL	AMBROSIAN
ACQUITTAL	ADVERTISE	ALARM-POST	AMBULANCE
ACQUITTED	ADVISABLE	ALBATROSS	AMBUSCADE
ACRIDNESS	ADVISABLY	ALCHEMIST	AMBUSHING
ACROBATIC	ADVOCATED	ALCOHOLIC	AMENDABLE
ACROPOLIS	AERODROME	ALECONNER	AMENDMENT
ACTUALITY	AEROMOTOR	ALERTNESS	AMIDSHIPS
ACTUARIAL	AEROPLANE	ALETASTER	AMOROUSLY
ACTUATION	AESTHETIC	ALGEBRAIC	AMORPHISM
ACUTENESS	AESTIVATE	ALGORITHM	AMORPHOUS
ADAPTABLE	AETIOLOGY	ALIENABLE	AMORTIZED
ADDICTING	AFFECTING	ALIENATED	AMOUNTING
ADDICTION	AFFECTION	ALIGHTING	AMPERSAND
ADDRESSED	AFFECTIVE	ALIGNMENT	AMPHIBIAN
ADDRESSEE	AFFIANCED	ALIMENTAL	AMPHIBOLE
ADDUCIBLE	AFFIDAVIT	ALIMENTED	AMPLENESS
ADDUCTION	AFFILIATE	ALINEMENT	AMPLIFIED
ADDUCTIVE	AFFIRMING	ALKALISED	AMPLIFIER
ADENOIDAL	AFFLATION	ALLAYMENT	AMPLITUDE
ADENOTOMY	AFFLICTED	ALLELUIAH	AMPUTATED
ADHERENCE	AFFLUENCE	ALLEMANDE	AMPUTATOR
ADJACENCY	AFFORDING	ALLEVIATE	AMUSEMENT
ADJECTIVE	AFFRONTED	ALLIGATED	AMUSINGLY
ADJOINING	AFOREHAND	ALLIGATOR	ANALGESIA
ADJOURNED	AFORESAID	ALLITERAL	ANALOGISE
ADJUDGING	AFORETIME	ALLOCATED	ANALOGIST
ADJUNCTLY	AFRICAANS	ALLOTTING	ANALOGOUS
ADJUSTING	AFTER-CARE	ALLOWABLE	ANALYSING
ADMIRABLE	AFTERGLOW	ALLOWABLY	ANARCHISM
ADMIRABLY	AFTERLIFE	ALLOWANCE	ANARCHIST
ADMIRALTY	AFTERMATH	ALLOWEDLY	ANATOMISE
ADMISSION	AFTERNOON	ALMOND-OIL	ANATOMIST
ADMISSIVE	AFTER-PART	ALMSHOUSE	ANCESTRAL
ADMISSORY	AFTERWARD	ALOES-WOOD	ANCHORAGE
ADMITTING	AGGRAVATE	ALONGSIDE	ANCHORING
ADMIXTURE	AGGREGATE	ALOOFNESS	ANCHORITE
ADOPTABLE	AGGRESSOR	ALPENHORN	ANCHOR-MAN
ADOPTEDLY	AGGRIEVED	ALTAR-TOMB	ANCIENTLY
ADORATION	AGITATION	ALTERABLE	ANCILLARY
ADORNMENT	AGONISING	ALTERABLY	ANECDOTAL
ADRENALIN	AGONISTIC	ALTERCATE	ANGEL-FISH
ADULATING	AGREEABLE	ALTERNATE	ANGELICAL
ADULATION	AGREEABLY	ALTIMETER	ANGLICISE

ANGLICISM	APPARATUS	ARTHRITIS	ATHLETICS
ANGLIFIED	APPEALING	ARTICHOKE	ATLANTEAN
ANGOSTURA	APPEARING	ARTICULAR	ATOMISING
ANGUISHED	APPEASING	ARTIFICER	ATONEMENT
ANGULARLY	APPELLANT	ARTILLERY	ATROCIOUS
ANGULATED	APPELLATE	ARTLESSLY	ATROPHIED
ANIMALISE	APPENDAGE	ASCENDANT	ATTACHING
ANIMALISM	APPENDANT	ASCENDENT	ATTACKING
ANIMATING	APPENDING	ASCENDING	ATTAINDER
ANIMATION	APPERTAIN	ASCENSION	ATTAINING
ANIMOSITY	APPETISER	ASCERTAIN	ATTAINTED
ANNEALING	APPLAUDED	ASCRIBING	ATTEMPTED
ANNOTATED	APPLE-JACK	ASHAMEDLY	ATTENDANT
ANNOTATOR	APPLE-JOHN	ASPARAGUS	ATTENDING
ANNOUNCER	APPLIANCE	ASPERATED	ATTENTION
ANNOYANCE	APPLICANT	ASPERSING	ATTENTIVE
ANNUITANT	APPLICATE	ASPERSION	ATTENUATE
ANNULARLY	APPOINTED	ASPHALTIC	ATTESTING
ANNULATED	APPORTION	ASPIRATED	ATTICISED
ANNULLING	APPRAISAL	ASSAILANT	ATTRACTED
ANNULMENT	APPRAISED	ASSAILING	ATTRIBUTE
ANOINTING	APPREHEND	ASSAULTED	ATTRITION
ANOMALISM	APPRISING	ASSAYABLE	AUBERGINE
ANOMALOUS	APPROBATE	ASSEMBLED	AUDACIOUS
ANONYMOUS	APPROVING	ASSENTING	AUGMENTED
ANOPHELES	AQUILEGIA	ASSERTING	AUSTERELY
ANSWERING	ARABESQUE	ASSERTION	AUSTERITY
ANTARCTIC	ARACHNOID	ASSERTIVE	AUSTRALIA
ANTECEDED	ARBITRARY	ASSESSING	AUTHENTIC
ANTEDATED	ARBITRATE	ASSIDUITY	AUTHORESS
ANTENATAL	ARBORETUM	ASSIDUOUS	AUTHORISE
ANTHELION	ARCHANGEL	ASSIGNING	AUTHORITY
ANTHOLOGY	ARCH-DRUID	ASSISTANT	AUTOCRACY
ANTIPATHY	ARCHDUCAL	ASSISTING	AUTOFOCUS
ANTIPHONY	ARCHDUCHY	ASSOCIATE	AUTOGRAPH
ANTIPODAL	ARCH-ENEMY	ASSOILING	AUTOMATIC
ANTIPODES	ARCHETYPE	ASSONANCE	AUTOMATON
ANTIQUARY	ARCH-FIEND	ASSORTING	AUTONOMIC
ANTIQUATE	ARCHITECT	ASSUAGING	AUXILIARY
ANTIQUELY	ARCHIVIST	ASSUETUDE	AVAILABLE
ANTIQUITY	ARDUOUSLY	ASSURABLE	AVAILABLY
ANTITOXIC	ARGENTINE	ASSURANCE	AVALANCHE
ANTITOXIN	ARGUFYING	ASSUREDLY	AVERAGELY
ANXIOUSLY	ARMADILLO	ASTHMATIC	AVERAGING
APARTHEID	ARMISTICE	ASTOUNDED	AVERTEDLY
APARTMENT	ARM'S-REACH	ASTRADDLE	AVOCATION
APARTNESS	ARRAIGNED	ASTRAKHAN	AVOCATIVE
APATHETIC	ARRANGING	ASTROLABE	AVOIDABLE
APERITIVE	ARRESTING	ASTROLOGY	AVOIDANCE
APHORISED	ARROGANCE	ASTRONOMY	AVUNCULAR
APISHNESS	ARROWHEAD	ASTROTURF	AWAKENING
APOCRYPHA	ARROWROOT	ASYMMETRY	AWARDABLE
APOLOGISE	ARSENICAL	ATAVISTIC	AWESTRUCK
APOLOGIST	ARSENIOUS	ATHANASIA	AWFULNESS
APOSTOLIC	ARTEMISIA	ATHEISTIC	AWKWARDLY
APPALLING	ARTHRITIC	ATHENAEUM	AXIOMATIC

B – 9

BABYLONIC
BACCHANAL
BACCHANTE
BACILLARY
BACKBOARD
BACKPIECE
BACKSIGHT
BACK-SLANG
BACKSLIDE
BACKSPACE
BACKSTAFF
BACKWARDS
BACKWATER
BACKWOODS
BADGERING
BADMINTON
BAGATELLE
BAILIWICK
BAKEHOUSE
BAKESTONE
BAKSHEESH
BALALAIKA
BALANCING
BALCONIED
BALD-PATED
BALEFULLY
BALKINGLY
BALLASTED
BALLERINA
BALLISTIC
BALLOT-BOX
BALLOTING
BALL-POINT
BAMBOOZLE
BANDAGING
BANDEROLE
BANDICOOT
BANDOLIER
BANDWIDTH
BANEFULLY
BANISHING
BANQUETED
BANQUETTE
BAPTISING
BAPTISMAL
BARBARIAN
BARBARISM
BARBARITY
BARBAROUS
BARBECUED
BARBERING
BAREBONED
BAREFACED
BARGAINED

BARLEY-MOW
BARMECIDE
BAROGRAPH
BAROMETER
BARONETCY
BARRELLED
BARRICADE
BARRISTER
BARTENDER
BARTERING
BASHFULLY
BASILICAN
BASILICON
BASKETFUL
BAS-RELIEF
BASTINADO
BASTIONED
BATH-BRICK
BATH-CHAIR
BATH-METAL
BATTALION
BATTENING
BATTERING
BATTLEAXE
BATTLE-CRY
BAWDINESS
BAYONETED
BAY-WINDOW
BEANFEAST
BEANSTALK
BEARDLESS
BEATIFIED
BEATITUDE
BEAU-IDEAL
BEAU-MONDE
BEAUTEOUS
BEAUTIFUL
BECALMING
BECKONING
BEDAZZLED
BEDECKING
BEDFELLOW
BEDLAMITE
BEDRAGGLE
BEDRIDDEN
BEDSPREAD
BEECHMAST
BEEFEATER
BEEFLOWER
BEEFSTEAK
BEELZEBUB
BEER-MONEY
BEFALLING
BEFITTING
BEFOGGING
BEFOOLING

BEFOULING
BEGETTING
BEGGARING
BEGINNING
BEGRIMING
BEGRUDGED
BEGUILING
BEHAVIOUR
BEHEADING
BEHOLDING
BELEAGUER
BELIEVING
BELITTLED
BELL-GLASS
BELLICOSE
BELL-METAL
BELLOWING
BELL-PUNCH
BELLYBAND
BELLY-ROLL
BELONGING
BELVEDERE
BEMOANING
BENEFITED
BENGALESE
BENIGHTED
BENIGNANT
BENIGNITY
BENZOLINE
BEREAVING
BERYLLIUM
BESEECHED
BESETTING
BESIEGING
BESMEARED
BESOTTING
BESPATTER
BESTIALLY
BESTIRRED
BESTOWING
BETHOUGHT
BETHUMBED
BETOKENED
BETRAYING
BETROTHAL
BETROTHED
BETTERING
BEVELLING
BEWAILING
BEWITCHED
BICKERING
BICYCLING
BICYCLIST
BIFURCATE
BIGOTEDLY
BILATERAL

BILINGUAL
BILLABONG
BILLETING
BILLIARDS
BILLOWING
BILLYCOCK
BILLY-GOAT
BIMONTHLY
BINDINGLY
BINOCULAR
BINOMINAL
BIOGRAPHY
BIOLOGIST
BIONOMICS
BIPARTITE
BIRTHMARK
BIRTHRATE
BISECTING
BISECTION
BISHOPRIC
BLABBERED
BLACKBALL
BLACKBIRD
BLACKCOCK
BLACKENED
BLACKHEAD
BLACKJACK
BLACKLEAD
BLACK-LIST
BLACKMAIL
BLACKNESS
BLADEBONE
BLAEBERRY
BLAMELESS
BLANCHING
BLANDNESS
BLANKETED
BLANKNESS
BLASPHEME
BLASPHEMY
BLATHERED
BLAZONING
BLEACHING
BLEAR-EYED
BLEMISHED
BLENCHING
BLESSEDLY
BLETHERED
BLIGHTING
BLINDFOLD
BLINDNESS
BLINDWORM
BLISTERED
BLOCKADED
BLOCKHEAD
BLOOD-BATH

BLOOD-HEAT
BLOODLESS
BLOODSHED
BLOODSHOT
BLOODWORM
BLOODYING
BLOSSOMED
BLOTCHING
BLUBBERED
BLUEBEARD
BLUE-BERRY
BLUE-BLACK
BLUE-BLOOD
BLUESTONE
BLUFFNESS
BLUNDERED
BLUNTNESS
BLUSTERED
BLUSTERER
BOANERGES
BOARDABLE
BOARHOUND
BOAR-SPEAR
BOASTLESS
BOAT-HOUSE
BOATSWAIN
BOB-SLEIGH
BOBTAILED
BODYGUARD
BOG-MYRTLE
BOLD-FACED
BOLOGNESE
BOLSHEVIK
BOLSTERED
BOMB-AIMER
BOMBARDED
BOMBARDON
BOMBASTIC
BOMBAZINE
BOMB-PROOF
BOMBSHELL
BOMBSIGHT
BONDSLAVE
BONDWOMAN
BONNETING
BONNINESS
BON-VIVANT
BOOBY-TRAP
BOOKISHLY
BOOKMAKER
BOOK-PLATE
BOOKSTALL
BOOKSTAND
BOOKSTORE
BOOMERANG
BOORISHLY

BOOTSTRAP
BORDERING
BORN-AGAIN
BORROWING
BOSPHORUS
BOTANICAL
BOTHERING
BOTTOMING
BOULEVARD
BOUNDLESS
BOUNTEOUS
BOUNTIFUL
BOURGEOIS
BOWER-BIRD
BOW-LEGGED
BOWSTRING
BOWSTRUNG
BOW-WINDOW
BOXING-DAY
BOX-OFFICE
BOYCOTTED
BRACKETED
BRACTLESS
BRAINLESS
BRAINWAVE
BRAKELESS
BRAKESMAN
BRAMBLING
BRANCHING
BRANCHLET
BRASS-BAND
BRASSERIE
BRASSIERE
BRAZENING
BRAZILIAN
BRAZIL-NUT
BREACHING
BREADLESS
BREAD-ROOM
BREAKABLE
BREAKDOWN
BREAKFAST
BREAKNECK
BREASTPIN
BREATHING
BREECHING
BREWHOUSE
BRIAR-ROOT
BRAC-A-BRAC
BRICK-CLAY
BRICKDUST
BRICK-KILN
BRICKWORK
BRICKYARD
BRIDECAKE
BRIDELESS

BRIDESMAN
BRIDEWELL
BRIDLE-WAY
BRIEFLESS
BRIEFNESS
BRIGADIER
BRILLIANT
BRIMSTONE
BRIQUETTE
BRISKNESS
BRISTLING
BRITANNIC
BRITTLELY
BRITTLING
BROACHING
BROADBEAN
BROADBILL
BROADBRIM
BROADCAST
BROADENED
BROADNESS
BROADSIDE
BROADWAYS
BROADWISE
BROCADING
BROKERAGE
BRONCHIAL
BROOD-MARE
BROOKWEED
BROTHERLY
BROWNNESS
BRUMMAGEM
BRUSHWOOD
BRUTALISE
BRUTALITY
BRUTISHLY
BRYTHONIC
BUCCANEER
BUCKBOARD
BUCKETFUL
BUCKETING
BUCKHOUND
BUCK'S-HORN
BUCKTHORN
BUCKTOOTH
BUCKWAGON
BUCKWHEAT
BUDGETING
BUFFETING
BUGLE-CALL
BULGARIAN
BULGINESS
BULKINESS
BULLFIGHT
BULLFINCH
BULLY-BEEF

BULWARKED
BUMBLE-BEE
BUMBLEDOM
BUMPINESS
BUMPTIOUS
BUOYANTLY
BURDENING
BURGEONED
BURLESQUE
BURLINESS
BURNISHED
BURROWING
BUSHINESS
BUTCHERED
BUTTERCUP
BUTTERFLY
BUTTERING
BUTTONING
BUXOMNESS
BUZZINGLY
BY-PASSAGE
BY-PRODUCT
BYSTANDER
BYZANTINE

C – 9

CABALLERO
CABLEGRAM
CABRIOLET
CACOPHONY
CADDIS-FLY
CADETSHIP
CAESARIAN
CAFETERIA
CAIRNGORM
CALABOOSE
CALCIFIED
CALCINING
CALCULATE
CALENDULA
CALIBRATE
CALIPHATE
CALLA-LILY
CALLIPERS
CALLOSITY
CALLOUSLY
CALORIFIC
CALVINISM
CALVINIST
CAMBERING
CAMCORDER
CAMPANILE
CAMPANULA
CAMP-FEVER
CAMPSTOOL

CANALISED	CARPINGLY	CELEBRATE	CHEAPNESS
CANCELLED	CARRIABLE	CELEBRITY	CHEATABLE
CANCEROUS	CARTESIAN	CELESTIAL	CHECKMATE
CANDIDACY	CARTHORSE	CELESTINE	CHECK-REIN
CANDIDATE	CARTILAGE	CELLARAGE	CHEEK-BONE
CANDIFIED	CARTOUCHE	CELLARMAN	CHEERLESS
CANDLEMAS	CARTRIDGE	CELLULITE	CHEESEFLY
CANDYTUFT	CARTWHEEL	CELLULOID	CHEESEVAT
CANE-CHAIR	CASHEWNUT	CELLULOSE	CHEMISTRY
CANE-SUGAR	CASHIERED	CEMENTING	CHEQUERED
CANKER-FLY	CASSEROLE	CENSORIAL	CHERISHED
CANKERING	CASSOWARY	CENSORING	CHEVALIER
CANKEROUS	CASTIGATE	CENSURING	CHICANERY
CANNON-BIT	CASTILIAN	CENTENARY	CHICANING
CANNONADE	CASTOR-OIL	CENTIGRAM	CHICKADEE
CANNONING	CASTRATED	CENTIPEDE	CHICKLING
CANONICAL	CAST-STEEL	CENTRALLY	CHICKWEED
CANONISED	CASUISTIC	CENTRE-BIT	CHIDINGLY
CANOODLED	CASUISTRY	CENTURION	CHIEFLESS
CANOPYING	CATACLYSM	CEREBRATE	CHIEFTAIN
CANTABILE	CATALEPSY	CERTAINLY	CHILBLAIN
CANTALOUP	CATALOGUE	CERTAINTY	CHILDHOOD
CANTERING	CATALYSER	CERTIFIED	CHILDLESS
CANTINGLY	CATALYSIS	CERTITUDE	CHILDLIKE
CANVASSED	CATALYTIC	CESSATION	CHILLNESS
CANVASSER	CATAMARAN	CETACEOUS	CHINA-CLAY
CAPACIOUS	CATAMOUNT	CHAFFERED	CHINA-ROSE
CAPACITOR	CATARRHAL	CHAFFINCH	CHINASHOP
CAPARISON	CATCHABLE	CHAFFLESS	CHINATOWN
CAPILLARY	CATCH-CROP	CHAGRINED	CHINAWARE
CAPITALLY	CATCHMENT	CHAIN-GANG	CHIROPODY
CAPITULAR	CATCHPOLE	CHAINLESS	CHISELLED
CAPRICCIO	CATCHWEED	CHAIN-MAIL	CHITTERED
CAPRICORN	CATCHWORD	CHAINWORK	CHOCK-FULL
CAPSIZING	CATECHISE	CHAIRLIFT	CHOCOLATE
CAPTAINCY	CATECHISM	CHALLENGE	CHOP-HOUSE
CAPTIVATE	CATECHIST	CHAMELEON	CHORISTER
CAPTIVITY	CATERWAUL	CHAMFERED	CHORTLING
CAPTURING	CATHEADED	CHAMPAGNE	CHORUSING
CARBONATE	CATHEDRAL	CHANDLERY	CHRISTIAN
CARBONISE	CAUCASIAN	CHANGEFUL	CHRISTMAS
CARBUNCLE	CAUSALITY	CHAPTERED	CHROMATIC
CARDBOARD	CAUSATION	CHAR-A-BANC	CHROMATIN
CAREENING	CAUSATIVE	CHARACTER	CHRYSALIS
CAREERING	CAUSELESS	CHARINESS	CHUCKLING
CAREFULLY	CAUTERISE	CHARIVARI	CHURCHILL
CARESSING	CAUTIONED	CHARLATAN	CHURCHING
CARMELITE	CAVALCADE	CHARLOTTE	CHURCHMAN
CARNALITY	CAVENDISH	CHARTERED	CICATRICE
CARNATION	CAVERNOUS	CHARTLESS	CICATRISE
CARNIVORA	CAVILLING	CHASEABLE	CIGARETTE
CAROLLING	CAVORTING	CHASTENED	CINERARIA
CAROUSING	CEASELESS	CHASTISED	CINGALESE
CARPENTER	CEILINGED	CHATTERED	CIPHERING
CARPENTRY	CELANDINE	CHAUFFEUR	CIPHER-KEY
CARPETING	CELEBRANT	CHEAPENED	CIRCUITED

CIRCULATE	COALFIELD	COLLIMATE	COMPASSES
CIRRHOSIS	COAL-HOUSE	COLLISION	COMPELLED
CIVILISED	COALITION	COLLOCATE	COMPELLING
CLAIMABLE	COAL-MINER	COLLODION	COMPETENT
CLAMBERED	COARSENED	COLLOIDAL	COMPETING
CLAMOROUS	COASTLINE	COLLOTYPE	COMPLIANT
CLAMOURED	COASTWISE	COLLUSION	COMPLETED
CLAPBOARD	COATFROCK	COLLUSIVE	COMPLEXLY
CLARENDON	COAXINGLY	COLLUSORY	COMPLAINT
CLARET-CUP	COBDENISM	COLONELCY	COMPLYING
CLARIFIED	COBDENITE	COLONISED	COMPONENT
CLARIONET	COBWEBBED	COLONNADE	COMPORTED
CLASSIBLE	COCHINEAL	COLORIFIC	COMPOSING
CLASSICAL	COCK-A-HOOP	COLOSSEUM	COMPOSITE
CLATTERED	COCKFIGHT	COLOUR-BOX	COMPOSTED
CLEANLILY	COCKHORSE	COLOURING	COMPOSURE
CLEANNESS	COCKINESS	COLOURIST	COMPRISED
CLEANSING	COCKROACH	COLOURMAN	COMPUTING
CLEARANCE	COCKSCOMB	COLTSFOOT	CONCAVELY
CLEAR-EYED	COCKSFOOT	COLUMBIAN	CONCAVITY
CLEARNESS	COCK'S-HEAD	COLUMBINE	CONCEALED
CLEAVABLE	COCOA-BEAN	COMBATANT	CONCEDING
CLEMENTLY	COCOA-PLUM	COMBATIVE	CONCEITED
CLENCHING	COCO-DE-MER	COMBINING	CONCEIVED
CLERGYMAN	CODIFYING	COMFORTED	CONCERNED
CLERK-LIKE	COEQUALLY	COMFORTER	CONCERTED
CLERKSHIP	COERCIBLE	COMICALLY	CONCIERGE
CLIENTELE	COETERNAL	COMINFORM	CONCISELY
CLIMACTIC	COEXISTED	COMINTERN	CONCLUDED
CLIMBABLE	COFFEE-BUG	COMMANDED	CONCOCTED
CLINCHING	COFFEE-CUP	COMMANDER	CONCORDAT
CLOAKROOM	COFFEE-POT	COMMENCED	CONCOURSE
CLOCK-GOLF	COFFERDAM	COMMENDED	CONCRETED
CLOCKWISE	COGITABLE	COMMENSAL	CONCUBINE
CLOCKWORK	COGITATED	COMMENTED	CONCURRED
CLOG-DANCE	COGNATION	COMMINGLE	CONCUSSED
CLOISONNÉ	COGNISANT	COMMISSAR	CONDEMNED
CLOISTERS	COGNITION	COMMITTAL	CONDENSED
CLOSENESS	COGNITIVE	COMMITTED	CONDENSER
CLOSETING	COHABITED	COMMITTEE	CONDIGNLY
CLOTH-HALL	COHEIRESS	COMMODITY	CONDIMENT
CLOTHYARD	COHERENCE	COMMONAGE	CONDITION
CLOUDLESS	COHERENCY	COMMOTION	CONDOLING
CLOUDLINE	COHERITOR	COMMOVING	CONDONING
CLOUT-NAIL	COINCIDED	COMMUNING	CONDUCING
CLOVE-PINK	COLCHICUM	COMMUNION	CONDUCIVE
CLUBBABLE	COLD-CREAM	COMMUNISE	CONDUCTED
CLUBHOUSE	COLLAPSED	COMMUNISM	CONDUCTOR
CLUSTERED	COLLARING	COMMUNIST	CONFERRED
CLUTCHING	COLLATING	COMMUNITY	CONFESSED
CLUTTERED	COLLATION	COMMUTING	CONFESSOR
COACHWORK	COLLEAGUE	COMPACTED	CONFIDANT
COAGULANT	COLLECTED	COMPACTLY	CONFIDENT
COAGULATE	COLLECTOR	COMPANION	CONFIDING
COAL-BLACK	COLLEGIAN	COMPARING	CONFIGURE
COALESCED	COLLIDING	COMPASSED	CONFINING

CONFIRMED	CONTINUED	CORNSTALK	CRAZINESS
CONFLUENT	CONTINUUM	COROLLARY	CREAM-LIKE
CONFORMED	CONTORTED	CORONETED	CREAM-LAID
CONFUCIAN	CONTOURED	CORPORATE	CREAM-WOVE
CONFUSING	CONTRALTO	CORPOREAL	CREDITING
CONFUSION	CONTRIVED	CORPOSANT	CREDULITY
CONFUTING	CONTUMACY	CORPULENT	CREDULOUS
CONGEALED	CONTUMELY	CORPUSCLE	CREMATING
CONGENIAL	CONTUSING	CORRECTED	CREMATION
CONGESTED	CONTUSION	CORRECTLY	CRENATURE
CONGRUENT	CONUNDRUM	CORRECTOR	CREPITANT
CONGRUITY	CONVENING	CORRELATE	CREPITATE
CONGRUOUS	CONVERGED	CORRODING	CRESCENDO
CONICALLY	CONVERSED	CORROSION	CRETINISM
CONJOINED	CONVERTED	CORROSIVE	CREVICING
CONJUGATE	CONVEXITY	CORRUGATE	CRIMELESS
CONJURING	CONVEYING	CORRUPTED	CRIMSONED
CONNECTED	CONVICTED	CORTICATE	CRINKLING
CONNECTOR	CONVINCED	CORTISONE	CRINOLINE
CONNEXION	CONVIVIAL	CORUSCATE	CRIPPLING
CONNIVING	CONVOKING	COSMOGONY	CRISPNESS
CONNOTING	CONVOLUTE	COSMOLOGY	CRITERION
CONNUBIAL	CONVOYING	COSSETING	CRITICISE
CO-NOMINEE	CONVULSED	COSTUMIER	CRITICISM
CONQUERED	COOK-CHILL	COTANGENT	CROCHETED
CONQUEROR	COOK-HOUSE	COTILLION	CROCODILE
CONSCIOUS	COOPERAGE	COTTER-PIN	CROOKBACK
CONSCRIBE	CO-OPERATE	COTTON-GIN	CROOKEDLY
CONSCRIPT	COOPERING	COTTONING	CROQUETTE
CONSENSUS	COPARTNER	COTYLEDON	CROSSBEAM
CONSENTED	CO-PATRIOT	COUNTABLE	CROSSBILL
CONSERVED	COPESTONE	COUNTDOWN	CROSS-EYED
CONSIGNED	COPIOUSLY	COUNTERED	CROSS-FIRE
CONSIGNEE	COPPERING	COUNTLESS	CROSS-HEAD
CONSIGNOR	COPPERISH	COUNTRIFY	CROSSNESS
CONSISTED	COPSEWOOD	COURT-CARD	CROSSROAD
CONSOLING	COPYRIGHT	COURTEOUS	CROSSTALK
CONSONANT	COQUETTED	COURTESAN	CROSS-WIND
CONSORTED	CORALLINE	COURTLIKE	CROSSWISE
CONSPIRED	CORALLITE	COURTSHIP	CROSSWORD
CONSTABLE	CORALLOID	COURTYARD	CROTCHETY
CONSTANCY	CORAL-REEF	COVERTURE	CROUCHING
CONSTRAIN	CORBELLED	COWABUNGA	CROWBERRY
CONSTRICT	CORDELIER	COWARDICE	CROW'S-FEET
CONSTRUCT	CORDIALLY	COXCOMBRY	CROW'S-FOOT
CONSTRUED	COREOPSIS	CRAB-APPLE	CROW'S-NEST
CONSULATE	CORIANDER	CRABBEDLY	CROW-STONE
CONSULTED	CORKSCREW	CRACKLING	CRUCIFIED
CONSUMING	CORMORANT	CRAFTSMAN	CRUCIFORM
CONTAGION	CORN-BREAD	CRAMP-IRON	CRUMBLING
CONTAINED	CORNCRAKE	CRANBERRY	CRUMPLING
CONTAINER	CORNELIAN	CRANKCASE	CRUNCHING
CONTENTED	CORNERING	CRAPULENT	CRUSADING
CONTESTED	CORNFLOUR	CRAPULOUS	CRUSTACEA
CONTINENT	CORN-POPPY	CRASSNESS	CRYPTOGAM
CONTINUAL	CORN-SALAD	CRAYONING	CUBICALLY

CUCKOLDED
CUDGELLED
CULMINATE
CULTIVATE
CULTURING
CULTURIST
CUMBERING
CUNEIFORM
CUNNINGLY
CUPBEARER
CUPRESSUS
CURBSTONE
CURIOSITY
CURIOUSLY
CURLINESS
CURLINGLY
CURRENTLY
CURRISHLY
CURRYCOMB
CURSORIAL
CURSORILY
CURTAILED
CURTAINED
CURTILAGE
CURTSYING
CURVATURE
CURVETTED
CUSHIONED
CUSTODIAN
CUSTOMARY
CUTANEOUS
CUTICULAR
CUTTER-BAR
CUTTHROAT
CUTTINGLY
CYCLOPEAN
CYCLORAMA
CYNICALLY
CYTOPLASM

D – 9

DACHSUND
DAEDALIAN
DAIRY-FARM
DAIRYMAID
DAISY-BUSH
DALLIANCE
DALMATIAN
DAMASCENE
DAMOCLEAN
DAMPENING
DAMPISHLY
DANDELION
DANDIFIED
DANGEROUS

DANNEBROG
DANTESQUE
DAREDEVIL
DARKENING
DARTINGLY
DARWINIAN
DARWINISM
DASHBOARD
DASTARDLY
DATUM-LINE
DAUNTLESS
DAVENPORT
DAY-LABOUR
DAY-SCHOOL
DAY-SPRING
DEACONESS
DEAD-ALIVE
DEADENING
DEAFENING
DEATH-BLOW
DEATHLESS
DEATHLIKE
DEATH-MASK
DEATH-RATE
DEATH-ROLL
DEATH-TRAP
DEATH-WARD
DEBARRING
DEBATABLE
DEBAUCHED
DEBENTURE
DEBOUCHED
DEBUTANTE
DECADENCE
DECAGONAL
DECALCIFY
DECALITRE
DECALOGUE
DECAMERON
DECAMETRE
DECAMPING
DECANTING
DECEITFUL
DECEIVING
DECENNIAL
DECENNIUM
DECEPTION
DECEPTIVE
DECIDABLE
DECIDEDLY
DECIDUOUS
DECILLION
DECIMALLY
DECIMATED
DECIMETRE
DECK-CHAIR

DECK-HOUSE
DECLAIMED
DECLARANT
DECLARING
DECLINING
DECLIVITY ,
DECOCTION
DECOLLETE
DECOMPLEX
DECOMPOSE
DECONTROL
DECORATED
DECORATOR
DECOY-DUCK
DECREASED
DECREEING
DECREMENT
DECUMBENT
DECUSSATE
DEDICATED
DEDUCIBLE
DEDUCTING
DEDUCTION
DEDUCTIVE
DEEPENING
DEEP-TONED
DEFALCATE
DEFAULTED
DEFAULTER
DEFEATING
DEFEATISM
DEFECTION
DEFECTIVE
DEFENDANT
DEFENDING
DEFENSIVE
DEFERENCE
DEFERRING
DEFIANTLY
DEFICIENT
DEFINABLE
DEFINABLY
DEFLATING
DEFLATION
DEFLECTED
DEFLECTOR
DEFLEXION
DEFOLIATE
DEFORMING
DEFORMITY
DEFRAUDED
DEFRAYING
DEISTICAL
DEJECTING
DEJECTION
DELEGATED

DELICIOUS
DELIGHTED
DELIMITED
DELINEATE
DELIRIOUS
DELIVERED
DELIVERER
DEMAGOGIC
DEMAGOGUE
DEMANDANT
DEMANDING
DEMARCATE
DEMEANING
DEMEANOUR
DEMI-MONDE
DEMISSION
DEMITTING
DEMOCRACY
DEMULCENT
DEMURRAGE
DEMURRANT
DEMURRING
DENIGRATE
DENOUNCED
DENSENESS
DENTATION
DENTISTRY
DENTITION
DEODORANT
DEODORISE
DEPARTING
DEPARTURE
DEPASTURE
DEPENDANT
DEPENDENT
DEPENDING
DEPICTING
DEPILATED
DEPILATOR
DEPLENISH
DEPLETING
DEPLETION
DEPLETIVE
DEPLETORY
DEPLORING
DEPLOYING
DEPLUMING
DEPORTING
DEPOSITED
DEPOSITOR
DEPRAVING
DEPRAVITY
DEPRECATE
DEPRESSED
DEPRIVING
DEPTHLESS

DEPUTISED	DETRAINED	DIGNITARY	DISGRACED
DERAILING	DETRIMENT	DIGRESSED	DISGUISED
DERANGING	DETRITION	DILATABLE	DISGUSTED
DERIVABLE	DEVASTATE	DILIGENCE	DISHCLOTH
DERIVABLY	DEVELOPED	DILUTEDLY	DISH-CLOUT
DERMATOID	DEVELOPER	DIMENSION	DISH-COVER
DEROGATED	DEVIATION	DIMORPHIC	DISHONEST
DERRING-DO	DEVIL-FISH	DINGINESS	DISHONOUR
DERRINGER	DEVILLING	DINING-CAR	DISHWATER
DESCANTED	DEVILMENT	DIPHTHONG	DISINFECT
DESCENDED	DEVIOUSLY	DIPLOMACY	DISJOINED
DESCRIBED	DEVISABLE	DIPTEROUS	DISLIKING
DESCRYING	DEVITRIFY	DIRECTING	DISLOCATE
DESECRATE	DEVOLUTED	DIRECTION	DISLODGED
DESERTING	DEVOLVING	DIRECTIVE	DISMANTLE
DESERTION	DEVONPORT	DIRECTORY	DISMASTED
DESERVING	DEVOURING	DIREFULLY	DISMAYING
DESICCANT	DEWLAPPED	DIRIGIBLE	DISMEMBER
DESICCATE	DEXTERITY	DIRTINESS	DISMISSAL
DESIGNATE	DEXTEROUS	DIRT-TRACK	DISMISSED
DESIGNING	DIABOLISM	DISABLING	DISOBEYED
DESIRABLE	DIAERESIS	DISABUSED	DISOBLIGE
DESIRABLY	DIAGNOSED	DISACCORD	DISOWNING
DESISTING	DIAGNOSIS	DISAFFECT	DISPARAGE
DESOLATED	DIALECTAL	DISAFFIRM	DISPARATE
DESPAIRED	DIALECTIC	DISAGREED	DISPARITY
DESPERADO	DIAL-PLATE	DISAPPEAR	DISPELLED
DESPERATE	DIAPERING	DISARMING	DISPENSED
DESPISING	DIAPHRAGM	DISAVOWAL	DISPENSER
DESPOILED	DIARRHOEA	DISAVOWED	DISPERSAL
DESPONDED	DICHOTOMY	DISBANDED	DISPERSED
DESPOTISM	DICHROMIC	DISBARRED	DISPLACED
DESTINING	DICKERING	DISBELIEF	DISPLAYED
DESTITUTE	DICTATING	DISBRANCH	DISPLEASE
DESTROYED	DICTATION	DISBUDDED	DISPORTED
DESTROYER	DICTATORY	DISBURDEN	DISPOSING
DESUETUDE	DIDACTICS	DISBURSED	DISPRAISE
DESULTORY	DIESINKER	DISCARDED	DISPROVED
DETACHING	DIETETICS	DISCERNED	DISPUTANT
DETAILING	DIETITIAN	DISCHARGE	DISPUTING
DETAINING	DIFFERENT	DISCLOSED	DISRATING
DETECTING	DIFFERING	DISCOLOUR	DISREGARD
DETECTION	DIFFICILE	DISCOMFIT	DISRELISH
DETECTIVE	DIFFICULT	DISCOURSE	DISREPAIR
DETENTION	DIFFIDENT	DISCOVERY	DISREPUTE
DETERRING	DIFFLUENT	DISCREDIT	DISROBING
DETERGENT	DIFFUSING	DISCUSSED	DISROOTED
DETERMINE	DIFFUSION	DISDAINED	DISRUPTED
DETERRENT	DIFFUSELY	DISEMBARK	DISSECTED
DETERRING	DIFFUSIVE	DISEMBODY	DISSEMBLE
DETESTING	DIGESTING	DISENGAGE	DISSENTED
DETHRONED	DIGESTION	DISENTAIL	DISSENTER
DETONATED	DIGESTIVE	DISENTOMB	DISSERVED
DETONATOR	DIGITALIN	DISFAVOUR	DISSIPATE
DETRACTED	DIGITALIS	DISFIGURE	DISSOLUTE
DETRACTOR	DIGNIFIED	DISGORGED	DISSOLVED

DISSONANT
DISSUADED
DISTANCED
DISTANTLY
DISTEMPER
DISTENDED
DISTILLED
DISTILLER
DISTORTED
DISTRAINT
DISTURBED
DISUNITED
DITHERING
DITHYRAMB
DIURNALLY
DIVAGATED
DIVERGENT
DIVERGING
DIVERSELY
DIVERSIFY
DIVERSION
DIVERSITY
DIVERTING
DIVESTING
DIVIDABLE
DIVIDEDLY
DIVISIBLE
DIVISIBLY
DIVORCING
DIVULGING
DIZZINESS
DOCK-CRESS
DOCTORATE
DOCTORING
DOCTRINAL
DODDERING
DODECAGON
DOGGINESS
DOGMATISE
DOGMATISM
DOGMATIST
DOG'S-TOOTH
DOG-VIOLET
DOLEFULLY
DOLTISHLY
DOMICILED
DOMINANCE
DOMINICAL
DO-NOTHING
DOODLEBUG
DOOR-PLATE
DOOR-STONE
DORMITORY
DOSS-HOUSE
DOUBTLESS
DOUGHTILY

DOVE'S-FOOT
DOWDINESS
DOWELLING
DOWERLESS
DOWNGRADE
DOWNINESS
DOWNRIGHT
DOWNWARDS
DRABBLING
DRACONIAN
DRAFTSMAN
DRAGGLING
DRAGON-FLY
DRAINABLE
DRAINPIPE
DRAMATISE
DRAMATIST
DRAWN-WORK
DRAY-HORSE
DREAM-LAND
DREAMLESS
DREAMLIKE
DRENCHING
DRIBBLING
DRIFT-LESS
DRIFTWOOD
DRINKABLE
DRINKLESS
DRIPSTONE
DRIVELLED
DRIZZLING
DROMEDARY
DROP-SCENE
DROPSICAL
DRUM-MAJOR
DRUMSTICK
DRUNKENLY
DRYSALTER
DUALISTIC
DUBIOUSLY
DUBITABLE
DUBITABLY
DUCK-BOARD
DUCK'S-FOOT
DUCTILELY
DUCTILITY
DUMB-BELLS
DUMBFOUND
DUMPINESS
DUMPISHLY
DUNGEONED
DUODECIMO
DUODENARY
DUPLICATE
DWINDLING
DYNAMICAL

DYNAMITED
DYSENTERY
DYSPEPSIA
DYSPEPTIC
DYSTROPHY

E – 9

EAGERNESS
EAGLE-EYED
EARLINESS
EARMARKED
EARNESTLY
EARPHONES
EARTHWARD
EARTHWORK
EARTHWORM
EASEFULLY
EAST-ENDER
EASY-CHAIR
EASY-GOING
EAVESDROP
EBONISING
EBULLIENT
ECCENTRIC
ECLIPSING
ECONOMICS
ECONOMISE
ECONOMIST
ECTOPLASM
EDELWEISS
EDITORIAL
EDUCATING
EDUCATION
EFFECTING
EFFECTIVE
EFFECTUAL
EFFICIENT
EFFLUENCE
EFFLUVIUM
EFFLUXION
EFFULGENT
EGLANTINE
EGREGIOUS
EGRESSION
EIDER-DOWN
EIDOGRAPH
EIGHTFOLD
EIGHTIETH
EIGHTSOME
EIRENICON
EJACULATE
EJECTMENT
ELABORATE
ELBOW-ROOM
ELDERSHIP

ELDER-WINE
ELECTORAL
ELECTRESS
ELECTRIFY
ELECTRODE
ELEGANTLY
ELEMENTAL
ELEVATING
ELEVATION
ELEVATORY
ELICITING
ELIMINATE
ELLIPSOID
ELOCUTION
ELONGATED
ELOPEMENT
ELOQUENCE
ELSEWHERE
ELUCIDATE
EMACIATED
EMANATING
EMANATION
EMBALMING
EMBANKING
EMBARGOED
EMBARKING
EMBARRASS
EMBATTLED
EMBEDDING
EMBELLISH
EMBEZZLED
EMBEZZLER
EMBODYING
EMBOSSING
EMBOWERED
EMBRACING
EMBRASURE
EMBROIDER
EMBROILED
EMBRYONIC
EMENDATOR
EMERGENCE
EMERGENCY
EMINENTLY
EMOLLIENT
EMOLUMENT
EMOTIONAL
EMPHASISE
EMPIRICAL
EMPLOYING
EMPOWERED
EMPTINESS
EMULATING
EMULATION
EMULATIVE
ENACTMENT

ENAMELLED	ENSNARING	ESPERANTO	EXCHANGED
ENAMOURED	ENTAILING	ESPIONAGE	EXCHANGER
ENCASHING	ENTANGLED	ESPLANADE	EXCHEQUER
ENCAUSTIC	ENTERTAIN	ESPOUSING	EXCISABLE
ENCHANTED	ENTHRONED	ESQUIRING	EXCISEMAN
ENCIRCLED	ENTHUSING	ESSENTIAL	EXCITABLE
ENCLASPED	ENTITLING	ESTABLISH	EXCLAIMED
ENCLOSING	ENTOURAGE	ESTAMINET	EXCLUDING
ENCLOSURE	EN-TOUT-CAS	ESTEEMING	EXCLUSION
ENCOMPASS	ENTRANCED	ESTIMABLE	EXCLUSIVE
ENCOUNTER	ENTREATED	ESTIMABLY	EXCORIATE
ENCOURAGE	ENTRECHAT	ESTIMATOR	EXCREMENT
ENCRUSTED	ENTREMETS	ESTOPPING	EXCRETION
ENDEARING	ENTRUSTED	ESTRANGED	EXCRETIVE
ENDEAVOUR	ENTWINING	ESTREATED	EXCRETORY
ENDLESSLY	ENUMERATE	ESTUARINE	EXCULPATE
ENDOCRINE	ENUNCIATE	ETERNALLY	EXCURSION
ENDORSING	ENVELOPED	ETHICALLY	EXCURSIVE
ENDOSPERM	ENVENOMED	ETHIOPIAN	EXCUSABLE
ENDOWMENT	ENVIOUSLY	ETHNOLOGY	EXCUSABLY
ENDURABLE	ENVISAGED	ETIOLATED	EXECRABLE
ENDURABLY	ENVOYSHIP	ETIQUETTE	EXECRABLY
ENDURANCE	ENWRAPPED	ETYMOLOGY	EXECRATED
ENERGETIC	EPAULETTE	EUCHARIST	EXECUTANT
ENERGISER	EPHEMERAL	EUCLIDEAN	EXECUTING
ENERVATED	EPICENTRE	EULOGIZED	EXECUTION
ENFEEBLED	EPICUREAN	EUPHEMISE	EXECUTIVE
ENFILADED	EPICURISM	EUPHEMISM	EXECUTORY
ENFOLDING	EPICYCLIC	EUPHONIUM	EXECUTRIX
ENFORCING	EPIDERMAL	EVACUATED	EXEMPLARY
ENGINE-MAN	EPIDERMIC	EVALUATED	EXEMPLIFY
ENGIRDING	EPIDERMIS	EVANESCED	EXEMPTION
ENGIRDLED	EPIGRAPHY	EVANGELIC	EXEMPTIVE
ENGRAVING	EPILEPTIC	EVAPORATE	EXERCISED
ENGROSSED	EPISCOPAL	EVASIVELY	EXFOLIATE
ENGULFING	EPISTOLIC	EVENTUATE	EXHALABLE
ENHANCING	EPITOMISE	EVERGLADE	EXHAUSTED
ENIGMATIC	EQUALISED	EVERGREEN	EXHIBITED
ENJOINING	EQUALISER	EVERYBODY	EXHIBITOR
ENJOYABLE	EQUALLING	EVIDENTLY	EXHORTING
ENJOYABLY	EQUIPMENT	EVOCATION	EXISTENCE
ENJOYMENT	EQUIPOISE	EVOLUTION	EX-OFFICIO
ENLARGING	EQUIPPING	EXACTABLE	EXOGAMOUS
ENLIGHTEN	EQUITABLE	EXACTNESS	EXOGENOUS
ENLISTING	EQUIVOCAL	EXAMINING	EXONERATE
ENLIVENED	ERADICATE	EXCALIBUR	EXORCISED
ENMESHING	ERECTNESS	EXCAVATED	EXPANDING
ENOUNCING	ERRAND-BOY	EXCAVATOR	EXPANSILE
ENQUIRING	ERRONEOUS	EXCEEDING	EXPANSION
ENRAPTURE	ERSTWHILE	EXCELLENT	EXPANSIVE
ENRICHING	ERUDITELY	EXCELSIOR	EXPATIATE
ENROLLING	ERUDITION	EXCEPTING	EXPECTANT
ENROLMENT	ESCALADED	EXCEPTION	EXPECTING
ENSCONCED	ESCALATOR	EXCEPTIVE	EXPEDIENT
ENSHRINED	ESCHEATED	EXCESSING	EXPEDITED
ENSLAVING	ESCORTING	EXCESSIVE	EXPENDING

EXPENSIVE	FADDINESS	FERRYBOAT	FIRSTBORN
EXPIATING	FAGGOTING	FERTILELY	FIRST-FOOT
EXPIATION	FAILINGLY	FERTILISE	FIRSTHAND
EXPIATORY	FAINTNESS	FERTILITY	FIRST-RATE
EXPLAINED	FAIRY-LAMP	FERVENTLY	FISH-CURER
EXPLETIVE	FAIRYLAND	FESTERING	FISHERMAN
EXPLICATE	FAIRY-LIKE	FESTIVELY	FISHINESS
EXPLOITED	FAIRY-TALE	FESTIVITY	FISH-KNIFE
EXPLORING	FALDSTOOL	FESTOONED	FISH-SPEAR
EXPLOSION	FALERNIAN	FETIDNESS	FISSILITY
EXPLOSIVE	FALLOPIAN	FETISHISM	FISTULOUS
EXPORTING	FALLOWING	FETTERING	FITTINGLY
EXPOUNDED	FALSEHOOD	FEUDALISE	FITTING-UP
EXPRESSED	FALSENESS	FEUDALISM	FIXEDNESS
EXPRESSLY	FALSIFIED	FEUDALITY	FLACCIDLY
EXPULSION	FALTERING	FEUDATORY	FLAGELLUM
EXPULSIVE	FAMISHING	FIBRELESS	FLAGEOLET
EXPUNGING	FANATICAL	FIBRIFORM	FLAGRANCY
EXPURGATE	FANCY-FREE	FICTIONAL	FLAGSTAFF
EXQUISITE	FANTAILED	FIDDLE-BOW	FLAGSTONE
EXTEMPORE	FANTASTIC	FIDGETING	FLAMBEAUX
EXTENDING	FARMHOUSE	FIDUCIARY	FLAMELESS
EXTENSILE	FARMSTEAD	FIELDFARE	FLAMINGLY
EXTENSION	FARROWING	FIELDSMAN	FLANNELLY
EXTENSIVE	FASCIATED	FIERINESS	FLARINGLY
EXTENUATE	FASCINATE	FIFE-MAJOR	FLATTENED
EXTOLLING	FASHIONED	FIFTEENTH	FLATTERED
EXTORTING	FASTENING	FILIATION	FLATTERER
EXTORTION	FATEFULLY	FILIGREED	FLAUNTING
EXTRACTED	FATHERING	FILLETING	FLAVOROUS
EXTRACTOR	FATHOMING	FILLIPING	FLAVOURED
EXTRADITE	FATIGUING	FILMINESS	FLEETNESS
EXTREMELY	FATTENING	FILTERING	FLESHLESS
EXTREMISM	FATTINESS	FILTRATED	FLEXITIME
EXTREMIST	FAULTLESS	FINANCIAL	FLICKERED
EXTREMITY	FAVOURING	FINANCIER	FLIGHTILY
EXTRICATE	FAVOURITE	FINANCING	FLINCHING
EXTRINSIC	FAWNINGLY	FINEDRAWN	FLINTLOCK
EXTRUDING	FEARFULLY	FINESSING	FLIPPANCY
EXTRUSION	FEATHERED	FINGERING	FLITTERED
EXUBERANT	FEATURING	FINICALLY	FLOATABLE
EXUBERATE	FEBRIFUGE	FINICKING	FLOODGATE
EXUDATION	FECUNDITY	FINISHING	FLOOD-MARK
EXULTANCY	FEDERATED	FIRE-ALARM	FLOOD-TIDE
EYEBRIGHT	FEELINGLY	FIREBRAND	FLOORLESS
EYE-OPENER	FEE-SIMPLE	FIREBRICK	FLORIDITY
	FEIGNEDLY	FIRECREST	FLOTATION
	FELONIOUS	FIRE-EATER	FLOUNCING
F – 9	FEMINISED	FIRE-GUARD	FLOWCHART
	FENCELESS	FIRE-IRONS	FLOWERING
FABRICATE	FENESTRAL	FIRELIGHT	FLOWERPOT
FACE-CLOTH	FENLANDER	FIREPLACE	FLOWINGLY
FACE-GUARD	FERMENTED	FIREPROOF	FLUCTUATE
FACSIMILE	FEROCIOUS	FIRESTORM	FLUIDNESS
FACTITIVE	FERRETING	FIREWATER	FLUKINESS
FACTORIAL	FERROTYPE	FIRMAMENT	FLUMMOXED
FACTORISE			

FLUORSPAR
FLURRYING
FLUSHNESS
FLUSTERED
FLUTE-LIKE
FLUTTERED
FLUXIONAL
FLY-BITTEN
FLYING-FOX
FLYING-JIB
FLY-POWDER
FOAMINGLY
FODDERING
FOGGINESS
FOG-SIGNAL
FOLIATION
FOLK-DANCE
FOLLOWING
FOMENTING
FOOLHARDY
FOOLISHLY
FOOLPROOF
FOOTBOARD
FOOT-FAULT
FOOTPLATE
FOOT-POUND
FOOTPRINT
FOOTSTALK
FOOTSTOOL
FOPPISHLY
FORAGE-CAP
FORASMUCH
FORBIDDEN
FORCELESS
FORCEMEAT
FORCE-PUMP
FOREARMED
FOREBODED
FORE-CABIN
FORECLOSE
FORECOURT
FOREDATED
FOREFRONT
FOREGOING
FOREIGNER
FORE-JUDGE
FORESHEET
FORESHORE
FORESHOWN
FORE-SIGHT
FORESTALL
FORETASTE
FORETOKEN
FOREWOMAN
FORFEITED
FORGATHER

FORGETFUL
FORGIVING
FORLORNLY
FORMALISE
FORMALISM
FORMALIST
FORMALITY
FORMATION
FORMATIVE
FORMULARY
FORMULATE
FORMULISM
FORMULIST
FORSAKING
FORTHWITH
FORTIFIED
FORTITUDE
FORTNIGHT
FORTUNATE
FORTY-FIVE
FORWARDED
FORWARDLY
FOSSILISE
FOSSORIAL
FOSTERAGE
FOSTERING
FOSTER-SON
FOUNDERED
FOUNDLING
FOUNDRESS
FOUR-HORSE
FOURPENCE
FOURPENNY
FOUR-SCORE
FOXHUNTER
FOXTAILED
FRACTIOUS
FRACTURED
FRAGILELY
FRAGILITY
FRAGRANCE
FRAGRANCY
FRAILNESS
FRAMEWORK
FRANCHISE
FRANCISCA
FRANGIBLE
FRANKNESS
FRATERNAL
FRAUDLESS
FRECKLING
FREEBOARD
FREELIVER
FREEMASON
FREESHEET
FREESTONE

FREE-WHEEL
FREIGHTED
FREIGHTER
FRENCHIFY
FRENCHMAN
FREQUENCY
FRESHENED
FRESHNESS
FRETFULLY
FRIBBLING
FRICASSEE
FRICATIVE
FRIGHTFUL
FRIGIDITY
FRITTERED
FRIVOLITY
FRIVOLOUS
FRIZZLING
FROCK-COAT
FROG-MARCH
FROGMOUTH
FROG-SPAWN
FROLICKED
FRONTAGER
FRONTWARD
FROSTBITE
FROSTLESS
FROWARDLY
FRUCTUOUS
FRUGALITY
FRUIT-CAKE
FRUIT-TREE
FRUSTRATE
FRUTICOSE
FRYING-PAN
FUGACIOUS
FULFILLED
FULGURITE
FULL-BLOWN
FULL-DRESS
FULL-FACED
FULL-GROWN
FULL-PITCH
FULL-SWING
FULMINANT
FULMINATE
FULSOMELY
FUMIGATED
FUNGICIDE
FUNICULAR
FUNNELLED
FUNNINESS
FURBISHED
FURIOUSLY
FURNISHED
FURNISHER

FURNITURE
FURROWING
FURTHERED
FURTHERER
FURTIVELY
FUSILLADE
FUSSINESS
FUSTIGATE
FUSTINESS

G – 9

GABARDINE
GABERDINE
GADDINGLY
GAINFULLY
GAINSAYER
GAITERING
GALACTOSE
GALANTINE
GALINGALE
GALLANTRY
GALLERIED
GALLICISE
GALLICISM
GALLINULE
GALLIVANT
GALLOPING
GALLOPADE
GALLSTONE
GALVANISE
GALVANISM
GALVANIST
GAMBOLLED
GAMMA-RAYS
GAMMONING
GANGBOARD
GANGRENED
GARDENING
GARIBALDI
GARLANDED
GARNERING
GARNISHED
GARNISHEE
GARNISHER
GARNITURE
GARRETEER
GARROTTED
GARROTTER
GARRULITY
GARRULOUS
GARRYOWEN
GARTERING
GAS-BURNER
GAS-CARBON
GASCONADE

GAS-COOKER	GIDDINESS	GOLDFINCH	GREEN-EYED
GAS-ENGINE	GIFT-HORSE	GOLDSMITH	GREENGAGE
GASEOUSLY	GILL-COVER	GOLF-LINKS	GREENHORN
GAS-FITTER	GILT-EDGED	GONDOLIER	GREENNESS
GASHOLDER	GIMLETING	GOODNIGHT	GREENROOM
GASIFYING	GIN-PALACE	GOOSANDER	GREENSAND
GAS-MANTLE	GINGERADE	GOOSEFOOT	GREENWICH
GASOMETER	GINGER-ALE	GOOSENECK	GREENWOOD
GASPINGLY	GINGER-POP	GOOSE-STEP	GREGORIAN
GAS-RETORT	GINGLYMUS	GOOSEWING	GRENADIER
GASTRITIS	GIRANDOLE	GORGONIAN	GRENADINE
GASTROPOD	GIRL-GUIDE	GOSPELLER	GREYBEARD
GATEHOUSE	GIRLISHLY	GOSSAMERY	GREYHOUND
GATE-MONEY	GIRONDIST	GOSSIPING	GREYSTONE
GATHERING	GLACIATED	GOTHAMITE	GRIEVANCE
GAUCHERIE	GLADDENED	GOUTINESS	GRILL-ROOM
GAUDINESS	GLADIATOR	GOVERNESS	GRIMACING
GAUNTNESS	GLADIOLUS	GOVERNING	GRIMALKIN
GAVELKIND	GLADSTONE	GRABBLING	GRIMINESS
GAZETTEER	GLAIREOUS	GRACE-NOTE	GRIPINGLY
GAZETTING	GLAMOURED	GRACILITY	GRISAILLE
GEARWHEEL	GLANDULAR	GRADATING	GRIST-MILL
GELIGNITE	GLARINGLY	GRADATION	GRITSTONE
GEMMATION	GLASSLIKE	GRADATORY	GRIZZLING
GENEALOGY	GLASSWARE	GRADGRIND	GROOMSMAN
GENERALLY	GLASS-WORK	GRADUALLY	GROPINGLY
GENERATED	GLASSWORT	GRADUATED	GROSSNESS
GENERATOR	GLENGARRY	GRADUATOR	GROTESQUE
GENIALITY	GLIDINGLY	GRANDAUNT	GROUNDAGE
GENTEELLY	GLIMMERED	GRAND-DUKE	GROUND-ASH
GENTILITY	GLIMPSING	GRANDIOSE	GROUNDING
GENTLEMAN	GLISSADED	GRAND-JURY	GROUND-IVY
GENUFLECT	GLISTENED	GRANDNESS	GROUNDNUT
GENUINELY	GLITTERED	GRANDSIRE	GROUND-OAK
GEOGRAPHY	GLOBE-FISH	GRAND-SLAM	GROUNDSEL
GEOLOGISE	GLOBOSITY	GRANULATE	GROVELLED
GEOLOGIST	GLORIFIED	GRANULOUS	GRUELLING
GEOMETRIC	GLOWERING	GRAPESHOT	GRUFFNESS
GERFALCON	GLOWINGLY	GRAPEVINE	GRUMBLING
GERMANDER	GLUCOSIDE	GRAPPLING	GRUNDYISM
GERMANISM	GLUEYNESS	GRASPABLE	GUARANTEE
GERMANIUM	GLUTINOUS	GRASSLAND	GUARANTOR
GERMICIDE	GLYCERIDE	GRASSLESS	GUARD-BOAT
GERMINANT	GLYCERINE	GRASS-PLOT	GUARDEDLY
GERMINATE	GNAWINGLY	GRATIFIED	GUARDLESS
GERUNDIAL	GOATISHLY	GRATINGLY	GUARDROOM
GERUNDIVE	GO-BETWEEN	GRATITUDE	GUARDSHIP
GESTATION	GODFATHER	GRAVELESS	GUARDSMAN
GESTATORY	GODLESSLY	GRAVEL LED	GUERRILLA
GESTURING	GODLINESS	GRAVEL-PIT	GUESSABLE
GET-AT-ABLE	GODMOTHER	GRAVENESS	GUESSWORK
GHOSTLIKE	GODPARENT	GRAVEYARD	GUEST-WISE
GHOST-MOTH	GOFFERING	GRAVITATE	GUIDE-BOOK
GIANTLIKE	GOLDCLOTH	GREATCOAT	GUIDELESS
GIBBERING	GOLDCREST	GREATNESS	GUIDE-POST
GIBBERISH	GOLDEN-ROD	GREENBACK	GUIDE-RAIL

GUIDE-ROPE
GUILDHALL
GUILELESS
GUILLEMOT
GUILLOCHE
GUILTLESS
GUINEA-PIG
GUMMINESS
GUN-BARREL
GUNCOTTON
GUNPOWDER
GUNRUNNER
GUSHINGLY
GUSTATORY
GUTTERING
GYMNASIUM
GYROSCOPE

H – 9

HABITABLE
HABITABLY
HABITUATE
HACKNEYED
HAGGARDLY
HAGGISHLY
HAGIOLOGY
HAGRIDDEN
HAILSTONE
HAILSTORM
HAIRBROOM
HAIRBRUSH
HAIRCLOTH
HAIRINESS
HALF-BLOOD
HALF-BOUND
HALF-BREED
HALF-CASTE
HALFCROWN
HALFPENNY
HALF-PRICE
HALF-ROUND
HALF-SHAFT
HALF-TIMER
HALLOWEEN
HALTERING
HALTINGLY
HAMADRYAD
HAMPERING
HAMSTRING
HAMSTRUNG
HANDBRACE
HANDCUFFS
HANDGLASS
HANDINESS
HANDIWORK

HANDPRESS
HANDSCREW
HANDSPIKE
HANKERING
HANSEATIC
HAPHAZARD
HAPPENING
HAPPINESS
HARANGUED
HARBINGER
HARBOURED
HARDBOARD
HARD-BOUND
HARDENING
HARDFACED
HARDIHOOD
HARDINESS
HARDSHELL
HARLEQUIN
HARMFULLY
HARMONICA
HARMONICS
HARMONISE
HARMONIST
HARMONIUM
HARNESSED
HARROVIAN
HARROWING
HARSHNESS
HARTSHORN
HARVESTED
HARVESTER
HASTINESS
HATCHBACK
HATCHMENT
HATEFULLY
HAUGHTILY
HAVERSACK
HAWK-EAGLE
HAWK-NOSED
HAWKSBILL
HAWSE-HOLE
HAYMAKING
HAZARDING
HAZARDOUS
HEAD-DRESS
HEADFRAME
HEADLINES
HEADLIGHT
HEADMONEY
HEADPHONE
HEADPIECE
HEADSTALL
HEADSTOCK
HEADSTONE
HEALINGLY

HEALTHFUL
HEALTHILY
HEARKENED
HEARTACHE
HEARTBURN
HEARTENED
HEARTFELT
HEARTHRUG
HEARTLESS
HEARTSICK
HEARTWOOD
HEATH-CLAD
HEATH-COCK
HEAVINESS
HEBRIDEAN
HECTOGRAM
HECTORING
HEDGELESS
HEEDFULLY
HEEL-PIECE
HEFTINESS
HEINOUSLY
HEIR-AT-LAW
HELIOGRAM
HELLEBORE
HELLENIAN
HELLENISE
HELLENISM
HELLENIST
HELLBOUND
HELLISHLY
HEMICYCLE
HEMSTITCH
HENPECKED
HEPATITIS
HEPTARCHY
HERALDING
HERBALIST
HERBARIUM
HERBIVORE
HERCULEAN
HEREABOUT
HEREAFTER
HERETICAL
HERITABLE
HERITABLY
HERMITAGE
HERONSHAW
HESITANCY
HESITATED
HETERODOX
HEXACHORD
HEXAGONAL
HEXAMETER
HEXASTYLE
HEXATEUCH

HIBERNATE
HIBERNIAN
HIDEBOUND
HIDEOUSLY
HIERARCHY
HIGH BLOWN
HIGH-FLIER
HIGHFLOWN
HIGH-FLYER
HIGH-TONED
HIGH-WATER
HILARIOUS
HILLINESS
HINDERING
HINDRANCE
HINDSIGHT
HINTINGLY
HIPPOCRAS
HISSINGLY
HISTOLOGY
HISTORIAN
HIT-AND-RUN
HITCH-HIKE
HOAR-FROST
HOARINESS
HOARSTONE
HOBGOBLIN
HOBNOBBED
HOCUSSING
HODOMETER
HOGBACKED
HOGGISHLY
HOLLANDER
HOLLOWING
HOLLYHOCK
HOLOCAUST
HOLOGRAPH
HOLSTERED
HOLYSTONE
HOMEBOUND
HOMESTEAD
HOMICIDAL
HOMOLOGUE
HOMONYMIC
HOMOPHONE
HOMOPHONY
HOMOPTERA
HONEY-BEAR
HONEYCOMB
HONEYLESS
HONEYMOON
HONEYWORT
HONORIFIC
HONOURING
HOOKNOSED
HOPEFULLY

HOPGARDEN	HUSBANDRY	IMITATIVE	IMPROVISE
HOP-PICKER	HUSHMONEY	IMMANENCE	IMPRUDENT
HOP-PILLOW	HUSKINESS	IMMEDIACY	IMPUDENCE
HOP-POCKET	HYBRIDISE	IMMEDIATE	IMPUGNING
HOPSCOTCH	HYBRIDISM	IMMENSELY	IMPULSION
HOREHOUND	HYBRIDITY	IMMENSITY	IMPULSIVE
HOROSCOPE	HYDRANGEA	IMMERSING	IMPUTABLE
HOROSCOPY	HYDRAULIC	IMMERSION	INABILITY
HORRIFIED	HYDROFOIL	IMMIGRANT	INAMORATO
HORSEBACK	HYDROLOGY	IMMIGRATE	INANIMATE
HORSE-BEAN	HYDROSTAT	IMMINENCE	INANITION
HORSEHAIR	HYDROXIDE	IMMODESTY	INAPTNESS
HORSELESS	HYMNOLOGY	IMMORALLY	INARCHING
HORSEMEAT	HYPERBOLA	IMMOVABLE	INAUDIBLE
HORSEPLAY	HYPERBOLE	IMMOVABLY	INAUDIBLY
HORSEPOND	HYPERICUM	IMMUNISED	INAUGURAL
HORSERACE	HYPHENING	IMMUTABLE	INAURATED
HORSESHOE	HYPNOLOGY	IMMUTABLY	INCAPABLE
HORSETAIL	HYPNOTISM	IMPACTING	INCAPABLY
HORSEWHIP	HYPNOTIST	IMPACTION	INCARNATE
HOSTELLER	HYPOCAUST	IMPAIRING	INCENSING
HOSTILELY	HYPOCRISY	IMPARTIAL	INCENSORY
HOSTILITY	HYPOCRITE	IMPARTING	INCENTIVE
HOT-HEADED	HYSTERICS	IMPASSION	INCEPTION
HOTTENTOT		IMPASSIVE	INCEPTIVE
HOUR-GLASS		IMPATIENS	INCESSANT
HOUSEBOAT	I – 9	IMPATIENT	INCIDENCE
HOUSEHOLD		IMPEACHED	INCIPIENT
HOUSELEEK	ICELANDER	IMPELLENT	INCLEMENT
HOUSELESS	ICELANDIC	IMPELLING	INCLINING
HOUSEMAID	ICHNEUMON	IMPENDENT	INCLUDING
HOUSEROOM	ICHTHYOID	IMPENDING	INCLUSION
HOUSEWIFE	ICONOLOGY	IMPERFECT	INCLUSIVE
HOUSEWORK	IDEALISED	IMPERIOUS	INCOGNITO
HOWSOEVER	IDENTICAL	IMPETUOUS	INCOMMODE
HUCKABACK	IDEOGRAPH	IMPINGING	INCORRECT
HUFFINESS	IDIOMATIC	IMPIOUSLY	INCORRUPT
HUFFISHLY	IGNORAMUS	IMPLANTED	INCREASED
HUMANISED	IGNORANCE	IMPLEMENT	INCREMENT
HUMANKIND	IGUANODON	IMPLICATE	INCUBATED
HUMANNESS	ILLEGALLY	IMPLORING	INCUBATOR
HUMBLE-BEE	ILLEGIBLE	IMPLOSION	INCULCATE
HUMBLE-PIE	ILLEGIBLY	IMPOLITIC	INCULPATE
HUMBUGGED	ILL-HUMOUR	IMPORTANT	INCUMBENT
HUMILIATE	ILLIBERAL	IMPORTING	INCURABLE
HUMMOCKED	ILLICITLY	IMPORTUNE	INCURABLY
HUMOURING	ILL-JUDGED	IMPOSABLE	INCURIOUS
HUNCHBACK	ILL-NATURE	IMPOSTURE	INCURRING
HUNDREDTH	ILLOGICAL	IMPOTENCE	INCURSION
HUNGARIAN	ILL-TIMING	IMPOTENCY	INCURSIVE
HUNGERING	ILLUMINED	IMPOUNDED	INCURVING
HUNKY-DORY	IMAGELESS	IMPRECATE	INDECENCY
HURRICANE	IMAGINARY	IMPRESSED	INDECORUM
HURRIEDLY	IMAGINING	IMPRINTED	INDELIBLE
HURTFULLY	IMBROGLIO	IMPROMPTU	INDELIBLY
HUSBANDED	IMITATING	IMPROVING	INDEMNIFY
	IMITATION		

INDEMNITY	INFURIATE	INSTANCED	INTONATED
INDENTING	INFUSIBLE	INSTANTLY	INTRICACY
INDENTION	INFUSORIA	INSTIGATE	INTRICATE
INDENTURE	INGENIOUS	INSTILLED	INTRIGUED
INDICATED	INGENUITY	INSTITUTE	INTRINSIC
INDICATOR	INGENUOUS	INSULARLY	INTRODUCE
INDICTING	INGESTION	INSULATED	INTROVERT
INDIGENCE	INGLENOOK	INSULATOR	INTRUDING
INDIGNANT	INGRAINED	INSULTING	INTRUSION
INDIGNITY	INGROWING	INSURABLE	INTRUSIVE
INDISPOSE	INHABITED	INSURANCE	INTUITION
INDOLENCE	INHERENCE	INSURGENT	INTUITIVE
INDRAUGHT	INHERITED	INTEGRANT	INUNCTION
INDUCTING	INHERITOR	INTEGRATE	INUNDATED
INDUCTION	INHIBITED	INTEGRITY	INUREMENT
INDUCTIVE	INHUMANLY	INTELLECT	INUTILITY
INDULGING	INITIALLY	INTENDANT	INVALIDED
INDULGENT	INITIATED	INTENSELY	INVECTIVE
INDURATED	INJECTING	INTENSIFY	INVEIGHED
INDWELLED	INJECTION	INTENSION	INVEIGLED
INEBRIATE	INJURIOUS	INTENSITY	INVENTING
INEBRIETY	INJUSTICE	INTENSIVE	INVENTION
INEFFABLE	INKBOTTLE	INTENTION	INVENTIVE
INEFFABLY	INKHOLDER	INTERBRED	INVENTORY
INELASTIC	INNERMOST	INTERCEDE	INVERSELY
INELEGANT	INNERVATE	INTERCEPT	INVERSION
INEPTNESS	INNKEEPER	INTERDICT	INVERTING
INERRABLE	INNOCENCE	INTERFACE	INVESTING
INERRABLY	INNOCUOUS	INTERFERE	INVIDIOUS
INERRANCY	INNOVATED	INTERFOLD	INVIOLATE
INERTNESS	INNOVATOR	INTERFUSE	INVISIBLE
INFANTILE	INOCULATE	INTERJECT	INVISIBLY
INFANTINE	INODORATE	INTERLACE	INVOICING
INFATUATE	INODOROUS	INTERLAID	INVOLUCRE
INFECTING	INORGANIC	INTERLARD	INVOLVING
INFECTION	INQUIRING	INTERLEAF	INWROUGHT
INFECTIVE	INSATIATE	INTERLINE	IRASCIBLE
INFERENCE	INSCRIBED	INTERLOCK	IRASCIBLY
INFERRING	INSENSATE	INTERLOPE	IRKSOMELY
INFERTILE	INSERTING	INTERLUDE	IRONBOUND
INFESTING	INSERTION	INTERMENT	IRONMOULD
INFIRMARY	INSETTING	INTERNING	IRONSMITH
INFIRMITY	INSIDIOUS	INTERNODE	IRONSTONE
INFLAMING	INSINCERE	INTERPLAY	IRRADIANT
INFLATING	INSINUATE	INTERPOSE	IRRADIATE
INFLATION	INSIPIDLY	INTERPRET	IRREGULAR
INFLECTED	INSISTENT	INTERRING	IRRIGATED
INFLEXION	INSISTING	INTERRUPT	IRRITABLE
INFLICTED	INSOLENCE	INTERSECT	IRRITABLY
INFLOWING	INSOLUBLE	INTERVENE	IRRITANCY
INFLUENCE	INSOLVENT	INTERVIEW	IRRITATED
INFLUENZA	INSPANNED	INTERWOVE	IRRUPTION
INFOLDING	INSPECTED	INTESTACY	ISINGLASS
INFORMANT	INSPECTOR	INTESTATE	ISLAMITIC
INFORMING	INSPIRING	INTESTINE	ISOLATING
INFRINGED	INSTALLED	INTIMATED	ISOLATION

ISOMETRIC
ISOSCELES
ISRAELITE
ITALICISE
ITERATING
ITERATION
ITERATIVE
ITINERANT
ITINERARY
ITINERATE

J – 9

JACARANDA
JACK-KNIFE
JACK-PLANE
JACK-SNIPE
JACKSTRAW
JACK-TOWEL
JACQUERIE
JANISSARY
JANSENISM
JANSENIST
JARRINGLY
JAY-WALKER
JEALOUSLY
JEERINGLY
JELLYFISH
JENNETING
JESSAMINE
JESTINGLY
JEWELLERY
JEWEL-LIKE
JITTERBUG
JOBMASTER
JOBSWORTH
JOCULARLY
JOINTEDLY
JOINT-HEIR
JOINTRESS
JOLLINESS
JOLLYBOAT
JOLTINGLY
JOSS-HOUSE
JOSS-STICK
JOURNEYED
JOVIALITY
JOYLESSLY
JOCUNDITY
JUDAS-TREE
JUDGEMENT
JUDGESHIP
JUDICIARY
JUDICIOUS
JUICELESS
JUICINESS

JUMPINESS
JUNIORITY
JURIDICIAL
JUSTICIAR
JUSTIFIED
JUTTINGLY
JUVENILIA
JUXTAPOSE

K – 9

KENNELLED
KENTLEDGE
KERBSTONE
KERNELLED
KIDNAPPED
KIDNAPPER
KILDERKIN
KILN-DRIED
KILOLITRE
KILOMETRE
KINGCRAFT
KINSWOMAN
KIPPERING
KISSAGRAM
KITCHENER
KITTENISH
KITTIWAKE
KNAVISHLY
KNEADABLE
KNEE-PIECE
KNIFE-EDGE
KNIFE-REST
KNIGHTAGE
KNIGHTING
KNITTABLE
KNOCKDOWN
KNOTGRASS
KNOWINGLY
KNOWLEDGE
KNUCKLING
KYMOGRAPH

L – 9

LABELLING
LABORIOUS
LABOURING
LABYRINTH
LACE-CORAL
LACE-FRAME
LACERATED
LACHRYMAL
LACTATION
LAGGINGLY
LAIRDSHIP

LAMB'S-WOOL
LAMELLATE
LAMENTING
LAMINATED
LAMPBLACK
LAMPLIGHT
LAMPOONED
LANCEWOOD
LAND-AGENT
LANDAULET
LAND-FORCE
LANDGRAVE
LANDOWNER
LANDSCAPE
LAND-SHARK
LANDSLIDE
LANGUIDLY
LANKINESS
LANTHANUM
LAODICEAN
LARCENOUS
LARGENESS
LARGHETTO
LASSITUDE
LASTINGLY
LATERALLY
LATHERING
LATTICING
LAUDATION
LAUDATORY
LAUGHABLE
LAUGHABLY
LAUNCHING
LAUNDERER
LAUNDRESS
LAURELLED
LAVISHING
LAWGIVING
LAWLESSLY
LAWMAKING
LAWMONGER
LAWNMOWER
LAY-FIGURE
LAZARETTO
LEADINGLY
LEAFINESS
LEAF-METAL
LEAF-MOULD
LEAFSTALK
LEAKINESS
LEAN-FACED
LEAPINGLY
LEARNABLE
LEARNEDLY
LEASEHOLD
LEASTWAYS

LEASTWISE
LEAVENING
LECHERING
LECHEROUS
LECTURING
LEERINGLY
LEGALISED
LEGENDARY
LEGER-LINE
LEGIONARY
LEGISLATE
LEISURELY
LEITMOTIF
LENGTHILY
LENIENTLY
LEPROUSLY
LESSENING
LETHARGIC
LETTER-BOX
LETTERING
LEUCOCYTE
LEVANTINE
LEVANTING
LEVELLING
LEVELNESS
LEVIATHAN
LEVITICUS
LIABILITY
LIBELLING
LIBELLOUS
LIBERALLY
LIBERATED
LIBERATOR
LIBERTINE
LIBRARIAN
LIBRATION
LICENSING
LICHENOUS
LIFEBLOOD
LIFEGUARD
LIGHTABLE
LIGHTENED
LIGHTLESS
LIGHTNESS
LIGHTNING
LIGHTSHIP
LIGHT-YEAR
LILACEOUS
LIME-JUICE
LIMELIGHT
LIMESTONE
LIME-WATER
LIMITABLE
LIMITEDLY
LIMITLESS
LIMNOLOGY

LIMOUSINE	LONG-FIELD	MAGNETISM	MARKET-DAY
LIMPIDITY	LONGINGLY	MAGNETITE	MARKETING
LIMPINGLY	LONGITUDE	MAGNIFICO	MARMALADE
LINCRUSTA	LOOSENESS	MAGNIFIED	MARMOREAL
LINEALITY	LOQUACITY	MAGNITUDE	MAROONING
LINEAMENT	LORGNETTE	MAHARANEE	MARQUETRY
LINEATION	LOUSINESS	MAHOMEDAN	MARROWFAT
LINGERING	LOUTISHLY	MAILCOACH	MARROWISH
LION-HEART	LOVE-APPLE	MAIL-GUARD	MARSHLAND
LIONISING	LOVE-CHILD	MAIL-TRAIN	MARSUPIAL
LIQUATING	LOVE-FEAST	MAIN-BRACE	MARTIALLY
LIQUATION	LOWERMOST	MAINFRAME	MARTINMAS
LIQUEFIED	LOWLANDER	MAINSHEET	MARTYRING
LIQUIDATE	LOWLINESS	MAJORDOMO	MARTYRDOM
LIQUIDISE	LOW-MINDED	MAJORSHIP	MARVELLED
LIQUIDITY	LOW-NECKED	MAKE-PEACE	MASCULINE
LIQUORICE	LUBRICANT	MAKESHIFT	MASSACRED
LIQUORISH	LUBRICATE	MALACHITE	MASSAGING
LISPINGLY	LUBRICITY	MALADROIT	MASSIVELY
LISTENING	LUBRICOUS	MALARIOUS	MASTERDOM
LITERALLY	LUCIDNESS	MALFORMED	MASTERFUL
LITERATIM	LUCK-PENNY	MALICIOUS	MASTERING
LITHENESS	LUCRATIVE	MALIGNING	MASTICATE
LITHESOME	LUCUBRATE	MALIGNANT	MATCHLESS
LITHOLOGY	LUCULLIAN	MALIGNITY	MATCHLOCK
LITHOTINT	LUDICROUS	MALLEABLE	MATCHWOOD
LITHOTYPE	LUMBERMAN	MALLEOLUS	MATERNITY
LITIGABLE	LUMBRICAL	MALMAISON	MATRIARCH
LITIGATED	LUMPISHLY	MAMMALIAN	MATRICIDE
LITIGIOUS	LUNISOLAR	MAMMALOGY	MATRIMONY
LITTERBUG	LUSTFULLY	MANNIFORM	MATRONAGE
LITTERING	LUSTINESS	MANACLING	MATTERING
LITURGIST	LUXURIANT	MAN-AT-ARMS	MAULSTICK
LIVERWORT	LUXURIATE	MANCUNIAN	MAUNDERED
LIVERYMAN	LUXURIOUS	MANDATORY	MAUSOLEUM
LIVIDNESS	LYMPHATIC	MANDOLINE	MAWKISHLY
LOADSTONE		MANDUCATE	MAXILLARY
LOAF-SUGAR	**M – 9**	MANGANESE	MAXIMISED
LOATHSOME		MANGINESS	MAYFLOWER
LOBSCOUSE	MACCABEAN	MANHANDLE	MAYORALTY
LOCKSMITH	MACCABEES	MANIFESTO	MEADOW-RUE
LOCOMOTOR	MACEDOINE	MANLINESS	MEALINESS
LODESTONE	MACERATED	MANNEQUIN	MEANDERED
LODGEABLE	MACHINATE	MANNERISM	MEANINGLY
LOFTINESS	MACHINERY	MANNISHLY	MEANWHILE
LOGARITHM	MACHINING	MANOEUVRE	MEASURING
LOGICALLY	MACHINIST	MANOMETER	MEATINESS
LOGISTICS	MACROCOSM	MANY-SIDED	MECHANICS
LOGOGRIPH	MADDENING	MARAUDING	MECHANISE
LOGOMACHY	MADREPORE	MARCASITE	MECHANIST
LOINCLOTH	MAELSTROM	MARCHPANE	MEDALLION
LOITERING	MAFFICKED	MARESCHAL	MEDALLIST
LOLLOPING	MAGICALLY	MARGARINE	MEDIAEVAL
LONGCLOTH	MAGNESIAN	MARGINING	MEDIATING
LONG-DOZEN	MAGNESIUM	MARINATED	MEDIATION
LONGEVITY	MAGNETISE	MARITALLY	MEDIATORY

MEDICABLE	METROLOGY	MIRTHLESS	MODERNIST
MEDICALLY	METRONOME	MISALLIED	MODERNITY
MEDICATED	MEZZANINE	MISATTEND	MODIFYING
MEDICINAL	MEZZOTINT	MISBECAME	MODULATED
MEDULLARY	MICACEOUS	MISBECOME	MODULATOR
MEGADEATH	MICROBIAL	MISBEHAVE	MOISTENED
MEGAPHONE	MICROCHIP	MISBELIEF	MOISTNESS
MEGASCOPE	MICROCOSM	MISCALLED	MOLECULAR
MEGASTORE	MICROFILM	MISCHANCE	MOLE-SHREW
MELANOSIS	MICROLITE	MISCREANT	MOLESTING
MELIORISM	MICROTOME	MISDATING	MOLETRACK
MELLOWING	MICROVOLT	MISDIRECT	MOLLIFIED
MELODIOUS	MICROWAVE	MISEMPLOY	MOLLUSCAN
MELODRAMA	MIDDLEMAN	MISERABLE	MOMENTARY
MELPOMENE	MIDDLINGS	MISERABLY	MOMENTOUS
MELTINGLY	MIDINETTE	MISFORMED	MONARCHAL
MEMORABLE	MID-STREAM	MISGIVING	MONARCHIC
MEMORABLY	MID-SUMMER	MISGOTTEN	MONASTERY
MEMORANDA	MIDWIFERY	MISGOVERN	MONDAYISH
MEMORISED	MIDWINTER	MISGUIDED	MONETISED
MENAGERIE	MIGRATING	MISHANDLE	MONEYLESS
MENDACITY	MIGRATION	MISINFORM	MONEYWORT
MENDELIAN	MIGRATORY	MISJOINED	MONGERING
MENDELISM	MILDEWING	MISJUDGED	MONGOLIAN
MENDICANT	MILESTONE	MISLAYING	MONKEYING
MENDICITY	MILITANCY	MISMANAGE	MONKEY-NUT
MENNONITE	MILITATED	MISMARKED	MONKSHOOD
MENSHEVIK	MILK-FEVER	MISNAMING	MONOBASIC
MENTALITY	MILK-FLOAT	MISPLACED	MONOCHORD
MENTIONED	MILKINESS	MISQUOTED	MONOCOQUE
MERCENARY	MILK-PUNCH	MISRATING	MONOCULAR
MERCILESS	MILK-TOOTH	MISREPORT	MONODRAMA
MERCURIAL	MILK-VETCH	MISRULING	MONOGRAPH
MERCUROUS	MILLBOARD	MISSHAPED	MONOLOGUE
MERCY-SEAT	MILLENARY	MISSHAPEN	MONOMANIA
MERGANSER	MILLENIAL	MISSIONER	MONOMETER
MERRIMENT	MILLEPEDE	MISSTATED	MONOPLANE
MERRINESS	MILLIGRAM	MISTAKING	MONOTONIC
MESMERISE	MILLINERY	MISTAUGHT	MONOTREME
MESMERISM	MILLIONTH	MISTIMING	MONSIGNOR
MESSENGER	MILLIPEDE	MISTINESS	MONSTROUS
MESSIANIC	MILLSTONE	MISTITLED	MOODINESS
MESSINESS	MILL-WHEEL	MISTLETOE	MOONCHILD
METABOLIC	MIMICKING	MISTUNING	MOON-DAISY
METALLING	MINCEMEAT	MITHRAISM	MOONLIGHT
METALLISE	MINCINGLY	MITIGATED	MOONRAKER
METALLIST	MINEFIELD	MNEMONICS	MOONSHINE
METALLOID	MINELAYER	MNEMOSYNE	MOONSHINY
METAMERIC	MINIATURE	MOANFULLY	MOONSTONE
METAPLASM	MINI-BREAK	MOBILISED	MORALISED
METEROID	MINIMISED	MOCKINGLY	MORBIDITY
METHODISM	MINISKIRT	MODELLING	MORDACITY
METHODIST	MINT-JULEP	MODERATED	MORDANTLY
METHOUGHT	MINT-SAUCE	MODERATOR	MORMONISM
METHYLATE	MINUTE-GUN	MODERNISE	MORTALITY
METHYLENE	MIRRORING	MODERNISM	MORTGAGED

MORTGAGEE
MORTGAGOR
MORTIFIED
MORTISING
MOSCHATEL
MOSS-GROWN
MOSSINESS
MOTHERING
MOTIONING
MOTOR-BOAT
MOULDABLE
MOULDERED
MOULD-LOFT
MOULD-WARP
MOUND-BIRD
MOUNTABLE
MOUSE-HOLE
MOUSE-HUNT
MOUSE-TAIL
MOUSETRAP
MOUSTACHE
MOUTHLESS
MUCKINESS
MUCKRAKER
MUCKSWEAT
MUDDINESS
MULLIONED
MULTIFORM
MULTITUDE
MUMCHANCE
MUMMIFIED
MUMMIFORM
MUNDANELY
MUNICIPAL
MUNITIONS
MURDERING
MURDERESS
MURDEROUS
MURKINESS
MURMURING
MURMUROUS
MUSCADINE
MUSCOVITE
MUSEFULLY
MUSHINESS
MUSICALLY
MUSIC-BOOK
MUSIC-HALL
MUSK-APPLE
MUSKETEER
MUSKINESS
MUSK-MELON
MUSK-SHREW
MUSSULMAN
MUSTACHIO
MUSTERING

MUSTINESS
MUTILATED
MUTINYING
MUTUALITY
MUZZINESS
MYSTICISM
MYSTIFIED
MYTHICISE
MYTHOLOGY

N – 9

NAILBRUSH
NAKEDNESS
NAMEPLATE
NARCISSUS
NARRATING
NARRATION
NARRATIVE
NARROWING
NASALISED
NASEBERRY
NASTINESS
NATURALLY
NAUGHTILY
NAUSEATED
NAVELWORT
NAVICULAR
NAVIGABLE
NAVIGATED
NAVIGATOR
NECESSARY
NECESSITY
NECKCLOTH
NECKLACED
NECK-PIECE
NECTARINE
NEEDFULLY
NEEDINESS
NEEDLEFUL
NEEDLE-GUN
NEFARIOUS
NEGATIVED
NEGLECTED
NEGLIGENT
NEGOTIATE
NEGROHEAD
NEIGHBOUR
NEOLITHIC
NEPENTHES
NEPTUNIAN
NERVELESS
NERVOUSLY
NEURALGIA
NEURALGIC
NEURATION

NEUROLOGY
NEUROPATH
NEUROTOMY
NEUTRALLY
NEVERMORE
NEWSPAPER
NEWTONIAN
NICKNAMED
NICTITATE
NIGGARDLY
NIGHT-CLUB
NIGHTFALL
NIGHT-GOWN
NIGHT-HAWK
NIGHT-LESS
NIGHT-LINE
NIGHTMARE
NIGHT-SOIL
NINETIETH
NIPPINGLY
NITRIFIED
NOBLENESS
NOCTURNAL
NOISELESS
NOISINESS
NOISOMELY
NOMINALLY
NOMINATED
NOMINATOR
NONENTITY
NONILLION
NONPAREIL
NON-SEXUAL
NONSUIITED
NORMALISE
NORMALITY
NORTH-EAST
NORTHERLY
NORTHWARD
NORTH-WEST
NORWEGIAN
NOSEPIECE
NOSTALGIA
NOSTALGIC
NOTEPAPER
NOTIFYING
NOTORIETY
NOTORIOUS
NOURISHED
NOVELETTE
NOVICIATE
NOVITIATE
NOXIOUSLY
NULLIFIED
NUMBERING
NUMERABLE

NUMERALLY
NUMERATED
NUMERATOR
NUMERICAL
NURSEMAID
NURTURING
NUTRIMENT
NUTRITION
NUTRITIVE
NUTTINESS
NYSTAGMUS

O – 9

OAST-HOUSE
OBBLIGATO
OBEDIENCE
OBEISANCE
OBESENESS
OBEYINGLY
OBFUSCATE
OBJECTIFY
OBJECTION
OBJECTIVE
OBJURGATE
OBLIGATED
OBLIQUELY
OBLIQUITY
OBLIVIOUS
OBLONGISH
OBNOXIOUS
OBSCENELY
OBSCENITY
OBSCURANT
OBSCURELY
OBSCURING
OBSCURITY
OBSEQUIAL
OBSERVANT
OBSERVING
OBSESSION
OBSTETRIC
OBSTINACY
OBSTINATE
OBTAINING
OBTRUDING
OBTRUSION
OBTRUSIVE
OBVERSION
OBVERSELY
OBVERTING
OBVIATING
OBVIOUSLY
OCCIPITAL
OCCLUDING
OCCLUSION

OCCULTISM
OCCUPANCY
OCCUPYING
OCCURRING
OCTAGONAL
OCTENNIAL
OCTILLION
ODALISQUE
ODDFELLOW
ODOROUSLY
ODOURLESS
OENOTHERA
OFFENSIVE
OFFERABLE
OFFERTORY
OFFHANDED
OFFICERED
OFFICIANT
OFFICIATE
OFFICINAL
OFFICIOUS
OFF-LIMITS
OFF-ROADER
OFFSPRING
OFTENNESS
OIL-COLOUR
OIL-ENGINE
OLEOGRAPH
OLEOMETER
OLEORESIN
OLFACTORY
OLIGARCHY
OLIGOCENE
OLIVE-YARD
OMBUDSMAN
OMINOUSLY
OMISSIBLE
ON-LICENCE
ONSETTING
ONSLAUGHT
OPALESCED
OPALISING
OPERATING
OPERATION
OPERATISE
OPERATIVE
OPPORTUNE
OPPOSABLE
OPPRESSED
OPPRESSOR
OPTOMETER
OPTOPHONE
OPULENTLY
OPUSCULUM
ORANGEADE
ORANGEMAN

ORANGE-PIP
ORATORIAL
ORBICULAR
ORCHESTRA
ORCHIDIST
ORDAINING
ORDINANCE
ORGANISER
ORGANZINE
ORGIASTIC
ORIENTATE
ORIFLAMME
ORIGINATE
ORPHANAGE
ORTHODOXY
OSCILLATE
OSCULATED
OSSIFYING
OSTEOLOGY
OSTEOPATH
OSTRACISE
OTHERNESS
OTHERWISE
OUT-AND-OUT
OUTBRAVED
OUTERMOST
OUTFACING
OUTGROWTH
OUT-JOCKEY
OUTLANDER
OUTLASTED
OUTLAWING
OUTLEAPED
OUTLINING
OUTLIVING
OUTMANNED
OUTNUMBER
OUT-OF-DOOR
OUTPACING
OUTPLAYED
OUTRAGING
OUTRANGED
OUTRIDDEN
OUTRIDING
OUTRIGGED
OUTRIGGER
OUTSAILED
OUTSPOKEN
OUTSPREAD
OUTSTARED
OUT-TALKED
OUTVALUED
OUTVOTING
OUTWARDLY
OUTWITTED
OUTWORKED

OVERACTED
OVERAWING
OVERBLOWN
OVERBOARD
OVERBUILD
OVERCLOUD
OVERCROWD
OVERDOING
OVERDOSED
OVERDRAFT
OVERDRAWN
OVERDRIVE
OVERHASTY
OVERJOYED
OVERLADEN
OVERLEAPT
OVERLYING
OVERNIGHT
OVERPOWER
OVERPROOF
OVERRATED
OVERREACH
OVERRULED
OVERSHOOT
OVERSIGHT
OVERSLEEP
OVERSPEND
OVERSTATE
OVERSTOCK
OVERTAKEN
OVERTHROW
OVERTRUMP
OVERVALUE
OVERWHELM
OVERWOUND
OVIPAROUS
OWNERSHIP
OXIDATION
OXIDISING
OXYGENATE
OXYGENIZE
OXYGENOUS
OYSTER-BED

P – 9

PACEMAKER
PACHYDERM
PACIFYING
PACKETING
PACKHORSE
PADLOCKED
PAGANISED
PAGEANTRY
PAINFULLY
PAINTBALL

PALANQUIN
PALATABLE
PALAVERED
PALE-FACED
PALISADED
PALLADIAN
PALLADIUM
PALLIASSE
PALLIATED
PALM-HOUSE
PALMISTRY
PALPITATE
PAMPERING
PANCAKING
PANDERING
PANEGYRIC
PANELLING
PANHANDLE
PANOPLIED
PANORAMIC
PANSLAVIC
PANTALOON
PANTHEISM
PANTHEIST
PANTINGLY
PANTOMIME
PAPARAZZI
PAPER-MILL
PAPILLARY
PARABOLIC
PARACHUTE
PARACLETE
PARAGRAPH
PARALYSED
PARALYSIS
PARALYTIC
PARAMEDIC
PARAMOUNT
PARASITIC
PARATAXIS
PARBOILED
PARBUCKLE
PARCELLED
PARCHMENT
PARDONING
PAREGORIC
PARENTAGE
PARGETING
PARHELION
PARLEYING
PARLEYVOO
PAROCHIAL
PARODYING
PAROTITIS
PARQUETRY
PARRICIDE

PARSIMONY
PARSONAGE
PARTAKING
PARTHENON
PARTIALLY
PARTITION
PARTITIVE
PARTNERED
PARTRIDGE
PASSENGER
PASSERINE
PASSIVELY
PASSIVITY
PASTORALE
PASTURAGE
PASTURING
PATCHOULI
PATCHWORK
PATENTING
PATERNITY
PATHOLOGY
PATIENTLY
PATRIARCH
PATRICIAN
PATRICIDE
PATRIMONY
PATRIOTIC
PATRISTIC
PATROLLED
PATRONAGE
PATRONESS
PATRONISE
PATTERING
PATTERNED
PAUPERISE
PAUSINGLY
PAYMASTER
PEACEABLE
PEACEABLY
PEA-JACKET
PEARLWORT
PEASANTRY
PECULATED
PECUNIARY
PEDAGOGIC
PEDAGOGUE
PEDALLING
PEDICULAR
PEDOMETER
PEEVISHLY
PEKINGESE
PELLITORY
PENALISED
PEN-AND-INK
PENCILLED
PENDRAGON

PENDULOUS
PENETRATE
PENHOLDER
PENINSULA
PENITENCE
PENNIFORM
PENNILESS
PENNYWISE
PENNYWORT
PENSIONED
PENSIONER
PENSIVELY
PENTAGRAM
PENTECOST
PENTHOUSE
PENURIOUS
PEPPERBOX
PEPPERING
PERCEIVED
PERCHANCE
PERCHERON
PERCOLATE
PERCUSSED
PERDITION
PEREGRINE
PERENNIAL
PERFECTED
PERFECTLY
PERFERVID
PERFORATE
PERFORMED
PERFORMER
PERFUMERY
PERFUMING
PERIMETER
PERIPHERY
PERISCOPE
PERISHING
PERISTYLE
PERJURING
PERMANENT
PERMEABLE
PERMEABLY
PERMEATED
PERMITTED
PERMUTING
PERORATED
PERPENDED
PERPETUAL
PERPLEXED
PERSECUTE
PERSEVERE
PERSIMMON
PERSISTED
PERSONAGE
PERSONATE

PERSONIFY
PERSONNEL
PERSPIRED
PERSUADED
PERTAINED
PERTINENT
PERTURBED
PERVADING
PERVASION
PERVASIVE
PERVERTED
PESSIMISM
PESSIMIST
PESTERING
PESTILENT
PESTOLOGY
PETERSHAM
PETRIFIED
PETROLEUM
PETTICOAT
PETTINESS
PETTISHLY
PETULANCE
PHAGOCYTE
PHALANGER
PHALAROPE
PHARISAIC
PHENOMENA
PHILANDER
PHILATELY
PHILIPPIC
PHILOLOGY
PHLEBITIS
PHONECARD
PHONETICS
PHONOGRAM
PHONOLOGY
PHOSPHATE
PHOSPHINE
PHOSPHITE
PHOTOCELL
PHOTOCOPY
PHOTO-PLAY
PHOTOSTAT
PHRENETIC
PHYSICIAN
PHYSICIST
PHYSICKED
PICKABACK
PICKETING
PICTORIAL
PICTURING
PIECEMEAL
PIECE-WORK
PIER-GLASS
PIETISTIC

PIGHEADED
PIGMENTAL
PIGNORATE
PIKESTAFF
PILFERING
PILLAR-BOX
PILLORIED
PILLOWING
PILOT-BOAT
PILOTFISH
PIMPERNEL
PINCHBECK
PINEAPPLE
PINIONING
PINNACLED
PIONEERED
PIPESTONE
PIPISTREL
PIQUANTLY
PIRATICAL
PIROUETTE
PISCATORY
PISCIFORM
PISTACHIO
PITCHFORK
PITCH-PINE
PITCHPIPE
PITEOUSLY
PITHECOID
PITHINESS
PITIFULLY
PITUITARY
PITYINGLY
PIZZICATO
PLACARDED
PLACATING
PLACE-KICK
PLACIDITY
PLAINNESS
PLAINSONG
PLAINTIFF
PLAINTIVE
PLANE-IRON
PLANETARY
PLANETOID
PLANTABLE
PLASTERED
PLASTERER
PLATEMARK
PLATE-RACK
PLATINISE
PLATITUDE
PLATONISE
PLATONISM
PLATONIST
PLAUSIBLE

PLAUSIBLY
PLAY-ACTOR
PLAYFULLY
PLAYGOING
PLAYGROUP
PLAYHOUSE
PLAYTHING
PLEACHING
PLEASANCE
PLENARILY
PLENITUDE
PLENTEOUS
PLENTIFUL
PLEURITIC
PLIGHTING
PLINTHITE
PLOUGHBOY
PLOUGHING
PLOUGHMAN
PLUMBLINE
PLUMB-RULE
PLUMELESS
PLUMPNESS
PLUNDERED
PLURALISE
PLURALISM
PLURALIST
PLURALITY
PLUS-FOURS
PLUTOCRAT
PLUTONIUM
PNEUMATIC
PNEUMONIA
PNEUMONIC
POCKETING
POETASTER
POGO-STICK
POIGNANCY
POINTEDLY
POINTLESS
POINTSMAN
POISONOUS
POKERWORK
POLARIZED
POLEMICAL
POLE-VAULT
POLICEMAN
POLISHING
POLITESSE
POLITICAL
POLLINATE
POLLUTING
POLLUTION
POLONAISE
POLYANDRY
POLYESTER

POLYGONAL
POLYGRAPH
POLYSTYLE
POLYTHENE
POMMELLED
POMPADOUR
POMPOSITY
POMPOUSLY
PONDERING
PONDEROUS
POOR-HOUSE
POPPYCOCK
POPULARLY
POPULATED
PORBEAGLE
PORCELAIN
PORCUPINE
PORRINGER
PORTATIVE
PORTENDED
PORTERAGE
PORTERESS
PORTFOLIO
PORTRAYAL
PORTRAYED
POSSESSED
POSSESSOR
POST-DATED
POST-ENTRY
POSTERIOR
POSTERITY
POST-HASTE
POST-NATAL
POSTPONED
POSTULANT
POSTULATE
POSTURING
POTASSIUM
POTBOILER
POTENTATE
POTENTIAL
POT-POURRI
POTTERING
POULTERER
POULTICED
POUNCE-BOX
POURBOIRE
POURPOINT
POWDER-BOX
POWDERING
POWERLESS
POWER-LOOM
POWWOWING
PRACTICAL
PRACTISED
PRAGMATIC

PRATINGLY
PRATTLING
PRAYERFUL
PRAYINGLY
PREACHIFY
PREACHING
PREAMBLED
PREBENDAL
PRECEDENT
PRECEDING
PRECENTOR
PRECEPTOR
PRECIPICE
PRECISELY
PRECISIAN
PRECISION
PRECLUDED
PRECOCITY
PRECURSOR
PREDATING
PREDATORY
PREDESIGN
PREDICANT
PREDICATE
PREDICTED
PREDOOMED
PRE-ENGAGE
PREFACING
PREFATORY
PREFERRED
PREFIGURE
PREFIXING
PREFORMED
PREGNANCY
PREJUDGED
PREJUDICE
PRELATURE
PRELUDING
PRELUSIVE
PREMATURE
PREMISING
PREMOTION
PREOCCUPY
PREOPTION
PREORDIAN
PREPACKED
PREPARING
PREPAYING
PRESAGING
PRESBYTER
PRESCIENT
PRESCRIBE
PRESCRIPT
PRESENTED
PRESENTLY
PRESERVED

PRESERVER
PRESIDENT
PRESIDING
PRESSGANG
PRESSMARK
PRESS-ROOM
PRESSWORK
PRESUMING
PRETENDED
PRETENDER
PRETERITE
PRETTYISH
PREVAILED
PREVALENT
PREVENTED
PREVISION
PRICELESS
PRICKLING
PRIDELESS
PRIESTESS
PRIMARILY
PRIMATIAL
PRIMITIVE
PRINCEDOM
PRINCIPAL
PRINCIPIA
PRINCIPLE
PRINTLESS
PRINTSHOP
PRISMATIC
PRIVATEER
PRIVATELY
PRIVATION
PRIVILEGE
PROBATION
PROBATIVE
PROBOSCIS
PROCEDURE
PROCEEDED
PROCESSED
PROCLITIC
PRO-CONSUL
PROCREANT
PROCREATE
PROCURING
PRODUCING
PROFANELY
PROFANING
PROFANITY
PROFESSED
PROFESSOR
PROFFERED
PROFILING
PROFITEER
PROFITING
PROFUSELY

PROFUSION
PROGNOSIS
PROGRAMME
PROJECTED
PROJECTOR
PROLIXITY
PROLOGUED
PROLONGED
PROMENADE
PROMINENT
PROMISING
PROMOTING
PROMOTION
PROMPTING
PRONENESS
PRONOUNCE
PROOFLESS
PROPAGATE
PROPELLED
PROPELLER
PROPHETIC
PROPONENT
PROPOSING
PROPRIETY
PROROGUED
PROSCRIBE
PROSECUTE
PROSELYTE
PROSINESS
PROSODIST
PROSPERED
PROSTRATE
PROTECTED
PROTECTOR
PROTESTED
PROTHESIS
PROTOTYPE
PROTOZOAN
PROTOZOIC
PROTRUDED
PROUDNESS
PROVENDER
PROVIDENT
PROVIDING
PROVISION
PROVISORY
PROVOKING
PROXIMATE
PROXIMITY
PRUDENTLY
PRUDISHLY
PRURIENCE
PRURIENCY
PSALMODIC
PSEUDONYM
PSORIASIS

PSYCHICAL
PSYCHOSIS
PTARMIGAN
PTOLEMAIC
PUBESCENT
PUBLICISE
PUBLICIST
PUBLICITY
PUBLISHED
PUBLISHER
PUCKERING
PUERILELY
PUERILITY
PUERPERAL
PUFF-ADDER
PUFFINESS
PUFFINGLY
PUGNACITY
PUISSANCE
PULLULATE
PULMONARY
PULMONATE
PULPINESS
PULSATING
PULSATILE
PULSATION
PULSATIVE
PULSATORY
PULSELESS
PULVERISE
PUNCHBOWL
PUNCTILIO
PUNCTUATE
PUNCTURED
PUNGENTLY
PUNISHING
PUPILLARY
PUPPYHOOD
PURCHASED
PURCHASER
PURGATION
PURGATIVE
PURGATORY
PURIFYING
PURITANIC
PURLOINED
PURPORTED
PURPOSELY
PURPOSING
PURPOSIVE
PURSUANCE
PURULENCE
PURVEYING
PUSHINGLY
PUSTULATE
PUTREFIED

PUTRIDITY
PUZZLEDOM
PYORRHOEA
PYRACANTH
PYRAMIDAL
PYROGENIC
PYROLATRY
PYROMANCY
PYROMANIA
PYROMETER
PYROXYLIC
PYROXYLIN

Q – 9

QUADRATIC
QUADRATED
QUADRILLE
QUADRUPED
QUADRUPLE
QUAKERISH
QUAKERISM
QUAKINGLY
QUALIFIED
QUARRYING
QUARRYMAN
QUARTERED
QUARTERLY
QUARTETTE
QUARTZITE
QUASIMODO
QUAVERING
QUEEN-POST
QUEERNESS
QUENCHING
QUERULOUS
QUIBBLING
QUICKENED
QUICKLIME
QUICKNESS
QUICKSAND
QUICKSTEP
QUICK-TIME
QUIESCENT
QUIESCING
QUIETENED
QUIETNESS
QUINQUINA
QUINTETTE
QUINTUPLE
QUITCLAIM
QUITTABLE
QUITTANCE
QUIVERING
QUIXOTISM
QUIZZICAL

QUOTATION
QUOTELESS

R – 9

RABBETING
RABBINATE
RABBINISM
RABBINIST
RABBITING
RABIDNESS
RACEHORSE
RACIALISM
RACIALIST
RACKETEER
RACKETING
RACONTEUR
RADIALITY
RADIANTLY
RADIATING
RADIATION
RADIATIVE
RADICALLY
RADIOGRAM
RADIOLOGY
RAFTERING
RAG-PICKER
RAIL-FENCE
RAILINGLY
RAIN-GAUGE
RAINMAKER
RAININESS
RAINPROOF
RAIN-WATER
RAMIFYING
RAMPAGING
RAMPANTLY
RAMPARTED
RANCIDITY
RANCOROUS
RANSACKED
RANSOMING
RANTINGLY
RAPACIOUS
RAPIDNESS
RAPTORIAL
RAPTUROUS
RAREE-SHOW
RAREFYING
RASCALITY
RASPATORY
RASPBERRY
RATEPAYER
RATIONALE
RATIONING
RAVELLING

RAVISHING
RAZORBACK
RAZORBILL
RAZOREDGE
RAZORFISH
REACHABLE
REACTANCE
READDRESS
READINESS
READJOURN
READOPTED
READORNED
READY-MADE
REALISING
REALISTIC
REALLEGED
REANIMATE
REANNEXED
REAPPLIED
REAPPOINT
REARGUARD
REARRANGE
REASONING
REASSURED
REAVOWING
REBAPTISE
REBELLING
REBELLION
REBINDING
REBLOOMED
REBOILING
REBOUNDED
REBUFFING
REBURYING
REBUTTING
RECALLING
RECANTING
RECAPTURE
RECASTING
RECEIPTED
RECEIVING
RECENSION
RECEPTION
RECEPTIVE
RECESSING
RECESSION
RECESSIVE
RECHARGED
RECHERCHE
RECIPIENT
RECKONING
RECLAIMED
RECLINATE
RECLINING
RECLOSING
RECLOTHED

RECOALING
RECOASTED
RECOGNISE
RECOILING
RECOINING
RECOLLECT
RECOMBINE
RECOMMEND
RECOMPILE
RECOMPOSE
RECONCILE
RECONDITE
RECONFIRM
RECONQUER
RECONVENE
RECONVERT
RECORDING
RECOUNTED
RECOUPING
RECOVERED
RECREANCY
RECREATED
RECREMENT
RECROSSED
RECRUITED
RECTANGLE
RECTIFIED
RECTIFIER
RECTITUDE
RECTORATE
RECTORIAL
RECUMBENT
RECURRENT
RECURRING
RECURVATE
RECURVING
RECYCLING
REDACTING
REDACTION
REDBREAST
REDDENING
REDEEMING
REDELIVER
RED-HANDED
REDINGOTE
RED-LETTER
REDOLENCE
REDOUBLED
REDOUBTED
REDOUNDED
REDRAFTED
REDRAWING
REDRESSED
REDUCIBLE
REDUCTION
REDUNDANT

RE-ECHOING
RE-ELECTED
RE-EMERGED
RE-ENACTED
RE-ENFORCE
RE-ENTERED
RE-ENTRANT
RE-EXAMINE
REFASHION
REFECTION
REFECTORY
REFERENCE
REFERRING
REFILLING
REFINEDLY
REFITMENT
REFITTING
REFLECTED
REFLOATED
REFLOWING
REFOLDING
REFORGING
REFORMING
REFORMIST
REFORTIFY
RE-FOUNDED
REFRACTED
REFRACTOR
REFRAINED
REFRAMING
REFRESHED
REFRESHER
REFULGENT
REFUNDING
REFURBISH
REFURNISH
REFUSABLE
REFUSENIK
REFUTABLE
REGAINING
REGARDANT
REGARDFUL
REGARDING
REGICIDAL
REGILDING
REGISTRAR
REGORGING
REGRANTED
REGRADING
REGRETFUL
REGRETTED
REGULARLY
REGULATED
REGULATOR
REHANDLED
REHANGING

REHASHING
REHEARING
REHEARSAL
REHEARSED
RE-HEATING
REHOUSING
REICHSTAG
RE-IGNITED
REMIBURSE
REINFORCE
REINSTALL
REINSTATE
REINSURED
REISSUING
REITERATE
REJECTING
REJECTION
REJECTIVE
REJOICING
REJOINDER
REJOINING
REJOINTED
REJUDGING
REKINDLED
RELANDING
RELAPSING
RELAXABLE
RELEASING
RELEGATED
RELENTING
RELETTING
RELEVANCE
RELEVANCY
RELIEVING
RELIGIOUS
RELIQUARY
RELISHING
RELOADING
RELUCTANT
REMAINDER
REMAINING
REMANDING
REMANNING
REMARKING
REMARRIED
REMEDYING
REMINDFUL
REMINDING
REMISSION
REMISSIVE
REMITTING
REMOULDED
REMOUNTED
REMOVABLE
RENASCENT
RENDERING

RENDITION	REQUIRING	RETENTION	RHYMELESS
RENEWABLE	REQUISITE	RETENTIVE	RHYMESTER
RENOVATED	REQUITING	RETEXTURE	RICE-PAPER
RENOVATOR	RE-READING	RETICENCE	RIDERLESS
REOPENING	RESCINDED	RETICULAR	RIDGE-POLE
REORDERED	RE-SCORING	RETICULUM	RIDICULED
REPACKING	RESEATING	RETORTING	RIGHTEOUS
REPAINTED	RESECTION	RETORTION	RIGHT-HAND
REPAIRING	RESELLING	RETORTIVE	RIGHTNESS
REPARABLE	RESEMBLED	RETOSSING	RIGMAROLE
REPARABLY	RESENDING	RETOUCHED	RING-FENCE
REPASSING	RESENTFUL	RETRACING	RINGLETED
REPASTING	RESERVING	RETRACTED	RING-OUZEL
REPAYABLE	RESERVIST	RETRACTOR	RING-STAND
REPAYMENT	RESETTING	RETREATED	RIOTOUSLY
REPEALING	RESETTLED	RETRIEVED	RITUALISM
REPEATING	RESHIPPED	RETRIEVER	RITUALIST
REPELLENT	RESIDENCE	RETRIMMED	RIVALLING
REPELLING	RESIDENCY	RETROCEDE	RIVERSIDE
REPENTANT	RESIDUARY	RETRODDEN	ROAD-HOUSE
REPENTING	RESIGNING	RETROFLEX	ROADSTEAD
REPERTORY	RESILIENT	RETROUSSE	ROARINGLY
REPLACING	RESISTANT	RETROVERT	ROCK-BASIN
REPLAITED	RESISTING	RETURNING	ROCK-BOUND
REPLANTED	RESOLUBLE	REUNIFIED	ROCK-CRESS
REPLEDGED	RESOLVENT	REUNITING	ROCKETING
REPLENISH	RESOLVING	REVALUING	ROCKINESS
REPLETION	RESONANCE	REVAMPING	ROGUISHLY
REPLY-PAID	RESONATED	REVEALING	ROISTERED
REPOINTED	RESONATOR	REVELLING	ROISTERER
REPORTAGE	RESORBENT	REVENGING	ROLLICKED
REPORTING	RESORBING	REVERENCE	ROMANCING
REPOSEFUL	RESORTING	REVERSELY	ROMANISED
REPOSSESS	RESOUNDED	REVERSING	ROMPISHLY
REPOTTING	RESPECTED	REVERSION	ROOMINESS
REPREHEND	RESPECTER	REVERTING	ROOTSTOCK
REPRESENT	RE-SPELLED	REVETMENT	ROPEMAKER
REPRESSED	RESPIRING	REVETTING	ROQUEFORT
REPRIEVED	RESPONDED	REVICTUAL	ROSACEOUS
REPRIMAND	RESTAMPED	REVIEWING	ROSE-APPLE
REPRINTED	RESTATING	REVISITED	ROSE-NOBLE
REPROBATE	RESTEMMED	REVIVABLE	ROSE-WATER
REPRODUCE	RESTFULLY	REVOCABLE	ROSINANTE
REPROVING	REST-HOUSE	REVOCABLY	ROTOGRAPH
REPRUNING	RESTIVELY	REVOLTING	ROTUNDITY
REPTILIAN	RESTOCKED	REVOLVING	ROUGHCAST
REPUBLISH	RESTORING	REVULSION	ROUGHENED
REPUDIATE	RESTRAINT	REVULSIVE	ROUGH-HEWN
REPUGNANT	RESULTANT	REWARDING	ROUGHNESS
REPULSING	RESULTING	REWORDING	ROUGHSHOD
REPULSION	RESURGENT	REWRITING	ROUNDED-UP
REPULSIVE	RESURRECT	REWRITTEN	ROUNDELAY
REPUTABLE	RETAILING	RHAPSODIC	ROUNDHEAD
REPUTABLY	RETAINING	RHEUMATIC	ROUNDNESS
REPUTEDLY	RETALIATE	RHINOLOGY	ROUNDSMAN
REQUESTED	RETARDING	RHUMB-LINE	ROUSINGLY

ROWDINESS
ROWELLING
RUDDINESS
RUFFIANLY
RUINATION
RUINOUSLY
RUMINATED
RUMMAGING
RUMOURING
RUPTURING
RUSSOPHIL
RUSTICATE
RUSTICITY
RUSTINESS
RUTHENIUM

S – 9

SACCHARIC
SACCHARIN
SACKCLOTH
SACRAMENT
SACRARIUM
SACRIFICE
SACRILEGE
SACRISTAN
SADDENING
SADDLE-BAG
SADDLEBOW
SAFEGUARD
SAFETY-PIN
SAFFLOWER
SAFFRONED
SAGACIOUS
SAGE-BRUSH
SAGITTATE
SAILCLOTH
SAILMAKER
SAILPLANE
SAINT-LIKE
SALACIOUS
SALE-PRICE
SALICYLIC
SALIENTLY
SALIFYING
SALIVATED
SALLOWISH
SALLYPORT
SALTATION
SALTATORY
SALTISHLY
SALT-MARSH
SALTPETRE
SALT-WATER
SALUBRITY
SALVARSAN

SALVATION
SAMARITAN
SANCTUARY
SANDALLED
SAND-BLAST
SAND-BLIND
SANDGLASS
SANDINESS
SANDPAPER
SANDPIPER
SANDSTONE
SANGFROID
SANHEDRIN
SAPIDNESS
SAPIENTLY
SAPPINESS
SARCASTIC
SARTORIAL
SASSAFRAS
SASSENACH
SATELLITE
SATIATING
SATIATION
SATINWOOD
SATIRICAL
SATIRISED
SATISFIED
SATURATED
SATURNIAN
SATURNINE
SAUCEBOAT
SAUCINESS
SAUNTERER
SAVOURING
SAVOURILY
SAXIFRAGE
SAXOPHONE
SCALELESS
SCALINESS
SCALLOPED
SCALLYWAG
SCANTLING
SCANTNESS
SCAPEGOAT
SCAPEMENT
SCAPULARY
SCARECROW
SCARFRING
SCARIFIER
SCATTERED
SCAVENGER
SCENTLESS
SCEPTICAL
SCHEDULED
SCHEMATIC
SCHILLING

SCHNORKEL
SCHOLARLY
SCHOLIAST
SCHOOLBOY
SCHOOLING
SCHOOLMAN
SCIENTIAL
SCIENTIST
SCINTILLA
SCISSORED
SCLEROSIS
SCLEROTIC
SCORBUTIC
SCORCHING
SCORIFIED
SCOTCHING
SCOTCHMAN
SCOUNDREL
SCRAGGILY
SCRAGGING
SCRAMBLED
SCRAMBLER
SCRAPPING
SCRAPBOOK
SCRAP-HEAP
SCRATCHED
SCRAWLING
SCREAMING
SCREECHED
SCREENING
SCREWBALL
SCRIBBLED
SCRIBBLER
SCRIMMAGE
SCRIMPING
SCRIMSHAW
SCRIPTURE
SCRIVENER
SCROLLING
SCROUNGED
SCROUNGER
SCRUBBING
SCRUM-HALF
SCRUMMAGE
SCRUPLING
SCRUTATOR
SCUFFLING
SCULPTURE
SCUMBLING
SCURRYING
SCUTCHEON
SCUTTLING
SEA-ANCHOR
SEA-BREACH
SEA-BREEZE
SEAFARING

SEA-LAWYER
SEA-LETTER
SEA-NETTLE
SEARCHING
SEA-ROBBER
SEA-ROCKET
SEASONING
SEA-SQUIRT
SEA-URCHIN
SEAWORTHY
SEBACEOUS
SECESSION
SECLUDING
SECLUSION
SECLUSIVE
SECONDARY
SECONDING
SECRETARY
SECRETING
SECRETION
SECRETIVE
SECRETORY
SECTARIAL
SECTARIAN
SECTIONAL
SECULARLY
SEDENTARY
SEDITIOUS
SEDUCTION
SEDUCTIVE
SEED-GRAIN
SEEDINESS
SEED-PEARL
SEEMINGLY
SEE-SAWING
SEGMENTAL
SEGMENTED
SEGREGATE
SEIGNIORY
SELECTING
SELECTION
SELECTIVE
SELFISHLY
SELVEDGED
SEMANTICS
SEMAPHORE
SEMBLANCE
SEMIBREVE
SEMICOLON
SEMIFLUID
SEMILUNAR
SEMINATED
SEMIVOCAL
SEMIVOWEL
SENESCENT
SENESCHAL

SENIORITY
SENSATION
SENSELESS
SENSITISE
SENSITIVE
SENSORIAL
SENSORIUM
SENSUALLY
SENTENCED
SENTIMENT
SENTRY-BOX
SEPARABLE
SEPARABLY
SEPARATED
SEPARATOR
SEPTEMBER
SEPTENARY
SEPULCHRE
SEQUACITY
SEQUESTER
SERENADED
SERIALISM
SERMONISE
SERRATION
SERVIETTE
SERVILELY
SERVILITY
SERVITUDE
SESSIONAL
SETACEOUS
SET-SQUARE
SEVENFOLD
SEVENTEEN
SEVENTHLY
SEVERABLE
SEVERALLY
SEVERALTY
SEVERANCE
SEXENNIAL
SEXUALITY
SFORZANDO
SHACKLING
SHADINESS
SHADOWING
SHAFTLESS
SHAKEDOWN
SHAKINESS
SHALLOWLY
SHAMBLING
SHAMELESS
SHAMPOOED
SHAPELESS
SHARPENED
SHARPNESS
SHATTERED
SHEAR-LEGS

SHEATHING
SHEEPCOTE
SHEEPFOLD
SHEEP-HOOK
SHEEPSKIN
SHEEPWALK
SHEER-HULK
SHELDRAKE
SHELLBACK
SHELLFISH
SHIELDING
SHIFTLESS
SHINGLING
SHINTOISM
SHIPMONEY
SHIPOWNER
SHIPSHAPE
SHIPWRECK
SHIRTLESS
SHIVERING
SHOEBLACK
SHOEBRUSH
SHOEMAKER
SHOPWOMAN
SHORELESS
SHOREWARD
SHORTCAKE
SHORTENED
SHORTFALL
SHORTHAND
SHORT-HOSE
SHORTNESS
SHORT-SLIP
SHOTPROOF
SHOULDERS
SHOVELLED
SHOVELFUL
SHOVEL-HAT
SHOVELLER
SHOWBREAD
SHOWERING
SHOWINESS
SHOW-PLACE
SHREW-MOLE
SHRIEKING
SHRILLING
SHRIMPING
SHRIMP-NET
SHRINKAGE
SHRINKING
SHROUDING
SHRUBBERY
SHRUBLESS
SHRUGGING
SHUDDERED
SHUFFLING

SIBILANCE
SIBYLLINE
SICCATIVE
SICKENING
SIDEBOARD
SIDEBURNS
SIDELIGHT
SIDE-TABLE
SIDETRACK
SIGHINGLY
SIGHTLESS
SIGHTSEER
SIGNAL-BOX
SIGNAL-GUN
SIGNALIZE
SIGNALLED
SIGNALMAN
SIGNATORY
SIGNATURE
SIGNBOARD
SIGNIFIED
SIGNORINA
SILENCING
SILICATED
SILICEOUS
SILKINESS
SILLINESS
SILVER-FOX
SILVERING
SIMILARLY
SIMMERING
SIMPLETON
SIMULATED
SINCERELY
SINCERITY
SINGINGLY
SINGLETON
SINISTRAL
SINLESSLY
SINUOSITY
SINUOUSLY
SIPHONAGE
SIPHONING
SISYPHEAN
SITUATION
SIXFOOTER
SIXTEENTH
SKEDADDLE
SKETCHILY
SKETCHING
SKEW-WHIFF
SKILFULLY
SKINFLINT
SKINNY-DIP
SKYDIVING
SKYROCKET

SLABSTONE
SLACKENED
SLACKNESS
SLANDERED
SLANTWISE
SLAPSTICK
SLATINESS
SLAUGHTER
SLAVE-LIKE
SLAVERING
SLAVISHLY
SLAVONIAN
SLEEPLESS
SLEIGHING
SLENDERLY
SLIDE-RULE
SLIGHTING
SLIMINESS
SLIP-COACH
SLIPPERED
SLITHERED
SLIVERING
SLOBBERED
SLOP-BASIN
SLOPINGLY
SLOUCH-HAT
SLOUCHING
SLOUGHING
SLOWCOACH
SLOW-MATCH
SLUMBERED
SMALL-ARMS
SMALL-BEER
SMALLNESS
SMARTENED
SMARTNESS
SMILELESS
SMILINGLY
SMIRCHING
SMOCKLESS
SMOKE-BOMB
SMOKELESS
SMOKINESS
SMOOTHING
SMOTHERED
SMUG-FACED
SMUGGLING
SMUTCHING
SNAFFLING
SNAIL-LIKE
SNAKE-BIRD
SNAKE-ROOT
SNAKEWEED
SNAKE-WOOD
SNATCHING
SNICKERED

SNIFFLING	SOUBRETTE	SPLENETIC	STAGNATED
SNIGGERED	SOULFULLY	SPLINTERY	STAIDNESS
SNIVELLED	SOUNDBITE	SPLINTING	STAINLESS
SNOWBERRY	SOUNDLESS	SPLIT-RING	STAIRCASE
SNOWBLIND	SOUNDNESS	SPOKESMAN	STAIRHEAD
SNOWBOARD	SOUP-PLATE	SPOLIATED	STAKE-BOAT
SNOW-BOUND	SOUTHDOWN	SPONSORED	STALACTIC
SNOWDRIFT	SOUTH-EAST	SPOON-BAIT	STALEMATE
SNOWFIELD	SOUTHERLY	SPOONBILL	STALENESS
SNOWFLAKE	SOUTHWARD	SPOON-FEED	STALKLESS
SNOW-GOOSE	SOUTH-WEST	SPORE-CASE	STAMMERED
SNOWSTORM	SOU'-WESTER	SPORTLESS	STAMMERER
SNUB-NOSED	SOVEREIGN	SPORTSMAN	STAMP-DUTY
SNUFFLING	SPACED OUT	SPOUT-HOLE	STAMPEDED
SNUGGLING	SPADEWORK	SPOUTLESS	STANCHING
SOAPINESS	SPAGHETTI	SPRAGGING	STANCHION
SOAPSTONE	SPANGLING	SPRAINING	STARBOARD
SOARINGLY	SPARENESS	SPRAWLING	STARCHING
SOBERNESS	SPARINGLY	SPREADING	STARGAZER
SOBRIQUET	SPARKLING	SPRIGGING	STARINGLY
SOCIALISE	SPASMODIC	SPRIGHTLY	STARLIGHT
SOCIALISM	SPATTERED	SPRINGING	STAR-SHELL
SOCIALIST	SPATULATE	SPRINGBOK	STARTLING
SOCIALITE	SPEAKABLE	SPRING-GUN	STATELESS
SOCIALITY	SPEAK-EASY	SPRINKLED	STATEMENT
SOCIOLOGY	SPEARHEAD	SPRINKLER	STATEROOM
SODA-WATER	SPEARMINT	SPRINTING	STATESMAN
SOFTENING	SPECIALLY	SPROUTING	STATIONED
SOJOURNED	SPECIALTY	SPUR-ROYAL	STATIONER
SOLARISED	SPECIFIED	SPUR-WHEEL	STATISTIC
SOLDERING	SPECKLESS	SPUTTERED	STATUETTE
SOLDIERLY	SPECKLING	SQUABBLED	STATUTORY
SOLEMNISE	SPECTACLE	SQUALIDLY	STAUNCHED
SOLEMNITY	SPECTATOR	SQUALLING	STAYMAKER
SOLICITED	SPECULATE	SQUASHING	STEADFAST
SOLICITOR	SPEECH-DAY	SQUATTING	STEADYING
SOLIDNESS	SPEECHFUL	SQUAWKING	STEAMBOAT
SOLILOQUY	SPEECHIFY	SQUEAKING	STEAMPIPE
SOLITAIRE	SPELLABLE	SQUEALING	STEAMSHIP
SOMETHING	SPERMATIC	SQUEAMISH	STEEL-CLAD
SOMETIMES	SPHERICAL	SQUEEZING	STEELYARD
SOMEWHERE	SPHINCTER	SQUELCHED	STEEPENED
SOMNOLENT	SPICINESS	SQUIGGLED	STEEPNESS
SONNETEER	SPIKENARD	SQUINTING	STEERABLE
SOOTINESS	SPILLIKIN	SQUIRMING	STEERSMAN
SOPHISTRY	SPINDLING	SQUIRTING	STELLATED
SOPHOMORE	SPINDRIFT	STABILISE	STERILISE
SOPORIFIC	SPINELESS	STABILITY	STERILITY
SORCERESS	SPINNAKER	STABLEBOY	STERNMOST
SORRINESS	SPINNERET	STABLEMAN	STERNNESS
SORROWFUL	SPIRALITY	STACKYARD	STERNPOST
SORROWING	SPIRITING	STAGE-PLAY	STEVEDORE
SORTILEGE	SPIRITUAL	STAGGERED	STEWARDLY
SOSTENUTO	SPLASHING	STAGHOUND	STEWARTRY
SOTTISHLY	SPLAY-FOOT	STAGINESS	STIFFENED
SOTTO-VOCE	SPLENDOUR	STAGNANCY	STIFFENER

STIFFNESS	STRANGELY	SUBMARINE	SUPERSTAR
STIGMATIC	STRANGLED	SUBMERGED	SUPERVENE
STILLBORN	STRANGLER	SUBMITTED	SUPERVISE
STILL-LIFE	STRAPPADO	SUBNORMAL	SUPPLIANT
STILLNESS	STRAPPING	SUBORNING	SUPPLYING
STILL-ROOM	STRAPWORK	SUBSCRIBE	SUPPORTED
STIMULANT	STRATAGEM	SUBSCRIPT	SUPPORTER
STIMULATE	STRATEGIC	SUBSERVED	SUPPOSING
STINGLESS	STREAKING	SUBSIDING	SUPPURATE
STINKBOMB	STREAMING	SUBSIDISE	SUPREMACY
STIPPLING	STREAMLET	SUBSISTED	SUPREMELY
STIPULATE	STRENUOUS	SUBSTANCE	SURCHARGE
STIRABOUT	STRESSING	SUBTENANT	SURCINGLE
STITCHERY	STRETCHED	SUBTENDED	SURFACING
STITCHING	STRETCHER	SUBVERTED	SURLINESS
STOCKADED	STRIATION	SUCCEEDED	SURMISING
STOCKDOVE	STRICTURE	SUCCENTOR	SURNAMING
STOCKFISH	STRINGENT	SUCCESSOR	SURPASSED
STOCKINET	STRINGING	SUCCOTASH	SURPRISED
STOCKINGS	STRIPLING	SUCCOURED	SURRENDER
STOCKLESS	STRIPPING	SUCCULENT	SURROGATE
STOCKWHIP	STROLLING	SUCCUMBED	SURVEYING
STOCKYARD	STROMATIC	SUCKERING	SURVIVING
STOICALLY	STRONG-BOX	SUDORIFIC	SUSPECTED
STOKEHOLD	STRONTIUM	SUFFERING	SUSPENDED
STOLIDITY	STROPPING	SUFFICING	SUSPENDER
STOMACHAL	STRUCTIVE	SUFFIXING	SUSPICION
STOMACHER	STRUGGLED	SUFFOCATE	SUSTAINED
STOMACHIC	STRUMMING	SUFFRAGAN	SWADDLING
STONECHAT	STRUTTING	SUFFUSING	SWAGGERED
STONE-COLD	STRYCHNIC	SUFFUSION	SWALLOWED
STONECROP	STUCCOING	SUGAR-BEET	SWANSDOWN
STONE-DEAD	STUD-GROOM	SUGAR-CANE	SWARTHILY
STONE-DEAF	STUD-HORSE	SUGARLESS	SWEET-CORN
STONELESS	STUDIEDLY	SUGAR-LOAF	SWEETENED
STONE-PINE	STUMBLING	SUGAR-MILL	SWEETMEAT
STONEWALL	STUPEFIED	SUGAR-MITE	SWEETNESS
STONINESS	STUPIDITY	SUGAR-PINE	SWEET-SHOP
STOOL-BALL	STUTTERER	SUGARPLUM	SWELTERED
STOPPERED	STYLISHLY	SUGGESTED	SWIFTNESS
STOP-PRESS	STYLOBATE	SULKINESS	SWIMMERET
STOP-WATCH	SUBAGENCY	SULPHURIC	SWINDLING
STOREROOM	SUBALTERN	SUMMARILY	SWINEHERD
STORESHIP	SUBCOSTAL	SUMMARISE	SWING-BOAT
STORMCOCK	SUBDEACON	SUMMATION	SWING-DOOR
STORM-CONE	SUBDIVIDE	SUMMING-UP	SWINGEING
STORMSAIL	SUB-EDITOR	SUMMONING	SWINGLING
STORTHING	SUBFAMILY	SUMPTUARY	SWINISHLY
STORYBOOK	SUBJACENT	SUMPTUOUS	SWITCHING
STOUTNESS	SUBJECTED	SUNBONNET	SWITCHMAN
STOVEPIPE	SUBJOINED	SUNFLOWER	SWIVEL-EYE
STRADDLED	SUBJUGATE	SUNSTROKE	SWIVELLED
STRAGGLED	SUBLIMATE	SUPERFINE	SWORDBELT
STRAGGLER	SUBLIMELY	SUPERHEAT	SWORDBILL
STRAINING	SUBLIMITY	SUPERPOSE	SWORD-CANE
STRANDING	SUBLUNARY	SUPERSEDE	SWORDFISH

SWORDHILT	TARANTULA	TESTATRIX	THWARTING
SWORD-LILY	TARDINESS	TESTIFIED	THYRISTOR
SWORDSMAN	TARNISHED	TESTIMONY	TICKETING
SYBARITIC	TARPAULIN	TESTINESS	TIDEGAUGE
SYCOPHANT	TARTAREAN	TETHERING	TIDE-TABLE
SYLLABARY	TASSELLED	TETRALOGY	TIDE-WATER
SYLLABIFY	TASTELESS	TETRARCHY	TIGER-LILY
SYLLABLED	TATTERING	TEXTUALLY	TIGER-MOTH
SYLLEPSIS	TATTOOING	THANKLESS	TIGER-WOOD
SYLLOGISE	TAUTENING	THATCHING	TIGHTENED
SYLLOGISM	TAUTOLOGY	THEOCRACY	TIGHTNESS
SYLPH-LIKE	TAWNINESS	THEOCRASY	TIGHTROPE
SYMBIOSIS	TAXIDERMY	THEOMACHY	TIMBERMAN
SYMBIOTIC	TAXIMETER	THEOMANCY	TIME-LAPSE
SYMBOLISE	TEACHABLE	THEORISED	TIMEPIECE
SYMBOLISM	TEASELLED	THEOSOPHY	TIME-SHARE
SYMBOLIST	TECHNICAL	THEREFORE	TIMETABLE
SYMMETRIC	TECHNIQUE	THEREFROM	TIMIDNESS
SYMPHONIC	TEDIOUSLY	THEREINTO	TIMOCRACY
SYMPHYSIS	TELEGRAPH	THEREUNTO	TINCTURED
SYMPOSIUM	TELEMETER	THEREUPON	TINDERBOX
SYNAGOGUE	TELEMETRY	THEREWITH	TINKERING
SYNCOPATE	TELEOLOGY	THERMIDOR	TINSELLED
SYNDICATE	TELEPATHY	THESAURUS	TIPSINESS
SYNODICAL	TELEPHONE	THICKENED	TIPSY-CAKE
SYNONYMIC	TELEPHONY	THICKNESS	TIREDNESS
SYNOPTIST	TELEPHOTO	THICK-KNEE	TITILLATE
SYNOVITIS	TELEPRINT	THICK-SKIN	TITIVATED
SYNTHESIS	TELESCOPE	THIGH-BONE	TITRATION
SYNTHETIC	TELLINGLY	THINKABLE	TITTERING
SYRINGING	TELLURIUM	THINK-TANK	TITTLEBAT
SYSTEMISE	TELLUROUS	THIRSTILY	TITULARLY
	TEMPERATE	THIRSTING	TOADEATER
	TEMPERING	THIRTIETH	TOADSTONE
T – 9	TEMPORARY	THORNBACK	TOADSTOOL
	TEMPORISE	THORNBUSH	TOAST-RACK
TABLATURE	TEMPTRESS	THORNLESS	TOLERABLE
TABLELAND	TENACIOUS	THRASHING	TOLERABLY
TABLE-TALK	TENACULUM	THREADING	TOLERANCE
TABULARLY	TENANTING	THREEFOLD	TOLERATED
TABULATED	TENDERING	THRESHING	TOLL-BOOTH
TACTICIAN	TENSENESS	THRESHOLD	TOMBSTONE
TACTILITY	TENTATIVE	THRIFTILY	TONSORIAL
TAILBOARD	TEPEFYING	THRILLING	TOOTHACHE
TAILORESS	TEPIDNESS	THROBBING	TOOTHLESS
TAILORING	TEREBINTH	THRONGING	TOOTHPICK
TAILPIECE	TERMAGANT	THROTTLED	TOOTHSOME
TALBOTYPE	TERMINATE	THROWSTER	TOPICALLY
TALKATIVE	TERRACING	THRUMMING	TORMENTED
TALLOWING	TERRIFIED	THRUSTING	TORMENTIL
TALLY-CARD	TERRITORY	THUMB-MARK	TORMENTOR
TALLYSHOP	TERRORISE	THUMB-NAIL	TORPEDOED
TALMUDIST	TERRORISM	THUMB-RACK	TORPIDITY
TAMPERING	TERRORIST	THUNDERED	TORPIFIED
TANGERINE	TERSENESS	THUNDERER	TORREFIED
TANTALIZE	TESTAMENT	THWACKING	TORSIONAL
TAP-DANCER			

TORTURING	TREPANNED	TWISTABLE	UNCHANGED
TORTUROUS	TRIATOMIC	TWITCHING	UNCHARGED
TOTTERING	TRIBALISM	TWITTERED	UNCHARTED
TOUCHABLE	TRIBESMAN	TWO-HANDED	UNCHECKED
TOUCH-HOLE	TRIBUNATE	TWO-MASTED	UNCLAIMED
TOUCHWOOD	TRIBUTARY	TYMPANIST	UNCLEARED
TOUGHENED	TRICKLING	TYPEMETAL	UNCLIPPED
TOUGHNESS	TRICKSTER	TYPICALLY	UNCLOGGED
TOWELLING	TRICUSPID	TYPIFYING	UNCLOSING
TOWN-CLERK	TRIENNIAL	TYRANNISE	UNCLOTHED
TOWN-CRIER	TRIGAMIST	TYRANNOUS	UNCLOUDED
TOWN-HOUSE	TRIHEDRAL		UNCOILING
TOWN-MAJOR	TRIHEDRON		UNCONCERN
TOWNSFOLK	TRILINEAR	**U – 9**	UNCORKING
TRACEABLE	TRILITHON	UGLIFYING	UNCOUNTED
TRACKLESS	TRILOBATE	ULCERATED	UNCOUTHLY
TRACTABLE	TRILOBITE	ULTIMATUM	UNCOVERED
TRACTABLY	TRINOMIAL	ULULATING	UNCROPPED
TRADEMARK	TRISECTED	ULULATION	UNCROSSED
TRADESMAN	TRITENESS	UMBELLATE	UNCROWDED
TRADE-WIND	TRIUMPHAL	UMBILICAL	UNCROWNED
TRADITION	TRIUMPHED	UMBILICUS	UNCURLING
TRADUCING	TRIVIALLY	UNABASHED	UNDAMAGED
TRAGEDIAN	TRI-WEEKLY	UNACCUSED	UNDAUNTED
TRAINABLE	TROOPSHIP	UNACTABLE	UNDECEIVE
TRAINBAND	TROUBLING	UNADAPTED	UNDECIDED
TRAIN-MILE	TROUBLOUS	UNADOPTED	UNDEFILED
TRAIPSING	TROUNCING	UNADORNED	UNDEFINED
TRAITRESS	TROUSERED	UNADVISED	UNDERDONE
TRAMPLING	TROUSSEAU	UNALLOYED	UNDERFEED
TRANSCEND	TROWELLED	UNALTERED	UNDERFOOT
TRANSFORM	TRUCKLING	UNAMENDED	UNDERGONE
TRANSFUSE	TRUCULENT	UNAMIABLE	UNDERHAND
TRANSIENT	TRUMPETER	UNAMUSING	UNDERHUNG
TRANSLATE	TRUNCATED	UNANIMITY	UNDERLAID
TRANSMUTE	TRUNDLING	UNANIMOUS	UNDERLAIN
TRANSPIRE	TRUNK-HOSE	UNASHAMED	UNDERLINE
TRANSPORT	TUGGINGLY	UNASSURED	UNDERLING
TRANSPOSE	TUMESCENT	UNBARRING	UNDERMINE
TRAPEZIUM	TUNEFULLY	UNBEKNOWN	UNDERMOST
TRAPEZOID	TUNNELLED	UNBENDING	UNDERPAID
TRATTORIA	TURBINATE	UNBINDING	UNDERPART
TRAUMATIC	TURBULENT	UNBLOCKED	UNDERPLOT
TRAVELLER	TURFINESS	UNBLUNTED	UNDERRATE
TRAVERSED	TURF-SPADE	UNBOLTING	UNDERSELL
TREACHERY	TURGIDITY	UNBOSOMED	UNDERSHOT
TREADMILL	TURNIP-FLY	UNBOUNDED	UNDERSIGN
TREASURED	TURNSTONE	UNBRACING	UNDERSOLD
TREASURER	TURNTABLE	UNBRIDLED	UNDERTAKE
TREATMENT	TURPITUDE	UNBRUISED	UNDERTONE
TREE-PIPIT	TURQUOISE	UNBUCKLED	UNDERTOOK
TRELLISED	TUTORSHIP	UNBUCKLES	UNDERVEST
TREMBLING	TWADDLING	UNCANNILY	UNDERWEAR
TREMULOUS	TWENTIETH	UNCAPPING	UNDERWENT
TRENCHANT	TWIDDLING	UNCEASING	UNDERWOOD
TRENCHING	TWINKLING	UNCERTAIN	UNDERWORK

UNDESIRED
UNDILUTED
UNDIVIDED
UNDOUBTED
UNDRAINED
UNDREAMED
UNDRESSED
UNDULATED
UNDUTIFUL
UNEARTHED
UNEARTHLY
UNEATABLE
UNELECTED
UNENGAGED
UN-ENGLISH
UNENVIOUS
UNEQUABLE
UNEQUALLY
UNEXCITED
UNEXERTED
UNEXPIRED
UNEXPOSED
UNFAILING
UNFEELING
UNFEIGNED
UNFITNESS
UNFITTING
UNFLEDGED
UNFOLDING
UNFOUNDED
UNFROCKED
UNFURLING
UNGALLANT
UNGIRDING
UNGRANTED
UNGRUDGED
UNGUARDED
UNGUMMING
UNHANDILY
UNHANDLED
UNHAPPILY
UNHARMFUL
UNHATCHED
UNHEALTHY
UNHEEDFUL
UNHEEDING
UNHELPFUL
UNHINGING
UNHITCHED
UNHOOKING
UNHOPEFUL
UNHORSING
UNHURTFUL
UNIFORMLY
UNIMPEDED
UNIMPLIED

UNINDUCED
UNINJURED
UNINSURED
UNINVITED
UNINVOKED
UNIPAROUS
UNISEXUAL
UNITARIAN
UNIVALENT
UNIVERSAL
UNJOINTED
UNKNOTTED
UNKNOWING
UNLASHING
UNLATCHED
UNLEARNED
UNLEASHED
UNLIGHTED
UNLIMITED
UNLOADING
UNLOCATED
UNLOCKING
UNLOOSING
UNLOVABLE
UNLUCKILY
UNMANNING
UNMANURED
UNMARRIED
UNMASKING
UNMATCHED
UNMERITED
UNMINDFUL
UNMOORING
UNMOULDED
UNMOUNTED
UNMOURNED
UNMUFFLED
UNMUSICAL
UNMUZZLED
UNNAMABLE
UNNATURAL
UNNERVING
UNNOTICED
UNOBVIOUS
UNOFFERED
UNOPPOSED
UNORDERED
UNORDERLY
UNPACKING
UNPAINFUL
UNPAINTED
UNPEGGING
UNPENNING
UNPERUSED
UNPICKING
UNPIERCED

UNPINNING
UNPITYING
UNPLAITED
UNPLANTED
UNPLEADED
UNPLEASED
UNPLEDGED
UNPLUGGED
UNPLUMBED
UNPOINTED
UNPOPULAR
UNPOTABLE
UNPRAISED
UNPRESSED
UNPRINTED
UNQUIETLY
UNREALITY
UNREBUKED
UNREFINED
UNREFUTED
UNRELATED
UNRENEWED
UNRESCUED
UNRESTFUL
UNRESTING
UNREVISED
UNREVIVED
UNREVOKED
UNRIDDLED
UNRIGGING
UNRIPENED
UNRIPPING
UNROLLING
UNROASTED
UNROUNDED
UNRUFFLED
UNRUMPLED
UNSADDLED
UNSALABLE
UNSAVOURY
UNSCANNED
UNSCATHED
UNSCOURED
UNSCREWED
UNSEALING
UNSEATING
UNSELFISH
UNSETTLED
UNSEVERED
UNSHACKLE
UNSHAPELY
UNSHEATHE
UNSHIPPED
UNSHRIVEN
UNSIGHTLY
UNSINKING

UNSKILFUL
UNSKILLED
UNSOUNDLY
UNSPARING
UNSPOILED
UNSPOTTED
UNSTAINED
UNSTAMPED
UNSTINTED
UNSTOPPED
UNSTRIPED
UNSTUDIED
UNSULLIED
UNTACKING
UNTAINTED
UNTAMABLE
UNTANGLED
UNTEMPTED
UNTENABLE
UNTHANKED
UNTIRABLE
UNTOUCHED
UNTRAINED
UNTRIMMED
UNTRODDEN
UNTUCKING
UNTUTORED
UNTWINING
UNTWISTED
UNUSUALLY
UNVACATED
UNVARYING
UNVEILING
UNVISITED
UNWAKENED
UNWARLIKE
UNWATCHED
UNWATERED
UNWEARIED
UNWEAVING
UNWEIGHED
UNWELCOME
UNWILLING
UNWINDING
UNWINKING
UNWITTILY
UNWOMANLY
UNWORLDLY
UNWORRIED
UNWOUNDED
UNWRAPPED
UNWREATHE
UNWRECKED
UNWRITTEN
UNWROUGHT
UPANISHAD

UPBRAIDED
UPHEAVING
UPHOLDING
UPHOLSTER
UPLIFTING
UPLIGHTER
UPPER-HAND
UPPERMOST
UPRIGHTLY
UPROOTING
UPSETTING
UPTURNING
USELESSLY
USHERETTE
USUALNESS
UTILISING
UTTERANCE
UTTERMOST

V – 9

VACCINATE
VACILLATE
VADE-MECUM
VAGUENESS
VAINGLORY
VALANCING
VALENTINE
VALIANTLY
VALIDATED
VALUATION
VALUELESS
VAMOOSING
VAMPIRISM
VANDALISM
VANISHING
VAPORISED
VAPOURING
VARIATION
VARIEGATE
VARIOUSLY
VARNISHED
VASSALAGE
VEERINGLY
VEGETABLE
VEHEMENCE
VEHICULAR
VELVETEEN
VENEERING
VENERABLE
VENERABLY
VENERATED
VENGEANCE
VENIALITY
VENTILATE
VENTRALLY

VENTRICLE
VENTURING
VERACIOUS
VERBALISE
VERBASCUM
VERBOSELY
VERBOSITY
VERDANTLY
VERDIGRIS
VERDUROUS
VERIDICAL
VERIFYING
VERITABLE
VERITABLY
VERMICIDE
VERMICULE
VERMIFORM
VERMIFUGE
VERMILION
VERMINOUS
VERRUCOSE
VERSATILE
VERSIFIER
VERSIFORM
VERTEBRAL
VESICULAR
VESTIBULE
VESTIGIAL
VESTRYMAN
VEXATIOUS
VIABILITY
VIBRATING
VIBRATION
VICARIATE
VICARIOUS
VICENNIAL
VICEREGAL
VICIOUSLY
VICTIMISE
VICTORIAN
VICTORINE
VIDEOTAPE
VIEWPOINT
VIGILANCE
VIGILANTE
VINACEOUS
VINDICATE
VINOMETER
VIOLATING
VIOLATION
VIOLENTLY
VIOLINIST
VIRGILIAN
VIRGINIAN
VIRGINITY
VIRTUALLY

VIRULENCE
VISCIDITY
VISCOSITY
VISCOUNTY
VISIONARY
VISITABLE
VISUALIZE
VITALISED
VITIATING
VITIATION
VITRIFIED
VITRIOLIC
VIVACIOUS
VIVIDNESS
VIVIFYING
VIZIERATE
VOCALISED
VOICELESS
VOL-AU-VENT
VOLLEYING
VOLPLANED
VOLTE-FACE
VOLTMETER
VOLUNTARY
VOLUNTEER
VOODOOISM
VORACIOUS
VOUCHSAFE
VULCANISE
VULCANISM
VULCANITE
VULGARIAN
VULGARISE
VULGARISM
VULGARITY
VULNERARY
VULTURINE
VULTURISH
VULTURISM
VULTUROUS

W – 9

WAGGISHLY
WAGNERIAN
WAGONETTE
WAILINGLY
WAISTBAND
WAISTBELT
WAISTCOAT
WAIST-DEEP
WAITINGLY
WAKEFULLY
WAKE-ROBIN
WALKABOUT
WALL-FRUIT

WALLOPING
WALLOWING
WALLPAPER
WALL-PLATE
WALL-SIDED
WALPURGIS
WANDERING
WAREHOUSE
WARNINGLY
WARRANTED
WARRANTEE
WARRANTOR
WASHBOARD
WASHERMAN
WASH-HOUSE
WASHINESS
WASHSTAND
WASPISHLY
WASSAILED
WASTELESS
WASTE-PIPE
WATCHCASE
WATCHFIRE
WATCHWORD
WATERBIRD
WATERBUCK
WATERBUTT
WATERCART
WATERFALL
WATER-FERN
WATER-FLAG
WATERFLEA
WATERFOWL
WATER-GALL
WATER-HOLE
WATERLESS
WATERLINE
WATERMARK
WATERMILL
WATER-POLO
WATER-RAIL
WATER-RATE
WATERSHED
WATERSIDE
WATER-TANK
WATER-VOLE
WATERWEED
WATERWORN
WATTMETER
WAVEMETER
WAXWORKER
WAYFARING
WAYWARDLY
WAYZGOOSE
WEAKENING
WEAK-KNEED

WEALTHILY
WEARILESS
WEARINESS
WEARISOME
WEATHERED
WEATHERLY
WEB-FOOTED
WEDGEWISE
WEDNESDAY
WEED-GROWN
WEEPINGLY
WEEVILLED
WEIGHABLE
WEIGHTILY
WEIGHTING
WEIRDNESS
WELCOMING
WELCOMELY
WELLBEING
WELL-HOUSE
WELL-TIMED
WELL-WATER
WESTERING
WESTERNER
WESTWARDS
WHALEBOAT
WHALEBONE
WHATSOE'ER
WHEEDLING
WHEELBASE
WHEREFORE
WHEREINTO
WHEREUNTO
WHEREUPON
WHEREWITH
WHETSTONE
WHICHEVER
WHIFFLING
WHIMPERED
WHIMSICAL
WHININGLY
WHINNYING
WHINSTONE
WHIPGRAFT
WHIPPER-IN

WHIPSNAKE
WHIPSTOCK
WHIRLIGIG
WHIRLPOOL
WHIRLWIND
WHISKERED
WHISPERED
WHISPERER
WHISTLING
WHITEBAIT
WHITEBEAM
WHITEFISH
WHITEHEAD
WHITE-HEAT
WHITE-IRON
WHITENESS
WHITENING
WHITETAIL
WHITEWASH
WHITEWING
WHITEWOOD
WHITTLING
WHIZZBANG
WHOLEFOOD
WHOLENESS
WHOLESALE
WHOLESOME
WHOSOEVER
WIDEAWAKE
WIDOWHOOD
WIELDABLE
WILLINGLY
WILLOWISH
WILSONITE
WINDHOVER
WINDINESS
WINDINGLY
WINDOW-BOX
WINEGLASS
WINEPRESS
WINE-STONE
WINKINGLY
WINNINGLY
WINNOWING
WINSOMELY

WINTERING
WIREDRAWN
WIREGUAZE
WISTFULLY
WITCH-HUNT
WITHDRAWN
WITHERING
WITHSTAND
WITHSTOOD
WITLESSLY
WITNESSED
WITTICISM
WITTINESS
WITTINGLY
WOEBEGONE
WOLFISHLY
WOLFHOUND
WOLFSBANE
WOLF'S-CLAW
WOLVERINE
WOMANHOOD
WOMANKIND
WOMAN-LIKE
WOMENFOLK
WOMENKIND
WONDERING
WONDERFUL
WOOD-ASHES
WOODBLOCK
WOODCHUCK
WOODCRAFT
WOOD-HOUSE
WOODINESS
WOODLAYER
WOODLOUSE
WOOD-NYMPH
WORDINESS
WORKHOUSE
WORKMANLY
WORK-TABLE
WORKWOMAN
WORLDLING
WORLDWIDE
WORMEATEN
WORM-WHEEL

WORRIMENT
WORSENING
WORST-CASE
WORTHLESS
WOUNDLESS
WOUNDWORT
WRANGLING
WREATHING
WRENCHING
WRESTLING
WRIGGLING
WRINKLING
WRISTBAND
WRONGDOER
WRYNECKED
WYCH-HAZEL

X – 9

XANTHIPPE
XYLOPHONE

Y – 9

YACHTSMAN
YANKEEISM
YARDSTICK
YAWNINGLY
YELLOWING
YELLOWISH
YESTERDAY
YGGDRASIL
YORKSHIRE
YOUNGLING
YOUNGSTER

Z – 9

ZEALOUSLY
ZIGZAGGED
ZIRCONIUM
ZOOGRAPHY
ZOOLOGIST
ZOOPHYTIC